**Blackburn**
College

Library
01254 292120

Please return this book on or before the last date below

The New Blackwell Companion to the City

Wiley-Blackwell Companions to Geography

Wiley-Blackwell Companions to Geography is a blue-chip, comprehensive series covering each major subdiscipline of human geography in detail. Edited and contributed by the disciplines' leading authorities, each book provides the most up to date and authoritative syntheses available in its field. The overviews provided in each *Companion* will be an indispensable introduction to the field for students of all levels, while the cutting-edge, critical direction will engage students, teachers, and practitioners alike.

Published:

A Companion to Economic Geography
Edited by Eric Sheppard and Trevor J. Barnes

A Companion to Political Geography
Edited by John Agnew, Katharyne Mitchell, and Gerard Toal
(Gearoid O Tuathail)

A Companion to Cultural Geography
Edited by James S. Duncan, Nuala C. Johnson, and Richard H. Schein

A Companion to Tourism
Edited by Alan A. Lew, C. Michael Hall, and Allan M. Williams

A Companion to Feminist Geography
Edited by Lise Nelson and Joni Seager

A Companion to Environmental Geography
Edited by Noel Castree, David Demeritt, Diana Liverman, and Bruce Rhoads

A Companion to Health and Medical Geography
Edited by Tim Brown, Sara McLafferty, and Graham Moon

A Companion to Social Geography
Edited by Vincent J. Del Casino Jr., Mary Thomas, Ruth Panelli, and Paul Cloke

Also available:
The New Blackwell Companion to the City
Edited by Gary Bridge and Sophie Watson

The Blackwell Companion to Globalization
Edited by George Ritzer

The Handbook of Geographic Information Science
Edited by John Wilson and Stewart Fotheringham

The New Blackwell Companion to the City

Edited by

Gary Bridge and Sophie Watson

⟨JW⟩WILEY-BLACKWELL

A John Wiley & Sons, Ltd., Publication

This edition first published 2011
© 2011 Blackwell Publishing Ltd

Blackwell Publishing was acquired by John Wiley & Sons in February 2007. Blackwell's publishing program has been merged with Wiley's global Scientific, Technical, and Medical business to form Wiley-Blackwell.

Registered Office
John Wiley & Sons Ltd, The Atrium, Southern Gate, Chichester, West Sussex, PO19 8SQ, United Kingdom

Editorial Offices
350 Main Street, Malden, MA 02148-5020, USA
9600 Garsington Road, Oxford, OX4 2DQ, UK
The Atrium, Southern Gate, Chichester, West Sussex, PO19 8SQ, UK

For details of our global editorial offices, for customer services, and for information about how to apply for permission to reuse the copyright material in this book please see our website at www.wiley.com/wiley-blackwell.

The right of Gary Bridge and Sophie Watson to be identified as the editor(s) of this work has been asserted in accordance with the UK Copyright, Designs and Patents Act 1988.

Library of Congress Cataloging-in-Publication Data

The new Blackwell companion to the city / edited by Gary Bridge and Sophie Watson.
     p. cm.
   Rev. ed. of: A companion to the city, 2000.
     Includes bibliographical references and index.
   ISBN 978-1-4051-8981-1 (hardback)
   1. Cities and towns. 2. Cities and towns–Cross-cultural studies. I. Bridge, Gary. II. Watson, Sophie. III. Companion to the city.
   HT111.C65 2011
   307.76–dc22

                                      2010041340

A catalogue record for this book is available from the British Library.

This book is published in the following electronic formats: ePDFs [978-1-4443-9511-2]; Wiley Online Library [978-1-4443-9510-5]; ePub [9-781-4443-9512-9]

Set in 10/12.5 pt Sabon by Toppan Best-set Premedia Limited
Printed and bound in Singapore by Fabulous Printers Pte Ltd

1   2011

Contents

List of Contributors

Julie Abraham, Sarah Lawrence College

Ash Amin, University of Durham

Sophie Body-Gendrot, Université Paris Sorbonne–Paris IV

Neil Brenner, New York University

Gary Bridge, Bristol University

Stephen Cairns, University of Edinburgh

Lesley Caldwell, University College London

Simon Carter, Open University

Allan Cochrane, Open University

Francis Dodsworth, Open University

Peter Droege, University of Liechtenstein

Susan S. Fainstein, Harvard University

Ruth Fincher, University of Melbourne

Ray Forrest, University of Bristol

John Friedmann, University of British Columbia

Matthew Gandy, University College London

Katherine Gibson, University of Western Sydney

Nina Glick Schiller, University of Manchester

Ian Gordon, London School of Economics

Stephen Graham, Newcastle University

Michael Harloe, University of Salford

Stephanie Hemelryk Donald, RMIT University, Melbourne

Andrew Hill, Open University

Kurt Iveson, University of Sydney

Jane M. Jacobs, University of Edinburgh

John Paul Jones III, University of Arizona

Maria Kaika, University of Manchester

Roger Keil, York University, Canada

Michael Keith, COMPAS, Oxford University

Lily Kong, National University of Singapore

Brian Ladd, State University of New York

Patrick Le Galès, Sciences Po, Paris

Christoph Lindner, University of Amsterdam

Setha Low, City University of New York

Peter Marcuse, Columbia University

Harvey Molotch, New York University

Frank Mort, Manchester University

Max Page, University of Massachusetts

Sue Parnell, University of Cape Town

Jamie Peck, University of British Columbia

Steve Pile, Open University

David Pinder, Queen Mary College University of London

Ato Quayson, University of Toronto

Jenny Robinson, University College London

Tyler Rooker, Shanghai University

Andrew Ross, New York University

Benjamin Rossiter, Victoria Walks Inc.

Evelyn S. Ruppert, Open University

Saskia Sassen, Columbia University

Mike Savage, University of York

Jeremy Seekings, University of Cape Town

Richard Sennett, New York University

Jessica Ellen Sewell, Boston University

Amrita Shah, freelance journalist and scholar

John Rennie Short, University of Maryland

AbdouMaliq Simone, Goldsmiths College London

Tom Slater, University of Edinburgh

Edward W. Soja, University of California Los Angeles

Rob Stone, University of British Columbia

Erik Swyngedouw, University of Manchester

Nik Theodore, University of Illinois at Chicago

John Urry, Lancaster University

Anthony Vidler, The Cooper Union

Daniel J. Walkowitz, New York University

Judith R. Walkowitz, Johns Hopkins University

Kevin Ward, Manchester University

Sophie Watson, Open University

Fulong Wu, Cardiff University

Wang Xiaoming, Shanghai University

Sharon Zukin, City University of New York

Preface

Cities are now where more than half of humanity live and urban processes affect the whole globe. The rates of growth, diversity of population, and complexity of their activities, as well as the scale of the problems (and possibilities) they pose, are breathtaking. This *Companion* seeks to capture the diversity and complexity of city life and to offer routes to understanding "the urban." The diversity is captured in the range of theoretical approaches and disciplinary perspectives that the contributors represent (including, amongst many others, geography, sociology, cultural studies, anthropology, history, and planning). With the exception of seven chapters, these are newly commissioned essays for this volume.

Since the publication of the first *Companion to the City* some of the ways of understanding the city and urban processes have changed in emphasis and new themes have emerged. We have sought to represent this with new sections on Materialities, Mobilities, and Affect. Although they have developed independently, if thought of together, materialities and mobilities further animate our understanding of cities, opening out the analysis to consider the life in what was hitherto thought of as inert (the material infrastructure of cities) and the importance of movements (of objects, or bacteria) previously considered insignificant. Affect too deals with forces and movements in the city (the emotions, affect, embodied agency) that have been overlooked in traditional urban analysis. We can see that the city is part constituted through the forces of materials, objects, microbes, and emotions – as well as humans and their projects and purposes.

Of course the more explicit and observable projects and purposes of humans are a vital part of city life and the outcomes of the cooperation and conflicts of these human activities are registered in the enduring themes of social division and difference; culture and public life; planning and politics (the other themes of this and the original *Companion*). There are also major global trends that occur across the themes. One would be the pervasiveness of the symbolic and actual power of markets across all elements of urban life, from the economic, through to the cultural, and even into the realms of welfare and support. This is of course particularly evident in the rapidly (albeit differentially) expanding metropolises of China and several chapters are concerned with various aspects of urbanization and urban growth in China. Another theme would be the increasing significance of networks. There is a continuing focus in urban studies on US and European cities and a number of chapters consider different aspects of urbanism in these countries. There are also a number of chapters that are concerned with the cities of the south, not just in terms of the analysis of the social and economic conditions of poor but rapidly growing cities, but in terms of challenging the influence of western modes of theorizing and analysis in the urban studies discipline.

Since the last *Companion to the City* a group of scholars – NYLON – in the UK and US (funded by the British Academy and New York University) met for three years to discuss urban questions from a cultural, historical, and social perspective, as these were articulated in the spaces of London and New York. Essays from most of these scholars appear here.[1]

This *New Companion to the City* has been conceived in relation to the second edition of the *Blackwell City Reader*. This latter volume comprises already published writings on the city which have been selected as representative of the oeuvre of texts on the city that we consider to have been most important and influential. The two texts in combination thus offer an overview of historical and contemporary thinking on the city. The *City Reader*, like the *New Companion*, reflects changing theoretical perspectives, as well as a shift in location of analysis away from the global north.

Note

1   Chapters by Frank Mort, Richard Sennett, Jane M. Jacobs, David Pinder, Michael Keith, Rob Stone, Gary Bridge, Sophie Watson, Harvey Molotch, Max Page, Andrew Ross, Judith Walkowitz, Daniel Walkowitz.

Acknowledgments

Putting together a *Companion* of this size of almost entirely newly commissioned chapters was a daunting, as well as an enjoyable, task. We would like to thank our contributors who made this book possible and who have been a delight to work with. We would also like to thank those who have helped make this book happen with incredible efficiency and speed, and whose work never gets to be seen: Annie Jackson, Hannah Rolls, and Ben Thatcher at Wiley-Blackwell. Without them the whole project would not have been possible.

Part I   City Materialities

The New Blackwell Companion to the City   Edited by Gary Bridge and Sophie Watson
© 2011 Blackwell Publishing Ltd

Chapter 1

Reflections on Materialities

Gary Bridge and Sophie Watson

Towards Active Urban Materialities

In the original *Companion to the City* there was a section of writings on city economies. In this new *Companion* some of those discussions are found here in Part I on
materialities, and to some extent Part II on mobilities. That is not to say that considerations of economic activity in the city are any less central than they have always
been but it is to say that ways of conceiving of economic activity and its relationships have shifted in interesting ways that open up new vistas in thinking about
what cities are and how they fit into broader economic processes across the globe.
One of the areas of discussion that have expanded over the last ten years since the
first *Companion* is to do with ideas of materials and materiality. This in itself is not
new. Marxist inspired analyses of the economy and what David Harvey called the
urban process in capitalism have been established for 40 years or more.

Historical materialism is one guiding framework that has informed the dominant
strand of urban analysis of long-term trends as well as the particularities of city life
in capitalism. Those insights were there when Marx was writing and can be seen
in his collaborator Friedrich Engels's analysis of capitalist urbanization in Manchester and London in the mid-nineteenth century. In *The Condition of the Working
Class in England in 1844* (sections of which are edited in the sister volume to this
Companion – *The Blackwell City Reader* 2nd edn) Engels identified material qualities of the city that are now the focus of sustained analysis (although in slightly
different ways). Engels went into close details of the material life of factory workers
in east Manchester – the poor quality of their dwellings, their clothes, their employer-
provided foodstuffs adulterated with non-food materials. Engels is also informed
by Marx's arguments about how materials, commodities, are imbued with the wider

The New Blackwell Companion to the City   Edited by Gary Bridge and Sophie Watson
© 2011 Blackwell Publishing Ltd

social relations of their production and the class exploitation and profit extraction from these materials. Objects as commodities are congealed forms of labor and that labor expresses the social relations of its organization and exploitation – literally materialized in the woven cotton produced in the factory but also evident in debased commodities, in the bulked-out food and the thinness of partition walls in the terraced housing in which the workers had to live. Materiality has been discussed in a number of ways that we consider in this section.

Another feature of Engels's observations that has contemporary resonance is his attention to the body. He describes in unrelenting detail the mutations to bodies that result from poor health, poor nutrition, and sub-standard accommodation. He catalogues the diseases that afflict the bodies he sees in the streets because of their miserable living conditions. And, rather more directly in terms of the processes of production that Marx was so concerned with, Engels shows how he is able to read from the distortions of body shape and limb development the particular interminably repeated task in the factory production process that the body was involved in. Objects, machines, and bodies are brought into a destructively intimate relationship.

The detailed divisions of labor that were found in the factory system describe a narrow, instrumental, tight relationship between objects and bodies. Contemporary understandings of materiality have loosened and expanded the idea of material human relationships. This suggests how objects can assemble human relationships in ways that are not just embedded and implicit (or mystified as Marx suggested) but more active and evident. There is a good deal of vitalist pragmatics here in thinking about objects acting back on humans and in suggesting a flatter relationship of significance between humans, objects, and other non-human actors. In fact much of actor–network theory or relational analysis sees objects not as solid lumpen things off which human activity can be understood but as processes themselves and co-constitutive of human/object/non-human actor relations (Latour 2005). In *Paris: Invisible City* (2006: 63, 64) Latour and Hermant see objects as keeping

> life in the big city together: objects despised under the label "urban setting," yet whose exquisite urbanity holds the key to our life in common … each of these humble objects from public toilet to rubbish bin, tree protector to street name, phone booth to illuminated signpost, has a certain idea of the Parisians to whom, through colour or form, habit or force, it brings a particular order, a distinct attribution, an authorization or prohibition, a promise or permission.

Here we have almost a sense of objects as alive and breathing in the city streets.

Chapter 6 by Matthew Gandy and Chapter 7 by Harvey Molotch capture the big stuff and small stuff of the material environment of cities. Gandy's research has been concerned with the materiality of the city and the way that big stuff such as urban infrastructure embeds social relations in its production and in its ongoingness, as it continues to assemble human and object relations in different ways. Gandy suggests how, far from being inert, urban infrastructures, in common with understandings of any landscape, bring into play complex layerings that involve experiences of space, different aesthetic sensibilities, memory, and indeed discourses and ideologies that connect powerfully to understandings of the public realm.

Figure 1.1 Sydney bridges. Photo S. Watson.

Harvey Molotch's chapter deploys similar assumptions to show how humans and materials co-produce in urban environments. They range from body and object relations such as subway turnstiles and public toilets through to the co-production of city neighborhoods, such as SoHo in Manhattan, where the occupation of former industrial lofts – large uncluttered spaces – facilitated an artistic practice involving large canvasses and art objects. These objects produced an art market in which the value of the objects raised the real estate value of the neighborhood which resulted in the displacement of the artists and the gentrification of the neighborhood (a process that Sharon Zukin noted in *Loft Living*, and which she discusses here in Chapter 49 on the retail landscape of lower Manhattan). Jane M. Jacobs and Stephen Cairns, in Chapter 8, illustrate how buildings as assemblages are held together in a continual process of building. Developing the approach from Science and Technology Studies (STS) they look at the socio-technical–material interrelations that continuously build the high rise. In the case of the Singapore residential high-rise buildings they study how this holding together involves a continuous process of maintenance and repair with inventories, purchase orders, observations, surveillance technologies – in combination with other actants such as wind, water, mould – that are working on the building in other ways.

The city can be seen as the site or arena where the continuities and co-effects of the social, the technical, and the material on each other and as an ongoing infra-structural ecology can be seen to greatest effect. This blending of the influence of actor–network theory and STS along with a revised view of the acting powers of the material raises issues of transhumanism, cyborg life, and a more distributed view of agency (between human, non-human, and technological actants). There is also the idea of performative enactments and events rather than linear causal change in terms of understanding urban processes (Amin and Thrift 2002; Latour 2005; Farias and Bender 2009). This view of urban life (in its broadest sense) powerfully and very usefully repositions the idea of the city as a supremely and exclusively human environment and achievement. At the same time it flattens the view of intentionality and rationality and power to such a degree that critical human political dilemmas and directions can be left hanging somewhat.

Neoliberalism, the Market, and the City

The focus on materiality is not just about the relationship between materials and humans but also between materials and the seemingly more dematerialized elements of the global economy. The links here were shown by a landmark study of Chicago by urban historian William Cronon (*Nature's Metropolis* (1991) – abstracted in the *Blackwell City Reader*). In fascinating detail Cronon shows how changing transport technology (boats to trains) meant that the volume of grain to be traded at the Chicago market, coupled with another technical innovation (the grain elevator), resulted in general grading of the quality of wheat the consistency of which had to be guaranteed by the newly formed Chicago Board of Trade. With these guarantees, paper contracts for quantities of different grades of wheat could be traded and, with the invention of the telegraph, this trading expanded across the US and increasingly across the globe. Furthermore paper contracts could be issued for quantities of grain "to arrive" at a certain date in the future. This gave traders opportunity to speculate on the future trajectory of grain prices. If they thought the price of grain would rise between their purchase of the paper contract and its completion they could sell the contract on later and make a profit simply on the movement of prices. Thus, the physicality of the commodity itself (in this case grain) combined with technical developments over its handling, movement, and categorization, along with technical developments in communications and institutional arrangements that supported a market for exchange over future states of the physical world (giving the price of grain in the future), created a futures market. The materiality of this process was intimately related to the more abstract and speculative trades that occurred in markets far away from the grain silos, the physical environment, and objects in which the grain was processed. But those abstract trades required physical infrastructure of communications, offices, and networks of human contacts for the market to operate. The expansion of this "market" also acted back on the urban fabric of Chicago, both in the immediate environment of the market and also in terms of Chicago's rising position in a developing urban hierarchy across the US.

The growth of markets and ever more remote and complex forms of abstraction over the trading of commodities has been one long-term trend in capitalist urbanization. The symbolic aspects of market abstraction have also become more powerful over time such that claims over market mechanisms have become hegemonic in all areas of life. The idea is that the pure competitive market model should be the preferred mechanism for the delivery not only of consumer products but also of public services through to large-scale urban infrastructures (from shopping malls to mass transit systems). This is a privileging of a certain idea of the market that has come to be known as neoliberalism (see Harvey 2005). It advocates unfettered market processes and a reduced role for governments. The underlying political message relies on the idea that markets are better at picking up on what Hayek (2007) called people's tacit knowledge, their wants and needs, than states are able to understand and plan for. The sustained critiques of neoliberalism have targeted its naivety about pure market processes that are in fact supported by governments and other institutional frameworks, in all kinds of ways. Also discussed is the overly extended idea of consumer sovereignty which is highly individualistic and ignores social needs and wider moral questions (Leitner *et al.* 2007).

Neoliberalism has impacted on cities and cities play a role in wider processes of neoliberal capitalism in a number of ways. The kind of speculative trading that Cronon showed in incipient form in the growing city of Chicago two centuries ago has expanded greatly since. This investment and speculative activity has grown as a proportion of all economic activity – the process of financialization. Financialization has grown disproportionately in certain cities that have command and control functions in the global economy. These global cities (traditionally London, New York, and Tokyo but now increasingly involving Shanghai, Mumbai, and others) are particular manifestations of neoliberal capitalism. They carry the institutional and sociological evidence of financialization – investment houses of the major banks and the producer services that support them (such as accountancy and legal services) and the highly paid professional workforces they employ. The economy of global cities themselves is increasingly bifurcated between highly paid professionals in the financial services sector and the poorly paid (often immigrant) labor forces that service the domestic, childcare, and consumption demand of the professional population: the two sides of the global city (as Saskia Sassen's research has established and as she argues in Chapter 18).

The continuities and discontinuities of global capitalism and global cities are also discussed in a comparison of London and New York in Chapter 4 by Susan Fainstein, Ian Gordon, and Michael Harloe. They trace the ups and downs of the global economy, the key roles played by these two finance capitals, and the economic outcomes for these two cities over the last 40 years. Economic bust and boom (and bust again) has accompanied a growing similarity between New York and London in terms of ever higher levels of social inequality and the clear emergence of a dual labor market, with high-earning private sector professionals at one end and an uneducated, low-paid class of workers servicing the demands of the professional class. These inequalities are likely to be even more marked as New York and London resume (banking) business as usual after the 2008 crash. However Fainstein, Gordon, and Harloe raise questions about the future limits to growth of the financial and producer services sectors as well as the continued dispersal (and regionalization) of activity away from the urban cores (regional urbanization is analyzed by Short in Chapter 3 and Soja in Chapter 59).

Aside from the particular effects on a few global cities, the effects of neoliberal economics on other layers of the urban hierarchy have been profound. First there are the distinctions between cities of the global north and south as the indebtedness of many countries of the global south and the neoliberal restructuring programs

they have been forced to adopt by the International Monetary Fund and World
Bank to meet debt requirements (under the so called Washington Consensus) provide
the context for increasingly uneven development and social inequalities.

Within cities of the global north and south there has been an increased marketization of their economies and politics. One such has been a shift of city governments
from a primary focus on social redistribution and collective consumption toward
business growth models and providing favorable financial environments for private
capital investment – what David Harvey noted some time ago as a shift from urban
managerialism to entrepreneurialism (Harvey 1989). This has extended into incentives to private companies to invest in elements of the public realm (such as the
public–private partnerships between central or local government and private firms
to fund infrastructure projects, for example, the expansion and renovation to the
London Underground system). This is a form of privatization which has been more
widely discussed in the urban context in terms of the privatization of public space
(Sorkin 1992; Mitchell 2003; and see Chapter 40 by Lily Kong and Chapter 41 by
Setha Low). The construction of shopping malls with private security forces has
meant the replacement of the more open and unpredictable space of the street. In
a growing number of cities urban redevelopment schemes for shopping and leisure
space have meant that new streets have been built but these are owned by private
developers rather than the municipal government: wholly privatized urban fabrics.

The influence of the market has been extended by these privatization processes
but it has also impacted on public spending and public services through the adoption of market mechanisms in these spheres, in the form of quasi markets in health
and environmental and social services. There have been moves away from municipal
governments being direct providers of services towards a purchaser (the municipality) and provider (a range of public, private, and voluntary sector agency) competing
for contracts to provide the service in a more post-Fordist regime of welfare. This
has impacted on city services (such as meals services to the elderly, garbage collection, and utilities being provided by contractees whose primary motive is profit
driven). These principles have even extended into the welfare sphere, for example,
with the spread of workfare schemes. These are symptomatic of a governance regime
in which market imperatives and market "disciplines" are pre-eminent in all areas
of life. In Chapter 2, Nik Theodore, Jamie Peck, and Neil Brenner identify and
analyze all these trends and their impacts on cities but also argue that there is a
form of neoliberal urbanization itself in which cities, their land ownership patterns,
built form, labor markets, and service provision often form the testing ground for
neoliberal experiments in all these spheres. They also encapsulate many of the divisions and social inequalities that result from unregulated markets.

Some of the divisions that come with the rise and decline of markets are captured
in the chapters by Xiaoming (Chapter 12), Forrest (Chapter 13), and Shah (Chapter
5). Wang Xiaoming analyzes the emergence of a real-estate market in Chinese cities,
one effect of which has been the loss of public space (albeit spaces that were also
controlled politically). Xiaoming traces the commodification of the city, through the
development of the real-estate market, the growth of the amount of space for car
use, and the negative impacts of car pollution on meeting-places in the city that had
existed previously, through to the growing separation and specialization of land use
via property submarkets and the growing dominance of residential space. He also

indicates the wider symbolic aspects of this process as the city itself becomes the subject of imagineering as billboards sprout up across the city selling images of the "ideal" house and the wider lifestyle and wider urban environment.

Ray Forrest's chapter provides some of the context and detail of the effects of the change from state to market in housing in Shanghai. He looks at inter-generational relationships and family strategies in coping with the changing incentives that come with the emergence of a market for housing. Forrest's chapter captures how global processes and economic change impact on family relations but also how family strategies can provide a coping strategy in an uncertain world. The effects of changes in the global economy and how they are registered on a city's geography and the everyday lives of its residents are captured in Amrita Shah's chapter on Ahmedabad in India. The decline of the cotton industry and the rise of the finance and service sector are accompanied by the effects on the built form and social geography in terms of de-industrialization and gentrification but also witnessed in the interweaving of myths and money in the cultural politics of the city.

Growing social divisions, neoliberal capitalism and urban landscapes come together in a particular way for Stephen Graham in his analysis of what he calls military urbanism. Graham's Chapter 11 suggests how control and surveillance technologies used in military combat can be used in cities to regulate populations, often within a discourse of the politics of security. Markets for military equipment meet forms of urban governance. He draws on the work of Giorgio Agamben (2005) and the states of exception where normal legalities do not hold as a testing ground for types of control and intervention. This results in the city being more and more like a military camp in terms of its direction of populations and treatment of social conflicts. On the other hand, Graham notes how urban infrastructures themselves are increasingly the target of military offensives in war in strategies of demodernization through the destruction of infrastructure and the creation of public health crises.

Urban Materialities of Nature

All the themes of materiality, neoliberalism, and globalization are brought together over concerns about nature and the environment, especially the issue of global warming. As Maria Kaika and Erik Swyngedouw usefully point out (Chapter 9), discussions of nature and the future of the environment have grown rapidly in the ten years since the publication of the first *Companion to the City* where their chapter was the only one to deal explicitly with environment/nature, a topic that is now widely distributed in several chapters across the *New Companion*. For many researchers, especially those coming from a neo-Marxist perspective, it is the logic of the working of capitalism itself that is inevitably leading to environmental catastrophe. The focus here is on the materiality of capitalist economic processes that seek to exploit raw materials for profit, aside from their wider environmental implications and connections. The exploitation of raw materials to produce products for consumption, and the growth of materialist culture across the world, mean that what Marx called "accumulation for accumulation's sake" (Marx 1967), without regard for the wider environment, continues apace. And that wider environment is social as well as physical. As we have seen, in his critique of the commodity form in the first chapter of *Capital*, Marx argued how the price of a commodity in market exchange hid all the social relations of the nature of its production: the congealed labor in the commodity was hidden and mystified. Those social relations, for Marx, were dominated by the exploitation of workers by capitalists and the confining of profit to the capitalist class. This results in many of the gross social inequalities that are evident in the divisions between the rich global north and the impoverished global south and also in increasing divisions within nations north and south as the competitive market model in neoliberal capitalism has been given full rein. From this perspective nature is transformed into the second nature of commodities in ways that are physically and socially unstable. Cities are not distinct or separate from nature, or somehow unnatural (Harvey 1993; Heynan *et al.* 2006). They represent processes of human transformation of the material environment, in the same way that rural agriculture and other, what might be seen as more natural, environments are transformed by human activity, including the demands of cities and their emissions. Preventing both environmental and social catastrophe requires a change of economic system to produce a more egalitarian outcome. As Kaika and Swynge-douw argue in their chapter, this is a call for "the egalitarian and democratic production of socio-ecological commons." They suggest it is thus a supreme irony that the market model itself is being promoted as the solution to the environmental crisis, through mechanisms such as carbon trading and the "polluter pays" principle. They suggest further, quoting Alain Badiou (2008), that ecology is the new opium of the masses, a way for governments and transnational corporations to impose various constraints and conformities on populations that preserve vested interests rather than change them.

There is another set of views that are technically led and accept the market model but suggest that the nature of the challenge will necessitate radical changes in industrial production, consumer lifestyles, and governance. Peter Droege's chapter reflects this approach. In Chapter 10 he argues that ending fossil fuel energy production, reversing deforestation, and significantly cutting material consumption in wealthier societies are necessary to ameliorate global warming. Droege emphasizes the implications for cities in this approach but also looks towards the possibilities of urban and regional solutions to energy production. These, he suggests, should be coupled with city-based initiatives that are within the remit of many types of municipal governments across the globe. They include initiatives on infrastructure standards to provide green infrastructure, urban land for food production and energy-autonomous buildings, repurchasing of municipal energy companies, and support to renewable energy projects through issuing bonds. Droege looks at a wide spectrum of energy saving including the operational use of energy and transport regimes but also consumable energy (energy requirements embedded in foodstuffs due to the energy used in their production).

Whether addressing global warming requires ultimately a replacement of the capitalist economy, or a series of sweeping measures within it, advocates of both approaches might agree that cities have a crucial role as the material assemblages of the transformative potential for the environment. Now that we have reached the point in human history where, for the first time, over 50 percent of the global population live in urban areas, the environmental future of the planet is increasingly an urban one. Cities are the concentrations of energy consumption and pollution. As

Figure 1.2 Rubbish trucks, Beijing. Photo S. Watson.

John Short amply illustrates in Chapter 3, the megalopolises of the US are the core regions of environmental impacts in the early twenty-first century. The megalopolis he discusses stretches over 52,000 square miles and encompasses the metropolitan regions of Boston, New York, Philadelphia, and Washington-Baltimore. It has a population of over 50 million but sprawled over a vast area and involving high energy use (in a nation that takes 25 percent of the world's energy). Nevertheless, as an alternative to this urban sprawl, higher density cities are increasingly being seen as the solution, rather than the main cause, of global warming. High-density, more compact settlements are seen as more energy efficient than the car-based, low-density, energy-sapping suburbs. A range of green technical innovations is more possible in urban environments, as Peter Droege's chapter demonstrates. Against the population control via ecological crisis arguments, one might raise the possibility that attention to energy audits and carbon footprints starts to open up new avenues of possible democratic accountability that are based on long-term goals. Energy audits reveal the inequalities that exist between cities and nations of the global north and south but also provide lessons for more sustainable cities in the future. The squatter settlements and slums that represent the greatest growth in urban built form into the future are indictments of the economic system but in their use of recycled materials and flexible form provide lessons for low-energy use in properly funded urban areas also.

Rethinking Urban Economies?

The possible reorientation of thinking that comes with the demands of sustainability might reflect how urban economies are conceived more widely. The classic model was to consider urban economies in terms of the dominant economic paradigm of neo-classical economics. The size and constitution of different cities came about as a result of the forces of agglomeration economies. The clustering of industrial production reduced supply costs, permitted specialized labor markets, and maximized potential markets. The externalities of increasing transport costs and pollution, growing labor market inflexibilities, and congestion brought diseconomies of scale that limited the size and distribution of cities. Within the city itself, land use was sorted according to the classical Bid Rent Model (see Alonso 1964) in which the ability and need to buy central city land varied between commercial, industrial, and residential users and so the price mechanisms sorted land use into different concentric zones.

The emergence of Marxist urban studies in the early 1970s onwards challenged all the assumptions of the neo-classical model. The aspects of agglomeration and labor market flexibility were interpreted as forms of accumulation of capital and exploitation of labor for which, from the Industrial Revolution onwards, cities were the centers of activity. The consequences of this we have already discussed in terms of human poverty, with Engels's observation of Manchester in the mid-nineteenth century. These conditions are reproduced across the world in cities of the south and the cities of the north that are seen as declining. This uneven development is a core element in the boom and bust nature of capitalist economic trends. Thus in cities of the north there are the global cities, with a section of the economy and urban space in forms of hyper accumulation (the financial centers such as the City of London) whereas the rest of the city around them and the rest of the national economy are much more mixed. There are cities that are successful in terms of the knowledge economy, through to former industrial cities and regions that are in prolonged decline (such as the rust belt cities of the northeastern United States). At the same time there are the rapidly emerging megacities of east Asia in economies that are growing apace but that combine elements of all stages of economic activity and social division and difference experienced by cities of the north over a much longer period. Thus the emerging megacity of the region of Hong Kong, Shenzen, Guandgzhou, Macau, and the settlements of the Pearl River delta, with a population way in excess of the 50 million of the megalopolis of the US, combines the infra-structure and the economic sectors and social enclaves to form a kaleidoscope of medieval and modern production systems, subsistence economies alongside world leading electronics and communications manufacture. There are the rapidly growing cities of sub-Saharan Africa where financial infrastructures are fragile and cities and nations are locked in a world economy through indebtedness and unequal trade based on prior colonial relationships and ongoing global forms of capital exploitation of raw materials and crops.

The global implications of these different economic timings and trajectories seem very evident in the question of the future of the environment. The nations of the global north, which have had a prolonged period of economic growth and development and have been the biggest energy users, are looking for cuts in activity and energy use from some nations of the global south that are going through more rapid economic growth in the present era. Discussions and disagreements occur at various climate summits over the degree to which the global north should help finance technologies to reduce carbon emissions in the global south and the economic and lifestyle measures required to cut emissions in the north. It can be argued that, as well as compensating for different histories of development as traditionally understood, a reconceptualization of the idea of development and economics is emerging. This includes discussions of no growth and negative energy impacts in the more market-oriented ideas, through to neo-Marxist analysis of what Swyngedouw and Kaika (2000) have called the production of the more equitable socioeconomic commons. This connects to arguments that the whole idea of economic and urban development has been dominated by western ideas and discourses. The importance of postcolonial analysis in urban studies has been understood for some time (see King 2003). Jenny Robinson has very usefully addressed the need for a postcolonial, alternative understanding of cities and development (Robinson 2005). She argues that urban analysis has looked too narrowly at certain forms of economic activity (finance, the knowledge economy, and creative industries) that skews the view urban economics has towards global cities, globalization, and the space of flows between globally connected cities. This has meant that certain sorts of cities and parts of those cities have received disproportionate analyses. Robinson calls for a reorientation towards the whole city and the ordinary, rather than extraordinary or global city. From the perspective and experience of cities of the south, the ordinary city contains a diversity of forms of economic activity (previously labeled formal and informal); a whole range of economic actors and institutions and ways of cooperating as well as competing. All of these hold profound lessons for what constitutes economic activity and significantly (in terms of global environmental issues) different models of how human life might be sustainable. Urbanists, as much as anyone, should look at the various forms of economic activity in a range of institutional settings and forms (including what has been called the social economy) in the ordinary cities of the global north and south.

Recent writing and research on the urban economies has suggested how market fundamentalism worked to control and order the wider social and cultural forces shaping cities. But, as we see in the other sections of this *Companion*, these social and cultural forces continue to open out new spaces and mobilities of engagement. Furthermore, we would suggest that this way of looking at the materiality of the city raises new questions about the relationship between democracy and the economic. New understandings of materiality suggest how the material environment (such as an urban infrastructure) can assemble human and non-human relations in ways that can open up new spaces for the public. The analysis of neoliberalism that has revealed the overly narrow idea of the market and the over-reliance on and idea of "pure" market activity (such as socially useless derivatives trading) unfettered by government activity or wider democratic norms, is more widely acknowledged and understood in the second decade of the twenty-first century than it was in the first. The challenge of global warming leads to an idea of nature that does not, and must not, sit outside the realm of democratic accountability and decision, and cities are the key arena for its political realization.

References

Agamben, G. (2005) *State of Exception*. Chicago: Chicago University Press.

Alonso, W. (1964) *Location and Land Use: Toward a General Theory of Land Use*. Cambridge, MA: MIT Press.

Amin, A., and Thrift, N. (2002) *Cities: Re-Imagining the Urban*. Cambridge: Polity Press.

Badiou, A. (2008) Live Badiou – Interview with Alain Badiou, Paris, December 2007. In *Alain Badiou – Live Theory*, ed. O. Feltham. London: Continuum, 136–9.

Cronon, W. (1991) *Nature's Metropolis: Chicago and the Great West*. New York: Norton.

Engels, F. (1987) [1844] *The Condition of the Working Class in England*. Harmondsworth: Penguin.

Farias, I., and Bender, T. (eds.) (2009) *Urban Assemblages: How Actor Network Theory Changes Urban Studies*. London: Routledge.

Harvey, D. (1989) From managerialism to entrepreneurialism: the transformation in urban governance in late capitalism. *Geografiska Annaler B* 71: 3–17.

Harvey, D. (1993) The nature of environment: dialectics of social and environmental change. In *Real Problems, False Solutions*, ed. R. Miliband and L. Panitch. A special issue of the *Socialist Register*. London: The Merlin Press, 1–51.

Harvey, D. (2005) *A Brief History of Neoliberalism*, Oxford: Oxford University Press.

Hayek, F. (2007) *The Road to Serfdom: Texts and Documents*. Chicago: University of Chicago Press.

Heynan, N., Kaika, M., and Swyngedouw, E. (eds.) (2006) *In the Nature of Cities: Urban Political Ecology and the Politics of Urban Metabolism*. London: Routledge.

King, A. (2003) *Postcolonial Urbanism*. London: Routledge.

Latour, B. (2005) *Reassembling the Social: An Introduction to Actor–Network Theory*. Oxford: Oxford University Press.

Latour, B., and Hermant, E. (2006) *Paris: Invisible City*. Trans. Liz Carey-Libbrecht. Available online at www.bruno-latour.fr/livres/viii_paris-city-gb.pdf (accessed October 18, 2010). Originally published in French in 1998, *Paris: ville invisible*. Paris: La Découverte-Les Empêcheurs de penser en rond.

Leitner, H., Peck, J., and Sheppard, E. (eds.) (2007) *Contesting Neoliberalism: Urban Frontiers*. New York: Guilford Press.

Marx, K. (1967) *Capital* (3 vols). New York: International Publishers.

Mitchell, D. (2003) *The Right to the City: Social Justice and the Fight for Public Space*. New York: The Guilford Press.

Robinson, J. (2005) *Ordinary Cities*. London: Routledge.

Sorkin, M. (1992) *Variations on a Theme Park: The New American City and the End of Public Space*. New York: Hill and Wang.

Swyngedouw, E., and Kaika, M. (2000) The environment of the city or the urbanisation of nature. In *The Companion to the City*, ed. G. Bridge and S. Watson. Oxford: Blackwell, 567–80.

Chapter 2

Neoliberal Urbanism: Cities and the Rule of Markets

Nik Theodore, Jamie Peck, and Neil Brenner

Market Rules

Neoliberal ideology rests on the belief that open, competitive, and "unregulated" markets, liberated from state interference and the actions of social collectivities, represent the optimal mechanism for socioeconomic development. Neoliberalism first gained prominence during the late 1970s as a strategic political response to the declining profitability of mass production industries and the crisis of Keynesian welfarism. In response to the breakdown of accumulation regimes and established systems of governance, national and local states throughout the older industrialized world began, if hesitantly at first, to dismantle the institutional foundations of the post-war settlement and to mobilize a range of policies intended to extend the reach of market discipline, competition, and commodification. In this context, neoliberal doctrines were deployed to justify, *inter alia*, the deregulation of state control over industry, assaults on organized labor, the reduction of corporate taxes, the privatization of public services and assets, the dismantling of social assistance programs, the enhancement of international capital mobility, and the intensification of interlocality competition. During the 1980s, neoliberalism was established as the dominant political and ideological form of capitalist globalization.

This, it must be stressed, is a dynamic order, one associated with mutating strategies of market rule. The neoliberal regime has proved to be remarkably adaptable in the face of institutional obstacles, deep-seated contradictions, and even profoundly challenging conjunctural events, such as the Asian financial crisis of 1997 and the global financial crisis of 2008–9. Reports of the death of neoliberalism have been issued on these and other occasions, only subsequently to be called into question in the face of some kind of resuscitation, reconstruction or rebirth (Peck

The New Blackwell Companion to the City Edited by Gary Bridge and Sophie Watson
© 2011 Blackwell Publishing Ltd

et al. 2010). This does not mean that neoliberalism is invincible, of course, but it does mean that the circumstances of its dynamic evolution and stubborn embeddedness warrant serious scrutiny, not least with reference to processes of urban development.

While neoliberalism is often equated with global pressures and imperatives, it always has been a multiscalar phenomenon: it reconstitutes scaled relationships between institutional and economic actors, such as local states and financialized capital; and it leads to the substitution of competitive for redistributive logics, while downloading risks and responsibilities to local actors and jurisdictions. This chapter considers one facet of these changing interscalar relationships – the connections between neoliberalization and urban transformation. We begin by presenting the methodological foundations for an approach to the geographies of what we term "actually existing neoliberalism." In contrast to neoliberal ideology itself, in which market forces are assumed to operate according to immutable laws no matter where they are unleashed, we emphasize the contextual *embeddedness* of neoliberal restructuring projects, insofar as they have been produced within distinctive national, regional, and local contexts defined by the legacies of inherited institutional frameworks, policy regimes, regulatory practices, and political struggles. These considerations lead to a conceptualization of contemporary neoliberalization processes as catalysts and expressions of an ongoing creative destruction of political-economic space at multiple geographical scales.

Although the neoliberal restructuring projects of the last three decades have failed to produce a coherent basis for sustainable capitalist growth, they have nonetheless profoundly reworked the institutional infrastructure and regulatory norms upon which Fordist-Keynesian capitalism was grounded. The concept of creative destruction is presented to describe the geographically uneven, socially regressive, and politically volatile trajectories of institutional/spatial change that have been crystallizing under these conditions. Accordingly, this chapter concludes by discussing the role of urban spaces within the contradictory and chronically unstable geographies of actually existing neoliberalism. Across the advanced capitalist world, cities have become strategic sites in the uneven advance of, and resistance to, neoliberal restructuring projects. Cities define some of the spaces within which neoliberalism takes root, as a geographically variable yet translocally interconnected project. But just as importantly, the urban realm is also a site of serial policy failure and sporadic resistance, and in this respect thus also highlights some of the potential limits and contradictions of the neoliberal project.

"Actually Existing Neoliberalism"

Neoliberal ideology rests upon a starkly utopian vision of market rule, rooted in an idealized conception of competitive individualism and a deep antipathy to sources of social solidarity. Yet there are serious disjunctures between this *ideology* of neoliberalism and its everyday political operations and societal effects (Harvey 2005). While neoliberalism aspires to create a utopia of free markets, liberated from all forms of state interference, it has in practice entailed a dramatic intensification of coercive, disciplinary forms of state intervention in order to *impose* versions of market rule and, thereafter, to manage the consequences and contradictions of marketization. Furthermore, whereas neoliberal ideology implies that self-regulating markets will generate an optimal allocation of investments and resources, neoliberal political practice has generated pervasive market failures, new forms of social polarization and economic insecurity, a dramatic intensification of uneven development, and recurrent crises within established forms of state regulation and governance (Brenner and Theodore 2002).

Crucially, the manifold disjunctures that have accompanied the transnational extension of neoliberalism – between ideology and practice, doctrine and reality, vision and consequence – are not merely accidental side-effects of this disciplinary project; rather, they are among its most diagnostically and politically salient features. For this reason, an essentialized and purely definitional approach to the political economy of neoliberal restructuring contains significant analytical limitations. We are dealing here less with a coherently bounded "ism," system, or end-state, than with an uneven, contradictory, and ongoing process of *neoliberalization* (Peck and Tickell 2002). Hence, in the present context, the somewhat elusive phenomenon that needs definition must be construed as an historically specific, fungible, and unstable process of market-driven sociospatial transformation, rather than as a fully actualized policy regime, ideological apparatus, or regulatory framework. Neoliberalization, in this sense, refers to the *prevailing pattern* of regulatory restructuring, one that is being realized across an uneven institutional landscape and in the context of coevolving political-economic processes. From this perspective, an adequate understanding of contemporary neoliberalization processes requires not only a grasp of their politico-ideological foundations but also a systematic inquiry into their multifarious institutional forms, their developmental tendencies, their diverse sociopolitical effects, and their multiple contradictions. While the ideology of neoliberalism rests on a deference to a singular, ahistorical, and uniquely efficient market, the infinitely more murky reality is that actually existing programs of neoliberalization are always contextually embedded and politically mediated, for all their generic features, family resemblances, and structural interconnections. Analyses of neoliberalization therefore confront this *necessary hybridity*, since it is not only difficult, but perhaps analytically and politically inappropriate, to visualize neoliberalism in ideal-typical terms, characterized by incipient or extant systemicity.

Moreover, rather than standing alone, neoliberalism tends to exist in a kind of parasitical relation to other state and social forms (neoconservatism, authoritarianism, social democracy, etc.), in the hybrid contexts of which the form and consequences of its associated restructuring strategies are shaped (Peck 2004). Just as the notion of a free-standing, self-regulating market has been exposed as a dangerously productive myth (Polanyi 1944), so too it is important to recognize that neoliberalism's evocation of a spontaneous market order is a strong discourse, rather than a rough approximation of the reality of neoliberal statecraft (Bourdieu 1998). Actually existing neoliberalisms, like actually existing markets, are inescapably embedded and context-contingent phenomena – even as their advocates' discursive representations routinely seek to deny this.

It follows that neither deep forms of neoliberalization, nor the tendential hegemony of neoliberalism at the global scale, necessitate simple convergence in regulatory forms and institutional structures. Instead, neoliberalization is both predicated on and realized through uneven development – its "natural state" is characterized by an unevenly developed and persistently unstable topography. Convergence on a unified and monolithic neoliberal end-state should not be anticipated, let alone held up as some kind of test of the degree of neoliberal transformation. Likewise, the long-run sustainability of any given neoliberal policy project (such as trade liberalization or welfare reform) is not required for there to be a neoliberalization of policy regimes; neoliberalization operates through trial-and-error experimentation, more often than not under conditions of crisis. Hence, the critical signifiers of deep neoliberalization will include: the growing influence of neoliberal structures, discourses, routines, and impulses within state formations; the intensification of regulatory restructuring efforts within neoliberal parameters; and the mutual inter-penetration and increased complementarity of neoliberal reforms.

In this context, the concept of actually existing neoliberalism underscores the ways in which neoliberal ideology systematically (mis)represents the real effects of such policies upon the macroinstitutional structures and evolutionary trajectories of capitalism. In this context, two issues deserve particular attention. First, neoliberal doctrine represents states and markets as if they are diametrically opposed principles of social and economic organization, rather than recognizing the politically constructed character of all economic relations. Second, neoliberal doctrine is premised upon a one-size-fits-all model of policy implementation which assumes that identical results will follow the imposition of market-oriented reforms, rather than recognizing the extraordinary variations that arise as neoliberal reform initiatives are imposed within contextually specific institutional landscapes and policy environments. Neoliberalism, in these respects, both exploits and produces socio-spatial difference. Uneven development does not signal some transitory stage, or interruption, on the path to "full" neoliberalization; it represents a co-evolving and co-dependent facet of the neoliberalization process itself.

The impacts of neoliberal restructuring strategies cannot be adequately understood through abstract or decontextualized debates regarding the relative merits of market-based reform initiatives, or the purported limits of particular forms of state policy. Rather, an understanding of actually existing neoliberalism requires an exploration of: first, the historically specific regulatory landscapes and political settlements that prevailed within particular territories during the Fordist-Keynesian period; second, the historically specific patterns of crisis formation, uneven development, and political contestation that emerged within those territories following the systemic crisis of the Fordist-Keynesian developmental model; third, the subsequent interaction of market-oriented neoliberal initiatives with inherited regulatory frameworks and patterns of territorial development; and fourth, the concomitant evolution of neoliberal policy agendas through their conflictual interaction with contextually specific political-economic conditions, regulatory arrangements, and "power-geometries."

Path-Dependent Neoliberalization

The notion of actually existing neoliberalism is intended to illuminate the complex, contested ways in which neoliberal restructuring strategies *interact* with pre-existing uses of space, institutional configurations, and constellations of sociopolitical power. Neoliberal programs of capitalist restructuring are never imposed in a pure form, on *tabulae rasae*, for they are always introduced within politico-institutional contexts that have been molded by inherited regulatory arrangements, institutionalized practices, and political compromises. It follows that there are always deep path-dependencies, as established institutional arrangements significantly shape the terrain, the terms, and the trajectory of market reform. In this context, pre- or non-neoliberal institutions should not be seen simply as anachronistic institutional residues; in their interpenetration with neoliberal forms of restructuring they will shape pathways and outcomes in ways that are distinctive, generative, and contradictory. It follows that each hybrid form of neoliberalization – each actually existing neoliberal formation – can be expected to be associated with its own emergent properties. Varieties of neoliberalism, then, are more than contingently variable; they represent distinctive yet interconnected conjunctural formations. This calls for situated analyses of specific hybrid formations *in connection*, not spurious assessments of degrees of divergence from a putative American norm, or naïve exercises in the cataloging of types of neoliberalism (Peck and Theodore 2007).

Neoliberal policy agendas have themselves been transformed through their interaction with inherited institutional landscapes and power configurations during the last three decades. Neoliberalism has evolved from a relatively abstract economic doctrine (its emergent form in the 1970s) and a means of dismantling Keynesian-welfarist arrangements (its prevailing form in the 1980s) into, most recently, a reconstituted form of market-guided regulation, intended not only to animate surges of financialized economic growth but also to manage some of the deep sociopolitical contradictions induced by earlier rounds of neoliberal policy intervention. Again, this is a strongly path-dependent trajectory: while first deployed as a strategic response to the crisis of an earlier political-economic framework (Fordist-Keynesian capitalism), neoliberal policies were subsequently modified qualitatively to confront any number of governance failures, crisis tendencies, and contradictions, some of which were endogenous to neoliberalism as a politico-regulatory project itself, and some of which followed from context-specific regulatory dilemmas confronting particular hybrid formations. The transition from the orthodox, radically anti-statist neoliberalisms of Reagan and Thatcher in the 1980s to the more socially moderate and ameliorative neoliberalisms of Blair, Clinton, and Schröder during the 1990s may therefore be understood as a path-dependent adjustment and reconstitution of neoliberal strategies in response to endogenous disruptions and dysfunctions. Even if, in an abstract sense, the broad contours of neoliberal projects exhibit a series of distinctive (or defining) features – such as an orientation to export-oriented, financialized capital, a preference for nonbureaucratic modes of regulation, an antipathy towards sociospatial redistribution, a structural inclination toward market-like governance systems or private monopolies – the actually existing neoliberalisms of today are markedly different from their early 1980s predecessors. Correspondingly, the stakes, sites, structures, and subjects of contemporary neoliberalization can be expected to be *meaningfully* different in, for example, Berlin, Johannesburg, and Chicago. These local neoliberalizations were each rooted in distinctive crises of, and reactions to, their respective, extant institutional orders, and they each signify unique conjunctural trajectories.

Creatively Destructive Neoliberalism

One way to grasp the path-dependent interactions between existing institutional forms and emergent neoliberal projects is to analyze actually existing neoliberalism with reference to two dialectically intertwined but analytically distinct moments – first, the (partial) destruction of extant institutional arrangements and political compromises through market-oriented reform initiatives; and second, the (tendential) creation of a new infrastructure for market-oriented economic growth, commodification, and capital-centric rule. Concrete programs of neoliberal restructuring tend to combine the rollback of alien institutional forms, through the dismantling of collectivist and progressively redistributionist systems and the contradictory deregulation of economies, along with the rollout of new modes of institutional regulation and new forms of statecraft (Peck and Tickell 2002). In this sense, neoliberalism should not be visualized as a coherent successor to Keynesian-welfarism in Fordist economies (or, for that matter, as a successor to developmentalist states in the global south) since, in practice, programs of neoliberal restructuring are substantially absorbed with, first, the long-running and always incomplete task of dismantling inherited institutional forms, and second, the challenge of managing the attendant economic consequences and social fallout. In contrast to the pristine discourses of competition and liberty that frame and legitimate neoliberal strategies, these forms of institutional reaction are not only more prosaic, they necessarily also entangle each and every neoliberal restructuring strategy with an enduring set of institutional legacies and coevolving conditions.

This is not just to make the point that neoliberal strategies echo domestic politics, that they are path dependent in some merely contingent manner, but rather to advance the stronger claim that neoliberal strategies are deeply and indelibly shaped by diverse acts of institutional dissolution – that the rollback dimension of neoliberalism, more than simply being a brush-clearing phase, is integral to its origins, dynamics, and logics. All actually existing neoliberalisms strongly bear the imprint of past regulatory struggles, which recursively shape political capacities and orientations and future pathways of neoliberal restructuring. And no single path or model should be considered paradigmatic (from which deviations can be measured), since actually existing neoliberalisms are conjuncturally specific and mutually (or relationally) constituted. Conceptually, this speaks to the nature of neoliberalization as an open-ended *process*, rather than a phase; politically, it underlines its character as a set of intersecting *strategies of restructuring*, rather than a stable and free-standing system.

Neoliberal Urbanization

The dynamic of creative destruction never occurs on a blank slate in which the "old order" is abruptly obliterated and the "new order" is unfurled as a fully formed totality. It occurs, rather, across a contested institutional landscape in which newly emergent "projected spaces" interact continually and conflictually with inherited regulatory arrangements, leading in turn to new, unforeseen, and often highly unstable layerings of political-economic space (Lipietz 1994). These recombinant amalgamations of inherited and emergent institutional arrangements also redefine the political arenas and stakes in and through which subsequent struggles over the regulation of accumulation, and its associated contradictions, will be articulated and fought out.

Clearly, the processes of creative destruction outlined above have been unfolding at a range of geographical scales and in a variety of institutional sites since the geoeconomic crises of the early 1970s. We argue, however, that *cities* have become strategically important arenas for neoliberal forms of creative destruction, as well as for resistance movements of various kinds. The central place of cities in Fordist-Keynesian systems of production and reproduction defines them as key arenas (if not targets) for neoliberal rollback strategies, while their strategic significance as loci for innovation and growth, and as zones of devolved governance and local institutional experimentation, likewise positions cities at the forefront of the neoliberal rollout. This is not to claim that the urban realm has achieved some form of scalar primacy in these neoliberal times, but it is to argue that cities have become critical nodes, and points of tension, in the scalar politics of neoliberalization. Table 2.1 illustrates some of the many politico-institutional mechanisms through which neoliberal projects have been promoted in North American and western European cities during the past two decades, distinguishing in stylized form their constituent destructive and creative moments.

Urban spaces have played strategically significant roles in successive waves of neoliberalization. During the initial ascendancy neoliberalism, cities became flashpoints both for major economic dislocations and for sociopolitical struggle, particularly in the sphere of social reproduction. They were also amongst the principal battlegrounds for struggles over the form and trajectory of economic restructuring during the protracted crisis of the Fordist-Keynesian growth regime. However, during the 1980s, when the rollback face of neoliberalism was often the dominant one, prevailing forms of urban policy shifted significantly. The subsequent consolidation of various forms of rollout neoliberalism since the early 1990s may be viewed as an evolutionary reconstitution of the neoliberal project in response to its own immanent contradictions and crisis-tendencies. On the one hand, the basic neoliberal imperative of mobilizing economic space as an arena for capitalist growth, commodification, and market discipline has remained the dominant political project for municipal governments. Indeed, state institutions have been drawn into ever more explicit forms of creative destruction of urban built environments (Weber 2002). On the other hand, the conditions for promoting and maintaining economic competitiveness have been reconceptualized by many elites to include diverse administrative, social, and ecological criteria. The institutionally destructive neoliberalisms of the 1980s have thus been unevenly superseded by new forms of neoliberal urbanization that actively address the challenges of establishing non-market forms of coordination through which to sustain market shares, competitive assets, and continued accumulation. Under these circumstances, neoliberal forms of institutional creation are no longer oriented simply towards the promotion of market-driven capitalist growth, but also towards the establishment of new flanking mechanisms and modes of crisis displacement, in order to insulate powerful economic actors from endemic failures in markets and governance regimes.

It follows that the creative destruction of institutional space at the urban scale does not take the form of a linear transition from a generic model of the "welfare

Table 2.1 Destructive and creative moments of neoliberal urbanization

Mechanisms of neoliberal urbanization	Moment of "destruction"	Moment of "creation"
Recalibration of intergovernmental relations	Dismantling of redistributive systems of central government support for municipal activities	Devolution of tasks and responsibilities to municipalities Creation of new incentive structures to reward local entrepreneurialism and to catalyze endogenous growth
Retrenchment of public finance	Imposition of fiscal austerity measures upon municipal governments	Creation of new revenue collection districts and increased reliance on local revenues, user fees, and other instruments of private finance
Restructuring the welfare state	Local relays of national welfare service provision are retrenched; assault on managerial-welfarist local state apparatuses	Expansion of community-based sectors and private approaches to social service provision Imposition of mandatory work requirements on welfare recipients; new (local) forms of workfare experimentation
Reconfiguring the institutional infrastructure of the local state	Dismantling of bureaucratized, hierarchical forms of local public administration Assault on traditional relays of local democratic accountability	"Rolling forward" of new networked forms of local governance based upon public–private partnerships and the "new public management" Incorporation of elite business interests in local development
Privatization of the local public sector and collective infrastructures	Elimination of public monopolies for the provision of municipal services (e.g. utilities, sanitation, mass transit)	Privatization of municipal services Creation of new markets for service delivery and infrastructure maintenance
Restructuring urban housing markets	Razing public housing and other low-rent accommodation Elimination of rent controls and project-based construction subsidies	Creation of new opportunities for speculative investment in central-city real estate markets Introduction of market rents and tenant-based vouchers in low-rent niches of urban housing markets
Reworking labor market regulation	Dismantling of traditional, publicly funded education, skills training, and apprenticeship programs for disadvantaged workers	Creation of a new regulatory environments to encourage contingent employment Implementation of work-readiness programs aimed at the conscription of workers into low-wage jobs Expansion of informal economies

Restructuring strategies of territorial development	Winding down of compensatory regional policies Increasing exposure of local and regional economies to global competitive forces Fragmentation of national space-economies into discrete regional systems	Creation of free trade zones, enterprise zones, and other "deregulated" spaces within urban regions Creation of new development areas, technopoles, and other "new industrial spaces" Mobilization of new "glocal" strategies intended to redirect economic capacities and infrastructure investments into "globally connected" agglomerations
Transformations of the built environment and urban form	Elimination and/or intensified surveillance of public spaces Destruction of working-class neighborhoods to make way for speculative redevelopment Retreat from community-oriented planning initiatives	Creation of privatized spaces of elite consumption Construction of mega-projects to attract corporate investment and reconfigure local land-use patterns Creation of gated communities, urban enclaves and other "purified" spaces of social reproduction "Rolling forward" of the gentrification frontier and the intensification of sociospatial polarization Adherence to the principle of "highest and best use" as the basis for major land use planning decisions
Inter-urban policy transfer	Erosion of contextually sensitive approaches to local policy-making Marginalization of "home-grown" solutions to localized market and governance failures	Diffusion of generic, prototypical approaches to "modernizing" reform among policy-makers in search of "quick fixes" for local social problems (e.g., workfare programs, zero-tolerance crime policies) Imposition of decontextualized "best practice" models derived from extrajurisdictional contexts
Reregulation of urban civil society	Destruction of the "liberal city" in which all inhabitants are entitled to basic civil liberties, social services, and political rights	Mobilization of "broken windows" policing Introduction of new discriminatory forms of surveillance and social control Introduction of policies to combat social "exclusion" by reinserting individuals into the low-wage labor market
Re-representing the city	Performative discourses of urban disorder, "dangerous classes," and economic decline	"Entrepreneurial" discourses and representations focused on urban revitalization, reinvestment, and rejuvenation. Celebration of self-actualizing "creative" growth

city" towards a new model of the "neoliberal city." Rather, these multifaceted processes of local institutional transformation entail a contested, trial-and-error searching process, in which an ascendant repertoire of experimental strategies is being
mobilized in place-specific forms and combinations (Brenner 2004). However, even
in their mature form, these strategies of localization often exacerbate the regulatory
problems they ostensibly seek to resolve – such as economic stagnation and under-
employment – leading in turn to further rounds of unpredictable mutation. Consequently, the manifold forms and pathways of neoliberal urbanization should be seen
not as coherent, sustainable solutions to the regulatory dilemmas and contradictions
of contemporary capitalism, but rather as deeply contradictory restructuring strategies that are destabilizing inherited modes of urban governance. The institutional
landscape of neoliberal urbanism is consequently a churning, dynamic one, the
continued turbulence of which is reflective of neoliberalism's *contradictory creativity*
– its capacity to repeatedly respond to endemic failures of policy design and implementation through a range of crisis-displacing strategies, fast policy adjustments,
and experimental reforms. The landscape of neoliberalization – its topographical
"surface" – is therefore both perpetually uneven and unstable.

Perhaps most crucially here, the urban scale is that at which the buck stops.
Unfunded mandates, the downloading of regulatory risks and fiscal discipline, and
a wide range of unmet needs resulting from the retrenchment of social-state and
redistributive systems, all have cumulatively negative consequences for cities, leading
to a widening chasm between devolved responsibilities on the one hand and diminished urban capacities on the other. This breeds a persistent state of competitive
anxiety amongst cities, coupled with the ever more desperate pursuit of investment
opportunities and (putative) development panaceas. New rounds of symbolic policy-making have ensued, many of which simultaneously reproduce and obfuscate
these underlying conditions of competitive vulnerability and fiscal-institutional incapacity, one example of which are the fig-leaf mantras of the "creative city." This
adds up to a slow-motion urban crisis, but one that has been (re)exposed in the
downstream consequences of the global economic downturn of 2008–9. The profitability of the financial sector may have been restored and economists may have
called a technical end to many national recessions, but amongst the many "lagging
indicators" one can anticipate an extended period of un(der)employment, social-
state retrenchment, and downward fiscal load transfers – with negative consequences for (most) cities. Irrespective of whether individual cities "choose" neoliberal
administrations, they will nevertheless be confronted by a deeply neoliberalized
operating environment.

Conclusion: From Neoliberalized Cities to Neoliberal Urbanism?

We live in an age in which both urban "problems" and urban strategies are framed
in neoliberal terms. But the logic of neoliberalism is not static. Cities have become
increasingly central to the reproduction, transmutation, and continual reconstitution of neoliberalism during the last three decades. Indeed, we contend that a
marked *urbanization of neoliberalism* has occurred, as cities have become strategic
targets and proving grounds for an increasingly broad range of neoliberal policy
experiments, institutional innovations, and political projects. Under these condi-

tions, cities have become the incubators for, and generative nodes within, the reproduction of neoliberalism as a living institutional regime.

It remains to be seen whether the powerful contradictions inherent within
the current urbanized formation of rollout neoliberalism will provide openings for
more progressive, radical-democratic reappropriations of city space, or whether, by
contrast, neoliberal agendas will be entrenched still further within the underlying
institutional structures of urban governance. However, it is worth recalling that just
as neoliberalism exploited, and drew energy from, the crises of the Keynesian
welfare state, so too might deepening crises within and around the neoliberal
project itself open up new strategic opportunities for both reformist and counter-
hegemonic movements. The 2008–9 economic crisis might prove to be such a
moment, exposing as it did the fundamental instability of neoliberalized regimes
of accumulation in the core zones of the world economy. There is nothing pre-
ordained about sites or fields of contestation against market rule, of course, but it
seems certain that the urban terrain will continue to be a decisive battleground.
Local struggles around affordable housing, living wages, and environmental justice
each in their different ways, for instance, expose pointedly relevant, progressive
alternatives to neoliberalism. Rolling back neoliberalism, however, will also entail
a pervasive reregulation of the city itself, in the form of measures to tackle the cor-
rosive effects of interurban competition and regressive redistribution. Beyond local
victories, the rules of the game must change. One of the keys to the transcendence
of neoliberalism is, therefore, the construction of new forms of urban solidarism,
between as well as within cities.

References

Bourdieu, P. (1998) *Acts of Resistance: Against the Tyranny of the Market*. New York: Free
 Press.
Brenner, N. (2004) *New State Spaces*. Oxford: Oxford University Press.
Brenner, N., and Theodore, N. (eds.) (2002) *Spaces of Neoliberalism: Urban Restructuring in
 North America and Western Europe*. London: Blackwell.
Harvey, D. (2005) *A Brief History of Neoliberalism*. Oxford: Oxford University Press.
Lipietz, A. (1994) The national and the regional: their autonomy vis-à-vis the capitalist world
 crisis. In *Transcending the State-Global Divide*, ed. R. Palan and B. Gills. Boulder, CO:
 Lynne Rienner Publishers, 23–44.
Peck, J. (2004) Geography and public policy: constructions of neoliberalism. *Progress in
 Human Geography* 28: 392–405.
Peck, J., and Theodore, N. (2007) Variegated capitalism. *Progress in Human Geography* 31:
 731–72.
Peck, J., and Tickell, A. (2002) Neoliberalizing space. *Antipode* 34: 380–404.
Peck, J., Brenner, N., and Theodore, N. (2010) Postneoliberalism and its malcontents. *Anti-
 pode* 41 (1): 94–116.
Polanyi, K. (1944) *The Great Transformation*. Boston: Beacon Press.
Weber, R. (2002) Extracting value from the city: neoliberalism and urban redevelopment.
 Antipode 34: 519–540.

Chapter 3

The Liquid City of Megalopolis

John Rennie Short

Introduction

Large city regions around the world are the principal hubs of economic and cultural globalization (Short 2004). In the US, for example, 10 megalopolitan regions, defined as clustered networks of metropolitan regions, have been identified (Table 3.1). Collectively these large city regions constitute only 19.8 percent of the nation's land surface yet comprise 67.4 percent of the population, and approximately three quarters of all predicted growth in population and construction from 2010 to 2040. The northeast area identified in this study, Megalopolis to use a term coined by Jean Gottmann (1961), is the largest of these regions in the country, responsible for 20 percent of the nation's gross domestic product.

The US Census identifies metropolitan counties that are functionally linked to a city through levels of commuting, population density, and population growth. Using the criterion of contiguous metropolitan counties I created a definition of Megalopolis that consists of 52,310 square miles stretching across 12 states, one district (District of Columbia), 124 counties, 13 metropolitan areas, and the four major metro regions of Boston, New York, Philadelphia, and Washington-Baltimore. Megalopolis spans 600 miles from north of Richmond in Virginia to just north of Portland in Maine and from the shores of the northern Atlantic to the Appalachians. Interstate 95 is its spine. As one vast conurbation that contains almost 50 million people, Megalopolis is the densest urban agglomeration in the US, one of the largest city regions in the world, and an important element of the national and global economy. This chapter is a condensed version of a larger study (Short 2007) and a more detailed analysis (Vicino *et al.* 2007), and a continuation of the theorizing provided by Hanlon *et al.* (2010). The display of data for such a large area creates

The New Blackwell Companion to the City   Edited by Gary Bridge and Sophie Watson
© 2011 Blackwell Publishing Ltd

Table 3.1　Megalopolitan regions in the US

Name	Largest metro	2000 population (million)
Southland	Los Angeles	20.96
Valley of the Sun	Phoenix	4.09
NorCal	San Francisco	11.56
Peninsula	Miami	12.83
Megalopolis	New York	49.18
Cascadia	Seattle	7.11
Gulf Coast	Houston	11.53
I-35 Corridor	Dallas	14.46
Midwest	Chicago	39.48
Piedmont	Atlanta	18.39

Source: after Lang and Dhavale 2005.

difficulties within the confines of a single text. The reader is directed to the electronic atlas of Megalopolis at http://www.umbc.edu/ges/student_projects/digital_atlas/instructions.htm where more than 60 maps of social and economic data are cartographically presented. The data display and analyses complement and contextualize the discussion presented here.

I employ the term *liquid city* to describe this urban region. Zygmunt Bauman (2005) describes the precarious life lived under conditions of constant uncertainty as "liquid life." He uses the term to refer to time and the question of identity in a rapidly changing world. I think it is appropriate to use *liquid city* with reference to the spatial incoherence of this built environment. Recent growth in Megalopolis, as in other urban regions around the world, large and small, has a liquid quality; it is constantly moving over the landscape, here in torrents, there in rivulets, elsewhere in steady drips, but always in the viscous manner of a semi-solid, semi-liquid, half-permanent, yet constantly changing phenomenon. Megalopolis, like many mega-urban regions, possesses an unstable quality that flows over political boundaries, seeps across borders, and transcends tight spatial demarcations; it is a process not a culmination, always in motion, rarely at rest, always in a state of becoming as well as being. Megalopolis is a large liquid metropolis whose boundary demarcation is always provisional, an approximation, the uncertain fixing of a constantly moving object.

Population Change in Megalopolis

In 1950 Megalopolis had a population of almost 32 million people. One in four of all US residents lived in this region. By 2000 the population had increased to over 49 million, 1 in 6 of the US population. Megalopolis is still the largest single concentration of population in the US. While there is an average of 80 people per square mile in the whole of the US, there are almost 930 people per square mile in Megalopolis.

In 1950 the population of Megalopolis was concentrated in the urban cores: over one in every two of the total population lived in the central cities. By 2000 much

Table 3.2   Areas of population loss in Megalopolis

	Population		Percent change
	1950	2000	
Baltimore	949,708	651,154	−31
Boston	801,444	589,141	−26
Philadelphia	2,071,605	1,517,550	−27
Washington, DC	802,178	572,059	−29

Source: US Census.

Table 3.3   Areas of population growth in Megalopolis

	Population		Percent change
	1950	2000	
Prince William Co., VA	22,612	280,812	1,142
Howard Co., MD	23,119	247,842	972
Fairfax Co., VA	98,557	969,749	884
Ocean Co., NJ	56,622	510,916	802
Loudoun Co.,VA	21,147	169,599	702

Source: US Census.

of the population and vitality of the region had shifted to the suburban counties. The region changed from a big city population to a much more fully suburbanized agglomeration. Two out of every three people now live in suburban counties. Table 3.2 highlights the loss in selected big cities and Table 3.3 indicates the levels of suburban county growth. It is important to note that the traditional "city–suburb divide" no longer suffices as a standard measure of comparison. Puentes and Warren (2006) identify what they call "first suburbs," defined as counties that were metropolitan counties adjacent to a metro core in 1950. These inner ring suburbs grew very quickly from 1950 to 1970, leveling off after 1990. Since the 1980s many of these suburbs have become suburbs in crisis as they lose population and experience declines in tax base and house prices (Hanlon 2009). The devalorization of these inner ring suburbs is the defining characteristic of what has been termed "suburban gothic" (Short et al. 2007).

While the 50-year data range shows decline in central city areas, since 1990 there has been a small but significant rebound in certain cities. Between 1990 and 2000 central city areas in New York such as the Bronx and Queens increased their populations by respectively 10.7 percent and 14.2 percent, representing absolute increases of 128,861 and 277,781. Boston increased its population from 562,994 in 1980 to 590,763 in 2006. New York and Boston, because of their growth in producer services and immigration flows, are experiencing a small population growth. Cities such as Philadelphia and Baltimore, with less buoyant economies, saw decline. In both cities the remaining population was proportionately more poor and black.

The racial mix of the Megalopolis population has changed. Whites have redistributed from the central cities to the suburbs. In 1960, 83.8 percent of the population of the central cities was white, but by 2000 this had declined to 42.4 percent. The whites became less urban and more of a suburban population. White flight left proportionately more blacks in the central cities and especially in the cities experiencing greatest economic difficulties. Blacks have doubled in population from 1960 to 2000 and now constitute 16.8 percent of the region's population. In 1960 blacks constituted 15.7 percent of the central city population, by 2000 this figure had increased to 27.4 percent. They have become the majority population especially in cities that have witnessed job and population loss. But there is also black suburbanization. In 1960 there were 773,160 blacks in the suburbs of Megalopolis but by 2000 this number had climbed to almost three million. Prince George's in Maryland, for example, a suburban county that borders Washington DC, has a majority black population. It is home to over half a million blacks who constitute two out of every three people in the county.

The Asian population has increased in numbers from a relatively insignificant 87,000 to over 2.3 million. Asians are found in the central cities as well as the suburbs. There are now almost six million Hispanics in Megalopolis, constituting 12 percent of the total population; three fifths are in the central cities, the remainder in the suburbs. The growth is particularly marked in the major metro areas of New York, Washington DC, and Boston. In selected cities and counties the Hispanic population has been the major driver of demographic growth.

Environmental Impacts

The US population leaves a heavy footprint on the earth. In Megalopolis there are now nearly 50 million people living at relatively low densities and consuming large amounts of energy. Compared to 1950, there are more people driving more cars to more places; more people running dishwashers, flushing toilets and using showers; more people in more and ever bigger houses. Whatever the measure used – automobile usage, water consumption, or waste generation – it is a similar story of increasing population growth in association with increased affluence and spiraling consumption producing a greater environmental footprint and increased strain on the natural systems that sustain and nurture life. As more population crams into the region, an incredible environmental transformation is wrought. Close to 50 million people, with the greatest environmental impact per head in the history of the world, now live in Megalopolis.

Economic Restructuring in Megalopolis

Over the past 50 years a major economic change has been the decline of manufacturing, the growth of services, and the growing importance of government. Manufacturing has long played an important role in the life of the region as a significant employer and major source of revenue. In 1900 Megalopolis had almost 1 in 2 of all manufacturing workers in the entire country. By 1950 this number had fallen to 1 in 3. By 1997, the numbers had fallen to 1,498,706, only 12.3 percent of the national total. There was a significant deindustrialization of the region in both absolute and relative terms. The region has lost over 1.5 million manufacturing jobs since 1958 and is no longer the manufacturing powerhouse of the US economy.

The region retains its primacy in selected producer services. Over 1 in 2 workers in the nation in the important sector of finance and insurance are located in Megalopolis while 1 in every 10 workers are based in the New York metro area. The figures are even higher for the subcategory of securities intermediation: 81 percent of all workers in the US in this category are employed in Megalopolis, with 33 percent located in the New York metro area. Although Megalopolis shed its manufacturing jobs, it is home to information processing sectors. Megalopolis contains 55 percent of all workers in the category of professional, scientific, and technical. It is the analysis of information rather than the manipulation of metal that is now the defining economic characteristic and leading economic sector in Megalopolis.

Economic growth is heavily dependent on the role of government, not only at the local and state level but especially at the federal level. Government spending influences private market decisions. The location of public highways, for example, has guided the form and level of private investment in suburban areas. The edge cities of out-of-town shopping malls and bedroom communities are as much creations of public spending as they are functions of private investment. Public investment provides an important container for private investment. Government spending also plays a role in the location of fixed-asset investments such as military bases and research centers. One of the fastest growing counties in Megalopolis is Montgomery County in Maryland. Its population grew from 164,401 in 1950 to 950,680 in 2008, a 578 percent increase, while the increase for Megalopolis as a whole was only 53 percent. The county has a concentration of federal research laboratories and regulatory agencies that in turn attract high technology companies, service industries, and vendors. Montgomery County is home to 19 major federal research and development and regulatory agencies, including the National Institute of Standards and Technology, the National Institutes of Health, the National Oceanic and Atmospheric Administration, the Naval Medical Center, the Nuclear Regulatory Commission, the Food and Drug Administration (FDA), the Department of Energy, the Walter Reed Army Medical Center, the US Army Diamond Labs, and the Consumer Products Safety Commission. The National Institutes of Health in Bethesda, for example, house 12 research institutes employing 20,000 workers and a budget of $28 billion. The National Institute of Standards and Technology employs 2,600 scientists at its primary site at Gaithersburg in Montgomery, developing measurement standards necessary to commercialize for industry. The FDA, headquartered in Rockville in Montgomery, employs 4,500 people. With this steady injection of federal dollars and the creation of secure and well-paid employment in the scientific research sector, it comes as no surprise that Montgomery ranks as the ninth most affluent county in Megalopolis with a median household income in 2007 of $92,440; the average for the nation was $50,740.

In the past 50 years Megalopolis has undergone a profound economic transformation that includes a decline in the amount of land devoted to agriculture, a marked loss of manufacturing employment, the growth of services, the rise of government as a powerful economic motor, the suburbanization of retail, and the overall shift of jobs from cities to suburbs. Each of these trends has distinct redistributional consequences, including the decline of blue-collar jobs and a weakening of organized labor, the rise of female employment participation rates, and the restriction of job opportunities for those trapped in the inner city by limited transport as more jobs suburbanize.

The Revalorization of Megalopolis

What underlies and embodies these population and economic trends is a profound revalorization of metropolitan space. Capitalism is a system always in motion. In their 1848 *Communist Manifesto*, Marx and Engels referred to the "Constant revolutionizing of production, uninterrupted disturbance of all social conditions, everlasting uncertainty and agitation ... All that is solid melts into air."[1] Almost a hundred years later, Joseph Schumpeter (1942) referred to the creative destruction at the heart of the capitalist system. Megalopolis is both a primary container and an important vehicle for such dynamism. The period immediately after World War II saw massive public and private investment in the suburban fringes. Capital reinvestment was fixed into the suburban landscapes in the form of houses, roads, factories, stores, and infrastructure. But, since the 1970s, there has been a revalorization that has remade Megalopolis into a new metropolitan form marked by growth and decline, expansion and contraction. From 1950 to around the mid-1970s, the primary dynamic of the US metropolis was a suburban shift. Since then, the picture has become more complex with at least four investment/disinvestment waves.

First, there has been a reinvestment in the central city. Downtown business interests responded to the postwar suburbanization of business and customers by initially promoting and supporting urban renewal programs as a way to maintain the commercial viability of downtown. Urban renewal programs of the 1950s and 1960s were attempts to stem the tide of decentralization and preserve downtown property values. The attempted solution not only failed, it exacerbated decline as downtowns became filled with unattractive, sterile, unusable spaces and a depressing collection of dead zones beneath elevated highways and busy intersections. A new strategy emerged in the 1970s and 1980s that focused more on building than demolition, on entertainment rather than production, and on public–private partnerships rather than a reliance on either private risk-taking or federal programs. Alliances of civic leaders, investors, and developers in cities across the nation sought to construct a new iconography of theme retail districts, cultural centers, convention centers, stadiums, festival malls, all in a reimagined downtown. The goal was to halt the devaluation of the downtown through its promotion as a place of fun, frivolity, shopping, and spectacle. The new downtown was imagined as a festival setting and was promoted as a cultural centrality in a splintering metropolis. In order to secure this new writing of the downtown, public money had to underwrite private projects and citizens had to be convinced that the benefits would ripple through the rest of the urban economy. A classic example is Baltimore's Inner Harbor. By the 1950s, much of the old port, right in the heart of the city, had become an abandoned space. A cluster of developments built between 1977 and 1981 made the Inner Harbor a festival setting: the World Trade Center and Maryland Science Center were built with state and federal funding; the Convention Center was funded with $35 million from state funds; Harborplace, built by the Rouse Corporation, provided retail outlets and restaurants in two large pavilions. The National Aquarium was built with $21 million from the city council. The Hyatt Hotel provided a downtown anchor after a $12 million public grant was made to Hyatt. There was a public underwriting of the whole redevelopment.

Secondly, and very much related to the first trend, there has been the return of people and capital to selected parts of the city, often given the general name of gentrification. The original definition of gentrification referred to housing that passed from lower to higher-income households. It has now taken on a number of different meanings to include the general sense of displacement of lower-income households and the arrival of new single-person and non-child households, the yuppies of popular discourse, in either new or refurbished dwellings.

The move back to the city has been explained by number of factors, including, on the demand side, the persistence of high-income jobs in central city locations, new forms of household formation with smaller households, and more single-person households and non-child households who place less emphasis on city school systems and more emphasis on accessibility to employment and urban recreation. On the supply side, Neil Smith (1996) identifies an investment opportunity created by the difference between the land value and the potential land value of an accessible inner-city location, given the changes in demand that we just outlined. This rent gap, as he terms the difference between existing and potential value, creates new opportunities for investment. In a detailed study of New York's Lower East Side he identifies turning points in the housing investment change that occurred slowly first around 1976 and reached its greatest extent in 1979–80. Gentrification often comes with displacement. Newman and Wyly (2006), for example, found that between 8,300 and 11,600 households are displaced each year in New York City. There was also reinvestment in the city that was unconnected to gentrification. Wyly and Hammel (2004) report that redlining, the practice of not lending to inner-city neighborhoods, was replaced by subprime mortgage lending to inner-city residents. This was the background to the subprime collapse and subsequent economic meltdown of late 2008.

New York is home to a number of gentrifying projects. Major construction projects, such as Towers on the Park which opened in 1988, and individual households buying up brownstone dwellings led to a distinct form of gentrification along the western corridor of central Harlem. In 1994 Harlem became a Federal Empowerment Zone that provided tax credits and federal and state monies. A large indoor mall opened in 2000 with chains such as Disney, Old Navy, and HMV that had previously ignored Harlem.

Just across the Hudson River from Lower Manhattan sits the small, formerly working-class city of Hoboken, just a quick ferry ride across from New York City's financial district. The process of gentrification began around 1980. Controls that maintained the presence of lower-income households, such as tenant protection and rent control, became more lax. The housing stock was effectively emptied of lower-income residents in favor of the higher-income households. As the bull market of the 1990s expanded the numbers of financial service workers in Manhattan and their remuneration, the process of gentrification accelerated in Hoboken and extended further out into such places as Newark and Jersey City.

Broad cycles of gentrification coincide with the cycles of the market, especially the rise and fall of business services that require downtown locations. The recession of the early 1990s saw limited gentrification in selected cities, the economic upturn of the late 1990s saw another cycle of gentrification, while the downturn of 2008 will no doubt see a curtailment of speculative growth.

Third, there is an effective disinvestment from the inner ring of selected working-class and middle-class suburban neighborhoods as the demand for many of these neighborhoods has shrunk. Many of the small, single-family house suburbs that were constructed and grew in population from 1950 to 1970 have been devalorized. The suburbs in crisis are most prevalent in metro areas where postindustrial contraction was not offset by an increase in well-paying service employment.

Fourth, the suburbs are also places of the wealthy, where new rounds of housing investment, brought about by the increasing wealth of the already wealthy, reinforce old established landscapes of privilege as well as creating new landscapes of consumption and exclusion. Affluent suburbs are home to the established wealthy as well as the new wealthy, to the understated rich as well as the conspicuously rich.

The net effect of these changes is places with very divergent experiences. Table 3.4 lists the five types of suburban places identified by principal components analysis and consequent grouping of component scores (Vicino *et al.* 2007): affluent, underclass, black middle class, immigrant gateways as well as the traditional suburbs, often termed Middle America. The affluent category includes such places as Scarsdale, New York, which had a median household income of $182,792 in 2000, almost four and a half times the median household income of the New York metropolitan area. The population of Scarsdale is highly educated, with 80 percent of the population being college graduates. Many members of the workforce in Scarsdale are managers and professionals, with 20 percent employed in finance, information, and real estate (FIRE), and 26 percent employed in the health and educational fields.

Camden, New Jersey, is example of an urban place that experienced tremendous industrial growth in the early twentieth century and subsequent marked decline. The gramophone was invented in the Nipper Building, home of the Victor Talking Machine Company, later the Radio Corporation of America (RCA). At its peak in the 1950s, RCA employed over 20,000 people in the city, spread over 50 buildings. By the 1960s the decline set in as manufacturing employment disappeared. The city lost jobs and population. Retail, and the middle class have moved out to suburban New Jersey. From a total of 125,000 in 1950, this city now has a population of almost 80,000 people. Almost half of the population is black, and 40 percent is Hispanic. The poverty rate increased from 20 percent in 1970 to 35 percent in 2000 and the median household income was $23,421 in 2000, less than half the median household income of the metropolitan area. Almost half the population did not graduate from high school.

Megalopolis is home to significant amounts of immigration from overseas. The foreign-born population has increased from 10 percent in 1960 to 20 percent in 2000, almost double the national average. Migrants are found in both central cities and in suburban areas; particular concentrations can be identified as immigrant gateways. One example is Tyson's Corner, Virginia, an archetypal edge city located off the Washington DC Beltway. The population of Tyson's Corner is 18,540 with almost 35 percent foreign-born, and 70 percent have four-year university degrees.

Table 3.4 Suburban places in Megalopolis

	Demographics	Income	Education and employment	Housing	Examples
Affluent places	Mostly white; married parents	Very high income; low poverty	College graduates; management occupations	Newer, large housing stock; high home-ownership rates	Scarsdale, NY; Chevy Chase, MD
Underclass places	Black; Hispanic; single-parent families	High poverty; low income	High school drop-outs	High rental; older housing stock	Camden, PA; Asbury Park, NJ
Black middle class places	Mostly black; some single-parent families	Middle income; low poverty	College graduates; high public-sector employment	Built after 1970s; high home-ownership rates	Bowie, MD; Mitchellville, MD
Immigrant gateway places	A quarter foreign born; Hispanic and other races high; mostly married couples with children	Low to middle income; some poverty	College graduates; some high school drop-outs; varied education levels	High rental; low home-ownership rates	Hoboken, NJ; Tyson's Corner, VA
Middle America places	Mostly white, married families; "1950s image" of suburbia	Low to middle income; low poverty	High school graduates; some college	Mostly home-owners; postwar bedroom communities	Levittown, NY; Dundalk, MD

Source: after Vicino et al. 2007.

This briefest of snapshots indicates the growing diversity of Megalopolis. As inequalities have widened, the difference between rich and poor places has increased. The suburbs, for example, are no longer just the preserve of the middle class; they contain rich and poor, black as well as white. And the increased levels of immigration have also created clusters of immigration gateways. Compared to the more homogeneous suburbs of the 1950s the revalorization of residential space, in association with increased immigration and marked inequality, creates a more complex residential mosaic.

Megalopolis as Political Entity

Marx made a distinction between a *class in itself* and *a class for itself*. A *class in itself* is shaped by economic and historic conditions, but, for a *class for itself* to emerge, there needs to be to a conscious sense of similar identity and an appreciation of a shared fate. Similarly we can identify a megalopolis that is an urban region in itself and for itself. While economic forces are creating Megalopolis as an urban region in itself, as housing and job markets extend out from one metro area to another in an increasingly interconnected network, many things operate in the political and cultural realms to inhibit the creation of the wider regional consciousnesses of an urban region for itself. The major cities of Megalopolis, for example, have separate regional news stations and different sports teams. Local school districts, different states and counties, metro TV markets, and fierce sport rivalries all work to suppress the creation of an urban regional consciousness. Megalopolis is a region in itself but not a region for itself.

Megalopolis is one of the most important urban regions in the US and indeed in the world. Its internal coherence has deepened as lengthening journeys to work, widening regional job markets, and dispersing housing markets effectively link the separate metros into overlapping fields of influence and interconnecting flows of people and goods. The region has become a region in itself. Whether it will become a region *for* itself, is a more debatable issue. Identities, allegiance, and political realities all work to balkanize Megalopolis.

There are some, public choice theorists being the most vocal, who would argue that political fragmentation is a healthy state of affairs. A large number of different municipalities allow residents to choose from a variety of tax loads, school districts, and forms of government. However, there are also problems associated with this fragmentation. We can consider two.

The first is a central city–suburban fiscal disparity. Central cities, especially those with shrinking populations, have a declining tax base and lower income population while the suburbs have an expanded tax base and a relatively affluent population. Cities have relied on the property tax as a source of revenue. With declining population and an out movement of businesses and higher-income households, the tax base shrinks while the concentration of poorer people places greater demand on service provision such as police, welfare, and social services. The older cities also have an ageing infrastructure that is expensive to maintain and replace. Central cities have to deal with the politics of economic decline while many suburbs contend with the management of growth. Municipal fragmentation that separates out poor cities from affluent suburbs reinforces the inequalities in US society.

A second related problem is public education. In the US, the federal government has a very limited role in providing funding and resources to public schools. School funding is dominated by state and municipal sources. States provide on average 50 percent of total school budgets, local districts around 45 percent, based on local property taxes, while the federal government only constitutes 5 percent. At the school district level, disparities in wealth feed directly into educational standards and performance. Poor school districts cannot afford to spend the same as richer school districts. The result is a range of school districts, some, more often in the affluent suburbs, platforms for success while others, especially in the cash-strapped central cities, are funnels of failure. The political fragmentation of the region into a large number of local governments has profound social outcomes.

Megalopolis Revisited

Gottmann's original Megalopolis, based on analysis of 1950 data, was the manu-facturing hub of the national economy, with substantial central city populations, few foreign-born inhabitants, and marked racial-ethnic segregation. The most sig-nificant changes in the intervening years include the relative shift of population from the central cities to the suburban counties, the loss of manufacturing jobs especially in the central cities, the growth of services, and the increase in the foreign-born population, especially in the selected central cities, although suburban counties also witnessed the absolute and relative increase in the foreign-born. Despite all these changes, racial segregation remains a stubborn fact of life in the nation's largest urban region.

I used the term *liquid city* to grasp the nature of this urban change. The term is useful, but it does need to be applied with caution. It should not, for example, be implied that all is flux. Fixed and frozen elements remain, such as elements of the built form and the persistent patterns of segregation, but they are constantly assailed by subsequent change and movement. Large fixed capital investments such as motorways and airports are anchored in place affecting subsequent flows of investment and movement. But flows there are. There are tensions between the fixed nature of the city and urban movements, especially the continual centrifugal forces in Megalopolis. Fixity and flow are in a constant dialectic as flows produce new places of fixed investment and concentration that in turn are undermined by new flows: structure and process, solid and liquid, stasis and flow, in a constant inter-connected reality. The term *liquid city* highlights the dynamic element of the dialectic.

The changes have wider cultural implications. Bauman (1992) also writes of a postmodern condition marked by a loss of certainty about conduct, the unpredict-ability of change, a lack of centeredness, the decline of grand narratives. The recent evolution of Megalopolis embodies this shift. As rapid changes restructure our cities, as more of our lives take place in a decentered metropolis, as city centers decline, as we follow space–time paths through the metropolis seemingly disconnected from our fellow citizens, and as our truly public spaces shrivel to a series of highly seg-mented places, then the oppressive and unsettling sense of continual change is made very real, the loss of grand narratives is made palpable, and the lack of center to social life is made visible. The postmodern condition thrives in Megalopolis.

In 1927 Patrick Geddes saw megalopolis, the idea, as a late stage in an inexorable decline (Defries 1927). In 1961 Gottmann, in contrast, saw Megalopolis, the place, as a harbinger of a new way of life. Which is correct, the gloomy formulation of Geddes or the sunnier claim of Gottmann? There answer rests on whether we can build livable humane cities that provide employment, hope, and sustainable futures. Megalopolis poses problems, major problems no doubt, but the forward edge of history lies in the collective and shared fate of such giant city regions as Megalopolis.

Note

1　See www.marxists.org/archive/marx/works/1848/communist-manifesto/index.htm (accessed 13 September 2010).

References

Bauman, Z. (1992) *Intimations of Postmodernity*. London: Routledge.

Bauman, Z. (2005) *Liquid Life*. Cambridge: Polity Press.

Defries, A. (1927) *The Interpreter Geddes: The Man and His Gospel*. London: Routledge.

Gottmann, J. (1961) *Megalopolis*. New York: Twentieth Century Fund.

Hanlon, B. (2009) *Once The American Dream: Inner-ring Suburbs in the Metropolitan United States*. Philadelphia: Temple University Press.

Hanlon, B., Short, J. R., and Vicino, T. (2010) *Cities and Suburbs: New Metropolitan Realities in the US*. London and New York: Routledge.

Lang, R. E., and Dhavale, D. (2005) Beyond Megalopolis: Exploring America's New Megalopolitan Geography. Metropolitan Institute of Virginia Tech. Census Report.

Newman, K., and Wyly, E. (2006) The right to stay put, revisited: gentrification and resistance to displacement in New York City. *Urban Studies* 43: 23–57.

Puentes, R., and Warren, D. (2006) *One-Fifth of America; A Comprehensive Guide to America's First Suburbs*. Washington DC: Brookings Institution Press.

Schumpeter, J. (1942) *Capitalism, Socialism and Democracy*. New York: Harper and Brothers.

Short, J. R. (2004) *Global Metropolitan*. London and New York: Routledge.

Short, J. R. (2007) *Liquid City: Megalopolis and the Contemporary Northeast*. Washington DC: Resources for the Future.

Short, J. R., Hanlon, B., and Vicino, T. (2007) The decline of inner suburbs: the new suburban gothic in the US. *Geography Compass* 1: 641–56.

Smith, N. (1996) *The New Urban Frontier: Gentrification and the Revanchist City*. London: Routledge.

Vicino, T. J., Hanlon, B., and Short, J. R. (2007) Megalopolis 50 years on: the transformation of a city region. *International Journal of Urban and Regional Research* 31: 344–67.

Wyly, E., and Hammel, J. (2004) Gentrification, segregation and discrimination in the American urban system. *Environment and Planning A* 36: 1215–41.

Chapter 4

Ups and Downs in the Global City: London and New York in the Twenty-First Century

Susan S. Fainstein, Ian Gordon, and Michael Harloe

The early 1980s initiated a new stage in the development of London and New York, as both cities entered a period of growth that, despite some fluctuations, continued at least up to the financial crisis and recession of 2008–9. While other economic sectors were dispersing geographically, certain industries involving financial activities and business services maintained their presence in the centers of these cities (Sassen 2001; Fainstein *et al.* 1992; Buck *et al.* 2002). This continuity resulted from a combination of two processes that increased the importance of sectors advantaged by their concentration in large, flexible, and internationally oriented agglomerations. One process was the rapidly expanding role of financial capital in a globalizing economy. The second, complementary to the first, was a strong tide of deregulation and vertical disintegration of corporations, generating new opportunities and markets for sophisticated producer services. Together the two gave rise to the invention of new markets for ever more arcane financial instruments and the amassing of huge pools of credit to underwrite increasingly speculative activities in financial derivatives, property development, mergers, and leveraged buy-outs. Physical proximity facilitated the face-to-face encounters among the principals, bankers, brokers, accountants, attorneys, and others necessary for deal-making – though more routine support functions continued to be hived off to cheaper domestic and offshore locations.

Other industries also flourished, generating more new jobs although less revenue than finance. New York and London continued to be centers of culture, information, tourism, higher education, and health services. Real-estate development, benefiting from the boom in financial and business services, constituted another growing industrial sector. The supply of offices grew, both to meet increased demand and because of speculation (Fainstein 2001), while housing markets soared, in terms of

The New Blackwell Companion to the City   Edited by Gary Bridge and Sophie Watson
© 2011 Blackwell Publishing Ltd

prices if not of output. Manufacturing, wholesale, and seaport employment were declining, but there was a notable growth in high- and low-end service jobs catering to an increasingly affluent minority.

The international flavor of the two cities resulted not just from their place in the global economy but also from their role as receptors of recent immigrants. Their metropolitan areas remained the largest in population in their respective nations, and thus they also comprised the largest markets for consumer products. At the same time, aggregate indicators of growth obscured the continuing increase in inequality that accompanied the boom.

Decline and Renewal

At the start of the last quarter of the twentieth century both cities seemed to be in decline. Population loss due to selective outmigration, a long established trend in London and more recently taking off in New York, was the most obvious indicator. Pessimism about the future resulted from the collapse of large sections of manufacturing industry, disinvestment in the built environment, the growth of the multi-faceted "inner city problem" resulting from large numbers of people trapped in poverty, and the failure of urban policies to reverse or alleviate such trends. The timing and details of the changes were not the same in both cities. Unlike New York in the 1970s, London had no fiscal crisis producing a contraction in government social spending, but in the 1980s the neoliberal Thatcher government cut public services and abolished the leftist Greater London Council (GLC), leading to a similar result. Thus, during the 1980s the effective governing bodies of both places (the city government in New York and the offices of the national government with responsibility for London) had redefined their mission from alleviating distress to stimulating economic growth. The social and ethnic composition of those most severely affected by decline differed, as did the nature of their political representation. But while such differences affected the intensity and timing of decline, a recognizably similar process seemed to be under way.

By the mid-1980s, however, the first signs of an improvement in economic performance began to appear. The indicators of revival and then a new economic dynamism from the mid- to late 1980s in the two cities had a great deal in common and pointed to a far-reaching restructuring of their space economies. First, there was the reversal, continuing through the 1990s and beyond the millennium, of population loss. In New York and a little later in London this gain resulted wholly from replacement of the outmigrating middle class by an even larger number of foreign-born newcomers and their children. New York gained more than 1.2 million inhabitants between 1980 and 2008, reaching an all-time population peak of 8.37 million (New York City Department of City Planning 2009). Similarly London between 1981 and 2008 added 800,000 residents, bringing its total population to 7.63 million. The upsurge in immigration to London lagged New York's by a decade, but the rate of increase had caught up by the late 1990s. Between 1986 and 2006, London's foreign-born population increased from 17.6 to 30.5 percent, though still behind New York's 36 percent. The two cities were also converging in terms of diversity. In 1986 most London migrants came from a few countries with strong historic and linguistic links to the UK; 20 years later there were large settled populations from other parts of Asia, Africa, Latin America, and the Middle East and many shorter-term migrants from across Europe (Gordon *et al.* 2007).

An equally significant change was the reversal of employment decline, though with large cyclical fluctuations. In both cities the turnaround also owed much to the fact that, as the older goods-related sectors shrank, the scale of ongoing job losses got overtaken by continuing expansion in office-based services.

New York experienced substantial job losses in the early 1990s, the early 2000s, and in 2008–9. By 2004, however, the city and the wider metro area had replaced all the jobs lost in the preceding decades (New York State Department of Labor 2009), although the city, unlike the metro area, never regained its 1969 peak. Rapid recovery from the 2001 downturn, resulting from a combination of the World Trade Center attack and national recession, stemmed from the special attributes of the city's economic base:

> Despite the magnitude of the losses, the sheer size of New York's economy kept the effects relatively small as a fraction of total economic activity, and the flexibility of markets in New York ... enabled the city to recover much of its economic vibrancy. (Chernick 2005: 3)

As in London, the strength of the area's economy rested on the financial and business services sector, but it continued to add jobs in fashion, cultural industries, and a variety of service occupations (Currid 2007). A sharp decline in the crime rate over the preceding two decades accompanied economic and population rises, and some of the city's increased attractiveness to people and businesses can be attributed to a changed perception of its safety.

There was a sharp downturn in London and the southeast of England in 1990, ahead of other regions in the UK. But in London this proved a briefer setback than in New York. Over the period 1981–2008 employment grew by almost 1 percent per annum on average, adding almost a million jobs (Gordon *et al.* 2009: Table 2.1). The factors which underlay this new era in London were similar to those in New York:

> London's historic position was of the economic, political and cultural capital of a centralised but outward looking nation. And it is the strengths established from that position – particularly flexibility, knowledge and international connections – which have become a key to its current role in a post-industrial UK facing a highly competitive global economy. (Gordon *et al.* 2009: 10).

In London, as in New York, crime rates fell, but with less significance since the change has been more modest than in New York, and perceptions of the city as dangerous were never as great.

In neither case can the revival of fortunes be very substantially attributed to the shift in local-level governmental priorities noted at the start of the 1980s, though the infrastructural developments associated with large-scale property development (Fainstein 2008) played enabling roles in accommodating the growth. More significant was deregulation (notably the "Big Bang" in the City of London) initiated from elsewhere (by finance capital, central banks, and national government). But the growth agenda has continued to be central to city governments. Significantly, in the London case, where restoration of a (stripped down) strategic authority brought back as its first elected mayor the formerly "leftist" leader of the ousted GLC, Ken Livingstone, there was a full commitment to a growth agenda, apparently as a means to secure from central government gatekeepers the necessary resources for infrastructure investment that the city could not itself fund (Gordon 2004).

Changing Labor Markets

The restructuring of the cities' labor markets consisted of a move from a "Fordist" (mass-production manufacturing) industrial organization to a much more flexible, postindustrial, and services-based labor market. The new jobs created in the two cities had many common features: for example, many tended to be occupied by women rather than men; expansion was in both well-paid positions for the highly qualified and low-level jobs for the less skilled (more in New York than London until the late 1990s), but fewer intermediate-level jobs for skilled manual and supervisory staff (Buck *et al.* 2002). In consequence, income inequality grew enormously in these two highly competitive cities.

As in New York, London's newly arrived workers were very diverse. On average they were better qualified than most Londoners, although a sharp divide separated the experiences of those from rich as compared to poor countries. Among the first group were many who came to London for a period of years, to work in, learn from, and help to further dynamize the leading sectors of the new economy. Among the second group, many had to start out at the bottom end of the job hierarchy, working for low pay, depressing the already low wages in this sector, and discouraging a growing proportion of other Londoners from seeking work.

Both cities have experienced considerable volatility in aggregate demand during this new era and at an individual level have provided less security to their workforces (Buck *et al.* 2002). Rates of labor turnover in the two cities have always been relatively high, and increased emphasis on flexibility has brought many jobs which are either short term or on a semi-casual basis. To some extent this flexibility has often fitted the preferences of (especially young) workers. In the context of barriers to entry into mainstream jobs, this might also be true for migrants, a significant proportion of whom in New York have worked in informal or under-regulated employment, as seems also to be the case among some of London's new cohorts of irregular migrants. Though volatility and insecurity can also affect highly paid workers, their chances of recovery are rather good in these cities, in contrast to the real risks of marginalization suffered by those at the bottom end of the market, who may both confront prejudice against their ethnic status and be easily dispensable at times of slack demand (Ehrenreich 1989; Sennett 1998; Buck *et al.* 2002; Gordon *et al.* 2009).

Urban Reinvestment

One of the most visible consequences of economic restructuring is the reinvestment in the built environment of the two cities. Mega-projects in London include Docklands development, facilities for the 2012 Olympics, and Crossrail – connecting the eastern and western ends of the metropolitan area. In New York, Battery Park City and three new sports stadiums, as well as renewed subway construction, constitute similar investments. Throughout both cities new offices, shopping, entertainment and leisure complexes, and luxury housing, together with the necessary (and largely publicly funded) infrastructure to support them, characterized the era. In contrast, relatively little investment has gone into construction of non-luxury housing. London has had a tightening housing market as demand outstripped the increase in supply. Consequently the differential between house prices in London and prices in the rest of the UK has continued to widen (while the rate of new building was considerably less than in the rest of the country). This pressure was accommodated by a rise in private renting and by increased sharing of accommodation. London's stock of subsidized housing decreased as a consequence of the Thatcher government's "right to buy" program to allow the purchase of council (i.e. public) housing by its occupants and its continuation under the subsequent Labour governments (Gordon *et al.* 2009: 50–7 and Table 4.7). In New York, despite the addition of 94,000 new or renovated units to the supply of affordable housing between 2002 and 2009, 200,000 units were withdrawn due to the expiration of rent regulation on housing built with various government subsidies (Fernandez 2009). Housing poverty became increasingly acute during the boom period, as the median rent burden rose from 41 to 44 percent of income for the bottom third of households (Bach and Waters 2008: 3).

The Social Consequences of Economic Change

The loss of skilled manual and supervisory jobs – evident throughout both national economies – has been amplified by the peculiar conditions which apply in the two cities, leading to the development of a polarized distribution of incomes and life chances. Evidently then, placement at the top of the world urban hierarchy does not result in a generally better quality of life for much of the populations of these cities. In the 1980s, as London and New York began their renaissance, scholarly attention turned to the impact of their economic transformation on their social structure and social divisions. Some sought to encapsulate these social changes in the image of the "dual city" – the suggestion that London and New York each contained, in the same urban and regional space, two increasingly separate economies, inhabiting increasingly segregated neighborhoods and social systems.

Detailed studies of the distributional consequences of economic change, however, lead us to a more complex conclusion. Above all, the changes benefited the financial and producer services industries, as well as associated higher-level consumer services and the people who occupied the high-level positions in these parts of the economy. For the middle mass, which constituted a far larger section of the metropolitan population, the outcome was more ambiguous. But by far the heaviest consequences of economic change have been experienced by those who were outside, on the margins of or at the bottom of the labor market. Growth resulted in an expansion of low-skilled, low-paid jobs, but in industries with a "missing middle," chances for upward occupational mobility are limited. Two groups in particular whose fortunes are closely linked have been noted in London. The first is the majority of new migrants, discussed above, who take entry-level service jobs. The second is the less skilled longer-term residents who are outcompeted by the new migrants (who may have significant qualifications but be downwardly mobile at least temporarily) and who in consequence are "bumped down" to lower-paid and even more insecure positions or become workless altogether (see Buck *et al.* 2002: ch. 6). One consequence of low-income employment, evident in both cities, is the rise in the average number of household members who are in full- or part-time work. In terms of poverty and inequality, a recent study (MacInnes and Kenway 2009) shows that London has the highest proportion of households in both the top and the bottom income deciles nationally. This kind of polarization seems to have increased as a consequence of the growth in the number of foreign-born, not simply as a result of the heightened service demands of the wealthy (Gordon *et al.*, 2009). And London has the highest poverty rate of any region in England with the level in inner London being the highest and in outer London the second highest.

New York City's income distribution resembles London's. The average income of families in the top quintile during the early 2000s was 9.5 times greater than the average income of families in the bottom fifth, up from a ratio of 7.6 in the late 1980s. Reflecting the enormous growth in income of those at the top, the gap between the highest quintile and the middle one has also increased, from a ratio of 2.6 in the late 1980s to 3.3 in the mid-2000s (Fiscal Policy Institute [FPI] 2008: 14), and the top 1 percent received 37 percent of adjusted gross income (FPI 2008: 17). Although income data is not available for the tri-state metro area, information on New York State indicates a similar pulling apart between the top and bottom. In 2008 the Bronx remained the country's poorest urban county, and the city's overall poverty rate was 18.2 percent, compared to the national rate of 13.2 percent (Roberts 2009).

By the early 1990s it was already clear that changes in UK policies had contributed to a marked convergence between the two cities, as growing income inequality in London brought it nearer to New York's situation (Fainstein *et al.* 1992). A later analysis (Buck *et al.* 2002) linked London's growth in inequality to a rise in unemployment rather than an expansion of low-waged positions, but that has changed remarkably with the expansion of low-waged services more recently. Nevertheless, the impact of poverty differs within the cities as a consequence of the more extensive availability in London of state-provided services, especially medical care, which is of crucial importance to the working poor. Furthermore, the provision of public housing and rent subsidies on a large scale has been particularly important in London and is quite low by comparison in New York.

Our previous surveys of London and New York in the early 1990s (Fainstein *et al.* 1992) and London at the millennium (Buck *et al.* 2002) made us wary of accepting any simple reduction of this complexity to an overall picture of a "dual" or a "polarized" city. However, it now seems clear that one consequence of London's dynamic economy over the past two decades – accompanied by a much more volatile labor market, the growth of both high- and low-level service employment, the rise of worklessness, and, crucially, the remarkable influx of migrants from the 1990s onwards – has been to create a city with strongly polarizing or dualistic characteristics. The growing competition for jobs resulting from increased immigration meant that the demand by affluent residents for locally provided services translated into an actual increase in low-status jobs. Sassen (2001), in the 1991 edition of her book, regarded this phenomenon as a feature of the global city era, largely on the basis of New York evidence. Her thesis was disputed by Hamnett (1994) among others, who showed that an enlarged low-wage sector was not a reality in London *at that time*. London, however, having converged with New York in the 1980s and 1990s in terms of overall income inequality, now also seems to be closer to it in terms of a polarizing labor market.

The study by Gordon *et al.* (2007) of London's recent migration noted above compares developments in London and New York, finding that during the 1980s in New York jobs at both ends of the pay scale outpaced the middle. The growth of global city roles made the city an uneconomic location for most kinds of routine jobs for less-qualified workers except for the low-level servicing jobs generated by the demands of the increasingly affluent. This was not actually true during this period for London, where the share of bottom-end jobs fell even while earnings in these jobs were growing faster than in the rest of the economy. One possible explanation of this difference was that New York's greater openness at that time to international migration produced a highly elastic labor supply for low-paying jobs. The more recent trends in migration in relation to wages and employment in the low-paid service sector of the London economy tend to support this explanation (Gordon *et al.* 2007: 57). The authors add that the key issue is not the increase in such low-paid jobs in London but the negative effects of the downward pressure on the earnings of established workers that the new migration has bought about (and the worklessness effect noted above).

The Future

In the first version of this chapter, written at the end of the 1990s, we noted that the recession early in that decade called into question the permanence of the 1980s revival. But in the period up to the credit crisis of 2008 this revival persisted and strengthened. An increasingly speculative, deregulated, and flexible global economy promoted the growth sectors of finance and business services along with high levels of office construction, the increasing treatment of housing as an investment asset, and booming consumption fueled by the rising asset values of this housing. After 2000 and up to 2007, the expansion of the London economy continued and, until the sub-prime crisis of 2007, it seemed as if London had embarked on a stable growth trajectory (Gordon *et al.* 2009). Likewise, New York after 2002 appeared to have momentum in its favor. As of the time of this writing, the 2007–9 downturn appears to be the consequence of cyclical rather than structural factors, and both cities are showing signs of returning to their previous course. In this context, however, a key consideration must be the long-term prospects for further growth in financial and producer services, together with those other economic sectors dependent on such growth. A second issue is whether financial and producer services growth will continue to center in London and New York.

The first point to note is the significance of changes in the regional space economy of which London and New York form a part. Although these core cities retain a unique importance no longer found in many other metropolitan regions, they nevertheless must rely on a narrower economic base than in the past. New York, which lacks London's governmental dominance, particularly suffers from a high level of specialization. New York experienced substantial job losses in the early 1990s and the early 2000s. In 2004 the city and the wider metro area had replaced all the jobs lost in the preceding decade (New York State Department of Labor 2009) although the city, unlike the metro area, never regained its 1969 peak. By 2000, financial services workers had increased their share of earnings in the city to 35 percent from 13 percent in 1960 (Federal Reserve Bank of New York 2006: 5).

Continued economic restructuring may bring fewer benefits to the core areas of the London and New York regions than in the past. An important issue concerns the future location of the existing financial and producer services industries and of possible future growth in them. Developments in transport, communications, and information technology continue to produce centrifugal tendencies, and the cost pressures in the urban cores are also significant in bringing about deconcentration. Until now, much of this outmigration has involved "back office" functions, leaving those activities which still require the advantages of agglomeration in the core. Further advances in information technology, however, may allow some of the latter also to decentralize. Changes in the organization of production and the other factors which have encouraged decentralization have already resulted in a new form of regional structure, with a development of relatively self-contained agglomerations outside the two core cities.

The continuing pre-eminence of London and New York as the world's leading global cities is indicated by a recent ranking of the leading financial centers of the world in terms of their competitiveness. This Global Financial Centres Index (GFCI) shows that London consistently ranks first among the centers surveyed, with New York following closely behind. Both are significantly ahead of the next strongest cities, Hong Kong and Singapore, though recently this gap has sharply narrowed. While the 2007–9 financial crisis generated a good deal of uncertainty and reduced confidence with a sharp fall in ratings for all centers, it is some measure of the limited effects of subsequent developments *on the international financial sector* that by September 2009 the GFCI ratings of all the major centers had risen back close to where they stood before the crisis began (City of London/Y/Zen Group 2009: 2).

The degree of protection that these two major financial centers themselves have enjoyed from the worst effects of recession as a consequence of the robust measures taken by the US and UK administrations to avoid a meltdown of their banking systems is indicated by the fact that employment trends in each have simply followed national trends. Much worse effects have been experienced in manufacturing centers, notably in the auto-cities of Detroit and the English Midlands. As far as the impact of the recession on employment in London's financial services is concerned, early fears of massive job losses have, at least up to the fall of 2009, not transpired. In 2007 about 354,000 people worked in the City of London in specialized "whole-sale" financial activities. There were about 30,000 job losses in 2008 and similar numbers were predicted for 2009. But by October 2009 the losses were projected to fall sharply to about 18,000 for the year, with a return to growth of perhaps 9,000 jobs in 2010 (*The Economist* 2009). The article further noted that City salaries and bonuses were also rising again due to the recovery of the markets in 2009. However, despite this recovery there were concerns expressed about the impact of stiffer regulation on financial services and the authors of the GFCI did not expect City jobs to return to their 2007 level for about a decade.

Likewise in New York the impact of the "Great Recession" proved less damaging than originally feared, at least in the short run. From August 2008 to August 2009, the city lost 96,739 private-sector jobs. These included about 36,000 finance and insurance jobs, which paid $280,872 annually on average in 2008, and over 10,000 construction jobs, which paid on average $68,119. Nevertheless, the total number of jobs still exceeded the number in 2000 by more than 100,000 (Haughney 2009). According to the city's Independent Budget Office (2009: 1), with the exception of the financial sector, losses were fewer than anticipated, and a sharp turnaround in Wall Street profits and compensation meant that tax revenues for 2010 were predicted to be nearly a billion dollars more than had been expected only six months earlier, resulting in less pressure on the city government to reduce its workforce.

Overall our chronicle of these two cities shows that their role as the headquarters of global capital (Friedmann 1986) has largely determined their destinies. In the last half century they have undergone substantial transformation as they have ridden the ups and downs of the global economy. In the aggregate, they are likely to continue to display substantial volatility as a world that is hostage to financial investment decisions will continue to see asset bubbles and deflations. The coordinating function played by investment banks means they will remain key players in the international network of financial flows. Their location, assuming they remain in these global cities, will mean both that these cities will harbor the world's wealthiest people, with whatever trickle-down advantages this might produce for the rest of their population in terms of employment, and that their income distribution will continue to show the enormous discrepancies between the top and the rest that have grown in the last 40 years of increasing financial ascendancy.

References

Bach, V., and Waters, T. (2008) *Making the Rent: Who's at Risk?* CSS Update Report. New York: Community Service Society.

Buck, N., Gordon, I., Hall, P., Harloe, M., and Kleinman, M. (2002) *Working Capital. Life and Labour in Contemporary London*. London: Routledge.

Chernick, H. (2005) Introduction. In *Resilient City*, ed. H. Chernick. New York: Russell Sage Foundation, 1–20.

City of London/Y/Zen Group (2009) *The Global Financial Centres Index*. London: City of London Corporation.

Currid, E. (2007) *The Warhol Economy*. Princeton, NJ: Princeton University Press.

Economist (2009) After the cull. *The Economist*, 392 (8653): 68.

Ehrenreich, B. (1989) *Fear of Falling*. New York: Pantheon.

Fainstein, S. S. (2001) *The City Builders*. 2nd edn. Lawrence: University Press of Kansas.

Fainstein, S. S. (2008) Mega-projects in New York, London and Amsterdam. *International Journal of Urban and Regional Research* 32 (4): 768–85.

Fainstein, S. S., Gordon, I., and Harloe, M. (eds.) (1992) *Divided Cities. New York and London in the Contemporary World*. Oxford: Blackwell.

Federal Reserve Bank of New York (2006) Challenges facing the New York Metropolitan Area economy. *Current Issues in Economics and Finance* 12 (1): 1–7.

Fernandez, M. (2009) As city adds housing for poor, market subtracts it. *New York Times*, October 15.

Fiscal Policy Institute (2008) *Pulling Apart in New York: An Analysis of Income Trends in New York State*. New York: FPI.

Friedmann, J. (1986) The world city hypothesis. *Development and Change* 17: 69–83.

Gordon, I. (2004) Capital needs, capital demands and global city rhetoric in Mayor Livingstone's London Plan. *GaWC Research Bulletin* 145, University of Loughborough.

Gordon, I., Travers, T., and Whitehead, C. (2007) *The Impact of Recent Immigration on the London Economy*. London: City of London Corporation.

Gordon, I., Travers, T., and Whitehead, C. (2009) *London's Place in the UK Economy 2009/10*. London: City of London Corporation.

Hamnett, C. (1994) Social polarisation in global cities: theory and evidence. *Urban Studies* 31(3): 401–24.

Haughney, C. (2009) Bloomberg has added jobs, and lost some, too. *New York Times*, October 15.

Independent Budget Office, New York City (2009) Fiscal Outlook. December. Available online at www.ibo.nyc.ny.us/iboreports/FiscalOutlookDec2009.pdf (accessed October 13, 2010).

MacInnes, T., and Kenway, P. (2009) *London's Poverty Profile*. London: CPF/NPI.

New York City Department of City Planning (2009) Current population estimates. Available online at www.nyc.gov/html/dcp/html/census/popcur.shtml (accessed November 30, 2009).

New York State Department of Labor (2009) Employment and unemployment data. Available online at www.labor.ny.gov/stats/laus.asp (accessed November 29, 2009).

Roberts, S. (2009) NY poverty data paint mixed picture. *New York Times*, September 29.

Sassen, S. (2001) *The Global City*. 2nd edn. Princeton, NJ: Princeton University Press.

Sennett, R. (1998) *The Corrosion of Character: The Personal Consequences of Work in the New Capitalism*. New York: Norton.

Chapter 5

Ethnography of an Indian City: Ahmedabad

Amrita Shah

Getting off a train at Ahmedabad's Kalupur Station you have to negotiate a mass of bodies sprawled in various postures waiting on the floor. By the time you pick your way through the tangle of limbs and luggage and emerge to stand on the steps looking out at the dizzying shininess of the metal trim, handlebars, and rear-view mirrors of what looks like a million two-wheelers, a gaggle of auto-rickshaw drivers will have materialized, seemingly out of nowhere – young, slightly built men with exchangeable faces shouting and gesticulating to get your attention. Should you respond to any one of them, the chosen one will take your bag from your weary shoulder and escort you outside. He will put your bag down on the unpaved ground and tell you to wait while he brings his vehicle. He will disappear, leaving you clueless with the dry heat singeing you like a flame. And then, suddenly he will reappear, grinning and rotating the handlebars of a green and yellow three-wheeler. You will settle in, noticing that the seat is broken, causing you to slip and slide a little. You will be dazzled by the glossy side panels laminated with alluring blow-ups of the driver's favorite film actress. And, as he hurtles you into the streets, unmindful of the traffic pouring in from the right and the left, you will begin to pray that you will reach your destination in one piece.

Ahmedabad is India's seventh largest city. It is an old city, established in 1411 by Sultan Ahmed Shah I. It was the city that Mahatma Gandhi made his home from 1915 to 1930, between the time he returned from South Africa and the time he set off on the historic Salt March which initiated the second phase of resistance against the British. In the heyday of the composite textile mill, it was also an industrial town, the second highest manufacturer of processed cotton fabric after Mumbai, which led to it being described as the "Manchester of the East." Between the mid-1980s and the late 1990s the city went into a decline. The mills closed down, unable

The New Blackwell Companion to the City   Edited by Gary Bridge and Sophie Watson
© 2011 Blackwell Publishing Ltd

to compete with the smaller, more efficient power looms and dyeing units that had come up on the outskirts of the city. The state of Gujarat, in which Ahmedabad is located, went through a period of political instability that had a detrimental effect on the city's development. But the most pernicious problem was communal violence: the city experienced outbreaks of violence in 1985–6, repeatedly through the decade of the 1990s, and then again in 2002. The last bout of violence is widely perceived as the worst incident of communal violence in independent India.

In terms of scale, the violence in 2002 was widespread, emanating from Ahmedabad and spreading rapidly through the state; official figures pegged the deaths at around a thousand but the toll is likely to have been much higher. The incident saw an extreme form of cruelty being unleashed not just on men but also on women and children. The victims were largely Muslims, who constitute the largest minority in the state (Bunsha 2006: xx). And the strong support the perpetrators of the violence appeared to have received from the state – controlled then and now by the Hindu chauvinist party, the Bharatiya Janata Party – and various authorities such as the police and the local judiciary have led many, notably Varshney (2002–3), to describe it as a pogrom.

The last seven years, however, have been a period of relative calm for the city. In 2005 the Indian government bestowed the status of a megacity on Ahmedabad, making it eligible for substantial funding under the Jawaharlal Nehru National Urban Renewal Mission – a program launched by the central government to develop urban infrastructure in the country. The declaration was a shot in the arm for the state government which has been seeking to overcome the negative publicity received by it for its role in the 2002 violence, not least by attracting large-scale investment to the state. The refurbishing of Ahmedabad, the state's principal city, fit well into its well-publicized campaign to turn Gujarat into a "world-class business destination" (*Vibrant Gujarat 2009*).

The computer-generated images on the official website of the city corporation recast Ahmedabad in the style of a generic modern western city. The plans, all of which are at various stages of completion, include a bus rapid transport system, lake development projects, a ring road, low-income housing, and a scheme to develop the river bank with walkways and entertainment and commercial complexes. The chief minister talks of turning Ahmedabad into Singapore, a dream that is shared by the city's influential businessmen, real estate developers, and the man and woman on the street. The drive from the station however reveals a city that is muddling along at its own pace, sometimes fast, sometimes slow, sometimes towards and sometimes even away from these glossy, futuristic dreams.

Traffic is sluggish outside Kalupur Station and the afternoon heat is suffocating.

Many of Ahmedabad's young women wear long white gloves to protect themselves from the sun. They also wind *dupattas*, or long scarves, around their heads, leaving just a slit open for the eyes. This cloth mask is a device to keep out dust and air pollution. Indian cities are highly polluted, partly because of the excessive reliance on private vehicles in the absence of reliable public transport systems. Ahmedabad at one time was one of the worst cases; in 2001, it was found to be the fourth most polluted city in the country. And the sight of these girl bandits racing across town on their scooters was a vivid and unsettling reminder of the perils of rapid growth. Over the last few years, however, pollution levels have dropped after buses and auto-rickshaws switched from petrol and diesel to the more environmentally friendly compressed natural gas (CNG). Ahmedabad was only the second city in the country, after Delhi, to make a mandated transition to CNG, replacing the fleet of black and yellow petrol-run auto-rickshaws with the environmentally conscious green and yellow colors of CNG. Pollution levels dropped dramatically. In 2008, the city had slid down to a respectable 50 on a pollution scale of polluted cities (*Economic Times*, August 10, 2008).

I ask my rickshaw driver if there had been any resistance from auto-rickshaw operators to the move, for, even taking into account the cash incentives offered by the state, adapting the vehicle to an alternative fuel was a costly affair. He shook his head vigorously to indicate that there had been no problem. In the long run, he argued, CNG was cost-effective. Once he and his colleagues had worked out the figures there was no need for resistance, he said. Indeed there was an air of relish in his manner as if this single action rather than merely improving the quality of air had opened up a whole new world of profitability. This line of reasoning, which measures profit and loss and ends with a willingness to invest in something new, seems to me a typical example of the city's famed pragmatism. "The spirit of Ahmedabad is utilitarian and materialistic" writes Gillion (1968: 35). Money is a central preoccupation for the city's people. The city has the second-oldest stock exchange in the country after Mumbai and contributes 14 percent of the total investments in all stock exchanges in India. Conversations in the city tend to revolve overwhelmingly around money, and actions and purchases are carefully monitored for their cost-effectiveness.

It is not the mere accumulation of wealth that is admired in the city, however, but the resourcefulness and ingenuity applied in its making. One gets the impression that money is something of a prize in a daily sport that is played in the city. Which is perhaps why so many of the stories about the city emphasize cleverness and trickery even when they seem to be purportedly about money. Take this fable, for example, which one is likely to find in most popular books about the city, including Pandya and Rawal (2002: 5). It tells of a guard at the Bhadra Gate who noticed a magnificently dressed lady slipping out of the city. "Who are you?" he asked. "I am the Goddess Lakshmi," the lady replied. The guard, stunned by the fact that he was face to face with the goddess of Wealth, nevertheless collected his wits and asked her to wait till he could get permission from the king to allow her to leave. She promised to wait and he sped away. As he ran however, the realization dawned on him that the city was doomed if the goddess was allowed to leave. So, in an act of supreme sacrifice, he beheaded himself. And this is how the city's prosperity was ensured and protected, says the fable, with Lakshmi still waiting for the noble guard's return at the Bhadra Gate. The story has been told to me by various people to emphasize various different aspects of the city's personality: one, the importance of wealth symbolized by the Goddess Lakshmi; and two, the guard's sacrifice as an example of the Ahmedabadis' dedication to their city. In my opinion, however, the guard's alertness and nimbleness of mind are equally the centerpiece of the story.

We have now cleared the gridlock outside the station and are speeding ahead on a wide and dusty road. A bleak jumble of sheds and bazaars rises up on our left. We pass a police station, a temple, a flock of schoolchildren, and then a gate about

20 feet tall and made of solid stone. There are 16 such gates scattered around the city. After the walls of the old city came down in 1922, the gates were left standing. No longer effective as protection against invaders, the gates have been appropriated for various uses – to be lit up as decoration by the city authorities, as landmarks, and even by hawkers to prop up their wares. We are skirting the old, walled city. Today much of it is a commercial area containing markets for automobile spare parts, electronics, fruit, ready-made garments, gold and silver jewelry, and second-hand textbooks. It is hard to walk or drive in these narrow congested lanes. But deep within, beyond the busy markets, is an area of unbelievable quaintness and beauty: narrow labyrinthine streets, temples, and old houses with intricately carved wooden facades.

There was a time, up until the early twentieth century, when almost the city's entire population was contained within the walls. People lived in houses designed typically with the toilet and washing area in the front and the kitchen and family space at the back. An atrium-like opening within the house funneled the hot air from the streets and provided a cooling effect all year round. A style of community life was nurtured within these streets that came to be known as the *pol* system. A pol consisted of a set of houses which were blocked off by a gate which would shut at night. Pol residents, though not necessarily related, developed intimate ties due to daily proximity. A blackboard served as a noticeboard for the common activities of the pol. Festivals were celebrated there with great gaiety and crises were jointly tackled.

Over time, the pols emptied. The rich were the first to leave. The big trader and mill-owning families of Ahmedabad moved out east, to Shahibaug, a neighborhood that took its name from a garden palace built by Shah Jahan, well known as the man behind the Taj Mahal, when he was serving as viceroy of Gujarat. The upper-caste middle class began to move out around the beginning of the twentieth century, setting up housing colonies on the western side of the Sabarmati river which borders the walled city at its northern end. Their place was taken by lower-caste Hindus, and violence broke out frequently between the new entrants and Muslim residents of the walled city, sparking off a further exodus (Patel 2002: 204–20). Walking around the old pols one finds many of the houses have been turned into godowns or are being used to run small businesses such as printing presses. There are many however who stubbornly refuse to move out. Like 69-year-old Upendra Adhyaru.

I meet Adhyaru on the occasion of Uttarayan, the annual kite-flying festival. He is seated in a comfortable wooden armchair on the top floor of his three-storyed house. A narrow steep staircase leads up to the airy rooms. Looking down one would think one is in a doll's house in a toy town. Any impression of fragility however would be misleading.

In the massive earthquake that hit Gujarat in January 2001, entire buildings came crashing down in the newer parts of Ahmedabad city to the west of the river. Adhyaru's ancient house, however, as he proudly points out, did not show so much as a crack.

Ironically, natural disasters appear to affect the newer parts of the city far more than the old pol area. In 2000 and in 2005 entire neighborhoods were flooded (in 2005 these included areas such as Jodhpur and Vastrapur in the west) mainly due to unplanned construction (Ray 2005: 3004–6) while the pols were unaffected.

There is a great deal of hustle and bustle about. Uttarayan is the most popular festival in Ahmedabad and the fervor with which it is celebrated in the walled city attracts visitors from all over the city and further. Adhyaru's sons have come with their wives and children and friends have been dropping in through the day. Preparations had begun some days before with the buying of the kites and the sharp *manjha* (the string used for hoisting kites) and the making of dry snacks and tea. In the night there will be a feast of *undhyu*, a traditional dish made by roasting vegetables in a mud pot underground that will be open to the residents of the pol and their guests. When I ask him about the changing life in the pols he admits that things are not as they used to be. Communal tension and the potential for it to erupt into violence is a perennial hazard for those living in the pols. So many of his neighbors have moved out. Strangers have taken their place. Those that are left behind have to deal with an assortment of problems, one being the difficulty in finding girls willing to marry boys living in the pols.

As far as he is concerned, however, he says there is nowhere else in the world where he would rather live. I ascend the stairs to the terrace. All around me, on every rooftop, are figures with their arms at work and their heads gazing up at a sky filled with colorful rectangles of paper. From the ground comes the metallic clanging of vessels being readied for the evening feast and it is easy to see why it would be hard to leave.

But there is a whole new city that has come up on the other side of the river. Ahmedabad was originally established on the eastern bank of the Sabarmati river. Over time, the population spread westward. Maps show the city in the shape of an expanding circle with the river dividing it in almost equal halves. The Ahmedabad Municipal Corporation was established in 1950 and grew from an area of 52.49 square kilometers in 1950 to 190.84 square kilometers in 1991; and its population from 2.8 million to 3.5 million. In 2006, the Gujarat government increased the area of the Ahmedabad Municipal Corporation to 500 square kilometers by merging seven municipalities. The move increased the city's population to approximately 4.5 million.

Middle-class housing colonies, universities, shopping complexes, offices, and slums came up on the west. Over the years, bungalows have given way to tall apartment blocks and malls, multiplexes, educational institutions, temple complexes, and a new High Court building have come up all over the west, particularly along the Sarkhej-Gandhinagar Highway that runs alongside the western edge of the city and connects it to the capital of the state, Gandhinagar. New expansions are also taking place thanks to the activities of the Ahmedabad Urban Development Authority (AUDA), constituted in 1978 by the Government of Gujarat under the provision of the Gujarat Town Planning and Urban Development Act, 1976, for the planned development of the peripheral areas of the city. AUDA's most recent and spectacular achievement has been the building of the 76-kilometer and 60-meter wide Sardar Patel Ring Road which now runs like a gleaming ribbon around the entire city.

But we are still on the east, passing neighborhoods with musical names such as Sarangpur, Raipur, Astodia, Khamsa, and Raikhad. The discovery of relics such as a sculpture from the eleventh or twelfth century of a two-armed Surya in the neighborhood, and references in ancient writings, suggest that a town by the name of Ashaval probably existed hereabouts prior to the establishment of fifteenth-century

Ahmedabad. Much has also been made of the possible existence of another such town, Karnavati, said to have been established by the Solanki ruler, Karnadeva, in the latter part of the eleventh century. Gujarat's ruling Hindu party is partial to this hypothesis and efforts have even been made to change the name of the city to Karnavati. The efforts have not succeeded but many private establishments including a popular club and an upscale car showroom bear the name Karnavati.

Much more is known about the city's Islamic origins, however. The history books describe Ahmed Shah, the founder of Ahmedabad, as being a man of vaulting ambition. It was his wish to be the progenitor of a great dynasty that is said to have led him to build Ahmedabad, a city which would serve to replace the old Hindu capital of Anahilvada Patan, 70 miles to the north, with a suitably grand capital of his own making (Gillion 1968: 14). To this end he initiated construction on a large scale. He built walls, gates, palaces, mosques, wide streets, marketplaces, and artificial lakes. The city he built evoked the admiration of several travelers. The sixteenth-century Persian work *Haft Iqlim*, for instance, called Ahmedabad a "grand beautiful town," and John Jourdain, a British traveler who visited it in 1611 on his travels through Arabia, India, and the Malay archipelago, called it "one of the fairest cities in all the Indies" (Shah 2007: 2).

Driving around Ahmedabad one can be surprised and delighted by the sudden glimpse of aged monuments that fuse Hindu craftsmanship and local motifs with Islamic plan geometry, pointed arches, domes, and *jaalis* (latticed screens) (Pandya and Rawal 2002: 104). Even buildings from Ahmed Shah's time still stand and are part of a vibrant evolving landscape, including the magnificent Jami Mosque (1424 CE) of which John Burton-Page writes: "The harmony of solids and voids in its noble façade makes it one of the loveliest mosques in India" (Burton-Page 1988: 32). The magnificence of Ahmedabad's architecture is widely acknowledged. In few cities is one likely to find the range of styles that is on display here: Sultanate, Moghul, Hindu, vernacular, colonial, modern, and contemporary. In the 1950s and 1960s Ahmedabad's wealthy mill-owners even invited internationally acclaimed architects such as Le Corbusier and Louis Kahn to build institutions and private homes in the city. The city has inspired several reputed local architects and is also home to the country's leading architecture school, the Center for Environmental Planning and Technology. But while Ahmedabad's builders made the city of brick, stone, wood, and cement, what gave it life was a substance that was far less concrete, something softer, more pliable, and more personal. That something was cloth.

If one were to take a detour and drive south one would pass the blue boards advertising the names of the various *chaalis* (housing complexes) and societies that came up more than a century ago to house laborers who had migrated to the city from villages in Gujarat to work in the cotton mills. Scattered around these are settlements inhabited by migrants from other states such as Uttar Pradesh and Rajasthan. In the beginning these colonies had houses which were little more than huts made of tin sheets. Now many of them have cement walls and tiled roofs. The interiors show varying degrees of gentrification. Some residents may have put in a bit of furniture and acquired small indulgences such as a television set. In other places the conditions are more basic – with low ceilings, bare floors, and makeshift kitchens – and not radically different from the kind of dwelling one may expect to find in rural Gujarat.

Interspersed between these colonies are large, open plots of land. One comes upon these plots suddenly and without warning. Many of them have the look of a war zone, with piles of rubble lying all around; others are overgrown with wild foliage and resemble a forest in the making. Locals walking you around the place can still recall the names by which these spots were once known: Silver Mill, Jubilee Mill, Sarangpur Cotton no. 2, and so on, names that remind you of a time past, of what was probably the most significant chapter in the city's life. In the grounds of the city museum at Paldi across the river, there is a large, imposing marble statue of the man who was responsible for chaperoning Ahmedabad into the modern industrial age. The figure is of a man with a thick walrus moustache and piercing, distant eyes. He is elaborately attired, in a turban, dhoti, shoes, a robe, with a medal on his pocket and is seated on an enormous chair shaded by a pavilion. The caption reads:

> The Honourable Rao Bahadur Ranchhodlal Chhotalal C.I.E. Born April 1824 died Oct 1898 aged 74 years. First Introducer of Cotton Mill Industry Into Ahmedabad. First Indian President of the Ahmedabad Municipality from 1884 to 1898.

Ahmedabad has always been a textile center. As far back as the fifteenth century, cotton, velvet, silks, and silver and gold brocade from the city were being exported through the nearby port of Cambay to faraway places such as the Middle East, Europe, and Africa. With the advent of the industrial age, the market for handlooms declined. In 1818, the first Indian cotton mill was established in Calcutta, followed by Bombay which went on to become the center of the Indian cotton textile industry. Ahmedabad, with its dry climate, was considered unsuitable for the manufacture of cotton textile. Yet Ranchhodlal, a former government clerk, went to great lengths, including borrowing money, to import and establish a mill in the city in 1861. Ahmedabad's traders and merchants decided to follow Ranchhodlal's lead and by 1901 there were 29 mills in the city, a number which rose steadily to 77 by 1939. The number of people employed in the mills was 77,859 and by the end of the 1970s the worker strength had gone up to 160,000 (Breman and Shah 2004: 44).

Manilal Somabhai Parmar, now aged 59, was part of this labor force. Manilal was born into a mill-working family. Both his parents were employed in the mills. As a teenager he too started filling in for absentees on a temporary basis, gradually easing his way in 1968 into a permanent job at the Jubilee Mills which had a work-force of about 3,000. In those days he said, it was assumed that mill-workers' children would follow in their parents' footsteps and he was fortunate to find a job in a mill which was associated with the reputed Calico brand. Every morning, Manilal would leave home at 6.45 for the 7 a.m. shift. The mill was close enough for him to walk and there was usually someone headed his way. It was an eight-hour shift with a half-hour recess and one of his family members would bring him lunch from home. "We workers would eat together," he recalls. "Some of us liked to smoke a bidi or chew pan. Sometimes we drank alcohol. It was a good life with a regular income. One felt respected by one's family and by people in one's hometown."

But that life was not destined to last. According to Breman, the first round of closures in the late 1970s and early 1980s resulted in a cutback of 40,000 jobs. By late 1996 the workforce had shrunk to 25,000 (Breman and Shah 2004: 64). In Manilal's case, from 1982 onwards production declined and pay was reduced by half. By 1987, there was a lock on the mill gates. Manilal sat at home for a few months hoping the mills would start again. Then, when it became increasingly clear that prospects of the mills reopening were bleak, he bought a hand cart and started peddling ice in his neighborhood making 25 rupees a day. For a while after that he sold slippers but that business proved unprofitable. Finally he got a job as a security man. "I don't have to do anything, just sit in front of a building, wearing a uniform," he says. The pay is almost a fourth of what he earned in the mills, but he has resigned himself to the situation. Many of Manilal's colleagues found work in the processing houses that had come up in the fast emerging industrial areas towards the south, areas like Naroda, Odhav, and Vatwa. Others went on to work in the diamond industry; 72 per cent of the world's diamonds are processed in India. The nerve center of the industry is a city called Surat, to the south of Ahmedabad. But about three decades ago, units for diamond cutting and polishing began to open in Ahmedabad, driven primarily by the existence of labor that had been released by the closing of the textile mills. The diamond polishing industry came up in a neighborhood called Bapunagar, an area of bleak wide streets and crowded back lanes.

In late February and early March, 2002, these industrial areas on the outskirts of the city saw the greatest amount of violence. Naroda Patiya, for instance, is a large colony of narrow lanes and cement huts populated by people of a lower economic class, many of them daily wage earners. In March 2002, a mob consisting of thousands descended upon the colony to rape, pillage, and kill. The stories that have emerged from Naroda Patiya are stories of the utmost inhumanity and bestiality. One incident in particular, which has been testified to by witnesses and even those accused of perpetrating the violence but which, because of the lack of other evidence one must accept as possibly apocryphal, even in its telling has become symbolic of the barbarism of this episode of violence and involves a fetus being put to death at the point of a sword (Bunsha 2006: 37).

I am at the Ellis Bridge, the oldest link between the old city in the east and the new city in the west. The bridge has been expanded in recent years and traffic flows swiftly on either side. But in the center, the old British-built bridge with its looped metal sides has been retained, a remnant from the past. To my left is the ashram where Gandhi lived and spun and struggled to free the country from colonial rule. In his autobiography Gandhi listed his reasons for choosing to set up home in Ahmedabad. One reason he gives is language: Gujarati was his mother tongue and there is a university called the Gujarat Vidyapith in the city which he set up to give primacy to the vernacular. Another reason for his preference is the fact that Ahmedabad is an ancient center for handloom weaving which made it, according to him, "likely to be the most favourable field for the revival of the cottage industry of hand-spinning" (Gandhi 1927: 329).

To my right are hoardings of various companies, the tops of modern residential and office blocks, and the recognizable tower of a revolving restaurant. Below me I can see the walls of the new riverfront development project taking shape. The Sabarmati glimmers below, flat and still in its sandy bed. Khilnani, remarking on Indian cities that did not fit the easy dichotomies of academic rhetoric – of traditional and modern, pre-industrial and industrial, eastern and western city – called

Ahmedabad "an exceptionally intriguing and neglected case" (Khilnani 1998: 112). I feel the past and the future hovering on the bridge. I don't think either are giving way.

References

Breman, Jan, and Shah, Parthiv (2004) *Working in the Mill No More.* New Delhi: Oxford University Press.

Bunsha, Dionne (2006) *Scarred: Experiments with Violence in Gujarat.* New Delhi: Penguin.

Burton-Page, John (1988, reprinted 2003) Mosques and tombs. In *Ahmadabad*, ed. George Michell and Snehal Shah. Mumbai: Marg Publications, 30–119.

Gandhi, M. K. (1927) *My Experiments with Truth.* Ahmedabad: Navjivan Publishing House.

Gillion, Kenneth L. (1968) *Ahmedabad: A Study in Indian Urban History.* Berkeley: University of California Press.

Khilnani, Sunil (1998) *Idea of India.* New Delhi: Penguin.

Pandya, Yatin, and Rawal, Trupti (2002) *The Ahmedabad Chronicle: Imprints of a Millennium.* Ahmedabad: Vastu-Shilpa Foundation for Studies and Research in Environmental Design.

Patel, Sujata (2002) Urbanization, development and communalisation of society in Gujarat. In *The Other Gujarat*, ed. Takashi Shinoda. Mumbai: Popular Prakashan, 204–20.

Ray, C. N. (2005) Mismanagement of floods in Gujarat. *Economic and Political Weekly* July 9: 3004–6.

Shah, Amrita (2007) *Vikram Sarabhai – A Life.* New Delhi: Viking-Penguin.

Varshney, Ashutosh (2002–3) Understanding Gujarat violence. *Items and Issues* (SSRC newsletter) 4 (1): 1–5.

Vibrant Gujarat 2009, Government of Gujarat publication.

Chapter 6

Landscape and Infrastructure in the Late-Modern Metropolis

Matthew Gandy

Introduction

If we extend our understanding of landscape to encompass the interconnectedness of space and of infrastructure to encompass the experience of space it is clear that these two domains are closely related. The spaces that have emerged from the intersection between landscape and infrastructure range from designed spaces such as parks or gardens to an array of incidental spaces that co-exist alongside utilitarian structures such as canals, power plants, and railroad tracks. Added to this range of material intersections we also encounter a diversity of imaginary or virtual explorations of urban space. Both landscape and infrastructure are now the focus of a renewed wave of urban analysis marked by themes such as the adaptive capacity of cities to climate change, the application of ecological ideas to urban design, or the reuse of former industrial spaces. Yet much of this emerging literature lacks historical perspective: an overriding emphasis on "policy relevance" has ironically precluded many possibilities for critically rethinking the role of landscape and infrastructure in the contemporary city.

The term "landscape," derived from the sixteenth-century Dutch word *landschap*, was originally used for the demarcation of land but has subsequently become associated with a way of seeing space from a distance. This sense of landscape as a visual panorama – developing initially through landscape art – has subsequently expanded and diversified in the modern era to include a variety of urban and industrial spaces and their representations in art, cinema, and literature. In analytical terms there has been a shift from an emphasis on the relationship between landscape and the idealized human subject – a genre closely associated with nineteenth-century romanticism – to a more nuanced and dynamic interpretation of the precise contexts within which landscapes are produced and experienced.[1]

The New Blackwell Companion to the City Edited by Gary Bridge and Sophie Watson
© 2011 Blackwell Publishing Ltd

The term "infrastructure" has been used since the 1920s to refer to the basic physical and organizational structures such as roads, power lines, and water mains needed for the material and organizational aspects of modernity. In analytical terms the study of infrastructure ranges from technical and engineering challenges facing the construction, maintenance, and functional characteristics of vital networks to neo-Weberian insights into the organizational capacities and legitimation challenges facing the modern state. More recently, the study of infrastructure has been extended to include multi-dimensional analysis of the horizontal and vertical composition of space, the interrelationships between visible and invisible domains, and the transition from integrated modes of service provision to more socially and spatially differentiated systems.[2]

Excavations

The use of stratigraphic metaphors depicts urban space as a succession of layers or traces. The presence of Victorian suburbs in London or Wilhelmine-era apartment blocks in Berlin, for example, attests to characteristic phases in city building. Yet the cultural and ideological contexts within which these urban forms emerged is harder to discern and provides a shadowy corollary to the physical structures themselves. At one level, therefore, the outward appearance of cities can clearly be related to historical developments such as legislative or political efforts to modify processes of capitalist urbanization and in some cases facilitate the reorganization of urban space itself.

Contemporary turbulence in the global economy invites a reassessment of the role of economic factors in the development of cities. The influential writings of Aldo Rossi, for example, emphasize the centrality of political and economic history to urban analysis and the complex dialogue between past and present. Drawing extensively on the ideas of Hans Bernoulli, Maurice Halbwachs, and Werner Hegemann, Rossi turns our attention towards "urban artefacts" and the degree to which urban form reflects incipient trends that may be realized under precise historical circumstances. He shows how the reconstruction of nineteenth-century Berlin, Milan, and other cities emerged through a combination of changes in land ownership and new patterns of political power.[3]

Urban form can be interpreted as an accumulation of the past viewed through the concerns of the present. For the Durkheimian sociologist Maurice Halbwachs, social beliefs have a "double character" derived from this interplay between past and present. "They are collective traditions or recollections," writes Halbwachs, "but they are also ideas or conventions that result from a knowledge of the present."[4] How are we to make sense of the role of memory in urban culture? Halbwachs makes a distinction between autobiographical memory and historical memory: the first is directly experienced whereas the second reaches the individual only through written records, photographs, festivals, or other forms of commemoration.

Urban landscapes present an accumulation of collective memory interspersed with the private realm of individual experience. In W. G. Sebald's novel *Austerlitz*, for example, we follow the main protagonist through a series of European cities as we grapple with the problem of memory. We enter a world where "everything is lapsing into oblivion with every extinguished life, how the world is, as it were, draining itself, in that the history of countless places and objects which themselves have no power of memory is never heard, never described or passed on."[5] Sebald poses the dilemma that no one individual can possibly grasp the full human significance of the objects or spaces that surround them; the emotional space of the city must remain largely impenetrable beyond the limited scope of our experience. We are constantly encountering things that we were not looking for so that urban landscapes take on a serendipitous quality of unexpected connections. Arriving in Antwerp, for example, the central protagonist of *Austerlitz* is transfixed by the bizarre architectural eclecticism of Louis Delacenserie's design for the city's main railway station, completed in 1905. The mix of colonial, Byzantine, and Renaissance symbols induces a kind of profound unease or historical vertigo that provokes associations between his fragile psychological state and hidden dimensions to Belgian history.[6]

The problem of memory, sentience, and the surfeit of information is explored in Mamoru Oshii's animation *Ghost in the Shell* [*Kōkaku Kidōtai*] (1995) where we are told that the "advent of computers and the subsequent accumulation of incalculable data has given rise to a new system of memory and thought." These cyborgian encounters with urban space unsettle distinctions between "living" and "non-living" through the autonomous and self-organizational capacities of technical networks. We are confronted by a series of tensions between technophile readings of the emerging body–technology nexus and more skeptical and critical accounts that question the social and political implications of the enhanced role of technological networks in everyday life.[7]

The rise of the networked city marks one of the critical technological mediations of urban space; an emerging dynamic that binds the human body to the city and at the same time reorganizes distinctions between private and public space. The gradual integration of networks presents one facet of the evolving relationship between urban infrastructure and the public realm. The term "public realm," which is repeatedly invoked in relation to both landscape and infrastructure, is rooted in the evolving relationship between politics and the urban arena.[8] The rationalization of space reflects in part the desire of the modern state to acquire some degree of political legitimacy but also the need to facilitate capitalist urbanization itself as cities anxiously jostle for competitive advantage. The emergence of legislative and institutional innovations such as eminent domain or new forms of municipal finance enabled the building of large-scale infrastructure projects and marked a radical extension of the coordinating capacities of the state.[9] Established relationships between technological networks, urban form, and the modern state are now undergoing a further phase of adjustment in response to the neoliberal impetus towards spatial disaggregation and emerging security discourses of resilience and control.

Whilst technological networks in the global North have been marked by a high degree of organizational and technical integration – notwithstanding more recent counter-trends observable in many cities – they are nonetheless structurally related to the more fragmentary patterns and relationships that have characterized the global South through both colonial and postcolonial phases of development. It makes little sense to regard dysfunctional infrastructure networks in terms of their regional context alone: nineteenth-century Bombay and Glasgow, for example, form part of a larger urbanization process. Current debates over the "adaptive capacity" of cities to flooding and other threats pose questions regarding the global interconnections between capital and investment: just as the threat of disease exposed the political dynamics of the industrial city, we are now encountering new intersections between "landscapes of risk" and differential capacities to respond.

Ideologies

Contemporary cities have generated a wealth of cultural representations often reworking long-standing themes such as alienation, questions of identity, or the use of multiple narrative structures to simultaneously uncover different facets of urban life. In the writing of Paul Auster, Don DeLillo, or Jonathan Raban, for example, the city often takes the form of a code to be deciphered. In DeLillo's *Underworld* (1997) it is waste that reveals the city in its full complexity and abject materiality: a garbage dump is described as "medieval-modern, a city of high-rise garbage, the hell reek of every perishable object ever thrown together."[10] Similarly, in films such as Robert Altman's *Short Cuts* (1993) or Alejandro González Iñárritu's *Amores Perros* (2000) different facets of the city are revealed through the dramatic intersection between ostensibly unconnected worlds. In Iñárritu's Mexico City a car crash creates a moment of violent collision between wealth and poverty whereas in Altman's Los Angeles it is an earth tremor that momentarily connects the city.

Among the most acute observers of late-modern landscapes is the writer J. G. Ballard who is fascinated by seemingly mundane spaces such as airports or shopping centers. In *Concrete Island* (1973) Ballard explores the consequences of a bizarre accident in which a bleary-eyed driver is inadvertently hurled from an elevated highway onto a patch of waste ground surrounded on all sides by busy roads from which he cannot escape:

> Gasping at the night air, he no longer tried to control himself. He leaned helplessly against the embankment, hands deep in the cold soil. A faint dew already covered his torn suit, chilling his skin. He looked up at the steep slope, for a moment laughing aloud at himself.[11]

Yet Ballard's repeated focus on middle-class anxiety has aroused the suspicion of neo-Marxian critics such as Fredric Jameson:

> Let the Wagnerian and Spenglerian world-dissolutions of J. G. Ballard stand as exemplary illustrations of the ways in which the imagination of a dying class – in this case the cancelled future of a vanished colonial and imaginary destiny – seeks to intoxicate itself with images of death that range from the destruction of the world by fire, water and ice to lengthening sleep or the berserk orgies of high-rise buildings or superhighways reverting to barbarism.[12]

What does Jameson's reading of Ballard tell us about the ideological parameters of late modernity? The adjective "Ballardian" is now widely used to refer to unsettling or dystopian dimensions to modern landscapes but one cannot resist the sense that Ballard himself clearly enjoyed being in the hotels, malls, and other spaces that he meticulously dissected in his novels. Jameson's critique of Ballard is reminiscent of earlier criticisms leveled at the Italian film director Michelangelo Antonioni for his move away from neo-realism towards the cinematic exploration of the psychological effects of modern Italian landscapes.[13] For Ballard, it is the fragility of modernity – and the institutional threads that enable everyday life – that drives his ironic neo-Hobbesian vision of the future. Science fiction writing can stage scenarios through which critiques of contemporary society can be explored. In response to real events such as the flooding of New Orleans, for example, Ballard observed that it is the virulent racism displayed towards the survivors of the calamity that is more shocking than technological failure or social breakdown.[14]

What, if anything, is distinctive about the contemporary urban landscapes that Ballard, along with other artists, writers or film-makers, has attempted to respond to? If we try to characterize contemporary cities the term "postindustrial" is potentially misleading since various types of industrial cities are still emerging, especially in regions experiencing very high rates of economic growth, whilst some of the fastest growing cities of the global South were never significantly based on industrial production but owe their size to other factors such as trade or accelerated rates of migration. At a global level we encounter a striking contrast between fast-growing cities where every available space is used and the phenomenon of shrinking cities where economic decline and depopulation have left an oversupply of housing and infrastructure. In parts of east Germany, for example, these empty or emptying spaces are so expensive to maintain that whole districts have been scheduled for demolition.[15] Similarly, in Russia, Ukraine, and other parts of the former Soviet Union, defunct urban-industrial complexes have also experienced widespread abandonment.[16]

Where cities are undergoing processes of reconstruction landscapes are often at the forefront of political conflict over urban iconography. These disputes range from "heritage" based attempts to recreate an imaginary past to "nativist" preoccupations with the restoration of ecological assemblages that might correspond with previous periods of environmental history or landscape design.[17] At the heart of these disputes are rival interpretations of historical "authenticity" and resistance towards social and cultural change. Recent objections to non-Christian religious symbols in parts of Europe, for example, form part of a wider ideological dispute over social and cultural diversity.[18] We can find historical parallels with the emergence of new forms of nationalism in the twentieth century culminating in the forcible erasure of Jewish culture through much of Europe so that the heterogeneous character of many European cities was destroyed. The historian Mark Mazower shows how the city of Salonica, now Thessaloniki, lost a fifth of its population in a matter of weeks during 1943 as the entire Jewish population were sent to Auschwitz: a city which had enjoyed a prenationalist medley of Christian, Muslim, and Jewish culture for centuries was, during the twentieth century, violently and irrevocably transformed.[19]

An uncertainty surrounding the relationship between landscapes and the historical present pervades many cultural explorations of cities in cinema, photography, and other art forms. The neo-romanticist fascination with ruins or abandoned spaces has featured prominently in European cinema and reveals a lineage between early explorations in Italian neo-realism such as Roberto Rossellini's *Viaggio in Italia* [*Journey to Italy*] (1953) to more recent examples in Andrei Tarkovsky's *Stalker* (1979) or Wim Wenders's *Der Himmel über Berlin* [*Wings of Desire*] (1987). These cinematic explorations of space and memory also extend to the global South through films such as Jia Zhang-ke's *Sanxia hoaren* [*Still Life*] (2006) and *Wuyong* [*Useless*] (2007). In the cinema of Zhang-ke the unsettling characteristics of landscape serve as a subtle critique of the political impetus towards accelerated modernity and urbanization: in the case of *Sanxia hoaren* it is the eerie landscapes of abandoned towns to be flooded by the construction of dams, whilst the documentary *Wuyong* culminates in a Paris fashion show by a little-known designer of women's clothes Ma Ke. Ma Ke's paradoxical arrival in the rarified world of *haute couture* is contrasted with the marginal zones within which Chinese workers undertake the mass production of clothes for export.

The visual saturation of urban space by new advances in materials science and digital technologies invites a re-examination of landscape aesthetics. Of particular interest is the emergence of neo-Kantian readings of urban and industrial landscapes where an emphasis on the "technological sublime" has developed as part of a wider attempt to expand our understanding of landscapes that appear to fall outside of, or in some cases contradict, established genres of interpretation.[20] The sublime has historically been used primarily in relation to the aesthetic experience of nature but the concept has been gradually extended to encompass the scale of human artifacts in the landscape such as machines or vast industrial installations. The application of the sublime to artificial or manufactured landscapes has become linked with the "technological sublime" yet the application of the term has been mainly restricted to specific national contexts or focused on large-scale transformations such as opencast mining or the construction of dams.[21]

Another aesthetic concept that has diffused through recent urban discourse is the "pastoral." Unlike the sublime, and its relation to an "interior landscape" of cognitive disorientation, the pastoral originates in cultural depictions of idealized rural settings. The pastoral genre has been closely associated with attempts to portray the lives of the poor – principally peasants and agricultural laborers – to social and economic elites. An early critique of the pastoral is provided by Raymond Williams, who distinguishes between the classical pastoral of bucolic harmony and the existence of "counter pastoral" representations of landscape wherein the relationship between the experience and representation of material landscapes is radically reconfigured to allow the authentic voices of those who work or produce landscapes to be acknowledged.[22] More recently, the idea of the pastoral has been extended to urban and industrial landscapes in three main ways: first, an "urban pastoral" has emerged out of "a degraded form of the *rural* pastoral" produced by cultural parodies of working-class life in a context of art-led processes of gentrification;[23] second, we find connections between the representation of postindustrial landscapes that combine the aesthetic qualities of the sublime with a new kind of synthesis between nature and culture in the late-modern metropolis;[24] and third, the ideological dimensions to the urban pastoral can be extended to touristic settings such as colonial appropriations of idealized landscapes.[25] In all these cases it is the disjuncture between the production, representation, and consumption of landscapes that is of interest. The presence of the "urban pastoral" is not restricted to the global North but extends to luxury developments in Buenos Aires, Mumbai, Shanghai, and a host of other cities that use the pastoral idyll as a means to create elite refugia that betoken rarefied forms of social and cultural separation. The idea of the urban pastoral helps to elucidate the cultural dimensions to global gentrification in new ways and at same time offers points of conceptual dialogue between neo-Marxian political economy and the latest developments in architecture and urban design.

The challenge to nature-based metaphors has been an integral element in post-positivist strands of urban analysis since the early 1970s yet there has been a recent resurgence of "scientism" in urban thought.[26] A welter of nature-based metaphors ranging from neo-Malthusian concerns with urban growth to new bio-physical conceptions of urban space are filtering through contemporary urban discourse. The current upsurge of nature-based metaphors deployed in urban design can be criticized as a regression towards pre-Kantian forms of mimetic adaptation and a loss of architectural nerve.[27] Equally, the expanding role of nature in urban design – especially for quasi-public spaces such as hotel atria, storefronts, and other features – reveals how artful arrangements of nature can serve as little more than elaborate architectural masks.[28] These shifts in the metaphorical reading of urban space reflect several interconnected developments: the increasing influence of biomorphic design facilitated by the growing sophistication of modeling techniques; the diffusion of ecological sensibilities – however ill-defined– through urban discourse; and the impetus towards "ecological modernization" and various attempts to subsume cities within the parameters of an ecological utilitarianism.

Conclusions

A critical engagement with landscape and infrastructure reveals our own subjectivities: we are not dispassionate observers but are actively engaged in the creation of meaning through thinking, talking, and writing. The meaning of urban space is always in a state of flux but its interpretation is not beyond our grasp: the questions raised in this essay are not a prelude to neo-romanticist mystification but rather an invitation to engage with the cultural and material aspects of urban experience through a renewed theoretical synthesis. The combination of landscape with infrastructure necessarily brings questions of aesthetics and cultural representation into our analytical frame and immediately unsettles a narrowly social scientific approach to the study of cities.

The material and conceptual intersections between landscape and infrastructure pose a range of issues that transcend disciplinary boundaries. Unresolved tensions include the status of the human subject in the contemporary city; the need to navigate between the realm of individual experience and the accumulation of collective memory; and the ideological uses of nature under contemporary processes of capitalist urbanization. Above all, these themes remain highly political: the choice of specific concepts or metaphors about urban space holds implications for acting as well as thinking.

Notes

1 The period since the mid-1980s has seen a resurgence of landscape as a focus for inter-disciplinary study. See, for example, Denis Cosgrove, *Social Formation and Symbolic Landscape*. Madison: University of Wisconsin Press, 1998 (1984); Stephen Daniels, Marxism, culture, and the duplicity of landscape. In Richard Peet and Nigel Thrift (eds.), *New Models in Geography*. London: Unwin Hyman, 1989, 196–220; W. J. T. Mitchell (ed.), *Landscape and Power*. Chicago: Chicago University Press, 2002; Antoine Picon, Anxious landscapes: from the ruin to rust. *Grey Room* 1 (2000): 64–83; and Simon Schama, *Landscape and Memory*. New York: Alfred A. Knopf, 1995.

2 New approaches to the study of urban infrastructure include Sabine Barles, *La ville délétère: médecins et ingénieurs dans l'espace urbain XVIIIe–XIXe siècle*. Seyssel: Champ Vallon, 1999; Matthew Gandy, The Paris sewers and the rationalization of urban space. *Transactions of the Institute of British Geographers* 24 (1) (1999): 23–44; Stephen Graham and Simon Marvin, *Splintering Urbanism*. London and New York: Routledge, 2001; Elizabeth Heidenreich, *Fliessräume: Die Vernetzung von Natur, Raum und Gesellschaft seit dem 19. Jahrhundert*. Frankfurt: Campus, 2004; Maria Kaïka and Erik Swyngedouw, Fetishising the modern city: the phantasmagoria of urban technological networks. *International Journal of Urban and Regional Research* 24 (2000): 120–38; Michelle Kooy and Karen Bakker, Technologies of government: constituting subjectivities, spaces, and infrastructures in colonial and contemporary Jakarta. *International Journal of Urban and Regional Research* 32 (2008): 375–91; Colin McFarlane, Sanitation in Mumbai's informal settlements: state, "slum," and infrastructure. *Environment and Planning A* 40 (2008): 88–107; Jochen Monstadt, Conceptualizing the political ecology of urban infrastructures: insights from technology and urban studies. *Environment and Planning A* 41 (2009): 1924–42; and Rosalind Williams, *Notes on the Underground: An Essay on Technology, Society and the Imagination*. 2nd edn. Cambridge, MA: MIT Press, 2008.

3 Aldo Rossi, *The Architecture of the City*, trans. Diane Ghirardo and Joan Ockman. Cambridge, MA: MIT Press, 1982 (1966). See also Manfredo Tafuri, *Architecture and Utopia: Design and Capitalist Development*, trans. Barbara Luigia La Penta. Cambridge, MA: MIT Press, 1976 (1973).

4 Maurice Halbwachs, *On Collective Memory*, trans. Lewis Coser. Chicago: University of Chicago Press, 1992 (1925/1941), 188. See also Andreas Huyssen, *Present Pasts: Urban Palimpsests and the Politics of Memory*. Stanford, CA: Stanford University Press, 2003.

5 W. G. Sebald, *Austerlitz*, trans. Anthea Bell. London: Penguin, 2001, 30–1.

6 Sebald further develops this exploration of Belgian colonial history in *The Rings of Saturn*, trans. Michael Hulse. London: Harvill, 1998 (1995).

7 See Matthew Gandy, Cyborg urbanization: complexity and monstrosity in the contemporary city. *International Journal of Urban and Regional Research* 29 (2005): 26–49 and Antoine Picon, *La ville territoire des cyborgs*. Paris: Les Éditions de l'imprimeur, 1998.

8 See, for example, J. Clarke, Dissolving the public realm: the logic and limits of neoliberalism. *Journal of Social Policy* 33 (2004): 27–48; Sudipta Kaviraj, Filth and the public sphere: concepts and practices about space in Calcutta. *Public Culture* 101 (1997): 83–113; and L. Lofland, *The Public Realm: Exploring the City's Quintessential Social Territory*. New York: Aldine de Gruyter, 1998.

9 See Susanne Frank and Matthew Gandy (eds.), *Hydropolis: Wasser und die Stadt der Moderne*. Frankfurt: Campus, 2006, 41–56; Matthew Gandy, Landscapes of disaster: water, poverty and urban fragmentation in Mumbai. *Environment and Planning A* 40 (2008): 108–30.

10 Don DeLillo, *Underworld*. London: Picador, 1997, 104.

11 J. G. Ballard, *Concrete Island*. London: Jonathan Cape, 1973, 24.

12 Fredric Jameson, Progress versus utopia: or, can we imagine future? In *Archaeologies of the Future*. London: Verso, 2005 (1982), 288.

13 Matthew Gandy, Landscapes of deliquescence in Michelangelo Antonioni's *Red Desert*. *Transactions of the Institute of British Geographers* 19 (2003): 218–37.

14 J. G. Ballard, Gewahlt ohne Ende. Interview with Evelyn Finger in *Die Zeit* (September 8, 2005).

15 Matthias Koziol, Dismantling infrastructure. In Philipp Oswalt (ed.), *Shrinking Cities*. Ostfildern: Hatje Cantz, 2006, 76–9.

16 Caroline Humphrey, Rethinking infrastructure: Siberian cities and the great freeze of January 2001. In Jane Schneider and Ida Susser (eds.), *Wounded Cities: Destruction and Reconstruction in a Globalized World*. Oxford and New York: Berg, 2003, 91–107.

17 See, for example, Gert Gröning, Ideological aspects of nature garden concepts in late twentieth-century Germany. In Joachim Wolshke-Bulmahn (ed.), *Nature and Ideology: Natural Garden Design in the Twentieth Century*. Washington, DC: Dumbarton Oaks, 1997, 221–48; and Stuart Hall, Creolization, diaspora, and hybridity in the context of globalization. In O. Enwezor, Carlos Basualdo, Ute Meta Bauer, Susanne Ghez, Sarat Maharaj, Mark Nash, and Octavio Zaya (eds.), *Documenta 11_Platform 3. Créolité and creolization*. Ostfildern-Ruit: Hatje Cantz, 2003, 185–98.

18 On the background to the 2009 Swiss referendum see Haig Simonian, Mosque vote threatens to isolate Swiss. *Financial Times* (November 23, 2009).

19 Mark Mazower, *Salonica: City of Ghosts*. London: HarperCollins, 2004.

20 See, for example, Scott Bukatman, The artificial infinite: on special effects and the sublime. In Linda Cooke and Peter Wollen (eds.), *Visual Display: Culture beyond Appearances*. Seattle, WA: Bay Press, 1995, 255–89; Paul Crowther, *Les immatériaux* and the postmodern sublime. In A. Benjamin (ed.), *Judging Lyotard*. London and New York: Routledge, 1992, 192–205; Eugène Freyssinet, On the sublime. *Arq: Architectural Research Quarterly* 5 (2001): 249–53; and George Hartley, *The Abyss of Representation: Marxism and the Postmodern Sublime*. Durham, NC: Duke University Press, 2003.

21 See, for example, David Nye, *American Technological Sublime*. Cambridge, MA: MIT Press, 1994; and Lori Pauli (ed.), *Manufactured Landscapes: The Photographs of Edward Burtynsky*. New Haven, CT: Yale University Press, 2003.

22 Raymond Williams, *The Country and the City*. Oxford: Oxford University Press, 1973.

23 Julian Stallabrass, *High Art Lite*. London and New York: Verso, 1999, 142.

24 See, for example, Vittoria DiPalma, Blurs, blots and clouds: architecture and the dissolution of surface. *AA Files* 54 (2006): 24–35; and Sandro Marpillero, Art as landscape architecture. *Lotus* 128 (2006): 64–75.

25 This argument is developed by Eyal Weizman in relation to occupied territories in Palestine. See Eyal Weizman, The politics of verticality: the West Bank as an architectural construction. In Klaus Biesenbach, Anselm Franke, Rafi Segal, and Eyal Weizman (eds.), *Territories: Islands, Camps and Other States of Utopia*. Berlin: KW Institute for Contemporary Art, 2003, 64–118.

26 Examples include Gunther Feuerstein, *Biomorphic Architecture*. Stuttgart: Axel Menges, 2002; Michael Hensel and Achim Menges (eds.), *Morpho-ecologies*. London: Architectural Press, 2006; Francesco Repishti, Green architecture. Oltre la metafora. *Lotus* 135 (August 2008): 34–41.

27 See Matteo Vercelloni, Mimesis, design and nature. *Lotus* 135 (August 2008): 86–95.

28 See Owen Hatherley, Living façades: green urbanism and the politics of urban offsetting. Monu (August 2009), 32–41, and Repishti, Green architecture.

Chapter 7

Objects and the City

Harvey Molotch

City life involves not just relations of people with one another or with environment in some generic sense of spatiality or natural resources. People live in a world of objects; the city can be thought of as a forest of artifacts. Buildings and their architecture as well as formal city plans have received much analytic attention in urban scholarship (see, e.g., Gieryn 2002; Brain 2008); my focus is on the artifacts, including those which are quite mundane. Some of these objects are privately acquired consumer goods (cars, jewelry), but some involve public infrastructures like subway turnstiles or traffic lights. I rely heavily on a series of recent research projects, mostly my own, to illustrate how objects function in city life.

The Background Issue

We run into many things and these contacts, even if fleeting, are of profound consequence. In dealing with, respecting, being stopped by, creating, judging, buying, altering, placing, using, and disposing of goods, people are simultaneously manipulating and deploying the make-up of their own selves. Without resorting to any version of ridiculous animism, it is possible indeed to see inanimate objects as "actants" – a word used, apparently independently, by the British anthropologist Alfred Gell (1998) and French sociologist Bruno Latour (2005) to properly recognize the inanimate as part of the persistent mutuality of the material and the social. Latour (and probably Gell, who died in the midst of his work) argues for symmetry of methodological approach between humans and objects. These scholars do not have some idealized vision of ontological equality (see Preda 1999). Instead, they treat the two realms as equal because indeed they are, in reality, bound up with one another. This means you can pick up the trail of sociality by focusing on the goods

The New Blackwell Companion to the City   Edited by Gary Bridge and Sophie Watson
© 2011 Blackwell Publishing Ltd

as much as the reverse. The goal becomes to attend to the material–social nexus as it occurs as ongoing process.

At a micro-level of the human–object interface, the objects forge the body and vice versa. We are more than tool *users*; as Nigel Thrift remarks: "the evidence suggests that organs like the hand, the gut, and the various other muscle and nerve complexes" and the brain itself have evolved in synch with tool use. Through this interpretation, "the human body is a tool-being" (Thrift 2007: 10). If we can understand "tools" as going beyond the narrow utilitarian sense, virtually all artifacts (whether a wrench or an oil painting) are, in some sense, tools and thus deeply human-making. Each object generates a particular choreography of movement and reinforces an "ensemble" (Elizabeth Shove's term [2003]) of other stuff with which it "goes" – whether in stylistic or mechanical terms. A desktop manual stapler, as opposed to paper clips or electric models, carries its own moments of thought: anticipating the downward sweep of palm on to a flat bar and then the discharge of staple through paper sheets that give way to the mighty thrust. Among the satisfactions is coming to see what were separate things in the world now conjoined as one. Some movements become reinforced, the hand sweep, maybe to arise again as a motor apparatus for a next product that will draw on its presence in the inventory of at-the-ready human capacities. Maybe it will be a recognizable disco gesture. Some people will have more trouble than others with the standard manual stapler and, compared to the electric model, be at a stapling disadvantage because their unsteady hand (Parkinson's perhaps) makes them "clumsy."

Focus on a specific object can reveal patterns of disease in ways that otherwise escape clinical or epidemiological analysis. In investigating prevalence of US AIDS infections, Bourgois and Ciccarone focus on the interaction of heroin type and the mechanics of the syringe used to inject it (Ciccarone and Bourgois 2003). In some parts of the USA – like San Francisco where the researchers were based – heroin users inject "Mexican black tar," which is a tacky, heavy type substance that gums up a syringe. For this reason, users rinse their syringe frequently to keep it from clogging, so much so that ethnographer Bourgois was worried that he might be infected by the splash from the users nearby.[1] But all the rinsing happens to have the positive consequence of removing blood traces from prior injections (and injectors), an act that decreases risk of AIDS. This maneuver, as well as other procedures needed to keep the stuff flowing through the syringe, results in significantly lower rates of AIDS infection among users of this type of heroin compared to the main alternative, which is in powder form. Bourgois and Ciccarone needed to explain geographic variation in AIDS infection among drug users and noticed a correlation between US region and type of heroin used. Through close attention to the syringe in action (something that could be done by the ethnographer Bourgois), the researchers were able to explain an outcome that might have otherwise remained elusive. The focus on an appliance in situ, along with an ecological correlation, contributes to a causal explanation.

As used by industrial designers, the term "affordance" indicates the capacity of an object to help people do something by virtue of its "interface" features – how it invites and facilitates doing some particular action. One of the pleasures and satisfactions of everyday life is meeting up with an affordance – experiencing the right "give" of a door or the "feel" of a lever whose downward motion signifies one's competence and capacity to move the world. Some types of affordance are probably universal, like the peelability of a banana skin, but others – like a kayak oar or cell-phone feature – are specific to a historic and social niche. As with the banana or kayak (or syringe), the object calls forth a particular behavioral repertoire that becomes intrinsic to worlds of sociality and production. The specifics of the goods distribute costs and benefits across social groups, nations, and the ecological system.

Building on some of the starts that others have made in trying to understand these amplifications, I discuss some projects and also point to implications for how to make use of thingness as method.

The Subway

In interviews and observations among New York city subway workers, Noah McClain and I focus on the instrumentation and workers' equipment under the city's streets (for a first result, see Molotch and McClain 2008). One of our prime artifacts is the turnstile, a mechanism to prevent people from riding for free. In his example of the automatic door-closer, Latour (1992) shows how this "helpful" object actually penalizes some individuals and classes of individuals, like package delivery people (see also Akrich 1992). The turnstile operates in the same way, making it difficult, for example, for food caterers to balance trays or people trying to move a chair from one location to another (see Figure 7.1). Just as interesting to us as the distribution of benefit, is the *dynamic* nature of the process: design, user-reaction, including "resistance" of sorts. Under conditions in the early and mid-twentieth century, many turnstiles were sufficiently simple (naive?) that even old or obese people could crawl under or climb over them (see Figure 7.2). In response, each "improvement" from the authorities altered who could and could not cheat the system and rearranged exactly how they could do so. Under some designs, crawling is foreclosed, but leaping still works, at least for the young and fit (this leap, actually a dive-leap tailored to the equipment, is said to have reappeared as a particular hip-hop dance move). The linkage of the more recent turnstiles to the Metrocard, which replaced coin-like tokens, generated the art of card-bending. A subtle twist of an exhausted card restores its functionality for one more ride at the machine. Now imposing young men, sophisticated in this technique (but not necessarily physically agile), gather up spent cards and then sell "swipes" to those looking for a discounted rate. It is not just illegal to sell swipes, but also to buy them, so the new system rearranges and expands the circle of criminality.

The fare-beating dynamic intersects, however, with other subway aspects. The most rigorous turnstiles, called "High Entry/Exit Turnstile" or "HEET" (see Figure 7.3) can cause human pile-ups, particularly when masses of teenagers, exuberant from just getting out of school, clog turnstile entries. Because of the difficulty of getting an injured person out of the system (like moving a gurney through the turnstile!) there is the further risk of delaying the trains for an extended period. As a solution, station agents can use buttons in their booths to unlock the doors, allowing anyone – with or without a Metrocard – to move through more quickly. This is an unauthorized but common response of the workers, however contrary to the rules. The HEET turnstiles also threaten orderly evacuation in case of emergencies like fire, a not uncommon event. In response to concerns of safety officials as well as those

Figure 7.1 Abandoned chaise. Photo Noah McCain.

alerted through journalistic reports, the Transit Authority installed Emergency Exit Doors. These doors are now used routinely for non-emergencies, opening up new possibilities for fare beaters to enter as others exit. As they do.

In these ways and others, public infrastructure instrumentation rewards some and penalizes others. In so doing, it marks off changing "publics" in the John Dewey sense, new conjoinings of people with a distinctive connection to the urban artifact. People thus meet with these set-ups as convenience or inconvenience, injustice or even, potentially, catastrophe. What we do not know much about is what these publics make of it: how much they blame the infrastructure or the nameable agencies behind it as against their own clumsiness. We see the muttering – but what is the muttering politics?

The Public Toilet

Sometimes the urban research object is one that tends toward taboo, and the silence itself becomes revelatory. Public toilets, albeit only haltingly, are finally gaining some traction in scholarly circles (see especially Greed 2003; Gershenson and Penner

Figure 7.2 New York subway turnstile, 1942. Photo courtesy of New York Transit Museum.

2009; Molotch and Noren 2010). The toilet is itself a kind of chair; according to architect scholar Galen Cranz, chairs evidently first arose to display status as in the throne and to offer respect as when people invite one to "have a seat" (Cranz 1999, see also Rudofsky 1980). As the chair became ubiquitous, musculature developed accordingly and people came to then *need* it. As the chair informs the mind and becomes intrinsic to social interaction, it alters (deforms, Cranz complains) the physique. The chair along with the pew and indeed the toilet snatches the body, creating a Latourian hybrid/Haraway cyborg. Those who do not use chairs (some for medical reasons, like Cranz), and children who "can't sit still" risk being labeled as deviant. For peoples who specialize in chair-sitting, it fosters the idea that those who crouch, eat on rugs, or squat when they defecate must indeed be primitive. And this is reinforced by other elements common to the squatting ensemble, like the use of water to cleanse rather than rubbing with toilet paper – the latter considered more decent.

In terms of public places, the toilet is indispensable – "the big necessity" as Rose George (2008) proclaims it. Here we have the striking reality of biology, in all its "bare life" (Thrift 2007: 69, citing Agamben 1998: 187 whose use differs from mine) entering into the scene of human volition. Given the way probably all people of the world are anxious about their personal waste, fear and anxiety graft on to

Figure 7.3 No entry HEET. Photo Noah McCain.

the array of particulars of the appliance. People must "go" and they take the immediate conditions very seriously. These conditions include who (if anyone) is adjacent
and precisely what "adjacent" – in spatial, aural, olfactory terms – means. How the
appliance articulates with extant notions of sanitation, security, and privacy further
modulates the nature of the experience and indeed whether it can happen at all.
The option is to just not leave home or immediate neighborhood rather than be
mesmerized into paruresis or some other, and more serious, elimination-related
ailment. The presence (or absence) of adequate facilities – including the details of
appliances provided by class, ethnicity, age, gender and cultural comfort – thus
structures urban life.

There are also implications for the methods of urban mobility. If rest rooms (of
the right sort) are at bus stations and subway stops, people can more easily do
without cars. Cyclists and pedestrians also benefit from appropriately located and
outfitted facilities. This effects how transportation systems shape the city as well as
the capacity to institute urban ecological reform (Greed 2003).

Making it easier for some people, say men, to relieve themselves, creates inequality in capacity to participate in public life by gender. Segregating genders with clear
signage and strong conventions against mixing reinforces the gender binary as a
critical basis of human classification – more so than class or age, for example. Racial

segregation in toilet use long marked off fear of the racial other in the US South, where it was more intensely enforced compared to other settings, like workplace or neighborhood. Caste in India works the same way and also, in a subtler and contested realm, how those with physical disability are dealt with – the quality of their accommodation and its degree of separation from others' facilities. Shifts in classification, altering benefits and losses to groups within these classifications, distributes comfort, dignity, and public capacity.

Changing Art

A work of art and city morphology can be seen as a single conjoined apparatus. Many have noted how artists cluster in bohemias and agree that this influences the art itself as creators mix and mingle, sometimes also with proximate dealers and patrons. There are agglomeration benefits in this creative sector just as there are in more quotidian sorts of industrial districts (Storper 1997). Collaborating with Mark Treskon, I have been working out other modes to see art and city as a blend (Molotch and Treskon 2009). A generation ago, Howard Becker (1984) remarked in his book, *Art Worlds*, that the height of the gallery's door determines the size of the art. Simple but true. Size also mattered, as Sharon Zukin (1982) documents in describing the rise of SoHo as the pre-eminent world center of contemporary art in the early 1980s. The studios were big and so was the art. But this happened not simply through aesthetic shifts in the history of art but through underlying changes in the urban system. It was not a simple consequence of government efforts at "gentrification" (government in fact, at least in the early phases, harassed the artists). Instead the process was indirect and heterogeneous.

As part of the era's deindustrialization, manufacturers left SoHo, but the city's zoning permitted only manufacturing. The combination caused the deserted buildings to plummet deeply in value. Artists then moved in illegally to live and work. Their studios were big and cheap. And illegality meant the artists would be offbeat, inventive, and risk-takers. Other compatible art world trends were in motion among artists working in more rural settings (Jackson Pollock's earlier drip paintings in his Long Island barn for example) to make big stuff, but the capacity to do so in an area close to the heart of Manhattan yielded a major shift in what art could be – and an appreciation by nearby critics and collectors of the result.

Of course, as the story is oft told, the success of the art brought in retail and high-end residential, eviscerating SoHo as a gallery district. This then led to art galleries moving on to the very cheap quarters of the Chelsea neighborhood, another deserted district not far away. Chelsea had even bigger spaces, encouraging still larger scales of work. This came to include installation projects – composites of found and created artifacts, including electronic and computer-generated displays. More than in SoHo, Chelsea, which had been used for warehouses, taxi storage structures, and utility services, had buildings with loading docks, full-open frontage, and industrial elevators. Following the SoHo pattern, rents began to rise, and indeed by some measures came to be even higher than the level for SoHo. But Chelsea thrives as an art gallery district, now the dominant venue in the world.

How is this possible? It survives because the price of art, as we have carefully worked out in our research, has risen faster than the price of space, even in the hot real estate market of the early twenty-first century. It also survives by changing the linkage between where artists live and work and where and how their art is shown. Chelsea is not a bohemia; artists live and work elsewhere, a pattern found in other parts of the world and indeed partly true for New York in its history as well. The new twist is a disconnect between art making and art showing facilitated by the nature of the real-estate market, the art market, and the art itself. Genres like installation art *do not exist* prior to their exhibition in a gallery (see Wharton and Molotch 2009). Wherever the artist lives or works, certain elements can be mocked-up, but they come together for the first time (sometimes even the last time) in the exhibition space. It may be that the work requires the active participation of gallery visitors to even exist – such as John Cage's incorporation of the footfall of gallery visitors and the sound of their openings and closings of cabinet doors and drawers as intrinsic to the work. Video art may rely for its impact on the scale and geometry and other particulars of the setting as well. But the artist can work in a small space, maybe just big enough for a laptop.

Galleries go on to accumulate as a "scene" (Currid 2007; Storper and Venables 2004), but not as a bohemia. Patrons, well heeled and/or young and flâneuresque, come to create buzz as they interact with the art – something long-noticed by analysts of shopping in prior times (Blumer 1969; Leach 1994). The bottom line is that the goods become the place as the place becomes the goods. Taking the goods as the point of analytic focus informs about aesthetics, sociability, and place making. And the future: the Chelsea gallery district could be doomed if art tastes shift away from big-scale toward miniatures, for example, or if some unanticipated big space buyers (bankruptcy specialists?) need and can pay for the space in a collapsing art market. Various scenarios are possible; the current point is that it will be the nature of the linkage between place and product, part of what I have elsewhere called the "lash-up" (Molotch 2003) that will inform what is co-produced.

Small City

Including materiality helps explain not only the way places change, but how they do not change – at least not in the sense of altering their "personality" or "tradition" compared to other cities and towns. Artifactual elements, as they accumulate both over the place and across time, show how historical recapitulations operate – making places durably different from one another, even under common conditions of industrialization (or capitalism or globalism).

A research group in which I participated (Molotch *et al.* 2000) contrasted the development of 17 different towns and cities in central and southern California. California has a more or less single "main street" of a freeway, Highway 101, that runs from the Mexican border to the boundary with the state of Oregon. Many jurisdictions, over time, have thus had to deal with the physical structure coming through – and their choices were very limited by the fact that state and national actors controlled the decision. Nonetheless, they could lobby, finesse, and alter the design through strategic actions. In our research, we came to focus in particular on the contrasting ways the cities of Ventura and Santa Barbara dealt with this hardware – two cities that were similar in at least some regards, but the "same thing" was a different phenomenon in the two places. It becomes methodologically possible to understand places through the different ways they dealt with the same type of exogenous project (see economist Albert Hirschman's classic work (1958), for the argument applied in a still larger context).

In Ventura, prior decisions of the city had come to favor spot industrialization at the waterfront to service oil companies, an industry equally active in Santa Barbara, but frustrated in that city by environmentally oriented residents. The industrial presence in Ventura lowered the amenity value of the coast thus making it cheaper, financially and politically, to acquire oceanfront land for road building. The freeway, in turn, undermined "higher uses" in the future, in particular hindering successive efforts to build ocean-related tourist facilities, or an amenity-based so-called "creative economy." These realities then reverberated throughout the cultural, political, and economic life of the locality, reinforcing place direction and sharpening its distinction from other coastal places. Beyond the big scale of oil and freeway were the small-scale details almost always overlooked in urban development studies. So in Ventura, the city, in "restoring" its historic Mission (the base of tourist development throughout California), mistakenly used an art nouveau tile, rather than the "Mexican" design otherwise thought correct by those in the know. This wrong tile can then be explicitly recognized as a sign of backwardness among the high cultural capital set and even those who do not have explicit knowledge, I think, perceive the "wrongness" without necessarily being aware. The city, in all its particulars and also as a sweeping gesture of landscape and topography "gives off," as Erving Goffman (1959) might say, and is hence imbibed by those within it. Its geography forms rounds and sounds of first-hand experience of co-present human and material vivacity, something that even the most sophisticated of communication technologies cannot provide.

Migrants, individuals, and now quite famously firms (Florida 2003) self-select as they move in and out. In the social and cultural multiplier effects of such exits and entries, they reinforce the meaning of local citizenship, the sense of what is right or wrong for the place, and the kinds of politics it should have to perpetuate its arrays of life. Each iteration of physical intervention gives direction to successive interventions to form a fixity over time – a tradition of place. There is a kind of grand path dependence of interacting parts, complex and additive in its structurating evolution. The place comes to be grasped through the details of experiencing it. And all this also rebounds into local elections and the disposition of the city budget, which further impact the next rounds of events and physical specificities.

Thing as Method

All these various examples point to the way the object can be a site of research strategy, useful as a consequential stop that can be, as a practical matter grabbed, held, and followed by the researcher. It also helps in a very practical sense of having something to facilitate interaction with research subjects when doing fieldwork or conducting interviews. People are quite willing and able to talk about the objects in their homes, for example, so this becomes a way into understanding family relations, social aspirations, health and economic problems, something the anthropologist Daniel Miller has done with especially good effect (Miller 2009). It eases

Figure 7.4 Kamehmeha. Photo Glenn Wharton.

awkwardness and leads into the content of lives and relationships without the need to ask directly about them.

Some people have the job of always working with objects – sculpture conservators are among them. Glenn Wharton, a conservator of public monuments, also with a background in social science, took on the restoration of a particular statue on the "Big Island" of Hawaii (Wharton 2009). It is arguably the state's most significant artifact, the original statue of King Kamehmeha (see Figure 7.4) – celebrated as "uniter" of the islands and commemorated on the official state seal and vast varieties of tourist souvenirs. Wharton used the opportunity not only to "preserve" the statue, but also to use its preservation to further ethnographic understanding of the present meaning of "Hawaiian." Local people, as it turned out, had been painting this nineteenth-century bronze figure in life-like colors at regular intervals for generations. No one had known that the artist who had designed the statue, a Bostonian living in Florence, had originally gilded it in gold leaf (with no paint, anywhere). The sinking of the ship carrying it from Europe left it at the mercy of the sea. When retrieved, its rescuers apparently made some repairs, including giving it a brownish paint job, perhaps to simulate the original bronze. For Wharton, "restoring" the statue meant either honoring the artist's original intent of gold leaf and bronze (hence obeying the traditional conservation canon) or taking into account the lived tradition of regular paint jobs. In response, Wharton set in motion a large-scale community project of deciding what to do and why.

The point for present purposes is that Wharton's task at hand (literally) forced debate among the locals as to what should be done and whose views should count in determining the statue's fate. This meant coming to terms with who is or is not a *bona fide* Hawaiian, in whatever sense, or otherwise entitled to a community voice. It also meant deciding what method would be used to decide: deferring to technical experts like Wharton? Holding a community-wide vote, as in a New England town hall ("mainland") convention? Or perhaps relying on local elders, something more akin to indigenous decision-making? Interviews and field observation about "what to do" with the statue revealed certain local fissures, such as those between "locals" (much use is made of that term in the islands) and "Honolulu" (the state capital which locals regard as intrusive and arrogant). "Local," as it turned out, counted for as much or more than "blood."

In this case study, the materiality was radicalized as method (the outcome by the way, was in favor of paint). Wharton did not just point to the object and ask about it in some general way, but brought up the treatment that was bound to change it. And in this way he could generate information about the contemporary social situation: people's attitudes toward life and heritage, their willingness and capacity to participate in continuing efforts at culture-building, and who should count as what in making the decisions. The statue is now all those things, including the reflexive decision by Wharton (and his funders) to put aside the professional canon.

For some contemporary artists, intervention or "provocation" is itself a medium; the graffiti artist is the well-known street variant. But other artists too make insertions into ongoing social pathways, including modes of organizational functioning. So the artist Hans Haacke, for example, created a 1971 show for New York's Guggenheim Museum depicting, on museum-lobby type plaques, the corporate identity of the museum's founders (Becker and Walton 1976). Successive plaques in the same series listed others in the Guggenheim corporate retinue, including those running the family's copper mining operations in Chile (Kennecott Copper). The brief statements of affiliations (and accompanying company revenues) ended with the fact of Salvador Allende's death and the restitution of corporate assets that followed – all inscribed in the same museo-dignified typeface and manner. The museum canceled the show and fired the curator who commissioned it. The Haacke installation thus displayed, through press commentary and actions taken, the power of capital over art. All objects are "congealed" social arrangements, as both Becker and Marx have said; in this case, the physical apparatus (and its voiding) performs those arrangements in a relatively transparent way. That is its beauty.

This all suggests a method: doing something with things (or at least raising the prospect of intervention) as a way to elicit cultural information. The researcher might propose something very modest, say a "Stop Sign" on the street corner, a particular gift for the school principal, or a new icon for the church recreation hall.

Or in the context of a private home, moving a lamp from one place to another (see Riggins 2004 for evidence of the importance of living room elements and their location). In sharp contrast to the "fly on the wall" idealization for the social science field worker, or strictures from the campus Human Subjects Committee in the US, the scholar who proposes (or enacts) changes in the local material world may garner information otherwise less accessible. Change the stuff and see who assembles.

Conclusion

This chapter shows how a focus on artifacts provides avenues for urban research. In a way we have become accustomed to understanding "tribal peoples" and rural dwellers through people's implements, so it is we can bring items of materiality into the sphere of urban studies. Goods are not merely mechanisms of showing off and displaying status (although they are indeed also that); they are instruments – whether privately or publicly consumed – through which urban life is made possible. Just as their production was the outcome of human projects, differentially undertaken by specific individuals and groups for their purposes, so it is they come to impact the nature of people's lives, including collective benefits and liabilities. They help shape cities and are no less a part of urbanism as a way of life than any other element.

Note

1   Bourgois explains that although his research team members used the "mantra" to one another, "Follow the needle," it was only after several weeks of receiving the splash that he happened on his explanation (personal email from Bourgois, November 5, 2008).

References

Agamben, Giorgio (1998) *Homo Sacer: Sovereign Power and Bare Life*. Stanford, CA: Stanford University Press.
Akrich, M. (1992) The de-scription of technical objects. In *Shaping Technology/Building Society: Studies in Sociotechnical Change*, ed. W. E. Bijker and J. Law. Cambridge, MA: MIT Press, 205–24.
Becker, Howard (1984) *Art Worlds*. Berkeley: University of California Press.
Becker, Howard, and Walton, John (1976) Speaking of art. In *Framing and Being Framed*, ed. Jack Burham and Hans Haacke. New York: New York University Press, 145–52.
Blumer, Herbert (1969) Fashion: from class differentiation to collective selection. *Sociological Quarterly* 10: 275–91.
Brain, David (2008) Beyond the neighbourhood: urban design and civic renewal. In *New Urbanism and Beyond: The Future of Urban Design*. New York: Rizzoli.
Ciccarone, D., and Bourgois, P. (2003) Explaining the geographic variation of HIV among injection drug users in the United States. *Substance Use and Misuse* 38 (14): 2049–63.
Cranz, Galen (1999) *The Chair*. New York: Norton.
Currid, Elizabeth (2007) *The Warhol Economy: How Fashion, Art and Music Drive New York City*. Princeton, NJ: Princeton University Press.

Florida, Richard (2003) *The Rise of the Creative Class and How It's Transforming Work, Leisure, Community and Everyday Life*. New York: Basic Books.

Gell, Alfred (1998) *Art and Agency*. Oxford: Oxford University Press.

George, Rose (2008) *The Big Necessity: The Unmentionable World of Human Waste and Why It Matters*. New York: Metropolitan Books.

Gershenson, Olga, and Penner, Barbara (2009) *Ladies and Gents*. Philadelphia: Temple University Press.

Gieryn, Thomas (2002) What buildings do. *Theory and Society* 31 (1): 35–74.

Goffman, Erving (1959) *Presentation of Self in Everyday Life*. New York: Doubleday.

Greed, Clara (2003) *Inclusive Urban Design: Public Toilets*. London: Architectural Press.

Hirschman, Albert (1958) *The Strategy of Economic Development*. New Haven, CT: Yale University Press.

Latour, Bruno (1992) Where are the missing masses? In *Shaping Technology/Building Society*, ed. Jack Burham and Hans Haacke. Cambridge, MA: MIT Press, 225–58.

Latour, Bruno (2005) *Reassembling the Social*. Oxford: Oxford University Press.

Leach, William (1994) *Land of Desire: Merchants, Power, and the Rise of a New American Culture*. New York: Vintage.

Miller, David (2009) *Stuff*. Cambridge: Polity Press.

Molotch, Harvey (2003) *Where Stuff Comes From*. New York: Routledge.

Molotch, Harvey, and McClain, Noah (2008) Things at work: informal social-material mechanisms for getting the job done. *Journal of Consumer Culture* 8 (1): 35–67.

Molotch, Harvey, and Noren, Laura (2010) *Toilet: The Public Restroom and the Politics of Sharing*. New York: New York University Press.

Molotch, Harvey, and Treskon, Mark (2009) Changing art: SoHo, Chelsea, and the dynamic geography of galleries in New York City. *International Journal of Urban and Regional Research* 33 (2): 517–41.

Molotch, Harvey, Paulsen, Krista, and Freudenburg, William (2000) History repeats itself, but how? City character, urban tradition and the accomplishment of place. *American Sociological Review* 65: 791–823.

Preda, Alex (1999) The turn to things: arguments for a sociological theory of things. *Sociological Quarterly* 40 (2): 347–66.

Riggins, Stephen (2004) Fieldwork in the living room: an autoethnographic essay. In *The Socialness of Things*. New York: Mouton de Gruyter, 101–47.

Rudofsky, Bernard (1980) *Now I Lay Me Down to Eat*. New York: Doubleday.

Shove, E. (2003) *Comfort, Cleanliness and Convenience: The Social Organization of Normality*. Oxford: Berg.

Storper, Michael (1997) *The Regional World*. New York: The Guilford Press.

Storper, Michael, and Venables, Anthony (2004) Buzz: face-to-face contact and the urban economy. *Journal of Economic Geography* 4 (4): 351–70.

Thrift, Nigel (2007) *Non-Representational Theory*. London: Routledge.

Wharton, Glenn (2009) The dynamics of participatory conservation: the Kamehmeha I Sculpture Project. *Journal of the American Institute for Conservation* 47: 159–73.

Wharton, Glenn, and Molotch, Harvey (2009) Installations. In *Conservation: Principles, Dilemmas, and Uncomfortable Truths*, ed. Alison Bracker and Alison Richmond. London: Elsevier, 210–22.

Zukin, Sharon (1982) *Loft Living*. Baltimore, MD: Johns Hopkins University Press.

Chapter 8

Ecologies of Dwelling: Maintaining High-Rise Housing in Singapore

Jane M. Jacobs and Stephen Cairns

This chapter considers the ways in which Science and Technology Studies (STS) has, to borrow a phrase from Bruno Latour (2005), reassembled the city. STS perspectives have drawn out previously backgrounded logics of the city and opened out a "cyborg urbanism" comprised of heterogeneous social and technical/material relations (Swyngedouw 1996; Gandy 2005). This chapter begins by giving a partial overview of the way STS approaches to the city have reassembled both urban studies questions and the city as an object of analysis. In such scholarship we are offered an entirely new way of thinking about city society and urban built environment, and one that, among other things, sidesteps an entrenched urban studies explanatory drama between social or environmental determinism. Certain veins of STS, notably those aligned with actor–network perspectives, do not even assume that there is a social world that confronts an "out there" non-human world. Rather they conceive of a process of being in the world in which the human and the non-human co-constitute what is.

This chapter elaborates an STS approach to the city by revisiting a much-documented example of urban transformation: the modernist-inspired, state-sponsored, high-rise housing program of post-independence Singapore. From the early 1960s onwards, the Singapore state, through the organizational bureaucracy of its Housing Development Board, has engaged in a project of "housing the nation," such that now over 80 percent of Singaporeans are housed in state-provided homes. The housing style selected by the island nation of Singapore for this program of housing development was the modernist-inspired residential high-rise, a housing type that maximized land-use and offered efficiencies of scale in terms of construction. The Singaporean high-rise offered an entirely novel housing system that restructured not only the built environment, but also the social worlds by which Singaporeans dwelt.

The New Blackwell Companion to the City   Edited by Gary Bridge and Sophie Watson
© 2011 Blackwell Publishing Ltd

Socio-technical Cities

A number of studies emerging from the general field of Science and Technology Studies have taken up urban infrastructures and urban objects as a focus, but often only in passing and metaphorically, or by default because that is where the technology under discussion was produced, made manifest or governed (as examples see Hughes 1983 and Coutard 1999). Such scholarship, although rich in urban case material, does not address an "urban question" or an "urban condition." It is intent on saying something about the co-evolution of large technological systems and society in general. Much of this work is only incidentally concerned with, for example, the links between the production and sustenance of systems and certain territorial articulations (such as a city) or territorially linked governance systems (such as urban planning). That said, some of the constructivist scholarship on technology and society has examined the ways in which technology shapes cities (see Tarr 1979), or the role of politics and cultural norms in shaping urban technologies, be they ones that never materialize or ones that become obdurate (see Rose and Tarr 1987; Aibar and Bijker 1997; Hommels 2005a, 2005b), although most of this work is historical.

It was not until Graham and Marvin's *Splintering Urbanism* (2001) that there was a contribution to the general field of socio-technical studies that dealt extensively with the contemporary city. *Splintering Urbanism* is also distinctive in its commitment to equalizing the emphasis between the nature of infrastructures and the nature of cities. As they argue (2001: 179), their study refuses to separate "the ontological status of 'infrastructure' or 'technology' from the 'urban' or the 'city.'" For Graham and Marvin "cities and infrastructures are seamlessly coproduced, and co-evolve." They demonstrate this co-evolution by investigating the relationship between contemporary restructuring of urban infrastructures (its unbundling and privatization) and the *parallel* social and material fragmentation of the urban condition, including injustices associated with access to and control of infrastructure. The theme of socio-technically linked urban injustice also frames much of the Marxian-inspired scholarship that comes under the name of political ecologies of the city, and which exposes the ways in which urbanization is also a matter of the technological transformation of nature (see as examples only Gandy 2002; Kaika *et al.* 2006; Swyngedouw 1996, 1997).

More recently, there has been a spate of urban scholarship explicitly influenced by actor–network theory (ANT). The city and urban processes, as objects of analysis, have had a faltering presence within ANT scholarship. For example, in 1981 Callon and Latour referred to the city in passing and metaphorically in order to illustrate their efforts to reassemble how large systems ("Leviathans") were understood. Rather than see large systems as integrated and whole, they conceived of them as resembling "a never-ending building-site in some great metropolis," where there was "no overall architect ... no design" and where

[e]ach town hall and each promoter, each king and each visionary claim to possess the overall plan ... [and where] whole districts are opened out and roads opened up ... houses razed to the ground, water courses covered over ... [d]istricts ... rehabilitated, other modern buildings ... destroyed. (Callon and Latour 1981: 295–6)

Latent in this suggestive quote are a number of the analytical tactics that have become hallmarks of actor–network approaches: an attention to the socio-technical, a grasp of the contingency of scale, and a sense of distributed agency. The limited instances of actor–network engagements with the city might in part be explained by the fact that an actor–network approach immediately and necessarily disaggregates a pre-formed object called "the city." As Callon and Latour imply, the city is not a coherent, fully integrated big system, it is something that is actualized differently in specific places and time. In his collaborative study with photographer Emilie Hermant, Latour offers a sustained investigation of the city of Paris conceived of as a building site and grasped by way of the ordinary, mundane, and often forgotten technical, representational, and infrastructural "problems" handled by thousands of city builders, be they engineers, technicians, civil servants, or inhabitants (Latour and Hermant 1998: 1). To uncover this invisible city Latour and Hermant actively deploy techniques such as tracking (of things and ideas and organizations), flattening (symmetry), de-scaling, redistributing, and connecting (see also www.brunolatour.fr/virtual/index.html).

In 2009 one of the first comprehensive collections of actor–network theory research on the city was published (Farías and Bender 2009). Their volume specifically explores how an actor–network perspective changes the types of questions asked of the city, as well as the nature of the settings and objects scrutinized. They offer up the useful notion of "urban assemblages" as a foundation for grasping the city anew. Urban assemblages, as conceived by Farías and Bender, comprise heterogeneous components (humans, organizations, tools, objects, technologies, texts, organisms) in contingently scaled relations. For them the city really is an "open building site," and one that is "relentlessly being assembled at concrete sites of urban practice" (Farías 2009: 2). This is not simply another way of seeing the city; it is, as Farías (2009: 13) notes, an "alternative ontology for the city" wherein the emphasis is always upon discerning how objects are being made and unmade at particular sites of practices. This making and unmaking does not simply occur in social hands (the constructivist social shaping of technologies). Rather, an actor–network perspective conceives of socio-technical process as enactments (performativities), what Farías (2009: 13) refers to as "heterogeneous ecologies of entities acting." This notion of a city-in-the-making has led to some exemplary studies of how city places and technologies (such as buildings) are assembled incrementally and contingently in and through planning and design practices and technologies, be they those that belong to the urban professional (the planner or the architect) or to the DIY amateur (Söderström 2000; Guy et al. 2001; Gieryn 2002; Tait 2002; Yaneva 2009; Guggenheim 2010). Although claiming new ground, the perspective activated in *Urban Assemblages* has much in common with Amin and Thrift's (2002) "reimagining" of the urban. The approach to the city taken by Amin and Thrift also attends to relationally produced forces. They look for these in the "neglected spatialities" of the city, in "hybrid, in-between figures" ("cyborgs") whose "continuous improvisation" reveals previously edited out networks of connection and influence (2002: 81).

One such neglected urban spatiality is that of repair and maintenance, as has been noted by Stephen Graham and Nigel Thrift. They argue for a "resurrection of the activities of repair and maintenance in the social sciences" (2007: 2). The city, they argue, not only "hosts" such work, but is to a large extent "defined" by the myriad functions of maintenance and repair. Repair and maintenance work is not simply a social response to social events (such as vandalism or accidental damage), it is needed because the things that constitute urban materiality act of their own accord with other non-human things like water, air, wind, and gravity (weathering, wearing, tearing, breaking, falling). Put simply, maintenance and repair is part of the social work that is required to offset the entropic destiny of the world. In talking about repair and maintenance in the city, Graham and Thrift also note that the nature of the "thing" being repaired is a complex hybrid of the material, the technical, the organic, and the social, hybrids that can have "a life of their own." They dub these hybrids forms of "ecology-in-action" and argue that through their "force of innovation" they are "pivotal" to how cities and urban life reproduce themselves (Graham and Thrift 2007: 5).

Socio-technical Housing

Although in 1997 Timothy Luke referred in passing to the necessity of a "housing machine" to contemporary human "cyborganization" (Luke 1997: 1368), only recently have we seen emerging points of convergence between STS approaches and housing studies. Michelle Gabriel and Keith Jacobs (2008), in a recent overview of the relevance of "post-social" thinking to housing studies, noted the resistance to such approaches. It is perhaps unsurprising that a disciplinary field largely dedicated to understanding the mechanisms by which social subjects are housed should resist displacing (or replacing) its humanist infrastructure. Furthermore, it was some time ago that housing studies emphatically set aside environmental determinism. More recently, a handful of studies have taken socio-technical analytical frameworks to the urban infrastructure of housing (Jacobs and Smith 2008). STS-inspired work has been undertaken on national housing policy frameworks (Murdoch 2000), the development of environmental housing technologies and behaviors (Hitchings 2003; Shove 2003; Lovell 2005), and to housing markets (Smith 2008). Our own research into the many afterlives of modernist-inspired, state-sponsored, high-rise housing has taken up a range of methodological tactics delivered by STS, and actor–network theory specifically, in order to better understand how such housing held in place in some contexts but fell apart in others (Jacobs 2006; Jacobs *et al.* 2007; Jacobs and Cairns 2008; Strebel in press; and see http://www.ace.ed.ac.uk/highrise/). The spirit of our methodology has been an exercise in avoiding the "vertiginous swing" (Latour 2005: 169) between a number of polarities: macro and micro; actor and system; technology and society. Our building ethnographies have assumed that a resident's action at a domestic window is as productive of a housing assemblage-in-action as a national housing policy statement or a universal housing technology standard. We have also assumed that words spoken about a housing system (by residents, policy-makers, activists) do not make sense without recourse to the building technologies themselves, just as the building technologies may be animated in new ways by words. And, just as we understand that what people say about housing is only part of what they might do with that housing, we also know that the force of people acting in and around a building is only one among many of the agents at work (think also of gravity, water, dirt, pests, mold, wind). Central then to our approach to housing has been to see it as a site of ongoing and active building work. By thinking of housing as housing-in-action we attune to how the social and technical assemble and act, creating the effect of housing that has form and stability, but also momentum.

Maintaining a Successful Housing Event

From its beginnings in 1960, Singapore's Housing Development Board (hereafter HDB), has been the main provider of housing for Singaporeans, nowadays accommodating well over 85 percent of the population in "owned" (long-term leasehold) flats. Constrained by land shortages, committed to the pragmatics of efficient delivery, and no doubt influenced by global trends in mass housing provision, it enthusiastically adopted the modernist high-rise as the architectural type for its post-independence program of universal housing provision (although this choice has always been justified pragmatically rather than aesthetically or ideologically). The HDB has routinely reflected with pride on the part it, and its housing program, has played in the making of modern Singapore, and the project has generated an extensive critical scholarship (see, as indicative examples only, Castells *et al.* 1990; Chua 1997).

Within the vast range of scholarship on Singapore's housing, little critical attention has been given the matter of repair and maintenance. Yet, from the outset, the HDB recognized that maintaining housing stock was as important as erecting it. It was understood that the high-rise, high-density housing type created special repair and maintenance responsibilities, especially with respect to elevator maintenance, water supply, common space care, and waste removal. Furthermore, the HDB also recognized that getting these aspects of repair and maintenance right was an essential part of convincing Singaporeans being forcibly relocated from kampongs and shop houses that high-rise, high-density living was acceptable and a "viable way of life" (Chong *et al.* 1985: 285). Of course, this was not just a technical matter and from the outset estate management in Singapore has comprised "social management" enacted through education campaigns on how to live in high-rise, high-density housing combined with more punitive regulatory frameworks of enforcement (Jacobs and Cairns 2008). The HDB's commitment to repair and maintenance was in part formulated by high-rise experiences elsewhere. In one official history of the HDB, *Housing a Nation* (Chong *et al.* 1985: 301), it is noted how estate management services had been "cautioned by the classic case of the Pruitt-Igoe Public Housing Project, which had moved from being a 'model public housing project' to a 'modern slum' … with no alternative but to demolish." In the view of the HDB, only good estate management could defend against the "national tragedy" of such a fate.

In the Singaporean housing system internal household repairs are carried out by (owner-occupier) residents, unless the occupant is on a social housing tenancy. In the very early days of the HDB, routine repair and maintenance of external spaces and fabric were handled centrally by laborers directly in its employ. By the 1960s repair and maintenance were decentralized to estate-linked area offices (later town councils) answering to a centralized Estates Management Department. Also, it was during the 1960s that the majority of repair and maintenance work was put out to private term contractors. In Singapore estate management comprises two key responsibilities: (1) repairs and maintenance of external common property parts of the building (stairs, corridors, open spaces) and building services (elevators, water pipes, soiled water extraction, external lighting, electricity, common TV antennae); (2) environmental services (removal of household garbage and debris, gardening). Repair and maintenance included remedial and routine maintenance, essential (emergency) maintenance as well as cyclical or preventative maintenance. In addition to these repair and maintenance cycles there is also a more comprehensive process of estate "upgrading," wherein an estate will undergo renovation and modernization works of a substantial nature (e.g. new elevator systems, the adding on of work rooms, alterations of windows, and drying technologies).

Emergency Repair

Within studies of science and technology, two specific types of socio-technical assemblages have attracted much analytical attention, these being the technological success and the technological failure. Latour (2005) articulates the heuristic value of this interest by arguing that successful technologies are significant because the socio-technical associations that hold them together are so seamlessly enmeshed they become invisible ("black boxed"), while the significance of failed technologies rests with the fact that previously invisible associations are, at the moment of failure, revealed. A specific study that has at its heart thinking about success and failure is Law and Callon's (1992) study of the life and death of an aircraft. In it, they show that the machine that fails is as interesting to technology studies as the machine that succeeds, for it is through the technology that fails that one can detect how "objects, artefacts, and technical practices come to be stabilized" (Law 1987: 111). There are many kinds of building technologies that can and do fail in the Singapore housing system, but one technology whose failure causes specific worry for tenants and estate managers alike is that of the elevator. The elevator is an utterly essential technology for high-rise housing and from the outset the HDB found the matter of elevator maintenance a core concern and "spared no effort" to ensure that the quality of elevator service was efficient, reliable, and secure and that there was a prompt maintenance service available at all times. Central to the worry around the elevator emergency breakdown was the prospect of residents being trapped in elevators because of a delay between the event of breakdown and the arrival of repair personnel. In a tropical climate such as Singapore, being trapped in a poorly ventilated elevator carriage is dangerous. And, in the early days of the HDB, residents new to the novel scales and circuits of high-rise housing expressed fears about elevators failing and plummeting to the ground. In short, there was a concern among HDB managers that frequent elevator failure, or slow responses to rescue in the event of elevator failure, might impact negatively on residents' views of the acceptability and viability of the high-rise living solution they were being offered. We can see some of this worry in the history of how elevator repair and rescue was managed by the HDB. By 1966 the HDB had set up an Emergency Repairs Unit to deal with electrical and sanitary repairs, but at this stage left elevator repair and rescue servicing to the elevator provider companies. By 1971 the HDB had enlarged and renamed its Emergency Repairs Unit, introducing the Essential Maintenance Service Unit (EMSU). At this point the EMSU assumed responsibility for a round-the-clock elevator rescue service in order to by-pass the unreliable services offered by elevator companies. In 1974 the stitching of technical elevator failure into a HDB-run system of elevator rescue and repair was enhanced by the introduction of VHF radio communication system so that the EMSU "nerve-center" could speak directly to elevator rescue and repair maintenance teams, allowing them to move from breakdown to breakdown and not return to a central station. Then, in 1979, the HDB spent some S$40 million to equip all its elevators with an automatic rescue device. This battery-operated device self-activates when the electricity supply to an elevator is interrupted and brings the elevator to the nearest landing to release any trapped passengers. The HDB was also concerned about instances of vandalism to elevators (from urinating in an elevator to damage to the physical surfaces and mechanisms). By 1978 the HDB was piloting a closed-circuit TV system integrated into the building's central TV antenna for elevator surveillance which also allowed residents to view their block's elevators on their own television sets. And by 1981, elevator engineers had successfully developed a telemonitoring system using a lift monitoring device (LMD) that continuously monitored the status of elevators (detecting faults and breakdowns, passengers trapped, as well as human misuse and abuse) and automatically notified the area receiving stations and then the Emergency Maintenance and Service Centre (a unit that was quickly given the less dramatic name of the Essential Maintenance Service Centre) (Figure 8.1). What finally came to be HDB's

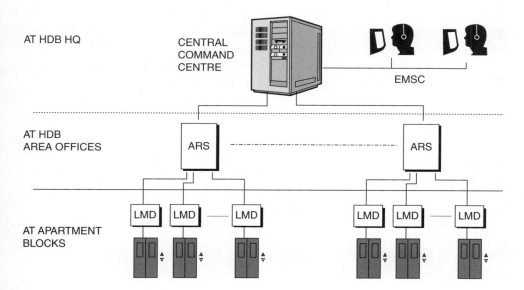

HDB's TELEMONITORING SYSTEM

AT HDB HQ

CENTRAL COMMAND CENTRE

EMSC

AT HDB AREA OFFICES

ARS   ARS

AT APARTMENT BLOCKS

LMD   LMD   LMD   LMD   LMD   LMD

EMSC = Essential Maintenance Service Centre
ARS = Area Receiving Station
LMD = Lift Monitoring Device

Figure 8.1 An HDB lift monitoring system. Courtesy of Housing and Development Board, Republic of Singapore.

Essential Service Centre routinely had its communication capacities upgraded and expanded (e.g. additional VHF stations and emergency phone-in switchboard positions) in the interests of better integrating the resident, the building, its technologies, and the repair and maintenance workers.

Cyclical Maintenance

The emergency repair is only one of the many socio-technical events that hold the Singaporean housing system in place. Much of the work of the HDB is directed at preventing such emergencies by way of what is called "cyclical repairs," which are developed in an anticipatory and preventative mode. Emergency repair is repair-after-failure. Cyclical repair is repair-before-failure, what is best termed maintenance. It happens whether the building or the building part needs it or not. It is intended to prevent or offset repair-after-failure, which is understood to be riskier and often more expensive, both financially and in terms of human safety and negative resident opinion. The cyclical repair systems of the HDB operate on a range of temporal cycles (Table 8.1). Routine is a technique for ensuring a stabilized mode of action in an organization (Miettinen and Virkkunen 2005) and acts as a storage system for organizational knowledge. In short, organizations remember by doing, although such doing is also supported by memory devices (files, spreadsheets, manuals, programs) which too require maintenance. As Star (1999: 382) noted, in big, complex, and multilayered infrastructures fixing and repair can only happen in modular increments. The temporal cycles adopted by the HDB order that incremental process in line with what has been learnt from the materials and technologies used in their housing (their performance in tropical Singapore) as well as technical or legal obligations (as specified in regulations). By dwelling on these routine cycles of maintenance we are reminded that the built environments of cities are not stable and fixed. Seeing the built environment as part of "slow time" (permanent) is an effect that ignores what Graham and Thrift (2007: 83) call "constant to and fro" of maintenance and repair (see also Latour and Yaneva 2008, on buildings that move).

Table 8.1 Cyclical maintenance routines for Bukit Ho Swee Estate

Building Element/Area	Activity	Maintenance Cycle
Public Areas (lift and stair lobbies, access corridors, concourse)	Sweep	Daily
Public Areas (lift and stair lobbies, access corridors, concourse)	Mop	Daily
Public Areas (access corridors)	Bulky rubbish removal	Daily
Service Chute Outlets (ground floor concourse)	Rubbish removal	Daily
Environs	Inspection: mosquito-born Dengue-fever breeding sites	Daily (during breeding season)

Table 8.1 (*Continued*)

Building Element/Area	Activity	Maintenance Cycle
Signage (lift and stair lobbies)	Inspection and repair if necessary	Daily
Rubbish Chute	Hosing	Weekly
Environs	Horticultural Services: shrub, hedge trimming	Weekly
Environs	Horticultural Services: grass trimming	Fortnightly
Lights	Inspection and repair if necessary	Fortnightly
Lifts	Inspection and repair if necessary: parts, oiling, emergency battery, UDD	Fortnightly
Water Pump	Inspection and repair if necessary	Fortnightly
Fire Equipment, Dry/Wet Risers	Inspection and repair if necessary	Monthly
Ventilation and Airconditioning Systems	Inspection and repair if necessary	Monthly
Public Areas (lift and stair lobbies, access corridors, concourse)	High pressure hose wash	Monthly
Environs	Horticultural Services: tree surgery	Ad-hoc (hotline)
Environs	Pest inspection: mosquito-born Dengue-fever sites, bee-hives, cockroaches	Ad-hoc (hotline)
Escalators (chain)	Replacement	5 yearly
Escalators (step rollers)	Replacement	7 yearly
Escalators (handrail rollers)	Replacement	7 yearly
Building Fabric	General repair, repainting, redecoration	7 yearly
Water Pump	Replacement	7 yearly
Lift (hoisting rope)	Replacement	7 years
Lift (emergency batteries)	Replacement	10–15 years
Rubbish Chute	Overhaul (including control panel replacement)	12 years
Water Tank	Relining	12 years
Roof	Replacement of waterproof membrane on concrete slab	14 years
Refuse Compactor	Replacement	15 years
Electrical Cabling	Replacement	20 years
Block (including plumbing, wiring, lifts, roof, doors)	Major upgrade	35 years

Source: Interview, Senior Property Officer, July 2007.

Checking

John Law (1987: 114), in talking about large-scale engineering, argues that various elements need to be "tamed" or "held in place" so that such an assemblage will not crumble. This, he says, requires not simply maintenance but also the "maintenance of vigilance and surveillance." We have already seen some of the (mechanized) systems of vigilance and surveillance that operate in the Singapore housing assemblage with respect to emergency elevator maintenance and repair. But the HDB, although enthusiastically embracing mechanization, has always admitted that a crucial part of estate management comprises "human resource." This commitment is embodied in the estate management staff position known initially as the housing maintenance inspector or, more recently, the property officer. This estate management professional has the job of inspecting, reporting on, and responding to the condition of the building and its surroundings. These officers have an allocated area of around 2,000–25,000 units, and attendant communal spaces. Their work is to determine what repairs are needed, to generate the work order for repairs, and to assess if the work is completed and to a standard considered appropriate. The basic currency of their work is the object called the "building defect." The building *defect* is obviously a building fault, although it is noteworthy that this term also carries with it the idea of something *defecting*. In the context of thinking of a large housing infrastructure as an assemblage then a defect is also at the same time a defection, something leaving the order needed for an assemblage to hold together as a successful housing infrastructure.

What constitutes a building defect? And how does a property officer come to know of a building defect? One way a property officer comes to know about a defect is if a resident reports it by way of the town center office. Property officers also find defects on their daily and weekly tours of those parts of the housing estate for which they are responsible. Here the instruments of vigilance and surveillance are specifically a choreographed route through the building (the block check), the human eye, the hand, the pen and notebook, the handheld mobile device. The "block check" is a routine walk around and visual assessment of a building in the care of a property officer. Strebel (in press) argues that such work routines are a largely overlooked aspect of how a building stays in place.

In 2007 we walked along with one such officer as she conducted a check of Block 22 in the Bukit Ho Swee housing estate (Figure 8.2). The checking of Block 22 is something that this property officer does every six weeks. Her work of the block check begins by riding the elevator to the top floor and then systematically walking down through the common deck corridors and stairways. As she moves along the corridor she is checking with her eyes, perhaps touching with her hand, all manner of things. The scope of what needs to be scanned and checked is determined by specifications and rules set down in an HDB technical manual she came to know through her three-month in-house training, and is reiterated through a one-month period of shadowing a more experienced property officer. This HDB-specific expertise augments a wider knowledge learnt by way of a degree in property management. This suite of training teaches the property officer how to recognize and deal with the building defect. Defects come in various forms. One category includes wear and tear resulting from the hot, humid climate such as peeling or mold-affected paint

Figure 8.2 Block check at Block 22, Bukit Ho Swee. Authors' photo.

or spalling concrete. Another category includes things that create risk in tropical conditions, such as uncovered water pools (created, say, by broken or missing gully drain covers or by residents leaving uncovered containers outside) that contribute to the incidence of insect-borne dengue fever. There are also those building defects that impact negatively on the residents' use of the building, such as broken lights, signs that are damaged or missing, elevator buttons that are broken (Figure 8.3). Finally, there is a range of "defects" that belong more to the way residents are living in the building than to the building and its performance. These include the graffiti of loan sharks shaming late-paying debtors, bulky items that have been left in common spaces (often stair landings), drying racks for washing that have been placed incorrectly so that they block corridor access or extend out beyond the exterior of the building, or pot plants or other objects that have been placed on external building walls and pose a risk of detaching and becoming what in Singapore is called "killer litter": litter which, with the help of gravity, can pose a danger to those below (Figure 8.4).

The first product of the block-check is a list of "defects" (Figure 8.5). The course of action in relation to these defects varies: repairing a non-aligned building technology is different to repairing a non-aligned resident, although to the property officer they do have some practical equivalence. In the case of the building defect, a repair works order is generated. In the case of the resident a more subtle approach is taken

Figure 8.3   Defects at Block 22, Bukit Ho Swee. Authors' photo.

Figure 8.4   Potential "killer litter," Block 22, Bukit Ho Swee. Authors' photo.

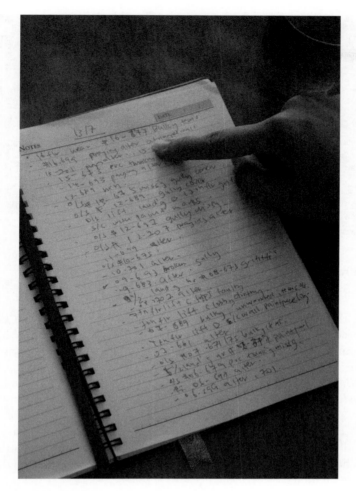

Figure 8.5 Working notebook. Authors' photo.

of sending out a circular or letter. The property officer has multiple roles with respect to the repair and maintenance of the building: inspector, repairer, and enforcer. She integrates this role through walking, looking, and noting. These inscriptions then mesh with other computerized systems such as the Total Property Management System (which is a computerized database for generating appropriately calculated specifications for ad hoc works orders), the Planned Maintenance System (which is the database that specifies the cyclical maintenance and replacement cycles), and the social management programs which, among other things, develop education campaigns about how to live in the housing provided (Figure 8.6).

The training of a property officer involves establishing background expectancies about what an HDB high-rise is like when it is in good repair so that they can know a defect when they encounter it (Garfinkel 1964; see also Strebel in press). Clearly, during the process of design and construction, HDB standards are embedded into the fabric of the houses and estates built. But, after the event of building, the prop-

Figure 8.6 Re-aligning residents, organisms, and elements through education posters. Source: HDB Jalan Besar Town Council, with permission.

erty officer, through her training, internalizes those standards. Then through the routine choreography of the block check, she carries these standards back into the built environment of the estate, placing them in contact with the building's perform-ance. The inscription of defects in a mobile document then allows the in-need-of-repair version of Block 22 to be carried back to the area office, where repair work orders or resident circulars can be generated. This routine piece of walking–looking–inscribing work actively stitches resident, building, town council, and maintenance professional together in a network directed at keeping this housing assemblage in place with all its components(human and non-human) performing as they should. The block check is an essential part of how the HDB ensures that HDB standards live on in the building.

Conclusion

This example of maintenance and repair on a large-scale housing assemblage shows well the relevance of often forgotten mundane process and phenomena. Latour (1988) refers to this as a strategy of "deflation," whereby scholarship can avoid, on the one hand, "kneeling" before the "big" explanations of political economy and, on the other, disappearing into relativist description. This middle-range tactic is of particular interest for housing studies where there has been tension between the relative merits of, on the one hand, political economy explanations concerned with questions of access and allocation and, on the other, detailed renderings of domestic life or resident satisfaction. Housing studies is also a useful example of how the social and the technical are often awkwardly dealt with in urban scholar-ship. It is, for example, possible to read political economy studies of a housing system that mention nothing of the housing itself (except perhaps in the most scant stylistic terms); just as it is possible to read resident satisfaction studies that appear to account for everything by way of the building design. We have tried in this chapter to offer some pathways out of these dualistic structures of thinking and being in urban studies. We have attempted instead to bring into view the to-and-fro effort that keeps this middling modernist, high-rise, high-density housing assemblage in place, and even allows for claims of success (a status denied similar high-rises in other national contexts). Through maintenance and repair the agencies of water, mold, and mosquitoes, for example, are kept in check, just as the agency of residents is managed. Furthermore, we see how the building is not simply a pre-designed and made container for a social world of domestic living. It too lives in its own way: expanding, crumbling, falling, wearing, tearing. The building (as the resident, as the mildew, as the Lift Monitoring Device) is but one component of a hybridized dwelling ecology requiring constant building work.

Acknowledgements

We would like to thank Mr Tay Yew Nguan, Corporate Development Department, Housing Development Board, Singapore, and Mr Derrick Ng and Ms Shan, Jalan Besar Town Council, Singapore.

References

Aibar, E., and Bijker, W. E. (1997) Constructing a city: the Cerdà Plan for the extension of Barcelona. *Science Technology Human Values* 22 (1): 3–30.

Amin, A., and Thrift, N. (2002) *Cities: Reimagining the Urban*. Cambridge: Polity Press.

Callon, M., and Latour, B. (1981) Unscrewing the big Leviathan: how actors macro-structure reality and how sociologists help them to do so. In *Advances in Social Theory and Methodology: Towards an Integration of Micro- and Macro-sociologies*, ed. K. Knoor-Cetina and A. V. Circourel. London: Routledge and Kegan Paul, 277–322.

Castells, M., Goh, L., and Kwok, R. Y.-W. (1990) *The Shek Kip Mei Syndrome: Economic Development and Public Housing in Hong Kong and Singapore*. London: Pion.

Chong, K. C., Phong, W. Y., Lim, K. L., and Lim, S. S. (1985) Estate management. In *Housing a Nation: 25 Years of Public Housing in Singapore*, ed. A. K. Wong and S. H. K. Yeh. Singapore: Maruzen Asia, 263–304.

Chua, B.-H. (1997) *Political Legitimacy and Housing: Stakeholding in Singapore*. London: Routledge.

Coutard, O. (ed.) (1999) *The Governance of Large Technical Systems*. London: Routledge.

Farías, I. (2009) Introduction. In *Urban Assemblages: How Actor–Network Theory Changes Urban Studies*, ed. I. Farías and T. Bender. London: Routledge, 1–24.

Farías, I., and Bender, T. (eds.) (2009) *Urban Assemblages: How Actor–Network Theory Changes Urban Studies*. London: Routledge.

Gabriel, M., and Jacobs, K. (2008) The post-social turn: challenges for housing research. *Housing Studies* 23 (4): 527–40.

Gandy, M. (2002) *Concrete and Clay: Reworking Nature in New York City*. Cambridge, MA: MIT Press.

Gandy, M. (2005) Cyborg urbanization: complexity and monstrosity in the contemporary city. *International Journal of Urban and Regional Research* 29 (1): 26–49.

Garfinkel, H. (1964) Studies of the routine grounds of everyday activities. *Social Problems* 11: 1–33.

Gieryn, T. (2002) What buildings do. *Theory and Society* 31: 35–74.

Graham, S., and Marvin, S. (2001) *Splintering Urbanism: Networked Infrastructures, Technological Mobilities and the Urban Condition.* London and New York: Routledge.

Graham, S., and Thrift, N. (2007) Out of order: understanding repair and maintenance. *Theory, Culture and Society* 24 (3): 1–25.

Guggenheim, M. (2010) Mutable immobiles: building conversion as a problem of quasi-technologies. In *Urban Assemblages: How Actor–Network Theory Changes Urban Studies,* ed. I. Farías and T. Bender. London: Routledge: 161–78.

Guy, S., Marvin, S., and Moss, T. (eds.) (2001) *Urban Infrastructure in Transition: Networks, Buildings, Plans.* London: Earthscan.

Hitchings, R. (2003) People, plants and performance: on actor–network theory and the material pleasures of the private garden. *Social and Cultural Geography* 4: 99–113.

Hommels, A. (2005a) Studying obduracy in the city: towards a productive fusion between technology studies and urban studies. *Science Technology and Human Values* 30 (3): 232–51.

Hommels, A. (2005b) *Unbuilding Cities, Obduracy in Urban Sociotechnical Change.* Cambridge, MA: MIT Press.

Hughes, T. P. (1983) *Networks of Power: Electrification in Western Society, 1880–1930.* Baltimore, MD: Johns Hopkins University Press.

Jacobs, J. M. (2006) A geography of big things. *Cultural Geographies* 13 (1): 1–27.

Jacobs, J. M., and Cairns, S. (2008) The modern touch: interior design and modernisation in post-independence Singapore. *Environment and Planning A* 40 (3): 572–95.

Jacobs, J. M., and Smith, S. J. (2008) Living room: rematerialising home. *Environment and Planning A* 40: 515–19

Jacobs, J. M., Cairns, S., and Strebel, I. (2007) "A tall story ... but, a fact just the same": the Red Road high-rise as a black box. *Urban Studies* 44 (3): 609–29.

Kaika, M., Heynen, N., and Swyngedouw, E. (2006) *In the Nature of Cities: Urban Political Ecology and the Politics of Urban Metabolism.* New York: Routledge.

Latour, B. (1988) The politics of explanation: an alternative. Available online at www.bruno-latour.fr/articles/article/032.html (accessed October 5, 2010).

Latour, B. (2005) *Reassembling the Social: An Introduction to Actor–Network Theory.* Oxford: Oxford University Press.

Latour, B., and Hermant, E. (1998) *Paris: ville invisible.* Paris: La Découverte.

Latour, B., and Yaneva, A. (2008) "Give me a gun and I will make all buildings move": an ANT's view of architecture. In *Explorations in Architecture: Teaching, Design and Research*, ed. R. Geiser. Basel: Burkäuser, 80–9.

Law, J. (1987) Technology and heterogeneous engineering: the case of Portuguese expansion. In *The Social Construction of Technological Systems: New Directions in the Sociology and History of Technology*, ed. W. E. Bijker, T. P. Hughes, and T. J. Pinch. Cambridge, MA: MIT Press, 111–34.

Law, J., and Callon, M. (1992) The life and death of an aircraft: a network analysis of technical change. In *Shaping Technology/Building Society*, ed. W. E. Bijker and J. Law. Cambridge, MA: MIT Press,: 290–308.

Law, J., and Singleton, V. (2000) Performing technology's stories: on social constructivism, performance and performativity. *Technology and Culture* 41: 765–75.

Lovell, H. (2005) Supply and demand for low energy housing in the UK: insights from a science and technology studies approach. *Housing Studies* 20: 815–29.

Luke, T. (1997) At the end of nature: cyborgs, "humanmachines," and environmental postmodernity. *Environment and Planning A* 29: 1367–80.

Miettinen, R., and Virkkunen, J. (2005) Epistemic objects, artefacts and organizational change. *Organization* 12: 437–56.

Murdoch, J. (2000) Space against time: competing rationalities in planning for housing. *Transactions of the Institute of British Geographers* 25 (4): 503–19.

Rose, M. H., and Tarr, J. A. (eds.) (1987) *Journal of Urban History* 14 (1). Special issue devoted to the city and technology.

Shove, E. (2003) *Comfort, Cleanliness and Convenience: The Social Organization of Normality*. Oxford: Berg.

Smith, S. J. (2008) Owner-occupation: at home with a hybrid of money and materials. *Environment and Planning A* 40: 520–35.

Söderström, O. (2000) *Des images pour agir: le visuel en urbanisme*. Lausanne: Payot.

Star, S. L. (1999) The ethnography of infrastructure. *American Behavioral Scientist* 43 (3): 377–91.

Strebel, I. (in press) The living building: notes on the art of the block check. *Social and Cultural Geographies* theme issue on *Practiced Architectures*.

Swyngedouw, E. (1996) The city as hybrid: on nature, society and cyborg urbanization. *Capitalism Nature Socialism* 7 (2): 65–80.

Swyngedouw, E. (1997) Power, nature and the city: the conquest of water and the political ecology of urbanization in Guayaquil, Ecuador: 1880–1990. *Environment and Planning A* 29 (2): 311–32.

Tait, M. (2002) Room for manoeuvre? An actor–network study of central–local relations in development plan making. *Planning Theory and Practice* 3: 69–85.

Tarr, J. A. (1979) Introduction to special issue on "The City and Technology." *Journal of Urban History* 5: 275.

Yaneva, A. (2009) *The Making of a Building: A Pragmatist's Approach to Architecture*. Bern: Peter Lang.

Chapter 9

The Urbanization of Nature: Great Promises, Impasse, and New Beginnings

Maria Kaika and Erik Swyngedouw

> Viewing the city as a process of continuous, but contested, socio-ecological change …
> unlocks new arenas for thinking and acting on the city. The tensions, conflicts and
> forces that flow with this process through the body, the city, the region and the globe
> show the cracks in the lines, the meshes in the net, the spaces and plateaus of resistance
> and of power.
>
> (Swyngedouw and Kaika 2000: 567)

The quotation above is taken from our contribution to the first edition of this
Companion. Our chapter was then the sole one to address the broad relationship
between nature and the city. In this *New Companion*, however, there are several
entries that cover different aspects of this relationship. While ten years ago we were
struggling to find references to theoretical and empirical contributions to substanti-
ate our claims, the past decade has witnessed an explosion of exciting research and
innovative ideas on nature and cities, some of which have redrawn the boundaries
of urban theory and practice (for reviews, see Keil 2003; Keil 2005; Braun 2005;
Cook and Swyngedouw 2011). This intense scholarly attention to urban socio-
ecological processes was set against remarkable changes not only in the environmental, but also the political-economic and socio-cultural conditions of cities.
Whilst the environmental "wedge" was evolving into a possible leverage for forcing
a more egalitarian urban living (Castree 2008), the neoliberal urban "revolution"
took ecological problems away from this politicized agenda, and promoted sustainable urban ecologies as a matter of individual consumer choice and market logic
(Krueger and Gibbs 2007).

A comprehensive review of the astonishing academic and political developments
of the last decade and of the insightful approaches to understanding the socio-

The New Blackwell Companion to the City   Edited by Gary Bridge and Sophie Watson
© 2011 Blackwell Publishing Ltd

ecological processes that shape urbanization, presents a challenge that lies beyond the scope of this chapter. We shall not return to historical analysis either, as we undertook this in our previous contribution (Swyngedouw and Kaika 2000). Instead, we wish to focus here on the paradoxical situation that, despite the extraordinary wealth of urban socio-ecological research, and the increasing attention paid to urban environmental problems on the part of policy-makers, experts, civil society organizations, and the like, the urban ecological conundrum has in fact become more intractable than ever. Over the last decade, we have witnessed Hurricane Katrina ransacking New Orleans, increasing carbon dioxide levels aggravating the threat of global warming, lack of access to basic resources (water, food, land, medicine) persisting as the number one cause of premature mortality in the megacities of the global south, and recurring quasi-epidemics (HIV, SARS, Avian and Mexican Flu) reshaping global and local geographies of uneven urban development. While some cities – mainly in the global north – have begun to clean up their act, others – notably in China, Africa, and India (where most of the toxic stuff has decamped) – have become festering sores of rapidly deteriorating socio-ecological conditions.

Set within the nexus of a growing awareness of the complexity of urban environments on the one hand, and a deterioration of urban socio-ecological conditions on the other, the aim of this chapter is twofold. First, to contend that urban socio-ecological research, having made great strides in retheorizing the city as a contested socio-natural process, contributed to pushing the urban environmental agenda onto the public stage. Second, to ask why, after a decade of intense scholarly and public attention to urban environmental concerns, relatively little has been achieved with respect to altering precarious socio-ecological conditions in both the cities of the global north and those of the global south.

We shall focus on four key perspectives that galvanized urban socio-ecological research over the past decade: urban metabolisms; the neoliberalization of urban environments; urban socio-ecological movements; and urban environmental imaginaries and discursive formations. We shall examine how each one of these perspectives has revolutionized urban theory and practice, and also how each has contributed in part to the political-ecological deadlock we are currently in. In the conclusion, we shall chart some of the intellectual pathways that might help to deal with this impasse, and insist, with renewed conviction, that renaturing urban theory is vital for urban analysis and urban politics as well as urban activism.

Urban Metabolism Redux

In his pioneering work *Nature's Metropolis*, William Cronon provides a brilliant historical-geographical analysis of how an intense socio-natural metabolic process transformed Chicago into a global metropolis (Cronon 1991). The term *metabolism* was originally used in a similar context by Karl Marx, when, back in the nineteenth century, he lifted it from scientific discourse to describe the process through which labor and capital produce and transform socio-natural landscapes: "man, through his own actions, mediates, regulates, and controls the *metabolism* between himself and nature" (Marx 1981 [1867]: 283, our italics). More recent approaches viewed the urbanization of nature as a process of continuous deterritorialization and reterritorialization of metabolic circulatory flows, organized through social and physical conduits or networks of "metabolic vehicles" (Virilio 1986). These processes are infused by relations of power and sustained by particular imaginaries of what Nature is or should be.[1] Under capitalism, the commodity relation and the flow of money suture these socio-ecological processes and turn the city into a metabolic socio-environmental process that stretches from the immediate environment to the remotest corners of the globe (Heynen *et al.* 2006).

Through this conceptual lens, urbanization is viewed as a process of geographically arranged socio-environmental metabolisms that fuse the social with the physical, producing a "cyborg" city (Swyngedouw 2006; Gandy 2005; Haraway 1991) with distinct physical forms and incongruous socio-ecological consequences. Recent monographs have substantiated, both empirically and theoretically, how cities and their human and non-human inhabitants across the globe are linked through networks and flows of technology and social relations of power for the circulation and disposal of water, energy, fat, chemicals, viruses, e-waste (Pellow 2007), household waste (Njeru 2006), redundant ships (Hillier 2009; Buerk 2006), ducts, pipes, cables, and channels (Graham and Marvin 2001). Gandy's *Concrete and Clay* narrates New York's urbanization process as a political-ecological construct (Gandy 2002), Kaika's *City of Flows* (Kaika 2005) considers the cultural, socioeconomic, and political relations through which urban socio-natural flows are cast and recast during modernity, Swyngedouw's *Social Power and the Urbanization of Water* (Swyngedouw 2004) excavates the relationship between cities and nature through the lens of water, Desfor and Keil examine the socio-ecological productions that shape Los Angeles and Toronto (Desfor and Keil 2004). Bakker (2003) follows the flow of water through the privatization politics of England and Wales. Davis excavates the peculiar ecologies of cities that should not be where they are (Davis 2002). Friedberg's majestic study demonstrates how green beans link African cities to Paris and London (Freidberg 2004). Klinenberg (2002) shows that heat can be a matter of life or death in Chicago, while Brechin (1996) narrates how San Francisco's elites rummaged through nature in search of earthly gain and power. Burrowing into the metabolic process of less visible, yet powerfully important socio-natural actants, Ali and Keil (2008) map how the SARS epidemic challenged global networks of urban governance, Bulkeley and Betsill (2005) search for the urban roots of carbon dioxide, Robbins (2007) reconstructs the networks of pollution and toxic waste that sustain the "green" suburban lawn, and Castro links water rights to citizenship in Mexico City (Castro 2006). Other, less dialectical, standpoints claim a greater sensitivity to non-human "actants," and critique and complement the above perspectives (Wolch *et al.* 2002; Hinchcliffe 1999), adding further insights into what is now a rapidly expanding body of thought.

The scholars cited above have resolutely debunked the myth that the city is where nature stops and convincingly argued that the urban process has to be theorized, understood, and managed as a socio-natural process. By doing so, they contributed to delegitimizing dominant twentieth-century perspectives on the city that ignored nature (mainly practiced in urban sociology), without falling into the trap of nature fetishism or ecological determinism. Moreover, by transcending the binary division between nature and society the urban metabolism perspective has shown that socio-ecological processes are intensely political, and confirmed that urban theory without nature cannot be but incomplete.

However, this body of thought has paid relatively little attention to the political opportunities such a perspective could bring, or to imagining radically different urban socio-ecological assemblages. Thus, although we may now be able to trace, chart, follow, and narrate the multiple socio-ecological lines that shape the urban process both locally and globally, precious little has been said about how to produce alternative, more equitable and enabling, urban socio-ecological assemblages. "What is required," Mark Whitehead argues (2005: 280), "is a political methodology of urban nature," that becomes an imperative since, as noted in the introduction, the development of a problematic of "urban natures" coincides with the consolidation of the neoliberal onslaught that engulfed the urban condition globally, albeit in highly diversified forms.

(Neo)liberalizing Urban Environments

The greatest of collectively produced socio-natural *oeuvres*, the city, has always been the playground and battlefield of what David Harvey terms "accumulation by dis-possession" (Harvey 2003: 137). However, the recent politics of neoliberalization extended dispossession and marketization from public spaces, parks, and collective environments to a new array of socio-natural objects – water, air, techno-natural infrastructures, carbon dioxide, and the genetic code, amongst others – which have now also entered the sphere of commodified quasi-objects and have become subjected to unchecked carousels of capitalist speculation.

This radical political-ecological reordering was facilitated by the institution of a new urban policy framework, which inserted the environmental question into urban policies via the logic of ecological modernization, and through the rhetoric of "sustainability." Despite the fact that the pioneering academic argument about "sustainable development" often incorporates the social – alongside the environment and the economy – as an integral part of the sustainable development "triad" (see Whitehead 2007), the current practice of "sustainable development" more often than not sidelines issues of justice and equality (Baker 2007; Keil 2007) through a new policy framework that promotes market-led, technocratic approaches to "greening" capitalism (Gibbs 2000; Mol and Spaargaren 2000; Heynen *et al.* 2007). The global bet for finding a technological fix to save the planet assembles complex, market-led, and probably unworkable "protocols" (like Kyoto) or nurtures new sinks for green capital investment.

As cities produce 80 percent of the world's greenhouse emissions (Bulkeley and Betsill 2005), greening capitalism becomes pretty much an urban question. Eco-cities are perhaps the most exemplary showcase of green capital investment. Abu Dhabi's Masdar City is portrayed as the first fully sustainable city and claims to be setting Abu Dhabi on a course to a post-carbon capitalist urbanization, albeit one that is now in jeopardy as the urban-financial crisis wreaks havoc in this erstwhile capitalist paradise. Dongtan, outside Shanghai, was conceived in 2005 as China's showcase for environmentally friendly eco-urbanization. A project of global scale and importance, designed by Arup, visualized through wonderful images (Dongtan had 150,000 Google hits in January 2010), commissioned by the Shanghai Indus-trial Investment Company (SIIC), supported by the British Prime Ministers Tony Blair and later Gordon Brown, promoted by both the Chinese President Hu Jintao and the city's Communist Party boss Chen Liangyu, Dongtan became the iconic lovechild of those who imagined the possibility of a new urbanity based on a new socio-ecological deal, sustained by market-based technological fixes. Yet the project has been stalled, while the first steps towards its materialization proved highly controversial. In April 2008 Chen Liangyu was sentenced to 18 years in prison over fraudulent land deals, while the SIIC's planning permissions have lapsed, along with the dream for a model global eco-city. Still, the project did confirm Shanghai's roaring success as a world city, and propelled it high on the list of cities where a new type of "sustainable" city–nature assemblages is imagined and possibly turned into real geographies.

As "sustainable development" evolves into a market logic that opens up new avenues for capital accumulation (Castree 2008; Himley 2008), the environmental question has become one that mobilizes diverse political energies. Indeed, the urban environmental question contributed to the formation of a highly selective "pluralization" of the state, whereby non-elected officials, experts, and private actors are being incorporated into the governance, delivery, and financing of sustainable cities (Swyngedouw 2009). Recent research has criticized these new forms of governance for excessively empowering business elites, for negating issues of democracy and accountability, and for "naturalizing the political" (Swyngedouw 2009). A considerable body of academic literature has also detailed how the new assemblages of money–materialities–governance for managing resources across the urban world redraw the socio-spatial choreographies of the flows of water, waste, food, etc., rearticulate patterns of control and access along class, gender, and ethnic lines, and reconfigure maps of entitlement and exclusion. At the other end of the spectrum, however, these same assemblages of capital–natures–cities–people have also given birth to all manner of struggles and contestation (Prudham 2004; Loftus 2006; Bakker 2000; Castro and Heller 2009; Olivera and Lewis 2004), ushering in a variety of tactics of resistance, rebellion, and imaginings of alternative urban socio-environmental practices. This is what we shall turn to next.

Urban Socio-Ecological Movements and the Struggles for Justice

In their book, *From the Ground Up*, Cole and Foster (2000) argue that involvement in an environmental justice movement can improve the lives of disadvantaged communities, as it can enhance their consciousness of patterns of injustice, and increase their "self-confidence," "capacity," and "expertise" (p. 153). The ways in which people across the world form or join movements of environmental justice and equality are indicative of the growing inclusion of urban environmental affairs in social struggles. These movements translate grievances into "repertoires of action," form collective identities, and influence "mechanisms" of injustice. The successful struggle of the Cochabamba people in Bolivia against Water International and the privatization of the city's water utility became an emblem of how social movements can successfully resist the neoliberalization of urban natures (Olivera and Lewis 2004).

However, intellectual engagement with socio-environmental justice struggles remains limited. Although we now have ample evidence on how the physical environment of place (e.g. factories, air quality, toxic sites) influences the day-to-day inequalities that communities are faced with (Sze 2006), little is known about how these place-specific physical environments can act as facilitators for – or barriers to – collective action (Leitner *et al.* 2008). For Nicholls (2009: 80), people's "sense of place" influences their "normative evaluations of what battles are worth fighting for, what battles are best left to others, who to cooperate with, and who to dispute." Therefore, socio-ecological movements cannot be understood outside their embedding in particular socio-spatial contexts. In order to understand their geographies, we need to focus on place as contested, scaled, in flux, and relational (Swyngedouw and Heynen 2003; Massey 2007).

Scale is indeed as important as place to the dynamics of social environmental movements. As these movements are embedded within a shifting political terrain, power relations are continually reworked within and between different political scales. This is exemplified through the growing, albeit still limited, interconnectedness of place-based urban socio-ecological movements and the internationalization of environmental politics (Carruthers 2008; Faber 2005; Pellow 2007). Yet, many of these urban socio-ecological movements remain locally based and inward-looking, preventing socio-environmental injustices to universalize from "Not in My Backyard" to "Not in Anyone's Backyard." Following Routledge (2007), we need to ask difficult questions about why most urban socio-ecological movements are primarily reactive rather than proactive; why their code word of choice is "resistance" (resistance to ecological degradation, to declining socio-ecological amenities, to privatization of common "resources"); why this "resistance" rarely translates into a demand for transformation and for producing equitable socio-ecological urban conditions; and why the imaginary of possible alternative urban natures is still impotent.

Urban Socio-Ecological Imaginaries: Discourses of Urban Natures

Despite the importance of the materiality of the urbanization of nature, neither urban environmental interventions nor the material practices of (in)justice and (in)equality can be understood without referring to the discursive practices that accompany and support them. Despite – or perhaps because of – the fact that social studies of science have convincingly rejected the possibility of fixing our knowledge about entities perceived as "natural" (Haraway 1992; Latour 1993), a variety of interpretations and representations of what "Nature" really is have been advanced, each of which aims to co-shape how to think about, and act on "Nature." For example, the representation of Nature as vulnerable, victim, or derailed, and therefore in need of saving or protecting, is based on "a political semiotics of representation" where "the represented is reduced to the permanent status of the recipient of action, never to be a co-actor in an articulated practice" (Haraway 1992: 313). This view of Nature has recently informed policies of environmental reconstruction that aim to revert Nature to its presumed pristine state, by dynamiting dams (US, France), or by producing new "pristine" urban natures in the form of urban rivers (Seoul) or public beaches (Paris). At the other end of the spectrum, Giddens's (1994) claim that we have reached "The End of Nature" paves the road for an entirely different way of engaging with nature, one that questions the notion of a lost and originally pristine nature (that needs to be recaptured), recognizes the irredeemable socialization of nature, and urges us to mobilize the courage to deploy new and different socio-ecological assemblages.

These imagined, scripted, and symbolically charged "Natures" are always necessarily inadequate, always leave a gap in the understanding and interpretation of the natures that are there materially, and which are complex, chaotic, often unpredictable, contingent, historically and geographically variable, and risky. Morton (2007), for example, argues convincingly that the proliferation of such conflicting meanings of Nature and associated policy derivatives, such as "sustainability," have turned Nature into an empty signifier. There is not, he insists, such a thing as a singular "Nature" around which an urban environmental policy or an environmentally sensitive intervention can be constructed and performed. Rather, there is a multitude of urban natures and a multitude of existing, possible, or practical socio-natural relations. "Nature" is a tapestry, a *montage* of meanings, held together with quilting points (*points de capiton*), like the upholstery of a Chesterfield sofa (see Swyngedouw 2010a).

However, despite general academic consensus on the impossibility of "fixing" the meaning of Nature, a growing global awareness of an "environmental crisis" that poses a possibly catastrophic threat to civilization as we know it, has led to an emergence of a global consensus over Nature as radically out-of-synch, singular, under threat, and in need of saving. This consensus has transformed, yet again, the signifying chains that attempt to provide a new "content" for Nature (Žižek 1989, 2008). Urging for techno-managerial and governance realignments that can save the planet, the discursive framing of Nature as singular has enormous implications for inequality and injustice in the city, as it annuls the properly political moment, ruptures hopes for environmental justice, whether in the form of procedural justice (through the removal of real debate and dissensus over what stands for equality) or the justice of capabilities (through disavowing more radical potential pathways to building a more socially and environmentally just society beyond the current status quo) (Swyngedouw 2010b).

Zimmerman contends that "in stressful periods, people are too willing to surrender to leaders promising to end humanity's alienation from nature" (Zimmerman 1993: 7). Indeed, while clouded in a rhetoric of immanent catastrophe and the need for radical change, technical fixes to environmental problems are currently highlighted as solutions, making sure that nothing really changes, contributing to what has been defined as a post-political urban condition (Žižek 1992/2002; Swyngedouw 2009, 2010b). Is this not the underlying message of, for example, former US vice-president Al Gore's missionary account of pending environmental catastrophe in *An Inconvenient Truth* (Gore 2007) or of the fourth report of the United Nation's Intergovernmental Panel on Climate Change (IPCC) on the human consequences of global climate change (IPCC 2009)? Both these narratives, in their very different representational ways (popular/populist on the one hand, "scientific" on the other), urge radical changes in the techno-organizational management of the socio-natural environment in order to assure that the world as we know it stays fundamentally the same (Žižek 2008). This sentiment is also shared by Frederic Jameson when he claims that "it is easier to imagine the end of the world than it is to imagine the end of capitalism" (Jameson 2003: 76), and leads Badiou (2008) to conclude that "ecology is the new opium for the masses."

Policiticizing Urban Environments: New Beginnings

Caught between the urge to retrofit urban socio-natures with "sustainable" technologies and "good" governance practices and the desire to "protect" a nature under threat, the controversies over urbanizing nature stand for a political inability to rearrange the socio-ecological coordinates of everyday life, and to produce radically new, and more equitable, urban socio-natural configurations. Whilst considering the extraordinary leaps that urban socio-ecological research has taken, we recognize that the urban ecological quandary remains as (if not more) acute than before. Although we now know a great deal more about the materiality and governance of the contested urbanization of nature, we are still faced with an extraordinary intellectual and practical challenge. We have traced the socio-ecological flows and power relations through which the urban becomes constituted, we have excavated how class tactics of dispossession and neoliberalization reframed both nature and the urban environmental question, we have charted the multitude of socio-environmental movements that come together around (un)just urban sustainabilities, and we have dissected the discourses on Nature in whose name the above are undertaken.

Still, the ecological mess is more real than ever and has to be taken seriously, but this would require a radical conceptual and political reframing. Attempts to mainstream the ecological problem have been marked so far by three distinct but interrelated processes. First, the ecological turn of capital and the marketization of "ecological" or "sustainable" products, which nevertheless carry dubious environmental credentials (e.g., clean hybrid car technologies using resources mined through environmentally disastrous processes in China and elsewhere). Second, the nurturing of particular discourses and policies as a panacea for environmental protection, notably "sustainability," environmental cost recovery, and the "polluter pays" principle. Third, the financialization/privatization of the environmental commons as the preferred mechanism to avoid the "tragedy of the commons." Carbon dioxide, forests, water and other resources, human and non-human genetic codes, and perhaps most importantly, the privatization of the greatest of all common ecologies, the urban process, are key examples.

Revisiting the meaning and politics of a common urban environment becomes imperative today, as we have entered a unique historical moment. For the first time, human–non-human interactions produce socio-ecological conditions that are inimical to the continuation of human and other life forms, and the urban environmental catastrophe is not one to come, it is already here. We are already living in it, particularly in the megacities of the global south. Henri Lefebvre's clarion call for a politics articulated around "the right to the city" has now become an urgent call for "the right to urban environments" and to the urban "commmonwealth" (see Hardt and Negri 2009).

Although the full ecological consequences of human socio-ecological labor remain partly unknown, the dominant scenario today is one of interventions articulated around the structural necessity to grow, to accumulate for accumulation's sake. Yet, this process has spiraled out of control with socio-ecological contradictions that are now plain to see. However, capitalism cannot and will not stand for an unconditional demand for a transformation to a different, egalitarian, socio-ecological order, despite the call to arms from a variety of elites, ranging from Prince Charles's dire warning that we have only 18 months left to do something to Al Gore's apocalyptic film *An Inconvenient Truth*.

The inability or incapacity to manage the (urban) commons of socio-ecological assemblages, not even in the elite's own interest, is an extraordinary situation. The point, here, is not to fall into the urge to save nature – which does not exist anyway as a stable marker or reference (Swyngedouw 2010a) – or to retrofit socio-ecological conditions (Kaika 2009) to an assumedly more benign earlier historical condition (which is of course an inherently reactionary demand) – but to call for an egalitarian and democratic production of socio-ecological commons. We contend that this would require recasting city/nature as a decidedly political project, and insist that recentering the political is a necessary condition for tackling questions of urban environmental justice and creating different socio-ecological urban assemblages, to recapture the urban as socio-ecological commons, as a collective and democratically produced *oeuvre*. But we also contend that recentering the political is not enough in itself. We also need to reassert the materialities of the natures we work with, respect the idiosyncrasies and particular acting of parts of nature, not all of which is or can be fully understood. We also need to engage head on with the condition that, despite intense struggle and despite growing understanding, precious little real change takes place. Whether we depict nature as a thing "out there" to be saved, or as a frontier to be conquered or ignored, it becomes imperative to ask questions about what visions of Nature and what urban socio-environmental relations we wish to inhabit. What quilting points can be mobilized? How can new political urban socio-ecological narratives be stitched together? What issues and whose voices are being silenced and who or what has the right to speak and to be heard?

Politically engaging urban ecological research and practice are about changing the frame through which things and conditions are perceived, transforming the conditions of impossibility, not simply to possible but to necessary ones. Imagining, again, urban environmental utopias that go beyond a neoliberal framework is imperative. We should dare to try again, to think anew, even if we have to fail again.

Note

1   When we use Nature (capitalized) it generally refers to a specific discursively constructed singular meaning or understanding of the natural world and what it is. The word nature (uncapitalized) refers to the sum total of the heterogeneous, diverse, and often whimsical things that comprise the physical environments of the world.

References

Ali, S. H., and Keil, R. (2008) *Networked Disease: Emerging Infections in the Global City*. Malden, MA: Blackwell.

Badiou, A. (2008) Live Badiou – Interview with Alain Badiou, Paris, December 2007. In *Alain Badiou – Live Theory*, ed. O. Feltham. London: Continuum: 136–9.

Baker, S. (2007) Sustainable development as symbolic commitment: declaratory politics and the seductive appeal of ecological modernisation in the European Union. *Environmental Politics* 16: 297–317.

Bakker, K. J. (2000) Privatizing water: producing scarcity: the Yorkshire drought of 1995. *Economic Geography* 76 (1): 4–27.

Bakker, K. J. (2003) *An Uncooperative Commodity: Privatizing Water in England and Wales.* New York and Oxford: Oxford University Press.

Braun, B. (2005) Environmental issues: writing a more-than-human urban geography. *Progress in Human Geography* 29 (5): 635–50.

Brechin, G. (1996) Conserving the race: natural aristocracies, eugenics, and the US conservation movement. *Antipode* 28 (3): 229–45.

Buerk, R. (2006) *Breaking Ships: How Supertankers and Cargo Ships Are Dismantled on the Beaches of Bangladesh.* New York: Chamberlain Books.

Bulkeley, H., and Betsill, M. (2005) *Cities and Climate Change: Urban Sustainability and Global Environmental Governance.* London: Routledge.

Carruthers, D. V. (2008) The globalization of environmental justice: lessons from the US–Mexico border. *Society and Natural Resources* 21: 556–8.

Castree, N. (2008) Neoliberalising nature: the logics of deregulation and reregulation. *Environment and Planning A* 40: 131–52.

Castro, J. E. (2006) *Water, Power and Citizenship: Social Struggle in the Basin of Mexico.* Basingstoke: Palgrave Macmillan, in association with St Antony's College, Oxford.

Castro, J. E., and Heller, L. (eds.) (2009) *Water and Sanitation Services: Public Policy and Management.* London and Sterling, VA: Earthscan.

Cole, L. W., and Foster, S. R. (2000) *From the Ground Up: Environmental Racism and the Rise of the Environmental Justice Movement.* New York: New York University Press.

Cook, I., and Swyngedouw, E. (2011) Cities, nature and sustainability. In *Cities and Social Change*, ed. E. McCann and R. Paddison. London: Sage.

Cronon, W. (1991) *Nature's Metropolis: Chicago and the Great West.* New York: W. W. Norton and Company.

Davis, M. (2002) *Dead Cities.* New York: The New Press.

Desfor, G., and Keil, R. (2004) *Nature and the City: Making Environmental Policy in Toronto and Los Angeles.* Tucson: University of Arizona Press.

Faber, D. (2005) Building a transnational environmental justice movement: obstacles and opportunities in the age of globalization. In *Coalitions Across Borders: Transnational Protest and the Neoliberal Order*, ed. J. Bandy and J. Smith. Oxford: Roman and Littlefield, 43–70.

Freidberg, S. (2004) *French Beans and Food Scares: Culture and Commerce in an Anxious Age.* New York and Oxford: Oxford University Press.

Gandy, M. (2002) *Concrete and Clay: Reworking Nature in New York City.* Cambridge, MA: MIT Press.

Gandy, M. (2005) Cyborg urbanization: complexity and monstrosity in the contemporary city. *International Journal of Urban and Regional Research* 29 (1): 26 –49.

Gibbs, D. (2000) Ecological modernisation, regional economic development and regional development agencies. *Geoforum* 31: 9–19.

Giddens, A. (1994) *Beyond Left and Right: The Future of Radical Politics.* Cambridge: Polity Press.

Gore, A. (2007) *An Inconvenient Truth: The Planetary Emergency of Global Warming and What We Can Do About It.* London: Bloomsbury.

Graham, S., and Marvin, S. (2001) *Splintering Urbanism.* London: Routledge.

Haraway, D. (1991) *Simians, Cyborgs and Women – The Reinvention of Nature.* London: Free Association Books.

Haraway, D. (1992) The promises of monsters: a regenerative politics for inappropriate/d others. In *Cultural Studies*, ed. L. Grossberg, G. Nelson, and P. Treichler. London: Routledge, 295–337.

Hardt, M., and Negri, T. (2009) *Commonwealth*. Cambridge MA: Harvard University Press.

Harvey, D. (2003) *The New Imperialism*. Oxford: Oxford University Press.

Heynen, N., Kaika, M., and Swyngedouw, E. (eds.) (2006) *In the Nature of Cities: Urban Political Ecology and the Metabolism of Urban Environments*. London: Routledge.

Heynen, N., McCarthy, J., Prudham, S., and Robbins, P. (eds.) (2007) *Neoliberal Environments: False Promises and Unnatural Consequences*. London: Routledge.

Hillier, J. (2009) Assemblages of justice: the "ghost ships" of Graythorp. *International Journal of Urban and Regional Research* 33 (3): 640–61.

Himley, M. (2008) Geographies of environmental governance: the nexus of nature and neoliberalism. *Geography Compass* 2: 433–51.

Hinchcliffe, S. (1999) Cities and natures: intimate strangers. In *Unsettling Cities: Movement/ Settlement*, ed. J. Allen, D. Massey, and M. Pryke. London: Routledge, 141–85.

IPCC (2009) *Climate Change 2007: Impacts, Adaptation and Vulnerability*. Working Contribution to the Fourth Assessment Report of the IPCC. Cambridge: Cambridge University Press.

Jameson, F. (2003) Future city. *New Left Review* 21: 65–79.

Kaika, M. (2005) *City of Flows: Nature, Modernity and the City*. New York: Routledge.

Kaika, M. (2009) Landscapes of energy: hydropower from techno-natures to retro-natures. *Harvard New Geographies* 2: 103–10.

Keil, R. (2003) Urban political ecology. *Urban Geography* 24: 723–38.

Keil, R. (2005) Progress report – Urban political ecology. *Urban Geography* 26: 640–51.

Keil, R. (2007) Sustaining modernity, modernizing nature: the environmental crisis and the survival of capitalism. In *The Sustainable Development Paradox: Urban Political Ecology in the United States and Europe*, ed. R. Krueger and D. Gibbs. London: Guilford Press, 41–65.

Klinenberg, E. (2002) *Heat Wave: A Social Autopsy of Disaster in Chicago*. Chicago and London: University of Chicago Press.

Krueger, R., and Gibbs, D. (eds.) (2007) *The Sustainable Development Paradox: Urban Political Economy in the United States and Europe*. New York: Guilford Press.

Latour, B. (1993) *We Have Never Been Modern*. New York and London: Harvester Wheatsheaf.

Leitner, H., Sheppard, E., and Sziarto, K. M. (2008) The spatialities of contentious politics. *Transactions of the Institute of British Geographers* 33: 157–72.

Loftus, A. (2006) The metabolic process of capital accumulation in Durban's waterscape. In *In the Nature of Cities: Urban Political Ecology and the Politics of Urban Metabolism*, ed. N. Heynen, M. Kaika, and E. Swyngedouw. London: Routledge, 173–90.

Marx, K. (1981 [1867]) *Capital: A Critique of Political Economy*, vol. 1. London: Penguin.

Massey, D. B. (2007) *World City*. Cambridge, Polity Press.

Mol, A. P. J., and Spaargaren, G. (2000) Ecological modernisation theory in debate: a review. *Environmental Politics* 9: 17–49.

Morton, T. (2007) *Ecology Without Nature: Rethinking Environmental Aesthetics*. Cambridge, MA and London: Harvard University Press.

Nicholls, W. J. (2009) Place, networks, space: theorising the geographies of social movements. *Transactions of the Institute of British Geographers* 34: 78–93.

Njeru, J. (2006) The urban political ecology of plastic bag waste problem in Nairobi, Kenya. *Geoforum* 37: 1046–58.

Olivera, O., and Lewis, T. (2004) *Cochabamba: Water War in Bolivia*. Cambridge, MA: South End Press.

Pellow, D. (2007) *Resisting Global Toxics: Transnational Movements for Environmental Justice*. London: MIT Press.

Prudham, S. (2004) Poisoning the well: neoliberalism and the contamination of municipal water in Walkerton, Ontario. *Geoforum* 35 3: 343–359.

Robbins, P. (2007) *Lawn People: How Grasses, Weeds, and Chemicals Make Us Who We Are*. Philadelphia, PA: Temple University Press.

Routledge, P. (2007) Transnational political movement. In *The Sage Handbook of Political Geography*, ed. M. Low, K. R. Cox, and J. Robinson. London: Sage, 335–49.

Swyngedouw, E. (2004) *Social Power and the Urbanization of Water: Flows of Power*. Oxford: Oxford University Press.

Swyngedouw, E. (2006) Circulations and metabolisms: (hybrid) natures and (cyborg) cities. *Science as Culture* 15 (2): 105–21.

Swyngedouw, E. (2009) The antinomies of the post-political city: in search of a democratic politics of environmental production. *International Journal of Urban and Regional Research* 33 (3): 601–20.

Swyngedouw, E. (2010a) Trouble with nature: ecology as the new opium for the people. In *Conceptual Challenges for Planning Theory*, ed. J. Hillier and P. Healey. Farnham: Ashgate, 299–320.

Swyngedouw, E. (2010b) Apocalypse forever? Post-political populism and the specter of climate change. *Theorie, Culture, Society* 27 (2–3): 213–32.

Swyngedouw, E., and Heynen, N. (2003) Urban political ecology: justice and the politics of scale. *Antipode* 34 (4): 898–918.

Swyngedouw, E., and Kaika, M. (2000) The environment of the city or ... the urbanisation of nature. In *A Companion to the City*, ed. G. Bridge and S. Watson. Oxford: Blackwell, 567–80.

Sze, J. (2006) *Noxious New York: The Racial Politics of Urban Health and Environmental Justice*. Cambridge, MA: MIT Press.

Virilio, P. (1986) *Speed and Politics: An Essay on Dromology*. New York: Semiotext(e).

Whitehead, M. (2005) Between the marvellous and the mundane: everyday life in the socialist city and the politics of the environment. *Environment and Planning D: Society and Space* 22 (6): 273–94.

Whitehead, M. (2007) *Spaces of Sustainability: Geographical Perspectives on the Sustainable Society*. London: Routledge.

Wolch, J., Pincetl, S., and Pulido, L. (2002) Urban nature and the nature of urbanism. In *From Chicago to LA: Making Sense of Urban Theory*, ed. M. J. Deer. Thousand Oaks, CA: Sage, 367–402.

Zimmerman, M. E. (1993) *Environmental Philosophy: From Animal Rights to Radical Ecology*. Englewood Cliffs, NJ: Prentice Hall.

Žižek, S. (1989) *The Sublime Object of Ideology*. London: Verso.

Žižek, S. (1992/2002). *Looking Awry: An Introduction to Jacques Lacan through Popular Culture*. Cambridge, MA: MIT Press.

Žižek, S. (2008) *In Defense of Lost Causes*. Verso, London.

Chapter 10

One Hundred Tons to Armageddon: Cities Combat Carbon

Peter Droege

The Future of Sustainable Urban Change

Sustainable development has taken on a sharp and well-defined meaning during the first decade of the twenty-first century, casting cities in a new light. Driven by accelerating climate change and exhaustible energy resource constraints, a search for urban and regional energy autonomy is rising to the top of international agendas. In turn, this search provides a welcome specificity in the meaning, policy, and guidance of sustainability in urban design. The rapid move from sustainability to survivability drives new ways of understanding the contemporary urban system as anachronism: a fossil fuel construct in search of rapid restructuring. This helps reexamine present local, provincial, and national planning guidance systems in their successes and failures; re-establishes urban and regional links; provides a new context for council, community, and business acceptance levels; and helps engender new models of institutional evaluation, feed-back, and learning. A radical transformation of city planning and development theory is in the making, in theory and in practice.

*   *   *

The global system of extracting and marketing toxic fossil and nuclear fuels is built on a central phenomenon: cities and their communities evolved as its captive client. Trapped in near-total dependency on these performance-enhancing substances the twentieth-century city bulked up like a prize-fighter on steroids. It reached its exalted status as dominant settlement form while making its population complicit in the global trade of oil, coal, gas, and radioactive material – and the related paraphernalia and techniques of delivering the drugs: coal and uranium mines, oil and

The New Blackwell Companion to the City   Edited by Gary Bridge and Sophie Watson
© 2011 Blackwell Publishing Ltd

gas fields, processing plants, pipelines, power generators, distribution networks, massive military interventions, overt and hidden political pressure – and the extensive financial systems to procure investments and extract the rising payments and profits.

By its very nature this energy system supported the rise of cities. Cities bulged as a direct consequence – and poisoned, paved, filled, or drained vast stretches of aquifers, rivers, and lakes in the process. Wetlands, bushlands, and grasslands disappeared at growing rates. Metropolitan regions grew, littered with highways and landfill sites. And they emerged as the narrative backdrop for countless human lives lost in income, class, and energy inequities. Mapped onto city geographies around the globe, misguided energy policy emerged as an obscene and avoidable tragedy, because decision makers ignored the abundant, local, and practically limitless, ubiquitous, and free source of the sun, embodied in solar, wind, water, and bio-energy.

When it comes to assessing the costs of this destructive process, its most menacing legacy is the atmosphere. The cocktail of anthropogenic carbon dioxide, nitrous oxide, methane, and chlorofluorocarbons that enriches the thin layer of terrestrial air is the global gaseous garbage pool resulting from generations of fossil fuel burning, cement production, and rapacious land management practice. The oceans serve as overflow receptacle. Much of this waste is being generated to support the material growth, management, and mobility of cities – and despite all green aspirations the gaseous sludge stream is growing day by day.

The atmosphere is oversaturated with waste, taking the viability of human life supports as benchmark. The alarm is struck in runaway Arctic and Greenland ice melts and African droughts alike. And yet, to the climate optimist, 100 tons of carbon dioxide combustion and land destruction waste still remain to be emitted for every person on earth, adding up to a total of 1,000 billion tons of atmospheric carbon waste generated since pre-industrial times. When discounting the other greenhouse gases or the effect of land clearing, every Australian or US denizen discharges close to 20 tons each year, given antiquated power systems and an insatiable appetite for consumption. The poorest countries manage not even a single ton. And one ton of carbon dioxide annual discharge is the worldwide per capita limit by 2050, if a calamitous two degree temperature rise is to be accepted (WGBU 2009).

But this gloomy prospect represents the more optimistic view. Since politically it is the most palatable position acknowledging a problem at all, the European Council adopted it as target in 1996. It is based on three erroneous assumptions: (a) a two degree rise is manageable; (b) a carbon dioxide concentration of 450 parts per million (ppm) can hold temperature to two degrees; and (c) the biosphere works like a controlled laboratory experiment, where a turn of the dial produces a predictable outcome. These fallacies are now exposed. First, a two degree Celsius (C) rise is unacceptable since it means the drowning of low-lying regions from Tuvalu to southern Florida, and evaporating water supplies for millions of urban and rural dwellers. Worse yet, it accepts the unraveling of features that helped stabilize climatic conditions for a large and somewhat advanced human civilization to evolve. These have already begun to shift or unravel at the 0.7 degree C rise experienced during the twentieth century. The point of no return beyond which no human intervention can halt the climatic cataclysm is likely to be reached below 450 ppm.

Even if a two-degree rise in global temperatures could somehow be regarded as "safe," as a policy-informing target the 450 ppm threshold is both arbitrary and unsuitable. This concentration carries a 50 percent risk of overshooting two degrees at the concentrations reached after 1,000 billion carbon tons emitted, i.e. the reaching of a 450 ppm carbon dioxide concentration level (Meinshausen 2005). And in other scientific surprises, the warming oceans have begun to slow their uptake of excess atmospheric carbon and turned significantly more acidic in the process. Such results may be fine for high-school laboratory experiments but are not acceptable if a foundation of the planetary food chain is wiped out: plankton.

Carbon City, City of Gas

These gigatons of carbon represent the evolution of industrial civilization and its cities, mapped upon the chemistry of the biosphere. A great gaseous city has invisibly risen in the skies, formed by burning fossil carbon at a madcap rate: of the nearly 330 billion tons of carbon dioxide released by fossil fuel burning and cement production since the middle of the eighteenth century, a full half has been emitted since the 1970s, still rising at the precipitous rate of 3.4 percent each year (Boden *et al.* 2009). A growing understanding of this lethal legacy, too large to be ignored even by the most myopic, is beginning to change the very evolution of the city, and of urban and regional planning. And it is not limited to small-town Austria or environmentally attuned San Francisco. On December 21, 2009 a CNN interview with New York Mayor Michael Bloomberg and Californian Governor Arnold Schwarzenegger focused on another spectacular failure of the United Nations Framework Convention on Climate Change Conference of the Parties (UNFCCC COP) process: the "Copenhagen COP(15) flop." A long-awaited breakthrough to global and shared commitments, seen as critical due to the expiration of the already weak and partial Kyoto Accord of December 1997 commitments in 2012, ended with the non-binding Copenhagen Accord of December 2009. The frustration expressed by Bloomberg and Schwarzenegger showed how mainstream urban and regional anxiety and hunger for a fundamental transformation have become. Both participants decried the failure to act and powerfully upheld the local capacity for change.

The warnings of the 1960s and 1970s were stark. Exemplary were the report to the Club of Rome (Meadows *et al.* 1972) – whose scenario of a trajectory to a twenty-first-century economic and social collapse was confirmed by Turner (2008) – and the Global 2000 Report (CEQ 1981). Yet both were dismissed when the time came to embrace effective global policies. They had only epitomized a much older tradition of environmental warnings. And with the dawn of the third millennium the face of the Apocalypse has become unnervingly detailed, even oddly familiar. Infernal prospects, Dantesque and even worse: the eternal hell of Planet Venus' 250 degree Celsius acidic sulphur-clouded atmosphere rises as plausible prospect for our still-blue planet in both Carl Sagan's and Stephen Hawking's dire warnings.[1] Unlike the Great Tribulation, the Mayan Day Zero, or the Norse Ragnarök, this cataclysmic prospect is as real as it is in human hands, like the possibility of a nuclear holocaust.

The failed Kyoto process aiming at modest global agreements has exposed the willingness of powerful actors and nations to accept genocide when asked to take responsibility for the vulnerable. It was built on a dream of universal consensus across diverse states of development and industrial interests. From 1997 it became focused on introducing emissions as a currency of fear and greed, in a misplaced application of US sulphur pollution trade legacy – instead of aiming at the polluting practices themselves. And yet the path to redemption is so clear, even banal. Three measures are key to averting the worst of this particular End Time: ending fossil fuel combustion, now subsidized with US$300 billion annually (Gelbspan 2000); reversing deforestation and the draining of wetlands; and cutting material consumption in wealthy countries.

Indeed, the need to lower fossil fuel energy consumed in goods and services is also critical. And given the advanced state of the atmospheric carbon bubble, bio-sequestration is emerging as a paramount if distant goal in making cities and city regions climate stabilizing: capable of taking up greenhouse gas from the atmosphere, rather than being merely carbon neutral. For both tasks – lifestyle changes and bio-sequestration – regional settings and partners emerge as a new and critical factor in building resilience. All of these imperatives seem still beyond the action radius of most cities. Much of public policy has been in denial for more than a generation: comparatively few governments dare to make an effective attempt at preventing a cataclysm, despite the overwhelming evidence.

The termination of fossil fuel burning through a combined effort in efficiency, demand reduction, and the rapid, widespread introduction of renewable energy sources addresses the greatest share in anthropogenic emissions. More than 85 percent of global primary commercial energy is supplied by non-renewable, toxic sources (EIA 1986), yielding 75 percent of emissions. Some 95 percent of motorized transport, essential to economies, cities, and the very dynamics of urban growth and lifestyles, is petroleum dependent (IPCC 2001). Peak oil – the inexorable arrival of the maximum point of oil production beyond which demand increasingly outstrips supply – exposes a structural flaw in the global urbanization architecture. All notions about urban change are being challenged by this. Global oil production capacity has likely been in peaking mode since 2006 (Schindler and Zittel 2008). And given continued demand trajectories, production downturn is likely going to be much sharper and more dramatic than predicted by most peak oil experts, due to the "net peak" effect: as reserves become scarcer it takes an increasing amount of energy to produce the dwindling resource. In 2000 it took one barrel of oil to extract 11 in the United States – down from a ratio of 1 : 100 in the 1930s (Cleveland 2004). As the point of peak is approached and passed, the rapidly decreasing production efficiency leaves substantially less in net usable production capacity than the 50 percent of total available resources usually depicted (Murphy 2009).

Vanguards of Change

Oil peak is still relegated to the far fringes of urban discourse, but climate change enjoys only a small but intensifying spotlight on the sustainability end of the stage. Indeed, given the extent to which global negotiations are captive to outdated powerful interests, attention has shifted to regional and local agendas in a search for paths from fossil and nuclear to renewable energy autonomy. Thousands of viable initiatives, programs, and projects are documented around the globe, some stretching back a generation. Among these, the call for energy autonomy is growing loud.

Figure 10.1 Texas A&M University house at the Solar Decathlon held in the Washington DC Mall in 2007. The Solar Decathlon is organized through the National Renewable Energy Laboratory of the US Department of Energy every two years and is testimony to simple technology largely available for more than a generation. Massive interests in the non-renewable energy industries work hard to keep this reality limited to marginal prototypes – increasingly unsuccessfully so. Photo by Jeff Kubina 2007.

Communities from Amsterdam to Boulder are in this race. Examples are especially rich in smaller communities, islands, and larger regions of lower population density (Radzi 2009) but not limited to these. The large southern German city of Munich is working to become energy self-sufficient, procuring solar and wind energy in the region, offshore in the North Sea and through Spanish joint ventures, and expanding its local and regional geothermal resources. Resentment against the lethal load of old infrastructure builds: in 2009 a lawsuit was being filed against coal-burning power producer Midwest Generation for its five antiquated Chicago and other Illinois plants.[2] The city of Sydney commissioned a plan to make the central business district independent from the State of New South Wales's near-total coal-based electricity network by 2030, using a network of "green transformers" – distributed gas-fired generators producing power for power, heat, cooling, and water recycling.[3] The city has seized the climate issue for some time, and sought to convert environmental complaints into green accolades.

But the neo-Dickensian nightmare of new and massive coal-fired generators still plays out on a daily basis, evidenced by power multinational Vattenfall's Moorburg plant in Hamburg, Germany. Centuries apart in technology and insight, and yet only a few hundred yards away in the shadow of the climate destabilizing behemoth,

Figure 10.2   A solar settlement – part of a surplus energy generating mixed-use development in the widely acknowledged Vauban district, city of Freiburg im Breisgau, Germany. It demonstrates with other related developments that simple market-shaping policies such as a renewable electricity feed-in tariff, combined with cost-saving energy efficiency measures, new storage, and grid technology, can bring about renewable energy autonomy in cities and regions swiftly and to the benefit of local prosperity and innovation. Photo by Claire 7373/Andrew Glaser 2007.

an enlightened International Building Exhibition, IBA-Hamburg, aims at improving social integration through broad regeneration programs in one of Germany's most needy, multi-ethnic urban neighborhoods. The program is designed to be carbon neutral by 2013: no new carbon dioxide emissions are to be caused by the construction or operation of projects.

San Francisco's 42nd mayor Gary Newsom continued a progressive legacy, from solar bonds to finance public solar installations to renewable mobility concepts throughout the greater Bay Area. Newsom rallied neighboring Oakland and San José to partner a commercial renewable electric car initiative, Better Place, and pursues regional food production and urban gardening initiatives, mapping unused public spaces from rooftops to surplus land. Indeed, the tools of social and technological change are well established. European communities from Austria's small-town green power giant of Güssing to the 272 communities across Spain's Navarre region experience greater demographic stability, employment, and living standards, as wind power overtakes nuclear in Spain, and solar electricity does the same in

Germany (Radzi 2009). The decarbonizing energy agenda is fast becoming an essential element in any urban regeneration and development strategy.

Calls for Carbon Stabilization

Some hopeful signs emerge, in this world frozen in symbolic action around emissions target negotiations, or narrowly focused on profiting from a rise in climate calamities. A groundswell of change in urban policy rises, especially significant in the movements around energy, currently cities' greatest conundrum. Energy efficiency and demand management have been loud if peripheral catch cries of urban policy since the 1970s, boosted by the International Council for Local Environmental Initiatives' (ICLEI) Local Agenda 21 drive for local environmental action[4] and other movements 20 years later, including its Cities for Climate Protection campaign, and, more recently, the city-geared efforts supported by the Clinton Climate Initiative known as the C40 – or 40 carbon-managing cities joining under this umbrella.[5] While not focused on cities in particular, the broader technical potential of reducing energy consumption has long been documented, by Amory Lovins, Harry Lehmann, and others (Hawken *et al.* 1999; Lehmann 2003; Lehmann and Peter 2009). It has been shown to range from 40 percent in transport to 60 percent in electricity generation, averaging 50 percent across residential, industrial, and commercial sectors in some industrial nations. Plans have been developed for cities to even eliminate emissions from fossil fuels (Lechtenböhmer 2009).

Yet, despite a great commitment to this critical cause, efficiency efforts have had disappointing results. Most major industrialized and industrializing countries experienced improvements in the energy intensity of their economies – but failed to sustain these, let alone approach potential improvements. The rise in absolute energy use has outstripped efficiency measures, with the demand rebound effect ensuring that supply capacity freed through efficiency is taken up by rising demand. This sobering response, eclipsed only by the difficulties in replacing the energy system itself, is not helped by a broad reluctance to impose tough efficiency standards without the support of major conventional energy generation, supply, and other interest groups.

Because their governance structures were developed in an energy-blind environment, most communities and cities found it difficult to grapple for effective action. Nancy Carlisle of the National Renewable Energy Laboratory at the US Department of Energy calls this the "planning gap," because it signals a widening chasm between what a community would need to do to become renewable energy based and what actually is being done: "[Communities] focus on short-term, incremental approaches instead of tackling the more challenging task of guiding the deeper transition to a 'renewable energy community'" (Carlisle and Bush 2009: 259).

A US survey of ten cities identified typical community challenges. First, greenhouse gas inventories are not standardized, making comparisons between communities problematic. Also, community emissions have broadly risen since 1990, with little hope of reaching even the mild Kyoto-like targets. Almost all the cities surveyed look to higher levels of government in obtaining help, but this attitude blunts local action, inhibiting local investment in energy projects of economic and environmental benefits (Bailey 2007).

Cultural and Organizational Dimensions

The dependence on centralized fossil fuel supplies structured the very form and function of cities and national economies. A simple supply–demand picture came to prevail, with environmental costs ignored. This externalized relation meant that the planning, development and design decisions shaping the very structure of cities and their built form came to be understood as removed from strategic energy decisions. This great energy blindness was mapped onto the decision-making apparatus and planning systems of local governments, especially since energy sources were relatively inexpensive. As a result relatively few cities control their own energy destiny. The very essence of the energy transformation is a shift from external and centralized supply structures of little choice and rising cost, to internal, ubiquitous, highly diverse, and largely cost-free sources providing great control and participation to individual users, turning passive consumers to producers – *prosumers*.

It is precisely here, in the organizational and programmatic frameworks of cities, where most recent change can be registered. The search for urban quality policies among US cities during the 1980s and 1990s revealed a striking arsenal of underused powers (Schuster *et al.* 1997: chapter 1). Expanding these areas of influence here reveals that urban governments have significant opportunities to guide emission control and even energy autonomy programs, with cities only using a fraction of this potential. Here is a summary of some seven of such tool sets.

The making of civic rules for infrastructure planning and construction is a traditional role of cities, but it has become seriously contested since the micro-economic reform years that commenced 20 years ago. Re-emerging from this paralyzing period is a focus on the very skill and craft of making effective regulations, and the art of policy design. The success of Barcelona's Solar Ordinance in informing policy in some 80 cities across Spain is an instructive example: here the provision of solar thermal and electricity supply was made mandatory (Puig 2008). Going beyond this, some communities have begun to embrace full renewable energy supply: virtually any combination of efficiency standards, climate targets, resource management, and national pricing support mechanism allows this.

Incentives for efficiency and renewable energy can be provided through taxation, pricing, and grid purchase policies. Affordable, well-reticulated public transport and support for cycling underpin intelligent commuter behavior when combined with disincentives to driving through the creation of car-free zones. Cities can also provide access to parts of the city for electric vehicles, provide production and market incentives for solar charging stations, and encourage solar car-share providers. Electricity is not only vastly cheaper than petrol as a transport energy source, but also significantly more efficient because it does not need the wasteful engine and transmission train of the internal combustion paradigm.

The facilities and stock controlled by the city – from infrastructure to the municipal buildings to street and traffic lights, vehicle fleets, and underused property – are a ready better-practice target. Government has a higher degree of accountability and hence an obligation to do better than the best of private industry. It is obliged to use its asset management and capital investment policy and practice to set an example to the community, going beyond vague exhortations to "do better in saving energy," or support of the voluntary green building rating tools. All new buildings should be developed as energy autonomous structures, while petrol-powered car fleets should be eliminated and replaced with bus tickets or electrical vehicles, and unused land opened to gardening cooperatives or solar farms.

Municipal assets also include institutional frameworks and organizations. Cities operating public utilities are blessed. These are powerful tools in projecting renewable energy and efficiency policies, developing local power infrastructure, and pursuing resource autonomy plans. Where no public power assets exist these can be acquired or reclaimed: Amsterdam had an opportunity to repurchase its municipal energy company two decades after its sale to a European power conglomerate. Municipal utilities are important assets in the fight against climate change and fossil fuel dependence. Other examples include the German municipal utility of Schönau and its fight against nuclear power (see http://100-gute-gruende.de and http://ews-schoenau.de); California's Sacramento and its long and successful battle to control the Sacramento Municipal Utility District; or Munich's historical utility embracing renewable electricity for all city apartments.

Long-term renewable power purchasing contracts, as bulk purchasing for end-consumer use, allow cities to act as non-profit agents to acquire renewable electricity at large-volume rates and to pass the savings on to the community by distributing the power without added price margin. In the absence of utility control, public bonds can support efficiency and renewable energy development finance. Here the development of policy-based virtual utilities may be an option for metropolitan areas or smaller city networks in alliance with regional or state government. Delaware's state Sustainable Energy Utility (SEU) was created in the mid-2000s, issuing bonds to fund efficiency and renewable energy development, retiring these from the income or savings generated. The SEU shows how to raise funds in the absence of a strong municipal capital asset or tax base (www.seu-de.org).

Cities can use bond finance, their own assets, public–private partnerships, contracting arrangements, or cooperatives to develop projects near or far. Useful examples include the city of Copenhagen's participation in the local offshore wind cooperative Middelgrunden, or Munich's investment in North Sea offshore wind assets and Spanish solar thermal capacity. Small town examples abound: the Bavarian village of Wildpoldsried developed wind and solar power assets that help them produce 380 percent of their own electricity demand in renewable power in 2008, generating millions of euros in income for the community thanks to Germany's enlightened feed-in tariff system (www.wildpoldsried.de).

Government-owned development corporations, too, can project energy and environment objectives. Sydney's Barangaroo Delivery Authority (BDA) pursued in its planning stages a carbon negative objective for an inner-city waterfront site. BDA managed to reduce development bids to 20 percent of normal energy consumption rates and hoped to counter the remaining fossil fuel content through the import of renewable energy, seeking to position the project as an active agent in the central business district's waste, water, and energy infrastructure. The aim was to facilitate advanced sewage mining, water recycling, and renewable energy tri- and quad-generation services in cooperation with public and private partners and to lower the site's carbon emissions equity balance to below zero (www.barangaroo.com). A regeneration example at a larger scale is the International Building Exhibition IBA-Hamburg and its climate neutral aspirations, expressed in its solar thermal network, biogas facilities, solar architecture experiments, and geothermal explorations (www.iba-hamburg.org). Another typical and well-regarded initiative is the residential new-town initiative Kronsberg in Hanover, conceived for the "green" EXPO of 2000 (www.secureproject.org/download/18.360a0d56117c51a2d30800078408/Kronsberg_Germany.pdf).

Traditional city government reflects nineteenth- and twentieth-century realities. They are organized into highly segregated and specialized units, very much like medieval guilds. A need for skills expansion has arisen, to support outcome-oriented practice and an institutional structure in which all units of government are focused on new aims: energy autonomy. Planning practice also changes dramatically in this environment. The mapping of renewable energy capacity, understanding energy flows, realizing what is available for renewable electricity and thermal energy conversion: this is the basis for local energy independence – by maximizing its potential within urban boundaries first, then seeking regional and wider resource access (Genske *et al.* 2009). Conventional urban planning is changing, too. Making infrastructure renewable, built areas self-sustaining, and parks biologically diverse and water managing, providing for electric vehicle infrastructure needs, planning for emissions reductions – these are the foci of new urban policy (Martinot 2009: Table 1).

Information provision is another underutilized municipal power. Articulate municipal agencies, activist support organizations, educational programs, and entities focused on improved energy practice are legion. But many have been too timid, content with early Local Agenda 21 and Cities for Climate Protection-style emissions estimation and target-setting exercises (www.iclei.org). Today autonomy from fossil and nuclear shackles is the most sensible goal remaining, regardless of climatic and cultural setting, level of development, or size of the city or community involved. It promises income generation, local prosperity, and jobs – investments are required, not unrecovered expenditures.

These benefits are local, and local organization is key. The powerful community self-help organizations and local area institutions in Dutch cities, Japanese *ku* governments, Swiss small town, district, and canton-level organizations, Chinese political neighborhood assistance and regulatory structures, are essential elements for self-reliant renewable energy development strategies. And physical assets abound. Just like streets, parking lots and roof tops can be developed as solar electric or thermal assets, port cities can transform their shipping areas as wind-power generation hubs, as the growing number of transformed Dutch harbors shows, in Amsterdam, Groningen, and Rotterdam.

When dense gardens and urban forests are developed, or wetland growth and surface water management is nurtured, this can significantly lower metropolitan carbon footprints. Regional links can harvest biomass, nurture carbon sequestering forests and energy farms, and help relocalize urban food supplies. The reconnection of city and region emerges as the driver of partnerships among long-separated neighbors: city cores, suburban rings, rural economies, and wider park, wetland, and waterway systems. Climate stabilizing – carbon absorbing – city regions represent the most advanced frontier of renewable city planning and development.

Paths to Urban Energy Autonomy

Energy autonomy is fast becoming a global vision (Scheer 2006). It demands local action. Each city must find its own path based on climate and weather, available resources, development history, degree of globalization or trade dependence, the relation to the region, governance capacity, and the manner in which civil society is engaged. Unlike the old fossil and nuclear power systems the technical tools to achieve energy autonomy are local: roof and facade surfaces for solar conversion into electricity and thermal energy, small wind power, heat pumps and deep geo-thermal sources, bio-methane capture and use, biomass – in autonomous islands or as distributed networks.

Only the pursuit of total renewable energy reliance is useful. This will cover all electricity and thermal consumption and transport energy – and also include con-sumed energy embodied in the goods and services procured. Most fractional targets aim at the direct use of emissions generated from operational energy use only. This approach is problematic because the targets are typically set arbitrarily and for political purposes; they are set too low and for too distant a time horizon; and they cover only a small band in the energy-use spectrum. In wealthy cities energy embod-ied in goods and services consumed represents up to 70 percent of household energy use – yet this lifestyle factor is not reflected in municipal statistics or policies (Lenzen *et al.* 2008).

Understanding embodied and imported fossil energy or emissions is crucial in assigning responsibility to consumers, and reducing the ecological footprint of urban dwellers. Consumption emissions are easy to understand yet their control is seen to go beyond the traditional scope of urban public policy. Yet embodied fossil fuel and carbon emissions can be countered with a wide array of measures – ranging from local food supply strategies to building local renewable energy powered indus-trial production capacity, to enhancing and promoting local and regional environ-mental and cultural qualities to lower the demand for international recreational travel.

A Dissident View on Global Urban Growth

Since 2007 United Nations population statistics have counted more than half of the world's population as urban (UNDESA 2009), while much of the growth occurred in the urban mega-slums in the structurally adjusted developing world (Davis 2005). Utter urban dependence on fossil energy and the inexorable decline in petroleum production capacity make growing urban expansion in this century unlikely, even when discounting climate change impacts. At this time there is no indication that governments or industry are moving fast enough to decrease energy demand in real terms, or in other ways fill the gap that will soon open between increasing demand and reduced low-cost fossil production. Even if enlightenment broke out and sound energy and environmental practices were to be widely embraced: the differences between the centralized and the more locally grounded renewable energy based framework mean that the very dynamics driving growth are going to shift. A time of global deurbanization and rerularization may lie ahead.

Notes

1 Sagan and Hawking quotes on http://350orbust.wordpress.com/2010/07/23/carl-sagan-and-stephen-hawking-on-effects-of-global-warming-the-runaway-greenhouse-effect-on-venus-is-a-valuable-reminder-to-take-the-increasing-greenhouse-effect-on-earth-seriously (accessed July 23, 2010).
2 Environmental News Service 2009 (www.ens-newswire.com/ens/aug2009/2009–08–27–091.html; accessed October 8, 2010).
3 See www.cityofsydney.nsw.gov.au/2030/theplan/ (accessed October 8, 2010).
4 www.gdrc.org/uem/la21/la21.html (accessed October 8, 2010).
5 www.iclei.org for Cities for Climate Protection; www.clintonfoundation.org for the Clinton Climate Initiative.

References

Bailey, J. (2007) *Lessons from the Pioneers: Tackling Global Warming at the Local Level.* Minneapolis, MN: Institute for Local Self-Reliance,

Boden, T. A., Marland, G., and Andres, R. J. (2009) Global, Regional, and National Fossil-Fuel CO^2 Emissions. Carbon Dioxide Information Analysis Center, Oak Ridge National Laboratory, US Department of Energy, Oak Ridge, TN. doi 10.3334/CDIAC/00001.

Carlisle, N., and Bush, B. (2009) Closing the planning gap: moving to renewable communities. In *100 Percent Renewable: Energy Autonomy in Action*, ed. P. Droege. London: Earthscan, 263–88.

Cleveland, C. J. (2004) Net energy from the extraction of oil and gas in the United States. *Energy* 30 (5): 769–82.

Council on Environmental Quality (CEQ) (1981) The Global 2000. Report to the President. Washington, DC: Government Printing Office.

Davis, M. (2005) *Planet of Slums*. London: Verso.

EIA (US Energy Information Administration) (1986) World Energy Outlook 1996–2006. Available online at www.eia.doe.gov/iea/overview.html (accessed October 8, 2010).

Gelbspan, R. (2000) The climate crisis and carbon trading. *Foreign Policy in Focus* 5 (20): 1–4.

Genske, D. D., Porsche, L., and Ruff, A. (2009) Urban energy potentials: a step towards the use of 100% renewable energies. In *100 Percent Renewable: Energy Autonomy in Action*. ed. P. Droege. London: Earthscan, 251–62.

Hawken, P., Lovins, A., and Hunter Lovins, L. (1999) *Natural Capitalism*. New York: Little Brown.

IPCC (Intergovernmental Panel on Climate Change) (2001). *Climate Change 2001: Mitigation. Contribution of Working Group III to the Third Assessment Report of the Intergovernmental Panel on Climate Change*. Cambridge: Cambridge University Press.

Lechtenböhmer, S. (2009) CO^2-free Munich. In *100 Percent Renewable: Energy Autonomy in Action*, ed. P. Droege. London: Earthscan, 86–92.

Lehmann, H. (2003) *Energy-rich Japan*. Aachen: Institute for Sustainable Solutions and Innovation (ISUSI).

Lehmann, H. and Peter, S. (2009) 100 percent renewable energy supply structure: scenarios, dynamic, costs. In *100 Percent Renewable: Energy Autonomy in Action*, ed. P. Droege. London: Earthscan, 71–86.

Lenzen, M., Wood, R., and Foran, B. (2008) Direct versus embodied energy: the need for urban lifestyle transitions. In *Urban Energy Transition*, ed. P. Droege. Oxford and Amsterdam: Elsevier, 91–120.

Martinot, Eric (2009) *Global Status Report on Local Renewable Energy Policies*. REN21/ISEP/ICLEI, working draft 12 June 2009. Tokyo: Institute for Sustainable Energy Policies.

Meinshausen, M. (2005) On the risk of overshooting 2°C. Paper presented at scientific symposium "Avoiding Dangerous Climate Change", Meteorological Office, Exeter, 1–3 February 2005. Available online at www.pik-potsdam.de/~mmalte/simcap/publications/meinshausenm_risk_of_overshooting_final_webversion.pdf (accessed October 8, 2010).

Meadows, Donnella H., Meadows, Dennis L., Randers, Jørgen, and Behrens, William H. (1972) *The Limits to Growth*. New York: Universe Books.

Murphy, D. (2009) The Net Hubbert Curve: what does it mean? Available online at http://netenergy.theoildrum.com/node/5500 (accessed October 8, 2010).

Puig, J. (2008) Barcelona and the power of solar ordinances: political will, capacity building and people's participation. In *Urban Energy Transition – from Fossil Fuels to Renewable Power*, ed. P. Droege. London and Boston: Elsevier, 433–49.

Radzi, A. (2009) 100 percent renewable champions – international case studies. In *100 Percent Renewable: Energy Autonomy in Action*, ed. P. Droege. London: Earthscan, 93–159.

Scheer, H. (2006) *Energy Autonomy: The Economc, Social and Tehcnological Case for Renewable Energy*. London: Earthscan.

Schindler, J., and Zittel, W. (2008) *Zukunft der weltweiten Erdölversorgung*. Berlin: Energy Watch Group/Ludwig-Bölkow-Stiftung.

Schuster, J. M., de Monchaux, J., and Riley, C. A. (eds.) (1997) *Preserving the Built Heritage: Tools for Implementation*. Hanover, NH: University Press of New England.

Turner, Graham (2008) *A Comparison of* The Limits of Growth *with Thirty Years of Reality*. Collingwood, Victoria: Commonweath Scientifc and Industrial Research Organisation.

UNDESA (United Nations Department of Economic and Social Affairs – Population Division) (2009) World Urbanization Prospects – The 2007 Update. United Nations. Available online at http://esa.un.org/unpd/wup/index.htm (accessed October 8, 2010).

WBGU (Wissenschaftlicher Beirat der Bundesregierung Global Umweltveränderung) (2009) Kassensturz für den Weltklimavertrag. Berlin. Available online at www.wbgu.de/wbgu_sn2009.pdf (accessed October 8, 2010).

Chapter 11

The New Military Urbanism

Stephen Graham

Introduction

As our planet urbanizes more rapidly than ever before, a new and insidious militarism is permeating the fabric of cities and urban life. Fueled by, and perpetuating, the extreme inequalities that have mushroomed as neoliberal globalization has extended across the world, this new military urbanism is a constellation of ideas, techniques, and norms of security and military doctrine. These are linked intimately into the militarized and neo-colonial predation of distant resources necessary to sustain richer and western cities and urban lifestyles. They fuse seamlessly with popular cultural worlds centered on militarized electronic entertainment, automobility, and urban lifestyles organized through new technologies that have military origins. And they relate closely to a proliferation of non-state insurgencies which appropriate the very architectures and circulations of cities as the means to launch their violence (see Graham 2009a).

In a world where full state-vs.-state wars are increasingly rare – for now – we are seeing instead a proliferation of violent struggles between state political violence and all manner of non-state insurgents, networks, and fighters. Warfare and political violence is now often organized on transnational scales while at the same time telescoping through the streets, spaces, infrastructures, and symbols of a rapidly urbanizing world. The practice and imagination of state and non-state political violence, as well as ideas of security, are thus inscribing themselves into the most intimate sites, spaces, and symbols of the planet's blossoming urban areas (Graham 2006). Indeed, war and organized political violence increasingly operate *through* the basic architectures and infrastructures of cities – the very same structures and systems that continually enable globalized urban life to operate. Perhaps unexpectedly, the most basic and banal of urban experiences, infrastructures or artifacts now

The New Blackwell Companion to the City   Edited by Gary Bridge and Sophie Watson
© 2011 Blackwell Publishing Ltd

are becoming fully inscribed into contemporary discussions surrounding geopolitics or international security. In the new military doctrine of "low intensity conflict," "assymetric war," "fourth generation war," or "military operations other than war," the prosaic and everyday sites, circulations, and spaces of the city become the main "battlespace" both at home and abroad.

As a collective, this new military urbanism operates by reworking the architectures, experiences, and cultures of cities in both the global north and the global south. Sometimes, such changes are manifest overtly in the repackaging of cities into archipelagos of fortified enclaves and the reorganization of militaries into urban counterinsurgency forces. More often, they emerge more covertly in the normalization of military techniques and paradigms as means to address civilian and social issues. Centered on the US–Israeli axis of military colonialism and high-tech securitization, this new wave of militarization works by folding all social and political problems – or at least their symptoms – into "security" issues requiring "hard" military solutions (Graham 2003).

The very breadth and power of the new military urbanism is such that, arguably, it is not since medieval times that ideas, techniques, and imaginations of political violence and "security" have centered so heavily on trying to (re)organize the basic architectures and experiences of urban life. Rather than castles, city walls, and siege warfare, however, the new military urbanism combines walls, fences, and barriers with biometric scanning. It adds killer robots and cyborg insects to the revitalizing sciences of urban fortification and "control architecture." And it blurs globe-straddling attempts to track people, information, money, and trade to a proliferation of more or less militarized or securitized camps, bases, security zones, and enclaves. Many of these, however – far from being split off from the world – are linked together through the very circulations and infrastructures that make neoliberal globalization possible.

Laced together with their own systems of connection and circulation, such enclaves and camps range across a wide spectrum. They encompass proliferating gated communities, offshore finance enclaves, and cruise ships for the überwealthy, as well as war prisons, torture and rendition camps, and military bases. They include export processing zones, refugee camps, logistics cities and the rapidly securitized financial cores of global cities. And they range from airport and port complexes, through "bubble-like" tourist enclaves, to fenced-off event spaces for political summits or mega-sporting events, or walled ethnic enclaves imposed by colonial powers. Georgio Agamben, the Italian philosopher, now even suggests that enclave-like camps are such a dominant architectural manifestation of power in today's world that they are more important than the more open terrain of cities (see Agamben 2005). In such a context it is necessary to outline the new military urbanism's four key foundations.

Foucault's Boomerang: Colonies Come Home

> War has … re-invaded human society in a more complex, more extensive, more concealed, and more subtle manner.
>
> (Liang and Wang Xiangsui 2002: 2)

First, as the circuits of the new military urbanism blur legal separations between the "homeland" cities and those on colonial frontiers, so both sets of cities become subject to similar logics of reorganization and (attempted) securitization. Colonial logics and geographies thus increasingly erupt within both domestic cities and those on colonial frontiers. Historian Lorenzo Veracini has diagnosed a dramatic contemporary resurgence in the importation of typically colonial tropes and techniques into the management and development of cities in the metropolitan cores of Europe and North America. Such a process, he argues, is once again working to gradually unravel "classic and long lasting distinctions between an outer face and an inner face of the colonial condition" (Veracini 2005).

It is important to stress, then, that the resurgence of explicitly colonial strategies and techniques amongst nation states such as the US, UK, and Israel in the contemporary period (see Gregory 2003) involves not just the deployment of the techniques of the new military urbanism in foreign war-zones but their diffusion and imitation through the securitization of western urban life. As in the nineteenth century, when European colonial nations imported fingerprinting, panoptic prisons, and Haussmannian boulevard building through neighborhoods of insurrection to domestic cities after first experimenting with them on colonized frontiers, colonial techniques today operate through what Michel Foucault termed colonial "boomerang effects." "It should never be forgotten," Foucault wrote:

> that while colonization, with its techniques and its political and juridical weapons, obviously transported European models to other continents, it also had a considerable boomerang effect on the mechanisms of power in the West, and on the apparatuses, institutions, and techniques of power. A whole series of colonial models was brought back to the West, and the result was that the West could practice something resembling colonization, or an internal colonialism, on itself. (2003: 103)

In the contemporary period, the military urbanism is marked by – and indeed, constituted through – a myriad of increasingly startling Foucauldian boomerang effects. For example, Israeli drones designed to vertically subjugate and target Palestinians are now routinely deployed by police forces in North America, Europe, and east Asia. Private operators of US "supermax" prisons are heavily involved in running the global archipelago organizing incarceration and torture that has burgeoned since the start of the "war on terror." Private military corporations heavily colonize "reconstruction" contracts in both Iraq and New Orleans. Israeli expertise in population control is regularly sought by those planning security operations for major summits and sporting events. And "shoot to kill" policies developed to confront risks of suicide bombing in Tel Aviv and Haifa have been adopted by police forces in western cities (a process which directly led to the state killing of Jean Charles de Menezes by London anti-terrorist police on July 22, 2005).

Meanwhile, aggressive and militarized policing against public demonstrations and social mobilizations in London, Toronto, Paris, or New York now utilizes the same "non-lethal weapons" as Israel's army in Gaza or Jenin. Constructions of "security zones" around the strategic financial cores of London and New York echo the techniques used in Baghdad's Green Zone. And many of the techniques used to fortify enclaves in Baghdad or the West Bank are being sold around the world as leading-edge and "combat-proven" "security solutions" by corporate coalitions linking Israeli, US, and other companies and states.

Crucially, such boomerang effects linking security and military doctrine in the cities of the west with those on colonial peripheries are backed up by the cultural geographies which underpin the political right and far-right, along with hawkish commentators within western militaries themselves. These tend to deem cities per se to be intrinsically problematic spaces – the main sites concentrating acts of subversion, resistance, mobilization, dissent, and protest challenging national security states.

Bastions of ethno-nationalist politics, the burgeoning movements of the far right, often heavily represented within policing and state militaries, tend to see rural or exurban areas as the authentic and pure spaces of white nationalism linked to Christian traditions. Examples here range from US Christian fundamentalists, through the British National Party to Austria's Freedom Party, the French Front National, and Italy's Forza Italia. The fast-growing and sprawling cosmopolitan neighborhoods of the west's cities, meanwhile, are often cast by such groups in the same Orientalist terms as the megacities of the global south, as places radically external to the vulnerable nation – threatening or enemy territories every bit as foreign as Baghdad or Gaza.

Paradoxically, the imaginations of geography which underpin the new military urbanism tend to treat colonial frontiers and western "homelands" as fundamentally separate domains – clashes of civilizations in Samuel Huntington's (1998) incendiary proposition – even as the security, military, and intelligence doctrine addressing both increasingly fuses. Such imaginations of geography work to deny the ways in which the cities in both domains are increasingly linked by migration and investment flows to constitute each other.

In rendering *all* mixed-up cities as problematic spaces beyond the rural or exurban heartlands of authentic national communities, telling movements in representations of cities occur between colonial peripheries and capitalist heartlands. The construction of sectarian enclaves modeled on Israeli practice by US forces in Baghdad from 2003, for example, was widely described by US security personnel as the development of US-style "gated communities" in the country. In the aftermath of the devastation of New Orleans by Hurricane Katrina in late 2005, meanwhile, US army officers talked of the need to "take back" the city from Iraqi-style "insurgents."

As ever, then, the imagination of urban life in colonized zones interacts powerfully with that in the cities of the colonizers. Indeed, the projection of colonial tropes and security exemplars into postcolonial metropoles in capitalist heartlands is fueled by a new "inner city Orientalism" (Howell and Shryock 2003). This relies on the widespread depiction amongst rightist security or military commentators of immigrant districts within the west's cities as "backward" zones threatening the body politic of the western city and nation. In France, for example, postwar state planning worked to conceptualize the mass, peripheral housing projects of the *banlieues* as "near peripheral" reservations attached to, but distant from, the country's metropolitan centers (Kipfer and Goonewardena 2007). Bitter memories of the Algerian and other anti-colonial wars saturate the French far right's discourse about waning "white" power and the "insecurity" caused by the *banlieues* – a process that has led to a dramatic mobilization of state security forces in and around the main immigrant housing complexes.

Discussing the shift from external to internal colonization in France, Kristin Ross points to the way in which France now "distances itself from its (former) colonies, both within and without." This functions, she continues, through a "great cordoning off of the immigrants, their removal to the suburbs in a massive reworking of the social boundaries of Paris and other French cities" (Ross 1996: 12). The riots of 2005 were only the latest in a long line of reactions towards the increasing militarization and securitization of this form of internal colonization and enforced peripherality within what Mustafa Dikeç has called the "badlands" of the contemporary French Republic (Dikeç 2007).

Indeed, such is the contemporary right's conflation of terrorism and migration that simple acts of migration are now often deemed to be little more than acts of warfare. This discursive shift has been termed the "weaponization" of migration (Cato 2008) – the shift away from emphases on moral obligations to offer hospitality to refugees toward criminalizing or dehumanizing migrants' bodies as weapons against purportedly homogeneous and ethno-nationalist bases of national power.

Here the latest debates about "assymetric," "irregular," or "low intensity war," where nothing can be defined outside of boundless and never-ending definitions of political violence, blur uncomfortably into the growing clamor of demonization by right and far-right commentators of the west's diasporic and increasingly cosmopolitan cities. Samuel Huntington, taking his "clash of civilizations" thesis further, now argues that the very fabric of US power and national identity is under threat, not just because of global Islamist terrorism but because non-white and especially Latino groups are colonizing, and dominating, US metropolitan areas (Huntington 2005).

Adopting such Manichean imaginations of the world, US military theorist William Lind has argued that prosaic acts of immigration from the global south to the north's cities must now be understood as act of warfare. "In Fourth Generation war," Lind (2004: 13–14) writes, "invasion by immigration can be at least as dangerous as invasion by a state army." Under what he calls the "poisonous ideology of multiculturalism," Lind argues that migrants within western nations can now launch "a homegrown variety of Fourth Generation war, which is by far the most dangerous kind."

Given the two-way movement of the exemplars of the new military urbanism between western cities and those on colonial frontiers, fueled by the instinctive anti-urbanism of national security states, it is no surprise that cities in both domains are starting to display startling similarities as well as their more obvious differences. In both, hard, military-style borders, fences, and checkpoints around defended enclaves and "security zones" superimposed on the wider and more open city, are proliferating. Jersey-barrier blast walls, identity checkpoints, computerized CCTV, biometric surveillance, and military-styles of access control protect archipelagos of fortified enclaves from an outside deemed unruly, impoverished, or dangerous. In the former case, these encompass green zones, war prisons, ethnic and sectarian neighborhoods, and military bases; in the latter they are growing around strategic financial districts, embassy zones, tourist spaces, airport and port complexes, sports event spaces, gated communities, and export processing zones.

Surveillant Economy

> What used to be one among several decisive measures of public administration until
> the first half of the twentieth century, [security] now becomes the sole criterion of
> political legitimation.
>
> (Agamben 2002: 2)

Second, the new military urbanism is sustained by a complex, transnational, but
poorly understood political economy. However, the colonization of urban thinking
and practice by militarized ideas of "security" does not have a single source. In fact,
it emanates from a complex range of sources. These encompass sprawling, transnational industrial complexes fusing military and security companies with technology,
surveillance, and entertainment ones; a wide range of consultants and industries
who sell "security" solutions as silver bullets to complex social problems; and a
complex mass of security and military thinkers who now argue that war and
political violence centers overwhelmingly on the everyday spaces and circuits of
urban life.

As vague and all-encompassing ideas about "security" creep to infect virtually
all aspects of public policy and social life, so these emerging industrial-security
complexes work together on the highly lucrative challenges of perpetually targeting
everyday activities, spaces, and behaviors in cities and the circulations which link
them together. The proliferation of wars sustaining permanent mobilization and
preemptive, ubiquitous surveillance within and beyond territorial borders mean that
the imperative of "security" now "imposes itself as the basic principle of state activity" (Agamben 2002: 2).

Amidst global economic collapse, markets for "security" services and technologies, which impose military-style systems of command, control, and targeting over
the everyday spaces and systems of civilian life, are booming as never before. It is
no accident that security-industrial complexes blossom in parallel with the diffusion
of market fundamentalist notions of organizing social, economic, and political life.
The hyper-inequalities and urban militarization and securitization sustained by
neoliberalization are mutually reinforcing. In a discussion of the US state's response
to the Hurricane Katrina disaster, Henry Giroux (2006: 172) points out that the
normalization of market fundamentalism in US culture has made it much more
"difficult to translate private woes into social issues and collective action or to insist
on a language of the public good." He argues that "the evisceration of all notions
of sociality" in this case has led to "a sense of total abandonment, resulting in fear,
anxiety, and insecurity over one's future" (ibid.).

"International expenditure on homeland security now surpasses established
enterprises like movie-making and the music industry in annual revenues" (*Economic Times* 2007). The Homeland Security Research Corporation (2007) points
out that "the worldwide 'total defense' outlay (military, intelligence community, and
Homeland Security/Homeland Defense) is forecasted to grow by approximately
50%, from $1,400 billion in 2006 to $2,054 billion by 2015." By 2005, US defense
expenditure alone had reached $420 billion a year – comparable to the rest of the
world combined. Over a quarter of this was devoted to purchasing services from a

rapidly expanding market of private military corporations. By 2010, such mercenary groups are in line to receive a staggering $202 billion from the US state alone (Schreier and Caparini 2005).

Meanwhile, worldwide "homeland security" spending outlay is forecasted to grow by nearly 100 percent, from $231 billion in 2006 to $518 billion by 2015. "Where the homeland security outlay was 12% of the world's total defense outlay in 2003, it is expected to become 25% of the total defense outlay by 2015" (Homeland Security Research Corporation 2007). Even more meteoric growth is expected in some of the key sectors of the new control technologies. Global markets in biometric technology, for example, are expected to increase from the small base of $1.5 billion in 2005 to $5.7 billion by 2010.

Crucially, the same constellations of "security" companies are often involved in selling, establishing, and operating the techniques and practices of the new military urbanism in both war-zone and "homeland" cities. Often, as with the EU's new security policies, states or supranational blocks are bringing in high-tech and militarized means of tracking illegal immigrants not because these methods are necessarily the best means of addressing their security concerns but because such policies might help stimulate their defense, security, or technology companies to compete in booming global markets for security technology. Moreover, Israeli experience in locking down its cities whilst turning the Occupied Territories into permanent, urban prison camps is proving especially influential as a source of "combat proven" exemplars to be imitated around the world. The new high-tech border fence between the United States and Mexico, for example, is being built by a consortium linking Boeing to the Israeli company Elbit whose radar and targeting technologies have been honed in the permanent lock-down of Palestinian urban life into highly militarized enclaves. It is also startling how much US counterinsurgency strategies in Iraq have explicitly been based on efforts to effectively scale up Israeli treatment of the Palestinians during the second intifada.

The political economies sustaining the new military urbanism inevitably center on cities as the main production centers of neoliberal capitalism as well as the main arenas and markets for rolling out new security "solutions." The world's major financial centers, in particular, orchestrate global processes of militarization and securitization. They house the headquarters of global security, technology, and military corporations, provide the locations for the world's biggest technological corporate universities which dominate research and development in new security technologies, and support the global network of financial institutions which so often work to violently erase or appropriate cities and resources in colonized lands in the name of neoliberal economics and "free trade."

The network of so-called "global cities" through which neoliberal capitalism is orchestrated – London, New York, Paris, Frankfurt, and so on – thus helps to directly produce new logics of aggressive colonial acquisition and dispossession by multinational capital working closely with state militaries and private military operators.

With the easing of state monopolies on violence, and the proliferation of acquisitive private military and mercenary corporations, the brutal "urbicidal" violence and dispossession that so often helps bolster the parasitic aspects of western city economies, and feeds contemporary corporate capitalism, is more apparent than ever (Kipfer and Goonewardena 2007). In a world increasingly haunted by the specter of imminent resource exhaustion, the new military urbanism is also linked intimately with the neo-colonial exploitation of distant resources to try and sustain richer cities and urban lifestyles. New York and London provide the financial and corporate power through which Iraqi oil reserves have been reappropriated by western oil companies since the 2003 invasion. Neo-colonial land-grabs to grow biofuels for cars or future food for increasingly precarious urban populations of the rich north in the poor countries of the global south are also organized through global commodity markets centered on the world's major financial cities. Finally, the rapid global growth in markets for high-tech security is itself providing a major boost to global financial cities in times of global economic meltdown.

Urban Achilles

> If you want to destroy someone nowadays, you go after their infrastructure.
> (Agre 2001: 1)

Penultimately, the new military urbanism rests on the way that the everyday architectures and infrastructures of cities – the structures and mechanisms that support modern urban life – are now being appropriated by state militaries and non-state fighters as primary means of waging war and amplifying political violence (see Graham 2009b). The very conditions of the modern, globalized city – its reliance on dense webs of infrastructure, its density and anonymity, its dependence on imported water, food, and energy – thus create the possibilities of violence against it and *through* it. Urban everyday life everywhere is thus stalked by the threat of interruption: the blackout, the gridlock, the severed connection, the technical malfunction, the inhibited flow, the network unavailable sign.

The potential for catastrophic violence against cities and urban life has changed in parallel with the shift of urban life towards ever-greater reliance on modern infrastructures. The result of this is that the everyday infrastructures of urban life – highways, metro trains, computer networks, water and sanitation systems, electricity grids, airplanes – may be easily assaulted and turned into agents of instantaneous terror, debilitating disruption, even demodernization. Increasingly, then, in high-tech societies dominated by socially abstract interconnections and circulations, both high-tech warfare and terrorism "targets the means of life, not combatants" (Hinkson 2005: 145). As John Robb (2007) puts it

> most of the networks that we rely on for city life – communications, electricity, transportation, water – are extremely vulnerable to intentional disruptions. In practice, this means that a very small number of attacks on the critical hubs of an [infrastructure] network can collapse the entire network.

Many recent examples demonstrate how non-state actors now gain much of their power by appropriating the technical infrastructure necessary to sustain modern, globalized urban life in order to project, and massively amplify, the power of their political violence. Insurgents use the city's infrastructure to attack New York,

London, Madrid, or Mumbai. Insurgents disrupt electricity networks, oil pipelines, or mobile phone systems in Iraq, Nigeria, and elsewhere. Somali pirates systematically hijacking global shipping routes have even been shown to be using "spies" in London's shipping brokers to provide intelligence for their attacks. Such actors can get by with the most basic of weapons, transforming airplanes, metro trains, cars, mobile phones, electricity and communications grids, or small boats, into deadly devices.

However, such threats of "infrastructural terrorism," while very real and important, pale beside the much less visible efforts of state militaries to target the essential infrastructure that makes modern urban life possible. The US and Israeli forces, for example, have long worked systematically to "demodernize" entire urban societies through the destruction of the life-support and infrastructure systems of Gaza, the West Bank, Lebanon, and Iraq since 1991 (Graham 2005). States have thus replaced total war against cities with the systematic destruction of water and electricity systems with weapons designed especially for this task – such as bombs which rain down millions of graphite spools to short-circuit electricity stations.

Ostensibly the means of bringing unbearable political pressure on adversary regimes, such purportedly "humanitarian" modes of war end up killing the sick, the ill, and the old almost as effectively as carpet bombing, but beyond the capricious gaze of the media. Such wars on public health are engineered through the deliberate generation of public health crises in highly urbanized societies where no infrastructural alternatives to modern water, sewerage, power, medical, and food supplies exist.

The devastating Israeli siege of Gaza since Hamas were elected there in 2006 is a powerful example here. This has transformed a dense urban corridor, with 1.5 million people squeezed into an area the size of the Isle of Wight, into a vast prison camp. The blockade, combined with continuing Israeli practices of infrastructural warfare, means that Gaza's weak, old, sick, and very young suffer particularly high rates of mortality. Everyone else is forced to live something approaching what Georgio Agamben (1998) has called "bare life" – a biological existence which can be sacrificed at any time by a colonial power which maintains the right to kill with impunity but has withdrawn all moral, political, or human responsibilities from the population.

Increasingly, such formal "infrastructural war," based on the severing of the lines of supply which continually work to bring modern urban life into existence as a means of political coercion, blurs seamlessly into economic competition and energy geopolitics. Putin's resurgent Russia, for example, these days gains much of its strategic power not through formal military deployments but by its continued threats to switch off the energy supplies of Europe's cities at a stroke.

The systematic demodernization of highly urbanized societies through air power is justified by "air power theory" which exists as the dark shadow of long-discredited modernization theory. This suggests that societal "progress" can be reversed, pushing societies "back" towards increasingly primitive states. Thomas Friedman, for example, deployed such arguments as NATO cranked up its bombing campaign against Serbia in 1999. Picking up a variety of historic dates that could be the *future* destiny of Serbian society, post bombing, Friedman urged that all of the movements and mobilities sustaining urban life in Serbian cities should be brought to a grinding halt:

It should be lights out in Belgrade [he said]. Every power grid, water pipe, bridge, road and war-related factory has to be targeted ... We will set your country back by pulverizing you. You want 1950? We can do 1950. You want 1389? We can do that, too! (cited in Skoric 1999)

In Friedman's scenario, the precise reversal of time that the adversary society is to be bombed "back" through is presumably a matter merely of the correct weapon and target selection.

The politics of seeing the bombing of infrastructure as a form of reversed modernization plays a much wider discursive role. It also does much to sustain and bolster the long-standing depiction of countries deemed "less developed," along some putatively linear line of modernization, as pathologically backward, intrinsically barbarian, unmodern, even savage. Aerial bombing aimed at demodernization thus works to reinforce Orientalist imaginations which relegate the "savage," colonized target population to an "other" time and space" (Deer 2006: 3). Indeed, Nils Gilman (2003: 199) has argued that, "as long as modernization was conceived as a unitary and unidirectional process of economic expansion" it would be possible to explain backwardness and insurgency "only in terms of deviance and pathology."

At its heart, then, the systematic demodernization of whole societies in the name of "fighting terror" involves a darkly ironic and self-fulfilling prophecy. As Derek Gregory (2003) has argued, drawing on Georgio Agamben's (1998) ideas, the demodernization of entire Middle Eastern cities and societies, through both the Israeli wars against Lebanon and the Palestinians, and the US "war on terror," are both fueled by similar "Orientalist" discourses. These revivify long-standing tropes and work by "casting out" ordinary civilians and their cities – whether they be Kabul, Baghdad, or Nablus – "so that they are placed beyond the privileges and protections of the law so that their lives (and deaths) [are] rendered of no account" (Gregory 2003: 311). Here, then, beyond the increasingly fortified homeland, "sovereignty works by *abandoning* subjects, reducing them to bare life" (Diken and Laustsen 2002: 1, original emphasis).

Virtual-Citizen-Soldiers

All efforts to render politics aesthetic culminate in one thing – war.
(Benjamin 1999: 241)

Finally, the new military urbanism gains much of its power and legitimacy by fusing seamlessly with militarized veins of popular, urban, and material culture. Very often, for example, military ideas of tracking, surveillance, and targeting do not require completely new systems. Instead, they simply appropriate the systems of high-tech consumption that have been laid out within and through cities to sustain the latest means of digitally organized travel and consumption. Thus, as in central London, congestion-charging zones quickly morph into "security" zones. Internet interactions and transactions provide the basis for "data mining" to root out supposedly threatening behaviors. Dreams of "smart" and "intelligent" cars blur with those of robotic weapons systems. Satellite imagery and GPS support new styles of civilian urban life as well as "precision" urban bombing. And, as in the new security initiative in Lower Manhattan, CCTV cameras designed to make shoppers feel secure are transformed into "anti-terrorist" screens.

Perhaps the most powerful series of civilian–military crossovers at the heart of the new military urbanism, however, are being forged within cultures of virtual and electronic entertainment, and corporate news. Here, to tempt the nimble-fingered recruits best able to control the latest high-tech drones and weaponry, the US military produces some of the most popular urban warfare consumer video games. Highly successful games like the US Army's *America's Army* or US Marines' *Full Spectrum Warrior* (see http://www.americasarmy.com/ and http://www.fullspectrumwarrior.com/ respectively) allow players to slay "terrorists" in fictionalized and orientalized cities in frameworks based directly on those of the US military's own training systems.

The main purpose of these games, however, is public relations: they are a powerful and extremely cost-effective means of recruitment. "Because the Pentagon spends around $15,000 on average wooing each recruit, the game needs only to result in 300 enlistments per year to recoup costs" (Stahl 2006: 123). Forty percent of those who join the army have previously played the game. The game also provides the basis for a sophisticated surveillance system through which army recruitment efforts are directed and targeted. In the marketing speak of its military developers, *America's Army* is designed to reach the substantial overlap in "population between the gaming population & the army's target recruiting segments." It addresses "tech-savvy audiences and afford[s] the army a unique, strategic communication advantage" (Lenoir 2003).

To close the circle between virtual entertainment and virtual killing, control panels for the latest US weapons systems – such as the latest control stations for "pilots" or armed Predator drones, manufactured by Raytheon – now directly imitate the consoles of the Sony Playstation 2, which are, after all, most familiar to recruits. The newest Predator control systems from Raytheon – leading manufacturer of assassination drones as well as a key player in the UK's E-borders consortium – deliberately use the "same HOTAS [hands on throttle and stick] system on a … video game." Raytheon's designer of unmanned aerial vehicles (UAVs) argues that "there's no point in re-inventing the wheel. The current generation of pilots was raised on the Playstation, so we created an interface that they will immediately understand" (Richfield 2006). Added to this, many of the latest video games actually depict the very same armed drones as those used in assassination raids by US forces.

Wired magazine, talking to one Predator "pilot," Private Joe Clark, about his experience directing drone assassinations from a virtual reality "cave" on the edge of Las Vegas, points out that he has, in a sense "been prepping for the job since he was a kid: He plays videogames. A lot of videogames. Back in the barracks he spends downtime with an Xbox and a PlayStation." After his training, "when he first slid behind the controls of a Shadow UAV, the point and click operation turned out to work much the same way. 'You watch the screen. You tell it to roll left, it rolls left. It's pretty simple,' Clark says" (Shachtman 2005).

Projecting such trends, Brian Finoki (2006) speculates about a near future when "video games become the ultimate interface for conducting real life warfare," as virtual reality simulators used in video gaming converge completely with those used in military training and exercises. Finoki takes the video game-like existence of the Las Vegas Predator "pilots," with their Playstation-style controls as his starting point. He speculates, only half ironically, whether future video gamers could "become decorated war heroes by virtue of their eye-and-hand coordination skills, which would eventually dominate the triggers of network-centric remote controlled warfare."

References

Agamben, G. (1998) *Homo Sacer: Sovereign Power and Bare Life*. Stanford, CA: Stanford University Press.

Agamben, G. (2002) Security and terror. *Theory and Event* 5 (4): 1–2.

Agamben, G. (2005) *State of Exception*. Chicago: Chicago University Press.

Agre, P. (2001) Imagining the next war: infrastructural warfare and the conditions of democracy. Radical Urban Theory. September14. Available online at www.rut.com/911/Phil-Agre.html (accessed June 2009).

Benjamin, W. (1999) The work of art in the age of mechanical reproduction. In *Illuminations*, ed. Hannah Arendt, trans. Harry Zohn. New York: Schocke, 217–52.

Cato (2008) The weaponization of immigration. Center for Immigration Studies, Washington, DC. February. Available online at www.cis.org/weaponization_of_immigration.html (accessed April 2010).

Deer, P. (2006) Introduction: the ends of war and the limits of war culture. *Social Text* 25: 3.

Dikeç, D. (2007) *Badlands of the Republic: Space, Politics and Urban Policy*. Oxford: Blackwell.

Diken, B., and Laustsen, C. (2002) Camping as a contemporary strategy: from refugee camps to gated communities. AMID Working Paper Series, 32, Aalborg University.

Economic Times (2007) Spending on internal security to reach $178 bn by 2015. December 27. Available online at www.twocircles.net/2007dec27/spending_internal_security_reach_178_bn_2015.html (accessed September 2010).

Finoki, B. (2006) War room. *Subtopia* blog, May 20. Available online at http://subtopia.blogspot.com/2006/05/war-room_20.html (March 2010).

Foucault, M. (2003) *Society Must Be Defended: Lectures at the Collège de France, 1975–6*. London: Allen Lane.

Gilman, N. (2003) *Mandarins of the Future: Modernization Theory in Cold War America*. Baltimore, MD: Johns Hopkins University Press.

Giroux, H. (2006) Reading Hurricane Katrina: race, class, and the biopolitics of disposability. *College Literature* 33.3: 171–96.

Graham, S. (2003) Lessons in urbicide. *New Left Review*, 19: 63–78.

Graham, S. (2005) Switching cities off: urban infrastructure and US air power. *City* 9 (2): 170–92.

Graham, S. (2006) Cities and the "war on terror." *International Journal of Urban and Regional Research* 30 (2): 255–76.

Graham, S. (2009a) *Cities Under Siege: The New Military Urbanism*. London: Verso.

Graham, S. (ed.) (2009b) *Disrupted Cities: When Infrastructure Fails*. New York: Routledge.

Gregory, D. (2003) Defiled cities. *Singapore Journal of Tropical Geography* 24 (3): 307–26.

Hinkson, J. (2005) After the London bombings. *Arena Journal* 24: 139–59.

Homeland Security Research Corporation (2007) Untitled report. Available online at www.marketresearch.com/vendors/viewVendor.asp?VendorID=2603 (accessed September 2010).

Howell, S. and Shryock, A. (2003) Cracking down on diaspora: Arab Detroit and America's "war on terror." *Anthropological Quarterly* 76: 443–62.

Huntington, S. (1998) *The Clash of Civilizations and the Remaking of World Order*. New York: Simon and Schuster.

Huntington, S. (2005) *Who Are We? The Challenges to America's National Identity*. New York: Simon and Schuster.

Kipfer, S., and Goonewardena, K. (2007) Colonization and the new imperialism: on the meaning of urbicide today. *Theory and Event* 10 (2): 1–39.

Lenoir, T. (2003) Taming a disruptive technology: open source, America's army, and the military-entertainment complex. Presentation, Stanford University, California, September 23. Available online at www.almaden.ibm.com/coevolution/pdf/lenoir.pdf (accessed March 2010).

Liang, Q., and Xiangsui, W. (2002) *Unrestricted Warfare*. Panama: Pan American Publishing.

Lind, W. (2004) Understanding Fourth Generation war. Military Review September–October. Available online at www.au.af.mil/au/awc/awcgate/milreview/lind.pdf (accessed ??)

Richfield, P. (2006) New "cockpit" for Predator? C4ISR Journal October 31. Available online at www.c4isrjournal.com/story.php?F=2323780 (accessed March 2010).

Robb, J. (2007) The coming urban terror. *City Journal*, summer. Available online at www.city-journal.org/html/17_3_urban_terrorism.html (accessed March 2010).

Ross, K. (1996) *Fast Cars, Clean Bodies: Decolonization and the Reordering of French Culture*. Cambridge, MA.: MIT Press.

Schreier, F., and Caparini, M. (2005) Privatising Security: Law, Practice and Governance of Private Military and Security Companies. Geneva Centre for the Democratic Control of Armed Forces (DCAF) Occasional Paper No. 6, March. www.smallarmssurvey.org/files/portal/...pdf/2005_Schreier_Caparini.pdf (accessed September 2010).

Shachtman, N. (2005) Attack of the drones. *Wired* 13 (6) June. Available online at www.wired.com/wired/archive/13.06/drones.html (accessed January 2010).

Skoric, I. (1999) On not killing civilians. Posted at amsterdam.nettime.org (May 6, 1999). Cited in Justitiële verkenningen (2005) Architectuur en veiligheid. Amsterdam: Ministry of Justice, 13. Available online at www.wodc.nl/images/JV1005_volledige%20tekst_tcm44-297536.pdf (accessed September 2010).

Stahl, R. (2006) Have you played the war on terror? *Critical Studies in Media Communication* 23 (2): 112–30.

Veracini, L. (2005) Colonialism brought home: on the colonialization of the metropolitan space. *Borderlands* 4 (1). Available online at www.borderlands.net.au/vol4no1_2005/veracini_colonialism.htm (accessed March 2010).

Chapter 12

The City's New "Trinity" in Contemporary Shanghai: A Case Study of the Residential Housing Market*

Wang Xiaoming, translated by Tyler Rooker

This chapter argues that since the end of the 1980s the city in China has been restructured through three mutually constitutive dimensions: a new valorization of the visual cultures of the urban, emergent new spaces, and a new structure of urban power. I will take the Shanghai residential housing market and its creation through the forces of advertising as a case study to explain the interrelationships of the three.

In 1949 the People's Liberation Army occupied Shanghai. A new Land Law was issued by the central government in 1950, declaring that all urban land was now state-owned. Within ten years, the Shanghai residential real-estate market met a similar fate to those in all other Chinese cities – it was completely eliminated.

But, in the mid-1980s, the paramount leader of the time, Deng Xiaoping, proposed that the Chinese government make significant efforts to re-establish the residential real-estate market.

Why? There were two main reasons:

1 A famine (1959–61) and the Cultural Revolution (1966–76) had seriously damaged the legitimacy of the Communist Party's political authority. The only solution was to increase the quality of people's lives, and a shortage of housing was one of the most urgent issues for urban residents.
2 In order to develop the economy, the government needed a large amount of funds. And the largest resource that could be translated into capital was land.

The re-establishment and expansion of the residential real-estate market from top to bottom was very rapid. In Shanghai, in less than 20 years the new market became one of the "pillar" industries (those deemed strategic to the economy in terms of

The New Blackwell Companion to the City   Edited by Gary Bridge and Sophie Watson
© 2011 Blackwell Publishing Ltd

defense, job creation, technology, or competitiveness) of the local economy. By 2009, the real-estate market was a leading driver of economic recovery in the post-credit crunch period, pulling the entire Chinese economy out of stagnation. The total amount of wealth that it created measured by currency was even more remarkable. This meant that land rapidly changed from an immobile "resource" to a "capital" with a price at which it could be bought and sold. Like the old American movie, *Man with a Million* (UK title *The Million Pound Note*) a "million-pound bill" has fallen from the sky. Therefore the main commodity in the re-established residential real-estate market is "land" not "apartments."

But the central position of land revealed the Chinese characteristics of the Shanghai (and national) residential real-estate market: Without the 1950 land law that transformed it from a "commodity" into a "resource" without compensation, land today could not have been transformed back into a "commodity." This was precisely the motivation and interest of the government in re-establishing the real-estate market in the 1980s. The remarketing of the 1980s was based on a 40-year non-market system, and was a rerelease of the energy of the system not, as is usually imagined, the destruction or elimination of the communist system itself. Because remarketing brings about profit without capital, how land was to be "sold" was completely decided by the government. In Shanghai, the first 50-year use rights for a parcel of land (in the Hongqiao area) was sold in 1988 to a Japanese real-estate company. The price was set very high: a calculation based on the area of housing subsequently built upon it, the land cost 3,500 yuan per square meter, while, at the time, the average monthly salary for Shanghai residents was less than 300 yuan.

In the passage of 20 years, the government has pushed through residential commodification to the degree that the current rate of private ownership of residential housing by Shanghai residents is much higher than Hong Kong, Tokyo, and London. Meanwhile, the average price of Shanghai housing has rapidly approached that of Hong Kong, Tokyo, and London (in August 2009, the average price of newly built residences surpassed 20,000 yuan per square meter [at 2009 rates there were approximately 6.8 yuan to the US dollar]). And the income of the average resident is only a fifth or less of that of residents in Hong Kong, Tokyo, and London. The market is harsh to consumers but massively profitable for governments and development companies (of which a large proportion are state-run companies).

Land in the city that can be used to construct residences was limited; a large majority of residents had to purchase or rent housing from the real-estate market; the low-rent housing and affordable housing planned by the government never materialized; the economy continued to develop, bringing increased pressure from inflation. The convergence of these various factors made the residential real-estate market in Shanghai very much like the stock market: despite dysfunction of the system and operations, it drew stampedes of individuals and groups. Hence, this market gradually revealed its capacity to transform and reorganize society.

First, it increased the speed of differentiation between different income levels (*jieceng*). In Shanghai, the people who were allocated relatively large residences by the government (often officials or others from high levels of society) before 1990 have benefited much more from the market than those who bought their own residences in or after 1990. Among those who used their own money to buy residences, those who could afford to buy two obtained more profits than those who could only buy one, and those who could buy three, obtained more profits than those who could only buy two. As for those investment groups (banks, large companies, funds), their large amount of capital meant that they could buy apartments by the building and then sell them by the unit, earning profits even further beyond the dreams of individual investors. Since the end of the 1980s, there has been a redifferentiation of social strata in China. The levels that previously occupied various dominant positions gained more and more overpowering advantages relative to the weaker levels below them. Hence, the massive wealth created by 30 years of economic growth was allocated among the various levels according to a pattern of "winner takes all" (*yingjia tongchi*). The re-establishing and expansion of the residential real-estate market was gradually ushered in by this "allocation." Eventually, the entire market became one of the important paths for this "allocation."

Second, it changed the composition of authority groups. Taking Shanghai as an example, in this city, the largest portion of an average person's private wealth is their residence. Today, the number and quality of residences held by almost all mid-level and above party and government officials are greater and better than for any other stratum (with the exception of a few capitalists). In other words, the expansion of the residential real-estate market has rapidly changed these party and government officials into wealthy people. The process of changing them into wealthy people often involves the buying and selling of residences, and inevitably involves variations of "trading money for power." Hence, those cadres who before the 1990s stood at arms' length from capitalists and submitted (even if often only passively) to the political situation, rapidly disappeared.

The more that officials become wealthy people, the more personal benefits become entangled with local economic affairs, and the more local bureaucrats and new capitalist groups (including local representatives of international capital) had to create fastidious unions that sought profits for groups, localities, and individuals. Over the last ten years in Shanghai, this type of union has been involved in increasingly serious clashes with upper-level and even central government authorities. The fact that residential prices rose in 2009 despite the economic downturn is an outstanding example. That is, the bubble in the residential market was large, and even the central government wanted to rein in prices, but the power of forces that extract profits from high prices was too strong, and they pushed the price of Shanghai housing even higher!

The profile of the residential real-estate market clearly drove and realized major changes in the structure of social power and allocation in the city, not only in terms of economic structure, but also in terms of political structure. Looking at its form, it seemed that the city was still governed by the original communist party municipal committee and the city government. But a careful analysis reveals that the political logic and social foundation of this governance has changed over the last 20 years. The combination of a highly autocratic market, an ambiguous but also dominant mainstream ideology, politics, economics, and high culture have almost completely merged with consumption in daily life. Now it is because of these factors that the governance described above has become more crucial. People often say that in mainland China today, Shanghai is the place that most preserves the characteristics of socialism and communist political authority. But from the above analysis, this is a misconception. With the expansion of the residential real-estate market, there was a new differentiation in urban space.

In Shanghai before the late 1980s, there was general coexistence and overlap between six types of space: first, public political space, for example squares where large-scale meetings took place, work locations for the communist party and government organs, and halls spread throughout various state-operated work units (factories, campuses, hospitals, etc.); second, industrial production space, including a portion that is extended to workers as residential space (workers' new villages); third, commercial space; fourth, the living space left over after residential space is detached from associated work units; fifth, transportation and other social service space, for example streets, hospitals, campuses, libraries, movie theatres, etc.; sixth, public socializing space, for example parks, small roads sometimes named as secondary access roads (because vehicle traffic is very low, this type of small road often – especially in summer – becomes a place for city residents to eat, chat, and even sleep), and chatting areas centered on small groceries or at lane entrances. From the 1950s to the 1980s, the proportions of these six spaces changed continually, and the directions of change varied. But there was one overarching trend. That was that the first two types of space went through significant expansion: a large number of meeting places were constructed; and a large number of small-scale enterprises were driven into small lanes and apartment buildings creating a situation where residence, workplace, and warehouses were jumbled together.

And today? After 20 years of "reform," Shanghai's public political space has shrunk noticeably. This shrinkage was not only physical, as in large-scale squares and meeting-places being made into commercial space; it was also abstract, as when the office/leisure areas of government organs expanded to constitute the majority of "public political space," making this a space without any "public" significance, instead becoming a "government affairs space." Industrial production space was reduced to an even greater degree. Almost all the various factories spread throughout the city center were closed; various industrial spaces in lanes and residential buildings were completely moved out; and even the large factories on the edge of the city center now are almost completely dismantled. Public socializing space also shrank considerably: the area of parks was encroached by the expansion of roads; small roads were enlarged and pervaded by automobile exhaust fumes; small groceries almost completely disappeared, and lane entranceways were replaced bit by bit with gates to residential apartment complexes so that, apart from the guards, no residents assembled there to chat.

What space expanded? One was commercial space, with large and small retail shops spreading throughout the city. Their appearance, sales methods, and even products for sale were more and more standardized: big-box retailers replaced small- and medium-scale department stores, shopping centers replaced large-scale department stores, and convenience store chains replaced small groceries. The largest expansion was in residential space. Almost all of the residential areas that used to be attached to *danwei* state-run work units (for example workers' new villages) were privatized to become ordinary residential areas. Even more impressive was a new combined space that was centered on residences; it often had a large area (some large-scale combined spaces have a land area that is larger than one square kilometer), was centered on a number of residential buildings, and gathered together shopping centers, restaurants, schools, banks, fitness centers, pet hospitals. Additionally, according to individual needs, roads were paved, post offices were established, bus stops were erected, and even subway stops were installed.

In this situation, the expansion of commercial space gradually became dependent on this new combined space, moving in directions dictated by it, and even taking shape in the space that it enclosed. Not only the distribution of commercial space, but that of transportation arteries (for instance subways and elevated roads) and other spaces (e.g., universities and banks) increasingly deferred and followed in the footsteps of this new space. In the last 20 years, this new combined space became the most important determinant of the change in Shanghai's urban space. It goes without saying that this new space was the result of the rapid expansion of the residential real-estate market, and that real-estate development companies were an important proponent. Along with the step-by-step encroachment by this space on other spaces (many of these residential areas are built on land of closed factories), real-estate developments determine the public service space, for example the planning and construction of transportation, medical, educational, and cultural infrastructure of the city. Effectively, the main planners of urban space are now real-estate development companies, the refashioning of the city is in the image of plans made by such companies.

Shanghai has become a peculiar form of "residential/consumer" city: residences and their complementary buildings that are increasingly tied to a consumer logic have become the main spatial form of the city. Urban space with this singular form has never appeared before in Shanghai. Before the 1950–70 era, the 1910–30 era involved foreign concessions that structured the spaces of the city; the Jiangwan New City area, and the two banks of the Suzhou River under China's jurisdiction. In all these areas, there were multiple forms of space coexisting, each not only with its own function, but with its own logic. Now, although in reality the majority of Shanghai residents spend most of their non-sleeping time not in their homes but in various office buildings, campuses, shops, or even in factories in the outskirts, they are forcefully disciplined by the spatial form of the city: *residences* are the center life space of Shanghai and Shanghai people.

The repartition of space in this way corresponded with a change of lifestyle for the entire city: Shanghai today is not a place where demonstrations are held, where the government organizes the public in mass meetings, where everyone chants support; it is a place that urges urban citizens only to be concerned with their own immediate interests, and not to think too much about other public affairs, a place that encourages everyone to idle away their after-hours time in front of the television, at the *majiang* (mah-jong) table, and in shopping centers. Of course, today's Shanghai is also a place where all employed people have become solitary individuals facing their bosses, worried that they will be replaced by others at any moment, where they can sleep soundly at night only once the front door is locked tightly, and where a happy and interesting life can be achieved only with shopping and travel. Individualization and spatial restructuring go hand in hand.

Over the past 20 years, this city has profoundly changed the lifestyle of residents, including their life aspirations, social ideals, and political attitude. Today's Shanghai people, compared to those from 20 years ago, are universally listless and at a loss. Although they are uneasy, and even full of dissatisfaction, they feel unable to do anything about it. They return home and put on their slippers in order to somewhat reduce the pressure of their lives. In the process of shaping the weak and tolerant ethos of urban citizens, the massive changes in urban constructed space have played an extraordinary role.

The transformation of urban space is manifested not only in a flood of new construction, but also in the dominant cultural production mechanism of the city, which also creates a new universe of visual representation in constructed space. The "visual" and the "real" are consequently mutually constituted. Take residential real-estate advertising in Shanghai as an example. In the last 15 years, this type of advertising has always been Shanghai's – and also other medium and large cities' – most eye-catching type of visual advertising (the second is automobile advertising). No matter where it appeared: on the street, on both sides of highways, on television screens, in newspapers and magazines, or even on the back of passenger seats in taxis and on the backs of airline boarding passes, the city makes sense of itself through the lexicon and grammar of a visual culture of real-estate imagery.

The following is an introduction to a few of the common advertising schemas, where the larger the scale of advertising, the more the schema follows these types:

Schema 1   The framing is selected very carefully, with attention paid to balance of the segments and matching of colors. Residences (usually their exteriors) are often put in one corner of the picture. Although it is eye-catching, other parts are even more prominent: foreign country (Europe or America) emotional appeal, complete community infrastructure, family life with beautiful wife and children, green environment.

Schema 2   The residential building is located in the center of the frame, while in the four surrounding directions are malls, offices, subway stations, parks, churches. Or, conversely, the residential area is the background, and different shops, city gardens, cafés, walkers, and even churches are included, almost as if the entire city has moved into the residential area.

Schema 3   The picture is like a windowframe, making viewers feel as if they are in the living room, looking out of the window at the exterior: river-banks, gardens, serene woods, brilliantly illuminated commercial areas. These are all the same as photographs framed on the wall, becoming part of the residence itself.

Schema 4   The residence is half-hidden or even invisible and the picture only includes the rural imagery of forests, blue skies, grasslands or ponds.

All these schemas work culturally through making equivalences: buying apartments is the same as buying wealth, safety, foreign country sentiments, a beautiful family, a bustling city, beautiful scenes outside the window, a life with distinction, a successful life. Even though it may be an advertisement for residences, what is revealed is not the residence itself but instead its "goodness" (*meihao*) with larger scope and more abstraction through equivalence.

It is certainly not only Shanghai's residential advertisements that make these equivalences. A famous advertisement in Beijing put it in even starker terms: it asserted "I am not selling an apartment, I am selling a life, and the apartment is complementary." In a sense, just as real-estate developers have become the primary planners of the city, residential advertisers also act as the primary priests of the city's residents: what they paint is not only an image of residences, but an image of lives and lifestyles for those who reside. The cartography of the advertisement provides not only a partial map but also a complete rendering of these lifestyles.

Shanghai today first emerges in the composite and allegorical fashion described above for residential advertising. It is echoed in other advertising (interior decoration, home furnishings, cosmetics), television sitcoms, commercial shop windows, and even in many online games. Many of the basic composite strategies used in residence advertising are deployed by other advertisements, of which a familiar example is automobile advertisements which stress outdoor scenery reflected in rearview and side-view mirrors. Broadly speaking, these advertisements, each selling different commodities, all do the same thing:

1   reduce the number of solitary images of streets, plazas, factories, fields, villages;
2   paint many partial pictures of a life world that is centered on residences and focused on interiors;
3   continue to induce a visual connection that makes equivalences between concrete products (cosmetics, furniture, cars) and the good life.

These methods, of course, arise from an autocratic market logic with Chinese characteristics. That is, the higher the price of residences, the more the real-estate market (or the automobile market for that matter) needs to popularize the following type of life consciousness: families and residences are the center of people's lives, and they are most connected to individual happiness. Those who make apartments the primary affair of their lives – no matter the motivation, whether "to live in a big house" or because "only houses keep their value" – are the consumers most needed by the market. And yet in the process of extending this market logic, in the process of spreading throughout the city a life image that makes residences central and far beyond their actual scope, a visual pattern that takes residences as fundamental viewpoints, a life world that is known through residences, and even a habit of perception that takes residences as life worlds have been born.

The vast changes in the urban space of Shanghai today have been "represented" mainly through this method of imaging. This representation is profoundly significant (and its limited content makes it highly focused) so that it is extremely clear. But precisely for this reason, in an era dominated by momentary fast-food culture, it has become a powerful allegory for the change in urban space, continuing to discipline Shanghai's urban citizens – especially the young – in terms of the perception of changes in space and how to understand new space. It goes without saying, this directly participated in the formation and strengthening of generally pessimistic perspectives of residents in post-1990s Shanghai – and of course, not only in Shanghai. The more that an individual feels reality is huge, and that "I" am very small, and hence "I" cannot grasp "my" own fate, but can only strive to adapt to reality, the more the disciplining of visual perception can be felt at the most basic levels, making one feel that life has always been this way, and if only one has a happy small nest, life will be satisfying.

Of course, for all of the above these changes constitute one another: change in the construction and production of space, the cultural representation of this space, and the entering of this representation into urban citizens' minds. All are produced simultaneously with the structure of social space and allocation where "winners take all." They are the basic conditions for the operation of this structure, or to put it another way, they are a part of this structure.

Note

*   The research on which this chapter is based is partly supported by Shanghai University's 211 project entitled "The Min-jian Situation of Chinese Society in Transformation."

Chapter 13

Residence Through Revolution and Reform

Ray Forrest

Introduction

In understanding the political economy of cities there is a tendency to construct narratives along a state–market continuum. This is particularly true of housing where explanations for system disruptions, social and spatial inequalities, and patterns of segregation are often rooted in accounts which emphasize shifts between private and public provision or the historic prevalence of particular modes of delivery and access. The neoliberal era accentuated this tendency, given its dominant overtones of market efficiency, state dependency, and public sector profligacy. This perspective, however, offers a rather limited view of how housing is experienced and access negotiated. People are reduced to recipients of luck or ill fortune, depending on income status, policy shifts, and the vagaries of place and time. It is structure heavy and agency light.

However, as Boltanski and Chiapello (2005) observe, several lived worlds are occupied, simultaneously or successively, with different and often competing value systems. They argue that people are not willing to sacrifice everything to the accumulation process of capitalism "precisely because they are not wholly identified with this regime, and have experience of different ones – for example, family attachments, civic solidarity, intellectual or religious life and so on" (p. 487). In their terms, it is this first, different regime of family attachments which is the main focus of this chapter albeit in a sharply different socio-political context, namely communist China over the last half century. What this chapter sets out to do is to show how the family unit negotiates, adapts to, and engages with significant social and political ruptures.

The New Blackwell Companion to the City   Edited by Gary Bridge and Sophie Watson

Academic and policy analyses often emphasize discontinuities, whether in relation to economic crises or political regimes, and in that sense privilege one lived world – capitalism, communism or whatever, above others. These other worlds, in this case family attachments and relations, may however mediate sharp changes in economic or political conditions and will themselves be transformed by that interaction. This is not to suggest therefore that family attachments and relations represent a domain of stability confronting and resisting a dynamic politics or economy. It is merely to suggest that accounts of structural change from this latter perspective may offer an additional lens through which to view societal transformations and one in which aspects of everyday life are more prominent. For example, as Turner and Rojek (2001: 77) observed:

> while sociologists might successfully construct an index of social dislocation (by reference to homicides, rape, family violence, divorce and so forth) it does not follow that individuals or social groups would necessarily or automatically experience the everyday world as disorderly. The round of everyday activities – sleeping, eating, talking and cleaning the household – *may* remain relatively normal and stable despite considerable dislocation.

Of course, there are few, if any, societies which have experienced such dramatic changes over the last half century or so than China. Indeed, this is precisely why the mediating role of family attachments is of particular interest in this context. Given the scale and severity of the structural shifts, and the pervasive intrusion of state powers, there would seem to have been little room for the family as an active influence in the residential sphere.

The changes associated with the Communist Victory, the Cultural Revolution, and the more recent reform period are reflected in the narratives as they traverse a pre-communist traditional and private housing system through the work unit system to the emerging, fragmented market system. They resonate closely with what Tang and Parish (2000: 17) have referred to as Chinese society's "strong geologically layered quality" in which the coming of age will have been for an older generation "during the 1950s, the golden age of Chinese Communism," for a middle generation "the 1966–1976 Cultural Revolution," and for the younger, during the reform period, when things were very different from the period of high socialism.

Shanghai has been at the heart of China's social and economic transformation, particularly in the reform era of the last two decades. In relation to housing provision, it has changed from a city in which state rental housing was the norm, provided mainly through the work unit system, to one in which private ownership dominates. It has also become a city in which new jobs are increasingly in the high technology, finance, media, and cultural sectors. The level of individual home ownership is now estimated at around 80 percent, a figure far in excess of many western European societies. However, a fully commercialized housing sector is still evolving and there remains considerable ambiguity over property rights. Moreover, as in the transitional economies of Eastern Europe, the housing sector has been in the vanguard of broader economic reforms and the massive transfer of properties from work units to individuals has involved highly variable benefits in terms of physical condition and asset values.

Research Background

There is not the space, nor is it appropriate, to offer a detailed methodological description of the research. In summary, this chapter draws on in-depth interviews with individual members of three generations of ten Shanghai families. In each case there is a member of an older, a middle, and a younger generation. Family members were interviewed separately and the construction of their housing history was used as the basic framework against which to explore more general experiences of social and economic change. It should also be noted in passing that all names used are fictitious.

It is not possible to represent the depth of evidence collected through the detailed interviews which amount to around 1,000 pages of transcription. And the inclusion of numerous verbatim quotes risks superficiality and would leave little room for discussion. The strategy adopted therefore has been to provide some general commentary from the study as a whole but to focus mainly on a few families. This also aids the narrative by making it possible to provide some additional background. For example, a brief profile of the Wang family captures the pattern and rapidity of social and economic change in Shanghai in microcosm. Old Wang (85) moved to the city in 1930 when she was six years old. Her husband died in 2006. She has three children, two sons aged 59 (Middle Wang) and 56 respectively and a daughter aged 57. From when Middle Wang was aged seven until she retired[1] Old Wang had worked as an embroiderer in a small clothing factory. Middle Wang had previously worked in a state-owned food enterprise but now worked as a driver for an art gallery. His wife is an assistant in a fashion boutique. Their only daughter, Young Wang, manages the marketing department of a small educational publishing company. They all live together in one privatized work unit apartment which has three bedrooms. They are not among the better off, new middle class of Shanghai but are an example of a typical Shanghai family in 2008 in terms of changing occupational profiles and living conditions.

In the communist era, housing distribution was based on the work unit system. Individuals were allocated to work units and most housing was allocated by the work unit. In the early period the accommodation consisted mainly of properties which had previously been privately owned. Gradually, work units built new housing, albeit of relatively low quality, and this was distributed according to various criteria including space per family member, work performance, and seniority and position in the party hierarchy. Some work units had more resources than others and thus the scale and quality of housing varied.

The *hukou*, or household registration system, was used as a means to control the supply of labor from the countryside to the city from the late 1950s. Household registration not only determined the right to live legitimately in a particular city but was linked closely to the housing distribution system. Stated simply, one household shared a *hukou*, and the household was defined by who was living together, so an extended family living in one living space would share a *hukou*. *Hukou* status was not only relevant to calculations about overcrowding and priorities for rehousing, but also to how many living spaces a family was allocated. As the reform era gathered pace in the late 1990s, the legacy of the *hukou* system affected the pattern of share out from compensation schemes due to redevelopment as well as the resources which could be realized and mobilized for market purchase. Against this necessarily brief background, the remainder of this chapter focuses on some of the ways families engaged with the social and economic changes and upheavals which engulfed them.

Making Space

For most of the twentieth century, the vast majority of households in Shanghai experienced extremely cramped living conditions. Large families shared small rooms, erected makeshift walls to create additional privacy, and converted balconies and yards to provide extra living quarters. Amenities were poor or non-existent and flush toilets a rarity. Even members of the more affluent households, some now living in chic new apartments in central Shanghai, for most of their lives endured what by western standards would be regarded as appalling living conditions. It should be stressed therefore that families strategized and negotiated about housing in conditions of serious constraint.

The older and middle generations were typically relatively large families compared to the "one child" generation which followed. Extended family living was common although it was often extended across space as family members came and went due to changes in work unit allocations, the forced mobilities of the Cultural Revolution, marriage, and childbirth. The dispersal of family members with, for example, husbands living separately from wives, or children being looked after by grandparents, was a common occurrence in order to maximize incomes and living space. In retrospect, at least, these separations which often involved many years apart, seemed to have been accepted as common if painful occurrences.

The shortage of space and the constant battle to adapt existing living quarters to changing space demands meant housing seems to have been a well-discussed theme among Shanghai families. Across all generations, there is remarkable recall about the size of an apartment or room (for example, 5 square meters or 10 square meters), how it was allocated, and who got what. This level of recall is also partly attributable to the rules in the socialist period for housing distribution in which the number of family members was divided into the available living space to determine rehousing priorities. But it also highlights the pivotal position of housing in overall life chances and the extent to which space scarcity was a preoccupation among families.

Housing is typically regarded as something which is allocated by a bureaucracy or acquired on the market. But space is also produced and exchanged through family actions and networks. This kind of activity is most manifest in the absence of adequate formal mechanisms – the visible shanty towns on the edge of rapidly expanding cities in the developing world. But the building of extensions, attic conversions, and the creation of basements are features of affluent cities and are an activity which is often neglected in terms of scale and significance in adapting to social changes. In Shanghai, and elsewhere in China, the conversion of space and informal exchanges were an important and necessary strategy to cope with shortages. These processes also operated across generations rather than, as is more typical in the western context, being associated with atomized households.

Sometimes acts of mutual assistance within the family were at the most basic level, involving an informally acquired piece of land and a makeshift construction.

Take this example from an account of Shanghai in the early 1950s. Old Li was able to be near his factory because he had managed to build a little shack on a patch of land, 10 square meters, and basically a place for sleeping in. He had been "lucky" enough to get this patch because his uncle already occupied it and there was enough space to build something for himself. "I bought simple stuff, like wood and thatch." His work unit was too poor to finance any house building at that time but he was able at least to use the public toilets and bathrooms in his factory. He lived there for ten years before he was allocated a small apartment when his factory relocated. He then gave the "bothy" back to his uncle as a marriage gift because his uncle's daughter had got married and needed somewhere to live.

When Old Wang got married she had a room in a Shikumen[2] dwelling which had to accommodate her mother, her husband, and the three children.

> We had to install an attic and some people lived upstairs ... As long as we had a place to live, as long as problems could be sorted out, it's okay ... you see, some people slept in the attic upstairs, some people slept the floor, and some slept in the bed ... problems were solved.

Their new living space was bigger and on the ground floor but Middle Wang needed marriage space – he was by then in his early thirties. When they moved in, they had installed another attic to accommodate his younger brother on his occasional visits. He had been sent to Jiang Xi province during the Cultural Revolution.[3] Middle Wang's solution was to take out the small attic, dig down "around 1.5 feet," and then rebuild the attic. "Now I could stand up straight and it was for marriage use."

Middle Wang felt guilty about his younger brother but the solution to that problem came through his father who had been living away from the family home since 1963, working as a miner in Nanjing. Under the rules, another family member could be offered work there – so the younger brother joined his father in Nanjing after several years. When his father was allocated an apartment by his work unit his mother and grandmother also moved to Nanjing. Middle Wang was left with the dug-out basement and attic all to himself and his wife. "I felt very happy having my own family home." His daughter was born shortly afterwards.

And there was Old Quan, who had been a well-known footballer in Shanghai and was constantly concerned to have a light, healthy living environment for his family. When the families living next door were moved to work elsewhere he managed to acquire three adjacent rooms so he "broke through the wall and combined them into one room." In his next dwelling, however, he had to take difficult decisions to prioritize family needs.

> My youngest son lived in the yard [which was converted into a room]; my wife and I lived in the living room with my granddaughter [his oldest son's], because my oldest son and his wife were working in Gansu, we put a bunk-bed in the living room; my elder son and his wife lived in another bedroom. But later since my youngest son was getting married, I kicked my elder son out.

The general point is that these informal activities in terms of space conversion as well as extensive self-build of "temporary" shacks were an important feature of

Figure 13.1   Entry door to privatized flat. Photo by Xiaohui Zhong.

Shanghai's changing urban morphology, particularly in the 1950s and early 1960s when officially deployed resources were woefully inadequate to keep pace with rising immigration. White (1978: 178), for example, draws on various sources to show the slow pace of housing investment in post-1949 Shanghai and the significant scale of self-building of simple dwellings.

Negotiating the Socialist System

A number of commentators (see, for example, Davies 2003) have written about the uneven opportunity structures for housing distribution within the socialist era with reference to the advantages of party membership or other means to acquire preferential treatment in a supposedly egalitarian system. These aspects are evident in some of the housing experiences in this study as are elements of simple good fortune. But, more significantly, it is the way strategies are played out across extended families which is striking because of the greater flexibility this created in the acquisition, retention, and exchange of living spaces. Swapping occurred between family members as well as between unrelated households. Another factor which appears regularly in the housing histories is a concern with the variable quality of education for children. When new housing was distributed via the work unit, its locational impact for schooling could outweigh considerations of space and quality. There are various tales of apartments being left empty or rented out because of the perceived inferiority of schools. For example, Middle Wang's opportunity to move from his childhood home came when his wife was allocated a two-room apartment by her work unit. It was twice the size of their current home with a separate bathroom and kitchen. But it was on the outskirts of Shanghai and at that time it would have meant losing their Shanghai household registration status.

> No [we never moved in], we exchanged it with another family ... like I said, our family's *Hukou* would have had to transfer to a non-Shanghai one which I knew would affect my child's future at some point, like going to school or something.

As it turned out, the registration boundaries were changed and the registration issue disappeared. However, Middle Wang was still concerned about the quality of schools on the outskirts.

As well as negotiating an exchange, he also managed to retain his old apartment. Middle Wang was now chief driver in his enterprise and had "got a bit of advantage." He wanted to keep the previous place because his younger brother (who had been working in Nanjing but whose *hukou* was still attached to the old, Shanghai apartment) had come back to Shanghai and was about to get married. "When they saw that my new apartment was located on the outskirt they agreed not to take away the old one." This was in 1985. Because he had a bigger apartment now, his mother and grandmother returned to live with them. They divided the bigger room into two, to create three bedrooms.

Some families did rather better than the Wangs in terms of entering the market era with nascent property rights over more than one apartment held by husband and wife or combinations of family members. Others were in less advantageous situations in terms of housing distribution but were already anticipating the impact of the new housing reform era and the demand for revalorized inner urban sites. Middle Yau was very explicit about his strategizing. He considered two options. He was excluded from the normal rules of exchange because

> in my case, my family lived in the old Shi Ku Men housing which belonged to the state, instead of any particular work unit. So I couldn't exchange it for something else. That's why my work unit distributed a room to me, not a real apartment. But I had to take it even though I didn't move in, because I could exchange it with others during the next distribution.

He was fortunate that his work unit was relatively wealthy and had built up a large stock of housing. He anticipated being able to capitalize on his seniority and gain a much better apartment with something to exchange. His second strategy anticipated the demolition of his current dwelling as urban redevelopment gathered pace and the prospect that his family would be paid compensation. "It was very likely that we and other families living in the old Shi Ku Men housing would come across such an opportunity." This is indeed what transpired. His mother and he received 428,000 *renmimbi* and he took his half to buy an apartment in the commercial sector. He also sold his allocated work unit housing for 40,000 RMB to pay for decoration.

Figure 13.2 New commercial housing neighborhood. Photo by Xiaohui Zhong.

Adapting to the Market

Middle Yau's considered strategy takes us on to the third theme in this chapter, namely the way in which Shanghai families adjusted to the housing reform era. Much has been written about the distributional consequences of the marketization and monetization of China's housing market (see, for example, Wang and Murie 2000; Davies 2003; Gustafsson *et al.* 2006). Again, consistent with research on the impact of housing reforms in Eastern Europe, the literature suggests a strong element of path dependency in terms of opportunities and outcomes. Those privileged in the socialist era through occupational status and political connections were often best placed to reap the rewards of the market as regards property asset values. In this context it should also be noted that whilst this chapter has emphasized the capacity of families to "creatively cope," typically in conditions of great adversity, the outcomes were not always positive. During the Cultural Revolution (1966–76), in particular, the experience of many was one of severe downward mobility in terms of housing and employment.

Nevertheless, it is evident that ingenuity and energy (and not just the mobilization of status and party networks) were employed to considerable effect during the socialist era to create opportunities which had not been anticipated when the reform period gathered pace. This was illustrated in the previous section in relation to the acquisition of multiple dwelling spaces, some being kept vacant. When those properties could be purchased from work units and subsequently traded, some families were able to acquire sufficient finance to achieve significant upward mobility. The other important mechanism, referred to by Middle Yau, was compensation for displacement as China's urban renewal gathered pace and old neighborhoods were torn down to be replaced by upscale apartment blocks and shopping malls. The payment of compensation and its distribution within the family then became a matter of negotiation and sometimes dispute. Leaving aside the issue of disrupted social networks and the social costs of displacement, these compensation payments often benefited poorer households in poor neighborhoods, rather than privileged cadres.

One of the striking features of these family housing narratives is an evident learning process – how to make the most of what is available and how to negotiate and maximize the opportunities in relation to whatever policies and practices are prevalent in a particular era. For most families, for most of the temporal span of the narratives, the space for negotiation was limited and the advantages gained enabled marginally enhanced subsistence and survival. Nonetheless, in their context, these gains were real and valued and experienced as such. The emergence of the market era, however, offered very different possibilities evidenced by the rapidly rising inequalities within cities and between urban and rural areas in China (He 2000; Logan *et al*. 1999). Here the experiences of the past of gaining first mover advantage and in negotiating between and around rules and regulations were quickly mobilized. Here is Middle Wang again:

> I thought there would be a long trend in privatizing work unit housing and you must do it quick. In China, things always work in the same way – you have to run ahead of the others when some new policies show up, you take the risks while you get most benefits.

He moved quickly and bought his apartment in central Shanghai from his work unit for 16,000 RMB. It was worth around 450,000 RMB in 2008.

And Middle Li reflected on her experience as a market pioneer.

MRS LI: There were not many estate agencies and I happened to see one, a newly opened one. I was their first customer, selling out my flat in Xin Ze road, their first deal. The agent looked very honest and I took him to see my flat, telling him that we wanted to sell it. It was on the twenty-fourth floor with a convenient neighborhood environment, very pleasing! The agent asked me what would be my preferable selling price. I gave him the price of more than 300,000 RMB,[4] as it was the work-unit housing for private use.

INTERVIEWER: How did you sell it as it was not permitted by the regulations?

MRS LI: We did that in secret through the estate agent. But in the late 1990s, work unit housing was to some extent being owned by the sitting tenant. As it was distributed to us, we had its property right … well, it was not a property right in a real sense, but the right of use which can be transferred to someone else. It has become common knowledge now, but ten years ago, people seldom talked about "property rights."

The Lis had bought two flats in the commercial sector and converted them into one. This had been financed through a complex, cross-family transaction involving shared compensation, the sale of two properties acquired at high discount from her husband's work unit, and then an exchange of properties with her parents-in-law.

The payment of compensation when older neighborhoods were demolished also led to the familiar story of some families hanging on till the last, hoping for larger payouts. It could also lead to protracted family disputes. Young Lu recalls the serious arguments which arose in her family when their Shi Ku Men house was demolished.

> My father's siblings thought that if my grandma continued to live with us, my parents would "pocket" her share of compensation. But that was not true … After consulting some lawyers, my father discussed this issue with my grandma, telling her that though we might have to use some of her money when buying this new apartment her name would not be written in any related documents, because in that case his siblings would fight for it after she dies; however, we promised to take good care of her during her old-aged life. But my uncles and aunts didn't believe us and thought we actually wanted to "steal" my grandma's money and might even send her to the rest-home. So they encouraged my grandma to buy her own housing and not live with us. So my grandma spent all her money [compensation] on the purchase of her current housing and they [her father's siblings] each gave out 30,000 RMB to support her.

Concluding Comments

The political and economic transformations in China have been intertwined with demographic and attitudinal changes. Family size has shrunk, by policy diktat and more recently from choice. A younger generation of urban Chinese is more individualistic and autonomous but in many ways more dependent on their parents for financial support, particularly in relation to education and housing. And over the three generations the place and role of housing has shifted from being a place for family gathering and communal living in tight-knit neighborhoods, through being intimately and functionally connected to the workplace, to its more contemporary version in which work and home locations are increasingly spatially separate. In terms of housing conditions it is a story of slow incremental shifts as regards increasing space and improved amenities as more housing is constructed.

An older generation emerged from a period in their own childhood when life was hard but relatively stable in traditional rural or semi-rural settings. Their entry to work and married life coincided with the establishment of a centrally planned economy and the emergence of the household registration system and the subsequent socialist transformation of the housing system. Further disruptions to family and working lives followed with the Cultural Revolution and *Shang shan, xia xiang* (literally, "up to the mountains and down to the villages") when high school students and young adults from urban areas were sent to the countryside. Almost all families were affected by this experience with sons, daughters, brothers, or sisters being sent away to often harsh and unfamiliar regions.

At the household level, there are important differences in relation to the relative prosperity of different work units and the use of informal contacts. As housing histories progress and as more housing is allocated according to family needs, complicated swaps and rearrangements occur via different family members. What is noteworthy is the way in which these informal arrangements via family, neighbors, and friends are overlain on an apparently rational, socialist allocation system. These informal processes remain as an important factor in the shaping of residential histories throughout the different periods.

The point of this chapter has not been to romanticize the resilience of the family domain in coping with adversity or destabilizing change, nor to underplay the scale of the suffering and hardships during China's various periods of social transformation. Moreover, the accounts of mutuality and reciprocity in the narratives are balanced by tales of conflict and tension among neighbors and family members. The aim rather has been to remind us that familism constitutes an important element of human agency across changing and often highly restrictive institutional and organizational contexts and, in Boltanski and Chiapello's terms (2005), draws on a set of values, which may mesh with, but are distinct from, other regimes. In this context, housing, whether as use value or exchange value, is a key site around which these different value systems conflict and coalesce.

Acknowledgment

This chapter draws on a research project "Housing assets and intergenerational dynamics in East Asian societies," funded by the UK Economic and Social Research Council in 2007–9 (RES-062–23–0187).

Notes

1   The mandatory retirement age in China is currently 60 for men and 55 or 50 for women.
2   Shikumen is a distinct housing type which is a fusion of a British terraced house and a traditional Chinese courtyard house. It was a dominant building form for the Chinese community from the middle of the nineteenth century until the communist victory in 1949. Denison and Ren (2006: 162) observe that "The primary consideration for the layout of the early Shi Ku Men was density with little concern for light, ventilation and the close proximity of neighbouring buildings."
3   During the Cultural Revolution, a period of around ten years (1966–76), some 17 million young people were sent from urban to rural areas to undertake manual labor as part of Mao's national campaign for socialist re-education to counter perceived bourgeois and capitalist tendencies. There are numerous detailed analyses of this period in contemporary Chinese history: of particular relevance to this piece is Zhou and Hou (1999).
4   At time of writing 1 CNY = 0.147 US$. At current exchange, 300,000 RMB is equivalent to around 44,000 US$.

References

Boltanski, L., and Chiapello, E. (2005) *The New Spirit of Capitalism*. London and New York: Verso.

Davies, D. (2003) From welfare benefit to capitalized asset: the recommodification of residential space in urban China. In *Housing and Social Change*, ed. R. Forrest and J. Lee. London and New York: Routledge, 183–96.

Denison, E., and Ren, G. Y. (2006) *Building Shanghai: The Story of China's Gateway*. Chichester: John Wiley-Academy.

Gustafsson, B., Li, S., and Zhong, W. (2006) The distribution of wealth in urban China and in China as whole in 1995. *Review of Income and Wealth* Series 52, 2: 173–88.

He, Q. (2000) China's listing social structure. *New Left Review* 5, September/October: 69–99.

Logan, J. R., Bian, Y., and Bian, F. (1999) Housing inequality in urban China in the 1990s. *International Journal of Urban and Regional Research* 23: 7–25.

Tang, W., and Parish, W. L. (2000) *Chinese Urban Life under Reform: The Changing Social Contract*. Cambridge, Cambridge University Press.

Turner, B. S., and Rojek, C. (2001) *Society and Culture: Principles of Scarcity and Solidarity*. London: Sage.

Wang, Y. P., and Murie, A. (2000) Social and spatial implications of housing reform in China. *International Journal of Urban and Regional Research* 24 (2): 397–417.

White, L. T. (1978) *Careers in Shanghai*. Berkeley: University of California Press.

Zhou, X., and Hou, L. (1999) Children of the Cultural Revolution: the state and the life course in the People's Republic of China. *American Sociological Review* 64 (1): 12–36.

Part II City Mobilities

Chapter 14

Reflections on Mobilities

Gary Bridge and Sophie Watson

Growth, connection/interconnection, networks, circulation, flows, movement, communication, all these are concepts which resonate with the city as the site of mobility and mobilities. As we set out to propose here, mobility/ies are central to understanding the ways that cities have developed since their origins many centuries ago, but the concept as a framing device has not been typically deployed in urban literature and analysis until recently. At the same time, the converse of this is equally pertinent, thus cities are also about the regulation of movement, control, segregation, exclusion, discipline, immobility, restriction, and so on.

Mobile Bodies

Thinking about cities through the lens of mobilities, we suggest, throws into sharp relief continuities and discontinuities over time/space, and underlines, once again, the ways in which many urban phenomena are not new, even if they vary in intensity or form in the current era.

Early to mid-twentieth-century urban analysis had mobility at its core. For Simmel (1948) and Benjamin (1999) the city is the site of excitement and movement, of the flow of images and commodities, and of affect and emotion. For Simmel this produces the blasé attitude in the urban citizen or the retreat from the city when mental life has become over-stimulated, while for Benjamin, the urban dweller, the *flâneur*, wanders through the Paris arcades, reveling in the phantasmagoria of new sights and sounds, of people passing by, and of new commodities. In the more pragmatic analysis characterized by the Chicago School's early urban sociology we similarly find the centrality of movement here deployed around city growth as analogous to the growth of plants. More recently mobility has been configured

The New Blackwell Companion to the City Edited by Gary Bridge and Sophie Watson
© 2011 Blackwell Publishing Ltd

around the figure of the nomad, where in social and cultural theory a nomadic metaphysics concerns cities in terms of flows, rhythms, and multiple lines of flight. As David Pinder elucidates in Chapter 19, Deleuze and Guattari's ideas of nomadic space as smooth open space without borders and enclosures, with its emphasis on lines and trajectories rather than fixities, have been influential. Though the nomad is potentially a figure of resistance and subversion, with the possibility of disrupting state spatial powers and orderings, and the means to take control and liberate subjects from mobile capitalism's global reach, as Hardt and Negri (2004) would contend, the conflation of nomadism with migration obscures the very nature of striated spaces, the unevennesses and differences, the enclosures and the boundaries, as Pinder argues here. In a different way also, Marx and Engels emphasize mobility, where the rapid movement of the population into towns and cities as a result of industrialization processes, is seen to lead to vast inequalities between the rich and poor, the bourgeoisie and the working class, mapped graphically onto city spaces.

The growth of cities is, of course, tantamount to a growth in their populations. Andrew Ross argues here (Chapter 15) that the capacity of cities to increase their population was considered to be a sign both of their prosperity and of tremendous technical and administrative achievement. Thus densely populated cities became synonymous with civilization and with progress, a perspective still influential in newly industrializing countries across the globe. The specter of overcrowding, traffic congestion, urban sprawl, slums, pollution, and the related serious consequences in terms of climate change, seem to have little effect in dissuading governments from supporting rapid urbanization, from Guangzhou to São Paolo. At the same time, there has been a long tradition of anti-urbanist sentiment, praising the glories of the rural idyll (Williams 1973), security and village community, *Gemeinschaft* (Tonnies 1955), and decrying the putative immoralities, miseries, insecurities, and dissociated social relations, *Gesellschaft* (Tonnies 1955) associated with city life. These have existed in tension in urban analysis and artistic/literary works (for example, Wordsworth and Dickens), at least since the early period of industrialization.

The rapid pace of urbanization in the west and the associated population growth were quickly deemed to be in need of governance – populations were seen as in need of regulation, management, and intervention, and discourses of concern around population growth and the movement of urban citizens began to proliferate. The origins of urban planning lay in the need to regulate the perceived negative impacts of population and overcrowding in cities, on the one hand, and the need to keep people moving – circulation – on the other. The urban poor represented the greatest threat to social harmony and to the health of the city. Not only were bodies subject to intervention, so also were the germs and microbes that they produced; thus public health initiatives proliferated hand-in-hand with planning intervention. Marx and Engels were quick to identify the requirements of capital for healthy and compliant workers, through water and sanitation initiatives, housing provision, and a modicum of social services. As Andrew Ross puts it: "The industrial city of the nineteenth century was the crucible for the emergence of population anxiety, and the subsequent humanitarian solutions codified in planning." As the twentieth century progressed, the Garden City movement with its displacement of urban citizens to model towns, the encouragement of home-ownership in the suburbs, and, in Britain, public

Figure 14.1 Shanghai building site. Photo S. Watson.

housing initiatives also, were all seen as vital to creating a stable population who would be unlikely to threaten the status quo through disruption and disorder.

Thus, anxiety concerning the potential for political unrest and the potentially negative social consequences of overcrowding, ill health, and poor welfare represented one motive for intervention. But of equal significance was a perceived need for the regulation of the population more generally. The police played a key role in the early modern period in social ordering, with a particular focus on the problems of vagrancy, pauperism, and labor, as Francis Dodsworth points out in Chapter 20. Drawing on Neocleous's (2000) work, he argues that "policing was concerned not only with practices of immobilization and discipline, but with mobilizing practices concerned with the production of order," where the former concern the control of disorder, and the latter are concerned with the production of an active and mobile workforce. Foucault's influence is evident in Dean's account (1999) which goes further in arguing that police are also "concerned with the regulation and enabling of certain flows (of money, goods, and people) and the fixation of particular (moral) attributes." In such accounts notions of urban civility and publicness are strongly embedded in the idea of a healthy urban environment in which such values can thrive.

A related narrative is that of the healthy body. Cities were long associated with disease and ill health, deriving on the one hand from immobilities – stagnant water, refuse, poor sanitation – and on the other, the rapid movement of disease through city spaces on account of the concentration and overcrowding of people in small, cramped, and poorly ventilated spaces. As Carter shows in Chapter 21, from the early days of Rome, through the medieval city to the present day, there has been a persistent connection between the city and infection. Taking the Black Death as one illustration, the juxtaposition of densely packed people, rodents, and fleas made for a rapid transmission of the disease between city dwellers, before distributing the radials of infection into the surrounding rural hinterland. Here too Foucault saw the measures deployed in combating the plagues as modes of controlling the borders of the city, restricting movement, and disciplining society (Foucault 1977).

Measures to restrict movement and travel shifted from the national level, as maritime trading presented threats of disease being carried from one part of the globe to another, as Carter explains here. Quarantine stations at the entrance to ports became familiar sites – in Sydney it is still possible to visit the quarantine station close to the northern entrance to the harbor where the last ship to be held was the *Nikki Maru* in 1972. Routinely passengers in modern airports are restricted from entering a country if they are suspected of disease, or in some cases, refused visas when known to carry particular viruses, such as HIV-positive applicants to travel to the United States until President Obama announced that all restrictions on people with HIV entering the United States was to be lifted as of January 4, 2010. At a more mundane level public health initiatives were core to local and national government policies from the early nineteenth century.

Global Flows

The notion of globalization is now almost commonplace, deployed by politicians and the person in the street alike. The newness of global processes remains somewhat disputed. Indeed some theorists (Hirst and Thompson 2009) contest the notion of a genuinely global economy, refuting the existence of a qualitatively new stage in the development of international capitalism, and arguing instead that it exhibits many similarities with earlier processes of internationalization. However, the majority of contemporary urban and social theorists point to the speeding up and intensification of globalizing processes in the latter quarter of the twentieth century, illustrated in the explosion of business air and rail travel on the one hand and international email traffic on the other. Urry (1999), for example, calls for a shift from the study of society as a set of bounded institutions to a focus on the physical, imaginative, and virtual movements in an increasingly unbounded world. Our own view is that the processes of connecting and interconnecting globally unfold at an uneven pace over time/space.

Globalization is typically deployed to describe a combination of economic, technological, environmental, socio-cultural, and political forces (Rennen and Martens 2003; Giddens 1999: Kawachi and Wamala 2007). An emphasis on the economic aspects of globalization is probably its most common use (e.g., Friedman 2000), where the focus is on the integration of national economies into the international economy through international capital and labor flows, trade and investment, and the spread of technology, particularly information technology (Castells 1996). Of relevance here is the reduction of barriers between national borders in order to facilitate the international flow of capital, goods and services – and to a lesser extent, labor. Much has been written on the economic, and also political power of transnational corporations, which takes many different and complex forms. Amin and Thrift (2002: 65) suggest that global firms "have become a 'constellation of network relations' incorporating entire social worlds of production, trade, organization and power play." Cities are increasingly exposed to decisions made at a distance, rendering local authorities vulnerable to the whims of international capital. Some cities are highly linked in and connected to international financial and industrial networks, while others are consigned to the margins, and this can shift and change seemingly overnight – as witnessed by the rapid rise of Shanghai as a financial center in the last decade, graphically represented by the building of the SWFC in 2007, now the second tallest building in the world, or the seemingly overnight property market crash of Dubai, the financial capital of the Middle East in 2009.

Globalization thus is an uneven process with highly differentiated social and economic effects. While some cities, or parts of cities, and the people who reside or work there, arguably, may benefit from connections and interconnections elsewhere, at the same time, other cities, regions, and localities suffer from increasing exclusion and marginalization from the key sites of power and wealth. Processes of globalization have undoubtedly contributed to growing divisions between the rich and the poor, both on a worldwide scale and between countries of the global north and global south (as we see in Part V, "City Divisions and Differences"). It becomes increasingly important to recognize that proximity and reach, distance and mobility, place and presence, shift the register of power in complex and unpredictable ways (Allen 2003), as each city is configured in relation to sites of power in different ways. As Sassen argues in Chapter 18, the global city is emblematic of the contradictory space of globalization, which is characterized by contestation, internal differentiation, and continuous border crossings. Without a place-bounded account of the global information economy, a whole array of activities and workers are evicted from the account – the night cleaners who are gone from the financial centers by the time the financial traders arrive for work in the morning, for example.

As far as cities are concerned cultural globalization is at least as significant in its effects. The tension between processes of homogenization where the global domination of American, and to a lesser extent European, culture has been seen to undermine local uniqueness and diversity – the similarity of waterfront developments or airports in cities across the world are a case in point – and the search for local uniqueness, individuality, and identity is now a familiar one. As Sassen (1998) points out, the large contemporary western city concentrates diversity with its multiplicity of cultures disrupting the dominant corporate culture as an immense array of cultures from around the world, each rooted in a particular village or town or country, are reterritorialized in the global cities, as a result of successive waves of migration. At the same time, the speed of internet communication, and the rapid transmission of images and digital information, and instantaneous communication between people anywhere in a variety of digital forms and media, have served to further break down cultural and – to a certain extent – social boundaries. The internet more than any other phenomenon has shrunk distances between people as communication across the globe is increasingly possible, opening up processes of cultural globalization through interaction and communication between people with very different lifestyles and from very different cultures. The widespread use of mobile phones in regions where landlines barely exist has similarly shrunk distances between people who are living across the globe from one another, to the extent that migrants now can keep up with daily life in their place of origin in ways that were unimaginable even a decade ago. At the same time, despite the increased potential for virtual forms of contact, co-presence and embodied encounters continue to matter, be it a migrant returning "home" to attend a wedding, or a business person establishing relations of trust through meetings with potential partners, or parties to a legal contract meeting to sign a document. This need to be co-present, Urry (2007) suggests, is even necessary from time to time for those involved in the virtual communities of the internet, even if this is simulated.

Transnational and Rural–Urban Migration

The massive movement people across the globe on the one hand, and the huge levels of rural–urban migration in Asia and the global south on the other, have changed cities in unprecedented ways. Ethnic and racial diversity is now the norm in the majority of global cities in the west, while cities in developing or newly developed countries and regions are marked by vast squatter settlements, homelessness, pavement dwellers, and other forms of temporary or inadequate housing as people leave country areas in search of employment or an income to survive. National and international movements of people are accompanied by increasing levels of regulation, restriction, and exclusion of certain categories of people, where access to citizenship rights is highly differentiated according to racial, social, religious, and economic criteria. At the same time these shifts have taken place with highly differentiated effects, where dominant narratives can be misleading, and where, we would argue, attention has to be paid to the specificities of place, history, politics, and culture to make sense of the complexities of the multicultural city. Diversity may be celebrated in its exotic manifestations such as music or food, in the same locality as a minority group is marginalized or subject to violence, diverse religious architectures may be welcomed or resisted (see Chapter 32 by Hill), street markets may thrive with a plethora of different goods on sale, or rapidly decline as ethnic minorities try to scratch out a living selling cheap goods (Watson 2006). While at the political/policy level the governance of multicultural populations can range from the French republican model within which difference is not tolerated in the public sphere, to strategies for the redistribution of social goods to address ethnic/racial urban inequalities, as is practiced in Canada.

More recently the notion of transnationality (as opposed to transnationalism, globalization, diaspora) has been deployed to situate "migrants and their transnational connectivities fully within the forces that are constitutive of the 'urban,'" and to draw attention to the mutual construction of the local, national, and global as Glick Schiller proposes in Chapter 16. This is a framework which allows us, she suggests, to situate the diversity of city inhabitants in "multiple, interpenetrating scales of relationality." Thus migrant individuals and groups are connected across a number of nation states and places in what Glick Schiller describes as a "transnational social field defined as a network of networks of unequal power." This has important effects on the cities as individuals are linked to a whole variety of social, religious, and economic institutions in their place of residence, as well as by strong affective, economic, and social links to their countries of origin or identification (in the case of second-generation migrants). There is no one pattern of how these networks and connectivities map out in any one place, though many cities exhibit similar concentrations of migrants in specific areas, with outmigration from inner city areas to more affluent suburbs as people become more established and economically secure. But even this pattern is more common in London than in Sydney or Paris for example, where new migrants are concentrated in outer suburban areas where the housing is cheaper.

Rural to urban migration is a worldwide phenomenon, causing increasing levels of urbanization and the growth of megacities (those over 10 million people) in Latin America, Asia, Africa, and India. The causes are manifold – natural disasters, such as famine and drought, unemployment, poor living conditions, war and conflict are key. Cities are seen, or imagined, to offer opportunities for employment and income, housing, healthcare, education and welfare services, protection from conflict and violence either real or imagined. There were 18 world megacities in 2000 including Tokyo at 26.4 million, Mexico City at 18.1 million, Mumbai 17.8 million, São Paolo 17 million, Shanghai 17 million. This number is predicted to increase to rise to 23 megacities by 2015 (UNFPA 2001), adding Hyderabad, Tianjin, and Bangkok amongst others, to the list. These cities are characterized by a number of problems including high levels of pollution and traffic, lack of clean water, extreme divisions between the rich and poor – with many in the latter category – poor power supplies, rubbish collection, and sewerage, lack of adequate housing, local gangs, drugs, and limited employment opportunities. Violence and exclusion of new migrants are a terrifying reality for many new arrivals to the city. In the context of Mumbai, Appadurai (2006) describes how rapid migration generates an uncertainty in the host country about "how many of 'them' are now amongst us." This uncertainty gathers momentum when there are large-scale movements, when risks are seen to be attached, or existing networks of social knowledge are threatened by rumor, terror, or social movements. In his view, the tip over into ethno-nationalism, and even violence, in democratic polities happens in the context of an "anxiety of incompleteness" when minorities, even in small numbers, are seen to threaten the sense of the nation as an unsullied national whole and a pure national ethnos. City governments are struggling to keep up with the pace of change, and strategies are deployed to marginalize and regulate new arrivals in ways that resonate with nineteenth-century social ordering in western cities described earlier.

Of course these negative and pessimistic narratives of migration to global megacities offer only one side of the story. Many migrants to cities find or establish employment opportunities, are adequately housed in public or private housing, and are integrated into social networks that sustain them. Class intersects with race/ethnicity in complex ways such that in the UK, for example, in 2010 the then Labour government's communities secretary, John Denham, was keen to assert that many white working-class families in cities were consigned to lives of poverty and marginalization, while the members of many Asian families were established in full-time education or employment (BBC News January 15, 2010). Tyler Rooker's chapter

(Chapter 17) details the lives of migrants in Shanghai who flow through networks and cluster according to home and kin relationships, integrating home lives, business, and technology in what he calls the "electronics city." His argument is that this group has congealed as an essential part of the informationalizing city, and thus is not as tenuously and precariously inserted in Chinese cities as migrants are typically assumed to be.

Not only is there the phenomenon of megacities resulting from massive population shifts, there are also several parts of the world where post-border cities have sprung up across the boundaries that delineate nation states. Referring to the boundary between the USA and Mexico, Dear and Lucero (2005, also extracted in the *Blackwell City Reader*, 2010) suggest that it is useful to think of the agglomeration of people and cities that have sprung up in this area over several decades as a megacity, which represents a form of urban growth without historical precedent. This border environment which has emerged out of tensions between the USA and Mexico represents a hybridization which encompasses both dislocation and deterritorialization. It is this hybridity which warrants the making of a new term – the post-border city. Chinese and Korean migrants in the Russian Far East; Koreans, Chinese, and Russians in Japan; and North Koreans in China represent similar kinds of populations arising from migration. Many of these cross-border migrants are temporary – such as short-term workers, traders, tourists, students, and business people, leading to urban populations in border regions which shift and change according to relative shifts in economic opportunities in the neighboring countries. According to Dear and Lucero, Bajalta California, as they term this agglomeration, offers a glimpse into a future where borders may no longer be consequential.

Mobile Cultures

Rapid movements of people, things, commodities, and information are culturally mapped in complex ways and registers, producing new cultural forms, artifacts and imaginations in city spaces. Cultural practices are intertwined with urban mobilities also in the processions, demonstrations, street performances, and tours enacted in city streets, constituting these as spaces of flow and fluidity at the same time as being enabled and constrained by them. The quintessential urban subject, the *flâneur*, inhabits her own psychic imaginative world as she ambles through the city streets with her private thoughts and interpretations of what she sees. The city is also the space of the affect, as we see in Part IV, where mobility is deeply implicated. Geographers in recent years have deployed the notion of psychogeography first defined by Guy Debord (1955) as the study of the laws and effects on the emotions, conscious and unconscious, and behavior of individuals. Psychogeography was developed originally by the Lettrist International and had connections to the Dadaists and Surrealists, and also Baudelaire's notion of the urban *flâneur* wandering through the city. Contemporary architecture was seen to restrict and constrain cities. David Pinder, in Chapter 19, traces the thinking of Constant in New Babylon where the mobility and fluctuation of the population in Deriveville – the drift city – forged a new city which would have no limits, frontiers or divisions. This is the notion of the city as produced by the very trajectories that move across it. Probably the most influential British writer who has drawn on psychogeographical ideas is Iain Sinclair, who has developed a body of work based on pedestrian exploration of cityscapes, such as in his book *London Orbital* (2002) where he traces London's M25 outer ring motorway on foot, detailing different sites on route.

A different kind of story of mobility is told by Daniel Walkowitz in Chapter 22. This is a story of movement as translation, as a cultural practice performed in one space (the UK) is transported and reconfigured in another place (the US) to produce a different form with different meanings. Obviously there is an infinite number of cultural practices from different arenas – film, theater, music, religion, dance, visual arts, and so on, which are transmogrified as they travel, change, and adapt across space, taking on new meanings and forms. Walkowitz's chapter here charts the relationship between music, dance, and urban geography in the history of English country dance, a dance form with origins in seventeenth-century England, which spawned square and contra dance in the United States. A key figure in its revival at the turn of the twentieth century was Cecil Sharp, who advocated the benefits of country dance as a counter-attraction to the popular commercial spaces of cabaret and music halls that were seen as having deleterious moral and physical effects on immigrant and working-class youth. What is interesting in this account is that a hundred years later, the dance form is thriving in the US while it languishes in London, where its revival originated.

Transport

That mobility is mediated through transport goes without saying. The continuing need for co-presence for social, economic, familial, and legal connections and the increasing importance of tourism, leisure, and educational travel (Urry 1999) mean transport is as important as ever in the global information and networked world. Even at a national level, the passenger miles traveled in the UK in the last decade of the twentieth century increased by 30 percent (Amin and Thrift 2002: 43). The continued use of the automobile in the west and the huge expansion of private car use in newly developing countries represent a persistent problem for cities in relation to pollution, congestion, road deaths, and quality of life, and impacts on the urban poor. Though cars facilitated the decentralization of populations to suburban areas, by the very same token, the increasing sprawl of suburban development in many parts of the world, cities such as Los Angeles and Phoenix representing graphic examples, has led to ever greater dependence on private transport. Nevertheless, as Brian Ladd points out in Chapter 23, automobiles have consistently been praised as vehicles of freedom, although this is a freedom which has become more and more subject to regulation and law enforcement through such practices as parking restrictions and congestion charges.

In the majority of countries across Asia, from Vietnam to India, until the last decade of the twentieth century, bicycles, motor bikes, and walking were the dominant mode of transport. Peng and Zhu (2007) show how the rapid rise of urban incomes in the Chinese city over the last decade has resulted in a parallel increase in vehicles on the road. Average vehicular speed has decreased over the same period, with many roads in total gridlock in the larger cities during rush hour. The common response by Chinese authorities has been to increase the supply of road infrastructure by expanding roads and developing light rail and bus rapid

Figure 14.2   Shanghai motorway. Photo S. Watson.

transit systems. Peng and Zhu argue that the needs of the urban poor, despite their growing numbers, have been largely ignored in transport policies. The emphasis on road expansion and rapid transit systems has brought few benefits to the poor, who cannot afford their own cars or the fares associated with the new forms of transport. The majority rely on walking or bicycles to get around, but processes of suburbanization result in many of the poorer households living far from their places of work, or from city centers, so the mobility of the urban poor is becoming severely limited. A similar set of issues is facing urban dwellers in countless cities in rapidly developing parts of the world.

New perspectives on everyday mobility, drawing on Bruno Latour (2005), have shifted analysis from the more common cultural perspective, where cars are represented as symbolic manifestations of various desires, to focus on the material practices of driving. Thrift (2002), echoing de Certeau, suggests a phenomenology of automobility, with its own practices of driving and "passengering." Thrift draws on Katz's (2000) work to reveal an extraordinarily complex everyday ecology of driving, going further to develop an argument that widespread use of the car was one of the key moments in the redesign of modern urban environments. In particular, cars he suggests are more and more like hybrid entities where intelligence and intentionality are distributed between human and non-human actors in ways that are increasingly inseparable. As car manufacture becomes more sophisticated through the application of ergonomics, the car becomes more wrapped up with the body. This way of thinking is indicative of the changing perspectives on mobilities that we have traced throughout this chapter.

References

Allen, J. (2003) *Lost Geographies of Power*. Oxford: Blackwell.

Amin, A., and Thrift, N. (2002) *Cities: Re-imagining the Urban*. Cambridge: Polity Press.

Appadurai, A. (2006) *Fear of Small Numbers: An Essay on the Geography of Anger*. Durham, NC: Duke University Press.

Benjamin, W. (1999) The arcades of Paris. In *The Arcades Project*, trans. Howard Eiland and Kevin McLaughlin. Cambridge, MA: Harvard University Press, 873–44.

Castells, M. (1996) *The Rise of the Network Society*. Oxford: Blackwell.

Dean, M. (1999) *Governmentality: Power and Rule in Modern Society*. London: Sage Publications.

Dear, M., and Lucero, H. (2005) Postborder cities, postborder world: The rise of Bajalta California. *Environment and Planning D: Society and Space* 23: 317–21.

Debord, G. (1955) Introduction to a critique of urban geography. Trans. K. Knabb. *Les Lèvres Nues* 6.

Foucault, M. (1977) *Discipline and Punish*. Trans. A. Sheridan. New York: Pantheon.

Friedman, T. (2000) *The Lexus and the Olive Tree*. New York: Anchor Books.

Giddens, A. (1999) *Runaway World*. London: Profile Books.

Hardt, M., and Negri, A. (2004) *Multitude: War and Democracy in the Age of Empire*. New York: Penguin.

Hirst, P., and Thompson, G. (2009) *Globalisation in Question*. 3rd edn. Cambridge: Polity Press.

Katz, J. (2000) *How Emotions Work*. Chicago: University of Chicago Press.

Kawachi, I., and Wamala, S. (2007) *Globalisation and Health*. Oxford: Oxford University Press.

Latour, B. (2005) *Re-assembling the Social: An Introduction to Actor–Network Theory*. Oxford: Oxford University Press.

Neocleous, M. (2000) *The Fabrication of Social Order: A Critical Theory of Police Power*. London: Pluto.

Peng, Z., and Zhu, Y. (2007) Urban transport in Chinese cities: the impact on the urban poor. In *The Inclusive City: Infrastructure and Public Services for the Urban Poor in Asia*, ed. A. Aprodicio, B. Laquian, and L. Hanley. Baltimore, MD: Johns Hopkins University Press, 144–70.

Rennen, W., and Martens, P. (2003) The globalisation timeline. *Integrated Assessment* 4 (3): 137–44.

Sassen, S. (1998) *Globalization and Its Discontents*. New York: The New Press.

Simmel, G. (1948) The metropolis and mental life. Trans. Edward Shils. In *Social Sciences III, Selections and Selected Readings*. Chicago: University of Chicago Press, 67–79.

Sinclair, I. (2002) *London Orbital: A Walk Around the M25*. London: Granta.

Thrift, N. (2002) Driving in the city. *Theory, Culture and Society* 21 (4/5): 41–59.

Tonnies, F. (1955) *Community and Association: (Gemeinschaft und Gesellschaft)*. London: Routledge and Kegan Paul.

UNFPA (2001) *State of the World Population*. Chapter 3. New York: United Population Fund Report.

Urry, J. (1999) *Society beyond Societies: Mobilities for the Twenty First Century*. London: Routledge.

Urry, J. (2007) *Mobilities*. Cambridge: Polity Press.

Watson, S. (2006) *Markets as Sites of Social Interaction: Spaces of Diversity*. Bristol: Joseph Rowntree Foundation and Policy Press.

Williams, R. (1973) *The Country and the City*. London: Chatto and Windus.

Chapter 15

"Nothing Gained by Overcrowding": The History and Politics of Urban Population Control

Andrew Ross

For most of recorded urban history, the capacity of cities to increase their populations was considered not only a sign of prosperity but also a great technical and administrative achievement. Indeed, densely populated cities have been synonymous with civilization itself – as visible monuments to the triumph of humans over nature. Cultures that boasted large urban centers have lessons in living to pass on; those that do not are largely obscure to us. Conversely, the sacking of cities in warfare is the most dramatic expression of domination of one civilization over another – a tradition very much alive during World War II (Dresden, London, Berlin, Hiroshima, Nagasaki) and in the more recent US threats against Vietnam and Iraq to "bomb" their capitals "back to the Stone Age."

While anti-urban sentiment had long been a reflex of elites seeking bucolic refuge from the sweaty mass, the onset of industrialization considerably magnified their doubts about the wisdom of living in high-density urban centers. Hitherto a source of pride for modernizing nations, urban population increase became an acute concern in the latter part of the nineteenth century. The newly teeming industrial city was perceived as a threat to the health of its inhabitants, raising their mortality rate and diluting their humanity. By the late twentieth century, rapid urbanization would be regarded as a threat to planetary life itself. As a result the swelling megacities of the global south are more likely to be seen today as symptoms of unsustainability than as feats of development.

This great reversal in the given wisdom about urban density is also the origin of modern urban planning. Population control is a primary principle of city, regional, and state planning. Programmatic campaigns to survey, segregate, decant, sterilize, or otherwise reduce urban populations have been at the heart of the planning policies by which state power came to be legitimized as a pastoral enterprise, responsible

The New Blackwell Companion to the City   Edited by Gary Bridge and Sophie Watson
© 2011 Blackwell Publishing Ltd

for the welfare of all. Over time, and especially since the mid-nineteenth century, these policies have been implemented in the name of various ideals: enlightened rationality, moral improvement, public health, good government, global economic competition, and planetary survival. Their impact has been generally uneven, reproducing or worsening the inequalities between groups that are stratified by race, gender, class, and sexuality. Ensuring that cities provide the most serviceable demographic profile for industry and other forms of economic profit is an underlying policy goal. From decade to decade, the needs of capital mutate, and the pressure on urban policy-makers to match those needs with the requisite workforce and consumer market segments is more and more visible. As the pace of global capitalist competition has intensified, so has the demand on city managers to produce the right population mix at the right time.

The industrial city of the nineteenth century was the crucible for the emergence of population anxiety, and the subsequent humanitarian solutions codified in urban planning. But the essential conditions for awakening that anxiety date to the supplanting of Europe's medieval "free" cities (Bruges, Florence, Lubeck, Ghent, Norwich, Venice, Bremen, Munich, York, Bordeaux, Toledo, Nottingham, Bologna, Barcelona) by the more centralized capital cities of the Baroque period, where the institutions of courtly power and trade were increasingly located on a permanent basis. The free cities were a creation of producer artisans seeking to locate themselves beyond the reach of feudal lords' rent and taxation (Pirenne 1927). Their founding, their governance through communes, and their growth through trade were declarations of independence, but their city walls, built initially for protection, would, in due time, become the bounded limits of real estate which merchant grandees and the religious orders came to dominate. Over time, the nascent capital cities of the Westphalian era of nation states supplanted the free cities in importance. These urban centers hosted the bureaucracies and mercantile houses that serviced the political, military, and economic needs of the courts, and they grew more and more monopolistic, drawing in populations in ever greater numbers (Mumford 1938).

The potential for extracting rent attracted the gentry, whose urban land-holdings became a new source of unearned increment. Profiting from the privatization of common lands (through enclosures) in the countryside, they reaped further dividends in rent from landless peasants who migrated to the cities. Evidence of urban overcrowding grew, and it was a direct result of rentiers' greed. Then as now, the rate of extraction from the poorest quarters was much higher than the profit from middle-class urban rents. The more congested the land, the higher the returns. Accordingly, the modest townhouse of the medieval city was subdivided over time, and became home to several families. The competition for urban space intensified, and overbuilding (especially through high tenement construction in cities like Edinburgh, Paris, and Berlin) was a natural outcome of land speculation in anticipation of further and greater rents. Furthermore, the demise of medieval guilds led to open labor markets, rendering the new urban working class more defenseless and precarious in the face of predatory employers and landlords.

With all of this urban growth, the notion of a "surplus" population began to circulate, though it was not strictly determined by considerations of physical space, sustainability, or even employability. The existence, in the cities and their environs, of "masterless men" (vagabonds or vagrants who were dispossessed of property, rights, or bonds to their social superiors) was a clear threat to the kind of social stability desired by elites, and this population would not be exploited as Marx's "reserve army" until the later development of industrial capitalism. A solution in the form of overseas resettlement was pursued. While it was primarily the appetite of mercantile and landed elites for accumulation which induced them to seek out foreign territories, the colonization of these lands was also perceived as an ideal destination for potentially insurgent groups. The New World colonies were an especially propitious location for absorbing peoples designated as surplus.

Each of the imperial powers of Europe invoked the Doctrine of Discovery to legitimize their seizure of land occupied by indigenous non-Christian peoples. Inspired by fifteenth-century papal bulls, the Discovery Doctrine assumed the superiority of Christian European civilization and the right of the "discovering" people to gain and exercise power and legal rights over native occupants. Even when the conquered appeared to be just as civilized (as demonstrated, for example, by the size and scope of Incan, Mayan, Zapotec, and Aztec cities) their heathen ways disqualified them, according to this doctrine. Though no northern American settlement could compete with the greatest Mesoamerican cities – Tenochtitlan, the ancient site of Mexico City, had an estimated population of 200,000 – some pre-Columbian cities, like Cahokia (located near modern East Saint Louis) may have reached a population of more than 20,000, while the irrigation complex of the Hohokam in the Salt River Valley (present day Phoenix) hosted as many as 40,000. Evidence of such dense urban centers contradicted settlers' claims that they had discovered vacant lands, and so the topic of pre-Columbian demography is a highly politicized field in the US where the Discovery Doctrine was expounded as international law in a series of Supreme Court decisions in the 1820s. Early European travelers' reports on Chinese cities marveled at their size and technical organization – Guangzhou alone had a million and half residents in 1800, more than the entire urban population of Europe combined (Frank 1988). Yet the resulting Sinophilia morphed into its opposite toward the end of the eighteenth century. Images of a China beset by economic stagnancy and spiritual sloth preceded and prepared the way for the campaign of European powers to open China's port cities to foreign domination and Christian religion (Adas 1989).

John Winthrop's 1630 exhortation to the Massachusetts Bay Colony pilgrims that they should build a "city upon a hill" set the model for Christian urbanism in the United States. His call was in keeping with a longstanding Christian equation of godliness with city living. Indeed, the revivalist promise of a new Jerusalem, attracting and increasing the faithful, pervaded the unquenchable spirit of American city-building throughout the eighteenth and nineteenth centuries (Sussman 1984). Conversely, the classification of cities as morally fallen was an invitation to revivalists to redeem their populations. In no small measure, this crusade to re-Christianize the lapsed city underpinned the reform efforts at urban improvement in the later nineteenth century.

Intolerable conditions in the Victorian industrial city were the occasion for these programs of conscience and uplift. First in Britain, and then in all the industrializing countries and their colonial centers of industry overseas, the centralizing advantages of steam power allowed owners to congregate their factory workforces in the most restrictive and congested arrangements, living atop one another in an environment befouled by soot and toxic effluvia from the factories. The lack of plumbing, sanitation, waste disposal, and open space bred pestilence, and mortality rates soared. By 1870, infant mortality on New York's Lower East Side, estimated to be the most densely populated place on the planet, was 240 for every 1,000 births. Thus was born the slum, and a vast literature sprang up to describe *How the Other Half Lives*, as Jacob Riis's 1890 photojournal famously put it. Whether in the form of government reports like Edwin Chadwick's *The Sanitary Conditions of the Labouring Population* (1842), or Henry Mayhew's contemporaneous travelogues "in the undiscovered country of the poor" (1861), or Charles Booth's later surveys of London poverty in the 1889 *Life and Labour of the People of London*, the portraits were of a living hell, and the tone was generally voyeuristic, rejoining a tradition of prurient moralism that dates to Juvenal's indictments of licentious Roman living. Alongside the paranoid fear of crowds, a persistent complaint of these commentaries was directed at the "unnatural" gender arrangements presented by the prospect of factory women, both at work and in the cramped, congregal sleeping quarters of their homes. Such conditions openly subverted the settled, middle-class picture of patriarchal family order (Wilson 1992).

Notwithstanding the offence to their morals, elites were more decisively persuaded of the need for social reform out of self-protection. Contagious diseases, after all, could not be contained within the lower orders. Nor could genteel women be fully protected from the city's intoxicating freedoms and the opportunity to succumb to debauchery and other forms of moral laxity (Walkowitz 1992). Last, but not least, there was the threat of insurgency, whether from spontaneous riots or in the form of an increasingly militant labor movement. Early efforts at reform were philanthropic, and chiefly based on beliefs in the civilizing influence of the environment. Nature, in the form of open parks, had to be brought into the city, and public space had to be created. Whether in the work of Fredrick Olmsted's Sanitary Commission, or in the emergent architectural model of the City Beautiful movement, the goal was to discipline and improve the moral character of the working poor through contact with model examples of environmental uplift (Boyer 1983). At the same time, the bourgeois suburb was born, where middle-class women would be encouraged to assert their dominion in the pastoral home, and where the patriarchal order, remote from the lures of illicit city street life, could be safeguarded.

In the laissez-faire climate of Victorian capitalism, where state intervention was generally eschewed, the demographic brunt of population control was primarily addressed by the ideology of social Darwinism. Malthus's epochal 1798 *Essay on the Principle of Population* continued to set the tone for Victorian anxiety about overpopulation, and it influenced not only Charles Darwin's theory of natural selection, but also those who translated his theory into the realm of social governance. According to the views of Herbert Spencer and other social Darwinists, all efforts to assist the poor majority were a waste of time and resources. Only the most resilient – and best equipped by nature – would subsist in the competition to survive; the rest were ill-suited to evolve any further. Yet the fear that the "less-fit" populations were "over-breeding" at a dangerous rate prompted reformers to propose more active solutions. One highly influential doctrine was the selective breeding philosophy of eugenics, conceived in the 1880s by Francis Galton, who suggested an accelerated schedule of breeding by the better born. However, putting eugenics principles into practice had to wait for laissez-faireism to be supplanted by a new paradigm of state intervention in the first decade of the twentieth century. By 1920, government reforms directed at "improving" the national gene pool through compulsory sterilization had become an established feature of progressive governance in the US, the country where eugenics had the widest appeal among elites because of fears that mass immigration was diluting the Anglo-Saxon racial stock. The closing of the immigration door in 1924 was a direct result of upper-class paranoia about what Theodore Roosevelt popularized as "race suicide."

The rise of professional urban planning was an alternative version of state responses to population anxiety. In this realm, the influence of Ebenezer Howard's concept of the Garden City can hardly be underestimated, for it is alive and well today, albeit in perverted versions, in the ethos of suburban developments all over the world. For reformers who fixated on population, the Garden City's *raison d'être* was summarized in the laconic slogan "Nothing Gained by Overcrowding," the title of a 1912 pamphlet by Raymond Unwin, its leading English practitioner. While Howard's and Unwin's passions for low-density towns in greenbelts were clear alternatives to the infernal Victorian city of industry, they were inspired by specific political beliefs; the independent anarchist commonwealth in Howard's case, and the utopian medievalism of the Arts and Crafts movement, in Unwin's case.

The Garden City concept was exported to administrators all over the British Empire, and, in the US, was embraced by the influential founders of the Regional Planning Association of America in the 1920s: Clarence Stein, Benton MacKaye, Lewis Mumford, and Henry Wright. As an exercise in public health, the general goal of the efforts to build garden cities was to decant populations away from the congested city, and to design neighborhood-based communities where sunlight, clean air, ventilation, and human-scale intercourse would facilitate biotic and civic life. As with most subsequent planning paradigms, the belief that improved design would produce "better" citizens was taken for granted, as was the benevolent paternalism of the planner experts. Without doubt, this belief runs through the entire planner lineage from Clarence Perry's "neighborhood unit" formula of 1929 through the urban renewal policies of the postwar period to the sustainable, mixed-use settlements of today's New Urbanism.

Exactly who constitutes a better citizen is a question shared both by the eugenics advocates and the expert planners. Indeed, it is difficult to avoid concluding that twentieth-century planners' efforts to move urban dwellers to a more wholesome and ordered environment were themselves a form of eugenics. Wielding new powers over land-use, such as zoning, planners now had the capacity not only to distribute population segments but also to effectively quarantine the more favored from contact with those considered undesirable. One result was to reinforce the racialization of urban space. Racial zoning was legally struck down in the US in 1917, discriminatory lending by government agencies was banned in 1948, and the 1965 Fair Housing Act barred discrimination in the sale, rental, and financing of dwellings, but local authorities, developers, banks, and homeowner associations continued to find legal and fiscal instruments with which to racially segregate the housing landscape. Armed in the war against blight first declared by Victorian reformers, the postwar advocates of urban renewal focused so much disproportionate attention on the elimination of densely populated black neighborhoods that the policies earned the sobriquet "Negro removal." Set up to analyze the urban insurgencies of the late 1960s, the Kerner Commission recommended a policy of "spatial decon-centration" for poor inner-city neighborhoods. Dispersing the population in this manner would defuse the threat of civil disorder but it also opened the way for gentrification of the central city by predominantly white professionals.

Postwar mass suburbanization was also planned as a way of defusing political threats. William Levitt, the most prominent suburban developer of the period, declared that "No man who owns his own house and lot can be a communist," because "he has too much to do." Employers, in flight from the trade union mili-tancy that had thrived in the spatial concentration of the industrial working class, were early movers to the suburbs. So, too, the spatial isolation and confinement of women to the home in the new suburbs were welcomed by defenders of traditional gender roles and justified by paeans to the more robust health of future generations.

Though the uneven consequences of urban decanting were magnified by market conditions in liberal capitalist cultures, they were directly enabled by government planning policies. In the UK, planners appealed directly to state paternalism: Patrick Abercrombie's Greater London Plan (1944), instrumental in the creation of many new towns, prescribed, quite confidently, the removal of one million inhabitants from the metropolis. In *Herrenvolk* democracies like apartheid-era South Africa, the creation of outlying black townships was an act of state policy. In communist states, urban populations were redistributed more explicitly in the name of egalitar-ian doctrine. A post-liberation plan to disperse the entire population of Shanghai, as punishment for the city's parasitical capitalist past, was averted only by the out-break of the Korean War (Tian 1996: 32). Nonetheless, the Maoist policy of "sending down" educated and skilled urbanites to underdeveloped regions began early and reached its heyday during the Cultural Revolution. To this day, population removal and redistribution is a central part of state planning as China's large cities are made over in the image of the western middle-class home-ownership. Though it is eroding, China's household registration policy (*hukou*), enacted in the 1950s to preempt rural migration to the cities, is still in force.

How did urbanist scholars respond to the mentality of population control? Pes-simistic thinkers like Oswald Spengler took the view that cities were subject to cycles of growth and decay – the bloated cities of the west were on the verge of collapse – and this sensibility fed into theories about the shrinkage and abandonment of large population centers. Early sociologists like Max Weber and George Simmel were critical of the impersonality and routine behavior fostered by city living, and believed that more holistic lifestyles, redolent of rural communities, were unlikely in this overstimulated urban environment. These German thinkers had an enormous influence on urbanists of the Chicago School such as Robert Park, Ernest Burgess, Roderick McKenzie, and Louis Wirth. Wirth's seminal "Urbanism as a way of life" (1938) diagnosed urbanization as the replacement of primary group relations (as observed by extended kin in a village community) by secondary contacts (as dem-onstrated by the voluntary associationalism of a densely populated urban environ-ment). These more superficial relationships were seen as depersonalized, segmented, transitory, and often predatory in nature. The underlying moralism of the Chicago School lay in this tendency to see people residing in great numbers as a potentially desperate condition of humanity. But their analyses of the spatial distribution of city populations leaned heavily on an evolutionary theory, derived from plant biology, about competition over land. Immigrant groups invade, succeed, and accommodate to environments in much the same way as plant species. This ecological approach dominated urbanist scholarship for several decades, and it reinforced the view that urban growth and demographic distribution were natural processes, not greatly influenced by vested social and economic interests. This belief dovetailed with the planning paradigm of pruning or thinning out density as a prudent exercise in "cultivating" the healthiest kind of population.

The 1960s saw backlashes against both the pruning practices of the planners and the evolutionism of the Chicago School. The former was crystallized in the figure of Jane Jacobs. Arguing that the decanting planners had forgotten the essential virtues of the city – the anonymity and intercourse of street life – she launched her momentous attack on both the Garden City ethos and the "tower in the park" doctrine of vertical dwelling championed by Le Corbusier. Top-down planners had practiced an "arrogant surgery" without the consent of populations, and their efforts to eliminate blight and overcrowding had only resulted, in her view, in soulless, sanitized, and empty downtown environments (Jacobs 1961). Champions of Jacobs's preference for the "creative disorder" of high-density urbanism paved the way for the repopulation of downtown centers by different class actors than those who had been displaced; artist bohemians and gays, with their unorthodox living arrangements, were the "pioneers," while more affluent and less diverse nuclear families would follow soon thereafter.

The second, more scholarly, response (though, like Jacobs, it had its roots in urban activism) took the form of Marxist-inspired critiques of the ecological approach. Proponents argued that there was nothing natural, linear, or evolutionary about urbanization. Cycles of investment and disinvestment drive the fortunes of cities, just as they shape the livelihoods of residents (Harvey 1973; Castells 1977). The organization of city space was the result of decisions about capital investment, whether in production or in land, and these investments were assisted and socialized by public policy-makers, including the planning profession. Populations that are critical to one era's mode of production – the industrial working class – may be dispensable in the next as and when more appropriate recruits – the "creative class" for example – are sought out. As massive sites of consumption, cities are also subject to population profiling to fill out the requisite market segments.

The Marxist analysis of urban space was shortly joined by an environmentalist awareness of the planetary limits to growth, and efforts at population reduction would play a prominent role in the response. Mid-century critiques of the overgrown megalopolis, like those of Lewis Mumford, rested on the assumption that cities had natural limits – beyond a certain size, they were "cancerous growths," and in that capacity actually had an anti-urban impact (Mumford 1938; Bookchin 1996). During the Cold War, they were also megadeath traps, and so urban deconcentration became part of the national security policy of all the major nuclear powers. But from the 1970s onwards, fears about the "population bomb" came to the fore of the agenda of policy-makers concerned about global environmental security. Population control programs had been initiated in many developing countries in the 1950 and 1960s – India, Pakistan, South Korea, Taiwan, and Turkey – but the various sterilization campaigns were stepped up in the 1970s under a concerted international crusade to reduce the fertility rate in "high-birth" countries. Little effort was made to conceal the coercive nature of these campaigns. The most high-handed was undertaken in India during the 1970's Emergency, when Sanjay Gandhi combined slum clearance with forced sterilization of more than 700,000 in Delhi, prompting a huge backlash at the polls (Connelly 2008: 314). China's equally controversial one-child policy has been most rigorously enforced in the cities; rural parents are allowed two tries at producing the sought-after son.

It has not always been easy to disentangle the worldwide programs of population control from the motives associated with eugenicists. In most cases, the "social others" are the ones who are charged with having too many children – the poor, minorities, immigrants, peasants. Then as now, action is provoked by scares about Euro-American birth rates falling below the replacement rate, and being inundated by populations of color. As for methods, there is no evidence that coercive policies – birth quotas, sterilization – are anywhere nearly as effective in lowering fertility rate as the more democratic factor of promoting women's access to education.

The recent phenomenon of "shrinking cities" in post-industrial Europe and North America has refueled this racially inflected genre of population anxiety. In more than half of the largest cities in the US, whites are now a minority. Conversely, intense urbanization in developing countries – with megacity populations in Mexico City, São Paolo, Mumbai, Lagos, Shanghai, Calcutta, Seoul, Jakarta, Manila, Bangkok, Tehran, Beijing, Karachi, and Cairo surpassing those in traditional metropolitan centers of the global north – has incited the same kind of eugenicist concern about overcrowding as the Victorian city once did (Davis 2006; Seabrook 1996). Solutions for bringing order to the slums and shantytowns of the global south are often prescriptions for ethnic cleansing, while quarantine zones for the affluent are built as fortified urban enclaves or as planned, and often gated, suburban communities. Supercharging these urban policies is the neo-Malthusian belief that a decent standard of living for all is simply not possible because it would pose an environmental threat to human survival on the planet. Indeed, there is a good deal of continuity between the crusade for global population control and the demand that newly industrializing countries drastically cut their carbon emissions. In response, state managers of these countries have appealed to the evolving doctrine of climate justice – each human being on Earth is entitled to the same share of carbon emissions. This new kind of right is most evident in the call for ecological reparations from northern governments and resource-extracting corporations.

In the global north, the moralistic focus of population anxiety has shifted from high-density inner cities to low-density suburban sprawl. Today's targets are the suburbanizing masses, whose auto-dependent and lawn-loving way of life is perceived as fundamentally selfish, claiming an unfair share of the world's energy budget (Duany *et al.* 2000; Bruegmann 2005). For those who can afford to be environmentally conscious, the smaller carbon footprint of compact urban residence is a growing factor in their choice of settlement. Dense cities that used to be seen as parasitical organisms, out of sync with nature, are now paragons of sustainability, carrying a much lower environmental load than the pastoral suburbs that were created as antidotes to urban ills. Indeed, statistical measures of sustainability such as the ecological footprint may soon displace traditional estimates of population density – housing units per acre or per square mile – as the standard assessment of urban living that planners and government authorities consider appropriate for the purposes of public health (Rees and Wackernagel 1994). Currently, corporate and state managers favor market models of carbon trading that allow those who are more wasteful to offset their larger footprints. If these models that foster selling the right to pollute come to prevail as a market fix for climate change, then the populations of rich countries or rich urban areas will continue to enjoy far more than their fair share of emissions at the cost of those in less affluent parts of the world.

In conclusion, the gathering political consensus about "smart growth," spear-headed by New Urbanist planning blueprints, regional mass transit schemes, and the embryonic market-based profile of a carbon-conscious era are the most recent twists in my account of the history of population and urbanism. At each stage of that history, dominant perceptions about the rectitude of population size and density have shifted, and always in a direction that suited the elite political temper of the time.

References

Adas, Michael (1989) *Machines as the Measure of Men: Science, Technology, and Ideologies of Western Dominance*. Ithaca, NY: Cornell University Press.

Bookchin, Murray (1996) *Limits of the City*. Montreal: Black Rose Books.

Booth, Charles (1889) *Life and Labour of the People of London*. London: Macmillan.

Boyer, Christine (1983) *Dreaming The Rational City: The Myth of American City Planning*. Cambridge, MA: MIT Press.

Bruegmann, Robert (2005) *Sprawl: A Compact History*. Chicago: University of Chicago Press.

Castells, Manuel (1977) *The Urban Question. A Marxist Approach*. Trans. Alan Sheridan. London: Edward Arnold. Original publication in French (1972).

Chadwick, Edwin (1965 [1842]) *The Sanitary Conditions of the Labouring Population*. Ed. M. W. Flinn. Edinburgh: Edinburgh University Press.

Connelly, Matthew (2008) *Fatal Misconception: The Struggle to Control World Population*. Cambridge, MA: Harvard University Press.

Davis, Mike (2006) *Planet of Slums*. London and New York: Verso.

Duany, Andrés, Plater-Zyberk, Elizabeth, and Speck, Jeff (2000) *Suburban Nation: The Rise of Sprawl and the Decline of the American Dream*. Berkeley, CA: North Point Press.

Frank, Andre Gunder (1988) *ReOrient: Global Economy in the Asian Age*. Berkeley: University of California Press.

Harvey, David (1973) *Social Justice and the City*. London: Edward Arnold.

Jacobs, Jane (1961) *The Death and Life of Great American Cities*. New York: Random House.

Mayhew, Henry (1861) *London Labour and the London Poor*. London: Griffin, Bohn.

Mumford, Lewis (1938) *The Culture of Cities*. New York: Harcourt, Brace.

Pirenne, Henri (1927) *Medieval Cities: Their Origins and the Revival of Trade*. Princeton, NJ: Princeton University Press.

Rees, William, and Wackernagel, Mathis (1994) *Our Ecological Footprint: Reducing Human Impact on the Earth*. Gabriola, BC: New Society.

Riis, Jacob (1890) *How the Other Half Lives: Studies among the Tenements of New York*. New York: Scribners.

Seabrook, Jeremy (1996) *Cities of the South: Scenes from a Developing World*. London and New York: Verso.

Sussman, Warren (1984) *Culture as History: The Transformation of American Society in the Twentieth Century*. New York: Random House.

Tian, Gang (1996) *Shanghai's Role in the Economic Development of China*. Westport, CT: Praeger.

Walkowitz, Judith (1992) *City of Dreadful Delight: Narratives of Sexual Danger in Late-Victorian London*. Chicago: University of Chicago Press.

Wilson, Elizabeth (1992) *The Sphinx in the City: Urban Life, the Control of Disorder and Women*. London: Virago.

Wirth, Louis (1938) Urbanism as a way of life. *American Journal of Sociology* 44 (1): 1–24.

Chapter 16

Transnationality and the City

Nina Glick Schiller

To speak of transnationality and the city is to challenge the paradigms that underlie most urban research and public policy. The term "transnationality" places cities within the synergies and tensions of the mutual construction of the local, national, and global. It also situates migrants and their transnational connectivities fully within the forces that are constitutive of "the urban." Sometimes used as a synonym for what I would call transnational social fields and others call transnationalism, the term "transnationality" can more usefully be used to signal the simultaneous social-cultural, economic, and political processes of local and cross-border participation, sociality, membership, connection, and identification. This reading of the term "transnationality" emphasizes the concept of nationality embedded yet problematized by the term. Transnationality invokes both social processes of connection and belonging (Ribeiro 1994). By theorizing transnationality and the city, this chapter contributes to the growing understanding that scholars need to situate cities and their diverse inhabitants in multiple, interpenetrating scales of relationality. These interpenetrating dimensions of connection and identification are produced and reproduced within both time and space (Amin and Graham 1997; Massey 2005; Mitchell 2003; Smith 2001).

Because migrants have been integral yet only intermittently acknowledged contributors to both the past and present of cities and their transnationalities, the relationship between migration and cities is a central theme in this chapter. Despite the fact that the study of migration and urban life has been closely linked since the emergence of the social sciences as organized disciplines of study, little work has been done about how the relationship between migrants and cities is shaped by and shapes the ways in which specific cities are constituted within transnational economic, social, cultural, and political processes. The division of labor among

The New Blackwell Companion to the City   Edited by Gary Bridge and Sophie Watson
© 2011 Blackwell Publishing Ltd

academic disciplines, which has divided the topics of cities, migration, and transnational processes into separate fields of research and theory, has mediated against
the comparative study of the transnationality of cities. In this chapter, I will first
look at past and current work in urban studies and migration to better understand
why transnationality and the city has so rarely been addressed. Next I will suggest
ways in which thinking comparatively about the relationships between migration
and cities can contribute to new understandings of both topics and the broader
subject of transnationality.

Defining Terms

The term "transnationality" is used far less often than "transnationalism," "global"
and "globalization," "diaspora," and "translocality," all of which, from the 1990s,
became prominent in the academic literature, although the meanings of these terms
is often conflated. The terminological confusion has been amplified by the fact that
scholars have used the terms "globalization" and "transnationalism" both to signal
the changing nature of the social world and as new analytical paradigms with which
to conceptualize social processes (Mittelman 1996; Beck and Sznaider 2006; Glick
Schiller 1999). After some intense debate and much confusion, most analysts have
agreed that there have been significant changes around the world in how life is
organized and experienced and that these changes have made new paradigms prominent. The new paradigms in turn shape how scholars think about the extent and
nature of current social transformations and their similarity and differences to past
historical conjunctures.

Currently, most analysts of cross-border processes, whatever terms they favor,
make the following points:

1   There are economic and cultural processes that bind localities, regions, and
    nation states around the world together and human mobilities have always been
    part of these processes.
2   These processes are not new but also do not proceed at a constant pace – there
    are ebbs and flows in this global intertwining and interpenetration.
3   During the recent interpenetration of geographic scales, nation states have not
    lost their significance but processes of governance have been restructured.
4   Governance has recently been reorganized within and across states so that the
    legal, financial, and military institutions of Europe and North America have
    become explicitly global, serving corporate and financial interests around the
    world and reducing even the semblance of sovereignty within many less powerful
    states.
5   The recent period has been shaped by the restructuring of processes of accumu-
    lation and rapid movement of capital and related but increasingly restricted
    movements of people.
6   The recent restructuring of capital has taken place with a specific rationale and
    logic that justify the reorganization of governance, economic and cultural pro-
    duction, distribution and consumption, and the constitution of self.
7   This project of transformation and legitimation has generated various forms of
    contestation, many of them centered on the city.

For the purpose of the argument I am making here about transnationality and cities, the term "transnationality" indicates cross-border connective processes that are both social and identificational, while the term "transnational" indicates the specific relationalities. These relationalities constitute networks that connect individuals or groups of people located in several specific nation states. Those who engage in a set of such relations constitute a transnational social field defined as a network of networks of unequal power that link individuals to one or more institutions that organize and regulate the daily economic, political, cultural, social, and religious activities of social life. In using the word social field, I build on the seminal work on social networks and fields done by the urban anthropologists of the Manchester School (Epstein 1967; Mitchell 1969). The utility of the concept of transnational social field is that researchers can study various social processes that contribute to place-making practices, identities, representations, and imaginaries without drawing a sharp binary between natives and foreigners.

People who have migrated are often central actors in building transnational social fields but some people who migrate and many people who have a family history of migration do not belong to transnational social fields. On the other hand, people who have no such personal or family history and are considered "natives" of a state often are part of transnational social fields. They enter these fields either through their relationships with people of migrant background who do participate in connections across borders or by establishing ongoing relationships based on various forms of communication and travel that cross borders.

None of these forms of relationality is new or dependent on recent technologies of communication. Regular connections including exchanges of documents and goods across different political regimes preceded the modern nation state; the social fields established through such relationship were made "transnational" with the advent of modern nation states and their border regimes. There have been ebbs and flows in the degree of social connections across the boundaries of states since the rise of states five millennia ago. Within this context, it is useful to use the term "globalization" to indicate the more recent situation of intensified penetration in which both the historic forms of networked connections intensify and transnationality, the processes of communication, commodification, identification, and shared affect, penetrate into all states (Eitzen and Zinn 2006).

Transnationality and Urban Studies

The initial social science of the city, such as that developed by members of the Chicago School of Sociology, often linked the nature of cities to their mix of diverse streams of people and ideas. From this perspective, processes of migrant incorporation were integral to urban life. Moreover, the founding generation of urban researchers noted that not only were industrial cities built by immigrants but also that these migrants tended to live across borders (Park and Miller 1921; Thomas and Znaniecki 1958 [1909]). Hence, research on migrant transnationality is as old as modern urban studies.

However, this classic scholarship of the city generally failed to address the broader historical transnational social processes that have given rise to urban life since the emergence of cities. Instead the past was placed in the realm of static tradition in contrast to the mobility and diversity of modernity. The imposition of this binary opposition precluded adequate theories of the transnationality of the city. Left unaddressed was the archeological and historical record, which documents that the rise of cities and their specific histories is a story of urban places serving as the crossroads of long-distance trade routes that linked together states and empires (Wolf 1982). Merchants and traders established transnational kinship, religious, and ethnic connectivities as they traveled and settled in response to ruling classes' demands for scarce and precious goods – indigo, frankincense, spices, silk, salt, and slaves – with which to validate their superior status.

Neither this global urban history nor those social theorists who recognized relationship between mobilities and urbanity adequately explored the varying ways in which cities were shaped within transnational processes including migration. Instead, theorization of urban life reflected the binary contrast of western social theory between traditional and modern, which was read through a technological division between the "pre-industrial" and "industrial cities" (Sjoberg 1960). Migrants were pictured as part of the urban industrial workforce but not theorized as constitutive of transnational processes within which cities are situated. Alternative efforts to theorize cities did little to address this problem. Neither Lefebvre's (2003 [1970]) theorization of urban space as generative of social transformation nor Castells's (1977) critique of this position, which emphasized capitalist development, left room for the transnationality of cities and transnational social fields. Similarly, although the urban scholars of the 1970s and 1980s, who spoke of the "postindustrial" city, the "post-Fordist/postmodern metropolis," and the "capitalist city," acknowledged globe-spanning economic or cultural processes, they did not adequately theorize transnational processes as constitutive of cities and paid little attention to migration (Scott and Soja 1996: viii; Smith and Feagin 1987; Waldinger and Bozorgmehr 1996: 4, 14).

This continuing analytic tradition was ruptured by the emergence of a global or world cities literature that reintroduced migrants as significant contributors to the life of certain cities and placed the urban within transnational processes and connections (Friedmann 1986; King 1991; Sassen 1991). However, global cities research and related work in cultural studies that specifically speaks of the transnationality of cities initially assumed that only a small set of cities was situated within transnational processes (Holston and Appadurai 1996). All other cities were confined within national terrains.

Subsequently, a new perspective on the spatialized restructuring of capitalist accumulation developed that critiqued but built upon the insights of the global cities literature (Brenner 1998; England and Ward 2007; Harvey 2006; Smith 1995). Examining the neoliberal restructuring of cities, these researchers argued that increasingly all cities and states were being rescaled in relationship to new forms of capital accumulation. They used the term "neoliberalism" for an agenda of "reforms" that, while instituted differently in different states and localities, legitimated certain kinds of restructuring in diverse places (Brenner and Theodore 2002). This restructuring included the privatization of formerly public resources, spaces, and forms of governance, the reduction of state efforts to equalize regional inequalities through public investments, and the reliance on increasingly precarious conditions of labor including short-term contracts and migrant labor with few or any rights. Urban scholars of neoliberalism emphasized that cities around the world increasingly competed for flows of international capital. They used the terms "scale," "rescaling," and "jumping scale," not for nested territorial geographies but to speak of interpenetrating relational processes within hierarchies of globe spanning power (Brenner 1998; Smith 1995; Swyngedouw 1997).

However crucial aspects of urban life including the agency of migrants and the role of contestatory social movements in urban transformations were neglected. The descriptions of urban restructuring often failed to highlight the way contradictions within the neoliberal restructuring of self and social relationality can produce aspirations for social justice and new social visions. As a result, some scholars of urban processes have rejected the global perspective on cities and their transnationalities offered by the literature on urban rescaling (Marston et al. 2005). Efforts to compare cities in terms of their economic, political, or cultural power are dismissed as colonialist European narratives that deny the vitality and viability of the cities of Africa and Asia. Instead, a recent urban scholarship, especially in geography, speaks of ordinary cities, "spatialities" linked by networks and transnational urbanism as a metaphor for cross-border connectivities (Leitner et al. 2007; Smith 2001; Robinson 2006). From this perspective, each city is unique with its own history and forms of sociality and comparison is ultimately not possible or desirable.

Arguing against this "flattened ontology" and in defense of concepts of scale and rescaling, Hoefle (2006) notes that ultimately such a perspective normalizes, naturalizes, and privileges the local. Researchers are left without an analytical lens with which to study the multiple ways in which the local and global are mutually constituting. Despite its intentions, the new localism, which can only approach the transnationality of the city in its local manifestations and struggles, is ultimately disempowering. Without a global perspective, it is difficult to build social movements across time and space.

Yet clearly place and time need to be theorized within discussions of the transnationality of cities. Researchers not only need to constantly situate their theorization of urban life in place and time but also develop a comparative analysis of cities. Inhabitants of specific cities must be understood not only to be constantly repositioning their city within fields of power that are transnational in their scope but also to be actors who are shaped by and shape the variations of transnationality produced within such repositioning.

This dialectic of place is not unique to cities. However, cities are good places to study these transnational processes and their outcomes comparatively. From a transnationality of cities perspective, cities serve not as bounded units of analysis but as analytical entry points from which to examine transnational processes. This is because cities usually are territorially based administrative units, and as such have various powers – regulatory, policing, taxation, and representational. These powers contribute to a commonality of experience that is generative of identity and loyalty. Analyzing cities through a comparative and global lens defines migrants and people of migrant background who live in a city as local actors rather than within binaries of native/foreign or citizen/outsider or legal/illegal. People of migrant background live within configurations of wealth, power, education, family, and forms of cosmopolitan sociabilities that are part and parcel of the varying transnationality of cities.

Migration and Urban Transnationalities

Migration scholars also have been hindered by the inability to examine the relationship between migrants' transnational social fields and their relationship to specific cities and ongoing urban transformations. One might expect that since migration is about movement across space, the transnationality of cities would be obvious within migration studies. This has not been the case. There is a vast scholarship of migration that describes the ways in which migrants live *in* cities. Increasingly this work has examined the social relations and identities that migrants maintain and construct as they live across borders and "simultaneously" settle into a new life and become reterritorialized (Levitt and Glick Schiller 2004). However, there has been too little comparative work done to examine the migrants' *varying relationships to* the positioning of cities. This is because migration scholars have been hindered by their methodological nationalism and ethnic lens (Glick Schiller and Çağlar 2009).

Methodological nationalism is an intellectual orientation "that approaches the study of social and historical processes as if they were contained within the borders of individual nation states" (Glick Schiller 2009a: 17; see also Beck 2000; Smith 1983; Wimmer and Glick Schiller 2002). The term "ethnic lens" refers to the propensity of migration researchers to rely on ethnic boundaries to define the unit of study and analysis for the study of immigrant settlement and transnational connection (Glick Schiller *et al.* 2006).

As a result of methodological nationalism and the ethnic lens, researchers often approach the terrain of the nation state as a single homogeneous national culture, while defining a migrant population as a community of culture, interest, and identity. This mode of study and analysis sets aside acknowledged internal regional and cultural differences within each nation state and ignores differences within national and ethnic populations along the lines of region, class, region of origin, gender, sexual orientation, identity, and linguistic, religious, and political differentiation.

Members of a migrating population settling in a specific neighborhood that is identified as an ethnic enclave and spoken of as a community stand in for the totality of the ways in which migrants and people of migrant background live not only in that city but in an entire country. In addition, the transnationality of an "ethnic group" is reduced to ties to and identification with a homeland. Sometimes it is the researcher herself who makes these discursive moves; in other cases the specificity of the local data is lost within more general discussions about parallel lives, ghettoization, cultural values, religious moralities, racism, or different national immigration policies and integrative strategies. Much is lost from this perspective including the multiple forms of sociability that migrants may have that connect them to persons locally, nationally, and transnationally but are not bound by shared ancestral identity. Also precluded are analyses of migrants' agency as it reshapes and is shaped by the transnational processes that construct neighborhood and urban life.

By homogenizing national and ethnic categories and using the national border as the boundary of social relationships, scholars and policy-makers make the native/foreign divide the primary area of concern in discussions of public policy and social cohesion. Those social theorists and public intellectuals who decry the pernicious political and moral effects of this binary differentiation have offered too few alternatives (Agamben 1998; Delgado Wise 2006). A theorization of transnationality and the city may not only contribute new perspectives on the constitution of urban life and local public policy but also offer broader horizons for social movements built around the right to the city.

Recently, in an effort to address urban variation, migration scholars who have done ethnographic work in specific cities have begun to write about the city as context (Brettell 2003; British Council n.d.). This approach resonates with seminal work that highlights the role of differential urban opportunity structures in fostering a variety of migrant pathways of incorporation (Collins 1980; Garbaye 2005; Rath and Kloosterman 2000; Ray 2003; Waldinger 1986). There have also been increasing numbers of studies that highlight migrant incorporations and transnational connectivities in a variety of cities (Çağlar 2006; Çağlar 2007; Itzigsohn and Saucedo 2002; Smith and Eade 2008). However, passing reference to contexts is insufficient. The challenge at hand is one of "variation finding," a method that would compare cities in terms of their positionality and transnationality in relationship to regional, national, and global hierarchies of power (Tilly 1984: 83).

A Comparative Perspective of the Varying Transnationality of Cities

To move beyond an acknowledgment of context and toward the comparative study of the transnationality of cities, I sketch an approach to the relationship between migrants' transnational social fields and the relative positionality of cities. The comparative material I briefly present develops the concept of the relative positionality and rescaling of cities and demonstrates the utility of this approach. Much of the current research on migrant settlement and transnational fields in specific cities can be rethought from this vantage point. Of particular use is the work on cities that are not global centers of power. Such work illuminates what is in fact specific to cities that have been dubbed global or world cities and how other cities have different forms of transnationality. Migrants contribute to, settle, and build transnational social fields within this range of contingencies, possibilities, and limitations.

Manchester, England, and the US metroplex of Dallas–Fort Worth are two upscaling cities where migrant transnationalities are contributing to efforts to reposition the city. After experiencing radical restructuring, the Manchester leadership chose to redevelop their city as a vibrant cosmopolitan center that could attract hi-tech workers into a youthful urban chic life style (Young *et al.* 2006). If they have any place in this aesthetic, migrants are reduced to providing the multicultural color that is envisioned as contributing to cosmopolitan consumption. However, migrant transnational networks and business interests produce more than multicultural sites and colorful neighborhoods. Transnational social fields built by people of migrant background have been playing a significant role and one not unacknowledged by Manchester developers.

An event in 2007 illustrated the significant relationship between migrants and the transnationality of Manchester. A private Pakistani airline, Airblue, initiated flights to Manchester Airport from Islamabad. As reported in Pakistan (*Pakistan Times* 2007), Airblue executives chose to make the Manchester–Islamabad route their first direct connection between Pakistan and the UK because of the large population in the Manchester area who originated from Mirpur, Pakistan, and continue to maintain dense family, economic, and cultural networks with this region. However the new air route was also of interest to travel agents, airport officials, and business and travel entrepreneurs in both cities. And it was welcomed by city leaders in Manchester who understand that their efforts to improve the competitive position of Manchester are linked to the success of its international airport, a development initiative threatened by cut-backs in the airline business. It is important to note that Manchester urban developers and political leaders found they needed the Pakistani migrants' transnational connections, at the same time that national authorities were defining these links as threatening to national security.

The efforts of corporate leaderships in the metroplex of Dallas–Fort Worth to welcome and utilize transnational ethnic networks of a highly skilled Indian work-force offer a parallel case of the synergies between migrant and urban transnationality and local urban transformation in an upscaling city (Brettell 2011). In the case of Dallas–Fort Worth, computer and electronic corporations have looked to Indian transnational organizations to recruit hi-tech professionals who otherwise would have chosen to settle in a more globally prominent city. Such recruitment contributes to the repositioning of the city and the success of its corporations within a highly competitive global industry. This corporate support of Indian organizations has encouraged them to invest in institutions of higher education in India, shaping the uneven terrain of development there. Caroline Brettell's (2011) insights into the specific instances of mutuality between a city's rescaling efforts and migrant path-ways of incorporation and transnational connection allow researchers to build a comparative analysis of urban transnationality. She demonstrates that an ethnic pathway of incorporation, which is the primary focus of migration scholarship, may be an outcome of the past and contemporary scalar positioning of particular cities.

This perspective is reinforced by comparative data from Philadelphia, Pennsylvania. Although south Asian professionals have been crucial actors in the restructuring of Philadelphia, ethnic organizations have not been a salient aspect of the local incorporation of the educated migrants who are a significant component of the staff and students of the University of Pennsylvania and its associated medical institutions (Goode 2011). Instead, in a city that has lost its prominent position, attracted much less financial capital than Dallas–Fort Worth, and achieved less global branding than Manchester, urban developers represent foreign professionals as a form of capital – in this case cultural capital. They are welcomed to the city not only as potential residents with ready cash but also as the cosmopolitan "creative class" that are key to the development of the "med-ed" complex on which the city leadership has pinned its hopes.

The examples from Dallas–Fort Worth, Manchester, UK, and Philadelphia, of the importance of people of migrant background to the efforts to redevelop and rescale non-"global" cities – sometimes acknowledged and sometimes not – also provide insights into opportunity structures and disparities that arise as a result of the development of hi-tech or knowledge industries. Working-class migrants may respond to increased employment in service industries, construction, and small businesses, providing the labor that makes urban redevelopment possible. At the same time, the efforts to create globe-spanning urban redevelopment, with costs differentially born by already impoverished residents, can create or intensify urban divides, inequalities, and tensions.

The repositioning struggles of a city also may shape whether different classes of migrants find their transnational ties encouraged or undermined, and whether forms of simultaneous local incorporation and transnational connection can find local support. At the same time, the subjective assessment that migrants make of the welcome they receive and the opportunities afforded within different cities and urban neighborhoods that become transnationally connected "hot spots" may influence the degree to which they settle and provide flows of capital and labor that are needed for cities to obtain or maintain competitive success (Van Dijk 2011). Monika Salzbrunn (2011) notes that the leadership of Senegalese Murids preferred New York City to Paris. New York offers a much wider scope for ethnic politics and recognition, as part of the city's historic transnationality. Subsequently, Murid investments in Harlem contributed to the city's efforts to maintain global predominance through cycles of neighborhood restructuring followed by gentrification.

Downscaled cities offer very different terrains of settlement and transnational connection than more successful cities. Manchester, New Hampshire, in the New England region of the United States, and Halle/Saale in eastern Germany provide two such examples (Glick Schiller *et al.* 2006; Glick Schiller and Çağlar 2011; Glick Schiller 2009b). Both were formerly industrial centers, their transnationality shaped by their circuits of production and distribution. Manchester, NH, lost its world-scale textile industries in the 1930s and Halle found its petrochemical industries dramatically reduced after German reunification in 1989. In this situation few migrants arrived and even fewer stayed; both cities counted only 4 percent of their population as foreign-born non-citizens in 2005.

Despite restructuring and rebranding efforts, and a certain degree of redevelopment of the city centers, both Manchester, NH, and Halle have been unable to improve their position nationally or globally and have remained dramatically downscaled cities. There were few local public or corporate resources to support migrant ethnic or transnational organizations. Migrants in both cities did respond to investment in the city centers by initiating a disproportionate number of the small businesses located there. However, the city center redevelopment did not fuel the influx of capital or technical talent necessary for "new economy" industries in either city. The international capital that did invest in these cities did not provide many opportunities for social mobility for the city's residents. Halle attracted a call center and multinational corporations owned small assembly plants offering non-unionized low-wage employment in the Manchester area.

Some residents, migrant and native alike, hoping to broaden their economic and social perspectives, sought networks within activities such as religious or sports organizations, often organized non-ethnically. In both cites, Nigerian pastors built religious networks that engaged both migrants and persons without migrant backgrounds in religious practices and Christian identities that were simultaneously local, national, and transnational.

Conclusion

Scholars need to do more than acknowledge the past and present transnationality of cities. A comparative analytical framework is needed that can highlight the varying ways in which the transnationality of cities is constituted and experienced. Such an approach to cities will allow both researchers and policy-makers to set aside the migrant/foreign divide and see migrants as actors contributing to and reshaping their urban environments and the transnational processes which constitute cities. In this scholarship of the relationship between cities and migration, a concept of the relative and changing positionality of cities is useful. This concept depicts residents of cities as engaged in rescaling processes that place cities within the simultaneous and ongoing construction of local, national, regional, and global scales.

The short sketches I have presented of the restructuring and rescaling projects of various cities indicate several different ways in which migrants are active agents in the neoliberal transformation of cites and their current transnationality. Migrants are integral parts of the labor force upon which the cities build their competitiveness, contribute to the comparative reassessment of the desirability of various cities and neighborhoods, and serve as agents of urban development that may lead to gentrification. They are actors within networks that provide various economic and social opportunities and disparities to urban residents. In addition, migrants in the past and present have linked residents of cities to alternative social visions, religious, political, and moral. The differing positionality of cities indicates that the degree and kinds of the transnationality of migrants and of cities is integrally part of the same process and must be analyzed together.

Migrants enter into urban life in different ways and have a differential impact in the restructuring trajectories of cities, depending on the city's scalar positioning. The urban developers, and corporate and political leaders of upscaling cities may find that the transnationalities of migrants of various classes are crucial components of their efforts to reposition their city within global fields of power. Cities that are downscaled are often unable to provide public or corporate support for ethnically based community organizations. Nor do they provide the opportunities for economic mobility for migrants or support for a strata of migrant professionals, who are usually the key actors in local ethnic politics and successful diasporic organizations found in "global cities" such as New York or London.

I close by noting that there is a politics to the approach to transnationality of cities offered here. Increasingly, there has been an effort to turn both highly skilled and unskilled workers into a contractual workforce who have few rights and protections and are seen as outside the body politic of the state to which they contribute their talents and labor. Although they are integrally part of cities, the nation states in which migrants work increasingly deny new arrivals the right to settle permanently, offering them at best only temporary legal status. Circular labor and remittances migrants send to "homelands" are celebrated while migrants' contributions to the transnationality of cities in which they are laboring is denied (World Bank 2006; Portes 2007).

In this conjuncture, cities can provide base areas for broader struggles not only for migrants' rights but also against all forms of social and economic inequalities. Increasingly city leaderships where migrants play central roles in urban restructuring and competitiveness see that their cities have different interests than those articulated in national agendas of anti-immigrant legislation. Through policies and narratives local urban leaderships acknowledge that migrants have rights in a city, whatever their official legal status. At the same time, in ways that vary with the positionalities of the city, people of migrant background and natives are able to join in common struggles, aspirations, and forms of conviviality and subaltern cosmopolitanism (Gilroy 2004; Salzbrunn 2011; Jeffrey and McFarlane 2008; Mitchell 2007). If the transnationality of cities is acknowledged, then demands for the "right to the city" by those being swept aside by urban restructuring can contribute to global struggles for social justice. These struggles will be both site-specific and able to critique a world of global disparities of wealth and power. Solidarities and alliances can be built that are simultaneously spatial and global.

References

Agamben, G. (1998) *Homo Sacer: Sovereign Power and Bare Life*. Trans. D. Heller-Roazen. Stanford: Stanford University Press.

Amin, A., and Graham, S. (1997) The ordinary city. *Transactions of the Institute of British Geographers* 22 (4): 411–29.

Beck, U. (2000) The cosmopolitan perspective: sociology of the second age of modernity. *British Journal of Sociology* 51 (1): 79–105.

Beck, U., and Sznaider, N. (2006) Unpacking cosmopolitanism for the social sciences: a research agenda. *British Journal of Sociology* 57 (1): 1–23.

Brenner, N. (1998) Beyond state-centrism? Space, territoriality and geographical scale in globalization studies. *Theory and Society* 28 (1): 39–78.

Brenner, N., and Theodore, N. (2002) Cities and the geographies of actually existing neoliberalism. In *Spaces of Neoliberalism: Urban Restructuring in North America and Western Europe*, ed. N. Brenner and N. Theodore. Oxford: Blackwell, 2–32.

Brettell, C. (2003) Bringing the city back: cities as contexts for immigrant incorporation. In *American Arrivals: Anthropology Engages the New Immigration*, ed. N. Foner. Santa Fe: School of American Research Press, 163–95.

Brettell, C. (2011) Scalar positioning and immigrant organizations: Asian Indians and the dynamics of place. In *Locating Migration: Rescaling Cities and Migrants*, ed. N. Glick Schiller and A. Çağlar. Ithaca, NY: Cornell University Press, 85–103.

British Council (n.d.) Migrant cites: a tale of eight cities. Available online at www.britishcouncil.org/fa/livingtogether-projects-working-across-borders-multilateral-projects-migrant-cities.htm (accessed October 2009).

Çağlar, A. (2006) Hometown associations, the rescaling of state spatiality and migrant grassroots transnationalism. *Global Networks* 6 (1): 1–22.

Çağlar, A. (2007) Rescaling cities, cultural diversity and transnationalism: migrants of Mardin and Essen. *Ethnic and Racial Studies* 30 (6):1070–95.

Castells, M. (1977) *The Urban Question*. Cambridge, MA: MIT Press.

Collins, T. W. (ed.) (1980) *Cities in a Larger Context*. Athens: University of Georgia Press.

Delgado Wise, R. (2006) Migration and imperialism: the Mexican workforce in the context of NAFTA. *Latin American Perspectives* 33 (2): 33–45.

Eitzen, D. S., and Zinn, M. B. (2006) Globalization: an introduction. In *Globalization: The Transformation of Social Worlds*, ed. D. S. Eitzen and M. B. Zinn. Belmont, CA: Thompson Wadsworth, 1–11.

England, K., and Ward, K. (eds.) (2007) *Neoliberalization: States, Networks, People*. Oxford: Blackwell.

Epstein, A. L. (ed.) (1967) *The Craft of Social Anthropology*. London: Tavistock.

Friedmann, J. (1986) The world city hypothesis. *Development and Change* 17 (1): 69–84.

Garbaye, R. (2005) *Getting into Local Power*. Oxford: Blackwell.

Gilroy, P. (2004) *After Empire: Melancholia or Convivial Culture?* London: Routledge.

Glick Schiller, N. (1999) Transmigrants and nation states: something old and something new in the US immigrant experience. In *The Handbook of International Migration: The American Experience*, ed. C. Hirshman, P. Kasinitz, and J. DeWind. New York: Russell Sage Foundation, 94–119.

Glick Schiller, N. (2009a) A global perspective on migration and development. *Social Analysis* 53 (3): 14–37.

Glick Schiller, N. (2009b) "There is no power except for God": locality, global Christianity, and immigrant transnational incorporation. In *Permutations of Order*, ed. B. Turner and T. Kirsch. Farnham, UK: Ashgate Press, 125–47.

Glick Schiller, N., and Çağlar, A. (2009) Towards a comparative theory of locality in migration studies: migrant incorporation and city scale. *Journal of Ethnic and Migration Studies* 35 (2): 177–202.

Glick Schiller, N., and Çağlar, A. (2011) Down-scaled cities and migrant pathways: locality and agency without an ethnic lens. In *Locating Migration: Rescaling Cities and Migrants*, ed. N. Glick Schiller and A. Çağlar. Ithaca, NY: Cornell University Press, 190–202.

Glick Schiller, N., Çağlar, A., and Guldbrandsen, T. (2006) Beyond the ethnic lens: Locality, globality, and born-again incorporation. *American Ethnologist* 33 (4): 612–33.

Goode, J. (2011) The campaign for new immigrants in Philadelphia: imagining possibilities and confronting realities. In *Locating Migration: Rescaling Cities and Migrants*, ed. N. Glick Schiller and A. Çağlar. Ithaca, NY: Cornell University Press, 143–65.

Harvey, D. (2006) *Spaces of Global Capitalism: Towards a Theory of Uneven Geographical Development*. London: Verso.

Hoefle, S. W. (2006) Eliminating scale and killing the goose that laid the golden egg? *Transactions of the Institute of British Geographers* 31 (2): 238–43.

Holston, J., and Appadurai, A. (1996) Cities and citizenship. *Public Culture* 8 (2): 187–204.

Itzigsohn, J., and Saucedo, S. G. (2002) Immigrant incorporation and sociocultural transnationalism. *International Migration Review* 36 (3): 766–99.

Jeffrey, C., and McFarlane, C. (2008) Performing cosmopolitanism. *Environment and Planning D: Society and Space* 26 (3): 420–7.

King, A. (ed.) (1991) *Global Cities: Post-imperialism and the Internationalization of London*. London: Routledge.

Lefebvre, H. (2003 [1970]). *The Urban Revolution*. Trans. N. Smith. Minneapolis: University of Minnesota Press.

Leitner, H., Sheppard, E. S., Sziarto, K., and Maringanti, A. (2007) Contesting urban futures: decentering neoliberalism. In *Contesting Neoliberalism: Urban Frontiers*, ed. H. Leitner, J. Peck, and E. Shepperd. New York: Guilford, 1–25.

Levitt, P., and Glick Schiller, N. (2004) Transnational perspectives on migration: conceptualizing simultaneity. *International Migration Review* 38 (3):1002–39.

Marston, S. A., Jones III, J. P., and Woodward, K. (2005) Human geography without scale. *Transactions of the Institute of British Geographers* 30 (4): 416–32.

Massey, D. (2005) *For Space*. Los Angeles: Sage.

Mitchell, J. C. (1969) *Social Networks in Urban Situations, Analyses of Personal Relationships in Central African Towns*. Manchester: Manchester University Press.

Mitchell, K. (2003) *Crossing the Neoliberal Line: Pacific Rim Migration and the Metropolis*. Philadelphia, PA: Temple University Press.

Mitchell, K. (2007) Geographies of identity: the intimate cosmopolitan. *Progress in Human Geography* 31 (5): 706–20.

Mittelman, J. (ed.) (1996) *Globalization: Critical Reflections*. Boulder, CO: Lynne Rienner.

Pakistan Times (2007) AirBlue flights to build Pakistan, UK stronger bonds. Available online at http://pakistantimes.net/2007/05/31/business1.htm (accessed April 2008).

Park, R., and Miller, H. A. (1921) *Old World Traits Transplanted*. New York: Harper.

Portes, A. (2007) Migration, development, and segmented assimilation: a conceptual review of the evidence. *Annals of the American Academy of Political and Social Sciences* Quick Read Synopsis 610: 270–2. Available online at http://ann.sagepub.com/cgi/reprint/610/1/266.pdf (accessed October 2009).

Rath, J., and Kloosterman, R. (2000) Outsiders' business: a critical review of research on immigrant entrepreneurship. *International Migration Review* 34 (3): 657–81.

Ray, B. (2003) The role of cities in immigrant integration. Migration Information Source. Available online at www.migrationinformation.org/feature/display.cfm?ID=167 (accessed July 27, 2007).

Ribeiro, G. L. (1994) The condition of transnationality. Paper delivered at American Anthropological Association Meetings, Atlanta, December 1.

Robinson, J. (2006) *Ordinary Cities: Between Modernity and Development*. New York: Routledge.

Sassen, S. (1991) *The Global City: New York, London, Tokyo*. Princeton, NJ: Princeton University Press.

Salzbrunn, M. (2011) Rescaling processes in two "global"cities: festive events as pathways of migrant incorporation. In *Locating Migration: Rescaling Cities and Migrants*, ed. N. Glick Schiller and A. Çağlar. Ithaca, NY: Cornell University Press, 166.

Scott, A. J., and Soja, E. (1996) *The City: Los Angeles and Urban Theory at the End of the Twentieth Century*. Berkeley: University of California Press.

Sjoberg, G. (1960) *The Preindustrial City, Past and Present*. Glencoe, IL: Free Press.

Smith, A. (1983) Nationalism and social theory. *British Journal of Sociology* 34: 19–38.

Smith, M. P. (2001) *Transnational Urbanism: Locating Globalization*. Oxford: Blackwell.

Smith, M. P., and Eade, J. (2008) *Transnational Ties: Cities, Migrations and Identities*. New Brunswick, NJ: Transaction Publishers.

Smith, M. P., and Feagin, J. (1987) *The Capitalist City: Global Restructuring and Community Politics*. Oxford: Basil Blackwell.

Smith, N. (1995) Remaking scale: competition and cooperation in pre-national and post-national Europe. In *Competitive European Peripheries*, ed. H. Eskelinen and S. Folke. Berlin: Springer Verlag, 59–74.

Swyngedouw, E. (1997) Neither global nor local: "glocalization" and the politics of scale. In *Spaces of Globalization*, ed. K. R. Cox. New York: Guilford Press, 137–66.

Tilly, C. (1984) *Big Structures, Large Processes, Huge Comparisons*. New York: Russell Sage Foundation.

Thomas, W. I., and Znaniecki, F. (1958 [1909]) *The Polish Peasant in Europe and America*. New York: Dover Publishing.

Van Dijk, R. (2011) Cities and linking hot spots: subjective rescaling, Ghanaian migration and the fragmentation of urban spaces. In *Locating Migration: Rescaling Cities and Migrants*, ed. N. Glick Schiller and A. Çağlar. Ithaca, NY: Cornell University Press, 104–22.

Waldinger, R. (1986) *Through the Eye of a Needle. Immigrants and Enterprise in New York's Garment Trade*. New York: City University Press.

Waldinger, R., and Bozorgmehr, M. (1996) The making of a multicultural metropolis. In *Ethnic Los Angeles*, ed. R. Waldinger and M. Bozorgmehr. New York: Russell Sage Foundation, 3–28.

Wimmer, A., and Glick Schiller, N. (2002) Methodological nationalism and beyond: nation state building, migration and the social sciences. *Global Networks* 2 (4): 301–44.

Wolf, E. (1982) *Europe and the People Without History*. Berkeley: University of California Press.

World Bank (2006) *Global Economic Prospects: Economic Implications of Remittances and Migration*. Washington, DC: World Bank. Available online at www-wds.worldbank. org/servlet/WDSContentServer/WDSP/IB/2005/11/14/000112742_20051114174928/ Rendered/PDF/343200GEP02006.pdf (accessed July 2009).

Young, C., Diap, M., and Drabble, S. (2006) Living with difference? The "cosmopolitan city" and urban reimagining in Manchester, UK. *Urban Studies* 43 (10): 1687–714.

Chapter 17

Migrants Making Technology Markets

Tyler Rooker

Introduction

Moving, floating peasant-workers, arriving, leaving, entering, and working – temporary and marginal. The image of migrants in China's cities is of a population of people in the process of motion between two places, the urban and the rural, uprooted (see Table 17.1). Migration in China is in some senses a new phenomenon: the urban population, including that in cities, prefectures, county-level cities, and towns was tightly controlled between 1960 and 1980, while rural villages and townships were left on their own as self-sufficient collectives expected to subsidize the project of urban industrialization. But in other senses the transition of China from a rural country to one dominated by massive cities of accumulation has been in process for hundreds of years, originating even before Western powers occupied and dictated trade from what would become centers of power in treaty ports. While a hexagonal pattern of marketing systems, creating distinct macro-regions, and a divergence between social-economic and administrative hierarchies of places continues to play an influence (Skinner 1964–5; Skinner 1977), the overall urbanization of China has eroded the salience of this model, mostly through migration and technological dissemination.

In this chapter, I extend the understanding of migration in China by examining the history of urban institutions and forms, emergent information markets, and population changes. First, I provide a genealogy of migration in China, as well as some estimates of their numbers including origins and destinations. Then I briefly review two emergent urban forms that are shaped by migration: Zhejiangcun, a "village" of migrants, mostly from rural Wenzhou, Zhejiang Province, established in Beijing during the late 1980s and 1990s; and *chengzhongcun*, or "villages amidst

The New Blackwell Companion to the City   Edited by Gary Bridge and Sophie Watson
© 2011 Blackwell Publishing Ltd

Table 17.1 Chinese terms for migrants

迁移人口	*qianyi renkou*	moving population
流动人口	*liudong renkou*	floating population
农民工	*nongmingong*	peasant workers
外来人口	*wailai renkou*	population arriving [in the city] from outside
外出务工者/员	*waichu wugongzhe/yuan*	people leaving [the village] to work for others
进城务工者/员	*jincheng wugongzhe/yuan*	people entering the city to work for others
打工妹/仔	*dagongmei/zai*	working girls/boys
暂住人口	*zanzhu renkou*	temporary population
边缘人	*bianyuan ren*	marginal figure

the city," usually rural villages that have been enclosed by city growth that now serve as residential and employment centers for migrants. As illustrated by this discussion, one could easily conclude that China's migrants remain tenuous and precarious parts of the city. I conclude, however, with research results on a new urban form in China, arising at the intersection of information technology, market reform, and migration – the "electronics city" (*dianzi cheng*, also known as "computer city") – an institution ubiquitous in China's cities. Migrants here flow through networks and cluster according to hometown and kin relationships but the persistence and diversity of this market, integrating lives, business, and technology, mark a new model for migration. By "stir-frying goods" and "carving out businesses," technology migrants have congealed as an essential part of the informationalizing city, but in the specific places of the electronics cities. Instead of a simple urban version of "information society" defined by structures of electronically processed information, electronics cities are an institution intricately tied to, and integrating, the informationalization of the city.

History and Context

In China, migrants are most commonly known as the "floating population" (*liudong renkou*). The concept refers to a group of people who "float" away from their home towns to new locations, most often for work but also for education, marriage, and family reunification. Hence there is an equivalence between hometown and belonging, between place and identity, that is understood to underlie all populations of China. The twin ideas of *xueyuan* and *diyuan*, or conditions and relationships determined by blood (reproduction) and place (geographic position), attributed by anthropologist Fei Xiaotong (1992 [1948]) to China's origins as a massively rural country, provide epistemological grounds for the concept that a population that is floating is *sui generis* from the local, stable population. This grounding of thought continues despite the upheavals of the nineteenth and early twentieth centuries, as well as two mid-twentieth-century wars, one a war of resistance against Japan and one a civil war, all of which involved massive population movements. Yet while structuring and facilitating centuries of sojourners and migrants in China, how do these ideas continue to work in the face of movement of over 100 million migrants and growing urbanization in China since 1990?

China's Communist Party established a system to track and monitor household registration, or *hukou*, after 1950. The relationship of this system, that became a key institution of urban governance starting from the 1960s and up to the present (Fan 2002), to the ontology of blood and place requires further examination. While the 1950s began with land reform in the countryside, in which landlords and rich peasants were forced to abdicate land to middle and poor peasants, and ended with the collectivization of all remaining private urban enterprises, the decade also reminded all leaders – from the central government to the local districts and towns – that a mass movement of people into industry and urban areas could bring about widespread famine and death (the aftermath of the Great Leap Forward). Indeed, the characterization of migrants as a "blind flow" (*mangliu*, a homonym for "hooligan" or *liumang*) originated in the State Council pronouncements from the period immediately preceding the Great Leap Forward (Chan and Zhang 1999). Hence, the 1958 *hukou* system that defined each individual and household in terms of origin (rural or urban) and job-type (agricultural or non-agricultural) was rigorously enforced starting from the 1960s (Cheng and Seldon 1994). Yet the connection between origins of blood and place and the *hukou* system cannot be overlooked. While the enforcement of the *hukou* was certainly harsher and more explicit than an underlying knowledge system that defines people by their hometown and kin relationships, the reinforcement of an epistemological system, by a governance system whose logic (or anti-logic) was visceral, in the deaths of 30 million in the Great Leap Forward is uncanny. Thus, that the *hukou* system dovetailed with the rural ontology of blood and place should not be overlooked. To take only one example: in a bustling industrial city like Shanghai, the urban population *fell* between the end of the 1950s and 1978 (Naughton 2007: 126) – a drastic illustration and boundary-making fact that underscores the complexity of discussing population movement in China today.

Despite the overlap of place and blood with the *hukou*, the institutional system of *danwei* – work units that organized both work and life in areas enclosed by walls and guarded from outsiders – was built in cities. The urban, non-agricultural *hukou* was housed in *danwei*, and entitled the urban population to eat grain and use capital subsidized by the collective countryside to build industrial China through producer cities (Henderson and Cohen 1984; Dittmer and Lu 1996; Bray 2005). Taking over the role of cities, hundreds of *danwei* organized the urban population, and identification was primarily with the *danwei*, rather than the city itself (Dutton 1998). As a total institution, *danwei* was a place for birth, life, and death, as changing jobs was rare. Over and above the fact that its residents' food, housing, education, and employment were dispersed through the *danwei* vis-à-vis the *hukou*, the city was populated by a largely unchanging population of "locals" (*bendiren*). While they differed amongst each other, in that the government level (central, provincial, municipal, etc.) determined the allocations and amenities granted the *danwei*, and in that "personalized particularism" (Walder 1986) by cadres made some more equal than others, urban citizens formed a new sense of an unchanging city, like the villages of rural China studied by Fei Xiaotong (see also Yan 1996) before 1978.

Deng Xiaoping's dictum to "reform and open" in 1978 was most acutely realized through the movement of population from the countryside into China's cities. In the early 1980s, the appearance of small markets for foodstuffs outside the ongoing rationing system made life bearable, while the provision of housing in the back-rooms and newly built partitions of farmers' homes offered shelter. First as a trickle of farmer-entrepreneurs then as a flood of temporary and service workers, the populations, labor markets, and economies of all of China's urban areas were fundamentally transformed, from centrally administered cities to market towns.

A key consequence of the presence of migrants in the city was the modification of the "urban public goods regime." This felicitous phrase, and documentation of some of the actual transitions under way, was coined by Solinger (1995). But migration occurred simultaneously with broad changes undertaken by local government officials dealing with intense decentralization of governance and policy-making, as well as transformations in *danwei* and suburban systems that simultaneously "ate away" and supplemented a public goods regime. This is a crucial context for understanding migration in China. As migrants entered cities from the countryside to take up various jobs, varying from manual labor for the city to high-tech private jobs, they contributed to and were influenced by an urban space that was moving from a loose coalition of mostly isolated *danwei* grouped together in the semblance of a "city," to a single unit responsible for planning, infrastructure, service and welfare provision, and population management. The explicit *buguan* ("not administer, not manage") philosophy of local officials with respect to migration was a descendant in part from Deng Xiaoping's urge to experiment with new processes and populations in the market (Zhu 2008). Hence, as local officials became policy enforcers, taking over that role from *danwei* staff, and providers of public goods in the first instance, they allowed migrant residence, work, and life in the city through various coping mechanisms. The institutionalization of these mechanisms, one might argue, is the new form of the public goods regime, now urban only in form since its constitution by off-post state workers and off-farm (rural) migrant workers integrates private actors and local government in a new constellation.

In the next sections, I give estimates of the number of migrants in China, as well as two examples of urban form – migrant enclaves and villages in the city – that have attracted significant scholarly and official attention in the search for an urban form of migration, especially in terms of a spatialization of blood and kin. Yet I conclude with research on an emergent institution that combines migration and technology with the city through informationalization, the name for China's specific engagement with information and communication technologies. The electronics city, in terms of social functions, organization of work, and practices, gives a model of migration with urban form in the twenty-first century. This is illustrated through two migrant practices in electronics cities that are discussed in detail.

Number of Migrants

Table 17.2 shows the number of floating population in 2008. These are estimates calculated using the 2005 National 1% Population Survey (State Council, Population Census Office and National Bureau of Statistics 2007) and the *China Statistical Yearbook 2008* (National Bureau of Statistics 2009). The 2005 survey obtained data from just under 17 million people, or 1.31 percent of the population. Using data on those residing outside their *hukou* registration, the author obtained proportions of migrants overall for China, as well as separating rates for inter-

Table 17.2   Estimated floating population, 2008

Area	2008 Population (NBS)	Estimated number of resident migrants	Estimated number of inter-provincial residential migrants
National	**1,321,290,000**	**151,367,344**	**51,480,924**
Beijing	16,330,000	6,038,864	3,601,821
Tianjin	11,150,000	2,267,393	1,260,129
Hebei	69,430,000	4,860,489	880,301
Shanxi	33,930,000	2,859,818	415,171
Inner Mongolia	24,050,000	4,412,892	707,223
Liaoning	42,980,000	6,564,691	1,125,642
Jilin	27,300,000	2,617,219	302,454
Heilongjiang	38,240,000	3,634,731	394,465
Shanghai	18,580,000	7,385,075	4,839,306
Jiangsu	76,250,000	11,115,678	4,313,354
Zhejiang	50,600,000	11,134,513	6,398,714
Anhui	61,180,000	4,019,432	343,776
Fujian	35,810,000	7,557,858	2,866,349
Jiangxi	43,680,000	2,987,179	252,969
Shandong	93,670,000	7,773,249	1,283,069
Henan	93,600,000	3,488,696	276,439
Hubei	56,990,000	4,623,222	453,086
Hunan	63,550,000	4,421,223	319,661
Guangdong	94,490,000	27,288,476	16,770,159
Guangxi	47,680,000	3,019,552	374,661
Hainan	8,450,000	997,954	297,906
Chongqing	28,160,000	2,237,414	352,183
Sichuan	81,270,000	5,651,171	493,747
Guizhou	37,620,000	2,429,415	383,580
Yunnan	45,140,000	3,441,678	816,451
Tibet	2,840,000	113,396	43,530
Shaanxi	37,480,000	2,371,224	377,989
Gansu	26,170,000	1,240,652	162,722
Qinghai	5,520,000	510,368	125,058
Ningxia	6,100,000	575,577	118,378
Xinjiang	20,950,000	2,255,978	1,069,666

Source: Calculated using State Council, Population Census Office and National Bureau of Statistics (2007) and National Bureau of Statistics (2009).

provincial versus intra-provincial migrants. Owing to the technical definition of floating population, and its origins in the *hukou* system, all people residing outside their *hukou* registration location are classified as "migrants." For a more detailed statistical picture, figures for each province, directly administered municipality, and autonomous region are given. Tables 17.3 and 17.4 highlight the five regions receiving the most migrants, and the five biggest senders of migrants. Notably, Guangdong Province is the destination for almost one third of all inter-provincial migrants (almost 17 million), followed closely by the area encompassing the Lower Yangzi River Delta (Shanghai, Zhejiang, and Jiangsu; 15.5 million). There is a regional

Table 17.3 Top five receiving locations for inter-provincial migrants

	Proportion of total inter-provincial (2005)	Proportion of total migrants (2005)	Proportion of total local migrants (2005)	Proportion of local population (2005)	Number of inter migrants (2008) (using national)	Number of inter migrants (2008) (using urban)
Guangdong	32.6%	11.1%	61.5%	17.7%	16,801,835	16,770,159
Zhejiang	12.4%	4.2%	57.5%	12.6%	6,377,611	6,398,714
Shanghai	9.3%	3.2%	65.5%	26.0%	4,768,331	4,839,306
Jiangsu	8.5%	2.9%	38.8%	5.7%	4,353,954	4,313,354
Beijing	6.8%	2.3%	59.6%	22.1%	3,492,918	3,601,821

Source: Calculated using State Council, Population Census Office and National Bureau of Statistics (2007) and National Bureau of Statistics (2009).

Table 17.4 Top five sending locations for inter-provincial migrants

	Proportion of total inter-provincial (2005)	Proportion of total migrants (2005)	Proportion of local population (2005)	Number of inter migrants (2008) (using national)	Number of inter migrants (2008) (using urban)
Sichuan	11.7%	4.0%	7.1%	6,016,907	5,783,057
Anhui	11.5%	3.9%	9.4%	5,915,316	5,742,995
Hunan	9.3%	3.2%	7.4%	4,794,623	4,677,818
Henan	9.0%	3.1%	4.8%	4,643,170	4,499,768
Jiangxi	7.4%	2.5%	8.6%	3,815,816	3,754,659

Source: Calculated using State Council, Population Census Office and National Bureau of Statistics (2007) and National Bureau of Statistics (2009).

flavor to inter-provincial migration, in that some of the top regions sending migrants to any particular destination will be located in adjacent provinces, i.e. Beijing has large numbers of Hebei and Shandong Province migrants, Shanghai has Jiangsu and Zhejiang migrants, and Guangdong has Hunan, Guangxi, and Jiangxi migrants. There are also "perennial sources" of migrants: namely, Henan, Anhui, and Sichuan Provinces – together, these provinces account for one third of all inter-provincial migrants in China (Hunan Province is also significant but 75 percent of its migrants travel to neighboring Guangdong).

A telling comparison is with the international migration situation as documented by the United Nations (2006) *Report of the Secretary General* (UN General Assembly 2006). In 2005, there were 190.6 million international migrants out of a total world population of 6.46 billion people, making migrants only 2.9 percent of the total world population. For China, the number of international migrants is listed as 596,000 people, less than half of 0.1 percent of its population. Compared to the "floating population," numbered at 151 million in 2008, or even the inter-provincial floating population, numbered at 51 million, the ongoing population movement in

China is truly unprecedented on a global scale, much less a national one. Detailed analysis of statistical data is not a further topic in this chapter, but the scale of China's migration, and its importance for global development and migration policy cannot be denied.

Zhejiangcun

China's "migrant enclaves" attracted significant attention starting in the 1980s and 1990s. The most significant enclave is Zhejiangcun, which typifies migrant enclaves in general. The prominent sources on Zhejiangcun are two contemporary scholars: Li Zhang (2001) and Xiang Biao (Xiang 1999; Ma and Xiang 1998). In fact, when Zhang was doing her doctoral research on Zhejiang migrants in Beijing, it was Xiang, then a Peking University graduate student, who introduced her to the migrant village and set up initial contacts (Zhang 2001: viii). In a non-trivial sense, Zhejiangcun (or Zhejiang "village"; Zhejiang is one of China's provinces) in Beijing is a traditional model of migration to the city (Zhao 2003). That is, Zhejiangcun is an enclave where migrants with ties of place and blood use chain migration to establish mutual support, production, and residence relationships based on the traditional model of rural society in China (Yan 1996). Hence the disappearance of migrant enclaves in the 2000s can be understood not only as the end of migrant-specific industries and urban places, but as a transformation in the organization of residence and work in the city.

Migrant entrepreneurs from rural Wenzhou began to appear in Beijing in the early 1980s, specializing in the clothing and textile industries. While initially numbering only six families in the area, Zhejiangcun grew to 100,000 migrants (and 14,000 local residents) in a rural area located on the cusp of Beijing's southern rural–urban boundary in Fengtai district. Interestingly, despite its name and the focus of scholars, almost *half* of the migrants resident and working in Zhejiangcun were not from Zhejiang: they were workers from Hebei, Sichuan, and Anhui (Ma and Xiang 1998: 571; Zhang 2001: 19). The Zhejiang entrepreneurs set up household enterprises that combined living and production in a single one-room structure, employing non-Zhejiang migrants as workers. They then sold the products in nearby markets established by local government reforms and on street corners. Other, similar enclaves existed in Beijing at the same time: Ma and Xiang (1998: 564) report migrants from Xinjiang, Henan, and Anhui clustering in similar "villages" (*cun*), each specializing in a particular industry (ethnic food, refuse collection, and household cleaning, respectively). Both authors stress chain migration and social networks based on hometown (and by extension kinship and friendship) in rural Wenzhou as key characteristics in the formation and success of Zhejiangcun.

The marginal nature of Zhejiangcun was intended: "the location and construction style ... can be read as the concrete materialization and externalization of Wenzhou migrants' marginalized, liminal, and unstable social status as 'strangers' in the city" (Zhang 2001: 86). In a city that was only beginning to recover its identity as such, local urbanites remained in the warm embrace of *danwei* throughout the 1980s, while local government was required only to provide marginal services. In the 1990s, *danwei* retreated, the city blossomed, and local government struggled to deal with a range of regulatory duties, running of enterprises (for revenue), and provisions of service. The demolition of Zhejiangcun in December 1995 must be viewed in this context – and it also must be remembered that the demolition was not total: only the residential/production compounds of the migrants were demolished, not their markets. Zhang highlights the fact that local officials in the area of Zhejiangcun opposed its demolition by city and central government officials. This curious puzzle and the absence of migrant enclaves today can be further understood by looking at contemporary *chengzhongcun*, the "villages amidst the city" that mostly appear in former rural–urban cusps of the urbanizing city.

Chengzhongcun

When Zhejiangcun was examined before and after demolition, its overall location in the socio-economic contexts of the city was not well understood. More recent studies have highlighted its location, a collection of villages on the cusp of the southern urbanized region of Beijing municipality. This type of a region, known as *chengzhongcun*, "villages amidst the city," has emerged as a specific type of place throughout urban China. Usually, scholars emphasize the role of *chengzhongcun* in providing cheap rental space for migrants, while urban officials view them as blights on the city in terms of planning, safety (*zhi'an*), and appearance (Zhang *et al.* 2003; Song *et al.* 2008). The case of enclaves of migrants from a particular area of China working and living together in an "enclave" is only one type of *chengzhongcun* (Qiu 2009). In fact, according to Le Zheng of the Shenzhen Academy of Social Sciences, there are no place-based enclaves in Shenzhen's numerous *chengzhongcun* (personal communication 2008). It can be difficult to recognize *chengzhongcun* due to the fact that those in highly urbanized areas, such as Zhongguancun in Beijing or Luohu district in Shenzhen, have been completely demolished and no original villagers or village housing remain.

Chengzhongcun are former villages mostly on the outskirts of urban areas that have been surrounded by and integrated with expansion of urban areas. Yet China's land laws, influenced by the *hukou* system, make *chengzhongcun* unique: urban land is owned by the state, making any built structure subject to planning and approval statutes set by the city and implemented by the urban district; rural land is owned by the collective, either village or township, and individual villagers are given individual plots, *zhaijidi*, on which they are free to build housing (Siu 2007; Hsing 2010). As they are integrated in the administrative structure of the city, the village and township governments of *chengzhongcun* are replaced by street and residents' committees, while village collective development companies (in which villagers hold shares) retain the right to build structures on the land free from the planning and infrastructure permissions required on urban land. These development companies engage mostly in renting to migrants and factories, which in the Pearl River Delta of South China shapes the "dormitory labor regime" extracting surplus female labor from the countryside (Pun and Smith 2007; Pun 2005). But in most of the rest of China, *chengzhongcun* function as the urban "workplaces" of migrants who circulate between rural home and urban work – a pattern that has become permanent (Zheng *et al.* 2009).

One of the best descriptions of *chengzhongcun* is as a sponge (Le 2007) that absorbs the flow of rural migrants into the city in times of flood, and squeezes them out in times of drought, as was explained by officials of Xiasha Village, Shenzhen, during the economic crisis in late 2008. But with respect to the city, the emphasis of scholars on the rental or housing functions of *chengzhongcun* is not accidental: to the extent that work and business go on, they are self-enclosed within a factory–labor regime rather than integrated with the city (Pun 2005). The relationships of blood and place that organized Zhejiangcun and other migrant enclaves in the 1980s and 1990s have become recruitment, information, and support networks that no longer define the urban or *chengzhongcun*: the rental market takes over the provision of housing, while the short labor cycle of three to five years for migrant workers implies that turnover and retraining occur again and again in staffing of migrant positions. Hence *chengzhongcun*, while ubiquitous in urban China and vital to migrant housing and labor reproduction, do not integrate migrants into the Chinese city through their residence and work there. To find migration integration, then, one must look at migrant workers and entrepreneurs in the information industry. It is there that is found a congealed urban form that plays a more multi-functional role in the city: the electronics city. While not providing housing, it takes on social functions, integration with the city, and creation of networks no longer based solely on blood and place.

Electronics Cities

Electronics cities in their current form opened in the late 1990s to replace the previous generation of converted storefronts, two- and three-storey warehouses, and hotels where computer and information technology products had previously been sold. Migrants from all over China, including rural and urban areas, come into the city and gather, not based on place or blood relationships, but based on technique, trade, and time in the city, in specific buildings clustered in certain parts of the city. In electronics cities, migrants work, selling, fixing, maintaining, refurbishing, customizing, and pirating, electronic information processing machines. The origins of migrants, in their initial trips to the city, choice of employees, and finding of customers, are not completely divorced from relationships of place and kin; however, significantly here, it is not these relationships that define electronics cities or migrant practices. Instead, they are based both on the consumer demand for electronics products and on the skill, market structure, ethos, and company organization of electronics cities populated by migrants. It is this mixture, consolidation, and new urban form that maintain an institutional continuity outside of *danwei* forms, technical learning/schooling, factory labor, and simple provision of housing.

Electronics cities are typically located in highly commercial areas adjacent to city centers and universities (e.g., Zhongguancun in Beijing, Xujiahui in Shanghai, Huaqiangbei in Shenzhen, Shipaicun in Guangzhou). They occupy massive 20-storey buildings, mostly occupying the bottom five or six floors as well as the entrances facing the street and exits suitable for picking up and dropping off of boxes of equipment. Different floors have different specialties. The typical layout of an electronics city is based on a functional differentiation between floors. That is, on the first floor are usually found specialty stores of particular brands (the Samsung store, the Dell store) as well as general stores and counters that are truly diverse: from basic electronics and motherboards to DIY computer assembly, hard drives, and pen drives. On the second floor are found notebook computers and more general stores. On the third floor are DIY components (discussed below). The fourth floor of an electronics city will have cameras and audio and video equipment. The fifth floor typically houses larger stock stores for photocopiers, notebook computers, and personal computers. Some electronics cities include restaurants and even supermarkets, which are located above the highest level of electronics (i.e., the sixth floor). Many electronics cities also have one storey underground that is typically filled with various countertops specializing in anything from smuggled personal game machines to digital cameras and ink cartridges.

Electronics cities can be defined by a dichotomy between storefront and storeroom. That is, especially for the stores located on the first and second floors, those facing entrances or directly in front of elevators and escalators, and those equipped with tables, chairs, and sofas, the general purpose of the store is to "front" or face the customer, display an aesthetically pleasing array of brands, goods, and company employees, and provide locations for customers to relax and negotiate deals. Directly contrasting this are stores where the general purpose is to provide a central location for company employees, store goods, and conduct bookkeeping. Using this dichotomy, one can classify different stores in terms of more or less "front" or "room." The specialty-store businesses, mostly on the first floor of the electronics cities, have little, if any, goods on hand, spend significant attention to store display cleanliness, up-to-date-ness, and employee appearance (most specialty-store employees wear uniforms with company logos). On the contrary, for DIY business and stores below ground or on the third floor or higher, appearance carries less weight. Many of these stores are crammed full of goods, wall-to-wall with motherboards, or stacked high with monitors or fax machines. While a glass table with chairs for customer negotiation might be present, there is also a computer (or several) for accounting, ordering, and accessing internet orders. Early in the day, many employees gather here but disperse before 10 a.m. to travel around "servicing the city" (Rooker 2005). In the evening, near closing time, employees at these "storerooms" recongregate to report on the day's activities, enter figures into the computer, plan the next day's business visits, play cards, smoke, and chat as those out servicing trickle back. In terms of the role of the store, as front or room, there exists a clear dichotomy for businesses.

This dichotomy, however, exists in a context of overall integration with the city. The electronics cities rely on this integration, both for customers and for everyday life. In the electronics cities, everyday practice is defined by the integration of multiple functions, only one of which is "selling goods." In most stores, the employees, from multiple locations in China, also spend the day learning trade, memorizing prices, ordering goods, chatting, and maintaining or fixing equipment. These migrants learn, socialize, make and remake relationships, and, ultimately, sell and fix electronic equipment. When migrant entrepreneurs share counters, leave boxes in aisles, "borrow" goods to sell at higher price, hide and sometimes flaunt cigarettes in the face of guards who randomly patrol, they engage in everyday practices that integrate the electronics cities as a whole. A sum total of migrant practices, tactics, goods, relationships, and places, electronics cities are salient as places that bring together a new urban form that is institutional. Unlike Zhejiangcun, there are no

Figure 17.1   Hilon Electronics City, Zhongguancun. Author's photo.

walls and place-based bosses. Unlike *chengzhongcun*, these are areas promoted by local officials, concentrated in commercial and business centers of cities. And, what is more important, in electronics cities the migrants do not rely on place or blood to create a new space for residence, work, exploitation, and resistance; instead, the migrants in electronics cities work in spite of hometown, learn new technologies, practice management and DIY, and start micro-enterprises over and over again. The emergence of electronics cities in the 1980s, the spread of information and communication technologies throughout the 1990s, and institutionalization of a new urban form in the 2000s coalesce here. Migrants flowed into cities, freed from the constraints of *hukou*, while urban residents became petty entrepreneurs, freed from the constraints of *danwei*. That ICTs would arise at this auspicious moment – an industry that has come to have a low threshold for entry, both technologically and financially – was a boon. Makeshift markets, this time truly resembling vegetable markets, arose on the streets of Beijing and Shenzhen in the 1980s and 1990s (and somewhat later in other cities). The entrepreneurs (this time college students, laid-off workers, and daring former officials) created makeshift Chinese versions of software, and on-the-fly solutions for hardware problems. This footprint, and its success, laid the blueprint firmly for the future and importance of the electronics cities – the scaled, one-stop shop agglomerations that emerged as 20 years of development changed the content but not the nature of business in urban China.

Figure 17.2   Store in Electronics City. Author's photo.

Practices that Matter: Chaohuo and Chuangye

The electronics cities are a context for, and shape, multiple practices through which migrants engage the city. These practices constitute everyday activity that centers on goods, the main objects circulating in and out of the electronics cities. It is these objects, too, and the networks of practices that encircle them, that informationalize the city. Here two crucial practices are described in depth. They deal, respectively, with the internal workings of electronics cities and the nature of migrant entrepreneurship with respect to electronics cities.

These two practices are found throughout the electronics cities and characterize them, even as they define the industry. One (*chaohuo*) is much more frequent than the other, occurring on a daily basis or even multiple times in a day for different stores; the other (*chuangye*) is a lifetime decision for a migrant, since it involves either leaving behind a former company or starting up one's own business with borrowed money and time away from home. Neither originates in the electronics cities. *Chuangye*, for example, has a rich history, being the title of a movie released at the end of the Cultural Revolution (1975). *Chuangye*, the movie, describes the history of Daqing, a city in Heilongjiang, located in the northeast area of China encompassing Manchuria, where oil fields were discovered in the late 1950s and early 1960s by the triumph of heroic entrepreneurs and workers despite class struggle and foreign (USSR) betrayal. (Daqing was made the focus of Mao's call for "industry to learn from Daqing" in 1964 [Song 2005]). Hence *chuangye* is an institutional practice that, in the process or carving out or opening up a business, industry, or job (*ye*), has heroic connotations in a context of difficult and hostile circumstances.

As noted by researchers of China's stock market, *chao* ("stir frying") can be used in relation to stocks and other goods that potentially can be cornered (Hertz 1998; Gamble 1997). *Chaohuo* in China's electronics markets now refers to the practice of advertising, marketing, and "selling" goods and services not directly provided by the stores or counters by directly engaging the customer. In this sense, migrants act as "intermediaries" between the vast expanse of customer needs and the intricate, overlapping networks of knowledge about who, where, and how goods and services are bought and made in the electronics cities. A migrant entrepreneur from Hunan working in a nondescript counter on the third floor of the Hilon Electronics City, for example, uses her hometown connection to another Hunan customer to attract his business (the customer wanted to buy a tabletop paper shredder). But it is the Hunan migrant's knowledge of the electronics city, that on the fifth floor were located stores that sold various types of shredder, and that the stores would sell on her behalf and give her the "profit" between a normal sales price and the price that she negotiated with her customer, that makes this sales transaction into an instance of *chaohuo*. Hence, inherent in the idea of *chaohuo* are ideas about the functioning of the market, knowledge of its operations, connections that enable the practitioner to secure the goods or services of the original producer, servicer, seller, or wholesaler, and skill in attracting customers and selling to them.

The knowledge of the market, in particular DIY, enables *chaohuo*. DIY means do-it-yourself (*zuzhuang*) computer assembly and involves putting together a computer from its fully manufactured parts. That is, a DIYer will install motherboard, CPU, memory, hard drive, CD-RW (DVD), networking card/modem, fan, video card, audio card in a computer case that includes power supply. Following this, a monitor, keyboard, and mouse are attached. With all components connected, the power is turned on and a Windows operating system (almost always pirated) is installed, along with BIOS and other drivers. The completed unit, tested and certified by the customer, is then reboxed and carried off, completing the DIY process. All components are selected based on the customer's wishes, making DIY also refer to the selection of the computer by the customer – an aspect not explored here. The key point is that DIY involves a large group of stores: a store specializing in DIY carries only a minimum of the required parts – perhaps a certain brand of motherboard and another brand of monitors. The DIYer must call in parts and components from throughout the electronics market, with price and quality determined according to the DIYer's knowledge of what the different stores offer. The vast majority of all stores and counters in electronics cities can and do DIY.

Chaohuo, then, is really just a larger application of DIY. A customer has a hard drive that has burned out, with valuable data needed for a sales presentation in two days. Walking into an electronics city, a simple inquiry to a DIY motherboard and monitor store turns into *chaohuo*: sitting the customer down, an Anhui migrant at the store calls his friend in Pudong, who tells him the number of a disk repair company in Xujiahui. Leading the customer through back alleys and up a cramped elevator, the Anhui migrant takes the customer to a seventeenth-floor specialist disk repair business, complete with dust-free room and thousands of "saved" hard drives in display cases from over a decade of migrant business. Another electronics city migrant, notable by his outsider accent, is negotiating help for a Shanghaiese woman attempting to retrieve deleted pictures from her mobile phone. The Anhui migrant, having introduced the customer to the technologist who will read data off the drive by the next day, takes note of the price (and so calculates his profit on the transaction) then leaves. Using his knowledge of the market, including not only people he can contact to find a reliable disk repair service but also the appropriate price and space for profit, this migrant has "stir fried" (*chaohuo*) the repair of the burnt-out disk. But DIY, and *chaohuo*, are not only individual practices – they are instituted processes that configure the electronics cities, and to which the electronics cities in general are configured. In this way, *chaohuo* is the informationalization of the city by migrants through the electronics cities.

Chuangye differs in that it is a practice that occurs much less frequently than *chaohuo*, which might occur several times in one day for successful businesses in the electronics cities. Usually glossed as "innovation," it extends deep into the nature of business and individual work. Looking at its use in the context of the 1970s movie (a movie, it turns out, that was criticized by Jiang Qing of the Gang of Four at the time), *chuangye* meant carving out a revolutionary new industry amidst difficult and hostile circumstances. For migrant workers in the electronic cities, an ongoing, often daily, topic for discussion, debate, and thought is: Why not *chuangye*? Why not stop working for others and become one's own boss? After all, "it is better to be the head of a chicken than the tail of a phoenix" (*ningwei jitou, budang fengwei*). This is a tactic of resistance, certainly, but it also must be understood as part of the ethos of electronics cities.

The carving out, starting up on one's own, away from the network of social connections that may have brought one into the electronics cities, is the importance of *chuangye*. And its success is measured against a ruthless context of thousands of other migrant entrepreneurs who are struggling to eke out an IT existence cheek by jowl. It is carved out of the market as a whole, in a niche well known to the migrant, making using of the market knowledge, customer relations, and technological skills acquired through years in the electronics markets. In the history of Zhongguancun, known as the Silicon Valley of China, all successful technology businesses are instances of *chuangye*. One famous entrepreneur, chronicled as one of Zhongguancun's heroes (Liu and Zhang 1998), related to me in an interview that Zhongguancun, the "zone" itself, had *chuangye* multiple times, going from an area defined by its concentration of academic institutions, to a place for the purchase of technology, and again to the base of innovative technology in China (Wang Wenjing, interview 2004). In this sense, then, *chuangye* in China's electronics cities occurs not in villages or at the margins of urban society, but directly in, and as part of, the city. It is only by carving out business from the urban informational electronics city that migrants can truly *chuangye*. That they do so, using both tactics of resistance and networks based in and through the electronics cities, points to the electronics city as a key organizer of migrant flows that, itself, is shaped by ongoing migrant practices.

Significance

Electronics cities are not just electronics markets, but migrant electronics markets. The relationships, new forms of living in the city, learning of technology, creation and reproduction of market knowledge, are all institutionalized in the built form of the electronics cities. Electronics cities are not located in Cartesian space, but in the informational city, which they both constitute and are constituted by. Hence, the city itself, even if only imagined as a node of global space flows, in fact directly influences the constitution of the electronics cities, in the first instance by the regional scale of migration – the location of a city dictates the extent to which migrants come to the city, though some migration (e.g., that from Sichuan and Anhui) will always be long-distance. The rise of ICTs in the late 1980s, and their spread and importance to life and business in the late 1990s and early 2000s, trans-formed the city not into a network society but into a society through which an increasing number of practices, communications, and activity involve the deploy-ment of ICTs. Hence, maintenance of these technologies is work that must be repeated over and over, tailored to specific requirements, and extended to large portions of the population. The possibility of this occurring depends on electronics cities, where migrant entrepreneurs and migrant workers *chaohuo* and *chuangye* the technology upon which "network society" depends.

As amply documented above, scholars have shown that "the city," narrowly defined, does not meet the material or social needs of migrants. *Danwei* meal tickets, both literally and metaphorically, were not issued to migrants; migrant clusters seem the natural consequences of a population of kin and place traveling to an unfamiliar and unaccepting (unfriendly) location. Hence the electronics cities play broad social roles that fit the unmet needs outlined by scholars. For one, the electronics cities are a means of subsistence, a place to buy cheap and sell dear, where anyone with moxie and gumption can eke out a living. These "cities" are, after all, also named "electronics markets." But at the social and cultural level, the level where migrants are viewed as second-class citizens, electronics cities are something else – a unique urban form that has arisen, exactly and coincidentally, with the flow of migrants into China's cities (this is another aspect of the importance of informationalization to electronic cities' migrants mentioned above).

A cursory understanding of the role of technology in the lives of migrants reveals conclusions along the lines of established theory on "network society," and the exclusion from the city of those viewed as lacking the *suzhi* to participate in modern Chinese society (Castells 2000; Qiu 2009; Anagnost 2004). As a hypermodern crossroads of consumption and production, China's electronics cities are fertile ground for testing the validity of this theory. If migrants from across China segregate along the lines predicted by *diyuan* in electronics cities, one would expect to find, e.g., Beijing bosses, Anhui ink replacers, Hebei photocopier maintainers, Hunan equipment recyclers, Dongbei computer DIYers, and Guangdong software pirates. If computer city migrants suffer under the burdens of socialist and capitalist exploi-tation, one would expect to find a new class of people fomenting a means to over-throw their oppressions. A true understanding of the city, the people, and the things that make it possible, disproves both conclusions. On the contrary, the electronics cities of China represent a new institutional form that secures the floating population, and enables them to play a crucial role in maintaining informational cities of China. The permanency and necessity of China's "information migrants" for the modern city contribute important ideas to the emerging world of information technology and movement. What is required, indeed demanded, is a thorough understanding of the role electronics cities play in shaping migrant lives and informationalizing – that is, informing – the city.

References

Anagnost, A. (2004) The corporeal politics of quality (suzhi). *Public Culture* 16: 189–208.

Bray, D. (2005) *Social Space and Governance in Urban China: The Danwei System from Origins to Reform*. Stanford, CA: Stanford University Press.

Castells, M. (2000) *The Rise of Network Society*. Oxford: Blackwell.

Chan, K. W., and Zhang, L. (1999) The hukou system and rural–urban migration in China: processes and changes. *China Quarterly* 160: 818–55.

Cheng, T., and Seldon, M. (1994) The origins and social consequences of China's hukou system. *China Quarterly* 139: 644–68.

Dittmer, L., and Lu, X. (1996) Personal politics in the Chinese danwei under reform. *Asian Survey* 36 (3): 246–67.

Dutton, M. (1998) *Streetlife China*. Cambridge: Cambridge University Press.

Fan, C. C. (2002) The elite, the natives, and the outsiders: migration and labor market segmentation in urban China. *Annals of the Association of American Geographers* 92 (1): 103–24.

Fei, X.-T. (1992 [1948]) *From the Soil: The Foundations of Chinese Society*. Berkeley, CA: University of California Press.

Gamble, J. (1997) Stir-fried stocks: share dealers, trading places, and new options in contemporary Shanghai. *Modern China* 23 (2): 181–215.

Henderson, G. E., and Cohen, M. S. (1984) *The Chinese Hospital: A Socialist Work Unit*. New Haven, CT: Yale University Press.

Hertz, E. (1998) *The Trading Crowd: An Ethnography of the Shanghai Stock Market*. Cambridge: Cambridge University Press.

Hsing, Y. T. (2010) *The Great Urban Transformation: Politics of Land and Property in China*. Oxford: Oxford University Press.

Le, Z. (2007) Basic problems with the development of Shenzhen's population [深圳人口发展的基本问题]. *SEZ Economy* 1: 13–16.

Liu, R., and Zhang, Y. (1998) *Knowledge Heroes: The 50 People Who Influenced Zhongguancun* [知识英雄：影响中关村的50个人]. Beijing: China Social Science Press.

Ma, L., and Xiang, B. (1998) Native place, migration and the emergence of peasant enclaves in Beijing. *China Quarterly* 155: 546–81.

National Bureau of Statistics (2009) *China Statistical Yearbook, 2008*. Beijing: China Statistics Press.

Naughton, B. (2007) *The Chinese Economy*. Cambridge, MA: MIT Press.

Pun, N. (2005) *Made in China: Women Factory Workers in a Global Workplace*. Durham, NC: Duke University Press.

Pun, N., and Smith, C. (2007) Putting transnational labour process in its place: the dormitory labour regime in post-socialist China. *Work, Employment and Society* 21 (1): 27–45.

Qiu, J. L. (2009) *Working-Class Network Society: Communication Technology and the Information Have-Less in Urban China*. Cambridge, MA: MIT Press.

Rooker, T. (2005) Technology as practice in the Silicon Valley of China. *International Journal of Technology, Knowledge, and Society* 1 (5): 129–38.

Siu, H. F. (2007) Grounding displacement: uncivil urban spaces in postreform South China. *American Ethnologist* 34 (2): 329–50.

Skinner, G. W. (1964–5) Marketing and social structure in rural China. *Journal of Asian Studies* 24 (1–3): 3–43, 195–228, 363–99.

Skinner, G. W. (1977) *The City in Late Imperial China*. Stanford, CA: Stanford University Press.

Solinger, D. (1995) China's urban transients in the transition from socialism and the collapse of the communist "urban public goods regime." *Comparative Politics* 27 (2): 127–46.

Song, L. (2005) *The Story of Industry Learning from Daqing* [工业学大庆始末]. Wuhan: Hubei People's Press.

Song, Y., Zenou, Y., and Ding, C. (2008) Let's not throw the baby out with the bath water: the role of urban villages in housing rural migrants in China. *Urban Studies* 45 (2): 313–30.

State Council, Population Census Office and National Bureau of Statistics, Department of Population Statistics (2007) *Data on the Sample Survey of 1% of the National Population in 2005* [2005年全国1%人口抽样调查资料]. Beijing: China Statistics Press.

UN General Assembly (2006) International migration and development. Report of the Secretary-General, May 18. Available online at www.unhcr.org/refworld/docid/44ca2d934.html (accessed August 28, 2009).

Walder, A. G. (1986) *Communist Neo-Traditionalism: Work and Authority in Chinese Industry*. Berkeley, CA: University of California Press.

Xiang, B. (1999) *A Community Transcending Boundaries: The Life History of Zhejiangcun in Beijing* [跨越边界的社区：北京浙江村的生活史]. Beijing: Sanlian Press.

Yan, Y. (1996) The culture of guanxi in a north China village. *China Journal* 35 (Jan.): 1–25.

Zhang, L., Zhao, S. X. B., and Tian, J. P. (2003) Self-help in housing and chengzhongcun in China's urbanization. *International Journal of Urban and Regional Research* 27 (4): 912–37.

Zhang, L. (2001) *Strangers in the City: Reconfigurations of Space, Power and Social Networks within China's Floating Population*. Stanford, CA: Stanford University Press,

Zhao, Y. (2003) The role of migrant networks in labor migration: the case of China. *Contemporary Economic Policy* 21 (4): 500–11.

Zheng, S., Long, F., Fan, C. C., and Gu, Y. (2009) Urban villages in China: a 2008 survey of migrant settlements in Beijing. *Eurasian Geography and Economics* 50 (4): 425–46.

Zhu, S. (2008) *Labor Migration and Economic Development: The Experience from You County in Hunan Province* [劳动力转移与经济发展：湖南省攸县外出务工模式研究]. Beijing: Economic Science Press.

Chapter 18

Analytic Borderlands: Economy and Culture in the Global City[*]

Saskia Sassen

What happens to place in a global economy? And how is globalization inscribed – in the spaces of the economy and of culture, in built form, and generally in space? I want to use these questions to argue that the dominant narrative about economic globalization is a narrative of eviction because its key concepts – globalization, information economy, and telematics – all suggest that place no longer matters. And they suggest that the type of place represented by major cities may have become obsolete from the perspective of the economy, particularly for the leading industries, as these have the best access to, and are the most advanced users of, telematics. It is an account that privileges the capability for global transmission over the concentrations of built infrastructure that makes transmission possible, that privileges information outputs over the work of producing those outputs, from specialists to secretaries, and the new transnational corporate culture over the multiplicity of cultural environments, including reterritorialized immigrant cultures, within which many of the "other" jobs of the global information economy take place.

The overall effect is to lose the place-boundedness of significant components of the global information economy. This loss entails the eviction of a whole array of activities and types of workers from the account about the process of globalization which, I argue, are as much a part of it as is international finance. And evicting these activities and workers excludes the variety of cultural contexts within which they exist, a cultural diversity that is as much a presence in processes of globalization as is the new international corporate culture. The terrain within which the dominant account represents economic globalization captures only a fraction of the actual economic operations involved. It reconstitutes large portions of the city's economy in "cultural" terms – the spaces of the amalgamated other, the "other" as culture. My purpose (Sassen 2001; 1998) is to reframe the terrain of the economy,

The New Blackwell Companion to the City Edited by Gary Bridge and Sophie Watson
© 2011 Blackwell Publishing Ltd

incorporating as an integral part the discontinuity between what is represented as economic and what is represented as cultural in the broad sense of the term – the "center" as economy and the "other" as culture. In so doing I reconstitute "the" economy as a multiplicity of economies with distinct organizational patterns. It also invites a rereading of the notion of a unitary economic system, a notion central to mainstream economic thought and encapsulated in the notion of "the" economy.

Recovering Place

How do we reintroduce place in economic analysis? And secondly, how do we construct a new narrative about economic globalization, one which includes rather than evicts all the spatial, economic, and cultural elements that are part of the global economy as it is constituted in cities? For me as a political economist, addressing these issues has meant working in several systems of representation and constructing spaces of intersection. There are analytic moments when two systems of representation intersect. Such analytic moments are easily experienced as spaces of silence, of absence. One challenge is to see what happens in those spaces, what operations (analytic, of power, of meaning) take place there.

One version of these spaces of intersection is what I have called analytic borderlands. Why borderlands? Because they are spaces that are constituted in terms of discontinuities; in them discontinuities are given a terrain rather than reduced to a dividing line. Much of my work on economic globalization and cities has focused on these discontinuities and has sought to reconstitute them analytically as borderlands rather than dividing lines. This produces a terrain within which these discontinuities can be reconstituted in terms of economic operations whose properties are not merely a function of the spaces on each side (i.e., a reduction to the condition of dividing line) but also, and most centrally, of the discontinuity itself, the argument being that discontinuities are an integral part, a component, of the economic system.

Methodologically, the construction of these analytic borderlands pivots on what I call circuits for the distribution and installation of economic operations. These circuits allow me to follow economic activities into areas that escape the increasingly narrow borders of mainstream representations of "the" economy and to negotiate the crossing of discontinuous spaces. Further, these circuits give us one possible representation of the materialization of global economic activity in a place.

These are the instruments through which I want to reread the city's economy in a way that recovers organizational, spatial, and cultural dimensions that are now lost in the dominant representation of that economy. I do this in three sections. The first is a brief discussion as to why cities are useful arenas within which to explore the limitations of this mainstream narrative. Secondly, I explain why crucial aspects of the most advanced sectors of the economy are place-bound, a fact disregarded in the mainstream account of the information economy, and especially its global dimension. Why does this matter? Because recovering place in the analyses of the economy, particularly place as constituted in major cities, allows us to see the multiplicity of economies and work cultures in which the global information economy is embedded. It also allows us to recover the concrete, localized processes through which globalization exists and to argue that much of the multiculturalism in large cities is as much a part of globalization as is international finance. The third section examines how space is inscribed in the urban economy, and particularly how the spaces of corporate culture, which are a representation of the space of power in today's cities, are actually contested spaces. The overall purpose is to bring these various elements together in an effort to move from an economic narrative of eviction to one of inclusion.

Why Focus on Cities in This Inquiry?

These questions can be usefully explored in large cities such as New York and Los Angeles, Paris and Amsterdam, or many other major Western European cities, for at least two reasons. First, cities are the sites for concrete operations of the economy. For now we can distinguish two forms of this. One is about economic globalization and place. Cities are strategic places which concentrate command functions and global markets, and, I add, production sites for the new, advanced information industries. The other form through which this concreteness can be captured is by an examination of the day-to-day work in the leading economic complex, finance and specialized services. Such an examination makes it clear that a large share of the jobs involved in finance, for example, are lowly paid clerical and manual jobs, many held by women and migrants. These types of workers and jobs do not fit the dominant representation of what the premier economic complex of our era is about.

Secondly, the city concentrates diversity. Its spaces are inscribed with the dominant corporate culture but also with multiple other cultures and identities. The slippage is evident: the dominant culture can encompass only part of the city. And while corporate power inscribes non-corporate cultures and identities with "otherness," thereby devaluing them, they are present everywhere. This presence is especially strong in our major western cities which also have the largest concentrations of corporate power. We see here an interesting correspondence between great concentrations of corporate power and large concentrations of "others." It invites us to see that globalization is not only constituted in terms of capital and the new international corporate culture (international finance, telecommunications, information flows) but also in terms of people and non-corporate cultures. There is a whole infrastructure of low-wage, non-professional jobs and activities that constitute a crucial part of the so-called corporate economy.

I now want to move to a rather straightforward account of the distinct ways in which place, and particularly the type of place represented by large cities, matters in today's global economy.

Place in the Global Economy

We can begin this inquiry by asking whether an economic system characterized by pronounced concentration of ownership and control can have a space economy that lacks points of intense agglomeration. Elsewhere (2001) I have argued at great length that the territorial dispersal of economic activity made possible by global telecommunications creates a need for expanded central control functions – if this dispersal is to occur under conditions of continued economic concentration. Globalization has engendered a new logic for agglomeration, a new spatial dynamic between dispersal and centralization. The neutralization of distance through telematics has as its correlate a new type of central place.

One way of capturing this is through the image of cities as *command centers* in a global economic system. The notion of command centers is actually one that lacks much content. In the specialized literature it is usually thought of in terms of the power and global reach of large corporations. I have sought to give it content, to capture the "production" of global command functions, the work of global control and management. Focusing on production rather than simply on the awesome power of large corporations and banks brings into view the wide array of economic activities, many outside the corporation, necessary to produce and reproduce that power. An exclusive focus on the power of corporations and banks would leave out a number of issues concerning the social, economic, and spatial impacts of these activities on the cities where they are located.

The domestic and international dispersal of loci of growth and the internationalization of finance bring to the fore questions concerning the incorporation of such growth into the profit-generating processes that contribute to economic concentration. That is to say, while in principle the territorial decentralization of economic activity could have been accompanied by a corresponding decentralization in ownership and hence in the appropriation of profits, there has been little movement in that direction. Though large firms have increased their subcontracting to smaller firms and many national firms in the newly industrializing countries have grown rapidly, this form of growth is ultimately part of a chain in which a limited number of corporations continue to control the end product and to reap the profits associated with selling on the world market. Even industrial home-workers in remote rural areas are now part of that chain.

This is not only evident with firms; it is also evident with places. Thus, the internationalization and expansion of finance have brought growth to a large number of smaller financial markets, a growth which has fed the expansion of the global industry. But top-level control and management of the industry have become concentrated in a few leading financial centers, especially New York, London, Tokyo, Frankfurt, Paris, and other such cities. These account for a disproportionate share of all financial transactions and one that has grown rapidly since the early 1980s.

The fundamental dynamic posited here is that the more globalized the economy becomes the higher the agglomeration of central functions in global cities. The extremely high densities evident in the downtown districts of these cities are the spatial expression of this logic. The widely accepted notion that agglomeration has become obsolete now that global telecommunication advances should allow for maximum dispersal, is only partly correct. It is, I argue, precisely the opposite in some of the leading sectors: because of the territorial dispersal facilitated by telecommunication advances, agglomeration of centralizing activities has expanded immensely. This is not a mere continuation of old patterns of agglomeration but, one could posit, a new logic for agglomeration.

Information technologies are yet another factor contributing to the new logic for agglomeration. These technologies make possible the geographic dispersal *and* simultaneous integration of many activities. But the distinct conditions under which such facilities are available have promoted centralization of the most skilled users in the most advanced telecommunications centers. Even though a few newer urban centers have built complex telecommunications facilities, entry costs are increasingly high, and there is a tendency for telecommunications to be developed in conjunction with major users, which are typically firms with large national and global markets (Castells 1989; Graham 2000). Indeed there is a close relationship between the growth of international markets for finance and trade, the tendency for major firms to concentrate in major cities, and the development of telecommunications infrastructures in such cities. Firms with global markets or global production processes require advanced telecommunications facilities. And the acceleration of the financial markets and their internationalization make access to advanced telecommunications facilities essential. The main demand for telecommunication services comes from information-intensive industries which, in turn, tend to be located in major cities which have such facilities.

Besides being command points, I see two additional ways in which major cities are strategic places in the global economy. One is as production sites for finance and specialized services, and the other is as transnational marketplaces for these products.

Production sites

Centralized control and management over a geographically dispersed array of plants, offices, and service outlets do not come about inevitably as part of a "world system." They require the development of a vast range of highly specialized services and of top-level management and control functions. These constitute the components for "global control capability" (Sassen 2001).

By focusing on the production of this capability, I am seeking to displace the focus of attention from the familiar issue of the power of large corporations over governments and economies; or the issue of supracorporate concentration of power through interlocking directorates or organizations such as the International Monetary Fund. I want to focus on an aspect that has received less attention, what could be referred to as the *practice* of global control: the work of producing and reproducing the organization and management of a global production system and a global marketplace for finance, both under conditions of economic concentration. This allows me to focus on the infrastructure of jobs involved in this production. Furthermore, while it is typical to think of finance and specialized services as a matter of expertise rather than production, the elaboration of, for example, a financial instrument requires inputs from law, accounting, advertising. There is a production complex in the advanced service economy that benefits from agglomeration. In addition, the actual production process includes a variety of workers and firms that are not usually thought of as being part of the information economy.

The growth of advanced services for firms along with their particular characteristics of production help to explain the centralization of management and servicing functions that fueled the economic boom of the 1980s in cities such as New York, London, Tokyo, Amsterdam, Toronto, and so on. The face-to-face explanation needs to be refined in several ways. Advanced services are mostly services for firms; unlike other types of services, they are not dependent on vicinity to the consumers served. Rather, economies occur in such specialized firms when they locate close to others that produce key inputs or whose proximity makes possible joint production of certain service offerings. Moreover, concentration arises out of the needs and expectations of the people likely to be employed in these new high-skill jobs. They are attracted to the amenities and lifestyles that large urban centers can offer. The accounting firm can service its clients at a distance, but the production of its service benefits from proximity to specialists of various kinds, lawyers, financial experts, programmers. In this sense then, one can speak of *production sites*.

Transnational marketplaces

Globalization does not *only* consist of instantaneous transmission around the globe; much of it takes place in markets and a key part of even the most digitalized market is likely to be located in a particular place. Cities are the location for many of the transactions in global markets for finance and specialized services. These are markets where firms, governments, and individuals from all around the world can engage in transactions that often bypass the "host" country.

Multi-site forms of organization in manufacturing, services, and banking have created an expanded demand for a wide range of specialized service activities to manage and control global networks of factories, service outlets, and branch offices. While to some extent these activities can be carried out in-house, a large share is not. High levels of specialization, the possibility of externalizing the production of some of these services, and the growing demand by large and small firms and by governments, are all conditions that have both resulted from, and made possible, the development of a market for freestanding service firms that produce components for "global control capability." This in turn means that not only large but also small firms can buy components of that capability, such as management consulting or international legal advice. And so can firms and governments from anywhere in the world. In brief, while the large corporation is undoubtedly a key agent inducing the development of this capability and is its prime beneficiary, it is not the sole user.

In brief, this focus on the *work* behind command functions, on *production* in the finance and services complex, and on market *places* has the effect of incorporating the material facilities underlying globalization and the whole infrastructure of jobs typically not marked as belonging to the corporate sector of the economy: besides the already mentioned work of secretaries and cleaners, there are the truckers who deliver the software, the variety of technicians and repair workers, and all the jobs having to do with the maintenance, painting, and renovation of the buildings where it all is housed.

This can lead to the recognition that there are multiple economies involved in constituting the global information economy. It allows for a valorization of types of activities, workers, and firms that have never been installed in the "center" of the economy or have been evicted from that center in the restructuring of the 1980s and have therefore been devalorized in a system that overvalorizes the "center." Globalization can, then, be seen as a process that involves several economies and work cultures. Yet it is in terms of the corporate economy and the new transnational corporate culture that economic globalization is represented. How can we expand the terrain for this representation to incorporate these conditions? And how can we make a new reading of the locations where corporate power is now installed, a reading that captures the non-corporate presences in those same sites?

Globalization and Inscription

Once we have recovered the centrality of place and of the multiple work cultures within which economic operations are embedded, we are still left confronting a highly restricted terrain for the inscription of economic globalization. Sennett (1992: 36) observes that "the space of authority in Western culture has evolved as a space of precision." And Giddens notes the centrality of "expertise" in today's society, with the corresponding transfer of authority and trust to expert systems (Giddens 1991: 88–91). Corporate culture is one representation of precision and expertise. Its space has become one of the main spaces of authority in today's cities. The dense concentrations of tall buildings in major downtowns or in the new "edge" cities are the site for corporate culture – though as I will argue later they are also the site for other forms of inhabitation, but these have been made invisible. The vertical grid of the corporate tower is imbued with the same neutrality and rationality attributed to the horizontal grid of American cities. Much has been said about the Protestant ethic as the culture through which the economic operations of capitalism are constituted in the daily life of people. Sennett (1992: 46–62) opens up a whole new dimension both on the Protestant ethic and on the American city by suggesting that what is experienced as a form of rational urban organization, the grid, is actually a far more charged event. It is the representation in urban design of a Protestant language of self and space becoming a modern form of power (Sennett 1992: 55).

We can recognize that the neutralization of place brought about by the modern grid contains an aspiration to a modern space of precision. This same aspiration is evident in the self-inscription of corporate business culture as neutral, as ordered by technology, economic efficiency, rationality. This is put in contrast to what is thought of as the culture of small businesses, or, even more so, ethnic enterprises. Each of these is a partial representation, in one case of the city, in the other of the economy.

The dominant narrative presents the economy as ordered by technical and efficiency principles, and in that sense as neutral. The emergence and consolidation of corporate power appears, then, as an inevitable form that economic growth takes under these ordering principles. The impressive engineering and architectural output evident in the tall corporate towers that dominate our downtowns are a physical embodiment of these principles. And the corporate culture that inhabits these towers and inscribes them is the organizational and behavioral correlate to these ordering principles. Authority is thereby "divorced from community"; "The visual forms of legibility in urban designs or space no longer suggest much about subjective life" (Sennett 1992: 37).

We can easily recognize that both the neutralization of place through the grid in its aspiration to a modern space of precision, *and* the self-inscription of corporate culture as neutral, as ordered by technology and efficiency, are partial representations of the city and of the economy. This inscription needs to be produced and reproduced, and it can never be complete because of all the other presences in the city which are inscribed in urban space. The *representation* of the city contained in the dominant economic narrative can exclude large portions of the lived city and reconstitute them as some amalgamated "other." The lived city contains multiple spatialities and identities, many indeed articulated and very much a part of the economy, but represented as superfluous, anachronistic, or marginal. Through immigration, for instance, a proliferation of, in their origin, highly localized cultures have now become presences in many large cities, cities whose elites think of themselves as cosmopolitan, that is, transcending any locality. An immense array of cultures from around the world, each rooted in a particular country or village, are now reterritorialized in a few single places, places such as New York, Los Angeles, Paris, London, and most recently Tokyo. Reterritorialized "cultures" are not the same as cosmopolitanism (Sassen 1998: chapter one). Subjective life is installed in a multiplicity of subjectivities, and this undermines the representation of the advanced modern economy as a space of neutrality, the neutrality that comes from technology and efficiency, the ordering principles of a modern economy.

The space of the amalgamated other is constituted as a devalued, downgraded space in the dominant economic narrative: social and physical decay, a burden. In today's New York or Los Angeles, this is the space of the immigrant community, of the black ghetto, and increasingly of the old manufacturing district. In its most extreme version it is the space of the "underclass, full of welfare mothers and drug addicts."

Corporate culture collapses differences, some minute, some sharp, among the different sociocultural contexts into one amorphous otherness, an otherness that has no place in the economy, that holds the low-wage jobs that are, supposedly, only marginally attached to the economy. It thereby reproduces the devaluing of those jobs and of those who hold the jobs. By leaving out these articulations, by restricting the referent to the centrally placed sectors of the economy, the dominant economic narrative can present the economy as containing a higher-order unity. The corporate economy evicts these other economies and its workers from economic representation, and the corporate culture represents them as the other. What is not installed in a corporate center is devalued or will tend to be devalued. And what occupies the corporate building in non-corporate ways is made invisible. The fact that most of the people working in the corporate city during the day are low-paid secretaries, mostly women, many immigrant or, in US cities, African-American women, is not included in the representation of the corporate economy or corporate culture. And the fact that at night a whole other workforce installs itself in these spaces, including the offices of the chief executives, and inscribes the space with a whole different culture (manual labor, often music, lunchbreaks at midnight) is an invisible event.

In this sense, corporate architecture assumes a whole new meaning beyond the question of the economy of offices and real-estate development. The built forms of the corporate economy are representative of its "neutrality" – of being driven by technology and efficiency. Corporate architectural spatiality is one specific form assumed by the circulation of power in the economy, and specifically in the corporate economy. Wigley (1992: 327) notes that the house is not innocent of the violence inside it. And we now have an excellent literature showing how the design of different types of buildings – homes, factories, "public" lobbies – is shaped not only by cultural values and social norms, but also by matters of power in its many instantiations.

The supposedly "rational" organization of office space illustrates certain aspects of Foucault's microtechnologies of power (Rakatansky 1992). But the changes in

the details of inhabitation – institutional practices, the types and contents of buildings – indicate there is no univocal relation between these and built form. I agree
with Rakatansky's observation that the play of ideologies in architectural form is
complex. And I would add that this conception is essential if we are to allow for
politics and agency in the built environment. Yes, in some sense, buildings are frozen
in time. But they can be reinscribed. The only way we can think of these towers
now is as corporate, if located downtown (and as failed public housing projects if
they are in poor ghettos). Can we reinscribe these corporate towers in ways that
recover the fact that they are also the workplace of a large non-corporate
workforce?

Another dimension along which to explore some of these issues is the question
of the body. The body is citified, urbanized as a distinctively metropolitan body
(Grosz 1992: 241). The particular geographical, architectural, and municipal
arrangements constituting a city are particular ingredients in the social constitution
of the body; Grosz adds that they are by no means the most important ones. She
argues that the structure and particularity of the family and neighborhoods are more
influential, though the structure of the city is also contained therein. "The city
orients perception insofar as it helps to produce specific conceptions of spatiality"
(1992: 250). The city contributes to the organization of family life, of worklife
insofar as it contains a distribution in space of the specific locations for each activity; similarly, architectural spatiality can be seen as one particular component in this
broader process of the organization of space. I would add to this that the structure,
spatiality, and concrete localization of the economy are also influential. In these
many ways the city is an active force that "leaves its traces on the subject's
corporeality."

But it is citified in diverse ways: it is inscribed by the many sociocultural environments present in the city and it, in turn, inscribes these. There are two forms in
which this weaves itself into the space of the economy. One is that these diverse
ways in which the body is inscribed by the diverse sociocultural contexts that exist
in the city work as a mechanism for segmenting and, in the end, for devaluing, and
they do so in very concrete ways. For example, research by the anthropologist
Philippe Bourgeois (1996) shows us the case of an 18-year-old Puerto Rican from
East Harlem who gets a job as a clerical attendant in an office in downtown Manhattan. He tells us that walking over to the copying machine, past all the secretaries,
is humiliating. The way he walks, the way he is dressed, the way he moves, all present
him to the office staff secretaries and managers as someone from the ghetto –
someone who "doesn't know the proper ways."

The other way in which this diversity weaves itself into the space of the economy
is that it re-enters the space of the dominant economic sector as merchandise and
as marketing. Of interest here is Stuart Hall's observation that contemporary global
culture is different from earlier imperial cultures: it is absorptive, a continuously
changing terrain that incorporates the new cultural elements whenever it can. In the
earlier period, Hall (1991) argues, the culture of the empire, epitomized by Englishness, was exclusionary, seeking always to reproduce its difference. At the same time
today's global culture cannot absorb everything, it is always a terrain for contestation, and its edges are certainly always in flux. The process of absorption can never
be complete.

One question is whether the argument developed earlier regarding the neutralization of space brought about by the grid, and the system of values it entails or seeks to produce in space, also occurs with cultural globalization. As with the grid, "global" culture never fully succeeds in this neutralization; yet absorption does alter the "other" that is absorbed. An interesting issue here that emerges out of my work on the urban economy is whether at some point all the "others" (at its most extreme, the informal economy) carry enough weight to transform the center. In the case of culture, one can see that the absorption of multiple cultural elements, along with the cultural politics so evident in large cities, have transformed global culture. Yet it is still centered in the west, its technologies, its images, as Hall argues. Thus absorbed, the other cultures are neutralized. And yet ... they are also present. We can perhaps see this most clearly in urban space, where multiple other work cultures, cultural environments, and culturally inscribed bodies increasingly inhabit a built environment that has its origins visibly in the corporate culture lying behind the grid. Here again, I ask, at what point does the "curve effect," as social scientists would put it, take hold and bring the center down?

In conclusion, we cannot restrict our account of the global information economy to global *transmissions* and information *outputs*. Likewise, we cannot restrict our representations of economic globalization to the new transnational corporate culture and the corporate towers it inhabits. Globalization is a contradictory space; it is characterized by contestation, internal differentiation, continuous border crossings. The global city is emblematic of this condition. In seeking to show that (a) these types of cities are strategic to economic globalization because they are command points, global marketplaces, and production sites for the information economy, and (b) that many of the devalued sectors of the urban economy actually fulfill crucial functions for the center, I try to recover the importance of cities precisely in a globalized economic system and thereby to make a countervailing argument. It is all the intermediary sectors of the economy (such as routine office work, headquarters that are not geared to the world markets, the variety of services demanded by the largely suburbanized middle class) and of the urban population (i.e., the middle class) that can leave and have left cities. The two sectors that have remained, the center and the "other," find in the city the strategic terrain for their operations.

Note

* Revised version of the 1992 Distinguished Visitor Lecture, Department of Art History, State University of New York, Binghamton, originally published in A. D. King (ed.) *Representing the City: Ethnicity, Capital and Culture in the 21st Century Metropolis* (London: Macmillan 1995).

References

Bourgeois, P. (1996) *In Search of Respect: Selling Crack in El Barrio*. Structural Analysis in the Social Sciences Series. New York: Cambridge University Press.

Castells, M. (1989) *The Informational City*. Oxford: Blackwell.

Giddens, A. (1991) *The Consequences of Modernity*. Oxford: Polity Press.

Graham, S. (2000) On global cities, telecommunications and planetary urban networks. In *Cities and their Cross-Border Networks*, ed. S. Sassen. Tokyo: United Nations University Press.

Grosz, E. (1992) Bodies–cities. In *Sexuality and Space*, ed. B. Colomina. Princeton Papers on Architecture. Princeton, NJ: Princeton Architectural Press, 241–53.

Hall, S. (1991) The local and the global: globalization and ethnicity. In A. King (ed.), *Current Debates in Art History 3. Culture, Globalization and the World-System: Contemporary Conditions for the Representation of Identity*. Binghamton, NY: State University of New York at Binghamton.

Rakatansky, M. (1992) Spatial narratives. In *Strategies in Architectural Thinking*, ed. J. Whiteman, J. Kipnis, and R. Burdett. Chicago: Chicago Institute for Architecture and Urbanism, and Cambridge, MA: MIT Press, 198–221.

Sassen, S. (1998) *Globalization and Its Discontents*. New York: New Press.

Sassen, S. (2001) *The Global City: New York, London, Tokyo*. New updated edn. Princeton NJ: Princeton University Press.

Sennett, R. (1992) *The Conscience of the Eye: The Design and Social Life of Cities*. New York: Norton.

Wigley, M. (1992) Untitled: the housing of gender. In *Sexuality and Space*, ed. B. Colomina. Princeton Papers on Architecture. Princeton, NJ: Princeton Architectural Press, 327–90.

Chapter 19

Nomadic Cities

David Pinder

With no timetable to respect, with no fixed abode, the human being will of necessity become acquainted with a nomadic way of life ... [The New Babylonian's] social space is unlimited. Because he [*sic*] is no longer "rooted" he can circulate freely: much more freely since the space he traverses endlessly changes shape and atmosphere with the result that it is constantly renewed.

Constant, New Babylon (1996 [1974]: 157, 165)

Introduction

Nomads and nomadism feature prominently in attempts by western critics, theorists, architects, planners, and others to come to terms with urban mobilities and their consequences. Nomadic metaphors are often mobilized to construct arguments about the states of cities and their futures. These frequently speak of anxieties about urban mobilities and the disorders they supposedly produce. The nomadic is construed as disturbing and threatening to the organization of urban life. It is an enemy of cities, what has to be overcome for the establishment of urbanism and architecture as disciplining practices. Nomads, along with other mobile figures often similarly associated with rootlessness and wandering, appear as sources of fear as well as targets for spatial disciplining and ordering (see Cresswell 1997, 2006; Sibley 1981, 1995). At the same time, however, nomadism appears with contrasting connotations. Notable in this regard has been the increasing significance within social and cultural theory of forms of "nomad thought" and "nomadic metaphysics," which center on movement, flux, and dynamism (Cresswell 2006; Adey 2010). Nomadic metaphors are here favored as a means of addressing cities in terms of movements, rhythms, flows, and lines of flight. These are typically distinguished

The New Blackwell Companion to the City Edited by Gary Bridge and Sophie Watson
© 2011 Blackwell Publishing Ltd

from "sedentarist" perspectives that privilege fixity, boundedness, and spatial order. Far from being derided as unruly, in some cases the nomadic is celebrated for its disruptive power, its resistance to hegemonic codes and spatial orderings, and for its associations with liberation.

In this chapter it is with those last connotations in mind that I approach the subject of nomadic cities. In so doing I am mindful of how much current nomad talk derives from quite particular experiences of mobility, especially those of privileged urban inhabitants who enjoy relatively smooth passage across spatial boundaries and borders in their global circulations through the "non-places" of airports, highways, hotels, rail stations, and the like. That point will be returned to later, with respect to the unlocated nature of many nomadic references and their elision of questions of power. But it is with the intention of providing critical perspectives on this subject and aspects of the politics of urban mobilities that the chapter takes its particular focus. In the next section I introduce my theme with reference to prominent forms of nomad thought derived in particular from the philosophers Gilles Deleuze and Félix Guattari. In subsequent sections, I turn to a vision of nomadic cities developed by the Dutch artist Constant during the 1950s and 1960s. The significance of this project that he entitled New Babylon has been increasingly well illuminated recently through exhibitions as well as historical and critical studies (Sadler 1998; Wigley 1998; Pinder 2005; van Schaik and Máčel 2005). What particularly concerns me here is how it presented mobility and specifically nomadism as an element of radical opposition to dominant forms of capitalist urbanism as well as of a free life to come. There is a need to understand this work in its context, including in relation to the work of other modernist and *avant-garde* architects at the time concerned with mobility and nomadism. But I also want to explore how, by following its mobilization of the figure of the nomad and some of the paths it has taken, it speaks in significant ways to broader questions about the politics of urban mobilities that have come to the fore in recent years.

Nomads, Nomad Thought, and Lines of Flight

Recent nomad thought has been significantly influenced and inspired by Deleuze and Guattari's *A Thousand Plateaus*. Through a range of historical and geographical materials, which include accounts of traveling workers who built Gothic cathedrals across Europe during the twelfth century, and who made political use of their mobility as well as their ability to strike, they present state power as arrayed against the nomadic, not to prevent movement but to control it through the construction of fixed and directed paths. State science is concerned with establishing "conduits, pipes, embankments, which prevent turbulence, which constrain movement to go from one point to another, and space itself to be striated and measured, which makes fluid depend on the solid, and flows proceed by parallel, laminar layers" (Deleuze and Guattari 1988 [1980]: 363). This includes with regard to the flow of labor that must be channeled and regulated. It is from the perspective of spatial ordering and striating that the nomad derives its elusive, threatening, and potentially subversive qualities that have so concerned many urban critics, planners, and reformers but that have also, for others, been the source of its appeal and strength.

A distinctive feature of nomad life for Deleuze and Guattari is its emphasis on lines, relays, and trajectories over points. "A path is always between two points, but the in-between has taken on all the consistency and enjoys both an autonomy and a direction of its own," they write. "The life of the nomad is the intermezzo. Even the elements of his dwelling are conceived in terms of the trajectory that is forever mobilizing them" (Deleuze and Guattari 1988 [1980]: 380). In that sense they distinguish between the nomad, who is "the Deterritorialized par excellence," and the migrant whose movement entails reterritorialization afterwards. They also distinguish between "sedentary space," which they describe as "striated, by walls, enclosures, and roads between enclosures," and "nomad space," which is "smooth, marked only by 'traits' that are effaced and displaced with the trajectory": "The nomad distributes himself in a smooth space: he occupies, inhabits, holds that space" (381). The opposition of the striated and smooth is in reality complex and entangled, however, with each being in mixture, tension, alternation, transversality, and superposition with the other. If the sea is "a smooth space fundamentally open to striation," then the city can be described as "the force of striation that reimparts smooth space, puts it back into operation everywhere" (481). Neither space is held to be intrinsically revolutionary or otherwise, and their meaning changes according to specific interactions and conditions. It is nevertheless clear that, for Deleuze and Guattari, the nomadic is associated with insubordination and with elements that resist, subvert, and interrupt state spatializations and orderings.

Their approach intertwines with work by other predominantly poststructuralist theorists who, from different positions and for different purposes, connect nomadism with practices that elude, undermine, or escape conventional codes and strategic operations (for reviews see Urry 2000; Cresswell 2006; Adey 2010). It also finds echoes in anthropological and geographical accounts of nomadic resistance to strategies of state power (for example, Scott 1998; Atkinson 2000). The practical and political dimensions of Deleuze and Guattari's nomadology are emphasized in particular by Sadie Plant, who positions them in relation to paths of radical contestation and subversion from the past and present, and who argues that the importance these philosophers attach to the tactics of the nomad can only be appreciated by attending to such "tales of radical dissent." These range from earlier assaults on bourgeois codes and conventions by the Dadaists – "One must be a nomad, pass through ideas as one passes through countries and cities," stated Francis Picabia in 1921 (cited in Breton 1981 [1922]: 216) – to the guerrilla tactics and nomadic "war machines" of autonomists and leftists in 1970s Italy, as manifest in waves of political protest and experiments such as those involving the Metropolitan Indians and Radio Alice. "Refusing settlement and resisting the authority of codification and order, the nomad's deterritorialization of the world interrupts every attempt to stabilize and encode it," writes Plant (1993: 88). The power of the nomadic for her thus lies in its resistance to being placed, its avoidance of categorization, its elusiveness, and its subversion of spatial and social identities.

Such nomadic perspectives have done much to inform critical thinking about cities in terms of their movements and trajectories, their processes of deterritorialization and reterritorialization, and their multiple lines of flight. As influenced especially by readings of Deleuze and Guattari, and also of Michel de Certeau (1984 [1980]) who dwells on the clandestine and swarm-like movements of ordinary people that cannot be fully captured by strategies of power, their significance for urban studies is commonly seen to lie in the terms broadly highlighted by Plant, that is in their associations with dissent, subversion, and subaltern power, and with deterritorializing, displacing, dispersing, and moving across striated spaces without reterritorializing or producing spaces of their own. Significant in that regard are Deleuze and Guattari's comments on nomadic space through the term *nomos*, to refer to a distribution in an open space without enclosures and borders. Against this were erected the fortifications of the city, hence *nomos* stands in opposition to the *polis*. But if the city is "striated space par excellence," they depict the smooth spaces arising from it as

> not only those of worldwide organization, but also of a counterattack combining the smooth and the holey and turning back against the town: sprawling, temporary, shifting shantytowns of nomads and cave dwellers, scrap metal and fabric, patchwork, to which the striations of money, work, or housing are no longer even relevant. (Deleuze and Guattari 1988 [1980]: 481)

They also note how it is possible to be an urban nomad and live smoothly within the city's spaces, in relation to which they cite "strange voyages in the city" and examples of nomadic transit that make the city "disgorge a patchwork, differentials of speed, delays and accelerations, changes in orientation, continuous variations" (482). These ideas will be drawn upon below but, in the next sections of this chapter, I want to turn to explore another way of thinking about cities from a nomadic perspective, one that gives a central role to the construction of space through a more totalizing and explicitly revolutionary attempt to imagine new cities and new ways of urban living.

Cities Made for Drifting

Becoming nomadic was central to how Constant imagined the transformation of cities and urban life in New Babylon. Born as Constant Nieuwenhuis (1920–2005), he embarked on this project shortly before he became a member of the Situationist International (SI) and he subsequently developed it, after his resignation from that group in 1960, in dialogue with other artists, architects, urbanists, and activists through the rest of that decade. Along with the Situationists and also others with whom he later had significant associations, notably Henri Lefebvre who became a strong admirer of his work, Constant understood urban spaces to be crucial terrains of political struggle. "The environment in which we live influences our activity, but reciprocally this environment is a product of our creative activity," he wrote. "This is why we must arrive at a conscious production of our environment with all the means that give rise to it" (Constant 2009 [1959]: 111). Previously regarded mainly as a painter, he now deployed maquettes, drawings, writings, lectures, and other means in an effort to outline a possible urban future in which both spaces and life were revolutionized. His project combined opposition to processes of capitalist urbanization and urban planning with an attempt to imagine that other city and other urban life. A key theme was the free movement of the population, whom he believed could become untethered from fixed abodes and free to create the spaces and trajectories of their lives. This would not simply be through the institution of new spatial designs or changes in transportation technologies, as some of his architectural contemporaries implied, but rather from fundamental social and spatial changes that would transform the very basis of the city.

The underlying supposition of New Babylon was that a new urban society was within reach, one based on the realization of what Marx termed "realm of freedom" beyond the "realm of necessity" (Marx 1967: 320). This would entail the socialization of land and the means of production, the rationalization of global production to overcome scarcity, the effective abolition of work through its automation, and the eradication of class division and rule. Urban inhabitants would for the first time be free to create their own lives, and would be relinquished from ties to particular places and schedules. A generalized creativity would become manifest in all areas of activity, in particular in the exploration and creation of the material spaces of this new life. "Starting from this freedom in time and space, we would arrive at a new kind of urbanization," stated Constant. "Mobility, the incessant fluctuation of the population, a logical consequence of this new freedom, creates a different relation between town and settlement" (1996 [1974]: 157). In calling the environment of this new nomadic life New Babylon, he stressed that it was completely different from traditional understandings of the city as a place of residence for a relatively stable and rooted population. That difference was conveyed by the title that he initially proposed for his project, Dériville. Literally "drift city," this promised a city made for the *dérives* through which the Situationists and their associates had explored cities on foot and experimented with mobile modes of behavior beyond the terrains of work and commercialized leisure (see Pinder 2005: 150–9). If those activities had given glimpses of other possible worlds within the urban spectacle, and if other pre-Situationist texts had explored ideas of mobile and passionate urban constructions that might be forged within it, or built upon its ruins, then New Babylon aimed to make palpable a more totalizing possible spatial and social transformation from which no one would be excluded. It was a city that would have no limits, frontiers, or divisions, its spaces being both the medium and the outcome of journeys open to all.

How to present this paradoxical idea of a city of drifting, a city that privileged lines over points and whose spaces were conceived in terms of the trajectories that mobilize them? Its architectural basis lay in multi-leveled urban sectors, raised off the ground to form vast networks. In maquettes and aerial drawings, these appear as relatively stable structures of social spaces and collective services, although they rejected ideas of permanence, and eschewed the nuclei of traditional settlements in favor of decentered chains that extend in all directions. In other depictions and accounts, everything seems to be in motion, not only the residents but also elements of the structures themselves. Internally the sectors are infinitely flexible, continually changing as the décor of a liberated urban life. This openness was crucial since Constant insisted that the environment had to be left undetermined to facilitate any movement and behavior by inhabitants, any change of place and mood. Spatial forms could not be decided in advance since, as he once put it in a lecture, "the people circulating in this enormous social space are expected themselves to give this space its everchanging shape, to divide it, to vary it, to create its always different atmosphere, and finally, to play their lives in the variety of these changeable

Figure 19.1   Constant, Figures in Space – Travel Sketch, 1965 (ink on paper, 30 × 42 cm), Gemeentemuseum, The Hague. © DACS 2010.

surroundings" (1964). The spaces are thus continually being shaped and transformed by inhabitants in motion whose appearance is often blurred or fleeting (see Figures 19.1 and 19.2). Such is the fluidity of this built environment that, at one point, he turns to metaphors of the sea in his suggestion that topographical surveys would require the kinds of symbolic notations used in a ship's log (1996 [1974]: 160).

Urban life is thus imagined as an endless journey through fluid and rapidly changing environments, through intensely stimulating spaces and atmospheres that afford unlimited adventures. Use is made of flexible architectural elements, climatic controls, audiovisual media, and telecommunications to facilitate nomadic wanders and to intensify experiences and encounters within even small areas. Spaces are not consumed passively but are shaped by the actions of those moving who in the process create "a collective poetry," for the "New-Babylonian nomad intervenes and marks the way of his passage" (Constant 1964). The friction, energy, creativity, bodily exertion, and sheer physicality involved in movement is apparent from the drawings, with their vigorous and scrambled lines, and from the internal spaces of the maquettes that are scoured, layered, labyrinthine, and apparently only snapshots of spaces always in process. If the emphasis is on journeys and trajectories, these are not smooth or necessarily fast flows. The changeability of the environment indeed ensures that wildly contrasting scenes and atmospheres can be experienced without much physical movement. Although Constant notes the occasional need for

Figure 19.2 Constant, Labyrisms, 1962 (lithograph from a series of 11, with texts by Carlheinz Caspari, 38 × 48 cm, edition of 79). © DACS 2010.

rapid relocations, he also refers to a slow flux, with the emphasis more on the adventures and pleasures of travel itself than on the destination. The contradictions posed by bringing together concepts of nomadism and cities are vividly conveyed by the tension apparent between the static forms of the maquettes and the fluid lines more easily evoked through the drawings and writings. In a commentary, Francesco Careri suggests the following formulation: "To design a city for a nomadic people that negates the city is a contradiction: New Babylon is this contradiction." He continues: "A double negative leads to a positive solution: a megastructural, labyrinthine architecture, based on the sinuous line of the journey of the nomad" (2002: 116).

Nomads and Political Fictions

When New Babylon was exhibited for the first time in its entirety at the Gemeentemuseum in The Hague, in 1974, Constant chose as the epigraph for his catalogue text a quotation from Vaïda Voivod III, the President of the World Community of Gypsies: "We are the living symbols of a world without frontiers, a world of freedom, without weapons, where each man may travel without let or hindrance" (cited in Constant 1996 [1974]: 154). This recalled the origins of the work, which had been inspired by an encounter with a group of gypsies in the Italian town of Alba, in December 1956. Ousted by the local council from the market-place where they usually stayed while passing through, and camping temporarily on land lent by the artist and SI co-founder Pinot Gallizio, their predicament led Constant, on returning to Amsterdam, to construct "Design for a gypsy encampment," a maquette made out of wood, metal spirals, and plexiglass. In contrast to dominant planning attempts to "order" the supposedly "disordered" spaces of Roma and gypsy-traveler communities through designs that ignore their preferences and intricate spatial codes by seeking to fix them in place (Sibley 1981; Bancroft 2005), the flexible partitions of this design were meant to evoke a fluid form that could be recomposed according to changing needs and desires. In subsequent years Constant extended the principle to embrace a wider understanding of nomadism as he outlined his vision for New Babylon "where, under one roof, with the aid of moveable elements, a shared residence is built; a temporary, constantly remodeled living area; a camp for nomads on a planetary scale" (Constant 1996 [1974]: 154). Meanwhile his interest in gypsy-traveler ways of life continued into the following decade, as he remained enthralled by the promise of free and continual movement as well as by associated music and dance.

Constant's concern with urban mobilities and specifically with figures and practices of nomadism was shared by a number of contemporaneous modernist and *avant-garde* architects who, like him, but from different perspectives, were rethinking urbanism in response to changing conditions, including those associated with migration, the uprooting of populations both violent and otherwise, the remaking of urban landscapes through spatial planning and urban renewal, and the development of technologies of transportation and communication. Organizing mobility had long been a key theme of modernist architecture and planning, with particular attention being given to installing appropriate machinery for differentiating and enhancing flows of traffic. By the 1950s, however, mobilities were being re-evaluated by a younger generation of modernists. Flexibility and openness became guiding principles for many as they broke with modernist orthodoxies through spatial designs that, so they argued, would allow inhabitants greater freedoms to move and to constitute their own environments. Not only were environments rethought in terms of the needs of increasingly mobile populations but also interiors, buildings, and cities themselves were mobilized through proposals for systems, space frames, megastructures, and even a more wholesale dissolution of architectural form through the deployment of portable constructions and personal units as in the remarkable projects of Archigram. It was in that context that many architects turned to the nomad, now frequently decked out in high-tech garb, their reclaiming of this figure marking an abrupt turn from its negative portrayal by many earlier urban critics and planners, therein lying part of its critical appeal (on this wider context, see Hughes and Sadler 2000; Pinder 2010).

Such references clearly play upon associations that are longstanding within modernity of mobility with freedom, emancipation, and innovation. A number of critics have recently raised concerns about such associations and nomad talk, however, in particular in relation to social and cultural theory. Janet Wolff, for example, in a much cited paper, objects to how the term "nomad," along with other travel metaphors, is usually deployed to suggest "ungrounded and unbounded movement" that "misleadingly implies a notion of universal and equal mobility" (Wolff 1993: 235, 236). Similarly Tim Cresswell notes how the "postmodern nomad" who wanders through much recent theory is "a remarkably unsocial being – unmarked by the traces of class, gender, ethnicity, sexuality, and geography." It is "abstract, dehistoricized, and undifferentiated – a mobile mass." He complains that nomad references have proliferated in some fields to the point of being subject to "vacuous generalizations," with "little attention [being] paid to the historical conditions that produce specific forms of movement, which are radically different" (Cresswell 2006: 53–4). This has led to calls for closer examinations of the relationships of power and meaning in specific geographical and historical circumstances, and of the frequently neglected ways in which nomadic metaphors are gendered as well as dependent on colonial discourses, thus having an orientalist provenance (see also Kaplan 1996: 85–91).

While largely targeting more recent writers and theorists, such criticisms bring into question the romanticization of both real and imagined nomads by Constant and others, revealing them to be part of a long tradition within the west that is the flip side of the marginalization and denigration that nomadic peoples have suffered at the hands of dominant powers. They highlight the need to think critically about how such nomads are depicted and how these metaphors, images, and figures work within arguments about cities and urban life. In this regard, Constant's depiction of anonymous New Babylonians, moving alone or *en masse*, often as wandering lines and blurs, traces and swarms, might seem to exemplify that evocation of ungrounded and unbounded movement that Wolff and others caution against. While he pays considerable attention to the mutually constitutive relationship between moving bodies and urban spaces, his references to nomads elide differences among those bodies and their abilities to move. In summoning the liberation of the "masses" and their creativity, it is assumed that all oppressive divisions will be swept away: New Babylon seems to be, as Hilde Heynen puts it, "a society without power relations." She nevertheless questions whether its imagined dissolution of all norms, codes, habits, and ties and embrace of the "law of transitory" provide an adequate basis for claims of a non-alienating and authentic urbanism (Heynen 1999: 172–3).

Constant's use of the term nomad might in this respect be contrasted with that of the poststructuralist feminist critic Rosi Braidotti (1994, 2006). Drawing on Deleuze and Guattari among others, she deploys the nomad as a politically informed image to rethink subjectivity in terms of embodiment and sexual difference, and describes it as a figuration of a situated and culturally differentiated understanding of the subject in ways that attend to the simultaneous intersection of axes of differentiation, even if it is a subject who "has relinquished all idea, desire, or nostalgia for fixity" (Braidotti 1994: 22). Yet, in doing so, she highlights its significance as a "myth" or "political fiction" that works against settled and conventional forms of thinking. She asserts that such political fictions currently have a vital role to play, based on her belief in "the potency and relevance of the imagination, of myth-making, as a way to step out of the political and intellectual stasis" of present times (4). This notion of political fiction is a useful way of thinking about Constant's mobilization of the nomad. It emphasizes the need to consider further the distinctive critical role it plays in his project, compared to how it is used in the works of others with which it is often associated, and how it is part of attempts to undermine settled codes and structures, even while it draws on and reproduces other ideological associations.

In particular it is necessary to situate Constant's references to nomadism within the critiques that he and other Situationists launched against the stultifying and constraining geographies of capitalist urbanization during the 1950s and 1960s, especially in the cities of western Europe where they were based, and against the techniques of state planning that they believed served to striate, channel, and regulate people and things according to notions of their "proper" place as defined by particular class interests. In this manner, Constant focused critical attention on the organization of urban mobilities as determined within social conditions of the time, and on how they might be remade. He attacked how functions and flows were channeled according to regimented planning doctrines, with circulation beholden to the dictates of utilitarian society, and in so doing considered how travel and modes of transport could be devoted not simply to ensuring efficient movement from one fixed point to another but also to facilitating and enhancing play, adventure, social encounters, and collective creativity. Most significantly he emphasized that freedom would not necessarily follow from spatial designs, however flexible and fluid, but also necessitated changing social conditions. Becoming nomadic entailed overturning both the spatial organizations of settlements and the social relations through which they are produced. Instead of the marginalization and involuntary displacement exclusion experienced by the gypsy-travelers he encountered at Alba, there would be a space without enclosures and frontiers, in which every place would be accessible to all and held in common.

Urban War Machines and Geographies of the Multitude

My focus in this chapter has been on attempts to imagine nomadic cities as spaces of liberation, a theme that I have briefly traced through some ideas and practices from specific geographical and historical contexts. In this concluding section I want to ask, what might be made of such visions of mobility from the different circumstances of the present? As I noted earlier, the common association between mobility and freedom, apparent in many of the references to nomadism discussed above, has been widely criticized. This has been especially on the grounds of its failure to consider unevenness and difference, in relation to which Wolff (1993: 235) put it succinctly: "we don't all have the same access to the road." But the road is also continually being recast and remade unevenly. When Constant turned to figures and practices of nomadism it was, as I discussed above, as part of an attack on what he perceived to be the deadening and oppressive forces of postwar urbanism and the power of capitalist development as well as modernist planning orthodoxies then reconstituting urban landscapes in dramatic ways. That was where its original critical appeal and force lay. If viewed from the contemporary perspective of what Raymond Williams (1989: 124) termed a "new nomad capitalism," however, which roams freely, demolishing spatial barriers as it erects new ones, and displacing and exploiting people as their environments melt into air, such visions of flexibility and fluidity as the medium of a nomadic life come to look rather different. As one critic of New Babylon puts it, "mobility is not simply a revolutionary force, disrupting bourgeois stability" since "capitalism is nothing if not dynamic, dependent upon mobility, on the elimination of distance, on breaking down all the Chinese walls standing in the way of the commodity" (McDonough 2001: 100).

Other contemporary perspectives may be gained from considering how ideas of nomadic spaces discussed in this chapter have been directly taken up more recently to inform interventions in urban arenas. Earlier I cited Sadie Plant's discussion of the practical and political dimensions of Deleuze and Guattari's nomadology where she connected it with forms of radical dissent during the twentieth century. A disturbing other side to her story, however, has recently been provided by the architect Eyal Weizman through his analysis of how the ideas of Deleuze and Guattari, along with other theoretical texts that give particular emphasis to mobility and to the significance of undermining fixed urban structures and codes, such as those by the Situationists and Bernard Tschumi, have been appropriated by institutions within the Israeli Defense Force (IDF). Vocabularies of nomadism, war machines, state apparatus, swarming, and deterritorialization became central to their efforts to rethink the operational theory for conducting warfare in urban areas and specifically in Palestinian cities from the mid-1990s. Thus the IDF referred approvingly to creating "smooth spaces," where it intended to operate as if borders did not affect it, in relation to the "striated spaces" of Palestinian areas with their walls, fences, ditches and roadblocks. "Walking through walls" – literally blasting through the walls of private homes in order to reach targets while avoiding the urban syntax of streets, courtyards and the like – became in Nablus, Balata, and elsewhere, a defining mode of military maneuver. Violent military techniques were framed and cloaked in theoretical resources originally intended for quite other kinds of spatial and social subversions (Weizman 2007: 185–218).

Weizman's aim is not to suggest that the theories are somehow responsible for such military aggression. Rather, it is to understand how they are made to perform for practical and tactical purposes, in this case when taken into the radically different political and ethical context of military research and training schools. That said, it should be noted that Deleuze and Guattari made much of the historical connections between nomads and violence themselves, associating the figure with armed rebellion, destruction, and the concept of the war machine. In reflecting on understandings of the nomad derived from their writings, and also that mobilized in Constant's work, it is necessary to acknowledge such associations as part of the "political density" of the figure and as issues that need confronting (Braidotti 1994: 25). Constant, after all, wished to overturn capitalist society and its spatial structures, and some of his images convey not only the destruction of the world war that he lived through as a young painter, or of later wars such as that in Vietnam, but also the upheaval of social change. The associations of nomads with rebellion are also what concerns Plant from the point of view of radical groups and movements. But the nomads of New Babylon as well as many of those discussed by Plant oppose state apparatus violence and look beyond it as they move to the rhythms of desire, festivity, play, and joy. And if Weizman points to one appropriation of such ideas then there are, of course, many actual and potential others, as the figure of the nomad is mobilized in different circumstances to inform different understandings of contemporary urban worlds and their possibilities.

To take one particularly influential example, Michael Hardt and Antonio Negri have recently deployed nomadism and rebellion as key concepts in their three-volume account of political energies of the "multitude" against the decentered global order that they term Empire (2000; 2004; 2009). Nomadism is for them, along with desertion and exodus, a means of class struggle and resistance in an era of imperial control, and they see it as expressing both refusal and a search for freedom. In its spontaneous forms they recognize that it often leads to a rootless suffering and misery. But they also present circulation as a means by which the multitude can constitute itself as an active subject, reappropriate spaces, and make new geographies. This circulation is one that they contrast radically with that tied to market exchanges and communication, which belongs to "the violence of imperial command," and they note that "only a radical act of resistance can recapture the productive sense of the new mobility and hybridity of subjects and realize their liberation" (Hardt and Negri 2000: 363–4). Their concern is particularly with the potential autonomy of the mobile multitude and the productive capacity of its circulation, and consequently with questions about how it can become a positive, political power. An essential moment to that process, and one that is vital in response to the "nomad capitalism" mentioned earlier, is taking control over its own movements so that the multitude gains the right to move and also, where appropriate, to stay put (Hardt and Negri 2000: 396–400).

Critics have taken their work to task for, among other things, a conflation of migration and nomadism with its presupposition of "smooth" global space (Bull 2004), and the "anaemic geographies" on which its abstract and at times seemingly mystical invocations of the multitude depend (Sparke 2005; Harvey 2009). Among the important questions it nevertheless raises are those about mobility as an active politics, and about the significance of battles over the imposition, control, repression, and organization of movements, including those movements of individuals, groups, and populations that are both necessary for capitalist production and also, from its perspective, deemed chaotic and threatening. More recently Hardt and Negri (2009) have turned to the metropolis as a key site of social and spatial struggle, suggesting that the metropolis is to the multitude what the factory was to the industrial working class. In their account of the metropolis in terms of the production of the common and of joyful encounter, and in their calls for these to be intensified through rebellion against hierarchies, divisions, and exploitation that also currently characterize it, nomadism is again being mobilized to speak of desires for other cities and other ways of living.

References

Adey, P. (2010) *Mobility*. London and New York: Routledge.

Atkinson, D. (2000) Nomadic strategies and colonial governance: domination and resistance in Cyrenaica, 1923–1932. In *Entanglements of Power: Geographies of Domination/Resistance*, ed. J. Sharpe, P. Routledge, C. Philo, and R. Paddison. London and New York: Routledge, 93–121.

Bancroft, A. (2005) *Roma and Gypsy-Travellers in Europe: Modernity, Race, Space and Exclusion*. Aldershot: Ashgate.

Braidotti, R. (1994) *Nomadic Subjects: Embodiment and Sexual Difference in Contemporary Feminist Theory*. New York: Columbia University Press.

Braidotti, R. (2006) *Transpositions: On Nomadic Ethics*. Cambridge: Polity Press.

Breton, A. (1981 [1922]) After Dada. In *The Dada Painters and Poets: An Anthology*, ed. R. Motherwell. Cambridge, MA: Harvard University Press, 204–6.

Bull, M. (2004) Smooth politics. In *Empire's New Clothes: Reading Hardt and Negri*, ed. P. Passavant and J. Dean. New York and London: Routledge, 217–30.

Careri, F. (2002) *Walkscapes: Walking as an Aesthetic Practice*. Barcelona: Editorial Gustavo Gili.

Certeau, M. de (1984 [1980]) *The Practice of Everyday Life*. Trans. S. Rendall. Berkeley, CA: University of California Press.

Constant (1964) Unpublished manuscript for a lecture given to the Conference for the Students Association at the Royal Academy of Copenhagen, 12 March 1964, no pagination. In the Constant Archive, Rijksbureau voor Kunsthistorische Documentatie (RKD), The Hague.

Constant (1996 [1974]) New Babylon. In *Theory of the Dérive and Other Situationist Writings on the City*, ed. L. Andreotti and X. Costa. Barcelona: Museu d'Art Contemporani de Barcelona/Actar, 154–69.

Constant (2009 [1959]) Contribution to *Forum* special issue on fusion of the arts and "Integration? ... of what?" In *The Situationists and the City: A Reader*, ed. and trans. Tom McDonough. London and New York: Verso, 110–11.

Cresswell, T. (1997) Imagining the nomad: mobility and the postmodern primitive. In *Space and Social Theory: Interpreting Modernity and Postmodernity*, ed. G. Benko and U. Strohmayer. Oxford: Blackwell, 360–79.

Cresswell, T. (2006) *On the Move: Mobility in the Modern Western World*. New York and London: Routledge.

Deleuze, G., and Guattari, F. (1988 [1980]) *A Thousand Plateaus: Capitalism and Schizophrenia*. Trans. B. Massumi. London: Athlone Press.

Hardt, M., and Negri, A. (2000) *Empire*. Cambridge, MA: Harvard University Press.

Hardt, M., and Negri, A. (2004) *Multitude: War and Democracy in the Age of Empire*. New York: Penguin.

Hardt, M., and Negri, A. (2009) *Commonwealth*. Cambridge, MA: The Belknap Press of Harvard University Press.

Harvey, D. (2009) *Commonwealth*: an exchange, with M. Hardt and A. Negri. *Artforum* November: 211–15, 256–62.

Heynen, H. (1999) *Architecture and Modernity: A Critique*. Cambridge, MA: MIT Press.

Hughes, J., and Sadler, S. (eds.) (2000) *Non-Plan: Essays on Freedom, Participation and Change in Modern Architecture*. London: Architectural Press.

Kaplan, C. (1996) *Questions of Travel: Postmodern Discourses of Displacement*. Durham, NC: Duke University Press.

Marx, K. (1967) *Capital*, vol. 3. New York: International Publishers.

McDonough, T. (2001) Fluid spaces: Constant and the Situationist critique of architecture. In *The Activist Drawing: Retracing Situationist Architectures from Constant's New Babylon to Beyond*, ed. C. de Zegher and M. Wigley. New York: The Drawing Center, and Cambridge, MA: MIT Press, 93–104.

Pinder, D. (2005) *Visions of the City: Utopianism, Power and Politics in Twentieth-Century Urbanism*. Edinburgh: Edinburgh University Press.

Pinder, D. (2010) Cities: moving, plugging in, floating, dissolving. In *Geographies of Mobilities: Practices, Spaces, Subjects*, ed. T. Cresswell and P. Merriman. Aldershot: Ashgate, 176–86.

Plant, S. (1993) Nomads and revolutionaries. *Journal of the British Society for Phenomenology* 24: 88–101.

Sadler, S. (1998) *The Situationist City*. Cambridge, MA: MIT Press.

Scott, J. (1998) *Seeing Like A State: How Certain Schemes to Improve the Human Condition Have Failed*. New Haven, CT: Yale University Press.

Sibley, D. (1981) *Outsiders in Urban Society*. Oxford: Blackwell.

Sibley, D. (1995) *Geographies of Exclusion: Society and Difference in the West*. London and New York: Routledge.

Sparke, M. (2005) *In the Space of Theory: Postfoundational Geographies of the Nation-State*. Minneapolis: University of Minnesota Press.

Urry, J. (2000) *Sociology Beyond Societies: Mobilities for the Twenty-First Century*. London and New York: Routledge.

van Schaik, M., and Máčel, O. (eds.) (2005) *Exit Utopia: Architectural Provocations 1956–76*. Delft: IHAAV-TV and Munich: Prestel.

Weizman, E. (2007) *Hollow Ground: Israel's Architecture of Occupation*. London and New York: Verso.

Wigley, M. (ed.) (1998) *Constant's New Babylon: The Hyper-Architecture of Desire*. Rotterdam: Witte de With/010 Publishers.

Williams, R. (1989) *Resources of Hope: Culture, Democracy, Socialism*. London and New York: Verso.

Wolff, J. (1993) On the road again: metaphors of travel in cultural criticism. *Cultural Studies* 7 (2): 224–39.

Chapter 20

Mobility and Civility: Police and the Formation of the Modern City

Francis Dodsworth

The management of mobility was a fundamental part of the emergence of the modern city, in terms of both its built form and its use. Of course, mobility was not purely an urban phenomenon, but questions and problems around mobility were particularly prominent in the urban context and, perhaps more importantly, the way these issues were dealt with played a fundamental role in shaping the modern city. The mechanisms for promoting certain kinds of mobility and for dealing with their consequences also developed in this period, contemporaneous with the formation of the city itself.

One of the most prominent mechanisms for this kind of social ordering is now commonly referred to by social scientists as a system of "police," a subject of study that was long neglected but is currently undergoing something of a renaissance (see, for example, Dubber 2005; Dubber and Valverde 2006, 2008; Neocleous 2000). In the early modern period, particularly in continental Europe, the term "police" meant much more than a force for the prevention and detection of crime, it encompassed the general regulation of the community for the health, wealth, and welfare of the population (Knemeyer 1980; Pasquino 1991, 2006). Although the term "police" was not in common use in England before the late eighteenth century, as Mark Neocleous (2000: 9–11) has pointed out, this was a question of translation rather than any distinction in terms of the rationale for government: what were termed questions of "police" in France or Germany were termed issues of "policy" in England. Despite this difference in terminology, however, the mechanisms of government employed in England and the concerns they addressed were quite similar to those on the continent (Dodsworth 2006, 2008; Neocleous 2000: 9–11) and it would be quite accurate to describe early modern English government as deploying "policelike powers" in Mariana Valverde's (2006) phrase. As Neocleous

The New Blackwell Companion to the City   Edited by Gary Bridge and Sophie Watson
© 2011 Blackwell Publishing Ltd

(2000: 5) rightly points out, we might in any case more profitably understand "police" in terms of a form of activity rather than an institution.

It has long been recognized that police power is concerned with the regulation of mobility. Classic studies of "social control" (Donajgrodzki 1977) stressed the concentration of police on the problems of vagrancy, pauperism, and labor and argued that the central purpose of modern paid police forces was to impose industrial discipline on the working class. Recently Mark Neocleous (2000: 6–7, 16–17) has revived these arguments, but with the important additional recognition that policing was concerned not only with practices of immobilization and discipline, but with mobilizing practices concerned with the production of order. For Neocleous (2000: xi, 16–17) the core of the police project is the administration of the class of poverty and he therefore conceives of immobilizing practices in terms of a concern with the prevention of disorder and sees mobilizing practices in terms of the fashioning of an active and mobile workforce, arguing that policing is essentially concerned with the creation of the working class and wage labor, not just with its administration. However, I think we can extend this beyond Neocleous's neo-Marxist emphasis on poverty, labor, and the laboring classes, which somewhat obscures other elements of the police project which were just as central to contemporaries.

Following the revival of interest in "police" occasioned by the late work of Michel Foucault, Mitchell Dean (1999: 93–4) argues that police in general is concerned with the regulation and enabling of certain flows (of money, goods, and people) and the fixation of particular (moral) attributes. Police and policelike powers have been used not only to control the poor and fabricate wage labor, but more generally to facilitate the flows of commerce, ensure the fair operation of markets (in both the literal and figurative sense), and more generally to enable the circulation of people and things through the city. Police powers were therefore engaged in the twin occupations of promoting mobility and stabilizing civil society by managing the consequences of commercial mobility, particularly the apparent growth of "luxury" amongst all classes and an increase in social mobility (on which see Dodsworth 2006, 2007).

Police power, then, was not simply negative in effect: equally important was the development of an increased sense of the importance of "civility" and "orderliness" and an attempt to establish these values in cities that were coming to be perceived as disorderly and uncivilized. Concomitantly there was an apparent increasing lack of toleration for anything which intruded on the "civilized" public sphere that reformers sough to create. From the late eighteenth century onwards reformers began to use the fabric of the city itself as a means of social ordering, making the city an engine of civility, and it was also in this period that they transformed the mechanisms and institutions with which they did so in order to render this process more effective. The desire to promote "healthy" flows of people and goods was, it appears, promoted by linking Harvey's idea that the health of the human body depended on the circulation of the blood to the vitality of the urban environment (Sennett 1994: 255–65). At the same time the exchange of ideas and goods were central to developing attempts to fabricate a distinct "public space," an act of urban engineering which sought to realize civil society in the city (Ogborn 1998). This civil society was itself to be civilized, a process driven by the twin developments of a culture of politeness (for a guide to which see Klein 2002) and a "culture of sensibility" (Barker-Benfield 1992) in which "disorder," dirt, excessive noise, and incivility in general became increasingly intolerable to those who sought to refine, cultivate, and civilize themselves and the environment within which they moved.

The significance of these developments for British urban history has recently been recognized (Joyce 2003), but there remains a sense in which "police" in the general sense was something that happened in continental Europe and that police in the English sense developed according to a distinct pattern. As such, although there are several new histories of the development of English police institutions (Beattie 2001; Harris 2004; Reynolds 1998) there remains little work on the relationship between the institutional history of police and broader concerns of urban and social ordering; only David Barrie's (2008) pioneering work on Scotland delves in any depth into the relationship between police reform and urban improvement. Social scientists have engaged with the relationship between the emergence of modern police institutions and the broader concerns of police as a system of governance, but they have focused primarily on police as a mechanism for governing social relations, be they capitalist wage relations (Neocleous 2000) or the manifestation of patriarchal power (Dubber 2005), and they have not paid sufficient attention to the material and spatial transformations involved in policing, which were themselves closely connected to institutional change.

My aim in this chapter is to trace the relationship between police reform and urban improvement in late eighteenth- and early nineteenth-century Manchester. The example of Manchester demonstrates that we do not have to restrict ourselves to analogies between the policelike powers of English government and European police science because in some parts of England there were bodies for the government of urban life that not only carried out a broad police function equivalent to that of their European counterparts, but which also took the name "police" and thereby identified themselves directly with this form of government. Here I explore the development of one such institution, the Police Commission introduced in Manchester in 1792, which was the principal governmental body in the town until the 1840s. The Police Commission allows us to explore the deployment of police power in early modern England and its role in shaping the rapidly developing city of Manchester, the "shock city" of the age which came in so many ways to define not only the industrial city but the "modern" city in general.

The Manchester Police Commission

Manchester's Police Commission was formally established in 1792 by an Act of Parliament "for cleansing, lighting, watching, and regulating the streets, lanes, passages and places, within the towns of Manchester and Salford ... [and] for widening and rendering more commodious several of the said streets" (32 Geo. III, c. 69). The Police Commission was established to run alongside a body called the Court Leet, a manorial court responsible for the government of the township of Manchester but which was now felt inadequate for the task (for more on Manchester's government in this period see Redford 1939–40; Turner 1994; Webb and Webb 1963 [1922]). In practice, Salford was administered separately to Manchester, a fact recognized in subsequent legislation in the 1820s. Further Police Commissions were established in Chorlton-under-Medlock (1822) and Hulme (1824), areas which were also adjoining to the township of Manchester and which became part of Manchester Borough Council in the 1840s.

The Police Commission was principally concerned with the "interior order and oeconomy of the town," most importantly safe passage of the streets and their maintenance in decent condition, as John Cross made clear in his address to the Grand Jury of the Court Leet in 1799 (cited in Earwacker 1889: 254–8). It is clear from this document that Cross addressed the jurors and officers of the Court Leet on matters concerning the Police Commission not only because they had a similar function, but because they were in fact the same individuals acting in different roles (Cross in Earwacker 1889: 254; Redford 1939–40: 97).

Unlike the old Court Leet, which appointed individual officers such as "market-lookers," scavengers, and constables to assess the quality of specific goods in particular markets and streets, and generally to maintain order in the town (see Dodsworth 2006), the Police Commission divided Manchester into 14 districts with responsibility for these districts divided equally amongst the 42 commissioners established by the 1792 Act. These commissioners were responsible for supervising the watchman appointed for their district and for checking on the activity of the companies hired to pave and light the streets. This focus on the watch function is important because as Reynolds (1998) makes clear the "new" crime-fighting police that developed in the early nineteenth century emerged directly from the eighteenth-century watchman, indeed most of the "new" policemen were simply the "old" watchmen in a new uniform, carrying out the same function. However, it seems that despite hiring dedicated watchmen the system still relied heavily on the voluntary energy of individuals committed to public service for their supervision and that this was not always forthcoming, hence Cross's concern to excite the Police Commissioners and Leet officers into activity.

Cross defined Manchester's problems as follows:

> During many wet and dark winter months, the streets have remained uncleansed and without lights; for some time no watchmen or patroles [sic] were appointed – Security and temptation were thus afforded to plunder: and none could pass through the streets in safety – Escaping personal violence, they were still in imminent personal danger, from the numerous unguarded cellars, pits and various obstructions that everywhere obstructed their passage … though innumerable buildings are everywhere rising up and crouded [sic] together, I am informed no party walls have been erected … the streets are still filled with annoyances … offenders are every day encouraged by the impunity with which their trespasses are committed. Not a street has been widened … on the contrary in many places by the act expressly designated to that end, we have seen recently erected spacious and substantial buildings. (Cross in Earwacker 1889: 256–7)

Ease and safety of mobility are clearly central to Cross's concern here, his aim being to establish the possibility of free passage through the streets without the danger of physical injury from either human or non-human assailants and maintaining the ease of traffic flow through the town.

Whether or not it was due to Cross's encouragement, the Police Commission certainly did become more active from 1799 when a German merchant, Charles

Frederick Brandt, became its treasurer and forced it into activity by appointing its first full-time police officer in 1804. His task was to oversee the night watch (the only aspect of their governmental duties actively carried out by the Commission who sub-contracted out all other services to private companies) and also to inspect the state of the paving and supervise the lighting and scavenging contractors (see Redford 1939–40; Webb and Webb 1963 [1922]: 259–63). The concern, then, was still with maintaining easy and safe passage through streets which should be clean and civilized. This period also saw houses numbered at public expense and more regular measuring of the extent of the town, something first carried out in 1753, both of which enabled the Commission to gain knowledge of the town and assess the quantity, quality, and density of building, the degree of coverage offered by the existing watchmen, lighting, and so on.

The Police Commission was reorganized in 1828 (9 Geo. IV, c. 117) and 1830 (11 Geo. IV, c. 47) to run on more formal lines, with the different functions of the Commission separated out into four different committees, with only the Watch, Nuisance, and Hackney Carriage Committee being directly administered by the Commission, the others once again being tendered out to private contractors. The watch function remained so central to their concerns that it was governed directly by the Commission itself. Importantly, the new, expanded watch force drew inspiration from the new Metropolitan Police in London, not only in its revised structure, but also following the wording of the Metropolitan Police instructions by focusing the attention of the watchmen on *the Prevention of Crime*" (Manchester Police Commission 1830: 3). Indeed, like the Metropolitan constabulary force, the Manchester watchmen were also to have the legal authority of special constables (Manchester Police Commission 1828: 69). It is clear that the Police Commission were well aware of developments in London from their frequent visits to the capital in order to get their Acts of Parliament passed, and they paid host to the Home Secretary Robert Peel, architect of the Metropolitan Police, at a dinner in Manchester on October 6, 1828 (Manchester Police Commission 1828: 153, 156–8). They also explored the police systems of Birmingham, Edinburgh, and Glasgow (Manchester Police Commission 1828–9) in their attempt to frame the best possible regulations for their own police department and actively utilized this information "by selecting from the Police regulations of London, Edinburgh and Glasgow, such parts as appeared applicable to the Police regulations of this Town" (Manchester Police Commission 1828–33: 407).

However, the Nuisance Department was also a part of this directly administered committee and this remained a general system of police with a primary concern being the circulation of people and goods through the city, with the Commission acting further on the city itself in order to achieve this. The Watch Department, like the Nuisance Department, was involved in the day-to-day maintenance of the new urban fabric the commission sought to create, being instructed not only to take "particular notice of any idle or suspicious person or persons, lurking within his round," examining "all persons carrying bundles, or furniture, through the streets," but also to ensure no ladders or wheelbarrows were left in the street (Manchester Police Commission 1830: 11–12).

Now the Police Commission were concerned not only with paving, lighting, and watching the streets so that they could be safely passed at all times of day and night, but they also set about widening streets and footpaths and rounding street corners, ensuring easy and safe passage for traffic through the town. They ensured doors opened inwards, cellar doors were closed and buildings were constructed according to the fire regulations (Manchester Police Commission 1828–33: 122, 250, 384–5 and throughout). One of the most pressing tasks for the reorganized Police Commission was the widening, draining, and solidifying of the streets: "For better securing the general convenience and health of the town the commissioners should be authorized to level pave and finish streets with soughs footways & c." (Manchester Police Commission 1828: 70). The Manchester Commission were particularly impressed in this regard by the condition of the "macadamized" streets of Birmingham which possessed "an Air of cleanliness and Comfort to which Manchester is an entire stranger, which may I think be in a great degree attributed to their Streets being all paved, and to the hilly nature of the ground on which the Town is built," presumably allowing a free circulation of air (Manchester Police Commission 1828–9: 4). The Mancunian observer "did not see a single wheelbarrow on the footpaths, nor of one instance of encroachment, or goods being sold in the streets except where the Market is held" (Manchester Police Commission 1828–9: 5).

The attempt to create this level of civility in Manchester necessitated the purchase of land and even buildings in the areas needing expansion, which were either added to the road or the footpath as needed. Another common practice was to round off the corners of major streets, easing the flow of traffic around the town. The rationale behind the attempted widening of Water Street in September 1830 was that it "was already a great thoroughfare and likely to become much more so," "the rapid increase of buildings in the interior of the Town renders it highly desirable that its leading avenues should be spacious, as well with a view to the health as the convenience of the Inhabitants, it was deemed desirable that that street be widened," illustrating the guiding principle that ease of passage for traffic and air, as well as light, were the prime motivators in the widening of the main streets (Manchester Police Commission 1828–33: 249). After the new act "no Street or Court should be laid out after the passing of the act of less than eight yards in width" (Manchester Police Commission 1828: 71).

The Act of Parliament Committee that was responsible for establishing this "New Police Bill" for Manchester (echoing the language of the debate taking place in London at the same time) expressed its concern over the licensing of carriages, dealers in second-hand goods and pawnbrokers, as well as leveling, paving, and draining the streets, preventing goods being thrown out of windows higher than the first floor, the selling of goods in the streets, flower pots projecting beyond the sides of houses, throwing stones, playing bat, "wantonly" cracking whips, chimney sweeps shaking their clothes, "the general prevention of singing ballads and songs or uttering obscene language in the streets or Markets or delivering or posting indecent placards or handbills," loitering in groups and obstruction of "passengers" (Manchester Police Commission 1828: 10, 17, 56, 70, 72–3). Overall, the Commission had powers over building regulations, the nightly watch, fire prevention, hackney carriages and other vehicles, and were authorized to make a variety of rules, orders, and bye-laws for the administration of the town including the maintenance of the highways, sewers, and drains and the prevention of bull- and bear-baiting, football in the streets, the use of fireworks, and the lighting of bonfires in the town. They were authorized to appoint surveyors, assessors, collectors, scavengers, lamplighters, and watchmen to enforce these regulations.

These regulations were concerned not only with enabling mobility and counteracting fears of stagnation, corruption, and miasma that were pervasive throughout the social imaginary, but with civilizing public space, creating a sphere free from noisy, obscene, and disturbing sensory invasions into the newly sensitized lives of the urban dweller. Civil society was being made truly civil and the civil made material. This was not a one-off act but an ongoing performance. Civilized, fluid spaces required maintenance to keep them in that condition, preventing vandalism of lights and blocking of pavements, moving on loiterers who congested the pavements or sidewalks and who created disturbances, likewise removing those more flagrant prostitutes who threatened to seduce the weak-willed passer-by. Street games, fireworks, and ballads likewise not only acted as a potentially dangerous obstruction or a distraction from one's proper business, but intruded, often coarsely, into the senses of those who wished to be free from such powerful impressions.

In order to maintain the streets in this civilized condition in 1832 the Nuisance Department of the Police Commission was separated from the other departments "in consequence of the great increase of business," particularly concerning encroachment occasioned by the explosion of building, demonstrating the developing importance of the nuisance function of the police (Manchester Police Commission 1831–4: 33). An inspector was appointed who was instructed to "frequently perambulate his district" to ensure that the streets were "kept in good order": that is properly swept, scraped, clear of snow, frost, or dirt by 9 a.m., either by dedicated scavengers or the house-owner, "more particularly to prevent persons beating door mats, shaking carpets, or leaving night-soil in the streets" (Manchester Police Commission 1838: 4–6). The very structure of the town was their concern, they were to "observe and report to the Committee any streets that are without tiles, or the doors of which are not properly numbered" and that "no encroachment, projection or obstruction is made in, upon, or over any footpath or street … and generally, that nothing is placed or done to prevent the free and uninterrupted passage of the footpaths and streets" (Manchester Police Commission 1838: 4–6). These inspectors formed a network of maintenance officers which operated constantly to ensure the systems created to encourage free movement did not themselves degrade.

So the streets were widened, cleaned, and constructed of a more permanent material, altering the upkeep of the town from the management of an environment defined in part by customary building and social practices and in part by rapid and unchecked development to one characterized by a sculpted, regulated space designed to produce or facilitate a polite, civilized, and commercial society. But this did not exhaust the Police Commission's attempts at urban transformation. The Police Commission further embedded themselves in the urban environment with the construction or renting of a series of buildings to house the watchmen and their other functionaries, literally manifesting themselves as a presence throughout the town. The expanding role and presence of the Police Commission can be read in the lists of property in the Commission's stock book which details everything from the Town Hall, houses and lockups, stores, wheelwright's shop, and smithy, to the ricks, boxes, and clothing of the watchmen. The list becomes increasingly comprehensive after 1829 (Manchester Police Commission n.d.). Perhaps most the most visible manifestation of police power was the new Town Hall the Police Commission built for themselves in 1825. This gave them a grand and permanent location from which to practice government, designed so that the entrance portico (now standing in Heaton Park) resembled the Erechtheion in Athens, while the dome was similar to the Tower of the Winds, sourced from Stuart and Revett's *The Antiquities of Athens* (1762). With this building the Police Commission were consciously creating democratic symbolism, "the sculpture on the façade of the building suggests that links with democracy were on Goodwin's [the architect's] mind, for in niches on the front were the figures of Solon and King Alfred, and in the attic were medallion portraits of John Locke, Solon and Matthew Hale," linking the ancient and modern English constitution to Athenian democracy (Parkinson-Bailey 2000: 59–60). No doubt the Commission sought to use this building to reinforce their claims to be representative of Manchester's population, something they had to construct a case for given the frequent accusations that they governed in the sectional interests of a Tory oligarchy (Turner 1994).

Conclusions

The creation of the Police Commission in Manchester saw the establishment of the first paid, hierarchically organized police system for the city, one modeled in part on the Metropolitan Police introduced in London in 1829. However, although the Manchester watchmen were now to be constables like their London counterparts and were told that their chief duties were to be the prevention of crime, they were just one element of a broader police function which encompassed urban reform in the most general sense. As such I would argue we need to think more carefully about the ways in which we bracket off English police history as separate and distinct from its European counterparts. It might be thought that Manchester is an unusual exception here, however the examples of Birmingham, Edinburgh, and Glasgow cited above, and the work of David Barrie (2008) on Scottish police, suggest otherwise. Indeed, as Webb and Webb (1963 [1922]) make clear, such systems of improvement were common in late eighteenth- and early nineteenth-century England. Even in London we can see considerable overlap between the interests of London police reformers (Reynolds 1998; Dodsworth 2008) and urban improvement being undertaken contemporaneously (Ogborn 1998). We need to recognize the interrelatedness of much urban and social reform in the late eighteenth and early nineteenth centuries. Even where institutional police reform took place separately, the newly reformed bodies were often intended to be complementary in operation to the grand projects of improvement that sought to bring modernity, civility, and politeness to the city.

The Manchester Police Commission, then, sought to reconstruct the city so as to facilitate the flows of people and goods, increasing the politeness, wealth, and civility of the town. The watchmen and nuisance inspectors were agents in this process of urban reform, essentially concerned with preventing the degradation of the newly civilized environment and its despoiling by those amongst the population who were yet to be converted to the cultures of sensibility or politeness. They were, however, only two elements in the process, which also saw the city itself deployed as a civilizing and mobilizing tool through the reshaping, cleaning, lighting, and patrolling of its streets and buildings. If we want to fully understand the role of police power in shaping the modern city and the societies that inhabit it we need to cast our gaze beyond the important factors of the labor process and social relations and reflect on its relationship to the material environment of the city and its maintenance as a space of mobility, commerce, and civility.

References

Barker-Benfield, G. J. (1992) *The Culture of Sensibility: Sex and Society in Eighteenth-Century England*. London: Chicago University Press.

Barrie, D. G. (2008) *Police in the Age of Improvement: Police Development and the Civic Tradition in Scotland, 1775–1865*. Cullompton: Willan.

Beattie, J. M. (2001) *Policing and Punishment in London: 1660–1750: Urban Crime and the Limits of Terror*. Oxford: Oxford University Press.

Dean, M. (1999) *Governmentality: Power and Rule in Modern Society*. London: Sage.

Dodsworth, F. M. (2006) Liberty and order: civil government and the common good in eighteenth-century England. CRESC Working Paper no. 21, August 2006. Available online at www.cresc.ac.uk/publications/ (accessed September 1, 2009).

Dodsworth, F. M. (2007) Police and the prevention of crime: commerce, temptation and the corruption of the body politic, from Fielding to Colquhoun. *British Journal of Criminology* 47: 439–54.

Dodsworth, F. M. (2008) The idea of police in eighteenth-century England: discipline, reformation, superintendence, c. 1780–1800. *Journal of the History of Ideas* 69 (4): 583–604.

Donajgrodzki, A. P. (ed.) (1977) *Social Control in Nineteenth Century Britain*. London: Croom Helm.

Dubber, M. D. (2005) *The Police Power: Patriarchy and the Foundations of American Government*. New York: Columbia University Press.

Dubber, M. D., and Valverde, M. (eds.) (2006) *The New Police Science: The Police Power in Domestic and International Governance*. Stanford, CA: Stanford University Press.

Dubber, M. D., and Valverde, M. (eds.) (2008) *Police and the Liberal State*. Stanford, CA: Stanford University Press.

Earwacker, J. P. (ed.) (1889) *The Court Leet Records of the Manor of Manchester (from the Year 1552 to the Year 1686, and from the Year 1731 to the Year 1846), vol. IX (1787)–1805*. Manchester: Blacklock and Co.

Harris, A. T. (2004) *Policing the City: Crime and Legal Authority in London: 1740–1840*. Columbus: Ohio State University Press.

Klein, L. (2002) Politeness and the interpretation of the British eighteenth century. *Historical Journal* 45: 869–98.

Joyce, P. (2003) *The Rule of Freedom: Liberalism and the Modern City*. London: Verso.

Knemeyer, F.-L. (1980) Polizei. *Economy and Society* 9: 172–96.

Manchester Police Commission (n.d.) Stock Book of the Commissioners of Police. Manchester Central Reference Library, Local Studies Unit, Archive Service, M9/30/7/1.

Manchester Police Commission (1828) Minutes of the Act of Parliament Committee, 1828. Manchester Central Reference Library, Local Studies Unit, Archive Service, M91/30/7.

Manchester Police Commission (1828–9) Reports of the Police Establishments in Various Towns. Manchester Central Reference Library, Local Studies Unit, Archive Service, M9/30/9/1.

Manchester Police Commission (1828–33) Proceedings of the Commissioners, 25 Aug. 1828–9 Jan. 1833. Manchester Central Reference Library, Local Studies Unit, Archive Service, M9/30/1/6.

Manchester Police Commission (1830) *Regulations for the Government of the Watch Department of the Manchester Police*. Manchester: Henry Smith.

Manchester Police Commission (1831–4) Proceedings of the Watch, Nuisance, and Hackney Coach Committee. Manchester Central Reference Library, Local Studies Unit, Archive Service, M9/30/5/2.

Manchester Police Commission (1838) *Instructions and Regulations for the Nuisance Department of the Commissioners of the Manchester Police*. Manchester: Clarke and Co.

Neocleous, M. (2000) *The Fabrication of Social Order: A Critical Theory of Police Power*. London: Pluto.

Ogborn, M. (1998) *Spaces of Modernity: London's Geographies, 1680–1780*. New York: Guilford Press.

Parkinson-Bailey, J. (2000) *Manchester: An Architectural History*. Manchester: Manchester University Press.

Pasquino, P. (1991) *Theatrum politicum*: the genealogy of capital – police and the state of prosperity. In *The Foucault Effect: Studies in Governmentality*, ed. G. Burchell, C. Gordon, and P. Miller. Hemel Hempstead: Harvester, 105–18.

Pasquino, P. (2006) Spiritual and earthly police: theories of the state in early modern Europe. In *The New Police Science: The Police Power in Domestic and International Governance*, ed. M. D. Dubber and M. Valverde. Stanford, CA: Stanford University Press, 42–72.

Redford, A., assisted by Russell, I. S. (1939–40) *The History of Local Government in Manchester*, 2 vols. London: Longman.

Reynolds, E. (1998) *Before the Bobbies: The Night Watch and Police Reform in Metropolitan London: 1720–1830*. London: Macmillan.

Sennett, R. (1994) *Flesh and Stone: The Body and the City in Western Civilization*. London: Penguin.

Turner, M. J. (1994) Gas, Police and the Struggle for Mastery in Manchester in the Eighteen-Twenties. *Historical Research* 67: 301–17.

Valverde, M. (2006) "Peace, order and good government": policelike powers in postcolonial perspective. In *The New Police Science: The Police Power in Domestic and International Governance*, ed. M. D. Dubber and M. Valverde. Stanford, CA: Stanford University Press, 73–106.

Webb, S., and Webb, B. (1963 [1922]) *A History of English Local Government: Special Bodies for Special Purposes*, vol. 4. London: Cass and Co.

Chapter 21

Disease and Infection in the City

Simon Carter

MAYOR (OF NEW ORLEANS):	I had Mackey make up a statement … a complete explanation of the facts as they stand. Before I give it to Neff here, I want a confirmation from you … that the disease can be contained, and there's no reason for panic.
DR. MACKEY:	Our only chance for full cooperation, Clint, is to inform the public.
MAYOR:	You agree?
LT. CMDR. CLINT REED: (PUBLIC HEALTH SERVICE)	NO! The minute he prints it, the men we're looking for will leave the city. Now, I told you once, and I'll tell you again. Anyone leaving here with … with plague endangers the entire country.
NEFF (NEWSPAPER REPORTER):	The entire country hasn't got it. We have. A woman died here last night. This problem lies right here in our own community.
LT. CMDR. CLINT REED:	Community? What community? – Do you think you're living in the Middle Ages?
NEFF:	Oh, come now.
LT. CMDR. CLINT REED:	Anybody that leaves here can be in any city in the country within ten hours. I could leave here today and be in Africa tomorrow. And whatever disease I had would go with me.
NEFF:	I know that.
LT. CMDR. CLINT REED:	Then think of it when you're talking about communities! We're all in a community … the same one!
LT. CMDR. CLINT REED:	… Give me a cigarette!
POLICE OFFICER:	Take the pack …
	(*Panic in the Streets*, Elia Kazan [1950])

The New Blackwell Companion to the City   Edited by Gary Bridge and Sophie Watson
© 2011 Blackwell Publishing Ltd

Introduction

The Elia Kazan film, *Panic in the Streets* (1950) depicts the city of New Orleans on the verge of a virulent and fatal epidemic of pneumonic plague. The central character, Dr Clint Reed (played by Richard Widmark) of the US Public Health Service, has to trace the source of the disease before a critical mass of local residents becomes infected and the city is decimated. Shot in a realistic documentary style, and paying close attention to public health procedures and practices, the film twists through run-down New Orleans locations, often using locals as bit-part actors and actual city locations as film sets: a waterfront packing plant; crowded bars; disorganized domestic environments; the city mortuary; a shipping office crowded with merchant seamen looking for work; a transnational merchant ship with a multi-national crew; and a crowded café with peeling paint on the walls. The film's central plot device, the search and hasty attempt to construct a borderland around infectious carriers of plague, is often juxtaposed to the hybridization of the global city itself – New Orleans is represented as a cacophony of different sensations with sounds, spaces, and even time mixing together and collapsing. Indeed, even the implied xenophobia of the film (the original plague-carrier was an illegal immigrant) is contrasted and neutralized by the continuous depictions of the ethnic, cultural, and global fusions going on within the city itself. The eventual confinement of infection provides a "happy ending" for the film but one that appears somewhat implausible given the narrative up to this point – the chances of producing a sanitized borderland around infection in this city (or in any similar city) seem to be slim.

This film can be said to encapsulate a number of themes relating to infection and disease in the city (see also Ali and Keil 2008: xx for a detailed discussion of disease in the global networked city). Three broad areas of inquiry are particularly worthy of attention. The first is the relationship between the "global city network" and microbial or viral traffic. Thus, to use the city in the film as an example, we can think of the global city as a node with inward flows of infection followed by an opportunity to amplify these before an outward redistribution of pathogens ("I could leave here today and be in Africa tomorrow. And whatever disease I had would go with me.") The second area is that of institutional governance and regulation often with a tension existing between local and national (and even international) officials about how to best disrupt those social and environmental interactions that might aid the spread of infection. The third field of inquiry is the thorny issue of the culture of civil society within the global city. For example how well do citizenship rights or the "multicultural fabric" hold up in the face of emerging pandemics? Should the lay publics be given unrestricted access to information about a pandemic? What if it might cause panic? How may rights be affected when an infection becomes overtly "racialized" as with SARS in Toronto or the re-emergence of tuberculosis (TB) in London?

This chapter will explore some of some of these questions from an historical perspective informed by Science and Technology Studies. From this position the historical city is a changing heterogeneous network – entangled within which are not only a variety of cultural entities (such as discourses about health and infection) but also technological artifacts (such as architectures, transport systems, health services, and technologies of control and surveillance). But of course, to begin with a dichotomy between cultural and technological artifacts is highly problematic. These are inherently intertwined into the many localized assemblages and orderings that make up the city.

The Medieval City and the "Black Death"

The issues outlined above seem particularly relevant today. The emergence of novel infections such as SARS and HIV, the threat of pandemic influenza, and the re-emergence in Europe and North America of previously controlled infections such as TB generate specific challenges (although in much of the world infections like TB were never controlled). Yet the connection between disease, infection, and cities is not a recent phenomenon. Thus taking the relationship between the "global city network" and microbial or viral traffic, we could point towards premodern or even ancient cities. Before the advent of industrialization, and the growth of modern cities, the largest city was ancient Rome – a city networked into the center of a global empire. Estimates of Rome's size are the matter of some debate, but at its largest (around 5 BCE) it is thought to have had between a half million (Storey 1997) and one million (Robinson 1992) residents. This would have given a population density that is comparable to some modern cities. While debates about ancient Rome's size continue, what is clear from historical records is that this was a spec-tacularly unhealthy place to live. Examination of tombstone inscriptions, held in the *Corpus Inscriptionum Latinarum*, reveal that the citizens of Rome enjoyed far shorter lives than those based in the rural areas of Hispania and Lusitania, or in the North African colonies. Around 70 percent of those in rural locations reached 30 years of age whereas for residents of Rome only 1 in 3 reached this age. Or to put this another way, every resident of Rome had a 1 in 20 chance of dying in any given year irrespective of their age (Macdonell 1913). Indeed this may be a some-what optimistic reading of the data as the most impoverished people living in Rome, and by implication the unhealthiest, would be unlikely to have tombstone inscrip-tions and so would be excluded from the analysis.

Rome may have been an extreme example of an insalubrious environment, but the conditions that made this city unhealthy could apply equally to the many urban centers that have grown up subsequently. As Cairns (1997) says, cities often are the "graveyards of mankind" due to their local ecologies of microbial and viral traffic. Hence, in scattered or dispersed communities, typically found in rural locations, infection either kills or immunizes all available victims rapidly, after which the contagion burns itself out. On the other hand, in a city environment, large numbers of people are likely to be in constant and close contact – immunity or the death of an individual is of little importance as there will always be fresh people who are still susceptible (especially children) to the infection. Indeed some have argued that diseases such as plague, leprosy, tuberculosis, and syphilis, conditions that still evoke repugnance in the social imaginary, were largely absent before the growth of urban centers and it was only because city environments were so favorable to these pathogens that they were able to flourish (McNeill, 1976).

A further example of the relationship between city networks and the spread of infection is the pandemic commonly referred to as the Black Death, which in the fourteenth century devastated Asia, North Africa, and Europe. Indeed, it is believed that the Black Death was one of the most deadly pandemics in history, having a mortality rate amongst the general population of between 30 and 60 percent in Europe and the Middle East. It is still not entirely clear what caused this pandemic or, indeed, the ways in which the Black Death was transmitted. But the most likely agent is still considered to be bubonic plague, caused by the bacillus *Yersinia pestis*, and spread by fleas and rodents (see McCormick 2003). The ecology of plague transmission is complex, with interlocking relationships between humans, bacilli, rodents, fleas, and their various environments. But it seems likely that a variety of different transmission pathways allowed the spread of the disease: for example, ships carried rats between city ports; the trade of goods such as grain, cloth, and bedding carried either rodents or fleas between cities; and the development of pneumonic plague (a form of bubonic plague) in some areas allowed the direct transmission of disease between humans.

Despite these complexities of transmission, the pattern of infection spread has been well established and is straightforward. The disease spread quickly along sea routes, appearing first in city ports and then passing more slowly along interior road and river trading routes to inland cities, where local city-based epidemics lasted between five and seven months. Medieval cities then formed the starburst amplification centers of infection, with each city-based epidemic distributing radials of infection into the outlying rural hinterland. It was the densely packed populations of humans, rodents, and fleas which coexisted in cities that allowed the Black Death to thrive. Thus, cities were the nodes in a global network of infectious flows that distributed plague. Hence, after first appearing near the Caspian Sea in 1346, the infection rapidly circled the Mediterranean, before spreading into Europe, China, and India. Very few regions of Europe were left untouched and by 1353 plague had reached as far north as Moscow and the Baltic. It was the truly global pandemic of its age. Plague illnesses continued to reappear sporadically over the next 300 years, following the same pattern of appearing first in cities before spreading along trade routes (Bowsky, 1971).

The example of the Black Death also illustrates the importance of taking account of institutional governance and the culture of civil society when considering infections in the "global networked city." Thus a variety of vigorous social and material measures, both formal and informal, were attempted to control the advance of the plague at different times and places in medieval Europe. One of the most common responses was flight from an infected city into its rural hinterland, especially for wealthy or privileged residents. Indeed, this was the typical response for aristocratic and royal families throughout Europe when the threat of plague loomed. However this did not always occur without incident. Thus during a plague outbreak at Lyon in 1628, the bourgeoisie of the city fled to their country estates. When the greater mass of Lyonnais inhabitants attempted to follow it was reported that they were driven back by stone-throwing peasants (Watts 1997). But as well as flight, in many European cities, the anticipated arrival of plague was often interpreted as a form of divine chastisement for the venial sins of locals. Public authorities sometimes attempted to respond by the prohibition of activities such as gambling and other lewd behaviors. But more extreme Christian reactions included banishing nonconformists or those following an irregular lifestyle. In some parts of Europe the casting out of non-conformists took more extreme forms including genocidal violence directed against Jews who were believed to be responsible for the spread of disease. Thus on Valentine's Day 1349, before the plague had even arrived, around 900 Jews were burned alive in Strasbourg (Watts 1997) – part of a more widespread pogrom against Jews throughout Provence, Switzerland, southern Germany, and the Rhineland. This led to the destruction of hundreds of communities and the violent death of thousands.

Other city authorities took what may be recognizable as more traditional health measures. Following a medical tradition based on the writings of Hippocrates and Galen, in which epidemics were thought to be caused by foul vapors, steps were instituted not so much to control contagion as to control the many odorous practices found within the city. However, city states in northern Italy adopted novel techniques in the fight against plague including instituting quarantines, imposing travel restrictions, passing laws restricting public gatherings, even for funerals or other religious assemblies, setting up "pest houses" to confine plague victims, burial of plague victims in special mass pits, appointing boards of officials (early health boards) to administer regulations, and by 1400 formulated special "licences to travel" to control access by individuals to plague areas – effectively a "proto-passport."

Italian city ports in this period were significant centers of maritime trading, with ships arriving from all parts of the known world. As such the cities of this region were particularly susceptible to plague. Thus the first modern quarantine was instituted in 1377 in the Venetian city colony of Ragusa. Initially this was enacted as a legal system to protect commercial networks and merchandise "rather than for medical aetiopathogenetic purposes" (Frati 2000: 103). At first the quarantine period for ships and individuals arriving from suspect areas was set to 30 days but this was later extended to 40 days when it was believed that the progress of the disease was unaffected by the shorter period. Soon the use of quarantine to control infection was accepted as the norm in other Italian city ports and in coming years quarantine was adopted more widely throughout Europe in attempts to control the spread not only of plague but other diseases such as cholera. Interestingly the 40-day period remained the norm for most quarantines irrespective of the disease that was to be controlled.

The measures adopted by the Italian cities in this period, for the most part, were not particularly effective. But what is of interest here is the enactment of legal instruments that conflated and commingled contemporary medical theory and municipal statutory practice. Local taxation was used to hire medical clinicians to advise and administer policies relating to the control of plague and health magistrates were appointed to oversee these policies. Thus confinement of plague victims in pest houses, or placing potential plague-carriers under quarantine, was sanctioned by medical theory and enacted within a legal framework. These novel ordering practices adopted by the Italian city states were the beginnings of state-sanctioned public health measures which, over the next few centuries, would be expanded throughout Europe (Park 1999).

For some commentators the enactment of plague control measures represents a turning point not only in the control of illness but also in the very ways in which people were ordered, controlled, and ruled in the early modern period (Watts 1997,

Carmichael 1986). This is very much the view taken by Foucault (1977) in describing the measures to combat plague in seventeenth-century Paris. Here he recounts how plague regulations produced an arrangement that attempted an absolute control over the city borders and movement within the city. The citizenry of the city were confined into their homes with the appointment of agents responsible for surveillance:

> Each street is placed under the authority of a syndic, who keeps it under surveillance; if he leaves the street, he will be condemned to death. On the appointed day, everyone is ordered to stay indoors: it is forbidden to leave on pain of death. (Foucault 1977: 195)

Foucault draws a comparison between these approaches and those used in previous eras to mark out, exclude, and confine lepers where the desire was to "purify" the city by the removal of a polluting or stigmatized sufferer. In contrast, the plague measures sought to create a "disciplined society" within the city where the sufferers were analyzed and observed: "each individual is constantly located, examined and distributed among the living beings, the sick and the dead – all this constitutes a compact model of the disciplinary mechanism" (Foucault 1977: 197). In this analysis the importance lay less in the effectiveness of the measures but was more about the "political dream" of a "disciplined society" that it offered: "in order to see perfect disciplines functioning, rulers dreamt of the state of plague" (Foucault 1977: 198).

The Regulation of Health in the Industrial City

The policies and plague regulations first used in Italian city states, and then much later by other cities, mark a change in the way that disease was addressed in the early modern city. Disease was now becoming an object of surveillance and analysis and subject to disciplinary techniques. Yet during the period that these measures were introduced, the plague had, for the most part, already disappeared from Europe. There was an isolated outbreak in Marseille in 1720 (Biraben 1975), and several epidemics in Russia throughout the eighteenth century (Melikishvili 2006), but for the most part the measures Foucault was writing about were a response to a menace that never materialized, to an "imminent but not yet actual, and really graspable, disaster" (Sontag, 1991: 175). This illustrates another important issue about the attempted management and control of urban diseases in the modern period: that the imagined threat, as much as the real threat of disease, inevitably produces new social and material orderings within the city itself.

However the scourge of disease and death in the rapidly growing cities of the eighteenth and nineteenth centuries was far from imaginary. With the coming of industrialization many cities, especially those in Britain, underwent rapid growth on an almost inconceivable scale. For example between 1801 and 1851 London's population more than doubled, rising from 960,000 to around two million. While some of this may have been due to the increasing birth-rates amongst city dwellers, the migration from rural to urban was also playing a significant role (Lawton 1986). A similar pattern of urban growth could be found around many of Britain's industrialized areas. Many of the developments to house the new urban populations were little more than the barest attempts to provide shelter, with small, cramped, back-to-back houses situated in small courtyard developments. Many such housing developments lacked sewers or were surrounded by paving stones with the result that access to these dwellings was through muddy courtyards and lanes filled with stagnant, unsanitary waste and water. While mortality rates in Europe had stabilized, and may have even begun to decline during the eighteenth and nineteenth centuries, urban mortality remained very high. Indeed rates in some cities actually increased in this period. The variety of fatal urban infections ranged from ever present scourges like tuberculosis to the sporadic epidemics of cholera, but also included often forgotten ailments such as the pneumonia-diarrhea complex responsible for the death of many children. High mortality rates were also compounded by the interactions of infection with other urban problems such as malnourishment and overcrowding.

The public revelation, in contemporary accounts from this era, of the conditions endured by the urban poor caused widespread public scandal. Indeed the founder of the Salvation Army, William Booth, produced a famous exposé of the conditions under which the urban poor lived and the very title of this work, *In Darkest England* (1890), established a link between the cramped and squalid conditions of the urban working classes and ill health. Similarly James Hole's *The Homes of the Working Classes* (1866) described the oppressive environmental conditions created by nineteenth-century urbanization when he warns of the "danger signal showing that we are infringing the laws of health in trying to live where the air will not support plants" (quoted in Creese 1966: 62).

Publications such as these provided a momentum for liberal reformers to tackle the problem of health and disease in the city. Many of the measures taken also provide good examples of how addressing health problems in the city also produces new social orderings. Thus one of the first attempts to reorder the city in Britain was the Public Health Act of 1875, which had an immediate material effect on the socio-spatial organization of British cities and without question rendered a new drawing of the industrial city's social imaginary. The 1875 Act cleared away "hidden slum courts" and brought into being the so called "bye-law" streets. These were streets where all the dwellings were required to have an exposed "street front." It was this piece of legislation that established the typical terraced housing aesthetic associated with many British industrial cities. The "bye-law street" was a significant socio-technical innovation because, by establishing regularity and order in housing patterns, it thus became far easier to provide services such as drainage and sewers. But it also had the effect of regulating and making visible the urban working classes.

Many diseases were able to thrive in the newly growing cities but one, TB, is worth considering because of the way it was able to exploit the newly expanding post-plague urban environments. This disease had a long history of co-existing with human populations but the growth of the modern industrial city clearly provided advantageous conditions for its spread. Modern epidemiological studies reveal three factors as the most important in the spread of TB. These are: crowding, especially when several people occupy the same room as was common in city slum areas; nutrition, with a poor diet making an individual susceptible to contagion; and working conditions, with workers exposed to dust-producing environments, such as mills, metal grinding, and masonry facilities, making their lungs inflamed and thus more susceptible to infection (Johnston 1999). Obviously an individual's exposures to all these exacerbating factors are dependent on socioeconomic status and are likely to be widely found in the early stages of urban industrial development. Here evidence indicates that, in the two centuries immediately before 1850, up to 20 percent of all deaths of adults were attributable to TB (Smith 1988). From the mid-nineteenth century TB began to go into decline. However, for the first half of the twentieth century it was still a major health problem with significant numbers requiring treatment. For example, in 1901 the annual death rate for TB in England and Wales was 128 per 100,000 people. In Britain, at the beginning of the twentieth century 1 in every 8 deaths was caused by TB. It was the most common cause of death amongst men and amongst women was only exceeded by heart disease as the major cause of death (Logan 1950). But more than the numbers of people that suc-cumbed and eventually died from TB was the fact that the disease also had a stub-born and mercurial hold on the collective imagination – it was both mysterious and terrifying (see Sontag 1991).

In the first decades of the twentieth century there was still much speculation about the reasons for the continuing high mortality from TB. One explanation that many lay people and clinicians found plausible was that the excitement and stress of modern urban life made individuals vulnerable to the disease. Thus Dr Vere Pearson, Chairman of the Joint Tuberculosis Council, addressed the 1937 Empire Conference on the Care and After-care of the Tuberculous, and stated that the three dangers to health "attending the development of big populations in big centres like London, New York, Buenos Aires" and other capital cities "were (1) the time and energy wasted in travelling, (2) the difficulty of getting to open spaces for recreation and (3) the anxiety associated with city environment in these days" (*The Times* 1937: 21). This belief, to a certain extent, also underpinned the most common course of treatment for TB sufferers – confinement to a sanatorium. The sanatorium was a descendent of the health spas found in Europe since the eighteenth century and followed a regime of rest or graduated exercise. The notion that partially sus-tained this belief in the value of the sanatoria cure was that the frenetic pace of modern city life may "exacerbate consumption and that removal to a salubrious environment could cure or arrest the disease" (Smith 1988: 97).

So what measures were used to thwart the progress of TB? While confinement in the sanatoria would in theory isolate the infectious individual, in practice most sufferers' stays were too brief to achieve this. About two thirds of admissions were to local-authority sanatoria, where a typical period of confinement was around three months. Patients were typically discharged still with active TB. Some argued that the only sure way of abolishing TB was to also abolish poverty but such proposals were generally regarded as naive (Bryder 1988: 146) and beyond any realistic pros-pect of achievement. Thus the control of TB typically was attempted through edu-cational messages that stressed TB could be avoided by self-responsibility and "healthy living." Characteristic of this approach was the 1925 film *The Invisible Enemy* produced by the National Association for the Prevention of TB. In this film a mother (from a rich family to stress that TB was not limited to the poor) asks a dark figure, representing death, what she had done to deserve losing her son to TB. The answer, providing scant consolation, was that she had failed to protect her son from germs, had not insisted on a "healthy diet" rather than sweets, and had not prevented him from over-excitement through too much hard work at school. The final scene of the film has the dark figure ordering parents to:

> Teach them the benefits of open air and the consequence of bad habits. Teach them to protect themselves from dirt. Hygiene in living, hygiene in the house ... It is a social duty from the point of national interest and general wellbeing. Prevention is better than cure ... Go and teach the truth: "The Fate of Each Man is in his own Hands." (Quoted in Bryder 1988: 147)

Conclusions

In conclusion we have seen how towards the end of the medieval period plague produced a new way of envisioning disease within the city – one that focused on disciplinary techniques of analysis and surveillance rather than simple "purification." These new ways of figuring the city in turn produced new social and material orderings within the city. New techniques of analysis and surveillance eventually and inevitably revealed the unhealthiness of some city environments and also revealed those "dark spaces" of the city in which observation was not possible. Thus, the slum clearances that followed the Public Health Act of 1875 were as much about being able to visually enumerate the city as they were about producing "public health." Within the twentieth century the fight against the tenacious and deadly disease of tuberculosis helped to further extend these ordering practices to within subjects themselves: now the city's energy and excitement became the cause of disease and it further became the "national" duty of the citizen to resist these through self-responsibility and "healthy living" – "the fate of each man is in his own hands."

In this chapter we have examined just two of the great epidemics that have devastated city populations over the last seven centuries. Of course it should be pointed out that there have been many others. But even with this limited examination we have seen how responses to actual, and imagined, threats to urban health have reshaped the institutional governance of, and civil society within, cities. At the time of writing many western cities have enjoyed decades of increasing health as the bacterial foes of the past have been vanquished. But in the epoch of the new millennium new viral threats loom into view – HIV at the end of the twentieth century and SARS and various influenzas in the first decade of the twenty-first century. It is still too premature to predict what threat these, and others, will pose to the global city dweller. But as Hinchcliffe and Bingham point out, "city, state, disease, and society are in process" (2008: 226). With the emergence of new viral threats it is inevitable that new viral orderings will also come forth. How these will shape our cities remains to be seen.

References

Ali, S., and Keil, R. (eds.) (2008) *Networked Disease: Emerging Infections in the Global City.* Oxford: Wiley-Blackwell.

Biraben, J. N. (1975) *Les hommes et la peste en France et dans les pays européens et méditerranéens.* Paris: Mouton.

Bowsky, W. (ed.) (1971) *The Black Death: A Turning Point in History?* London: Holt McDougal.

Bryder, L. (1988) *Below the Magic Mountain: A Social History of Tuberculosis in Twentieth-Century Britain.* Oxford: Clarendon Press.

Cairns, J. (1997) *Matters of Life and Death: Perspectives on Public Health, Molecular Biology, Cancer, and the Prospects for the Human Race.* Princeton, NJ: Princeton University Press.

Carmichael, A. (1986) *Plague and the Poor in Renaissance Florence.* Cambridge: Cambridge University Press.

Creese, W. (1966) *The Search for Environment: The Garden City – Before and After.* New Haven, CT: Yale University Press.

Foucault, M. (1977) *Discipline and Punish: The Birth of the Prison.* Trans. Alan Sheridan. London: Allen Lane.

Frati, P. (2000) Quarantine, trade and health policies in Ragusa-Dubrovnik until the age of George Armmenius-Baglivi. *Medicina nei Secoli* 12 (1): 103–27.

Hinchcliffe, S., and Bingham, N. (2008) People, animals, and biosecurity in and through cities. In *Networked Disease: Emerging Infections in the Global City*, ed. S. Ali and R. Keil. Oxford: Wiley-Blackwell, 214–29.

Johnston, W. D. (1999) Tuberculosis. In *The Cambridge World History of Human Disease*, ed. K. F. Kiple. Cambridge: Cambridge University Press, 1059–68.

Lawton, R. (1986) Population. In *Atlas of Industrializing Britain, 1780–1914*, ed. J. Langton and R. Morris. London: Routledge, 10–30.

Logan, W. P. D. (1950) Mortality in England and Wales from 1848–1947. *Population Studies* 4 (2): 132–78.

Macdonell, W. R. (1913) On the expectation of life in ancient Rome, and in the provinces of Hispania and Lusitania, and Africa. *Biometrika* 9: 366–80.

McCormick, M. (2003) Rats, communications, and plague: toward an ecological history. *Journal of Interdisciplinary History* 34: 1–25.

McNeill, W. H. (1976) *Plagues and People.* New York: Doubleday.

Melikishvili, A. (2006) Genesis of the anti-plague system: the tsarist period. *Critical Reviews in Microbiology* 32: 19–31.

Park, K. (1999) Black Death. In *The Cambridge World History of Human Disease*, ed. K. F. Kiple. Cambridge: Cambridge University Press, 612–16.

Robinson, O. F. (1992) *Ancient Rome.* London: Routledge.

Smith, F. (1988) *The Retreat of Tuberculosis.* London: Croom Helm.

Sontag, S. (1991) *Illness as Metaphor with AIDS and its Metaphors.* New York: Penguin.

Storey, G. R. (1997) The population of ancient Rome. *Antiquity* 71 (274): 966.

The Times (1937) Tuberculosis in the Empire. May 4, 21.

Watts, S. (1997) *Epidemics and History: Disease, Power and Imperialism.* New Haven, CT: Yale University Press.

Chapter 22

Urban Choreographies: Dance and the Politics of Space

Daniel J. Walkowitz

You take an aerobics class now in a gym, the movements, the music is way too loud, number one. And the movements tend to be really violent; it's very staccato kind of stuff. And our, you know, the dancing we do here is aerobic, but it doesn't have that kind of jarring ... I think it's more centered on a heartbeat than the driving rhythms of a machine, which I think is what drives the modern music.

(Thom Yarnel, Pinewoods, Mass., August 2000)

Leading contemporary country dance teachers in London and New York highlight two developments in the contemporary urban recreational folk dance communities. First, they note the irony that English Country Dance (ECD) – a dance form with origins in seventeenth-century England that spawned square and contra dance in the United States – thrives in New York (and the US) today while, comparatively, it languishes in London (and the UK) where its revival originates. As the choreographer and leader of the ECD community in Scotland, Nicholas Broadbridge, sums up the problem:

There's very little dance technique taught in Britain now which is very sad. But in the days when dance technique was taught, when I grew up, people learned to dance carefully and properly. And that is the kind of dancing I found in Berea [College, the folks arts center in Kentucky]. (Smith *et al.* 1999–2009)

Colin Hume, a British computer programmer by day and leading choreographer and caller by night, gets right to the point: "I hate to admit it, but I do think English Country Dancing is thriving more in the States" (Smith *et al.* 1999–2009).

The second observation is one that is readily apparent to any visitor to either a London or New York ECD dance and bespeaks them both: the dance community

The New Blackwell Companion to the City   Edited by Gary Bridge and Sophie Watson
© 2011 Blackwell Publishing Ltd

consists mostly of white, middle-aged and older people. How will the dance community recreate itself and draw from the broader community are constant questions among dancers and dance organizers. As Gene Murrow, a leading New York dance teacher and musician, observes:

> in no way does Pinewoods camp reflect, to use the politician's phase, "the look of America." We do not. The ethnic and social backgrounds of the people who come to English dance week especially, I think, is very different. And that intrigues me and interests me and sometimes worries me. (Smith *et al.* 1999–2009)

By examining the relationship between music, dance, and urban geography in the history of ECD as a cultural practice, this chapter seeks to understand some of the developments that underlie this worry. The geographer Adam Krims, in his study of geomusicology, highlights the spatialized importance of particular musical forms, noting how different forms of music and dance speak different languages with particular social and cultural meanings (Krims 2007). Following Krims, this chapter pays special attention to what might be called geo-kinesthetics, the spatialized location of dance forms. Like music, dance is historically situated, but it is even more closely aligned with social spaces. Music can be transported everywhere on one's personal recorder; dance as a group activity is typically located in a place, be it a ballroom or a club. This chapter illustrates the particular and historically contingent place of modern cultural forms in the city by focusing on ECD in New York, in contrast to its experience in London. The comparison illustrates both the spatialized meanings of cultural practices in contemporary cities and the specific historical context that shape its different trajectories.

English Country Dance

ECD, both as a dance form and in its music, conveys very particular social and political messages. The dance embodies what Cecil Sharp, the leading English revivalist in the early twentieth century, called "gay simplicity." Couples dance in sets of two, three, or four couples or in long lines (for "as many as will") with men across from their partner. The figures, which the popular film dramatizations of Jane Austen novels reproduce, resemble square or contra dancing, the genre's more robust American cousins. Couples typically dance with an adjacent couple for 32 bars of music and then repeat the figures with other couples as each proceeds up or down the line. Musical embodiment is at the heart of the dancing messages though: one dances at arms' length on the ball of the foot with a forward motion to the baroque and renaissance music of masters such as Corelli and Purcell. There is no intimate physical contact, and to a contemporary audience the classical tunes and the dancing bodies signify bourgeois or upper-class propriety and taste.

The cultural meaning of ECD is also spatialized and the dance and its venues represent a counterpoint to meanings associated with other dance forms such as popular ballroom and club dancing. At the turn of the twentieth century, for example, social reformers worried about the deleterious moral and physical effect of music halls and cabarets on immigrant and working-class youth. They worried about unchaperoned commercial spaces that served alcohol, and about the intimate turning dances and the "tango craze" that invited vertigo and loss of social control. Dance revivalists advanced counter-attractions to these commercial venues: chaperoned urban spaces – contact points – in which social revitalization could take place, such as schools, playgrounds, and settlement houses. Folk dance and, most especially, the restrained English country dances, promised a safe healthy alternative in safe supervised spaces. As Cecil Sharp argued to English education authorities, teach English language first, but then teach immigrant working children English folk songs as their "national inheritance." It will, he continues, "make the streets a pleasanter place … and do incalculable good in civilizing the masses" (Sharp 1907: 174–5). In the US, Jane Addams, writing three years later, echoed Sharp: "The public dancing halls filled with frivolous and irresponsible people in a feverish search for pleasure, are but a sorry substitute for the old dances on the village green in which all of the older people of the village participated" (Addams, in Lausevic 1998: 27). Addams did not have to go to England to find support for such views; a cadre of American psychologists and advocates for physical culture shared her perspective. The influential developmental psychologist G. Stanley Hall celebrated folk dancing as "one of the pure expressions of pure play," recapitulating evolutionary development of "race history" (Hall 1905: 160).

One century later, this social and moral language of the early dance revivalists is still echoed in the sentiments of recreational ECD enthusiasts. Dancers observed by the author both as a participant and as a part of the Smithsonian Folklife and Cultural Heritage Center's ECD Video Documentation Project speak a remarkably uniform language with their bodies. Take the example of Pat Ruggiero, a librarian-cum-dancer from Virginia. On the dance floor, Ruggiero's dignified carriage is the predominant body language. In an interview, she candidly acknowledges her preference for the constrained sexual narrative in ECD dancing that makes it a safe place for her of historical imagining:

PAT RUGGIERO: I start with a dignified demeanor, arms quiet at the side, economy of motion, move through the space without any flailing of arms, without any embellishment to the figures, without any unnecessary gestures. Oh, and in body motion, I try to eliminate from my own motion, dancing or not, a lot of twentieth-century ways of conducting ourselves that I no longer care for. Either [the] smarmy sort of gliding across the floor, or jiggles or thrusts, or little coy affectations of the head, and I try to eliminate all of those so I don't look like a twentieth-century person dancing. I don't like it.

Q: Why? What don't you like about it?

P. R.:   … It's very overtly physical, and I prefer a reticence in my interactions with people. And so rather than thrust some limb or do some coy or flirtatious thing that would draw someone toward me – that's not what I want in my interactions, so I want to be honest in my interactions with people, and I prefer a certain aloofness, a certain reticence – so I keep my body tight. So I hold my body in reticence.

(Smith *et al.* 1999–2009)

By holding her "body in reticence" as she "moved through space," Ruggiero told a gendered class story that echoed in many dancers and whose signifiers could be seen and heard through dress, carriage, and music.

Modern ECD

While the embodiment expressed by Ruggiero is fundamental to the ECD, contemporary commentators see differences in the style and vibrancy of the dance in New York and London. Observers point, for instance, to differences in social interactions on and off the dance floor which they attribute to national character: British reserve or American brashness (i.e., American dancers look their partners in the eye more than their British equivalents). "National character" does not, however, account for the apparent similarity in the dancing for the first two thirds of the twentieth century. Neither does it account for a difference in the politics of sound: the tempi, orchestration, and the energy, pace, and flow of the dance as mirrored in the energy, pace, and melodic line in the music. In the UK, according to dance caller Michael Barraclough, "As audiences dwindle and clubs have to cut costs there is a significant trend towards two piece bands for club dances. This will typically be a violin + accordion or piano or keyboard." In contrast, US dancer/dance historian Allison Thompson notes that the "typical band line-up" at an American dance event consists of a "piano plus a few melody instruments (violin, concertina, flute/recorder, clarinet) with sometimes guitar/mando[lin] filling in the middle but also acting from time to time as melody. Percussion, if any, is typically hand-percussion (bodhran, bones, triangle)" (Thompson 2006). Thompson goes on to note that the relatively robust American dance band allows instrumentalists to trade lead roles playfully and to energize the dancers with riffs and tune variants while the band creates a strong melodic line. In contrast, the English dance band sound, which has traditionally been dominated by the accordion (often with percussion from a drum), sounds relatively thin and places greater emphasis on the beat. The raw energy it produces does feel more in keeping with the less fussy "knees-up" dancing of Britain that mixes the older "gentry" historical dances with traditional village dances and squares.

The origins of the differences within the contemporary New York and London dance communities reflect their distinct historical experiences of World War II, the Cold War, and a Second Folk Revival in mid-century. Again, while my focus will be on New York and in trying to understand contemporary New York dancers' concerns with the social character and future of the dance community, the London comparison helps to illustrate the historical context in which cultural forms are located in urban space.

London

The "decline" of the ECD in England observed by choreographer-callers like Colin Hume and Nicholas Broadbridge with which we began can be traced to the mid-century impact of a Second Folk Revival, this one, coming from the US to England, reversing the flow of the first one a half century earlier led by Sharp. At the 1935 International Folk Festival at Cecil Sharp House, Douglas Kennedy, president of the

English Society (EFDSS) was transfixed by what he saw as the raw energy of the peasant dances from other lands and vowed to bring that "fire" to the English dance. Kennedy proceeded to de-emphasize the Playford dances (dances published in *The English Dancing Master* by John Playford, and later by his son Henry and John Young in 18 editions beginning in 1651) that had been his predecessor's stock in trade and until then, the hallmark of ECD. In its place Kennedy substituted a new focus on traditional village dances, squares, and reels, many of which he published in seven volumes of the *Community Dance Manual* (Walkowitz 2010).

Kennedy's new focus reshaped the EFDSS repertoire and the character of a typical country dance evening in mid-century England. Cecil Sharp had worked tirelessly to train a corps of teachers who could carry on his work, and indeed, Kennedy was a member of his demonstration team. De-emphasis on Playford-style dances meant less attention and encouragement to the training of historical ECD dance teachers and musicians and EFDSS never developed the formal apprentice programs for teachers and musicians that subsequently arose in American dance communities like New York.

The Second World War brought further changes as well to the repertoire and the dance community. Because the war decimated the ranks of male dancers, Kennedy imposed a couples-only policy at dances over the protests of many women. At the same time, American soldiers based in the UK encouraged a new passion for square dancing. To entice them to these events, EFDSS ran many square dances in the immediate postwar era. The postwar era also brought American folksingers and folk collectors to England who quickened a new enthusiasm for collecting and spurred the rise of a vital folk song culture of folk clubs, folk festivals, and traditional "popular" village dances. This new folk movement of song and dance reinforced the passion for square dancing and traditional reels and jigs, and created a boisterous ceilidh-like "knees-up" atmosphere with little concern for dance styling.

As important as the transformation of the country dance, though, were changes in the dance community. Since its inception, EFDSS had been an elite group of affluent middle-class professionals. But the entry of young enthusiasts of skiffle music and new folk clubs in the 1950s and 1960s democratized the English folk movement, and in time, the EFDSS dance community as well. By the 1960s, the country dance community in England was younger and represented a broader social base than it had in the past. At the same time, ECD was a national English (and not British) dance tradition with less apparent traction for young people attracted to the Celtic nationalist revival. Thus, in London, the Second Revival became the cultural expression of a British counter-politics, of young people who marched for nuclear disarmament and identified with American jazz and radical folksingers while opposing American (and British) Cold War politics (Walkowitz 2010).

Nonetheless, Playford enthusiasts did persevere in England. However, newcomers encountered less teaching of the older historical dances and fewer experienced part-ners from whom to learn. In practice, the community of Playford dancers aged over time, with their numbers ever diminishing. As the new century dawned, at Cecil Sharp House ECD dancers were mostly octogenarians who had danced since mid-century. Without an infusion of new dancers, the group had become an increasingly small and insular band numbering perhaps two dozen, if all ever came on the same night. In 1998, unable to find a musician (in all London!) to replace their accordionist who had tired of commuting in from Oxfordshire, the group folded.

New York

In contrast to London, the New York ECD community remained fairly unchanged until the late 1960s, and it remained a relatively privileged group of Anglophiles in mid-century, its members drawn mostly from the professional-technical class with upper "middle-class" incomes. Representatives of both the working class and corporate echelons were notably absent. Its leadership remained firmly in the hands of teachers who were English-born, trained personally by Sharp, and devoted to his legacy. May Gadd, whom Sharp had certified, arrived to direct the American Branch of the English Folk Dance Society in 1926 and remained firmly in charge until she retired in 1972 at the age of 82.

Gadd led a like-minded ECD community, however, that celebrated traditional and socially conservative values, especially relative to the political and social upheavals in the Greenwich Village community where the American branch was based. The Second Folk Revival originates in the US. Lead Belly, Woody Guthrie, Jean Ritchie, Muddy Waters, John Lomax, and Pete Seeger and the Weavers, among others, led a revival of the "songs of social significance," and an International Folk Dance movement with evenings of dances "from many lands" blossomed at much the same time. But compared to its British counterpart, the American Country Dance Society was quite resistant to the Second Folk Revival, and nowhere would this be more apparent than in New York's country dance community. Indeed, the Cold War was especially virulent in the US and arguably nowhere more so than in New York City, which headquartered the American Communist Party and had an active radical community. So while New York's substantial left-wing community embraced songs of the "common man" [sic] and "peasant" dances from around the world as an expression of international proletarianism, ECD stood aloof, trumpeting an alternative national tradition. Indeed, in Cold War New York, any association with the Second Folk Revival and the internationalism of International Folk Dance was suspect if not politically dangerous. So, not surprisingly, the leaders of the ECD in New York kept the Second Folk Revival at arms' length and the candle of the Sharp tradition of Playford dances continued to burn brightly. Working from the Country Dance Society offices in Greenwich Village only a few blocks from the political and cultural ferment of beatnik and hippie folksingers in Washington Square Park, Gadd insisted that overt "politics" be kept out of the dance community (Walkowitz 2010).

By the late 1960s, the infusion of young people from International Folk Dance, a "contra boom," and the counter-culture began to change the ECD community in New York. Thanks to the new enthusiasts, American contra dance gained equal footing alongside the Playford tradition in the Country Dance and Song Society (CDSS) as a home for English and American country dance, although ceilidh dance gained no traction in the US. Never subject to the explicitly couple-only policy that marked the London experience, the New York dance community sustained a rich, Playford-historical dance tradition and corps of teachers to advance it.

The Politics of Space

Although New York ECD flourished and London ECD languished by the end of the twentieth century, both groups of dancers voiced concerns that the aging and uniform social character of the dance community as white and affluent threatened the future of the tradition. In Colin Hume's words, "We're not attracting that many young people ... There are a few other people, but mainly it tends to be the middle class." Nicholas Broadbridge adds "I would have to say I think it's [the dance community] middle class and middle aged." And Thom Yarnal, a New York dancer who had moved to Wisconsin to manage a regional theater, notes the dominant place of whiteness as well: "we're a pretty affluent group of people; we're pretty white." He concludes, though, with the question often left unstated: "What accounts for it? Um, you know, I don't know" (Smith *et al.* 1999–2009).

The musical and kinesthetic languages the music and dance expressed in both New York and London spaces suggest some answers. While they may have had different accents, the music and dance sent similar and, as we shall see, unwelcoming class, racial, and gendered messages to many prospective members – the black, Hispanic, and Asian majorities of the city. The New York case, which continues to thrive, illustrates the problem most graphically.

The social profile of the New York dance community changed in the 1970s. Dancers who took the floor at Metropolitan Duane Hall from 1970s to the present were still white and affluent. The nature of whiteness had changed, however, to include white ethnic Jews and Italians (Jacobson 1998). Survey data from the early twenty-first century confirms this impression: only 36.9 percent of respondents claim British ancestry; Jews, who were largely absent a half century earlier, now make up 27.5 percent of the group (Walkowitz 2001–2). Aside from a few African Americans and people of East Asian and Japanese descent, everyone at dances was white.

While the class background of dancers has broadened since Cecil Sharp's visit, it remains pre-eminently middle class and urban. Class and racial homogeneity of the community persists: most "folk" remain professional-technical workers or in the arts – the majority (56.3 percent) are professors, teachers, librarians, social workers, nurses, and doctors, but there was also a fair representation (14.3 percent) of crafts, theatrical, and musical people. In a reflection of the changing character of work in the late twentieth century, a substantial number (10.1 percent) worked in the computer world. Not surprisingly, this professional-technical group is older, well established, and highly educated. The average dancer reports a comfortable household income of $80,000, nearly twice the national average, virtually all are college educated (88.3 percent), and more than half (60.2 percent) have graduate degrees (Walkowitz 2001–2).

The new cohort in the ECD dance community, however, also occupies a particular cultural and political niche appropriate to the dance form and the dance spaces of ECD. Part bohemian, part bourgeois – they resembled the "bobos" caricatured by the journalist-social critic David Brooks (Brooks 2000). With one foot – perhaps only a large toe – back in the counter-culture, they have, as dancer and anthropologist Jennifer Beer observes, "dropped out of the achievement races and just want to hang out and dance and make music" (Beer 2000).

In interviews, dancers repeatedly testify to a professed "spiritualism" (they do not describe themselves as "religious"). ECD, they claim, takes them to another social and emotional space. Yarnal is a good representative of this view. He loves ECD for its "other-worldly" quality. "It doesn't have anything to do with the twentieth century, as far as I'm concerned. It takes you to a different place and it takes you mentally and physically" (Smith *et al.* 1999–2009). Similarly, Glenn Fulbright, a retired professor of music from Kentucky, finds the music the "most transporting experience I have." After doing a dance, he feels "like I've been to church" (Smith *et al.* 1999–2009). Invoking its access to a sacred place suggests how the music associates with highbrow culture. Indeed, tunes by Corelli, Purcell, and other classical and baroque composers functioned as a signifier of this particular class fraction's "distinctiveness" and its status.

Participants repeatedly claim that the dance and music transports them to a "safe" social space as well. Even though the heyday of the counter-culture has passed, many dancers believe that the CDSS community still serves as an alternative social space, a respite from the prevailing "speed-and-greed" culture in which they might thrive as affluent professionals, technical and cultural workers, yet find alienating. Yarnal points out that people on the ECD dance floor express themselves in ways that would be ridiculed elsewhere: "the kind of gestures that we do in dancing, you just don't do on the street." The dance might be "modern," but is a world of its own away from "answering cell phones and running around." As Gene Murrow explains it, doing "English country dancing to beautiful acoustic music in a beautiful setting with people we feel comfortable with" makes the ECD dance community "a haven" from "the hurly-burly of the twenty-first-century American speed-and-greed culture." Indeed, as the descriptor "haven" suggests, dancers saw themselves as in a separate social and cultural space. As Baltimore's Mary Alison (pseudonym) explained:

> This is a refuge from the rest of the world ... [P]eople here are among their tribe, and out in the real world, you often are not. You're trying to find your way among a lot of people with different values, and people that don't necessarily share your interests and share your common history ... [Here] they're entering into a community that's accepting of them and that basically wants them here. (Smith *et al.* 1999–2009)

But the invocation of "community" celebrates bonds and coherence that often blur the exclusionary social boundaries of the group. "Community" is a historically contingent experience: they change their principles of inclusion and commitments to collective experience over time. In this respect, the folklorist John Bealle has emphasized how the neoliberal embrace of privatization in the 1990s may have weakened the communitarian ties of the counter-cultural expression of community in important ways (Bealle 2005). The shift compels a revisit to the New York dance community to look more closely at the inclusive or exclusive character of the social, political, and cultural messages the music and dance gave to the space in which it was performed.

Spatialized Urban Culture

New York's Duane Hall exudes a "distinctive" culture with class signifiers. Affluent, well educated, and well employed, these dancers also describe themselves as environmentalists, speak positively about the influence of feminism, and claim to be "spiritual" rather than religious (Walkowitz 2001–2). The Playford-inspired music, drawn from highbrow, classical composers, operates as another signifier of class and race – identification with the northern European white bourgeoisie and court. Dress, which is also more bourgeois and formal than "country," conveys a similar message. At fancy-dress balls, some women wear garlands in their hair, but they accompany ball dresses or designer "peasant" dresses à la Laura Ashley. Although most men simply wear white, ruffled shirts with knickers/kneebreeches at balls, some put on tuxedos or elaborate eighteenth-century aristocratic costumes.

The dancing body, with its gendered and racialized meanings, gives these class and culture signifiers human form. To be sure, most dancers are less explicit than Pat Ruggiero about eschewing the sexual meanings of the twentieth century, but the controlled dance form illuminates the bodily component of what they mean by feeling safe. In ECD, except for the "final waltz," the couple generally dances at arms' length, and the American tradition is to change partners after every dance.

One dancer is unusually articulate and vocal about the related sexual and class meanings of the dance. Jennifer Beer, drawing upon her professional background as an anthropologist, describes Ruggiero's views on styling as "gendered whiteness." Beer also places the body language in a class context: "[T]here's a certain containment in the way you handle your body all the time that is definitely a class mark … [I]t's a structure that allows sexuality, but in a very middle-class, contained kind of way, a safe way." Then in a particularly revealing comment, she added, "You don't show off your butt or your breasts the way you might in, say, in some African dances, where you let it all hang out" (Smith *et al.* 1999–2009).

Beer's candid reference insightfully suggests how ECD in the new millennium stands in opposition to central elements of a more lusty cross-class and intra-ethnic alternative urban black youth culture. The music, dress, and comportment of the dancers combine to mark the dance spaces in New York as white, elite, and "proper." The sound and dancing body move with fluid grace that contrasts with what dancer Thom Yarnal finds to be the "jarring" aerobic music and movement experienced in the urban sports clubs (Smith *et al.* 1999–2009). Thus, the cultural politics of the ECD space is a "respite," a "safe" alternative to black hip-hop and rap youth culture which has come to dominate urban culture outside the dance halls (Bennett 2001).[1]

The classical music's romantic and lyrical tones and the dances' "easy" walking and skipping style at a slow pace contrast with the "thrusting hips" and "jarring" aerobic music that ECD devotees associate with urban sounds. ECD dancers' discomfort with the materialist "speed-and-greed" culture cannot easily be disentangled from anxieties about the cultural expressions of the dominant black urban youth (Nugent 2007). "Whiteness" has changed, but it has not obliterated the exclusionary politics of race nor the politics of space. As an alternative, ECD offered its New York members contained sexual physicality limited to hand holds and eye contact, reliance on classical music and the privileging of English dance as the root of Anglo-Americanness. The physical and cultural space of the dance, then, was an alternative urban space, but the music and the dancing body advanced Anglo-Saxon cultural hegemony. Seeking a wider community, New York dancers invested their spaces with cultural signifiers that marked them as a "distinctive" world apart.

Note

1   The London experience merits further study, but the ceilidh dance also speaks more to white rural culture than to the urban culture of Asian and Afro-Caribbean Londoners.

References

Bealle, John (2005) *Old-Time Music and Dance: Community and Folk Revival*. Bloomington: Indiana University Press.

Beer, Jennifer (2000) Email to the author, Dec. 11.

Bennett, Andy (2001) *Cultures of Popular Music*. Buckingham: Open University Press.

Brooks, David (2000) *Bobos in Paradise: The New Upper Class and How They Got There*. New York: Simon & Schuster.

Hall, G. Stanley (1905) *Adolescence*. London: Sidney Appleton.

Jacobson, Matthew Frye (1998) *Whiteness of a Different Color: European Immigrants and the Alchemy of Race*. Cambridge, MA: Harvard University Press.

Krims, Adam (2007) *Music and Urban Geography*. New York and London: Routledge.

Lausevic, Mirjana (1998) A different village: International Folk Dance and Balkan music and dance in the United States. PhD dissertation, Wesleyan University, Department of Music.

Nugent, Benjamin (2007) Who's a nerd, anyway? Someone very, very white for one thing. *New York Times Magazine* July 29: 15.

Sharp, Cecil (1907) *English Folksong: Some Conclusions*. London: Novello and Co.

Smith, Stephanie, Walkowitz, Daniel J., and Weber, Charles (1999–2009) *English Country Dance Video Documentation Project*. Washington, DC: Center for Folklife and Cultural Heritage, Smithsonian Institution. Interviews with Jennifer Beer, Nicholas Broadbridge, Glenn Fulbright, Colin Hume, Gene Murrow, Patricia Ruggiero, Thom Yarnal.

Thompson, Allison (2006) Email exchange on the ECD listserv, March 30, with a response from Michael Barraclough, March 31.

Walkowitz, Daniel J. (2001–2) ECD dancer survey. Unpublished, in possession of the author.

Walkowitz, Daniel J. (2010) *City Folk: English Country Dance and the Making of Modern Liberalism*. New York: NYU Press.

Chapter 23

Cities on Wheels: Cars and Public Space

Brian Ladd

Cars changed cities: that seems obvious. Automobiles have given people an astonishing degree of individual mobility. They have also become leading causes of pollution, carbon-dioxide emissions, death, and the destruction of urban parks, homes, and neighborhoods. They dominate urban streets and squares, and these (perhaps along with parks) are cities' main public spaces. Streets and squares have long been used for transportation, but also for commerce, for recreation and socializing, and for political communication and organization. During the twentieth century, most of these uses receded in favor of transportation and, to a greater or lesser extent, most other modes of transportation have yielded to the private automobile in cities around the world. The result is urban public space divided between the interior comforts of the vehicles and the noisy, polluted, and dangerous environment they create outside – with a great deal of urban land also devoted to the storage of cars. In most US cities, and many others, private automobiles are the nearly exclusive form of transportation. Even where they are not (as in New York or London or many cities in poorer lands) they are, in effect, the default mode, used by those who have a choice and setting the agenda for urban and transportation planning.

How did automobiles come to dominate cities? Have cars caused, or merely completed, a transformation in the understanding and use of urban public space? It is easy to see a kind of technological determinism at work: a glance at the history of the twentieth century seems to show that automobiles transformed cities. In 1900, cars were new and few. Soon, however, their growing numbers and their mechanical power gave them the upper hand in the streets, and compelled other users to get out of the way. But, of course, people had chosen to put these cars on the streets. Thus an alternative but closely related interpretation stresses individual choice as the cause of the automobile's triumph: the new machine was suited to what people

The New Blackwell Companion to the City   Edited by Gary Bridge and Sophie Watson
© 2011 Blackwell Publishing Ltd

wanted, so they embraced it, cherishing its advantages while tolerating its drawbacks. This view, too, seems obvious in some ways. But historical causation is rarely so simple.

A different interpretation argues that people's choices were thwarted by powerful interests. Since the 1970s, many Americans (and more than a few others) have believed that the nearly complete disappearance of their once-ubiquitous streetcars was the result of a conspiracy led by the giant automaker General Motors to acquire and shut down streetcar companies, leaving people with no practical alternative to buying cars. General Motors (GM) did, in fact, buy many failing local transit companies (through a subsidiary) and was, in fact, convicted of an antitrust violation for requiring the subsidiary to buy GM buses. It was not convicted of conspiring to destroy streetcar systems, but belief in the GM conspiracy theory persists and has had to be debunked repeatedly (Jones 2008: 61–8; Ladd 2008: 153–9). By the car-choked 1970s, many Americans could not understand why the removal of streetcars would have ever made sense. They had forgotten that by the 1920s, most streetcar companies were losing customers and money, cutting service, and earning a reputation as rude and ruthless monopolists. The new technology of motor buses, cheaper to buy and operate (at least in the short run) and more compatible with the growing number of private cars, was hailed as the wave of the future – whereas streetcars recovered their luster decades later, when broken-down buses, stuck in traffic, left a sour impression.

The fact that streetcars were removed from the great majority of cities worldwide shows that the conquest of city streets by the automobile was far too general a phenomenon to be blamed on any conspiracy. To reject the conspiracy theory can easily lead us back to the conclusion that the triumph of the car was the product of many individual choices (for example, Bottles 1987). Certainly we must acknowledge that people chose – often eagerly – to drive cars. But it does not necessarily follow that the inherent appeal of cars explains their triumph. We can consider a wide range of intermediate explanations between a conspiracy and a free-market choice, once we recognize that people's individual choices are neither wholly constrained (as the conspiracy theory would have it) nor wholly free – that, as Matthew Paterson (2007: 72–6) argues, "individual agency" does not operate free of "structure or cultural discourse." The notion that people simply choose what is best for them is an abstraction sometimes used by economists; real circumstances are more complicated. In particular, urban transportation policy was far from a free market, with governments maintaining roads used by transit companies that were either regulated monopolies (as was typical in the US) or government-run (in many other lands). In other words, people's individual choices were mediated, influenced, and restricted by politics.

Motorists versus Pedestrians

Peter D. Norton has investigated one key turning-point: the conflict between urban pedestrians and motorists during the 1920s in the United States – the first place where automotive traffic threatened to overwhelm city streets. (American rates of auto ownership far exceeded those of any other country during the first half of the century. Similar conflicts emerged at the same time in a few European cities, and eventually in many cities around the world.) During this decade, American cities addressed the growing problem of pedestrian fatalities by banning pedestrians from city streets, except on sidewalks and at designated crossings – an unprecedented segregation of street space that labeled pedestrian wanderers as "jaywalkers" and lawbreakers (Norton 2007, 2008). The removal of streetcars (mainly in the 1930s and 1950s, in most cities around the world) followed a similar logic: the purpose of street space came to be defined as the unconstrained movement of automobiles, and streetcars were an obstruction, as were passengers walking to and from the streetcars. These new rules made cities more attractive places to drive, and less desirable places to get around any other way.

Norton concludes that automotive interests won the struggle for control of the streets because they effectively mobilized their economic muscle for political ends. His history reminds us that people don't make their transportation decisions in a vacuum. People had many reasons for wanting cars, but often they made their choices amid rules that effectively encouraged driving. Nor can official promotion of motoring be separated from the undeniable fact that cars and highways have long been more fashionable than any alternative. A striking but by no means unique example is the case of Jakarta in the 1950s, where Indonesia's President Sukarno, eager to project a modern image, decreed not only an ambitious freeway program but also the removal of streetcars from city streets, against the advice of the city's mayor (Silver 2008: 95).

The power struggle described by Norton, and its later equivalents in other lands, had profound implications for the organization of urban public space. The priority given to traffic flow meant that streets were not understood to be places of communal assembly, places to meet and socialize, or places of commerce, except to the extent that the rapid movement of motor vehicles was understood to serve the interests of rapid commercial exchange. As the efficient movement of motor vehicles became the chief purpose of city streets, their design and operation were put in the hands of a new breed of traffic engineers, who reorganized streets with the goal of removing all obstacles to speeding cars. Because the engineers were rarely charged with protecting the interests of pedestrians, bicyclists, or transit riders, nor of street peddlers or playing children or gossiping neighbors, they typically treated those street users simply as obstructions to traffic. For the engineers, a city was simply a traffic system, so the ideal city was one in which motor traffic flowed freely.

Traffic engineers did prove successful in enabling far more cars to flow, far more rapidly, than municipal leaders had believed possible when they faced early traffic jams in the 1910s and 1920s. Urban life and commerce, that is, continued to function despite far greater numbers of automobiles. American experts developed sophisticated methods of collecting traffic statistics, charting motorists' journeys, and designing more efficient traffic lanes, and many European, Asian, and Australian cities engaged their services after the middle of the century (Ladd 2008: 126).

The engineers' model of traffic flow was the freeway: the limited-access, intersection-free, automobile-only road. Freeways were originally designed for rural areas, but urban traffic planners soon embraced their promise of rapid travel. American cities built a few during the 1920s and 1930s, and after mid-century every US city built a network of freeways, as did many cities in other lands. The construction of

Figure 23.1   A US suburban freeway. Author's photo.

these roads usually required the destruction of parks, housing, and neighborhoods, and their presence disrupted adjacent areas with noise, pollution, and barriers to access. Organized opposition to proposed urban freeways emerged in many places (Mohl 2004; Ladd 2008: 104–29). These freeway revolts – some successful, most not – became the catalyst of urban resistance to the incursion of automobiles in the 1960s and 1970s. Urban freeways remain controversial; a few short stretches have even been demolished. Freeway advocates saw in them a technocratic ideal of free movement and, more broadly, a reorganized city that gave priority to speed. For opponents, the freeway was the death knell of compact and walkable neighborhoods, a subsidy to suburban commuters, and the final surrender of the city to the automobile.

The Transformation of the Street

A recognition that car-friendly policies are the products of political struggle still leaves us with the question of where the division between pro-car and anti-car factions came from. How did the forces that Norton calls "motordom" establish their power in the first place? In order to understand the arrival of the automobile, then, we need to understand the culture of city streets at the turn of the twentieth century, when automobiles suited emerging tastes and needs – but not everyone's tastes and needs.

When automobiles were invented at the end of the nineteenth century, European and North American cities were already geared to mobility, with new technologies (notably railways) promoting the growing demands of commerce and industry. Major city streets were becoming extraordinarily crowded, a sometimes frightening maelstrom of fast-moving vehicles, horse-drawn vehicles, and people engaged in commuting, communicating, buying, and selling. Profound changes in the uses of city streets thus predated the automobile, as pedestrian commuters, strollers, children, and peddlers were forced to make way for more and faster vehicles of various kinds: wagons and carriages, horse-drawn and then electric trams, bicycles, and, in some places, steam railroads. The commercial and social uses of streets, that is, were being subordinated to the needs of transportation.

But this change in function was not driven entirely by transportation needs. It was part of a broader transformation of urban culture that left its imprint on city streets. The increased mobility of people and goods reflected fundamental changes in the economic order of society, a vastly increased scale of production and commerce that made cities larger, more diverse, and more volatile places. The social geography of western cities also changed. Especially in larger and more densely populated cities, the wealthy and powerful classes increasingly disapproved of, or at least felt uncomfortable with, the behavior of the urban poor on the streets. Some of their fears were explicitly political, notably in Paris, where the urban crowd was the catalyst of several revolutions. In other places, an abhorrence of the sanitary or moral habits of the urban poor prompted urban leaders to impose new regulations on public behavior (Winter 1993; Brown-May 1998; Nead 2000).

Long before the automobile age, many prosperous English and American city dwellers escaped the discomforts of city life by moving to new suburbs (Fishman 1987). Even where the classes remained in closer proximity to one another, urban elites were, in various ways, limiting their physical contact with the poor. Since automobiles were, at first, affordable only to the wealthy, they served both as tokens of wealth and as tools of segregation in the streets. Peter C. Baldwin's (1999) analysis of Hartford, Connecticut, reveals how nineteenth-century reformers' ambitious efforts to improve the moral climate of the city's streets later yielded to more modest attempts to segregate undesirable activities and undesirable people in streets and neighborhoods less frequented by the respectable classes. When Hartford's middle class acquired automobiles in the 1920s, the new machines merely helped them to do what they had increasingly been doing during the previous decades: move quickly through the streets while protecting themselves from distasteful activities and unwanted contact with strangers. It had long been the poor who were more likely to socialize and do business in the streets, rather than in shops and clubs and drawing rooms. Changing patterns of commerce, residence, and transportation made the street an even more exclusive preserve of the poor, and thus a place where the wealthier classes felt less comfortable and to which they had less allegiance.

In other words, it can be argued that the transformation of city streets (as described by Norton for the United States in the 1920s) was completed, but was not caused, by the arrival of the automobile or by automotive interests. In the automotive era, streets in many cities have become largely devoid of pedestrians – because people chose to be in cars, but also, and more fundamentally, because a changed economy and society placed less value on the kinds of personal contact that took place in the street.

The Automotive City

This analysis suggests that cars were symptoms, or results, or perhaps the means of urban transformation, but not its cause. That is true only up to a point. Even if the social and political chasm between motorists and non-motorists was not new, the power and speed of the new machines expanded the spatial and social distance between them. In other words, although the arrival of automobiles was only part of a broader transformation of urban public life, the very presence of cars – that is, the ways people used them – itself changed cities. The bodily experience of a motorist's encounter with city streets and with fellow citizens differs quite sharply from that of a passenger in a slow-moving or open vehicle, and differs even more profoundly from that of a pedestrian. The protection afforded by a car, and the accompanying sense of power, have, of course, always been among the attractions of urban motoring, transforming personal encounters into unequal tests of power, and enabling motorists to act on aggressive impulses that were not new, but may previously have been suppressed. It is difficult to know just how much automobiles have changed urban social interaction, but it is clear that someone who experiences city streets from within a closed car will perceive the city differently from a pedestrian or transit rider, and will have different expectations of city life (Thrift 2004).

Even as we acknowledge that automobiles have impoverished, even brutalized, personal interaction in city streets, it is a mistake to recall the pedestrian city as a place of democratic encounters among equals. It is even more sentimental to think that these encounters were reliably civil or pleasant. Some citizens gladly climbed into their cars in order to avoid physical contact with strangers or social inferiors. On the one hand, then, it is possible to argue that cars promoted social peace by averting conflict. On the other hand, some social critics have argued that we are all the poorer for having deprived our bodies of contact with strangers on city streets (Jacobs 1961; Sennett 1994). Others have suggested that a society is certainly different, if not necessarily poorer, when citizenship is effectively equated with the command of a motor vehicle (Urry 2007: 130; Seiler 2008; Koshar 2008).

Automobiles have always been praised as vehicles of freedom; and the high price of that freedom has always been decried. John Urry has described automobility as a "peculiar combination of flexibility and coercion" (2004: 27) because the choice to drive puts a motorist at the mercy of powerful forces and complex systems. In crowded urban spaces, the limitations and contradictions of automotive freedom become peculiarly apparent. The urban motorist is dependent on a complicated machine and on the availability of a parking space, must negotiate a thicket of traffic regulation and law enforcement, and can enjoy automotive freedom only to the extent that fast roads are available. Non-motorists – whether they are a majority (as in the wealthiest countries) or a minority, as in poorer lands – are, of course, excluded from the freedom brought by the automobile as well as the citizenship that is implicitly equated with driving. They are unavailable, invisible, or seen as lesser citizens – even, perhaps, by themselves.

Figure 23.2 A Rome street. Author's photo.

A perverse result of automotive freedom has been the transformation of mobility from an opportunity into a necessity, a phenomenon that has been labeled "enforced mobility" (Linder *et al.* 1975). The automobile has enabled millions of people to live, work, and socialize in widely separated places. This individual mobility has accelerated the deconcentration of cities – which in turn promotes automobile dependence. This dependence has a behavioral or psychological component: the car's convenience makes it a habitual choice, and the relative inconveniences of walking or bicycling or taking a train or bus (or living in a walkable neighborhood) loom large in the typical car-owner's views about alternative modes of transportation. More important, for cities, is the structural component of automobile dependence. Increased reliance on cars is the inevitable result of political decisions to build cities for the convenience of motorists and to the detriment of all others – to site development around highways and parking lots, so ensuring the wide separation of living, working, shopping, and recreation (Newman and Kenworthy 1999; Dupuy 1999a, 1999b; Ladd 2008: 159–67). The assumption that automobiles were generally available turned this tendency toward urban sprawl into a self-reinforcing process promoted by pro-car attitudes and by auto-friendly urban development.

Although today's decentralized cities are not entirely a product of the automobile, only the widespread ownership of private cars freed cities from the centralizing tendencies of both walking (which put a premium on proximity) and railways (which concentrated activity in central hubs). Auto-centered urban development is most apparent in those cities and suburbs that are entirely a product of the automotive age: places designed with room for fast driving, acceleration, and turns, and also providing ample space to park cars. These cities typically separate residential, industrial, and commercial uses to an extent never dreamed of by nineteenth-century urban planners eager to protect people from urban smoke and noise. The result is a city spread out over a vast area, one in which private automobiles become a virtual necessity, because distances are too great for walking, and destinations are too scattered for any form of mass transit to be rapid or economical. The advantages and (especially) costs of this urban sprawl have been much debated (Gillham 2002; Squires 2002; Bruegmann 2005; Bogart 2006). For motorists, it offers extraordinary mobility, as long as an adequate supply of roads is provided. It also requires a great deal of driving, with all the attendant (if disputed) costs in energy use, environmental degradation, and social separation.

Auto-dependent urbanization has become the international norm. Some cities in developed countries have attempted to reclaim urban space for pedestrians and alternative modes of transit, with results that are impressive in some particular instances but which have made only a small dent in the broader growth of automobile use. Meanwhile, the world's most rapidly growing cities are, with few exceptions, seeing (and encouraging) rapid increases in driving. The most dramatic case is China, where, in the early twenty-first century, urban car-ownership and use is skyrocketing, and is being promoted by government policies, including extensive urban freeway construction; and where many cities have been turning street space over to the motoring minority in ways that recall the United States in the 1920s (Campanella 2008: 217–39; Sperling and Gordon 2009: 205–34).

One frequently hears that cars have destroyed cities – a development that some lament and others celebrate. Certainly the automobile has been a crucial tool in the transformation of crowded industrial cities into something quite different, and it has contributed to the breakdown of urban–rural differences that once defined city life. Many people believe that the advantages of the decentralized, auto-oriented city are well worth the price. What others see as the erosion of urban life by cars is, for them, welcome evidence of liberation from spatial constraints. Rapid mobility (especially by automobile) and electronic communications have made physical location less important for many urban functions. In 1963 the urban planner Melvin Webber described the automobile's contribution to the new "community without propinquity" in which people's social and occupational contacts are no longer circumscribed by physical proximity (Webber 1963). The internet age has seen this view propounded again and again, although it remains unclear just how eager people are to liberate themselves from physical space and from bodily contact with friends and strangers.

These new technologies have certainly not induced a mass abandonment of cities. On the contrary, people (especially the young) continue to flock to the cities in search of economic or social opportunities – in wealthy countries and even more so in poor ones. A growing proportion of the world's population is living in urban areas, even if many of those areas – particularly the more car-centered ones – look quite unlike older cities. They differ in their separation of residential, industrial, and commercial functions, and in their dependence on automobiles to get people from one destination to another. It is an open question whether their suitability to automobiles makes them better suited to twenty-first-century human beings. Automobiles have become indispensable tools of urban life, but their speed, emissions, and need for space also make them a fundamental urban problem. There will long be controversy over continued attempts to adapt cities for the convenience of motorists, and over the importance of preserving automobility in more sustainable forms. Cities' current auto-centric form will shape, but not necessarily determine, a future that may be less auto-centric.

References

Baldwin, P. C. (1999) *Domesticating the Street: The Reform of Public Space in Hartford, 1850–1930*. Columbus: Ohio State University Press.

Bogart, W. T. (2006) *Don't Call it Sprawl: Metropolitan Structure in the 21st Century*. Cambridge: Cambridge University Press.

Bottles, S. L. (1987) *Los Angeles and the Automobile: The Making of the Modern City*. Berkeley: University of California Press.

Brown-May, A. (1998) *Melbourne Street Life: The Itinerary of Our Days*. Kew, Victoria: Australian Scholarly/Arcadia.

Bruegmann, R. (2005) *Sprawl: A Compact History*. Chicago: University of Chicago Press.

Campanella, T. J. (2008) *The Concrete Dragon: China's Urban Revolution and What it Means for the World*. New York: Princeton Architectural Press.

Dupuy, G. (1999a) From the magic circle to automobile dependence. *Transport Policy* 6: 1–17.

Dupuy, G. (1999b) *La dépendance automobile: symptomes, analyses, diagnostic, traitements*. Paris: Anthropos.

Fishman, R. (1987) *Bourgeois Utopias: The Rise and Fall of Suburbia*. New York: Basic Books.

Gillham, O. (2002) *The Limitless City: A Primer on the Urban Sprawl Debate*. Washington, DC: Island Press.

Jacobs, J. (1961) *The Death and Life of Great American Cities*. New York: Vintage.

Jones, D. W. (2008) *Mass Motorization and Mass Transit: An American History and Policy Analysis*. Bloomington: Indiana University Press.

Koshar, R. J. (2008) Driving cultures and the meaning of roads: some comparative examples. In *The World Beyond the Windshield: Roads and Landscapes in the United States and Europe*, ed. C. Mauch and T. Zeller. Athens: Ohio University Press, 14–34.

Ladd, B. (2008) *Autophobia: Love and Hate in the Automotive Age*. Chicago: University of Chicago Press.

Linder, W., Maurer, U., and Resch, H. (1975) *Erzwungene Mobilität*. Cologne: Europäische Verlagsanstalt.

Mohl, R. A. (2004) Stop the road: freeway revolts in American cities. *Journal of Urban History* 30: 674–706.

Nead, L. (2000) *Victorian Babylon: People, Streets and Images in Nineteenth-Century London*. New Haven, CT: Yale University Press.

Newman, P., and Kenworthy, J. (1999) *Sustainability and Cities: Overcoming Automobile Dependence*. Washington, DC: Island Press.

Norton, P. D. (2007) Street rivals: jaywalking and the invention of the motor age street. *Technology and Culture* 48: 331–59.

Norton, P. D. (2008) *Fighting Traffic: The Dawn of the Motor Age in the American City*. Cambridge, MA: MIT Press.

Paterson, M. (2007) *Automobile Politics: Ecology and Cultural Political Economy*. Cambridge: Cambridge University Press.

Seiler, C. (2008) *Republic of Drivers: A Cultural History of Automobility in America*. Chicago: University of Chicago Press.

Sennett, R. (1994) *Flesh and Stone: The Body and the City in Western Civilization*. New York: Norton.

Silver, C. (2008) *Planning the Megacity: Jakarta in the Twentieth Century*. London, Routledge.

Sperling, D., and Gordon, D. (2009) *Two Billion Cars: Driving Toward Sustainability*. New York: Oxford University Press.

Squires, G. D. (ed.) (2002) *Urban Sprawl: Causes, Consequences, and Policy Responses*. Washington, DC: Urban Institute Press.

Thrift, N. (2004) Driving in the city. *Theory, Culture and Society* 21: 41–59.

Urry, J. (2004) The "system" of automobility. *Theory, Culture and Society* 21: 25–39.

Urry, J. (2007) *Mobilities*. Cambridge: Polity Press.

Webber, M. M. (1963) Order in diversity: community without propinquity. In *Cities and Space*, ed. L. Wingo. Baltimore, MD: Johns Hopkins University Press, 23–54.

Winter, J. (1993) *London's Teeming Streets 1830–1914*. London: Routledge.

Part III   City Affect

The New Blackwell Companion to the City   Edited by Gary Bridge and Sophie Watson
© 2011 Blackwell Publishing Ltd

Chapter 24

Reflections on Affect

Gary Bridge and Sophie Watson

In the first edition of the Blackwell *Companion to the City* no section was organized around the theme of affect. Rather our choice was to deploy the notion of city imaginaries. We argued that cities were not simply material or lived spaces, they were spaces of the imagination and representation, and how they were envisioned had effects. Two themes were pursued on the interrelationship: how the city affects the imagination and how the city is imagined. The effect of the city on the imagination, it was suggested, contains a tension between the conditions of the city as stimulating or constraining the imagination – they can be places that encourage creativity or they can consolidate it in the collective imagination as tradition and authority. Forms of collective imagination can be both positive and negative, where prejudiced imaginaries of the "other" can be a source of racism, for example, and western imaginaries of the city, we suggested, are overwhelmingly visual in nature (the colonial gaze, the watching *flâneur*). Nevertheless within this framing of "city imaginaries," affect made its presence felt, through notions of fragmented subjectivity and over-stimulation, through the notions of anxiety, fear, and the uncanny, or through notions of the city as spaces of fantasy and self-realization. The difference was that affect was not mobilized at center stage.

Affect and Emotion

The fact that affect was chosen to organize a number of different contributions in the *New Companion*, including some chapters which could have sat comfortably in a section called "City Imaginaries," reflects a significant growth of interest in the concept within urban studies, geography, and social/spatial analysis, reflected for

The New Blackwell Companion to the City   Edited by Gary Bridge and Sophie Watson
© 2011 Blackwell Publishing Ltd

example in the inauguration of a journal specifically devoted to new research in the area: *Emotion, Space and Society*. As the editors of the new journal argue: "While emotions have always been profoundly present in academic studies, it is only relatively recently that their import has been widely, or at least openly, felt and discussed as a topic in its own right" (Davidson *et al.* 2008: 2). Deborah Thien (2005), drawing on Williams (2001), offers five explanations for the increasing attention paid to emotions: the influence of critical theory and feminist debates on notions of rationality; a greater increase in interest in the body as discursive (following Foucault), as phenomenological (drawing on Merleau-Ponty), and as hyper-real (drawing on Baudrillard); the dominance of consumer culture with its commercialization of emotions (in women's magazines, for example); a rise in therapeutic culture; and new political debates concerning emotions, responsibility, and democracy. Various other explanations could be suggested, such as the rise in the popularity of fundamentalist religions, the legacy of Thatcherism's promulgation of the individual, the economic exclusion of many from access to wealth or economic wellbeing.

Emotion and affect are sometimes used interchangeably, and sometimes also the notion of feeling. Many writers criticize the distinction, which Henderson (2008) argues is of little use both politically and socially. Affect is by no means a straightforward term to define. Inherited from Freud's psychoanalytic theory, where it encompasses instincts, drives, and emotions, it is variously deployed in relation to emotion and feelings – or for Matthis (2000) a matrix of the two. Ben Anderson (2006: 734) makes the distinction between affect, feeling, and emotion "as three different modalities enacted from heterogeneous processes of circulation, expression and qualification." The point he emphasizes here is that the rational cannot be reduced to a range of discrete internally coherent emotions which are coterminous with the mind of an individual. Rather, he suggests, we need to be attuned to "affect as a transpersonal *capacity* which a body has to be affected (through an affection) and to affect (as the result of modifications)" (p. 735); affects are "*beings* whose validity lies in themselves and exceeds any lived" (Deleuze and Guattari 1994: 164). Drawing on Massumi (2002), Anderson proposes that "being affected – affecting emerge from a processual logic of *transitions* that take place during spatially and temporally distributed encounters" at different levels in capacity, where this is thought of as "a change in which powers to affect and be affected are addressable by a next event and how readily addressable they are" (Massumi 2002: 15). To put this another way, the interconnections between affect, bodies, and their encounters are always embroiled in the materialities of space/time (Anderson 2006: 736). Further, movements of affect are expressed through visceral and postural shifts in bodies, often described as feelings, such as the blush of a body through shame (Probyn 2005), or shaking with anger.

Nigel Thrift (2004: 57), drawing on Bruno (2002) argues for approaches which work with "a notion of broad tendencies and lines of force: emotion as motion, both literally and figurally," and as a form of thinking and intelligence about the world. Or, in Thien's words "affect is the *how* of emotion … (in both the communicative and the literal sense) the motion of emotion" (2005: 451). Thrift (2004), like a number of others (e.g., Gatens 1999), finds Spinoza's challenge to Cartesian rationality and the mind/body distinction helpful here. In Spinoza's monist philosophy mind and body are of one substance and everything consists of thinking and doing at the same time, expressed in two different registers emerging at different levels of intensity in particular instances. This way of thinking posits affect as an attribute of the body which structures encounters so that bodies are disposed for action in a particular way (Thrift 2004: 62).

Sarah Ahmed (2008: 10) similarly argues against the notion that emotion or affect stand apart from an object in the world; they are, rather, implicated in it. Her starting point is the messiness of experience, where bodies unfold into the world within "a drama of contingency." If we were to think of being in the city here we might say that we are oriented towards sites and spaces in relation to how we are affected by them. Shared views of particular sites, objects, spaces, as good or happy are produced through a shared orientation to these as positive, and once places are invested with positive affect, they accumulate yet further positive affective value as they are shared as such by others. Taking the political/policy implications of this, we might suggest that once places are imbued with positive affect, they also become valued by wider agencies, such as institutions of the local state, who invest in them in pragmatic (financial, strategic investment, management, etc.) ways, thus enhancing their potential yet further.

City Affect

It should be clear from the preceding discussion that there are subtle and complex distinctions in the deployment of the notion of affect in the social/spatial literatures. We have only sketched the brief contours of the debate here (see also Davidson *et al.* 2005) which are useful for our purposes. Let us turn now to the more specific field of the city and urban studies. Cities can be seen as "maelstroms of affect" (Thrift 2004: 57) or as sites of "intensities of feeling" (see Massey *et al.* 1999), from anger to fear (Watson 2008), passion to boredom, revealed in major events, such as at football matches, or in the commonplace activities of everyday life. Affect circulates through built forms, city sites, city events, and representations of it. For AbdouMaliq Simone, in Chapter 31, affect is exhibited through exaggeration and the baroque in Kinshasa where the precariousness of existence appears to gives rise to a highly decorated discourse full of ironies and *double entendre* and where the movements of the body are accentuated to the obscene. But as Thrift (2004) pointed out, until the early twenty-first century, affect remained remarkably absent from urban studies with of course major exceptions. Thrift attributes its neglect to the dominance of a Cartesian analysis, its demarcation in the cultural arena, or the complexity of defining this register in print (p. 58). Though this is largely true it is all too easy to forget that some of the writings of some of most influential thinkers on the city in the first half of the twentieth century, such as Simmel, Jacobs, Benjamin, and Sennett (the latter two acknowledged by Thrift indeed) on the one hand, and the mammoth opus of modernist literary writings on the city, such as Joyce and Woolf, on the other, are very much imbued with affect.

How, briefly, is affect central to these seminal writers on the city? For Simmel, in *Metropolis and Mental Life* (2010 [1903]), the city in its complexity and abundance of sensory data is a space which contributes to our sense of fragmented subjectivity or overload. In his exploration of the relation between the subject's inner life and the city he suggests that in the modern metropolis the individual becomes saturated with stimuli from which s/he seeks to retreat:

> There is perhaps no psychic phenomenon which is as unconditionally reserved to the city as the blasé outlook. It is at first the consequence of those rapidly shifting stimulations of the nerves which are thrown together in all their contrasts and from which it seems to us the intensification of metropolitan intellectuality seems to be derived. (Simmel 1948: 14)

In Chapter 28 of this volume, Lindner considers how relevant Simmel's thinking is to the contemporary global city through Wong Kar-Wai's film set in Hong Kong. He proposes the notion of the post-metropolitan attitude to describe the state of radical detachment depicted there that he suggests is far more extreme, alienating, and destructive than the blasé attitude explored by Simmel.

Walter Benjamin has long interested scholars of the city for his attention to the city as a site of bedazzlement, spectacle, pleasure, and consumption. In the *Arcades Project* (1999), where he describes the glittering emporium of the Paris arcades, he evokes the synesthesia of sights and sounds in urban spectacle (or phantasmagoria) with its heady mix of commodities which has an effect on class relations, diverting expectations from social solidarity to individualized consumption. Buck-Morss (1989) makes the point that culture, aesthetics, and the psychoanalysis of desire are not just entrained and commodified by separate processes; they are there at the beginning of his analysis. Thus, desire, aesthetics, and fantasy are brought right to the heart of the capitalist economy, and the city provides the space to explore their interrelations: "On the walls of these caverns, their immemorial flora, the commodity, luxuriates and enters, like cancerous tissue, into the most irregular combinations. A world of secret affinities: palm tree and feather duster, hair dryer and Venus de Milo" (Buck-Morss 1989: 395). A key metaphor in this text is mirror reflections both for the sparkle of the commodities and the deceptive masks of passers-by whose eyes are like "veiled mirrors."

Jane Jacobs and Richard Sennett "do affect" in a rather different mode, though the concept is equally present. Jane Jacobs's book *The Death and Life of Great American Cities* (1962) is best known for its arguments in favor of mixed land uses and active streets where different people are constantly passing by, enacting informal surveillance to keep the street safe, which is diminished by the separation of land uses into separate zones so popular with urban planners in the postwar period. But her analysis is also strongly embedded in an understanding of emotions and she is well attuned to the ways in which fear inhibits movement, as people withdraw from the streets that they imagine to be dangerous and violent, making the streets more unsafe by that very retreat. Sennett's preoccupation with the loss of public space, the decline of fully urban civil relationships with the rise of secularism and consumer capitalism, and urban planning initiatives which emphasize order and homogeneity, runs through much of his early work (e.g., 1970; 1974). But probably his most significant book for our purposes here is *Flesh and Stone* (1994), where in particular the chapter on the Venice Ghetto pays attention to the ways in which fear, anxiety, and disgust underpinned the segregation of the Jews into the ghetto in the sixteenth century. As Sennett puts it:

In that real Venice, the desire for Christian community lay somewhere between dream
and anxiety. The impurities of difference haunted the Venetians ... When they were
shut inside the Ghetto, the Venetians claimed and believed they were isolating a disease
that had infected the Christian community, for they identified the Jews in particular
with corrupting bodily vices. Christians were afraid of touching Jews: Jewish bodies
were thought to carry venereal diseases as well as to contain more polluting powers.
(Sennett 1994: 317)

These works aside, we would argue that literary texts do, as it were, affect with
considerably more depth and complexity than most academic scholarship (with
notable exceptions), particularly in the modernist period. On the subject of fiction,
and more specifically, James Joyce's *Ulysses*, Raymond Williams in his seminal work
The Country and the City (1973) writes that

the forces of the action have become internal and in a way there is no longer the city,
there is only a man walking through it. The substantial reality, the living variety of the
city, is in the walker's mind ... The history is not in this city but in the loss of a city,
the loss of relationships. The only knowable community is the need, the desire, of the
racing and separated forms of consciousness. (Williams 1973: 243–5)

In her essay on Joyce, Woolf, and the city Johnson (2000) goes to some length to
chart the work of these authors and how it interrogates the effect of cities on the
mental life of those who live there, while also insistently figuring the cities of Dublin
and London in significantly material terms (p. 61). But it is Woolf more than Joyce,
she argues, who explores mental life, subjectivity, and the city. In this essay our
attention is drawn in particular to *The Years* (1998 [1937]) and a scene where the
protagonist Martin Pargiter is gazing at St Paul's Cathedral and as he looks up "all
the weights in his body seemed to shift. He has a curious sense of something moving
within his body in harmony with the building; it righted itself; it came to a full stop.
It was exciting – this change of proportion" (p. 244). As Johnson explains, Pargiter
is connecting the pleasure with his private fantasy – that of being an architect rather
than living on his father's private inheritance (p. 67). Woolf's novels are rich with
such exposition of subjectivity formed and reformed in the spaces of the city, where
affect is "in motion" and implicated in the buildings and streets encountered. So
also we find Peter Walsh in *Mrs Dalloway*:

down his mind went flat as a marsh, and three great emotions bowled over him;
understanding; a vast philanthropy; and finally, as if the result of the others, an irre-
pressible, exquisite delight; as if inside his brain, by another hand, strings were pulled,
shutters moved, and he, having nothing to do with it, yet stood as the opening of
endless avenues down which if he chose he might wander. He had not felt so young
for years. (Woolf 2000: 87)

Rereading this text once again, some years after being immersed in more recent
scholarship on affect, it is striking how little literary insights have informed urban
studies over the years.

In *Writing the City*, Preston and Simpson-Housley (1994: 2) suggest that "the
city has always been an important literary symbol, and the ways in which a culture

Figure 24.1   Beijing street. Photo S. Watson.

writes about its cities is one means by which we may understand its fears and aspirations."

Cinematic Cities

Affect in the city has also been central to cinema narratives since their inception. James Donald (1999: 132) argues that modern cinema has had the effect of exposing people to complex representations of modern urban experience – the dangers, fears, and eroticism of the streets, at the same time as placing people above it, thereby creating a panoramic vision of the city. The cinema, he suggests, embodies people's visual experience of the city, while providing a distanced perspective of rational vision:

> The modern city and its cinematic projection can be seen in the terms of a dramatic encounter between the irrational and instinctual forces, the fearful elements of the city, the unconscious and the uncanny, on the one hand, and the powers of reason, vision and control, that is to say conscious powers, on the other. (Donald 1999: 132)

Figure 24.2 Waiting for the bus, Shanghai. Photo S. Watson.

The new global city, for Donald, now exceeds our field of vision as it is more and more implicated in global communication networks and virtual spaces. For Lindner, in this volume, this global city is best understood as the post-metropolis, where violence, both in material and cultural forms, has become an endemic feature of everyday urban life.

Stephanie Donald, in Chapter 27, considers one such global city, Beijing, where she suggests that affect arises "through, or despite, the powerful nexus of political power, longstanding urban community, and cultural energy that shapes the city's daily life." Her focus is on urban civility and the imaginative landscape of Beijing where stories of everyday affect can be narrated – the home and family, the uncertain lives of the young and transient, and the non-places of modern work. For Donald the city/film connection is strongest when it exposes the ragged edges and immediacy of urban geography with the intimacy of strangers. She selects three films which are not distributed beyond the video compact disc (VCD) market in China to capture the affect of Beijing as both politically organized and socially constrained. Lesley Caldwell in a related vein (Chapter 29) looks at two Italian films by the Italian director Mario Martone, set not in a global city, but in Naples, which illustrate the centrality of place in constituting an understanding of the self. This director, she argues, uses the images and sensations of this city as a way to externalize the protagonists' introspective fantasies, thus presenting the public arena as the repository of both individual and collective history. This cinematic strategy thus opposes the argument made by some analysts (e.g., Morley and Robins 1993) that emphasizes the modern condition as a universalizing experience where the construction of individual identity is dislocated from any one place.

Spaces of Affect

Affect and its effects in the city have been explored in a variety of sites and spaces over the last decade or more. Fear offers one such illustration. Fear of others who are defined as different, as strangers, is an inherent part of city life; at the same time, and often in the same place, that difference, unassimilated otherness (Young 1990), may be acknowledged and even celebrated. What changes over time are the subjects to whom such fear is attached, the response to the Jewish presence in Venice, mentioned earlier, being a graphic case in point. Fear of dangerous others has very real material effects in the city, leading to what Bauman (2003) calls mixophobia and the exclusion of unknown others in residential or gated communities, or the use of CCTV cameras in everyday city streets (Watson 2008). Psychoanalytic understandings of fear in the city have proved useful. Sibley (1995) draws on Kristeva's "simple logic of excluding filth" to explain the way borders between those inside and those outside are constructed. For him stereotypes are formed through the splitting of the self and the world into good and bad objects (a Kleinian notion) where the bad self is associated with fear and anxiety over the loss of control, which is then projected onto bad objects. By splitting off the part of ourselves that we fear and detest, the foreigner within, we avoid the things we cannot face. According to Kristeva (1991: 95), the foreigner "the hidden face of our identity, the space that wrecks our abode" can only be defined in a negative fashion. Stereotypical views of people arise in a conflict situation when a community that represents itself as the norm feels threatened by those who are perceived as distant and threatening, illustrated by Sibley in the treatment of gypsies.

Fear is deeply implicated in Freud's notion of the uncanny, which has seeped into a good deal of urban literature over the last decade. Of the uncanny Freud writes:

> There is no doubt that this belongs to the realm of the frightening, of what evokes fear and dread. It is equally beyond doubt that the word is not always used in a clearly definable sense, and so it commonly merges with what arouses fear in general. (Freud 1985 [1919]: 123, quoted by Pile 1996)

The uncanny is the familiar rendered strange: the strangely familiar (Borden *et al.* 1996) although this is not always uncanny. In Chapter 25, Pile deploys the uncanny to understand the horror of the film *Cloverfield*, as well as many of the stories that were told about the attack on the World Trade Center. Drawing on Nicholas Royle's account (2003), he unpacks the different forms that the uncanny can take:

> such as silence, darkness, the inexplicable, being buried alive, déjà vu, the double (lookalikes) or doubling, coincidences and repetitions, fate or inevitability, crowds, ghosts, crowds of ghosts, automatism, the inanimate becoming animate (or vice versa)

(especially dolls), cannibalism (being eaten) and other taboos, the evil genius, death. (Pile, this volume, 296–7)

Many of these forms are to be found in Freud's own experience of the uncanny, which he sees more generally as deriving from a number of possible experiences such as an unintentional return, a feeling of helplessness, being lost and endlessly returning to the same point, coincidences that seem to mean more than mere chance and so on.

Pile argues that, looking simply at the form of the film, *Cloverfield* ought to be uncanny. But he also finds it helpful in considering his material to deploy another Freudian term in his analysis, the compulsion to repeat – in this case the events of 9/11. This connects also with Chapter 26, by Max Page, which illustrates forcefully how New York's destruction has repeatedly and obsessively been envisioned by writers and film-makers over at least two centuries as a spectacle to enjoy. According to Page, 9/11 was its own form of New York disaster movie played out live on every screen in the world, which Americans watched over and over again for days afterwards Thus, as Pile points out, *Cloverfield* repeats the trauma of 9/11, but it does so among a blizzard of already circulating images of 9/11, and thus is not able to shock its audiences enough or provide new ways of seeing 9/11, which is already, as it were, a repetition. And as Page suggests, drawing on Žižek (2002: 17), America got what it had always fantasized about which was the biggest surprise of all.

Finally, affect is mediated through the senses, with corporeal and also psychic effects each circulating through the other in interconnected loops. John Urry, in Chapter 30, explores how the senses operate in "open cities" elaborating a "sensuous geography" which connects together analyses of body, sense, and place (Rodaway 1994). In the hierarchy of the senses, he argues, visual is at the top, where the intimacy of eye contact was given early urban expression in the figure of the *flâneur* in the pavement cafés of nineteenth-century Paris. The visual sense enables people to take possession of diverse environments and people at a distance. Andrew Hill (Chapter 32) also argues for the importance of visuality to understand why certain religious buildings have assumed such levels of spectacularity. He finds useful Lacan's analysis of visuality where he discusses the way in which painting functions as a "trap for the gaze" (1994: 89), constituting a lure which serves to attract, hold, and pacify the spectator's vision. Hill deploys this notion to understand how spectacular religious architecture functions as a trap for the gaze, that derives from the desire to instil in the spectator a sense of the power of religion and its ability to draw in and hold whoever casts their eyes upon it. Urry extends his exploration of the visual to incorporate the senses of smell and touch, which have found their way also into Lefebvre's (1991: 197) ideas around the production of different spaces being bound up with smell. Smell, he suggests, is a subversive sense in that it cannot be wholly banished, and reveals the artificiality of modernity; for example, a smell-free city is intimately linked with the workings of the drainage system or rubbish collection, whose fragility can be tested in adverse economic conditions, as the famous British winter of discontent in 1979 so clearly demonstrated.

We have seen in this essay that affect is mediated and functions in a variety of ways. The chapters presented in this section give a taste of this very rich and developing field in urban studies.

References

Ahmed, S. (2008) Sociable happiness. *Emotion Space and Society* 1 (1): 10–13.

Anderson, B. (2006) Becoming and being hopeful: towards a theory of affect. *Environment and Planning D: Society and Space* 24: 733–52.

Bauman, Z. (2003) *Liquid Love: On the Fraily of Human Bonds*. Cambridge: Polity Press.

Benjamin, W. (1999) *The Arcades Project*. Trans. Howard Eiland and Kevin McLaughlin. Cambridge, MA: Harvard University Press.

Borden, I., Kerr, J., Pivaro, A., and Rendell, J. (eds.) (1996) *Strangely Familiar: Narratives of Architecture in the City*. London: Routledge.

Bruno, G. (2002) *Atlas of Emotion: Journeys in Art, Architecture and Film*. New York: Verso.

Buck-Morss, S. (1989) *The Dialectics of Seeing*. Cambridge, MA: MIT Press.

Davidson, J., Bondi, L., and Smith, M. (eds.) (2005) *Emotional Geographies*. Aldershot, UK: Ashgate.

Davidson, J., Smith, M., Bondi, L., and Probyn, E. (2008) Editorial introduction. *Emotion, Space and Society* 1 (1): 1–13.

Deleuze, G., and Guattari, F. (1994) *What Is Philosophy?* London: Verso.

Donald, J. (1999) *Imagining the Modern City*. London: Athlone Press.

Freud, S. (1985 [1919]) The uncanny. In *Art and Literature: Jensen's "Gradiva," Leonardo da Vinci and Other Works*. Penguin Freud Library, vol. 14. Harmondsworth: Penguin.

Gatens, M. (1999) *Collective Imaginings*. London and New York: Routledge.

Henderson, V. (2008) Is there hope for anger? The politics of spatializing and (re)producing an emotion. *Emotion Space and Society* 1 (1): 28–37.

Jacobs, J. (1962) *The Death and Life of Great American Cities*. London: Jonathan Cape.

Johnson, J. (2000) Literary geography: Joyce, Woolf and the city. *City* 4 (2): 199–214.

Kristeva, J. (1991) *Strangers to Ourselves*. Trans. L. Roudiez. New York: Harvester Wheatsheaf.

Lacan, J. (1994) *The Four Fundamental Concepts of Psychoanalysis: Seminar XI*. London: Penguin.

Lefebvre, H. (1991) *The Production of Space*. Oxford: Blackwell.

Massey, D., Allen, J., and Pile, S. (eds.) (1999) *City Worlds*. London: Routledge.

Massumi, B. (2002) *Parables for the Virtual: Movement, Affect and Sensation*. Durham, NC: Duke University Press.

Matthis, I. (2000) Sketch for a metapsychology of affect. *International Journal of Psycho-analysis* 81 (2): 215–27.

Morley, D., and Robins, K. (1993) No place like *Heimat*: images of home (land) in European culture. In *Space, and Place Theories of Identity and Location*, ed. E. Carter, J. Donald, and J. Squires. London: Lawrence and Wishart, 3–31.

Preston, P., and Simpson-Housley, P. (1994) *Writing the City: Eden, Babylon and the New Jerusalem*. London: Routledge.

Pile, S. (1996) *The Body and the City: Psychoanalysis, Space and Subjectivity*. London: Routledge.

Probyn, E. (2005) *Blush: Faces of Shame*. Minneapolis: University of Minnesota Press.

Rodaway, P. (1994) *Sensuous Geographies*. London: Routledge.

Royle, N. (2003) *The Uncanny*. Manchester: Manchester University Press.

Sennett, R. (1970) *The Uses of Disorder: Personal Identity and City Life*. New Haven, CT: Yale University Press.

Sennett, R. (1974) *The Fall of Public Man*. New York: Alfred A. Knopf.

Sennett, R. (1994) *Flesh and Stone*. London: Faber and Faber.

Sibley, D. (1995) *Geographies of Exclusion: Society and Difference in the West*. London: Routledge.

Simmel, G. (2010 [1903]) *The Metropolis and Mental Life*. Trans. Edward Shils. In *The Blackwell City Reader*, ed. G. Bridge and S. Watson. 2nd edn. Chichester: Wiley-Blackwell, 103–10.

Thien, D. (2005) After or beyond feeling? A consideration of affect and emotion in geography. *Area* 37 (4): 450–6.

Thrift, N. (2004) Intensities of feeling: towards a spatial politics of affect. *Geografiska Annaler* 86B (1): 57–78.

Watson, S. (2008) Security in the city. In *Security: Sociology and Social Worlds*, ed. S. Carter, T. Jordan, and S. Watson. Manchester: Manchester University Press.

Williams, R. (1973) *The Country and the City*. London: Chatto and Windus.

Williams, S. J. (2001) *Emotion and Social Theory: Corporeal Reflections on the (Ir)rational*. London: Sage.

Woolf, V. (1998 [1937]) *The Years*. London: Penguin.

Woolf, V. (2000) *Mrs Dalloway*. Harmondsworth: Penguin.

Young, I. (1990) *Justice and the Politics of Difference*. Princeton, NJ: Princeton University Press.

Žižek, S. (2002) *Welcome to the Desert of the Real*. London: Verso.

Chapter 25

Intensities of Feeling: *Cloverfield*, the Uncanny, and the Always Near Collapse of the City

Steve Pile

Introduction: *Cloverfield* and the Destruction of New York (Again)

Cloverfield, the movie, was premiered on January 16, 2008 and went on general release the day after. It was not the biggest or best movie of 2008, though it is to date the largest grossing January release ever – taking about $40 million in the first weekend alone, eventually taking $170 million (easily recouping the £30 million spent on it). My interest in this movie is its undisguised re-presentation of some of the key visual and experiential tropes of the attack on the World Trade Center on September 9, 2001. The puzzle for me lies in two directions: first, why "repeat" 9/11, if only in fantasy; and, second, how is it that the trauma of 9/11 can be so accurately re-presented? One way I seek to think this through is by using Freud's notion of the uncanny. The uncanny is a likely candidate for understanding the horror both of a monster flick such as *Cloverfield*, and also of many of the stories that were told about the attack on the World Trade Center. The problem is that uncanniness does not quite cover *Cloverfield*, nor indeed 9/11 after 9/11. So, I turn to Freud's notion of the "compulsion to repeat," to see if this has some purchase on the re-presentation of a trauma – as in *Cloverfield*'s case – in only a slightly modified form. The product of this investigation is to help us rethink the relationship between cities and affect, and how we view cities as sites where there are "intensities of feeling" (see Massey *et al.* 1999).

Cloverfield as a Repetition of 9/11 (or Not)

Before the release of *Cloverfield*, a cunning poster, trailer, and viral marketing campaign presented the audience with the central conceit of the movie – you would be

The New Blackwell Companion to the City   Edited by Gary Bridge and Sophie Watson
© 2011 Blackwell Publishing Ltd

Figure 25.1 *Cloverfield* (2008), directed by Matt Reeves. Ref: CLO036AA; PARAMOUNT PICTURES / THE KOBAL COLLECTION.

"in" something, but you would not have any idea what was going on most of the time. It looked like *Blair Witch* meets *Godzilla*, set in New York. The poster ominously intoned, "Some thing has found us": in its foreground stood a decapitated Statue of Liberty, behind lay a wake in the Hudson that led to the path that the something had cut through the buildings. "Some thing" was attacking and destroying "Us" (that is, them). Even the title of the movie was cryptic and somewhat rustic, turning out to be a (US) Department of Defense designation for the attack, but seemingly referring to anything but a monster or a site of destruction.

The movie purports to be the found contents of a digital SD card, like those used by many DVD camcorders: document #USGX-8810-B467 found at incident site US-447 (formerly known as Central Park). The initial images inform us, by watermark, that what the audience is to see is the "Property of the US Government." It also says "Do Not Duplicate." The film knows, in other words, that it is in many

Figure 25.2 Screenshot from *Cloverfield* (2008), directed by Matt Reeves, produced by J. J. Abrams and Byron Burk.

ways a duplicate. Cinematically, it duplicates both a *Blair Witch Project* (1999) style and also a Godzilla-like attack on New York (compare *Godzilla* 1998). As interestingly, it also duplicates specific visual and experiential aspects of the 2001 attack on the World Trade Center, as shown in Jules and Gédéon Naudet's documentary film *9/11* (released September 11, 2002). Now, back to the movie.

The first images from the SD card show Central Park, at 6.42 a.m. on April 27 from a vantage-point high in one of the tower blocks that line the park. The camera approaches the scene: New York's high-rises form a wall abutting the dark greenery of the tree-tops. A thin row of lights marks the road the separates park from city. Columbus Circle hasn't yet fully woken up. It seems to have been raining, the city is shrouded in a gloomy mist. Shots of the interior of the apartment and of the bedroom establish the camera, and its point of view, as personal, intimate, and profoundly ordinary. The camera is the point of view: what people see, it sees. It records what is going on, but only as people see it. What we see is two lovers, Rob and Beth, messing around, with the camera becoming a "toy" through which they can enjoy one another. Camera off. Camera on. The images jar and grate as the camera is turned off and on again. The ever-present timestamp tells us that it is now 6.43 p.m. on May 22. The camera is not pointed anywhere, as a man – who turns

Figure 25.3 Screenshot from *Cloverfield* (2008), directed by Matt Reeves, produced by J. J. Abrams and Byron Burk.

Figure 25.4 Screenshot from *Cloverfield* (2008), directed by Matt Reeves, produced by J. J. Abrams and Byron Burk.

Figure 25.5 Screenshot from *9/11*, directed by Jules Naudet, Gédéon Naudet, and James Hanlon, produced by Richard Barber, Mike Haley, Bruce Speigel, and Mead Stone.

out to be Rob's brother Jason – tries to operate it. Off screen, a woman – Jason's girlfriend Lily – shouts a warning. The scene comes into focus. They are preparing for some kind of party for Rob (although explicitly not a wedding). Then, suddenly, we're back on April 27, at 11.14 a.m., on a train going over a bridge on the Hudson. We see Beth, smiling. To Rob, she says, "You have no clue." And back to Jason on May 22, 6.45 p.m.

Already, in the opening "phrases" of the movie, we see jumps in time and space, disorientating visual and audio information. Images from the previous recording on the SD card sometimes interrupt the flow of current events: sequences from April 27 incongruously appear in the interstices between sequences on May 22, in those moments between on and off – deliberately duplicating a home-movie video-tape experience (rather than a digital SD one). While on, the camera is turned around, sometimes giving the audience a visual roller-coaster ride – much as some had done in the *Blair Witch Project* before, people left the cinema because they felt physically sick. The camera's ability to see is drastically limited by the ability of the person holding the camera to work it. The ability is not simply technical, it is also experiential: people's perception and comprehension lag behind the unfolding events, and the camera lags behind the people. These lessons *Cloverfield* learned from 9/11. They were not the only ones.

Rob's farewell party is a fraught affair. The relationship between Rob and Beth is tense. By now the camera is in the hands of Rob's friend, Hud. Late into the party, there's a loud yet strange crash from somewhere off in the distance; car alarms nearby go off. A startled Hud yelps "What the hell was that?" The camera

Figure 25.6 Screenshot from *9/11*, directed by Jules Naudet, Gédéon Naudet, and James Hanlon, produced by Richard Barber, Mike Haley, Bruce Speigel, and Mead Stone.

Figure 25.7 Screenshot from *9/11*, directed by Jules Naudet, Gédéon Naudet, and James Hanlon, produced by Richard Barber, Mike Haley, Bruce Speigel, and Mead Stone.

looks in the general direction of the noise, but it's too dark to see anything. The party-goers are screaming in alarm, but calm descends quickly as people pull themselves together. They turn to the TV, a newsreader talks of a possible earthquake in lower Manhattan – "Tanker Capsizes Near Statue of Liberty" reads the headline. "That's really close, man," Hud murmurs, to no one in particular. A few from the party, including Hud (and the camera) head for the roof to get a better look.

"What do you think? Is it another terrorist attack?" asks one woman, as they ascend the stairs. No one answers. The question is mute. On the roof, there's the distant sound of police sirens. People stop to share their experiences. Barely audibly, a man in the background shouts "A terrorist attack!" Hud approaches Rob. "Huh. Man. What is going on? Maybe you should have left town a little bit earlier, right?" he jokes. They hear a loud explosion, and Hud swings his camera (just too late) to capture it. In the near distance, we can see a fireball. Hud inexpertly zooms in. The fireball is now large enough to envelop one of lower Manhattan's taller buildings. Huge chunks of burning debris have been thrown in all directions, resembling the terrifying explosive effects of a catastrophic volcanic eruption. Everyone runs for cover, as the firebombs rain upon the neighborhood. The camera seems to panic too, as Hud races down the staircase.

Onto the streets. The noise of people shouting and screaming is deafening, as they rush in all directions, uncertain where to go. The streets have a surreal quality, lit only by the orange glow of streetlamps. Hud quickly gathers himself, and points the camera towards the noise. Five or six blocks down, a plume of dust is visible. Hud zooms in. People are running in fear. Hud just catches something as it destroys the top of another building, in another huge fireball. What looks like a ball bounces towards him (and the camera), crashing past him. It's the smashed-in head of the Statue of Liberty, which grinds to a halt only meters from where they are standing. (This scene was inspired by the poster for *Escape from New York*, 1981.)

Cries of "Oh my God" briefly drown out the car alarms. Someone dashes over to the decapitated Liberty, and takes her picture: others quickly follow. They are interrupted by yet another loud crash. Hud swings himself and the camera around. He just about focuses the camera on another plume of dust, as something huge appears to walk across the street. Another crash, more dust, as a tall building (resembling the Woolworth Building) collapses.

The collapse of this building is important. It is not knocked over by the barely visible terror, it falls with gravity – straight down, as if it had been deliberately demolished that way to minimize the disruption to adjacent buildings. The people stand, watching. But then they see a wall of dust rushing towards them. They turn. They flee. Hud, and his friends dive into a delicatessen, the large window allowing them to see the wall of dust overtake the people as they run. There is banging and crashing from outside. Amidst the chaos, Hud tells Rob, "I saw it. It's alive." Despite Rob's pleas, Jason insists on going outside. The streets are now foggy with dust. Fires, damaged buildings and debris are all around. People are slowly walking through the streets, like zombies.

People are choking in the dust. Bits of paper flutter down, like cherry blossom from trees. From here on, *Cloverfield* is split into two basic sections: the first is an attempt to leave Manhattan island, to escape the monster; the second is Rob's ultimately futile struggle to rescue Beth from her apartment on the 57th floor of the Time Warner Building (more on this below).

Several features of *Cloverfield* bear comparison to *9/11* (2002), a film by Jules and Gédéon Naudet (also directed by James Hanlon). On September 11, 2001, Jules and Gédéon were doing a documentary about a "probie" fire-fighter, Tony Benetatos, in New York. By July 2001, the "probie" had been assigned to Engine 7, Ladder 1, in TriBeCa, Lower Manhattan. The morning of September 11, the filmmakers had split up to follow different stories: Jules was riding with the Battalion Chief Pfeifer, following a crew as they did routine checks of the gas-mains; Gédéon, the lead cameraman, was following Tony – of course, completely unaware of what was going to happen.

As the fire-crew checked the grills with gas meters, they heard a plane go over. It was about 8.46, so unusual to hear a plane at that time. But it also sounded low and close. They all look up. Jules is just in time to catch a plane as it smashes into the World Trade Center. Unknown to them at the time, American Airlines Flight 11 had been deliberately flown into World Trade Center 1, the north tower, under the control of Mohamed Atta. Jules zooms in, as the plane explodes in a fireball of dust and debris. Off camera, someone is shouting "Oh shit! Holy shit!"

The fire-fighters immediately jump in the fire engine and set off for the World Trade Center. The sound is dominated by the fire alarm, as Chief Pfeiffer calls in the report. People in the streets had stopped, looking up at the gaping hole in the burning north tower. The fire-crew park outside Tower 1, and prepare to go in. Jules follows them. Inside, there are screams, but the foyer is foggy with dust. Other fire-crews quickly assemble, and prepare to walk themselves and their gear up to the 78th floor and beyond. Jules assumed that Gédéon must be amongst them somewhere, following Tony up the stairs. Gédéon was with Tony, only Tony had been ordered to stay at the fire-house and was now answering desperate phone-calls and anxiously watching the news. Someone in the streets says to no one in particular, "It's something out of *Towering Inferno*, like a movie."

At 9.03 a.m., Jules is in the foyer of Tower 1 when United Airlines Flight 175 strikes Tower 2, the south tower. At 9.59 a.m. the south tower collapses. Jules is filming as a wall of dust overtakes the foyer of the north tower. He and the fire-fighters are overwhelmed. Gédéon, meanwhile, is now walking through the streets: he films a piece of an aeroplane engine that had crashed completely through the south tower. Debris lies everywhere. Paper flutters through the air, as if in a ticker-tape parade. But Gédéon is unable to reach the World Trade Center. Back at the station, Tony is watching the news – "it's clearly not an accident," the newsreader says. Live pictures show the burning towers. The area around the collapsed World Trade Center resembles a ghostly netherworld. Shocked and dazed, people walk down the streets like zombies.

Just as Rob rushes around Manhattan looking for Beth, while Hud records the events, so Jules and Gédéon attempt to find one another, while recording events as they unfold. Jules recalls "I think the whole world knew more than we did." News reports were able to gain an overview, a perspective, with more information than was available "on the ground" of Ground Zero. Similarly, Rob and Hud have almost no idea what's going on, except in those moments when they either break to watch TV or talk to the military – though everything, at this point, is speculation (as they say on TV, at these moments).

So, *Cloverfield* repeats 9/11: the gravitational collapse of a tall building; the wall of dust; the shock and panic of spectators; the lack of a perspective or overview; the eye being just too late to see what's (really) going on; the fear of an attack, perhaps by terrorists, but certainly by the unknown. It repeats the rushing around, fearing for others. It repeats the experience of being lost; lost in terrifying events. It repeats death and destruction – death and destruction in New York. The movie ought to be scary; it ought to make the hairs stand up on the back of your neck, as the familiar is rendered strange and horrific – the very definition of the uncanny, perhaps.

Cloverfield and the Uncanny

Of the uncanny, Freud says:

> There is no doubt that this belongs to the realm of the frightening, of what evokes fear and dread. It is equally beyond doubt that the word is not always used in a clearly definable sense, and so it commonly merges with what arouses fear in general. (2003 [1919]: 123)

In his essay on the uncanny, Freud seeks to specify what the uncanny might be. His analysis roams largely over particular forms of literature – that deal with "negative emotions" such as fear and repulsion – as he searches for a common "thought" that lies beneath them. What he discovers is that the uncanny "is that species of the frightening that goes back to what was once well known and had long been familiar" (2003 [1919]: 124).

This contracted specification has been distilled even further by urban theorists (Vidler 1992). The uncanny is the familiar rendered strange: the strangely familiar (Borden *et al.* 1996). But Freud reminds us: "not everything new and unfamiliar is frightening" (2003 [1919]: 125). The familiar rendered strange, to be sure, is not always uncanny. As important, for understanding *Cloverfield*, there are questions that hang over the strangely familiar renderings of horrific moments, or perhaps the familiarly strange. But such combinations and recombinations of strange and familiar take us further and further away from the problem. How are we to understand that species of frightening that is the uncanny?

Looking simply at form, *Cloverfield* ought to be uncanny. Nicholas Royle's book helpfully unpacks the different forms that the uncanny can take, such as silence, darkness, the inexplicable, being buried alive, déjà vu, the double (look-alikes) or doubling, coincidences and repetitions, fate or inevitability, crowds, ghosts, crowds of ghosts, automatism, the inanimate becoming animate (or vice versa) (especially dolls), cannibalism (being eaten) and other taboos, the evil genius, death (2003). Many of these forms can be found in Freud's own real-life experience of the uncanny. He writes:

> Strolling one hot summer afternoon through the empty and to me unfamiliar streets of a small Italian town, I found myself in a district about whose character I could not long remain in doubt. Only heavily made-up women were to be seen at the windows

of the little houses, and I hastily left the narrow street at the next turning. However, after wandering about for some time without asking the way, I suddenly found myself back in the same street, where my presence began to attract attention. Once more I hurried away, only to return there again by a different route. I was now seized by a feeling that I can only describe as uncanny, and I was glad to find my way back to the piazza I had recently left and refrain from any further voyages of discovery. (2003 [1919]: 144)

Freud sees the shock of the uncanny as being built out of many potential experiences: the unintentional return, a feeling of helplessness, being lost in such a way that you return to the same place again and again, unintended repetition that gives the impression of the inevitable or fate, a coincidence that appears to have greater meaning than mere chance, and the lure of superstition as if hidden forces were at work.

Cloverfield, simply, ought to be uncanny.

From my short summary above, we can think about the dust that engulfs the people on the streets, creating a haunting silence as crowds of seeming ghosts stumble almost aimlessly through the grey-white streets. Silence. Haunted. Ghosts. Zombies. Buried alive. Or the decapitation of the Statue of Liberty, with her face torn by some inexplicable force. Severed heads. Castration. The inexplicable. The survivors search for a way to reach Beth, they encounter by chance the military, parasites from the monster's back, the monster itself, in Central Park. Lost. Eaten alive. Chance.

As Rob nears the tower Beth is living in, he sees that it has fallen against a neighboring tower. This, of course, both replicates and inverts the gravitational collapse of other buildings in the movie. The movie "doubles" 9/11 both by repeating the collapse of the twin towers, but also by showing how the towers should have collapsed. Inside Beth's leaning tower, the walls and floors of the building resemble a carnival's "house of horror": normal ways of getting around buildings are thrown into disorder (so much so that the actors themselves felt nauseous on set). In this sequence, the archaic fear of falling is played to good effect, especially as the monster storms about below, threatening to topple the building while they are in it. The chaotic unreality of the leaning building is matched by the chaotic destruction by the monster below. To this is added the visual chaos of the hand-held point-of-view camera work. The audience is in amongst the chaos, as experienced by very frightened, and very vulnerable, characters. Helpless. The inevitable. Fate.

For Freud, the uncanny is not simply fear in general, however. There are two basic sources for uncanny experiences and feelings. First, there is a sense of the supernatural. Second, there are childhood anxieties. These can be, of course, intimately interwoven while also being distinct from one another. Freud's point is that beliefs in the supernatural or occult can linger in the mind, even if such beliefs are consciously and explicitly abandoned. Similarly, childhood fantasies and anxieties can be repressed or forgotten, yet they may persist in the dark places of the mind. A classic example would the children's blurring of the boundary between the animate and inanimate, leading to confusion over what is alive and what is not. This can be turned to good effect in horror stories by bring inanimate or dead creatures to life – dolls and ghosts are a particularly good examples. In *Cloverfield*, Rob and the others are clearly presented by a supernatural force, tapping quietly into both the idea that there are natures that are beyond visible nature, and childish anxieties about monsters, especially ones that lurk in dark shadowy places (such as the Hudson River, apparently).

Somehow, all this uncanny-work by the makers of *Cloverfield*, as well as the referencing of the horrific events of 9/11, didn't quite have the desired effect. *Cloverfield*, for many, was simply too much like 9/11: see for example these reactions, as documented on Wikipedia:

> Todd McCarthy of *Variety* called the film an "old-fashioned monster movie dressed up in trendy new threads," praising the special effects, "nihilistic attitude" and "post-9/11 anxiety overlay," but said, "In the end, [it's] not much different from all the marauding creature features that have come before it." Scott Foundas of *LA Weekly* was critical of the film's use of scenes reminiscent of the September 11, 2001 attacks in New York City and called it "cheap and opportunistic." ... Manohla Dargis in the *New York Times* called the allusions "tacky," saying, "[The images] may make you think of the attack, and you may curse the filmmakers for their vulgarity, insensitivity or lack of imagination," but that "the film is too dumb to offend anything except your intelligence." She concludes that the film "works as a showcase for impressively realistic-looking special effects, a realism that fails to extend to the scurrying humans whose fates are meant to invoke pity and fear but instead inspire yawns and contempt." Stephanie Zacharek of *salon.com* calls the film "badly constructed, humorless and emotionally sadistic," and sums up by saying that the film "takes the trauma of 9/11 and turns it into just another random spectacle at which to point and shoot." Michael Phillips of the *Chicago Tribune* warned that the viewer may feel "queasy" at the references to September 11, but that "other sequences ... carry a real jolt" and that such tactics were "crude, but undeniably gripping." He called the film "dumb," but "quick and dirty and effectively brusque," concluding that despite it being "a harsher, more demographically calculating brand of fun," he enjoyed the film. (http://en.wikipedia.org/wiki/*Cloverfield*#Reception. Last accessed December 22, 2009)

To be enjoyed, *Cloverfield*'s audience, the snarling reviewers imply, must be tasteless or dumb. Anyone with a wit of geopolitical sense would find the proximity of the movie to the events of 9/11 sickening and, intellectually at least, offensive. From a Freudian perspective, the likeliest audience would be those who are closer to beliefs in the supernatural and/or closer to their childhood anxieties. The movie's (best) demographic, thus, would be the even-faintly superstitious young (which is generally, of course, the horror movie's target demographic: witness the success of *Paranormal Activity*, 2009). Grudgingly, however, the critics admit that *Cloverfield* is a gripping monster flick, with realistic special effects. Something about this movie, then, *works* – perhaps despite its intentions to be uncanny, perhaps despite its allusions to 9/11.

Freud observes something else about the uncanny. It is important that beliefs in the supernatural or occult linger despite rational protests to the contrary and/or that childhood anxieties persist in the shadows of the mind despite our ignorance of them, but it is also important that these beliefs and anxieties have enough force to return, to come back, to repeat:

In the unconscious mind we can recognize the dominance of the *compulsion to repeat*, which proceeds from instinctual impulses. This compulsion probably depends on the essential nature of the drives themselves. It is strong enough to override the pleasure principle and lend a demonic character to certain aspects of mental life; it is still clearly manifest in the impulses of small children and dominates part of the course taken by the psychoanalysis of victims of neurosis. (2003 [1919]: 145)

The compulsion to repeat is a common theme in Freud's work. I want to set to one side the argument that it is associated with instinctual impulses and drive theory – yet keep the idea that there is some kind of compulsion in repetition (which may or may not be instinctual, which may or may not be *a* drive). But what is being repeated? And, what might be the force that lies behind *Cloverfield*'s compulsion to repeat?

Trauma, the Compulsion to Repeat, and the Always Near Collapse of the City

I have indicated that *Cloverfield* marks a compulsion to repeat. It repeats many things, of course, but I have already shown that it repeats 9/11. Of course, *Cloverfield* also falls into a long line of fantasies of the destruction of New York. Max Page (2008) points out that New York's destruction has been envisioned by writers and film-makers over at least the last two centuries. New York has been repeatedly, compulsively, destroyed and spectacularly so. The destruction of New York is a spectacle – a vision to behold as well as to enjoy. Most often, the destruction of the city, or the threat of its destruction, is carried by the Empire State Building, rather than the twin towers. Thus, both *King Kong* (1933) and the aliens in *Independence Day* (1996) head for the symbol of New York itself. So, while each age produces new ways of expressing its fears and anxieties, certain consistencies remain. The tall building offers less of a vantage point from which to see destruction than a measure of the destructive force itself. The larger the force, the bigger and the more spectacular the fall. In *Cloverfield*'s poster, the monster seems not only to have decapitated the Statue of Liberty, but also the twin towers themselves, as the beast lands in Battery Park.

According to Page, one reason that 9/11 looked to some "just like a movie" (see above) is that it did look just like a movie. Even more so now. It feels all too familiar. As Joanne Faulkner argues,

It would seem that there is very little about the events of September 11, 2001, that has not already been said or imagined. Our understanding of these events, and especially the attacks on the Twin Towers, has been overdetermined by the seemingly endless repetition of (by now) iconic images: of planes perforating the clear, tranquil surface of those seemingly impenetrable buildings and thus opening a rupture in the Western consciousness, the reparation of which is not yet in sight. (2008: 67)

Cloverfield repeats the trauma of 9/11, but it does so amongst a blizzard of already circulating images of 9/11. *Cloverfield*'s problem was less its plagiarizing of real-life horror and trauma, than the fact that it could not sufficiently shock its audiences with new ways of seeing or understanding 9/11. Nor, indeed, could it get itself out from under the thick history of always-already being destroyed New York. Less interesting than its "dumb" or "crass" repeating of 9/11, is its spectacular compulsion to repeat 9/11. As important, 9/11 is itself a repetition.

9/11 was not the first time that foreign-based terrorists had attacked New York. At 12.01 p.m. on September 16, 1920, 100 pounds of dynamite on board a wagon exploded on Wall Street. Also on the wagon was about 500 pounds of cast-iron weights. These cut through everything in their way. The effect was devastating: 38 people were killed and a further 400 injured. Initially, it wasn't clear to the FBI that it was in fact a terrorist attack. However, many were quick to blame anarchists and communists. Suspicion fell, particularly, on Italian anarchists who were known to be responsible for a series of bomb attacks across America. The FBI, however, were unable to identify the perpetrators.

By 1993, terrorists had traded up from a wagon to a car. On February 26, 1993, a bomb made of 1,500 pounds of explosive was detonated in the car park under the north tower, Tower 1. The intention was to bring the north tower crashing into the south tower, thereby toppling both towers in one horrific go. The bomb killed six people and injured a further 1,042, but it did not bring the north tower down. Indeed, the strengthening of the foundations of the north tower led, ironically, to the survival of dozens of people on 9/11. Four men were convicted of the bombing in March 1994, and a further two in November 1997. Though the attack was planned by Ramzi Yousef, the terrorist cell received some finance from his uncle, Khaled Shaikh Mohammed. It is possible that the World Trade Center was not the prime target, however Khaled Shaikh Mohammed is allegedly the mastermind behind the attack of September 11 (amongst other spectacular terrorist acts). Although he had been held in Guantanamo Bay, Khaled Shaikh Mohammed currently faces a criminal trial in a Manhattan federal court.

New York has seen its destruction before. As importantly, it has seen buildings destroyed before. As Page says, the attack on the World Trade Center "was the most perfect and horrific demolition job: two quarter-mile-tall towers exploding, then imploding, one-acre floors falling each through the next, two hundred times over" (2008: 199). Jeff Byles agrees; he also think that the collapse of the World Trade Center looked like a demolition (2005: 250). The idea that the collapse of the World Trade Center resembles a demolition is itself a repeated theme. Some have even built conspiracy theories on similarities between the collapse of the World Trade Center and known demolitions.

One remarkable, if not uncanny, coincidence is that Minoru Yamasaki was the architect of both the Pruitt-Igoe housing project and the twin towers. Pruitt-Igoe – that is, the Captain W. O. Pruitt Homes and the William L. Igoe Apartments – were opened in central St Louis between 1954 and 1955 at a cost of about $36 million. At 3 p.m. on March 16, 1972, 33 buildings in the complex were demolished. Charles Jencks famously observed that this was "the day Modern architecture died" (1991 [1977]: 9), a statement that many took to mark the end of modernity itself. Ironically, perhaps, the collapse of the twin towers marked the end of postmodernity – as history returned with a vengeance.

Freud is at pains to point out that not everything that is horrific is uncanny. Frightening experiences are not necessarily uncanny experiences. For him, the key

Figure 25.8   People protesting about a 9/11 cover-up. Author's photo.

to understanding the feeling of the uncanny is the reappearance of something – whether the source is (supposedly) long-discarded beliefs in the supernatural or repressed childhood anxieties and fears. The secret of the uncanny is "actually nothing new or strange, but something that was long familiar to the psyche and was estranged from it only through being repressed" (2003 [1919]: 148). Something that should have remained hidden has broken cover. What broke cover in *Cloverfield* was less a series of supposedly uncanny effects than a repressed fear of inevitable collapse. What *Cloverfield* – and all the other many destructions of New York – returns to is the relationship between the seeming permanence of (especially tall) buildings and their "unimaginable" potential for disintegration.

So strong is this repression of death, destruction, and disintegration that New York is already rebuilding the twin towers, not as an exact copy, but with one tower stretching 1,776 feet into the sky. Nicknamed the Freedom Tower (a nickname now dropped), it was to stand for an ideal that could not be vanquished or tarnished by acts of terrorism. Instead, it might properly stand for arrogance and the repression of "unimaginable," yet inevitable, future attacks – and future collapse.

Conclusion: Cities and Intensities of Feeling

Arguably, urban studies is founded on an interest in the relationship between affect and city life (see for example Simmel 1997 [1903]). A major theme within the explorations of urban affects has been the underlying anxieties and fears of city life and the responses of urbanites to those fears. Terms such as blasé attitude, indifference, and cynicism have come to be seen as the hallmarks of urban psychological

Figure 25.9   Artist's impression of the rebuilt World Trade Center. Courtesy of Skidmore, Owings, and Merrill LLP.

life (see also Simmel 1990 [1900]: 228–57). It is not simply the mental life of cities – the affect that underlies social interactions between urbanites – that is impacted by the affect of city, however. Affect is found, also, in its built form and in the representations of the city and its life. On this basis, cities are better characterized not by their physical structures, but by the way affects circulate through forms, representations, and events. Even if this is the case, this is not that easy to discern or track. One lesson from 9/11 and *Cloverfield* is that the blizzard of images and re-presentations of an event can mask, very quickly, the affects that motivate the blizzard of images and re-presentations.

The extreme visibility of the events of 9/11 has led to a spectacle of death and destruction that is, through its circulation and repetition, shorn of its power to shock and horrify. *Cloverfield* failed to shock not because it wasn't far enough away from the images of 9/11 but because it tried to be too close to them. The all-too-familiar images of collapse are now the means of repressing the fear of collapse. The unimaginable events of 9/11 are already covered over in a thick layer of imaginable destructions. This is not unusual. It has happened before and will happen again. In

New York. And in other cities too. Cities everywhere are spectacles of horror but, in spectacularizing that horror, they learn to draw a veil over the traumas that define, at least in part, the affect of city life.

References

Borden, I., Kerr, J., Pivaro, A., and Rendell, J. (eds.) (1996) *Strangely Familiar: Narratives of Architecture in the City*. London: Routledge.

Byles, J. (2005) *Rubble: Unearthing the History of Demolition*. New York: Three Rivers Press.

Faulkner, J. (2008) The innocence of victimhood versus the "innocence of becoming": Nietzsche, 9/11, and the "falling man." *Journal of Nietzsche Studies* 35–6: 67–87.

Freud, S. (2003 [1919]) The uncanny. In S. Freud, *The Uncanny*. Trans. D. McLintock. Harmondsworth: Penguin Books, 123–62.

Jencks, C. (1991 [1977]) *The Language of Post-Modern Architecture*. New York: Rizzoli International Publications.

Massey, D., Allen, J., and Pile, S. (eds.) (1999) *City Worlds*. London: Routledge.

Page, M. (2008) *The City's End: Two Centuries of Fantasies, Fears, and Premonitions of New York's Destruction*. New Haven, CT: Yale University Press.

Royle, N. (2003) *The Uncanny*. Manchester: Manchester University Press.

Simmel, G. (1990 [1900]) *The Philosophy of Money*, 2nd edn. London: Routledge.

Simmel, G. (1997 [1903]) The metropolis and mental life. In *Simmel on Culture: Selected Writings*, ed. D. Frisby and M. Featherstone. London: Sage, 174–85.

Vidler, A. (1992) *The Architectural Uncanny: Essays In The Modern Unhomely*. Cambridge: MA: MIT Press.

Chapter 26

The Future of New York's Destruction: Fantasies, Fictions, and Premonitions after 9/11[*]

Max Page

Two contradictory phrases were spoken over and over again on September 11, 2001, and during the weeks and months following. On the one hand: "It was unimaginable." On the other: "It was just like a movie." The sight of the twin towers falling was, in fact, both: utterly incomprehensible and, at the same time, wholly recognizable. If the first phrase reflected our daily experience living in relative safety in the world's one remaining superpower, the second emanated from our well-trained popular-culture imaginations, shaped by what we see when we turn on the television, go to a movie, or play a video game. By the millions, we have read these books, watched these movies, played these games, and found an electric thrill in watching the skyscrapers of Manhattan topple. Despite repeated observation that the events of September 11 were unimaginable, our culture has been imagining and even rehearsing these events for decades.

America's writers and image-makers have pictured New York's annihilation in a stunning range of ways. Earthquake, fire, flood. Meteor, comet, Martian. Glacier, ghosts, atom bomb. Class war, terrorism, invasion. Laser beams from space ships, torpedoes from Zeppelins, missiles from battleships. Apes, wolves, dinosaurs. Environmental degradation, nuclear fallout, "green death." American culture has been obsessed with fantasizing about the destruction of New York. At each stage of New York's advance over the past two centuries, visions of how the city would be demolished, blown up, swallowed by the sea, or toppled by monsters have proliferated in painting, graphic arts, cartoons, literature, photography, postcards, films, and computer software. These visions have been not only the purview of elite artists and novelists but a common narrative, inscribed in all popular forms of communication and culture. Visions of New York's destruction resonated with some of the most

The New Blackwell Companion to the City   Edited by Gary Bridge and Sophie Watson
© 2011 Blackwell Publishing Ltd

Figure 26.1 *Amazing Stories* magazine 3 (10) January 1928. Frank R. Paul as illustrator at www.frankwu.com.

longstanding themes in American history: ambivalence toward cities, the troubled reaction to immigrants and racial diversity, the fear of technology's impact, and the apocalyptic strain in American religious life. Furthermore, these visions of the city's end have paralleled the city's economic, political, racial, and physical transformations. Projections of the city's end reflected and refracted the dominant social issues. Each era in New York's modern history has produced its own apocalyptic imagery that explores, exploits, and seeks to resolve contemporary cultural tensions and fears. (See especially Rozario 2007 and Yablon 2010.)

But no amount of history, no rehearsals, could prepare New Yorkers for September 11 and the days, months, and, for some, years of grief and worry that followed. Usually, the rest of the country has feared New York, rather than New Yorkers fearing their city. New York, ascending to dominance by the early nineteenth century, became the most feared city of all. In New York, Americans saw the poor, immigrants, and people of all races. In New York, crowding, crime, disease, and radicalism were not only found but nurtured and propagated.

Figure 26.2 Cover from the August 5, 1950 edition of *Collier's* magazine, featuring an illustration by Chesley Bonestell for the article "Hiroshima USA."

Figure 26.3 Screenshot from *Planet of the Apes* (1968), directed by Franklin J. Schaffner, produced by Arthur P. Jacobs.

Within the city, fear has always been present. To nineteenth-century New Yorkers, who may have been told stories of the city's burning during the seven-year British occupation in the Revolutionary War, who lost friends and family members to the cholera epidemics of the 1830s, who perhaps watched the burning of much of lower Manhattan in 1835, or who later saw rioting mobs rage through the city in 1863, the notion that the city was forever was absurd. And in the twentieth century, the city at the height of its power was hardly immune to fears of sudden catastrophe, the distinct possibility of nuclear attack. September 11 bombed the city back to the atomic age, when a roar in the sky could instantly evict daydreams from New Yorkers' minds and substitute apocalyptic visions.

September 11 was its own form of New York disaster movie, played out live on every screen in the world. And in the days afterward, Americans voluntarily submitted themselves to watching the horror of the destruction of the twin towers, of people jumping to their deaths, of a great pile of collapsed skyscrapers burning, smoking, filling the air with toxic clouds and paper. This was the ultimate, all-encompassing disaster movie, which Americans watched for days on their television and computer screens.

Even as America and the world immersed itself in the picture of New York under attack, we rebelled against fictional accounts of the same scenes. The reality was so awful that it was simply no longer enjoyable to imagine it. My heart-pounding flights as a college student on Microsoft's *Flight Simulator* became unimaginable. My proposal for an exhibition at the New York Historical Society entitled "Destroying New York," which I was proofreading and was ready to mail out on the morning of September 11, and which I had pitched successfully as a "fun" exhibition, was now unseemly and insensitive. What had been not only acceptable but enjoyable and profitable on September 10 – thinking of new ways to set the heart palpitating by watching New Yorkers die – a day later was offensive and unpatriotic. Even selling pictures of the Trade Center as it was before 9/11 was deemed profiteering, although many were selling mementos honoring the towers and the people who worked in them. Profiting from real and imagined disaster – one of the engines fueling the New York destruction genre for two centuries – immediately became an outrage.

As the shockwaves of 9/11 rippled through American society, the culture of violence came under scrutiny. Because so much of that culture had centered on New York, the chorus for changing films and television shows was all the more powerful: to modify a violent film centered on New York now was a patriotic act, a necessary salve on the wounds of Americans in the name of a united front against terror.

Within days of 9/11, popular-culture producers of all types instituted an unofficial self-censorship to protect consumers from reminders of the attacks. Video game producers altered content (including scenarios of terrorist attacks on New York and Washington) in order "to avoid stirring emotions unnecessarily and unwillingly offending the public," as one executive said. On September 14, 2001, Microsoft announced that it would delete the World Trade Center from its 2002 edition of *Flight Simulator*. The attacks of September 11 brought out of the woodwork many devotees of *Flight Simulator* and their guilty secret: the lure of flying into the World Trade Center was a central appeal of the program. Months later, when Kabul fell, journalists found a reference to Microsoft's *Flight Simulator* in an Al-Qaeda member's home. The Marxist hip-hoppers Coup, who had sought to highlight their critique of capitalism by imagining the destruction of the Trade Center, quickly backpedaled, insisting that the image was "not supposed to be realistic in its depiction. The Coup advocates change, but change through peaceful means, never through violence." The CD liner image, completed in July, was quickly altered for a November release. The new cover had a less offensive image of a martini glass filled with flaming gasoline.

Movies filmed in New York but not yet released before 9/11 faced a dilemma: move forward with the World Trade Center as part of the skyline, or digitally edit out the towers. The poster for *Spider-Man* was edited to remove the reflection of the twin towers from Spider-Man's eyes, and a scene was removed (though seen by millions in promotional trailers before 9/11) in which a web hanging between the twin towers catches a helicopter. Film-makers adopted similar editing strategies in films including *Zoolander*, *Serendipity*, *Men in Black II*, *People I Know*, and *The Time Machine*. They claimed that they were simply trying to avoid offending and disturbing audiences unnecessarily. It seems equally likely that filmmakers worried that the sight of the towers would detract from the narrative and undermine the escapist pleasure that is the essence of big Hollywood films.

Commentators across the political spectrum predicted that the attacks of September 11 would finally be the straw that broke the back of a culture of violence. For years, the rising tide of "disaster porn" had provoked worried efforts from reformers, from both the left and the right. Studies seemed to back up what many feared: that the violence of movies and video games could provoke violent behavior among the nation's youth. The prevalence of video cameras made it easier to capture images of crimes and natural disasters as they were happening. The corporatization of news meant that sensational reports and footage of disasters of all types made the top of evening newscasts.

In the wake of 9/11, journalists and theorists, news commentators and politicians realized that the language of the disaster movie had shaped the initial, unscripted response to 9/11, and they were appalled. "This is not a movie," argued Anthony Lane, a film critic for the *New Yorker,* in an impassioned essay just two weeks after 9/11. "What happened on the morning of September 11th," Lane argued, "was that imaginations that had been schooled in the comedy of apocalypse were forced to reconsider the same evidence as tragic." Perhaps, he suggested, "the disaster movie is indeed to be shamed by disaster." Lane expressed what many intellectuals and commentators feared in the wake of 9/11: that our culture had immersed itself in violent movies over the past generation, effectively dulling our ability to comprehend real disaster. September 11, he argued, might represent "not only an official rebuke to that license but the fiery end of the ride" (Lane 2001).

Leon Wieseltier, the literary editor of the *New Republic,* underscored Lane's critique with a blistering attack on those who would seek, after 9/11, a "balm in culture." According to Wieseltier, analogies between Ground Zero and the work of Frank Gehry, or Piranesi, or other architects of the "fragment" were not simply in bad taste but an inevitable product of a society that preferred to flee from a confrontation with evil and find solace in pat sentiment. A year later, nearing the first anniversary of September 11, Wieseltier was appalled by how thoroughly the actual date and horrors perpetrated on that date had been supplanted by "September 11," a media phenomenon that quickly moved the reality of the tragedy into a realm of sentiment and emotion. "The media," he wrote a year later, "is greedy for tears." September 11 "was the deadening of September 11. It was deadened, like all images and ideas that are hallowed, by repetition, and also by sentiment, which is what our popular culture uses to drive away lasting significance. The American heart is the bouncer at the door of the American mind." You can almost hear him pounding the table and insisting that popular culture had no business trying to portray 9/11. It would only sentimentalize and sterilize the tragedy (Wieseltier 2001, 2002).

The critic Slavoj Žižek had little time for these debates over whether 9/11 had been or would be made "just another media spectacle ... a catastrophe version of the snuff porno movies." Instead, he wondered, "Where have we already seen the same thing over and over again?" The disaster movies were, in Žižek's thinking, the unconscious reflection of our repressed knowledge that "we live in an insulated artificial universe ... [that] generates the notion that some ominous agent is threatening us all the time with total destruction." Just as people who live behind the walls of gated communities are sure that crime is on the rise "out there," so too does our own isolation – from the world but also from classes and races within the United States – breed a profound fear of what might be threatening us. Our very well-being in a world of inequality and violence paradoxically haunts us with "nightmarish visions of catastrophes." "America got what it fantasized about, and that was the biggest surprise" (Žižek 2002: 17, 33, 16).

All this debate and rapid response by film studios and record companies might seem to indicate that the ship of American culture had taken a sharp turn away from the disaster spectacles of the previous decade. But it was a shortlived detour. *Collateral Damage* – a typically violent Arnold Schwarzenegger vehicle – had been scheduled to open in October 2001; it was delayed, but only until March 2002. On the other hand, Sony Pictures Entertainment accelerated the release of *Black Hawk Down*, an extremely violent film about a failed rescue effort in Somalia in 1993, from March 2002 to December 2001, in a bid to exploit the jingoistic sentiment aroused by the invasion of Afghanistan.

Audiences responded as they always had, proving film studios and directors wrong in their calculations. Film critics attacked as dishonest and even cowardly movie-makers who used postproduction editing to eliminate potentially disturbing images. As one fan wrote, "We're giving up our culture to protect ourselves from pain." Some audiences felt duped by retouched skylines. Directors who chose to leave in the twin towers – such as Sam Raimi, director of three *Spider-Man* films (the first of which was released in 2002), and Cameron Crowe, director of *Vanilla Sky* – were praised. Martin Scorsese, in *Gangs of New York,* chose to leave the World Trade Center in the final scene of the movie, in which the characters view Manhattan from Brooklyn and see the city of 1863 transforming before their eyes into the city of 2002.

Within months, violence and disasters made their way back onto screens. Not many movie-makers were willing to show New York's destruction explicitly on screen immediately after 9/11, however. If the desire for – and the profit in – violent movies and videos could not be quelled, at least the location of the disaster could be changed. Hollywood could avoid criticism while feeding audiences the disaster imagery they craved, by shifting the destruction to other cities. Los Angeles has competed with New York in the disaster genre for several decades, and now it found new life, or death. The hit television series *24* subjected the city to an atomic bomb and bioterrorism. Baltimore was destroyed in *The Sum of All Fears* in 2002. San Francisco fell to the *Hulk* in 2003, and again in *X-Men: The Last Stand* (2006). In *Category 6* (2004), a made-for-television film, three storms converged over the Midwest and headed northward to decimate Chicago (after doing a fair bit of damage in Las Vegas and leveling the St Louis Arch). And "because people love scary wind," the film brought in 16.68 million viewers. It almost bested another kind of disaster show, the ABC series *Lost*, about a group of badly behaved people stranded on an island after a plane crash. Another made-for-television disaster movie, *10.5* (2004), is centered on the west coast. In an opening scene the Space Needle in Seattle tips over and crashes after the city is hit with a 7.9 magnitude earthquake. But the worst is yet to come, as aftershocks of 8.4 and higher head south. The Golden Gate Bridge is destroyed, and Los Angeles's towers tumble down as the "big one" rumbles through southern California and finally does what many have joked about for years: turns the coast of California into an island.

The tide had turned. Now it was acceptable to speak about what people had felt even on that morning – that the sight of the World Trade Center towers collapsing was horrifyingly beautiful. Within less than a year, in the world of art and culture, New York was no longer safe, despite the changes to album covers and films and software, and despite a trend toward picturing other cities in disaster movies. The early prediction that American culture would stay away from imagining New York's destruction (and from violence in general) was quickly proved wrong. How long ago those solemn declarations seem. After a brief lull, projecting New York's end was back in style.

Back to Normal: The Resilience of the Disaster Theme

If culture-makers needed any inspiration to return to the theme of the city's end, policy-makers, politicians, and scientists helped by creatively imagining horrible destruction arriving in New York. Blowing up a chlorine tank, spreading pneumonic plague throughout the city, bombing the Holland Tunnel, releasing a "suitcase" nuclear bomb in Times Square or dirty bombs in the subway, attacking the Indian Point nuclear power plant, launching a terror attack in Shea Stadium, destroying the Brooklyn Bridge – the list of scenarios offered up to a frightened public went on forever. The city, state, and federal governments contributed with mock terror attacks, reports of unreadiness, and plans for evacuation. The Bush administration played the fear card like a good Hollywood screenwriter. Plots were floated, terror alerts were raised, headline fonts were enlarged, nervous New Yorkers were quoted. And then holes would begin to appear in the stories.

The attack was not imminent; it was only in the planning stages, or a passing comment by a man on the streets of Cairo. In July 2006, just as the Bush administration was in the midst of a counter-offensive to rescue its final two years from utter political disaster, it announced that a plot to bomb the Holland Tunnel in order to flood lower Manhattan had been foiled. As it turns out, none of the suspects was in the United States, and there were no real plans, only words. Such "truth-based" scenarios provided fodder and inspiration for popular culture-makers.

On the other hand, when a real disaster of sorts hit – a blackout that struck New York and a large part of the northeast in August 2003, just a month before the second anniversary of 9/11 – the experience taught the city and nation new lessons. The almost universal calm that accompanied the blackout was in stark contrast to reactions to the 1977 blackout, the worst in the nation's history; that episode had led to utter chaos in the city, with looting, riots, and arson taking over whole neighborhoods. The city was far less fragile than it had seemed after 9/11. Similarly, when a man blew up his Upper East Side home in the summer of 2006 rather than let his wife have it in their divorce settlement, the disaster registered for a day or two, inspiring more jokes about the value of Manhattan real estate than concerns about the possibilities of post-9/11 catastrophe. Disasters that struck other people – New York is nothing if not a catalogue of daily pain, violence, crime, and collapse – became, once again, entertainment for everyone else. As in the good old bad old days, New York had about a minute to be concerned with threats and daily disasters.

Or people had a couple of hours to watch it on the screen. Though film-makers made forays to other cities, the power of New York as the locus of the culture's destructive fantasies was remarkably resilient. After that brief era of editing out the twin towers, or avoiding destruction in and of New York, Americans rushed back to that theme with gusto. The films came at an accelerating pace: *Spider-Man* and *Spider-Man II* (2002 and 2004), *Batman Begins* (2005), *Skycaptain and the World of Tomorrow* (2004), *The Day After Tomorrow* (2004), *Superman Returns* (2006), *X-Men: The Last Stand* (2006), and television shows *10.5* (2004), *Category 6* (2004), and *Heroes* (2006), to name just a few. Perhaps the finale to several years of battling over whether or not to show New York's destruction, or to show the twin towers, came in a fluffy comedy in the summer of 2006, *Click*, starring Adam Sandler as a man who gets a "universal remote" that allows him to fast-forward through his life. For just a brief second, in a scene set in 2021, we see the skyline of the city two decades from now. At the tip of lower Manhattan stands not one Freedom Tower (based on the initial design by David Childs after control had been wrested from the architect Daniel Libeskind) but two. A feeling that the site needed twin towers to "restore" the skyline and deny the terrorists victory seemed to have found a supporter in Hollywood.

The End of the World as We Know It: Environmental Fears and the End of New York

The shackles restraining American culture from one of its favorite activities – imagining new ways to demolish New York – were quickly shattered. Just a year or two after 9/11, new themes began to emerge. The most powerful of these was global warming, which scientists unanimously predicted and right-wing politicians stridently repudiated. Natural disaster, and the subgenre of climate change, has always been a popular theme – as we have seen in works as diverse as *Deluge*, the *Twilight Zone* episode "The Midnight Sun," *Meteor*, and *Deep Impact*. All these dramas demonstrate the persistent fear that natural forces on the earth or beyond will end New York's fragile existence.

In the early years of the twenty-first century, natural disaster became environmental disaster, caused by human action or inaction. Some earlier works had hinted at human culpability. But now the movies and stories showed humans provoking not degradation – not a natural, steady state of decline – but a dramatic shift in the earth's fortunes that would lead to cataclysmic shifts in the earth's atmosphere.

> In this unearthly light many tall structures of the metropolis, which had as yet escaped the effects of undermining by the rushing torrents in the streets, towered dimly toward the sky, shedding streams of water from every cornice. Most of the buildings of only six or eight stories had already been submerged, with the exception of those that stood on high grounds in the upper part of the island.

This is an excerpt from the astronomer Garrett P. Serviss's novel *The Second Deluge* (1912: 133). The disaster is inevitable; the best humans can do is to recognize the coming calamity and be resourceful enough to survive. That scene, minus the biblical overtones, and with the addition of human environmental depredation as the root cause, could have been a summary of a scene from the 2004 film *The Day After Tomorrow*. The makers of that film consciously launched it into the global warming fracas and the 2004 election. The story is built on a scientific theory that global warming would lead not to a steady warming and gradual melting of glaciers but rather force a tipping-point, causing rapid cooling and the onset of an ice age.

Waters rush through the canyons of Manhattan in *The Day After Tomorrow* (2004). As the ice age rapidly sets in, survivors try to get inside the New York Public Library. To establish his catastrophe as worldwide, the director Roland Emmerich piles in an assortment of disaster scenarios – hurricanes, tornadoes, ice age. Devastation hits every corner of the globe. And yet Emmerich comes back, as film-makers always do, to New York City. The city's destruction brings it all home in a horrible – and horribly beautiful – frozen dream.

The fear of global warming proved fertile ground for a variety of culture-makers. Hurricane Katrina, which hit New Orleans at the end of August 2005, fueled the global warming debate in several ways. Katrina raised the fear of more frequent and more violent hurricanes which could devastate coastal cities. But it also offered dramatic images of what global warming would mean: flooded coastal cities as waters rise. Though New Orleans is a unique case in the United States – a city that sits below the water line, artificially protected by a system of levees – its submersion sent scientists, journalists, and artists scurrying to picture the future of their cities. Katrina also revealed the utter impotence of the federal and state governments either to prepare for the hurricane by building up adequate levees or to respond adequately to disaster.

Images of New Orleans in a future of continued global warming and rising waters were soon paired with visions of a flooded New York. They appeared in *Harvard Magazine*, in *Vanity Fair*, on the History Channel, and in newspapers. The image of New York under water appeared in former vice president Al Gore's 2006 movie *An Inconvenient Truth*. One of the most powerful images of the film shows the impact of melting Arctic glaciers through a satellite view of New York if the ocean level were to rise just a few feet. The edge of Manhattan would be at Broadway, with the World Trade Center memorial site deep under water. While seeking to sound a loud alarm about the threat of global warming, the film-makers wanted to avoid being marginalized for hyperbole. The shrinking of Manhattan Island – to roughly its dimensions of the eighteenth century before a succession of infills widened the island significantly – was a good choice: dramatic and suggestive of far greater tragedy (say, if the ocean levels rose ten feet) without overwhelming audiences with apocalyptic imagery. In an escapist disaster movie, audiences demand drama and realism; in a documentary, accuracy and caution win out.

No such caution is seen in the visionary paintings of Alexis Rockman, an artist who has spent a decade imagining and painting a submerged New York, a future environmental wasteland. In one work Central Park is half tropical jungle, half Arctic glacier, ringed by decaying skyscrapers; Times Square and Washington Square are submerged with palm trees growing out of the buildings' windows. The culmination of this decade-long exploration is *Manifest Destiny*, completed in 2004. In an 8 by 24 foot mural first exhibited in the Brooklyn Museum of Art, Rockman painstakingly depicts a panoramic view across the East River to Brooklyn in the year 5000, after three millennia of global warming and environmental degradation. Rockman calls *Manifest Destiny* a "very traditional history painting." This is a history painting for the future: global deluge caused by global warming, he suggests, will be our history if we cannot change our ways. The oil barrel – a cause of global warming – floats along, providing a haven for the creature that would surely persist: the cockroach. New York, once the exemplar of civilization, now becomes its graveyard. Beneath the waters lies a necropolis, a dead city that was unwilling or unable to curb its consumption and pollution. Tunnels and an oil tanker, a stealth bomber and a submarine – these are all that remain of the grand vision that animated this city.

Welcome Back, King Kong

Artists and writers of every era – each with their own world of cultural and social concerns – returned to New York, to destroy it, to entertain their audiences, and to define their stances on the social concerns of the day. New York's death is a storyline that plays through every type of fiction American culture has produced. As varied as the media are, the narratives play in two consistent if harmonically different keys. One is the dark, minor key of alarm and warning, lessons and political arguments, fear and premonition of real disaster. The other is the key of celebration and entertainment, homage and love for the city. These two registers mark the two ends of the American ideological composition: a persistent embrace of progress and modernism, utopia and ascent, but also a suspicion of failure, and the harsh truth of the jeremiad. American identity has been built on a "culture of calamity" (Rozario 2007). That culture has been built on imagining our greatest city's end.

The balance between love and hate has swung wildly in the works of artists and writers of different political and class stripes. But love and hate are two sides of the same coin. American culture has destroyed New York because it is so unimaginable for Americans not to have this city. It is a healthy playing out of our fears onto the screen. As E. B. White wrote, "New York is to the nation what the white church spire is to the village – the visible symbol of aspiration and faith, the white plume saying the way is up!" (White 1977: 123). The white plume we saw on Tuesday,

Figure 26.4 "That Liberty Shall Not Perish from the Earth" (1917).

September 11, 2001, was the billowing debris of two massive towers falling down, taking with them thousands of lives. This was a conscious choice of the perpetrators – to make our fantasies and our nightmares horrible reality, to turn gleaming symbols of the city into burning sites of terror. September 11 is not the endpoint of this essay, nor of the imagination of New York's end. The memory of September 11 may have shifted the tone and content of portrayals of New York's destruction. But the ongoing – perhaps unending – war on terrorism, and New York's continued importance in American life, at the very least ensure that our culture will continue to spin stories of New York's end.

If you were worried about New York's future in the aftermath of 9/11, you could take heart in late 2005: just like old times, the city was being destroyed at a theater near you. The best thing for New York might have been the sight of King Kong tramping through the streets of Manhattan on his way to a fateful appointment at the top of the Empire State Building. For if there is one thing that symbolizes New York's pre-eminence, it is that so many still want to imagine the city's end.

Rather than bemoan the degradation of our insensitive culture, perhaps we should celebrate these fantasies. New York has been destroyed for so long that it is somehow reassuring to see the tradition continue. Even as we watch New York being demolished in a darkened screening room, we are already anticipating the aftermath – not the postapocalyptic landscape, but the scene after the lights go up. What we crave from these tense Hollywood films of menace and devastation is, in fact, reassurance that the city has survived. For New Yorkers, that means walking out of the movie theater and into a still extant, and robustly alive, city of New York. For those beyond the city, we expect the relief of watching that skyline behind David Letterman, as reliable as ever.

It is important to remember that New York has always been better at celebration than at fear. New York has always prided itself on humming – ticker-tape parades down Broadway, the tall ships at the Bicentennial, that memorable V-J Day kiss caught by Eisenstaedt in Times Square – these are New York's emotional landmarks.

All this life explains why we continue to destroy New York in books, on canvas, on movie screens, and on computer monitors: because it is so unimaginable for us, in reality, not to have this city. We have played out our worst fears on the screen and in our pulp fiction because, as the city's oracle, E. B. White, wrote in the shadow of the atomic bomb: "If it were to go, all would go – this city, this mischievous and marvelous monument which not to look upon would be like death" (White 1977: 132).

So the makers of American popular culture flirt with causing real disaster if they move their sets and canvases to other cities. When New York is no longer destroyed – on film, in flight-simulator software, in video games, paintings, and books – that will be a sign that the city no longer dominates America's, and the world's, imagination.

And if New York is no longer the setting of our worst fears then it may no longer be the home of our greatest hopes. And that would truly be the beginning of the city's end.

Note

* This essay is derived from Max Page, *The City's End: Two Centuries of Fantasies, Fears, and Premonitions of New York's Destruction*. New Haven, CT: Yale University Press, 2008.

References

Lane, Anthony (2001) This is not a movie. *New Yorker* September 24: 79.
Rozario, Kevin (2007) *The Culture of Calamity: Disaster and the Making of Modern America*. Chicago: University of Chicago Press.
Serviss, Garrett P. (1912) *The Second Deluge*. New York: McBride, Nast.
White, E. B. (1977) Here is New York. In *Essays of E. B. White*. New York: Harper and Row. Originally published in *Holiday* magazine, 1948.

Wieseltier, Leon (2001) Ruins. *New Republic* November 26.

Wieseltier, Leon (2002) A year later. *New Republic* September 2.

Yablon, Nick (2010) *American Ruins: An Archaeology of Urban Modernity, 1830–1920*. Chicago: University of Chicago Press.

Žižek, Slavoj (2002) *Welcome to the Desert of the Real! Five Essays on September 11 and Related Dates*. London: Verso.

Chapter 27

Public Spaces? Branding, Civility, and the Cinema in Twenty-First-Century China

Stephanie Hemelryk Donald

Ordinary Affect

In her study on affect in America, *Ordinary Affects* (2007), Kathleen Stewart looks for the exceptional moments of being in the everyday experiences of emotion. She thereby makes connections between what is intimate and what is public, what is internal and what is external, and what is expressed best through juxtaposition, repetition, and the accumulation of details. She lays the ground for a discussion of urban affect, wherein events, the environment, the talk, and the policies that govern a city's everyday are as much a factor in the emotional registers in which life is lived, as are the personal engagements between family members, friends, and lovers. None of these can be separated.

> One day Sissy's husband, Bud, came home talking about a real smart guy who told him that the economy is going bust. Something about how the price of gold would go way up and they'd have to print up a whole different kind of money – red money. Bud thinks that this means that the color of the money will be red, but Sissy thinks the guy's talking about communist money somehow. (Stewart 2007: 107)

In this short discussion of city and cinema in China, the focus is on the national capital, Beijing, where the color of money is indeed red, at least in 100 yuan notes, and where communism is a far more complicated descriptor than Sissy or Bud might imagine. Affect in Beijing arises through, or despite of, the powerful nexus of political power, longstanding urban community, and cultural energy that shapes the city's daily life. China (and Beijing as the urban face of the nation) has been described by Lijia Zhang as a cage, that "has grown so large, we can hardly feel its limits" (2008: n.p.), succinctly pointing to the reality of bearable authoritarianism, with nationalist

---

The New Blackwell Companion to the City   Edited by Gary Bridge and Sophie Watson
© 2011 Blackwell Publishing Ltd

characteristics (Hughes 2006: 113–15). The triangulation of cinema, civility, and branding are effective conceptual mechanisms for paying attention to these factors in accounting for the city's publicness, or lack of it, as that mimics the quotidian encounter of people and politics. Civility in Beijing is most obviously palpable in the parks on a Sunday morning, where people gather to dance, exercise, sing, or perform for one another. Older people pay only two yuan for entry (and some parks are free to senior citizens), allowing them to spend much of their time outside and in the pavilions in the company of friends and acquaintances. In the past several years there has been a notable element of nostalgia in these gatherings, with large groups, up to 200 people in Tiantan Park on one of my visits in 2007, gathering regularly to sing old songs from the revolutionary era, their equivalent of 1980s anthems, as it were. The civility of shared values is, as elsewhere, a strong element of publicness in Beijing, and it inflects the use of available spaces for convivial sociality. The difficulty in describing Beijing's public life is that it does not easily fit with the ideal models of publicness, autonomy, and civility which European thought attaches to those notions. The city is highly convivial, and somewhat anarchic in its just-in-time approach to everyday sociability, and yet it is also a highly managed authoritarian space. The "structure of attention" (Donald 2006: 64–5) through which one reads Beijing must recognize that whilst politics and the influence of the state are always present, and structurally relevant to almost every aspect of daily life, they are nonetheless not the sum of the energy and spatial organization of the city. Effective moments of cinema arise when a film-maker observes the tragedy or comedy in quotidian moments, and thereby illuminates the patterns of social relations and the effects of state power that together form the character of the city itself.

Beijing is not an easily cinematic city. The monumentality of its formal architecture creates a landscape of power that is indisputable, but impossibly scaled as a background to intimacy. Nonetheless, there is an imaginative landscape in Beijing where stories of ordinary affect can be told. Everyday Beijing offers three key locales for storytelling: the intimacy of home and family, generally the cramped family living space in a modern apartment, or older courtyard-laneway home (*hutong*); the indeterminacy of the young and transient, located in the laneways themselves, on demolition and building sites, and in the non-places of modern work environments, such as the backstage living spaces of Jia Zhangke's *The World* (China 2004) (Donald 2009), and, of course, the many city parks. From Zhang Yuan's essay on homoerotic desire in *East Palace, West Palace* (China 1996) to documentaries on ageing passions and the politics of dance partners in Lina Yang's *The Love of Mr An* (China 2007) and Ning Ying's *For Fun* (China 1993) from her *Beijing Trilogy* (2001), all are set in the city parks. There are also films, many of which are not distributed beyond the VCD market in China, which capture the affect of Beijing as both politically organized and socially constrained. I will look in more detail at three such films in this discussion, *Beijing Bastards* (Zhang Yuan, China 1993), *Beijing Bicycle* (Wang Xiaoshuai, China 2001), and *The Concrete Revolution* (Guo Xiaolu, China 2004). The first is a quasi-documentary, quasi-fictional account which treats the aftermath of Tiananmen through the experience of a young group of musicians, including the Tiananmen generation hero, Cui Jian. The second is a story about an encounter between a migrant worker and a school student, and deals with the spatiality of class-based opportunity in the city. The third is a documentary which also is interested in the scales of class in Beijing, particularly through the eyes of those caught up in the development of the city for the Olympics.

1989, 2008, 2009

At the end of the film *Beijing Bicycle* (*shiqisui de danche*, or *The Bicycle of a Seventeen Year Old*), the main protagonist, Guei, walks through the streets carrying his smashed bicycle over his shoulder. He walks past the crowds, against the traffic, with little hope other than his stubbornness to protect him. An innocent, he has been the recipient of ill treatment and bad luck, and, rather in the manner of the young second-generation migrant teenagers in *La Haine* (Kassowitz, France 1995), he has finally lost control. In *La Haine*, the one character most likely to escape the Paris projects is Hubert, but in the end he picks up a gun and takes aim at the police. Guei, a determined and impressive escapee from provincial poverty, has attacked the Beijing teenager who kicked and stamped on his bicycle until it buckled. He has done so with a concrete brick that has fallen out of the crumbling *hutong* laneway in which a drama between local boys has raged, and caught him in the middle. The person may or may not be dead, and Guei may be about to be imprisoned or executed for murder. We are not told. All we do know is that as a migrant worker in Beijing, Guei has briefly enjoyed the freedom of the city streets, cycling as a courier from one job to the next, earning the price of his bike, and refusing to succumb to the everyday prejudices against outsiders (*waidiren*). Here, in the final scene, he is still displaying a courageous and stubborn belief in his right to walk the city streets in any direction he chooses, and to take his means of income and the symbol of his autonomy along with him, broken or not. Life must go on, even if there is no real hope that it might.

A decade earlier, Zhang Yuan shot the semi-documentary feature, *Beijing Bastards* (*Beijing zazhong*). The film, self-consciously post-Tiananmen, is also concerned with how young people occupy Beijing, what spaces they use, and the degree to which external forces inhibit their movement. In one scene the police shut down a rock concert or "Party." In another, one of the young musicians talks to his girlfriend about having an abortion, leaving her shocked and weeping under a concrete flyover. It is, however, in the sequence in which we see hundreds of anonymous Beijingers cycling in the rain past Tiananmen Square, that Zhang reminds us of the ordering power of the state over urban space. There is no overt mention of the conflict that took place in the square three years earlier on June 3–4. There is simply the juxtaposition between suppressed history, expressed through the beating of the rain against the windows of the musicians' van (and thus too on the eye of the camera that is capturing the scene), and the stolid cyclists, shrouded in yellow rain capes, moving in one direction around the square.

2008 was the year in which Tiananmen was supposed to have been forgotten, an unfortunate hiccough on the journey to urban renewal and prosperity. Brand China had reached its apogee. It was the year in which the city both fulfilled its ambition to showcase great achievements in urban modernization and nonetheless refused to acknowledge how that same regeneration rubbed out historical formations of civility and memory (Lovell 2009: 16–17). In 2008, everyone in the world with access to broadcast media learned of the city's relevance and power to impress, but arguably, no one was truly introduced to the city as a living environment and a place of sophisticated sociability and complex human engagement. Brand China (Ramo 2007), as evidenced in brand Beijing that year, was insistent, demanding, and powerfully contained within its own mixed logic of success and victimhood. Everything was on the best possible track, and anything that went wrong was attributed to western media, Tibetan exiles, and unnamed terrorist elements. This was essential for the maintenance of the brand. As worker after worker attests in Xiaolu Guo's interviews with migrant workers in her film, "Beijing is good, my life here is good, the Olympics will be good." All place-brand campaigns rely on the support of internal as well as external stakeholders. That may be highly qualified in practice by cynicism, transitory levels of self-interest, and the contingencies of unexpected events. Whilst China's torch relay dented the image of China in Europe, the same debacle was used to build a wave of national pride and indignation at home, which carried through to the Olympics, until they in turn recaptured global admiration at Chinese aesthetic competence, mass organization, and sporting talent. Externally, no one could reasonably suggest that China's grasp of the modern media event was anything but superb. As primary host, it was Beijing that won that attention and thereby reiterated its metonymic status as the idea of China.

2009 was the year of anniversaries, of the founding of the People's Republic of China in 1949, of the May 4 nationalist movement in 1919, and of the massacre of Tiananmen in 1989. Only the first was formally celebrated in Beijing. Nationalist modernity was discussed as a matter of academic interest by those who see the link between the waves of change effected or marked by mass demonstrations. All open debate about Tiananmen was stifled on the mainland. The main difference between June 4, 2009 and, say, February 4 in the same year was that there were more security checks at the subway stations, more gossip amongst 40-somethings, and far less access to social networking sites on the internet. Individual intellectuals, with a record of independent historical thinking, were followed by the police. During a meeting 40 miles outside the city on June 5, a conversation amongst 10 people was interrupted by the arrival of two police cars. The officers stood outside their cars smoking. The people inside glanced out of the window, some more nervous than others. The principal speaker guessed that he was the person in whom the police were interested. He decided to grab some lunch, before heading back into town and so deflecting the problem.

These things happen. Life went on. One colleague said that there was no need to remember June 4, the effects of the clampdown were still evident in every interaction on the city streets. In the terms of this essay, his feeling was that the structure of affect of contemporary Beijing continues to be profoundly shaped by the expectations of power and control created by the massacre of Beijing civilians in 1989.

Remember Tankman, the Beijinger with his shopping bags outside the Beijing Hotel who politely stood in front of armored cars, which equally politely refused to run him down? This same friend wants to set up a photo-shoot of Beijingers today giving way to four-wheel drive vehicles outside the Beijing Hotel, and perhaps photoshop Tankman into the scene, a lone remaining figure of dissent. The trouble with his plan is that younger Beijingers today, the very few who get to see the Tankman image at all, think that it's been photoshopped already. But in June 2009, the older people still danced in the parks and flew kites into the powerlines. Uighurs still sold huge slabs of fresh sesame cake for 30 yuan on Workers' Stadium Road. And in 2001, cinema offered us the image of Guei, a migrant tankman in his own narrative, walking against the traffic. Life goes on.

Anyone who has lived in a place, left it, and then come back, months, years, or decades later, will remark that, whilst things both change and stay the same in different measure, there is no perfect return. Nor is the vulnerability of one's ownership and emotional purchase on place particular only to large towns or major cities. The phenomenon does have different manifestations however according to who you are, where you have been, and why you are returning. In Beijing there are the "sea turtles" (*haigui*, Chinese returning to the motherland to take part in the economic revolution of the reform era, or students returning after an overseas education), the foreign ex-pats who come and go, the migrant workers who live in the backways of Beijing's modernization program, the "lost" generation who returned to the city after nearly ten years in the hinterland in the 1970s, and the post-1980s (*80hou*) generation, criticized as selfish by their elders until they showed extraordinary national solidarity with the victims of the Wenchuan earthquake in May 2008. These people will negotiate their own space in the city and make it work for them as best they can. Their paths will cross in so far as the city's structure allows them to do so. They will not be immune to the past or to the politics that shape the present, but, as Negt and Kluge (2007) argued in describing the mystification at the core of organized collective experience within capitalism, they may or may not know or accept that this is the case. Often, they simply do not know what happened 10 or 20 years earlier. Or they feel that whatever it was that an earlier generation demanded, has been achieved. Life goes on. The cage has grown big enough to be comfortable. Mystification has worked again. Sometimes, the very act of remembering the past makes the present impossible to bear. This is the conundrum of the affective structure of Beijing, a city that is wise and knowing and experienced, but also politically quietened to the point of acquiescence.

The Map Room

> Maps on a wall transform the wall itself, turning it into a permeable surface that can be entered in different ways and travelled through ... The wall of the map room is a porous site, loaded with the multiple fantasies and the strata of history projected onto it ... There also, the wall is a screen – the filter of a private, public voyage.
>
> (Bruno 1998: 275)

Beijing's city map is easily recognizable to anyone who has visited or lived in the city, and presumably to many who have not. Like the films of New York, the map of Beijing is a traveling palimpsest of the city's affective power worldwide. Its apparent simplicity: the ring roads and grids, the square projection, and its central focus in Tiananmen and the Forbidden City make the city legible. Indeed, the map of Beijing sums up its brand identity too. It is strongly organized, with firm lines and a defined center. The remaining network of *hutongs*, the suburban projects where residents from destroyed *hutongs* now reside, the restful eight-storey courtyards from the 1970s, are not the emphases of the map. It is therefore easy to get lost unless one stays on the main roads, but it is only possible to live in the city if one adventures below the surface.

The affective relationship between cinema, experience, and the urban environment was eloquently addressed in Giuliana Bruno's famous *Atlas of Emotion*, a book, as she herself described it, which allows her to share her "sentimental geography" (1998: 26) with the world of scholarship. In Bruno's book, cinema is both subject to and a creator of the haptic experience of urban space. Seminal too, and I confess a personal favorite, is James Donald's *Imagining the Modern City* (2005) a book which travels through three cities of Europe with cinema leading the way, and with an acute sense of masculine style in company. Important also is Jonathan Crary's *Suspensions of Perception: Attention, Spectacle, and Modern Culture* (1999), a treatise on the role of vision in the emergence of modern sensibilities. In all these books there are suggestions of the authors' individual intellectual journeys described through sentimental attachment to certain images and passages of film. The works are exemplary because they are both learned and close to the core of each writer's passion. They thus demonstrate affect in the realization of their scholarship, as much as in the telling juxtapositions that they effect through their observations. In Crary, it is Georges Seurat's *Cirque* (1891) which seems to fascinate him the most – a painting which exudes the movement and precision of an artiste (the bareback rider on the circus horse) and yet simultaneously, in Crary's argument, shows Seurat at work dissolving that certainty into the fragments of attention characteristic of modernity. The rider's trained insouciance makes us, sophisticates of the modern city, giddy.

In Bruno's atlas, her many examples coalesce into the vision of the map room. The map room might be just that, a fine room in a great house or national museum specifically maintained to give wall space to maps. They represent the world beyond the room itself. They give structure, scale, and scope to the imaginations of those who look at them, offering histories of empire and exploration, documents of development and change, possibilities for travel and orientation. Sometimes the maps were made in three dimensions, requiring huge spaces for storage and display. The story of the extraordinary Coronelli globes created for Louis XIV of France in 1683 is in part about their creation and in part about finding public spaces equivalent to their dimensions. These globes, one of the earth and one of the heavens, are each nearly 4 meters in diameter. The globes were created as a gift to the king, to commend his power, whilst educating the viewer in the intricate vagaries of the world as it was then known. The globes are decorated with detailed pictures as well as maps, and the illustrations are accompanied by explanations. Thus, the South Pacific, at the time the tail end of the French sphere of influence and very much the target of Chinese expansionary trade agreements, is decorated with images of French warships, Japanese vessels, and notes on the speed of the prevailing winds (Richard 2006: n.p.).

The globes are, finally, housed at the new Bibliothèque Nationale Française in Paris, adding an extraordinary map room to that mirrored edifice to contemporary French letters and modern education. The contemporary map room is multiply realized, in ordinary atlases, in books of maps published as sidelines by museums, and in sites online designed to facilitate touristic adventure. There is a growing academic literature on place-branding and how the web whets the appetite and defines the expectations of what a place is "like." In the eighteenth century women who could not travel themselves read books to get a taste of what they were missing. Now, place-branding campaigns are premised on the expectation that multiple media platforms deliver an idea of place to millions who will never visit the city in question. Thus of course it was for the Beijing opening ceremony in 2008, an important year for mediated versions of the Symbolic in China.

Donald's essays on the modern city are compelling for the way they treat both the uneven city that one traverses on foot and the edited rendition of that same uncertainty in a city traversed by the cinematic eye. The walker is not merely a *flâneur/se*. S/he is also vulnerable to the unexpected moment, the confrontation, the excitement, or the disappointment of humanity on the urban streets. In film, the act of cinematic rendering of place could conceivably smooth over the uncertainty of urban engagements, as indeed it does in films that self-consciously brand space in a hagiographic fashion. But city-film is strongest when it exposes the ragged edges and immediacy of urban geography and the intimacy of strangers. In the map room of the moving image, there are films that inspire adventurous imagining, and there are others which mundanely follow the brand, without catching at the contradictions that make a place-brand something worth visiting in the first place.

The opening sequence of *Beijing Bicycle* is a briefing session for a line-up of migrant workers. (Think of that first scene in *The Usual Suspects*.) These are the fortunate few who have been given a job at a courier company. They stand hopefully in front of a large wall map of Beijing. From northwestern and central provinces, their accents are thickly non-standard. The manager assures them that he will cut their hair and put them in uniform, and thus prepared they will go forth and conquer the city grid so clearly delineated behind them on the map. As Guei discovers as the film unfolds, however, the experience of Beijing is only partly captured in those assured axial pathways in the city. The life of the courtyard passageways, and the brutal emptinesses of unfinished buildings are where life happens, and indeed where his own hopes of conquering the city are destroyed. As he flees from attackers, their actual target, another 17-year-old called Jian, screams, "Why are you following me?" Guei screams back, "I don't know how to get out of here."

In *The Concrete Revolution*, there is also an opening sequence featuring the Beijing map. This time, however, it is filmed in close up, and the narrator tells us of the way in which the city changes shape as more *hutongs* are pulled down, and high-rises erected in their place. It is as though the maps in the map room are moving, and the stories they tell cannot be trusted. The voice-over speaks not on behalf of a migrant trapped in the unfamiliar territory of a local gang, but of a Beijinger, a confused old man who can't find his way home.

Brand Beijing

The Beijing that we encountered in Zhang Yimou's masterly opening ceremony at the Bird's Nest Stadium at 8 p.m. on August 8, 2008, showed neither intimacy nor chance at play. Evidently this was not a film as such, but the crafting of the event drew on Zhang's signature as a cinematographic magician, and was designed primarily for screen: televisions, DVD players, and computers. The pre-emptive vision of urban meaning in this national spectacle was both spectacular and spectacularly over-determined. The Olympic statement of China's place on the world stage was an exercise in exquisite overkill, and as such, conveyed very little of the more varied intelligence and energy of the city in which the Games took place. There was much order, glory, and elegance in the Beijing ceremonies, but scant humanity. There were Confucian scholars aplenty, but no hint of the red, glorious, brightness (*hongweiliang*) in cultural explosions of the 1960s, or indeed of any other innovation of the last 50 years. In a movement of utter irony, the Party, whose very legitimacy these Games supported, was evident in the organizational structure of the event, but not in the story itself.

The asymmetrical relationship between historical memory and urban space on the one hand and national brand management and media event on the other, was compounded on the evening of the opening when Beijingers congregated on the streets and in the main squares of the city to celebrate their Olympics, but were shortly urged to return home and to stay behind quickly erected crash barriers. Even at the Olympic park, located directly north of Tiananmen and the Forbidden City in concordance with the city's axial layout, crowds, mostly without tickets, clustered to catch the mood and see the architecture over the first days of the Games, but found themselves shepherded by crash barriers along pavements and roadways. There was nothing to see apart from men selling flags. They usually did not know which flag belonged to which country anyway. Anything blue, red, and white counted as the United States. The crowds dwindled. The Bird's Nest was visible but the freeway between the ticketless onlookers and the stadium area did not set it off to full advantage. Everything made better viewing back home on the TV. Maps of the site were available but as there was no access even to the environs of the key arena, they seemed obtuse. Tickets were very hard to buy despite the ticket touts, and despite the fact that huge swathes of empty seating eventually led to the *laladui* phenomenon (ladies in yellow T-shirts bussed in to cheer and make up the numbers on screen). The gap between the screening of the Beijing Olympics and the walking city in that first week of the 2008 Olympics, was very great.

The designer of the Bird's Nest, Ai Weiwei, pulled out of the project before the opening. And indeed, the building was/is beautiful, but it also resembled a cage. This is not because Ai's design failed to escape the monumentality of the blocks of downtown Tiananmen, but because the meaning of the architecture was redefined by the intrinsic presence of the state which had commissioned it. But, as ever in Beijing, ordinary affect is not wholly subject to power. A photographer based in Beijing, Ben McMillan, was on the site throughout the weeks of the Olympics and Paralympics competition. He created a series of motion capture sequences in the open spaces around the Bird's Nest and inside the venues (http://gallery.me.com/bm.photography#100153&bgcolor=black&view=grid). These sequences show that Chinese spectators did have fun in the quasi-public spaces that were available to them. They played in the fountains, laughed at the camera, and took up what we might term affective room in a recorded memory of their day out at the Olympics.

For Bruno, Crary, and Donald, affect is what drives the eye and the intellect to understand spatial relationships and to appreciate the structures within which unstructured engagement occurs. Structure is created by the solid architectures of the city, by cinematic representations, and is best evidenced and reproduced in the everyday social civilities which these engender or make visible. The city's "ordinary affect" is available to the observer, walker, and map-reader, and it is created when someone splashes in a fountain and laughs at the foreigner with a tripod, rides the wrong way round Tiananmen, or shrugs when, again, he is followed when he talks to old friends about old times and what they meant. Brand China is, ironically, constituted by these subtleties of affect. Even as the state creates the conditions for nothing untoward to occur, everything that does happen produces a stronger affect by virtue of the wonder of people's commitment to the expression of life itself.

In 2003–4 a colleague and I administered an online and face-to-face survey, which tried to tease out some notion of affect in world cities. We did so to test internal and external responses to brand identity, against the professional decisions of branding teams who were at work in key Asian cities. The survey employed various elicitation techniques, including a section on color. Simply, the respondents were given a large palette of colors and a list of cities, and asked to match the color that best described the city. Colors could be used more than once if necessary, not all cities had to be matched, and respondents could base their choice on direct experience, cinematic experience, or other forms of cultural hearsay. We wished to probe the degree to which a city's character was understood in emotional registers, and how people responded to the idea of place in terms of affect, whether or not they had been there in person. We were most interested in Shanghai, Hong Kong, and Sydney (Donald and Gammack 2007), but included other cities in the list as well. The responses across all cities were surprisingly uniform, with very little variance. Beijing, which was on the list but not our original focus, came up as "black" in almost every returned survey (just under 400 in total). I presented this finding in a workshop on creative cities in Kaohsiung (Taiwan) in 2006, noting also that Hong Kong had returned as "red," Shanghai as "brown," and London as "grey or pink." The Beijing "black" caused predictable hilarity in a predominantly Taiwanese meeting, and some irritation on the part of two visiting scholars from the mainland.

But what was the underlying reason for the choice of black? Reasons given in the free form box ranged from pollution to politics. Yet, three years later, in 2008, Beijing was the city of bright lights, blue skies, fireworks, orchestrated brilliance, and overwhelming spectacle. Again, we are faced with the contradictions between the national brand campaign that the Olympics represented, and the ordinary affect of everyday encounters, that are both individually experienced and also part of a pattern of sociability and the structures of power through which Beijingers encounter the present.

References

Bruno, G. (1998) *Journeys in Art, Architecture and Film*. New York: Verso.

Crary, J. (1999) *Suspensions of Perception: Attention, Spectacle and Modern Culture*. Cambridge MA: MIT Press.

Donald, J. (2005) *Imagining the Modern City*. London: Continuum Collection.

Donald, S. H. (2006) The idea of Hong Kong, structures of attention in the city of life. In *Urban Space and Cityscapes*, ed. C. Lindner. London: Routledge, 63–74.

Donald, S. H. (2009) Global Beijing: *The World* is a violent place. In *Globalization, Violence and the Visual Culture of Cities*, ed. C. Lindner. Oxford and New York: Routledge, 122–34.

Donald, S. H., and Gammack, J. G. (2007) *Tourism and the Branded City: Film and Identity on the Pacific Rim*. Aldershot: Ashgate.

Hughes, C. R. (2006) *Chinese Nationalism in the Global Era*. London: Routledge.

Lovell, J. (2009) Prologue: Beijing 2008 – the mixed messages of contemporary Chinese nationalism. In *Beijing 2008: Preparing for Glory, Chinese Challenge in the "Chinese Century,"* ed. J. A. Mangan and J. X. Dong. London and New York: Routledge, 8–28.

Negt, O., and Kluge, A. (2007) *Public Sphere and Experience: Towards an Analysis of the Bourgeois and Proletarian Public Sphere*. Minneapolis and London: University of Minnesota Press.

Ramo, J. C. (2007) *Brand China*. London: The Foreign Policy Centre. Available online at http://fpc.org.uk/fsblob/827.pdf (accessed April 6, 2009).

Richard, H. (2006) *Les globes de Coronelli*. Paris: Bibliothèque Nationale de France, Seuil.

Stewart, K. (2007) *Ordinary Affects*. Durham, NC, and London: Duke University Press.

Zhang, Lijia (2008) China's growing cage: the legacy of Tiananmen. The China Beat. Available online at http://thechinabeat.blogspot.com/2009/06/chinas-growing-cage-legacy-of-tiananmen.html (accessed April 6, 2009).

Chapter 28

The Postmetropolis and Mental Life: Wong Kar-Wai's Cinematic Hong Kong

Christoph Lindner

Film and the Global City

This chapter is about visual culture and the urban environment. It is also about globalization and violence. Engaging with these issues as they relate to cinematic Hong Kong, my focus is Wong Kar-Wai's 1995 film *Fallen Angels* – a mood study of urban emptiness and disconnection set in pre-handover Hong Kong and centered on an emotionally detached hit-man and his desensitized female agent. In particular, my discussion of the film considers some of the ways in which Georg Simmel's notion of a "blasé metropolitan attitude" (Simmel 2002: 14), which he associates with the rise of the modern metropolis in the late nineteenth century, can be reconfigured in the context of the global city. I begin, therefore, by revisiting Simmel's classic essay of 1903, "The metropolis and mental life," before recalibrating Simmel's thinking in light of contemporary urbanism and, in particular, Edward Soja's (2000) work on the phenomenon of the postmetropolis. It is important to clarify, however, that I am not suggesting *Fallen Angels* constitutes any kind of realistic representation of contemporary urban life. Cinematic cities should never be confused with their brick-and-mortar counterparts, although they do frequently influence our perception of real cities in profound and powerful ways. Rather, my position is that Wong's cinematic treatment of Hong Kong offers a poignant example of the impact of globalization on the urban imaginary – what is best understood in Soja's terms as "the mental or cognitive mappings of urban reality and the interpretive grids through which we think about, experience, evaluate, and decide to act in the places, spaces, and communities in which we live" (Soja 2000: 324).

From a methodological point of view, this chapter can accordingly be characterized as working at the intersection of three interrelating fields: critical spatial studies,

The New Blackwell Companion to the City   Edited by Gary Bridge and Sophie Watson
© 2011 Blackwell Publishing Ltd

globalization studies, and film studies. Critical spatial studies, which emerged in the late 1960s and early 1970s following the work of thinkers like Kevin Lynch (1960), Michel Foucault (1972), and especially Henri Lefebvre (1992), draws on geographical and philosophical concepts of space to address a wide range of developments in contemporary society and culture. Globalization studies, which has its roots in sociology and economics and has been gaining momentum ever since the early 1990s with publications like Saskia Sassen's *The Global City* (1992), involves the study of transnational exchange in all its forms, but especially those associated with capitalist societies. And film studies, at least the version that I am comfortable reconstructing here, can be broadly understood as the analysis of cinematic production focusing on both the formal-aesthetic and social-ideological dimensions of the medium (Dyer 2000), and has been around since at least the publication of Walter Benjamin's 1935 essay on the work of art in the age of mechanical reproduction (Benjamin 1970). None of these fields is new, but I would argue that combining them together as I attempt to do in this chapter does enable some fresh insights into the category of critical analysis we are calling "the city."

Metropolis to Postmetropolis

Writing at the turn of the twentieth century, the German sociologist Georg Simmel famously suggests that the inhabitants of cities tend to develop a "blasé metropolitan attitude" (Simmel 2002: 14) in order to cope with the anonymity, intensity, and velocity of modern urban life. For Simmel, the modern city is overwhelming and relentless in its assault on the senses and the blasé attitude, which is characterized by a posture of disinterest, serves as a form of protection against the mental invasions of the city:

> Thus the metropolitan type ... creates a protective organ for itself against the profound disruption with which the fluctuations and discontinuities of the external milieu threaten it. Instead of reacting emotionally, the metropolitan type reacts primarily in a rational manner ... Thus the reaction of the metropolitan person to those events is moved to a sphere of mental activity which is least sensitive and which is furthest removed from the depths of the personality ... There is perhaps no psychic phenomenon which is so unconditionally reserved to the city as the blasé outlook ... This incapacity to react to new stimulations with the required amount of energy constitutes in fact that blasé attitude which every child of a large city evinces. (Simmel 2002: 12–4)

Crucially, Simmel posits the blasé individual, not unlike the figure of the roving *flâneur* theorized by Walter Benjamin (1997), as a kind of modern intellectual capable of abstraction and rationality, but also deeply implicated in the urban spectacle. And like Benjamin's *flâneur*, Simmel's blasé individual is specifically linked to the great cities of capitalist modernity (Paris, Berlin, Vienna, London) and reflects their cold, impersonal system of commodity exchange.

Such a view of the metropolitan individual as a blasé observer/participant in the urban scene certainly informs many cultural responses to the rise of the modern city and is evident in popular works ranging, for example, from Edgar Allan Poe's proto-modern short story "The man in the crowd" (1840); to Jacob Riis's ghetto photography of 1880s New York; to classic noir films like the *Maltese Falcon* (1941) and *The Big Sleep* (1946) and their clichéd use of the jaded figure of the hard-boiled detective. But to what extent is Simmel's thinking still relevant in our late-capitalist urban era? In other words, what happens to the blasé metropolitan individual when confronted by life in the contemporary global city?

One answer – and this is the idea explored by Wong Kar-Wai's film and its representation of Hong Kong – is that the lived experience of the global city can lead to a state of radical detachment that is far more extreme, alienating, and destructive than the blasé attitude described by Simmel. This state of radical detachment, which marks an accentuation or intensification of the dynamic of estrangement first explored by Simmel in the early twentieth century, is what I want to call the blasé *postmetropolitan* attitude, and here I am indebted to Edward Soja's notion of the postmetropolis.

Soja develops the term postmetropolis to describe the future-oriented urbanism of our late-capitalist age of globalization, and suggests that the term can "be used interchangeably with *postmodern metropolis* and be interpreted as an expression of what some now call *postmodern urbanism*" (Soja 2000: xiii). From the fractal city to the simcity, and from the cosmopolis to the exopolis, the postmetropolis can take on many forms (Soja 2000: 154–5). My interest here, however, is not in individual constructions of postmetropolitan spaces, but rather in the overarching concept of the postmetropolis itself – in the idea that the late twentieth century saw the emergence of a new kind of city specific to postmodernity and representing the "product of intensified globalization processes" (Soja 2000: 152). In this sense, the postmetropolis can be broadly understood as the city produced by, and organized around, the transnational circulation of capital and labor, what sociologist Manuel Castells has identified as the techno-informational "space of flows" enabling our network society (Castells 2000: 409), and what philosopher Paul Virilio has otherwise condemned as the "city of panic" (Virilio 2005: 85).

As we will see, the idea of the contemporary city as a space of both flow and fear has a certain resonance with Wong Kar-Wai's cinematic Hong Kong. For now, what I want to suggest is that the film *Fallen Angels* offers an extreme and fictionalized example of the blasé postmetropolitan attitude, an attitude linked not to the great cities of western modernity, but instead to a transnational network of globalized city-spaces. In the case of Wong's film and its cinematic re-imagining of the postmetropolis, this attitude leads beyond the relatively harmless posture of intellectual indifference described by Simmel to much more disturbing patterns of nihilism and violence.

Hong Kong Cool

To illustrate exactly how this blasé postmetropolitan attitude is expressed in Wong's work, I want to discuss a key scene from *Fallen Angels* in some detail. The scene, which comes towards the beginning of the film, establishes the professional relationship between two central characters: the hit-man (Leon Lai) and his female agent (Michelle Reis) who plans and organizes his hits. At this point in the film, the female agent and the hit-man have never met in person. All of their work together is done

Figure 28.1 Lethal calculations: the agent maps the killer's route (*Fallen Angels*, directed by Wong Kar-Wai, produced by Jeffrey Lau, courtesy Kino International).

through mail-drops, faxes, and other forms of distanced and depersonalized communication. They are connected only by dead bodies and dirty money.

The scene begins with a close-up shot of the female agent's face as she slowly walks through a busy Hong Kong restaurant at night (Figure 28.1). The restaurant and its customers remain an indistinct blur of lights, shapes, and colors in the background. The agent's face is cropped by an angular haircut that reinforces the tight framing of the camera. She moves in slow motion towards the door as her eyes covertly scan the scene, planning a route which the hit-man will later use to reach his targets. Her pouting expression conveys a mixture of boredom, annoyance, and disdain. Although the shot lasts for only around 20 seconds, it captures perfectly the dynamic at work in Wong's film between the postmetropolis and mental life. Behind the agent's disinterested exterior is an active, analytical mind busy making lethal calculations in which the city and its inhabitants are reduced to a series of spatial obstacles needing to be either circumnavigated or eliminated.

The film then cuts to an interior shot showing the agent at home in her cramped, cluttered bedsit where she watches TV while preparing the information and instructions needed by the hit-man to execute the job. A fax machine next to her bed serves as a visual and thematic link to the hit-man, whom we see in the next shot receiving her telecommunication. The shot introducing the hit-man is visually interesting in the way it splits the screen in half. The left side of the screen shows the bare and impersonal warehouse space that serves as his office and home. The right side of the screen shows the city outside, where an elevated train rushes past the window. The accelerated city and its noises are deliberately contrasted against the empty, still space of the killer's office-home, creating a sense of discomfort and loneliness. At the same time, however, Wong's framing of the shot clearly emphasizes the shared

Figure 28.2 "Because I'm cool": the hit-man as killing machine (*Fallen Angels*, directed by Wong Kar-Wai, produced by Jeffrey Lau, courtesy Kino International).

geometry of the interior and exterior spaces. The long, narrow shape of the room is picked up and paralleled by the lines of the train track, emphasizing the hit-man's symbolic connection to the city, as well as commenting obliquely on the intensely anonymous, dehumanized condition of life in the postmetropolis.

The last part of the scene follows the hit-man as he travels across Hong Kong to the restaurant where his targets are hiding out. It ends in a slow-motion shooting spree, in which the hit-man bursts into a back-room gambling den and kills all of the occupants without any trace of emotion whatsoever (Figure 28.2). Throughout, his movements remain functional and robotic. Reminiscent of the decelerated action that distinguishes John Woo's cinematic style, Wong's use of slow motion here enables the camera to linger over the violence, effectively aestheticizing the spectacle of mass murder. This is reinforced by Wong's choice of music for this scene: a hybrid Chinese-English indie-rock song, performed by Hong Kong-based musical nomad Nogabe Randriaharimalala, in which the chorus, repeated in English throughout the scene, proclaims "because I'm cool." The double meaning of "cool" is highly relevant in the sense that it both describes the hit-man's emotional numbness and references the scene's stylized treatment of violence.

The lead-up to this moment of violence is significant too. Riding across the city in a public bus, the hit-man appears to be just another weary, late-night passenger on his way to some dead-end job. By placing the hit-man in this mundane public space, Wong invites us to understand this deeply antisocial figure not as an exceptional or aberrant presence in the city, but rather as somehow prototypical – at least in terms of appearance and attitude – of its everyday inhabitants. Given the purpose of the journey and the multiple deaths to which it leads, this is a disturbing insight and suggests in an exaggerated way that, just as many globalization scholars have

argued (Sassen 1992; Harvey 2006), asociality has become an increasingly prominent and endemic feature of everyday life in global (and globalizing) cities.

It is therefore interesting that the hit-man's face only appears in the city-bus shot
as a reflection in the driver's rear-view mirror (Figure 28.3) – a hovering, ghostly
form gliding past a lurid nocturnal streetscape that, in its overexposed spectacle of
consumer decadence and excess, recalls both the retro-futuristic Los Angeles of
Ridley Scott's cyberpunk classic *Blade Runner* (1982) and the sleazy, threatening
New York of Martin Scorsese's *Taxi Driver* (1976). The juxtaposition of the hit-
man's blank face with disorienting images of urban frenzy reinforces the idea that,
in order to function in such an intense and chaotic environment, the individual must
retreat psychologically from the city even as he immerses himself in its spaces and
experiences.

However, what particularly interests me about this entire extended scene, which
begins with the extreme close-up of the female agent's face and ends with the shoot-
ings in the restaurant, are the links Wong Kar-Wai makes between globalization and
violence. The hit-man is a lethal product of the late-capitalist city of speed and flash –
a dehumanized killing machine who profits from the extreme commodification of
human life, and whose professional success not only hinges on an illicit flow of
information and capital, but also depends on the smooth navigation of a hyper-real
urban landscape.

The female agent is likewise connected to this late-capitalist cityscape. She is
plugged into its networks of communication and transportation, and similarly
dependent on its culture of anonymity and hyper-mobility. These ideas are graphically expressed in the shot showing her at home, in her semi-transient bedsit, where
the scene is illuminated by the dull, monochromatic glow of the television set, tuned

Figure 28.3   Reflections in a city bus: the hit-man rides to work (*Fallen Angels,* directed
by Wong Kar-Wai, produced by Jeffrey Lau, courtesy Kino International).

to the BBC World News service, and where she inspects a plane ticket while a money-counting machine rifles through thick wads of American cash. This confluence of money, information, and travel signals more than just the transnational circulatory system of globalization. It also evokes both Hong Kong's colonial condition (suggested by the disembodied voice of British authority droning monotonously in the background) and Hong Kong's emergent postcolonial identity, tied as it is to the fast flow of people and money in the hybrid spaces of the Sino-western city.

Most significant, however, is the way both the hit-man and his agent adopt a blasé attitude in their encounters with the global city – an attitude characterized here by a near-total socio-psychological disassociation. The implication, if we follow Simmel's thinking, is that this attitude marks a strategic response to the hostile, oppressive urban environment the characters inhabit – partly the result, in this film at least, of being habitually assaulted by the city's neon-washed consumer nightscape.

In other words, the violent, antisocial, and quasi-suicidal attitudes presented in Wong's film develop partly in response to the look and feel of the global city. As such, Wong's aesthetic treatment of Hong Kong is a critical feature of the film's urban commentary. Throughout the film, the city is marked by images of confinement, enclosure, estrangement, distortion and – interestingly – discoloration. In fact, as David Bordwell (2000), Peter Brunette (2005), and Ackbar Abbas (1997) have all noted, Wong's visual style in *Fallen Angels* is dominated by the use of harsh neon lighting with its jarring, nauseating colors. In fact, virtually every shot in the film contains an exposed neon light bulb, as if to suggest that the global city's ubiquitous artificial illumination directly contributes to the derangement and isolation of its blasé postmetropolitan inhabitants.

Global Hong Kong

To bring my discussion around to the topic of global Hong Kong, which is the final destination of this chapter, I next want to discuss the film's final scene. Like the scene discussed above, this one is also set at night and also begins with an extreme close-up of the female agent's face. This time she is seated in a restaurant eating noodles while smoking a cigarette – a form of double ingestion that serves as a visual statement about her unbalanced state of mind. The look on her face is totally blank, almost lobotomized, and her head gently rolls and bobs involuntarily as she eats. She has the appearance of a heavily medicated mental patient. The scene then cuts to an exterior shot of the agent riding silently on the back of a motorcycle with a mute man she has just met in the restaurant. The mute character belongs to a parallel plot line in the film that explores the voicelessness and invisibility of Hong Kong's unemployed, and this moment of intersection between the two lines of narrative – the story of the hit-man and his agent and the story of the mute and his efforts to subvert the capitalist system (which involves breaking into shops at night and forcing passers-by to consume goods and services against their will) – marks a convergence of the film's preoccupation with the disposability of human life in our throw-away society and the inescapability of globalized consumer culture. The camera goes on to follow the motorcycle as it races along deserted Hong Kong streets, before entering a long tunnel beneath the city. As the motorcycle emerges

Figure 28.4 Hong Kong skyscrapers: the closing shot (*Fallen Angels*, directed by Wong Kar-Wai, produced by Jeffrey Lau, courtesy Kino International).

from the tunnel in the early dawn light, the film ends with a panning low-angle shot of Hong Kong skyscrapers set against a dawning sky (Figure 28.4).

This final shot can be read as a deeply ambivalent statement about the global city. While it may be tempting to interpret the ending as an uplifting moment of human connection in a film that is otherwise all about disconnection, it is important to note that the scene features a voice-over commentary by the female agent in which she specifically explains this moment of physical and psychological *rapprochement* as a fleeting, meaningless encounter.

The final image of the skyscrapers, however, is what really interests me in this scene, partly because it is the film's only shot of open space and natural light. The closing shot therefore provides a welcome relief from all the neon discoloration and spatial enclosure dominating the rest of the film. At the same time, however, the superimposition of the skyscrapers over the tunnel (and the street-life to which it connects) suggests that overlying the everyday city is the corporate architecture of globalization: faceless, impersonal, unemotive. The message, as I read it, is that this architectural uncanny, and the economic system it embodies, is what overhangs the future of this city and its inhabitants, which is a significant (and prescient) statement considering that the film was released just two years before the handover of Hong Kong in 1997.

In this sense, Wong's work can accordingly be seen as belonging to a wider, transnational body of contemporary film-making concerned with exploiting but also critiquing the paranoid, carceral urbanism of globalization. It is a line of critique that extends in several directions and includes films as diverse as Mathieu Kassovitz's *La Haine* (1995) and its dramatization of the politics of exclusion in the Parisian *banlieues*; Danny Boyle's *Trainspotting* (1996) and its exploration of addiction and decay in Edinburgh's post-industrial urban slums; David Fincher's *Fight Club* (1999) and its crisis of masculinity in the menacing sprawl of Los Angeles; Fernando Meirelles and Katia Lund's *City of God* (2002) and its spectacularizing of gang-warfare and drug-trafficking in the *favelas* of Rio de Janeiro; and even Sofia Coppola's *Lost in Translation* (2003) and its touristic driftings across the disorientating landscape of Tokyo.

What these films have in common beyond their portrayal of the contemporary city as a place of radical isolation, runaway consumption, and spatial estrangement, is that each explores – in its own way – the figure of the blasé postmetropolitan loner. These loners may be fictional characters, but I would argue that they represent expressions – albeit distorted, exaggerated, and stylized – of the impact of globalization on the lived experience of the city and, in particular, the extent to which violence, in both material and cultural forms, has become a prominent and endemic feature of everyday urban life in the global era. This last idea is taken to conceptual and visual extremes in *Fallen Angels*, where the late-capitalist city's pervasive culture of death reduces all human life to a disposable commodity, but it also informs all the other films cited above.

By using the figure of the blasé postmetropolitan individual to explore links between globalization and violence, contemporary cinema reflects a real development that is becoming increasingly evident in cities around the world. As recent work on this subject has shown (Lindner 2010), there is a growing trend towards violence in global and globalizing cities that extends well beyond the mass-mediated examples of the 9/11 attacks in New York and Washington, the London transport bombings, the Mumbai hotel sieges, and the Paris *banlieue* riots, to include less obvious – yet equally important – examples such as São Paulo's state of undeclared civil war, the architectural excesses of Shanghai and Bejing, the aesthetic defacements of post-unification Berlin, and the escalating siege mentality gripping African cities like Lagos and Johannesburg. Not all these cities may yet constitute postmetropolises in the exact sense that Soja gives to the term, but the intensification of globalization processes they are experiencing combined with the extreme forms of social and psychological disconnection they can engender – registered so powerfully in contemporary visual culture through the figure of the blasé postmetropolitan individual – suggest that they are moving in this direction. *Fallen Angels* should therefore be seen not just as a dystopian urban fantasy, but also as an insightful, if imaginative, commentary on the violence inherent in the contemporary urban condition.

References

Abbas, A. (1997) *Hong Kong: Culture and the Politics of Disappearance*. Minneapolis: University of Minnesota Press.

Benjamin, W. (1970) The work of art in the age of mechanical reproduction. In *Illuminations*, trans. H. Zohn. London: Jonathan Cape, 219–53.

Benjamin, W. (1997) *Charles Baudelaire: A Lyric Poet in the Era of High Capitalism*. Trans. Harry Zohn. London: Verso.

Bordwell, D. (2000) *Planet Hong Kong: Popular Cinema and the Art of Entertainment*. Cambridge, MA: Harvard University Press.

Brunette, P. (2005) *Wong Kar-Wai*. Chicago: University of Illinois Press.

Castells, M. (2000) *The Rise of the Network Society*. Oxford: Blackwell.

Dyer, R. (2000) Introduction to Film Studies. In *Film Studies: Critical Approaches*, ed. J. Hill and P. Church Gibson. Oxford: Oxford University Press, 1–8.

Foucault, M. (1972) *The Archeology of Knowledge*. London: Tavistock.

Harvey, D. (2006) *Spaces of Global Capitalism*. London: Verso.

Lefebvre, H. (1992) *The Production of Space*. Oxford: Blackwell.

Lindner, C. (ed.) (2010) *Globalization, Violence, and the Visual Culture of Cities*. London: Routledge.

Lynch, K. (1960) *The Image of the City*. Cambridge, MA: MIT Press.

Sassen, S. (1992) *The Global City: New York, London, Tokyo*. Princeton, NJ: Princeton University Press,

Simmel, G. (2002) The metropolis and mental life. In *The Blackwell City Reader*, ed. G. Bridge and S. Watson. Oxford: Blackwell, 11–19.

Soja, E. W. (2000) *Postmetropolis: Critical Studies of Cities and Regions*. Oxford: Blackwell.

Virilio, P. (2005) *City of Panic*. Trans. J. Rose. Oxford: Berg.

Chapter 29

Imagining Naples: The Senses of the City

Lesley Caldwell

In this article I discuss two movies by the Italian director Mario Martone which illustrate the centrality of place in constituting an understanding of the self. In emphasizing the characters' links with the city of Naples, Martone provides a cinematic exploration of the workings of the past in the present as containing both an individual and a social reality. He uses the images and sensations of the city as an externalization of the protagonists' introspective fantasies, and, in so doing, presents the public arena as the repository of both individual and collective history. When Susan Sontag describes Walter Benjamin as "not trying to recover his past, but to understand it: to condense it into its spatial forms, its premonitory structures" (1979: 13), she identifies one of the many echoes that resonate between Martone's work and Benjamin's own account of Naples, written in 1924.

A different strand in recent work on location and identity has involved some questioning of previously assumed links between place and the understanding of self. This work registers the transformation of perceptions of local and national, individual and collective ideas about self and other, occasioned by the dislocations, migrations, movements, and diasporas of the twentieth century. It emphasizes the modern condition as a universalizing experience which has had the effect of partially detaching the individual from any continuous sense that identity has connections with a particular place (Carter *et al.* 1993; Morley and Robins 1993). Martone's two movies not only set the narratives in a particular city, they use images of Naples to represent personal, individual memory and to begin to think about the memories of past generations of Italians and a different Italy. In this way, they highlight some of the changes in Italian society since World War II.

The New Blackwell Companion to the City   Edited by Gary Bridge and Sophie Watson
© 2011 Blackwell Publishing Ltd

A Neapolitan Director

Martone's first feature-length movie *Morte di un matematico napoletano* (hereafter *Death of a Neapolitan Mathematician*, 1990) is a movie with a distinctly local ambience organized around the symbolic importance of city space. His next film, *L'amore molesto* (1995), also assigns a primacy to the city. Both movies, through their narratives and through their representation of Naples, explore the links between place and identity. The city is strongly signaled as desired, the intimate possession of a creative artist who has attempted to represent his own city, one with a strong, lasting grasp on the European imagination, in a distinctively different way. The massing of details, fragments, and impressions, as it were, from the inside, extends considerably the complex of associations brought to mind by the idea of "Naples." In this respect these movies form part of a more general cinematic, cultural, and political opening which happened in Naples during the 1990s.

The European art cinema has often been regarded as a tool for the elaboration of the personal issues of its directors as they are articulated through the creativity of movie-making (Bordwell 1985; Neale 1981). This tradition has emphasized the director as the authorizing presence and the condition of coherence for a form of movie-making whose ambiguities often stress a self-conscious narration and an overt concern with psychological states.

The concentration on visual style, character, and the interiorization of dramatic conflict in Martone's two movies asserts the links between personal, psychological identity and its local and regional roots. Memory and time appear as possessing both personal and collective attributes and meanings. The crowded allusions to which they give rise, materially and geographically, but also mentally, form the focus for a set of interlocking concerns – the lives of the characters and their relation with the past of the city in the diegesis, the transformations in Naples, and in Italy, from the 1950s to the 1990s, and the director's younger self and interest in his city.

Each movie identifies one central character as its focus, a man in the first, a woman in the second. Through their encounters with themselves and their past in the streets of Naples, the city is established as the other major protagonist, a setting through which the emotions and conflicts of living are encountered, enacted, recognized/misrecognized, and thought about by the characters themselves, but also by the spectator. The shifting between past and present registered through physical locations becomes a visual rendering of states of mind, and of a process of self-realization. The characters, Renato the mathematician, and Delia the daughter, are played by two actors with long associations with Naples and with the theater. This offers Martone, a theater director himself, another area for exploration: the overlap of actor and role (Martone 1995: 14).

Versions of Naples

Some of Martone's themes in these first two feature-length movies mirror the preoccupations Sontag proposes as central to Walter Benjamin:

> Benjamin had adopted a completely digested analytical way of looking at the past. It evokes events for the reactions to the events, places for the emotions one has deposited

in the places, other people for the encounter with oneself, feelings and behaviour for intimations of future passions and failures contained in them. (1979: 9–13).

Benjamin's own account of Naples written with his lover Asja Lacis, emphasizes "the interpenetration of buildings and action" (p. 169). Furthermore,

> What distinguishes Naples from other large cities is that each private attitude or act is permeated by streams of communal life; similarly dispersed, porous and commingled, is private life. To exist, for the northern European the most private state of affairs, is here a collective matter. So the house is far less the refuge into which people retreat, than the inexhaustible reservoir from which they flood out. (1979: 167).

This idea of Naples as a city which shapes private lives through the dominance of public spaces is an image which brings together architecture, geography, and people. Since the center of Naples contains one of the highest territorial densities in Europe, this further adds to a set of dramatically shifting parameters between lives conceived in conventional private terms and their existence in a public domain. Until the postwar period and the extension outwards of the speculation of the 1960s, a geographical separation of poverty from wealth, a separation of classes in a separation of zones or areas, was strictly limited. In Naples it was one of higher and lower, with the rich above the poor, and the poor often, literally, below ground.

The vertical organization of Naples and the architectural choices that have followed its physical forms certainly contribute to the particular social relations identified by Benjamin, but Martone has mainly chosen not to represent this, just as other familiar images of the city – the volcano, the bay, the ruins of antiquity – are also absent from his movies. The touristic picture of Naples, part of a legacy predating the photograph and the film, stresses this combination of geographical, natural, and architectural features, and such associations have been the basis of many other cinematic representations, often shaping them as a kind of residuum of the folkloric (Bruno 1997: 47–9). Various commentators, including the director himself, have insisted that these movies represent an attempt to engage with an alternative tradition, and, by rendering Naples from the inside, to introduce another reality (Fofi 1997; Martone 1997).

In the first film, *Death of a Neapolitan Mathematician*, Naples appears uncharacteristically empty, in *L'amore molesto* it is full and noisy. In both, the encounter of character and city embodies the space of individual experience and precipitates the decisions following upon it. An intimacy and a distance between the two protagonists of each movie – the character and the city – are constructed by the camera's way of locating them relationally in the pro-filmic space. But this is also the construction of a mental space, a space of thought, rumination, association, and sensation first for the characters, then for the spectators. Artistic choices in the construction of the personal narratives emphasize them as narratives of the city. Naples emerges both as dreamlike terrain and as a constellation of different and distinctive cultural arenas and groups, a visual reinforcement of the claim that "the mental and the social find themselves in practice in *conceived* and *lived* space" (Lefebvre 1996: 197).

In offering a sense of the very different lives of Neapolitans of different classes and genders in an earlier period and in the nineties, these movies stress the perception of what Lefebvre and Régulier (1986; reproduced in Kofman and Lebas 1996) have described as a city's "rhythms," as fundamental. In their delineation of some general characteristics of Mediterranean cities, "persistent historical links ... fated to decline, to explode into suburbs and peripheries," they propose that such cities have more discernible rhythms than others, rhythms that are both "historical and daily," "closer to the lived" (p. 228).

Naples is an obviously Mediterranean city, a city of immense beauty and reputation, which has been pictured as containing and encouraging a fullness and extravagance, elsewhere already considered impossible or lost. The idea that lives of passion and melodramas of raw emotions exist in the midst of wretchedness, squalor, and misery, condenses an array of beliefs, fantasies, prejudices, and expectations about "the Neapolitans." Naples, as a place where Europe's Other is to be met within its own territory, is one of its most longstanding myths. It is often regarded as changing and loosening up the outsider who encounters the combination of city and people together (Goethe 1987, and many others). Martone's representation of a local Naples ultimately also serves to confirm this view.

The simultaneity of a visible past written into a present is one theme that Martone's movies develop, and one which links him directly with Roberto Rossellini who conveys a similar sense of Naples in *Viaggio in Italia* (1953). Starring his then wife Ingrid Bergman and George Sanders, this study of a marriage and how it was affected by a northern couple's exposure to Naples and its environs, made the city and its environs the other character whose influence becomes decisive. Bazin said of this movie, "It is a Naples filtered through the consciousness of the heroine ... Nevertheless, the Naples of the movie is not false ... It is rather a mental landscape at once as objective as a straight photograph and as subjective as pure personal consciousness (quoted in Brunette 1987: 160). In *Viaggio*, Catherine's (Bergman's) journey becomes that of the spectator (Kolker 1983: 132) and in each of Martone's movies something similar is involved. *Death of a Neapolitan Mathematician* is a loose interpretation of the last week of the life of Renato Caccioppoli (1904–59), a well-known mathematician, the son of a Neapolitan surgeon and a woman known as the daughter of the Russian anarchist Bakhunin. Renato was a well-known intellectual and political figure, with a colorful history, first of antifascism, and later, of relations with the Italian Communist party (PCI). Played by the Tuscan stage actor Carlo Cecchi, who has a long association with Naples, Renato is shown at work and at meetings in the university, in restaurants, at the opera, with friends, comrades, ex-wife, brother and, crucially, alone. Warmth, concern and conviviality in the life of a leftist bourgeois intellectual in the 1950s are set beside the solitude of the man and his progressive withdrawal from the world around him. The passing of the days of his last week lived within the streets and spaces of the old center of Naples provides the film's structure, and a certain labyrinthine aspect of the city conveyed through the streets and the angles of the buildings, becomes the condition of its representability.

L'amore molesto is based on a book by Elena Ferrante. It recounts the events following the return to Naples of Delia/Anna Buonaiuto, a designer of comics living in Bologna. Delia returns the day after her birthday on hearing the news of her mother Amalia's mysterious death in the sea. The daughter seeks out the facts of her mother's last few days, meets up with her father, her uncle, a petty criminal

type – her mother's possible long-term lover – and his son, her childhood companion. She imagines, remembers, invents, and encounters her loved, known mother,
along with other possible mothers and other possible selves. It is the return to Naples
which proves decisive for this engagement with the past and its shaping of her
present and future. The film's notionally investigative structure is a personal journey
in which a noisy, modern Naples is the setting for a fraught internal encounter. The
encounter with the mother in the mind is occasioned by the encounter with the city,
a city often associated with the maternal and the feminine (Gribaudi 1996; Ramondino 1991).

In the spaces of its buildings and streets, its language and its sounds, its inhabitants and their customs, its relationship to an illustrious set of traditions, and its
place in a national culture (although, in the case of the latter, it is largely to be
inferred from the well-nigh complete absence of any explicit reference to it) a city
which is simultaneously local and particular, national and general is pictorialized.
In the first movie the status of Naples as an intensely cosmopolitan city ties it to a
particular Italian and European past. In the second, local intensities, bodies, words,
sounds, and images are immersed in the more general anonymity of shops, transport, cars, and crowded streets. The appropriation of the body of one by the eye
of another, and of course the eye of the camera, is common to both, but, in the first,
the concentration of looks is more from camera and spectator to (male) actor and
city; in the second, the looks at, and between, the characters, especially at Delia,
the heroine, record an invasive intimacy, a visual aggression and an awareness of
bodies through a regime of looking that renders the physicality and sensuality of
Naples through an explicitly hierarchical relation between the sexes.

As a central component of both movies, time figures in three different ways.
There is the severely proscribed time in which the events of each narrative
emerge – a week in the first film, two days in the second; the pace of the
movies – slow thoughtful, distanced, and introspective in the case of the first, frenetic, noisy, overbearing, and externalized in the second. Finally there is the presence
of an earlier historical era within the temporality of each movie. Through this juxtaposition of a filmic present, and a remembered past, the different renderings of
time make available different ways of living and thinking. "Pastness" forms an
intractable aspect of Mediterranean cities and their associations, and this is utilized
by Martone as the terrain for a kind of public and personal memoir where the past
both facilitates and constrains the life of the present.

Death of a Neapolitan Mathematician

In *Death* the movie reveals a Naples of the 1950s, still existent today, a living recollection, in stone and buildings, of a different Naples and a different Italy from that
of the movie's construction. Renato's visual confinement within a small area of the
city center suggests the mathematician's despairing evaluation of his life and himself,
but Martone's use of an intensely personal Naples makes the overall mood one of
nostalgia rather than despair. Piantini (1993) sees the civility and behavior of family
and friends and the shots of Naples which express such conviviality and warmth as
creating a regret for the passing of the 1950s. The movie is shot in a golden light,
described by Roberti (1992) as a permanent sunset, and its color spectrum provides

a setting of gentleness, luminosity, warmth, and beauty, that is markedly at odds both with the suicide of the hero and with the associations of enclosure and entrapment sometimes conveyed by the camera angles. It lends support to the sense in which thinking about the life of the man is the occasion for an essay about the city and its past, and the director and his. For the character Naples is ultimately confining, loving but irrelevant. The man of thought, mathematics, politics, music, culture is permanently clad in an old raincoat that echoes the feel of the street and the color of the buildings. "Fantastic reports by travellers have touched up the city. In reality it is grey: a grey red or ochre, a grey-white. Anyone who is blind to forms sees little here" (1992: 169). Martone explained the film's color as the suggestion of Bigazzi, the cinematographer, who, in sorting out locations, had been struck by the yellowness of Naples. "I was immediately convinced because this yellow seemed to gather together another instance of the double aspect of the city, the comforting yellow of the sun's rays, and the pallid dusty yellow of illness" (Roberti 1992: 132). The emptiness and silence may act as signifiers of the inner despair of the man, but, paradoxically, they register the richness and beauty of the city itself.

The local sites in this movie are mostly confined to a particular area of Naples, that of Via Partenope, Via Chiaia, and the Spanish quarter. Palazzo Cellamare, where the protagonist, Renato Caccioppoli, lived, is shot from inside, outside, by night, by day; a constant visual reference. It may have once been the home of Goethe, but, far more significantly, Martone himself lived his adolescence there, and it is still his family home. His Naples, like that of his mathematician, is part of the intense intellectual, artistic, musical, and commercial culture that has long distinguished the city; but it is not one that has seen much cinematic attention.

> How is a field of memory formed? It needs frontiers, milestones, seasons … Otherwise, days flood in, each erasing the previous one, faces are interchangeable, pieces of information follow, and cancel one another. It's only in a defined space that there is room for an event, only in a continuum that beginnings come into view and ruptures occur.
> (Pontalis 1993: 79)

Martone's use of the city/person connection in this movie depends upon an inversion of the traditional theatricality and spectacle of Naples, mentioned by Benjamin, but the movie echoes him in another: "buildings and action interpenetrate in the courtyards, arcades and stairways. In everything they preserve the scope to become a theater of new, unforeseen constellations" (Roberti 1992: 169). As Renato withdraws, the city becomes the theater for the staging of the troubled mind of a ruined political and intellectual hero and it is no suprise that Renato is reading Beckett with friends the night before his death.

L'Amore Molesto

The second movie makes the modern anonymous city the external impetus for the uncovering of a particular personal history which is part of a social one. The story of Delia, her mother, and family figures is also an account of a Naples of women's work, men's violence and jealousy, of poverty, postwar shortages and hardship, and of the differences and similarities between the nineties and earlier decades. While the wish that guides the narrative of *L'amore molesto* appears as the clarification of the circumstances of the mother's death, questions of past and present are here laid, the one upon the other, from sequence to sequence, in an attempt to capture the fluidity and apparent randomness of individual mental processes through the cinematic codes of editing and color.

L'amore molesto contains a fantasy or a memory of a possible past event, but, overall, this seems less significant than the more general accession of Delia to her younger self through the recollection of a former Naples and the encounter with a present one, both ordered on gendered lines. The gestures, assumptions, and behavior of the old men seem ludicrous and inappropriate, but their continuity in relations between the sexes is underlined by the persistent looking of the young men in the streets and on public transport. The fantasies, memories, recollections, flashbacks, the status of the possible personal pasts of the protagonist, Delia, remain open, and in this too, the film's structure offers an analogy with the mind and the kaleidoscopic transformations provoked in fantasy by memories. That they originate in a vital, gutsy Naples does nothing to detract from this oneiric sense.

The relation of past and present in the second movie is a complexly shifting affair; the female character involves a less directly personal dimension for the director, and the movie inscribes a Naples described by him as "sometimes unknown disquieting and foreign" (Martone 1995), a Naples of the margins, not only the geographical margins – Delia's father lives in the periphery – but peopled with the old, whose language, gestures, and behavior Martone has identifed as setting them apart "like an ancient tribe barricaded inside the hostile modern city" (1995).

Noise is one of the most notable elements of contemporary Naples and constant sound is the accompaniment of most of the second film, especially its exterior scenes. The sounds of dialect and the level and timbre of the voices, together with the omnipresence of the car and other modes of transport, carry the sensation of the modern city. The exceptions are the scenes signaled as memory and the past. In *L'amore molesto* the physical and architectural aspects of Naples more often appear in Delia's memories, most of which are staged below ground, a reference to the social conditions of her family, though also available to a symbolic reading given the film's engagement with memory.

A cool color spectrum is employed throughout, and in the tinted sequences that signify memory or recollection or fantasy, Amalia, the mother, is always in blue except in the scenes of her death, imagined by Delia on the rail journey away from Naples. In them, Amalia, wearing the red lingerie the old admirer had returned to the daughter earlier in the film, dances round a fire on the beach, first laughing, then crying, finally walking into the sea as the old man sleeps. Delia imagines these scenes of her mother's enjoyment, and discovers a facet of her own, as, once more dressed in the gray/blue suit, she shares the beer offered to her by the young men.

This is one of the few Italian movies to feature the mother–daughter relation and it makes its embeddedness in Naples central, so that a general interrogation of the maternal and what it means also runs through the film. "There still exists today a series of stereotypes in the Italian imagination; Naples as a female city, a belly city, a city of the heart: in short, a mother city ... the city willingly accepts the image of mother which is frequently assigned to it" (Niola 1994, quoted and translated by

Green 1999). A fantasy of shifting identifications in the condensation of memories, events, and sexual encounters of both mother and daughter is continually alluded to through their clothes. The mother's birthday present was a clinging red dress which Delia wears for most of the film, replacing the gray/blue suit in which she arrived. In fantasy, and in the time of the film, red and blue garments move between mother and daughter, paralleling visually the intricacies of the relationship. For Delia/Anna Buonaiuto, encountering the city and its inhabitants forces a revisiting of her mother, and herself, and her own past. The intensity of the individual situation emerges through the amalgam of social meanings, experiences and knowledge comprised in the images of the city.

In its public spaces, after an absence of three years, and immediately following her mother's death, Delia becomes a sexualized body, almost as a present from her mother. Her decision to wear the dress is queried by her old uncle, "We've just buried your mother!" She replies, "Don't you like it? I was depressed. I wanted to give myself a present." In this dress the female protagonist negotiates the streets of Naples and her own mind, as it gathers around her the accumulated connotations of such a garment. Putting it on parallels the revival of memories of family and self, but it also bequeaths to Delia a sexual persona and a bodily enjoyment. In it, the relation with the dead mother and with her own and her mother's sexuality is revived.

An economy of sex is introduced in the stark contrast of the individualized woman's body and the masses of other bodies, and Bo reads the corporeality of Naples as the frame across which *L'amore molesto*'s taking on both of bodies and of love develops (1997: 15). It is this connectedness that the movie appears to insist upon, even in the midst of the everyday violence of the remembered domestic scenes. Through the involvement in the city as repository of her past life and that of her family, especially her mother, Delia's own life appears to become a life more vital and available for living. The exchanges between mother and daughter and their inscription in the red garments propose a potentially conservative and unchanging account of the place of sexuality in the lives of these women of different generations – Delia, after all, inherits her mother's position as the object of the look – yet what is released by the mother's death and the daughter's return appears as the possibility of a fuller life rather than its opposite. That Naples and the South should be its propeller contributes to those myths about the transformations that city has been associated with facilitating.

Conclusion

In *Civilisation and its Discontents* Freud first imagines (1930: 70) the layering of one famous Rome upon another as paradigmatic of the mind, but then dispenses with the possibility of the city as metaphor and rejects the idea that, outside the mind, the same space can contain different contents. Through the visual evocation of Naples in different decades as they are held in the characters' individual memories, Martone establishes the link between place and person over time and offers an exploration of the relation between body and mind, feeling and thought. Like Freud's Roman ruins, the residues and results of individual and collective mental life are evident in the filmed spaces of the city.

Apart from period, the past these movies explore is radically other in terms of class, cultural norms, and customs, quarters of the city, family relations, sex, and intellect.

Martone speaks of the double aspect of Naples: warmth and generosity, and harshness and toughness; and the two movies, in revolving around the one or the other, offer a double-sided vision of the city (Roberti 1992: 130). The fluctuating aspects of masculinity and femininity, and of what might be called the maternal function, are represented as a quality of the city itself, where, like human sexuality, there is little neat confinement or traditional division between rationality, the mind, and the male (ostensibly the territory of *Death*), and emotionality, the body, and the female (that of *L'amore molesto*).

The different emotional registers constitute an ongoing investigation of life and living, as complexly inscribed in the simultaneity in the mind, of a person's past and present places. But Martone also claims that the individual trajectories of these characters offer access to "the sense, feel, atmosphere of Naples," something he sees as residing "not in ethnic roots, but in the movement between the people of the city, given through its cinematic representation" (Addonizio *et al.* 1997: 341).

The lives of the two protagonists may be incommensurable in terms of family and domestic life, but the rhythms of Naples and of the South are consistent across the cinematic imaging. Language, cityscapes, noise, bodies, the presence of death – the first movie ends with a funeral, the second begins with one – reveal, at the same time, a regional city of the South, and an Italian city like any other. In the emotional geography the movies map, external differences shape internal scenarios, locally and nationally.

References

Addonizio, A. *et al.* (1997) *Loro di napoli: il nuovo cinema napoletano 1986–1997*. Palermo: Edizioni della Battaglia, in collaboration with FICC, Bologna.

Bo, F. (1997) Una Iucida vertigine. *Cinecritica* 2 (8): 13–25.

Bordwell, D. (1985) *Narration in the Fiction Film*. London: Methuen.

Brunette, P. (1987) *Roberto Rossellini*. London: Oxford University Press.

Bruno, G. (1997) City views: the voyage of movie images. In *The Cinematic City*, ed. D. Clarke. London: Routledge, 47–60.

Carter, E., Donald, J., and Squires, J. (eds.) (1993) *Space and Place Theories of Identity and Location*. London: Lawrence and Wishart.

Fofi, G. (1997) Introduction. In Addonizio *et al.*, 3–8.

Freud, S. (1930) *Civilisation and its discontents*. In *Standard Edition*, vol. 21. London: The Hogarth Press and the Institute of Psychoanalysis, 59–148.

Green, P. (1999) Neapolitan bodies in Italian cinema. Che c'è di nuovo nel nuovo cinema napoletano? Paper given to movie studies seminar, Birkbeck College, University of London, May.

Goethe, J. W. (1987) *Italian Journey*. London: Penguin.

Gribaudi, G. (1996) Images of the South. In *Italian Cultural Studies: An Introduction*, ed. D. Forgacs and B. Lumley. Oxford: Oxford University Press, 72–87.

Kofman, E., and Lebas, E. (eds.) (1996) *Henri Lefebvre. Writings on Cities*. Oxford: Blackwell Publishers.

Kolker, R. P. (1983) *The Altering Eye: Contemporary International Cinema*. Oxford: Oxford University Press.

Lefebvre, H. (1996) Introduction to Kofman and Lebas, ch. 18.

Lefebvre, H., and Régulier, C. (1996) Rhythmanalysis of Mediterranean cities. In Kofman and Lebas, 228–40 (ch. 23).

Martone, M. (1995) *Le due anime del cinema italiano contemporaneo: the two souls of Italian cinema*. Handout to Department of Italian, University of Warwick.

Martone, M. (1997) Interview in Addonizio *et al.*, 79–103.

Morley, D., and Robins, K. (1993) No place like Heimat: images of Home(land) in European Culture. In Carter *et al.*, 3–31.

Neale, S. (1981) Art cinema as institution. *Screen* 21 (1): 11–40.

Niola, M. (1994) *Totem e ragù*. Naples: Pironti.

Piantini, L. (1993) Sulla morte di un matematico napoletano. *Cinema Nuovo* 42 (1): 26–7.

Pontalis, J. B. (1993) *Love of Beginnings*. London: Free Association Books.

Ramondino, F. (1991) *Star di casa*. Milan: Garzanti.

Roberti, B. (1992) Lui, una città, dei compagni di strada, nel tempo. Conversazione con Mario Martone. In *Morte di un matematico napoletano*, ed. F. Ramondino and M. Martone. Milan: Ubulibri, 130–6. Reprinted from *Filmcritica*, 425, April, 1992.

Sontag, S. (1979) Introduction. In W. Benjamin, *One Way Street and Other Writings*. London: NLB, 7–28.

Chapter 30

City Life and the Senses

John Urry

Introduction

In this chapter I develop an issue interestingly expressed by Popper when he characterizes "closed societies" as a "concrete group of individuals, related to one another ... by concrete physical relationships such as *touch, smell,* and *sight*" (1962: 173; emphasis added). In the following I explore, not the senses powerful within closed societies, but how such senses operate in "open societies" and especially in what we might call "open cities." Which senses dominate and what role do they play in producing the spatializations of city life within the "West" (for an alternative account of sensing nature, see Macnaghten and Urry 1998: ch. 4)?

Rodaway usefully elaborates a "sensuous geography" which connects together analyses of body, sense, and space (1994). As well as the *social* character of the senses emphasized by Simmel (Frisby and Featherstone 1997), Rodaway shows that the senses are also spatial. Each sense contributes to people's orientation in space; to their awareness of spatial relationships; and to the appreciation of the qualities of particular micro- and macro-spatial environments. Moreover, each sense gives rise to metaphors which attest to the relative importance of each within everyday life. With regard to sight, it is often said that "we see" something when we understand it; someone who does not understand a topic is said to be "blind"; farsighted leaders are said to be "visionary"; while intellectuals may be able to "illuminate" or "shed light on" a particular topic. By contrast those who cannot understand some issue remain "in the dark" (and see Hibbitts 1994: 240–1).

Rodaway further suggests that there are five distinct ways in which different senses are interconnected with each other to produce a sensed environment: *co-operation* between the senses; a *hierarchy* between different senses, as with the visual sense during much of the recent history of the West; a *sequencing* of one sense which has to follow on from another sense; a *threshold* of effect of a particular sense which has to be met before another sense is operative; and *reciprocal* relations of a certain sense with the object which appears to "afford" it an appropriate response (1994: 36–7).

Visuality

The hierarchy of the senses within western culture over the past few centuries has placed the visual at the top (Rorty 1980). This was the outcome of various developments. These included new ecclesiastical styles of architecture of the Middle Ages which allowed increasingly large amounts of light to filter through the brightly colored stained-glass windows. The medieval fascination with light and color was also to be seen in the growth of heraldry as a complex visual code denoting chivalric identification and allegiance (Hibbitts 1994: 251). In the fifteenth century linear perspectivism enabled three-dimensional space to be represented on a two-dimensional plane. There was also the development of the science of optics and the fascination with the mirror as a popular object found in grand houses and later in urban shops. Also there was the growth of an increasingly "spectacular" urban legal system with colorful robes and elaborate courtrooms.

Most significant was the invention of the printing press which reduced the relative power of the oral/aural sense and enhanced the seeing of the written word, as well as pictures and maps (Hibbitts 1994: 255). Jay summarizes the significance of this visual sense within the broad sweep of western culture: "with the rise of modern science, the Gutenberg revolution in printing and the Albertian emphasis on perspective in painting, vision was given an especially powerful role in the modern era" (1986: 179). Marshall McLuhan similarly argues that "as our age slips back into the oral and auditory modes ... we become sharply aware of the uncritical acceptance of visual metaphors and models by many past centuries"; to be real a thing must, he says, be visible (1962: 238).

Simmel makes two important points about this visual sense. First, the eye is a unique "sociological achievement" (Frisby and Featherstone 1997: 111). Looking at one another effects the connections and interactions of individuals. Simmel terms this the most direct and "purest" interaction. It is the look between people (what we now call "eye-contact") which produces extraordinary moments of intimacy. This is because "[o]ne cannot take through the eye without at the same time giving"; this produces the "most complete reciprocity" of person to person, face to face (Frisby and Featherstone 1997: 112). The look is returned, and this results from the expressive meaning of the face. What we see in the person is the lasting part of them, "the history of their life and ... the timeless dowry of nature" (Frisby and Featherstone 1997: 115). By contrast the ear and the nose do not reciprocate – they only take but do not give.

This intimacy of eye contact was initially given urban expression in nineteenth-century Paris, with its sidewalk cafés in which lovers could be "private in public" (Berman 1983). This intimacy was enhanced by the streams of anonymous city-dwellers and visitors, none of whom would return the look of the lovers. They remained wrapped in the intimacy of their particular face-to-faceness, surrounded by the rush, pace, and anonymity of the city life going on all around them.

Second, Simmel notes that only the visual sense enables possession and property; while that which we hear is already past and provides no property to possess (Frisby and Featherstone 1997: 116). The visual sense enables people to take possession, not only of other people, but also of diverse environments. It enables the world to be controlled at a distance, combining detachment and mastery (see Robins 1996: 20). By seeking distance a proper "view" is gained, abstracted from the hustle and bustle of everyday city life (see Hibbitts 1994: 293).

This power of possession is best seen in the development of photography. Adam summarizes: "The eye of the camera can be seen as the ultimate realisation of that vision: monocular, neutral, detached and disembodied, it views the world at a distance, fixes it with its nature, and separates observer from observed in an absolute way" (1995: 8). Photography is thus a particularly powerful signifying practice which reproduces a dominant set of images and, at the very same time, conceals its constructed character (see Berger 1972; Sontag 1979; Albers and James 1988; Urry 1990). It also gives shape to the very processes of movement around the city (see Urry 1990: 137–40). Photographic practices thus reinforce the dominance of the visual gaze, including that of the male over the bodyscape of women within the city. By contrast, Irigaray argues that for women "investment in the look is not as privileged in women as in men. More than other senses, the eye objectifies and masters. It sets at a distance, and maintains a distance" (1978: 50; and see Heidegger on the "modern world picture," 1979: 134).

This visual sense is moreover increasingly mediatized, as it shifts from the printing press to electronic modes of representation, and from the camera to the circulation of digital images. Such transformations stem from the nineteenth-century process by which there was a "separation of the senses" and especially the visual sense from touch and hearing (see Crawshaw and Urry 1997, on such a sequencing of the senses). The autonomization of sight enabled the quantification and homogenization of visual experience. Many new objects of the visual began to circulate in the city – including commodities, mirrors, plate-glass windows, postcards, photographs, and so on. These objects displayed a visual enchantment in which magic and spirituality were displaced by visual appearances and surface features, reflecting in the city the mass of consumers passing by.

In the twentieth-century city, most powerful systems of modern incarceration involve the complicity of sight in their routine operations of power. "Distancing, mastering, objectifying – the voyeuristic look exercises control through a visualization which merges with a victimization of its object" (Deutsche 1991: 11). It is argued that we live in a "surveillance society," even when we are apparently roaming freely through a shopping center or the countryside (Lyon 1994). Virilio has particularly emphasized the novel importance of video surveillance techniques to changing the morphology of the contemporary city and hence of the trust that the public now have to invest in such institutions of surveillance (1988). It has been calculated that one is "captured" on film 20 times during a walk through a major shopping center. What is striking about such CCTV techniques is their ordinariness, much akin to the child playing video games in an arcade or on a home computer (Robins 1996: 20–1; and see the film *Sliver*).

Thus the city both is fascinated with, and hugely denigrates, the visual. This ambivalence is reflected in the diverse discourses surrounding travel. On the one hand, we live in a society of spectacle as cities have been transformed into diverse and collectable spectacles. But on the other hand, there is denigration of the mere sightseer to different towns and cities. The person who only lets the sense of sight have free rein is ridiculed. Such sightseers are taken to be superficial in their appreciation of environments, peoples, and places. Many people are often embarrassed about mere sightseeing. Sight is not seen as the noblest of the senses but as the most superficial, as getting in the way of real experiences that should involve other senses and necessitate much longer periods of time in order to be immersed in the site/ sight (see Crawshaw and Urry 1997, for further detail).

The critique of the sightseer is taken to the extreme in the analysis of "hyper-reality," forms of simulated experience which have the appearance of being more "real" than the original (Baudrillard 1981; Eco 1986). The sense of vision is reduced to a limited array of features, it is then exaggerated and it comes to dominate the other senses. Hyper-real places are characterized by surface which does not respond to or welcome the viewer. The sense of sight is seduced by the most immediate and visible aspects of the scene, such as the facades of Main Street in Disneyland. What is not experienced in such hyper-real places is a different visual sense, the baroque (Jay 1992; Buci-Glucksmann 1984). This involves the fascination for opacity, unreadability, and indecipherability. Jay seeks to celebrate

> the dazzling, disorientating, ecstatic surplus of images in baroque visual experience ... [the] rejection of the monocular geometricalization of the Cartesian tradition ... the baroque self-consciously revels in the contradictions between surface and depth, disparaging as a result any attempt to reduce the multiplicity of visual spaces into any one coherent essence. (1992: 187)

He talks of baroque planning seeking to engage all the senses as found in some carnivals and festivals (1992: 192). This partly parallels Sennett's critique of the blandness of the "neutralised city" which is based upon fear of social contact with the stranger involving the various senses (1991). Sennett advocates the positive uses of disorder, contradiction, and ambiguity in the development of contemporary cities (and see Robins 1996: 100–1).

Likewise feminists have argued that the concentration upon the visual sense overemphasizes appearance, image, and surface. Irigaray argues that in western cultures "the preponderance of the look over the smell, taste, touch and hearing has brought about an impoverishment of bodily relations. The moment the look dominates, the body loses its materiality" (1978: 123; Mulvey 1989). This emphasis upon the visual reduces the body to surface, marginalizes the multiple sensuousness of the body and impoverishes the relationship of the body to its environment. And at the same time the visual overemphasizes masculinist efforts to exert mastery over the female body, particularly through the voyeurism effected via the pornographic picture (Taylor 1994: 268). By contrast a feminist consciousness emphasizes the dominant visual sense less and seeks to integrate all of the senses in a more rounded way, which does not seek to exert mastery over the "other" (Rodaway 1994: 123). Other writers have particularly emphasized the significance of aural traditions in women's lives – especially within socially dense urban areas – to talking and listening, telling stories, engaging in intimate detailed dialog or gossip and the use of the metaphor of "giving voice" (Hibbitts 1994: 271–3).

Smell and Touch

I turn now to these other senses and their complex relationships with visuality. I begin with nineteenth-century urban England. In 1838 the House of Commons Select Committee argued that, because there were whole areas of London through which no thoroughfares passed, the lowest class of person was secluded from the observation and the influence of "better educated neighbours" (Stallybrass and White 1986: 134). Engels noted how the social ecology of the industrial city had the effect of "hiding from the eyes of wealthy gentlemen and ladies ... the misery and squalor that ... complement ... their riches and luxury" (cited in Marcus 1973: 259). It was claimed that the "lower" classes would be greatly improved if they became visible to the middle and upper classes. There are parallels here with the rebuilding of Paris and its hugely enhanced visibility which resulted from replacing the medieval street plan with the grand boulevards of the Second Empire (see Berman 1983).

In Britain visibility was increasingly viewed as central to the regulation of the lower classes within the new cities. As the "other" classes were now seen in the massive cities of nineteenth-century Britain, the upper class desperately tried not to touch them (unless of course they were prostitutes or domestic servants who were deemed available for touching by upper-class men). The concepts of "contagion" and "contamination" were the tropes through which the upper class apprehended nineteenth-century city life (Stallybrass and White 1986). As the "promiscuity" of the public space became increasingly unavoidable, so the upper and middle classes sought to avoid touching the potentially contaminating "other," the "dangerous classes."

This was in turn reflected in the development of Victorian domestic architecture which was designed to regulate the flows of bodies, keeping servants apart from the family "below stairs," adults apart from children who were in the nursery, and male children apart from female children. As a contemporary argued, there were:

> two currents of "circulation" in a family dwelling ... There is the activity of the master and his friends, which occurs on the most visible, genteel and accessible routes, and there is the "circulation" of the servants, tradesmen and everyone else who provides the home with services, and this should take place in the least conspicuous and most discreet way possible. (quoted in Roderick 1997: 116)

More generally, the upper class mainly sought to gaze upon the other, while standing on their balconies. The balcony took on special significance in nineteenth-century life and literature as the place from which one could gaze but not be touched, could participate in the crowd yet be separate from it. It was one of the earliest examples of replacing the city of touch with the city of visibility (see Robins 1996: 20). According to Benjamin the balcony demonstrates superiority over the crowd, as the observer "scrutinizes the throng" (1969: 173). The later development of the skyscraper, beginning in 1880s Chicago, also enabled those inside to gaze down and across the crowd, while being insulated from the smells and the potential touch of those who were below. In Chicago the avoidance of the smells of the meat processing industry was a particularly important spur to building skyscrapers up into the light.

And there are parallels with the way in which the contemporary tourist bus gives a bird's eye view, in but not of the crowd, gazing down on the crowd in safety, without the heat, the smells, and the touch. It is as though the scene is being viewed on a screen, and sounds, noises, and the contaminating touch are all precluded because of the empire of the gaze effected through the windows of the bus. Thus the dominance of sight over the dangerous sense of smell has been effected through a number of physical objects and technologies, such as the balcony, the skyscraper, and the air-conditioned bus.

Smell was thus significant in the cultural construction of the nineteenth-century western city. It demarcated the unnaturalness of the city. Stallybrass and White argue that in the mid-nineteenth-century "the city ... still continued to invade the privatised body and household of the bourgeoisie as smell. It was, primarily, the sense of smell which enraged social reformers, since smell, whilst, like touch, encoding revulsion, had a pervasive and invisible presence difficult to regulate" (1986: 139). Smells, sewers, rats, and the mad played key roles in the nineteenth-century construction of class relations within the large cities. Later, in the 1930s, George Orwell noted powerful odors along the road to Wigan Pier (1937: 159).

As the nineteenth-century upper class repressed reference to their own lower bodily functions, they increasingly referred to the simultaneous dangers *and* fascinations of the lowlife of the "other," including the smells of the slum, the ragpicker, the prostitute, the sewer, the dangers of the rat, below stairs, the kneeling maid and so on (Shields 1991 on lowlife in nineteenth-century Brighton). The upper class in nineteenth-century British cities experienced a particular "way of sensing" such cities, in which smell played a pivotal role. The odors of death, madness, and decay were thought to be ever-present in the industrial city (Tuan 1993: 61–2; Classen *et al.* 1994: 165–9, on the class and ethnic structuring of such smellscapes). There was thought to be a distinctive "stench of the poor" in Paris (Corbin 1986: ch. 9). There was a pronounced rhetoric of the delights of the "open air," that is air that did not smell of the city, for those apparently confined to living within nineteenth-century cities.

Lefebvre more generally argues that the production of different spaces is crucially bound up with smell. He says that "where an intimacy occurs between 'subject' and 'object', it must surely be the world of smell and the places where they reside" (1991: 197). Olfaction seems to provide a more direct and less premeditated encounter with the environment; and one which cannot be turned on and off. It provokes an unmediated sense of the surrounding townscapes. Tuan argues that the directness and immediacy of smell provides a sharp contrast with the abstractive and compositional characteristics of sight (1993: 57).

One way of examining smell is in terms of the diverse "smellscapes" which organize and mobilize people's feelings about particular places (including what one might also call the "tastescapes" of different gastronomic regimes). This concept brings out how smells are spatially ordered and place-related (Porteous 1990: 369). In particular, the olfactory sense is important in evoking memories of specific places, normally because of certain physical objects and their characteristic smells which are thought to inhabit certain places (see Tuan 1993: 57). And even if we cannot name the particular smell it can still be important in helping to create and sustain one's sense of a particular place or experience. It can generate both revulsion and attraction; as such it can play a major role in constructing and sustaining major distinctions of social taste.

Rodaway summarizes the power of smell in relationship to place as "the perception of an odour in or across a given space, perhaps with varying intensities, which will linger for a while and then fade, and a differentiation of one smell from another and the association of odours with particular things, organisms, situations and emotions which all contribute to a sense of place and the character of places" (1994: 68). Toni Morrison writes in the *Song of Solomon* of how

> On autumn nights, in some parts of the city, the wind from the lake [Superior] brings a sweetish smell to shore. An odo[u]r like crystallized ginger, or sweet iced tea with a dark clove floating in it ... there was this heavy spice-sweet smell that made you think of the East and striped tents ... The two men ... could smell the air, but they didn't think of ginger. Each thought it was the way freedom smelled, or justice, or luxury, or vengeance (1989: 184–5).

Simmel argues that the sense of smell is a particularly "dissociating sense," transmitting more repulsions than attractions (Frisby and Featherstone 1997: 119). He talks of "olfactory intolerance," suggesting for example that hostility between Germans and Jews has been particularly generated by distinctions of smell (see Guérer 1993: 27). More generally he thought that the "effluvia" of the working class posed a threat to social solidarity (Frisby and Featherstone 1997: 118). This became more pronounced during the twentieth century as domestic hygiene had been very unevenly introduced, so reinforcing class attitudes of social and moral superiority based upon smell. The stigma of odor has provided a constant basis of stratification, resulting from what Simmel terms the "invincible disgust inspired by the sense of smell" (cited in Guérer 1993: 34).

Modern societies have apparently reduced the sense of smell by comparison with the other senses (Lefebvre 1991). Premodern societies had been very much characterized by distinctions of smell (see Classen *et al.* 1994, on the significance of aroma within the classical world). In modern societies there is an apparent dislike of strong odors and the emergence of various technologies, objects, and manuals which seek to purify smells out of everyday life. These include the development of public health systems which separate water from sewerage and which involve channeling sewage underground away from both the nose and the eye (Roderick 1997). Corporeal functions and processes came to occupy a "proper place" within the home; they were increasingly spatially differentiated from each other and based upon the control and regulation of various bodily and piped fluids. In particular as water came to be piped separately from sewage so it was possible to wash the whole body much more frequently; bath and shower technologies were developed and also came to be given a "proper place" within the home. A lack of smell came to indicate personal and public cleanliness. Domestic design develops so as to exclude animal and related smells.

More generally, Bauman argues that "Modernity declared war on smells. Scents had no room in the shiny temple of perfect order modernity set out to erect" (1993: 24). For Bauman modernity sought to neutralize smells by creating zones of control in which the senses would not be offended. Zoning became an element of public policy in which planners accepted that repugnant smells are in fact an inevitable byproduct of urban-industrial society. Refuse dumps, sewage plants, meat process-ing factories, industrial plants and so on are all spaces in which bad smells are concentrated, and are typically screened off by being situated on the periphery of cities. Domestic architecture developed which confined smells to particular areas of the home, to the backyard, and the water closet. This war of smell within modernity was carried to the extreme in the Nazi period, when the Jews were routinely referred to as "stinking" and their supposed smell was associated with physical and moral corruption (Classen *et al.* 1994: 170–5).

But smell is a subversive sense since it cannot be wholly banished (Bauman 1993). Smell reveals the artificiality of modernity; it shows, following Latour, that we have never been really modern (1993). The modern project to create a pure, rational order of things is undermined by the sweet smell of decomposition which continu-ously escapes control and regulation. Thus the "stench of Auschwitz" could not be eliminated even when at the end of the war the Nazis desperately tried to conceal what had happened through ridding the camps of the stench of death (Classen *et al.* 1994: 175). Bauman submits that decomposition has "a sweet smell," exerting its revenge upon a modern world which cannot be subject to complete purification and control (1993).

The ways in which smells emanate from diverse objects, including especially the human body, result in the social significance and power of diverse hybrids such as sewage systems, notions of hygiene, and new discourses and technologies of domes-tic architecture. More generally Roderick argues that, although there are all sorts of *smelly* substances within houses and apartments (such as sewage, dirty water, and gas, as well as the *dangerous* flows of electricity and boiling water), modernity has sought to confine their flows to various channels. But of course these flowing substances are always threatening to seep through the walls of these channels and to enter the "home," analogous to the way that blood does not stay within its own vessels (Roderick 1997: 128). Much women's work within the home has been based upon taking a special responsibility for these dirty fluids, somewhat paralleling Grosz's characterization of the female body as "a leaking, uncontrollable, seeping liquid; as formless flow; as viscosity, entrapping, secreting" (1994: 203). Men only enter the scene when the seepage gets out of hand and it is they who climb along the vessels of the house, to clean and repair the pipes that flow above the ceilings and behind the walls, which confine the dirty and the dangerous.

Conclusion

Thus I have considered some of the ways that vision and smell form and reform themselves to constitute the evolving spatiality of the nineteenth- and twentieth-century city (I have not considered the non-western city, see Edensor 1998). With more time I would have developed similar analyses of the acoustic sense, which like smell cannot be turned on and off. According to Simmel "the ear is the egoistic organ pure and simple, which only takes but does not give" (Frisby and Featherstone 1997: 115). Within the contemporary city there appears to be a reinvigorated oral culture reflected in musak, loudspeakers, ghetto blasters, telephone bells, traffic, mobile phones, sex chat lines, and so on (see Hibbitts 1994: 302–3). I would also have considered further the sense of touch. I noted how cities have been transformed so as to avoid what Canetti terms "the touch of the unknown" (1973), to replace the city of touch with the radiant city. But it should also be noted that people necessarily move among bodies which continuously touch and are touched, in a kind of reciprocity of contact (see Robins 1996: 33). Unlike the seeer who can look without being seen, the toucher is always touched (see Grosz 1994: 45).

Invoking the senses challenges much of our understanding of city life. On the basis of an account of the microspatiality of those in a city confined to a wheelchair, Massey points to the significance of the diverse senses: "there are local landscapes of sense other than vision. Try imagining – and designing – a city of sound and touch, a city that plays to all the senses" (and we might add, a city that plays to taste and smell; see Massey 2002: 474).

References

Adam, B. (1995) Radiated identities: in pursuit of the temporal complexity of conceptual cultural practices. Theory, Culture and Society Conference, Berlin, August.

Albers, P., and James, W. (1988) Travel photography: a methodological approach. *Annals of Tourism Research* 15: 134–58.

Baudrillard, J. (1981) *For a Critique of the Economy of the Sign*. St Louis: Telos.

Bauman, Z. (1993) The sweet smell of decomposition. In *Forget Baudrillard?*, ed. C. Rojek and B. Turner. London: Routledge, 22–46.

Benjamin, W. (1969) *Illuminations*. New York: Schocken.

Berger, J. (1972) *Ways of Seeing*. Harmondsworth: Penguin.

Berman, M. (1983) *All That Is Solid Melts Into Air*. London: Verso.

Buci-Glucksmann, C. (1984) *Baroque Reason: The Aesthetics of Modernity*. London: Sage.

Canetti, E. (1973) *Crowds and Power*. Harmondsworth: Penguin.

Classen, C., Howes, D., and Synnott, A. (1994) *Aroma: The Cultural History of Smell*. London: Routledge.

Corbin, A. (1986) *The Frail and the Fragrant*. Leamington Spa: Berg.

Crawshaw, C., and Urry, J. (1997) Tourism and the photographic eye. In *Touring Cultures*, ed. C. Rojek and J. Urry. London: Routledge, 176–95.

Deutsche, R. (1991) Boys town. *Environment and Planning D: Society and Space* 9: 5–30.

Eco, U. (1986) *Travels in Hyper-Reality*. London: Picador.

Edensor, T. (1998) *Tourists at the Taj*. London: Routledge.

Frisby, D., and Featherstone, M. (eds.) (1997) *Simmel on Culture*. London: Sage.

Grosz, E. (1994) *Volatile Bodies: Towards a Corporeal Feminism*. Sydney: Allen and Unwin.

Guérer, A. le (1993) *Scent: The Mysterious and Essential Powers of Smell*. London: Chatto and Windus.

Heidegger, M. (1979) *One-Way Street and Other Writings*. London: New Left.

Hibbitts, B. (1994) Making sense of metaphors: visuality, aurality, and the reconfiguration of American legal discourse. *Cardozo Law Review* 16: 229–356.

Irigaray, L. (1978) Interview with L. Irigaray. In *Les Femmes, La Pornographie et L'Erotisme*, ed. M.-F. Hans and G. Lapouge. Paris: Minuit.

Jay, M. (1986) In the empire of the gaze: Foucault and the denigration of vision in twentieth century French thought. In *Foucault: A Critical Reader*, ed. D. Hoy. Oxford: Blackwell, 175–204.

Jay, M. (1992) Scopic regimes of modernity. In *Modernity and Identity*, ed. S. Lash and J. Friedman. Oxford: Blackwell, 178–95.

Latour, B. (1993) *We Have Never Been Modern*. Hemel Hempstead: Harvester Wheatsheaf.

Lefebvre, H. (1991) *The Production of Space*. Oxford: Blackwell.

Lyon, D. (1994) *The Electronic Eye: The Rise of the Surveillance Society*. Cambridge: Polity Press.

Macnaghten, P., and Urry, J. (1998) *Contested Natures*. London: Sage.

Marcus, S. (1973) Reading the illegible. In *The Victorian City: Images and Reality*, vol. 1, ed. H. Dyos and M. Wolff. London: Routledge and Kegan Paul, 257–76.

Massey, D. (2002) Living in Wythenshawe. In *The Unknown City: Contesting Architecture and Social Space*, ed. Iain Borden. Cambridge, MA: MIT Press, 458–75.

McLuhan, M. (1962) *The Gutenberg Galaxy*. London: Routledge.

Morrison, T. (1989) *Song of Solomon*. London: Picador.

Mulvey, L. (1989) *Visual and Other Pleasures*. London: Macmillan.

Orwell, G. (1937) *The Road to Wigan Pier*. London: Victor Gollancz.

Popper, K. (1962) *The Open Society and its Enemies*. London: Routledge and Kegan Paul.

Porteous, J. (1990) *Landscapes of the Mind: Worlds of Sense and Metaphor*. Toronto: Toronto University Press.

Robins, K. (1996) *Into the Image*. London: Routledge.

Rodaway, P. (1994) *Sensuous Geographies*. London: Routledge.

Roderick, I. (1997) Household sanitation and the flows of domestic space. *Space and Culture* 1: 105–32.

Rorty, R. (1980) *Philosophy and the Mirror of Nature*. Oxford: Blackwell.

Sennett, R. (1991) *The Conscience of the Eye*. London: Faber.

Shields, R. (1991) *Places on the Margin*. London: Routledge.

Sontag, S. (1979) *On Photography*. Harmondsworth: Penguin.

Stallybrass, P., and White, A. (1986) *The Politics and Poetics of Transgression*. London: Methuen.

Taylor, J. (1994) *A Dream of England*. Manchester: Manchester University Press.

Tuan, Y.-F. (1993) *Passing Strange and Wonderful*. Washington, DC: Island Press.

Urry, J. (1990) *The Tourist Gaze*. London: Sage.

Virilio, P. (1988) The work of art in the age of electronic reproduction. Interview in *Block* 14: 4–7.

Chapter 31

The Politics of Urban Intersection: Materials, Affect, Bodies

AbdouMaliq Simone

Coming To Deal

They show up, although they are not sure quite why; still with a sense of necessity – activists, city councilors, local thugs, entrepreneurs, fixers, religious figures, NGO workers, and some concerned citizens. In the back banquet hall of an old restaurant food and drinks are served, and there is no real agenda. It is late, and no one knows quite what the outcome will be. But a deal will be hammered out; no one will like it very much; no one knows quite how it will be enforced or what the long-term implications will be. It is likely people will return soon, perhaps not here, but to some other fairly anonymous place that everyone knows. Still, it is an occasion when no particular expertise or authority prevails; there are openings to make things happen across a landscape of gridlock, big money, and destitution.

These are gatherings that take place across many cities of the world; usually at off-hours and usually under somewhat vague pretenses and aspirations. Nevertheless, it is an urban politics at work, engaged in the arduous task of bringing some kind of articulation to increasingly divergent policy frameworks, administrative apparatuses, money streams, and authority figures that intertwine at abstract levels but whose mechanics of interdependency are too often opaque within day-to-day routines of navigating and governing cities.

Competencies and jurisdictions are often demarcated and institutionalized in ways that entail clear limits to what any given agency, organization, or company is entitled and available to do. Therefore, projects and programs that require the application of many different kinds of entities at various times often require administratively complex negotiations and scheduling pertaining to the way these entities work together and apply their abilities to a particular site of intervention.

The New Blackwell Companion to the City   Edited by Gary Bridge and Sophie Watson
© 2011 Blackwell Publishing Ltd

Organizational structures tend to emphasize the efficient replication of responses through standardization. For what they do has to be applied to many different kinds of clients and situations. So those who can offer, for example, the ability to put together construction crews, cartage, waste removal, cut-rate overtime, supplementary finance, political connections, and media spin in one, on the surface, seamless package are vital to municipal administrations, and have to be rewarded in ways that are often difficult to accommodate within prevailing rules and norms.

Urban heterogeneity is not simply a diverse composition of readily discernible income levels, life styles, aspirations, and settlement histories. Almost all the major cities of the global south continue to be replete with districts where different capacities, inclinations, purchasing power, and orientations are thoroughly intertwined in dense proximity. Here, precise categorizations of what people are – their class backgrounds, their ways of making decisions and using available resources – are highly under-coded.

Even when classifications are generated in well-elaborated local vernaculars, these tend to continuously change – so it is not clear who is poor and what criteria constitute the poor, or middle class, for there are prolific gradations. This relative absence of certain categorization tends to make people more willing to pay attention to each other, to take certain risks in their affiliation, and to try out various ways of using local spaces. From this willingness stem a plurality of local economies – i.e., different scales at which things are made, distributed and sold – from furniture, textiles, foodstuffs, building materials, and household items. Different potentialities of consumption are concretized through the ability to access different quantities of goods and services within a district. This doesn't mean that everyone necessarily gets along or talks to each other. It is not a social economy based on easy reciprocities and well-honed collaboration. Rather, it stems from often highly opportunistic maneuvers that use the very tensions incumbent in such heterogeneity to continuously remake temporary accords, deals, and trade-offs that remake the local built and social environment, and where the remaking precipitates new tensions and accommodations.

This ability to mobilize certain potentialities inherent in the heterogeneity of the city is usually incumbent in those operations that are able to manipulate the networked effects that scale enables. Yet frequently, such operations emerge from highly localized yet intensive positions within specific sectors or neighborhoods that capitalize on apparently incommensurable relations – i.e., the intersection of social identities, functions, and domains that usually wouldn't be expected to work together. So deals that can connect, for example, religious leaders, gangsters, financiers, professionals, journeymen, and civic associations begin to cover a lot of ground and spread out across other territories. While big players such as multinational consultancy firms, technicians, contractors, and property developers may have the size and coverage to deliver unrivaled efficiencies, they may not have sufficient local knowledge to expedite getting things done.

Between What Is and What Is Not: Navigating Urban Politics

In Africa, ordinary citizens have a major role producing the built environment, particularly those who take over pre-existing buildings and transform them to suit the needs of emerging and underserved communities. These "projects" emphasize agency and desire and lend voice to multiple, overlapping languages – of politics, aesthetics, irony, and hope. This does not minimize the difficulty of living in spaces stripped of even the most basic amenities, hostages to sewage and detritus, state violence or extreme divides of wealth and power. Yet, they highlight the way that notions of "regularity" and "tenure" – basic elements of stabilization and coherence – are enacted and secured through highly mobile interrelationships between labor, the spaces that house it, and the activities and sites residents depend upon for their livelihood. Inhabitation does not mean a clear separating out of work and home, of marketing and producing, of clear demarcations among various modalities of social exchange.

At the same time in many African cities, as indicated before, it is often not clear who residents "really" are. The relationships that produce the conditions of their existence are increasingly difficult to trace and account for. Hundreds of new words and gestures appear in cities on a weekly basis. "Time zones" proliferate – where some individuals live literally in the end of days (the Apocalypse), others in some futuristic warp, and still others in an endless present of putting bread on the table. Actions can be excessively generous or cruel without apparent reasons, as is the coupling of bodies and materials. The interrelationships of these conditions give rise to urban actors to which the usual attributions perhaps make little sense.

All of these intersections of varying usages of space and materials within intense proximity cannot be apprehended – in the sense of both being understood and being captured – by prevailing frameworks of law or state policy. But they, nevertheless, are subject to such apparatuses, fall under their purview, and are compelled to have some kind of a relationship with them. The everyday tensions and challenges that arise from the elements of these intersections working or not working together are managed largely by the improvised mechanisms necessary to deal with constantly shifting dilemmas.

At times, dilemmas are simply lived out in highly fractured performances, where residents dramatize the inability to be discernible subjects or citizens of any kind. Take the city of Kinshasa, widely expected to grow from its estimated population of 10 million to become Africa's largest city in the next 20 years. Its annual budget of US$ 23 million means that almost nothing can be done – no capital investment, no municipal services. Personal effort almost alone is the vehicle to survival.

Kinois live between veracity and exaggeration, the empirical and the baroque. Like everywhere, many topics are not easily talked about, and allusion and euphemism abound. But there is also a pervasive matter-of-factness and precision in people's speech. A woman will quickly arrive at the number of loaves of bread she has sold in the past six months; a resident in Bayamu will point out the overcrowded tenements on a random street and tell you the various prices of the rooms without hesitation. Minute details are invoked with great confidence. Whether the content of the assertions are really true is not the point here. Rather it is the attention to detail. How many sticks of cigarettes did a child street vendor sell on a particular night on a particular block in comparison with the 10 other kids working the same turf? How many glasses of whiskey did the commanding police officer buy the night before for the relatives of the *chef du quartier*? What is the exact time the manager of the warehouse for the beer company Primus arrived at the house of the sister of the head of state?

A drug wholesaler in Matete, in a matter of 15 minutes, identifies the different routes that heroin, cocaine, and amphetamines enter the city, with an outline of the prices entailed in the many transactions along the way. He can recite the consumption patterns of each of his 657 clients and generates a rapid analysis of exactly how his prices have fluctuated according to different supply trajectories over the past three years, as well as the full names of hundreds of people associated with the various policing authorities he has had to pay off.

All of the details are recited without emotion or hesitation, as if whatever is being spoken about is fully within the natural order of things and could have easily been spoken about with equivalent authority by anyone else. Everything that occurs may somehow be important, if not now, then later on. In a city of few luxuries, and where survival requires constant decisions about what is really important in the hundreds of conversations, events, and words that surround the individual on a daily basis, this almost promiscuous attention to the mundane would seem to be impractical, if not impossible. In a city of incessant trickery, where everyone is trying to take some advantage of each other, it would seem more rational for people to ignore much of what is going on and focus on what really matters – i.e., to the specific details of their current situation. But where individuals are implicated in the lives of both so many known and unknown others, and where it is difficult to get a handle on what is likely to take place in the very immediate future, this kind of paying attention is a constant means of hedging one's bets. It is a way of finding new angles to earn money, and get information and opportunity.

This approach to the empirical, of taking into account the smallest details of transactions of all kinds, makes it possible for individuals to also act as authorities in many matters. It is the basis from which people can speak to various situations, on the street, in the bus, bar, or office so as to possibly shape the outcome. In this way they do not leave themselves vulnerable to the impact of other people's actions. It provides them with a basis to intervene in situations that on the surface would not seem to be their "business" or concern. This is not the act of nosey arrogance, but stems more from the uncertainty as to what one's "business" really is, after all. For the boundaries between matters that concern an individual directly and those that may have only a tangential relevance are often fuzzy. No matter how distant they might be, it is often not clear what events will come back to haunt one. And so it is often better to be proactive in advance – not with the speech of opinion but with "facts," which in the end may be nothing more than speculation rendered with cold calculation.

At the same time, Kinshasa is renowned for being a city of fakery and exaggeration. Despite the capacities for resilient interactions with others, for changing gears, and finding new opportunities in new affiliations and scenarios, the daily grind for most Kinois is a repetitive search for small money, for drinking beer, and going to church. The details are banal and there is not much basis to make claims for anything else. The precariousness of existence would seem to indicate an overarching need to be precise, to keep things focused and functional. But this is where the exaggeration kicks in. What could be expressed in a simple phrase becomes a highly decorated discourse full of ironies and *double entendre*. The movements of the body, particularly the hips and the buttocks, during dance, exaltation, and everyday meandering are accentuated to the obscene.

Music is everywhere, and is perhaps the one constant of Kinois life. Rooted in the rumba, it changes only slightly as it becomes the key instrument of what residents have in common. Thus, it is the backdrop against which they can safely display a sense of singularity and express the raw desire to exceed whatever the individual experiences themselves to be. For in the daily grind of looking for money, of dealing with hundreds of others where words must be chosen carefully, of boarding over-crowded vans, and carving out small spaces of safety and health, individuals are always having to "rub shoulders" with others, always having to signal that one knows one's place, even if there are no clear maps to refer to. And so always the obverse is not far away in this practice, the sense that all of these bodies in close proximity – barely arranged and activated in ways that provide a functional separa-tion, a set of functional roles and responsibilities – could converge in some wild assemblage.

Thus the exaggeration of the body and speech – particularly the exaggeration of the sexual – becomes the mechanism to handle a kind of permanent state of excita-tion that the city by its very definition offers. When the reproduction of family life becomes increasingly difficult, when having a chance in life means having to leave the country and go somewhere else, and when working hard at school or work promises almost nothing, there are few mechanisms to counter individual desires to simply abandon the familiar forms of selfhood and belonging. At the same time, the dangers of physical desire are well known. The seemingly endless stories of jealousy and witchcraft, the rampant problems of sexual abuse and HIV, and the long history of the use of physical violence in the city on the part of authorities of all kinds, make the expression of desire dangerous. So the often baroque forms that personal expression assumes, particularly in front of the music, become a way of dealing with this dilemma, but in a way that has little to do with personal efficacy, talent, or skill.

For example, Werrason, aka "King of the Forest", remains Kinshasa's foremost band leader – a position he has maintained now for over a decade. By all conven-tional aesthetic parameters, Werrason cannot really play musical instruments, dance, or sing – yet he is at the top. While there is a long history that can be told about this, what Werrason's voice and words convey (when he actually does use them, which is increasingly less frequent as he turns over much of the work to the sup-porting cast) is the rawness of that expression of desire, full of its complications, full of its burdens. Yet, it remains a powerful invocation of something that cannot be captured or tamed, something that cannot be made into aesthetics, even if the image of Werrason dominates all kinds of advertisements. It is an expression that ends up counting for a lot in Kinshasa because it can't be counted. It can't be subsumed as a social event or a pure uninhibited cry for life. Rather, it is full of the detritus of the city, and yet it doesn't care, it proceeds to act as if there is nothing in its way.

Keeping the City in Line?

Despite the precarious conditions under which the majority of urban residents in Africa live, the urban fabric is always changing, driven by the relative lack of "cemented" trajectories and networks of relations among materials, people, events, and space. This is a process partly driven by a complex municipal politics of everyday regulation, where different actors who share communities, quarters, or districts attempt to work out incessantly troublesome connections between land, housing, services, and livelihood that are not held in any stable and consistent relationship with each other (Magnusson, 2006). Cities must continuously rework how people, things, infrastructures, languages, and images are to be intersected and pieced together. These are efforts that self-conscious planning may provide representations of but which are generated by maximizing the vast potentials within the city itself – potentials for relations among all kinds of things for which there exist no prior maps, inclinations, or even apparent possibilities.

So called modern cities have always taken the energies, experiments, and styles of their different human and non-human inhabitants and "contracted" them, both in the sense of truncating these practices and establishing contractual relationships defining the rights and responsibilities of urban citizens. This "contraction" may provide urban actors with new opportunities for looking, understanding, and organizing themselves. It may provide a framework for how to pay attention to all that goes on in the city and for understanding what it is possible to do and how to do it. But it also takes from them sensibilities, inclinations, and a vast set of provisional "accomplishments" for working with others and using the city and "repackages" them in ways that are then difficult to recognize and be reclaimed as their own.

Therefore we are left with the seemingly endless conundrum of development paradigms where governing cities is the issue of the political management of complex trade-offs that must be made by all cities in a context of sometimes painful global exposure. The trade-offs concern to what extent, for example, fiscal soundness takes precedence over the equitable delivery of urban services, or the extent to which managerial proficiency supersedes expanded popular participation in decision-making. The critical issue is how these trade-offs are defined? Who is involved in negotiating them? What are the appropriate forms of community organization and mobilization in a context where urban government is increasingly less capable of meeting the demands of all citizens? How does one combine, relate, and balance different forms of participation, negotiation, contestation, and partnership to ensure vibrant politics and constructive collaboration to solve real problems. Part of the problem is that not enough attention is paid to the hundreds of small deals, small transactions, and provisional accommodations worked out in backroom banquet halls, behind food stalls in night markets, in glitzy rundown casinos, and in the courtyards of neighborhood mosques – all places where different claims, tactics, and senses of things intersect.

This process of intersection doesn't necessarily mean that everyone has to take each other into consideration, has to meld their actions into some kind of hybrid way of doing things that incorporates bits and pieces of the actions and interests of everyone. Part of every intersection is the prospect that things will not come together and take something from each other; rather that some fundamental divides and impossibilities of translation will remain. The idea of local intersection among heterogeneous actors, materials, and affect here means that accommodations – in the form of giving rise to new consensually determined ways of speaking, relating, deciding, distributing, sharing, and so forth – do not necessarily take place. This absence doesn't mean that people are not paying attention to each other or taking each other seriously, but that the differences of others are not experienced as conditions necessitating some kind of challenge or motivation for any particular group to now enact their lives in a different manner.

Instead there is the simultaneous performance of ways of doing things that have no obvious concurrence or fit. In "neighborhoods" of actions and styles that appear to operate at cross-purposes, it is these very cross-purposes that provide a concrete manifestation of the different things that can be done and imagined in any given place. It is a materialization of different possibilities, different routes in and out toward the rest of the city; it is a reiteration of the possibility that specific prospects can be pursued by individuals and groups without them being perceived as threats and competition to others and that their effectiveness need not be predicated on having to somehow appeal to or subsume what others are doing.

Spaces of Intersection

Jean-Luc Nancy (1991) has stated that contemporary political existence shifts its focus from sovereignty to intersection. Sovereignty was a means of completion, of finishing the identity of territories and subjects – as something excessive to identities in that it frees them from the persistent mundane flows of continuous interaction that necessarily destabilizes and renders incomplete any version or articulation of identity, and converts them into an immutable reference. Intersection, on the other hand, refers to an incessant process of acting without a model, and is thus an environment also in the making. Instead of consolidating clearly discernible and bounded territories as platforms of action and interaction, there is a process of "spacing out," of generating, enfolding, and extending space in which mapping is always behind, struggling to "catch up."

At one level, both northern and southern cities appear to become more cosmopolitan – i.e., settings for the accelerated incorporation of cultural and economic diversity. But cosmopolitanism, to a large extent, implies the intersection or concordance of established identities, cultural values, and so forth. What is instead taking place, to use Agamben's (1995) language, is a progressive "exodusing" from such distinct positions – where residents who are both citizens and strangers, indigenes and migrants, are displaced from clearly elaborated identities.

The ramifications of such displacement are substantially different for African and northern cities even if in fundamental ways they are experiencing a "common moment." The space for the insertion of Africans into northern cities is opened up by the progressive abandonment of industrial and low-paid service jobs by a declining population base who can afford the risk to realign themselves to the uncertain terrain of an expanding "new economy." As Sassen (2003) has well documented, this new economy, in its need for the proximity of differentiated skills, knowledge bases, and experiences, engenders complex transactions requiring an expansion of low-skilled services. In most African cities, migration is triggered largely by the inability of cities to absorb a slow but discernible increase in a skilled urban population and the inability to expand economies due to a long-term shortage of investments in human capital and industry.

While remittances may constitute an increasingly important form of reinvestment, the more an African presence is spread across and instituted in northern cities, despite the efforts made to curtail immigration, the less those remittances will mean in terms of potential "development resources." Rather, remittances will increasingly serve as a kind of welfare allotment to households "left" behind. On the other hand, the more that urban Africa entrenches itself elsewhere and the more informal political rule and economic dynamics become at home, the more African cities may serve as contexts for the triggering and steering of transnational illicit economies.

Yet, if one looks at the old "African quarters" of the continent's major cities, such as New Bell in Douala, Ikeja in Lagos, Treichville in Abidjan – all mixtures of old money, ambiguous entrepreneurship, migration, and worn but still viable infrastructure – they continue to "work" in many ways. They embody a wide range of capacities to operate in many places at once and accommodate many different types of people and activities at the same time. This accommodation, despite all the polarization taking place in cities, remains a living capacity.

Intersecting agents seek to continuously maintain a capacity to mobilize whatever is available in order to access new opportunities and vantage points, as well as ways of manifesting themselves. As such, these worlds exist as fundamental spaces of argument – i.e., of political disputation where distances among groups who remain largely strangers to each other are activated and maintained for their productive capacities, rather than simply to reiterate differentiation.

Living Architectures

Pheng Cheah (2003) has written about the "spectral nationality" that hangs over and haunts peoples of the postcolony. That no matter how the course of nationhood in much of the global south has found itself dissipated and fractured by war, indebtedness, exploitation, or nearly comprehensive incorporation in the circuitries of global capital, a dream-image of a way of life whereby a people exceeds the particularities of their local circumstances and relations is concretized in and through the locus of nationality. Indeed, the challenge of cities remains how to draw lines between different ways of doing things, different walks of life.

Too often architecture has deployed various built environments as registers of fear, of keeping people in a certain line and state of hesitancy. The emphasis has been on "strange attractors" such as monuments, shopping malls, skylines, and big projects that often turn into "dead zones" – making claims on space that rule out a wide range of uses.

What, then, does a daily living architecture point to? Cities are rambunctious in the contrarian inclinations of their inhabitants – their bravado and overwrought caution, their furtive impatience and hard-fought stabilities. These inclinations make their mark on the built environment and provide varied opportunities for the management of decay, repair, and regeneration. The concrete demonstrations of those who save for years, who spend profusely, who consolidate place and position, who circulate through prolific versions of renewal and opportunity, elaborate a field of adjustments and compensations, an intricate economy of calibration where households, plots, enterprises, associations, and networks carve out niches that are partially folded into each other – even if only barely.

Places, people, and times have their definitions. Sometimes these definitions are malleable; sometimes they are worn down by the wear and tear of always having to articulate themselves in a crowded field of competing claims; and still sometimes they persist loud and clear only because they are willing to live in unprofessed complicities with challenges of all kinds. Distinctions of privilege and access – to services, thoroughfares, land, labor, and decision-making – may have progressively been spatialized in cities, but in many cities of the postcolonial world, they remain thoroughly entangled, capable of being apparent and making their mark but in intersecting orbits, not on their own. The concrete signs of modernity and economic wellbeing across many districts continue to run "interference" for the often messy improvisations forced upon the poor, whose residential areas frequently remain out of sight, ensconced in the residues of colonial spatial plans that kept them from the geometrical grids.

Building lines, plot size, distribution points, service reticulations continue to be systematically violated – sometimes in the interest of greed – but more often as mechanisms to maintain the viability of diverse kinds of residencies in close proximity. Equations that link training to skill, skill to occupation, occupation to set modalities of entrepreneurship, and entrepreneurship to specific forms of spatial encapsulation can themselves be thoroughly mixed up. Districts known for furniture production, auto repair and parts, printing, floral decoration, textiles, or ceramics usually contain a wide range of plant sizes, technologies, specializations, and degrees of formal and informal organization. There are many venues and instances of collaboration and clustering, as there are differentiated approaches and competition. Still, even under the rubric of a common sector, these activities are difficult to organize as associations, chambers, or unions – subsumed to a formalized set of business practices and representations.

This doesn't mean that rationalizations of various kinds aren't necessary. Legality, land use planning, and spatial regulation can be important instruments to sustain economic and social vitality – but usually only as a means of mediating among different ways of doing things, of drawing plausible lines of connection and mutual responsibility, rather than as the imposition of order and imagination. They can become a means for the diverse capacities and practices within districts to become more visible to each other – take each other into consideration and make productive use of their respective knowledge and potentials. These instruments then are an aid to the ways in which such urban districts have largely governed themselves in the past – i.e., through maintaining navigable thresholds and compelling economic motivations for different kinds of residents to be continuously involved in each others' lives.

The seemingly wide divergences between contemporary economic spaces – between traditional markets and hypermarkets, shopping malls and streets full of small shops and stalls – poses many challenges to how such lines of articulation and mutual implication can be drawn. Big projects cast long and ominous shadows over vast numbers of small enterprises and labor markets even as they promise to accelerate new job creation. Different temporalities are involved, and so the cost savings and efficiencies anticipated by expanded scale also tend to flatten the intricate gradations once available to residents in terms of how they balanced their management of shelter, education, mobility, proximity to work and social support, opportunistic chances, and household consumption; how they "paced" themselves over time and calculated what kind of time they had to work with.

These gradations didn't so much stand alone as class positions or characteristics of neighborhoods, but were more provisional markers that provided clues for how households, associations, and networks might collaborate, how they would use available resources of all kinds. So the challenge is how to redraw the lines of connection. Here the day-to-day struggles of municipal politics remain critical. This means finding fiscal formulas to give different economic scales and residential possibilities their own space; even if it centers on mandating cross-subsidies that tie the enhanced profitability of large-scale property development to the continuous renewal of local economies across the city which themselves fight for potentials of articulation in different versions of the "large scale."

References

Agamben, G. (1995) We refugees. *Symposium* 49: 114–19.

Cheah, P. (2003) *Spectral Nationality: Passages of Liberation from Kant to Postcolonial Literatures of Liberation*. New York: Columbia University Press.

Magnusson, W. (2006) The city of God and the global city. CTHEORY: Theory, Technology and Culture, 29. Available online at www.ctheory.net/articles.aspx?id=520 (accessed February 23, 2008).

Nancy, J.-L. (1991) *The Inoperative Community*. Ed. Peter Connor, trans. Peter Connor, Lisa Garbus, Michael Holland, and Simona Sawhne. Minneapolis: University of Minnesota Press.

Sassen, S. (2003) *Cities in a World Economy*. Thousand Oaks, CA: Pine Forge Press.

Chapter 32

The City, the Psyche, and the Visibility of Religious Spaces

Andrew Hill

For the three great monotheisms – Islam, Judaism, and Christianity – scopic desire is profoundly troubling. It figures as integral to fleshy wants, threatens to swerve into idolatry, and distracts the individual subject from the demands of the pious life and the worship of Allah-God-YHWH. If – as James Elkins elaborates in his fascinating *The Object Stares Back: On the Nature of Seeing* (1996) – vision and scopic desire are deeply disconcerting devices (morally and existentially), these three faiths appear all too aware of what is at stake here.

And yet while scopic desire may be acutely threatening to the three monotheisms, this should not be equated with their possessing a simple "injunction against the visual." Rather, the functioning and expression of scopic desire is something to be exploited and harnessed – as evinced in the histories of religious artistic practices and material culture. Indeed, if we turn to the built environment, the history of religious architecture – from Chartres, to Mecca, to the Temple on the Mount, to the Hagia Sophia (to confine ourselves just to the three monotheisms) – contains some of the most spectacular, most visually compelling buildings ever to have been built. And yet there is a paradox at play here – the first in a series of paradoxes this chapter will highlight that are foregrounded by thinking about the relationship of this architecture to questions of visuality. For, whilst it might be contended that buildings are "non-representational" – and as such present no challenge to God's status as the Creator, or threaten to descend into idolatry – it can equally be contended that they present acts of creation so dramatic and lasting that they might be said to offer the most serious challenge to this status.

Why though have religious buildings assumed these levels of spectacularity? Why this grandiloquence when there is nothing that predetermines that these structures should appear this way? Indeed, within the monotheisms there are branches that

The New Blackwell Companion to the City   Edited by Gary Bridge and Sophie Watson
© 2011 Blackwell Publishing Ltd

renounce the desire for spectacular, highly visible structures, as embodied in the simplicity and typically small scale of the Methodist chapel, or in the case of Islam, those contemporary critiques of the desire to construct spectacular, visually striking mosques, that emphasize that all that is required for a structure to act as a mosque is a *mihrab* indicating the direction of Mecca, and facilities for *wudu* (washing before prayer). See for example the debate around the 1989 Aga Khan Awards for architecture, in which the economist Mahdi Emandjara accused the Egyptian architect Abdel Wahed el-Wakil, "of trying to transplant Western and Judaeo-Christian ideas about 'sacred art' into Islam," arguing that "Islamic architecture was not sacred; the mosque was just a place for praying and teaching" (quoted in Eade (1996: 226).

It is the role played by the visibility of religious architecture that I want to explore in this chapter in regard to its significance for the terms in which this architecture functions as marker of the presence of the religious within the urban environment, and the way in which this intersects with questions of politics (in regard to the diverse manifestations the latter can take). For if politics is fundamentally about the exercise and functioning of power, in their attempts to assert their divine truth upon the world, religions are profoundly political entities.

A Lure, a Technique of Intimidation

My starting point is Lacan's analysis of visuality in *The Four Fundamental Concept of Psychoanalysis* ([1964] 1994). Here, Lacan discusses the way in which painting functions as a "trap for the gaze" (p. 89), constituting a lure which serves to attract, hold, and pacify the spectator's vision. I want to suggest that the spectacularity of religious architecture can be understood in similar terms, with the intention of functioning as a version of this trap for the gaze, that derives from the desire to instill in the spectator a sense of the power of religion and its ability to draw in and hold whoever casts their eyes upon it.

In this respect religious architecture accords with a second process Lacan outlines in his discussion of visuality. Namely, this architecture can be understood as functioning as "a technique of intimidation" ([1964] 1994: 100) that entails the "over-valuation that the subject always tries to attain in his appearance," a process evinced in animals in stages of sexual competition and combat in which the, usually male, animal may expand or swell up – namely create a spectacle at the level of the visual (that Lacan designates the Imaginary), intended to supersede or achieve an "over-valuation" of their presence at the Real (p. 107) (see Figure 32.1).

Such an analysis raises the questions though of religion's relationship to the Real – a question that is particularly apposite given that the power of religions is premised upon their seeking, as Jacques Alain Miller (2006) contends, to give meaning to that dimension of experience which Lacan designates the Real – the raw, unmediated dimensions of the world. Indeed, the very "belief" which monotheisms call for people to exercise in them, and the appeal of which constitutes the kernel of their power, emanates precisely from the accounts they offer of the Real and those dimensions of experience which seem otherwise incomprehensible (herein lies the opposition between religion and science and the knowledge generated by the latter).

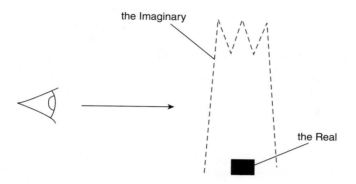

the Imaginary

the Real

Figure 32.1

In so doing, the spectacularity of religious buildings can be understood as functioning as a means of seeking to assert – over and above the claims they are able to make about the validity of belief in them – the power of religion. Rather than simply constituting a testament to the power of religious belief – as religious architecture has often been conceived as doing – the visibility of these structures points to an underlying insecurity on behalf of the religions (or, it might be contended, an insecurity amongst those who constructed them in the name of religion) – signifying an unease that the claims made about the power of religion are not enough by themselves, and that they require the techniques of intimidation manifest in the form of these buildings to buttress and support their assertions. This split function of religious architecture – as testifying at once to both the power and the insecurity of religion – is a theme that will be returned to a number of times in what follows.

If we are (still) struck with wonder now at these structures, we need to imagine the position they occupied in the eras of their construction and completion – both in terms of their visual presence in less developed urban environments (see Figure 32.2), but also in terms of the economic resources expended upon them, and their relationship to the relative wealth of the societies that produced them. (And in regard to this point it is worth thinking not only about the most spectacular examples of religious architecture, but the more typical too – as in the case of the vast number of village churches that litter the rural landscape of Europe – and the place they must have occupied in the visual economy of the societies that produced them.) Indeed, the visions of excess that religious architecture has presented us with accord with Bataille's analysis in *The Accursed Share* ([1949] 1991) of "general economy" and the excessive, unproductive, and non-recoverable dimensions economies possess that generate nothing in the way of wealth but find their outpouring in one of two forms – in luxury, the arts, the sumptuous, and the spectacular, or destructiveness and war. While subsequent centuries of building developments have served to diminish the prominence of these structures – an exaggerated example of this process is St Patrick's Cathedral (1858–78) in Manhattan, which at its completion dominated the surrounding area, but came rapidly to be dwarfed by the skyscrapers of midtown (see Figure 32.2) – this is still visible in examples such as Ely Cathedral (on which work began in 1083) as it rises above East Anglia's fenland flats.

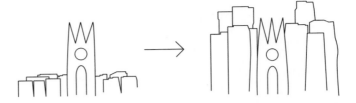

Figure 32.2

At the same time the spectacularity of these structures is bound up with their "permanence." Whilst the durability of buildings is in some sense a fantasy – witness the destruction of religious buildings to be discussed below – buildings are typically imagined as lasting if not permanent presences. Indeed, their ongoing presence functions as a key metonym of the continued salience of the religious – even at moments of the purported decline in religion's significance, or its marginalization within societies – as was claimed to be taking place in the west in the decades prior to the September 11 attacks. The attacks and the subsequent "war on terror" prompted a rapid reappraisal of these assertions.

The ongoing presence of religious architecture serves to emphasize how, whilst cities may alter and develop radically as the societies around them do, the presence of religion persists. In this respect the medieval churches of the City of London are particularly notable, as vestiges of the old city nestling amongst the changing architecture of one of late capitalism's nodal sites, oblivious to what is taking place around them.

Interiors and Exteriors

This question of permanence takes us beyond the visual, to the material status of these structures. The visual and the material are fundamentally bound together – as Michael Taussig (1993: 135) makes clear, there is no "pure" appearance, no possibility of a visible "entity without materiality." Whilst it is the materiality of religious buildings that provides the physical basis for the visibility of these structures, this is not a simple unilinear relationship, with a building's visibility able to contribute significantly to its durability and capacity to continue to exist in material form, through establishing it as a "landmark" that cannot be removed or altered without an outcry.

At the same time the relationship between the visible and the material lies at the heart of the relationship between the exterior and interior of buildings – a relationship that reveals much about the visibility of religious spaces in the urban environment.

While exteriors can constitute a lure or trap for the gaze, they also offer a means of restricting or shutting out the view of outsiders, whilst at the same time establishing a fixed boundary between the interior of buildings and the world outside. The latter function is fundamental to the conception of architecture Lacan presents in his seminar from 1959–60 *The Ethics of Psychoanalysis* (1992: 135–6). Here Lacan discusses how architecture is "organized around emptiness," presenting a means of enclosing, framing, and dividing up space, with space – as Lacan discusses elsewhere

(1962–3) – constituting a primary dimension of the Real. In so doing Lacan foregrounds the way in which religious architecture provides an exemplar of this enclosing function – the example Lacan cites as embodying "the sacred emptiness" of architecture, is St Mark's Cathedral in Venice. Lacan's analysis suggests an overlap between the Real of space as enclosed by architecture, and the encounter with the Real of religious belief. Indeed, following Lacan's analysis, religious buildings can be configured as presenting "holders" or "containers" of belief that serve to locate belief within a bounded space. This confluence of the Real of space and belief's encounter with the Real perhaps lies behind the awe an atheist (such as myself) can still experience inside religious buildings.

The interior of religious buildings serves to add to the sense in which these spaces constitute a dimension of the Real, with their scale contributing to the heightened experience of the Real of space, and the decoration and ordering of these interiors acting as a means of drawing the spectator back to the contemplation of the space. Strikingly different approaches to this latter aim are apparent in, for example, the voluptuous, "overwhelming" decor encountered in Catholic churches of the Baroque and the sense of massive "emptiness" achieved by the single, vast space of a structure like Istanbul's Suleiman mosque (1550–7). At the same time these interiors – which often provide little means for the spectator inside to see outside of them – serve to seal those inside them off from the outside world, creating a sense of their being contained inside the sacred space and emphasizing the exceptionalism of the space and its difference from the surrounding urban environment. Indeed, a function of stained glass can be said to be to allow light in whilst limiting the spectator's vision out and imbuing the outside with the quality of the sacred in the guise of visions of saints and disciples.

At the same time, as Catherine Belsey attests in her discussion of Lacan's conception of architecture, the "civilizing power" of architecture is found in the way in which it "affirms the power of culture to keep the Real in its place" (2002: 33). In regard to religious architecture, this architecture can be identified as fulfilling a dual role: at once providing a means of establishing the presence, in spatial terms, of the religious within the city, whilst at the same time serving to limit or contain religion's presence there. As such we might speculate that the efforts of monarchs to construct religious buildings are ambivalent, revealing a dual desire both to display their religiosity, and to seek to restrict the sacred to these spaces, so that the monarch's secular power remains supreme everywhere else. (Here I am reading the monarch's power as secular rather than divinely adorned, whatever the claims made about it being so.)

Indeed, it can be argued that a "truly" or utopian religious society would require no religious buildings, as the sacred is present everywhere. Indeed, such an outlook can be traced in the type of critiques of the significance of buildings in Islam pointed to above. In such terms the paradoxical status of religious buildings is evident again in their presenting spectacular markers of a failure of religions – in revealing the limitations of the presence of the religious in society.

Al Walid's Golden Spike, the "War on Terror"

The role of religious buildings as containers of belief leads us in the direction of religion's relationship to conflict and violence. James Hillman (2004: 178–217) identifies the ties between violence and belief as an integral feature of monotheism.

As Hillman asserts, monotheistic belief sanctions and encourages the recourse to violence in the assertion of the rightness of the one divine truth, which must not be allowed to be challenged or contested. (Other notable analyses have pointed to the broader relationship between violence and religion, including Freud ([1913] 2001, [1927] 1991) and Girard ([2005] 1972).

Carl Raschke (2004: 18–19) highlights the way in which this extends into the present, with monotheism having, "spawned sixteen year old suicide bombers and descendants of Holocaust survivors who would easily annihilate the 'others' who trace their holy lineage to Ishmael rather than Isaac." The reference to Ishmael and Isaac is significant. As Hillman (2004: 186) asserts, it is Abraham's/Ibrahim's willingness to sacrifice Isaac/Ishmael that at once underpins and binds together the three monotheisms in their relationship to violence – in the guise of an act that for each faith is taken as presenting an exemplar of true belief.

Viewed in such terms religious spaces, as spaces of belief, constitute metonymic sites of this violence. Indeed, in Judaism Abraham's act is identified with a specific site – the Foundation Stone, located in the Dome of the Rock, Jerusalem. In Islam this act is identified as taking place at an unspecified site. As the holiest site in Judaism and the third holiest in Islam, the Dome of the Rock has figured historically as one of the most contested religious sites in the world. This site of the binding of Isaac presents a paradigmatic site for the ethno-religious tensions that have historically marked not just Israel-Palestine, but the relationship between the monotheisms more broadly.

As markers of the presence of different ethno-religious groups, and testaments to the power of competing religions, religious buildings have repeatedly been caught up in ethno-religious conflicts. This has reached its most extreme form in the outright destruction of religious buildings, as embodied in the emblematic (and perhaps apocryphal) instance from 708 of Al Walid I's sublime acting out of the aggression the monotheisms have exhibited towards each other, in initiating the destruction of the church that stood on the site of what would become the Umayyad Mosque in Damascus, by driving a golden spike into its walls. A more recent instance of this urge to destroy – beyond the three monotheisms – is provided by the destruction of the Babri Mosque in Ayodhya by Hindu nationalists in 1992, who wanted to replace the mosque with a *mandir*, which led to riots across India.

And yet destruction is not the only means by which religious buildings have figured in ethno-religious conflicts. They may be taken over by opposing groups and continue to be used for religious purposes as in the case of the Hagia Sophia following the fall of Constantinople in 1453 to Sultan Mehmad II, and in the myriad instances from the Reconquista in which mosques were transformed into Christian places of worship, including, perhaps most notably, Cordoba's Mezquita (itself built on the site of a church, incorporated into the mosque). Where the destruction of another religion's buildings constitutes a means of denigrating an opposing faith, this process of appropriation can be read as a part tribute to the achievement of the religion responsible for initially constructing the building.

The position of religious architecture in conflict situations has acquired renewed significance in the wake of the September 11 attacks and the subsequent "war on terror" – a conflict imbued with religiosity on both sides (Hill 2009: 25, 39–40). In the west this has witnessed a renewal in the long-running association of Islam with violence, giving rise, as Gabriele Marranci (2004: 113) suggests, to the conception of mosques as, "the lions' den, in which bearded fanatical throat-cutters are meeting to organize the next plot against Western civilization." At the same time the period since the September 11 attacks has witnessed numerous attacks upon mosques in the west, and the spread of opposition to the construction of new mosques in western societies – most notably in western Europe, including both countries with longer established (including the UK and France) and newer (including Spain and Italy) Muslim populations. Alongside the broad opposition to the construction of new mosques, the particular visibility of minarets has served to generate considerable controversy about their construction, as evident most starkly in Switzerland, where in November 2009 a referendum resulted in the banning of new minarets.

The opposition to mosque building has found its most dramatic expression in response to plans for and the construction of large-scale, highly visible structures. In the opposition surrounding these developments much is typically made of the ties between Islam and violence and the role played by mosques in promoting hatred and violent activity. However, large-scale, highly visible buildings are typically far easier to monitor and police than the smaller-scale, "hidden" structures these buildings often replace. Instead, the hostility with which these developments have been met can be understood in terms of their constituting highly visible markers of the presence of Islam that feed attendant fears of Islamization, with, for those who oppose them, the very visibility of these structures assuming the guise of a technique of intimidation of the type outlined earlier in this chapter. Here the proposed mosque development at Abbey Mills in East London presents a particularly pertinent example. Opposition to the development – which would have constituted the UK's largest capacity religious building – highlighted the mosque's location close to the principal site of the London Olympics. As a widely circulated email opposing the development anxiously declared, such a location would render the mosque visible to "people flying in from all over the world for the 2012 Olympics," who will "see it as the biggest landmark in London" (Greater London Authority 2007).

The hostility displayed towards Muslim places of worship evident since the September 11 attacks reached an apogee of a kind in the call made by US Republican Congressman Tom Tancredo, in July 2005, that if Islamic terrorists launched a nuclear attack on the United States, the latter should retaliate by "bombing Mecca" (Fox News 2005). Whilst this may appear an isolated and far-fetched example, the very fact that such an assertion is made at all by a member of the then governing political party is symptomatic of the levels at which such ideas circulate and the simultaneous fear and aggression Islam motivates. While the relations between Islam and the west lie at the heart of the "war on terror," as this conflict has spread it has served to unlock other ethno-religious tensions that have in turn led to places of worship coming under attack. Since the invasion of Iraq in 2003, the country has witnessed numerous attacks upon religious sites by opposing Sunni and Shia groups, as in (perhaps most spectacularly) the destruction of the golden dome of the Shia Al Askari shrine in Samarra, as well as attacks upon the Christian minority in Iraq's places of worship.

In the light of these events it is worth asking the question, what if the September 11 attacks had been upon a religious building? How would this have shaped the response to the attacks? What if a future attack takes place upon St Peter's in Rome, or perhaps more appositely, a "mega-church" such as the (archetypal) Willow Creek Community Center in South Barrington, Illinois?

The Triumph of Nowhere

Religious spaces need to be understood then as fundamentally bound up with the history of religions as political entities and the violence underpinning their assertions of power and claims to legitimacy. I want to close this chapter, however, with an example of a profoundly unspectacular contemporary religious space that seemingly enacts a break with these historical associations – the multi-faith prayer rooms found in shopping malls, hospitals, and airports across the globe.

Visually, what is striking about these spaces is how unprominent, how banal and unnoticeable they typically are. Indeed, contained within the mega-structures they inhabit they often lack a visibly identifiable exterior at all. These spaces constitute a renunciation of the techniques of intimidation identified with the spectacularity of religious architecture in this chapter, and the assertions of power that underpin these techniques. In this way these spaces offer a conception of the religious that accords with the modernity of the structures they appear in, one in which the religious takes second place to, or is subsumed by, the practices of modernity these buildings serve: consumption, international travel, and (medical) science.

It can be argued that the very banality of the appearance of these prayer rooms constitutes a precondition for their use as multi-faith sites, in presenting a means by which these spaces negotiate the problem of identifying with one particular faith over another. And yet such a contention raises the question of what form a spectacular multi-faith building might take? This is a question that points to the absence of prominent multi-faith structures across the world, an absence that not only suggests a fundamental lack of desire for such buildings both historically and in the present, but raises doubts about whether such structures are even possible given the competing claims to supremacy and possession of the divine truth so integral to the monotheisms.

Indeed, in the absence of an identifiable historical relationship with the locations they inhabit – and hence of a specific relationship to any one religion – these prayer rooms can be said to present a version of the type of "non-places" Marc Auge (1995) in his oft-cited analysis identifies as so prevalent in late modernity. Auge's analysis in turn points to a fundamental incompatibility between the conception of space in late modernity – as empty and lacking historical resonance – and the sanctity of religious sites and the claims made for their privileged status.

Indeed, in the renunciation of their importance these prayer rooms appear to assert, these spaces present an antidote to the declarations of supremacy and rhetorics of fundamentalism that have dogged the history of religions, and assumed such prominence again in the wake of the September 11 attacks.

References

Auge, M. (1995) *Non-places: Introduction to an Anthropology of Supermodernity*. London: Verso.

Bataille, G. ([1949] 1991) *The Accursed Share*, vol. 1: *Consumption*. New York: Zone.

Belsey, C. (2002) Making space: perspective vision and the Lacanian Real. *Textual Practice* 16 (1): 31–55.

Eade, J. (1996) Nationalism, community and the Islamization of space in London. In *Making Muslim Space in North America and Europe*, ed. B. Metcalf. London: University of California Press, 217–33.

Elkins, J. (1996) *The Object Stares Back: On the Nature of Seeing*. London: Harvest.

Fox News (2005) Tancredo: If they nuke us bomb Mecca. 18 July. Available online at www.foxnews.com/story/0,2933,162795,00.html (accessed August 3, 2009).

Freud, S. ([1913] 2001) *Totem and taboo*. In *The Standard Edition of the Complete Psychological Works of Sigmund Freud*, vol. 13. London: Vintage, 1–162.

Freud, S. ([1927] 1991) *The future of an illusion*. In *The Penguin Freud Library*, vol. 12. London: Penguin, 183–241.

Girard, R. (2005) *Violence and the Sacred*. London: Continuum.

Greater London Authority (2007) Email whipping up communal hatred to influence online Evening Standard poll. Press release, April 4. Available online at http://legacy.london.gov.uk/view_press_release.jsp?releaseid=11471 (accessed July 17, 2009).

Hill, A. (2009) *Re-Imagining the War on Terror: Seeing, Waiting, Travelling*. Basingstoke: Palgrave Macmillan.

Hillman, J. A. (2004) *Terrible Love of War*. New York: Penguin.

Lacan, J. (1962–3) Seminar X: anxiety. Unpublished, translated by Cormac Gallagher.

Lacan, J. ([1964] 1994) *The Four Fundamental Concepts of Psychoanalysis: Seminar XI*. London: Penguin.

Lacan, J. (1992) *The Ethics of Psychoanalysis: Seminar VII*. London: Routledge.

Marranci, G. (2004) Multiculturalism, Islam and the clash of civilizations theory: rethinking Islamophobia. *Culture and Religion* 5 (1): 105–17.

Miller, J. A. (2006) The symptom, knowledge, meaning and the Real. The Symptom 7. Available online at www.lacan.com/symptom7_articles/miller.html (accessed July 17, 2009).

Raschke, C. (2004) Radical Islam and the specter of the desert: otherwise, the call of theory. *Journal for Cultural and Religious Theory* 5 (2): 15–19.

Taussig, M. (1993) *Mimesis and Alterity: A Particular History of the Senses*. London: Routledge.

Part IV City Publics and Cultures

The New Blackwell Companion to the City   Edited by Gary Bridge and Sophie Watson
© 2011 Blackwell Publishing Ltd

Chapter 33

Reflections on Publics and Cultures

Gary Bridge and Sophie Watson

The nature of public life and its particular blends of cultures, as ways of life and forms of aesthetic expression, are defining elements that differentiate cities and give each one its distinctive atmosphere. Yet publics and cultures, deeply entwined as we would argue they are, have complex, sometimes conflictual, relationships that define the politics of the urban (the topic of Part IV of this volume). Here we trace the complexities of those relationships between cultures and publics and the ways that they combine or draw together different spatial scales and temporal trajectories into the particularities of place. We suggest that publics (visible or invisible) are vital in reproducing cultures. We also explore how the notion of the public realm in the city, as one that transcends culture into forms of political will, now exceeds the static space of "properly" constituted debate. Rather, it involves the formation of multiple publics in an ongoing process of openings and closures of publicness that circulate and implicate subjectivities, bodies, and materials in various ways. This brings out several contemporary themes in understanding publics and cultures – public as process, as multiple and involving forms of connection and communication that do not just involve humans. These themes include understanding the importance of affect and emotion alongside, or opposed to, rationality in public discourse. This means paying attention to bodies as well as minds in the constitution of publics. It also suggests how the public is constituted through materials as well as social action and discourse, which leads to questions about the role of buildings and urban infrastructure and services as part of the public realm. The impact of globalization and a complex ensemble of influences and interests at different spatial scales and locations have opened up the question of the geography of contemporary publics which cities encapsulate through their diversity and concentrations of difference.

The New Blackwell Companion to the City Edited by Gary Bridge and Sophie Watson
© 2011 Blackwell Publishing Ltd

Public Reason in the City?

In the earliest systematic analysis of the city by the Chicago School of urban ethnography, in the context of mass immigration to Chicago in the early twentieth
century, the relationship between publics and cultures was drawn in a certain way.
The School was most concerned with ethnicity and culture and the way that different immigrant groups reacted or adapted to life in the growing metropolis. This
resulted, they argued, in a blend of traditional cultural attributes and adaptations
to the new environment in which different ways of life and social mores left the city
as a "mosaic of little worlds" (Park *et al.* 1925). But this linked to the School's less
discussed ideas on the public and rationality that Park argued was the ability to be
understood by a community. Thus urban publics as well as communities could be
represented by the urban mosaic. Building a wider public beyond these communities
could be seen as a major challenge given the social distance and social segregation
of one from another.

The experience of being in public amongst strangers in the city perpetuated urban
divisions through forms of blasé behavior and indifference. This is what Richard
Sennett explains as the "mask of rationality" that Georg Simmel (1950 [1903]) had
previously identified as mutual indifference between urban dwellers in public to
protect themselves from the unbearable nature of emotional contact and over-
stimulation in the city. These ideas of rationality in the city contrasted with arenas
of political philosophy that saw the very idea of a public as the capacity to stand
apart from one's interest and assumptions or social mores of the community. As
Sennett points out in his chapter, both Hannah Arendt (1958) and Jürgen Habermas
(1984) had an idea of rationality as the ability to transcend interests and partial
perspectives from community through rational discourse. Sennett puts forward the
alternative approach to urban publics (which his own work has done so much to
establish – Sennett 1974) which is that the importance of the public in the city is
performative rather than rational. This is the idea that differences can be overcome
in public discussion through style of public address and bodily behavior that cut
across or disrupt social and cultural divisions. That is why Sennett stresses the edges
or boundaries and the "uses of disorder" between communities as the crucial space
in which the public might be established (Sennett 1970). In a previously published
piece now extracted in the *Blackwell City Reader* (2nd edn. 2010) Sennett suggests
how the capacity to dramatize difference through encounter in the spaces of the city
often gets closed down by urban infrastructure and architecture that inserts boundaries rather than borders. He argues that buildings are over-determined in their
specifications and that architecture should plan for change and flexibility. Buildings
should, in this sense, be incomplete, and technologies (such as time-based traffic
restrictions) could help open up the spaces of encounter against the prevailing trend
of the privatization of space through car use and the loss of dedicated public space.

Seeking to overcome the divisions between ideas of the rational and the performative in the constitution of the public in the city, Gary Bridge (2005) has drawn
on the work of American pragmatist philosopher John Dewey (who once taught
Robert Park and greatly influenced the Chicago School) to suggest how performative
bodies and rational discourse are interleaved as forms of communication in a continuum of human intelligent response to the environment. Dewey saw body-minds,

emotion, and cognitive reflection as part of the same intelligent system of human organisms communicating to deal with the diverse impulses of their environment. These are forms of what Dewey called "transactions" involving mediatized communication as well as face-to-face encounter, transaction implying that the subjects and objects involved were not rounded out and complete but in process. This idea of the subject in process links to Sennett's argument for the public as process, and to a wider idea of subjectivity beyond the subject formed through public discourse (Habermas 1996; Benhabib 1996). The test of this public discourse is its ability to address the consequences of actions in which the participants in the discourse are not themselves directly affected (Dewey 1927). The point Bridge makes is that this form of qualified impartiality can come about from the sheer diversity and intensity of impulses (including affect, bodies, emotion, and "thinking") that urban life affords.

The diversity of impulses of the city includes its material and non-human environment. The vitality of the material environment is a theme that crosses this *Companion*. In relation to publics and cultures it involves how materials are cultural and act back on culture and how what Ash Amin calls the "situated surplus" of the material environment predisposes relations in public (Amin 2007, 2008; and see his Chapter 55 in this volume). This connects to the importance of the technological and the non-human in various "assemblies" that constitute publics outside the realm of professional politics (such as laboratories and supermarkets) or over interests in the environment (a river): how things can make publics (Latour and Weibel, 2005).

Figure 33.1 Temple of Heaven, Beijing. Photo S. Watson.

As overwhelmingly dense and intricate assemblages of actor networks, cities are concentrations of the possibilities of new publics and new spaces of the public, in this way (Farias and Bender 2009; Amin and Thrift 2002; and also Chapter 6 by Gandy and Chapter 8 by Jacobs and Cairns in this volume).

Spaces of Publicness

The significance of the intersection of the public realm (in terms of publicly provided services along with urban planning) and public space is brought out in Chapter 36 by Kurt Iveson and Ruth Fincher in which they use political philosopher Nancy Fraser's ideas of justice as a combination of redistribution and recognition to which they add "encounter" in public as a key ingredient. Iveson and Fincher pursue these ideas through the example of the public library as a space that is produced by a form of redistribution through tax-based public funding which in its micro-arrangements can facilitate forms of convivial encounter that might have more portent for political commitment to a public realm as part of the ongoing constitution of a wider public.

This constitution of the public through the intersection of infrastructure, public services, and spaces of publicness is subject to the constellation of forces of rapid urbanization in Chinese cities. In this context, discussions of the public and culture that have prevailed thus far, based on the examples of cities of the north, seem somewhat one-dimensional in comparison. The Chinese city, as Michael Keith points out in Chapter 35, is not one of transition from planning to markets but one of the construction of markets within different micro-political, legal, and cultural contexts within the same city (in this case Shanghai) that result in different experiences of housing and urban services and result in new and differentiated types and experiences of citizenship. Forms of citizenship have become a significant question for urban cultures and publics as part of the wider discussion over the scales of citizenship and effective representation and responsibility in the processes of globalization (Isin 2000) and the rise of post-Westphalian, postnational constellations (Habermas 1996; Fraser 2009). What Keith's chapter suggests is how forms of citizenship are being fashioned in the conditions of rapid urbanization within city neighborhoods as well as in nation states or beyond them.

This collision of culture (as ways of life and modes of aesthetic expression) and forms of urban governance has received a good deal of attention in the literature on cities. Certain theoretical perspectives on this issue are indebted to the work of the Frankfurt School and their ideas of the commodification of culture and the prominence of culture industries in late capitalism, captured so well originally by Benjamin (1999) in his analysis of the Paris arcades. There are different theoretical and political interpretations that all acknowledge the promotion of (certain) cultural aspects of each city in that image-making at an international level and as an ingredient in forms of urban regeneration within individual cities. Lily Kong, in Chapter 40, sums this up as the "governance of culture" and gives two examples of cultural projects (in Singapore and Hong Kong) that expose the mixed fortunes of the initiatives of the central and local state in urban cultures that in one case come up against class dynamics, as well as isolation between the cultural practitioners that question the veracity of cluster theories. Kong shows how cultural projects can be much more

contested than their promotion would suggest, but also how a contestation is important if cultural activities are not to be frozen or commodified in ways that more
resemble theme parks. The non-conforming and contestatory elements of cultural
production cannot be managed in any smooth way, or at least require different
forms of governance.

The locational characteristics of these schemes are not just of parochial interest.
As Setha Low argues in Chapter 41, "it is through embodied space that the global
is integrated into the spaces of everyday life where attachment, emotions, and morality come into play. Embodied spaces are sites of translocal and transnational space
and place as well as personal experience and perception." Low conveys how one
such context of embodied space, Moore Street Market in Brooklyn, assembles and
enacts the transnational connections through the sounds and smells of the market,
the different types of music playing on radios, the intimacies of body movements
of the Puerto Rican pensioners and Latino vendors. These embodied movements
are in part determined by class and ethnic dispositions and bodily deportments that
in some sense pre-orientate the possibilities of encounter in public. Yet these selfsame
encounters constantly renew and possibly alter the nature of those dispositions.

Bodies/Publics

The importance of body as a form of disposition or habitus (to use Pierre Bourdieu's
language) connects to other themes raised in this section on publics as well as issues
of affect from Part III. The first is the significance of the presentation of bodies
involving body shape, clothes, and styles of movement (what Erving Goffman 1971
called body gloss). Bourdieu (1984) has noted how different types of gait and inclination of the head can express class position. How bodies present certain social/
class dispositions is important in how people come into the co-present public and
react to others. So much is communicated before a word is spoken and this has
consequences for thinking about the public in terms of social interaction in the
"public" spaces of the city. Also important is body performance. Related to presentation, this is the way that bodies convey information and receive it from others.
Sennett has shown the importance of this for public, or theatrical, forms of communication that act as a reference point for wider forms of public discussion beyond
particular interests. But bodies can also be barriers to communication through the
pre-discussion communicative content of their presentation (in various racialized,
classed, or gendered ways). Yet it is possible that these same bodies can break down
divisions by forms of disarming conduct in spaces of the city that (unlike Sennett's
example) are more mundane and are not specifically the spaces for public discussion
or communication. Sophie Watson seeks to show this potential to "rub along" in
city spaces such as markets and public swimming pools and suggests its importance
for publics in her book *City Publics: The (Dis)Enchantments of Urban Encounters*
(Watson 2006).

A third strand in the relationship between bodies and publics is emotion. Bodies
are often conveyed as the repositories and most visible registers of emotion. Emotion
has always been set against reason. If discussion in public requires the use of reason
then emotions might be judged to have no place in publics. Simmel's "mask of
rationality" was a protection from the sheer emotional possibilities of encounter in

Figure 33.2   Beijing public park. Photo S. Watson.

the city. Sennett suggests how the emotions are important in body performance in the publics of the city, but he sets that against the idea of rationality and the public. Much of the burgeoning discussion of the importance of emotion in sociology and geography takes a similar route of separating out emotion from rationality: emotion as an alternative or something that gets out from under the dictates of rationality, especially as those might discipline and control through the body (as Foucault argued). Rossiter and Gibson's Chapter 43 ties together bodies, performance, and emotion in their example of the artists who lived behind a shop window during a Melbourne art festival and the way that this transposition of the public and the private disrupted normal communication and brought out qualities of tenderness and concern in the audience for the well being of the "art-stronauts" behind the plate glass window.

A fourth element of bodies and publics is the way that bodies translate affect. Again referring to Anderson's definition of affect (see Chapter 24, p. 278) as the transpersonal capacity a body has to be affected, affect is decidedly non-rational but might be important for considerations of the public. In Chapter 25, Pile, drawing on Freud's work from which the idea of affect emerges, discusses how cities are full of affect, of hauntings or feelings of unhomeliness or the uncanniness of being lost but finding yourself in the same place again and again. The mood of the city and the way the body senses that mood can be important in setting the tone for urban encounter and publics that may or may not result from that. Sense, as well as linguistic representation, might be significant for urban publics. Some of this is conveyed by Rob Stone in Chapter 39 on the aural environment of a city and how this registers mood and affect. Fascinatingly his discussion reverses this relationship when listening to student black-cab drivers learning "The Knowledge" (a mental map of London streets and the best routes through them). When they challenge each other to relate routes from various origins to destinations the sound of their voices and interruptions is an aural register of the intensity and complexity of the city itself.

What Stone's chapter also does, we argue, is to suggest the intimate interrelatedness of the talk of the city and its sensory environments such that the context and setting of talk become part of the constitution of the validity of that talk in public. This is part of a larger concern we suggest with the relationships between everyday practices, the active nature of urban environments and publicness and publicity. The city is comprised of body practices, materials, and discourse. Judith Walkowitz captures excellently these interrelations in Chapter 37. The history of the Soho district in London reveals what she suggests is the selective nature of the discourses of cosmopolitanism. On the one hand Soho and some of its buildings are treated as "a treasured relic of a sturdy national past" and at other times are scripted as though they are "full of deracinated and questionable objects, bodies and practices." Soho's mix of sex industry, international cuisine, entertainment venues, and architectural heritage is differently discoursed depending on the historical period of political motivation. The ambiguities of the interrelations of bodies, practices, buildings, and discourse make for an ambiguous cosmopolitanism.

This ambiguity of bodies, publicness, and urban spaces is also evident in Frank Mort's chapter on the twentieth-century post-Victorian social and sexual geography of Soho and neighboring areas of London (Chapter 38). Mort reveals how bodies, practices (especially sexual practices), and high politics and public life come together in postwar Soho, especially in the case of the Profumo affair in which the Tory Minister for War, John Profumo, was forced to resign from government in 1963 after admitting an affair with call girl, Christine Keeler, who was also having a sexual relationship with a Russian spy. This involves several forms of public – the public as political, as the revelation of private deeds into the public realm (as a scandal), and the role of publicity and the media in that process. Private and public worlds of Soho sexual practices and venues, Westminster and the gentlemen's clubs of Pall Mall and the then more marginal areas of Notting Hill (where a number of Keeler's Afro-Caribbean lovers lived) collide in ways that reveal the significance of the social and sexual geographies of the city. Mort's chapter is also suggestive of the temporal lags and resonances of the city in that an avowedly post-Victorian idea of modern London is constructed through postwar comprehensive urban planning and international media portrayals of swinging London, that at the same time clash with persistent Victorian gentlemanly practices and an assuredly Victorian moral discourse.

The practice, performance, and discourse of the public come together in John Paul Jones III's chapter on the street politics of Jackie Smith (Chapter 42). By occupying the sidewalk outside the Lorraine Motel in Memphis, where Martin Luther King was assassinated and which has now been converted into a civil rights museum, Jackie Smith provides passers-by with an alternative discourse on the museum. She argues that it should be a community resource and ongoing source of activism for the poor African American neighborhood in which it sits, rather than have these ideas fixed in the wider politics of the city and nation. Jones suggests how Jackie Smith and the museum present alternative discourses of the legacy of the civil rights movement which are held in productive tension by the street outside the museum that separates them. In terms of the arguments we pursue here we might say that they encompass competing rationalities. Jackie Smith's involve her body physically, occupying the street space over a protracted period of time in a way that acts instantaneously but also relates symbolically to the street marches and protests of the civil rights movement itself. The protest literature she hands out and the arguments she makes to passers-by who engage with her are in the tradition of linguistic action and rationality in the discussions of the public. The museum itself represents the institutionalization of the civil rights discourse into an educative, symbolic, and political function in the city and in the US more widely, but one that is subject to all the compromises that come with that institutionalization. These competing discourses can be seen as part of a wider public discourse over the proper legacy and ongoing project of the civil rights movement.

Publics in Process and Urban Democracy

The contrasts offered by the Jackie Smith case encapsulate wider questions in the formation of the public in terms of democratic practice more extensively both as an ethos of open debate and participation and also as the requirement of the will of the people to be realized effectively (Barnett 2003). Much of the discussion of the public and the city has been concerned with questions of access to and participation in the public. This has favored discussions of radical or agonistic politics (Mouffe 2005). On the other hand, discussions of urban politics and governance have been concerned more with institutional questions of how power gets exercised in the city and the different theoretical interpretations of that (Marxist, liberal, poststructuralist, pluralist). Part IV of this *Companion*, on city cultures and publics, and Part VI, on city politics and planning, represent the realities of this division but it is one that we would want to speak across by bringing these themes into engagement with each other in these reflections on both sections.

What we have sought to do in work elsewhere is to open up the terrain between for example, the performative elements of democratic inclusion (via bodies, emotions, and non-discursive action) with forms of rationality (Bridge 2005) and the idea of public space and the constitutive micro-politics of the public (Watson 2006). This relates to the capacity of cities both to close down and to open up the possibilities of the public. Much of the discussion has been concerned with how public space is being lost from cities through forms of privatization (Sorkin 1992; Mitchell 2003). This comes about through the replacement of city streets with shopping malls with their own private security forces and ultra surveillance systems as well as the creation of new city streets (in mega-developments) that are owned by private companies. These privately owned and regulated environments are where control is exercised over the forms of encounter and the diversity of people that might be significant for the formation of a public. They are often associated with urban redevelopments on "heritage" sites or waterfronts that turn urban spaces into theme parks with their glossy image and production of a singular (sellable) discourse that

Figure 33.3 Community garden, Kingston, Jamaica. Photo S. Watson.

overrides other urban histories and voices (Sorkin 1992; Zukin 2010). The commodification of creative energies and cultures in this way is, as we have seen, illustrated by Lily Kong's example of cultural projects in Hong Kong and Singapore. Even where the environments are not total in this sense, ordinances and bye-laws can prevent certain forms of behavior or engagement in public. Alongside this there are forms of privatization of public infrastructure (through private finance initiatives) to encourage private investment in public infrastructure. All of this can be seen as a growing marketization of the public and indicative of forms of neoliberal governance (discussed in Parts I and VI of this *Companion*).

Discussions of neoliberalism combined with Michel Foucault's ideas on the disciplinary society and forms of governmentality (for example, Foucault 1977) lead to the conclusions that the possibilities of the public are pre-empted by systems of power that produce certain forms of political subjectivity, rather than allow such subjectivities to flourish in new forms of political engagement and new publics. This is why ideas of insurgent publics and agonistic politics have had such influence over framings of democratic practice and politics: they are seen as being the only alternatives in a political and institutional system that is seen as being so compromised by the dictates of neoliberal capitalism. We argue that cities do display the inequalities and stark divisions of neoliberal urbanism but also that institutional forms and political subjectivities are not so wholly closed off or rounded out as might be assumed. By shifting our focus from singular notions of public space we might see how public baths, living rooms, internet-supported education (Watson 2006), and all the more mundane, everyday spaces of encounter (whether co-present or not) might be sites where new engagements are made, that even in these micro-spaces involving bodies and talk, construct new transnational links and political agendas, just as Setha Low suggests for Moore Street Market in Brooklyn. By shifting our focus from publics and markets and questioning the degree to which specific public or market activities are (or are not) open and democratic we might raise interesting questions about how complete, or structural, institutional forms might be, or whether institutions can be flexible and incomplete, in the way Sennett has argued the practice of architecture and the form of buildings should be (Sennett 2009) or as political institutions might be, as Roberto Unger has argued (Unger 2007). Keith's chapter suggests how citizenship can be an unstable category and institutional form, within the same city. Walkowitz's, Mort's, and Jones's chapters suggest how the same physical space of the city can be discoursed differently. Iveson and Fincher suggest how micro-space can permit new forms of encounter, Rossiter and Stone show how new forms of encounter can be artistically produced.

What we suggest from all these chapters is that the possibilities of the public come from aspects of city life that mean that subjectivities are in process and radically incomplete. The city has spaces (some of them unremarked and ostensibly unremarkable) and just as significantly we argue, rhythms, that open up political possibilities. This is evident in Rob Stone's chapter on the affect of acoustics and how aural rhythms might change the nature of encounter. There are retreats from this incompleteness in the form of indifference first suggested by Simmel, or in stereotyping, demonizing, and forms of stigmatization, but the city and its rhythms are always producing new spaces and ambiances and openings. This is the sense of the city that novelists, rather than social scientists, often pick out. Similar to the Moore Street Market is the Gowanus district of Brooklyn, the subject of several of Jonathan Lethem's novels (in particular *The Fortress of Solitude* [2004]) in which he recounts the social diversity and micro politics of the neighborhood of his youth. This part of Brooklyn has been gentrified in recent years and a good deal of that social diversity has been lost. Yet in an interview (Wood 2010) Lethem argues that possibilities are generated by the

> intangible essence of the place which hovers between my body and the buildings and the streets ... I guess I'd call myself a kind of addict of that process. Because it's the unfinished quality that's surprising. Being able to come back here and feel like it was still alive came from realizing that gentrification didn't mean that it was somehow sealed in amber now, but that frictions and juxtapositions are still being generated here.

The Brooklyn that he loves, Lethem says, is marked by "a definitive incompleteness" (Wood 2010). It is the definitive incompleteness of the city that gives new possibilities for the public.

References

Amin, A. (2007) Rethinking the urban social. *City* 11 (1): 100–14.
Amin, A. (2008) Collective culture and urban public space. *City* 2 (1): 5–24.

Amin, A., and Thrift, N. (2002) *Cities: Re-imagining the Urban*. Oxford: Polity Press.

Arendt, H. (1958) *The Human Condition*. Chicago: University of Chicago Press.

Barnett, C. (2003) *Culture and Democracy: Media, Space and Representation*. Edinburgh: Edinburgh University Press.

Benhabib, S. (1996) *Democracy and Difference*. Princeton, NJ: Princeton University Press.

Benjamin, W. (1999) *The Arcades Project*. Trans. Howard Eiland and Kevin McLaughlin. Cambridge, MA: Harvard University Press.

Bourdieu, P. (1984) *Distinction: The Social Critique of the Judgement of Taste*. London: Routledge and Kegan Paul.

Bridge, G. (2005) *Reason in the City of Difference: Pragmatism, Communicative Action and Contemporary Urbanism*. London: Routledge.

Dewey, J. (1927) *The Public and Its Problems*. New York: Henry Holt & Co.

Farias, I., and Bender, T. (eds.) (2009) *Urban Assemblages: How Actor–Network Theory Changes Urban Studies*. London: Routledge.

Foucault, M. (1977) *Discipline and Punish*. Trans. A. Sheridan. London: Allen Lane.

Fraser, N. (2009) *Scales of Justice: Reimagining Political Space in a Globalizing World*. New York: Columbia University Press.

Goffman, E. (1971) *Relations in Public: Microstudies of the Public Order*. New York: Basic Books.

Habermas, J. (1984) *Moral Consciousness and Communicative Action*. Cambridge, MA: MIT Press.

Habermas, J. (1996) *Between Facts and Norms*. Cambridge: Polity Press.

Isin, E. (2000) *Democracy, Citizenship and the Global City*. London: Routledge.

Latour, B. and Weibel, P. (eds.) (2005) *Making Things Public: Atmospheres of Democracy*. Cambridge, MA: MIT Press.

Lethem, J. (2004) *The Fortress of Solitude*. London: Vintage Books.

Mitchell, D. (2003) *The Right to the City: Social Justice and the Fight for Public Space*. New York: Guilford Press.

Mouffe, C. (2005) *On the Political*. London: Routledge.

Park, R. E., Burgess, E. W., McKenzie, R. D., and Wirth, L. (1925) *The City*. University of Chicago Studies in Urban Sociology. Chicago: University of Chicago Press.

Sennett, R. (1970) *The Uses of Disorder*. Harmondsworth: Penguin.

Sennett, R. (1974) *The Fall of Public Man*. New York: Norton.

Sennett, R. (2009) Quant: The Public Realm. Available online at www.richardsennett.com/site/SENN/Templates/General2.aspx?pageid=16 (accessed October 2, 2010).

Simmel, G. (1950 [1903]) The metropolis and mental life. In *The Sociology of Georg Simmel*, ed. and trans. K. Wolff. London: Free Press, 409–24.

Sorkin, M. (1992) *Variations on a Theme Park: The New American City and the End of Public Space*. New York: Hill and Wang.

Unger, R. (2007) *The Self Awakened: Pragmatism Unbound*. Cambridge, MA: Harvard University Press.

Watson, S. (2006) *City Publics: The (Dis)Enchantments of Urban Encounters*. London: Routledge.

Wood, G. (2010) The writer who lives on the streets of Brooklyn. *The Observer Review* (London) Jan. 10: 4–5.

Zukin, S. (2010) *Naked City: The Death and Life of Authentic Urban Places*. Oxford: Oxford University Press.

Chapter 34

Reflections on the Public Realm*

Richard Sennett

What I would like to lay out is several ways in which in the last century concepts of public life have changed and now need to change again, including my own concepts of the public realm. At the time of the French Revolution when political philosophers used the word public they tended to try to get hold of what it meant for a society to shift from court-based power to urban power, from court to city. And "le publique" would no longer be a public that referred to the workings of royal power but was instead something that was self-constituting. Probably the most significant moves made to understand that shift in political philosophy were made by Kant and Hegel in terms of equating the public with the impersonal. And the problematic, for Hegel in particular, was "how could an impersonal realm be self-constituting?"

Hegel's answer to this dominated most of nineteenth-century thinking about the public realm. He tried to give an account of the self-constituting impersonal public by making an equation between the impersonal and the rational. Basically what it meant was that the public realm was a realm of political action bordering on state power and the citizen's participation was in the realm of the state rather than civil society. That is, he made a distinction between the public and the civil, where civil society is the realm of partial interests. It is also the realm of face-to-face associations which, Hegel argued, are inherently irrational because they lack the properties of having a universalizable law. Civil society is one of fractures and partialities. And that equation of the impersonal to the rational in terms of laws which apply to everyone was not a useful way of trying to understand the public realm from the nineteenth century – it permeates Mill, it permeates Marx. It makes a separation between the public and civil society.

The New Blackwell Companion to the City   Edited by Gary Bridge and Sophie Watson
© 2011 Blackwell Publishing Ltd

Simmel's Mask of Rationality

In our century the story I want to begin to pick up is the way in which in thinking about the public realm this separation of the public and the civil was eroded. We owe this in particular to Simmel 90 years ago both in his *Philosophy of Money* and various Berlin lectures, and the one we all know (and his earliest), *The Metropolis and Mental Life*. What Simmel tried to do was to drag the issue of impersonal rationality back into civil society, and specifically to the city, as the fundamental institution of civil society. And you may remember the peculiar way this occurs. Looking around the Berlin of his time what Simmel observed in others, and certainly felt in himself, was the fact that this enormous, dense city provoked in people at the bottom level a sense of psychic over-stimulation. At the physical level people living in the city were threatened with a kind of chaos of multiple stimulations. Nobody, he said, could live as an animal in the city, meaning by that that no one could live by his or her senses in the city. In order to deal with this psychic over-stimulation, the intensity of urban life he observed in Berlin at that time, Simmel formulated the notion of the mask of rationality. That is, he redefined the issue of rationality not as a question of law, but as the kind of qualities of behavior which would lead people to be able to manage their physical sense impressions. What he means by "rational" is rather neutral exchanges between people in a state of equilibrium among strangers.

Simmel argued that the impulse to trade using money for instance was not at the heart of urban life – something that had to do with the accumulation of profit – but had to do with a way of balancing out relations between strangers in public so that they did not have to deal with each other face-to-face emotionally and so on. Money and all kinds of rational trades based on money stood for Simmel as a medium for ironing out this terrible chaos of stimulation in the city. He looked at money as a psychological transaction rather than as an economic one, which seems very bizarre to us now. But the notion more largely with Simmel is that when people are faced with the condition of density and diversity they have to take refuge from it, they cannot live in it. And they take refuge from it by forms of impersonal relations in which the players know the value of what they are doing (as it were), in which there is very little room for interpretation and in which the relations are equilibrated. So that people for instance will see on the street somebody who has had a heart attack and they will know to walk around that person rather than to try to ask the person what has happened. It is that kind of notion of indifference as a defense mechanism that Simmel argued had a rationality to it which is the rationality of equilibrating impersonal exchange.

On the positive side what Simmel did was to show that rationality was a social construct in everyday life and that that begins to distinguish a man of our time rather than a man of Hegel's time. That rationality is a reaction to something else – it is a social construction. It is not a property of state law – urban rationality as in Hegel – nor even, as in Weber, is rationality a property of civic action. It is something that is rooted in the inability of people to live in cities openly as animals. The negative of this Simmelian notion of the mask of rationality is that information is exchanged in this way but communication is lowered, particularly communication that transcends self-interest as well as communication of an emotional sort. The way in which you create an impersonal public realm is by lowering, as it were, the amount of information given. What this mask does is restrict the amount that people can know about you. It is reduced to information that can be codified and exchanged like money.

Importantly what is missing in this notion of the urban mask is that people never get beyond self-representations to each other. By that I mean that when Simmel looked on the streets of Berlin, what he saw his fellow urbanites doing in public was identifying themselves to others in such a way that the others would know that they were not going to be invaded. For example, people would never come up to a stranger and begin talking in a wild way or without introducing why they were saying what they were saying. The notion would be that in the public realm you would always identify yourself in such a way that the anxiety about the other was damped down by giving them clues about who you are. Probably the most brilliant of all Simmel's insights in this regard was his notion that this kind of city rationality would be more effective if it operated by the eye than by the mouth. That is, that this is a visual order rather than an oral one. You can create that sense of exchange on the street more easily if you do not speak but take clues from each other about how to look. So it is a privileging of the visual over the verbal in the name of this peculiar thing that he called urban rationality that I am calling the mask of rationality. And that is how, in my reading of Simmel, what we think of as the modern problem of public order, of the public realm, takes shape.

What Simmel gave to us as urbanists was a notion of impersonal life as being caught between the bodily experience which was unmanageable, and a kind of self-repression through rationality which gradually constricted the urban realm so that it was a realm of neutral information rather than full self-exposure which operated by more visual than verbal cues. To give you just a practical idea of what he meant by the notion of strangers meeting on the street: they know what to do to pass each other. They know how to manage their eyes so that they do not stare into each other. All of these are codes for managing the insanity of over-stimulation, an irrational that is their exchange relationship.

Getting Beyond the Mask of Rationality: Notions of the Public for Arendt and Habermas

So there, in my view, is where our problem in thinking about what is the public realm began – with this very particular theory. The problem in the twentieth century that theorists of the public realm have had to deal with is not the first or positive part of Simmel's achievement – that is the notion that rationality is an essential construct – but the second or more negative part of this theory, which is that rationality in this form is repressive. It is in general a problem that appears in Freud for instance, and it appears in all the permutations of negative dialectics that inform the Frankfurt School. For urbanists it has inspired two very different responses particularly after World War II. One of them is a trajectory that is embodied in the writings of Hannah Arendt and Habermas. The other is a trajectory that is much more social-scientific embodied in the writings of people like Erving Goffman, Clifford Geertz, and some of my own writing. I would like to give you a brief account of how each of these two schools have tried to deal with Simmel's negative – that is the problem of the public realm being a realm of repression.

Arendt interestingly was a very close reader of Simmel, and what she tried to argue was that the public realm need not fall into this kind of Simmelian self-repression. What it meant for Arendt is that there is a kind of space, a metaphoric space in society, which transcends self-interest. Arendt went back to some of the Hegelian notions about the refusal of civil society as the location for the public realm. Particularly she refused the notion that labor constitutes anything that we can call public life. The argument that is made in *The Human Condition* is that there has to be a space in society where people no longer have to speak in the name of their labor, most of which she found to be labor which was oppressed, where they were free from representing themselves as economic animals and where they were free from fear of speaking. When that could happen and people were freed from the fear of speaking, they entered the public realm. That is, she reversed the Simmelian notion of sight and speech and argued that the public realm was a realm in which we had to privilege speech over sight.

That is what this idealized agora and the idealization of Athens itself is about in Arendt. It is a space that is no longer a visual space but a place for speech. The notion of it is quite humane in a way, in that if what we have is spaces of self-representation à la Simmel, then of course in a capitalist society the people who have the most power will be the ones who colonize the public realm. It is an idealization of entering and leaving civil society in order to empower everybody with speech, and this is why Arendt insists that the public realm has to be founded above all on equal rights of discourse. It is also why the whole constitutionalism in Arendt is founded on the notion of free speech. That is the public realm.

In some ways the Habermasian picture of the public realm is richer than Arendt's because he does not want to particularly exclude questions of labor and economy from the public. The whole trajectory of Habermas's project is to try to find a way to bring that aspect of civil society back into the discussion of what is the public realm, and also to look at impersonality in a slightly different way from Arendt. For Arendt the impersonal meant, as it does to John Rawls, the fact that you cannot identify how rich somebody is and what they do for a living. In other words, there is a veil of ignorance which is cast over the conventional means of categorizing people in the public realm. For Habermas the impersonal means much more that the conditions of talking about interest, fully revealing oneself to other people, gradually mean that people begin talking about what interest is, rather than about defending their own interest. There is a kind of idealization in Habermas's work, that the more interactive one's discourse becomes the more the very process of speaking to others begins to work against the simple representation of self-interest. This is what the theory of communicative interaction is all about in regard to the public realm, which then begins to make people separate or objectify the nature of interests from their own interests. Thus public space for Habermas is a realm which forces people to discuss what the objects of interests are, rather than simply say, "I am your employer – do as I say." That is why he put so much emphasis on newspapers, for instance, and letters to the editor in newspapers – these kinds of things are terribly important to him. It is why when the internet first began Habermas was wildly excited about it because this looked to him like a public realm of the sort that fits this theory of communicative interaction. What he most liked about it was that people could talk to each other in different ways, like the possibility of altering their own identities, and so on. There was some capacity not simply to be classified by speech. But the assumption that is rather different from Arendt's is that the more diversity there is in the public realm, and the more there is a mixture of interests, the more objectifying the process of discourse is going to be. Thus it is a way of recovering the notion of rationality in another form, where in this case, diversity leads to rationality via its objectification of interests.

Now what I would say about both Hannah Arendt and Habermas is that when they use the term "public realm" what they are talking about is an activity, which is first, an activity that is clarified by communication with strangers, and second, it is purified of self-interest through the effort to speak and hear clearly. That may seem like a nice nostrum but what it means, and I think the edge that it has, is that it supposes that discourse among strangers is more complete and objective than discourse among intimates. That is, you do not think as rationally and you do not speak as rationally to those whom you love as to those who are strangers to you – that is the cutting edge of this. This is why Hannah Arendt rejected psychoanalysis and why she thought that politics and psychology could never be reconciled, because the moment that one speaks to a stranger with whom one has no affective relationship is the moment in which one can also leave oneself. So that it is a privileging of the public over the private That is how Simmel's negative is dealt with, by arguing that impersonality is a fuller system of meaning than private life. The public person is fuller, more rational, more complete, and more liberated than the person in private life.

Putting Aside the Mask of Rationality: Performativity in the Public Realm

The second response to Simmel – in thinking about the public realm – has a very old name to it; it could be called a school of *teatro mundi* or theater of the world and, as I said, it is represented variously in my writings and in those of Erving Goffman and Clifford Geertz. What it tries to do on the one hand is cut free discussions of public life from questions about rationality – to push this whole issue to the side. Instead it tries to focus on the problem of how strangers express themselves to each other, that is, how they communicate emotionally with people whom they do not know. It is the parallel problem between the way in which an actor or an actress comes on stage and moves strangers to believe he or she is about to die of sickness or is just about to murder his or her mother or whatever, and enacts the problems which people face in everyday life – of making themselves credible speakers to people they do not know. This is not about communicating information but about communicating something that, we might say, has a rhetorical force, but even more that there is a credible scene in which what is spoken is something that the other has to take in and respond to.

One way to think about this – and that is what Goffman's theory of role playing, and my, or Geertz's, notions of theatricality are about – is the idea that other people can act information so that it becomes believable, moving, and arousing to other people. To give you a specific example of this, you will remember something many people quote who have read Habermas's work on the public sphere – the discussion of newspapers and coffee houses. What he focuses on is the fact that in these newspapers which were read in coffee houses for the first time during the eighteenth century you have cheap mass-produced instruments of communication among strangers. A different way of looking at that as a public activity is the kind of thing I tried to do in *The Fall of Public Man*, which is to understand what happened when people discussed with each other what they read in the papers – how did they go about doing that? And what I found is that these places – these coffee houses – are the origins of our modern insurance companies. For example, Lloyds of London began as a coffee house and maybe it has stayed that way. For information to be freely exchanged and for people to believe what they heard, even though they might be of very different classes – you had a kind of theatrical activity – which was that people spoke in these coffee houses in imitation of what they heard in theaters, so that they had powers of eloquence which they literally borrowed from theatrical speech as a way to convince others that the information they were giving them was credible. It is a realm in which there is the privileging of speech over the eye – and of course where this is between somebody who is a tailor and somebody who might he a baronet looking at each other, then they obviously know that they are not in the same realm. But by using this highly artificial language that is similar, this highly theatrical language, they have a kind of common speech which creates an "as if" as though they are in the same realm – and this is literally a suspension of disbelief.

This kind of analysis of role playing in public is what this other tradition of public life is about. In terms of cities this kind of approach to the public domain is much more tied to the material conditions of daily life, which we can understand if we think back to Renaissance practitioners of *teatro mundi* like Inigo Jones, for instance, in London. Inigo Jones would try out architectural designs on stage that he thought about in terms of "is this a space in which people can move around believably, and does it work as an architectural space?" This long tradition of thinking about whether the kinds of spaces in which people are noticing others who are different and are reacting to them, which has strangers paying attention to them and so on, is part of what this tradition of *teatro mundi* has been about. So it is a much more visually oriented way of thinking about the public realm à la Habermas and Arendt.

In my own work I argue that the spaces which are most possessed of these powers – provoking role playing and this *teatro* of public life – are multifunctional rather than monofunctional – an argument I made in *The Uses of Disorder*. That is to say, that disorder in public is something that provokes the impulse, the freedom to be disorderly in public, and provokes more vivacity in public spaces. Thus the privatization of space occurs by making it monofunctional. What I have argued is that there is a very complex relation between convention and disorder of public space and that the more that that play between the disorder of public spaces and conventional behavior can be exploited and encouraged, the more public life is enhanced.

The second thing I would say about this tradition of *teatro mundi* is that by design it is more attuned to engage with the question of difference and make the question of difference concrete – certainly more than Arendt, and I also think, Habermas have done. In Arendt, the whole notion of the public realm is one that transcends difference by design. That is to say when you enter into the public, you take off the particularities of being black, a woman, or poor and you enter into the community of equalization of speech in which self-reference is seen as a violation of the norms of politics. Habermas's notion is that with fuller communicative interaction the differences do not go away, but they do not matter to people, so it does not have that Arendtian fiction of the agora. For Habermas, if you have a vivid public realm, eventually if there is enough interaction, a poor black will feel himself/ herself entitled to speak openly to a rich white. So for Habermas the whole politics of the public realm is to make that kind of entitlement, that kind of growing together so that one thinks about what race is or class is without self-reference, occur more and more.

By contrast other writers, and in this regard I think of Erving Goffman and Clifford Geertz most, tried to emphasize the ways in which the conventions of behavior with others in public depend on people dealing with and acknowledging the differences of others in terms of age, race, class, sexual preference, and so on. In this case, the notion is that people are self-dramatizing with respect to their differences in the public realm. That is what they mean by public behavior – it is a kind of self-dramatization which they think is good.

I have taken a rather different tack on this question of difference in public life. What I have been interested in with regard to this question of difference is how people portray themselves to others not, as it were, in the centers of places, but at the edges. This is why my analysis is focused not on the hub of communities, on central business districts or places like Trafalgar Square, but on all those seemingly dead edges where one community, one difference, meets another. And as a practicing urbanist what I try to do is bring those spaces where the differences touch alive. That is, for me, if you take the dramatization of difference seriously, the place where it really matters – not where you meet a whole lot of people like yourself but where you are reluctant to meet those who are *unlike* you. The deficit about this *teatro mundi* is that it has contained within it nevertheless a certain kind of political indifference, for example as in the work of Albert Speer. What Goffman, Geertz, and I have failed to address in our work is what a liberated politics is – what is a liberating theatricality in the city and what is a repressive one?

I lay all this out to say that this, I think, represents so far how a modern conception can resume a public realm that is composed of people looking on each other, who are strangers and who are impersonal. What is interesting is the fact that the seemingly self-repressive qualities of the public realm that Simmel perceived, and that Freud perceived in another way, (or that Horkheimer and Adorno perceived after World War II) took two very different paths. One of them, focused on *the public realm as an action* (the Arendtian, Habermasian approach), tended to try and look to recover once again the Hegelian notion (but in very different ways) that the public and civil society were at least separable. And the other – the *teatro mundi* way of looking at the public realm – focused on civil society to be sure, but tried to throw out the whole preoccupation with rationality and impersonality which marked most of the century, and tried to discover a kind of self-dramatization as a principle of creating a public life. My own approach was to focus on territory – on the issue of boundaries rather than centers and to focus on the peculiar balance between theatricality and disorder in public space itself.

Now we have to take a different tack I think because a century after Simmel two rather different questions about conceiving the public realm have come into being.

As discussed earlier, for Simmel the problem was psychic over-stimulation, yet it would be very difficult to argue that most modern cities are psychically over-stim-ulating places. In contrast the problem is precisely creating the stimulus of being in the public. And it seems to me that this is going to require a whole different set of thoughts about what the logic is of getting people together who are stimulated by the presence of others, because of the very practical things like the fact that auto-mobiles are probably the ultimate piece of technology for isolating people from the stimulation of difference – you die if you get too stimulated by it. Similarly the cities we know now tend to be much more outward than inward – differences tend to separate and they are not edges between communities which can be made interactive because there is too much space between them.

A whole range of questions arise as to how to create a public realm in which people will tolerate being stimulated by the other, and this is not just a matter of capitalist domination. The destimulation of the city is something that has also tapped that Simmelian fear of being overwhelmed by difference and there is a con-fluence of causes between power and desire. So that issue of stimulation, rather than over-stimulation, needs to be faced. And the other issue for a new public realm does not concern politics alone, as much as political economy, and the need to focus not on global markets but on the transformation of bureaucracy that has occurred in the last 20 years – both in work and the welfare state, because that transformation of bureaucracy is intensely privatizing and individualizing. The body politic has been rent asunder by the way in which people work, by the relationship to their needs and political economy. There is a long discussion we could have about what these changes in the bureaucracy of work and the changing bureaucracy of the welfare state mean, but the essential point is that the effect on individuals is intensely privatizing. So in thinking about a strong public realm the question is to think about how to countervail this, and the question for us as urbanists is, can powers of place of the public do that work? That is, is place a really meaningful element in countervailing the individualizing effects of these great changes in the work and welfare bureaucracies? For me the issue that now faces us is how this impersonal realm of the public can be conceived in collective terms rather than in terms of issues of rationality. That is ultimately a more political project and also a more open-ended one.

This is a summary of the main currents in thinking about public life in this and the last century. Maybe now the things that have occupied me and earlier genera-tions have come to an end and something else more addressed to the conditions of contemporary capitalism has to grow up as a sense of what public life is.

Note

*   This lecture was delivered as a plenary session of the "Cities at the Millennium" confer-ence in London at RIBA, December 1998.

Chapter 35

City-zenship in Contemporary China: Shanghai, Capital of the Twenty-First Century?

Michael Keith

If for Walter Benjamin Paris was the capital of the nineteenth century and for some eminent geographers and urbanists Los Angeles the iconic city of the late twentieth then is Shanghai to capture the exemplary urbanism of the twenty-first century? You might think so from the manner in which the Chinese metropolis of some 20 million people, host of the 2010 World Expo, has been the focus of representational hype in recent years in writing, film, and art.[1] In a growing stream of serious journalism and academic description, Chinese urbanism in general and the experience of Shanghai in particular, are held up to represent the future of the city. Indeed just after the globe went urban, with just over half the world's population now living in cities, a flurry of interest has focused on the dynamism of contemporary Chinese life.[2] Perhaps then, if the future of the world rests on the shoulders of China's 1.3 billion people then the fate of Shanghai assumes even greater symbolic weight.

In trying to represent a "generic urbanism" of the mid-twenty-first century the director Michael Winterbottom, in his critically acclaimed film *Code 46*, draws on photographic fragments of Kuala Lumpur, Shanghai, Hong Kong, and India and "joined up bits of those cultures into the culture" of the governance DNA of the city.[3] But it is the glossy exteriors of the new architecture of Shanghai that are used to convey a sense of the future. In the film the principal protagonist (played by Tim Robbins) flies into Shanghai across the Dubai desert. In Winterbottom's dystopian future the city exemplifies the metropolitan heart of the system; citizens are allowed inside, denizens remain at the gates, albeit that the boundaries of this Shanghai are marked by the twenty-first-century turnpikes of the 14-lane highway that separates the old city from the new airport.

The narrative of the film plays both to a sense of science fiction futures and the traditional genre of the *Bildungsroman* in which the characters arrive in the city

The New Blackwell Companion to the City   Edited by Gary Bridge and Sophie Watson
© 2011 Blackwell Publishing Ltd

and discover themselves as they explore the metropolis (see Donald 2005). A fragile sense of becoming maps the cartography of the persona and the spiritual journey of the protagonists. In Goethe and in Dickens this sense of discovery links an understanding of being modern to a sense of being metropolitan as the strangeness of the city is rationalized, mapped, and re-imagined. A similar sense of bewildering excess greets every first-time arrival in Shanghai. It is an excess that is captured by both the scale of the city and by the immersion in new sights, sounds, smells, words, and textures. In an obvious way this newness questions what it means to live in the city in ways that recall other historical moments when the shock of the new was identified with particular forms of metropolitan experience. Famously, at the turn of the twentieth century, Georg Simmel identified modernity with the *sensorium* of the city (Simmel 1997 [1923]). The innocent arriving from the countryside in *fin de siècle* Berlin, Vienna, Paris, or London was confronted by the technologies of the industrial revolution that challenged the sense of self as well as any understanding of the spaces and society in which they had arrived. The concatenation of print, lights, sound, and crowds bombarded the senses of the city dweller and a notion of urbanism arose partially through the editing down of this overload into a comprehensible narrative of city life.

Simmel's modernity challenged what it meant to be human and what it meant to be urban. Similarly, today's travelers arriving in Shanghai can easily believe that they have flown into the future. The architecture of the international airport in the new Pudong is designed by Paul Andreu. He is the airport builder of the present, whose architecture sits at the edge of twenty-first-century engineering skills (or just beyond in the case of the Charles de Gaulle terminal 2 in Paris that collapsed in 2004 killing four people after innovation exceeded technological competence). From the airport you can reach the city center in 15 minutes on the Maglev (magnetic levitation) connection that travels at 431 kilometers per hour and makes the Japanese bullet train look tardy and transforms the surrounding Pudong landscape into a city panorama on fast forward.

But equally we might ask what it means to know both the cities of China in particular and the megacities of the twenty-first century in general. The ethnographic certainties of area studies specialists and the privileging of the ethnographic experience of particular cities sit uneasily alongside the pace of change that confronts the indigenous or vernacular informant. Just as the modern city was defined by its facility for disorientation, the twenty-first-century megacity challenges both our understanding of what it means to be metropolitan and the very basis of urban knowledge. The city changes so fast it confounds apprehension, as my *laoshi* (teacher) in Beijing commented in an interview: the opening of a series of new metro lines in Beijing immediately before the 2008 Olympic Games "reinvented the city," made it knowable through an alternative technology of movement and a different calculus of time and mobility.

As a researcher arriving in the autumn of 2006 on the first of 14 research field visits, to me the surface veneer of the city appeared extraordinary; a sensory overload that at times feels like a twenty-first-century version of Simmel's urbanism a hundred years earlier. In Winterbottom's film, on arrival Robbins's character is transported to Jin Mao tower, where he checks in at the Grand Hyatt, an hotel which starts 50 stories up in the air and goes up to a rooftop bar 50 stories higher again. *Wallpaper* magazine describes the building as a cross between a "Buddhist pagoda and a Gotham style skyscraper" (*Wallpaper* 2006: 20) and its beautifully vertiginous atrium creates an effect (though not a design replica) similar to Frank Lloyd Wright's New York Guggenheim, only this time the spiral takes the eye down all 100 floors. The attempt to mimic a pagoda structure is ironic: as Leo Ou-fan Lee has commented (2009) the pagoda itself was designed to atone for sins; the scale of Jin Mao Tower implies an extraordinary penance. And so the combination of the present-day practices of architectural corporations and the city imaginary of transnational futures comes together as Winterbottom's camera flits across the city's new financial district of Pudong and the narrative develops as Robbins's protagonist tries to unpick the DNA of the city that joins its stunning architectural artifacts to its social fabric (a hybrid language of *papelles*, *khidafiz*, and *cerveza*) and political economy (including a migrant cosmopolitanism).

The film's beauty is not quite matched by its unfulfilled narrative promise. But it does perversely provide a powerful sense of what it means to arrive in today's Shanghai and an intimation of what some might see as the tensions implicit in making sense of the city and making a space to live in its urbanism; tensions that foreground forms of being and modes of becoming, strangeness and familiarity, ethnographic proximity and appropriate critical distance. Should we call this Chinese urbanism, megacity urbanism or merely the twenty-first century's expression of global capitalism? How does its future inhabit our present? Methodologically, one of the many challenges of contemporary urban sociology is to find a medium that can do justice to the novelty and dynamism of China's change whilst situating it within a firmly global context; a sense that the received wisdom of narratives of economy, globalization, and urbanism might learn from the Chinese experience without turning its extraordinary form into something either naively celebratory or complacently dystopian.

Our research project considered the dynamics of an economic sociology in contemporary China. It aspired to an approach that is largely dialogical, developed jointly with colleagues in China's academy and drawing on the work of researchers from universities in London and China.[4] We have collaborated with Wang Xiaoming at Shanghai University, a specialist in cultural studies and analysis of city change. Xiaoming is part of a collective of individuals behind the Chinese journal *Dushu* (*Writings*) that has received increasing attention in the west (Mishra 2006). Early research visits to China to set up the project in late 2006/early 2007 involved not only the standard bibliographic research of urban studies writing in English but also interviews with Xiaoming and some of his colleagues who edit or write for the paper, such as Wang Hui[5] and Cui Zhiyuan. Collectively, they and the school of writers associated with them have become known in China as the new left, a term initially used against them pejoratively but that they have in turn embraced. They are known for their critique of the marketization process in China, and particularly for their analysis of the genealogical development of the interplay of economy and culture in approaches that are openly interdisciplinary in their nature. In part their work might be seen as decoupling modernity from neoliberalism. Their scholarship involves an embrace of novelty, change, and the global circulation of ideas and ethics. It involves equally a trenchant analysis of the balance sheet of recent changes; recognizing both the outstanding pace of economic growth and the release from poverty of over 400 million people in the last decade and the promotion of extremes of inequality that confront the Shanghai visitor as colonial echoes resonate along the riverfront architecture of Shanghai's Bund, where the Hong Kong and Shanghai Bank's first headquarters and a replica of Big Ben remind the viewer of another past. And for the purposes of this chapter one of the tensions identified in writing by some of these individuals involved a form of theorizing that embraced both the path dependencies of city change in China and the particularities of new and rapidly changing urban cultures. In particular the study of the cultures of urbanism is qualified by an ability to know the rapidly evolving megacity of 10–20 million people and the languages of rights and belonging that are qualified by reinstating the centrality of local governmentalities of property relations at the heart of a model of urban citizenship.

In this complex tapestry of past and present the need to find a language that does justice to the city's economic, social, and political landscape is challenging. In part, Wang Xiaoming's work focuses on the power of description and the moral imperative of portraying the nature of contemporary culture before subjecting it to political or ethical analysis and ethical prediction. In a sense he asks what it means to be modern in today's China. In the 1970s Chen Jingrun, a Chinese mathematician, was the first to generate an arithmetic proof of Golbach's Conjecture, the proposition dating from the eighteenth-century work of Christian Golbach, a German schoolteacher, that every even number greater than two is the sum of two primes. Chen Jingrun's work won international recognition. As a symbol of the "modern" in the China of the 1980s Chen Jingrun was acclaimed nationally. Xiaoming asks whether the same would be true in the twenty-first century, if knowledge so free of commodity value sits easily with more materialistic definitions of the modern in twenty-first-century China (Wang Xiaoming 2003).

A cultural study of the city juxtaposes the myths of the modern in today's urban China with its more prosaic realities. The modern in Shanghai is commonly taken to be exemplified by the members of the middle class; the new rich who garner air space and press coverage. Yet, as Xiaoming points out, the city is shaped as much by more numerous but less visible forces. To take just one example, in the case of more than two million migrant workers from the countryside who form the bulk of the unskilled workforce, and do not always have citizenship rights in the city, "plannners of Shanghai's municipal development often ignore them as if they did not exist" (Wang Xiaoming 2003: 277). And yet the demands of more than two million households shape the markets of street vendors, the global networks of migrant labor, the consumption patterns in video and pirated DVD markets, and the shape of the unregulated city. Only an empirical engagement with this more penumbral world can generate an understanding of how it is, let alone what it will become.

Inspired by the first generation of Birmingham's school of cultural studies, Xiao ming contextualizes the ability of the intellectual to "intervene" in the shaping of the new world but valorizes their power to describe it. This power of description is matched by a moral imperative that outlines the thinking that narrates the new Chinese realities through a veil of ideological distortion that masks some of the less nuanced realizations of modernization and marketization in today's China. The modern in China is consequently contradictory and complex in nature, not simply a linear move from one historical moment to the next and certainly not a Whiggish progress from communism to capitalism. Xiaoming speaks with an ambivalence that senses that the processes of modernization bring together all the best and worst about Shanghai's past with all that is best and worst in the cultural traffic of globalization. In his writing there is a sense of the contradictory and nuanced nature of modernization that explicitly rejects simplistic dichotomies of traditional/modern, closed/open, conservative/reformer, market/planned, socialism/capitalism, communist/anticommunist:

> [A]s long as openness is not viewed as a paradise, and modernization is seen as a necessary process that brings both gains and losses, we can say that China is not only being modernized but is already half way down the road of globalization. But it is difficult to avoid thinking here of Krylov's fable of the cart pulled simultaneously in three different directions by a swan, a pike and a crayfish. (Wang Xiaoming 2003: 286)

The academic imperative to describe reinforces a sense of a cultural studies obligation to analyze the mediating stories that narrate and distort realities of the nature of Chinese modernization, drawing on notions of ideology developed from Marcuse (personal interview with Wang Xiaoming, January 2007). It implies a more ambiguous take on China's new urbanism and a resolutely synthetic engagement with both the unseen city and the protagonists who theorize the newly regenerated metropolis. And in some similar ways, for Cui and his contemporaries a theory of marketization demands a complementary theory of rights and of political formation in the structuring of property markets in particular (Cui forthcoming). Markets are consequently considered in terms of the interplay between state and market regulation. Cui returns to Enlightenment traditions of liberal thought that interrogate the central role of property rights in structuring the liberal subject and the work of J.-P. Proudhon, F. Lassalle, and J. S. Mill that addresses this problematic in another age. In a "back to the future" synthesis of philosophical scholarship and a political history of the present, it is Cui's fascination with political economies of the Enlightenment that leads him to re-examine the thinking that confronted the greed of Europe's industrialization. He has a particular concern with the writing of Henry George (the nineteenth-century American political economist) whose work on land tax focused on the social responsibility to develop land for its use value rather than acquire it and bank it for its accumulation value.

China's moves towards a new economy are taking place in the shadow of the catastrophic excesses of Russian *perestroika* and east European kleptocratic privatization. What became known as the "Washington Consensus" that normalized "neoliberal orthodoxies" of economic policy in the late twentieth century took the market as a natural phenomenon. Cui's work is important in part for the ways in which he attempts both a diagnostic understanding of how new markets, and property markets in particular, are being constructed and also because of his fascination with a return to eighteenth- and nineteenth-century political economy to think how markets might be made otherwise. So a description of the evolving city in China involves interrogating and describing the ways in which new markets are socially and politically constructed. This is not just an ahistorical exercise that normalizes the processes of market completion or the teleological transition from socialism to market economy. The market is historically contingent, institutionally uneven, and framed by global power and differential regimes of local regulation.

In the looking-glass world of today's China, the move towards marketization represents in part a move away from monopoly ownership of land by the state to variations on contingently commodified land rights (Haila 2007; Wu 2002). Buying property in China for development normally involves the purchase not of land per se but of the right to use the land (either commercially or residentially) for a fixed period of time (most commonly for 50 or 70 years respectively). For Cui, an understanding of the development of markets has to begin from an understanding of their ethical, legal, and philosophical construction, a deconstruction that prefigures an engagement with the forms of new market that are being developed in today's China (personal interviews with Cui Zhiyuan, September 2006, December 2006). Cui's work consequently demonstrates the manner in which the past might inhabit the present slightly differently in thinking about the evolving economies of tomorrow's cities, fusing the cultural forms of China and the west in creating something novel, itself a form of cultural as well as mercantile exchange. Consequently it speaks to debates that consider the importance of property rights as at times pluralized, ambiguous, or fuzzy (Ho 2001).

There have been valuable attempts to capture the breadth of studies of the city in China (e.g., Logan 2002; Ma 2006; Solinger and Chan 2002; Shenjing *et al.* 2006; Wu 2006) or summarize the particular trends in local urban change. But at times such literature – when written by scholars from China or from the west – places the city in China in a taxonomy of metropolitan change across the world, a metropolis driven by analytical lenses shaped by concepts of globalization or gated communities or consumption or gentrification. Alternatively some attempt to consider the city in China as a moment in a teleological transition towards capitalism (Walker and Buck 2007). Such work may have considerable value. But what if we try to understand how the particular trajectories of China's cities speak to the condition of the twenty-first century; how might an urban scholarship of the west learn from China rather than categorize, appropriate, and narrate China's cities through the narratives of western urban studies?

In this context it might be worth considering how an understanding of freedom is recast at the interface of urbanism, citizenship, and property rights in ways that bring together realizations of modernity in the city (Hsing 2010). On the one hand we have the tradition of the arrival in the city, its sensorial overload, its multi-mediated empirical excess and we might ask how Simmel would respond to the phenomenal forms of megacities in general and urban China in particular. In this tradition it is the very "unknowability" of the city that is at the heart of its attraction; its social and economic dynamism is causally linked to the technological limits of attempts to govern, rationalize, and control its form. This is the city of Winterbottom's rather than Koolhaas's generic urbanism, it is also the invisible city of migrant labor and street-life China (Dutton 1999).

On the other hand, there are the particular realizations of citizenship rights that in China owe their lineage to the attempts in the 1950s to regulate excessive flows of people to the metropolis and the focus on rural development that characterized Mao's socialism and were structured by the *hukou* system. From the 1950s the *hukou*, effectively a rights-bearing residential registration certificate in a particular city, comes to define a new regime of urban citizenship (Wing Chan and Li Zhang 1999; Wu and Treiman 2004). With the opening up and reform of China the ability to dwell in the city is restructured by the reform of the old *danwei* units (that controlled workplace and homeplace simultaneously) into unevenly structured markets in commodity housing and real estate. As *danwei* are streamlined into profit- and loss-making enterprises, their previous roles of providing social welfare are abandoned. Local state organizations have started to take on some of these welfare responsibilities. The extent to which this is a change from the past will be partly determined by the salience of the various urban *danwei* systems. The synthesis of residence, community governance, (reformed) *hukou* system, and nascent commodity housing generates an assemblage of welfare, citizenship rights, governmentality, and institutionally contingent market forms of housing in the cities of today's China (Krug and Hendrischke 2008). So the emergent megacity of China needs to be understood as simultaneously both material and cultural, a synthesis of regimes of power and government, economy and society, market and hierarchy. Unevenly distributed forms of market institutionalization mesh with a developing form of political reform, an emergent local state capitalism. This speaks to some very old traditions of urban thought. Heidegger's speculation about the possibility of dwelling in the city is recast as simultaneously about both the political regulation of the rights of the city and the creative attempts to make a home, to sculpt a place to live in the city out of the old *danwei* that are commoditized, the new residential districts or *xiao qu* that are simultaneously a site of community governance (Bray 2005, 2006), or the villages in the city (*chenzhongcun*) where rural property rights of ownership in tracts of land encircled by metropolitan change allow family networks to build some of the most intensive and residentially dense sites of development, hosting migrant workers in extraordinary densities in the handshake apartments (*woshou fang*) of Shenzhen, Beijing, Guangzhou, and Shanghai.

This second tradition speaks to the forms of emergent urbanism in cities across the globe but it also makes us think how China's new urbanism takes us back to thinking about dwelling, freedom, and culture as simultaneously about objects and material cultures, the liquid cultural forms of the city and the bricks and mortar alongside one another, not divided into separate disciplines of urban culture and housing studies. But these particular trajectories of a specifically twenty-first-century urban China cannot exoticize its subject matter; alongside the path from socialism towards the socialist market economy there is also a prehistory of vernacular modernities that infest China's cities. Shanghai itself is a product of the contact zones of the colonial and the postcolonial city. In a beautifully written book Leo Ou-fan Lee (1999) has described how in the period from 1930 to 1945 the encounter between Shanghai, modernity, and the colonial present mapped the city through a cultural traffic that played back and forth between what it meant to be modern and what it meant to be Chinese. A cartography of cinemas, theaters, clubs, and bars generated a cultural traffic between west and east, past, present, and future that speaks to the present in ways that might urge us to think carefully about descriptions of the cultural formation of today's megacity.

So one message to emerge from some of the writing by Chinese scholars must be about the manner in which an urban sense of "learning from China" involves a notion of this traffic; that shapes the landscapes of twenty-first-century Shanghai

and China's new economy but not as a teleological endpoint of capitalist development nor simply as a new territorialization of the western market. A history of
Shanghai's present involves an understanding of governance forms at a distance and
up close; an invocation of globalization Chinese-style and urbanism Chinese-style
as neither an end-point of history nor a unique form of geography but instead as
an extraordinary moment in the routed transformation of contemporary urbanism.
In understanding whether Shanghai is to be the capital of the twenty-first century
it might be essential to work out the ways in which it is simultaneously haunted by
the twentieth century and structured by the dynamics of here and elsewhere. To
begin to understand how Shanghai's future inhabits our present it may be essential
to rethink the manner in which urbanism's past inhabits its present in the genealogy
of what it means to be modern and to be urban.

Rather than transform Shanghai into either a utopian or a dystopian exemplar
of some form of generic urbanism, both engagement up close and the critical
distance of academic inquiry might make us think slightly differently about the
global cultural traffic of ideas about the ethics and practices of property rights,
economic growth, and the social construction of markets, as well as about the
palimpsests that reveal the city's hidden pasts that define its unhomely or uncanny
present. In such urbanism the trajectories of the temporal and the cartographies
of ideas might reveal some equally interesting material about how we can learn
from the ways in which the Chinese experience speaks to what it means to be
metropolitan.

Notes

1   See for example Deyan Sudjic's fascinating but problematic piece on Shanghai: *The Speed
    and the Friction in the Urban Age Project*. Available online at www.urban-age.net/
    0_downloads/UABulletin1June2005.pdf
2   See for example Ross 2006 and Hutton 2007 for two of the more high-profile recent
    discussions of the economic transition of today's China.
3   www.indiewire.com/people/people_040806winter.html
4   "Risk cultures in China: an economic sociology." ESRC funded project by Scott Lash and
    Michael Keith.
5   For an introduction to Wang Hui's work see Wang Hui 2006.

References

Bray, David (2005) *Social Space and Governance in Urban China: The Danwei System from
    Origins to Reform*. Stanford, CA: Stanford University Press.
Bray, D. (2006) Building community: new strategies of governance in urban China. *Economy
    and Society* 35 (4): 530–49.
Cui, Z. (forthcoming) *Wrestling with the Invisible Hand: Soft-Budget-Constraint and Vertical
    Conflict Over Property Rights*. Cambridge, MA: Harvard University Press.
Donald, J. (2005) The enigma of arrival. In *The Glittering Tart: Imaging Sydney*, ed. Cath-
    erine Simpson and Anthony Lambert. *Scan* 2 (1) April (online journal http://scan.net.au/
    scan/journal/display.php?journal_id=47, accessed July 2010).
Dutton, M. (1999) *Streetlife China*. Cambridge: Cambridge University Press.

Haila, A. (2007) The market as new emperor. *International Journal of Urban and Regional Research* 31 (1): 3–20.

Ho, P. (2001) Who owns China's land? Policies, property rights and deliberate institutional ambiguity. *China Quarterly* 166: 394–421.

Hsing, You-Tien (2010) *The Great Urban Transformation: Politics of Land and Property in China*. Oxford: Oxford University Press.

Hutton, W. (2007) *The Writing on the Wall: Why We Must Embrace China as a Partner or Face It as an Enemy*. London: Simon and Schuster.

Krug, B., and Hendrischke, H. (2008) Framing China: transformation and institutional change through co-evolution. *Management and Organization Review* 4 (1): 81–108.

Logan, J. (ed.) (2002) *The New Chinese City: Globalization and Market Reform*. Oxford: Blackwell.

Ma, L. (2006) The state of the field of urban China: a critical multidisciplinary overview. *China Information* 20: 363–89.

Mishra, Pankaj (2006) China's new leftist. *New York Times* October 15.

Ou-fan Lee, L. (1999) *Shanghai Modern: The Flowering of a New Urban Culture in China, 1930–1945*. Cambridge, MA: Harvard University Press.

Ou Fan Lee, Leo (2009) Contemporary architecture in urban China. Paper delivered at Designing China workshop, Shanghai workshop, University of California Irvine, August.

Ross, A. (2006) *Fast Boat China; Lessons from Shanghai*. New York: Pantheon Books.

Shenjing He, Zhigang Li, and Fulong Wu (2006) Transformation of the Chinese city, 1995–2005: geographical perspectives and geographers. Contributions. *China Information* 20 (3): 429–56.

Simmel, G. (1997 [1923]) The metropolis and mental life. In *Simmel on Culture: Selected Writings*, ed. D. Frisby and M. Featherstone. London: Sage, 174–87.

Solinger, Dorothy, J., and Kam Wing Chan (2002) The China difference: city studies under socialism. In *Understanding the City: Contemporary and Future Perspectives*, ed. John Eade and Christopher Mele. Oxford: Blackwell, 204–21.

Walker, R., and Buck, D. (2007) The Chinese road: cities in transition to socialism. *New Left Review* 46: 39–66.

Wallpaper (2006) *Wallpaper City Guide: Shanghai*. London: Phaidon.

Wang Hui (2006) *China's New Order: Society, Politics and Economy in Transition*. Cambridge, MA: Harvard University Press.

Wang Xiaoming (2003) A manifesto for cultural studies. Trans. Robin Visser. In *One China Many Paths*, ed. Chaohua Wang. London: Verso, 274–91.

Wing Chan, K., and Li Zhang (1999) The hukou system and rural–urban migration in China: processes and changes. *China Quarterly* 160: 818–55.

Wu, Fulong (2002) China's changing urban governance in the transition towards a more market-oriented economy. *Urban Studies* 39 (7): 1071–93.

Wu, Fulong (ed.) (2006) *Globalization and the Chinese City*. London: Routledge.

Wu, X., and Treiman, Donald J. (2004) The household registration system and social stratification in China: 1955–1996. *Demography* 41 (2): 363–84.

Zhang, Li, and Zhao, Simon X. B. (1998) Re-examining China's urban concept and the level of urbanization. *China Quarterly* 154: 330–81.

Chapter 36

"Just Diversity" in the City of Difference

Kurt Iveson and Ruth Fincher

Introduction: Planning, Publics, and the Right to the City

How can urban social planning contribute to the development of justice in contemporary cities? While progressive and even utopian impulses form part of the roots of modern urban planning as a technology of governance, it is clear that a variety of injustices have continued to persist in those cities where planning has been practiced. What is more, the persistence of these injustices has not been the result of planners failing to have enough influence over urban change. Rather the very application of planning has itself frequently ignored people's rights to the city and contributed to injustice.

While urban planning has quite different histories in the many cities where it has been practiced, critiques of its application and impact across these different contexts have nonetheless identified some common concerns. Central among these concerns is that one of the core values by which modern town planning was meant to contribute to justice has in fact had the opposite effect. Planning was meant to identify and then act on behalf of a universal "public good" or "public interest." And yet, time and time again it has been shown that planners have marginalized the interests of groups such as women, children, ethnic minorities, the disabled, the poor, and others when they have claimed to be acting for all. In doing so, planning has in fact worked to provide a powerful mask of universality for those whose particular interests have been privileged at the expense of such groups.

For those who nonetheless believe that planning can still be a valuable tool in the struggle for justice and the rights to the city, it is therefore crucial to identify a new framework for its application in contemporary cities. Quite rightly, many efforts in this direction have emphasized the need for planning frameworks to take

The New Blackwell Companion to the City   Edited by Gary Bridge and Sophie Watson
© 2011 Blackwell Publishing Ltd

adequate account of *diversity* of cities, by identifying and working with the many publics which inhabit them. In doing so, it is hoped that the injustices associated with attempts to identify and impose a universal public interest can be overcome.

However, much discussion about planning with diversity has focused on planning processes rather than planning ambitions or broad social goals. The discussion overwhelmingly has been about the need for planners to involve and consult with different publics and groups in decision-making processes. It is our view that a parallel focus on the broad social goals of planning is crucial if planning is to make a meaningful contribution to justice in cities. Like a number of other scholars (such as Heather Campbell (2006), Michael Dear (2000), Susan Fainstein (2005)), we are critical of the emphasis on procedure and process over ends and outcome in the so-called "communicative turn" in planning. We join them in calling for a focus on "what is to be done" as well as "how it is to be done."

Reflecting on the question of "what is to be done," Susan Fainstein (2005: 126) argues that "[t]he 'what' for urban planners is the 'right to the city' described by Henri Lefebvre." She goes on to argue that Lefebvre's concept of the right to the city is useful because it:

> raises questions of who owns the city, not in the sense of direct individual control of an asset but in the collective sense of each group's ability to access employment and culture, to live in a decent home and suitable living environment, to obtain a satisfying education, to maintain personal security, and to participate in urban governance.

Lefebvre's original articulation of the right to the city (first published in 1967: see Lefebvre 1996) is very much of its time and place – 1960s Paris, where the working classes and migrants were finding themselves increasingly banished to the *banlieues* on the outskirts of the city and denied access to certain parts of the city. But despite the particular context in which it was developed, the notion of a right to the city has struck a chord among those concerned with achieving justice or citizenship in cities. In invoking Lefebvre's notion of the right to the city, Fainstein is one of a number of contemporary thinkers in the planning and urban studies fields who have continued to draw insights from the concept (see also Amin and Thrift 2002; Deutsche 1999; Harvey 2003; Isin 2000; Mitchell 2003; Purcell 2008; Soja 2010). The appeal of the concept beyond the context of its initial formulation derives from the importance that Lefebvre ascribed to space for progressive politics and social justice. Spatiality, insisted Lefebvre, was not simply symptomatic of social relations but formative of them. And as such, attempts to address injustice and inequality would have to change space.

Developing the notion of a right to the city to usefully inform contemporary planning efforts requires coming to grips with the nature of diversity in the city. This will be crucial in efforts to work towards the core promise of the right to the city – the notion that all urban inhabitants have a right to full participation in urban life as equals. Following the argument presented more fully in our recent book (Fincher and Iveson 2008), we set out a framework of three broad, intersecting, and mutually defining goals for planning in pursuit of rights to the city – redistribution, recognition, and encounter. These three goals or "social logics" can usefully be applied in determining what should be done in the planning realm.

Our paper proceeds now in three sections. First, we outline our perspective on the nature of diversity in cities to which planning frameworks should respond. Second, we set out how the social logics of redistribution, recognition, and encounter respond to this diversity. And third, we illustrate our approach with a discussion of planning for public library provision in the UK and Australia, showing how these three logics interact in this particular case. In focusing on public libraries, we are also drawing attention to the significance of public spaces beyond the street for achieving rights to the city in cities of difference.

Different Kinds of Difference

In the 40 years since social movements and radical scholars launched the first attacks on the assumptions and outcomes of urban planning, the *diversity* of cities and their inhabitants has become a core topic of concern for planning thought and practice, and for urban theory more generally. Of course, planning's radical critics did not speak with one voice, either with regard to their diagnoses of planning's ills or their suggested remedies. But in retrospect, it is possible to say that their cumulative effect was to challenge the assumption that expert planners knew what was best for cities and their diverse populations. The voices of dissent were widely interpreted as being the voices of groups whose particular views, experiences of the city, and expectations had been marginalized in the planning process, which seemed to be premised on (and sought to impose) a homogeneity across the diverse urban field.

However, in debates about the injustices which have been the result of dominant approaches to urban planning, the nature of urban diversity and its implications for planning have been far from clear. Reflecting back on the ways in which the diversity of cities has been conceptualized in these discussions, Loretta Lees (2003: 613) has observed that "[the] diversity of different 'diversities' is often under-theorised." This point has significant implications for any attempt to develop new approaches to urban planning. As Hugh Stretton (1970) argued in his critique of planning in Australia, while the homogenizing impulses of planners were a problem, the just response could not be a simple embrace of "diversity." "Any decent intellectual," argued Stretton, "despises the difference of more and less and reveres the difference of originality" (1970: 11). Addressing attacks on the conformity of planned suburbs, he noted: "Before we all got the same houses, the contrasts of mansion and slum did not signify individual differences of desire, nor a tenth of the free choices we have now" (1970: 11). The point is that for planning to promote a "just diversity" in cities, it will need to do more than "accommodate" or "embrace" diversity as such. Rather, it will need to disentangle the different kinds of diversity characterizing city life and distinguish between those forms of diversity that are just and those that are unjust.

There are at least three intersecting and yet distinct kinds of diversity which characterize urban life and which set the context for the pursuit of "just diversity." The first is the difference of rich and poor, whereby the characteristics of the city exacerbate the fact that some people have more and some fewer material resources and opportunities. The second is the difference of status, whereby some people's identities (and their associated ways of inhabiting the city) are devalued in relation to others in the city. The third is the difference of hybridity, whereby no individual can be reduced to any one group identity, because each has a range of potential identities and identifications that constitute their urban presence.

The difference of rich and poor is unjust when it is a product of processes which persistently distribute resources and opportunities unequally, such that class inequalities take hold. The difference of status is unjust when some identities are positioned hierarchically with respect to others, such that some groups experience normative censure, punitive regulation, or violence on the basis of their shared attributes. The difference of hybridity is unjust when some individuals find their opportunities to explore potential identifications and shared projects with others curtailed.

Redistribution, Recognition, and Encounter as Goals for Planning

Each of these forms of difference has a spatial dimension. Planning in pursuit of the right to the city is planning that seeks to craft outcomes which address these different kinds of diversity and promote a "just diversity." Planning responses to the different forms of diversity should be geared towards achieving what Nancy Fraser (2004) has called "parity of participation," by which she means a situation in which all members of a given polity are able to interact with one another as peers. Defined in this way, parity of participation is not solely a matter of procedural equity, but rather refers to the social conditions required for decision-making processes to be conducted among equals. Fraser herself, of course, has identified redistribution and recognition as goals for progressive politics, and we believe that these two goals form the appropriate responses to the first two forms of difference in cities identified above.

Redistribution is a key goal if planning is to help craft a just diversity in cities. It has long been a goal for some urban planning efforts, although Fraser's (2000: 107) point that calls for egalitarian redistribution have declined relative to other forms of progressive politics in recent times is surely applicable to urban planning. In urban planning, mechanisms designed to address inequitable distribution of resources and opportunities have usually been informed by concepts of spatial or locational disadvantage. The concept of locational advantage (or disadvantage) draws on the idea that where a person lives affects their opportunities, and contributes substantially to their wellbeing or difficulties. A location, region, or place will be seen as disadvantaging if the "bundle" of services and facilities it offers its residents is substandard. Here, redistributional planning has been envisaged as an alternative to markets for providing more just spatial arrangements of resources, infrastructure, and services across urban locales, whereby citizen entitlement to equitable allocations of resources rather than market power shapes outcomes.

When maldistribution has been understood as a production of locational disadvantage, planning interventions have focused on trying to equalize the opportunities a person has or doesn't have in his/her area to use facilities and services like schools, hospitals, parks, libraries, public transport, and so on, by providing a relatively equal distribution of such facilities and services. Here, we are generally referring to the physical location of services. But of course physical proximity to a facility or service does not necessarily make it *accessible*. As such, redistributional efforts in planning must also focus on accessibility, in the sense that potential users of such a facility or service feel that it is appropriate to their needs and they are welcome as users. Adequate provision of accessible services means also that services for "the public" should not inadvertently exclude certain people or groups. Of course, one of the ways that planning has sought to make services and infrastructure accessible is to make access a matter of right rather than consumer power. But place-based planning, in the services it provides, as well as in other ways, may exclude groups of people who don't fit in. We have long known this and used it in discussions of "not in my backyard" responses to the location of community facilities, but the matter links redistributive planning to the concept of recognition in reducing injustice. To ensure that accessibility is achieved, we must acknowledge the importance of recognizing group differences in pursuit of redistribution.

Indeed, **recognition** has emerged as a goal for urban planning at least partly in response to the limitations of redistribution as a strategy for achieving justice in cities. The devaluing and stigmatization of some urban identities and ways of life is one of the principal forms of injustice in cities. Disputes over all sorts of urban issues are instigated by groups who argue that their particular values and needs ought to be taken into account in the shaping of cities. Political claims of this nature, based as they are on the needs and values of particular groups (such as "women," "young people," "British Asians," etc.), have come to be known as "identity politics." When such groups feel that their very identities and ways of being in the city are unfairly denigrated or stigmatized, justice is fundamentally a matter of status and has an inter-subjective dimension: the pursuit of equality involves working against "cultural patterns that systematically deprecate some categories of people and the qualities associated with them" (Fraser 1998: 31).

The notion that justice involves the recognition of cultural differences has been the most widely articulated and debated response to the claims of identity politics. The proper model of recognition remains a contentious matter in social and political theory. Important questions are posed by the notion of recognition: what is the nature of the "identity" to be recognized? And who or what does the recognizing? In urban planning, we can distinguish at least two models of recognition: an affirmative model and a relational model. The affirmative model of recognition is based on an essentialist reading of identity. Here, different identities are considered to be the product of pre-existing differences between those who belong to distinct groups, and recognition is considered to be a matter of defining, acknowledging, and/or protecting group distinctiveness. Recognition, in this form, establishes and maintains boundaries between groups in order to protect their members from any social norms or institutional arrangements which prevent them from "being themselves." Here, the capacity of group members to "be themselves" is measured with reference to a model of selfhood derived from a set of characteristics and orientations considered to be essential and unique to the group in question. We are all no doubt familiar with the kind of "group checklist" planning informed by this approach, where recognition takes the form of identifying and consulting with an ever-expanding list of "special needs" groups.

However, it is relatively easy to show that different identity groups are in fact internally differentiated, that they have unstable rather than immutable boundaries. Any individual is likely to "belong" to many such groups, and the meaning of belonging is always far from settled. Responding to this problem is not simply a matter of refining some checklist of identity groups to make it more accurate (such as the breaking up of the group identity of "women" into groups of "white women," "women of color," "young women," "lesbians," "bisexual women," etc.). Rather, it is a matter of pursuing a relational form of recognition, whereby claims for recognition are adjudicated according to whether they address matters of *status relations* rather than identity as such (Fraser 2003). That is to say, claims for recognition should not be supported on the grounds that they help to sustain a group's distinctiveness *per se*. Rather, we should support those claims for recognition which seek to address institutionalized patterns of cultural value which give a particular group a subordinate status in relation to others.

Encounter, our third goal for urban planning, has emerged in response to critiques of essentialist identity politics which sometimes arise in pursuit of recognition. Those who argue for a more fluid and relational approach to diversity suggest that public policy (including planning) should not work to reify identity groups. Rather, it should be geared towards ensuring that people have opportunities to explore those aspects of themselves and their relationships with others which are not fully contained within any one identity category. That is, "parity of participation" as proposed by Fraser (2004) is not to be reduced to a matter of people being able to "be themselves" in relation to some group identity. Rather, urban inhabitants must also have opportunities to become someone else through encounters with the strangers with whom they share the city, to explore their own hybridity (Deutsche 1999, Tajbakhsh 2001).

Of course, encounters can take many forms, not all of which will contribute to justice and the right to the city by working against reification of identity! We are arguing for planning to foster *convivial* encounters, whereby those who share (and pass through) urban spaces have opportunities to build shared identifications with one another as strangers rather than as members of a particular identity group. Such identifications may emerge through fleeting encounters, or through more purposeful activities. As Paul Gilroy (2004: xi) puts it, the concept of conviviality:

> introduces a measure of distance from the pivotal term "identity" ... The radical openness that brings conviviality alive makes a nonsense of closed, fixed, and reified identity and turns attention toward the always-unpredictable mechanisms of identification.

Lisa Peattie (1998: 248) has pointed out that such activities are within the domain of urban planning:

> Conviviality can take place with few props: the corner out of the wind where friends drink coffee together, the vacant lot which will become a garden. But it must have some sort of material base – the right-shaped corner, the piece of vacant land and a couple of rakes – and it must have the rules that permit it. Conviviality cannot be coerced, but it can be encouraged by the right rules, the right props, and the right places and spaces.

Planning can work to establish the infrastructure upon which such conviviality might be built, whilst at the same time deploying the "light touch" needed so as not to privilege or impose particular forms of interaction, a delicate task indeed and one usefully discussed using the example of planning to retain alternative arts spaces in gentrifying locales of Amsterdam (Shaw 2005). Importantly, such planning is not simply a matter of providing grand "public spaces" where strangers can mingle in crowds (Amin 2002). Rather, it is a matter of resourcing situations and institutions through which people can make contact on the basis of shared activities and interests which might transcend fixed identities such as gender, race, and class. As we shall argue in a moment, spaces such as public libraries can be just as significant here as open public spaces – indeed, public spaces may have significant limitations as spaces for encounter (Watson 2006).

Of course, the task for planning, in real time and real places and politics, is rather complicated precisely because the different forms of diversity to which redistribution, recognition, and encounter respond do not exist in isolation, but rather intersect. Rarely will one of these goals be adequate on its own to address injustice. Indeed, if anything the histories of planning have shown that when one of these goals is pursued in isolation from the others, it may well have harmful consequences. We have already noted that efforts to redistribute resources are not likely to address important questions of accessibility if they fail to take account of group differences. Similarly, efforts to provide spaces for convivial encounters will exclude many of those most in need if they are too closely connected with certain forms of consumption (such as eating and drinking, as Sharon Zukin (1996) has pointed out in her writing on policies designed to promote certain forms of conviviality which amount to no more than "pacification by cappuccino").

In this context, some may wonder about the analytical utility of separating these three goals. Indeed, this issue was at the core of the vigorous debate between Iris Marion Young, Nancy Fraser, and others over the best way to conceptualize justice and injustice (Young 1997; Fraser 1997). While we believe that forms of diversity and their associated forms of injustice are typically intertwined, we nonetheless agree with Nancy Fraser that it is useful to distinguish between them analytically, to give us some socio-theoretical and political purchase on complex problems. The analytical categories of redistribution, recognition, and encounter are useful for the matters to which they draw our attention, even as we recognize their indivisibility as norms and logics identified in planning practice.

Redistribution, Recognition, and Encounter in Practice: The Public Library

In this section we provide one brief and highly condensed snapshot of how our three social logics might be applied to thinking about planning for justice and the right to the city: the case of public library provision in cities. In focusing on this "everyday" space, we seek to illustrate our claim that the *analytical separation* of these logics is useful precisely in its utility for showing the fundamental necessity for them to be *pursued simultaneously*. As we shall see, this is not without its difficulties.

The provision of metropolitan public library networks in many cities in the western world is fundamentally shaped by the *redistributional* paradigm in planning, which places emphasis on the role of the state in addressing questions of locational disadvantage and accessibility through direct provision of services and infrastructure. To the extent that access to resources for information, knowledge, and communication has been considered important, public library networks are intended to facilitate access equally to all regardless of income and status. (In the 1970s, one celebrated analysis of how this intention plays out locally was made by Levy *et al.* (1974) about public library planning in Oakland, California.)

A decade or so ago, the decline of the public library was widely thought to be upon us, a product of the rapid rise of the internet and the simultaneous decline of the public sector associated with neoliberal forms of urban governance and policy. However, in recent years public libraries have enjoyed a resurgence in many cities across the United Kingdom, Australia, and the United States. This resurgence can be attributed, at least in part, to the successful ways in which library advocates have worked closely with policy-makers and planners to develop new visions for public libraries which are concerned with matters of recognition and encounter alongside matters of redistribution in library provision.

One of the key ways in which public library services have changed in many cities over the past few decades is via the targeting of library collections, services, and spaces to recognize the needs of particular groups. Many metropolitan library networks have come to realize the limitations of uniform provision across neighborhoods, whereby "equality" is to be achieved through offering the same standardized collections and services regardless of the population characteristics of a given neighborhood. So, for instance, where a library is located in a locality of high unemployment or minority ethnic concentration, the library's collections and services are organized (in consultation with these user groups) to recognize their particular needs. In the process, libraries have often become institutions through which such groups have been able to launch campaigns to raise awareness of their concerns and justice claims.

But successful libraries have done more than recognize the needs of particular identity groups. They have also very effectively enhanced their status as a valued space of encounter in the city, which offers the potential for new forms of conviviality and identification which transcend fixed identity categories. To step into a public library is to step into a space that is shared with "strangers," in the form of other library users and library staff. As such, the forms of encounter that might occur between these strangers are mediated by the normative expectations about how a library should be used that are extant in any given library – what we might call a library's "library-ness" (Bryson *et al.* 2003). One of the remarkable features of "library-ness" most commonly identified in research on contemporary public libraries concerns the diversity of uses and users that libraries can accommodate. Reading newspapers, checking community notices, checking email, surfing the internet, doing homework, relaxing with a coffee, attending lectures and community meetings, listening to live or recorded music, discussing a book with staff or other users, flirting, meeting and making friends ... all of these activities are taking their place in many public libraries alongside more conventional activities such as consulting reference material and borrowing books or audio-visual resources.

In the course of these various activities, forms of encounter can vary enormously. Users might remain silent for their entire stay and have only non-verbal interactions with one another, they might have brief chats with other users and staff whom they may or may not recognize, they might form more regular or lasting connections and relationships with others. All of these encounters are significant. They are premised on the capacity of those who use the library to mutually negotiate their common status as *library users* in the moments of their encounters. This is a process of mutual (if temporary) *identification* which transcends fixed identity categories.

This is not to say that users stop being "young people," or "elderly," or members of a particular ethnic community or community association, etc., when they use a library – indeed, it is precisely in relation to such identities that people may in fact come to the library in the first place. But once they are there, they also become library users. And as such, people who may otherwise be very different from one another, and who may not encounter each other in any other context, are drawn into a momentary relationship as they share library space.

In public libraries, then, the successful pursuit of redistribution has in part relied on a simultaneous pursuit of recognition and encounter. Conversely, the potential for public libraries to recognize group needs and provide spaces of encounter is fundamentally a matter of redistribution. Free and open access to libraries and their resources, facilities, activities, and spaces is fundamental to the forms of "library-ness" we have discussed above. A survey of library users and non-users in Australia found:

> an almost universal perception that libraries are places where all people have a right of access, regardless of their circumstances or backgrounds ... The heritage of free use and the public ownership of libraries mean that nobody is turned away, and users feel that all others have a right to be there, creating a sense of equity and entitlement, and thereby neutralising any sense of marginalisation or exclusion. (University of Technology Sydney and State Library of New South Wales 2000: 8)

As Alstad and Curry (2003) note, in the end, supporters of public libraries must resist the logic of commercialization which has been applied to other forms of urban infrastructure provided by the state – any introduction of a "user pays" logic would significantly undermine both the recognition of group needs and the convivial aspects of library-ness we have discussed. It is crucial that access to public libraries is simultaneously understood as a matter of citizenship, with its associated notions of universal rights of access, as well as identity and strangerhood.

There are, of course, some tensions to be managed between these three social logics. The first relates to the interior design of library spaces. Some libraries have embraced a "libraries within libraries" approach to library use, by establishing different spatial zones for different activities (such as computer use, group discussion, quiet reading and contemplation, etc.). Such a strategy is justified on the grounds that it can help to diversify the user groups who come to public libraries. But this strategy presents its own problems:

> How is the historic universalism of the public library to be squared with managerial requirements to separate out different user groups and their needs, particularly in a more culturally segmented and multi-media society? (Warpole 2004: 22)

Functional segregation may in fact work to prevent some of the forms of encounter that have been associated with public libraries in the discussion above:

the library may also represent the only place where ... different social and age groups come into contact, and this contact may well have more positive than negative consequences. Total segregation is unlikely to represent the best solution. (Warpole 2004: 20)

This tension has no simple solution. There is a fine balance between the use of design to foster diversity, and the use of design to "solve" conflict by separating different user groups in a way that isolates them from one another. Where distinct zones are created, they should not be so clearly defined and bounded that they become "no-go" areas for other users, thus preventing the potential for encounter (University of Technology Sydney and State Library of New South Wales 2000: 23). Where libraries decide to establish distinct zones, such spaces should be established in conjunction with shared open spaces which have a life of their own, through which all users are likely to pass and/or linger, and which are by definition not associated with any one user group.

Second, co-location with commercial or government facilities is often considered a useful way to heighten the exposure of public libraries to a variety of potential users who may not otherwise use the library (Bryson *et al.* 2003: 30). But, once again, this spatial strategy potentially has significant drawbacks. Co-location might compromise the highly valued neutrality and accessibility of libraries, which are fundamental parts of their library-ness (Goulding 2004: 5). For instance, where public libraries are co-located with government agencies, levels of trust/mistrust in government among some users may deter them from visiting the library. Similarly, where public libraries are co-located in commercial premises (such as retail arcades or entertainment quarters), tensions may arise when ideals of universal access confront commercial concerns for establishing secure spaces for consumption.

Concluding Remarks

In this discussion, we have sought to respond to the call for urban planning to articulate a vision of "what should be done" in order for it to make a contribution towards justice and the right to the city. Our case study demonstrates how this can be done through planning public space – in this case, public libraries. Drawing on discussions from critical theory concerning "parity of participation" and from urban theory about the "right to the city," we have set out three broad social goals for urban planning: redistribution, recognition, and encounter. These three goals are intended as elements of an analytical framework that can be applied both to identify instances of injustice, and to adjudicate between different policies designed to address those instances of injustice. These goals do not add up to a neat vision of the good city – they propose no formulaic outcome that will benefit urban dwellers. Indeed, while in some cases these goals might coincide, sometimes they may need to be held in tension with one another. It may be in some situations, for example, that a strong focus on recognition reduces the redistributive potential of a given planning action, or that facilitating encounter means that some groups are excluded from a place for a time. One of the values of our framework is that it can identify such tensions, by keeping sight of the diverse and sometimes disjunctive dimensions of endeavors seeking rights to the city.

References

Alstad, C., and Curry, A. (2003) Public space, public discourse and public libraries. *LIBRES* 13 (1). Available online at http://libres.curtin.edu.au/libres13n1/ (accessed January 6, 2008).

Amin, A. (2002) Ethnicity and the multicultural city. *Environment and Planning A* 34 (6): 959–80.

Amin, A., and Thrift, N. (2002) *Cities: Reimagining the Urban*. Cambridge: Polity Press.

Bryson, J., Usherwood, B., and Proctor, R. (2003) *Libraries Must Also Be Buildings? New Library Impact Study*. Sheffield: The Centre for Public Libraries and Information in Society, Department of Information Studies, University of Sheffield.

Campbell, H. (2006) Just planning: the art of situated ethical judgement. *Journal of Planning Education and Research* 26 (1): 92–106.

Dear, M. (2000) *The Postmodern Urban Condition*. Oxford: Blackwell.

Deutsche, R. (1999) Reasonable urbanism. In *Giving Ground: The Politics of Propinquity*, ed. J. Copjec and M. Sorkin. London and New York: Verso, 176–206.

Fainstein, S. (2005) Planning theory and the city. *Journal of Planning Education and Research* 25 (2): 121–30.

Fincher, R., and Iveson, K. (2008) *Planning and Diversity in the City: Redistribution, Recognition and Encounter*. Basingstoke: Palgrave.

Fraser, Nancy (1997) A rejoinder to Iris Young. *New Left Review* 223: 126–9.

Fraser, N. (1998) Social justice in the age of identity politics: redistribution, recognition and participation. Tanner Lectures on Human Values 19. Available online at www.tannerlectures.utah.edu/lectures/documents/Fraser98.pdf (accessed October 2, 2010).

Fraser, N. (2000) Rethinking recognition. *New Left Review* 3: 107–20.

Fraser, N. (2003) Social justice in the age of identity politics: redistribution, recognition and participation. In *Redistribution or Recognition? A Political-Philosophical Exchange*, ed. N. Fraser and A. Honneth. London and New York: Verso, 7–109.

Fraser, N. (2004) Institutionalizing democratic justice: redistribution, recognition and participation. In *Pragmatism, Critique, Judgement: Essays for Richard J. Bernstein*, ed. S. Benhabib and N. Fraser. Cambridge, MA: MIT Press, 125–48.

Gilroy, P. (2004) *After Empire: Melancholia or Convivial Culture?* London: Routledge.

Goulding, A. (2004) Libraries and social capital, *Journal of Librarianship and Information Sciences* 36 (1): 3–6.

Harvey, D. (2003) The right to the city. *International Journal of Urban and Regional Research* 27 (4): 939–41.

Isin, E. (2000) Introduction: democracy, citizenship and the global city. In *Democracy, Citizenship and the Global City*, ed. E. Isin. London: Routledge, 1–21.

Lees, L. (2003) The ambivalence of diversity and the politics of urban renaissance: the case of youth in downtown Portland, Maine. *International Journal of Urban and Regional Research* 27 (3): 613–34.

Lefebvre, H. (1996) *Writings on Cities*. Oxford: Blackwell.

Levy, F., Meltsner, A., and Wildavsky, A. (1974) *Urban Outcomes: Schools, Streets, and Libraries*. Berkeley: University of California Press.

Mitchell, D. (2003) *The Right to the City: Social Justice and the Fight for Public Space*. New York: Guilford.

Peattie, L. (1998) Convivial cities. In *Cities for Citizens*, ed. M. Douglass and J. Friedmann. Chichester: John Wiley & Sons, 247–253.

Purcell, M. (2006) *Recapturing Democracy*. New York: Routledge.

Shaw, K. (2005) The place of alternative culture and the politics of its protection in Berlin, Amsterdam and Melbourne. *Planning Theory and Practice* 6 (2): 149–69.

Soja, E. (2010) *Seeking Spatial Justice*. Minneapolis: University of Minnesota Press.

Stretton, H. (1970) *Ideas for Australian Cities*. Adelaide: Hugh Stretton.

Tajbakhsh, K. (2001) *The Promise of the City: Space, Identity, and Politics in Contemporary Social Thought*. Berkeley: University of California Press.

University of Technology Sydney and State Library of New South Wales (2000) *A Safe Place to Go: Libraries and Social Capital*. Sydney: University of Technology Sydney and State Library of New South Wales.

Warpole, K. (2004) *21st Century Libraries: Changing Forms, Changing Futures*. London: Commission for Architecture and the Built Environment, Royal Institute of British Architects, Museums and Libraries Archives.

Watson, S. (2006) *City Publics: The (Dis)enchantments of Urban Encounters*. London: Routledge.

Young, Iris Marion (1997) Unruly categories: A critique of Nancy Fraser's dual systems theory. *New Left Review* 222: 147–60.

Zukin, S. (1996) *The Cultures of Cities*. Oxford: Blackwell.

Chapter 37

The Emergence of Cosmopolitan Soho

Judith R. Walkowitz

Recent scholarly debates have tended to focus on cosmopolitanism as a form of privileged, aesthetic, and ethical thinking beyond the nation *or* as material knowledge gained by transnational migrants through adverse daily routines (Williams 1976: 137; Anderson 2001; Cheah and Robbins 1998; R. Walkowitz 2006). By and large, historians have remained marginal to these debates, as has cosmopolitanism's own sedimented history as a genre of urban knowledge and material practice in specific metropolitan environments. There is an urban cultural history of cosmopolitanism to be written, and one good place to begin is London's West End at the end of the nineteenth century, when cosmopolitanism emerged as a key descriptor of the locale. This study reveals how commercial venues set the stage for competing and overlapping modes of cosmopolitanism; it also illuminates how a discourse of Old and New London altered the fortunes of a cosmopolitan space.

My focus is late Victorian and Edwardian Soho, a district of potentially unsettling diversity at the margins of the West End. An old district whose street patterns date back to the seventeenth and eighteenth centuries, its population numbered 24,000 residents in 1901 (Census 1902: RG 13/100–01; RG 13/97; RG 13/98). In the three decades leading up to World War I, Soho became increasingly visible as a meeting ground of bad and good cosmopolitanism. "Soho stories" depicted the district as a plague spot of international crime, subversive politics, and sex and/or an attractive stage set for bodily pleasures, appetites, and modern technologies of the self. The social investigator Charles Booth pronounced Soho to be as markedly "cosmopolitan" as other London neighborhoods were "curiously insular and self-contained" (Booth 1902: 185). Another contemporary, Count Armfelt, also described Soho as the center of "Cosmopolitan London," the "cherished home of foreign artists, dancers ... and the sanctuary of political refugees ... and defaulters of all nations"(Armfelt 1990 [1902]: 241). By advancing selective elements of the social

The New Blackwell Companion to the City   Edited by Gary Bridge and Sophie Watson
© 2011 Blackwell Publishing Ltd

landscape, these cultural expressions had material consequences, particularly for the local commodity culture/leisure industry emerging at the turn of the century.

Urban Cosmopolitanism and New London

Material and representational factors created Soho's cosmopolitanism. One driving force in Soho's transformation was the building of an improved New London along Soho's borders. Economic and physical changes followed in the wake of this new development. But just as important to Soho's fortunes was the new valuation of Soho as a relic of Old London filled with literary memories. These historical associations not only enhanced Soho's cachet as a bohemian space of taste and culture but proved to be valuable resources for ethnic entrepreneurs who endeavored to sell their cosmopolitan product to a metropolitan market.

In the last decades of the nineteenth century, a central commercial district devoted to cosmopolitan pleasure was built along the "street improvements" of Regent Street, Shaftesbury Avenue, and Charing Cross Road and the older sedimented landscapes of Oxford Street and Leicester Square. Nineteenth-century street improvements plowed through the central rookeries of Old London, displacing thousands of residents from the noisome slums that resisted police supervision. However, new roadways and mass transit systems also transported new social actors into the district, including legions of service and theatrical workers who assisted and entertained suburbanites and tourists descending on the West End to visit the shops and the shows (Rappaport 2000; J. Walkowitz 2003).

Popular print culture ascribed a bourgeois version of cosmopolitanism to the department stores, variety theaters, hotels, and luxury restaurants built along Soho's imposing commercial peripheries. This version of cosmopolitanism conveyed the West End's reputation for sensory indulgence, privileged mobility, and worldly command of goods, ideas, and bodies. Journalists and writers frequently remarked on the dramatic materializations of foreign cultural artifacts along these thoroughfares, linking them to a visual culture featuring women as spectacles and increasingly as spectators (J. Walkowitz 1998; J. Walkowitz 2003; Weightman 1992). Cosmopolitan attractions seemed to embody the international status of London, not only as an imperial capital but also as the "greatest city of the world," as an international finance center and tourist attraction with a supporting range of urban and cultural amenities (*The Times*, quoted in Smith 1999: 25; Driver and Gilbert 1998).

The same journalists viewed Soho, with its foreign refugees and irregular economies of sex and crime, as the epitome of a different cosmopolitanism: a debased condition of sexual transgression, displacement, and degeneration. In practice, cosmopolitanism in its glossy, pleasurable sense depended on close proximity to the dangers and enticements of the second set of meanings (J. Walkowitz 2003). By the turn of the century, both modes of cosmopolitanism began to migrate into *fin-de-siècle* Soho as it developed its own versions of cosmopolitan pleasure around nightlife and food culture.

Cosmopolitan Soho

West End thoroughfares cemented Soho's identity, but they also opened up Soho, as the leisure industries along Soho's boundaries eventually penetrated inward. The monumental cityscape of the boulevards consolidated Soho's identity as an intact relic of Old London: a muddy accumulation of old bricks and stones, yet increasingly viewed as a treasured remnant of a national past. At the same time, West End development forged a New Soho, remaking the old Georgian space into a modern site of doubtful commerce and industry, employing a new cosmopolitan workforce of immigrants. Rather than segregate and contain Soho, the late Victorian thoroughfares laid bare "the foreign quarter of the metropolis ... for the inspection of the world at large" (*Pall Mall Gazette* 1887).

The building of Regent Street in the 1820s radically transformed the parish of St Anne Soho, creating a north/south spine demarcating the fashionable West End from plebian London to its east (Summerson 1991). Once an early modern space of fashionable commerce and residence, marked by a French émigré presence, Soho increasingly became a proletarian and "cosmopolitan" district, notorious for its declining urban fabric, its foreignness, its doubtful trades, and its political dissidents. Tailoring workshops and culinary businesses attracted new settlements of European immigrants eager to find employment. As the cockney population began to desert Soho, its winding streets were repopulated by Italian, French, and German immigrants, some of them refugees of failed revolutions, most of them economic migrants. By the 1890s, Eastern European Jews moved in and represented the largest ethnic enclave. In 1900, the vicar of St Anne Soho declared that two thirds of his parish (8,000 out of 12,000) was foreign (*Cassell's Saturday Journal* 1900). Throughout the twentieth century, Soho would remain heterogeneous and polyglot and no ethnic grouping exerted cultural or political predominance (Black 1994; Summers 1989; Tames 1994).

Soho also underwent a geographic remapping. It expanded westward, informally annexing the eastern edge of St James's parish that had been detached from the West End by the building of Regent Street in the 1820s. Its parallelogram shape was secured in 1887 with the construction of Charing Cross Road as its eastern boundary. Even though the bordering thoroughfares visually marked Soho's identity, Soho's boundaries were not fixed by law or governance; there were no district or administrative boundaries, and no official consensus on where to establish its limits.

"The Worst Street in London"

Events in 1906 brought Soho's reputation for dangerous cosmopolitanism into sharp relief. At the center of the dispute were two representatives of official London. In October of that year, Inspector McKay of the Metropolitan Police "C" division vilified Greek Street, Soho, as the "worst street in London" before the Royal Commission on the Police. Localizing Greek Street as the home of the "vilest reptiles" in London, McKay conflated political refugees with the purveyors of cosmopolitan vice (quoted in Summers 1989: 158–9; McLaughlin 2000: 136–9; Eade 2000: 67–8). The next day, Reverend J. H. Cardwell of St Anne Soho came to the defense of the hardworking, foreign residents of Greek Street and denounced McKay's testimony as "absurd calumny." "I will say that there is not a single disreputable character in Greek-street. I will even go so far as to say that there is scarcely one in the whole of Soho" (*Evening Standard* 1906).

McKay's rendition of Greek Street's dangerous heterogeneity signaled Soho's demographic shift from French to "cosmopolitan" as well as the presence of political refugees who owed no allegiance to any nation. For over a hundred years, French political exiles had followed the example of the Huguenots and found a refuge in dingy Soho. By 1848, a more diverse set of political émigrés began to arrive, including Karl Marx and his family, who rented two rooms on the fourth floor of 28 Dean Street from John Marengo, an Italian-born cook (Ashton 1986: 99). After 1871, Italians, Swiss, and Russians, many of them anarchists, swelled the population of political émigrés in and around Soho, spreading north of Oxford Street, where an overflow of Soho developed, as émigrés endeavored to remain as close to Soho's radical clubs, restaurants, and news shops as they could. The intensive policing of these political dissidents helped to reconfigure Soho's status as a refuge for rootless, dangerous cosmopolitanism (Shpayer-Makov 1988).

Compounding Soho's infamy as the "cosmopolitan home of arson and murder" was its equally unsavory reputation as a center of "cosmopolitan vice." Soho's sex trade gained extensive publicity through a series of local anti-vice campaigns spearheaded by Reverend Cardwell, the defender of Greek Street's honor in 1906. Newly arrived in Soho in 1891, Cardwell found St Anne's parish to be full of brothels, the police indifferent, and respectable workers "literally driven out of house and home to make room for the traders in vice who can afford to pay exorbitant rents" (quoted in Summers 1989: 157; Cardwell 1911: 19–20). Cardwell claimed that one in six houses in Soho was a disorderly house and that Soho's sex trade was largely controlled and staffed by foreigners. By stressing the "organized" and foreign nature of Soho vice, both the police and the social reformer strengthened the case for a police crackdown (Petrow 1994: 166–74). By 1896, Soho's infamy was so well-established that the *Sun* began a paragraph on a "Soho incident" with the observation, "Soho seems determined to sustain its pre-eminence as a centre of disturbance" (*The Sun* 1896).

Cardwell's anti-vice crusade generated some unintended negative consequences: it amplified Soho's notoriety as a "perfect little paradise for pimps" and incited police supervision of the district by the likes of Inspector McKay (quoted in Summers 1989: 155). While targeting criminals, Cardwell also endeavored to "disabuse the public of erroneous [negative] impressions of Soho." To this end, he defended respectable Sohoites in all their ethnic heterogeneity. In 1900, when asked by a *Cassell's* reporter if his parish was more "Continental than English," he proudly catalogued his exotic flock "as if they were a special collection" (McLaughlin 2000: 137). He praised the Latin residents as well as the Jews of Soho, who had "invaded" the district close to Piccadilly and Regent Street. He even stood up for local anarchists. "Our Soho anarchists are not what the public imagine." They are not desperadoes, not "drinking, good-for-nothing fellows." For the most part they are "decent, moral living people" (*Cassells Saturday Journal* 1900).

Poverty Studies and Local History of Old Soho

Cardwell also countered the dark picture of Soho poverty and overcrowding circulated by his fellow philanthropist, Robert Sherwell of the West London Mission. In *Life in West London* (1897), Robert Sherwell presented Soho as an impoverished

"Outcast London" located at the margins of the wealthy West End. While mindful of Soho's "terrible social evils," Cardwell insisted that Sherwell had blackened Soho's reputation and confused Soho's geographic identity by blurring the boundaries between Soho and adjacent dark poverty spots to the east of the parish (quoted in *Cassell's Saturday Journal* 1900).

Instead of assembling his own sociological profile of Soho, Cardwell opted for an alternative system of urban knowledge: a topographical history of Soho that summoned up the glory days of the Georgian past. Compiled by St Anne's clergy and parish workers, *Two Centuries of Soho* detailed the rise and progress of Soho's firms, institutions, and amusements over two centuries. Rather than dwell on the present "horrors" of Soho, the book tried to stir up "parochial patriotism," not only among residents but among "those engaged in business, who spend their working days in the parish" (Cardwell 1898; Cardwell 1911: 22–4).

As a work of "local history," *Two Centuries* embraces the empiricist method and imaginative geography of Victorian topographical guidebooks that interwove past history and geographic description, superimposing literary and historical associations on to streets and districts. Building on the Romantic attachment to ruins as material memory, topographical guides exploited a paradigmatic Victorian ambivalence about the "improving" modern city. By juxtaposing the cityscapes of Old and New London, the straight, rational thoroughfare set against a meandering alley, they transmuted the remnants of Old London into "heterotopic" spaces for modernity (Nead 2000: 5–6; Melman 2006: 6–9; Mandler 1997; Samuel 1994).

By the late nineteenth century, Soho occupied a special status in this story of Old and New. More than any other central district, declared the editor of *Old and New London*, Soho revealed "the past history and character" of London: "we fancy that no city in Europe can more thoroughly tell the story of its own past than can Soho testify to the glories of other days which still surround its decaying and decayed houses with a halo" (Thornbury 1887: 173). The destruction of Old London led to a new appreciation of the Georgian material legacy that remained, including the urban fabric of grimy Soho (Olsen 1976; Zemgulys 2008).

Two Centuries capitalized on these late Victorian recalibrations of history and heritage styles (Cardwell 1903; Cardwell 1898). It charts the dynamic convergence of Old and New London as Soho's philanthropic institutions adapted to the changing social face of the population under their care. It presents the landscape of late Victorian Soho as studded by hospitals, schools, missions, medical dispensaries, workingmen's clubs, trade societies, churches, and clubs for working boys and girls. By comparison, the book's section on business firms, occupying two thirds of the volume, is more backward-looking, its entries restricted to those solid English firms already in existence at the beginning of Queen Victoria's reign. Violin-makers and silversmiths were the "two arts inseparably connected with our parish from the period of its first foundation to the present" (Cardwell 1898: 223). By the 1890s, only a few Huguenot silversmith firms persist, but Cardwell is able to enumerate the continuation of many other "old-fashioned," substantial and "high class" businesses catering to the carriage trade that had "carried on with little or no change in [their] character" (Cardwell 1898: 185).

Despite Reverend Cardwell's publicist efforts, a story of displacement, fraudulence, and decay adheres to *Two Centuries'* story of Soho's *fin-de-siècle* industrial production. On Wardour Street, where Sheraton once had his showrooms, the tradition of furniture-making continues; but like so much else in Soho, this trade has acquired a shady, declining reputation. Furniture-makers had to struggle to compete with cheaper machine-made articles: "craftsmen skills" were obtained "at a greater cost than the machine-made article" (Cardwell 1898: 187). However, Soho tradesmen could turn artisan skills to good use when consumers developed a "new interest for old things," notably for old Georgian fittings and furniture, signified by "Chippendale," "Sheridan" and "Adam" (Cardwell 1898: 189). As a result, Wardour Street became the center of the production of fake antiques, of "furniture of uncertain age" that were "probably not so venerable in years as in appearance" (Cardwell 1898: 188–9).

The changing fortunes of Soho's urban fabric also yields a mixed historical lesson, revealing a heterogeneous combination of high and low, sacred and profane, foreign and native-born, the world of letters and the pleasures of the flesh. We learn, for example, that part of St Patrick's Church (1791) had previously belonged to Carlisle House, an elegant aristocratic residence that was converted for commercial use in 1760. Here, Mme Cornelys, a "foreign adventuress," hosted the Soho masquerade, attracting the cream of London society to her "Temple of Festivity" (Cardwell 1898: 37). The bohemian social world of Georgian Soho also surfaces in the history of the Westminster General Dispensary, located in the same Gerrard Street house previously tenanted by the Turk's Head tavern, where Dr Johnson, Boswell, Reynolds, and their friends assembled weekly for their renowned Literary Club (Cardwell 1898: 67–8).

Interior material fragments of Soho's buildings also evoke memories of a lost fashionable and cultivated past. *Two Centuries* draws attention to the beautiful mahogany staircase, paneling, and wall painting to be found inside the premises of Wilson and Son, tin plate workers, at 75 Dean Street. The wall painting is attributed to Hogarth and is in a "good state of preservation." "Soho once abounded in beautiful specimens of wall painting, but for the most part they have been neglected or destroyed, and few now remain to tell of the faded glory of the past" (Cardwell 1898: 263).

In *Two Centuries*, Cardwell shows himself to be more invested in Soho's Georgian past than in broadcasting the active contributions of new immigrants to modern Soho. Apart from the extensive labors of philanthropists and the persistence of artisan firms dating back to Georgian days, Cardwell can discern no signs of cultural energy or enterprise in contemporary Soho. His local histories are backward-looking, summoning up the ghosts of old Bohemia to create an inspirational romance of old Soho that was long enduring. But recent immigrants are not the only social actors ignored by Cardwell's local studies. Cardwell's inventory of Soho celebrities is notably silent about the turn-of-the-century bohemians who had already rediscovered its streets and restaurants. His life stories do not feature Oscar Wilde, Whistler, Symons, and other francophile intellectuals who gravitated to the Soho of the 1890s, nor does it map out the Soho resorts where they drank absinthe, had sex in upper rooms, discussed symbolism, contemplated suicide, or pursued other doubtful practices (Brooker 2004; Kaplan 2005). Soho's artists and writers are safely "dead and gone," embedded in a sanitized Georgian past. Nonetheless, Caldwell's nostalgic portrait of old Bohemia provided journalists and ethnic entrepreneurs with exactly the kind of cultural capital to remake Soho's modern cosmopolitan reputation.

Cosmopolitan Catering in Soho

In 1906, the *Caterer and Hotel-Keeper*, the main trade journal for the restaurant and hotel industry, exploits this romantic history in a food travelogue of Soho (*Caterer and Hotel-Keeper* 1906b; 1906c; 1906d; 1906e; 1906f; 1907a; 1907b). Its seven-part series, "Soho and its restaurants," presents Soho not as a parish, or part of a police or sanitary district, but as a bounded cultural zone dedicated to food. Mindful of recent media scandals, the *Caterer* acknowledged that "the darker social problems of Soho … are perhaps more complicated and difficult than in any other district," but it pronounces these problems to be "outside the scope of these articles" (*Caterer and Hotel-Keeper* 1906b: 263).

"Soho and its restaurants" introduces readers to this "fascinating district on the northern border of theatre land," and it delineates three distinctive features of Soho. It highlights its cosmopolitanism, signified by the profusion of foreign provision shops with French, German, Italian, and Austrian names above their lintel and displays of gastronomic wares that were "startling" to British taste (*Caterer and Hotel-Keeper* 1906b: 264). It briefly notes a second feature, Soho's centuries-old history as refuge for outcasts and rebels who provided the original clientele for the restaurants. But it quickly moves on to underscore Soho's distinction as the home of a "splendid bohemia" of the distant past. Surveying the contemporary street scene, the *Caterer* can discern no physical sign of Soho's former glory as a "noble Bohemia," apart from the picturesque little restaurants of various nations. Greek Street, so vilified by Inspector McKay, is "enlivened by the presence of about ten restaurants – French, German, Austrian, Italian, and English," the sole reminder of the street's commercial heyday when it was the site of Wedgwood's showroom (*Caterer and Hotel-Keeper* 1906c: 304–5).

The *Caterer* praises the picturesque eateries along Old Compton Street that allow theater-goers to test out foreign food, especially French cuisine, in agreeable surroundings for "remarkably small cost" (*Caterer and Hotel-Keeper* 1906b: 265). Here it signals an expanding market niche in Soho: the purveying of after-theater suppers for play-going couples, part of the expansion of middle-class heterosexual nightlife in the metropolis. As it moves on to other venues, it discerns the tendency of Soho restaurants to deviate from French to Italian catering. Gerrard Street, once the home of "such celebrated English literary artists" as Dryden and Burke is "now connected with Italian catering rather than with pictorial or literary art" (*Caterer and Hotel-Keeper* 1906d: 339.).

The "wily" "intelligent aliens" of Soho, rather than Cardwell's tradesmen and philanthropists, become the protagonists of the *Caterer*'s narrative (Paul 1898: 64). Mr Ucceli of the Boulogne Restaurant in Gerrard Street is one such hero. A "native of Italy," "he is better described as a Cosmopolitan than as an Italian, for he has spent far less time in Italy than out of it." His movements follow the well-established pattern of Italian catering workers who found their way to London after a probationary period in the international hotel circuit. Mr Ucceli found his market niche in Soho by providing an economic version of the silver service and haute French cuisine available to wealthy patrons in West End establishments. Thanks to Mr Ucceli's careful management, the Boulogne is able to use wholesome materials to make tasty, varied, well-cooked luncheons for 1s/6d and still turn a profit (*Caterer and Hotel-Keeper* 1906f: 542–4).

The *Caterer* features the Boulogne as an example of a new culinary practice in the heart of London. It prints its menu in French; it organizes its meal in conformity to the standards of service, order of courses, and assemblage of dishes established by Escoffier (Burnett 2004; Mennell 1985). Its tables are covered with white cloths, its waiters wear evening dress. But the Boulogne deviates from the reigning gastronomic orthodoxy by supplementing French fare with Italian specialties such as macaroni. The result is a hybrid cuisine, neither the ordinary peasant fare previously consumed by culinary workers in their native land nor the international French cuisine available in the grand hotels across Europe and in the West End (Barber and Jacomelli 1997).

By profiling the rags-to-riches cosmopolitan career of Mr Ucceli, the *Caterer* refigures Soho's reputation from a center of dangerous cosmopolitanism to a safe zone of cultural consumption of economical, exotic pleasures. Rather than threaten the integrity of the nation, the *Caterer*'s version of Soho cosmopolitanism ratifies London's capacity to master and contain unsettling multiplicity within a specialized enclave of cosmopolitan difference (Eade 2000: 6). To domesticate Soho's eateries, the *Caterer* anoints them as the colorful inheritors of the "splendid Bohemia" of the Georgian past. It casts Soho's ethnic entrepreneurs as the heroes of the story, as honest counterpoints to Soho's dangerous gang of international criminals and dynamiting anarchists. And it publicizes their hybrid food culture as part of a campaign to modernize the conservative culinary taste of the "great British public" (*Caterer and Hotel-Keeper* 1906a: 16).

The Cosmopolitan Fate of Old Soho

In 1914, national attention once again focused on a Soho street in peril. The street in question was Dean Street, and this time the threat emanated from the property market rather than from international crime or vice. On January 5, *The Times* warned its readers that "London is in imminent danger of losing a beautiful and most interesting old house of the early Georgian period." It identified the endangered house as 75, Dean Street, Soho, "believed to have been the residence of Hogarth's father-in-law, Sir James Thornhill" (*The Times* 1914a). *The Times* made its case for preservation on two grounds: the building's historical associations with Thornhill and Hogarth and its intrinsic beauty. Mr Mulliner, the new proprietor, had arranged for its cleaning and restoration, hoping to attract a suitable institutional benefactor. As no civic-minded individual or body of persons came forward, Mulliner was now negotiating with a commercial buyer who intended to demolish the house. For several weeks, *The Times* kept up a spirited campaign to prevent the destruction of "Hogarth's Soho House" (*The Times* 1914b; *The Times* 1914c). In response, the Commissioner of Works issued the first preservation order under the Ancient Monuments Act of 1913, placing "Soho's Hogarth House" under protection for 18 months, until Parliament could decide whether to purchase it for the nation (Hobhouse 1971: 6–8).

The landmark status of "Hogarth's Soho House" seemed to depend on the dual claim that it was a "beautiful house with Hogarth associations." Although a precious relic of the English past, its historical value also derived from the blending of English and Venetian artistic traditions: the mural painting is "one of the few relics of a time when the artists of our smoky city took their inspiration from [sunny] Venice" (*The Times* 1914a). Campaigners won the support of May Morris and Walter Crane, leaders of the Arts and Crafts movement, who believed that historical interest in old buildings and locales fostered social conscience and civic patriotism (Morris 1914).

Nonetheless, questions remained about the building's historical provenance, particularly about its "Hogarth associations." *The Times* acknowledged that research into the rate books yielded no evidence of Thornhill's residence on Dean Street; it turned instead to topographical histories as "collateral evidence" (*The Times* 1914c). A second sticking point was 75 Dean Street's location in Soho. Preservationists might claim that Soho deserved their attention because it was an old district vulnerable to large-scale modern "developments" in the property market. But urban planners, such as Lawrence Gomme, believed that Soho had lost its claims to being an historic area by allowing itself to become an overcrowded slum (Gomme 1914: 323).

Commentators felt obliged to negotiate the irony of preserving this "noble piece of Old London" in "one of the most curious and foreign districts in London" where it was an island of peace "hemmed in by a babbling sea of foreign tongues" (*The Times* 1914c). *The Times* also alerted readers of the destructive impact of the cosmopolitan capital of the present day. It would be a "thousand pities," it warned, if these stately chambers fell into "vandals' hands" and were "broken up and carried piecemeal to some foreign country with a stronger sense of tradition and beauty" (*The Times* 1914b).

This was indeed the ironic denouement and fate of 75 Dean Street. The attempt to preserve a building under the Ancient Monuments Act of 1913 proved to be "tragically abortive" (Hobhouse 1971: 27). The building fell victim to the conflicting claims over national interest and private property, but also to the shady market in antiques and salvages that had evolved out of the Wardour Street trade. H. H. Mulliner, the building's owner, was a "connoisseur" and director of the decorating firm of Lenygon and Morant, the leading importer of English "olde worlde" rooms across the Atlantic (Harris 2007: 104). Between 1912 and 1914, Mr Mulliner presented himself as a patriotic benefactor of Hogarth's Soho House, only desirous of finding a buyer who would cover his out-of-pocket costs. When he realized that the preservation order did not involve compensation or governmental purchase, he petitioned against the order. He disputed the historic value of the building, notably the family association with Thornhill and Hogarth. The House of Lord's Select Committee upheld his petition against the order.

World War I temporarily postponed the destruction of the building, but, shortly after the Armistice, the transatlantic trade in antiques and period rooms resumed and the building's interior treasures were shipped off to America. But the spurious 'olde English' Hogarth association continued to enhance the commercial value of the interior artifacts. In 1925, to great public acclaim, the staircase and paneling of the "Hogarth house" were donated to the Art Institute of Chicago, only to be de-accessioned as a fraud in 1997 (Harris 2000: 19–21).

Hogarth's Soho House provides a fitting book end to the McKay/Cardwell dispute over Soho's dangerous cosmopolitanism. These controversies illuminate the competing versions of cosmopolitanism that migrated into turn-of-the-century Soho and their troubling relation to any stable meaning of Englishness. On the one hand Soho was imagined to be filled with deracinated and questionable objects, bodies, and practices; on the other hand, it was a treasured relic of a sturdy national past. Old world charm and contemporary exoticism combined to establish Soho's positive cosmopolitan reputation as a modern space of taste and refinement. But its historic urban fabric proved to be as mutable and transportable to other countries as the immigrant refugees who arrived on English shores and settled in Soho. Old Soho, it seems, could be as inauthentic as Soho's Franco-Italian cuisine, the product of an earlier moment of assimilated cosmopolitanism and modern historic invention. And its new cosmopolitan migrants proved themselves capable of the same strategies of adaptive self-fashioning as the worldly, privileged connoisseurs of Old Soho's Georgian treasures.

References

Anderson, Amanda (2001) *The Powers of Distance: Cosmopolitanism and the Cultivation of Detachment*. Princeton, NJ: Princeton University Press.

Armfelt, Count (1990 [1902]) Cosmopolitan London. In *Edwardian London*, ed. G. R. Sims. 4 vols. London: Village Press, vol. 1, 241–7.

Ashton, Rosemary (1986) *Little Germany: Exile and Asylum in Victorian England*. Oxford: Oxford University Press.

Barber, Peter, and Jacomelli, Peter (1997) *Continental Taste: Ticinese Emigrants and Their Café-Restaurants in Britain, 1847–1987*. Occasional Paper, Camden History Society. London: Camden History Society.

Black, Gerry (1994) *Living up West: Jewish Life in London's West End*. London: London Museum of Jewish Life.

Booth, Charles (1902) *Life and Labour of the People in London*. 3rd edn., vol. 2: *Religious Influences*. London: Macmillan.

Brooker, Peter (2004) *Bohemia in London: The Social Scene of Early Modernism*. Basingstoke: Palgrave Macmillan.

Burnett, John (2004) *England Eats Out: A Social History of Eating Out in England from 1830 to the Present*. Harlow and New York: Pearson/Longman.

Cardwell, John Henry (1898) *Two Centuries of Soho: Its Institutions, Firms, and Amusements*. London: Truslove and Hanson.

Cardwell, John Henry (1903) *Men and Women of Soho, Famous and Infamous: Actors, Authors, Dramatists, Entertainers and Engravers*. [London]: Truslove and Hanson.

Cardwell, John Henry (1911) *Twenty Years in Soho. A Review of the Work of the Church in the Parish of St Anne's, Soho from 1891 to 1911*. London: Truslove and Hanson.

Cassell's Saturday Journal (1900) In the slums of Soho: a chat with Rev. Cardwell. August 8: 902. Westminster Archives, newspaper clippings, vol. 14.

The Caterer and Hotel-Keeper (1906a) Open-air cafés. July 16: 13.

The Caterer and Hotel-Keeper (1906b) Soho and its restaurants. June 15: 262–66.

The Caterer and Hotel-Keeper (1906c) Soho and its restaurants. July 16: 304–6.

The Caterer and Hotel-Keeper (1906d) Soho and its restaurants III: Gerrard Street, Dryden, and the origins of coffee houses. August 15: 338–40.

The Caterer and Hotel-Keeper (1906e) Soho and its restaurants IV: Gerrard Street (continued) – the Literary Club and the Italian element. November 15: 480–82.

The Caterer and Hotel-Keeper (1906f) Soho and its restaurants V: Gerrard Street (continued) – a notable cosmopolitan career. December 15: 542–44.

The Caterer and Hotel-Keeper (1907a) Soho and its restaurants VI: Lisle Street. February 15: 84.

The Caterer and Hotel-Keeper (1907b) Soho and its restaurants VII: Leicester Square. March 15: 112–13.

Census (1902) *Census of England and Wales, 1901.* London: HMSO.

Cheah, Pheng, and Robbins, Bruce (1998) *Cosmopolitics: Thinking and Feeling Beyond the Nation.* Minneapolis: University of Minnesota Press.

Driver, Felix, and Gilbert, David (1998) Heart of empire? Landscape, space and performance in imperial London. *Environment and Planning D: Society and Space* 16: 11–28.

Eade, John (2000) *Placing London: From Imperial City to Global City.* Oxford: Berghahn.

Evening Standard (1906) Topics of the day: the worst street. October 20. Westminster Archives, Newspaper clippings, vol. 14.

Gomme, George Laurence (1914) *London.* Philadelphia and London: J. B. Lippincott Company.

Harris, John (2000) What might be called a frame-up: The Hogarth House. *British Art Journal* 1 (1): 19–21.

Harris, John (2007) *Moving Rooms.* New Haven, CT, and London: Yale University Press for the Paul Mellon Centre for Studies in British Art.

Hobhouse, Hermione (1971) *Lost London: A Century of Demolition and Decay.* London: Macmillan.

Kaplan, Morris B. (2005) *Sodom on the Thames: Sex, Love, and Scandal in Wilde Times.* Ithaca, NY: Cornell University Press.

Mandler, Peter (1997) *The Fall and Rise of the Stately Home.* New Haven, CT: Yale University Press.

McLaughlin, Joseph (2000) *Writing the Urban Jungle: Reading Empire in London from Doyle to Eliot.* Charlottesville: University Press of Virginia.

Melman, Billie (2006) *The Culture of History: English Uses of the Past, 1800–1953.* Oxford and New York: Oxford University Press.

Mennell, Stephen (1985) *All Manners of Food: Eating and Taste in England and France from the Middle Ages to the Present.* Oxford: Blackwell.

Morris, May (1914) Arts and Crafts: the future of 75, Dean-Street. Letters to the Editor. *The Times* January 26: 6.

Nead, Lynda (2000) *Victorian Babylon: People, Streets, and Images in Nineteenth-Century London.* New Haven, CT: Yale University Press.

Olsen, Donald J. (1976) *The Growth of Victorian London.* New York: Holmes & Meier.

Pall Mall Gazette (1887) Charing-Cross Road. February 26: 1–2.

Paul, Howard (1898) A dinner at Kettner's. *Caterer and Hotel Keeper* February 15: 64.

Petrow, Stefan (1994) *Policing Morals: The Metropolitan Police and the Home Office, 1870–1914.* Oxford: Oxford University Press.

Rappaport, Erika Diane (2000) *Shopping for Pleasure: Women in the Making of London's West End.* Princeton, NJ: Princeton University Press.

Samuel, Raphael (1994) *Theatres of Memory.* London: Verso.

Sherwell, Robert (1897) *Life in West London: A Study and a Contrast.* London: Methuen.

Shpayer-Makov, Haia (1988) Anarchism in British public opinion, 1880–1914. *Victorian Studies* 31 (4): 487–516.

Smith, Tori (1999) "A grand work of noble conception": the Victorian memorial and imperial London. In *Imperial Cities: Landscape, Display and Identity*, ed. Felix Driver and David Gilbert. Manchester: Manchester University Press, 21–39.

Summers, Judith (1989) *Soho: A History of London's Most Colourful Neighbourhood*. London: Bloomsbury.

Summerson, John (1991) *Georgian London*. London: Pimlico.

The Sun (1896) Soho incident. July. Westminster Archives, newspaper clippings, vol. 15.

Tames, Richard (1994) *Soho Past*. London: Historical Publications.

Thornbury, George Walter (1887) *Old and New London, Etc*. London: Cassell & Co.

The Times (1914a) Georgian house in Soho. January 9: 9.

The Times (1914b) No. 75, Dean Street. January 14: 9.

The Times (1914c) The preservation of No. 75, Dean-Street. January 17: 2.

Walkowitz, Judith R. (1998) Going public: shopping, street harassment, and streetwalking in late Victorian London. *Representations* 62: 1–30.

Walkowitz, Judith R. (2003) The "Vision of Salome": cosmopolitanism and erotic dancing in central London, 1908–1918. *The American Historical Review* 108 (2): 337–76.

Walkowitz, Rebecca L. (2006) *Cosmopolitan Style: Modernism Beyond the Nation*. New York: Columbia University Press.

Weightman, Gavin (1992) *Bright Lights, Big City: London Entertained, 1830–1950*. London: Collins & Brown.

Williams, Raymond (1976) *Keywords: A Vocabulary of Culture and Society*. New York: Oxford University Press.

Zemgulys, Andrea (2008) *Modernism and the Locations of Literary Heritage*. Cambridge and New York: Cambridge University Press.

Chapter 38

Modernity and Gaslight: Victorian London in the 1950s and 1960s

Frank Mort

It has become a commonplace to insist that England is an "old country"; its culture constrained by a deference towards the past and its versions of national identity transfixed by the weight of history that is productive and disabling in equal measure. Recent arguments that erupted among historians about the significance of the nineteenth century for our own period pointed to the way that "Victorianism" in particular has provided an ever-burgeoning set of objects and images that shape contemporary urban culture: heritage sites and domestic interiors, fashion and popular literature, and even the interior spaces of memory. Public commentators often argued about the implications of this obsession with the Victorian past, variously seeing it as part of a self-fulfilling culture of national decline or as a source of historical energy and strength, but they were all agreed about its power (Wright 1985; Hewison 1987; Samuel 1994). What was equally significant about this heritage debate was how historians identified London as the privileged site of a reinvented Victorianism. Whether they focused on Dickensian images of the nineteenth-century metropolis, on the contemporary meanings of crumbling, soot-blackened London brick, or on the frisson of horror produced by the retelling of the Jack the Ripper murders by local East-End historians, it was overwhelmingly the English capital city that provided them with an urban optic to view the nineteenth-century past.

These uses of Victorianism and their embeddedness in urban culture are not new. Since the early twentieth century, when public intellectuals like Lytton Strachey and Virginia Woolf launched a modernist assault on the negative legacy of the nineteenth century, multiple and contradictory readings of the Victorians, and of London as the paradigmatic Victorian city, have functioned as an active set of cultural resources for different groups of social and political actors (Strachey 1920; Woolf 1974). These interpretations of recent history have rarely been simply academic; social

The New Blackwell Companion to the City   Edited by Gary Bridge and Sophie Watson
© 2011 Blackwell Publishing Ltd

commentators have understood nineteenth-century urban culture as an active presence in the development of contemporary English society, while their readings of the connections between the Victorian past and the present have generated distinctive understandings of current problems and anxieties, as well as providing blueprints for the future.

My focus is on the contested meanings of London's Victorian legacy in the years from the end of World War II to the early 1960s. This is a period that historians have conventionally defined as avowedly *post-Victorian* in many areas of society, politics, and culture. Stories of economic growth and technological innovation, the rise of consensus politics and the welfare state, the impact of mass affluence, and the reshaping of class and social hierarchies, along with the modernization of personal and sexual relationships are among the familiar master-narratives of progressive social advancement that are told about the postwar period (Marwick 1998; Hennessy 2006). Taken together these accounts have stressed a definitive break with the nineteenth-century past, documenting the final abandonment of economic liberalism, the end of empire, and the demise of Victorian social morality. I want to revise this view of the postwar years as marking a radical break with the nineteenth-century, showing how the processes of capital city change continued to be marked by the extended cultural reach of Victorianism, in ways that had implications for English society more generally.

Two general methodological points are worth stressing at the outset. First, following the recent pioneering work of cultural historians, I understand modern London as a city produced by the material fabric of its built environment, by a distinctive social and economic geography, and also by a dense lexicon of urban representations that are shaped by a wide variety of textual and iconographic resources (Stedman Jones and Feldman 1989; Walkowitz 1992; Nead 2000). Second, drawing on my own analysis of the legacy of the nineteenth-century metropolis, I argue that postwar interpretations of Victorianism were invariably historically contingent (Mort 2006). What different groups of urbanists chose to prioritize as Victorian was highly selective; their choices reflected current social preoccupations as much as any desire to excavate an objective nineteenth-century past. Moreover, their sense of historical periodization was often equally eclectic; events or moments in what historians would now call the long nineteenth century were frequently kaleidoscoped together, including urban images and environments from the Edwardian period as well, so that chronological cut-off points separating and defining different historical moments fluctuated widely. Despite these differences, almost all postwar commentators and policy-makers were agreed that the Victorian city could not be ignored in assessing the needs of contemporary Londoners.

The most significant blueprint for modern London, in the aftermath of wartime enemy bombing by the German Luftwaffe and all its attendant social dislocations, was the implementation of a planning-inspired vision for the capital in the 1940s. Driven by Labour politicians both at Westminster and at the London County Council, working in close alliance with the enhanced power of the planning profession, this represented the most systematic attempt to reorder London's physical and social environment since Christopher Wren's grandiose vision for the rebuilding of the city after the Great Fire of 1666. Self-consciously progressive, planning in its most expansive form identified London as a paradigmatic metropolis of the future.

Insisting that the capital would need to serve multiple functions in the postwar years ahead, planners simultaneously envisaged London as a modern imperial metropole for the newly invented Commonwealth, a contemporary world city functioning as a hub for international communications, finance, and culture, and a supra-urban conurbation, with a hinterland dominating most of southern England (Forshaw and Abercrombie 1943; Corporation of London 1944).

All of these plans began by confronting the serious problems posed by the destruction of much of the metropolitan core of the capital, including the City of London and the inner East End, by enemy bombing. From that centrifugal point they fanned out across the nineteenth-century suburbs, the proposed Green Belt, and the envisaged new towns beyond. Comprehensively addressing major aspects of London's physical and social geography, they envisaged large-scale population movements, organized coherent transport systems, and instituted social and industrial zoning, together with a series of long-term environmental measures. Despite financial and political constraints, this postwar planning moment represented a major paradigm shift away from ad hoc urban policy-making towards a much more coordinated vision for London. Given that similar schemes for modern urban redevelopment were replicated across other English cities, planners were cast as key professional players in the implementation of the postwar social contract, founded on the principles of increased state intervention, extended citizenship rights, and the power of expert knowledge (Cullingworth 1962; Mandler 1999).

How did the doyens of the planning profession view Victorian London? Overwhelmingly, as an obstacle to the future success of a modern metropolis because the nineteenth-century city represented an affront to cherished beliefs about urban progress on account of its decrepit infrastructure, its chaotic and disordered development, and its dysfunctional social and moral uses. Planners drew on the strategy of social zoning familiar from American cities, twinning it with the home-grown traditions of English town planning, to produce an appropriate sense of modern social geography. Planning blueprints of this sort enshrined both a coherent understanding of orderly and integrated urban functions such as transport, housing, and leisure provision, on one hand, and an equally strong sense of matter and people out of place, on the other (Matless 1993: 167). For the most part nineteenth-century London was cast as the antithesis of a streamlined English modernism.

The high noon of this planning discourse produced some of the most notorious schemes for the demolition of large tracts of the Victorian West End. Pronouncing Gilbert Scott's elaborate neo-classical government buildings fronting Whitehall as an "inefficient ... slum," the *Architect's Journal* laid out ambitious plans for their wholesale demolition and replacement by modern, functional office blocs (Anon. 1962: 733). Schemes of this sort received serious attention from national politicians and civil servants keen to promote an efficient bureaucracy; they were agreed that the dilapidated condition and antiquated atmosphere of Victorian public buildings made them feel like a "mausoleum" (Macmillan 1969: 492). Very few of the capital's conservationists and burgeoning residents' associations believed nineteenth-century London was worthy of preservation until the mid-1960s. Campaigners and urban settlers focused their attention on the built environment of the Georgian city in prestige areas such as Mayfair, following a conservationist tradition that had been established in the early years of the twentieth century.

Planners and public moralists targeted their anxieties about the Victorian West End on Soho's cosmopolitan neighborhood, east of Mayfair and north of Whitehall. Historically Soho was the home of English bohemianism and political radicalism, the focal point for a plethora of European and Jewish migrant and artisanal cultures, and the longstanding centre of London's thriving sex trade. In reality, much of Soho's infrastructure had been laid out in the early eighteenth century as part of the commercial and residential expansion of the district north of the royal court of St James's, but for many urban reformers postwar Soho came to epitomize the worst excesses of a Victorian inner-city area, where moral and material blight went hand-in-hand. The *County of London Plan*, produced by the architects John Forshaw and Patrick Abercrombie (1943) for the London County Council, set the tone for many subsequent schemes. With a sidelong glance at the area's sexually dubious atmosphere, they noted that any proposed new development would have to address what they euphemistically described as "deteriorated mixed ... use" (Forshaw and Abercrombie 1943: 24). The answer was a stricter rationalization of commercial functions; the restaurant trade would henceforward define the district's local economy, with a hoped-for marginalization of its other irregular activities. Forshaw and Abercrombie championed orderly commerce as the most effective form of counter-publicity to offset the area's disreputable reputation. Ten years later, private-sector developers laid out much more radical proposals for the eradication of Victorian Soho. An architectural consortium, appropriately called the Glass Age Development Committee, advocated the "clearance" of eighteenth- and nineteenth-century streets and buildings on a grand scale. Their ambition was to replace most of Soho with six high-rise glass towers, each housing 1,500 residents, air-conditioned shopping and office precincts, glassed-in arcades, enhanced by canals and water gardens, underground car parking, and "spacious open-air entertainment areas" (Glass Age Development Committee 1955: 56).

Modernist schemes for Soho's redevelopment remained largely confined to the drawing-board, but they represented a different approach to the rebuilding of the West End and the City of London in the 1950s from that championed by the planning profession. They were spearheaded by financiers, speculative developers, and a group of commercially minded architects. Their vision for London opened a new phase of what novelist Peter Ackroyd, evoking Dickens, has described as that living monstrous, voracious, intensely commercial London (Ackroyd 2000: 584). Historians who have charted the story of the capital beyond the 1950s have argued that this commercial ethic consistently won out over planned initiatives. The property boom of the subsequent decade, together with the later bursts of free-market entrepreneurialism associated first with the political project of the Thatcher governments in the 1980s and then with the power of global capital, all reinforced assumptions that private-sector development triumphed over coordinated planning in most central areas of the city (Hall 1989; White 2002).

Developers and entrepreneurs have also been credited with putting in place the material infrastructure for some of the major postwar changes to sexuality and personal life that finally ended the legacy of Victorian social morality. Transformations associated with permissiveness in the 1960s, involving the reorganization of the sex industry, the fashion and youth markets, and egalitarian forms of cosmopolitan culture, have all been linked to changing portfolios of property ownership and retail use centered on the West End and adjacent areas (Booker 1969; Breward 2004). One very familiar version of this story is the idea of swinging London. When the young American journalist Piri Halasz published her famous article advertising London as a swinging metropolis, as the cover story for *Time* magazine in 1966, she introduced a neologism that fixed the capital in the world's imagination for years to come. Halasz's notion of London as the swinging city *par excellence* was a celebration of the youthful talent and switched-on urban personalities who paraded along Chelsea's King's Road and Soho's Carnaby Street, but she also laid out influential arguments about London as a post-Victorian city. For Halasz and for many commentators who followed her lead, "with it" life in the English capital was now more meritocratic and certainly more relaxed; it represented a loosening of nineteenth-century inhibitions and social hierarchies. If Britain had "lost an Empire," *Time* concluded, it had "recovered a lightness of heart lost during the weighty centuries of world leadership." London now led the field in the "art of living" and in the "special quality" that was the hallmark of all "great cities; civility in the broadest sense" (Halasz 1966: 32, 41; see also Raban 1974).

Arguments of this sort about London as an exemplary modern metropolis of the 1960s have become part of the dominant historical accounts of the postwar city, just as they have shaped wider debates about the social and cultural modernization of English society. One major problem with such explanations is the Whiggish ideal of progress implied by the supposed abandonment of Victorian values and the energetic take-up of more liberal codes of culture and social morality. A related issue is the linear notion of progressive urbanism implied by this interpretation, as the material fabric and the culture of the nineteenth-century city are understood to have been displaced by more modern rebuilding schemes and related forms of social advancement. Yet this is only part of London's postwar story; a different version of events charts the ongoing presence of Victorianism in the immediate postwar years, and even into the 1960s. This nineteenth-century legacy was not simply regressive; it played an active role in the modernization of contemporary urban relationships and it suggests a more complex account of social change than the one outlined by the idea of swinging or permissive London.

We might begin our alternative history of the postwar city with the role of royalty and the upper class. The coronation of Elizabeth II in 1953 recentered London in the national imagination and across the world. The coronation was itself a piece of royal tradition that owed much to the reinvention of monarchy during the late Victorian period. As a London spectacle it was Janus-faced; it looked forward to an optimistic future symbolized by the idea of a new Elizabethan age but it was also a revivalist myth, the last great imperial display, in a world where British influence on the international stage was being heavily squeezed by the new superpowers. Geographically, the coronation redirected public attention back towards the metropolitan central area, after the planning-inspired expansion of suburban and "greater London" in the 1940s. The Queen's coronation procession followed a route through the nineteenth- and early twentieth-century metropolis (the Mall, Admiralty Arch, Oxford Street, and back down Whitehall) which had first been perfected for the funeral of Queen Victoria and the coronation of Edward VII.

Coronation London also gave pride of place to the leaders of elite metropolitan society, continuing the renaissance of upper-class manners and mores that had begun in the late 1940s. Historians have argued that the political and social power wielded by the upper class was substantially curtailed in the immediate postwar period under the combined democratizing effects of World War II, the Labour government's program of social redistribution, and the changing dynamics of public life (McKibbin 1998). Yet many of society's rituals and some of its personalities underwent an energetic revival and a partial transformation during the postwar years, especially in the West End which functioned as the parade ground for socialites, ranging from the Queen's sister Princess Margaret to visiting international celebrities. This renaissance was encouraged by the dynamic forms of cultural conservatism linked to the coronation and to the Conservative Party's General Election success of 1951, which ushered in a thirteen-year period of Tory political hegemony. The reappearance of key milestones of London's Victorian and Edwardian social season, such as the Chelsea Flower Show, Wimbledon tennis, and the presentation of debutantes at court, centered on the display of leisured wealth and royal patronage in the capital city, as they had done a century earlier.

The revival of patrician culture was closely associated with the re-emergence of elite personalities who had dominated London life before 1914. Prominent among these metropolitan characters was the figure of the man-about-town. As London's distinctive rendering of the Parisian *flâneur*, the enthusiastic postwar reinvention of the man-about-town by young, upper-class dandies testified to the continuing power of elite culture in a country that was now supposedly democratic and increasingly egalitarian. Being a man-about-town in 1950s London was quintessentially about masculine forms of privilege. The world of Pall Mall's gentlemen's clubs, court and society functions in St James's and Mayfair, fashionable consumption in Jermyn Street, and all of the West End's varied night-time amusements was on offer to men-about-town. Like the late Victorian gent or "swell," they claimed imaginative rights to the whole of the city that embraced both high- and low-life versions of the capital's pleasure economy. A number of leading society figures also extended their itineraries into London's homosexual spaces, showing how the man-about-town displayed significant sexual fault-lines that rendered his personality potentially dubious or problematic. Much further down the capital's social hierarchy, Teddy Boys empowered by nascent consumer culture fashioned their own styles of leisured gentlemanliness. Their take-up of Edwardian styles of dress and display in inner-city districts like Lambeth and Islington, that lay adjacent to the world of West-End high society, showed how young working-class men drew on the resources of the past to fashion the first postwar youth subculture (Fyvel 1961).

The counterpoint to the revival of London's elite culture was the way that a number of society figures and their society settings were seen to be implicated in the capital's underworld or its *demi-monde*, via their sexual tastes or politically motivated actions. A series of highly publicized metropolitan cases variously involving sex, treason, espionage, and high politics punctuated the decade from the early 1950s. Exposés of sexual scandal centered on show trials of the upper-class characters Lord Montagu of Beaulieu and Michael Pitt-Rivers, along with their friend Peter Wildeblood, for homosexual offences with two young working-class airmen (Wildeblood 1957; Waters 1999). Even more spectacular was the Profumo affair in

1963, which undermined the Conservative government as a result of the sexual entanglement of the Minister for War, John Profumo, with call-girl Christine Keeler (Keeler 2001; Swanson 2007). The Profumo affair had a double plot that coupled sex and espionage; it therefore needs to be seen in relation to the other genre of public scandal dominating the postwar years, the high-profile cases of spying that involved sexually deviant characters, especially homosexual men, as security threats. The most prominent episodes in this latter category were the defections of the Foreign Office officials Guy Burgess and Donald Maclean to the Soviet Union in 1951, together with the fall-out from the Vassall spy scandal in 1962–3, involving the exposure and trial of the Admiralty clerk John Vassall for stealing military secrets for the KGB (Driberg 1956; Home Office 1963).

All of these incidents highlighted particular problem zones in the inner city and they were characterized by the association of high and low cultures that were seen to be dangerously interrelated in London's central areas. Coverage of the cases in the national press in part evoked a nineteenth-century urban topography; over-worlds collided with underworlds that were depicted in *chiaroscuro* half tones and shadows, reviving images and characters that were familiar from Victorian urban encounters. Men-about-town and other society figures made regular appearances in the scandals, personalities who were frequently shown to be compromised by their association with low-life or disreputable characters. The episodes also pushed together competing beliefs about pathological forms of masculinity and sexually wayward femininity, set against the norms of marriage and family life. Many of the incidents probed the psychology and motivations underpinning the nature of evil, treason, sex, and passion – forms of human behavior that were seen to be stimulated by the capital's urban environments. On a more contemporary note, a number of these scandals brought into play anxieties about the capital's immigrant cultures, and especially about the way that cosmopolitan areas were being transformed by the impact of Caribbean migration.

This was by no means the first time that metropolitan scandals had functioned as conduits for wide-ranging social problems. Throughout the nineteenth century a succession of murder trials and sexual intrigues had allowed different groups to engage in struggles over meaningful stories about urban danger and moral truth (Israel 1997; Erber and Robb 1999). The scandals that erupted during the immediate postwar years were influenced by earlier events and drew heavily on their cultural and political resources. But they also orchestrated decidedly contemporary versions of social morality that functioned as major interpretative devices within English society. Overwhelmingly, these postwar incidents dramatized quintessentially modern anxieties that eventually led to changes in social mood and in attitudes towards sexual mores and criminal conduct, as well as to some of the key markers defining national identity. Yet the cases were in no sense unproblematically forward-looking. The characters who dominated them were not the familiar range of progressive reformers or go-ahead entrepreneurs that historians have associated with permissive or swinging London. What shaped these transgressive incidents were some very traditional elements within public life: sex, treason, and political scandal.

The Profumo affair in particular pushed together many of the contradictory pressures towards tradition and innovation that characterized English society in the early 1960s, orchestrating them in a London setting. Running throughout the spring and summer of 1963, the scandal fatally compromised John Profumo, who was forced to resign from Harold Macmillan's government as a result of his sexual affair with Keeler. Keeler's other lovers at the time included a number of Caribbean men, and as a result the elite world of English politics was drawn into an uneasy relationship with West Indian migrant culture. Most significantly of all, Keeler's rumored affair with the naval attaché and Soviet spy Eugene Ivanov coupled high-society sex and miscegenation fears with the geopolitics of the Cold War. Meanwhile, her close relationship with her mentor, the society osteopath and playboy Stephen Ward, who committed suicide at the height of the scandal, focused public attention on the sexually ambiguous status of upper-class English masculinity. Circulated as world news by the international media, the case was described by Lord Denning in his judicial review of the affair as a "sensation that captured the attention of the world" (Denning 1992: v).

Profumo was a London-centered event; at almost every stage, the case was shaped by London's social relationships and environments. Its erotic encounters and scandalous incidents were stimulated by the city's historically distinctive architectural and spatial layout. In particular, the interrelated worlds of metropolitan society, clubland, and Tory high politics were crucial settings for the incubation of the affair, as they had been in many earlier sensational sex cases. Members of Macmillan's government who intervened politically in the scandal or who were embarrassed by it moved regularly between Westminster, Pall Mall's clubland, and diplomatic and embassy functions hosted in Belgravia and Mayfair. All of these settings were located in the compressed metropolitan spaces of London's central area and they were easily accessible to each other by chauffeur-driven car, taxi, or even on foot.

The Houses of Parliament and the imposing government offices lining Whitehall were situated only a short distance from Soho. This dramatically polarized social geography had major consequences for English public life. Politicians like Profumo, whose ostensible brief was national security, were in a constant dialogue with the sexual worlds on their doorstep, not just as problems demanding official solutions but also as erotic entertainment which provided them with the frisson of excitement. Dangerous sexualities pressed hard on government, especially when public figures brought London's *demi-monde* into the heart of the state through their personal liaisons.

Soho featured in the Profumo affair as the setting for amorous night-time encounters between prominent men-about-town such as Profumo and Ward and sexually available women like Keeler. In this sense the story had a familiar ring; entanglements involving senior ministers in extra-marital affairs with glamorous young showgirls replicated the structure of many Victorian and Edwardian sex cases (Montgomery Hyde 1986). But Christine Keeler was more culturally and geographically mobile than traditional courtesans or kept women had been; she used the resources of female sexuality to cross and recross social and sexual boundaries. In the early 1960s her constant desire for sexual experimentation propelled her beyond a string of society boyfriends and casual encounters and into a series of affairs with Caribbean lovers, especially Antiguan Johnny Edgecombe. Her interest in West Indian men, coupled with Stephen Ward's own fascination with exotic slumming, shifted the scandal's centre of gravity towards the new spaces of cosmopolitan

London, located in Notting Hill, with their distinctive atmosphere of racial and cultural disturbance.

Notting Hill in the early 1960s was London's wild west. Three miles beyond Soho down the Bayswater Road, its nineteenth-century squares and imposing middle-class villas had become decaying flats and rooming houses where Caribbean immigrants now made their homes. For planners and social workers it was one of London's "twilight zones," containing a "motley collection of people" ranging "from the top to the bottom of the social scale" (Glass 1964: xx–xxi). During the first stage of the migration cycle young, single West Indian men were the subject of endless local fascination and anxiety. Exotic food, calypso music, drugs, and above all the sexual behavior of the newcomers turned Notting Hill into an informal cultural laboratory and a place of racialized conflict. The district produced a different version of cosmopolitanism from that experienced in Soho, shifting the idea away from its European and Jewish associations and towards the Caribbean. Culturally as well as politically the impact of the West Indian newcomers was double edged. Extending the idea of London as a multicultural city, they also encouraged a defensive, territorial sense of Englishness among many poor whites, and it was these tensions that erupted dramatically in the Notting Hill riots of 1958.

The social and sexual impact of the Profumo affair as a modern scandal was generated by the London settings that were exposed in relationships of corrupt and unhealthy dependence. Anxieties about the racialized forms of transgression epitomized by the Profumo, Keeler, and Edgecombe triangle became a major focus for media attention as events pointed to disturbing connections between the Caribbean cultures of Notting Hill and the West End's social elites. This was the focus of a wide-ranging debate about the consequences of permissive morality. In all the flurry of argument about the meaning of permissiveness that erupted during the scandal, one issue was recurrent: a widely held belief that the rapidly changing environments of metropolitan London occupied a pivotal role in shaping broader social and sexual changes. Permissiveness understood in this way did not refer to the conventional markers of sexual liberalization (progressive entrepreneurs, the enhanced power of sexual experts, or shifts in personal habits and beliefs) but to a dynamic realignment of people and spaces in the capital city.

Harold Macmillan turned to this theme as the crisis unfolded. Deeply anguished about the scandal's consequences for public life, he struggled to understand how and why John Profumo had behaved so indiscreetly. He sensed that part of the answer lay in London's changing social environments; as he saw it Profumo and his associates moved within a raffish society where no one really knew anyone anymore. Macmillan grasped that the metropolitan settings covered by the scandal were not the venues of conventional society assignations, nor even those of the West End's established cosmopolitans and bohemians. What characterized the new social landscapes was their deliberate cultural ambiguity, with a lack of any clear separation between licit and illicit activities. In his Edwardian youth and interwar manhood, he recalled, "you could be absolutely sure that you could go to a restaurant with your wife and not see a man that you knew having lunch with a tart … It was all kept separate, but this does not seem to happen these days," he complained (Horne 1988: 495). For Macmillan, the early twentieth-century confidence of the man-of-the-world now no longer held; people and places collided in an alarming fashion.

The Profumo affair along with the other scandals that dominated postwar London life produced an atmosphere of crisis that was brought about by infraction of the rules of morality, law, or custom. Metropolitan London featured as a major part of the anxieties released by these episodes because the environments that they pushed together generated an extremely powerful atmosphere of moral disturbance. The incidents represented a crisis of place and location, bringing to a head public concerns and social fantasies about the city that ultimately reshaped the character of public and private life. But the changes they introduced were not straightforwardly modernizing; stories of wayward or dangerous sexuality, acted out in quasi-Victorian locations that juxtaposed metropolitan overworlds and underworlds, appeared on first reading to confirm a backward-looking agenda. Yet in almost every instance the effect of these episodes was to destabilize traditional moral and sexual certainties via social personalities and urban settings that drew heavily on the resources of the past. What these scandalous events highlight is the continuing force and adaptability of nineteenth-century cultural forms and urban environments in a period that was repeatedly characterized as post-Victorian. Such uses of history problematize established understandings of postwar modernization and they complicate conventional periodizations that have been used to distinguish nineteenth- from twentieth-century London. Recognizing the continuing impact of the Victorian past in the postwar period involves historians and urbanists in constructing a more complex narrative of social change as part of a revision of the history of the modern city.

References

Ackroyd, P. (2000) *London: The Biography*. London: Chatto & Windus.

Anon. (1962) Loving modernisation or expedient desecration. *Architect's Journal* 136 (13) September 26: 733.

Booker, C. (1969) *The Neophiliacs: A Study of the Revolution in English Life in the Fifties and Sixties*. London: Collins.

Breward, C. (2004) *Fashioning London: Clothing and the Modern Metropolis*. Oxford: Berg.

Corporation of London (1944) *Report to the Right Honourable the Lord Mayor etc. on the Preliminary Draft Proposals for Post War Reconstruction in the City of London*. London: Batsford.

Cullingworth, J. (1962) *New Towns for Old: The Problem of Urban Renewal*. London: Fabian Society.

Denning, A. (1992) *The Denning Report: The Profumo Affair; with a New Introduction by the Author*. London: Pimlico.

Driberg, T. (1956) *Guy Burgess: A Portrait with Background*. London: Weidenfeld & Nicolson.

Erber, N., and Robb, G. (eds.) (1999) *Disorder in the Court: Trials and Sexual Conflict at the Turn of the Century*. Basingstoke: Macmillan.

Forshaw, J., and Abercrombie, P. (1943) *County of London Plan*. London: Macmillan.

Fyvel, T. (1961) *The Insecure Offenders: Rebellious Youth in the Welfare State*. London: Chatto & Windus.

Glass, R. (1964) Aspects of change. In *London: Aspects of Change*, ed. Centre for Urban Studies. London: MacGibbon and Kee, xiii–xlii.

Glass Age Development Committee (1955) The Soho Project – 3, *Official Architecture and Planning* February: 56.

Halasz, P. (1966) Great Britain. *Time* April 15: 32–41.

Hall, P. (1989) *London 2001*. London: Unwin Hyman.

Hennessy, P. (2006) *Having It So Good: Britain in the Fifties*. London: Allen Lane.

Hewison, R. (1987) *The Heritage Industry: Britain in a Climate of Decline*. London: Methuen.

Home Office (1963) *Report of the Tribunal Appointed to Inquire into the Vassall Case and Related Matters*. Cmnd. 2009. London: HMSO.

Horne, A. (1988) *Macmillan: 1957–1986. Volume II of the Official Biography*. London: Macmillan.

Israel, K. (1997) French vices and English liberties: gender, class and narrative competition in a late Victorian sexual scandal. *Social History* 22 (1): 1–26.

Keeler, C. (2001) *The Truth at Last: My Story*. London: Sidgwick & Jackson.

Macmillan, H. (1969) *Tides of Fortune, 1945–1955*. London: Macmillan.

Mandler, P. (1999) New towns for old: the fate of the town centre. In *Moments of Modernity: Reconstructing Britain 1945–64*, ed. B. Conekin, F. Mort, and C. Waters. London: Rivers Oram, 208–27.

Marwick, A. (1998) *The Sixties: Cultural Revolution in Britain, France, Italy, and the United States c. 1958–c. 1974*. Oxford: Oxford University Press.

Matless, D. (1993) Appropriate geography: Patrick Abercrombie and the energy of the world. *Journal of Design History* 6 (3): 167–78.

McKibbin, R. (1998) *Classes and Cultures: England 1918–1951*. Oxford: Oxford University Press.

Montgomery Hyde, H. (1986) *A Tangled Web: Sex Scandals in British Politics and Society*. London: Constable.

Mort, F. (2006) Scandalous events: metropolitan culture and moral change in post-Second World War London. *Representations* 93 (Winter): 106–37.

Nead, L. (2000) *Victorian Babylon: People, Streets and Images in Nineteenth-Century London*. London and New Haven, CT: Yale University Press.

Raban, J. (1974) *Soft City*. New York: E. P. Dutton.

Samuel, R. (1994) *Theatres of Memory*, vol. 1: *Past and Present in Contemporary Culture*. London: Verso.

Stedman Jones, G., and Feldman, D. (eds.) (1989) *Metropolis – London: Histories and Representations since 1800*. London: Routledge.

Strachey, L. (1920) *Eminent Victorians*. London: Chatto & Windus.

Swanson, G. (2007) *Drunk with the Glitter: Space, Consumption and Sexual Instability in Modern Urban Culture*. Abingdon: Routledge.

Walkowitz, J. (1992) *City of Dreadful Delight: Narratives of Sexual Danger in Late-Victorian London*. London: Virago.

Waters, C. (1999) Disorders of the mind, disorders of the body social: Peter Wildeblood and the making of the modern homosexual. In *Moments of Modernity: Reconstructing Britain 1945–1964*, ed. B. Conekin, F. Mort, and C. Waters. London: Rivers Oram, 134–51.

White, J. (2002) *London in the Twentieth Century: A City and its People*. London: Penguin.

Wildeblood, P. (1957) *Against the Law*. Harmondsworth: Penguin.

Woolf, V. (1974) *Moments of Being*, ed. J. Schulkind. London: Chatto & Windus.

Wright, P. (1985) *On Living in an Old Country: The National Past in Contemporary Britain*. London: Verso.

Chapter 39

The Doing Undone: Vagrancies for the Acoustic City

Rob Stone

The tram roared and swung down Goldhawk Road towards Young's Corner. Julia, in the front seat was pleasurably aware of the feeling of height and authority that such a position seemed to give her, almost as though she were driving the great swaying, clanging thing herself. There came the grinding of brakes, Julia's body adapted itself to the slowing rhythm of the tram ... The bell clanged, the driver pushed his shining brass lever, the tram, with the screaming of wheels on the rails, went on round the curve and down the Chiswick High Road, taking up its part again in the orchestra of Greater London. And what an orchestra – Julia, with no actual thought, was yet aware of it through all her consciousness. It was too insistent all around her, with its stringed instruments and its brass instruments, its bass notes as of gongs, its sudden sharps both of sound and colour – in twanging bells and in the thin fine young green leaves of the plane trees flickering in the sunlight – for anyone as alive as Julia not to be aware of it. She did not think of it as the voice of London, but she did think of it as the voice of life. And she was herself not only part, but the very central core of life.

(F. Tennyson Jesse, *A Pin to See the Peepshow* (1934): 10)

Whistling Walking

It is some time in the early autumn; morning and bright. Dazzling. Lambchop have just released their new album *Nixon* (2000). Earphones in, I sit happily upstairs at the front of a No. 53 bus heading along Old Kent Road from Elephant and Castle to New Cross. On London FM radio, Robert Elms articulates his enthusiasm for "Up With People" – the album's best-known track. With the schooled seductions of his familiar and accommodating introduction, "Good Morning London", his voice beams. Today, with its simple, entrancing chord pattern and its clapping, the rhythm of "Up With People" is the shining-faced character of the city, its sunlight

The New Blackwell Companion to the City Edited by Gary Bridge and Sophie Watson
© 2011 Blackwell Publishing Ltd

and its citizens. Yet, the thesis of "Up With People" is a melancholy one about loss. A kind of counter-narrative, if such a thing is possible, to its buoyancy. It remembers a booming sound, perhaps pushing up against one's feet, and emanating from an "underground." The same thing, it proposes, now seems sponsored by something chilling; a welfare state of the soul. There are sophisticated textural allusions to blues, soul, and country in the song, to help anchor this rather rheumy elegism. But there is movement in the song's enriching confection of musical glances. Through these glances, London recognizes itself; I think. And, I wonder to myself exactly whose narcissism that recognition depicts; if this song and my listening might represent some theory of this part of the city. Might it be possible to write from here?

"Up With People" can't say everything about the dense and rapidly changing demographics of Old Kent Road, which is now what Limehouse was. It will fall short, as all good theories must. However, in that fallibility it will also fall across and unto. One of its limitations, possibly its most productive, will be the very musicalness of its rhetoric. Timbre, melody, pitch, interval, rhythm, are things which are of exciting but only partial use in exploring an acoustic ecology, especially one that is organized (which can't be the word) from hoots, hums, drones, and rumbles, from murmurs, babblings, and spattered glints of conversation, fractions of overheard personal stereo, rustlings, the ringing of phones and the mercurial mood of passengers. Maybe "Up With People" can't be made to say everything about the incidental character of commuting, or its grander tides. Maybe it can't embrace detailed histories of municipal road management, or track the patterns of social sorting that occur in urban transport systems. Maybe an entirely adequate layering of languages, accents, and their textures lies beyond it.

Maybe not. The traffic column stalls. I climb down from the happy bus and, as I do, am arrested by the sound made by the entry note of a clarinet from a well-known concerto floating out of a parked, white truck. For a fleeting instant, in a sudden and grinning euphoria, I am looking at a man listening to Radio 3 as he unloads boxes of fruit. I feel for the city, corporeally, affected. Everything is lifted and connected.

Then, it is not. For in that same instant, knowing an error, I find myself regarding only the deflated outline of my own abruptly dejected prejudices. I have mistaken the sound of the hydraulic lift that lowers the loading deck of the truck for the plangent clarinet. They can sound remarkably similar, sometimes. Why was it that, of all the specific minor affects, I felt pleasant surprise in translating the misprized, misidentified Mozart as the accompaniment to this man's labor? Listening to the city helps one live in error, in a very liberating way. Listening frequently throws up such contrary, literally misleading facets of the city's architecture. They are the objects of an aural cartography, its attachments and affective coordinates. It is important to understand what such signifiers discourse upon, and what they might argue, certainly, as they extend and endure in ways very different from the suggestions made by the concrete and clay of more recognizable urban land-marking. Rather than decoding, however, what these deceits require is "further encryption" (Wood 1992).

The character of change in the constitution, perception, and experience of the most recognizable urban spatial fabrics was radically altered during the middle decades of the twentieth century. A statement like this is almost too true to be true.

Yet, it remains hard to ignore the ways that a host of theorists of modern cultural change in the twentieth century have, whilst acknowledging precursory events from the nineteenth century, oriented themselves towards that dynamic period between the wars as one when vivid, characterizable outlines of change appear to manifest. In this process of alteration, one identifiable force has been, if not exactly neglected, certainly not accorded the same kind of pervading influence as the manifold descriptions of the forms of modern novelty depicted by the fine arts, industrial design, architecture, and so forth. The combined advent at this time of telephony, microphony, gramophony, broadcast radio, and the cinematic synchronization of images with sound, represents a technical ground for the exploration of what Tom Levin notably described as the "acoustic dimension" of modernity (1984). A simple account of the emergence and refinement of such technology is, as Levin also suggests, clearly not sufficient as a way of understanding the changes in urban sensibility and sociability that came about in its context. Subjective techniques of aural attention have as much, and in most circumstances more, to contribute to the conceptualization of urban sound, whilst obviously admitting that these listening practices may never have come about without the existence of such technologies. The M-49 Neumann microphone, for example, certainly had an enormous impact in crafting the aural signatures of competing commercial recording companies in the years immediately after World War II. Yet, taken alone, its role in constelling the sounds of musical voices and instruments and the places they occurred has little to say of the nature of the kind of inhabitable, aurally modern spaces that such recordings offered to those most charmed by and cathected to them. A detailed history of a microphone can occasion, but perhaps not sustain, for instance, an investigation into the political implications of the often utopic, but always fantastic, mutation and redistribution of spaces that gramophone records and radio broadcasts achieve. It can't sustain a discourse on the myriad intersubjective encounters convened by records and radio in parlors or pubs. It can't account for the way that coughs or creaks in recordings might precipitate personal epiphanies or cascading, affective calamities in listeners. It can't account for delinquent aesthetic interests in the ways that scratches or dust, particular forms of audio inadequacy, hums or interference might be composed. Such a history might fall, as I say, across and unto these anecdotal, seemingly uninfluential things, however – in the process, figuring for them an interpretative power.

In part, the limitations of a technologically focused investigation become foregrounded because of a distracting or deferring quality that subjective attention to sound brings to the redefinition of the hitherto held conventions at work in understanding the physiology of space. Theodor Adorno, once commenting on the shuffling sound made by his slippers as he moved about his room changing records on the turntable, was moved to remark that his slippers were monuments, monuments mind, to idleness (1974 [1951]: 110). His interest in a memorial to an underappreciated intellectual disposition was obviously of more significance to him at this point than the next gesture he was to make in his ongoing critique of the contemporary grasp of Beethoven.

Much of what might constitute a bibliography on sound and urban space is found in literature, critical theory, poetry, architectural projects, cinema of all kinds, experimental music and its criticism, and a variety of other kinds of performative practices, all of which have been developed in both minor and more rhetorically elevated manners. As theoretical listenings, this body is, thankfully, frequently marked by idiosyncratic digressions like Adorno's. That capacity for usefully eccentric world-views to articulate curiously hybrid, allotropic objects of interest at the site of the intersection of sound with visually narratable space has brought with it a necessity to fundamentally reorganize the precepts of critical stances in order to render them capable of correctly voicing the things of significance that are revealed at those intersections. There is a sense in which that eccentricity is able to appropriately furnish the constitutive space that exists between subjects and their often rather surprising objects that arise from their aural attention. There is more than a handful of classic gestures that have been made towards this material/psychological impression of urban space. Frantz Fanon's essay on the formation of a specific type of revolutionary consciousness through the process of attempting to listen to disrupted radio broadcasts in Algeria is one example (1989 [c. 1965]). Cornelius Cardew's definition of the practices that might lead to forms of uncommodifiable music is another (1971). Julia Kristeva's mobilization of acoustic metaphors in providing practical models for the apprehension of the spatialization of subjectivities, makes a different kind of contribution (1984 [c. 1974]; 2001). The practice of humming in order to find eigentones in ancient, urban stairwells that was suggested by early, Canadian members of the Acoustic Ecology movement offers a further means of investigation (Schafer 1977). Adrian Stokes's architectural historical practice of listening to the diminuendo of buses, trains, and fountains (1947), even Alain Corbin's view of the practical role of bells in the nomic organization of French provincial urban and rural space (1998), each of these vantages on the world stand upon radical creative-cognitive innovation in the form of their imagined reconstitution of mappable space. The effect of these re-imaginings of space has been to unmoor some of the qualities of recognized, stable, urban spatial tropes and to hitch them to the textural organization of other perceptual concerns. Such practices, again of necessity, are forced into the position of having to rethink and devise new kinds of archive and theoretical prefigurations, new critical deportments and intentions, and new types of aurally-visually, spatially confectable materials. An overheard conversation in a queue in which someone is plunged into an embarrassed confusion over the correct amount of change would be a triviality were it not for the fact that such complex affective events represent powerful and common details in everyday urban existence. Questions arise from it, like how might a recent history of aurally precipitated embarrassment be pursued? Is flustered confusion a possibly productive intellectual environment to inhabit and explore? What would its objects be, and how would they be composed? How does one deal with the suddenly available, material components of such a situation – the hot, red skin, the effects of sudden clumsiness, a desire to vanish or to beat oneself, staccato speech, a kind of blindness, the uncertainly choreographed movements of security staff? A connected cartography of discomfiture like this is made plausible by its aural dimension, and it is the aurality that convenes these disciplinary novelties.

There are other examples of such classic gestures besides those I have briefly referred to. What is clearly a shared stake amongst them is an animated concern with the *practice* of listening, its doing, and what that doing undoes. What is also at stake in each of these instants, in their varying ways, is a kind of dwelling within a useful *mésalliance* of reifications with affects, and the disputable space that is produced by that conflation. By this I mean, the way that the practice of an aural-izing reflection on urban cartography has, via its choice of attachments, shown itself able to extend what might be ordinarily available to that cartography into a psy-chological realm. This is a realm where symptoms, discharges, and sensibilities, as much as the design of street furniture, are included in an expected area of proper competence. Here, cartographic acts like dating, attribution, and provenance, quan-tifiability, statistical distributions, and the ways these might be converted into legends, suddenly sit in disputed terrains where Lukácsian (for instance) ideas about the reifying mechanisms involved in the manufacture of common, class-specific purviews vie with Freudian (for example) notions of the ways in which affects, subjective, corporeally registered responses to phenomena open onto historical nar-ratives which might be easily perceivable functions of a publicly available record, but might just as easily be buried by mountainous psychical overdeterminations of an utterly Delphic nature.

The point of this is to say that, in the work of Fanon, Cardew, Kristeva, Stokes, even Corbin, reifications and affects do not vie with each other at all. Rather, mutu-ally, they produce an arena in which it is possible to swap about the contrapuntal grounds of a diagnosis of urban cultural processes. In their work, attending to the poetics of acoustic architectures as they have, a pretext has been figured in which the illuminations offered by what Adrian Rifkin has called the sound-plan of the city might be preserved in its open-ended, enigmatical constitution (1993). Adorno, again, is useful in observing this. Perhaps his most famous utterance about the sound of the city, New York in particular, was made in 1938. He told of a man strolling along a subway station whistling a tune derived from one of Brahms's concertos. Working through his aesthetic irritation at this, as an affectation, he used the anec-dote as a way of staging a criticism that landed heavily on the shoulders of the American, commercial, music recording industry. With other forces, Adorno said, the insufficiency of recording techniques had conspired to reduce the overall, tex-tural, philosophical significance of Brahms's music to a "whistleable ditty." In that description of whistling, he supplied a detail of an aural cartography, the *ad hoc* production of a transient, nearly unseizable urban space, the significance of which was uniquely apprehendable by the morphology of Adorno's own intellectual history. The figuring of his affect here, his irritation, energized an intensely written essay that tried to show the ideological complexity of this whistling as a reification, whilst at the same time seeking out the allegorical grounds of his own affrontedness by itemizing the minutiae of his attachment to Brahmsian musical texture (Adorno 1976; 1991 [c. 1938]).

It is, perhaps, not surprising that it fell to Roland Barthes to give a civic dimen-sion to this considered, questioning mode of urbanity (Barthes 1989). Wherever it lies, one thing is true: the *grain* of acoustic material – whether it be recorded, or divined from live performance – does not lie in the material itself. The grain appears as the epiphenomenon of an acute, heightened engagement with a personal agenda of concerns that is lent a structuring context by given sound. In his reprising interest in the idea of the grain, Barthes asked for an almost reticent, deliberately uninflu-ential form of askesis. Discriminating against a ferally adrenalized mode of *hearing* that finds its confidence in the readily recognized, Barthes argued for a manner of *listening* that demanded a ratcheting-up of the input of creative energies to inter-subjective encounters of all kinds. His metaphor for this was the Lacanian psycho-analyst's couch and the drama of the ever-enigmatic analyst prompting the labor of the analysand to struggle against the acceptance of redactive platforms. In his proposal of this as the basis for a compact of municipal civility, Barthes may well have considered his responsibilities to be challenging, even utopian. The fact remains that the sound of the city fits his prescription extremely well.

Affets réels

The Knowledge is at once a complexly figured, socio-geographic episteme, and one of London's great monuments. It is the form of recalling and understanding the layout of the city that professionally qualifies London's black-cab drivers to do their job. The Knowledge is something performed, as it were, continually, lending an intellectual motility to the fabric of London's streets. It is judged by the efficiency with which cab drivers get to their given destinations. It is visible not only in the smart movement of the city's taxis, but also in the numerous mopeds that students of The Knowledge use to make themselves familiar with the correlation of the city to its A–Z. Both taxi and moped have very recognizable acoustic signatures. The mopeds, however, are compelling. Their riders, clad in dislimning, all-weather gear, made grimy by the streets, are frequently to be seen paused at the roadside, studying maps fixed to the handlebars of their bikes, rehearsing and devising mutterable mnemonics for themselves that will connect roadways with instrumental, personalized, narrative images, and this helps them through their examinations. In some senses, these students of the city are too familiar to Londoners. They, and their sound, are almost transparent. The term apprentice does some kind of disservice to them. Invariably they look like people who are in a process of professional change. As figures in an urban landscape, they signify unknown prehistories, and seem simultaneously to be both lost and in the process of finding themselves.

If the Route: The Great Learning of London is a radio performance work designed and documented by the artist film-maker Beatrice Gibson and the composer Jamie McCarthy (2006–7). It explores the aural, anecdotal dimensions of The Knowledge. One of its starting points is some observations on the process of coming to knowledge. In particular, these are ones made by Confucius in *The Great Learning*, as articulated by the composer Cornelius Cardew in his score for *Paragraph 1 of the Great Learning*. Once greatly admiring of it, Cardew became increasingly disillusioned with Confucius's text as his interests in Chinese politics changed over time. Much in the manner of Adorno, though verbally (if not musically) lacking his nuanced interpretative agility, Cardew found in it something worthy of the severest criticism. It is the image of social stasis promoted by *The Great Learning* that irked him. Over time, Cardew became profoundly moved by the notion of revolutionary self-criticism, and took this as the cognitive, aesthetic basis of a revolutionary sociability. He found Confucius's prescription of a means of learning that insisted on coming to an awareness of the unchallengeably enduring order of things to be irretrievably bourgeois. In the end, he rejected Confucius and, after trying to repair it, his own work also. It is striking that he should have done this. The various paragraphs of *The Great Learning* that he scored, and which together constitute a monument in the canon of experimental music, were intended to enable collaborative, democratic, improvised music and social interaction. This was a musical practice that tried to push away received ideas about what music should sound like, and replace them with a mutual, politicized sociability that, in the end, and as a result of its working, could produce utterly new and appropriate modes of sound-making. The musicians he had in mind should be untrained in the conventional, conservatoire manner, or at the very least prepared to embark on a demanding critical process of removing the effects of that training.

The image of stasis and its rejection are an important trope in the structure of *If the Route …* , existing as an affecting/ideological counterpoint in several ways. The dominating, early part of Gibson and McCarthy's performance piece is constructed from the textured voices of student cab drivers. Gibson had managed to gain access to the schools where The Knowledge is taught, no easy thing, and in part, the work stands as a witness to Gibson's sociable capacities. The pedagogical structures of The Knowledge are intriguing, quite apart from the simple labor of repeatedly schlepping about town on a small cc moped. There are competitive games. One of these, Calling Over, involves a pair of students working together. One will ask to be taken from one place to a specific destination. The other narrates that route. Gibson and McCarthy invented another game, one that involves students working in larger groups. Again a destination is stated and one of the number starts to describe a route. If others in the group can think of a more efficient way, they can take control of the route by naming the next intersection, and so on until they either reach the destination or are themselves interrupted. The sound made in the practice of these exercises is as aurally compelling as the mopeds are visually so. Gibson and McCarthy persuaded a group of these students to perform these exercises live, and it is this texture of sometimes ordered, sometimes disputing, voices that gives rise to a vivid image of the city in the work. With as many as ten pairs of students speaking together, it is impossible at times to hear more than an approximate acoustic image of staccato *vocalise*. At other times a particular street name might be framed by a moment's silence, and be suddenly connected arbitrarily to another named by a different pair, which may be very distant from the first. This informal montage of place names has its own hallucinatory effects on cartography. But, it also produces something like a musical structure, which can be subject to a technical musicological vocabulary – it is a language of grains and clusters, rather than notes and rhythms. At times there are crescendos, scripted only by the sneakiness of a topographic question, and at others diminuendos and long silences prompted by a thoughtful wrestling with orientation.

In the early part of the performance, these quietnesses and silences are inhabitable, and the image of the city in gravid repose filling these silences is hard to deny. Later in the piece, the structure of these silences is mimicked in a score for music to be played by a small group of string players. There is a cinematic character to this music, as it starts to vie with the latency of the city for the audience's attentions, threatening a displacement or supplanting of that dream. And, the score is quite self-conscious in its affectations. There is much of Samuel Barber in there, a powerfully put rhetoric of stasis.

I have gone into some detail here regarding the technical structure of *If the Route …* for a reason. More than a cartography, the piece seems to suggest itself as an aural essay in the aesthetics of urban sociability. The silences are more complex than they appear. When describing a journey from one place to another, a knowing-ness (a deportment which is more than a mere knowledgeability) is articulated as much by sophisticated acts of preterition – detours, roadworks, time-sensitive con-gestions are bypassed without remark – as it is by remembering a one-way system or a neat shortcut. What are also left unuttered are the myriad little stories, some personal, some public, which cab drivers come to know as part of their appreciation and sustenance of The Knowledge, and which occasionally become available as part of an in-car entertainment for passengers, welcome or otherwise. More, aestheti-cally, the timbre of the voices is not merely musical, either. The way that the tenor of the exercises, the phatic gestures of assertion and giving way, repeat the social mores of the traffic column has its own metaphoric facility. In the formation of The Knowledge as an expedient knowledge for a specific, proprietorial, closed caste within London's petite bourgeoisie, competition and helping one another, claiming space and conceding it, are the figures of a contradictory social and professional politic.

If the Route ... does not venture the kind of conceptual symphonism seen at work in older images of the city, in the ways that say Walter Ruttmann did in making his film *Berlin* in 1927, or F. Tennyson Jesse did in describing the somatic identifica-tion of the sound of the city with the inner life of her chief female protagonist during the opening passages of *A Pin to See the Peepshow* (1934). These do connect his-torically in some ways with Gibson and McCarthy's piece, however. Both of these are visions produced at the moment of the impact of new sound technologies in constellating urban social space. Both of them imagine an older, perhaps stereo-typed, set of subjects of commuting. Yet, these subjects are involved in complicated, philosophical, and not always entirely legible social transactions. The subjects that appear in both of these texts are odd and sometimes have an extraneity about them. Aspects of them are produced, as it were, extra-diegetically. In one scene in *Berlin*, Ruttmann edits together images of a prostitute plying outside a department store with those of a sewing machine running off garments. A blunt remark about fashion and the sex industry, with the needle of the sewing machine standing as a coarse metaphor for mechanicalized eroticism, is overtly made and may have had predict-able affective results in the audience. What is harder to lend credence to is the fact that, in sharing an acoustic signature, the image of the sewing machine and the sound of the film projector (they are the same mechanism) offered a sudden impres-sion of the synchronized sound that was to soon appear to so startlingly transform the arenas of public entertainment. That prescient subject of modernity may have only been the projector's operator and, indeed, may not have been in any position to recognize this aural coordination of images. The possibility of such an aural-urban subjecthood exists nevertheless. Supplying outline to that subjecthood – the autobiographical and perceptual details – makes peculiar demands on any discipline that cannot embrace the apparent cognitive eccentricities of its students. Similarly, the dark shadow that follows the libidinally joyous way that Jesse's character Julia Almond (a portrayal of Edith Thompson, a shop assistant in a London clothes shop, in the notorious Thompson/Bywaters murder case of 1924) is entranced by the city and its music, is present only if the reader knows she is going to be hanged. This is made more piquant as it is for her proximity to, not her guilt in, a murder that

Julia is charged. Jesse's production of the particular character of Julia's guilt, though, is as a subject of British jurisprudence and its moralities. But it is also a guilt made just as much of consuming personal vanity, adultery, and uncontrollable ardency. This is how the young and old Julia is a figure of a peculiar urban modernity. She is made of mixed and conflicting intentions and desires, subject to almost overpowering affects, yet capable of reflection upon them – certainly as she reflects on what she sees as the outrage on her body soon to be committed by law. With both of these figures of early aural modernity, Ruttmann's and Jesse's, we are asked to suspend prejudice so that it may be examined, and that perhaps some rapprochement with the autobiographical mechanisms by which subjects come into unusual forms of being might be made. Taking this speculative, improvisatory role in the fashioning of the figured aural elements of the city, being prepared to make and unmake errors, cultivating some form of responsibility for that, means that, with luck, the sound of the city need never become a discipline.

The status of these proudly eccentric, anecdotal, autobiographical details, which never amount to an idea of a coherent historical motor, bear on *If the Route ...* in a powerful way. I suppose at some level, I must have known that London's cab drivers come from all sorts of different class, cultural, and ethnic backgrounds. I must have known that they could be shy, sharp, funny, and affable, and subject to the gamut of human heroisms, humors, and fallibilities. I must have known that they were people. I must have been aware that the cheerily abrasive London cabbie, who wears the same Londonisms as Robert Elms's voice, comes from Turkey, or Latvia, or India, and likely always has done. But, it wasn't until I watched the audience of the first public performance of *If the Route ...* and listened to them listening to a city spoken, it wasn't until I watched similar and other sentiments appear to fleet through that audience as they reached some comprehension, some strained remembrance, that I glimpsed that constellated complexity in the London cab driver as an urban fact. What is important about this, to me at least, is that all of this registered as a kind of kinaesthesia; a set of memories and revelations about the city, some shared, some personal, some strange even to me. And, augmented as an enigmatically composed, corporeal reality, they provide something from which it is possible to write.

References

Adorno, T. W. (1974 [1951]) *Minima Moralia*. London: Verso.

Adorno, T. W. (1976) *Introduction to the Sociology of Music*. New York: Seabury Press.

Adorno, T. W. (1991 [c. 1938]) On the fetish-character in music and the regression of listening. In *The Culture Industry*, London: Routledge, 29–61.

Barthes, R. (1989) Listening. In *The Responsibilities of Forms*. New York: Hill and Wang, 245–60.

Cardew, C. (1971) Towards an ethic of improvisation. In *Treatise Handbook*. London: Edition Peters, xvii–xxi.

Corbin, A. (1998) *Village Bells: Sound and Meaning in the Nineteenth-Century French Countryside*. New York: Columbia University Press.

Fanon, F. (1989 [c. 1965]) This is the voice of Algeria. In *Studies in a Dying Colonialism*. London: Earthscan, 69–97.

Jesse, F. T. (1934) *A Pin to See the Peepshow*: London: Heinemann.

Kristeva, J. (1984 [c. 1974]) *The Revolution in Poetic Language. New* York: Columbia University Press.

Kristeva, J. (2001) *Melanie Klein*. New York: Columbia University Press.

Levin, T. (1984) The acoustic dimension: notes on cinema sound. *Screen* 25 (3): 55–68.

Rifkin, A. (1993) *Street Noises: Parisian Pleasure 1920–1940*. Manchester: Manchester University Press.

Schafer, R. M. (ed.) (1977) *European Sound Diary*. Vancouver: ARC Publications.

Stokes, A. (1947) *Inside Out: An Essay in the Psychology and Aesthetic Appeal of Space*. London: Faber and Faber.

Wood, D. (1992) *The Power of Maps*. New York: Guilford Press.

Chapter 40

Sustainable Cultural Spaces in the Global City: Cultural Clusters in Heritage Sites, Hong Kong and Singapore

Lily Kong

Introduction

Global cities are highly networked nodes, with multiple and intensive global flows of people, goods, services, ideas, and images. They are economic and financial centers. Simultaneously, the most global of cities are also centers of great and diverse cultural and social activity. The financial troubles that have shaken the world in recent years pose very serious questions about the sustainability of economic practices. While much attention is given to economic issues, countries would do well to also address the cultural and social sustainability of their cities.

One way of addressing these issues is to examine the urban spaces that bear evidence of the economic and cultural flows that characterize the global city. Such analyses can tell us much about the global city's economic and cultural condition. The focus in this chapter will be on the spaces of culture that contribute to the character of global cities. These spaces may take monumental and iconic proportions (such as grand theaters and museums), or they may be reinvented local places, drawing on place-based heritage (such as artist clusters in abandoned factory and warehouse spaces). Global cities need both types of cultural spaces to give them character and identity, and the vibrancy and viability of these spaces are markers of the vitality of global cities. Indeed, many of these spaces have been useful in urban imaging strategies, projecting the image of their cities as alive with arts and culture. Yet, not all are successful or sustainable spaces for culture.

In this chapter, I examine one type of cultural space in two global cities in Asia – Hong Kong and Singapore – analyzing the ways in which local places are reinvented and turned over to cultural use, evaluating the impetuses for their reinvention and their success and sustainability as cultural and social spaces (see Kong 2007, 2009a, 2009b for analyses of the monumental cultural projects in these two cities).

The New Blackwell Companion to the City   Edited by Gary Bridge and Sophie Watson
© 2011 Blackwell Publishing Ltd

Through analyses of these spaces, I draw larger conclusions about the governance of culture and urban space in these cities, the value and harnessing of heritage for sustainable cultural management, and the usefulness of cluster theory in offering a sustainable approach to managing cultural spaces (the theory propounds that the shared knowledge, embedded relationships, and enhanced interactions in clusters will be a boost to cultural creativity, ideas, energies, and activities (Mommaas, 2004; O'Connor, 2004)). Ultimately, on the basis of these analyses, we gain insights into the cultural and social sustainability of these cities.

Context

The chapter is situated within the literature on culture-led urban regeneration and cultural/creative economy, in which cultural investment is valued because of the contributions to urban and economic regeneration, because culture is "a source of prosperity and cosmopolitanism," and because it stands cities in good stead in international urban competition (Comedia 2003). Concomitantly, cultural investment can be

> a means of spreading the benefits of prosperity to all citizens, through its capacity to engender social and human capital, improve life skills and transform the organizational capacity to handle and respond to change ... [and] a means of defining a rich shared identity ... thus engender[ing] pride of place and inter-communal understanding, contributing to people's sense of anchoring and confidence. (Comedia 2003)

Cultural investment in urban and economic growth often takes the form of investment in the production of space for cultural use, and in many cities, this takes monumental proportions. Examples that come quickly to mind include Beijing's National Theater and the Guggenheim Museum in Bilbao, to name but two. These cultural icons have successfully constituted part of urban imaging strategies. Additionally, cultural investment has also entailed the remaking of local places through (re)inventing place-based heritage. Such sites have increasingly become clusters of cultural/creative activities (e.g., Keane 2007, ch. 8), which, together with the heritage value of the sites, hold much promise for the cultural life of the cities.

Just how much such strategies actually address issues of cultural identity and creativity, social interaction, understanding, and inclusion, is however often questionable. Stevenson (2004: 126) argues that "the 'social' of social inclusion has become synonymous with the economy to such an extent that participation in society (full citizenship) can only be achieved through participation in the economy." In this way, culture becomes implicated in reproducing inequalities as opposed to automatically revitalizing the public sphere (Miles and Paddison 2005: 836). Similarly, Evans (2005) is concerned that the measures of impact are all too often focused on economic impacts rather than long-term sustainability; Johnson and Thomas (2001) believe that effects such as enjoyment, appreciation, and such "softer" aspects of the arts' impact are left insufficiently acknowledged and promoted. In fact, Keith Bassett (1993: 178) had made this argument as early as the 1990s, that economic regeneration does not necessarily mean that there is also cultural regeneration, which involves community self-development and self-expression. To achieve such cultural sustainability, there has to be the ability to create local cultural content and embed indigenous idioms in cultural "products," as well as the possibility of creating unique cultural forms that underscore a local sense of identity and nation-hood, particularly in the face of globalizing and potentially homogenizing forces. Where there is cultural sustainability, there should also be a nurturing of cohesion and a development of common identity, without suggesting a simultaneous xeno-phobic rejection of external influences (Bailey *et al.* 2004: 49). Indeed, cultural sustainability emphasizes the ability of culture to "forge a productive diversity for the human species" as well as to "nurture the sources of cohesion and commonal-ity," recognizing culture to be "the glue of similarity ('identity,' literally) that grounds our sociability" (*IJECESS*). In this way, it fosters social sustainability, working through systems, structures and programs to allow "our participation as autonomous yet social beings" (*IJECESS*), promoting healthy social interaction, protection of the vulnerable, and respect for social diversity. In short, it is imperative that sustainability goes beyond economic terms, and considers issues such as cultural imagination and creativity, social inclusion and cohesion, and community develop-ment (Ng *et al.* 2001; Scott 2004).

Additionally, it is important to add to the agenda the environmental sustainability of urban cultural spaces, that is, their sustainability as valuable repositories of human (personal and social) meaning, and as liveable, rejuvenated spaces. This is especially pertinent when addressing the ways in which historical spaces are pre-served/conserved and reused. Environmentally sustainable heritage sites remind users of the history of the place through its preserved/conserved elements, while sustaining new uses in sensitive and responsive ways.

In the following sections, I draw on the cases of Cattle Depot Artist Village, a disused cattle slaughterhouse in Hong Kong, and selected adaptive reuse shophouses in Singapore's Chinatown to examine the sustainability of cultural spaces in these cities. Certainly, these are not the only cultural spaces in the two cities, and their conditions do not represent the entire spectrum of promises and perils in their cul-tural life. Nevertheless, they represent one type of urban cultural space in the two cities, and offer important perspectives into the kinds of challenges and possibilities that such spaces hold in the making of global cultural cities.

Cattle Depot Artist Village, Hong Kong

The origins of the 1.7-hectare Cattle Depot Artist Village, as its name implies, lie in its past as a cattle slaughterhouse, the oldest in the former British colony. First constructed in 1908 in Kowloon's Ma Tau Kok Road, it fell into disuse in 1999, and was then reopened in 2001 as Cattle Depot Artist Village. The site is labeled a third grade historical monument,[1] and is made up of five blocks of red-brick, mainly single-storey buildings. The original 32 arts practitioners (six arts groups and about ten individual artists) occupying Cattle Depot were resettled from Oil Street, where they had occupied a government general supply depot for about a year. In the late 2000s, only about 15 of the 19 units at Cattle Depot have been occupied on one-year leases, housing performing arts groups, visual arts exhibition venues run by non-profit arts organizations, and some individual artists. Activities include alterna-tive theater, multi-media performances, new media production and installation arts, arts education, arts criticism, arts policy research, and international cultural exchange.

For the Cattle Depot artists, the heritage buildings offer a unique opportunity for a meaningful and creative experience. Yet, the very heritage conditions that give it meaning are also constraining, particularly when interpreted to an extreme by over-zealous implementation of policy decisions. On the social barometer, the site has also not succeeded in generating an organic sense of social inclusion though some of the artist occupants have begun in recent years to invest considerable effort in generating public awareness and participation. While such collaborative efforts by some tenants may suggest synergies and collaboration within the cluster, and hence a sense of community, identity, and shared purpose, the relationships are in fact somewhat partial and periodic rather than wholesome and sustained. The movement away of artists over time without replacement also diminishes the potential of the site. Under these circumstances, the artists continue to try and push the boundaries with their art, with many undertaking experimental work, thus seeking to develop local art and finding space for indigenous expression. Nevertheless, the lack of clarity of official responsibility with different government offices each with some responsibility for the site, and hence the broken chain of governance, makes it difficult for the full potential of the site to be realized. In what follows, the environmental, social, and cultural conditions surrounding the Cattle Depot Artist Village and the gaps in governance will be elaborated, to demonstrate the importance of the governance of culture and urban space if cities are to have sustainable cultures and spaces.

Various artists in Cattle Depot have expressed satisfaction with their beautiful and unique site, extolling its spaciousness in highly built-up Hong Kong. One artist describes the sense of liveability using words such as "relaxing," "more healthy," "like having a vacation." The heritage value of the site also appeals to some occupants' sense of pride. Yet, this positive evaluation of the environment quickly gives way to a recognition of the practical difficulties of occupying a heritage site, for Cattle Depot's facilities were not made for arts use. Tenants shared how they had to do much on their own to improve the place, from putting in partitions between units to prevent rain from getting indoors, to renovating space at their own expense into a black box, including putting in lighting, audio systems, and stage controls. They also had to put up with frequent blackouts prior to 2002, which disrupted performances, and had to live with restrictions on putting nails into walls and repainting walls.

Even while these inconveniences could be tolerated, tenants complained about other less comprehensible prohibitions, for example, restrictions on the placement of plants outside the units in the shared public space within the compounds of the complex. Even sculptures – works of the artists – are not allowed, nor may theater groups perform. Photography is prohibited. "How can the place come alive with a spirit of art, if everything has to be kept indoors, and preferably behind doors?" one artist asks. It is difficult to understand these restrictions except to see them as the actions of over-zealous implementers, rendering the very heritage conditions that give the site meaning a constraining rather than an enhancing role.

For Cattle Depot to exist as a socially sustainable site, two dimensions of its social existence need to be addressed. The first is the internal dynamics within the cluster; the second is its relationships with society and community beyond it. Relationships within the cluster are partial and uneven. Whereas some report interactions with neighbors in the cluster, others complain that other tenants appear "invisible," returning only once every week or two, often keeping to themselves. In fact, some space had been sublet to other groups to store props, which reduced the possibilities for interaction. Further, the policy not to accept new tenants when old ones move out does nothing to help enliven the place. The policy reflects the underlying official attitude – a lack of certainty as to future plans for the place, with inertia resulting. Below the official surface, however, some new artists have obtained space by sharing units with the original lessees. Such subletting thus circumvents the effects of official (in)action.

In recent years, as a reaction against official policy, five of the units at Cattle Depot formed a group to liaise with the authorities. The idea was first mooted in 2006 when the Arts Development Council (ADC) wanted to turn Cattle Depot into a performing arts space and to move all the visual arts groups and individuals to a new project in Shek Kip Mei (the Jockey Club Creative Arts Center). The tenants did not want to move. In the face of an increasingly aggressive approach by the ADC, five of the groups got together to present their case to ADC. The five – named G5 – included two visual arts groups, one multimedia group, and two theater groups. The internal dynamics strengthened as a result of a common "enemy," and the members of the group have since extended their cooperation to take on other causes, such as an attempt to secure a collective grant for their activities, to secure a "live" rental system to allow the inflow of new tenants, to set up a board to oversee the management of the artist village, and to run an arts festival, turning themselves into the Cattle Depot Arts Festival Association. Some of these efforts have given the groups a sense of purpose, even if they have yet to fully rejuvenate the cultural and artistic life of the village.

With regard to the interface with a larger community and society, a recurrent view among tenants is the need for the arts space to be an integral part of community life and rhythm, and to be part of the warp and woof of Hong Kong social and cultural life. Unfortunately, its relationship with the immediate surrounding community is not healthy. As one artist put it: "Their image of this place is not good. People living across the street have no idea what kind of space this is. They think we are the scum of society." This may be rooted in the fact that the surrounding housing is low-cost high-rise housing catering to the lower socio-economic classes for whom the arts mean little. For the site to be socially sustainable, it is imperative that it is able to attract people who value its existence and appreciate its offerings. While those who are especially interested in the arts – the "culturally interested," as one artist put it – do sometimes visit, it is "not yet a space for passersby." Indeed, another artist describes it as "a bit dead," acknowledging the need to make the place "more lively and vibrant." This has been achieved to some extent through an event called October Contemporary, a month-long event first held in 2007 to promote contemporary visual art in Hong Kong. Eight of Hong Kong's leading art spaces and institutions worked together to present talks, workshops, exhibitions, and performances under an overarching theme. Three of the groups at Cattle Depot participated, and some of the events were held there as well. There has also been a book fair which has helped to draw in the crowds. As one artist put it, "That was the first time that Cattle Depot was really used in a way that it should be used, and that was quite nice." While successful for the period of the event, the momentum and liveliness are unfortunately not sustained throughout the year; for as long as the space is treated as private space, with security guards at the entrance and the requirement that visitors show their IDs and sign in at the doors for the best part of the year, the space is unlikely to be particularly welcoming. Thus, despite ideas such as October Contemporary, the Cattle Depot Arts Festival and the book fair, the village generally does not project a sense of inclusivity, nor will the artists find sustainability and encouragement for their art from a "general public." This state of affairs is expressed in quite depressing terms by one of the artists:

> I drew 19 crows on the wall ... some of them are facing out, just like some of the artists are moving out. And why I drew 19 crows is because we have 19 units here. I choose crows because it is a metaphor. From the word crows, if you take down the "r," you can see cows. And crows, you have a feeling that it is related to dying, going to die I mean. Because the government, they won't extend here, I think it is not sustainable, you can't see good prospects here. The exhibition ... I took a big corner and just drew some crows on the wall, and I placed some blue pigment on the floor. The blue pigment, though the color is very beautiful, it is poison.

In evaluating the challenges confronting the sustainability of Cattle Depot Artist Village, it seems impossible to ignore the fact that the lack of clarity of official responsibility, the broken chain of governance, and the lack of will have hampered the realization of the site's potential. One of the members of G5 explained how the Government Property Agency (GPA) manages the site, just as it does all other vacant government properties, treating it as workshop space for the artists, refusing to open it to the public. On the other hand, the government agency responsible for arts and culture – the Home Affairs Bureau – sees it as an artist village, but does not have direct oversight of the compound. The Tourism Commission, on its part, has put up a sign outside labeling the site "Cattle Depot Artist Village," contradicting the GPA's refusal to allow the artist community to put up a permanent banner stating the same because it is not supposed to be an artist village! A temporary sign is allowed, and the request has to be repeated every two months. Reflecting this stance, official maps of Hong Kong label the site "Cattle Depot Quarantine Center." The case thus demonstrates clearly how a site with much potential to support the sustainable development of arts and culture in Hong Kong cannot deliver better because the governance of culture and urban space is fractured.

Chinatown, Singapore

In a city-state where about three in four in the population are ethnically Chinese, the notion of a "Chinatown" seems misplaced. This inscription of "Chineseness" in a specific place has its roots in colonial urban planning, when a town planning committee in the early 1820s marked out separate quarters for the different "native" communities, including one for the Chinese on the south-west bank of the Singapore River. The colonial legacy has persisted in post-independence Singapore. Rather than an anachronistic place name in a predominantly Chinese city, government agencies have sought to retain (or indeed, remake) the area as a quintessentially Chinese site. In particular, the urban conservation and tourism agencies (Urban Redevelopment Authority and Singapore Tourism Board respectively) have colluded in the scripting of a "Chinese" landscape, from the businesses that are encouraged to the activities performed to street furniture.

Our current gaze is trained on two streets within Chinatown, particularly, the upper storeys of a row of eight shophouse units along Smith Street and two at adjacent Trengganu Street. They have been occupied since 1998 by non-profit arts groups and artists, including specialists in Cantonese Opera, Beijing Opera, Teochew Opera, music, theater, calligraphy, and literary arts. This occupancy was made possible by the National Arts Council's (NAC) Arts Housing Scheme, which provides affordable spaces converted from old buildings through a subsidy scheme. Tenants pay 10 percent of the rental charged by Singapore Land Authority, while the NAC subsidizes the remaining 90 percent. Because many of these properties are in close proximity to one another and house new uses in old buildings, they have come to form "adaptive reuse arts belts." The premises may be used by artists and arts groups as offices and studios, for rehearsals and performances.

Based on the occupants selected for the Chinatown arts belt, there was clearly a deliberate attempt on NAC's part to gather all those arts groups related to traditional Chinese arts and culture, as well as Chinese and/or bilingual theater groups, at this historically Chinese enclave. This was part of the rewriting of the Chinatown landscape in the 1990s (Yeoh and Kong 1994) as the Urban Redevelopment Authority embarked on the conservation of the city's historical districts, and struggled to give attention not only to architectural conservation but to the life and spirit of the conserved area too. Chinatown was among the first areas thus affected, and the somewhat forced effort to showcase Chinatown as a distinctively Chinese cultural area is evident in the authorities' (then) vision of Chinatown as a site of traditional trades such as herbalists, temple idol carvers, and effigy makers, "vibrant" performances of puppetry shows, lion and dragon dances, Chinese lantern quizzes, and trishaw rides. The NAC's concentration of Chinese arts groups and artists in Chinatown was part of the overall effort. The outcome has been nothing short of dismal. Critics have lambasted the strategies as "sterile," "static," and "uninteresting," turning Chinatown into a superficial theme park (Yeoh and Kong 1994; forthcoming).

In the same way that the attempt to use Chinese heritage as a uniting, reviving principle has not worked for the remaking of Chinatown, the potential benefits of clustering for the arts groups have similarly not been realized. Despite the clustering of cognate arts groups in close proximity, there is hardly any interaction, let alone collaboration. Members of one of the opera groups interviewed did not even know which other groups and artists were their neighbors. The calligraphy and seal carving group members reported infrequent interactions with other groups, at best occasional attendance at community activities. Some politely explained it in terms of their different interests and activities. However, the leaders of one of the literary groups went so far as to dismiss the other cultural groups as unworthy of her attention, describing them as "a minority of people who are simply interested superficially in the arts but have no foundations or capacity to involve themselves in the spreading of Chinese culture." The intra-cluster social and cultural interactions are thus quite non-existent, making co-location unhelpful in enhancing the development of creative synergies. Whereas cluster rhetoric assumes and extols physical propinquity as a positive factor in the development of social relations and cultural creativity (Mommaas 2004; O'Connor 2004), the evidence in this particular case cannot be further from the theory, and reliance on clustering for a sustainable social and cultural existence is simply not borne out.

Not all cultural clusters have positive internal dynamics, but some can nevertheless be beneficial for the tenants and their arts (Kong 2009b). In the case of the Chinatown arts belt however, even this has not been achieved. For one, despite the intended effect of locating the arts groups in the "hearth" of a Chinese community, the location has not helped to draw in a public interested in Chinese arts. Whereas the calligraphy society had previously opened the space to visitors daily, in the hope that their small exhibitions might be attractive, they have since stopped and taken their exhibitions elsewhere for lack of visitors. Most other groups take their activities off site, whether it is performances at the Victoria Theatre, or reading clubs at the National Library and even public housing estates. As a member of one literary group opined: "Chinatown has become a leisure, food and relaxation paradise. There is nothing cultural about that." She describes how they "used to go to a pavilion and recite poetry" but it ended because the reactions of the audience were "pretty cold, because they don't know what you are doing. ... If you sang pop songs, then yes they can understand." It is no wonder that attempts to contact the groups via various means proved highly challenging. On one of my several futile visits, a neighboring shopkeeper silently pointed to the padlock on the doors of one of the associations to indicate their normal and expected absence.

The idea of remaking Chinatown into a quintessentially "Chinese" landscape was a flawed one in the first place (Yeoh and Kong 1994). The preferred traditional businesses are not economically sustainable in the modern age, and the efforts to turn Chinatown into a place more Chinese than it ever was rendered it a re-engineering effort doomed to failure (Yeoh and Kong forthcoming). Within this context, the gathering of Chinese arts groups there did not at all draw on a "natural" constituency and community to engage with and involve. Neither did the arts groups and artists have any connections prior to their relocation to the common site. Many accepted the premises because of the rental subsidy, not because of the location in Chinatown, or because of any attraction in co-locating with other "similar" groups. There is thus a real issue of a culturally and socially sustainable existence in Chinatown, an existence sustained only by the financial attraction of a rental subsidy. Even so, this attraction is questionable, for as one opera group shared, the subsidized rental comes with a string attached: an obligation for the group to put on a performance once or twice yearly. This exacts its own costs. For the group in question, performance space has to be rented and opera directors and musicians brought in from overseas at significant costs because the Singaporeans who can take on the roles are "very old, and the young ones are not very professional." The very cultural sustainability of the art form is thus in question, which the combined strategies of developing cultural clusters, leveraging on heritage roots, and offering subsidized rentals cannot collectively address.

Conclusion

In as much as global cities should be concerned about their economic and environmental vitality and sustainability, so too should they be concerned about the sustainability of their cultural and social life. A city is only heralded as truly global when it has a vivacious social rhythm and vibrant cultural life, in addition to its necessary role as a business and financial center. This requires that cities have sufficient lively and sustainable cultural spaces supporting the vitality expected of global cities. While selective in its cases and therefore painting only a partial story, this chapter is a reminder that simply having a heritage to draw on and the application of a theory about clustering are alone insufficient conditions for the creation of sustainable cultural spaces. Specifically, the examples of Cattle Depot in Hong Kong and Chinatown in Singapore allow us to draw three conclusions.

First, whereas cluster theory suggests that geographical propinquity generates fruitful relationships amongst constituents of a cluster, yielding externalities, the evidence principally suggests otherwise here. In both the Hong Kong and Singapore cases, interactions are infrequent, if they occur at all. Similarly, collaborations are rare or non-existent. The need to counter external forces – official pressures in Hong Kong's case – helped to draw some constituents together for collective action. There was no such impetus in Singapore's case. Clustering in and of itself does not necessarily provide conditions to support mutual growth and sustainable development.

Second, the clusters in question here are located in heritage sites, a phenomenon common to other parts of the world as well. Despite the potential to draw on the cultural capital that heritage bestows, these cases demonstrate how heritage can be a liability rather than the asset it is assumed to be. Whether it exacts (un)reasonable constraints on activities and behavior (as in Cattle Depot), or it fossilizes and essentializes the meanings of a place (as in Chinatown), the heritage location has detracted from the clusters' success in these cases. The lessons that can be drawn from these analyses relate to the need for sensitive management of the environment and appropriate harnessing of the past.

Finally, the governance of culture and urban space plays a critical role in contributing to the sustainability of cultural and social life. The case of Cattle Depot demonstrates clearly how a site with much potential to contribute to the sustainable development of arts and culture in Hong Kong cannot deliver better because the governance of culture and urban space is fractured. Responsibilities overlap, with different agencies adopting different stances, and evidently little inter-agency coordination. On the other hand, in Singapore, the alignment across agencies is quite total, with the URA, STB, and NAC all publicly working in the same direction with respect to Chinatown. Unfortunately, the coordination of effort yields negative effects because an inappropriate approach to Chinatown's conservation is repeated across agencies.

Ensuring the sustainability of cultural and social life in global cities is deeply rooted in efforts to ensure the sustainability of cultural spaces. In cities like Hong Kong and Singapore which are better associated with business and finance than with arts and culture, organic development is not impossible, though perhaps less common than in the well-established global cities of London and New York. Without suffocating any organic grassroots efforts, concerted effort and coordinated action on the part of public agencies and cultural actors can go a long way in contributing to the making of sustainable cultural spaces.

Note

1   This refers to "buildings of some merit," where "preservation in some form would be desirable and alternative means could be considered if preservation is not practicable" (Antiquities and Monuments Office, Hong Kong).

References

Antiquities and Monuments Office, Leisure and Cultural Services Department, Hong Kong, www.amo.gov.hk/en/built3.php (accessed November 16, 2009).

Bailey, C., Miles, S., and Stark, P. (2004) Culture-led urban regeneration and the revitalisation of identities in Newcastle, Gateshead and the north-east of England. *International Journal of Cultural Policy* 10 (1): 47–65.

Bassett, K. (1993) Urban cultural strategies and urban cultural regeneration: a case study and critique. *Environment and Planning A* 25 (12): 1773–88.

Comedia (2003) Releasing the cultural potential of our core cities: culture and the core cities. Available online at http://www.corecities.com/coreDEV/comedia/com_cult.html (accessed June 8, 2008).

Evans, G. (2005) Measure for measure: evaluating the evidence of culture's contribution to regeneration. *Urban Studies* 42 (5–6): 959–83.

IJECESS, International Journal of Environmental, Cultural, Economic and Social Sustainability website http://ijs.cgpublisher.com/about.html (accessed June 8, 2008).

Johnson, P., and Thomas, B. (2001) Assessing the economic impact of the arts. In *The UK Cultural Sector*, ed. S. Selwood. London: Policy Studies Institute, 202–16.

Keane, M. (2007) *Created in China: The New Great Leap Forward*. London: Routledge.

Kong, L. (2006) Creative clusters: arts and cultural activities in Singapore. Paper presented at conference on *Creative Cities, Creative Economies*, Shanghai, 16–18 October.

Kong, L. (2007) Cultural icons and urban development in Asia: economic imperative, national identity and global city status. *Political Geography* 26 (4): 383–404.

Kong, L. (2009a) Making sustainable creative/cultural space: Shanghai and Singapore. *Geographical Review* 99 (1): 1–22.

Kong, L. (2009b) Beyond networks and relations: towards rethinking (creative) cluster theory. In *Creative Economies, Creative Cities: Asian-European Perspectives*, ed. L. Kong and J. O'Connor. Dordrecht: Springer, 61–75.

Kong, L. (2009c) Creative economy, global city: globalizing discourses and the implications for local arts. In *Cultural Expression, Creativity and Innovation*, ed. H. K. Anheier and Y. R. Isar. Cultures and Globalization Series. London: Sage, 166–75.

Miles, S., and Paddison, R. (2005) Introduction: the rise and rise of culture-led urban regeneration. *Urban Studies* 42 (5–6): 833–39.

Mommaas, H. (2004) Cultural clusters and the post industrial city: towards the remapping of urban cultural policy. *Urban Studies* 41 (3): 507–32.

Ng, M. K., Cook, A., and Chui, E. W. T. (2001) The road not travelled: a sustainable urban regeneration strategy for Hong Kong. *Planning Practice and Research* 16 (2): 171–83.

O'Connor, J. (2004) A special kind of city knowledge: innovative clusters, tacit knowledge and the creative city. *Media International Australia incorporating Culture and Policy* 112: 28–49.

Scott, A. J. (2004) Cultural products industries and urban economic development. *Urban Affairs Review* 39 (4): 461–90.

Stevenson, D. (2004) "Civic gold" rush: cultural planning and the politics of the Third Way. *International Journal of Cultural Policy* 10 (1): 119–31.

Yeoh, B., and Kong, L. (1994) Landscape meanings: state constructions and lived experiences in Singapore's Chinatown. *Habitat International* 18 (4): 17–35.

Yeoh, B., and Kong, L. (forthcoming) Singapore's Chinatown: nation building and heritage tourism in a multiracial city. In *Gateways to the Urban Economy: Ethnic Neighbourhoods as Places of Leisure Consumption*, ed. Volkan Aytar and Jan Rath.

Chapter 41

Spatializing Culture: Embodied Space in the City

Setha Low

Introduction: Moore Street Market, Brooklyn, New York City

At lunch, the Moore Street Market is a lively locale, housed in a squat, white cement building that looks more like a bunker than an enclosed food market with its barred windows and unmarked doorway. The deserted street in the shadow of the looming housing projects seems oddly quiet for a busy Monday morning. Upon entering, however, carefully stacked displays of fresh fruit, yucca, and coriander, passageways lined with cases of water and soda, and high ceilings with vestiges of the original 1940s architecture of wooden stalls, bright panels, and ceiling fans reveal another world. Puerto Rican salsa music emanating from the video store competes with Dominican *cumbia* blaring from a radio inside the glass-enclosed counter of a narrow restaurant stall where rice, beans, *empanadas*, and *arroz con pollo* glistening with oil and rubbed red spice are arrayed. The smell of fried plantains fills the air-conditioned air as Puerto Rican pensioners gather at the round white metal tables with green umbrellas open to offer intimate places to sit and talk. A young boy in a Yankees T-shirt orders lunch for his Columbian mother who is hesitant to pass the security guard perched at the entrance who might ask for her immigration papers. She remains outside in the blazing Brooklyn sun, selling flavored ices while searching for a spot on the crowded sidewalk near the subway entrances or under the train tracks that shade local businesses and shoppers from the nearby hospital.

Doña Maria shuts her metal screened stall, locking away her Seven Saints' oil, plastic flowers, and white first communion dresses. She tells me about her most recent trip to Mexico City and her success at obtaining the special orders, botanicals and medicinal potions for regular customers. She continues recounting her many careers starting when she worked in the homes of white middle-class households

The New Blackwell Companion to the City   Edited by Gary Bridge and Sophie Watson
© 2011 Blackwell Publishing Ltd

that still lived in the neighborhood, and culminates in the recent threat of market eviction by the city, and her reluctance to join the remaining vendors to keep the market open. While Doña Maria and other Latino vendors have been struggling to hold on to their businesses, African American residents who live in the projects across the street – many of whom are female, unemployed, and poor – cannot find their preferred foodstuffs at Moore Street as they did in the past before it became a "Puerto Rican" market. Further, illegal immigrants, many of whom sell their wares on the streets, cannot rent a market stall because the Economic Development Corporation (EDC) of New York City refused to rent out empty stalls.

This chapter employs Moore Street Market as an illustration of how an urban public space links anthropological analyses of the body in space, the global/local power relations embedded in space, the role of language and discursive transformations of space, and the material and metaphorical importance of architecture and urban design. Anthropologists have struggled with a conception of space and place that does not lock people in locations, but is more process-oriented, and person-based, and allows for agency and new possibilities. One way to solve this problem is to posit that space and place are always embodied. Their materiality can be metaphoric and discursive, as well as physically located and carried about. Introducing embodiment into spatial analysis enables the exploration of their social construction and production at diverse global and local scales. The body (bodies), conceptualized as embodied space(s), incorporates metaphors, ideology, and language, as well as behaviors, habits, skills, and spatial orientation derived from global discourses and faraway places – especially for the migrant – and yet is grounded at any one moment in an urban location such as Moore Street Market.

This chapter argues that it is through embodied space that the global is integrated into the spaces of everyday urban life where attachment, emotions, and morality come into play. Embodied spaces are sites of translocal and transnational space and place as well as of personal experience and perception. From this theoretical and methodological perspective, Moore Street Market can be understood as a place where people spend the day listening to music from their homeland, eating lunch, and working at stalls where they make their livelihoods, while simultaneously being enmeshed in networks of relationships, transnational spaces and circuits, and ways of being, that extend from the built environment of the market to where they migrated from where, in many cases, the products that they sell come from, and where other family members remain, supported from the profits of their commercial endeavors.

Spatializing Culture: A Theoretical and Methodological Project

This project draws upon the work of French social theorists who incorporate the physical body and body discipline in their analyses of how power is exercised and flows through the body, built environment, and spatial practices. Michel Foucault (1975; 1984) approaches the relationship of power and space by positing architecture as a political technology for working out the concerns of government through the spatial "canalization" of everyday life. The aim of such a technology is to create a docile body through the surveillance, enclosure, and organization of individuals in space (Rabinow 1982; 1989). Michel de Certeau (1984) sets out to show how peoples' ways of operating constitute the means by which users reappropriate space organized by techniques of sociocultural production. By tracing out the operations of walking, naming, narrating, and remembering the city, he develops a theory of lived space in which spatial practices elude the discipline of urban planning. Henri Lefebvre (1991), on the other hand, views space as a social product that masks the contradictions of its own production. He deconstructs this illusion of transparency by explicating how social space is made up of a conceptual triad of spatial practices, representations of space, and representational spaces. Although the theoretical scope and object of study in each are quite different, the body and body practices are a significant component in each.

Unfortunately these social theories were too abstract or overly categorical to use in the ethnographic study of the Costa Rican plaza. Instead I have utilized the social processes of the social production of space (King 1976; Lefebvre 1991) and the social construction of space (Berger and Luckman 1967; Rodman 1992; Richardson 1984) to explain how culture is spatialized. In my analysis, the social production of space includes all those factors – social, economic, ideological, and technological – that result, or seek to result, in the physical creation of the material setting. The materialist emphasis of the term social production is useful in defining the historical emergence and political/economic formation of urban space. The term social construction then can be reserved for the phenomenological and symbolic experience of space as mediated by social processes such as exchange, conflict, and control. Thus, the social construction of space is the actual transformation of space – through peoples' social exchanges, memories, images, and daily use of the material setting – into scenes and actions that convey meaning. Both processes are social in the sense that both the production and the construction of space are contested and fought over for economic and ideological reasons, and understanding them can help us see how local conflicts over space can be used to uncover and illuminate larger issues (Low 2000).

In this dyadic "co-production model," planning, design, funding, and construction as well as the flow of global capital, labor, and ideas encompass the political economic forces of social production that shape the built environment, encoding it with intentions and aspirations, uses and meanings that are themselves contentiously appropriated, produced, and reproduced by users and residents. For example, while professional designers and political elites may negotiate and enact competing future images of the city, these are rarely consistent with the daily spatial experiences and understandings of urban residents and workers. Interventions that physically shape the landscape attract opposition because they produce socio-spatial forms that reference deep and still unresolved or unresolvable conflicts among political economic forces, social actors, and collectivities (Low and Lawrence 2003: 20).

I conclude that in Parque Central and Plaza de la Cultura, Costa Rican plazas in the center of the capital city, San José, there is a relationship between what is experienced and socially constructed by the users, and the circumstances that socially produced the space and its current physical form and design (Low 2000). Further, the architectural design and furnishings of these plazas are subject to symbolic interpretation and manipulation by the users in such a way that the designs and material conditions of these two worlds become cultural representations to the users themselves. Thus the contestation of the design, furnishings, use, and atmosphere of a plaza becomes a visible, public forum for the expression of cultural conflict, social change, and attempts at class-based, gender-segregated, and age-specific social control.

An illustration of how the co-production model works analytically can be seen in a conflict over the design and style of the kiosk (bandstand) in Parque Central, the colonial central plaza in San José, Costa Rica. From 1990 through 1992 the city held a series of town meetings to discuss replacing the 1944 modernist cement kiosk with a replica of the original Victorian wooden one that had previously burnt down. Many Josefinos argued that the Victorian kiosk was a better representation of Costa Rican cultural values because it evoked a nostalgic image of bourgeois decorum and *cultura* ("culture," see Richardson 1982; Low 2000). Others, however, argued that the 1944 kiosk was part of the city's patrimony and should not be destroyed, but instead preserved and improved. Ultimately governmental representatives and the Minister of Culture backed the historic preservation forces even in the face of the locally opposed demonstrations, town meetings, and the majority of citizens who voted for replacing the existing kiosk with the Victorian model. The cement kiosk was restored as the central design element in a redesigned plaza that opened in 1994. What is illustrative about this vignette is: (1) the cultural importance of the design of the kiosk, as shown by the fact that citizens staged demonstrations and the government responded with a series of open town meetings; (2) how these two images of a kiosk were materially produced in different historical and political periods and retained symbolic meanings from the periods of their material production; (3) how these spatial representations took on new social meanings in the struggle between citizen-based working-class groups and middle-class historic preservation forces in San José; and (4) how this conflict highlights the importance of urban space as a strategy for understanding peoples' negotiation of cultural politics and representations of those politics.

Unfortunately the co-production model that I developed is limited by its binary structure. It does not adequately consider other important spatial dimensions, that of the body and group and the transnational and translocal spaces of the global economy. Further, the co-production model does not directly address how language and discourse influence the meaning and politics of the built environment. In my own field experience, gated community residents' discourse of fear plays a critical role in sustaining the spatial preference for, meaning of, and cultural acceptance of walled and guarded developments (Low 2003). Yet these insights have not been incorporated in socio-spatial theory. To develop a more powerful notion of "spatializing culture" it is necessary to incorporate these additional dimensions of spatial practices and meanings.

Embodied Space

Spatial analyses often neglect the body because of difficulties in resolving the dualism of the subjective and objective body and distinctions between its material and representational aspects. The concept of "embodied space," however, draws these disparate notions together, underscoring the importance of the body as a physical and biological entity, as lived experience, as a center of agency, and a location for speaking and acting on the world.

I use the term "body" to refer its biological and social characteristics, and "embodiment" as an "indeterminate methodological field defined by perceptual experience and mode of presence and engagement in the world" (Csordas 1994: 12). Embodied space is the location where human experience and consciousness take on material and spatial form (Csordas 1988; Merleau-Ponty 1962, 1964). After identifying the inherent difficulties in defining the body and cultural explanations of body experience, I trace the evolution of anthropological approaches to embodied space.

The space occupied by the body, and the perception and experience of that space, contract and expand in relationship to a person's emotions and state of mind, sense of self, social relations, and cultural predispositions. In western culture we perceive the self as "naturally" placed in the body, as a kind of pre-cultural given. Westerners imagine experiencing the world through a "social skin," the surface of the body representing "a kind of common frontier of society which becomes the symbolic stage upon which the drama of socialization is enacted" (Turner 1980: 112).

Human beings are embodied and everyday life dominated by the details of corporeal existence, but Bryan Turner (1984) cautions that biological reductionism distracts from focusing on the ways in which the body is also inherently social and cultural. Terence Turner (1995) argues that while there is an individual organism biologically, it depends on other individuals and the environment for reproduction and sustenance, such that even this biological individuality is relative, depending on other social beings.

Feminists take this critique even farther by exploring the epistemological implications of knowledge as embodied, engendered, and embedded in place (Duncan 1996). By disrupting the binary mind/body by positionality (Boys 1998), and focusing on the situated and colonized body (Scott 1996), states of mind become loosened from the location of social and spatial relationships (Munt 1998). Donna Haraway argues that personal and social bodies cannot be seen as natural, but only as part of a self-creating process of human labor. Her emphasis on "location" and "situatedness," positions in a web of social connections, eliminates passivity of the female body and replaces it within a site of action and of agency (Haraway 1991).

The majority of anthropologists emphasize the intrinsically social and cultural character of the human body. Marcel Mauss (1950) argues that acquired habits and somatic tactics, what he calls the "techniques of the body," incorporate all the "cultural arts" of using and being in the body and the world. The body is at the same time the original tool with which humans shape their world, and the substance out of which the world is shaped (Mauss 1950, also see Csordas 1994). Pierre Bourdieu (1977) employs the term *habitus* to characterize how the body, mind, and emotions are simultaneously trained, and uses this concept to understand how social status and class position become embodied in everyday life (Bourdieu 1984). *Habitus* also explains how moral virtues are acquired through the coordination of bodily acts and social demeanor with emotional states, thoughts, and intentions (Mahmood 2001).

For this reason, I am proposing the concept of embodied space as the location where human experience and consciousness take on material and spatial form. Embodied space offers a useful framework for understanding the creation of place through spatial orientation and movement. A number of anthropologists helped to explicate this concept through their work on proxemics (Hall 1968), phenomeno-logical understandings of space (Richardson 1984), and spatial orientation and field of action (Munn 1996).

Edward Hall (1966, 1973) established the field of proxemics, the study of space as an aspect of culture. He postulates that humans have an innate distancing mecha-nism, modified by culture, that helps to regulate contact in social situations. Con-ceptualized as a bubble surrounding each individual, personal space varies in size according to the type of social relationships and situation. Appropriate spatial vari-ations in social relations are learned as a feature of culture, and patterns vary by culture. In proxemics, the body is a site of spatial practice with multiple screens for interacting with others and the environment.

Miles Richardson (1982, 1984) addresses how body experience and perception become material by considering how experience is transformed into a symbol and then remade into an object, such as an artifact, a gesture, or a word. Individuals use objects to evoke experience, thus, molding experience into symbols and then melting symbols back into experience. In his work, embodied space is being-in-the-world, that is, the existential and phenomenological substance of place: its smell, feel, color, and other sensory dimensions.

Nancy Munn (1996) brings these ideas of culturally determined personal space and being-in-the-world together by considering "space/time" as a symbolic nexus of relations produced out of interactions between bodily actors and terrestrial space. Drawing in part upon Lefebvre's concepts of field of action and basis of action, she constructs the notion of a mobile spatial field that can be understood as a culturally defined, corporeal-sensual field stretching out from the body at a given locale or moving through locales. Her theory goes beyond Hall's concept of proxemics with culturally constituted spatial orientations and interpersonal distances and Richard-son's phenomenological understanding of being-in-the-world by constructing the person/actor as a truly embodied space, in which the body, conceived as a moving spatial field, creates its own place in the world.

Adding embodied space to an analysis of the social construction and social pro-duction of space solves a myriad of problems. The actor as a mobile spatial field, a spatio-temporal unit, with feelings, thoughts, preferences, and intentions as well as out-of-awareness cultural beliefs and practices, creates space as a potentiality for social relations, giving it meaning and form, and ultimately through the patterning of everyday movements, produces place and landscape (Pred 1986; Massey 2005; Rockefeller 2010). The social construction of space is given material expression through a person/spatio-temporal unit, while social production is understood as both the practices of the person/spatio-temporal unit and global and collective social forces.

Language

In a letter that accompanied the publication of *Proxemics* (Hall 1968) Dell Hymes (1968) criticizes the limited use of linguistic theory to understand body space. He comments that if current linguistic theory was taken as model, it would not place primary emphasis on phonological units but on grammatical relationships, and chides linguists for not undertaking transcultural proxemic ethnography as well as transcultural descriptive linguistics. More recent critiques of the use of language models dispute whether experience can be studied at all, because experience is mediated by language, and language itself is a representation. This tension between language and experience and the subsequent dominance of semiotics over phenomenology is resolved by Paul Ricoeur (1991) in his argument that language is a modality of being-in-the-world, such that language not only represents or refers, but discloses our being-in-the-world (Csordas 1994: 11).

Alessandro Duranti (1992, 1997) corrects these omissions through his empirical investigation of the interpenetration of words, body movements, and lived space in Western Samoa. He examines the sequence of acts used in ceremonial greeting, explicating that the words used cannot be fully understood without reference to bodily movements (Duranti 1992). The performance of ceremonial greetings and the interpretation of words are understood as located in and at the same time constitutive of the sociocultural organization of space inside the house (Duranti 1992). His theory of "sighting" embodies language and space through an interactional step whereby participants not only gather information about each other and about the setting but also engage in a negotiated process at the end of which they find themselves physically located in the relevant social hierarchies and ready to assume particular institutional roles (Duranti 1992: 657). Duranti thus reinterprets embodied space within a linguistic model that includes language, spatial orientation, and body movement.

Duranti expands the concept of embodied space by integrating language, body movement, spatial orientation, inhabited space, and distant homelands as expressions of cultural connectedness and socialization. His ideas when combined with the spatial orientation insights of Munn (1996) provide a fleshed-out theory of embodied space that, when combined with insights about translocal spaces, brings the distant homelands into the space of one's body and communicates it to others.

Transnational/Translocal Spaces

Another dimension that the co-production model did not adequately capture is the importance of transnationality and translocality in contemporary understandings of space and place. By transnational spaces, I mean the socio-spatial impact of the globalizing economy, and how people move across borders creating new transnational spaces and territorial relationships (Schiller *et al.* 1992; Ong 1999; Smith 2001; Rothstein 2007). This process of cultural globalization creates translocal spaces and forms of public culture embedded in the imaginings of people that dissolves notions of state-based territoriality (Gupta and Ferguson 1992; Appadurai 1996a).

The critical spatial issue in global debates is the presumed deterritorialization of places of work and community as a by-product of post-Fordist forces and economic restructuring (Sassen 1991, 1996b; Low 2002; Smart 1999). Manuel Castells (1989, 1996) captures this transformation in his analysis of the network city, one in which the space of flows supersedes the local meaning of places. Thus, global space is conceived of as the flow of goods, people, and services as well as capital, technology, and ideas across national borders and geographic regions, resulting in the deterritorialization of space, that is, space detached from local places.

The globalization/deterritorialization model, however, does not focus on the horizontal and relational nature of contemporary processes that stream across spaces and does not express their "embeddedness in differently configured regimes of power" (Ong 1999: 4). Aihwa Ong (1999) prefers the term transnational to denote movement across spaces and formations of new relationships between nation states and capital. She defines transnational spatial processes as situated cultural practices of mobility that produce new modes of constructing identity and result in zones of graduated sovereignty based on the accelerated flows of capital, people, cultures, and knowledge.

Within anthropology, transnational space most often is used to describe the way that immigrants "live their lives across borders and maintain their ties to home, even when their countries of origin and settlement are geographically distant" (Schiller *et al.* 1992: ix), and it is through detailed ethnographies of the rhythms of daily life in transnational migrant communities, that a sense of transnational space emerges (Mountz and Wright 1996; McHugh 2000). There is also a tendency to conceive of transnational spaces as sites of resistance, and to depict cultural hybridity, multi-positional identities, border crossings, and transnational business practices by migrant entrepreneurs as conscious efforts to escape control by capital and the state. Roger Rouse (1991) defines this change as a new kind of social space created by the experiences of working-class groups affected by capitalist exploitation. By breaking down community to encompass more than a single, bounded space, he imagines a social terrain that reflects the cultural bifocality of migrants and describes a fragmented reality made up of circuits and border zones. This reformulation of transnational space as fluid and fragmented, produced by people on the move, complements studies of the sovereignty and citizenship and the reconsideration of the nation state as a spatial entity or territory (Sassen 1996a). Arjun Appadurai (1996a, 1996b), for example, describes a world where minorities and migrants are flowing into nation states, threatening the stability of ethnic coherence and traditional rights. There is increasing pressure to maintain the nation state in territorial terms, while at the same time, it is increasingly apparent that territory, in the sense of states, nations, territories, and ideas of ethnic singularity, is disintegrating into translocality.

Both transnationality and translocality offer a critical approach to spatiality and the production of space. What is important for this discussion is that these new forms of spatiality center on the individual and his/her movement (the spatio-temporal axis) throughout the world, focusing on how the individual moves on his/her own trajectory while at the same time acknowledging the underlying importance of political economy and global capital in the production and reproduction of the pathways. The challenge is to look at space outside, across, and beyond the nation state, while at the same time retaining an ethnographic perspective that situates these transnational/translocal spaces in the bodies of people with feelings and desires.

The addition of transnational/translocal space complicates the picture because of the magnitude of these spatial and personal transformations and the creation of an entirely new social space. But if a theory of space and place remains centered on the spatio-temporal unit(s), the articulation of transnational and translocal space to specific people and practices becomes clear. These spaces are not abstract, but

socially constituted through the social relationships and the spatiality of those relationships in various geographic locations. Transnational/translocal spaces are
embedded in language and movement as in Duranti's Samoan example as well as
the geopolitical locations that a person travels from or to. But in all cases, these
spaces are produced by the individual, through his/her movements, thoughts, and
imaginings. In this sense, the global is located in embodied space, negotiated and
given meaning through individual agency and social and spatial relationships in
specific cultural and political contexts.

Conclusion: Returning to Moore Street Market and Urban Public Space

I want to return briefly to the Moore Street Market example, and offer a more
embodied analysis of the site. It begins with an analysis of the social production of
the market that was built during the first half of the twentieth century, when New
York City's Department of Markets identified the "food problem" as one of adequate, affordable, and safe supply, and constructed a network of markets to be
managed by the city in an effort to feed its millions of residents. By 1941, the
Department of Markets, with support from the WPA (Works Projects Administration) had constructed nine enclosed markets in three boroughs of New York City
to relocate push-cart vendors and open-air markets that were thought to be health
and fire hazards. These enclosed markets reflected Mayor LaGuardia's (1934–45)
desire to sweep vestiges of immigrant life off the streets as part of an effort to
modernize the city. Thus, Moore Street Market was designed by the municipal
government to relocate vendors out of sight, make high-quality food available at
low cost, encourage immigrants to become small merchants through paying rent
and taxes, and in the process, Americanize the vendors through incorporation into
a municipally controlled food distribution system that was a symbol of New York
City's modernity.

Four of these enclosed markets remain today – on Arthur Avenue in the Bronx,
Essex Street on the Lower East Side, La Marqueta under the elevated tracks in East
Harlem, and the Moore Street Market in Brooklyn. They are no longer symbols of
progress, and instead, have been socially constructed as ethnic markets whose social
and cultural importance within their respective communities is in tension with their
economic viability.

Moore Street Market was a thriving, culturally diverse – mostly Irish, Jewish,
and Italian – immigrant market in its heyday. Although the neighborhood had a
significant Puerto Rican population by 1960, as late as the early 1970s some of the
original vendors remained. The market and the neighborhood changed during the
1970s and 1980s. A resident involved in community building today blames the city
for turning the neighborhood into a "dumping ground," and then turning their back
on the problems caused by a conflation of poverty and underdevelopment.

In 1995, the architectural firm of Hirsch/Danois won a competition to upgrade
the market. Plans included adding bright graphics and dropped-canopy ceilings and
relocating the coolers – previously scattered casually about the floor – to the basement. But by March 2007, the Economic Development Corporation (EDC)
announced that market would close on June 15, 2007 to make way for affordable

housing. The vendors were not given prior notice of EDC's plans, and had difficulty organizing a defense.

Moore Street Market vendors were represented in the press as underdogs fighting an impersonal municipal administration intent on destroying a neighborhood cultural and social institution:

> The 70-year old Moore Street Market was always more than just a place to do business, they said. It is part of the fabric of Williamsburg life, with periodic cultural events and tiny shops and stalls that hearken back to the days before glitzy shopping malls and sterile big-box stores. (Gonzalez 2007)

The conflicting use of language and metaphor by city officials and the private developers who would benefit from building affordable housing – "it's not supporting itself; too tired and rundown," in response to the sympathetic media coverage as "an asset to the community and a haven for Latino social life" – drew political attention from US Representative Nydia Velazquez and State Assemblyman Vito Lopez who teamed up to fight for the market's survival. *States News Service* announced in December 2007 that Nydia Velazquez had secured $3.2 million in federal funding in the Omnibus Appropriations bills, including $235,000 for Project for Public Spaces "for efforts to preserve and revitalize the Moore Street Market in Brooklyn."

In 2008, Moore Street Market vendors were made up of Latino populations from Puerto Rico, Dominican Republic, Ecuador, Mexico, and Nicaragua. All merchants – both owners and employees – were first-generation immigrants. Puerto Rican merchants immigrated to New York in the 1940s, while Dominicans, Mexicans, and Nicaraguans immigrated in the 1980s. Ethnic and national identities were spatialized in the market with Puerto Rican vendors located in its social and economic heart, a central area near the café that sells Caribbean food and plays *salsa* music, while the relatively new Nicaraguans and Mexican vendors were located in stalls along the periphery. These first-generation immigrants all kept their ties to their homeland alive through music, food, family relationships, and visits home. As the example at the beginning of this chapter illustrates, vendors like Doña Maria travel back and forth from Mexico bringing goods from Mexico for sale and carrying gifts and merchandise to local families in Mexico.

The vast majority of customers at the Moore Street Market are older Puerto Rican men and women. This group uses the market for day-to-day social interactions whose regularity is valued and prioritized over the purchase of food. In fact, for the senior Puerto Rican men in particular, buying food seems to be a pretext for the socializing that takes place among the vendors and customers. Often the same group of men moved slowly from one end of the market to the other, perching on the "No Sitting" barriers and at the tables in the café area, sometimes taking a tour outside the market onto Moore or Humboldt Streets, only to return later. The senior Puerto Rican women, on the other hand, were almost always in motion. They often arrived in pairs, chatting as they selected their vegetables. If they stopped for a snack, it was often eaten leisurely, but while standing. Once their purchases were complete, they moved on and out of the market. Unlike the male customers, the senior Puerto Rican women most often shop at one stand and leave, rather than making a tour of the entire space. On weekends, the crowd in the market remained overwhelmingly Puerto Rican with other Latino customers shopping, but not necessarily joining the family groups seated at the café tables, eating *sancocho* and other specialties.

It is in the movement of these bodies – differentiated by gender, age, class, ethnic and national identity – and their everyday activities: conversations, purchases, leisure time spent listening to Latino music, eating homemade food – that these vendors and their clients make the market space what it is. And it is also through the embodied space of their social relationships that the market is transformed into a translocal/transnational space. Moore Street Market for most of its users is both a cultural home in Brooklyn and a native homeland located in the same space/time continuum.

The market was socially produced by the political machinations of New York City institutions and officials, and these municipal institutions continue to play a role in its physical condition and architectural form, while still posing a challenge to the market's continued existence. At the same time, the meanings of the market are socially constructed differently by the African American residents who live nearby, tourists who visit, the officials who want to close it, the media who want a story, and the regulars who see it as their place. Even the language and metaphors of state officials and the media, as well as the "talk" of its visitors and neighbors, contribute to a series of differential renderings of the space as at "the center of the Latino community" to a place that is "forlorn, decaying and deteriorating." These contradictory discourses and meanings are bought together through the embodied space of the market and the people who use it. In this sense, the market is a form of "spatialized culture" that encompasses multiple publics and conflicting meanings, contestations, and negotiations in the ongoing creation of this urban public space.

References

Appadurai, Arjun (1996a) *Modernity at Large: Cultural Dimensions of Globalizations*. Minneapolis: University of Minnesota Press.

Appadurai, Arjun (1996b) Sovereignty without territoriality: notes for a postnational geography. In *The Geography of Identity*, ed. P. Yeager. Ann Arbor: University of Michigan Press, 40–58.

Berger, Peter, and Luckman, Thomas (1967) *The Social Construction of Reality*. New York: Doubleday.

Bourdieu, Pierre (1977) *Outline of a Theory of Practice*. Cambridge: Cambridge University Press.

Bourdieu, Pierre (1984) *Distinction*. Cambridge, MA: Harvard University Press.

Boys, Jos (1998) Beyond maps and metaphors. In *New Frontiers of Space, Bodies, and Gender*, ed. R. Ainley. London: Routledge, 203–17.

Castells, Manuel (1989) *The Informational City: Information, Technology, Economic Restructuring and the Urban-Regional Process*. Oxford: Blackwell.

Castells, Manuel (1996) The net and the self: working notes for a critical theory of the informational society. *Critique of Anthropology* 16 (1): 9–38.

Certeau, Michel de (1984) *The Practices of Everyday Life*. Berkeley: University of California Press.

Csordas, Thomas (1988) Embodiment as a paradigm for anthropology. *Ethos* 18: 5–47.

Csordas, Thomas (1994) *Embodiment and Experience*. Cambridge: Cambridge University Press.

Duncan, Nancy (1996) (Re)placings. In *BodySpace: Destabilizing Geographies of Gender and Sexuality*, ed. N. Duncan. London: Routledge, 1–10.

Duranti, Alessandro (1992) Language and bodies in social space: Samoan ceremonial greetings. *American Anthropologist* 94: 657–91.

Duranti, Alessandro (1997) Indexical speech across Samoan communities. *American Anthropologist* 99 (2): 342–54.

Foucault, Michel (1975) *Discipline and Punish: The Birth of the Prison*. New York: Vintage.

Foucault, Michel (1984) Des espaces autres. *Architecture, Mouvement, Continuité* October: 46–9.

Gonzalez, J. (2007) Brooklyn's La Marqueta buys time. New York Daily News, June 13. Available online at http://www.nydailynews.com/news/2007/06/06/2007–06–06_brooklyns_la_marqueta_buys_time.html (accessed December 3, 2010).

Gupta, Akhil, and Ferguson, James (1992) Beyond "culture": space, identity and the politics of difference. *Cultural Anthropology* 7 (1): 6–23.

Hall, Edward T. (1966) *The Hidden Dimension*. New York: Doubleday.

Hall, Edward T. (1968) Proxemics. *Current Anthropology* 9 (2): 83–95.

Hall, Edward T. (1973) Mental health research and out-of-awareness cultural systems. In *Cultural Illness and Health*, ed. L. Nader and T. W. Maretzki. Washington, DC: American Anthropological Association, 977–103.

Haraway, Donna (1991) *Simians, Cyborgs, and Women: The Reinvention of Nature*. New York: Routledge.

Hymes, Dell (1968) Letter. *Current Anthropology* 9 (2–3): 100.

King, A. (1976) *Colonial Urban Development: Culture, Social Power and Environment*. London: Routledge and Kegan Paul.

Lefebvre, Henri (1991) *The Production of Space*. Oxford: Basil Blackwell.

Low, Setha (2000) *On the Plaza: The Politics of Public Space and Culture*. Austin: University of Texas Press.

Low, Setha (2002) *Theorizing the City*. New Brunswick, NJ: Rutgers University Press.

Low, Setha (2003) *Behind the Gates: Life, Security and the Pursuit of Happiness in Fortress America*. New York and London: Routledge.

Low, Setha, and Lawrence-Zuñiga, Denise (2003) *The Anthropology of Space and Place: Locating Culture*. Oxford: Blackwell.

Mahmood, Saba, (2001) Feminist theory, embodiment, and the docile agent. *Cultural Anthropology* 16 (2): 202–36.

Massey, Doreen (2005) *For Space*. Los Angeles: Sage Publications.

Mauss, Marcel (1950) *Les techniques du corps: sociologies et anthropologie*. Paris: Presses Universitaires de France.

Mauss, Marcel (1979) *Sociology and Psychology*. London: Routledge and Kegan Paul.

McHugh, Kevin (2000) Inside, outside, upside down, backward, forward, round and round: a case for ethnographic studies in migration. *Progress in Human Geography* 24 (1): 71–89.

Merleau-Ponty, Maurice (1962) *Phenomenology of Perception*. New York and London: Routledge and Kegan Paul.

Merleau-Ponty, Maurice (1964) *The Primacy of Perception*. Evanston, IL: Northwestern University Press.

Mountz, Alison, and Wright, Richard A. (1996) Daily life in the transnational migrant community of San Augustín, Oaxaca, and Poughkeepsie, New York. *Diaspora* 5 (3): 403–28.

Munn, Nancy (1996) Excluded spaces: the figure in the Australian Aboriginal landscape. *Critical Inquiry* 22: 446–65.

Munt, Sally R. (1998) Sisters in exile: the lesbian nation. In *New Frontiers in Space, Bodies and Gender*, ed. R. Ainley. London: Routledge, 3–19.

Ong, Aihwa (1999) *Flexible Citizenship. The Cultural Logics of Transnationality*. Durham, NC: Duke University Press.

Pred, Allan (1986) *Place, Practice, and Structure: Social and Spatial Transformation in Southern Sweden – 1750–1850*. Totowa, NJ: Barnes and Noble.

Rabinow, Paul (1982) Ordonnance, discipline, regulation: some reflections on urbanism. *Humanities in Society* 5(3–4): 267–78.

Rabinow, Paul (1989) *French Modern: Norms and Forms of Missionary and Didactic Pathos*. Cambridge, MA: MIT Press.

Richardson, Miles (1982) Being-in-the-plaza versus being-in-the-market: material culture and the construction of social reality. *American Ethnologist* 9: 421–36.

Richardson, Miles (1984) Material culture and being-in-Christ in Spanish America and the American South. *Built Form and Culture Conference Proceedings*, October 18–20. Lawrence: University of Kansas.

Ricoeur, Paul (1991) *From Text to Action: Essays in Hermeneutics II*. Evanston, IL: Northwestern University Press.

Rockefeller, Stuart (2010) *Starting from Quirpini: The Travels and Places of a Bolivian People*. Bloomington: University of Indiana Press.

Rodman, Margaret (1992) Empowering place: multilocality and multivocality. *American Anthropologist* 94 (3): 640–56.

Rothstein, Frances Abrahamer (2007). *Globalization in Rural Mexico*. Austin: University of Texas Press.

Rouse, Roger (1991) Mexican migration and the social space of postmodernism. *Diaspora* 1 (1): 8–23.

Sassen, Saskia (1991) *The Global City*. Princeton, NJ: Princeton University Press.

Sassen, Saskia (1996a) *Losing Control? Sovereignty in an Age of Globalization*. New York: Columbia University Press.

Sassen, Saskia (1996b) Whose city is it? Globalization and the formation of new claims. *Public Culture* 8 (2): 205–24.

Schiller, Nina Glick, Basch, Linda, and Blanc-Szanton, Cristina (1992) *Towards a Transnational Perspective on Migration: Race, Class, Ethnicity and Nationalism Reconsidered*. New York: New York Academy of Sciences.

Scott, Joan (1996) *Feminism and History*. Oxford: Oxford University Press.

Smart, Alan (1999) Flexible accumulation: across the Hong Kong border. Petty capitalists as pioneers of globalized accumulation. *Urban Anthropology* 28 (3–4): 373–406.

Smith, Michael Peter (2001) *Transnational Urbanism*. Malden, MA and Oxford: Blackwell.

Turner, Bryan S. (1984) *The Body and Society*. Oxford: Basil Blackwell.

Turner, Terence (1980) The social skin. In *Not Work Alone*, ed. J. Cherfas and R. Lewin. London: Temple Smith, 112–40.

Turner, Terence (1995) Social body and embodied subject: bodiliness, subjectivity, and sociality among the Kayapo. *Cultural Anthropology* 10 (2): 143–70.

Chapter 42

The Street Politics of
Jackie Smith

John Paul Jones III

genealogical practice transforms history from a judgment on the past in the name of
a present truth to a "counter-memory" that combats our current modes of truth and
justice, helping us to understand and change the present by placing it in a new relation
to the past.

(Jonathan Arac, *Postmodernism and Politics*, xviii)

On April 3, 1968, Martin Luther King, Jr., together with Jesse Jackson and Ralph
Abernathy, arrived in Memphis, Tennessee to lend their support for striking garbage
workers. They stayed at the historically Black Lorraine Motel, located adjacent to
the city's Black business district on the outskirts of downtown Memphis (Figure
42.1). The next day, while standing on the balcony outside his room, King was shot
down by a bullet fired from across the street. The instant was captured in a famous
Joseph Louw photograph (Figure 42.2), an image that immediately became an
emblem of the 1960s. Today, the Lorraine is both a shrine to the fallen civil rights
leader (Figure 42.3) and the site of the nation's first civil rights museum.

The transformation of the Lorraine took many years. Following King's death, it
continued to operate as a motel, but not surprisingly, it drew more curiosity seekers
than guests. By the 1970s it was a run-down building badly in need of repair, an
embarrassment for the city of Memphis not unlike Dealy Plaza was for Dallas. In
the early 1980s, a local Black official, D'Army Bailey, and the mayor of Memphis,
Dick Hackett, put into place a fundraising project to save the Lorraine. By the late
1980s, the nonprofit Lorraine Civil Rights Museum Foundation had assembled
some nine million dollars from the City of Memphis, Shelby County, and the State
of Tennessee, as well as from various private sources. The renovation project

The New Blackwell Companion to the City   Edited by Gary Bridge and Sophie Watson
© 2011 Blackwell Publishing Ltd

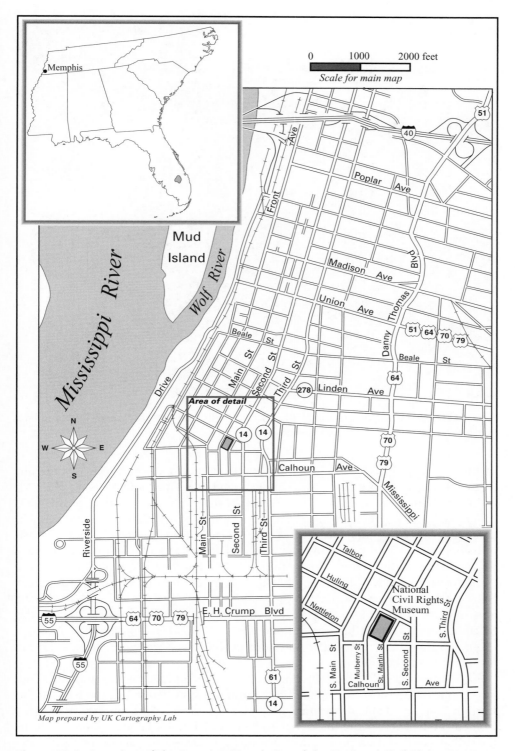

Figure 42.1 Location of the Lorraine Motel, site of the National Civil Rights Museum in Memphis, Tennessee.

Figure 42.2 King's assassination at the Lorraine. Photo by Joseph Louw/Time and Life Pictures/Getty Images. Used with permission.

involved removing one wing of the old motel to create a portion of the museum (Figure 42.4), while preserving the wing containing King's room, number 306.

Inside the main area visitors are treated to a short introductory film, to traveling galleries celebrating African-American contributions to art, education, and science, and to displays recounting the history of the US civil rights movement. The showcase of the museum is a series of hands-on exhibits combining audio, video, and interactive audience participation. These cover the Montgomery bus boycott, the court case, *Brown v. Board of Education*, the desegregation of Little Rock's Central High School, the March on Washington, and the Memphis garbage strike. Visitors can also view the site of King's death, either from the brick-inlay courtyard below the balcony, complete with historic automobiles of King's era (Figure 42.5), or from room 306, faithfully redecorated to represent the way it was when King spent his last night in the Lorraine.

The National Civil Rights Museum attracts some 100,000 visitors annually. One year, while on a visit to Memphis, I too planned a visit. Rounding the back of the Lorraine on foot from downtown Memphis, I suddenly and unpreparedly confronted the balcony, a site intertextually linked to Louw's famous photograph. In the stillness of that moment I noticed a woman (Figure 42.6), Jacqueline Smith. She struck a discomforting presence across the street from the museum, sitting on a

Figure 42.3 Historical marker describing the significance of the Lorraine Motel.

Figure 42.4 The National Civil Rights Museum. At left is the entrance to the museum.

Figure 42.5 The balcony outside the preserved wing of the motel. The automobiles reference the cars captured in Joseph Louw's photograph (Figure 42.2).

Figure 42.6 Jacqueline "Jackie" Smith protests the Lorraine's transformation into a museum.

tattered old couch, with handmade placards in protest of what she called the "Civil Wrong Museum." Rather than continue into the museum, I crossed the street to talk to her, asking about her protest. Thus began a series of visits I have made to the Lorraine over several years, never once violating her request that I boycott the museum. This chapter is about her story.

Jackie's Protest

Jackie's protest operates at several levels. Listeners – at least those who cross the street to talk to her, for she is under a court injunction not to disrupt the museum's operations – will first learn that she is against the use of the site as a civil rights museum. For her, civil rights is an ongoing, everyday struggle that must be practiced (Figure 42.7); it should not be petrified, canonized, and memorialized in a series of interactive exhibits. Jackie believes that a civil rights museum is an all-too-comforting experience for visitors, implying that civil rights were won with desegregated buses, schools, and lunch counters. Among his other writings, as a rationale for her protest, Jackie points to King's final sermon, in which he rejects eulogies and awards, affirming instead actions such as feeding the hungry, clothing the naked, and counseling those in prison. Jackie maintains that the Lorraine should be used in ways consistent with King's philosophy, particularly by helping those living in the deteriorated community in which it is located, which she notes is characterized by unemployment, poor housing, drugs, and crime. Accordingly, Jackie maintains that the Lorraine should house a homeless shelter, a medical clinic, a job-training center, and a drug rehabilitation facility. Jackie goes on to record the rationale for her protest:

Figure 42.7 Jackie asks Memphis residents and visitors to boycott the museum.

That's why I'm protesting ... that would be the main reason and the fact that the way King said he wanted to be remembered is simply being ignored in favor of bricks and mortar, lifeless, been set up and done for appearances, does not solve the social problems, does not get to the root of our problems, and that's what King was all about, he was about serving humanity, and helping, that was his basic philosophy and I don't see that being focused on. All I see being focused on is how many tourists did we get, how much money did we make, what is the tally, that's what I see, the bottom line, somebody sitting back trying to make a dollar. ... I just think the reason for having a museum at the site of Dr. King's death for educational purposes lacks substance because we have a run-down neighborhood, poverty, homelessness, crime, drug abuse, all these ills that plague our society. I just feel that those problems are more important because we need to be trying to eradicate them.

Those who linger to speak with Jackie can also hear her offer a detailed political-economy critique of land development in the area around the Lorraine. She cites explicit and de facto redlining, castigates the nearby gated communities alongside the Mississippi river that house such luminaries as Memphis's favorite daughter, actress Cybill Shepherd, and laments the use of the Lorraine by the city's White establishment as a stimulant for gentrification. As Jackie notes, "Blacks have lived and operated business in this area for years. Now they want to tear the buildings down and replace them with high-rent apartments they know we can't afford." "Where are we supposed to go?" she asks. Tracing a story common to many US cities, Jackie offers that the Lorraine's development "is just a ploy to get the Blacks out of the neighborhood. It's one of the biggest landgrabbing conspiracies. It's urban renewal, all over again, but now it goes by the name of gentrification." Jackie will also hold forth about the 1979 strategic plan that still guides changes in the built environment around the hotel. The plan predicted that rising rents would substantially alter the neighborhood's racial composition:

They [urban planners] predicted that by year 2000 there would be only 21 percent of African-Americans in the area even though at the time that they wrote the report there were 79 percent African-Americans in the area. And within that report they had the number of condominiums and townhouses they had planned on building and they had how much they would cost, and so the report was broken down to income levels, and see by that they made their prediction that there would be only 21 percent African-Americans in this area, because they know we can't afford the apartments and townhouses and condominiums that they built. And so that's how they came up with the figures, and I'm telling you, you've probably gone around and looked around for yourself and you see all the new apartments that have sprung up and they look like they've been here for years but they have not, they've been building on them now since the early eighties. So it's not a matter of my thinking, it's a matter that we know for sure what has taken place in this area, and we had ... neighborhood meetings with some of the planners of this area and they just simply told us what was going to transpire in this area. And so that's when I began to speak out against what was going on because, hey, Dr. King was assassinated here. I mean you going to mistreat the poor people that live down here, you going to push them aside in order to gentrify the neighborhood? And that's exactly what they're doing.

Finally, Jackie offers a cultural critique of the museum. She protests turning King's death site into a "partyhouse" by the city of Memphis. Who, she asks, would organize champagne brunches and courtyard dancing (Figure 42.8) in such a sacred space? She protests using the Lorraine to attract tourists to Memphis, and its emergence as an obligatory stop for conventioneers (Figure 42.9), some of whom are treated to black-tie galas under the balcony of room 306. She critiques the interactive exhibits as a form of entertainment inappropriate for the Lorraine; she argues that everything one could learn in the museum – and more – is already contained in the public library; and, noting the lack of historical authenticity of the museum's exhibits, she laughs at the pilgrims who throw themselves in a fit of emotion on the automobiles under the balcony, cars in which King never actually rode:

> Well one thing I see is that the Lorraine is being separated from its history. They are trying to turn it into something that it was not and I think that's a mistake. I think the Lorraine should be set up to deal with today's problems, to deal with today's

Figure 42.8 The museum is a site for some of the city's cultural events.

Figure 42.9 The street between Jackie and the museum is regularly traversed by vehicles, such as this one, carrying tourists.

discrimination, crime, poverty and that sort of thing. But they have turned the Lorraine into just another place for entertainment, parties. I don't think it's right to turn the death site of Dr. King into a place to party. I really think that that's wrong. He didn't come here to die, so why should somebody take death and capitalize off of it and turn that site where he died into a place to party? To me that is totally wrong, distasteful, and I don't think that is the proper way to honor the memory of a man like Dr. King.

What is most remarkable about Jackie's protest is its duration. Jackie was the night manager and the last resident of the old Lorraine Motel. In January 1988, the building was condemned for the museum project, but she locked herself in her room and refused to leave, even after the water and electricity had been turned off. She and the local government entered into a 50-day siege that ended when Jackie was forcibly evicted from the building on March 2, 1988. She was deposited on the sidewalk outside the Lorraine, and from that moment forward, day and night, she has been living in protest outside the museum, a large sign recording the number of days (Figure 42.10). Not the weather, harassment by local officials, nor racist acts against her life, have deterred her. She turned 47 years old when the protest entered its eleventh year, but through my various visits I have never heard her express any doubt about her actions; as she puts it, "I am too stubborn to give up."

As a result of her everyday presence, Jackie has herself become an institution, even, a tourist attraction in her own right (Figure 42.11). Some visitors will stop to hear her story for the first time, but summer in Memphis is the site of scores of reunions among African Americans whose families extend from Chicago to the

Figure 42.10 The sign records the number of consecutive days Jackie has protested. This photograph was taken in 1995. As of this writing, she is still there.

Figure 42.11 Memphis visitors inquire about the protest.

lower Mississippi delta, and both the museum and Jackie have become an annual affair for many of these families. Local friends and neighbors will also drop by frequently.

Street Politics

Jackie's protest encourages a range of reflections relevant to the nature of politics, space, and memory. Traditionally conceived by urban researchers in electoral and institutional terms, politics for Jackie emerges from, and is practiced at, a deeply personal level. Her vigil sharply contrasts civic and personal politics, effectively demonstrating how the strategies of capital and state institutions can be counter-manded, if not overturned, by the persistent, everyday tactics of those located on the margin. Jackie thus reminds us of other "bottom up" urban politics, including the protestations of graffiti artists, parade and carnival demonstrators, and alterna-tive media activists. And yet, unlike many of these forms of protest – but like King himself – she explicitly taps a reservoir of religious discourse, demonstrating its critical resourcefulness over and against the secularized discourses of the state. In opposition to the language of community development espoused by city officials, planners, and developers, Jackie poses deconstructive-style questions: What pre-cisely is meant by "community," or by "development"? Defined by and for whom?

In another vein, Jackie reminds us of Henri Lefebvre's admonition that space is never neutral, but is a product literally filled with ideology. Seeing the Lorraine in these terms enables us to understand Jackie's protest as "spatial praxis" – a specifi-cally geographic form of political action. On the one hand, the target of her protest is the Lorraine, and through this site she makes connections to the wider spaces of Memphis that the museum fails to serve. On the other hand, her continuous spatial presence across the street from the Lorraine illustrates that her chosen forms of protest – witnessing, testifying, and vigilance – are themselves deeply geographic practices; in other words, the "eye of power" has location and direction. Jackie's protest also tells a story about the "social construction" of history, by which is not meant that history is in the mind, but that it is only available to us through socially mediated forms of experience and interpretation. In this space in particular we learn that the social authority to determine what will be history, and how it will be honored, is typically bound to the state apparatus, as it is with so many memorials, museums, and state-sanctioned parades. But through Jackie we equally learn that no commemoration is ever fully sealed, since no history is ever without subjects who experience, interpret, and learn from it differently. Jackie shows us, in other words, that the Lorraine is not a tombstone. Her presence taps a surplus of meaning that exceeds the authorial intentionality of Lorraine's creators. It is in fact this excess that enables and makes meaningful her spatial praxis, for she demonstrates that for both space and history, as in all things political, there is always the potential for reinterpretation, and hence always a potential oppositional moment.

Finally, in asking Memphis visitors to make a choice between her activist vision for the Lorraine and the institutionalized memorialization of civil rights put forth by the museum's curators, she implicitly poses the question: "What does it mean to be political?" I have listened as scores of visitors have interacted with her, with this question just below the surface. Some will side with the museum, and encourage

Jackie to find more productive pursuits for her energies. Others will applaud her vision and offer both moral and, occasionally, material support. And I have struggled with both responses: how can one measure Jackie's vision for the museum over and against its arguable educational benefits, which include the visits of as many as 50,000 school-age visitors each year? One answer to this question is to conceive of the productive politics of this space as located in the street that separates Jackie from the museum, that interstitial space that juxtaposes and puts into sharp relief one version of African-American history to another. On the one hand is an attempt to preserve the memory of civil rights so that the struggle is not forgotten; on the other hand is Jackie's effort to activate that memory for the unfinished project of civil rights. Seen in this way, perhaps visitors like me return to Memphis because of the dialectical and co-constitutive tensions produced by the structure of the Lorraine and Jackie's critical presence. And, perhaps Jackie's legacy will be, if not the transformation of the Lorraine, more critical reflection on the politics that reside in this and other spaces of memory.

Epilogue

This chapter first appeared in the original *The Blackwell Companion to the City* (2000). It is printed here with a few updated figures.

Jackie's protest continues to this day – late 2009 – now well over 20 years. Readers can keep track of her through the website, www.fulfillthedream.net.

Acknowledgments

This paper was presented at the Inaugural International Conference in Critical Geography (Vancouver), the Association of American Geographers (Boston), the Southeastern Division of the Association of American Geographers (Memphis), and the Cities at the Millennium Conference (London), as well as at the University of Wisconsin, the University of Toledo, Clarion University, University of Wales at Aberystwyth, Southwest Texas State University, and the University of Kentucky's African American Studies and Research Program. My thanks to Nick Blomley, Gary Bridge, Bernadette Caldwell, Tim Cresswell, Margo Kleinfeld, Geraldine Pratt, Tobie Saad, Gerald Smith, Gerald Thomas, Sent Visser, and Sophie Watson for these invitations. I also want to thank Deborah Dixon, Owen Dwyer, Wolfgang Natter, and the audiences at these presentations for offering insights and comments. I am of course most of all indebted to Jackie. Readers may contact her by writing to PO Box 3482, Memphis TN 381730482.

Chapter 43

Walking and Performing "the City": A Melbourne Chronicle

Benjamin Rossiter and Katherine Gibson

"The street level is dead space. ... It is only a means of passage to the interior" – summed up Richard Sennett, two decades ago, his analysis of the most impressive and spectacular urban developments of his time, ushering in the new era of the post-modern metropolis.

(Bauman 1994: 148–9)

Today's action is, after all, different: it is, mostly, about *passing* from here to there, as fast as one can manage, preferably without stopping, better still without looking around. Beautiful passers-by hide inside automobiles with tinted windows. Those still on the pavement are waiters and sellers at best, but more often dangerous people pure and simple: layabouts, beggars, homeless conscience-soilers, drug pushers, pickpockets, muggers, child molesters and rapists waiting for the prey. To the innocent who had to leave for a moment the wheeled security of automobiles, or those others, still thinking of themselves as innocent, who cannot afford that security at all, street is more a jungle than the theater. One goes there because one must. A site fraught with risks, not chances; not meant for gentlemen of leisure, and certainly not for the faint-hearted among them. The street is the "out there" from which one hides, at home or inside the automobile, behind security locks and burglar alarms.

(Bauman 1994: 148)

Perhaps it's the fear that Richard Sennett and Zygmunt Bauman are right that drives the City of Melbourne to host a regular International Arts Festival in which all and sundry (and especially those who can't afford the ticket prices of the undercover shows) are enticed out on to the streets of the central city with the offer of free entertainment – street theater, food stalls, fireworks, and displays. The tinted glass is wound down, automobiles, security locks and burglar alarms abandoned, respectables and "deviants" intermix and the luxuriously wide (automobile, or was it cart,

The New Blackwell Companion to the City   Edited by Gary Bridge and Sophie Watson
© 2011 Blackwell Publishing Ltd

determined) streets of Bauman's Melbourne are reclaimed and enlivened becoming home, for a brief few weeks, to *flâneurs* and *flâneuses* momentarily released from their otherwise largely suburban experience.

It was during this short burst of urban self-consciousness that I ventured out with family in tow to "take in the sights/sites." Not, of course, without the usual generational trade-off: walking the streets and enjoying the ambience with a specific look-in on the Urban Dream Capsule – a group of five male performance artists locked up in a department store window for the duration of the Arts Festival – in return for a visit to a city movie complex to see *Independence Day* – the latest Parental Guidance-rated Hollywood blockbuster with a prerelease hype that had captured the eight- and ten-year-olds' interest enough to motivate a tenuous companionability. So it was that through an afternoon and evening I walked in a city experiencing it from the street, from the theater seat, and from the street again – materiality and representation jostling for priority.

In recollecting this day two different stories of the city stand out in stark contrast. One is the prevalent narrative of urban decay, immanent doom, and civic destruction told once again in the filmic representation of North American cities in *Independence Day*. Picking up on the apocalyptic tone adopted by many contemporary commentators of the "postmodern city," the movie shows civil disorder, hysterical masses, and sexuality gone awry as a shadow is cast over the cancerous, "sprawling giantism" of late twentieth-century urbanism by huge alien cities hovering in the sky (Mumford 1961: 618). One by one, each earthly metropolis is engulfed in a fiery blast emanating from the airborne monstrous craft. The city streets that for some, such as Bauman, have already become uninhabitable (except by the layabouts, beggars, homeless, drug pushers, etc.) or for others, such as Michael Sorkin (1992) and Paul Virilio (1991) have been rendered obsolete by the dominance of the screen interface and the fiber-optic superhighway, are finally erased, decimated, and consumed by the aliens' fireballs. The modern city as a physical presence is rendered irrelevant and the technologically mediated "posturban" age is upon us. The central characters, a cast of souls who regain their masculinity and/or morality in an all-American way through violence and the exercise of force, abandon the cities and flee – not to the traditional anti-urban utopia of a lush green rural Eden, but to a secret hypertechnical military installation buried deep under the dry brown desert.

As each set of events necessary to the blockbuster genre was roughly welded together, laughs of incredulity burst forth from the teenagers sitting behind us indicating that even they could tell that this was a stupid (but not therefore unentertaining) movie. What was so compelling for this *flâneur/se* trapped in its web by a necessary familial transaction was the movie's resonance with the familiar modernist morality tale that underpins much cultural commentary and discourse upon postmodern urbanism. As it is told and retold in movie or in social theory the story of an urban/moral order under threat, of accelerating mayhem in the streets, ultimate physical destruction, and rebirth of a technologically mediated social order in which the street is invalidated as a social space repeatedly constitutes and reinforces the power of deep-seated anti-urban sentiments that in turn inform so much of our urban experience and practice.

So what a shock to return to the street and to resume walking in a city in the throes of celebrating the urban. It was early evening and people were everywhere, milling around, not seemingly going anywhere, but being sociable, entertained, and present. Here was another, very different city story – space occupied, not ceded to a narrative of despair or destruction. It is this other image that we want, in this chapter, to dwell upon and explore for its potential.

Walking (in) the City

The practice of walking and the reflection on urban walks contribute to a counter-discourse of the urban. This counter-discourse finds its power in relational opposition to those god's-eye conceptions of city form and changing structure that have been motivated by the modernist quest for lawful spatial order and captured by the organizing narrative of capitalist urbanization (Gibson-Graham 1996: ch. 4). Walter Benjamin, Roland Barthes, and Michel de Certeau among others have drawn upon this ambulatory counterpoint in their representations of the urban.

> The ordinary practitioners of the city live "down below," below the thresholds at which visibility begins. They walk – an elementary form of this experience of the city; they are walkers, *Wandersmanner*, whose bodies follow the thicks and thins of an urban "text" they write without being able to read it … The networks of these moving, intersecting writings compose a manifold story that has neither author nor spectator, shaped by fragments of trajectories and alterations of spaces: in relation to representations, it remains daily and indefinitely other. (de Certeau 1984: 93)

De Certeau invites us to walk in the city and to allow the "long poem of walking" to reveal and confuse what has been concealed and clarified by urban theory. Working against the "imaginary totalizations" produced by those who seek to render the city readable and therefore ultimately controllable, he encourages pedestrians to be producers of their own urban texts, to construct and occupy urban space inventively. Perhaps the metaphor of walking possesses the power to unsettle the narrative of (post)modern urban decay and civic disarray?

> This city can be known only by an activity of an ethnographic kind: you must orient yourself in it not by book, by address, but by walking, by sight, by habit, by experience; here every discovery is intense and fragile, it can be repeated or recovered only by memory of the trace it has left you: to visit a place for the first time is thereby to begin to write it: the address not being written, it must establish its own writing. (Barthes 1982: 33–6)

As he meandered on foot through the (for him) "practically unclassified" streets of Tokyo guided only by impromptu drawings and gestures that elevated new ways of seeing and writing over old ways of speaking and reading, Barthes reflected that the "rational is merely one system among others" of knowing a place (1982: 33). His observations on Tokyo prompt us to challenge representations of a perceived coherence of the urban as embodied in the map, guide, telephone book, or indeed panopticon pronouncements on the "postmodern" (western) city. Barthes writes of the trace left by the city in one's memories – of the feel of the pavement, the orientation of objects in space, the smells and tastes – its writing on/in you. And here he touches upon topics written about so lucidly by Benjamin: "autobiography has to do with time, with sequence and what makes up the continuous flow of life. Here, I am talking of a space, of moments and discontinuities. For even if months and years appear here, it is in the form they have at the moment of recollection" (Benjamin 1978: 28).

In "A Berlin chronicle" Benjamin (1978) describes his own introduction to the city, recollecting street images and associated emotions, school spaces, friendships of his childhood and youth, buildings, and happenings in context. His urban writings represent a denarrativized city – a city temporarily released from the discursive structures imposed by history and rationality. He celebrates distracted thought and absent-minded strolling, straying, hovering, daydreaming, and idling as bodily/intellectual practices which are counter and subversive to the notion of productivity. Walking for Benjamin is a practice of remembrance. Memory is the "medium of past experience" just as the ground is the medium in which dead cities lie buried. Benjamin validates the power of imaginary maps and alerts us to the chance that "valuable things" left "lying around" the streets might be found, like objects long forgotten in an attic, and incorporated into the individual's experience of walking/knowing (in) the city (1978: 20). He places value on these discarded, little used, or seemingly unimportant urban activities and spaces that are rarely seen to hold significance in conventional urban discourse. For Benjamin to dig and dig again in the same and new places reveals "hidden treasures" lying buried deep in one's memory (1978: 24–6). At the same time the "art of straying" and losing oneself in the city enables the mind to be more receptive to deceased experiences flashed into the present by involuntary memories. Walking might be seen as an invitation to allow sudden flashes of illumination and chance stumblings across hidden treasures to reshape urban knowledge, possibly invigorating pro-urban sentiments and writing different scripts for the "postmodern city."

We are interested in the enabling potentialities of re-presenting the city from the street – from the perspective of the walker and the street inhabitant. The trope of walking offers us ways of representing the city and constituting contemporary urban experience that might unsettle both the anti-urban apocalypticism of much contemporary urban thinking and the preoccupation with spatial ordering that has channelled urban representations and experience into the constricting binarisms of public/private, home/street, residential/non-residential. It allows new spatializations of the city to emerge and loosens the hold of historicist narratives of restructuring and postmodern decay. The body is reintroduced to the urban, but not in its capacity to occupy at various times private/residential space or public/industrial or commercial space, or to move between point A and point B as commuter or householder intimately linked to the functioning of capitalist production or reproduction. The body is introduced as a sensual being – smelling, remembering, rhythmically moving, jostling with other bodies – and in the process constituting active, perhaps multiple, urban subjectivities. The walker becomes lost, allows the city – street signs, bars, cafes, billboards, passers-by – to "speak" to her as does a bird call in the wild or a twig crackling under foot in a forest (Benjamin 1978: 8–9). The speech act of walking creates stories, invents spaces, and opens up the city through its capacity to produce "anti-texts" within the text. The ambulatory occupation of urban space permits a myriad of unrealized possibilities to surface, triggering emotions and feelings that may lie dormant in many people.

The invitation to stroll, daydream, look about, and wander aimlessly through city space was offered to Melburnians during their International Arts Festival. Precisely because the city itself often appears in contemporary texts as an outmoded fragment or ruin of its former self, the strategy of enticing people on to the streets during the festival could be read as a recognition of the real abandonment of public civic space and therefore as a rearguard action by the City, or it could be seen as an intervention that operated completely outside this discourse of despair. We prefer the latter reading because on the day that our chronicle documents, flashes of illumination emanating from a boxed treasure suggested that walking in the city is an activity that turns up even greater possibilities for destabilization and re-enchantment than at the time that Benjamin was writing.

Performing (in) the City

> In a world where privacy is vanishing, come see your future. For sixteen days of the Festival, five of Melbourne's street performers will be hermetically sealed behind the glass walls of Myer's Bourke Street Windows! ... these intrepid art-stronauts will translocate their entire lives to the heart of the city in a 24 hour a day, nonstop, incubation event. Without a curtain in sight. Watch them eat, sleep, entertain, perform – in our very own biosphere experiment that is at the cutting edge of performance art.
>
> (Melbourne Festival Guide 1996: 38)

In a flash of recognition and then misrecognition it becomes clear that the Myer department store windows – home every Christmas to a wondrous scene of moving mechanical gnomes, fairies, elves, and assorted fairy story characters – is occupied by grown living men! The crowd gathered in front of the windows is not mainly kids and their Christmas-shopping parents, but Melburnians of all ages and backgrounds gathered to observe the "Myersphere experiment." When we push our way to the front of the crowd it is "getting-ready-for-bed" time. Some of the five bald men are in their striped pyjamas – others are still in their day suits. One is in the window/room that contains the bathroom basin, shower (with partial screen) and exercise equipment, cleaning his teeth. He turns round to the crowd, my son bares his teeth and has them scrubbed – albeit through the "pane of separation" (Kermond 1996). The smudge of toothpaste on the inside surface remains in place all evening – a trace of the communicative act.

The Urban Dream Capsule (UDC) took the 1996 Melbourne Festival by surprise. By the time the art-stronauts (Andrew Morrish, Bruce Naylor, Nick Papas, Neil Thomas, and David Wells) emerged after 16 days of sealed isolation in the four adjoining shop windows, an estimated 200,000 people had viewed them for varying lengths of time. Even more had contacted them via fax, telephone, and email. At any time of day or night the crowd outside the windows never seemed to drop below 50. Sometimes it was cast in the subject position of "audience" to be "entertained" by the "elaborate synchronised ritualisation of everyday activities" (shaving heads in the morning, preparing meals, showering, and preparing for bed). "People are transfixed by the spectacle, bonded by a sneaky sense of voyeurism coupled with outright fascination" (Scott-Norman 1996).

At other times members of the crowd actively communicated with the performers. On one occasion two people shouted through the glass to Neil Thomas (the mas-

Figure 43.1 Art-stronaut Andrew Morrish has his daily headshave under the watchful eye of early morning shoppers (photo: Angela Wiley; from *The Age*, October 19, 1996).

termind of the performance), "We've got a house-warming present for you." They proceeded to attach a very small plant, perhaps a sweet pea, in a tiny square pot about a metre from the ground. Thomas looked truly delighted. He wrote a sign which read "Please take care of our garden" and attached it to the inside of the window. Not long after someone else watered it. "The experience has been full of surprises, says Thomas. People turning up regularly with notepads to write messages on; people concerned about whether the capsulites were eating and sleeping enough; big burly guys, the type Thomas says don't usually go in for performance art, getting a charge out of the experience" (Schembri 1996b).

Partially conceived as an exposé of the increased technological surveillance of urban lives and the loss of privacy, the Myersphere experiment turned the disciplinary power of panopticon vision into a game. The UDC transformed a common tactic of the urban marginalized – occupation and performance – into an acceptable art form. Just as teenagers entertain themselves by acting up for the security cameras strategically placed in shopping malls and railroad stations, the capsulites acted up 24 hours a day under the constant gaze of countless Big Brothers. Out of harsh coldblooded scrutiny and visual invasion, those under surveillance generated love, humor, and identification.

Perhaps the potential for this inversion to take off as a model for urban interaction was infectious. When early the next year students of the city campus of RMIT University of Technology occupied the administration building for 19 days to protest the introduction of fee-paying courses, the television screen replaced the glass of the Myer store window. Media coverage of the sit-in produced images of recognition and resonance with the previous year's public occupation. The televised scenes of students on the second floor receiving food and supplies on a rope paralleled the UDC deliveries of food through their "backstage" door. Their window performances were more raucous and less polished, but nevertheless served to highlight issues of resources and survival for young people.

The languages of science and cyberspace were harnessed in the promotion of the UDC. The performers were scientific experimental subjects – their everyday life, the object of scientific observation by the crowd cast here as "researchers." They in turn cast themselves as scientific observers of the crowd: "There's a score where we imagine that we're in an alien bathysphere that has landed in Myer and we're there to observe. So it's like we're at the bottom of the sea – the sealife is floating by and we're taking notes" (cited in Schembri 1996a). And as experimental scientists testing out the usefulness of the internet as a performance aid: "I don't know if this is good to say, but being honest, part of this thing was to check out whether the Internet was an interesting form of communication, and I just don't think it is. If you want to get real, come down and see the show. You can't beat that" (cited in Schembri 1996b).

As authentic scientists, the five bald men were open to discovery. In representational or naturalistic theater actors perform with a fictional "fourth wall" between them and the audience – while the audience sees the actors, the actors appear not to see the audience (McGraw 1980: 141; Whitmore 1994: 60). Street performers, performance artists, and comedians often tilt at this convention moving through this fictional wall to variously shock and engage. In accordance with their exploratory mission, the UDC placed themselves behind an actual fourth wall and discovered that it proved to be quite porous. They found that the plate-glass window, described by Richard Sennett in terms of its "strong power of isolation" and its ability to divide the "physical senses" through the way it insulates those inside "from sound and touch and other human beings" outside (1990: 109), was indeed permeable. Sociality could cross the boundary, it could osmose through the tinted glass and transform scientific practice into playful intercourse. And in this experiment, even this paneful communication was more compelling than the cyberspace variety.

For many, the UDC was a treasure to be stumbled over, providing a fleeting interchange and welcome laugh in an otherwise impersonal space. For us it provides inspiration for thinking the city outside the hegemonic frames of inherited urban theory. We are not only interested in the ways in which it worked to unsettle prevalent urban "stories" such as that of the diminished privacy and increased technological surveillance of contemporary urban life. We are also intrigued with the way in which it destabilized binary modes of thinking the city and in the process helped to interpellate and constitute very different urban subjects. In bringing the private, domestic realm on to the streets this "public exposition of the mundane" (*The Age*, Nov. 5, 1996, editorial) took just a little step further than do TV soapies, docudramas like *Sylvania Waters*, and infotainment shows such as *Burke's Backyard* and *The Home Show* toward demystifying the private and rendering the practice of individual self-management a public "entertainment." The "audience" admired the apartment's decor and were concerned that the art-stronauts were getting enough to eat and enough sleep, and were cleaning their teeth before they went to bed.

Figure 43.2 In their "living room" the Urban Dream Capsule art-stronauts perform for a Festival audience (photo: Penny Stephens; from *Sunday Age*, November 3, 1996).

At the same time the very act of living on the street in Melbourne's Central Business District in an environment that dripped affluence (a brightly lit interior with all the mod-cons, comfortable beds, paintings on the wall, a well-stacked refrigerator) spoke to two current political concerns – the homeless and the Postcode 3000 invasion. Among the audience were, indeed, real street inhabitors, people who through force of circumstance and sometimes inclination actually do live on the streets of Melbourne. And rubbing shoulders with them, no doubt, were the new residents of modern apartment blocks and office conversions who have been actively recruited by the City to move into Postcode 3000 to "revitalize" the urban center (and perhaps constitute a force to agitate for the clean-up of street people in the area). For the homeless and homed to comfortably share the same space and stand, for a nanosecond at least, as one in a space that is usually premised on the exclusion of "undesirables" is a rare experience. For a moment, imaginary battle lines between "illegitimate" occupants and the "legitimate" residents might have been forgotten in the interpellation of all concerned as a heterogeneous "we." Perhaps such a collective positioning of the performers and crowd would have stirred the question as to why the ethic of care that was being actively generated for the UDC dwellers might not extend to those who actually live on the streets.

Certainly we need not ignore the extent to which the UDC inhabitants, unlike people living on the streets, were permitted to dwell in city space *because* they were performers. Nor need we overlook the ways in which elements of the performance appeared as a spectacle of consumption that worked to advertise the store and its wares – particularly as, following the UDC's success, the window space continued to be used as a live advertising space exhibiting anything from models in underwear to cooking demonstrations. But to recognize the existence of these forces does not annul the alternative power and challenging nature of the performance.

In some small way the UDC enabled a degree of sustained interaction over 16 days that had the capacity to alter the way the city is experienced and thought. In observing this interaction, many people appeared to possess a sense of contentment in being involved, even if it was simply watching others in their communication with members of the UDC. People owned the UDC, participated in the performance, and permeated its glassed boundary. As they became attached to the UDC, the city became more inhabitable. By openly inhabiting the uninhabitable, the UDC challenged the imagined fixed spatiality of the domicile upon which the city is dependent. It troubled the perceived solidity of public/private and home/street boundaries. Perhaps as a consequence of the performance, the city appeared less of a place to be wary and more of a place to belong or occupy.

"Street theater and freak shows, [Thomas] said, have strong parallels" (Kermond 1996). Certainly the UDC was a freak occurrence, a flash of intense brilliance in an already full-with-brilliance International Arts Festival. For any one of the 200,000 visitors to the site an illumination of very ordinary acts rendered extraordinary was produced. Straying past this city site people were captured and drawn into its excess, energy, and unknowability. By the end of the third day the performers also stumbled across this secret: "Yesterday we had our first serious meeting, expressing concerns about burn-out, over-excitement, disorganisation. Then all promptly performed like maniacs for eight hours without stop. It's not really tiring. It's inspiring. The audience fuels our energies as we fuel theirs. Behind the window, it's performer's heaven" (Thomas 1996).

The overexcitement and stimulation of the city is something that urban commentators from Simmel on have observed and been wary of. In the quest for order, control, and a homogeneous conception of civility such subversive emotions and affects have often been deemed dangerous. Perhaps now, however, this (feminized) energy is less threatening? As political theorists cast around for new postmodern models of citizenship such as Iris Marion Young's "the being together of strangers" (1990: 232) and Alphonso Lingis's "the community of those who have nothing in common" (1994) we can see here a glimpse of a new civility of excess. Interpellated as communicators across technology, physical barriers, social and cultural difference, the crowd and the UDC modeled new forms of address and care: "And the biggest surprise? 'What this show has done is put people in a space where they're very beautiful,' Thomas says in the draped-off area behind the capsule (where the toilet is). 'People are really smiling and they're very loving. It's just brought out that side'" (Schembri 1996b: B10). "'People come along and do the most amazing drawings for us,' he says. 'There's this incredible sense of comradeship and love and care that comes through the windows, and also through the e-mail and the fax – and that's like 'Wow! I don't mind seeing that'" (Schembri 1996b).

Conclusion

The poetics of walking permits encounters with city fragments and seemingly "unimportant" urban activities – the practices of urbanism that are not neatly folded

into forceful stories of capitalist urbanization, social polarization, urban consolidation, and dead city syndrome. How are we to think of these entertaining but ultimately "unimportant" experiences? One way is to critically address the discourse
which discursively "discards" these urban treasures placing them in a position of
marginality on the urban terrain. In the face of the alien spaceships in *Independence
Day* urban street performances appear quixotic, small, and ineffectual. Similarly, in
the face of apocalyptic pronouncements on the state of cities and city life "under
late or postmodern capitalism" the transformative potential of walking and performing appears weak, powerless, and foolish. But these are representations all.

In the distracted state of watching and interacting with the UDC perhaps the
shock defense of urban fear and alienation produced by dominant urban narratives
was pierced in many of the UDC's diverse audience? Perhaps the "rhetoric of
walking" allowed new conversations to begin between urban subjects and a rewriting of the urban text to commence? It was not only the speech/performance acts of
the UDC that confronted and sidestepped dominant images of the city, but also the
feelings and speech that flowed on the footpath between the walkers momentarily
arrested by the brilliance of what caught their eyes. Straying in city space exposed
walkers to the things that are concealed by the concept city of urban planning and
theory. Stories such as those that can be composed around the UDC have the power
to rewrite the city. They can contribute to a vision of the city as a site of potentiality, not imminent destruction; of civic sensibility as caring of others, not competi-
tively self-interested; of urban structures as permeable and diverse, not rigid and
limited and of urban narratives that lean toward enabling futures, not nostalgic
pasts.

References

The Age (Melbourne) (1996) Editorial. Nov. 5.
Barthes, R. (1982) *Empire of Signs*. Trans. Richard Howard. New York: Hill and Wang.
Bauman, Z. (1994) Desert spectacular. In *The Flâneur*, ed. K. Tester. London/New York:
    Routledge, 138–57.
Benjamin, W. (1978) A Berlin chronicle. In *Reflections: Essays, Aphorisms, Autobiographical
    Writings*, ed. P. Demetz, trans. E. Jephcott. New York: Schocken Books, 3–60.
Certeau, M. de (1984) *The Practice of Everyday Life*. Trans. S. Rendell. Berkeley: University
    of California Press.
Gibson-Graham, J. K. (1996) *The End of Capitalism (As We Knew It): A Feminist Critique of
    Political Economy*. Cambridge, MA: Blackwell.
Kermond, C. (1996) Suffering the pane of separation. *The Age* (Melbourne), Oct. 19: A5.
Lingis, A. (1994) *The Community of Those Who Have Nothing in Common*. Bloomington:
    Indiana University Press.
McGraw, C. (1980) *Acting is Believing: A Basic Method*. New York: Rinehart and Winston.
Mumford, L. (1961) *The City in History*. Harmondsworth/Ringwood: Penguin.
Schembri, J. (1996a) The window of opportunities. *The Age* (Melbourne), Oct. 11: 5.
Schembri, J. (1996b) Opening the urban dream (time) capsule. *The Age* (Melbourne), Nov.
    1: B10.
Scott-Norman, F. (1996) Bald, bold and an act with more front than Myer. *The Age*
    (Melbourne), Oct. 26: A31.

Sennett, R. (1990) *The Conscience of the Eye: The Design and Social Life of Cities*. New York: Alfred A. Knopf.

Sorkin, M. (ed.) (1992) Introduction. In *Variations on a Theme Park: The New American City and the End of Public Space*. New York: Hill and Wang, xi–xv.

Thomas, N. (1996) Behind life's window, tired means inspired. *The Age* (Melbourne), Oct. 21: B3.

Valentine, G. (1993) (Hetero)sexing space: lesbian perceptions and experiences of everyday spaces. *Environment and Planning D: Society and Space* 11: 395–413.

Virilio, P. (1991) The overexposed city. In *The Lost Dimension*, trans. D. Moshenberg. New York: Semiotext(e).

Whitmore, J. (1994) *Directing Postmodern Theater: Shaping Signification in Performance*. Ann Arbor: University of Michigan Press.

Young, I. M. (1990) *Justice and the Politics of Difference*. Princeton, NJ: Princeton University Press.

Part V City Divisions and Differences

The New Blackwell Companion to the City   Edited by Gary Bridge and Sophie Watson
© 2011 Blackwell Publishing Ltd

Chapter 44

Reflections on Division and Difference

Gary Bridge and Sophie Watson

Urban divisions and differences have been the focus of urban analysis from the earliest days of the Chicago School to the present. Variously registered in relation to class, economic and social status, politics, sex/gender, race, ethnicity, religious affiliation, they have been typically viewed as a bad thing which should be alleviated and remedied through urban policy initiatives. The nuances of the two terms are bifurcated, with divisions denoting difference as a negative force separating one from another, clearly a binary notion, while differences are seen as more fluid, offering positive potentialities and possibilities. The former is more typically deployed in relation to the socio-economic/political realm, the latter in relation to culture and bodies – though there are many points in between. Of concern has been how these divisions and differences in cities are managed and regulated, and how they are solidified and materialized in built form. Division emphasizes notions of inequalities, segregation, and stratification, while representations of difference are more likely to highlight variegated socio-spatial urban textures, where city differences can be read, imagined, and experienced in a plethora of ways. The field is a rich one ranging from studies of the ghetto, cities in conflict, urban poverty, and residential enclaves on the one hand to studies of gentrification, gay quarters, and ethnic neighborhoods on the other. Central to most urban studies is the argument that urban processes, particularly capitalist urban processes (these days more commonly articulated as neoliberal), inevitably involve socio-spatial inequalities of some kind.

Thinking Divisions Relationally

There has been a strong tendency within urban writing to date for analysis in this field to suffer from two particular failings. One is the trope of binary thinking. Here

The New Blackwell Companion to the City Edited by Gary Bridge and Sophie Watson
© 2011 Blackwell Publishing Ltd

dominant groups and institutions in cities – populated by the rich, the middle classes, the long established (in the west often white) nationals (except where Aboriginal or native populations are concerned), able-bodied, straight men – are taken as the given who do or don't accept or welcome "others," generally cast as the poor, the working class, and minorities who may be migrants, women, gays, particular ethnic groups, disabled, and so on. To the former is attributed the prerogative to allow or disallow difference from the so-called norm, which is often so obscured as to be naturalized as given. Rather than difference itself being constitutive of, and central to, the ways in which a specific city has been developed and made, it is always necessarily situated on the outside looking in, something to be dealt with in positive or negative ways. The second problem is that division and difference are usually mobilized as static forces and attributes, which appear in a particular form and which, as such, must be accommodated, rather than being seen as produced within a complex intersection of flows, networks, and technologies in specific places, at particular moments and conjunctures. This approach not only serves to embed difference yet further in often unproductive ways, but also leaves notions of the dominant group, the norm, as unchanging, fixed, homogeneous, and unaffected by the complex forces and relations that produce differences. In this way of thinking those not produced within discourses of difference are almost forgotten and outside analysis – the rich, men, able-bodied, straight individuals and groups within cities – with of course notable exceptions. This paradigm has a further global dimension – that of north and south, also represented in terms of developed and developing countries and parts of the world. Here the paradigms of global north/western thinking are imposed universally on places where different histories and politics require different paradigms, as Robinson and Parnell argue here in Chapter 46.

Intrinsic to questions of division and difference is the question of power, though power tends to be more firmly located in urban divisions, which foreground the spatialization of inequality, than within the notion of differences, whose particular salience in postmodernist accounts renders relations of power slightly out of view, since power is everywhere existing in capillary networks that can sometimes be hard to grasp. The more recent turn to "post-human" urban theory has shifted power even further from view with its shift of focus from social inequalities fixed in territory and bounded spaces to a more networked, mobile, relational, and fluid understanding of the urban. Mike Savage proposes a way out of this impasse through a recovery of Bourdieu's "lost urban sociology" (Chapter 45). Savage suggests that a productive route is to link Bourdieu's field theory, where relational power struggles are clearly marked in the urban landscape itself, to a Deleuzian attention to both immanence and the processes of becoming, deterritorialization, and to the importance of "re-territorialization" and the ways in which processes become sedimented in physical features, and define a striated space where fixed locations can be seen as the sediment of intensive flows. This, he suggests, allows us not to abandon social inequalities but instead to see them as processes in flux, where people, objects, and identities are differently sifted and patterned through complex mechanisms allowing some to move more freely than others. Such an analysis thus brings back power, but in a very different guise.

Divisions in cities are always and inevitably political. They are also intrinsic to city life – an ineradicable part of living with people who differ from one another in

Figure 44.1   Bicentennial Park, Glebe, Sydney. Photo S. Watson.

a myriad of ways. This is the agonistic terrain on which Mouffe, amongst others, insists, which is not to say that encounters across difference are not differently mediated and expressed within different discourses of risk, uncertainty, ignorance, and empathy (Watson 2006). Political divisions in some cities around the world have produced conflicts amongst urban citizens of extreme kinds, where everyday violence is a familiar occurrence. In Britain, an ESRC research project on cities in conflict is focusing on Jerusalem, Belfast, Nicosia, Berlin, Beirut, and Kirkuk, and seeks to understand how cities have been shaped by ethnic, religious, and national conflicts, at the same time as absorbing, resisting and potentially playing a role in transforming these conflicts, through particular forms of urban fabric and architecture. Central to the study is the argument that control and resistance through territorial separation and bordering is at the core of state-related ethno-national and religious conflict, materialized in borders in divided cities and through policing and management. Mike Dumper and Wendy Pullan (2009), who are in charge of the Jerusalem team, suggest that while cities can be divided, populations share the same place temporally with the same space used at different times by different ethnic groups, not necessarily leading to conflict. Other urban analysts are rather more pessimistic. Oren Yiftachel (2006) conceptualizes the Israeli regime as an ethnocracy which promotes a dominant project of "ethnicization" throughout Israel/Palestine, which has constructed ethno-class identities and a stratified form of citizenship through the process of expansion, development, and politicization in the different regions Israel/Palestine. Security has increasingly been central to political analysis and intervention in post-conflict cities, yet Alice Hills (2009) argues that the concept of order is more meaningful to urban citizens, and that this depends far more on tactics already in place than on reconstruction efforts. Looking at cities such as Kinshasa, Baghdad, Basra, and Kabul, she finds that as security is increasingly ghettoized, people make their own rules for survival.

Segregated Spaces, Changed Spaces

One the most stark and persistent social divisions in any city has been the high levels of residential segregation – usually described as ghettos – experienced by the African American population in US cities. Massey and Denton (1993) discuss this hyper-segregation of African Americans across US cites as a form of apartheid. Analyzing segregation indices over an extended period, they show how black neighborhoods are the spatial testament of continued racial discrimination in US cities, and that even where segregation indices are falling, this only occurs in cities where the black population represents a small proportion of the metropolitan area. It is not uncommon for the public response to racial segregation to blame the communities themselves for what they see as the prevailing values, low levels of achievement, and crime concentrated in these neighborhoods. Liberals in contrast have linked disadvantage with broader social factors such as racial discrimination and social class subordination and have argued for affirmative action and anti-discrimination legislation. Wilson (1987) suggests that liberals have lost ground to the conservatives who use an accusatory, cultural framing of the underclass argument. Instead he uses the notion of underclass to explain how poverty and disadvantage of urban African Americans (historically a product of racial discrimination) are now also located in the workings of the US economy with the loss of manufacturing employment and the lack of government retraining initiatives to make up for that loss. This results in a growing underclass of the underemployed and unemployed overall, but one in which African Americans have been disproportionately affected.

Negative discourses of the ghetto tend to permeate media representations, but there are many counter-narratives. These are the social imaginaries of marginalized concentrations of poor and underprivileged groups as Sharon Zukin points out here in Chapter 49. But what she also points to is the vibrancy of street life, the gatherings of poets, the "cultural flowering" of the 1920s when, despite the impoverished living conditions, the African American community spawned a plethora of sites of jazz, dance, nightlife, preaching, and politics. What is often forgotten also, is the active engagement of gays, also marginalized from mainstream city neighborhoods, as George Chauncey documents in *Gay New York* (extracted in the *Blackwell City Reader*). Here were located key spaces which were vital for forms of expression that allowed the gay community to flourish. Thus gay identity intersected with racial identity and politics to affect the ways that gay identity was played out.

Though most commonly deployed in the contemporary American context, the ghetto has a long history, beginning with the formation of the Jewish ghetto in Renaissance Venice. Richard Sennett (1994) tells the story of a people who were segregated but who then made new forms of community life out of their segregation, suggesting that Jews gained a certain degree of self-determination there. There are echoes here of Peter Marcuse's point (2000) that walls in cities not only act as boundaries of exclusion, they can also act to protect. Thus, self-segregation behind walls or more permeable boundaries and marking of territory, can also be a form of resistance by less powerful groups. This speaks to the necessity of reading built environments and technologies in nuanced ways. Nevertheless, there are many instances in which the materiality of cities codifies and instantiates different forms of exclusion of those positioned as threatening or "other" to more wealthy and powerful groups, to which the growth of gated communities and residential enclaves in cities across the globe exists as a powerful testimony.

Divisions can also be starkly materialized in urban artifacts such as bollards, barriers, or the militarized spaces of Fortress LA so powerfully drawn by Mike Davis (1990) 20 years ago. Borders and boundaries may also be constituted in symbolic, less visible or material ways, though equally powerful in their effects. The Jewish *eruv*, now a feature of many cities such as Sydney, Washington, and London, which delineates a space of free mobility for Orthodox Jews on the Sabbath, illustrates this clearly. The erection of a connected wire to symbolically enclose a particular locality is mobilized to redefine the activities permitted in semi-public space for the purposes of the Sabbath in order that activities normally allowed only in the private domain can be performed. What brings the *eruv* into being is a series of rituals, a performativity, where new identities, spaces, social practices, and notions of the private are constituted. Despite the *eruv*'s lack of visibility, this claim over formerly neutral space by a religious group has been fiercely contested in a number of localities, where for its opponents the *eruv* "stains" the wider space in which it operates (see Watson 2006; Cooper 1998). Don Mitchell (2004) draws our attention to spaces of exclusion which are constructed through legal injunction, where exclusion zones can be set at a micro scale around buildings but also around persons and can move with them through the city. Through an analysis of what he calls "bubble laws" Mitchell (2004) shows how people can be excluded from behaving in certain ways within an eight-foot floating bubble around the person. His argument is that these laws represent a profound sort of privatization of space in the public realm as well as supporting a form of hyper-individualism that is representative of a broader neoliberal politics.

Gentrification represents another form of social practice where divisions are enacted through housing practices which have strong social effects. Explanations for the transformation of working-class districts into middle-class ones (with varying degrees of displacement) have ranged from Marxist arguments about capital disinvestment then reinvestment in inner urban neighborhoods to close the "rent gap" (Smith 1996) through to more cultural explanations of an anti-suburban generation seeking the social diversity and architectural cache of downtown neighborhoods, and convenience to inner city professional employment (Ley 1996). Whereas gentrification involves class politics within the residential neighborhood, across the different districts of the city, the spatial divisions between home and work has meant that, in the US context at least, the class politics of the union and employment was often offset by the politics of community and residence and ethnic loyalties – resulting in a series of "urban trenches" that prevented wider class mobilization (Katznelson 1981). For Neil Smith (1996), segregation and control of urban space is part of a wider class politics in which the middle classes "re-take" the city from the poor and displaced, in what he calls a politics of revenge and urban reorganization – the revanchist city. In Chapter 50 Tom Slater similarly argues that gentrification has to be recognized as a powerful form of displacement from below which widens class inequality in cities, rather than seeing it as an expression of taste or choice on the part of the middle classes. And, as Zukin shows here, gentrification has frequently been fostered by state and city governments, which in the case of Harlem ironically re-presents the self-same spaces of the former "ghetto" as sites and places of fine architecture and cultural distinction.

Bodies and Identities

How built forms inscribe difference and division provides one lens for thinking the city; how bodies enact difference and how embodied difference is spatialized in cities is another. There are various different ways in which bodies/sex/gender and cities have been thought. In the early days of feminist analysis, historians sought to uncover the ways women's sexuality was feared, particularly through the figure of the prostitute, and regulated, through the bourgeois Victorian family (Walkowitz 1992). While feminist sociologists and geographers argued that cities mapped patri-archal/capitalist power relations to produce and reproduce gender relations through, in particular, the separation of home/work, center/periphery, city/suburb, and through residential and urban design and architecture (Hayden 1980; McDowell 1997; Watson 1988). Though in part aiming to destabilize binary categories, such thinking also served in part to perpetuate them. Over the years the analysis has become more complex, such that attention has increasingly been paid to differenti-ated meanings of spaces and modes of resistance and to the complex interconnec-tions and co-constitution of bodies and cities. Elizabeth Grosz (1992), for example, seeks to examine how different cities actively produce the bodies of their inhabitants as distinctive bodies with particular physiologies, affective lives, and concrete behav-iors. Elspeth Probyn (1996) positions the self as a point of departure moving through multiple migrations. A more Deleuzian approach opens up possibilities for thinking through the technologies and materialities of city/body through which networks and flows settle and unsettle, configure and disrupt bodies in city spaces in unpredictable and fluid ways. Jessica Sewell's emphasis in Chapter 52 is on both the materiality of the city, and the complexity of practices – the possibilities for resistance and transgression – within it. She thus analyzes the physical, imagined, and experienced cultural landscapes and how they interact to construct gendered spaces.

Explorations of gays/lesbians and the city have followed a similar path. As Julie Abraham points out in Chapter 51, early nineteenth-century literature on the emerg-ing modern cities of London and Paris told stories of lesbians and gays and revealed associations between same-sex desire and intrigue, fear of unknown others, politics, radicalism, and crime. By the twentieth century, discourses had shifted to position homosexuals as the "worst outcome of the nervous strain of modern life." By the 1970s and 1980s studies had begun to highlight gays' marginality in the city, or saw cities as the safe havens where sexuality could be more easily expressed on the one hand, or of celebrated gay spaces on the other. The celebratory turn reached its apotheosis in the work of Richard Florida (2005) who went so far as to propose the notion of the gay index to describe the often observed phenomenon of a correlation between the concentration of gay men – not lesbians – and a city's creativity and vibrant cultural economy. In recent years several writers have shifted the terrain to place gays more centrally in city narratives, rather than cast to the margins in a frame of difference/division, intervening to disrupt binary thinking in much the same way that Nina Glick Schiller suggests in relation to migrant studies (see Chapter 16). George Chauncey's (1994) *Gay New York*, for example, gives a wonderful account of the complexity of gay lives during twentieth-century New York, weaving these with explorations of the African Americans of Harlem and the bohemians of Greenwich Village. Julie Abraham insists that homosexuality of cities cannot be subsumed within the framework of city divisions and differences, even if it is useful to describe particular gay communities in particular cities. Instead the focus must be the "broader web of the history of homosexuality of cities" which challenges the bifurcated mode of analysis within much urban studies.

Differentiating Globally

Edward Said (1978), in his renowned text *Orientalism*, famously critiqued the west's attitude to the east which he perceived as a constellation of false assumptions based on a "subtle and persistent Eurocentric prejudice against Arab-Islamic peoples and their culture" (Windschuttle 1999). In his view, a longstanding western tradition of false and romanticized images of Asia and the Middle East had served as an implicit justification for European and American colonial and imperial ambitions. Visions of the dominant elite, whether it be in class, race, or gender terms, of different others have long been striking in western perspectives imposed on the rest of the world, once mobilized in terms of the developed versus the under-developed or developing world and now sometimes mobilized in a discourse of global north/global south. This binary thinking, of course, describes very real differences, particularly in relation to economic and political power and questions of inequality, but it brings its own dangers of constructing homogeneity across space when heterogeneity between and within cities and nations in relation to global connections, flows, information, on the one hand, and local socio-cultural, economic, and material realities on the other, offers a far more realistic picture. In this sense, urban analysis of different cities across the globe increasingly needs to be alert to specificity and to the interplay of local/global in any one place, to make any sense at all of what is going on. Though the colonial days of importing western models of urban planning and knowledges to countries across the world should be long gone, there remains a very common trope within urban studies and analysis of imagining, seeing, and constructing the world from one standpoint – that of the richer, more powerful and dominant nations.

That said there is an identifiable shift in the field, exemplified here in Chapter 46 by Jenny Robinson and Sue Parnell. Indebted also to Edward Said's notion of how learning can move across different countries, they deploy the idea of traveling theory to draw attention not just to the multiplicity of urban experiences across the world, but to suggest that urban theorization itself needs to be able to build accounts of different cities that are disparate and divergent while at the same time being situated in common circuits of production, experience, and meaning. Reflecting on what the travels of neoliberal theories and policies have meant for city development, they propose a geographical imagination of neoliberalism as a spatially restricted component of governmental landscapes. Rather than being a universal paradigm, it is reconfigured in different contexts by a wide range of agents and technologies as "assemblages" of rule and even resistance. Such is the diversity of urban contexts and outcomes, there needs to be, they suggest, a wider understanding of neoliberalization than that initially specified in its northern idiom.

Studies of different cities make Robinson and Parnell's broader point abundantly clear. Ato Quayson's study of Oxford Street in Accra (Chapter 48) reveals the overall spatial logic that has governed the city's expansion from the areas of European influence along the coast from the early 1900s to the present day. Here he focuses on the different ways in which people in this commercial space have grasped opportunities for self-fashioning and profit-making in the face of the processes of transnationalism and globalization. What is revealed in this space is that the street is both a typical African commercial street and also the chimerical projection of Ghanaian cosmopolitan desire, one illustration of which is the adverts which imagine a different kind of blackness to what it is to be African in the local context. The reality of African cities as also marked by race, class, and inequality is no more stark than in the former apartheid cities of South Africa with their profound residential segregation on the basis of race. What Jeremy Seekings draws attention to in Chapter 47 is the persistence of racial segregation and deep social and economic inequality in post-apartheid South Africa, at the same time as the cities are undergoing important processes of transformation as former victims of apartheid take control of remaking the city.

Deep social and economic inequalities are glaring in many of the cities cut out of the dominant circuits of capital, information, and connections, and global comparisons attest to vast differences in income and wealth: more than 80 percent of the world's population lives in countries where income differentials are widening; the poorest 40 percent of the world's population accounts for 5 percent of global income and the richest 20 percent accounts for three-quarters of world income. At least 80 percent of the world's population lives on less than $10 a day and, according to UNICEF, 25,000 children die each day due to poverty. But it is important at the same time to highlight the large gaps between the rich and poor in cities in the "global north" also. For example, in 2007–8, 13½ million people in the UK were living in households below the low-income threshold of 60 percent or less of the average (median) British household income in that year, which represents one fifth (22 percent) of the population. In the US, as a consequence of sub-prime lending, and in the UK, mortgage repossessions have been rising sharply since 2004 and, by 2008 in the UK they were six times the level of 2004, with a resulting increase in homelessness for this group.

We have argued in this essay, as is explored in the chapters which follow, that divisions and differences take many different forms and are constituted in many different ways across a complex network of flows, spaces, powers, histories, cultures, practices, institutions, and so on. There are other dimensions to such complexity, and the last we shall mention here is that of temporality. The ways that cities are experienced, subjectivities produced, and inclusions and exclusions mobilized, can also be analyzed in relation to times of day and night. As Sassen (1991)

Figure 44.2   Repossessed house in Phoenix, Arizona. Photo S. Watson.

has pointed out, the global city is the site of night-workers and cleaners, who are frequently migrants, the poor, and the marginalized, who benefit little from the financial centers that they are helping maintain. Sophie Body-Gendrot, in Chapter 53, explores the ambivalent phenomenon of nights in the city, the positive and negative representations, the diversity of lives, and the contradictory perceptions. Focusing on Paris at night, she offers a different lens which reveals the city after dark as a contradictory space of desire and violence, or carousing and work, and as the last frontier of the city acting as a space of resistance to competitive, consumer-oriented standards of living and the opportunity for alternative choices.

References

Chauncey, G. (1994) *Gay New York: Gender, Urban Culture and the Making of the Gay Male World 1890–1940*. New York: Basic Books.

Cooper, D. (1998) *Governing out of Order: Space, Law and the Politics of Belonging*. London and New York: Rivers Oram.

Davis, M. (1990) *City of Quartz*. London: Verso

Dumper, M., and Pullan, W. (2009) Conflict in cities and the contested state. Editorial. *Jerusalem Quarterly* 39 (autumn): 1–3.

Florida, R. (2005) *Cities and the Creative Class*. New York: Routledge.

Grosz, E. (1992) Bodies–cities. In *Sexuality and Space*, ed. B. Colomina. New York: Princeton Architectural Press, 241–54.

Hills, A. (2009) *Policing Post-Conflict Cities*. London: Zed Books.

Hayden, D. (1980) What would a non-sexist city be like? In *Women and the American City*, ed. C. Stimpson, M. Nelson, and K. Yatrakis. Chicago: University of Chicago Press, 167–84.

Katznelson, I. (1981) *City Trenches: Urban Politics and Patterning of Class in the US*. New York: Pantheon Books.

Ley, D. (1996) Urban geography and cultural studies. *Urban Geography* 17 (4): whole issue.

Marcuse, P. (2000) Cities in quarters. In *A Companion to the City*, ed. G. Bridge and S. Watson. Oxford: Blackwell, 101–14.

Massey, D., and Denton, N. (1993) *American Apartheid: Segregation and the Making of the Underclass*. Cambridge, MA: Harvard University Press.

McDowell, L. (1997) *Capital Culture: Gender at Work in the City*. Oxford: Blackwell.

Mitchell, D. (2004) The SUV model of citizenship: floating bubbles, buffer zones, and the rise of the "purely atomic individual." *Political Geography* 24 (1): 77–100.

Probyn, E. (1996) *Outside Belongings*. London: Routledge.

Said, E. (1978) *Orientalism*. New York: Pantheon.

Sassen, S. (1991) *The Global City*. Princeton, NJ: Princeton University Press.

Sennett R. (1994) *Flesh and Stone*. London: Faber and Faber.

Smith, N. (1996) *The New Urban Frontier: Gentrification and the Revanchist City*. London: Routledge.

Walkowitz, J. (1992) *City of Dreadful Delight: Narratives of Sexual Danger in Late Victorian London*. Chicago: University of Chicago Press.

Watson, S. (1988) *Accommodating Inequality*. Sydney: Allen and Unwin.

Watson, S. (2006) *City Publics: The (Dis)enchantments of Urban Encounters*. London and New York: Routledge.

Wilson, W. J. (1987) *The Truly Disadvantaged*. Chicago: University of Chicago Press.

Windschuttle, K. (1999) Edward Said's "Orientalism" Revisited. *The New Criterion* 17 (5): 30.

Yiftachel, O. (2006) *Ethnocracy: Land and Identity Politics in Israel/Palestine*. Philadelphia, PA: Pennpress.

Chapter 45

The Lost Urban Sociology of Pierre Bourdieu

Mike Savage

Urban studies currently face a dilemma. There is a striking lack of dialogue between popular theoretical frameworks on the one hand, and empirical urban studies on the other. Urban theory is increasingly concerned with mobility, networks, liquidity, and fluidity, and has sought to reorient urban analysis away from a tired urban sociology which delineates the city in terms of its fixed territorial properties (for example, Amin and Thrift 2002; Graham and Marvin 2001; Urry 2007; Sheller and Urry 2006; Gandy 2005). These new interests admirably explore the technological dimensions of distributed or networked urbanism, instantiated in devices such as transport and communication, and in flows such as those of money, sensory perceptions, objects, and people. On the other hand, numerous empirical urban studies emphasize inequalities and stratification. Some writers identify that the "spatialization of class" appears as endemic within the current urban fabric (Parker *et al.* 2007). Whether marked in the exclusionary practices of the middle class in suburban locations (notably in gated communities), or in the revanchist politics of gentrification, or in wide-ranging processes of ghettoization and residualization, the socio-spatial sedimentation of social inequalities seems intrinsic to urban process (see, for example, Butler and Watt 2007; Blokland and Savage 2008; Ellison and Burrows 2006; Atkinson 2006; Atkinson and Blandy 2007; Parker 2003).

Urban studies needs to find a way of staging a more effective dialogue between these two currents. This is, however, singularly difficult. The sociology of stratification continues to be focused on an employment aggregate approach which concentrates on occupational classes (see the discussion in Crompton 2008) and has little ready means of dealing with the spatiality of social inequality. Marxist-inspired urban analyses, for instance that associated with the regulation school, have developed powerful analyses of neoliberal restructuring and urban governance but have

The New Blackwell Companion to the City   Edited by Gary Bridge and Sophie Watson
© 2011 Blackwell Publishing Ltd

largely stayed clear of sociological debates about how inequality can best be conceptualized.[1] By contrast, "post-human" urban theorists find it difficult to bring a focus on human inequalities within their purview in a developed or elaborated way. On occasion, their concerns are seen to displace conventional sociological categories such as that of social class (see notably Latour 2005, who calls for an "associational sociology").

In the face of this stand-off, I will suggest here that Pierre Bourdieu's social theory retains the potential for effectively recharging urban studies, so long as this is interpreted within the frame of field analysis. A few writers such as Loic Wacquant (2007, 2008), Chris Allen (2008a, 2008b), Tim Butler (Butler and Robson 2003), Paul Watt (e.g., 2008), as well as myself (e.g., Savage *et al.* 2005a, Savage *et al.* 2010) have argued that Bourdieu's conception of field, *habitus*, and capitals is a theoretically powerful way of reorienting urban theory in ways which take account of the significance of flows and mobility, yet which embeds these in processes of social stratification. Currently, however, this work remains marginal within urban studies. In part this is due to the perception of Bourdieu as a reductive sociologist with limited geographical concerns. This reputation is partly deserved due to the way that Bourdieu – especially in his later political writings pitched against neoliberalism – seems to defend conventional national models (see, notably, Bourdieu and Wacquant 1999). In this chapter I therefore seek to recover Bourdieu's "lost urban sociology," the elements of his thinking which allow a more effective and productive engagement with current spatial theory.

A central argument here is that rather than focusing on the concept of *habitus* (as in the attempt to consider Bourdieu's legacy for urban studies by Hillier and Rooksby 2002 and Painter 2000), we need to turn to his field analysis, as a form of inquiry which offers a ways of operationalizing the kind of relational strategies which Doreen Massey (2005) rightly sees as essential to an adequate theory of spatiality. In the first section I therefore situate Bourdieu's thinking in the longer-term problems that field analysis has encountered in recent years. In the second section I recover Bourdieu's "lost urban sociology" through a detailed account of how he saw the relationship between field analysis and urban studies at different moments in his career. I concentrate especially on his shift from a more structural to a more spatialized mode of analysis in his later work, and reflect on his interests in a distinctive urban sociology.

Pierre Bourdieu's Field Analysis

Bourdieu's intellectual project can be seen as involving a battle on two fronts, against positivist sociology on the one hand, and what he saw as the excesses of the "cultural turn" on the other. In seeking an anti-positivist social scientific position, "field theory" became increasingly important to him, as a means of recognizing the complex interplay between social and physical space. Only with the recent translation of his early rural sociology has it become apparent to English-speaking readers that Bourdieu was interested in spatiality at the outset of his research career. In the studies of his home region of Béarn in southwest France, conducted between 1959 and 1960, Bourdieu used a form of "total description" (Bourdieu 2008: 2) to explore the dilemma of the oldest sons who were unable to marry as farm daughters left the countryside, so leaving the men stranded in declining family farms. He sees the ultimate mark of the social deprivation of these men in terms of their fixity, their inability to leave their family homes. The masculinism of Bourdieu's account is worthy of note here: his concern is explicitly with the parlous situation of the unmarried men, rather than the women who remain ciphers in his work.

His account draws strongly on the organization of rural mobility, which he sees as part of a wider opposition between *bourg* (town) and *hameaux* (hamlets or farms) which was being eroded as peasants increasingly shopped and used the local services of the towns rather than relying on their own domestic resources (Bourdieu 2008: 68). He states that

> In traditional society, spatial dispersion was not experienced as distance, because of the strong social density linked to the intensity of collective life. Nowadays, given that collective work and neighbourhood festivals have disappeared, peasant families feel their isolation concretely. (Bourdieu 2008: 70)

Although peasants become dependent on the services provided by the town, they are culturally distant and alienated from it, and hence "at the very centre of his universe, the peasant finds a world in which, already, he is no longer at home" (Bourdieu 2008: 75). This image of the inability to belong is evocative, and is a forerunner of his concepts of cultural capital which at this time he had not yet developed (see Robbins 2005). He links this tension to the linguistic divide between French-speaking town-dwellers and Béarnese-speaking farmers. He emphasizes how this organization of space is not reciprocal. The town-dweller reacts against the "primitive" peasant, confirming a sense of urban sophistication. But peasants are dependent on the town, and are forced into a deferential acceptance of its power, even whilst acknowledging their own difference from urban life, thus underscoring their own subordination based on fatalism. In this formulation, which is now 50 years old, many recent themes are articulated which have surfaced in the class analysis influenced by Bourdieu's work (e.g., Skeggs 1997; Savage 2000; Savage *et al.* 2005a), especially the idea that it is precisely the marginalized who are unable to act collectively to redress their grievances. It is clear that Bourdieu sees this as related to the spatial organization of social relationships.

In this early work, the concept of field is absent. Indeed, Bourdieu's early interest in field analysis, originating in the early 1970s, appeared to mark a break with this interest in the organization of space. In the early formulations, such as that in *The Rules of Art* and in papers published in the early 1970s (Bourdieu 1994), the concept has two, somewhat contrasting sources of appeal. Firstly, it allowed him to retain elements of the structural analysis which he had championed during the mid-1960s whilst ditching what he saw as its problematic "objectivist" baggage. This affiliation is especially clear in his 1976 lecture where he laid out, for the first time, elements of his field analysis, in a form which echoed Althusserian structuralism:

> Fields present themselves synchronically as structured spaces of positions (or posts) whose properties depend on their position within these spaces and which can be analysed independently of the characteristics of their occupants (which are partly determined by them. (Bourdieu 1993b: 72)

Secondly, the concept of field allowed him a means of taking on the positivist methodology of Lazarfeld, who, as he explains in his *Sketch for a Self-Analysis* (Bourdieu
2007), he had battled with during the 1960s as he developed his first cultural analysis. Rather than seeking to delineate the power of "causal" variables, Bourdieu saw
fields as a means of delineating social relationships through their spatial organization, where he became interested in using multiple correspondence analysis, a
method developed in the 1960s by the French mathematician Jean-Paul Benzecri,
which located individuals and variables as co-ordinates in geometric space. This
was the method which he took up in *Distinction* as a means of demonstrating the
opposition between "high" and "low" culture, and between the cultural practices
of "intellectuals" and "industrialists," through the use of visual maps and diagrams
(see Bennett *et al.* 2009 for a recent example in the British case).

   Bourdieu notes in *Distinction* that:

> The mere fact that the social space ... can be presented as a diagram indicates that it
> is an abstract representation, deliberately constructed, like a map, to give a bird's eye
> view ... Bringing together ... positions which the agents can never apprehend in their
> totality and in their multiple relationships, social space is to the practical space of
> everyday life, with its distances which are kept or signalled, and neighbours who may
> be more remote than strangers, what geometrical space is to the "travelling space" of
> ordinary experience. (Bourdieu 1985: 169)

This evocation of "neighbours who may be more remote than strangers" emphasizes
all too clearly how Bourdieu saw his field analysis, originating out of his structuralist
thinking, as an anti-humanist strategy for breaking from any determinism implied
by physical or geographical space.[2]

   A similar concern to map out abstract field relations is evident too in the papers
on aspects of the artistic and literary fields which were collected in English in 1993
under the title of *The Field of Cultural Production* (Bourdieu 1993a). Although
diverse in focus, ranging from abstract theoretical statements to case studies of
Flaubert and Manet, the emphasis is constantly on seeing fields as defined by position taking, "spaces of the possible." In none of these studies are actual urban
examples given. This invokes apparently a-spatial analyses, which appear to leave
space as taken for granted, a backdrop to social action.

   However, it is interesting that, in his later work, Bourdieu returned to the relationship between social and physical space in a rather different register. Influenced
by his working through of phenomenological sociology (most clearly demonstrated
in *Pascalian Meditations* [2000]), as well as by his fieldwork of the 1980s reported
in *The Weight of the World* (1999), and also by the example of his collaborator,
the urban sociologist Loic Wacquant, we can detect a reorientation of the concept
of the field, in which the properties of social space are partly inferred from the
analysis of physical space, and in which an interest in the relationship between the
social and spatial is of greater analytical interest.

   Some of Bourdieu's later work retains the formalist field analysis which is evident
in his writings from the 1970s (e.g., Bourdieu 2005), but there is also a new concern
to reflect on the nature of physical space. The reasons for this move become more
explicit in *Pascalian Meditations,* where he notes how certain properties of social
space are derived from physical space.

> Just as physical space, according to Strawson, is defined by the reciprocal externality of positions ... the social space is defined by the mutual exclusion, or *distinction*, of the positions which constitute it ... Social agents, and also the things insofar as they are appropriated by them and therefore constituted as *properties,* are situated in a place in social space. (Bourdieu 2000: 134, italics in the original)

Bourdieu here invokes the irretrievably corporeal nature of both physical and social space, the way that shapes on the ground are associated with the organization of fields and the distribution of capital. This marks a return to the spatial sensibility which is evident in *The Bachelors' Ball,* but which subsequently disappears in his early formulations of field analysis. This renewed interest in physical spatiality is clearly articulated in *The Weight of the World*:

> As bodies (and biological individuals), and in the same way that things are, human beings are situated in a site (they are not endowed with the ubiquity that would allow them to be in several places at once), and they occupy a place. The *site (le lieu)* can be defined absolutely as the point in *physical space* where an agent or a thing is situated, "takes place," exists: that is to say either as a *localization* or, from a relational view-point, as a *position*, a rank in an order. (Bourdieu 1999: 123)

This insistence is now part of Bourdieu's concern to demonstrate that fields matter concretely, that the relational power struggles they illuminate *cannot but be marked in the urban landscape itself.* This is a different emphasis to the apparently a-spatial structuralism of his earlier conception of field. He now argues that this process of "translation" is also one of "naturalization," in which the conflicts and tensions which his field analysis reveals abstractly are occluded to social agents because of the way they are mundanely marked on physical space.[3] Processes of misrecognition are thereby associated with the way that social categories become naturalized through being embedded in fixed, physical, devices. Thus, physical space is the concretization of social space.

Bourdieu's thinking here is probably related to the interview testimonies collected as part of *The Weight of the World*, many of which told stories of suffering integrally related to people's accounts of how they are fixed in deprived locations. He thus returns to the tension between spatial fixity and mobility which he first examined in the later 1950s. Whereas, in his field analysis of *Distinction*, the powerful and the powerless could be detected as occupying different "zones" of social space, he becomes more aware that seeing fields in these terms, as if the powerful and disadvantaged are two competing rugby teams each with their own formation on a fixed pitch, is problematic. It overstates the ability of the powerless to form a coherent team at all. Returning to his more fluid conceptions of spatial organization evident in his youthful rural sociology, he now recognizes that "the lack of capital intensifies the experience of finitude: it chains one to a place" (Bourdieu 1999: 127).

Anticipating the arguments of Zygmunt Bauman (1998) and Manuel Castells (1996), he identifies the tension between the mobility of the powerful and the fixed-ness of the disadvantaged as integrally related to the difficulties of imagining change. In this analysis, the ability to have "a place of one's own" becomes almost a precondition for social existence (again, a return to the concerns of his earlier rural sociology). Thus, in his invocations of the problems of living in Jonquil Street, Bourdieu talks about how urban decline is associated with de-industrialization and how this loss of place is itself related to the racism and fragmentation of urban experience.

Throughout this book, Bourdieu deliberately refuses to abstract the nostalgic accounts of his respondents from their physical location. In his cameo introductions to collections of interviews, he deliberately starts by sketching the physical environment from which the accounts were generated (e.g., Bourdieu 1999: 6, 60).

It is this concern with how social space is both modeled on spatial exclusion, yet also shapes the urban landscape by differentiating between those with, and those without, the capacity to place themselves, which Bourdieu (2001) develops in his last substantial study, *The Social Structure of the Economy*. In developing an analysis of the housing market which is explicitly critical of the assumptions of neo-classical economics, Bourdieu seeks to establish how forms of capital are implicated in the very organization of the housing stock (see, further, Wacquant 2008). His stress now is on how housing is "doubly linked to space" in that it is necessarily built uniquely in a given location and is also subject to distinctively local markets, yet also how it is produced by universalizing market forces. He goes on to insist on the need for local analyses, where the local is not seen as a manifestation of "larger" processes, but where the dynamic between universalizing forces which range over physical space, and local particularity, are central. Bourdieu now goes beyond his earlier emphases on how different zones figure as habitats for those with different amounts of capital. Rather, he seeks to deconstruct the distinction between "center" and "periphery" by seeing these terms as themselves the product of, and themselves at stake in, the organization of the field itself. Here, the ability of the bureaucratic state to define itself as located outside any particular site, as conveying universal value, is fundamental to its ability to constitute itself as a powerful agent within the field. He further insists, however, that the necessarily located existence of actual people striving for decent housing prevents any simple implementation of a universalized plan.

What we now see, therefore, is that the capacity to define one's actions transcends the local as a central political battle. Here his concern to criticize neoliberal markets is rooted in a resistance to its universalizing procedures, as well as a recognition that simply defending local particularity will fail to grasp the wider processes at work.[4] Through this reformulation of field analysis, Bourdieu's thinking has certain resonances with that of Latour (who is also concerned with the contingent formation of immutable mobiles which are thus able to constitute themselves as "obligatory points of passage"). Latour's emphasis on an associational sociology which is premised on the flatness of the social world and which refuses to privilege social forces as being of ontological importance has its counterpart in Bourdieu's insistence that power resides in the capacity to constitute itself as above location. In what follows, I want to argue further that elements of this form of field analysis can be elaborated in a way which allows these issues of mobility and intensity to be taken up in an empirically effective way.

The Radicalization of Field Analysis

We have seen how, in his later work, Bourdieu spatializes his conception of field through seeing space itself as an object of contestation rather than as a given. My final suggestion here is that elements of complexity theory – which are already current in urban theory – can be reconciled with Bourdieusian field analysis in a way which might be empirically productive in developing urban analysis.

Contemporary urban theory largely starts from Henri Lefebvre's (1990) insistence on the constructed nature of social space, which in his case is linked to a Marxist insistence on the power of capitalism to produce "abstract space." Lefebvre's Hegelian analysis lacks a concept of field relations, and thereby proves problematic in recognizing how contestation takes place, other than through the invocation of the role of artistic *avant gardes*. This weakness is linked to historicist elements of Lefebvre's thinking, whereby capitalist forces have their own efficacy within an "expressive totality." More recent theorists have emphasized relationality – the reciprocal relations between different groups, objects, sentiments, and ideas – as central to urban theory, and it is this which makes Bourdieu's field analysis, which is also concerned with relationality, so potentially appealing. The most challenging attempt to elaborate conceptions of power within urban thinking has been from those drawing on the increasingly influential social theory of Gilles Deleuze and Felix Guattari, in which conceptions of spatiality, or "geophilosophy," are vital (see, generally, Amin and Thrift 2002; Massey 2005; Gandy 2005). Deleuzian social theory is often seen as concerned to overcome dualisms between the human and technical, through its insistence on the "desiring machine" and the "body without organs" (see for instance Gandy 2005). Deleuze's starting point is immanence, the importance of thinking beyond existing concepts, through recognizing the process of "becoming" as one which breaks from structure and form. This emphasis on the figure of the rhizome allows a critical perspective on the arboreal metaphor which characterizes linear thinking. This rhizomatic thinking seems different to Bourdieu's advocacy of the field, yet I want to suggest some unexpected parallels.

Although concerned with "de-territorialization," Deleuze also addresses the importance of "re-territorialization," the way that intense processes become (literally) sedimented and etched into physical features. This insistence is also linked to his differentiation between smooth (intense) space and striated (marked) space (on which see also Osborne and Rose 2004). They claim not that fluidities and mobilities somehow eradicate the importance of territoriality, but rather that fixed location can be seen as the sedimented product of intensive flows.

> The first articulation chooses or deducts, from unstable particle flows, metastable molecular or quasi molecular units (substances) upon which it imposes a statistical order of connections and successions (forms). The second articulation establishes functional, compact, structures (forms) and constructs the molar compounds in which these structures are simultaneously actualized (substances). (Deleuze and Guattari 1987: 46)

The challenge, then is to radicalize field analysis to recognize the tensions between intensive and extensive, smooth and striated, space. As De Landa puts it, in elaborating Deleuze and Guattari:

> A space is not just a set of points, but a set together with a way of binding these together into *neighbourhoods* through well defined relations of *proximity* or *contiguity*. In our familiar Euclidean geometry these relations are specified by fixed lengths or distances which determine how close the points are to each other ... there exist other spaces, however, fixed distances cannot define proximities since distances do not remain fixed. A topological space, for example, may be stretched without the neighbourhoods which define it changing in nature. (De Landa 2002: 22)

This involves reading fields as de-centered processes, involving intensities and dynamic features, in ways which might cut against a focus on key ("arboreal") variables or determinants. Here localization cannot be taken as given but is itself subject to field processes. This is close to the way that Wacquant defines a field as "relational configuration endowed with a specific gravity which it imposes on all the objects and agents which enter into it" (Wacquant 1992: 17). These concerns suggest new strategies for urban analysis. Rather than assume, along with Bourdieu and Wacquant (1999), that fields are contained within national boundaries, we might more usefully explore how struggles over scale are part of field dynamics, and that situated urban case studies might be better able to probe these issues.

Conclusions

During the last three decades, leading urban theorists have rightly argued for the need for a de-centered urban sociology, one which does not reify the urban or assume fixed territorial boundaries. They have then faced the problem of retaining space and place as significant categories of analysis when such fluidities are held to be of defining importance. One result, usually unintentional, has been to make it unclear how urban studies inform analyses of the kinds of persistent and deepening inequalities which mark the current urban landscape.

I have argued here that we can best deal with this impasse through invoking, and radicalizing, a tradition of field analysis which recognizes how power operates through abstraction from location, and which is attentive to the resulting dialectic of de- and re-territorialization. I recognize that my yoking of Bourdieu's field theory with Deleuze and Guattari's social thought and aspects of complexity theory is unusual, and might even be regarded as perverse. Yet I hope to have at least intimated that there is the potential of radicalizing field analysis so that we do not read it as relying on the invocation of fixed positions in geometric space. We can read diagrams not as representational maps, but as indicators of flows and forces. We are thus in a position to be able to use such methods to think about "a language of forces, densities, potentialities, virtualities" (Amin and Thrift 2002: 81) in a way which avoids a return to a purely linguistic or textual formulations. Through linking these concerns also to Bourdieu's own remarkable corpus of work, we can explore how to avoid abandoning concerns with inequality and social division. Rather than treating class, gender, and other social inequalities as variables, we can instead see them as processes in flux. Through examining the clustering, sifting, and sorting of people, objects, and identities in physical and social space, through investigating the mechanisms which allow some to move more freely than others, and also through examining the clustering and patterning of actions, we have the potential for enriching contemporary urban theory and recharging our understanding of social inequality.

Notes

1 For the sociological debate, see for example Scott *et al.* 2000; Savage *et al.* 2005b; Bottero 2005. An interesting example of this lack of engagement is Jamie Peck's (2005) powerful critique of Florida's idea of the "creative class," which makes trenchant points about

Florida's misunderstanding of urban dynamics, but does not discuss how class itself should be conceptualized.

2 See further on this, Martin's (2003: 29) comment that "a field theory is not simply a spatial model – while a field is, as Bourdieu (1993a: 72) says, a structured set of positions, and positions can often be understood in spatial terms ... not all sets of relative positions can be understood as a conventional space (since 'distances' may not work according to spatial logic)."

3 He discusses the *"naturalization effect"* produced by the long-term inscription of social realities in the natural world. Thus historical differences can seem to have arisen from the nature of things (we need only think of the "natural frontier"). This is the case, for example, with all the spatial projections of social difference between the sexes (at church, in school, in public, and even at home) (Bourdieu 1999: 124).

4 "The perfectly commendable wish to see things in person, close up, sometimes leads people to search for the explanatory principles of observed realities where they are not to be found (not all of them, anyway), at the site of observation itself. The truth about what happens in the 'problem suburbs' certainly does not lie in these usually forgotten sites that leap into the headlines from time to time" (Bourdieu 1999: 181).

References

Allen, C. (2008a) *Housing Market Renewal and Social Class*. London: Routledge.

Allen, C. (2008b) Gentrification research and the academic nobility: a different class? *International Journal of Urban and Regional Research* 32 (1): 180–5.

Amin, A., and Thrift, N. (2002) *Cities: Re-Imagining the Urban*. Cambridge: Polity Press.

Atkinson, R. (2006) Padding the bunker: strategies of middle class disaffiliation and colonization in the city. *Urban Studies* 43 (3): 819–32.

Atkinson, R., and Blandy, S. (2007) Panic rooms: the rise of defensive homeownership. *Housing Studies* 22 (4): 443–58.

Bauman, Z. (1998) *Globalization*. Cambridge: Polity Press.

Bennett, T., Savage, M., Silva, E., Warde, A., Gayo-Cal, M., and Wright, D. (2009) *Culture, Class, Distinction*. London: Routledge.

Blokland, T., and Savage, M. (eds.) (2008) *Networked Urbanism: Social Capital and the City*. Aldershot: Ashgate.

Bottero, W. (2005) *Social Stratification*. Cambridge: Polity Press.

Bourdieu, P. (1985) *Distinction*. London: Routledge.

Bourdieu, P. (1993a) *The Field of Cultural Production*. Cambridge: Polity Press.

Bourdieu, P. (1993b) *Sociology in Question*. London: Sage.

Bourdieu, P. (1994) *The Rules of Art*. Cambridge: Polity Press.

Bourdieu, P. (1999) *The Weight of the World*. Cambridge: Polity Press.

Bourdieu, P. (2000) *Pascalian Meditations*. Cambridge: Polity Press.

Bourdieu, P. (2001) *The Social Structure of the Economy*. Cambridge: Polity Press.

Bourdieu, P. (2005) The political field, the social science field, and the journalistic field. In *Bourdieu and the Journalistic Field*, ed. R. Benson and E. Neveu. Cambridge: Polity Press, 29–47.

Bourdieu, P. (2007) *Sketch for a Self-Analysis*. Cambridge: Polity Press.

Bourdieu, P. (2008) *The Bachelors' Ball*. Cambridge: Polity Press.

Bourdieu, P., and Wacquant, L. (1999) On the cunning of imperialist reasoning. *Theory, Culture and Society* 16 (1): 41–58.

Butler, T., and Robson, G. (2003) *London Calling*. Aldershot: Ashgate.

Butler, T., and Watt, P. (2007) *Understanding Social Inequality*. London: Sage.

Castells, M. (1996) *The Rise of the Network Society*. Oxford: Blackwell.

Crompton, R. (2008) *Class and Stratification*. 3rd edn. Oxford: Blackwell.

De Landa, M. (2002) *Intensive Science and Virtual Philosophy*. London: Continuum.

Deleuze, G., and Guattari, F. (1987) *A Thousand Plateaus*. London: Continuum.

Ellison, N., and Burrows, R. (2006) New spaces of (dis) engagement? Social politics, urban technologies and the re-zoning of the city. *Housing Studies* 22 (3): 295–312.

Gandy, M. (2005) Cyborg urbanization: complexity and monstrosity in the contemporary city. *International Journal of Urban and Regional Research* 29 (1): 26–49:.

Graham S., and Marvin, S. (2001) *Splintering Urbanism: Networked Infrastructures, Technological Mobilities and the Urban Condition*. London: Routledge.

Hillier, J., and Rooksby, E. (2002) *Habitus: A Sense of Place*. Aldershot: Ashgate.

Latour, B. (2005) *Re-imagining the Social*. Oxford: Blackwell.

Lefebvre, H. (1990) *The Social Production of Space*. Oxford: Blackwell.

Martin, J. (2003) What is field theory? *American Journal of Sociology* 109 (1): 1–49.

Massey, D. (2005) *For Space*. London: Sage.

Osborne, T., and Rose, N. (2004) Spatial phenomenotechnics: making space with Charles Booth and Patrick Geddes. *Society and Space* 22: 209–28.

Painter, J. (2000) Pierre Bourdieu. In *Thinking Space*, ed. M. Crang and N. Thrift. London: Routledge, 239–59.

Parker, S. (2003) *Urban Theory and Urban Experience: Encountering the City*. London: Routledge.

Parker, S., Uprichard, E., and Burrows, R. (2007) Class places and place classes: geodemographics and the spatialisation of class. *Information, Communication and Society* 10 (6): 902–21.

Peck, J. (2005) Struggling with the creative class. *International Journal of Urban and Regional Research* 29 (4): 740–70.

Robbins, D. (2005) The origins, early development and status of Bourdieu's concept of cultural capital. *British Journal of Sociology* 56 (1): 13–30.

Savage, M. (2000) *Class Analysis and Social Transformation*. Milton Keynes: Open University Press.

Savage, M., Bagnall, G., and Longhurst, B. (2005a) *Globalisation and Belonging*. London: Sage.

Savage, M., Warde, A., and Devine, F. (2005b) Capitals, assets and resources. *British Journal of Sociology* 56 (1): 31–48.

Savage, M., Allen, C., Atkinson, R., Burrows, R., Méndez, M.-L., and Watt, P. (2010) Focus article. *Housing, Theory and Society* 27(2): 115–61.

Scott, J., Crompton, R., Devine, F., and Savage, M. (2000) *Renewing Stratification Theory*. Oxford: Blackwell.

Sheller, M. and Urry, J. (2006) *Mobile Technologies of the City*. London: Routledge.

Skeggs, B. (1997) *Formations of Class and Gender*. London: Sage.

Wacquant, L. (1992) Towards a social praxeology: the structure and logic of Bourdieu's sociology. In *An Invitation to Reflexive Sociology*, by P. Bourdieu and L. Wacquant. Cambridge: Polity Press, 1–60.

Wacquant, L. (2007) *Urban Outcasts*. Cambridge: Polity Press.

Wacquant, L. (2008) Relocating gentrification: the working class, science and the state in recent urban research. *International Journal of Urban and Regional Research* 32 (1): 198–205.

Watt, P. (2008) The only class in town? Gentrification and the middle-class colonization of the city and the urban imagination. *International Journal of Urban and Regional Research* 32 (1): 206–11.

Urry, J. (2007) *Mobilities*. Cambridge: Polity Press.

Chapter 46

Traveling Theory: Embracing Post-Neoliberalism Through Southern Cities

Jenny Robinson and Sue Parnell

Introduction

If the paradigmatic cities of twentieth-century urbanism were firmly located in northern, wealthy countries, the cities that stand for the cutting edge of twenty-first-century urban experiences may not be primarily, or at all, found in these contexts. This shift in the primary locus of the urban has to change the way we think and write about cities. Leading urbanists and policy-makers regularly draw attention to some distinctive trends in this new century of urbanization. Firstly, they point to the emergence of extremely large, megacities, mostly – although not all – in contexts outside of the US–European nexus which shaped the thinking of twentieth-century urban observers, and secondly, they point to some of the distinctive – often alarming – experiences of the majority of the world's urban population: slums, weak states, the absence of public infrastructure, environmental degradation, and lawlessness.

There are then compelling, if somewhat stereotyping, headline reasons for imagining an urban studies whose reference points more effectively incorporate the experiences and challenges of urbanization and urban life in "most of the world" (Chatterjee 2006), where living conditions militate against building positive livelihoods and may even undermine life itself. We are encouraged by the growing attention to these issues in the literature. High-profile urban writers increasingly draw insights from the specific experiences of poorer cities (Smith 2002; Gandy 2005; Davis 2007; Harvey 2009); urban studies journals specifically encourage and look to a growing contribution from scholars working in and on poorer cities and beyond the US–EU academic networks (Seekings and Keil 2009); scholars whose theoretical work is inspired by these contexts are increasingly seen as central to new developments in the field (Simone 2004; de Boeck and Plissart 2004; Roy and Alsazaar

The New Blackwell Companion to the City   Edited by Gary Bridge and Sophie Watson
© 2011 Blackwell Publishing Ltd

2003); and there has been a significant increase in attentiveness by many scholars to the located specificity of the insights they are generating through research in any given national or local context. The claims of generations of urbanists working in and on poorer contexts – or previously third world, developing, postcolonial cities – to have their insights and findings treated as contributions to a wider theorization of cities rather than as part of a separate and unincorporated intellectual project, are coming, it seems, to fruition (Southall 1973; Mitchell 1987).

In this chapter we want to press this agenda further. We proceed on the assumption that the case for such a strong international theorization of cities has been well received (Simone 2004; Roy and Alsazaar 2003; Robinson 2006). We build on this to suggest more precisely how a postcolonial, international, and comparative urban studies might be taken forward in practice and to offer some examples of what it might look like substantively. When viewed from the global south what sorts of things could be learnt in relation to specific debates within urban studies? And how might the center of gravity of urban theory be shifted to give greater weight to the pressing urban realities of our times? In order to explore the pertinence of viewing urban theory from the new urban epicenter – the global south – we have selected to review urban neoliberalism, a theoretical topic of importance for writers working on both poorer and wealthier cities, which has been tracked in many different contexts.

Subtending our agenda here is a wager that the future of urban studies will need to address new modes of urbanism emergent in diverse situations. Given their numerical and increasingly economic dominance, it is likely that the politics and practices of urban development in rapidly urbanizing and fast expanding Asian contexts, for example, will increasingly shape the styles and practices of other urban situations, especially in Africa and Latin America. At the very least, the many circuits which tie cities together across the globe – of architects and planners (King 2004; McNeill 2009), policy-makers and consultants (Peck 2002; Saunier 2002; McCann forthcoming), firms and workers (Kelly 2000; Taylor 2004) – mean that the origins and tracks of the phenomena and relationships that inform contemporary urban expectations are likely to draw not only from established urban regimes of the global north, but also from experiences in other rapidly growing cities. Thus the flow of ideas about cities is likely to become ever more multi-directional and varied and the global salience of theory generated by the traditional hubs of urban studies will be eroded and diffused. Here is an invitation, then, to spawn theories which, as they travel, are able to inspire relevant and innovative ways of thinking about what to do in cities that face monumental developmental challenges, but also the opportunities of being only half built. In this regard we argue that the dominance of certain theoretical approaches to urban neoliberalism may be out of kilter with this intent, perhaps even muting more stimulating emergent debates on the urban roles of government and civil society. We feel this is especially so in the African context, where pervasive informality and deep poverty exist in many cities with virtually no formal institutional state capacity. In such contexts there is a particular need to reinvent the paradigms from which we understand and engage "the urban" (Parnell *et al.* 2009).

In thinking about traveling theory we are of course quickly indebted to Edward Said's (1983) thoughtful account of how learning might happen across different contexts – especially across contexts with deeply intertwined and power-laden histories. Learning is thus not innocent of the circuits and journeys which have preceded us here, and inspiration from different contexts is usually enmeshed in the already given languages of theory's travels, far too commonly in languages indebted to sites of research and discursive endeavor located in well-resourced and historically powerful countries that (generally) communicate in English. In this sense, our theoretical language is often significantly out of step with the ambitions and reach of urban experiences today. But this is not a fatal flaw so much as a condition of theoretical existence in a postcolonial intellectual milieu, and certainly in an intellectual landscape profoundly mediated by the realities of geopolitics and inequality. It establishes a rubric for theoretical labor, in which it is necessary to be on the alert for parochial assumptions embedded in the writings of knowledge producers in powerful contexts (Chakrabarty 2000) and to the inevitable limitations of apparently universal concepts as they travel (Connell 2007).

The strategies we propose, then, in the ways of traveling theory for cities, include:

- Bringing scholars, scholarship, and urban experiences from different places into conversation with one another, to highlight the localization of existing theory, to provoke opportunities to disembed parochial assumptions and to disturb the universalist aspirations of theoretical claims;
- following the international/transnational circuits of various aspects of city life, to catch their resonances with multiple contexts, and to attend to the diverse ways in which often quite similar processes or phenomena are interpreted, experienced, and localized;
- building the foundations for a more careful and more strongly international urban comparativism, including much more extensive empirical research on lesser known cities, from which we would be able to build wider, theoretical claims about contemporary urban experiences from the concerns and politics of diverse, even divergent, urban contexts.

We insist then that theory – and urban theory – is both globally and locally generated and is not necessarily universally relevant; that it, like the city experiences it aims to describe, moves along specific tracks, often requires various kinds of interpretation and reworking in its travels if it is to be useful, and usually finds itself transformed in the process – if only in terms of the changes in meaning it may acquire along the way. As we seek to reconstitute theory in a manner that is responsive to the shifting distribution of the world's population it is not just the multiplicity of urban experiences that must be absorbed. Rather, the changing portals from which theory is constructed and the dramatically shifting terrain with which theory must engage in practice must also be acknowledged. Given the increasing complexity of cities, our hunch is that an international urban theorization needs to be capable of building accounts of a world of cities that is disparate and divergent, and yet entrained in common circuits of production, experience, and meaning. Such a theorization would do well to construct itself as substantially limited in its ambitions and as necessarily fallible and revisable in relation to different experiences if it is to be useful to the task of understanding twenty-first-century urbanisms. With this call for a more nuanced approach in mind, we trace neoliberalism's travels, opening up possibilities for its theorization against a wider range of contexts and reflecting on what direction post-neoliberal theories about development in cities might take if the intellectual space for more divergent alternatives were created.

The Routes of Theorizing Urban Neoliberalism

The idea of "urban neoliberalism" has attracted substantial theoretical attention in many different parts of the world, and so is a useful concept through which to begin to consider the potential for new trajectories. It also articulates deep political cleavages in cities and in urban theory, and this is one important reason why it deserves close attention: the concepts we bring to analyses of neoliberalism (and its alternatives) have implications for political action in particular cities. In the urban studies literature nuanced and careful assessments of the reformulations of neoliberalism coexist with incisive political commentary and usually committed opposition to the, often debilitating, effects of neoliberal innovations in urban governance (e.g., Brenner and Theodore 2002; Leitner, Peck, *et al.* 2007).

Attempts to understand the travels of neoliberalism and the processes of urban neoliberalization grapple with conceptualizing the powerful global circuits of neoliberal policies in relation to their coproduction through (always) hybrid localizations (for Brenner *et al.* 2010a) or dis/articulations (as in Ong 2006). This makes the geographies of neoliberalism – the relations amongst the circuits, systems, localities, and institutional nodes which frame processes of neoliberalization – a central issue in the theorization of this phenomenon. For us, these geographies draw our attention to some important questions concerning the political meaning of neoliberalism in different places. But the extensive travels of theories of neoliberalism, and their dominance within the canon of urban studies as a whole, also suggest that a more self-conscious placing of this body of theory might be helpful. Certainly established scholars pressing for the continuing utility of the theory of neoliberalization in understanding contemporary processes of urban change are increasingly eager to attend to evidence from around the world (see especially Peck *et al.* 2010). We want to press this further by a more radical questioning of the overall importance of neoliberalism to urban politics – its absence or oversight, rather than its differentiation or rejection. We suggest, based on a somewhat different geography of theorizing, that neoliberalization needs to be understood alongside other forces that shape cities, and that at the limit it may not be a useful analytical optic.

In this regard, Aihwa Ong's Deleuzian-inspired engagements with Asian contexts have led her to postulate the idea of neoliberalism as the exception to dominant systems of economic and political regulation, suggesting that we also pay attention to those people and places excluded from the ambit of neoliberal forms of rule. By these she means to draw attention to the dynamics of neoliberalization in places where "neoliberalism itself is not the general characteristic of technologies of governing" (Ong 2006: 3). This offers us a geographical imagination of neoliberalism as a spatially restricted component of governmental landscapes. Is this Asian-inspired assessment more widely relevant to contemporary forms of capitalist production and social regulation? James Ferguson, considering the experiences of various capitalist enterprises across Africa, proposes the idea of an "extractive neoliberalism", with socially "thin" forms of regulation in sequestered securitized zones, in contrast to the socially "thick" models of national development that framed the post-independence era in many African countries. Suggestively he writes that

> where capital has been coming to Africa at all, it has largely been concentrated in spatially segregated, socially "thin" mineral-extraction enclaves. Again, the "movement of capital" here does not cover the globe; it connects discrete points on it. Capital is *globe-hopping*, not *globe-covering*. (Ferguson 2006: 38)

Furthermore, he proposes that these systems of production built on exceptions to neoliberalism may well be more central to contemporary capitalism than often acknowledged, as the securitized enclaves for the production of oil in militarized zones of the Middle East, notably Iraq, share many features with their counterparts in Africa (Ferguson 2006: 206–7). By this logic the creation of a whole new gated city outside of Luanda in Angola is not analogous to the gated communities that emerge from the neoliberal retreat of the state as in the USA or Dubai (Davis 2007), but may reflect the new urban form of an absent and utterly incapacitated state that arises out of very different circumstances than those that gave rise to neoliberalism.

Such a discontinuous geography of neoliberalization suggests the importance of social and governmental processes that are not well connected to the circuits of neoliberalization. It also poses the question to us of the limits or exceptions to neoliberalism as theory. Certainly sophisticated theorists insist that neoliberalism is only one of many diverse processes shaping particular urban policy outcomes (Leitner, Sheppard, *et al.* 2007: 22), noting "the intensely contradictory blending of neoliberal and extra-neoliberal elements" (Brenner *et al.* 2010b: 216). But as Leitner, Sheppard, *et al.* also suggest, we need to "develop an understanding of when neoliberalism, or its contestants, has been transformed to the point where it is no longer recognizable as such" (2007: 10). In what sense, then, and where, is neoliberalization as object of theorization likely to disappear as a relevant analytic? And where might an insistent focus on the multifaceted applications and outcomes of neoliberalism mask outwardly similar but structurally unrelated processes of change?

A number of writers have pointed to the political valency of neoliberal techniques. Especially, but not only, Foucauldian and Deleuzian-inspired writers find it helpful to decompose "neoliberalism" into its constituent technologies ("policies, forms of enterprising subjectivity, economic or political-economic theories, norms of accountability, transparency and efficiency, and mechanisms of quantification or calculative choice"), and to explore the ways in which these travel variously through specific circuits, and are reconfigured in different contexts, by a wide range of agents, as specific "assemblages" of rule or even resistance (Hoffman *et al.* 2006: 10). Stephen Collier has explored the ways in which neoliberal technologies have been drawn on to reframe calculations of central–local state budgetary allocations in the post-socialist context. He observes that "the entire substantive bestiary of Soviet social modernity – heating pipes, apartment blocks (etc.) – are coded into a distribution coefficient" (Collier 2005: 386). He turns the tables on neoliberalism's critics by suggesting that they "can intervene not by humanizing neoliberal technology but by engaging in the (neoliberal) project of technologizing humanism: of finding better ways to satisfy human needs with scarce resources" (Collier 2005: 389). In this sense, the neoliberalism which is associated with specific capitalist class projects, and which is mobilized to regulate and enable new rounds of capitalist accumulation to the detriment of the poor, certainly disappears into a reconfigured project of residual social provisioning and collective service delivery.

In a similar vein, Larner's (2000) reading of New Zealand's radical neoliberalizations proposes an accommodation with welfare provisioning and feminist politics and Ferguson (2007) indicates the ways in which neoliberal technologies enable poverty alleviation strategies in South African cities. Parnell (2007) also explores this in relation to the specific provision by sub-national governments of a basic level of subsidy for urban services for the poor or indigent, something she ascribes to the expansion of the state rather than the devolution of responsibilities under a neoliberal induced ideology of reform.

Decomposing neoliberalism and exploring its radical (re)contextualization in a very wide range of different political projects might well result in the disappearance of a coherent (even if differentiated and patterned) neoliberalism as a relevant analytical lens. This does not mean that one is left with a purely localized and contingent account of urban policy and politics. For, as theorizations of neoliberalization remind us, the tracks and circuits of urban policy formation and circulation are profoundly power-ridden. There are, as Brenner *et al.* are concerned to remind us, certainly patterns to these circulations, sharp gradients of power involved in their promotion and adoption, and policy circulations are no doubt profoundly structured by unequal resourcing, the disciplining of capitalist expectations, and national scale macro-regulation (Brenner *et al.* 2010a). But then, looking out from any given city, (neoliberal) policy circuits are already hybrid, and perhaps nowhere more so than in the highly fragmented urban spaces of the global south where governance regimes are fluid and contested, and where much of the city itself is informally constituted. Although we should certainly acknowledge that the plight of many poor cities has been profoundly exacerbated by macro-economic neoliberalism in the form of structural adjustment policies, it is in these poorer cities that theories of urban neoliberalism are possibly least helpful in illuminating the contemporary urban condition and where theoretical counterpoints are most urgently sought. This imperative to build theory that speaks to the project of creating more inclusive cities draws us to the interface between neoliberal agendas and those of wider urban policy.

Developmentalism is a persistent fellow traveler of any neoliberal policy ambition or innovation in poorer city contexts, and this is increasingly evident at the urban scale. To the extent that even the most powerful of international agencies is dependent on persuasion and not coercion in the adoption of policy innovations at the local level, changes have taken place in the expectations of international development institutions inclined to promote participation, social development, and poverty reduction (Watts 2002). In relation to cities, the World Bank, for example, has been traditionally weak and relatively uninterested in promoting investment at this scale (World Bank 2001), although it has recently announced that "the urban" is the critical site of all future development (Peirce 2010). A substantial proportion of their efforts in this regard are currently channeled through the Cities Alliance, a collaboration with the United Nations Centre for Human Settlement (UNCHS), including developing country participation in its governance (states and social movements). Certainly the themes and technologies of neoliberalization are not absent from the policies and approaches advocated by this organization, but it would be rather conspiratorial to reduce the aims of their programs of slum upgrading and strategic planning capacitation to the cause of advancing neoliberalism, rather than to supporting improvements in urban governance and much-needed service delivery in many poor country cities.

If the circuits of policy are themselves already hybridized, and the consequences of their localization not necessarily associated with the restructuring of neoliberal agendas so much as developmentalism or other ambitious global and national projects, a further site at which neoliberalism might disappear is the moment of articulation of circulating policies with local agents. Here the subtle and complex power relations of policy adoption and the unintended consequences of implementation need to be appreciated, as do the many diverse agendas informing any particular appropriations of ostensibly neoliberal policies. It is the case, for example, that most African countries refuse to adopt a strong urban policy. The reasons for this are poorly understood and documented (see Turok and Parnell 2009, on South Africa; Pieterse 2008 for some more general reflections). But what this does mean is that urban scholars and policy advisors are in a relatively unpowerful position in the supposed circulation of powerful ideas.

In many contexts, city managers lack capacity, resources, and authority to proceed in the absence of central government support (Rakodi 2005), and international policy innovations may well be enthusiastically adopted only to be swerved to serve divergent local agendas (see Myers 2005 for some examples in the field of sustainable urban planning). The personal investment of many officials who benefit from the circuits of policy debate, workshops, and stakeholder forums means that enthusiastic and competitive positioning for involvement in the latest international policy initiative promoting neoliberalism does not necessarily translate into its effective adoption or implementation. It cannot be assumed that relatively powerful agents are imposing their will on those with fewer resources, or that circulating knowledges impose themselves on local agents: shared agendas, independently derived local enthusiasms, and subtle reconfigurations of meaning are all at play (see Salskov-Iversen *et al.* 2000; Harrison 2001; and Green 2003 for some examples of these points; for further discussion see Robinson 2011). Thus, in these moments of appropriation, adoption, or attempts at shaping agendas, it could be that something entirely different is happening in the train of prolific policy circuits – not neoliberalization, then, but the appropriation of neoliberal agendas to local pathways, or perhaps even the privatized appropriation of the benefits of the policy circuit itself. In the many cities of the global south, where little or no substantive research has been undertaken, discerning a clear adoption of or divergence from neoliberalism's pathways is not possible. In generalizing, then, it is all too easy to extrapolate and theorize from well-trodden, carefully documented cases where researchers and graduate students are thick on the ground and the evidence of neoliberalism's intended, unintended, and differentiated manifestations are accessible.

It is thus our suggestion, that in some – most? – urban places we might be observing far more than the path-dependency of neoliberalization. Taking seriously the suggestion that neoliberalization is just one of many processes shaping places (and circulations), we might indicate that diverse and divergent pathways are not adding to the emergent "syndrome" of neoliberalization (Brenner *et al.* 2010a) but to a range of different trajectories of accumulation and political regulation in cities. Béatrice Hibou's excellent account (2004) of the ways in which neoliberal agendas of privatization have been appropriated to advance a more thoroughly informalized (and criminalized) form of state regulation in some African states, advancing elite interests, indicates one distinctive pathway which may well exceed existing theorizations of urban neoliberalization, if not broader understandings of how city politics might work.

There are many vantage points from which the concept of neoliberalism ceases to have explanatory value. Looking out from developmentalist neoliberalisms, the complex urban processes to be theorized, the patchy information available about relevant urban dynamics, and the multiple circulating policy discourses which accompany the international development project, create messy accounts of urban change. Regardless of whether they emanate from scholars, practitioners, or politicians, these processes are not easily attributable to something called neoliberalism. Moreover, the varied actions in cities can no longer be understood as contributing to the transformation of a system-like project called neoliberalization. This is not (necessarily) "an embrace of unprincipled variety and unstructured contingency" (Brenner *et al.* 2010b: 203) – certainly systems of exploitation and circuits of power and knowledge actively frame the experiences of all cities and we agree that we need to try to understand these. Thus policy outcomes may well be part of systems and tendencies, of programmatic attempts to change the world, countries or cities, of capitalism's dynamics and capitalist ambitions. But these may not be about neoliberalization. One result of this is that neoliberalism and projects of neoliberalization may not take the form of a system which can be apprehended as such – no matter how differentiated and tendentious it is considered to be. A corollary to this is that it may not be helpful for political resistance to inequality, poverty, peremptory and violent power, exclusions, and exploitation in urban processes to be effected under the sign of anti-neoliberalism, and, conversely, it may well be imperative to creatively contribute to institutional elaborations of policy interventions, incorporating neoliberal technologies to achieve urgent developmental and/or progressive redistributive ends. We suggest the value of a progressive politics beyond a focus on neoliberalism and anti-neoliberalism, if not one which is after neoliberal politics (of which, by all accounts, we have not yet seen the end), then certainly one which is intellectually more ambitiously post-neoliberal.

Conclusion

While the broadest accounts of cities have been disadvantaged by longstanding divisions between understandings of cities in poorer and wealthier areas, or in different regions, or in different locations within wider systems, there is a growing awareness that under conditions of globalization and postcolonialism, new, more international, forms of urban theorizing are essential to reflect the increasing diversity of urban life and the complexity of the challenges of city governance. We have argued that existing, albeit sophisticated, theorizations of urban neoliberalization and associated assessments of urban politics, need to be further reconfigured to take account of this diversity. Specifically, we question the extent to which the diversity of urban outcomes with which neoliberal policy circuits are associated necessarily contributes to a wider project of neoliberalization initially specified in its northern idiom. We suggest that this opens up important spaces for urbanists to contribute to present projects concerned to forge alternative forms of urban development, and to consider alternative starting points for theorizing urban processes.

References

Brenner, N., and Theodore, N. (eds.) (2002) *Spaces of Neoliberalism*. Oxford: Blackwell.

Brenner, N., Peck, J., and Theodore, N. (2010a) After neoliberalization. *Globalizations* 7 (3): 327–45.

Brenner, N., Peck, J., and Theodore, N. (2010b) Variegated neoliberalization: geographies, modalities, pathways. *Global Networks* 10 (2): 182–222.

Chakrabarty, D. (2000) *Provincialising Europe*. London: Routledge.

Chatterjee, P. (2006) *The Politics of the Governed: Reflections on Popular Politics in Most of the World*. New York: Columbia University Press.

Collier, S. (2005) Budgets and biopolitics. In *Global Assemblages: Technology, Politics, and Ethics as Anthropological Problems*, ed. A. Ong and S. J. Collier. Oxford: Blackwell, 373–90.

Connell, R. (2007) *Southern Theory: The Global Dynamics of Knowledge in Social Science*. Sydney: Allen and Unwin.

Davis, M. (2007) *Planet of Slums*. London: Verso.

de Boeck, P., and Plissart, M. (2004) *Kinshasa: Tales of the Invisible City*. Brussels: Ludion.

Ferguson, J. (2006) *Global Shadows: Africa in the Neoliberal World Order*. Durham, NC: Duke University Press.

Ferguson, J. (2007) Formalities of poverty: thinking about social assistance in neoliberal South Africa. *African Studies Review* 50: 71–86.

Gandy, M. (2005) Learning from Lagos. *New Left Review* 32: 37–53.

Green, M. (2003) Globalizing development in Tanzania: policy franchising through participatory project management. *Critique of Anthropology* 23: 123–43.

Harrison, G. (2001) Post-conditionality politics and administrative reform: reflections on the cases of Uganda and Tanzania. *Development and Change* 32: 657–79.

Harvey, D. (2009) Reshaping economic geography: the *World Development Report 2009*. *Development and Change* 40 (6): 1269–77.

Hibou, B. (2004) From privatising the economy to privatising the state: an analysis of the continual formation of the state. In *Privatising the State*, ed. B. Hibou. London: Hurst and Company, 1–46.

Hoffman, L., De Hart, M., and Collier, S. (2006) Notes on the anthropology of neoliberalism. *Anthropology News* September: 9–10.

Kelly, P. F. (2000) *Landscapes of Globalization. Human Geographies of Economic Change in the Philippines*. London: Routledge.

King, A. (2004) *Spaces of Global Cultures: Architecture, Urbanism, Identity*. London: Routledge.

Larner, W. (2000) Neoliberalism: policy, ideology, governmentality. *Studies in Political Economy* 63: 5–24.

Leitner, H., Peck, J., and Sheppard, E. (eds.) (2007) *Contesting Neoliberalism*. New York: Guilford Press.

Leitner, H., Sheppard, E., Sziarto, K., and Maringanti, A. (2007) Contesting urban futures: decentering neoliberalism. In *Contesting Neoliberalism*, ed. H. Leitner, J. Peck, and E. Sheppard. New York: Guilford Press, 1–25.

McCann, E. (forthcoming). Urban policy mobilities and global circuits of knowledge: towards a research agenda. *Annals of the Association of American Geographers*.

McNeill, D. (2009) *The Global Architect: Firms, Fame and Urban Form*. London: Routledge.

Mitchell, J. C. (1987) *Cities, Society, and Social Perception. A Central African Perspective*. Oxford: Clarendon Press.

Myers, G. (2005) *Disposable Cities: Garbage, Governance and Sustainable Development in Urban Africa*. Burlington, VT: Ashgate Publishing.

Ong, A. (2006) *Neoliberalism as Exception: Mutations in Citizenship and Sovereignty*. Durham, NC: Duke University Press.

Parnell, S. (2007) Urban governance in the south: the politics of rights and development. In *A Handbook of Political Geography*, ed. K. Cox, M. Low, and J. Robinson. London: Sage, 595–608.

Parnell, S., Pieterse, E., and Watson, V. (2009) Planning for cities in the global south: a research agenda for sustainable human settlements. *Progress in Planning* 72: 232–40.

Peck, J. (2002) Political economies of scale: fast policy, interscalar relations, and neoliberal workfare. *Economic Geography* 78: 331–60.

Peck, J., Theodore, N., and Brenner, N. (2010) Postneoliberalism and its malcontents. *Antipode* 41: 94–116.

Peirce, N. (2010) The World Bank and cities: dawn of a new era? *Washington Post* (January 3). Available online at http://citiwire.net/post/1602.

Pieterse, E. (2008) *City Futures: Confronting the Crisis of Urban Development*. London: Zed Books.

Rakodi, C. (2005) The urban challenge in Africa. In *Managing Urban Futures*, ed. M. Keiner, M. Koll-Schretzenmayr, and W. Schmid. Aldershot: Ashgate, 47–72.

Robinson, J. (2006) *Ordinary Cities: Between Modernity and Development*. London: Routledge.

Robinson, J. (2011) The spaces of circulating knowledge: city strategies and global urban governmentality. In *Mobile Urbanism: Cities and Policymaking in the Global Age*, ed. E. McCann and K. Ward. Minneapolis: University of Minnesota Press.

Roy, A., and Alsazaar, N. (eds.) (2003) *Urban Informality: Transnational Perspectives from the Middle East, Latin America, and South Asia*. Lanham, MD: Lexington Books.

Said, E. (1983) *Travelling theory*. In *The World, the Text, and the Critic*. Cambridge, MA: Harvard University Press, 226–47.

Salskov-Iversen, D., Hansen, H. K., and Bislev, S. (2000) Governmentality, globalization and local practice: transformations of a hegemonic discourse. *Alternatives: Global, Local, Political* 25 (2): 183–223.

Saunier, P.-Y. (2002) Taking up the bet on connections: A municipal contribution. *Contemporary European History* 11 (4): 507–27.

Seekings, J., and Keil, R. (2009) The International Journal of Urban and Regional Research: An editorial statement. *International Journal of Urban and Regional Research* 33 (2): i–x.

Simone, A. (2004) *For the City Yet to Come: Changing African Life in Four Cities*. Durham, NC: Duke University Press.

Smith, N. (2002) New globalism, new urbanism: gentrification as global urban strategy. *Antipode* 34 (3): 427–50.

Southall, A. (1973) Introduction. In *Urban Anthropology: Cross-Cultural Studies of Urbanization*, ed. A. Southall. New York: Oxford University Press, 3–14.

Taylor, P. (2004) *World City Network: A Global Urban Analysis*. London: Routledge.

Turok, I., and Parnell, S. (2009) Reshaping cities, rebuilding nations: the role of national urban policies. *Urban Forum* 20: 157–74.

Watts, M. (2002) Alternative modern: development as cultural geography. In *Handbook of Cultural Geography*, ed. K. Anderson, M. Domosh, S. Pile, and N. Thrift. London: Sage, 433–53.

World Bank (2001) *Urban Policy and Economic Development: An Agenda for the 1990s.* World Bank Policy Paper. Washington, DC: The World Bank.

Chapter 47

Race, Class, and Inequality in the South African City

Jeremy Seekings

The Apartheid City

The "apartheid city" in South Africa stands out as an extreme example of urban social engineering. Urban segregation was pervasive across the colonial world, some other cities in colonial and even postcolonial Africa were subject to massive forced removals or restrictions on urbanization that compared to South Africa under apartheid (Freund 2001; Burton 2005), and ghettos are certainly not uniquely South African. Nonetheless, the apartheid city was distinctive in several important respects.

Firstly, its basis was not simply the usual binary division between "white" ("European") and "black" ("native," "Bantu" or "African"), or citizen and subject, or colonial and colonized, with some ambiguity surrounding people of mixed descent as well as African people of high status. Instead, statutory "racial" classification demarcated also separate "coloured" as well as "Indian" populations: the category "Indian" referred to the descendants of people brought from South Asia, mostly as indentured workers in the late nineteenth century; "coloured" encompassed an arbitrary mix of people, including the descendants of the indigenous Khoi and San populations of the Western Cape, people descended from slaves brought to the Cape from Malaysia and Indonesia, and people of "mixed-race" (Christopher 2002; Posel 2001). This rigid classificatory system was combined with strict prohibitions on interracial marriage and sex, removing the possibility of assimilation or other forms of boundary-crossing.

Secondly, residential segregation was especially thorough, and controls on urbanization unusually severe. Residential segregation (under the Group Areas Act) resulted in towns that were mercilessly divided into separate "white," "coloured," "Indian," and "African" areas. Hundreds of thousands of people were forcibly removed, especially in the 1960s, into racially designated "group areas" (Western 1981; Field 2001). Residential segregation was linked to the systematic regulation of social interaction in both public spaces (especially municipal facilities). In addition, "influx control," i.e., restrictions under the "pass" laws on where African people could live and work, served both to limit the growth of the urban African population and to determine where African workers could live if they were allowed into the cities. Many male African workers were confined to overcrowded migrant hostels, whilst shack settlements were largely prohibited from the cities and towns in "white" South Africa. Family accommodation for African people in the cities was limited to the small and standardized "matchbox" housing in highly planned townships such as Soweto. Unemployed African men and most African women and children were excluded from the apartheid city through mass arrests, prosecutions, and deportations.

The apartheid city was thus highly ordered spatially, with the archetypal design illustrated tellingly by Davies (1981; see also Lemon 1991; Christopher 1994: 103–40). Figure 47.1 illustrates this for the port city of Cape Town. The historic city center, the Southern Suburbs stretching down the Cape Peninsula and the Northern Suburbs curving along low hills inland to the northeast – the axes indicated by black lines – were almost entirely set aside for white settlement. African settlements were successively removed eastwards, away from the city center, to the areas marked as "A." The coloured population was the primary victim of forced removals from the 1960s through to the 1970s, subjected to relocation from what became uniformly white areas to more distant areas, especially on the sandy Cape Flats to the southeast (marked "C").

Thirdly, and perhaps most importantly of all, the purpose of racial segregation was not simply to separate "racial" groups but also to ensure a clear racial hierarchy in which "poor whites" would be lifted, economically and socially, above almost all non-white people. The consequence of this was that inequality in South African cities took on a caste-like form, with largely impermeable boundaries between castes. Caste shaped class in that someone's racial classification shaped the range of possible class positions open to him or her, although each caste comprised a set of classes. At the same time, class shaped the caste system, in that some aspects of racial discrimination and segregation served the interests of some sections of the bourgeoisie (notably the gold-mining houses and many commercial farmers) and many white South African workers (who restricted competition from black workers for better-paid employment).

Urban segregation therefore also entailed ghettoization. South Africans classified as white lived in relatively prosperous neighborhoods with good municipal infrastructure and lucrative pockets of commercial activity. Rapid economic growth under apartheid resulted in suburbanization. South Africans classified as coloured or Indian were removed to less-serviced neighborhoods, where poverty, drugs, and gangs were rife. "Townships" for the African population were provided with minimal infrastructure on the grounds that African people were temporarily resident in "white" South Africa, and would and should return to the rural areas in due course. In addition, any infrastructure should be funded out of revenues raised from within these poor neighborhoods. Policing was thorough, but services were minimal (with electrification only in the 1980s). In most townships, African people were not

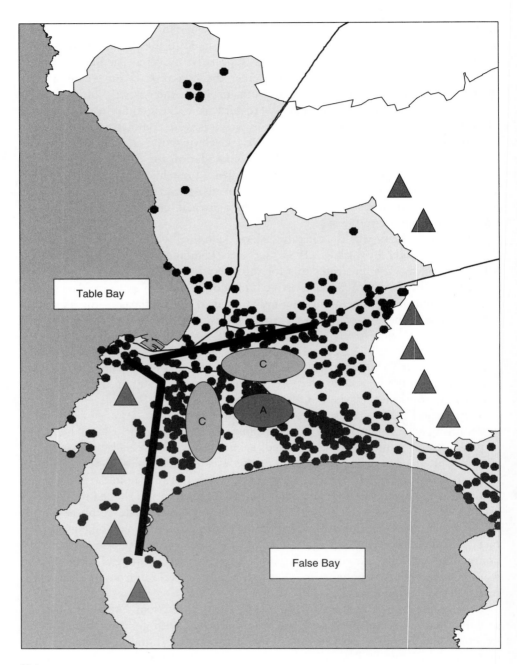

Note:
Triangles indicate mountains.
Dots indicate the distribution of the population in 2001.
The bold black bars indicate areas demarcated for "white" occupancy under apartheid.
"A" and "C" refer to areas demarcated for African and coloured people respectively.

Figure 47.1 Cape Town: African townships and coloured "group areas" in the mid-twentieth century.

permitted to own their houses. Restrictions on construction meant that, at least from the 1970s, housing in coloured, Indian and African neighborhoods was severely overcrowded, and shacks proliferated in backyards (Swilling *et al.* 1991).

The most impoverished ghettoes in apartheid South Africa were located not in the city, however, but in the supposed rural areas in the "bantustans," i.e., the supposedly self-governing (and even "independent") "homelands" set aside for African people so that the denial of South African citizenship might be more defensible. Urbanization was "displaced" (Simkins 1983; Murray 1987) into slums such as Phuthaditjaba (on the border with Lesotho), whose population grew from 24,000 in 1970 to (officially) 342,000 in 1991 (Nattrass 2000). Only a few of these slums were in commuting distance of cities in "white" South Africa (see Lelyveld 1986: ch. 5).

Economic growth and change brought changes in the class structure of South Africa which in turn shaped political conflict. Skill shortages in the late apartheid period led to the steady relaxation of the "colour bar" in employment, especially in the service sector. Growing numbers of African men and women moved into better-paid employment (Crankshaw 1997). At the same time, deagrarianization together with a stagnant demand for unskilled labor in urban areas meant that open unemployment rose rapidly. Influx control kept many, but not all, unemployed people in "rural" slums. Continuing racial segregation and ghettoization helped to forge the political coalition in African townships that drove the "township revolt" against the apartheid state in the 1980s: upwardly mobile, skilled workers and the nascent African middle class, forced to remain in infrastructurally deprived and ever more overcrowded townships, and repeatedly denied dignity; semi-skilled workers suffering from industrial stagnation; rural immigrants contesting influx control; and growing ranks of young unemployed. Mass unemployment also helped to fuel defiance of the state in many of the quasi-urban slums in the bantustans (Seekings and Nattrass 2005).

The Persistence of Inequality after Apartheid

In 1990, Nelson Mandela was released from prison, the African National Congress (ANC) and other organizations were unbanned, and negotiations over political change began. Four years later, in 1994, the country held its first democratic elections, won by the ANC. By 1994, almost all legislation which discriminated on explicitly racial grounds had been abolished: people could now vote in elections, live or attend school anywhere, do any work, and marry and have sex, all without regard for racial classification. Inequalities, however, remained: the legacy of the past could not be undone overnight.

Researchers, political leaders, and (of course) poor South Africans themselves had long been aware of the persistence of poverty but accurate data had only become available for the first time in 1993. Using the standard and ungenerous international poverty measure of US$1 per person day (adjusted for local purchasing power), one in four South Africans lived in (deep) poverty in 1994, whilst as many as one half had incomes below the more generous poverty line favored in South Africa itself. One in six South Africans was not expected to survive to the age of 40 – a proportion that was to grow as the AIDS pandemic reduced life expectancy by one quarter. At the same time, a minority of South Africans, almost all white, enjoyed evident prosperity. Inequality meant that the poverty gap, defined as the aggregate amount by which poor people's incomes are below the poverty line as a proportion of the total income in society, was very small. A perfectly targeted transfer of only 5 percent of national income from rich to poor would have sufficed to eliminate poverty, even using the higher South African poverty line set above US$1 per person day. Given that the top household income decile, i.e., the richest 10 percent of households, earned almost exactly one half of the national income, they would only have to forsake one tenth of their aggregate incomes to have eliminated poverty (Seekings and Nattrass 2005).

The transition to democracy, marked by democratic elections in 1994, was unsurprisingly accompanied by high hopes that income poverty and inequality would be reduced. The votes of poor people had helped to ensure victory for the ANC, which had campaigned around the promise of "a better life for all." Its election manifesto – the Reconstruction and Development Programme (RDP) – identified "attacking poverty and deprivation" as "the first priority of the democratic government"; all South Africans should enjoy "a decent living standard and economic security" (ANC 1994). The 1996 constitution also recognized socioeconomic rights to health care, "sufficient food and water," and income security, albeit subject to the availability of resources, as well as education. These and other rights were said to be based on the "democratic values of human dignity, equality and freedom."

The performance of the democratic ANC-led government following the 1994 elections is a matter of some debate. On the one hand, the ANC itself cautiously lauds its success, at least in "laying the foundations" for the elimination of poverty (South Africa 2003, 2007). On the other hand, a series of critical commentators have argued that the ideals of 1994 have been betrayed repeatedly, as the ANC has adopted "neoliberal" policies that reproduced the inequities of the past. "Apartheid did not die," in the words of John Pilger (2006). In this view, the racialized inequities of apartheid gave way to new "market" inequities, as the post-apartheid political elite embraced (or was embraced by) global neoliberalism. Neoliberalism was seen to be especially rampant in South African cities, which offered appropriate spaces for global capitalism to circumvent possible restrictions arising from national politics. Neoliberalism is said to have made Cape Town, for example, into "one of the most – if not *the* most – unequal cities in the world" (McDonald 2008: 42; emphasis in the original). The deep inequalities that were nurtured by apartheid, through direct, coercive, and inegalitarian intervention, are now being reproduced, it is argued, precisely because the state has withdrawn from playing an active role in the regulation of markets, i.e., the state is withdrawing from any commitment to decommodification. Scholars pointed to policies such as the privatization of or introduction of user-charges (and cost-recovery) for municipal services, the delegation to the private sector of house-building, and the proliferation of gated communities and business-led improvement districts (McDonald and Pape 2002; Beall *et al.* 2002; Harrison *et al.* 2003; McDonald 2008).

There is indeed strong evidence that both income poverty and inequality worsened in the years immediately following the transition to democracy in 1994. Income poverty and inequality worsened disproportionately in South Africa's cities as the urban elite and middle classes prospered whilst rapid rural-to-urban migration combined with rising unemployment rates to swell the ranks of the urban poor. In the early 2000s, however, income poverty seems to have declined, in part due to a modest decline in unemployment, but primarily because of the expansion of public welfare programs (Van der Berg *et al.* 2008; Leibbrandt *et al.* 2009; Seekings 2011).

Delineating the class structure of South Africa – or of South African cities – is not straightforward, given the limits of both the available data and the theoretical understanding of what constitutes a meaningful conception of class in a context such as South Africa's. Using data on occupations, income from wealth and business activities, and household composition, the class structure can be understood in terms of ten classes, which can be combined into three composite categories. The composite "upper class" category comprises households with substantial earnings from wealth or business, or including people in professional or managerial occupations. A middle category encompasses households that include people in semi-professional, supervisory, and skilled occupations, as well as semi- and unskilled workers outside of domestic work and agriculture. It also includes households with modest earnings from wealth or business (labeled "petty traders" for convenience). A lower category comprises households in which workers are in unskilled occupations in the marginal sectors of domestic work and agriculture or in low-income self-employment, together with a systematically disadvantaged "underclass" trapped in unemployment (Seekings and Nattrass 2005: chapters 7 and 8). In 1993, on the eve of the first democratic elections, the upper classes accounted for 12 percent of the total population of households but 45 percent of the national income. The middle category accounted for 48 percent of households and 45 percent of national income. The lower classes accounted for 41 percent of households, but only 10 percent of national income. Household incomes in the upper category were, on average, more than 15 times larger than household incomes in the lower category (Seekings and Nattrass 2005: 254).

Fifteen years later, the class structure shows limited changes. Figure 47.2 shows the distribution of households and income in 2008, using data from the first wave

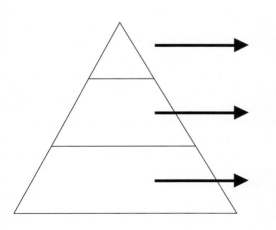

3 "upper" classes, defined by occupation (managerial or professional), wealth, or (substantial) business activity:
14% of households, 46% of income
(17% / 49% in metro areas)

4 classes in a middle position: the semi-professional class, intermediate class, core working class, and petty traders:
38% of households, 34% of income
(44% / 34% in metro areas)

3 "lower" classes: the marginal working class, underclass (defined in terms of systematic disadvantage in the labor market), and a residual "other" category:
48% of households, 20% of income
(39% / 17% in metro areas)

Figure 47.2   The class structure of South Africa, 2008 (calculated from NIDS data).

of the National Income Dynamics Study. Figures in brackets refer to the six major metropolitan areas only. Whilst the data from 1993 and 2008 are not precisely comparable, they suggest that the upper classes have maintained their privileged position, and perhaps even grown slightly. The middle category has, however, shrunk in terms of its share of the total population of households, and the lower category has grown in terms of its shares of both the total population of households and the national income. Many households in the lower category have benefited from the government's social assistance programs (as well as housing programs). Inter-class income inequalities have declined somewhat since 1993, but remain large: households in the upper category have, on average, incomes three and a half times larger than households in the middle category, and approximately eight times larger than households in the lower category.

A comparison of data from 1993 and 2008 suggests that there has been some continued social polarization in post-apartheid South Africa. Such a conclusion is supported by an additional detail. The "core working class" – defined as households dependent on semi-skilled and unskilled workers in sectors other than agriculture and domestic work – seems to have shrunk very dramatically across this 15-year period, perhaps by as much as two thirds. The effect of this has been muted for reasons suggested by Borel-Saladin and Crankshaw (2009), on the basis of their analysis of somewhat older occupational data from censuses. They found, in the case of Cape Town, that there was significant deindustrialization in the late apartheid and early post-apartheid periods. The decline of middle-income jobs in occupations such as artisan, machine operator, and driver between 1980 and 2001 was matched, however, by rising employment of middle-income clerks, and sales and personal service workers. Household and labor force data suggest, however, that *formal* semi- and unskilled employment has declined in general, possibly because of the effects of labor market institutions and regulations. This has also been partly offset by rising low-income *informal* employment. The decline of lower-paid, semi- and unskilled but formal working-class occupations has entailed some polarization.

The lower cluster of classes has grown in terms of both its share of the total population of households and its share of national income. The former is explained primarily by the growth of the "underclass," i.e., households who (to borrow from Wilson 1987) are "truly disadvantaged": households without any working members, disadvantaged not only by their lack of skills but also by their lack of social capital, in a labor market in which connections are imperative in the face of very high unemployment (with the unemployment rate standing at about 35 percent, down from a peak of 40 percent in the early 2000s) (Seekings and Nattrass 2005). The growth in the lower cluster of classes' share of national income reflects primarily the expansion of government social assistance programs.

Insofar as the class structure has changed, it has not resulted in any major diminution of interpersonal inequality. The social structure has changed, however, in terms of the relationship between race and class. The lower cluster of classes remains entirely African, but the higher cluster of classes has continued to diversify in racial terms. Improved educational opportunities for African people combined with government policies that promoted affirmative action (in both public and private sectors) and "black economic empowerment" (meaning primarily transfers of capital from white to black, and especially African, people) meant accelerated upward mobility of some African people into the upper classes (Seekings and Nattrass 2005). In Johannesburg, by 2001, the "middle class" was evenly divided between white people, on the one hand, and black (i.e., African, Indian, and coloured) people on the other (Crankshaw 2008: 1697). Nationally, and in cities such as Johannesburg, the distribution of income within the African population has become as unequal as for the population as a whole, i.e., including all racial categories (Leibbrandt *et al.* 2009; Seekings 2011). Nowhere is the deracialization of the elite and middle class more apparent than in urban shopping malls (see, for example, Nkuna 2006).

The Persistence of Segregation

Given that the class structure remains largely unchanged, and highly unequal, whilst deracialization is limited to the upper cluster of classes, one might expect that racial segregation would have declined only in higher-income neighborhoods. Initial studies of post-apartheid segregation found that the pace of desegregation was very slow indeed (Christopher 2001, 2005): the "post-apartheid" city should perhaps be viewed as a "neo-apartheid" city, with the overwhelming majority of people living in mono-racial areas.

There are exceptions to this general pattern. In Johannesburg, in the early 1990s, the inner city was rapidly transformed as African people moved in and white residents moved out (Morris 1999). In Cape Town, a handful of neighborhoods were established for low-income African people in the midst of middle-class suburbia (notably Imizamo Yethu, Masiphumelele, and Westlake on the Cape Peninsula, and Marconi Beam in northern Cape Town; see Saff 1998) – although, in general, public housing projects have been located on low-cost land on the urban periphery. Lower-middle-class private housing developments provide an opportunity for racial integration (for example, Summer Greens in Cape Town: see Broadbridge 2001). On occasion, the state has explicitly sought to create mixed neighborhoods by allocating new houses to both coloured and African people (for example, in Delft, see Oldfield 2004; Millstein 2007; and Westlake, see Lemanski 2006a). Overall, however, the post-apartheid city remains heavily segregated.

To describe the contemporary South African city as a "neo-apartheid" city reflects one of its dimensions, the persistence of segregation, but distracts attention from a second, that the consequence of rapid metropolitan growth is that a large proportion of the segregated city comprises neighborhoods that did not exist when statutory residential segregation was abolished during the transition to democracy. Figure 47.3 shows the pattern of segregation in post-apartheid Cape Town. The expansion of the city has entailed the reproduction of segregation in newly developed neighborhoods: predominantly white suburban neighborhoods, often gated and walled, on the northern and northeastern periphery of the city or down the Cape Peninsula to the south (indicated by the black arrows); the rapid expansion of overwhelmingly African neighborhoods in an easterly direction (marked "A"), and the slower growth of coloured neighborhoods in pockets around the former coloured "group areas" (marked "C"). Only in one area – Delft (marked "C/A") – has there been significant racial integration of coloured and African people.

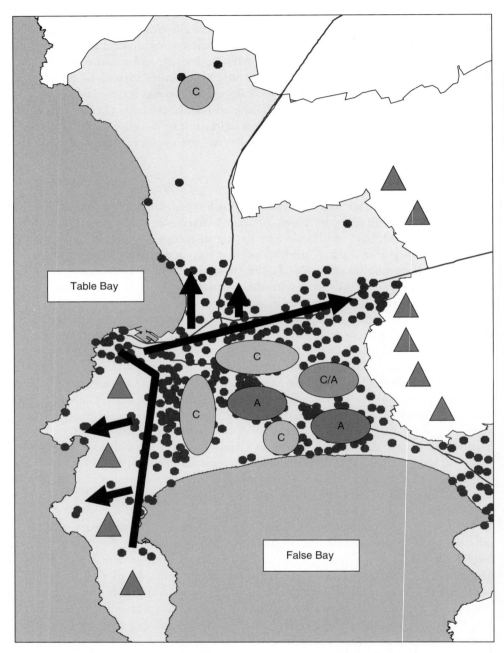

Figure 47.3 Cape Town: expansion at the end of the twentieth century.

Economic factors are clearly part of the explanation of segregation in new as well as old neighborhoods. As Besteman (2008: ch. 2) emphasizes in the case of Cape Town, coloured and African people face severe economic obstacles in moving into formerly white neighborhoods where the prices of housing and land are inflated. As in the United States, access to higher-paid employment does not mean that the upwardly mobile can put down deposits on property. In Cape Town, the gaps between each step on the housing ladder are so large, relative to incomes, that getting onto one step does not mean that it is easy to ascend further (Lemanski 2011). Economic factors might be buttressed by racism on the part of richer, white South Africans. Johannesburg's city center transformed rapidly because, when African people began to move in, white residents fled to the city's gated and walled northern suburbs. Employers followed them, and Johannesburg's northern neighborhoods themselves were soon transformed into a new "edge city" that was largely independent of the former central city (Beavon 2004; see also Saff 1998; Lemanski 2006b). The continuing separation of rich and poor neighborhoods reflected also the failures of public planning (Watson 2002; Harrison *et al.* 2008).

These explanations are not entirely adequate, however. For one thing, as Crankshaw (2008) emphasizes, many early studies underestimated the extent of desegregation in richer neighborhoods. In Johannesburg, he found, somewhere between one quarter and one third of the residents (excluding domestic workers) of Johannesburg's middle-class northern neighborhoods were African, coloured, or Indian by 2001, and the proportion was higher still in formerly white neighborhoods in the south of the city. Novels provide the most vivid illustration of the growth of the suburban African upper classes. There are echoes of Pierre Bourdieu in Kopano Matlwa's novel *Coconut*. Matlwa (2007) describes Ofilwe (or "Fifi," as she prefers to be called), who lives in the Little Valley Country Estate with her newly rich (African) family. Ofilwe speaks English (the "TV language") at home, and attends a formerly white school. Every Sunday her family goes to the Silver Spoon Coffee Shop (in the Little Square Shopping Centre) to eat Traditional English Breakfasts. The central moral issue at the heart of novels such as *Coconut* is the dilemma that arises when newly rich African people seek to emphasize their own status, relative to other African people, whilst themselves encountering white racism and social exclusion. The fact that embourgeoisement is accompanied by such a dilemma does little, however, to mitigate the divides of class-segregated cities.

There has been less desegregation in most cheaper areas of the post-apartheid city, but economic explanations do not suffice in such areas, especially in Cape Town where segregation persists among similarly poor African and coloured populations. Despite the emergence of a housing market in even low-income neighborhoods, segregation is reproduced to a far greater extent than would be expected given patterns of income distribution. One reason for this is that opportunities exist in most cities for many upwardly mobile people to find better housing within the overall racial pattern of the city. In Johannesburg, a prosperous middle class lives in elite suburbs *within* Soweto, and can shop at the massive Maponya Mall ("where South Africa's vibrant and trendy Sowetan community gather to shop, socialize, eat, and to see and be seen": see www.maponyamall.co.za). Cape Town's Khayelitsha is home to far fewer middle-class people than Soweto, but it too now contains gated communities built for African teachers and other relatively high-income households.

Similarly, prosperous coloured families can extend their existing houses or build large new properties within the broad confines of formerly coloured neighborhoods. The precise motivation for such patterns is unclear, but is likely to entail a mix of economic constraint and social preference. Post-apartheid Cape Town thus increasingly comprises a patchwork of differently classed neighborhoods within broadly mono-racial areas of the city.

Another reason for continued segregation in the city is the mechanism by which plots and houses have been allocated in the massive new public housing projects that have contributed greatly to the expansion of every major South African city. Most public housing has been earmarked for residents of specified informal settlements, with disregard for city-wide waiting-lists. When a number of informal settlements are pressing claims to public housing, complex negotiations are undertaken to allocate certain numbers of sites to each "community." Moreover, continued immigration into informal settlements generally means that the allocation of houses to the "community" fails to solve the "problem," and additional housing projects need to be earmarked to the (new) members of the existing "community." In a situation where, for a mix of reasons, informal settlements are both almost entirely African and politically militant, new housing projects are as mono-racial as the older parts of the city. People living in the backyards of formal townships or sharing overcrowded housing with older kin are rarely able to mobilize the collective political pressure required to ensure an allocation of new houses or plots. The consequence is that most new neighborhoods remain unmixed by various criteria, including racially.

Whatever the reasons, the persistence of racial segregation in most parts of the city has important social and perhaps political consequences. Many urban South Africans remain extraordinarily ignorant about their fellow-citizens. In Cape Town, for example, white and coloured people remain deeply ignorant about the city's growing African population, whilst the many unemployed people in African (and coloured) neighborhoods have little contact with their richer and white fellow citizens (see Besteman 2008, ch. 3; Bray et al. 2010). Urban politics remains highly racialized, with white, coloured, and Indian voters supporting the opposition Democratic Alliance whilst urban African voters supported the ANC (at least until 2009, when a section of the ANC split to form the Congress of the People, taking a significant minority of the urban African vote).

Decommodification

The post-apartheid city remains deeply divided by class and, for the most part and for whatever reason, race also. A series of studies suggest that these inequalities are linked to "neoliberal" policies with regard to urban infrastructure, housing, and services. The privatization or commercialization of municipal services, and the accompanying emphasis on cost-recovery, have allegedly led to the denial of basic social and economic rights to the poor. Whereas racial discrimination underlay the fragmented and unequal apartheid city, now neoliberalism and class underlie the fragmented and unequal post- (or neo-) apartheid city – although these inequities have been challenged by militant urban social movements. In this view, the pervasive application of neoliberal principles has not only prevented the decommodification required to realize the progressive ambitions of the RDP and constitution, but has even rolled back the partial decommodification that preceded the transition to democracy (McDonald and Pape 2002; Beall *et al.* 2002; Harrison *et al.* 2003; McDonald 2008).

This argument ignores important aspects of post-apartheid policy. It relies overmuch on the form in which public services are provided and the discourse sometimes used by public officials. It pays too little attention to the actual distribution of public services or to the financing thereof. Whilst post-apartheid service delivery is indeed characterized by an emphasis on cost-recovery and private–public partnerships, these are underpinned by highly redistributive financing, such that rich taxpayers (and ratepayers at the municipal level) finance heavily public schooling, health care, and municipal services for the poor. High-income neighborhoods typically receive better-quality services than low-income ones, but they pay a disproportionate share of the cost of services city-wide. In other words, there has been a widespread and rising decommodification of service provision for poor people in many parts of South Africa's major cities.

Access by the poor to these public services has improved since the end of apartheid. In Cape Town, for example, only 33 percent of African households lived in formal housing in 1996; by 2003, 55 percent did so. In 1996, about two thirds of African households had their refuse removed by the council at least once a week; by 2003 this proportion had risen to 87 percent. The improvement of service delivery is even more striking when it is presented not in terms of percentages of the relevant population, but in absolute numbers, because in-migration from rural areas accelerated population growth. Between 1996 and 2001, for example, the absolute number of African households in Cape Town increased by 50 percent. Over this period the actual number of African households with weekly refuse removal doubled, even though the proportion only rose by about 20 percentage points. Since the transition to democracy there has been a massive improvement in services in poorer parts of the city, and this has *not* been funded along market principles.

The most important element of decommodification in South Africa is the government's set of social assistance programs. The ANC inherited a system of unusually generous non-contributory pensions and grants payable to categories of deserving poor: the elderly, disabled, and single mothers. After 1994 the ANC government expanded this system, such that it entailed the redistribution of approximately 3.5 percent of national income by the late 2000s. In the six major metropolitan areas, approximately one half of all households receive one or more government grants. Among the lower cluster of classes, the proportion is close to two thirds.

Post-apartheid South African cities are certainly characterized by deep economic and social inequalities as well as spatial fragmentation. But they are also cities undergoing important processes of partial transformation. Most importantly, African people may have been the victims of apartheid, but they are now active agents in the remaking of the city, playing major roles in both the desegregation of higher-income neighborhoods and the reproduction of segregation in lower-income areas, as well as – through the mechanisms of representative democracy as well as direct action – in the continued uneven decommodification of municipal infrastructure and services.

References

ANC (1994) *The Reconstruction and Development Programme*. Johannesburg: African National Congress.

Beall, Jo, Crankshaw, Owen, and Parnell, Susan (2002) *Uniting a Divided City: Governance and Social Exclusion in Johannesburg*. London: Earthscan.

Beavon, Keith (2004) *Johannesburg: The Making and Shaping of the City*. Pretoria: University of South Africa Press.

Besteman, Catherine (2008) *Transforming Cape Town*. Berkeley: University of California Press.

Borel-Saladin, Jacqueline, and Crankshaw, Owen (2009) Social polarisation or professionalisation? Another look at theory and evidence on deindustrialisation and the rise of the service sector. *Urban Studies* 46 (3): 645–64.

Bray, Rachel, Gooskens, Imke, Kahn, Lauren, Moses, Sue, and Seekings, Jeremy (2010) *Growing Up in the New South Africa: Childhood and Adolescence in the New South Africa*. Cape Town: Human Sciences Research Council Press.

Broadbridge, Helena (2001) Negotiating post-apartheid boundaries and identities: an anthropological study of the creation of a Cape Town suburb. Unpublished PhD thesis, Stellenbosch University.

Burton, Andrew (2005) *African Underclass: Urbanisation, Crime and Colonial Order in Dar es Salaam*. Oxford: James Currey.

Christopher, A. J. (1994) *The Atlas of Apartheid*. Johannesburg: Witwatersrand University Press.

Christopher, A. J. (2001) Urban segregation in post-apartheid South Africa. *Urban Studies* 38 (3): 449–66.

Christopher, A. J. (2002) "To define the indefinable": population classification and the census in South Africa. *Area* 34 (4): 401–8.

Christopher, A. J. (2005) Further progress in the desegregation of South African towns and cities, 1996–2001. *Development Southern Africa* 22 (2): 267–76.

Crankshaw, Owen (1997) *Race, Class and the Changing Division of Labour under Apartheid*. London: Routledge.

Crankshaw, Owen (2008) Race, space and the post-Fordist spatial order of Johannesburg. *Urban Studies* 45 (8): 1692–711.

Davies, R. J. (1981) The spatial formation of the South African city. *GeoJournal Supplement* 2: 59–72.

Field, Sean (ed.) (2001) *Lost Communities, Living Memories: Remembering Forced Removals in Cape Town*. Cape Town: David Philip.

Freund, Bill (2001) Contrasts in urban segregation: a tale of two African cities, Durban (South Africa) and Abidjan (Côte d'Ivoire). *Journal of Southern African Studies* 27 (3): 527–46.

Harrison, Philip, Huchzermeyer, Marie, and Mayekiso, Mzwanele (eds.) (2003) *Confronting Fragmentation: Housing and Urban Development in a Democratizing Society*. Cape Town: University of Cape Town Press.

Harrison, Philip, Todes, Alison, and Watson, Vanessa (2008) *Planning and Transformations: Learning from the Post-Apartheid Experience*. London: Routledge.

Leibbrandt, Murray, Woolard, Ingrid, and Woolard, Christopher (2009) A long-run perspective on contemporary poverty and inequality dynamics. In *South African Economic Policy under Democracy*, ed. Janine Aron, Brian Kahn, and Geeta Kingdon. Oxford: Oxford University Press, 270–99.

Lelyveld, J. (1986) *Move Your Shadow: South Africa, Black and White*. London: Abacus.

Lemon, Anthony (ed.) (1991) *Homes Apart: South Africa's Segregated Cities*. London: Paul Chapman.

Lemanski, Charlotte (2006a) The impact of residential desegregation on social integration: evidence from a South African neighbourhood. *Geoforum* 37: 417–35.

Lemanski, Charlotte (2006b) Desegregation and integration as linked or distinct? Evidence from a previously "White" suburb in post-apartheid Cape Town. *International Journal of Urban and Regional Research* 30 (3): 564–86.

Lemanski, Charlotte (2011) Moving up the ladder or stuck on the bottom rung? Homeownership as a solution to poverty in South Africa. *International Journal of Urban and Regional Research* 35 (1).

Matlwa, Kopano (2007) *Coconut*. Johannesburg: Jacana.

McDonald, David (2008) *World City Syndrome: Neoliberalism and Inequality in Cape Town*. New York: Routledge.

McDonald, David, and Pape, John (2002) *Cost Recovery and the Crisis of Service Delivery*. Pretoria: Human Sciences Research Council Press.

Millstein, Marianne (2007) Challenges to substantive democracy in post-apartheid Cape Town: the politics of urban governance transformations and community organising in Delft. PhD thesis, University of Oslo.

Morris, Alan (1999) *Bleakness and Light: Inner-city Transition in Hillbrow, Johannesburg*. Johannesburg: Witwatersrand University Press.

Murray, Colin (1987) Displaced urbanisation: South Africa's rural slums. *African Affairs* 86: 311–29.

Nattrass, Nicoli (2000) Wage strategies and minimum wages in decentralized regions: the case of the clothing industry in Phuthaditjhaba, South Africa. *International Journal of Urban and Regional Research* 24 (4): 873–88.

Nkuna, L. (2006) "Fitting-in" to a "classy place": the zone and youth identity. In *Globalisation and New Identities: A View from the Middle*, ed. P. Alexander, M. Dawson, and M. Ichharam. Johannesburg: Jacana, 261–74.

Oldfield, Sophie (2004) Urban networks, community organizing and race: an analysis of racial integration in a desegregated South African neighbourhood. *Geoforum* 35 (2): 189–201.

Pilger, John (2006) *Freedom Next Time*. London: Bantam.

Posel, Deborah (2001) Race as common sense: racial classification in twentieth-century South Africa. *African Studies Review* 44 (2): 87–113.

Saff, G. (1998) *Changing Cape Town: Urban Dynamics, Policy and Planning During the Political Transition in South Africa*. Washington, DC: University Press of America.

Seekings, Jeremy (2011) Poverty and inequality in South Africa, 1994–2007. In *After Apartheid: Reinventing South Africa*, ed. Ian Shapiro and Kahreen Tebeau. Charlottesville, VA: University of Virginia Press.

Seekings, Jeremy, and Nattrass, N. (2005) *Class, Race and Inequality in South Africa*. New Haven, CT: Yale University Press.

Simkins, Charles (1983) *Four Essays on the Past, Present, and Possible Future of the Distribution of the Black Population of South Africa*. Cape Town: Southern African Labour and Development Research Unit, University of Cape Town.

South Africa (2003) *Towards a Ten Year Review*. Pretoria: Policy Co-ordination and Advisory Services, the Presidency.

South Africa (2007) *Mid-Term Review*. Pretoria: The Presidency.

Swilling, Mark, Humphries, Richard, and Shubane, Khehla (eds.) (1991) *Apartheid City in Transition*. Cape Town: Oxford University Press.

Van der Berg, Servaas, Louw, Megan, and Yu, Derek (2008) Post-transition poverty trends based on an alternative data source. *South African Journal of Economics* 76 (1): 58–76.

Watson, Vanessa (2002) *Change and Continuity in Spatial Planning: Metropolitan Planning in Cape Town under Political Transition*. London: Routledge.

Western, John (1981) *Outcast Cape Town*. London: George Allen and Unwin.

Wilson, William Julius (1987) *The Truly Disadvantaged: The Inner City, the Underclass and Public Policy*. Chicago: University of Chicago Press.

Chapter 48

Oxford Street, Accra: Spatial Logics, Street Life, and the Transnational Imaginary

Ato Quayson

Accra's gradual urbanization began with its selection as capital of the then Gold Coast Colony by the British in 1877. The population rose steadily from a mere 19,999 in 1891 through 135,926 in 1948 to 337,000 by 1960, three years after Independence. Accra's currently estimated population of 2.5 million masks a long and complicated process of urban evolution. A comparative study of certain neighborhoods and commercial areas reveals the overall spatial logic that has governed the city's expansion from the areas of European influence along the coast from the early 1900s to the present day. Furthermore, the specific focus on Oxford Street in Accra that is adopted in this chapter allows us to highlight specific questions regarding the ways in which people have grasped opportunities for self-fashioning and profit-making in the face of the processes of transnationalism and globalization. This cannot be pursued without a careful understanding of the spatial logics that have governed the evolution of the city in the first place.

While cross-border migration between countries in West Arica was extremely common and was seen as an extension of internal migration it was colonialism that set the essential character for both internal migration and external migration in Ghana. By 1960 about 12 percent of Ghana's population was made up of migrants from the subregion, many of whom came to work on cocoa farms. After the expulsions following the Aliens Compliance Order in 1969 and definitely by the mid-1970s the country moved from being a country of immigration to one of net emigration. By 1983 Ghanaians constituted 81 percent of all ECOWAS (Economic Commission of West African States) nationals resident in Nigeria with Niger a very distant second at 12 percent, followed by Togo and Benin, both at 3 percent each. The expulsions from Nigeria triggered a second wave of Ghanaian migration, with many of those sent out of Nigeria coming back to the country for only a short time

The New Blackwell Companion to the City   Edited by Gary Bridge and Sophie Watson
© 2011 Blackwell Publishing Ltd

before finding their way to Libya, Germany, Holland, Canada and other places. To quote Takyiwaa Manuh:

> What has now emerged in Ghana is a culture of migration, which is reflected in popular drama, song texts and popular TV programmes and the popular TV series *Greetings from Abroad* which features Ghanaians in different destinations on a weekly basis. The precariousness of the migrant dream does not seem to be reflected in the national imaginary on migration, as week after week, dramas are produced on television propagating the message that migration is a solution to the problems of ordinary working people … migration is a privatized investment scheme, to enable Ghanaians themselves to supply the necessary capital for national regeneration. (2006: 24–5)

Thus, given the realities of African migration that have intensified since the early 1980s a new question regarding Africanness may be posed: what does it mean to be African in Accra whilst contemplating New York, London, Amsterdam, Milan, or Hong Kong? As we shall see in the final section, the ideas of "blackness" and "Africanness" are themselves problematized by the advertisements that proliferate on places like Oxford Street. With specific reference to the highly creative cellphone adverts on the street, their main aim seems to be to proffer an invitation for people to consume locally inflected communication products as a way of being "logged into" a transnational imaginary, but done in such a way as to render the precise location of the implicit zeitgeist of such an imaginary irrelevant.

Changing Places: African Studies and the Location of the City

Studies of African cities may be divided into four main categories: (1) descriptive social science often closely aligned to policy oriented approaches; (2) that inspired by the dependency school; (3) that of a largely neo-Marxian tendency; and (4) studies of the urban esoteric and the ineffable. These categories are by no means mutually exclusive, and have as orientations been incarnated in different guises in studies of African cities. Due to the particular political emphases of the British policy of indirect rule, which as much as possible sought to govern through native customary structures, urban studies of the colonial period and well into the post-Independence period focused predominantly on questions of detribalization and retribalization and the impact of large-scale labor movements on urban tribal sentiments (Kilson 1974; Abrams 1978). These were inspired by anthropological and labor economics approaches and by variants of modernization theory. These lines of enquiry intersected with studies of the politicization of ethnicities in African towns that in their turn held longstanding interest for African urban scholars (Banton 1957; Cohen 1969; Lonsdale and Berman 1992; Osaghae 1995, Ndegwa 1997; Parker 2000). The idea that urban ethnicity is not homogeneous but is shaped by and in its turn helps shape transnational and global processes is taken up by other scholars to problematize the ethnicity-as-political-identity approaches. Thus James Ferguson (1999) argues that cosmopolitanism and localism are by no means static concepts but are rather styles adopted by urban dwellers that help establish specific connections along a rural–urban continuum of social and cultural formations.

The scourge of structural adjustment programs from the mid-1980s to the early 1990s was to inspire neo-Marxian analyses that detailed the impact of International Monetary Fund (IMF) and World Bank policies on the overall weakening of urban formations, the upsurge of unemployment, and the expansion of the informal economy (Hart 2006; Freund 2007). The most recent emphasis in African urban studies has been the interest in seeing the African city as a space of the irrational or the uncanny, whereby the city is never fully understood but is grasped by its denizens as the space of a systematic delirium (Castoriadis 1987) where the esoteric world rules the universe of social transformations (De Boeck and Plissart 2004; Simone 2004). This tendency comes from the desire to define alternative modernities for the African, thus leading to a revaluation of witchcraft and juju, both of which were previously considered only marginal to urban social life. While noting the various tendencies within African urban studies discourse my interest is in trying to show that in the specific case of Accra the pursuit of different urban and town planning policies from the early colonial period has produced what Frederic Jameson describes in terms of multi-synchronicities: "The co-existence of various synchronic systems or modes of production, each with its own dynamic, or time scheme" (1981: 82).

Accra's urban planning phases may productively be read as physical, in terms of the urban fabric of roads, buildings, public parks, and so forth, as well as emotional and affective, in terms of how people have reacted to the unfolding urban fabric. Each phase of Accra's urban planning was not simply superseded by subsequent forms of urban forms. Rather, such phases were only partially assimilated to an organic urban structure (driven by a singular modernist agenda). Ordinary people's response to these impartial assimilations was to try and "privatize" the city. Why is it, for example, that a vendor of cold drinks decides to set up a table at a slow intersection, with children in tow, and thus converts that site into a market for the immediate gratification of the pressing and universally acknowledged need for regular fluid intake in a tropical country? Or that a second-hand clothes vendor deploys the wall of one side of a government building to display his wares, reminding everyone of how precarious the boundary is between public and private and between local and transnational? This process of privatization is further compounded by the fact that there are several ethnicities that lay claim to the city. Whereas at independence the indigenous Gas formed 70 percent of the population, they are now a mere 15 percent and dwindling fast. Yet Accra's peculiarity is not "African" in any straightforward sense, but constituted by the historical interchange and conversion of local sentiments and experiences through and into transnational realities. And these transnational realities are both African, with respect to the interchange between Ghana and other African countries, and well beyond Africa itself, in terms of the dissemination of the Ghanaian diaspora in London, New York, Toronto, and elsewhere. The influences from the outside world also means that Accra's urbanism has been at once intimately local and remotely global (Piot 1999).

The Evolution of Accra

From the 1900s to the late 1940s colonial urban planning in Accra was driven essentially by two impulses, namely sanitation control and disaster management. Because the livelihood of the indigenous coastal neighborhoods was inextricably tied to the sea (fishing and the processing and storage of fresh fish, ferrying goods in boats to and from cargo ships at the port, etc.), it was initially extremely difficult for the colonial authorities to convince residents of the wisdom of decongestion. The British efforts were in line with colonial concerns with sanitation in other parts of Africa (Swanson 1977; Burke 1996). Indeed the early flashpoints in colonial/ indigenous relations in Accra centered on the institution of various administrative mechanisms for overseeing indigenous sanitation (Quarcoopome 1993). First the bubonic plague of 1908 and then the influenza epidemic of 1918 allowed the British colonial administration to persuade people that it was in their interest to move out of the congested coastal neighborhoods to newly developed outlying areas such as Tudu and Adabraka from the 1920s. By the 1950s both of these neighborhoods were well incorporated into the Central Business District. The big earthquake that hit the city on June 22, 1939 was also to provide a boon for colonial urban planners. Several low-cost housing developments were to follow in the wake of the earthquake, leading to a further decongestion of the immediate coastal neighborhoods of Ga Mashie and Nleshie and the development of areas such Mamprobi, to the west of the old city core along the coast and Kaneshie, some eight miles inland to the northwest.

The land use and urban planning products of these early sanitation-and-disaster-management processes were later to be rationalized by the colonial administration in two major planning documents of the 1950s (Acquah 1958; Trevallion and Hood 1958), both of which integrated the hitherto piecemeal urban development initiatives initially sponsored by the Canadian Governor Gordon Guggisberg (1919–27) into a more coherent template of urban planning. Even though the main tenets of the plans were to be adopted by the post-Independence government of Kwame Nkrumah, new political realities and further demographic and population pressures on the city led to a gradual abandonment of the colonial era plans. With the wave of migrants from different parts of the country attracted to the promise of largely non-existent jobs in the city, new residential neighborhoods and townships developed in a mixture of state planning and private innovation. Thus from the early 1970s to the mid-1990s neighborhoods such as Medina and Kasowa were to evolve into full-blown peri-urban "dormitory" townships on the outskirts of the metropolitan area, with a mixture of low-cost and unplanned housing that were to feed workers into the city center and further compound land use pressures.

The interracial children of Europeans and Africans furnished the first cohort of colonial-era elites, with well-known political and cultural figures such as James Bannerman, Henry Richter, and Carl Reindorf among others providing a wealth of historical evidence of the transnational vitality of these early mullatoes, as they were called in the historical record. These mullatoes were both merchant princes and educated elites, and in their commercial, political, and other networks mediated the early processes of proto-transnationalism and globalization for Accra. These mediations have continued to the present day, but, as we will see later, have also been vastly augmented by the expanding diaspora of Ghanaians abroad and by the ways in which they are helping to change ideas about ethnicity, gender relations, social identity, and urban space.

With certain qualifications, the paradigmatic nature of western urban planning was also to make its effect felt directly on Accra and other colonial cities like it. A document entitled *Accra: A Plan for the Town*, originally commissioned by the colonial government in 1954 but only presented to Kwame Nkrumah in 1958, had as one of its primary stated objectives the incorporation of parks, gardens, and monuments to reflect the urban logic of central London itself. Account was also to be taken of the specific natural ecological advantages enjoyed by the city: "no one can deny the appeal of palm trees, colourful vegetation, white sand, and the roar of the Atlantic surf" (Trevallion and Hood 1958: preface). The appeal to the natural advantages of the city as a justification for the 1958 plan was patently false. For what it actually did was to rationalize a series of piecemeal urban planning projects that had been instituted by the colonial government since the early 1900s. Apart from expanding the housing stock, increasing the number of roads and highways, and redesigning the Central Business District, the plan also sought to protect the essentially European parts of the city, several of which had a role to play in the later evolution of Oxford Street. Indeed, like other colonial towns, the European areas of Accra were ringed round by a veritable *cordon sanitaire* of parks, building restricted areas, and empty spaces. This was specifically achieved by placing the former racecourse as a buffer between Ridge Residential Area (formerly an exclusively European residential area) and Osu to the east. To the west the land that extended north from Accra Polytechnic to the Holy Spirit Cathedral, covering some 20.8 hectares was acquired as a building-free zone. The north of the residential area was protected by 118.35 hectares of what was originally assigned specially for dairy farming. The ultimate purpose of the disposition of these lands by the colonial government was to separate the European residential area from the African settlements at Adabraka and Labadi (see Odame-Larbi 1996; also Drakakis Smith 1987 and King 1976). Thus the urban experiments in European cities took a specifically segregationist inflection when transplanted onto the colonies. Postcolonial regimes were to take this blueprint and while by no means fulfilling its vision, still retained its essential lineaments in subsequent city planning. As we shall see, the economic nature of Oxford Street at Osu derives directly from the overall disposition of residential areas in the city that dates from the colonial period.

Spatial Logics and the Features of an Urban Fragment

The common division between commercial and residential streets is not directly pertinent to Oxford Street, for the spatial logics that govern it transcend what we might understand through the exclusive lens of the residential or commercial street. To unravel these spatial logics we have to think of the phenomena on the street – social, economic, cultural, historical, and political – as first and foremost intersectional. And despite the invocation of its namesake in London, the intersectionality of the phenomena on the street is only partly that between the global and the local; more suggestively, it is the conjuncture between variant and sometimes quite contradictory forms of economic activities and how they coalesce to define a particular spatial fix that produces Oxford Street's peculiar intersectionality.

The name Oxford Street is partly a chimerical projection of popular desire, for it is not the real name of the street under discussion and does not appear on any official maps of the city. Rather, it is part of a much longer road, officially called Cantonments Road. It is not clear how exactly the nickname originated, but it

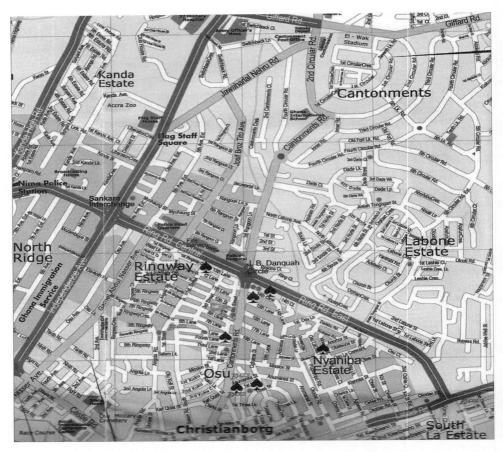

Figure 48.1 Map of Accra showing Cantonments Road and its immediate environs. Source: Accra City Map. Surf Publications 2003.

appears to have been popularized after the return to the country of various diasporic Ghanaians particularly from London following the end of military rule and the restoration of democracy in 1992. Oxford Street is roughly the mile-and-a-half of Cantonments Road that stretches between Mark Cofie to the south and Danquah Circle to the north. Cantonments Road itself stretches from the Oxford Street area and, merging with Fourth Circular Road, joins Airport Road to form a crucial south–north axis connecting some of the most important neighborhoods in the city. The farther south one goes along Cantonments Road and its connecting streets the closer one gets to the sea, and, more significantly, to Christiansborg Castle, the current seat of government.

Apart from locals to the street, many others come from the various workplaces that populate the area. Oxford Street and its immediate environs are dominated by a concentration of foreign missions, businesses, and restaurants, including until a couple of years ago what was the United States embassy (now moved into a grand fortress-like structure at the Cantonments neighborhood), the embassies of Egypt and Côte d'Ivoire, the Goethe Institute, and several internet cafés, electronic goods shops, and large grocery stores. There are also a large number of high-end restaurants, many of them Chinese, and the extraordinarily popular fast-food restaurants, Frankie's, Papaye, and Osu Food Court. Ryan's, an exclusive Irish pub with a largely white clientele reputed to be "the best Irish pub outside Dublin" is also walking distance from the street. Significant also in the evolution and maintenance of the specific commercial character of Oxford Street is its relative proximity to government buildings such as the State House, the Kwame Nkrumah Conference Centre, the Accra Sports Stadium, and the ministries. This enclave contains the headquarters of all government departments. Combined with the upwardly mobile neighborhoods we noted earlier, this is what lends Oxford Street the sense of a 24-hour hub of commercial activity, irrespective of the fact that it is in actuality not the most densely populated commercial part of town. That distinction is still reserved for the Central Business District.

The proximate neighborhoods to Cantonments Road (see Figure 48.1) include the Ringway Estates, East Ridge, Labone Estates, Cantonments itself, and Kanda, further to the northwest of the Oxford Street area. Several of these neighborhoods were planned as high-cost low-density housing to accommodate senior civil servants and expatriates during the colonial period. These areas are generally well appointed, with good access roads, excellent links to water and electricity supply, and a generally pleasant ecological to built ratio (lots of trees both along the avenues and within the house plots). The neighborhoods that touch on Cantonments Road have been the preferred residential areas of the ruling elites, their local satellites, and their international collaborators since the colonial period. Cantonments Road in general then has always been an important urban corridor traversed by these elites, members of which also own significant locations on Oxford Street, thus making its later conversion into an active economic hub always part of its potential.

The transnational evocativeness of Oxford Street derives partly from its implicit mimesis of the opportunities for urban self-fashioning replicated in many cities across the world, as it is in the contradictory structural features of the commercial boulevard, especially that between authenticity and imitation on the one hand, and between legal sale and fugitive vending on the other. On entering the street from the north side (that is, from Danquah Circle, see maps in Figures 48.1 and 48.2) one is struck by how crowded it looks with both vehicles and people, many large commercial buildings, and a proliferation of large billboards advertising everything from cellphone company products (MTN: "Everywhere You Go"; Tigo: "Express Yourself") to the United Emirates Airlines, and from Nescafé to sanitary pads (Femcare: "Confidence between Your Legs") and DStv ("Glow More"). There is a clear sense of entering a space where there is a permanent and insistent "invitation to treat" also found on passenger vehicles decorated with mobile and unpredictable slogans and mottoes that are both colorful and complex.

Cars and pedestrians, both Africans and foreign, mingle freely on the street, with mobile vendors attempting to do brisk business as they run alongside the private cars and commercial vehicles trying to make a sale. The items they carry vary: red snapper caught fresh from the sea is sold by women at the seashore itself. Then there are the more commonly young male vendors of fresh fruit from bananas,

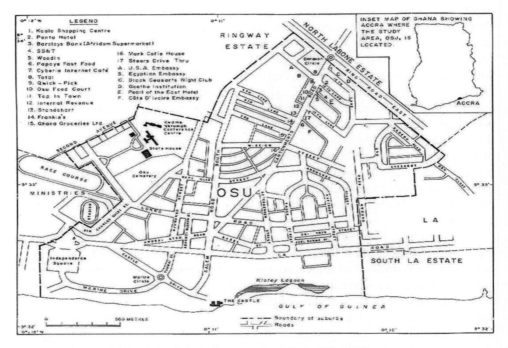

Figure 48.2 Map showing the study area, Osu, and surrounding areas.

pineapples, and oranges, to fresh coconuts and imported apples and grapes, and vendors of manufactured products from dog chains and flashlights to soccer balls.

Until the late 1980s it was the vitality of its night life that defined Oxford Street for most city-dwellers; currently it is the popularity of the fast-food joints on the street that has secured its fame. For unlike commercial streets elsewhere in the world, Accra's Oxford Street is defined not so much by fashion as by fast-food places which are transforming the take-out food habits of the general population. Whereas food from roadside stalls serving an assorted range of offerings such as rice and beans, kenkey and fish, and the delicious *kelewele* (ripe plantain marinated in a light mix of ginger, chilli peppers, and salt then fried) still remain popular as staple take-home meals of choice, it has now become increasingly common for the aspiring classes to travel from all across the city to Oxford Street to buy beefburgers, fried chicken and chips, and the obligatory sodas. More importantly, meals for funerals and other communal occasions, in the past prepared by women in the extended family and providing an important occasion to exchange gossip about who was doing what within the extended family system, have now been overtaken by the preference for prepackaged foods from outlets such as Papaye, Osu Food Court, and Frankie's. It has been almost impossible to attend a funeral in Accra in the last few years without being served a prepackaged meal. And prepackaged meals also feature significantly at government departmental end-of-year parties.

Despite the fact that it is the fast-food culture on Oxford Street that defines its local popularity it is really the number of banks that reveals its links to economic globalization. With five major banks (and growing), all with the now obligatory

ATM cashpoints in this mile-and-a-half stretch, the banking activity on the street seems to outstrip even that on the high street. And I do not refer here merely to the global financial nexus. There is something more banal and yet more complex. Given the specific concentration of variant activities on Oxford Street it is not so much the sheer number of banks that is pertinent to the globalized character of the street but the way in which they allow us to see the replication of a particular relation of capitalist exchange identifiable on the commercial boulevard elsewhere, namely that between money, specifically cash, and ephemeral consumption. The relationship is most clearly exemplified in the peculiar link to be seen between fast-food and cash-points in many globalized cities, be it London, New York, Paris, Istanbul, or Johannesburg. Wherever you see the big yellow arched M of McDonald's you are likely to find a cashpoint no more than 100 meters away, since most major fast-food joints until fairly recently resolutely insisted exclusively on cash for customer transactions. Indeed it is cash that dominates all transactions on the street and not credit cards. Very few stores and enterprises in Accra generally have proper facilities to process credit card transactions. Furthermore, given that most Ghanaians prefer *not* to put their money in banks (too much hassle and not enough trust are the primary reasons) the banks on Oxford Street are really there to serve the interest of the many businessmen and tourists who traverse the street on a daily basis.

Tigo Cellphone Adverts: Consuming the Transnational, Locally

As noted, Oxford Street is dominated by large advertising billboards. The Tigo cellphone company illustrates well the intersection of the translation of transnational images for local consumption. The Tigo adverts also play a subtle game of problematizing the intersection of Africanness and blackness by unsettling the question of what qualifies as black youth and how this is to be imagined in the modern day. Tigo is a subsidiary of Millicom International Cellular SA. According to the Millicom website the parent company originated in 1979 during the early days of the cellular industry as part of a phone company in Sweden. In 1982 Millicom, along with others in the industry, came together to form a company that later evolved into Vodaphone. Tigo Ghana is one of 16 Millicom subsidiaries in Central and South America, Africa, and Asia. With a current subscriber base of 2,741,122 users it is the second largest cellphone company in the country after MTN. Others that operate in the country are Kasapa, OneTouch (taken over in 2008 by Vodaphone), and Zain. Each cellphone company styles its adverts with a focus on distinguishing thematics to mark themselves off from their competitors. Thus whereas OneTouch, the originally government owned company, models itself on a thematic of familial harmony, MTN focuses on the theme of fun-filled youth activity and the inherent attractiveness of the movement involved in "getting somewhere" in contrast to that of those standing still. Tigo strikes a more distinctive cosmopolitan and transnational tone. This is well captured in their billboards, but in ways that are not entirely straightforward.

The pictures of the Tigo billboards in Figures 48.3 and 48.4 were taken in the summer of 2006, at the height of the soccer World Cup held in Germany, for which Ghana had qualified for the first time in its history. Both giant billboards were on either side of the same tall pillar at the entry into Oxford Street from Danquah

Figure 48.3   Tigo billboard. Author's photo, used with permission.

Circle. The first thing we note about the billboards is how unGhanaian the models in the pictures are compared to those on the MTN and OneTouch billboards. Note-worthy is the hue of their skin, which suggests immediately that they are of mixed-race origins. They also wear well-known fashion labels. In these billboards this is marked by the young woman in the yellow Calvin Klein T-shirt. Other billboards have a young man in a green Abercrombie and Fitch T-shirt in the foreground of the frame. Significantly also the models sport either dreadlocks or some form of highly expressive hairdos, such as the one of the young woman at the foreground of Figure 48.3. The overall sense conveyed by their skin hue, their fashion sense, and their gestures and demeanor is that these are black youth well versed in an urban youth chic that might be found in every large metropolis in the world today. This urban youth chic would not be exclusive to black youth either. An initial suspicion that the Tigo billboards were self-consciously referring to a transnational rather than a local circuit of imagery was later borne out by the discovery that the firm in charge of their outdoor advertising was called Creative Eye and that their brief was markedly different from that of any of the other cellphone companies. Creative Eye was founded in Dar es Salaam, Tanzania, in the early part of 2006

Figure 48.4 Tigo billboard. Author's photo, used with permission.

and had been specifically charged by Tigo with creating images of "Pan-African" black youth for its outdoor advertising. The particular billboard adverts in Accra were also run in Tanzania in the same period. The idea of Pan-Africanism being deployed here seems to have no relationship whatsoever to the ideals first espoused by Kwame Nkrumah, Gamel Abdel Nasser, and other charismatic African statesmen of the 1960s. Rather, it pertains to an image of black youth that allows it to be assimilated to various categories of fashion that are (a) not easily localizable, and (b) not limited to an exclusive black ethnic identity. The precise content of the images may have something to do with the roots of Creative Eye itself, since Dar es Salaam and East Africa in general are well noted for their multicultural mix, having been home to an active South Asian community from the 1880s, along with various waves of Islamic and Arab trading influences from at least the fourteenth century onwards. Swahili, the *lingua franca* of the region, is a hybrid mix of Arabic, Persian, and local words and has a long and distinguished literary tradition. Furthermore, it turns out that though the concept for the billboards was put together by Creative Eye, the assembling of the images into the generic format that we see on Tigo billboards was outsourced to a firm in Bangalore. That the people at

Creative Eye would choose such a placeless image of African youth makes complete sense in view of the fact that their understanding of what constitutes an "African" is subject to the highly hybridized and diasporic context of East Africa itself. For, given the waves of mass migrations that have defined sub-Saharan Africa since at least the sixteenth century, either in Africa or overseas, the modalities of what constitutes an African or indeed black identity are increasingly being put under scrutiny (Appiah 1992, 2006; Hill 2001, 2007). It would be too much to say that the Tigo adverts are fully conscious of such debates, but there is no doubt that in their image-making they have opted for a version of Africanness that would not be easily assimilated to a normative blackness. In addition to the transnational image of black youth in the billboard images, there is also evidence of a Caribbean flavoring to the collage, registered in the coconut trees and the clear blue skies that seem to envelope the entire frame.

What we see then is that the Tigo billboards create a generic image of blackness that performs a series of operations. Tigo invites its users to be part of a transnational image of blackness that is generalized enough so as to partake of an African and postmodern cosmopolitan semiotic simultaneously. The postmodernist ethos derives from the absolute replicability of that image across a series of cosmopolitan sites, whether these are in Africa itself or well outside its shores. And the evocation of the Caribbean provided by the palm trees and the blue skies situates the image within another intersecting grid of blackness, one associated with the diasporic black "brethren." It is the simultaneities of identities – African, Caribbean, Euro-African, etc. – and the invitation to local Tigo product consumers to imagine themselves within the images proffered by the billboards that is the central performative effect sought after. The semiotic efficacy of the Tigo adverts operates on multiple levels, starting from the direct invitation to consumption, which is no different from any other invitation to consumption proffered by the many multinational companies in Ghana, from Coca-Cola to Barclays to Adidas, but also proffering an invitation to self-fashioning through a pathway of transnational enchantment. The force of the invitation to such self-fashioning comes from being asked to imagine oneself as participating in a transnational circuitry of image-making by consumption of these particular products. And from the evidence of the Tigo adverts this does not reside exclusively within the particularity of being black or indeed ethnic. In this discourse blackness and ethnicity are just two commodifiable vectors of self-fashioning. In this instance transnational enchantment also invokes visions of prosperity and leisure (the blue-skied beaches of the Caribbean), a general idea of prosperity that is not that distant from the prosperity narratives such as those to be seen in evangelical discourses in the country for example (Gifford 2004).

Conclusion: Capitalism as Systematic Delirium

Given its name, Oxford Street is really the chimerical projection of Ghanaian cosmopolitan desire. But there are other ways in which it is chimerical: on the one hand it is geographically located in a particular part of Accra, and is a typical African commercial street that mixes the ethos of the bazaar with the qualities of WalMart or Marks and Spencer or Gap. And yet it is not of Accra at all, since in its form it also harbors the repetitively compulsive attraction to the ephemeral that is an intrinsic part of the commercial boulevard elsewhere in the world. Most importantly, it conceals within its form some of the most acute contradictions of globalization. This is captured in the fact that the adverts on the street imagine a different kind of blackness that may have very little to do with what it is to be African in the local context. To uncover this logic we are obliged to read the African commercial street in new ways. Oxford Street offers an excellent starting point.

Acknowledgments

A special thank you to my research assistants over the years, Barbara Archampong, Evans Mensah, and Vera Edu and to my friends and interlocutors in Accra, Jeeba Jehu-Appiah, Irene Odotei, and Nat Amarteifio, among others. I also want to thank Manor, who made a delightful film of the street for me and the incomparable Kwaku Sakyi-Addo, who interviewed me on my research for his TV series *Kwaku One on One*, in which he productively stimulated me to clarify the terms of my research.

References

Abrams, Philip (1978) Towns and economic growth: some theories and problems. In *Towns in Societies: Essays in Economic History and Historical Sociology*, ed. P. Abrams and E. A. Wrigley. Cambridge: Cambridge University Press, 9–33.

Acquah, Ione (1958) *Accra Survey: A Social Survey of the Capital of Ghana*. London: London Universities Press.

Appiah, Anthony Kwame (1992) *In My Father's House: Africa in the Philosophy of Culture*. New York: Oxford University Press.

Appiah, Anthony Kwame (2006) *Cosmopolitanism: Ethics in a World of Strangers*. New York: W. W. Norton.

Banton, Michael (1957) *West African City: A Study of Tribal Life in Freetown*. Oxford: Oxford University Press.

Burke, Timothy (1996) *Lifebuoy Men, Lux Women: Commodification, Consumption, and Cleanliness in Modern Zimbabwe*. Durham, NC: Duke University Press.

Castoriadis, Cornelius (1987) *The Imaginary Institution of Society*. Trans. Kathleen Blamey. Cambridge: Polity Press.

Cohen, Abner (1969) *Custom and Politics in Urban Africa: A Study in Hausa Migrants in Yoruba Towns*. London: Routledge and Kegan Paul.

De Boeck, Filip, and Plissart, Marie-Françoise (2004) *Kinshasa: Tales of the Invisible City*. Ghent: Ludion/Tervuren: Royal Museum for Central Africa.

Drakakis Smith, D. (1987) *The Third World City*. London: Methuen.

Ferguson, James (1999) *Expectations of Modernity: Myths and Meanings of Urban Life on the Zambian Copperbelt*. Berkeley: University of California Press.

Freund, Bill (2007) *The African City: A History*. Cambridge: Cambridge University Press.

Gifford, Paul (2004) *Ghana's New Christianity: Pentecostalism in a Globalizing African Economy*. Bloomington: Indiana University Press.

Hart, Keith (2006) Bureaucratic form and the informal economy. In *Linking the Formal and Informal Economy: Concepts and Policies*, ed. Basudeb Guha-Khasnobis, Ravi Kanbur, and Elinor Ostrom. Oxford: Oxford University Press, 21–35.

Hill, Lawrence (2001) *Black Berry, Sweet Juice: On Being Black and White in Canada*. Toronto: HarperPerennial.

Hill, Lawrence (2007) *The Book of Negroes*. Toronto: HarperCollins.

Jameson, Frederic (1981) *The Political Unconscious: Narrative as a Socially Symbolic Act*. London: Methuen.

Kilson, Marion (1974) *African Urban Kinsmen: The Ga of Central Accra*. London: C. Hurst and Company.

King, Anthony (1976) *Colonial Urban Development*. London: Routledge.

Lonsdale, John, and Berman, Bruce (1992) *Unhappy Valley: Conflict in Kenya and Africa*. Oxford: James Currey.

Manuh, Takyiwaa (2006) *An 11th region of Ghana? Ghanaians Abroad*. Accra: Ghana Academy of Arts and Sciences.

Ndegwa, Stephen N. (1997) Citizenship and ethnicity: an examination of two transition moments in Kenyan politics. *American Political Science Review* 91 (3): 599–616.

Odame-Larbi, Wordsworth (1996) Spatial planning and urban fragmentation in Accra. *Third World Planning Review* 18 (2): 193–215.

Osaghae, Eghosa E. (1995) *Structural Adjustment and Ethnicity in Africa*. Uppsala: Nordic African Institute.

Parker, John (2000) *Making the Town: Ga State and Society in Early Colonial Accra*. Portsmouth, NH: Heinemann.

Piot, Charles (1999) *Remotely Global: Village Modernity in West Africa*. Chicago: Chicago University Press.

Quarcoopome, Samuel S. (1993) The impact of urbanization on the socio-political history of the Ga Mashie people of Accra: 1877–1957. Unpublished PhD thesis, Institute of African Studies, University of Ghana.

Simone, AbdouMalik (2004) *For the City Yet to Come: Changing Life in Four African Cities*. Durham, NC: Duke University Press.

Swanson, Maynard (1977) The sanitation syndrome: bubonic plague and urban native policy in Cape Colony, 1900–1909. *Journal of African History* 18 (3): 387–410.

Trevallion, B. A. W., and Hood, Alan G. (1958) *Accra: A Plan for the Town*. Accra: Government Printer.

Chapter 49

Harlem Between Ghetto and Renaissance

Sharon Zukin

Harlem occupies a special place in the cultural geography of New York City and indeed in the social imaginary of all cities with marginalized concentrations of poor and underprivileged groups. Because of its history as a racial ghetto that attracted both talented and enterprising men and women of African descent and unskilled, perpetually poor, equally stigmatized others, Harlem developed as a spiritual home of the "black cultural sublime" (Gates 1997: 10). In the early years of the twentieth century, immigrants from the Caribbean, migrants from the rural south, and members of a sophisticated black bourgeoisie, all living in the same crowded area of the city, created cosmopolitan fusions across ethnic lines. Popular and experimental forms of jazz, fiction, poetry, and visual art that were made in Harlem in the 1920s and 1930s shaped the fluid language of modernism, marking the district for cultural innovation, on the one hand, and social exclusion, on the other.

Initially built for the middle class, Harlem's physical and social environment steadily deteriorated throughout the 1900s. Capital investment after World War II was mainly subsidized by the state in the form of public housing projects for the working poor. After 1970, the proportion of residents dependent on state welfare payments increased, especially in "the projects," as did the numbers of unemployed, drug addicts, and dealers. During the 1980s, however, the city government established loan programs to rehabilitate shabby housing and encouraged the formation of community-based, nonprofit development corporations. In the 1990s, the state put in place a new model of public–private investment, using both a federally funded enterprise zone and a business improvement district funded by local commercial property-owners; for a variety of reasons, this resulted in a burst of new residential construction and the growth of new types of stores. Though the area's redevelopment in the early years of the twenty-first century would certainly not have occurred

The New Blackwell Companion to the City Edited by Gary Bridge and Sophie Watson
© 2011 Blackwell Publishing Ltd

without direct input by the state, it also relied on the cultural image of the Harlem Renaissance that was fostered by the media and middle-class tastes. In crucial ways, though, this image contradicted Harlem's historic authenticity as a "dark ghetto" (Zukin 2009).

Ghettoization

Between 1905 and 1920 Harlem became a home for men and women who were not welcome to live in other areas of the city because of their skin color, the most visible sign of race (Osofsky 1963). Blacks were lured uptown to Harlem after a period of overbuilding when landlords and real-estate agents could not rent vacant apartments to whites. Immigrants from Russia and Italy and migrants from Puerto Rico lived in different parts of the neighborhood close to blacks but each forming its own enclave economy. The growing concentration of African Americans, however, created a complex "black metropolis" of different occupations and social classes (Drake and Cayton 1993 [1945]) as well as a tourist attraction for whites who wanted to "go slumming" in an "exotic" locale (Erenberg 1981; Heap 2009). Night clubs and bars provided jobs for blacks, especially during Prohibition in the 1920s and 1930s, but most owners and managers were white, and the clubs themselves were usually segregated. The nightlife economy also featured illicit and even illegal activities involving drugs, alcohol, and prostitution that were kept out of white neighborhoods by zealous property-owners and the police.

In the daytime, Harlem had a vibrant street life. Street vendors and small stores on 125th Street or Lenox Avenue shared space with sidewalk preachers and political speakers advocating Black Nationalism, emigration "Back to Africa," and other Afrocentric movements. On Sundays, families walked along Seventh Avenue to the great black churches. Artists and intellectuals met at the public library on 135th Street or in private apartments, where gatherings might include the poet Langston Hughes, the novelist Zora Neale Hurston, or social theorist and activist W. E. B. DuBois. During this extraordinary era of the Harlem Renaissance, the district was at the peak of its celebrity (Lewis 1981; Douglas 1995; Abdul-Jabbar 2007).

At the same time, Harlem residents suffered from high rates of disease, unemployment, and overcrowded housing. Despite the prosperous entrepreneurs and entertainers who lived on Strivers' Row, most Harlem residents worked as domestic servants or unskilled labor, and their poverty deepened during the Great Depression. In the 1930s, black consumers protested against the high prices for shoddy goods in local stores, which were mostly owned by whites, and white merchants' refusal to hire blacks for any but the most menial jobs. They also complained about mistreatment by the police who were still almost entirely white. Riots broke out in 1935, when a white shop clerk in a five-and-dime store accused a Puerto Rican teenager of shoplifting, and again in 1944, when a black soldier was shot and wounded by a white police officer.

After World War II, white families moved to new homes in the suburbs, but developers refused to sell houses to blacks or Latinos. The US government neither pushed for the suburbs' racial integration nor helped residents of the cities' ethnic neighborhoods to get mortgage loans from banks (Massey and Denton 1993). When the federal, state, and city governments began a massive program of slum clearing and building apartments for low-income families, the New York City Housing Authority placed a large number of the high-rise, high-density projects in Harlem (Bloom 2008). These "towers in the park" offered better housing than tenants had before, but they symbolized private developers' disregard for blacks and their stigmatization by the state as well.

A riot broke out in Harlem in 1964 because of distrust between black residents and the police, and another in 1968, after the assassination of Martin Luther King, Jr. During these tense years, social movements like the Black Panthers and (Puerto Rican) Young Lords pressed for improvements in housing, jobs, and schools and publicly expressed hostility to whites. Whites in turn became fearful of violence. Many white store owners closed their businesses, and white visitors stopped coming to shows at the Apollo Theater. The opening of an historical exhibition, "Harlem on My Mind" at the Metropolitan Museum of Art, was denounced by blacks as an example of whites' cultural imperialism; whites then denounced blacks for anti-white racism and anti-Semitism (Schoener 1979; Kimmelman 1995).

By the mid-1970s, absentee landlords were abandoning buildings instead of trying to maintain them at the low rents most Harlem residents could afford. These buildings were then vandalized by drug addicts and colonized by gangs, and taken over by the city government. Many were boarded up or torn down, leaving vacant lots. Middle-class Harlemites left for better neighborhoods in Brooklyn or Queens and even in the suburbs. They benefited from the civil rights laws which gradually opened more places for blacks in higher education and led to the hiring of more non-whites in the private sector. But Harlem was still considered a "dark ghetto," in the words of the psychologist Kenneth Clark (1965), where residents' social pathology reflected their inability to overcome white racism. During the 1980s, when other New York City neighborhoods began to be gentrified, no one could imagine Harlem meeting with such a fate (Schaeffer and Smith 1986).

The "Second" Harlem Renaissance

The steady growth of a new black middle class after the 1960s gradually created a pool of people who were willing to move to Harlem though they could afford to live elsewhere. Unlikely as it might seem, these black gentrifiers and a smaller stream of whites described the unique lure of Harlem in terms of the cosmopolitan aesthetics of the Harlem Renaissance. Like white gentrifiers, middle-class blacks were attracted by nineteenth-century townhouses of architectural distinction that they could buy for much lower prices in Harlem than in other areas of the city. They chose to ignore the real danger of crime and the neighborhood's physical deterioration as well as the lack of good public services and high-quality stores. Some of them bought houses at auction from the city government for only one dollar; the uncommonly low price was meant to encourage middle-income home-buyers, but since banks were unwilling to loan money in Harlem, and few purchasers could afford to make the necessary renovations on their own, most of the city-owned houses were not sold. Harlem's gentrifiers, therefore, required deep pockets and an extraordinary dedication to the neighborhood.

Besides gentrifiers who invested their own funds in Harlem, African American cultural entrepreneurs created new institutions, including the Studio Museum and the National Black Theater, that were funded by the state (the National Endowment for the Arts, the New York State Urban Development Corporation, and the New York City government), private foundations, and large corporations. More than a billion dollars of "shallow subsidies" for housing for middle-income residents were also put in place during the 1980s and 1990s by Mayor Edward I. Koch and new local community development corporations, led by the Abyssinian Baptist Church. In contrast to black gentrifiers, who were upper-middle-class professionals, financial managers, and entertainers, black middle-income residents tended to be school-teachers, government employees, or sales clerks. Together, they formed a small but significant base of home-owners that became stronger after crime rates began to fall in the mid 1990s.

For almost 20 years, though, gentrifiers had to weigh Harlem's deep cultural attraction against terrible living conditions. An advertising executive who grew up in the South and bought a four-family house in Harlem in 1998 tells of a common experience when he says there was a "state of emergency" with drug dealers when he moved in (Garb 2001). Walking on Lenox Avenue now, though, he feels he is a part of the "second" Harlem Renaissance. "When I walk these streets," he says, "and think that Langston Hughes lived here and Duke Ellington and all the others, it's wonderful. I can feel all of that history alive again."

As this language suggests, the dominant narrative of the "first" Harlem Renaissance highlights those parts of Harlem's culture that most people aspire to today: the affluence of Strivers' Row rather than poverty and vice, good times at the Cotton Club rather than at tenement rent parties, the aesthetics of Langston Hughes and Duke Ellington instead of the more critical racial politics of W. E. B. DuBois or Marcus Garvey. These images appeal to both middle-class blacks and whites who learned about the Harlem Renaissance in school.

State-Sponsored Renaissance

In contrast to the cultural flowering of the 1920s, the "second" Harlem Renaissance of the early 2000s was sponsored by the state and promoted by the media. Mayor Koch's housing subsidies, followed in the 1990s by Mayor Rudolph Giuliani's war on crime, offered safer streets and better housing for residents who were willing to take a risk. Articles in the mainstream media, beginning with the *New York Times*, drew attention to the architectural beauty of Harlem's nineteenth-century town-houses and to the restoration of these properties undertaken by upper-middle-class and celebrity black home-buyers such as the writer Maya Angelou and the professional basketball player Kareem Abdul-Jabbar, and these articles circulated widely on the internet. From the late 1990s, the real-estate section of the Sunday *New York Times* also began to feature occasional interviews with white home-buyers who said they were attracted to Harlem because they could buy larger homes of architectural distinction there, at lower prices than elsewhere in Manhattan or in the gentrified neighborhoods of Brooklyn. Articles and videos on the architectural restoration projects of Harlem's new home-buyers were posted on websites and cable TV. Nearly all of this media coverage spoke of a "new" or "second" Harlem Renaissance, nurtured by a "return" to Harlem by middle-class blacks from different ethnic and geographical origins.

Just as important, the "new" Harlem Renaissance reflected state subsidies for commercial redevelopment, with loans to new businesses made by the federal empowerment zone established by the US Congress in 1994. Empowerment zones use state-backed bonds to aid new business development in low-income districts; they also eliminate or reduce taxes and other payments in return for hiring local residents. Proposed by the Clinton Administration and influenced by Harlem's long-time Congressional representative Charles Rangel, the Upper Manhattan Empowerment Zone (UMEZ) covers both northern Manhattan and the Bronx, but the major share of state investment has been made in Harlem. Unlike earlier efforts to improve the area, UMEZ was oriented from the beginning toward "making markets" rather than expanding social programs. This goal expressed the pro-market view of centrist Democrats, including President Bill Clinton, as well as the pro-business politics of the Republican governor of New York State, George Pataki, and the Republican mayor of New York City, Rudolph Giuliani. It also complemented the emerging consensus in the 1990s on welfare reform, which ended social welfare payments to many men and especially single mothers, and required them to get a job, as well as the new private-sector role in managing commercial streets through business improvement districts (BIDs). UMEZ started out with a capital fund of $300 million: one third from the federal government, one third from the state, and one third from the city.

The empowerment zone's first big project was Harlem USA, a 275,000 square foot shopping and entertainment complex, which opened on 125th Street in 2000. Harlem USA was remarkable in many ways. It was a large, new, glass-fronted shopping center in one of Central Harlem's most prominent locations, near the historic Apollo Theater. Most stores around it were small, cheap, and individually owned: discount stores selling clothing and sneakers, smoke shops selling cigarettes and lottery tickets, take-out food shops, and providers of services like hair braiding and check cashing, as well as street vendors of incense and bootleg CDs. There were no movie theaters. In contrast to this extremely modest commercial landscape, the new Harlem USA offered a nine-screen multiplex showing first-run films; a modern bookstore and café, Hue-Man Books, owned by three African American women entrepreneurs; branches of well-known chain stores and a bank. The key to the whole development was the use of public-sector funding in the form of loans supported by bonds to leverage loans from the private sector and other state agencies. The resulting arrival of chain stores and banks, so taken for granted in other neighborhoods, led to an enormous amount of media coverage.

But luring developers and chains was not easy. Though a 50,000 square foot supermarket opened on East 125th Street in 1999, supported by the nonprofit Abyssinian Development Corporation, local merchants complained about the competition. Neither public nor private entrepreneurs found it easy to line up commitments by big commercial tenants despite lower rents than elsewhere in Manhattan and a residential population of underserved consumers.

UMEZ also provided loans to new cafés and boutiques that would attract a middle-class clientele. With the help of one of these loans, Settepani café, owned by an Italian-American bakery owner and his Ethiopian wife, opened on Lenox Avenue in 2001. A *New York Times* profile (Leland 2003) described it as a setting for "a new Harlem gentry in search of its latte," meeting and greeting each other in the "pale mist curling from pastel-hued scoops of gelato in porcelain bowls," and Set-tepani's outdoor café quickly became a meeting place for gentrifiers, journalists, and business owners. But with its handsome red awnings, panini, and lattes, the café aroused divided reactions in the community. For Harlem's emerging middle class, Settepani brought a needed amenity. For struggling, low-income residents, however, especially if they were black, Settepani put a public face on the displacement they feared (see Taylor 2002; Jackson 2005; Hyra 2008).

Nevertheless, both Settepani and Harlem USA represent the kind of change the city government desired. They illustrate the neighborhood's dual rezoning in 2005 for construction of high-rise apartment houses on the avenues and continued gen-trification of brownstone houses on the side streets, and anchor the commercial gentrification that will attract more affluent, highly educated residents, both black and white.

Commercial Gentrification

For many years, the biggest chain stores avoided US cities, especially their low-income ghettos. Their business model is based on customers who drive to the store, which would require a large plot of expensive urban land for a parking lot. Chain stores also depend on frequent deliveries of merchandise by truck, and city streets are too congested to allow this kind of flow. Most chain store executives, moreover, live in suburbs, and fear cities as dangerous. Together with rising crime rates from the 1960s to the 1990s and a perception that all ghetto dwellers are poor, this fear conditioned an avoidance of urban locations.

UMEZ appeared, though, just when views of inner-city business opportunities were changing. A professor at Harvard Business School, Michael Porter (1995), argued that residents of inner-city areas represented a pent-up demand for goods. He urged big stores to take advantage of both these captive consumers and their central locations. The US Department of Housing and Urban Development (1999) supported Porter's view. By the end of the 1990s, lower crime rates, higher land prices in more desirable neighborhoods, and over-saturation of suburban markets persuaded chain stores to take a good look at the incentives UMEZ offered for locating in Harlem. In the new climate of "making markets," UMEZ approved more than $335 million in grants, loans, and bonds between January 1995 and May 2006.

For the first time, moreover, the black community in New York City was able and willing to participate in business development. Many African Americans had begun to respect the Republican view, adopted by the Clinton Administration, that the poor should be weaned from dependency on government aid. Black leaders had grown tired of trying to tear down the wall of public disapproval and investors' apathy that circled the dark ghetto, and a new generation of African American lawyers and MBAs was eager to become entrepreneurs. These professionals had little in common with the separatist movements of the past that had advocated either black capitalism or black power. Some even joined the Republicans, breaking the strong political ties African Americans had forged with the Democratic Party during the New Deal. UMEZ offered an opportunity for businesses and Republican Party leaders to circumvent the networks forged for years by Harlem's black politicians.

The empowerment zone's strategies, the ambitions of a new generation of black entrepreneurs, and the changing attitudes of retail chains transformed Central Harlem's commercial landscape (Zukin *et al.* 2009). In 1995, only 3 percent of more than 600 stores were branches or franchises of chains. In 2000, there were fewer stores, but 7 percent of them – twice as many as in 1995 – were connected to chains. By 2006, with many old buildings torn down or boarded up for redevelopment, and new stores occupying larger spaces, only 300 stores remained, but 16 percent of them – almost three times as many in total as in 1995 – were chains.

Not all of Harlem's residents were happy about the new shopping opportunities, for they saw them as a sign of gentrification. "At a June [2002] town hall meeting at the Schomberg Center for Research in Black Culture," a reporter writes in the *Village Voice* (Little 2002), "audience members heckled forum speakers, including representatives from banks, UMEZ, the city's Housing Preservation Department (HPD), and the public housing authority. One elderly woman, whose voice was stronger than the fragile fist she threw in the air, screamed: 'Where the hell are the politicians?'" A few years later, when a developer told a conference audience, "There's very little real estate speculation going on in Harlem right now," a woman in the audience shouted out, "Ha! There's nothing but speculators running around up there." Then the owner of a small store complained that he could not meet the competition from "corporate big-box stores" (Vitullo-Martin 2006).

UMEZ loans also fostered new cafés, restaurants, boutiques, and services (Zukin *et al.* 2009). Some offered spa treatments and cosmetic products oriented toward African Americans or Afrocentric art and décor; others, like Settepani, featured the transnational aesthetic of upscale consumption. Though there were only a modest number of these stores in Central Harlem, their share of storefront space rose from zero in 1995 to 10 percent in 2006. At the same time, the share of traditional, cheap, locally owned stores fell from 84 to 74 percent.

Like chain stores, the opening of boutiques in Central Harlem shows the impact of state-managed redevelopment. Five of a sample of 15 new entrepreneurial retail businesses that opened between 2000 and 2006 received UMEZ loans, and three of those five also received help from the Clinton Foundation, the former president's organization whose office is on 125th Street (Zukin *et al.* 2009). A sixth new retail merchant received a loan from the US Small Business Administration; the other nine relied on their own capital and that of outside investors. UMEZ funding was not easy to get. A successful loan application required a prospective merchant to fill out many bureaucratic forms, develop a coherent business plan, and show access to other sources of financing. As these requirements suggest, many of Harlem's new retail entrepreneurs were members of the new black middle class. They had college, master's, and law degrees and had already established themselves in financial, administrative, or professional careers. Unlike previous generations of small shopkeepers in Harlem, these store owners had access to solid funding, often from wealthy black investors, performers, and professional athletes.

Not all of the new retail entrepreneurs were black, however, or came from the Harlem community. Slightly fewer than half of all the owners and co-owners of the 15 stores in the research sample were Harlem natives or residents. The others included a restaurateur from India, a café owner from France, and an art gallery owner from Chicago. Because of Harlem's history of contentious racial politics, it is crucial, though, for new entrepreneurs to construct a personal narrative that connects them with the black community. The Ethiopian co-owner of Settepani is often interviewed in the media; the African American owners of Carol's Daughter, a cosmetics firm, and Harlem Vintage, the area's first wine store, network with community organizations; the Liberian co-founders of Nubian Heritage, another cosmetics company with a flagship spa in Harlem, are described as former street vendors who began by selling "their wares along the sidewalks of 125th Street" (www.nubian-heritage.com). In fact, they majored in business at Babson College in Boston. They did sell their home-made products on the street, but they also organized street vendors into a distribution network.

Onward to the New Harlem

Though the state and city governments deny that they have fostered gentrification, many Harlem residents feel under attack by the forces of upscale change. Until the economic crisis broke out in 2008, renovation of townhouses and construction of new apartment houses – and far less crime than in the past – continued to change Harlem's streets. Despite the continued majority of a black, mainly low-income population, the area attracted increasing numbers of white middle-class residents, including many students, who patronized the new boutiques, restaurants, and cafés whether they had an Afrocentric, Afro-French, or Italian theme.

Two redevelopment plans adopted by the city council in 2008 stirred huge resentment for further diluting the community's historic black identity: first, Columbia University's acquisition of a large site in West Harlem, from 125th to 135th Streets, to expand its campus and second, the City Planning Commission's rezoning of 125th Street, from Broadway to Second Avenue, for high-rise commercial and residential buildings. Both plans had been discussed for years, with some concessions being made, at least in principle, to demands for affordable housing and jobs. But Columbia's $7 billion expansion, designed by the distinguished architect Renzo Piano, will take up all of a 17-acre site, and the rezoning, like others in a series of nearly 90 zoning plans adopted since 2002 by the Bloomberg Administration, will likely raise rents along Harlem's major commercial thoroughfare and displace most remaining small individually owned stores. A compromise gave developers the right to build taller buildings if they would reserve storefront space for arts and cultural facilities, but these may include commercial movie chains.

"Soon it will all be millionaires and the native people won't be able to live in their homes," warned Shikhulu Shange, the African-born owner of the Record Shack, a well-known music store on 125th Street, when he spoke at the City Planning Commission's hearing on the rezoning plan. "Soon there won't be any black-owned businesses." Soon, in fact, Shange would know the consequences of rezoning first hand. Threatened with losing his sublease in 1995 when the store that held the main lease wanted to expand, he lost the space forever in 2007 because the black church that owned the building sold it to a developer, and he ended up hawking CDs on the street. "What we have built, they want it now," Shange told the hearing. "They want the culture" (Harpaz 2007; Edozien *et al.* 2008; Williams 2008).

The economic crisis halted sales of luxury apartments in Harlem and put capital investment at risk. But the state's support for commercial redevelopment and the many new buildings that are already in place strengthen the image of a new, upscale community and weaken the cultural authenticity of the old one. Though few long-time residents wish to return to the dark ghetto's worst days, the cosmopolitan entrepreneurialism of the new Harlem Renaissance imposes a new image and a different sort of authenticity.[1]

Acknowledgment

Some of the research for this chapter comes from a study conducted by the author and five students in the PhD program in sociology at the Graduate Center of the City University of New York. The author wishes to thank Valerie Trujillo, Danielle Jackson, Peter Frase, Tim Recuber, and Abraham Walker, and also to express appreciation to Babette Audant, Bahar Aykan, Aneta Kostrzewa, Yvonne Liu, and Soniya Munshi, who worked with us on a preliminary stage of the project.

Note

[1] Several items listed in the References will be helpful to readers who wish to know more about current issues in "black-on-black" gentrification: the book on Harlem and Chicago by Derek Hyra (2008), and the books on Harlem by John Jackson, Jr. (2005) and Monique Taylor (2002). Mary Pattillo's ethnographic study of the gentrification of a low-income, African American neighborhood near the University of Chicago (Pattillo 2007) offers rich material for comparison. For a contrary view, Lance Freeman's study (2006) of Harlem and a neighborhood in Brooklyn argues that the negative effects of gentrification have been greatly exaggerated. For more detail on the processes described in this chapter and comparison with changes in other New York City neighborhoods, see Zukin 2010 and Zukin et al. 2009.

References

Abdul-Jabbar, K., with Obstfeld, R. (2007). *On the Shoulders of Giants: My Journey Through the Harlem Renaissance*. New York: Simon and Schuster.

Bloom, N. D. (2008) *Public Housing That Worked: New York in the Twentieth Century*. Philadelphia: University of Pennsylvania Press.

Clark, K. B. (1965) *Dark Ghetto: Dilemmas of Social Power*. New York: Harper & Row.

Douglas, A. (1995) *Terrible Honesty: Mongrel Manhattan in the 1920s*. New York: Farrar Straus and Giroux.

Drake, St C., and Cayton, H. R. (1993 [1945]) *Black Metropolis: A Study of Negro Life in a Northern City*, rev. edn. Chicago: University of Chicago Press.

Edozien, F., Kronfeld, M. J., and Geller, A. (2008) New-look Harlem clears a big hurdle. *New York Post* March 11.

Erenberg, L. A. (1981) *Steppin' Out: New York Nightlife and the Transformation of American Culture, 1890–1930*. Chicago: University of Chicago Press.

Freeman, L. (2006) *There Goes the 'Hood*. Philadelphia: Temple University Press.

Garb, M. (2001) If you're thinking of living in West Harlem: brownstones in Manhattan, at a discount. *New York Times* February 25.

Gates, H. L., Jr. (1997) Harlem on our minds. *Critical Inquiry* 24 (1) (autumn): 1–12.

Harpaz, B. J. (2007) Harlem's tourist appeal remains strong despite change. Available online at http://www.usatoday.com/travel/news (December 20).

Heap, C. (2009) *Slumming: Sexual and Racial Encounters in American Nightlife, 1885–1940.* Chicago: University of Chicago Press.

Hyra, D. S. (2008) *The New Urban Renewal: The Economic Transformation of Harlem and Bronzeville.* Chicago: University of Chicago Press.

Jackson, J. L., Jr. (2005) *Real Black: Adventures in Racial Sincerity.* Chicago: University of Chicago Press.

Kimmelman, M. (1995) Art view; culture and race: still on America's mind. *New York Times* November 19.

Leland, J. (2003) A new Harlem gentry in search of its latte. *New York Times* August 7.

Lewis, D. L. (1981) *When Harlem Was in Vogue.* New York: Knopf.

Little, R. G. (2002) The new Harlem: who's behind the real estate gold rush and who's fighting it? *Village Voice* September 18–24.

Massey, D. S., and Denton, N. A. (1993) *American Apartheid: Segregation and the Making of the Underclass.* Cambridge MA: Harvard University Press.

Osofsky, G. (1963) *Harlem: The Making of a Ghetto.* New York: Harper & Row.

Pattillo, M. (2007) *Black on the Block.* Chicago: University of Chicago Press.

Porter, M. (1995) The competitive advantage of the inner city. *Harvard Business Review* 73 (3): 55–71.

Schaeffer, R., and Smith, N. (1986) The gentrification of Harlem? *Annals of the Association of American Geographers* 76: 347–65.

Schoener, A. (1979) Introduction to the new edition. In *Harlem On My Mind*, ed. A. Schoener. 2nd edn. New York: Dell.

Taylor, M. (2002) *Harlem Between Heaven and Hell.* Minneapolis: University of Minnesota Press.

US Department of Housing and Urban Development (1999) *New Markets: The Untapped Retail Buying Power in America's Inner Cities.* Washington, DC: US Department of Housing and Urban Development.

Vitullo-Martin, J. (2006) First fully market-rate apartments come to Harlem. *New York Sun* March 2.

Williams, T. (2008) Longtime Harlem fixture now sells CDs on street. *New York Times* October 9.

Zukin, S. (2010) *Naked City: The Death and Life of Authentic Urban Places.* New York: Oxford University Press.

Zukin, S., Trujillo, V., Frase, P., Jackson, D., Recuber, T., and Walker, A. (2009) New retail capital and neighborhood change: boutiques and gentrification in New York City. *City and Community* 8 (1): 47–64.

Chapter 50

Gentrification of the City

Tom Slater

Introduction

In 1951, Ruth Glass took up a post as Director of Social Research at University College London. Her sustained intellectual and critical engagement with the postwar upheavals that resulted in the formation of the British welfare state led her to immersion in the writings of Marx and Engels, and encouraged her gradual switch from urban planning to urban sociology. The links between housing and class struggle in London (particularly in Islington, where she lived) became her long-term research interest, and concerns about the accelerating rehabilitation of Victorian lodging houses, tenurial transformation from renting to owning, property price increases, and the displacement of working-class occupiers by middle-class incomers led her to coin the term "gentrification" in 1964. By the time Glass passed away in 1990, gentrification had not only generated a large international literature; it had become a word around which class struggles and urban social movements (fighting for the rights of those at the bottom of the urban class structure in a variety of contexts) could mobilize and gain visibility and political momentum. This remains the case today, and that large literature has now morphed into an immense body of scholarship, one so large that it makes summaries, syntheses, and concise critique a considerable challenge. Consider, for instance, that there have been six special issues of journals on the topic of gentrification since 2003!

As Ruth Glass intended, "gentrification" simply yet very powerfully captures the class inequalities and injustices created by capitalist urban land markets and policies. The rising house expense burden for low-income and working-class households, and the personal catastrophes of displacement, eviction, and homelessness,

The New Blackwell Companion to the City   Edited by Gary Bridge and Sophie Watson
© 2011 Blackwell Publishing Ltd

are symptoms of a set of institutional arrangements (private property rights and a free market) that favor the creation of urban environments to serve the needs of capital accumulation at the expense of the social needs of home, community, family. Neil Smith (2002: 445) has outlined precisely why it is important to retain an analytical commitment to the critical intent behind Ruth Glass's coinage: "Precisely because the language of gentrification tells the truth about the class shift involved in the 'regeneration' of the city, it has become a dirty word to developers, politicians and financiers."

Over the years there have been numerous deliberate attempts to avoid the language of gentrification completely, and more recently some attempts to gentrify the term itself, putting a positive gloss on a word that was coined to signify a worrying trend, one that raises vital, normative questions about the future of urban places. As Glass went on to say in her famous essay: "London ... may acquire a rare complaint ... [It] may soon be faced with an *embarras de richesses* in her central area – and this will prove to be a problem, too" (Glass 1964: 141).

Gentrification commonly occurs in urban areas where prior disinvestment in the urban infrastructure creates opportunities for profitable redevelopment, where the needs and concerns of business and policy elites are met at the expense of urban residents affected by work instability, unemployment, and stigmatization. It also occurs in those societies where a loss of manufacturing employment and an increase in service employment has led to expansion in the amount of middle-class professionals with a disposition towards central city living and an associated rejection of suburbia. Considerable time, energy, and ink have been consumed arguing over whether it is the quest for profit or the expansion of the middle classes that offers the best explanation of gentrification. Initially a reflection of exciting theoretical and ideological contests, it is argued here that this is now a stale, turgid debate, despite some attempts to persevere with it (Hamnett 2003; Butler 2007). But whilst it would be analytically tedious to spend this chapter immersed in this debate, it would be disrespectful and politically questionable to ignore it completely. Therefore, this chapter offers both a *temperature check* and a *prognosis* – a condensed, introductory, and critical glimpse of the literature for newcomers to the topic, together with some thoughts on where gentrification research might go if the literature is to be of increasing political salience or consequence. In particular I want to argue that a commitment to viewing the most serious consequence of gentrification – displacement – "from below" (i.e., in the terms of those who experience it) is essential if critical scholarship on gentrification is to overthrow the mainstream scholarship that does nothing more than parrot and perpetuate the status quo (widening class inequality in cities) with so much appeal to the media and to neoliberal policy elites.

Invitation to a Debate

The title of this chapter matches that of the first edited collection on the topic published in 1986, edited by Neil Smith and Peter Williams. Whilst every chapter in the collection has become a classic in its own right, particular conceptual insights can be gained from reading the editors' eloquent introduction, especially when placed in the context of how the literature has unfolded since the mid-1980s. In recent years there has been considerable disagreement over how to define gentrification; in short, whether gentrification should refer only to the residential rehabilitation described by Ruth Glass, or whether it refers to a much more large-scale production of urban space for middle-class consumers, involving *inter alia* "new-build" developments on vacant land (Davidson and Lees 2005). It is unfortunate that those insisting that we go no further than the fine details of Ruth Glass's original definition (Boddy 2007) did not consult the words of Smith and Williams written over 20 years ago:

> If we look back at the attempted definitions of gentrification, it should be clear that we are concerned with a process much broader than merely residential rehabilitation ... [A]s the process has continued, it has become increasingly apparent that residential rehabilitation is only one facet ... of a more profound economic, social, and spatial restructuring. In reality, residential gentrification is integrally linked to the redevelopment of urban waterfronts for recreational and other functions, the decline of remaining inner-city manufacturing facilities, the rise of hotel and convention complexes and central-city office developments, as well as the emergence of modern "trendy" retail and restaurant districts ... Gentrification is a visible spatial component of this social transformation. A highly dynamic process, it is not amenable to overly restrictive definitions. (Smith and Williams 1986: 3)

It is also worth noting the account provided by Saskia Sassen in a book that was influential well beyond the field of gentrification:

> Gentrification was initially understood as the rehabilitation of decaying and low-income housing by middle-class outsiders in central cities. In the late 1970s a broader conceptualization of the process began to emerge, and by the early 1980s new scholarship had developed a far broader meaning of gentrification, linking it with processes of spatial, economic and social restructuring. (Sassen 1991: 255)

To label as anything other than gentrification the construction of upmarket housing aimed at young professionals in or on formerly working-class industrial spaces (for example, vacant dockyards or warehouses), and to use a term like "revitalization" or "regeneration" to characterize the implosion of low-income public housing projects in favor of mixed-income developments, is analytically erroneous and politically conservative. Kate Shaw provides an especially helpful and vivid account of what gentrification is today when she calls it

> a generalised middle-class restructuring of place, encompassing the entire transformation from low-status neighbourhoods to upper-middle-class playgrounds. Gentrifiers' residences are no longer just renovated houses but newly built townhouses and high-rise apartments. Their workplaces are as likely to be new downtown or docklands office developments as warehouse studios. Gentrification extends to retail and commercial precincts, and can be seen in rural and coastal townships as well as cities ... Designer shops, art galleries, bars and restaurants form the background to a landscape of people in semi-public space (tables on the footpath they must pay to occupy) watching the passing parade and sipping chardonnay from a boutique winery, beer from a microbrewery, coffee from organic beans grown in the developing country *du jour*. (Shaw 2008: 2)

In terms of sheer geographical scale we are dealing with a quite different urban phenomenon than what was observed in the 1960s (Lees *et al.* 2008: 128–61). As implied in my introduction, where Ruth Glass does remain important and relevant is less in the empirical details of 1960s Islington, and more in her critical perspective on class transformation, and her deep commitment to social justice.

Following their claim that gentrification was an intrinsic part of something much larger than residential rehabilitation, Smith and Williams offered readers an "invitation to a debate," or more accurately a set of debates, that ran through the pages of the book. They set out five related themes that occupied the analytical attention of the book's contributing authors, where differences of opinion were clear. Three in particular have come to dominate the ensuing literature:

1   Production-side versus consumption-side explanations.
2   Is there a "new middle class" and what is its role?
3   What are the costs of gentrification today and in the future?

Almost a quarter of century later it is instructive to wed social and epistemological critique and consider the nature and extent of knowledge on each of these three themes as the gentrification process has unfolded in different societies. Due to space limitations I cannot cover here all the important themes in gentrification inquiry,[1] so the rest of this chapter thus offers readers a fresh invitation to the gentrification debates in an attempt to provide a solid point of departure for further intellectual engagement. I will conclude with some comments on where gentrification research might go if it is to be of political salience and analytical coherence.

Production-side versus consumption-side explanations

As is clear following a careful read of the entire Smith and Williams collection, the production-side versus consumption-side explanation was a heated and fast-moving debate by the mid-1980s, even if, as the editors quite rightly stated, "few are arguing an exclusively production-based or consumption-based argument" (Smith and Williams 1986: 5). But what are those arguments? To cut a long story as short as possible, it is absolutely vital to register that *both* arguments emerged in reaction to the obfuscations of 1970s neoclassical economists' take on gentrification as a natural, inevitable market adjustment process, something to be celebrated as part of an apparent middle-class return to the central city from suburbia (Lipton 1977; Wheaton 1977; Kern 1981; LeRoy and Sonstelie 1983; Schill and Nathan 1983). Those prioritizing a production perspective rejected the neoclassical view that gentrification was an expression of the changed consumption choices among certain sections of the middle class, and instead emphasized the role of capital and its institutional agents (public and private) in creating gentrifiable spaces (Smith 1979; Clark 1987; Engels 1994; Hammel 1999). Gentrification through a production lens explains the process as a consequence of the uneven investment of capital in certain land uses, its devaluation through use and systematic disinvestment, and the opportunities for profitable reinvestment created by these capital flows. The most important and influential theory in this tradition is Neil Smith's (1979) rent-gap thesis, as provocative and convincing today as it was when it was first elaborated.[2] Those explaining gentrification from a consumption perspective reacted to simplistic neo-classical accounts of demographic changes and lifestyle preferences by illustrating how changes in the industrial and occupational structure of advanced capitalist cities, occurring as they did at a time of significant social and cultural upheaval (post-1968), produced an expanding pool of gentrifiers with a disposition towards central-city living, and an associated rejection of suburbia for the blandness and monotony it symbolized (Ley 1986; Hamnett 1991; Butler 1997).[3] Arguably the most important analyses in this tradition have come from the pen of David Ley, worked into his *magnum opus* in 1996 that thoroughly explored gentrification in six Canadian cities, a book particularly memorable and admirable for exemplary fusion of quantitative measures with qualitative accounts.

A very influential survey of the literature by Chris Hamnett (1991) portrayed Neil Smith and David Ley as polar opposites and the *de facto* representatives of mutually exclusive production and consumption explanations respectively, and ensured that a generation of scholars saw gentrification in stark binary terms of production or consumption, supply or demand, structure or agency, economics or culture. Whilst Hamnett's article had its strengths, especially in outlining why academic interest in gentrification is so intense, its legacy was obstructive. I have argued elsewhere (Slater 2006) that the production-consumption (or Smith–Ley) debate in gentrification research is the most overdrawn and misrepresented contest in the history of urban studies. Both analysts are not nearly as one-sided in the explanation of gentrification as many newcomers to the topic might think. To argue that David Ley ignored economic transformation in Canadian cities in his work is nothing short of preposterous, and the same can be said for any writing which gives the impression that Neil Smith ignored the cultural aspects of gentrification in his writings on New York's gentrification. Despite crucial interventions suggesting ways to work through competing theoretical tensions (Clark 1992; Lees 1994), analytical energy was sapped by irritating dualisms and irksome squabbling about whether it was Smith or Ley who had the most convincing explanation. By the mid- to late 1990s, many researchers lost interest (see Bondi 1999), and now any essay pressing the same dualisms should be treated with the utmost suspicion. A solid explanation of gentrification in any context must recognize the importance of production and consumption factors, and how they work together to result in neighborhood expressions of class inequality (Ley 2003). It does not matter whether production or consumption is viewed as more important in driving gentrification, so long as neither is completely ignored. Most important of all, writing on gentrification must not get caught up in what is now an old debate. If it must be revisited, it is essential to consult the original essays of those associated with competing explanations, in order to guard against further misrepresentation and theoretical confusion.

Is there a "new middle class" and what is its role?

The changing class structure of capitalist societies has for several decades been a major research theme in urban sociology, where the debate essentially boils down to the longitudinal *character* of the class structure (how many people fit into certain pre-defined class categories), and to a lesser extent how class struggles and class differences are reconfigured and redefined in the context of wider macroeconomic, social, and cultural transformations (see Butler and Watt 2007, for an excellent summary). In the context of gentrification research, when Smith and Williams (1986) noted an emerging concern with a "new middle class" and pointed out that a number of chapters in their collection "touch on this issue" (p. 7), they could not have foreseen the astonishing mushrooming of scholarship examining the growth, life, and times of the gentrifying middle classes that we have seen since the mid-1990s. This scholarship emerged for two reasons; first, to probe far deeper than the sweeping neoclassical generalizations that gentrification is a natural outcome of shifts in the trade-offs between accessibility and space that make central city locations more attractive for wealthier households; and second, as a challenge to Marxist political-economic explanations that were seen to focus narrowly on cycles of investment and fluctuations of urban land rent, to the neglect of human agency. As Damaris Rose memorably put it,

> "gentrifiers" are not the mere bearers of a process determined independently of them. Their constitution, as certain types of workers and as people, is as crucial an element in the production of gentrification as is the production of the dwellings they occupy. (Rose 1984: 56)

A rare point of agreement among analysts of gentrification is that *class* should be the central focus (Wyly and Hammel 2001). The overwhelming research response has been to investigate the growth and behavior of the middle classes, and particularly *why* they are seeking to locate in previously disinvested neighborhoods. Over the years there has been increasing theoretical sophistication in research undertaken in many different countries that seeks to understand middle-class gentrifiers – a very diverse, ambivalent group that cannot be reduced to popular slanders of "yuppies," not least because the negative connotations of that term are at odds with the "marginal" economic position of some gentrifiers (Rose 1984), and the left-liberal politics that many gentrifiers demonstrate at the ballot box (Ley 1994). Furthermore, even so-called "yuppies" have limited choices in the housing market.

Probably the most sophisticated attempts to understand the practices of gentrifiers have come from those who have drawn upon the work of Pierre Bourdieu in his classic book *Distinction* (1984), particularly his concern with understanding and explaining the middle-class *habitus*.[4] In a striking study of the "loft living" movement in Montreal, Podmore (1998) argues that the gentrified district is nothing short of the spatial expression of a new middle-class *habitus*. Butler with Robson (2003) use this theoretical approach to develop the notion of a "metropolitan *habitus*" in London, drawing on fieldwork in six very different neighborhoods and relating middle-class fractions to various forms of capital (with particular emphasis on social capital). Bridge (2006: 65) interprets their work as even "suggesting a series of mini-habituses," but in his own work (Bridge 2001a) has argued that the *habitus* concept, derived from what he sees as Bourdieu's passive and oversocialized view of human action, means that it needs to be wedded to rational action theory if we are to interpret why gentrifiers invest their cultural, social, and economic capital in areas considered to be "risky" by investors and real-estate agents. This is in fact the underlying research question of all those analysts who are uneasy with both neoclassical and Marxist explanations of gentrification: why do gentrifiers seek to locate in areas that have been subjected to disinvestment and are affected by territo-rial stigmatization? Furthermore, since much available evidence reveals that gentri-fiers view living in the central city as "a mark of distinction in the constitution of an identity separate from the constellation of place and identity shaped by the suburbs" (Ley 1996: 211), some researchers have directed their attention to how this social distinction marked out on the streets of gentrifying neighborhoods. This strand of inquiry investigates what has become known as the *gentrification aesthetic* (Bridge 2001b), an effort to reveal the aesthetic strategies that gentrifiers (and those who produce space for them) employ to distinguish themselves from other social class groups. A classic essay in the Smith and Williams collection by Jager (1986) on Victorian landscapes in gentrifying Melbourne built upon the pioneering work of Zukin (1982) on loft development in lower Manhattan to pave the way for subsequent investigations that sought to explain the economic valorization of the gentrification aesthetic, or the ways in which places once deemed hip, authentic, trendy, and subversive quickly become appropriated, manufactured, and mass-produced kitsch for higher-earning groups (Mills 1988; Ley 2003).

Class is not the only axis of difference towards which researchers have focused their attention. Since the early 1980s, coinciding somewhat with the advent of both postmodernism and the cultural turn in the social sciences, considerable analytical energy has been expended towards the intersections of fine-grained class positions with other dimensions of difference, such as gender, sexuality, and race/ethnicity. There is no space here for a lengthy summary,[5] other than to point out that some of this work has become extremely influential; Castells (1983) on gay gentrification in the Castro in San Francisco and Rothenberg (1995) on lesbians creating social spaces in Park Slope, New York City; Rose's pathbreaking (1984) article on gentri-fication as an outcome of professional women seeking support networks and oppor-tunities unavailable in the suburbs; Bondi (1991) and Warde (1991) on gentrification as an expression of professional women responding to changing structures of patri-archy; Taylor (2003) on black gentrification in Harlem, New York City; and Pat-tillo's (2007) ethnographic portrait of the black middle class resettling in Chicago's South Side. Whilst there is much to admire in work that retains a spirit of social critique in interpreting the residential peregrinations of different types of gentrifier (Talja Blokland's eloquent 2003 study of a Rotterdam neighborhood being an exemplar of this spirit), my own view is that this area of research, as well as being somewhat saturated, has become less critical in recent years, anchored in thinly veiled empathetic sentiments for middle-class gentrifiers that serve to blot out any other human agents involved in the process (Butler 2007), such as those "producing space for progressively more affluent users," as Hackworth (2002) terms it, and, crucially, working-class groups on the receiving end of urban policies that favor middle-class settlement at the expense of housing affordability.

What are the costs of gentrification today and in the future?

Displacement from home and neighbourhood can be a shattering experience. At worst it leads to homelessness, at best it impairs a sense of community. Public policy should, by general agreement, minimize displacement. Yet a variety of public policies, particu-larly those concerned with gentrification, seem to foster it. (Marcuse 1985: 931)

Two chapters in Smith and Williams focused directly on the question of displacement, a reflection of what was a lively debate in the early 1980s, and the subject of highly sophisticated inquiries that have not lost their (varying) political bite with the passage of time. Many of the articles in early collections on gentrification such as Laska and Spain (1980), Schill and Nathan (1983), and Palen and London (1984) were concerned with displacement and much greater attention was paid to the effects of gentrification on the working class than to the characteristics of the new middle class that was moving in. Although there was not necessarily agreement on the severity and extent of the problem (Sumka 1979), displacement was undoubtedly a major theme, in terms of how it was defined (Grier and Grier 1978), how it was measured (Schill and Nathan 1983), and how it was central to a rounded understanding of the entire process (LeGates and Hartman 1986; Marcuse 1985; Nelson 1988).

Concerns over displacement reached their apex in a remarkable publication written for community organizations and their advocates, but one that turned out to be far more wide-reaching in scope and influence. *Displacement: How to Fight It* (Hartman *et al.* 1982) was perhaps the key publication that emerged as part of the San Francisco-based "Anti-Displacement Project," a national campaign to protect affordable housing occupants from the displacement pressures of profiteering reinvestment in America's cities during the 1970s.[6] The Anti-Displacement Project derived much of its energy from a monumental early 1970s struggle over the construction of San Francisco's Yerba Buena Center, a substantial convention, performing arts and public space complex in that city's South of Market area. To create Yerba Buena, the San Francisco Redevelopment Agency displaced over 4,000 poor elderly tenants from single room occupancy hotels (SROs) in South of Market, in a particularly brazen case of what Hartman (1974) appropriately called "land grab." Something of the experience of displacement was later captured in retrospect by Hartman with poignant eloquence:

> For many pensioners, accustomed to forty-dollar- and fifty-dollar-per-month rents, relocation was a terrifying experience ... For older people in particular, personal friendships are perhaps the most important aspect of day-to-day life. Loss of familiar faces in the streets and in the hotel lobbies, of people to talk to, eat, drink, and play cards with is a severe shock. Similarly, the loss of stores, restaurants, and other commercial institutions can rob people of an important basis of stability, a place to obtain credit, to meet friends. (Hartman 2002: 66)

The situation was abysmal, but the fight against the callous obliteration of a working-class quarter of San Francisco, led by a tenants' organization with the support of nonprofit legal organizations, saw some impressive gains. After protracted litigation battles, half the units torn down in South of Market were replaced, and subsidized for permanent low-rent occupancy by federal and state sources and the city's hotel tax, with the tenants' organization acting as developers and managers of much of the new housing. The slogan of the social movement against Yerba Buena said it all: "We Won't Move."

Displacement: How to Fight It began with these words, as much an exposé of the dubious language of urban planning and policy (and neoclassical land theory) as a rallying cry to community activists:

Moving people involuntarily from their homes or neighborhoods is wrong. Regardless of whether it results from government or private market action, forced displacement is characteristically a case of people without the economic and political power to resist being pushed out by people with greater resources and power, people who think they have a "better" use for a certain building, piece of land, or neighborhood. The pushers benefit. The pushees do not. *The Anti-Displacement Project also regards it as fundamentally wrong to allow removal of housing units from the low–moderate income stock, for any purpose, without requiring at least a one-for-one replacement. Demolition, conversion, or "upgrade" rehab of vacant private or publicly owned lower-rent housing should be just as vigorously opposed as when those units are occupied.* (Hartman *et al.* 1982: 4–5, emphasis in the original)

Rereading these stirring words nearly three decades on, in the context of the latest round of research on displacement that has emerged from the United States (after a protracted period of dormancy), one cannot help be struck by the contrasts. In that latest round, three quantitative studies of displacement have become very high profile: by Vigdor (2002) in Boston, by Freeman and Braconi (2004) in New York City, and a national study by three urban economists (McKinnish *et al.* 2008). These studies analyzed data on household mobility drawn from various government housing databases and found that low-income and lesser-educated households exit gentrifying neighborhoods at significantly lower rates than comparable households in non-gentrifying neighborhoods. The conclusion of each study was that critics of gentrification have got it all wrong, for large-scale displacement is negligible and gentrification has a positive side that should be encouraged by urban policy, as it brings better services and amenities to neighborhoods affected for so long by disinvestment. Newman and Wyly explain the impact of these studies:

The new evidence on gentrification and displacement … has rapidly jumped out of the obscure scholarly cloister to influence policy debates that have been ripped out of context … [and] used to dismiss concerns about a wide range of market-oriented urban policies of privatization, home-ownership, "social mix" and dispersal strategies designed to break up the concentrated poverty that has been taken as the shorthand explanation for all that ails the disinvested inner city. If displacement is not a problem, many are saying, then regeneration (or whatever else the process is called) is fine too. Perhaps it will even give some poor people the benefits of a middle-class neighborhood without requiring them to move to a middle-class community. (Newman and Wyly 2006: 25)

Elsewhere (Slater 2006, 2009) I have advanced a step-by-step methodical critique of these studies, which are analytically defective when considered alongside Peter Marcuse's (1985) conceptual clarity on the four distinct forms of displacement in gentrifying neighborhoods: direct last-resident displacement, direct chain displacement, exclusionary displacement, and displacement pressure (see Slater 2009 for a detailed elaboration of each). It is no coincidence that those who have been pressing the view that displacement is negligible and that gentrification is not as troubling as the extensive literature suggests have all missed Marcuse. When conceptual verification is brought to bear on the declamatory discourse of the media reaction to this scholarship,[7] claims that gentrification is a panacea for abandonment and class/ethnic segregation become deeply problematic. Furthermore, the magnitude of dislocation taking place on the new frontiers of gentrification and displacement in the global south such as in Shanghai (He 2007), Quito (Swanson 2007), and Mumbai (Whitehead and More 2007) offers compelling evidence for an argument that intellectual and moral concerns over displacement must not dissipate at precisely the moment they are urgently needed on both scientific and political grounds. It is only by uncovering the mechanisms that create different forms of displacement that any attempt to legitimize or naturalize housing turbulence at the bottom of the urban class structure (e.g., Hamnett 2008) can be effectively refuted.

Conclusion: From "Policy Relevance" to Relevant Politics

In this essay I have attempted to bring the reader up to date on the state of play with respect to three crucial areas of inquiry in gentrification research. This leaves us with an obvious question, appropriate for a conclusion: where do we go from here? The answer depends largely on whether one adopts a critical or a mainstream approach to urban studies (for an outline of the differences between these approaches, see Brenner *et al.* 2009). If one adopts the former approach (from a starting point of being opposed to gentrification), a careful analytical indictment of the mainstream research output (typified by scholarship concluding that gentrification is acceptable if it is "managed" by policy) is necessary but not sufficient. Such an indictment needs to be coupled with further research that seeks to document displacement[8] (in any or all of its forms) "from below," in the sobering terms of those who experience it. The absence of qualitative accounts of displacement is striking and shocking when juxtaposed with quantitative measures, or with all those accounts of the trials and tribulations of the new middle class. It is the civic duty of critical urbanists to understand and intuitively sympathize with those whose problems they examine. If the pain, bitterness and even the humiliation that come with being forced out of one's home is not a central component of critical studies of gentrification, then it is unlikely that critical studies will make much difference. Critical researchers must be with, and ultimately stand with, those whose problems they analyse, describe, and explain.[9]

The authors of *Displacement: How to Fight It* made no secret of their rejection of the neoclassical dictum of "economically optimal" or "highest and best use" of particular land parcels, arguing that competitive bidding for land fails to take into account the fortunes of those who occupy it rather than own it. The deleterious influence of neoclassical land theory on urban policy and planning also led to Chester Hartman's (1984) call for a "right to stay put." That essay is a spirited example of what is becoming an endangered species in urban studies – spirited policy critique with a call for urgent reform (as opposed to vague and inconsequential "policy relevance" that characterizes many policy evaluations of "urban regeneration"), seen most clearly in Hartman's rejection of conventional cost–benefits thinking in housing policy, in favor of an understanding of displacement costs as emotional, psychological, individual and social:

> In seeking a new place to live, the displaced tend to move as short a distance as possible, in an effort to retain existing personal, commercial, and institutional ties and

because of the economically and racially biased housing-market constraints they face. What they find usually costs more, has less adequate space, and is of inferior quality. Involuntary residential changes also produce a considerable amount of psychosocial stress, which in its more extreme form has been found analogous to the clinical description of grief. (Hartman 1984: 305–6)

Hartman's blend of the analytical and the political, the intellectual and the emotional, in my view now serves as a touchstone, foreshadowing the insights of the nascent (Lefebvrian) Right to the City movement and of an emerging political philosophy for a "right to place" (Imbroscio 2004). It also foreshadows the insights of one of the more striking studies of displacement to appear in quite some time, written by a medical doctor, Mindy Fullilove, who equates displacement with a clinical condition called root shock (the title of her book):

Root shock, at the level of the local community, be it neighborhood or something else, ruptures bonds, dispersing people to all the directions of the compass. Even if they manage to regroup, they are not sure what to do with one another. People who were near are too far, and people who were far are too near. The elegance of the neighborhood – each person in his social and geographic slot – is destroyed, and even if the neighborhood is rebuilt exactly as it was, it won't work. The restored geography is not enough to repair the many injuries to the mazeway. (Fullilove 2004: 14)

Just as there are valuable theoretical lessons to be learned from critical studies of the formation and constitution of middle-class gentrifiers, so there are from poignant accounts of love and loss in the context of the devastation of displacement.[10]

Notes

1 A comprehensive critical treatment of a literature over 40 years old can be found in Lees *et al.* (2008).
2 The rent gap is the shortfall between the actual economic return from a land parcel given its present use (capitalized ground rent) and the potential return if it were put to its optimal, "highest and best" use (potential ground rent). As the rent gap grows larger, it creates lucrative profit opportunities for developers, investors, and home-buyers.
3 Contrary to the "back to the city" rhetoric of the 1970s (see Laska and Spain 1980), most gentrifiers came from other central city neighborhoods, not the suburbs.
4 Helpfully defined as "[T]he way society becomes deposited in persons in the form of lasting dispositions, or trained capacities and structured propensities to think, feel, and act in determinate ways, which then guide them in their creative responses to the constraints and solicitations of their extant milieu" (Wacquant 2005: 316).
5 A detailed elaboration of this literature can be found in Chapter 3 of Lees *et al.* (2008).
6 The obstacles were formidable – this was a time of optimistic "back-to-the-city" pronouncements nationwide, when gentrification was viewed by the media and city officials as a welcome remedy for decades of redlining, disinvestment, and "white flight." Rarely did public discourse focus on what we might call the downside of upscale.
7 Take for example the headline in *USA Today*: "Studies: gentrification a boost for everyone" (Hampson 2005), under which coverage of Lance Freeman's (2005) work appeared. *Time* Magazine featured the study by McKinnish *et al.* (2008) under the headline: "Gentrification: not ousting the poor?" (Kiviat 2008).

8　It is telling that the chapter on gentrification written by Chris Hamnett in the first *Companion to the City* did not contain the word "displacement."

9　I am grateful to Peter Marcuse for this point.

10　Lees *et al.* (2008) is a comprehensive critical introduction to the literature. The monographs by Smith (1996) and Ley (1996) are essential reading for any serious analyst of gentrification, and read together they provide a rounded theoretical platform for further inquiry. Zukin's (1982) work on loft living in lower Manhattan is a lesson in historical materialism; Clark's (1987) classic book is the definitive work on the history, theoretical roots, and empirical expression of rent gaps, based on his research in Malmö, Sweden. Butler with Robson (2003) is a comprehensive treatment of the role of the new middle class in London's gentrification. Hartman *et al.* (1982) is the most important and most comprehensive treatment of urban displacement ever written.

References

Blokland, T. (2003) *Urban Bonds: Social Relationships in an Inner City Neighbourhood.* Cambridge: Polity Press.

Boddy, M. (2007) Designer neighborhoods: new-build residential development in non-metropolitan UK cities – the case of Bristol. *Environment and Planning A* 39: 86–105.

Bondi, L. (1991) Gender divisions and gentrification: a critique. *Transactions of the Institute of British Geographers* 16: 290–8.

Bondi, L. (1999) Between the woof and the weft: a response to Loretta Lees. *Environment and Planning D: Society and Space* 17 (3): 253–5.

Bourdieu, P. (1984) *Distinction: A Social Critique of the Judgement of Taste.* London: Routledge.

Brenner, N., Marcuse, P., and Mayer, M. (2009) Cities for people, not for profit: introduction. *CITY: Analysis of Urban Trends, Culture, Theory, Policy, Action* 13: 176–84.

Bridge, G. (2001a) Bourdieu, rational action and the time-space strategy of gentrification. *Transactions of the Institute of British Geographers* 26: 205–16.

Bridge, G. (2001b) Estate agents as interpreters of economic and cultural capital: the gentrification premium in the Sydney housing market. *International Journal of Urban and Regional Research* 25: 87–101.

Bridge, G. (2006) The paradox of cosmopolitan urbanism: rationality, difference and the circuits of cultural capital. In *Cosmopolitan Urbanism*, ed. J. Binnie, J. Holloway, S. Millington, and C. Young. London: Routledge, 53–69.

Butler, T. (1997) *Gentrification and the Middle Classes.* Aldershot: Ashgate.

Butler, T. (2007) For gentrification? *Environment and Planning A* 39: 162–81.

Butler, T., with Robson, G. (2003) *London Calling: The Middle Classes and the Remaking of Inner London.* London: Berg.

Butler, T., and Watt, P. (2007) *Understanding Social Inequality.* London: Sage.

Castells, M. (1983) *The City and the Grassroots: A Cross-Cultural Theory of Urban Social Movements.* Berkeley: University of California Press.

Clark, E. (1987) *The Rent Gap and Urban Change: Case Studies in Malmo, 1860–1985.* Lund: Lund University Press.

Clark, E. (1992) On blindness, centrepieces, and complementarity in gentrification theory. *Transactions of the Institute of British Geographers* 17: 358–62.

Davidson, M., and Lees, L. (2005) New-build "gentrification" and London's riverside renaissance. *Environment and Planning A* 37 (7): 1165–90.

Engels, B. (1994) Capital flows, redlining and gentrification: the pattern of mortgage lending and social change in Glebe, Sydney, 1960–1984. *International Journal of Urban and Regional Research* 18 (4): 628–57.

Freeman, L. (2005) Displacement or succession? Residential mobility in gentrifying neighborhoods. *Urban Affairs Review* 40: 463–91.

Freeman, L., and Braconi, F. (2004) Gentrification and displacement: New York City in the 1990s. *Journal of the American Planning Association* 70 (1): 39–52.

Fullilove, M. T. (2004) *Root Shock: How Tearing Up City Neighborhoods Hurts America, And What We Can Do About It*. New York: One World/Ballantine Books.

Glass, R. (1964) Introduction: aspects of change. In *London: Aspects of Change*, ed. Centre for Urban Studies. London: MacKibbon and Kee, xiii–xlii.

Grier, G., and Grier, E. (1978) *Urban Displacement: A Reconnaissance*. Washington, DC: US Department of Housing and Urban Development.

Hackworth, J. (2002) Post-recession gentrification in New York City. *Urban Affairs Review* 37: 815–43.

Hammel, D. J. (1999) Gentrification and land rent: a historical view of the rent gap in Minneapolis. *Urban Geography* 20 (2): 116–45.

Hamnett, C. (1991) The blind men and the elephant: the explanation of gentrification. *Transactions of the Institute of British Geographers* 16 (2): 173–89.

Hamnett, C. (2003) Gentrification and the middle class remaking of inner London, 1961–2001. *Urban Studies* 40 (12): 2401–26.

Hamnett, C. (2008) The regeneration game. *The Guardian*, June 11. Available online at www.guardian.co.uk/commentisfree/2008/jun/11/housing (accessed October 18, 2010).

Hampson, R. (2005) Studies: gentrification a boost for everyone. *USA Today* April 20.

Hartman, C. (1974) *Yerba Buena: Land Grab and Community Resistance in San Francisco*. San Francisco: Glebe Books.

Hartman, C. (1984) The right to stay put. In *Land Reform, American Style*, ed. C. Geisler and F. Popper. Totowa, NJ: Rowman and Allanheld, 302–18.

Hartman, C. (2002) *City for Sale: The Transformation of San Francisco*. Berkeley: University of California Press.

Hartman, C., Keating, D., and LeGates, R. (1982) *Displacement: How to Fight It*. Washington, DC: National Housing Law Project.

He, S. (2007) State-sponsored gentrification under market transition: the case of Shanghai. *Urban Affairs Review* 43: 171–98.

Imbroscio, D. L. (2004) Can we grant a right to place? *Politics & Society* 32: 575–609.

Jager, M. (1986) Class definition and the aesthetics of gentrification: Victoriana in Melbourne. In *Gentrification of the City*, ed. N. Smith and P. Williams. London: Unwin Hyman, 78–91.

Kern, C. R. (1981) Upper-income renaissance in the city: its sources and implications for the city's future. *Journal of Urban Economics* 9: 106–24.

Kiviat, B. (2008) Gentrification: not ousting the poor? *Time* Magazine June 29.

Laska, S. B., and Spain, D. (eds.) (1980) *Back to the City: Issues in Neighborhood Renovation*. New York: Pergamon Press.

Lees, L. (1994) Rethinking gentrification: beyond the positions of economics and culture. *Progress in Human Geography* 18 (2): 137–50.

Lees, L., Slater, T., and Wyly, E. (2008) *Gentrification*. New York: Routledge.

LeGates, R., and Hartman, C. (1986) The anatomy of displacement in the US. In *Gentrification of the City*, ed. N. Smith and P. Williams. London: Unwin Hyman, 178–200.

LeRoy, S. F., and Sonstelie, J. (1983) Paradise lost and regained: transportation innovation, income, and residential location. *Journal of Urban Economics* 13: 67–89.

Ley, D. (1986) Alternative explanations for inner-city gentrification: a Canadian assessment. *Annals of the Association of American Geographers* 76 (4): 521–35.

Ley, D. (1994) Gentrification and the politics of the new middle class. *Environment and Planning D: Society and Space* 12: 53–74.

Ley, D. (1996) *The New Middle Class and the Remaking of the Central City*. Oxford: Oxford University Press.

Ley, D. (2003) Artists, aestheticisation and the field of gentrification. *Urban Studies* 40 (12): 2527–44.

Lipton, S. G. (1977) Evidence of central city revival. *Journal of the American Institute of Planners* 43: 136–47.

Marcuse, P. (1985) To control gentrification: anti-displacement zoning and planning for stable residential districts. *Review of Law and Social Change* 13: 931–45.

McKinnish, T., Walsh, R., and White, K. (2008) *Who Gentrifies Low-Income Neighborhoods?* Working Paper No. W14036. Cambridge, MA : National Bureau of Economic Research.

Mills, C. (1988) Life on the upslope: the postmodern landscape of gentrification. *Environment and Planning D: Society and Space* 6: 169–89.

Nelson, K. (1988) *Gentrification and Distressed Cities: An Assessment of Trends in Intrametropolitan Migration*. Madison: University of Wisconsin Press.

Newman, K., and Wyly, E. (2006) The right to stay put, revisited: gentrification and resistance to displacement in New York City. *Urban Studies* 43 (1): 23–57.

Palen, J., and London, B. (eds.) (1984) *Gentrification, Displacement and Neighborhood Revitalization*. Albany: State University of New York Press.

Pattillo, M. (2007) *Black on the Block: The Politics of Race and Class in the City*. Chicago: University of Chicago Press.

Podmore, J. (1998) (Re)reading the "loft living" habitus in Montreal's inner city. *International Journal of Urban and Regional Research* 22: 283–302.

Rose, D. (1984) Rethinking gentrification: beyond the uneven development of Marxist urban theory. *Environment and Planning D: Society and Space* 1: 47–74.

Rothenberg, T. (1995) "And she told two friends": lesbians creating urban social space. In *Mapping Desire: Geographies of Sexualities*, ed. D. Bell and G. Valentine. London: Routledge, 165–81.

Sassen, S. (1991) *The Global City: New York, London and Tokyo*. Princeton, NJ: Princeton University Press.

Schill, M., and Nathan, R. (1983) *Revitalizing Americas Cities: Neighborhood Reinvestment and Displacement*. Albany: State University of New York Press.

Shaw, K. (2008) Gentrification: what it is, why it is, and what can be done about it. *Geography Compass* 2: 1–32.

Slater, T. (2006) The eviction of critical perspectives from gentrification research. *International Journal of Urban and Regional Research* 30: 737–57.

Slater, T. (2009) Missing Marcuse: on gentrification and displacement. *CITY: Analysis of Urban Trends, Culture, Theory, Policy, Action* 13: 292–311.

Smith, N. (1979) Toward a theory of gentrification: a back to the city movement by capital, not people. *Journal of the American Planning Association* 45 (4): 538–48.

Smith, N. (1996) *The New Urban Frontier: Gentrification and the Revanchist City*. London and New York: Routledge.

Smith, N. (2002) New globalism, new urbanism: gentrification as global urban strategy. *Antipode* 34 (3): 427–50.

Smith, N., and Williams, P. (1986) Alternatives to orthodoxy: invitation to a debate. In *Gentrification of the City*, ed. N. Smith and P. Williams. London: Allen & Unwin, 1–10.

Sumka, H. (1979) Neighborhood revitalization and displacement: a review of the evidence. *Journal of the American Planning Association* 45: 480–7.

Swanson, K. (2007) Revanchist urbanism heads south: the regulation of indigenous beggars and street vendors in Ecuador. *Antipode* 39 (4): 708–28.

Taylor, M. (2003) *Harlem: Between Heaven and Hell*. Minneapolis: University of Minnesota Press.

Vigdor, J. (2002) Does gentrification harm the poor? In *Brookings-Wharton Papers on Urban Affairs*. Washington, DC: Brookings Institution Presss, 133–173.

Wacquant, L. (2005) Habitus. In *International Encyclopedia of Economic Sociology*, ed. J. Beckert and M. Zafirovski. London: Routledge, 315–19.

Warde, A. (1991) Gentrification as consumption: issues of class and gender. *Environment and Planning D: Society and Space* 9: 223–32.

Wheaton, W. (1977) Income and urban residence: an analysis of consumer demand for location. *American Economic Review* 67: 620–31.

Whitehead, J., and More, N. (2007) Revanchism in Mumbai? Political economy of rent gaps and urban restructuring in a global city. *Economic and Political Weekly* June 23: 2428–34.

Wyly, E., and Hammel, D. (2001) Gentrification, housing policy, the new context of urban redevelopment. In *Research in Urban Sociology*, vol. 6: *Critical Perspectives on Urban Redevelopment*, ed. K. Fox Gotham. London: Elsevier, 211–76.

Zukin, S. (1982) *Loft Living: Culture and Capital in Urban Change*. Baltimore, MD: Johns Hopkins University Press.

Chapter 51

The Homosexuality of Cities

Julie Abraham

When in 2001 the gay American novelist, memoir writer, and essayist Edmund White announced that "Paris is a big city," he justified his claim by citing, "A reckless friend [who] defines a big city as a place where there are blacks, tall buildings and you can stay up all night." Though he committed himself to "the strange corners of Paris … rather than to the classic headquarters of the Gallic tradition," the portrait of the city he offered in *The Flâneur* was founded on the work of those mid-nineteenth- and early twentieth-century icons of late twentieth-century urban studies, the poet Charles Baudelaire and his chief interpreter, the essayist Walter Benjamin, as well as organized around the figure they both portrayed as the representative modern urbanite. And although he identified "blacks" as those people whose presence marks the urban spot, he claimed "be[ing] gay and cruis[ing]" as "an extension of the *flâneur*'s very essence, or at least its most successful application" (2001: 1, 52, 145).

In 1999 Samuel Delany, another gay American novelist, memoir writer, and essayist, writing about New York City in *Times Square Red, Times Square Blue*, attached his work to that of iconic mid-twentieth-century urban planner Jane Jacobs. He offered the sexual encounters between men he describes at the center of his city as models of the "contact" Jacobs described, in *The Death and Life of Great American Cities*, as the basis of urban order, "fundamental," as Delany emphasized, to cosmopolitan culture … [and] quality of life" (1999: 198–9).

At the turn of the twenty-first century, literary and/or gay commentators such as White and Delany were not the only ones so definitively joining gays and cities. University of Toronto social scientist Richard Florida received widespread attention in the United States and internationally, in the media and from local governments as well as among economists, urban planners, and sociologists, for

The New Blackwell Companion to the City Edited by Gary Bridge and Sophie Watson
© 2011 Blackwell Publishing Ltd

his *The Rise of the Creative Class* (2002) and *Cities and the Creative Class* (2005). An extraordinary amount of that attention was paid to his references to gays (Letellier 2005). Rejecting "the greatest of the modern myths about cities … that *geography is dead*," he insisted that place still matters, because it matters economically. But the economic potential of any given urban place, he proposed, also invoking Jacobs, depends on its social and cultural qualities. Places that offer a "community life" of interest to creative people will thrive economically, and such places can be identified by the presence of gays – a presence codified in his "gay index" (Florida 2005: 28, 29).

White, Delany, and Florida not only place gays in the city, but via their uses of Baudelaire, Benjamin, and Jane Jacobs, within the modern "great city",

> the metropolis of the second half of the nineteenth century and of the first half of the twentieth century … the place where new social and cultural relations, beyond both city and nation in their older senses, were beginning to be formed. (Williams 1997: 44)

This European "great city" has been identified as the home of "blacks" of various colors – the Irish, Africans, South Asians, or Arabs – since the first attempts to address the explosive urbanization of the modern world in accounts of Paris, London, and new industrial centers such as Manchester, in the first half of the nineteenth century. The Jews would become model urban strangers for late nineteenth- and early twentieth-century sociologists, and thus provide a framework for the

Figure 51.1 Souvenirs of New York City, 2007. Author's photo.

Chicago School's identification of "the city" with "the ghetto" by the mid-twentieth century in the United States. Yet as White's, Delany's, and Florida's early twenty-first-century writings indicate, homosexuality remains equal to if not more powerful than "race," as a mark of the great city.

As I have argued in *Metropolitan Lovers*, over the course of the past two centuries modern understandings of same-sex desires and of cities developed interdependently (Abraham 2009). Homosexuals became simultaneously model citizens of the modern city and avatars of the urban, that is, models of the city itself. More familiar claims – that cities produce homosexuals or their identities, or, conversely, that cities are produced by homosexuals; that cities have been the salvation of gays, or that gays might be the saviors of cities – have been derived from and supported this history. Understandings of historical change, fears of illegible persons and places, convictions about the workings of social groups, conflicts over divisions between public and private lives, and assumptions about the street and the home, have all been worked out within this framework. But most significantly, the interdependent development of modern understandings of same-sex sexuality and of cities has determined who is seen as homosexual and how homosexuals are seen, as well as what is seen as urban and how cities are seen.

Although Edmund White writes about gay men who live in the Arab neighborhoods of Paris in *The Flâneur,* those men are not Arabs. Samuel Delany, himself African American, writes about a multi-racial group of men having sex with other men in New York City in *Times Square Red, Times Square Blue.* But in both White's and Delany's works, as in Richard Florida's studies, the homosexuals are all male. Florida's gays also all have financial resources. Which is to say that the history of the homosexuality of cities has been woven through racial, gender, and class divisions. Since the 1970s, an image of gays as white and wealthy as well as male has come to dominate accounts of contemporary urban life in which "gays" are routinely contrasted with "blacks." Nonetheless, the belief that same-sex desires are profound threats to "proper" racial and class divisions was a powerful force shaping identifications of homosexuality and the city. And the homosexuality of cities has never been exclusively male. In different cities, at different moments, lesbians or gay men have been in turn more or less salient figures – more or less useful to the construction and maintenance of central understandings of the great city.

This process has taken different forms over the past two centuries. But overall, the history of the homosexuality of cities has had, in very broad terms, three phases.

In the first phase, the terms of debate about the great city were being established. From the first decades of the nineteenth century, as the literature of the modern city was emerging in Paris and London, accounts of same-sex desire and the persons who might experience such desires were embedded in descriptions of and debates about urban life. Fantastic stories of lesbian intrigue became the pretext for disquisitions on the values and rules of city living. The sexual and moral excesses lesbianism was thought to embody could represent, and neutralize, each of the apparently opposed terms that made up the paradigms – pleasure/gold; vice/capital; nature/history – within which explanations for the social upheavals of the cities were being sought. At the same time, fears of the unknown others unavoidable in urban crowds, of the illegibility of strangers on the street, could be articulated through stories of men who desired other men as well as stories of the schemes of criminals and political radicals, uniquely at home in the city. These also all turned out to be the same stories. Most spectacularly, in the case of Oscar Wilde, even the storyteller himself was revealed as at once a political radical, a criminal, and homosexual.

During the second phase of this history, homosexuality was a pivotal subject for those concerned with the social life of cities. From the later decades of the nineteenth century through the mid-twentieth century, on both sides of the Atlantic, for a wide range of hostile commentators, homosexuals represented the worst outcome of the nervous strain of modern life most fully felt in cities. Consequently, to those decrying the pressures of modernization, they most fully represented city life. At the same time, homosexuals were increasingly understood by literary writers, sexual scientists, social scientists, and gay advocates alike, as simultaneously the most isolated of individuals and indistinguishable from one another, inseparable from their group. This paradoxical understanding of perverts in groups meant that homosexuals were ideal subjects through whom social fears of and desires for both isolation and communal life in the city could be mapped. But queers themselves were also practically as well as theoretically engaged in efforts to ameliorate the difficulties and to intensify the distinctions of urban life. From the 1890s, activists such as Jane Addams worked for the improvement of urban conditions with a vision of the city as a site for new social forms. By the 1920s novelists and gay advocates such as Radclyffe Hall were articulating the distinctiveness of gay life through the distinctiveness of urban life, efforts which meshed with sociologists' investments in the city as the peculiar location of "the criminal, the defective, and the genius."

In the third phase of this history, homosexuals emerged as a political as well as a social and cultural force in the United States in the decades after World War II, in the context of the rapid suburbanization of white Americans and the deindustrialization of American cities. Homosexuality and urbanity had fused as subjects. Homosexuals and urbanites shared the qualities that made both types un-American. And subsequent defenses of homosexuals and of the city employed the same terms – in part as a result of the arguments about the necessity of shared public life that those defenses also shared. Consequently, when the city was re-imagined as a theater and a ghetto, from the 1950s to the 1970s, gays could represent the theatricality of the city and the city as ghetto. By the 1980s, a romance of the gay community elaborated by gay advocates and urban planners alike meant that "gay San Francisco" – seen as making urban meaning from aesthetic and communal rather than economic values – could be presented as the model for a revival of the postindustrial, postmodern city.

Straight as well as gay commentators have used ideas about homosexuals to negotiate their own places in "the city," from the mid-nineteenth century to the present. Most recently, gay as well as straight commentators have used the identification of homosexuals with cities as a means of talking about place itself. Queers can be called on, by their exclusion, to signal the significance of place. Place still matters: they are still threatening queers in the countryside of the United States. But queers can also signal, by their presence, the insignificance of place. Place no longer matters. Not only are there same-sex couples in the suburbs of America these days (a sure sign of the end of suburban difference), but it is possible to be an American-style homosexual in almost any "great city" of our globalized world (a sure sign of the end of global difference).

The homosexuality of cities is not then a subject that can be encompassed within the framework of "city divisions and differences." In fact, our late twentieth-century language of difference and division, with their corollaries, "polarization, inequality, and fragmentation" or "power, resistance, and celebration of identity," are fundamentally beside the point. Even the histories of queer communities, or LGBT individuals, in particular cities, have been shaped by the broader web of the history of the homosexuality of cities. The fact that "homosexuals" as a group do not fit into a model of the city divided and polarized is worth examining however, because that failure to fit – like the history of the homosexuality of cities in all of its details – illuminates fundamental patterns in accounts of the great city and the fundamental persistence of the great city model within contemporary urban debates. It is not an accident that White and Delany were so recently writing about Paris and New York, so frequently presented as capitals of the nineteenth and twentieth centuries respectively – or that their work meshes so well with Florida's prescriptions for the future of the postindustrial, postmodern city.

Within the context of the homosexuality of cities, the model of the city divided and polarized can be seen not just as an artifact of contemporary political concerns but as a core pattern of urban study from the early nineteenth century onwards. The literature of the city has been fascinated with the social margins since its inception. In the bifurcated terms of modern urban study established in the earliest accounts of the modern city by figures as different as Baudelaire and Friedrich Engels, the underclass is invariably presented as the group within the city that is definitively urban. Elite men have routinely written about the city by presenting themselves as uniquely knowledgeable about, even immersed in, but never subject to, the limits of the lives of non-elite others. The elites themselves, or the middle classes they purport to instruct, are never full subjects of discussion.

Edmund White's elite status echoes that of the classic urban commentator. Samuel Delany clarifies those conventions of great city studies even as he blurs them. He identifies himself as a gay African American college professor from a family of professionals who goes out onto the street – the natural home of the economic, racial, ethnic, and sexual "lower" classes – to pursue his research. Their exclusion of women as urban actors is far from peculiar to their homosexual interests. At the same time, both White and Delany actually articulate the sexual interests that remain implicit in many earlier versions of this model. As gay men, they have the capacity to embody both aspects of the divided city, to be both elite and marginal. For that reason, their reprise of that earlier model highlights another very significant but implicit aspect of the earlier work, which is the yearning of the elite commentator for union or identification with the truly urban underclass without any loss of his own elite status. Finally White and Delany, with their focus on the sexual, do not just bring sex to the surface. They also illustrate a key aspect of the role of homosexuality in urban discourse, and thereby illuminate a key pattern of that discourse, which is the obfuscation of the economic by the sexual – or in the original mid-nineteenth-century terms, capital by vice – in accounts of the conditions of the city.

In late twentieth- and early twenty-first-century discussions of cities, the equation of homosexuality and urbanity has been played in two apparently opposite ways, with gays presented as representatives of both simulated cities and authentic urbanity.

Both of these developments depend upon the identification of homosexuals with the great city, and on the persistence of that modern metropolis within analyses of post-modern urbanity.

One of the key anxieties accompanying the development of the modern city, traceable from the writings of Balzac in the 1830s and Engels in the 1840s to those of Georg Simmel at the turn of the century, was that authentic human relations would not be possible in the rapidly expanding urban centers they were observing, because of the problem of legibility in the city, the necessary reliance on appearances in the rush of urban life, and the indifference to others generated by the crowd. Hence the identification of the great city with artifice. Ironically, the modern city that produced this fear of artifice is now seen in retrospect, in turn-of-the-twenty-first-century discussions of the urban, as the site of an authentic, even quintessential, urbanity. As Elizabeth Wilson notes, in the 1990s "urbanists of various kinds drew on concepts of the good city … a nineteenth-century metropolis such as had been described and explored by Baudelaire and Benjamin," the city "of the flâneur, the pedestrian city, the city of many villages … cities of pleasure and civility" (1997: 133). This embrace of the great city model was in part a response to new anxieties about urban artifice, about inauthentic persons and relations in the late twentieth century. It did not however allay those anxieties. They were instead dispersed into fear of a postmodern city inauthentic in itself, where the very buildings might be false – a city suburbanized, Disneyfied, malled, or theme-parked out of existence.

Insofar as anxieties about the postmodern simulated city are an extension of anxieties about artificiality in the modern city, and insofar as homosexuals have long represented the artificial modern city, gays can appear as iconic residents of the simulated city. In a moment that has a peculiar resonance among the "friends of Dorothy," even as it restates the difference between city and heartland central to gay and urban identities, geographer Edward Soja introduces his discussion of Los Angeles as "simcity" under the heading, "Toto, I've got a feeling we're not in Kansas anymore" (1999: 94) For sociologist Sharon Zukin, gay people offer a key example of the commodification of city culture (1995: 263–4). What does the simulation of urbanity produce among the residents of Disney's new urbanist Celebration, according to cultural critic Andrew Ross, but fear of homosexuality (1999: 114–15).

Iconic residents of the simulated city, gays could nevertheless, and simultaneously, function as a defense against artificiality. Because of their long association with the now "authentic" modern great city, they could serve as icons of an authentic urbanity (Ross 1999: 114–15). Thus Ross begins his report on community in Celebration with the gays of Celebration (1999: 115). Art historian Rosalind Deutsche, countering Soja's analysis of Los Angeles as the model for our postmetropolitan future, bases her advocacy of a new "reasonable urbanism" on a reading of a British gay novel, Neil Bartlett's *Ready to Catch Him Should He Fall* (1990). And the only optimistic sign in *Hollow City* (2000), Rebecca Solnit and Susan Schwartzenberg's account of San Francisco's real-estate market run amok, is the gay candidate Tom Ammiano's mayoral campaign.

In the United States, the role of gays in accounts of the city has in fact reached the height of contradiction. Gays are pursued by city governments and real-estate developers precisely for their capacity to simulate, and thereby stimulate the revival of, an authentic (that is, modern) urbanism in postmodern cities. Their presence marks a place as urban and, it is hoped, that place then becomes a "city." This is the development that has as its theoretician Richard Florida. To support his analysis, Florida presents "the city" as the quintessential site of human creativity, offering as evidence a twentieth-century urban history that runs from the Chicago School's Robert Park to Jane Jacobs, and thereby makes clear his commitment to a great city model. Florida, in effect, systematizes the status of gays as place markers. Gays have been transformed from the urban saviors they were identified as in the 1980s into pure signs of urbanity, and as such, signs of "the city's" potential for survival. Only truly urban cities, Florida argues, the kind occupied by gays, will persist as such, that is, as distinct places. By the same token, struggling cities can be revived only if they can become the kind of places his gays represent.

Florida's presentation of gays as signs of urbanity exemplifies a cultural development that can be traced in the past decade in the United States and internationally. After the city of Chicago set up rainbow painted pylons on North Halsted Street in 1997 to mark out Boystown as a gay neighborhood, gay historian George Chauncey noted that this gesture gave evidence of Chicago's status as a "world-class city" (Acosta 2001). Invocations of the presence of gays as evidence of world-class city status have also been central to the development of international gay tourist circuits, from Sydney to Madrid (Giorgi 2002; Markwell 2002). In Berlin, the mayor, Klaus Wowereit, a gay native son who came to power in 2001 and was re-elected in 2006 in a city rapidly losing its industrial base, offered himself as a promising sign of urban life. Focusing Berlin's economic plans on tourism he announced, "We are poor but sexy" (Landler 2006).

This evolution of gays from urban saviors to urban signs is not solely an effect of their ongoing identification with great cities and the recent embrace of great cities as models for authentic city life. Two other mutually reinforcing factors have contributed. One is the definitive recasting of the great city as a site of non-economic values, as the city of the *flâneur* rather than of industry, Paris rather than Manchester. The other is an intensification of the association of gays with consumption.

Gay men were already being described in *Esquire,* as early as 1972, as "the new artisans ... always on the cutting edge of culture and urban living," with "child-free lives [that] allow them more time to pursue personal ... and artistic interests." This fantasy of gay urban life, Michael Bronski argues, was easily conflated with "the consumerism of the 1970s and 1980s" (1998: 154–5). That conflation is now taken for granted. Geographer Richard Walker recently asserted both that "Gay liberation jump-started the yuppie era and its celebration of personal indulgence" in San Francisco in the 1970s, and that in the 1980s, "The yuppie consumer culture ... usher[ed] in ... gay sensibilities in architecture, dress, and the arts" (1998: 12, 15). In 2005, when sociologist Judith Stacey wanted to present contemporary Los Angeles as "the paradigmatic metropolis of postmodernism," she invoked both consumption and gays, each representing the other: "no city better symbolizes sexual excess, consumer culture, and the anti-thesis of family values" and "no population" is more representative of this city, she writes, than "the gay male denizens who crowd the bars, beats, and boutiques of West Hollywood," Los Angeles' gay ghetto (2005: 1914, 1915).

The most widely purveyed images of LGBT consumption remain images of moneyed white gay men, as in the United States, in the Bravo cable television show

Queer Eye for the Straight Guy (2002–7), where gays gave purchasing goods a veneer of style and culture. The conflation of assumptions about gay men, consumption, and the city was encapsulated in the term "metrosexual" – an import from Britain, first appearing there in the mid-1990s and quickly flaring in the US media after the turn of the century. A metrosexual was supposed to be a new type of man, a heterosexual with the style, the grooming habits, and the cultural capital as well as the interest in shopping ascribed to gay men. "Metro" mediated between homo and hetero – the city representing the homosexual without sexual implications, the homosexual as an accomplished consumer (St John 2003).

Such conflation of homosexuality, consumption, and the city has become so pervasive that LGBT hostility to the consumption-focused "gay life" now being sold to us all can take the form of hostility to the city itself (Sinfield 1998: 70, 103). People who might otherwise see themselves as "gay" and "urban," like the men from the Philippines interviewed by Martin Manalansan in New York City in the 1990s for his study *Global Divas*, self-consciously reject "American gay urban life" despite having moved to US cities to pursue their same-sex desires (2003: 22, 23). Reactions against popular images of gay urban life fuel gay men's journeys back and forth across urban/suburban and national borders, whether they are Americans who live in the suburbs of northern New Jersey and commute into New York City to pursue their "gay" lives, or Mexicans living in *zona rosa* in Mexico City, on the south side of Puerto Vallarta, or in Guadalajara, and traveling back and forth to Los Angeles (Brekhus 2003; Cantu 2002). Such reactions also justify the self-conscious commitment of many North American lesbians and gay men to suburban lives that they understand as less "gay" because they are suburban.

What has developed from the conflation of homosexuality, consumption, and cities is, in effect, a self-perpetuating system ensuring that the gays who are taken to represent modern urbanity in Chicago, Madrid, and Sydney remain a familiar moneyed, white, and male group. Reinforcing pre-existing gender, race, class, and national divisions among LGBT persons, this system, at the same time, continually emphasizes, to those it appears to favor, the hostility of the world in which they live, and so the possibility that they will be punished for their desires.

Hostility is in fact fundamental to the cultural usefulness of the homosexuals who represent modern urbanity in Chicago, Madrid, and Sydney – as well as that of the media gays of *Queer Eye* and the spectral homos hovering behind the metrosexual. The history of their oppression, as much as the incomes with which these men are credited, is where their value lies. Richard Florida is among the many who still cheerfully invoke the wealth of childless male same-sex households that supposedly allows them to "devote larger portions of their income to the purchase and development of amenities" (2005: 189). But the welcome these supposedly wealthy gays are offered in Chicago or Madrid or Sydney is, equally, based on the premise that they cannot expect to be accepted everywhere. Gay tourists, for example, are explicitly reminded by the cities and the companies seeking to profit from their travel that their sexuality is not accepted "at home": tours can then be sold to them as necessary journeys to rare spaces of freedom (Giorgi 2002; Puar 2002).

Hostility is also the premise of many of the urbanists who have recently posed gays as the hope of the city. Rosalind Deutsche, in her argument for a "reasonable urbanism" modeled on gay fiction, emphasizes the violence against gays that novelist Neil Bartlett describes in London in the 1980s (1990). Richard Florida's explanation for the role of gays as metropolitan signs is explicitly predicated on gay vulnerability. "As a group," he explains, "gays have been subject to a particularly high level of discrimination ... To some extent, homosexuality represents the last frontier of diversity in our society, and thus a place that welcomes the gay community welcomes all kinds of people" (2005: 41).

The "creative class" Richard Florida's cities need to attract for their own economic survival is, of course, interested in more than economic values. It is in fact the manifestation of other than economic values in urban settings that his "gay index" tracks. Gays not only give consumption a veneer of style but, at the same time, give cities increasingly turned over to consumption a veneer of authenticity. That veneer of authenticity rests in the end not just on the identification of homosexuals with the now authentic great cities of the nineteenth century, but again on the history of gay oppression. It is that history – with the possibility of enduring hostility it conveys – that connects homosexuals to what are, after style, perhaps the two other most highly prized non-economic values in the postmodern city: "diversity" and "feeling."

However familiar, even ideal (wealthy, white, male) gays might seem, their status as members of an oppressed minority allows their presence to serve as evidence of urban diversity. It is their oppression, moreover, that secures the continuing identification of gays with feeling. Their own feelings for each other, after all, are so intense as to lead them to defy social hostility. More to the point, that intensity is carried over into their commitment to the city, and to the communities that they supposedly journey to cities to seek, in their flight from social hostility elsewhere.

Consequently, heterosexuals are not just moving to US cities these days but to what were once considered gay ghettos – Chelsea in New York City, Boystown in Chicago, the Castro in San Francisco – in pursuit of authentically urban experiences (Zernike 2003; Rich 2004; Brown 2007). Gay enclaves are being gentrified. The cities in which gays serve as signs of authentic urbanity will, perhaps, remain distinct places. But the gays, the cities, and the experiences of social difference they all offer will be safely limited.

References

Abraham, Julie (2009) *Metropolitan Lovers: The Homosexuality of Cities*. Minneapolis: University of Minnesota Press.

Acosta, Marcel, and Hinkle, Jeffrey (2001) Branding queer identity: Chicago's North Halsted district. *Planners Network* 146: 12–13.

Bartlett, Neil (1990) *Ready to Catch Him Should He Fall*. London: Serpent's Tail.

Brekhus, Wayne H. (2003) *Peacocks, Chameleons, Centaurs: Gay Suburbia and the Grammar of Social Identity*. Chicago: University of Chicago Press.

Bronski, Michael (1998) *The Pleasure Principle: Sex, Backlash, and the Struggle for Gay Freedom*. New York: St Martin's Press.

Brown, Patricia Leigh (2007) Gay enclaves, once unique, lose urgency. *New York Times* October 30: A1.

Cantu, Lionel (2002) *De Ambiente*: queer tourism and the shifting boundaries of Mexican male sexualities. *GLQ* 8 (1–2): 139–66.

Delany, Samuel R. (1999) *Times Square Red, Times Square Blue*. New York: New York University Press.

Deutsche, Rosalind (1999) Reasonable urbanism. In *Giving Ground: The Politics of Propinquity*, ed. Jean Copjec and Michael Sorkin. New York: Verso, 175–206.

Florida, Richard (2002) *The Rise of the Creative Class*. New York: Basic Books.

Florida, Richard (2005) *Cities and the Creative Class*. New York: Routledge.

Giorgi, Gabriel (2002) Madrid *en transito*: travelers, visibility, and gay identity. *GLQ* 8, (1–2): 57–80.

Landler, Mark (2006) Berlin mayor, symbol of openness, has national appeal. *New York Times* September 23: A4.

Letellier, Patrick (2005) Interview with Richard Florida: success depends on gays. *Advocate* June 7: 22.

Manalansan, Martin F., IV (2003) *Global Divas: Filipino Gay Men in the Diaspora*. Durham, NC: Duke University Press.

Markwell, Kevin (2002) Mardi Gras tourism and the construction of Sydney as an international gay and lesbian city. *GLQ* 8 (1–2): 81–99.

Puar, Jasbir Kaur (2002) Circuits of queer mobility: tourism, travel, and globalization. *GLQ* 8 (1–2): 101–38.

Rich, Motoko (2004) Edged out by the stroller set. *New York Times* May 27: F1, F10.

Ross, Andrew (1999) *The Celebration Chronicles*. New York: Ballantine.

Sinfield, Alan (1998) *Gay and After*. London: Serpent's Tail.

Soja, Edward W. (1999) Inside exopolis: scenes from Orange County. In *Variations on a Theme Park*, ed. Michael Sorkin. New York: Hill and Wang, 94–122.

Solnit, Rebecca, and Schwartzenberg, Susan (2000) *Hollow City*. New York: Verso.

Stacey, Judith (2005) The families of man: gay male intimacy and kinship in a global metropolis. *Signs* 30 (3): 1911–35.

St John, Warren (2003) Metrosexuals come out. *New York Times* Style section, June 22: 1.

Walker, Richard A. (1998) An appetite for the city. In *Reclaiming San Francisco: History, Politics, Culture*, ed. James Brook, Chris Carlsson, and Nancy J. Peters. San Francisco: City Lights, 1–19.

White, Edmund (2001) *The Flâneur: A Stroll Through the Paradoxes of Paris*. New York: Bloomsbury.

Williams, Raymond (1997) Metropolitan perceptions and the emergence of modernism. In *The Politics of Modernism: Against the New Conformists*, ed. Tony Pinkney. London: Verso, 37–48.

Wilson, Elizabeth (1997) Looking backward, nostalgia and the city. In *Imagining Cities: Scripts, Signs, Memories*, ed. Sallie Westwood and John Williams. New York: Routledge, 125–36.

Zernike, Kate (2003) The new couples next door, gay and straight. *New York Times* August 24: A16.

Zukin, Sharon (1995) *The Cultures of Cities*. Oxford: Blackwell.

Chapter 52

Gendering Urban Space

Jessica Ellen Sewell

The city is a material thing – it is made up of buildings and infrastructure as well as people and activities. Many forms of difference within the city are expressed materially – difference visibly shapes neighborhoods and creates divisions. We can locate wealth and poverty by district, block, and building. Differences of nationality, ethnicity, and race are similarly locatable; Chinatowns and other ethnic districts are called out on maps and become important elements of our cognitive maps of the city. Class and ethnicity also mark the physical landscape of the city. The scale of housing units, expense and type of materials, and upkeep of buildings let us know who lives within, whether renters with unkempt lawns or the rich, guarded by doormen and the gates of private communities. Signage and style give us clues to ethnicity; we can read national background not only from the languages on storefronts, but also in the design of houses and gardens and the ways of using the front yard or stoop. As a form of difference in the city, gender functions differently. It cross-cuts other categories; we do not have men's and women's residential districts, but gender is an important category structuring all residential districts, across class and race.

To see and understand gender within the city, the standard set of tools for how to understand difference in the city does not always serve us well. Instead, we must look at how spaces within the city are imagined and experienced, how they are conceptualized as gendered, and how practices confirm or complicate that gendering. The idea that gender should be understood as a practice through which women experience and resist patriarchal norms has been a mainstay of gender geography and women's history since the 1990s (Bondi and Rose 2003). However, the materiality of the city and the role that it plays in gendered urban practices are only rarely explicitly addressed within this literature. In contrast, scholars who study the material aspects of the city – architecture and urban form – have mostly focused

The New Blackwell Companion to the City Edited by Gary Bridge and Sophie Watson
© 2011 Blackwell Publishing Ltd

on how the city expresses patriarchal power and contrains women (Hayden 1980; Matrix 1984; Roberts 1991; Weisman 1992), without taking account of the possibilities for resistance and transgression. To explore gender in urban space in a way that fully takes account of both the materiality of the city and the complexities of practices within it, I analyze physical, imagined, and experienced cultural landscapes and explore how they interact to construct gendered spaces (Sewell 2011). By analyzing these dimensions of the gendering of space separately and then overlaying them on each other, it becomes possible to see how ideology, experience, and the built environment sometimes reinforce and at other times contradict each other, making space for resistance and change.

The physical landscape is the built environment and its spaces. While we often think about urban space in abstract terms, as districts or zones, for example, the physical city underlies those abstract spaces. Streets, infrastructure, and buildings make certain kinds of uses possible or probable, and define physical boundaries that are then overlaid with social and cultural ones. The physical landscape also serves as a concretization of cultural values. For example, expensive materials let us know that the people and activities attached to a space have high cultural value. Design languages also communicate to us whether we are the intended users of a space; dark wood and leather, for example, mark a restaurant or executive lounge as a space for men (Kinchin 1996). At a larger scale, the physical landscape constrains and shapes our movement through and use of spaces.

The imagined landscape is the landscape as conceived of and understood by individuals within a group. While each individual may have a slightly different understanding of the landscape, it is most useful to focus on the shared aspects of these imaginings, and particularly the culturally dominant imaginings, those that have the most currency and the most influence on the shaping of physical space. Aspects of the imagined landscape include commonly shared notions of neighborhoods and their character; expectations and preconceptions about the type of people, activities, and buildings that should or will be found in a certain area; personal feelings about which places are safe or unsafe, pleasant or uncomfortable, interesting or dull; and the memories and conceptions of the city one uses to navigate and use space. One form of imagined landscape is ideology, the ideal structure of activities in space for which planners and other experts strive. But the filter through which individuals make sense of the space around them is also a form of imagined landscape (de Certeau 1984; Pred 1992).

The experienced landscape is the physical landscape as experienced in daily practice. Experienced landscapes, like imagined landscapes, are personal, but many people with shared social characteristics will share similar experiences. Any given physical landscape will correspond to several imagined landscapes and several experienced landscapes, as women and men, rich and poor, workers and tourists, will all experience the same place somewhat differently. It is through everyday experience that the structure of the physical landscape has social effects, as we struggle, for example, to live in a house designed for a nuclear family (Hayden 1980), or to navigate public transportation designed for able-bodied people not burdened with strollers (Matrix 1984). At least equally importantly, it is through everyday experiences that contradictions between the physical and the imagined landscape, or between different imagined landscapes, are manifest. It is at the level of the experienced landscape that individuals negotiate gender in the city, as they make use of and contradict the ways that space is imagined as gendered, in the process often changing the meanings of that space.

In the remainder of this essay, I apply this approach to one example of gendered urban space, the downtown shopping district. While this one space cannot stand in for the entire city, the extent of research that has been dedicated to it, as well as its centrality in discussions of gender and public space, make it a prime example of a complexly gendered urban space, through which and within which gendered norms have been contested.

Downtown Shopping Districts

The territory most often identified as women's space in the city is the downtown shopping district, focused on department stores and large dry goods stores. This district came into being in the second half of the nineteenth century, in the context both of the expansion of consumer goods and of the increasing separation of residential, work, and retail space within cities. By the late nineteenth century, the majority of workplaces were no longer in the same buildings as residences, and most workplaces were entirely separated from middle- and upper-class residential districts. Much office work in particular moved into specialized tall buildings in the downtown, which was well served by public transportation. Downtowns also typically contained an entertainment district of theaters and spectacular restaurants, as well as the shopping district. Shopping, entertainment, and office districts were each imagined in different gendered ways – with shopping seen as entirely feminine, offices as distinctly male, and entertainment a space in which women should be escorted and elite – but of course women actually were active participants in all of these spaces, and as I will argue, their experiences of these spaces helped to complicate the meanings of the gendered downtown shopping district.

These downtown districts were typically imagined at the turn of the century as entirely separate. The power of this imagination is such that many scholars have treated the downtown shopping district, and in particular department stores within them, as if they were isolated. However, in fact, shopping, entertainment, and office districts often overlapped significantly (Sewell 2003). All three activities were dependent on high accessibility by public transportation and banks, but had different requirements. While ground-floor locations, with windows to show goods, were essential for shops, they were not important for other uses. As the real-estate ideal for shops was expensive, the most financially efficient building type maximized use by combining ground-floor shops topped by multiple stories of cellular offices, accessed through a separate entrance that segregated the spaces intended for shopping women and office workers. Similarly, many downtown theaters and restaurants had offices above. In some cases, all three downtown districts were accommodated in the same building. For example, the Flood building in downtown San Francisco housed shops aimed at women on its ground floor, offices upstairs, and a grand downtown café with multiple dining rooms and live entertainment in the basement.

Within the downtown, the shopping district was the area defined by department stores and other shops focused on a female clientele, often concentrated on a single street, such as Broadway in New York City, State Street in Chicago, or Oxford Street in London. The sidewalks of this street were lined with show windows, displaying goods in increasingly elaborate ways and creating the leisure activity of window shopping. The stores containing these windows were similarly opulent and impressive. Department stores in particular had inventive shop-window displays and striking architecture. However, their interiors were significantly more opulent and spectacular than their exteriors. Their elaborate interior space was usually organized around a grand central atrium, sometimes lit through a stained glass window, which was filled with lights, music, goods, and decorations to the point of overwhelming shoppers with stimulation. Through their architecture and their wide range of goods and services, department stores served as microcosms of the downtown shopping district, potentially negating the need for shoppers to go anywhere else. In addition, their overwhelming displays and centrally focused design sometimes made it difficult, then as now, to find the exit. While enclosing women within the department store was economically desirable for store-owners, it also served an ideological purpose, reinforcing the idea that women shoppers were removed from the public streets of the downtown, and ensconced instead in a privatized feminine public space, a feminine island within the more masculine city.

Imagining downtown shopping districts

Downtown shopping districts, and the department stores that anchored them, were imagined in multiple and often contradictory ways in their nineteenth-century and early twentieth-century heyday, but all of the imaginings were bound up with gender. A dominant mode of imagining the shopping downtown, that promoted by department store owners and managers and other city boosters, is as a middle-class feminized space (Abelson 1989; Leach 1984; Domosh 1996). For middle-class women, making goods at home became increasingly unfashionable, and shopping became both a necessary task and a source of pleasure. Guidebooks described downtown shopping districts and department stores as peopled entirely by women shopping for leisure. The men who shared the sidewalks with women and worked and shopped in the stores were invisible. Department stores in particular, the anchor of downtown retail districts, were imagined by the 1890s as an entirely female space, in which women shoppers were served by female clerks (Abelson 1989; Benson 1986; Leach 1984). Similarly, the presence of non-elite women was largely unremarked in boosters' descriptions of the downtown.

This imagining of the downtown shopping district as a safe, middle-class space made it a space of freedom for many women, even as it naturalized gender and class differences and reinforced the idea of women as emotional, illogical, and useless (because they were consumers not producers). As Leach (1984) and others have argued, the shopping district functioned as a foothold in public space for women (Domosh 1996; Friedberg 1993). Leach argues that the downtown shopping district was emancipatory, that women's presence in public, combined with the experience of being treated as a powerful, individual, consumer, helped to transform women's sense of themselves and their relationship to the city. Erika Rappaport similarly argues that shoppers in London's West End participated in a new feminized public realm, one marked by pleasure and freedom (Rappaport 2000). Women made use of their power within the downtown to mobilize it as a political space as well, convincing shop owners to mount pro-suffrage window displays (Sewell 2003; Enstam 1998: 167). Even the English suffragettes who destroyed shop windows did so in the context of their rights to the downtown shopping district, arguing that they were reminding retailers that because they depended on women shoppers, it was their duty to support women's voting rights (Rappaport 2000: 217). In addition to empowering elite shoppers, the stores of the downtown shopping district, particularly the department stores, created many new jobs for women, primarily working-class clerks, but also middle-class managers and professionals (Leach 1984; Benson 1986). This not only provided independence for many women, but also increased the presence of women in the downtown, further strengthening women's claim to public space.

Within the downtown shopping district, women shoppers' vision was the prize for which shops competed. The displays in show windows competed to amaze and surprise, not merely displaying goods, but turning them into elaborate pictures, setting up lifelike dramas, or surprising viewers with the vanishing woman and other elaborate mechanical displays. The perfect transparency of window glass, which allowed these displays to pull shoppers into the stores, was achieved through expert lighting and air circulation. Within the stores, elaborate displays made use of multiple colors (many of them newly available in the late nineteenth century because of the invention of aniline dyes), elaborate lighting, and the sheer spectacle of excess. Through spectacle, shoppers were, shop-owners and advertisers believed, drawn into stores and seduced into purchases. Because of the primacy of the shopper's vision within the downtown shopping landscape, the downtown shopping district also, Anne Friedberg (1993) has argued, allowed women to function as *flâneuses*. As they window-shopped, women were able not only to be observers – possessors, not objects, of the gaze – but also to be mobilized as they strolled along the street. Just as Leach argues that the role of being a consumer gave women new social power, Freidberg argues that women's consumer gaze gave women new agency. Department stores themselves even made use of the idea of the *flâneuse* in their marketing, presenting themselves as a safe space through which women could experience the modern city and its thrills (Rappaport 2000). The act of shopping both allowed women to roam the city on their own and entailed many other activities in addition to shopping, such as eating in tea rooms and attending matinees. The physical separation between the shopping district and polite residential districts meant that women shoppers not only walked the streets of the downtown, but also rode regularly on public transportation, thus becoming part of other public spaces in the city.

These narratives of female empowerment emerge from the downtown shopping district being imagined as essentially a safe female world, a polite space where middle-class women could respectably participate in the public space of the city and native-born working women could respectably earn a living. However, it was also a district predicated on women's supposed irrationality and inability to control their passions. The striking window displays, lavish interiors, and elaborate buildings of the district reflected the idea that women were irrational beings, controlled by their passions, which could be easily manipulated through spectacle (Abelson 1989). As a San Francisco guidebook described the scene in the shopping district in 1904,

"Some are lured by the fragrant aroma or tempting window exhibition into the sanctuary of ices and candies; others succumb to the florist, and thus money circulates by the caprice of feminine fancy" (Keeler 1903: 37). Before the 1890s, when the majority of department store employees were still male, the sexualized desire for goods that is expressed in this quotation, in the rhetoric surrounding kleptomania (Abelson 1989), and in Emile Zola's *The Ladies' Paradise*, which describes a fictionalized Bon Marché, was compounded by the idea that shopping women were passionate about the good-looking young men working in the stores as well (Domosh 2001; Scobey 2002).

The emotional passion of women's potential relationship to goods fed into a second, contrasting imagining of the downtown shopping district and the women who peopled it, one which saw the district as immoral and sexualized, not polite and safely feminine (Domosh 2001; Scobey 2002). In the 1860s and 1870s anxieties about consumer society were embodied in the "New York Woman," the denizen of the downtown shopping district, whose absence from the home, lack of self-mastery, interest in displaying herself, and association with consumption rather than production made her morally repugnant (Domosh 2001). This association was reinforced by the architecture of the stores within the district, which were theatrical and opulent both inside and out, creating a stage on which shopping women displayed themselves, in clear violation of the norms of respectability. The geography of the downtown shopping district further fed this imagining, as it combined the department stores and other shops offering frivolous goods and smooth-talking salesmen with a landscape of amusements such as theaters and restaurants, which further stoked the image of the district and its denizens as superficial and morally suspect. In some cities, such as New York, the fancy stores and high-class amusements of the downtown were also cheek by jowl with much less respectable, although still elite, brothels and gambling rooms (Scobey 2002).

While the idea that the downtown shopping district and the women who peopled it were immoral was clearly a negative imagining of the district, shopping women's self-display and individualistic consumption can also be seen as granting them a new sort of power. David Scobey (2002) argues that women on New York's Ladies' Mile were able to recast the sexual and moral boundaries of women's sphere while also enjoying the pleasure of being the center of attention. This was only possible because Ladies' Mile, like other downtown shopping districts, was understood to be segregated by class as much as, if not more than, by gender. It is within the context of a safely elite space that women were able to experiment with self-display, helping to create, Scobey argues, a new heterosocial bourgeois public sphere that celebrated leisure, consumption, and spectacle as civilizing practices (2002: 58).

Experiencing downtown shopping districts

The downtown shopping district as experienced was much more of a space of mixture than admitted in dominant imaginings. Because the buildings of the district often contained offices and the district overlapped significantly with office and entertainment districts, the people on the downtown streets were rarely if ever all female or all middle class. This was particularly the case on major thoroughfares, whose role as a transportation corridor meant that they were frequented by workers and others on their way to nearby locations beyond the center of the downtown. Not only did shopping women share the street with shop clerks, factory workers, service workers, and male office workers, but they also increasingly shared the street with female office workers, as the jobs of typist and secretary became increasingly feminized. While this strengthened the association of women with the downtown, it undercut the polite, middle-class nature of downtown's femininity. To some extent, different users were segregated by time of day, with workers on the streets in the morning and evening and elite shoppers at midday, but some mixture was always present. This had always been the case in industrial cities, as Mary Ryan (1990) points out, but the idea that the street should be segregated, always present, became increasingly powerful as other parts of the city became more specialized. The power of the ideal of segregated space and its contradiction with reality was such that in many cities a strong effort was made by elites, particularly elite women, to clean up the downtown, removing people and activities that did not correspond to a middle-class ideal (Baldwin 1999).

The extent to which women experienced the shopping district as a space of mixture varied significantly by their class and race position, as did their ability to navigate that mixture without compromising their respectability. My own research on San Francisco shows that the stores that catered to a lower-middle-class clientele tended to be located along Market Street, the spine of the transportation network, and to the west of the central downtown area, in a highly mixed area (Sewell 2011). Similarly, Sharon Wood (2005: 24–5) describes a mixture of shops, factories, offices, and saloons in the more working-class portion of downtown Davenport, Iowa. In San Francisco the elite shops were along Grant Avenue and in the vicinity of Union Square, much more removed from the industrial and working-class area south of Market and the bustle of Market Street itself. In addition, while the lower-status shops shared buildings and blocks with offices, the elite shopping was more single-use (Sewell 2011). Thus for shoppers whose trips focused on higher-end goods, their experiences more closely approximated the ideal of a gender- and class-segregated shopping district. However, these class-based areas overlapped, and elite women also traveled by streetcar, and thus their trips downtown inevitably entailed some contact with men, immigrants, and the lower classes.

Class differences in women's experiences of the downtown shopping district went beyond simple geography, however. Equally significant is how experiences were shaped by the class power of individual women. For elite women, their status, marked through their clothing and their purchasing power, gave them relatively free rein throughout the downtown: in stores, where they were comfortably served by shopgirls just as they were served by maids at home; in tea rooms, where they could afford to spend money on expensive sweets; in high end restaurants, most of which served liquor; and even, with a male escort, in elite saloons (Sewell 2011; Scobey 2002). For poorer women, the chance of being mistaken for a prostitute or otherwise compromising their respectability was higher, so the range of downtown establishments they could comfortably visit was fewer. When elite women shopped, they were able to purchase what they wished and to demand full service from stores, using them as a sort of women's club. In contrast, lower-middle-class women only visited more elite stores on occasion, whether to make a purchase, use the writing room, or listen to music, but their class status made them conscious of being visitors to these spaces, with less ownership than their elite sisters. They more often patronized discount department stores and other stores during sales, which meant dealing with unpleasant crowds and below-par merchandise, making shopping a chore more than a pleasure (Sewell 2011).

The Consequences of Heterogeneity

While the experience of class and gender mixture on the streets has often functioned as a source of anxiety, there is much to suggest that the mixture of the downtown can also be a source of not only pleasure but also power for women. It was precisely the mixture of men and women of all classes on the downtown streets, combined with women's claims on this space as shoppers and as workers, that made it a prime location for suffrage activity, for example, which required women to convince men to vote for women's rights (Sewell 2003, 2011). Women's presence in the downtown, the symbolic heart of the city, also gave them a new claim to citizenship based on their rights as individuals (and individual consumers), rather than as mothers (Sewell 2011). The successful movement of much leisure shopping from the downtown to the shopping mall in the postwar United States weakened women's ties to the downtown and moved women shoppers to a privatized space that limited free speech and political expression (Cohen 1996).

The experience of heterogeneous space also provides an opportunity for women to experience the freedom of anonymity in the city. Elizabeth Wilson suggests that the impulse to sort and segregate the city even functions in part as a desire to contain women, who gain real power from the chaotic city (Wilson 1991). In the contemporary context, Julie Podmore explores the consequences of the heterogeneity of the Boulevard St-Laurent in Montréal, which houses a wide variety of land uses and attracts a range of class, age, and ethnic groups to its diverse shops, bars, and restaurants (Podmore 2001). She argues that this street functions as a space of safety for lesbians, who find that the character of this street as a "space of difference" makes it a comfortable place to be out about their sexuality. This is not a lesbian territory per se, just as the turn of the century downtown was not exclusively a middle-class women's territory, but the experience of mixture, combined with Boulevard St-Laurent's popular imagining as a space of difference, allows it to function as an important landmark in lesbians' daily lives.

Physical, Imagined, and Experienced Gendered Spaces

While I have focused in this essay on the downtown shopping district, using the approach of examining physical, imagined, and experienced spaces and the convergences and slippages between them can be fruitful for examining the relationship between gender and a wide range of urban spaces, including spaces of leisure, transportation, and work. The relationship between the physical spaces within which men and women work, and how their organization reflects gendered power structures, explored by scholars such as Angel Kwolek-Folland (1994), how workplaces are imagined as spaces of solidarity, sexuality, or gender privilege (Enstad 1999; Boyer 1998; McDowell 1997), and how the spaces encountered on a daily basis by workers are experienced, can provide us with rich understandings of gendered cities. Likewise, examinations of how leisure spaces are built, imagined, and experienced can lead us to better understand the role of urban leisure in the construction of gender, whether the early twentieth-century dance halls and nickel-odeons that Peiss (1986) pinpoints as sites where working-class women articulated new, sexualized gender roles, or the playgrounds that Anke (2007) argues were a site for the creation of feminist community in Midwestern American cities in the 1960s and 1970s. Paying attention to both the material reality of the city and the multiple gendered ways in which it is imagined and experienced will allow us to paint a richer picture of how gender infuses all aspects of urban space.

References

Abelson, E. S. (1989) *When Ladies Go A-Thieving: Middle-Class Shoplifters in the Victorian Department Store*. New York: Oxford University Press.

Anke, A. (2007) *Finding the Movement: Sexuality, Contested Space, and Feminist Activism*. Durham, NC: Duke University Press.

Baldwin, P. C. (1999) *Domesticating the Street: The Reform of Public Space in Hartford, 1850–1930*. Columbus: Ohio State University Press.

Benson, S. P. (1986) *Counter Cultures: Saleswomen, Managers, and Customers in American Department Stores, 1890–1940*. Urbana: University of Illinois Press.

Bondi, L., and Rose, D. (2003) Constructing gender, constructing the urban: a review of Anglo-American feminist urban geography. *Gender, Place, and Culture* 10 (3): 229–45.

Boyer, K. (1998) Place and the politics of virtue: clerical work, corporate anxiety, and changing meanings of public womanhood in early twentieth-century Montréal. *Gender, Place, and Culture* 5 (3): 261–76.

Cohen, L. (1996) From town center to shopping center: the reconfiguration of the community marketplace in postwar America. *American Historical Review* 101 (4): 1050–81.

de Certeau, M. (1984) Walking the city. In *The Practice of Everyday Life*. Trans. Steven Rendall. Berkeley: University of California Press, 91–110.

Domosh, M. (1996) *Invented Cities: The Creation of Landscape in Nineteenth-Century New York and Boston*. New Haven, CT: Yale University Press.

Domosh, M. (2001) The "Women of New York": a fashionable moral geography. *Environment and Planning D: Society and Space* 19: 573–92.

Enstad, N. (1999) *Ladies of Labor, Girls of Adventure: Working Women, Popular Culture, and Labor Politics at the Turn of the Twentieth Century*. New York: Columbia University Press.

Enstam, E. Y. (1998) *Women and the Creation of Urban Life: Dallas, Texas, 1843–1920*. College Station: Texas A&M University Press.

Friedberg, A. (1993) *Window Shopping: Cinema and the Postmodern*. Berkeley: University of California Press.

Hayden, D. (1980) What would a non-sexist city be like? In *Women and the American City*, ed. C. R. Stimpson, E. Dixler, M. J. Nelson, and K. B. Yatrakis. Chicago: University of Chicago Press, 167–84.

Keeler, C. (1903) *San Francisco and Thereabouts*. San Francisco: The California Promotion Committee.

Kinchin, J. (1996) Interiors: nineteenth-century essays on the "masculine" and the "feminine" room. In *The Gendered Object*, ed. P. Kirkham. Manchester: Manchester University Press, 12–29.

Kwolek-Folland, A. (1994) *Engendering Business: Men and Women in the Corporate Office, 1870–1930*. Baltimore, MD: Johns Hopkins University Press.

Leach, W. J. (1984) Transformations in a culture of consumption: women and department stores, 1890–1925. *Journal of American History* 21 (2): 319–42.

Matrix (eds.) (1984) *Making Space: Women and the Man Made Environment*. London: Pluto Press.

McDowell, L. (1997) *Capital Culture: Gender at Work in the City*. Oxford: Blackwell.

Peiss, K. (1986) *Cheap Amusements: Working Women and Leisure in Turn-of-the-Century New York*. Philadelphia: Temple University Press.

Podmore, J. A. (2001) Lesbians in the crowd: gender, sexuality and visibility along Montréal's Boul. St-Laurent. *Gender, Place, and Culture* 8 (4): 33–55.

Pred, A. (1992) Languages of everyday practice and resistance: Stockholm at the end of the nineteenth century. In *Reworking Modernity: Capitalisms and Symbolic Discontent*, ed. A. Pred and M. J. Watts. New Brunswick, NJ: Rutgers University Press, 118–54.

Rappaport, E. (2000) *Shopping for Pleasure: Women in the Making of London's West End*. Princeton, NJ: Princeton University Press.

Roberts, M. (1991) *Living in a Man-Made World: Gender Assumptions in Modern Housing Design*. London: Routledge.

Ryan, M. P. (1990) *Women in Public: Between Banners and Ballots, 1825–1880*. Baltimore, MD: Johns Hopkins University Press.

Scobey, D. (2002) Nymphs and satyrs: sex and the bourgeois public sphere in Victorian New York. *Winterthur Portfolio* 37 (1): 43–66.

Sewell, J. (2003) Sidewalks and store windows as political landscapes. In *Building, Image, and Identity: Perspectives in Vernacular*, vol. IX, ed. A. Hoagland and K. Breisch. Knoxville: University of Tennessee Press, 85–98.

Sewell, J. (2011) *Women and the Everyday City: Public Space in San Francisco, 1890–1915*. Minneapolis: University of Minnesota Press.

Weisman, L. K. (1992) *Discrimination by Design: A Feminist Critique of the Man-Made Environment*. Urbana: University of Illinois Press.

Wilson, E. (1991) *The Sphinx in the City: Urban Life, the Control of Disorder, and Women*. Berkeley: University of California Press.

Wood, S. (2005) *The Freedom of the Streets: Work, Citizenship, and Sexuality in a Gilded Age City*. Chapel Hill: University of North Carolina Press.

Chapter 53

Nights in the Global City

Sophie Body-Gendrot

Introduction

Night is a multifaceted, socially constructed, and highly ambivalent phenomenon, with objective, subjective, natural, and cultural dimensions. In a city, itself a problematic geographical and social entity, both positive and negative representations of darkness are magnified. The study of nights in the city has been little explored, it is both elusive and fundamental and it is perceived by some as the "last frontier of the city" (Gwiazdzinski 2005). There is not one night but multiple nights, illuminated and gloomy nights, nights for revelry and duty, for the partygoers and the homeless, for rest and unrest. The evidence of night breaks into the day for the best and for the worst.

Throughout the centuries, authorities, law enforcers, and more recently media, have constructed representations of urban nights as times and places of threats or potential risks. Their goal was (and still is) to impose order, via silence and inactivity, in order to ensure safety for the citizens. But night is not just the continuity of the day, it marks a mental and biological rupture, based on an imaginary construction with a social translation. Everywhere, resistances to the idea that cities should be sleepy hollows can be found, all the more so when the necessities of the global economy require that cities never sleep.

This tentative work, still in the making, is informed by several seminars conducted by L. Gwiazdzinski from 2004 to 2008 and by my personal interest in this issue over the years. The seminars involved the testimonies of night professionals, the discussions of scholars from various disciplines, and the support of the French Ministry of Housing and the City in 2008. This explains why French examples are predominant in this chapter.

The first section of the study reviews the evolution of the conceptions and perceptions of urban nights. The second section analyzes the representations of darkness

The New Blackwell Companion to the City   Edited by Gary Bridge and Sophie Watson
© 2011 Blackwell Publishing Ltd

in cities and profiles the diversity of solutions it entails. The third section, by contrast, presents voices from nights' users and lovers which lead to considerations of this time of night as a conquest over the rigidity of daytime. The fourth section focuses on the contradictions in the perceptions of night.

The Diverse Perceptions of Urban Nights.

We may start with man's biological clock sending signals of the physical necessity to rest after a day's labor. Darkness is then interpreted as a signal to stop action. Darkness indeed disorganizes perceptions since 80 percent of them come from eyesight. Therefore, before technological innovations took place, nights were permeated with a sense of fear *of* the night and *in* the night (of specific places, individuals, and groups), anticipating death.

History and sciences

In Renaissance Tuscan and Flemish cities, drums, trumpets, bells, and horns warned residents that the day was ending (Cabantous 2009: 31). The heavy doors of the historic cities were then closed, so that sleeping dwellers would better be protected. Historians have also led us to understand how much scientific discoveries in the use of light have changed urban perceptions.

Scientific progress indicates indeed a slow conquest which accelerated in the twentieth century. After thousands of years of repose inflicted by the constraints of darkness, people contrived to make use of fire in order to have darkness gradually recede into light. People were then learning to progressively tame their fears of night. Yet with fire came the threat of destruction and disasters, as numerous cities were built out of wood. Thus Glasgow and Amsterdam in 1652, London in 1666, Madrid in 1734, Paris and other French cities suffered major fires (Cabantous 2009: 47) not to mention Chicago and San Francisco which were also devastated in their early development. Domestic accidents remained a major risk all along, but the use of oil lamps, torches, and candles helped cities, their streets and their homes come out of the dark ages still prevailing in the hinterland.

While Greek cities such as Antioch and Ephesos learned early how to make use of light, the Middle Ages remained dark. The French King, Philip V, in 1318 passed an ordinance ordering candles to burn at his castle door all night: murders had indeed become too frequent and grievances were growing. Subsequently, night watchmen patrolling the streets appeared as well as street lanterns. King Louis XI ordered Parisians to "have weapons in their homes, to watch over the walls and to set bright torches and lanterns at the cross roads" (Gwiazdzinski 2005: 80–1).

Such ordinance, however, was not enforced and the rates of nightly homicides remained high before modern times. The police lieutenant of King Louis XIV in 1662 had the mission of providing the city and suburbs of Paris with lanterns and torch-bearers. City-dwellers were asked to light their streets and crossroads with candles. Guards carrying bells would signal when to start the lights in Paris and keep them lit until 2 a.m. Street lamps appeared in 1744, and the use of gaslight was generalized after 1798. City residents in the nineteenth century were the first to imagine that urban nights could be artificially lit. Baron Haussmann ordered 14,000 gaslamps to illuminate the streets of Paris after 1852.

Electric lighting was widespread after 1900. Large cities competed from that moment on to attract visitors with splendid night entertainments. The first advertisements were seen on the Eiffel Tower during the Universal Exhibition in 1900. The rise of skyscrapers in American cities (the first one built in 1882 in Chicago) embodies this transition to modernity, with their vast skylines continuously lit, used as city brands. The break between the day and the night gradually vanished and new landscapes emerged, capturing the urban imaginary. After 1945, nine homes out of ten were equipped with electric lighting in New York, and in Paris all gaslamps were removed from the streets after 1962. But not without negative side effects. According to scientists, lit towers and street lights have been detrimental to many bird species (owls, bats, migratory birds, etc.) and how light is used in cities is more and more questioned.

Geography

L. Gwiazdzinski (2005: 151), a French geographer, has studied the various periods during which daily activities continue in cities after dark. According to his typology, pre-night extends from 8 p.m. to 1.30 a.m., characterized by night leisure and the stretching of daytime. The core of night takes place between 1.30 a.m. and 4.30 a.m. when those exerting surveillance, working night shifts, or enjoying darkness make use of the city. In most European countries, transportation has almost stopped in railway stations, bus stations, and airports. Then, from 4.30 a.m. to 6 a.m., dawn is about to conquer urban space. Night addicts ready to take a rest will come across early risers.

In his typology of night people, Gwiazdzinski distinguishes (1) solitary people studying, writing, dreaming, walking, or locking themselves in; (2) partygoers, citizens committed to political meetings and the like; (3) "street artists" and performers; (4) young tribes running from one disco to another, to parties and to bars; (5) people at work including burglars, prostitutes, and drug dealers; (6) the homeless and drifters (2005: 160). One could add those going out at night to let their steam off and those not distinguishing night and day or alternating their uses.

Art

Such typologies are supported by art and literary work. *Night Falcons* painted by Edward Hopper in 1942 evokes perfectly the solitude of the urban night. American photographer Weegee took pictures of night murders, fires, and accidents; he titled his book published in 1945 *The Naked City*. Writers, along with travelers, journalists, and script-writers have translated subjective and objective perceptions of night into countless books, reviews, *films noirs*, comic strips, and images.

Sociology

The sociologists of the Chicago School have devoted numerous case studies of gangs, of girls in dance halls, of prostitutes; of criminals, all night people drifting

from bowling alleys to saloons, to clubs or specific spaces where information circulates, tricks are elaborated, coalitions are made. C. Shaw (1930), a former parole
officer, wrote the life-story of Jack, a 16-year-old delinquent ripping off drunk
clients when the bars in Chicago closed around 2 a.m. R. and C. Block (1995)
confirm that the peak of thefts in Chicago occurs around 2 a.m. when patrons
are drunk and thieves can easily escape via the elevated rail system or poorly lit
parking lots.

Nights of All Dangers?

Representations of dangerous nights vary according to the legacy of different cultures. In the United States, an example in point of the ambiguities associated with
this concept is offered by the way people revel at night. From colonial America to
current times, collective feasts unveil indeed contradictory wishes for order and
chaos, inertia and change, observes A. Lherm (2002). Drinking, fights, leisure,
waste, loose morals marked New England nights and thus threatened the foundations of the civic order in the eyes of colonial authorities. Consequently, as early as
1618, Virginia forbade partying, dance, card games, and music on Saturdays and
Sundays. After 1730, the authorities of Massachusetts decided that people could let
steam off only on Friday nights so they would not spend too much time "merrying"
(2002: 420).

Halloween

During the nineteenth century, elites feared the potential nocturnal violence of
immigrant working classes when they met in their neighborhoods for festive
events.

Halloween is a case in point. It was first celebrated by Scottish, English, and Irish
communities in America, and like Santa Claus, was reinvented in the nineteenth
century and reappropriated by American folklore. It had to adjust to the economic
and social changes of industrial and urban America and nocturnal Halloween
became a medium for acculturation and social control, Lherm (2002: 701) remarks.
The feast was well accepted and the North American nocturnal environment in the
nineteenth century was indeed crowded and reflected the diversity of a multicultural
population.

During the 1930s and most of all, the 1950s, Halloween offered the opportunity
to reinvent a lost, enchanted, communal world in opposition to a conflictual and
disquieting modernity. Later, the myth reflected the tensions dividing American
society: loose morals were denounced, rumors spread (for example, the risk of
criminals inserting razor blades in apples; between 1965 and 1972, the *New York
Times* and other media circulated such stories which never happened). Eager to
keep the upper hand on social control, the adults reappropriated for themselves
the use of the October night and pledged to make Halloween a safe night for
children. However, some religious groups were only too happy to denounce the
pagan feast. Halloween then appears as the sounding board of a fast-changing
society, getting scared of such changes and tired of constant adjustment in behaviors
and values.

What happens?

According to French philosopher and architect, P. Virilio (2004) numerous catastrophes – plane crashes, fires, black-outs, and major failures – occur during dark hours. Eighty percent of dysfunctions in public services in France occur at night when only 20 percent of the staff is at their job (Gwiazdzinski 2005).

Risks in the city at night are obviously increased by troublemakers and delinquents making use of darkness to break conventional norms and cause law-abiders to worry. Such threats have led cities to light public spaces and adopt crime prevention measures, CCTVs and all the paraphernalia meant to make spaces defensible (Newman 1975). Yet it should be emphasized that, in France at least, "for obvious reasons, daytime remains the major moment for diverse offences and crimes due to its multiple opportunities for frictions, delinquency, busy and reactive populations" (Cabantous 2009: 165).

Urban riots in America

In reports on the racial violence which inflamed American cities in the 1960s, one is struck, J. Janowitz (1969) remarks, by the spirit of carnival at night, which marks the first stages of riots: they commonly start after an incident with the police in the black ghetto, and night makes a favorable context for rumor propagation and all forms of unrest as well as easing all ways out. During the summer of 1967, 150 American cities experienced riots, between 1964 and 1968, 329 riots inflamed 260 cities (Kerner Commission 1968).

French urban unrest

In France, since the beginning of the 1980s, numerous incidents and clashes between young people and the police have started after dark. Take for instance the disorders which spread in 200 French cities in the fall of 2005. Numerous Muslim families live in localities northeast of Paris, and at Ramadan they get together at the end of the day to share the only meal they are allowed to take. The triggering incident occurred after a soccer game, when three young men took a shortcut to hurry home, wanting to avoid police control because they carried no ID with them. They found shelter in a nearby electricity substation and two of them were fatally electrocuted. After the news of their deaths spread, policemen were accused of being the cause of deaths. As usual, to express their pain and their anger, local youths set cars on fire. Fires carry both physical and symbolic meanings: the destruction of goods valuable to others for their mobility but also the threat that powerless young men carry (Body-Gendrot 2007).

In this context, the role of the media is all but neutral. For E. Balibar (2006), the movement narrowly depends, in order to spread, on the reflection of its own image via the media. Viewers seeing similar images, night after night, make sense out of them, generalizing from isolated incidents and taking them out of the specific contexts to which they belong. For journalists with TV ratings in mind, reporting on such events necessitates a sensational narrative, the incorporation of hundreds of parochial incidents into the construction of a global danger, and providing the audience with actual targets and opponents.

Firm responses were taken both at the national level and by cities. A state of emergency was pronounced by decree on November 9, 2005 for almost two months. It allowed curfews in sensitive cities (but only 5 percent of them took this option), along with a string of police measures that stretched to daytime.

Violence between young people in night-time leisure zones

A most innovative study on conflicts taking place between young people in nightspots in various European cities has been financed by the European Commission (Recasens 2007). As there has been no previous investigational work on this issue, this study will be quoted at length as it summarizes numerous findings developed in other field researches. It focuses on the development of night-time leisure and conflicts in five European cities (14 case-studies); in addition, it rates the efficiency of measures adopted by various social and institutional players faced with this phenomenon in their cities.

In Bologna (but also in other cities of southern Europe), conflicts usually arise after 11 p.m. or midnight, when the consumption of alcohol or drugs is at its peak. Starting around 9 p.m., "small groups of friends meet, usually at home then they go out to drink something in a bar or pub. Around midnight they go to the disco, entering in the long and complex process of selection and admittance" (Selmini 2007: 107, 111). In Barcelona, "the closing time of discos marks the partying route of those who want to prolong the night by going onto other clubs and bars which are still open (after-hour bars), in public spaces or private houses." Large amounts of alcohol are often consumed in after-hours bars by the most night-loving public when the discos close. In the summer, informal places open, such as raves, which are alternative nightspots, and last all night (Barruti and Rodriguez Basanta 2007: 146–7).

Leisure spending in night economies is a rather recent phenomenon in Europe. It reveals a social and spatial segmentation due to class inequalities and to the presence of sub-cultures in cities. There are very few violent incidents among middle-class young people going into leisure venues downtown (Recasens 2007: 23; Marlière 2007: 47).

Comparing nightlife in British cities, P. Hadfield (2006) remarks that violence between young people during leisure time poses one of the greatest threats to public order in Britain today. In Italy, Portugal, or Spain, alcohol misuse is of low priority to decision-makers and scholars. The uses and meaning of alcohol are both socially constructed and historically contingent. In countries such as Spain or France, alcohol is woven into the cultural fabric of everyday (and every night) life, and being drunk is frequently considered as a sign of weakness, he observes. The use of public space is also different. For Hadfield (2007: 181), in cities like Bologna and Barcelona, one finds

a certain continuity of culture wherein the young follow patterns established by previous generations in their appropriation of the public realm. The spontaneous assembly of large crowds of people in city squares and parks in order to socialize thus involves ... elements of familiar and positively-sanctioned leisure activities that do not necessitate commercial exchange ... (i.e. licensed leisure).

But in the last 15 years, institutional concern about young people's behavior fueled by media alarm campaigns has emerged and more attention has been paid to the association of alcohol or drug consumption, night-time leisure zones, and risks. Cross-national similarities relate to tensions between various groups of young people, between them, the police, bouncers, security guards, and residents when conflicts take place in public spaces, at the periphery and with disco-owners. This point is specifically salient, as it raises the issue of the exclusion of certain groups of youths from leisure places.

> Leisure in private establishments in the urban context is, in a way, the container of our society because it perpetuates segregation and ratifies discrimination by excluding the poor, undesirable and marginalized. Youth violence is merely the consequence of the competitive consumer order that reigns at urban leisure venues in the heart of the so-called post-industrial society. (Marlière 2007: 55)

The leisure-time scenario is an age-old concept that represents business for entrepreneurs and a way of letting off steam for their clients (Recasens 2007: 25–6). In the second half of the 1990s, it became a flourishing economic activity, a consumer commodity, and a screen for access which triggers conflicts. But the image of insecurity and violence that has been sought in night-time leisure has been exaggerated; such violence is a minority occurrence while social conflicts are more common.

Benevolent Nights

The change from light to darkness allows norms of daylight to be shaken and the tyranny of rules to be alleviated.

A special atmosphere for night employees

As opposed to the daytime, when autonomy and mental independence are most praised, solidarity is often a must in the teams of nightshift workers. A special atmosphere and strong friendship are provided and shared by working people. It is obvious for some occupations that take place in hospitals, mail sorting offices, surveillance centers, police stations, or street festivals and entertainment.

According to A. Vega (2000: 25–8), a night-lover and senior nurse, "working nights" gives the opportunity to make numerous decisions, it gives a lot of leverage, the weight of hierarchy is light, all the resources and knowledge accumulated with experience on the job are mobilized when unanticipated events occur. In the first part of the night, she observes, the nurses are afraid of committing mistakes, then a pause takes place around 11 p.m. It is the time when unexpected encounters among working people may happen, the exchange of secrets, the sharing of ethical problems or memories. After 3 a.m. "everything becomes kind of weird ... The ghosts slide stealthily between dark masses, along the corridors." The most difficult time probably takes place just before dawn, due to fatigue. Patients emerge from sleep, they require special care or the delivery of their drugs. At dawn, the staff is in a hurry to leave, the day has arrived.

This night solidarity in work is supported by other studies. Trust and friendship are reported among policemen, firemen, typesetters, and the like working on night shifts (Gathérias 2000: 62; Lipset *et al.* 1962; Chetkovitch 1997).

Time for mutual enhancement

One should mention also the testimony of a French bouncer. The bar he worked in on the Left Bank was owned by a legendary figure in France, the Franciscan Abbé Pierre, who devoted his life to the poor. The bouncer avows that in his eight years of night work, he confessed more people than in a church! After the bar closed, he would open a meeting-place for night birds (where the rule forbade sleep) in a nearby street. There, a surgeon would meet a housewife or a drifter: all kinds of people came, eager to talk and appreciate their diversity enhanced by the magic that the night bestows on people. These witnesses claim that nights are peaceful, creative, and benevolent. If the air of city makes people free, so does the night.

Safer cities

Segregation and poverty combine to make environments and Otherness threatening for those who do not belong. But if control is exerted by institutions at the top, it is also exerted at the bottom by communities, civic organizations, and all kinds of communal actors. The interaction of the two processes makes sense. What comes to mind are self-help practices such as Neighborhood Watches which emerged in the 1960s in the United States. The thirty million Americans volunteering for Neighborhood Watch see themselves as the "eyes and ears" that will make street life safer. But unlike Jane Jacobs's (1961) praising of the density and diversity of streets for good prevention, the Neighborhood Watch concept is mostly a middle-class one and less representative of neighborhoods with young people, immigrants, and poor minorities.

In minority neighborhoods, organizations' responses to the drug dealers taking hold of their streets and public parks is to organize. At the beginning of the 1990s, one night every other month, in Chicago, the residents in a given neighborhood would get together, sit around tables on the sidewalks and take back their streets to have their area look like other safe areas. Older women such as the Grey Panthers are part of such vulnerable community organizations (Body-Gendrot 2001: ch. 5).

Ethical Issues Set by the Cities that Never Sleep

How to reconcile the city that sleeps, the city that carouses, and the city that works? Does it constitute a dilemma that should be on the agenda of all local authorities so that possible antagonisms and conflicts are looked at and anticipated?

Economic constraints

Recent economic studies focus on the benefits and liabilities of cities that never sleep, in large part due to the globalization and the communication techniques that allow continuous linkages of time and space.

The headquarters of firms set in global cities may organize their production on various sites of the planet, ignoring the time differences and negating the barrier of night. A typical example is the way stock exchanges operate: the flow of information, with its associated financial exchanges, is viewed as a matter of survival for firms which are both rival and complementary economical actors; these global agents use their global cities (New York, London, Tokyo, and many other cities in a smaller scale) to optimize their profits by ignoring the night (Sassen 1991).

More generally, in cities that never sleep, consumers are happy to buy a magazine or a bottle of milk, play basketball or even golf, or listen to jazz or dance at any time. Along with the day-workers, though, they rely on shadow workers (mostly immigrants) who are willing to clean cars or office towers, to iron suits, to provide catering or buildings security, to transport parcels ...

But when we leave the domain of information data and dollars, the night work is felt far differently: for example, the constraints of processing the mail in the central United Postal Service in Louisville, Kentucky, has proved difficult to organize because of lack of employees volunteering for night service. It requires substantial inducements and the help of the city to solve the problem, in the form of shelters to avoid long commuting time and to recover from work exhaustion (*New York Times*: November 1, 1998). "While usually consumers enjoy services provided twenty four hours on row and employers make profit out of their investments, a lot of employees do not find working night hours attractive" (Presser 2003: 21).

A high price to be paid

Two American surveys (US Dept of Commerce 1998; US Dept of Labor 2002) showed that when a household has no child, it can generally manage the stress generated by night work. By contrast, with children, the risks of divorce increase, particularly when the mother works after midnight. Her lack of sleep has an impact on the couple and on the children.

Researchers have questioned nurses and other women opting for night work. They accept to work after midnight to be able to have dinner with their children and put them to bed before leaving. These mothers have usually four or five hours' sleep. However, after a while, their memory is failing, their work is less competitive, and they experience frequent fits of anger (Hattery 2001).

Conclusion

Leisure and dreams vs. labor and economic progress? Freedom vs. merchandized workforce? Aren't such night antagonisms the mirrors of daylight's? Like Janus, whether night or day, human activities offer two opposed faces, irritating and inseparable. Concerning entertainment and personal choice, night activity is rich.

But should its negative aspects be accepted as a fate? Aren't societies empowered enough to judge and make choices?

Before the energy revolution, drastically supplementing the human production force, darkness was not mastered on a significant scale, and night was granted as a time for rest and risk. Industrialized societies have now created activities offering a full range of services available to all citizens, whether for entertainment or work, providing them with security, safety, catering, financing, traveling, home energy ...

Such services, along with a lot of production lines which never stop, require people at work 24/7. Many of those at work have no other choice but to accept: in that respect, they fit into the socialist pattern of blue-collar workers (and employees today) selling their labor in order to (barely) survive. For them, the price tag is the ruin of their health, the decay of their family life, and, being perceived as mere commodities, the erosion of their dignity.

Undoubtedly, nightlife is an object of desire for those who can afford to rest during daytime or who feel that the reward they get from night justifies their choice. But for the armies of those without choice, isn't it time to question the pertinence of the continuous stretching of day activities into night?

One answer could be that generous benefits could reward those submitted to such a regime. Unfortunately, experience has shown that social and wealth improvements do not generally result from this approach. Another possibility is offered by the prospects of a greener world. Those who support this approach contest excessive production modes, which squander natural resources and produce too much greenhouse gas. If the goal of hyper-production, associated with forced productivism, and unfair distribution is to be drastically changed for the purpose of a sustainable world, will not this choice include a greater respect for human life in all its aspects? Then night – or rather nights – would be the last frontier of the city indeed, a necessity, an evidence of resistance to competitive, consumer-oriented standards of living, and the opportunity for other choices.

References

Balibar, E. (2006) Uprisings in the banlieues. *Lignes* November 21: 50–101.

Barruti, Mila, and Rodriguez Basanta, Anabel (2007) Violence in nightspots: a case study in Catalunia. In *Violence Between Young People in Night-Time Leisure Zones: A European Comparative Study*, ed. A. Recasens. Brussels: VUBPress, 141–72.

Block, R., and Block, C. (1995) Space, place and crime: hot spot areas and hot spot places of liquor-related crime. In *Crime and Place*, ed. J. Eck and D. Weisburd. Monsey, NY: Criminal Justice Press.

Body-Gendrot, S. (2001) *Villes: la fin de la violence?* Paris: Presses de Sciences Po.

Body-Gendrot, S. (2007) Urban "riots" or urban violence in France? *Policing* 1 (4): 416–27.

Cabantous, A. (2009) *Histoire de la nuit. XVIIe–XVIIIe.* Paris: Fayard.

Chetkovitch, C. (1997) *Real Heat: Gender and Race in the Urban Fire Service.* New Brunswick, NJ: Rutgers University Press.

Gathérias, F. (2000) Le policier la nuit. *Les annales de la recherche urbaine* 87, September: 59–62.

Gwiazdzinski, L. (2005) *La nuit, dernière frontière de la ville.* La Tour d'Aigues: Editions de l'Aube.

Hadfield, P. (2006) *Bar Wars: Contesting the Night in Contemporary British Cities*. Oxford: Oxford University Press.

Hadfield, P. (2007) Young people, alcohol and nightlife in British cities. In *Violence Between Young People in Night-Time Leisure Zones: A European Comparative Study*, ed. A. Recasens. Brussels: VUBPress, 173–90.

Hattery, A. (2001) Tag-team parenting: costs and benefits of utilizing non-overlapping shift work in families with young children. *Families in Society, the Journal of Contemporary Human Services* 82 (4): 419–27.

Jacobs, J. (1961) *The Life and Death of Great American Cities*. Harmondsworth: Penguin.

Janowitz, J. (1969) Collective racial violence. In *Violence in America: The History of Crime*, ed. T. Gurr. Newbury Park, CA: Sage, 261–86.

Kerner Commission (National Advisory Commission on Civil Disorder) (1968) *Report*. New York: Bantam.

Lherm, A. (2002) La fête d'Halloween dans les îles britanniques et les pays nord-américains du XVIIè siècle à nos jours. Doctoral dissertation, Université de Paris I.

Lipset, S. M., Trow, M., and Coleman J. (1962) *Union Democracy*. New York: Anchor Books.

Marlière, E. (2007) Violence between young people going out at night in Paris and the surrounding region. In *Violence Between Young People in Night-Time Leisure Zones: A European Comparative Study*, ed. A. Recasens. Brussels: VUBPress, 31–58.

Newman, O. (1975) *Defensible Spaces*. New York: Collins.

Presser, H. (2003) *Working in a 24/7 Economy. Challenges for American Families*. New York: Russell Sage Foundation.

Recasens, A. (ed.) (2007) *Violence Between Young People in Night-Time Leisure Zones: A European Comparative Study*. Brussels: VUBPress.

Sassen, S. (1991) *The Global City*. Princeton, NJ: Princeton University Press.

Selmini, R. (2007) Violence among young people in leisure time. The case of the city of Bologna. In *Violence Between Young People in Night-Time Leisure Zones: A European Comparative Study*, ed. A. Recasens. Brussels: VUBPress, 89–114.

Shaw, C. (1930) *The Jack-Roller: A Delinquent Boy's Own Story*. Chicago: Chicago University Press.

US Department of Commerce (1998) *Marital Status and Living Arrangements*, Current Population Reports, Series P20–514. Washington, DC: US Government Printing Office.

US Department of Labor (2002) *Workers on Flexible and Shift Schedules in 2001*. USDL 02–225 April 18.

Vega, A. (2000) Nuits blanches à l'hôpital. *Les annales de la recherche urbaine* 87, September: 25–8.

Virilio, P. (2004) *Ville panique. Ailleurs commence ici*. Paris: Galilée.

Part VI City Politics and Planning

The New Blackwell Companion to the City   Edited by Gary Bridge and Sophie Watson
© 2011 Blackwell Publishing Ltd

Chapter 54

Reflections on Politics and Planning

Gary Bridge and Sophie Watson

The sheer variation of cities across the globe, their differential rates of growth or decline, and ways they are inserted into, and influence, wider national and international economic and cultural processes, makes trying to analyze urban planning and politics a bewildering task. Without denying this variation, and also avoiding the kinds of models that in the past have been orientated exclusively towards the experience of cities of the north, we would argue that it is possible to pick out some themes that resonate across the contemporary urban world. These themes are: various manifestations of the tension between the plan and political imagination, and its object, the city; the rise of entrepreneurialism, privatization, and the dominance of the market in discussions of neoliberal governance; the idea that the market has driven the political out of the city; the question of political subjectivity and the possibilities for the re-assembling of politics in the city.

Planning Imaginaries

One theme in urban planning is the tension or separation between imaginings of the city and the pace and scale of its socio-cultural-material developments. This is paralleled by tensions between the politics/planning of striving to see the city as a whole or in parts, as an entity, or as networked and porous, open to and extending over a range of spatial scales. Whole city visions dominated the western planning imagination in which the city was thought of as either an organism or a machine. For example, despite its political eclecticism, Ebenezer Howard's Garden City project saw the city as an organism which would draw on features of the countryside and the city, would be self-sustaining financially and to some degree in terms of food supplies, and would consist of a balanced socially mixed population (Howard

The New Blackwell Companion to the City   Edited by Gary Bridge and Sophie Watson
© 2011 Blackwell Publishing Ltd

1902). The city would be self-contained, entire unto itself. Similarly the Chicago School of urban ecology saw the city as a social organism in which the organic metaphors (from plant ecology) of invasion, succession, disorganization, and reorganization into "natural areas" loomed large. Although the different parts of the organism might not cohere, they were thought to be coordinated as a whole by the metabolic beat of the city. Totalizing city visions also infuse modernist architect Le Corbusier's machinic idea of the city in which the different specialized commercial, residential, and industrial zones were connected by rapid transit highways with residential zones of homes as machines for living in (Le Corbusier 1971). This is the classic conception of modernism in planning, deploying a certain idea of rationality (Boyer 1983) which conceives the city in terms of instrumental efficiency and clarity of geography and purpose. The power of this rationality is the claim to be able to see the city as a whole and be separate from its confusing constituent parts. Anthony Vidler, in Chapter 57, illuminates these themes very strongly. Vidler analyzes how Le Corbusier, master architect and planner, makes use of the new technology of the airplane and the relatively new technology of the camera to present aerial photographs of Le Marais in central Paris which are used to trump other (on-the-ground) plans for the area. It is against this envisioning that other (anti-rational, psychogeographic) mappings of the city, from the Situationists particularly, were posed (discussed by Vidler, but see also Chapter 19 by David Pinder and the introduction to Part II, Chapter 14).

The physical separation and superiority of vision that Vidler illustrates is a claim to the power of the expert. This opens up another theme in urban politics and planning, the tension between expert knowledge (often couched in terms of discourses of rationality) and lay or everyday knowledge. More and more in late modernism the authority and influence of expert knowledge (in science, in politics, more recently in economic analysis) has been challenged. Ash Amin, in Chapter 55, speaks to this challenge, which he characterizes as a move from a "knowing" planning tradition to a more deliberative one. The city cannot be fully known, and in any case knowing and intention are distributed much more widely than the expert planning idea assumes. It is a theme that one of the editors of this volume has pursued in a related way in trying to understand rationality from a perspective (informed by philosophical pragmatism) in which emotion and non-discursive elements come into rational deliberation (Bridge 2005, 2008). Also drawing on philosophical pragmatism, Amin seeks to expand the idea of non-cognitive deliberation to material and non-human relations in which what he calls the "situated surplus" of the material environment informs human intentionality and deliberation in the first place. This gives us a renewed idea of the public realm that takes in the materiality of the city and technical and non-human assemblages.

The continuum of expert to lay knowledge, or rather the politics of its separation, also runs through Peter Marcuse's Chapter 56, looking at the main historic currents of urban planning. What he calls the "deferential technicist approach" is very much in the planner-as-detached-expert mode either in terms of science and planning as engineering, or in terms of design expertise or contractual efficiency. All these involve a certain expert rationality, "knowing" planning that does not challenge existing power relations in any way. Social reform planning seeks to compensate for the negative effects of the capitalist economy through social welfare initiatives – initially to do with poor health of the working class in cities but expanded into a wider welfare model. This reform model increasingly included public participation (more "lay" knowledge – including most deliberative models) but in ways that Marcuse argues do not challenge the status quo. This is left to social justice planning in which lay knowledge and experience is used to envisage alternative societies (utopian planning) or to mobilize for wholesale social and economic change (critical and radical planning).

The tension between what constitutes expert and lay knowledge is also crossed by the struggle and separation between the plan and its object – the city. That tension and separation were particularly telling in colonialism in which western plans and models were imposed on various cities of the south (discussed in detail by King 2003). More recently it has been investigated, for example, in a detailed analysis of the modernist planning of Brasilia and the social and cultural adjustments that took place to deal with the inappropriateness of the plan (Holston 1989). As Jenny Robinson has argued powerfully, western models of development have also dominated the thinking about cities of the south more generally. She has a call to provincialize the cities and the models that have been established as iconic, in order to make space for an idea of the ordinariness of all cities so as to be able to see their diversity and the different ways in which urban life can, and is, being improved on the ground across the cities themselves (Robinson 2005).

The western planning imagination can also fail to grasp the realities of cities of the north as well. This is the point that Edward Soja makes in Chapter 59. He argues that planners are still informed by models of the city as a distinct metropolis which have long ago been subsumed by forms of regional urbanization. Soja argues that density convergence across whole regions breaks down traditional distinctions between city and suburbs, as do patterns of activity and communications. They also act as massive agglomeration economies that have global significance on which existing models of urban planning and constricted forms of political jurisdiction have little purchase. These arguments relate strongly to Short's conception of liquid urbanization of the megalopolis in Chapter 3. These processes are of course writ large in the rapidly growing cities of East Asia (as Friedmann, Wu, Xiaoming, Kong, Keith, Forrest, and Rooker analyze in various ways in this *Companion*).

The Changing Shape of Urban Governance

It is not just that the city as the object of planning and politics lacks the locational coherence that traditional planning models and political structures were established to address, but that the processes they encompass now raise significant challenges for the structures and mechanisms of urban governance. Roger Keil identifies this as "transnational urbanization" in Chapter 62. Both Keil and Soja see the city as unbounded in this sense. Cities are unbounded in terms of the mobility of disease that Keil discusses, for instance the circulation of Severe Acute Respiratory Syndrome (SARS) through a particular network of cities in 2003. Networks can reveal urban vulnerability as the flipside of the benefits of connectivity and can pose huge problems for urban governments. That vulnerability can emerge in urban infrastructures, with power supply failures, through to the targeting of infrastructure as a strategy of demodernization in modern warfare (discussed by Stephen Graham in

Chapter 11). Keil also discusses infrastructure as a part of transnational urbanization in that many major urban infrastructures are financed internationally and so
non-local owners have a greater influence and involvement in urban governance
issues – or glocal governance. These infrastructures themselves often serve an international as well as a local use. In this sense, parts of the material environment for
which urban government has traditionally had responsibility is now open to the
interests and investments of actors who do not have any democratic accountability
for other urban services and structures in these cities.

The unevenness of investment results in cities that are laden with infrastructure
and those that lack sufficient infrastructure. Stark infrastructural inequalities exist
within many cities of the south – divided, as they often are between the formal
infrastructure and economy of the core city, or suburbs housing professional workers
and the informal infrastructure and housing of the slums and squatter settlements
that surround the core. Mike Davis has powerfully detailed the scale of poverty of
the cities of slums (Davis 2007). Others have explored the ways in which various
networks of organizations (formal, informal, public, private, third sector, *in situ*
organizations) have cooperated to try to supply the basics of life and prospects for
improvement through to investigations of individualized tactics of survival in these
most deprived of circumstances in the urban world (see Chapter 46 by Robinson
and Parnell, Chapter 47 by Seekings, and Chapter 48 by Quayson).

Subject to international investment and in part to facilitate international companies and their workforces, large infrastructure projects are also seen to enhance the
competitiveness of the city vis-à-vis other cities. In a process first identified by David
Harvey (1989) there has been a shift in urban government from managerialism to
entrepreneurialism, another major theme in thinking about urban politics and planning. Rather than being a concern with how to represent voter interest, provide
urban services or coordinate city activities, the emphasis became more and more on
supporting business and providing the kind of environment that would attract
inward investment and enhance the city's image and attractiveness compared with
other cities. This was first registered as an increased focus on the economic development side of urban government, whatever the political hue of the administration.
It also saw a greater emphasis in the 1980s and 1990s on imagineering, in positioning and promoting the city as a commodity itself in the game of inter-urban competition: the myriad of examples of this was caught in the literature on place
marketing (Kearns and Philo 1993; Rutheiser 1996). This has led to a whole consultancy industry on how best to sell your city, based on indices of its attractiveness
and creative diversity (Florida 2005) which has been roundly critiqued (Peck 2005).
Along with this was the creeping privatization of the functions and services provided
by city hall. In large projects public–private partnerships became more common, in
which private investors and private interests were more and more part of investment
in infrastructure and other large public assets. As well as privatization of the public
realm, public authorities were acting more as private entrepreneurs. The market (or
quasi-market) model was taken into public services as city government took a post-
Fordist turn with an increasing separation between purchaser and provider functions in which the local authority or municipal government became the purchaser
of services put out to tender to a range of public, private, and third sector providers
who competed for the contracts that were frequently awarded on the basis of lowest

tender. The users of these services were treated more as consumers and less as citizens.

The increasing focus of city government on supporting economic development and using market models and market mechanisms to dispense the business of government also affected the nature of urban policy to a much greater degree from the 1980s and 1990s. The conceptual framing of urban policy in terms of urban renaissance, or regeneration again put the emphasis on economic development and property-led urban renewal with an implied trickle-down from core business economic activities through to welfare and public services. This has impacted socially in debates on social mix or balanced community policies which many urban researchers argue is a form of state-supported, and in some cases, state-sponsored gentrification (Lees 2003; Smith 2002). Attracting middle-class residents back to the inner city has been seen in policy circles as a way of either raising local revenues (in some countries such as the US), or raising the prospects for real estate, or increasing revenue on leisure and consumer businesses. There is also an implied social benefit for the poor from these policies in that middle-class residents are assumed to take an advocacy role and also to demand higher standards of services and neighborhood amenity that also benefits poorer residents. What this model fails to take into account is the impact of gentrification in terms of direct displacement of poorer households and other indirect forms of displacement that come with affordability problems and loss of suitable retail and services (Marcuse 1986; Slater 2006; Atkinson 2004). Furthermore it is not at all clear whether middle-class mobilization has the spillover advocacy effect assumed or whether in fact middle-class residents cooperate within themselves to improve and protect the particular services, or neighborhood schools, or outlets from which they directly benefit most (Butler 1997). These developments can be seen in a wider context as gentrification has been generalized in cities across the globe (Smith 2002). Neil Smith has seen this as a form of revanchist urban politics (Smith 1996) in which the middle classes and elites take back the city both physically, in term of the gentrification of inner urban neighborhoods, and in the wider symbolic politics and framing of urban policy. It could be argued that there is a convergence here between cities of the north and those of the south in the politics of the elites in the central city dominating the whole city polity, in ways that have been seen in cities of the south during the colonial period and beyond.

Kevin Ward, in Chapter 63, helps us understand the context for these changes involving elite politics and business-led urban policy, but also specific mechanisms for the transfer of certain policy formulae across cities. Policy learning and policy transfer he sees as being either event-led or visit-led. Event-led initiatives are ones where there are key conferences, seminars, or colloquia involving urban professionals, academics, and business representatives across cities where certain policy and strategy ideas are discussed and disseminated. Visit-led transfer occurs when business, government, and cultural representatives from one city visit another as an example of best practice or how-to learning from certain urban strategies or initiatives. Ward argues that both types of contact between city elites have been hugely influential in the spearheading and sedimenting of certain assumptions, not just about certain policy initiatives, but about what is possible and not possible in policy terms overall. Ward also makes the point that these networks and initiatives can

Figure 54.1   A neighborhood market. Photo S. Watson.

shape whole swathes of the city and their activities. The example he uses is central Birmingham, UK, in which certain streetscapes and the central cultural quarter were redesigned to make a new landscape for culture, leisure, and consumption. This illustrates how the political economy and the cultural politics of place are brought together in ways that facilitate business and consumption-oriented activities. The institutional urban politics of this are that the state plays a facilitative role in what Ward and others have identified as new forms of statecraft that involve private sector models and financing.

What the changing aspects of urban government discussed here point to is the overall impact of neoliberal capitalism in the late twentieth and early twenty-first century: the idea that the pure market competitive model should be unfettered by public planning and in fact should be supported by government to distribute goods and services (including public services) in the most efficient way according to those principles. Like Kevin Ward's discussion of policy tourism, Allan Cochrane's analysis of European Union (EU) policy-making on urban issues (Chapter 64) emphasizes the importance of fast policy transfers between cities. Cochrane shows the growing importance of multi-level governance in urban affairs. State institutional networks do still matter, even in this market dominated neoliberal world. For example, the policy networks and soft influence of EU initiatives seek to support a polycentric and balanced urbanism across EU states. This contrasts with the promotion of a more competitive and uneven relationship between cities advocated by other policy networks involving global players such as the World Bank (in the guise of stimulating innovation and inter-urban competition). That unevenness is demonstrated in cities of the south in which informal housing and economic activity in the slum neighborhoods have increasingly been seen in policy circles as examples of entre-preneurialism that must be supported and encouraged in various ways. This is in the most constrained macro-economic circumstances in terms of debt repayments and the Washington Consensus involving the World Bank and the International Monetary Fund, that demanded structural adjustment programs that reduced welfare spending and directed national economies towards raw material exports. What Allan Cochrane's chapter also re-emphasizes, in terms of a theme identified earlier, is that despite institutional differences the overall framing of welfare inter-ventions has shifted in a neoliberal direction. This is shown in support to business in the hopes that there will be welfare spillovers, with the key urban terms being city competitiveness, megaprojects, cultural initiatives, and place marketing.

The loosening of the relationship between city government and the urban land-scape is illustrated by Patrick Le Galès in Chapter 65, in which he makes the point that the city is governed to different extents. Looking at the governance of European cities Le Galès notes how the growth of regional urban systems (see also Chapter 59 by Soja in this section and Chapter 3 by Short), the mobility and temporariness of certain populations, the rise of long-distance commuting (where home and work are in different political jurisdictions), and writing off and non-governing of what are defined to be "lawless" inner or outer urban neighborhoods, mean that different parts of the city and its residents are differently governed and governed to a greater or lesser extent.

Being differently governed connects to considerations of how certain city spaces and subjects are constructed through policy and planning discourse as "outside" or "other" in ways that reinforce control and conformity (see the discussion of Foucault's notion of governmentality below). Dikec (2007), for example, has exam-ined the discursive construction of the French state through the othering of certain poor and immigrant neighborhoods in the *banlieues* of Paris.

Subjectivity and the "Post Political" City?

As well as the construction and marketing of urban landscapes, the structure of cities is influenced by the differential effects of market processes. This is seen with particular acuity in Chinese cities in the move from a state-planned environment to one which is opened up to the market (for example in real estate) but within a still strongly state-directed context. John Friedmann (in Chapter 60) and Fulong Wu (in Chapter 61) deal with these changes with comparable conclusions. With the intro-duction of market forces the traditional system of home–work residential complexes (*danwei*) where the whole of someone's work and domestic life was lived in the past, is being broken up as employment becomes more geographically dispersed and precarious and more socially separating in terms of occupational status. State involvement and control are maintained in the new residential developments through neighborhood committees and residents' associations which form what Friedmann calls the "invisible architecture" of governance in rapidly changing Chinese cities. Both Wu and Friedmann note how traditional migration controls via neighborhood registration systems (that can now lead to forms of differentiated citizenship as Michael Keith observes in Chapter 35) are often overwhelmed by the scale of rural–urban migration. The new residential developments can take many different forms that introduce further status distinctions into the city, as Wu's chapter illustrates in the contrasting designs of different residential complexes, from large apartment blocks through to luxury villas in gated communities. Neighborhood governance is in tension with many of the pressures of marketization in terms of increasing social distinctions and divisions, contrasting neighborhood types, separation of home and work, and greater mobility. Whether the invisible architecture will help ensure a sense of community or neighborhood affiliation is highly questionable given all the forces of differentiation and fragmentation that comes with market processes. Both Friedmann and Wu doubt whether neighborhood governance will forge a "neighborhood type" of person when subject to these market pressures.

The shaping of social mentality and a new personality is a question that Wu raises (in the context of Simmel's classic discussion of the metropolis and mental life) at the end of his chapter, but it relates to a much broader set of issues than we are concerned with in this section and throughout this *Companion*. That is the relation between the city and subjectivity, in this case political subjectivity. The question Simmel raised was how the experience of public life in the city produced a certain defensiveness in residents. To protect themselves from the over-stimulation of the city they hid behind a "mask of rationality" that bred a certain indifference to others. This was a reduction of the possibilities of the political.

More recently, since Foucault's work on disciplinary power, the analysis has moved to how forms of government, and for us the urban environment itself, have

Figure 54.2 New residential blocks, Yunmeng, Hubei. Photo S. Watson.

been directed to produce certain forms of political subjectivity or lack of it. Foucault sees forms of governmentality to do with the "conduct of conduct" and the production of the liberal subject (see also Rose 1999, and in an urban context Osborne and Rose 1999). Here is an argument that sees neoliberalism going all the way down into the shaping, not just of "good" cities (as Evelyn Ruppert argues in Chapter 58) but of "good" citizens. The production of the right kind of citizen is written into the discourse and design of city spaces, in the case of Ruppert's chapter, the Yonge-Dundas intersection in downtown Toronto. She reveals how the space is moralized and how discourses "that activate the space are written into its production." Thus certain activities (for example short-lease discount stores), and the personalities and behaviors that are discursively produced to be associated with them, are written as being outside the rationality and logic of the space for the city as a whole. The governance of subjectivity in the city is not new and other chapters have dealt with this in a historical context and in terms of the interrelationship between city spaces, mobility, the control of population, and political subjectivities (see, for example, Chapter 20 by Dodsworth and Chapter 15 by Ross).

A constellation of forces have been considered in this chapter: the rise of the entrepreneurial city, the dominance of technicist planning, the privatization of the public, and indeed the crowding out of the political and political contestation by the market. Erik Swyngedouw has related some of this to what he calls the post-political city (Swyngedouw 2009) in which what passes for politics and policy is a long way from any idea of political contestation. Urban governance and urban policy get reduced, as Cochrane argues in Chapter 64, to the management of troublesome populations, or further, as Ruppert's chapter shows, the planning out of these populations in the production of urban spaces themselves. In this framework, urban politics becomes professional management in alliance with liberal elites in support of the capitalist city under the guise of deliberative democracy. This depoliticization of the city involves the loss of the public (something Sennett (1974) identified long ago) and confusion between the public and the private.

The response to this presumed triumph of neoliberalism, we would argue, has developed in several directions. The first acquiesces to market processes but seeks to insert frameworks, regulations, and corrections that compensate for the market. This response crosses over Marcuse's categories of deferential technicist and social reform planning. It looks to socializing various hitherto assumed characteristics of the market, such as forms of social entrepreneurialism, and to include sectors other than the private sector (especially the third sector) as institutions that can provide some element of a redistributive welfare function in the city. These networks are born out of harsh necessity in cities of the south.

The second direction has been agonistic and oppositional. This has been to argue that the political is at root endlessly conflictual and that the more obvious attempts to achieve political consensus usually fold into the dominant liberal (more likely neoliberal) hegemony (Mouffe 2005; Laclau and Mouffe 1985). In its critique of consensus in the urban field this has also aligned with the alternative neo-Marxist political discourse that points to the distance between capitalism and social justice. These arguments have been most obvious in the use of Henri Lefebvre's work. Lefebvre contrasts the politics of the capitalist city with the idea of the right to the city as the right to urban life itself (Lefebvre 1996). What this means is that urban residents should be able to participate in shaping the city, its economy, its built form, its social purpose. From a neo-Marxist perspective Lefebvre's work emphasizes the distance between the actually existing capitalist city and the city of social justice, that distance providing a source of theoretical and practical critique of the existing system. These ideas have been examined and advanced in thinking about democracy in an urban context recently (Purcell 2008). The latest development in merging the neo-Marxist and agonistic models is seen in discussions of the post-political that Swyngedouw has so well expressed. Nevertheless this does involve an ontologizing of politics as "the political" and a separating off of this alternative space away from "democratic" politics as usual in the thrall of liberal capitalism (Barnett 2005, 2008). It suggests that the political outruns the social and is constituted separately to it. The post-political constitutes the idea of "the people" that is manufactured and commodified rather than full of any genuine dissent. Kaika and Swyngedouw (in Chapter 9) suggest how this manufacturing of consent can occur even over global environmental concerns as the environmental crisis becomes the new disciplining device to shut down dissensus and push the market as solution. It sees the triumph of a form of narrow instrumental rationality in the service of neoliberal capitalism.

A third direction of response to neoliberalism has been to resist this move to ontologize politics but rather to seek to deepen democracy and to see the sphere of politics and even political institutions as open to oppositional politics and ongoing genuine contestation as well as consensus (Barnett 2008). This approach emphasizes the democratic possibilities that exist already, in the institutional structure, in cultural expression, in the spaces of the city, and to seek to expand these possibilities in terms of deliberative democracy. John Dryzek has characterized this as the pressures for democratization that he sees as combining in various ways through social movements and globally linked environmental movements (Dryzek 2006). Jürgen Habermas has suggested the possibilities in the processes of globalization and the post-national constellations in which "the people" are not a population in a territory, but the emergence and circulation of certain discourses. Habermas's canon (1984, 1987, 1996) has explored how the narrow instrumentalities of capitalist rationality can be exceeded by the communicative rationality of human expression and how that communicative rationality can be effectively institutionalized. Nancy Fraser (2009) has explored the issues in terms of the efficacy of democratic will at different spatial scales. Seyla Benhabib (1996) and Iris Marion Young (2000) have thought about ways in which the politics of difference and the incompleteness of subjectivity are vital democratizing impulses. In Iris Marion Young's case, the idea of the city as a coming together of strangers was still important for the idea of political democracy. Current concerns extend to questions about the extent to which the materiality of the city and its non-human elements contribute to prefacing and predisposing political engagements in the first place. This brings us full circle to Ash Amin's Chapter 55, and the possibilities of a shift from urban planning as expert "knowing" to planning as "deliberation" involving lay knowledge.

Deliberative planning has a strong tradition and has been much discussed and practiced in various cities (Forester 2000; Hoch 1984a, 1984b; Healey 1997). It draws on a pragmatist tradition that Bridge (2005) has argued elsewhere is significant in thinking about communicative action (discursive, emotional, non-discursive) in its widest sense as a stimulus for democratic participation and the continued importance of cities for this. But this is part of a wider claim for the possibilities of radical democracy in terms of democratic accountability in the economy as well as in society and politics. It also takes, we would argue, another impulse of pragmatism, which is to suggest that those problems that become the focus of attention become more tractable in terms of solutions or change. And the city might have renewed political importance in two ways here. The first is as the arena for the coming together of various social movements that are part of the pressure for democratization, and the second is in connecting up political agendas that make for a more sustained "will" in terms of urban change. This connecting up is an act of political imagination in which groups feel responsibility for the effects of actions that they themselves are not directly affected by – John Dewey's notion of the constitution of the public (Dewey 1927). This also points in the direction of pluralism but, rather than the pluralist city politics of an earlier era (see Dahl 2005), one that has radical potential in the way different interests can be connected up within and across cities. What all these approaches are suggesting is that a fuller form of democratic participation and accountability is needed across all areas of life and across difference (the economy, society, and politics) and that the city is still the place where those possibilities can be best imagined.

References

Atkinson, R. (2004) The evidence of the impact of gentrification: new lessons for urban renaissance? *European Journal of Housing Policy* 4 (1): 107–31.

Barnett, C. (2005) The consolations of neoliberalism. *Geoforum* 36 (1): 7–12.

Barnett, C. (2008) Political affects in public space: normative blindspots in non-representational ontologies. *Transactions of the Institute of British Geographers* n.s. 33: 186–200.

Benhabib, S. (1996) *Democracy and Difference*. Princeton, NJ: Princeton University Press.

Boyer, C. (1983) *Dreaming the Rational City*. Cambridge, MA: MIT Press.

Bridge, G. (2005) *Reason in the City of Difference: Pragmatism, Communicative Action and Contemporary Urbanism*. London: Routledge.

Bridge, G. (2008) City senses: on the radical possibilities of pragmatism for geography. *Geoforum* 39 (4): 1570–84.

Butler, T. (1997) *Gentrification and the Middle Classes*. Aldershot: Ashgate.

Dahl, R. (2005) *Who Governs? Democracy and Power in an American City*. 2nd edn. New Haven, CT: Yale University Press.

Davis, M. (2007) *Planet of Slums*. London: Verso.

Dewey, J. (1927) *The Public and Its Problems*. New York: Henry Holt & Co.

Dikec, M. (2007) *Badlands of the Republic*. Oxford: Wiley-Blackwell.

Dryzek, J. S. (2006) *Deliberative Global Politics*. Cambridge: Polity Press.

Forester, J. (2000) *The Deliberative Practitioner*. London: MIT Press.

Fraser, N. (2009) *Scales of Justice: Reimagining Political Space in a Globalizing World*. New York: Columbia University Press.

Florida, R. (2005) *Cities and the Creative Class*. New York: Routledge.

Habermas, J. (1984) *The Theory of Communicative Action*, vol. 1: *Reason and the Rationalisation of Society*. Trans. T. McCarthy. London: Heinemann.

Habermas, J. (1987) *The Theory of Communicative Action*, vol. 2: *A Critique of Functionalist Reason*. Trans. T. McCarthy. Cambridge: Polity Press.

Habermas, J. (1996) *Between Facts and Norms*. Cambridge: Polity Press.

Harvey, D. (1989) From managerialism to entrepreneurialism: the transformation in urban governance in late capitalism. *Geografiska Annaler B*. 71: 3–17.

Healey, P. (1997) *Collaborative Planning: Shaping Places in Fragmented Societies*. London: Palgrave Macmillan.

Hoch, C. (1984a) Doing good and being right: the pragmatic connection in planning theory. *Journal of the American Planning Association* 50: 335–45.

Hoch, C. (1984b) Pragmatism, planning and power. *Journal of Planning Education and Research* 4: 86–95.

Holston, J. (1989) *The Modernist City: An Anthropological Critique of Brasilia*. Chicago: University of Chicago Press.

Howard, E. (1902) *Garden Cities of Tomorrow*. London: S. Sonnenschein & Co.

Kearns, G., and Philo, C. (eds.) (1993) *Selling Places: The City as Cultural Capital – Past and Present*. Oxford: Pergamon.

King, A. (2003) *Postcolonial Urbanism*. London: Routledge.

Laclau, E., and Mouffe, C. (1985) *Hegemony and Socialist Strategy: Towards a Radical Democratic Politics*. Trans. W. Moore and P. Cammack. London: Verso.

Le Corbusier (1971) *The City of Tomorrow and its Planning*. 3rd edn. London: Architectural Press.

Lees, L. (2003) Policy (re)turns: Urban policy and gentrification, gentrification and urban policy. *Environment and Planning A* 35 (4): 571–4.

Lefebvre, H. (1996) Right to the city. In *Writings on Cities*, selected and translated by E. Kofman and E. Lebas. Oxford: Blackwell, 63–177.

Marcuse, P. (1986) Abandonment, gentrification and displacement: the linkages in New York City. In *Gentrification of the City*, ed. N. Smith and P. Williams. London: Unwin Hyman, 153–77.

Mouffe, C. (2005) *On the Political*. London: Routledge.

Osborne T., and Rose, N. (1999) Governing cities: notes on the spatialisation of virtue. *Environment and Planning D: Society and Space* 17 (6): 737–60.

Peck, J. (2005) Struggling with the creative class. *International Journal of Urban and Regional Research* 29 (4): 740–70.

Purcell, M. (2008) *Recapturing Democracy: Neoliberalism and the Struggle for Alternative Urban Futures*. New York: Routledge.

Robinson, J. (2005) *Ordinary Cities: Between Modernity and Development*. London: Routledge.

Rose, N. (1999) *Powers of Freedom: Reframing Political Thought*. Cambridge: Cambridge University Press.

Rutheiser, C. (1996) *Imagineering Atlanta: The Politics of Place in the City of Dreams*. London: Verso.

Sennett, R. (1974) *The Fall of Public Man*. New York: Norton.

Slater, T. (2006) The eviction of critical perspectives from gentrification research. *International Journal of Urban and Regional Research* 30 (4): 737–57.

Smith, N. (1996) *The New Urban Frontier: Gentrification and the Revanchist City*. London: Routledge.

Smith, N. (2002) New globalism, new urbanism: gentrification as global urban strategy. *Antipode* 34 (3): 428–50.

Swyngedouw, E. (2009) The antinomies of the post political city: in search of a democratic politics of environmental production. *International Journal of Urban and Regional Research* 33 (3): 601–20.

Young, I. M. (2000) *Inclusion and Democracy*. Oxford: Oxford University Press.

Chapter 55

Urban Planning in an Uncertain World

Ash Amin

Introduction

How should city planners act in an urban environment that is daily shaped by distant forces and hidden interdependencies that generate unpredictable and unexpected outcomes? Cities have become sprawling entities and plural universes with complex relational dynamics that make them difficult to map, track, and coordinate. They are increasingly made and unmade through these relational dynamics, which include the returns of repetition, inertia, and legacy, and the unanticipated lurches produced by emergent combinations or perturbations transmitted across an entire network space. They are thoroughly enmeshed in global processes over which they have little control, exposed to transnational flows of one kind or another, world-level or distant developments, decisions taken at various spatial scales, and the circulations of virtual, symbolic, and material inputs.

As the sum of multiple geographies of formation, cities increasingly defy the staples of territorially based planning. City planners face the dual challenge of intervening effectively in an urban system geared for novelty and surprise, as well as finding grip in a meshwork of connections and flows with multiple nodes of authority and authorizing capacity (De Landa 2006). They confront the problem of acting without purchase, exactly at a time of high public expectation in face of mounting unpredictability and risk linked to rapidly spreading hazards such as pandemics, global warming, economic turbulence, large-scale human displacement, and transnational warfare. This problem is by no means unique to urban planning. It is symptomatic of the general difficulty of finding expertise, authority, and grip in a multi-polar and interconnected world that is not only risk prone but also regulated by its own internal dynamics.

The New Blackwell Companion to the City   Edited by Gary Bridge and Sophie Watson
© 2011 Blackwell Publishing Ltd

In *Acting in an Uncertain World,* for example, Callon *et al.* (2009) address the problem of responding to major science-led hazards that, on the one hand, require specialist knowledge and decisive action, but on the other hand, also possess a life of their own or are perceived differently by publics from experts and the authorities. They analyze the fraught and contested history of response in France to controversies such as nuclear waste disposal, bovine spongiform encephalopathy (BSE), and muscular dystrophy, which traditionally have been tackled in a closed and dirigiste manner by the state, based on assuming that experts and politicians know best. Callon *et al.* criticize this approach, arguing that publics must be seen as knowledgeable subjects and stakeholders, that expertise is only ever partial and circumstantial, that interests are never neutral or impartial, and that risks are compound, mutable, and non-programmable. They propose, instead, an approach based on a science and politics of concerns made public, active stakeholder involvement, distributed responsibility, and the enrolment of expert and lay knowledge, acting in an open, experimental, and democratic manner in an uncertain world and staying close to developments as they unfold.

In some senses, the globalization of risk and hazard itself is forcing a shift in state practice, but in contradictory directions. One the one hand, faced with the threat of, say, an unforeseen terrorist attack, a sudden health pandemic, a catastrophic climatic event, or a market shock with uninsurable losses, states have begun to scale back on promises of avoidance or universal protection, choosing instead to prepare publics to live in a crisis-prone environment, to mobilize all manner of knowledge, lay and expert, to build resistance and resilience, and to redefine their own role as crisis managers rather than crisis avoiders. A logic of preparedness and shared responsibility is replacing a logic of avoidance and centered authority (Dillon 2008). On the other hand, states have moved fast to introduce – and make permanent – emergency measures that allow them to intervene unilaterally with warlike authority and conviction (Ophir 2007; Graham 2009; Amoore and de Goede 2008). This change follows a logic of meeting uncertainty with unconstrained state power, free from democratic accountability, on permanent alert, ready to strike before being attacked, reliant on an elaborate infrastructure of surveillance, conformity, and counter-attack. The steps to stop, search, and lock up suspects, prop up ailing markets, build tidal defenses, close down borders, wage war with aberrant states, roll out mass vaccination programs, are all acts of certitude and determinacy, reassertions of centered authority.

The kind of thinking advanced by Callon *et al.*, thus, is both reflected in, and contradicted by, current state practice. However, it resonates strongly in urban planning theory, which, though less concerned with the issues of risk and uncertainty, has long grappled with the problem of how best to intervene democratically in the variegated, open and multi-polar city. Planning theory has shifted away from a "knowing" towards a "deliberative" tradition in recent years. The former – epitomized by the projects of modernist planning – endeavored to observe the city from a privileged vantage point, know the pulse that beats through urban life, intervene through a central authority, and roll out a plan of the good life. So, for example, it acted to save cities from disaster, lift the masses out of want and poverty, and re-engineer the urban fabric to meet the goals of modernity. The latter, in contrast, pointing to the mutability and multiplexity of the city and to the arrogance and mistakes of the knowing tradition, has chosen to work through micro-practices, seeking to weave a way through multiple voices, conflicting demands, and contradictory developments. It sees knowledge as situated, problems as complex, outcomes as temporary, and interventions as catalysts rather than solutions, defining planning as the art of intermediation, working pragmatically through opposing interests and concerns, making things visible, and intervening in relational dynamics for communal local advantage.

The knowing tradition has by no means disappeared. It persists in the vanities of strategic urban plans, large architectural impositions, design-led urban regeneration, massive infrastructure projects, sweeping slum clearances, new megacity developments in countries such as China. It does not lack powerful protagonists – political, professional, and corporate – but conceptually the deliberative tradition seems to have come to the forefront due to the ideas developed over the last 20 years by an influential body of planning theorists such as John Friedmann, John Forester, Leonie Sandercock, Patsy Healey, Andreas Faludi, Luigi Mazza, Bent Flyvberg, Judy Innes, Alessandro Balducci, and Jean Hillier. These theorists have mounted compelling critiques of the knowing tradition, revealed the complexities of the contemporary city, elucidated an epistemology of relational and situated knowing, articulated the principles and practices of deliberative/pragmatic planning, and worked closely with communities, activities, and urban leaders on specific projects and urban plans. They have formed a school of thought with solid theoretical and philosophical foundations and clear principles and practices of intervention.

The deliberative tradition calls upon planners to: act as intermediaries who can harness lay knowledge, broker agreements, and speak for the disempowered; address issues of common concern, seek pragmatic solutions, and work with imperfections, incertitude, and constitutive disagreement; redefine strategic planning as the articulation of "motivating visions" (Healey 2007) and diagrams of possibility (Hillier 2007) rather than as a blueprint of action; accept that interventions are specific, partial, and experimental, and not total, systemic, or certain; and intervene with care and modesty in trajectories that are democratically and deliberatively constructed. In short, the approach to issues of immediate public concern as well as developments beyond the horizon is a blend of visionary sketching and democratic consultation.

Although I am sympathetic to the arguments and proposals of the deliberative tradition and also believe that the relationally constituted city requires a negotiated approach (Amin and Thrift 2002; Amin 2007), two aspects of its thinking strike me as problematic regarding the urgency to act decisively in an uncertain world that generates grave hazards and risks. The first concerns what counts as a stakeholder and intermediary in urban life. My claim is that the deliberative tradition makes light of non-human and non-cognitive inputs, an omission that not only overstates the potential of inter-human deliberation but also limits thinking on how the materiality of cities – brick, stone, metal, wires, software, and physical space – is implicated in the regulation of uncertainty. The second concerns the skepticism of the deliberative tradition towards expert judgment and programmatic intervention, which raises the important question of how to respond effectively to serious hazards and risks without recourse to the authoritarian excesses of the knowing tradition. Is it possible to act with authority in an uncertain urban environment without compromising stakeholder involvement and the mobilization of diverse knowledges? This chapter addresses these two issues in turn.

Material Culture

Thus far, the deliberative tradition has remained decidedly humanist. Its address to power is based on empowering communities, building social voice, intermediating between diverse interests, and organizing for agonistic engagement between stakeholders. The ambition is to rehumanize the city by returning authority and control to the citizens and residents of a city; to ensure that decision-makers are not allowed to fall into rule-based, depersonalized, or centralized governance of urban life. The full spectrum of urban affairs, from civil defense and waste or traffic management to economic planning, cultural management, and housing allocation, is expected to be subjected to democratic audit, measured for human consequence, and placed under the scrutiny of the city's many communities.

It is hard to disagree with much of this, not only because it makes democratic sense, but also because much damage – to those without rights, power, or means – has been done as a consequence of centralized planning. The unfortunate legacy of urban monoculture (consumption only, production only, spectacle only, gentrification) – sprawl, erosion of the commons, social and spatial marginalization of the poor or minorities, heavy policing of difference and dissent, ejection of migrants and itinerants – might have been avoided without such planning. The question I wish to pose, instead, is whether the humanism of deliberative thinking is able to deliver its ambition, whether the unspoken assumption that it is conscious/deliberating human actors – in and beyond the city – who make and unmake urban social life is valid. It is a question that goes to the heart of the determinants of social life – including human rationality, behavior, and culture – in a city. My argument is that urban material culture, that is, the entanglements of humans and non-humans that make up social practice and associational life, profoundly affects urban possibility. Conscious deliberations form a small part of an urban society supported by, and made through, a "pre-cognitive" and "trans-human" environment that brings into play many actants and structuring rhythms.

Nigel Thrift and I (2002) have argued that cities might be thought of as machinic entities; engines of order, repetition, and innovation (sparked by the clash of elements and bodies) that drive the urban experience, including what humans make of themselves, others, and their environment. The urban environment is a meshwork of steel, concrete, natural life, wires, wheels, digital codes, and humans placed in close proximity and it is the rhythms of the juxtapositions and associations – coming together in symbolic projections, cultural routines, institutional practices, regulatory norms, physical flows, technological regimes, experience of the landscape, software systems – that surge through the human experience. The machinic rhythms of the city, I would argue, blend together the human and the urban condition, making people subjects of a specific kind, with their demeanor and outlook (compared to that of humans in other time-spaces) formed by their inhabitation of the urban environment and, most importantly, its inhabitation in them, fixed through these rhythms. Such material ordering of urban being is by no means confined to local inputs, but includes others of various spatial composition and provenance that form part of the spatially dispersed meshwork in which cities exist as nodes regulated from many directions (e.g., government bureaucracies, internet traffic, weather systems, commodity chains).

The precise details of such ordering are far from fully understood. However, some of the behavioral pushes, in our times of experiencing the city of extreme urban global exposure and hybridization, might include an adaptability to multiple sensory, technological, and environmental inputs, an ability to inhabit many time-spaces of dwelling, meaning, and community, and to cohabit with significant others that include non-humans, and a requirement to negotiate a world fully revealed, with all its risks and opportunities, delights and disenchantments. Urban planners, including deliberative planners, can hardly be described as unaware of the city's material environment. If anything, a central professional imperative is to manage social life through interventions in the city's physical, technological, and natural environment (e.g., zoning regulations, infrastructure projects, land and building planning decisions, policies towards housing, public space, and the economy, urban landscape and architecture projects). My point, instead, is that the material environment tends to be treated as an exogenous factor serving or affecting human practice, rather than as an intrinsic component of human being in the city, threaded into the social conscious and unconscious (Amin and Thrift forthcoming).

This difference is vividly revealed in the treatment of the role of public space in urban civic culture. Humanist planning (deliberative or other) has long looked for ways of enhancing civic behavior by altering the terms of human interaction in public space. Typically, interventions have ranged from facilitating leisurely circulation and mingling in open spaces such as parks, squares, shopping malls, and marinas, to planning for social diversity and interaction in neighborhoods, housing estates, and schools. In recent times of urban social fracture and fragmentation, it has been hoped that schemes such as pedestrianized streets, well-managed parks, open-air events, community gardens, and mixed housing schemes can help to rebuild a sense of the shared commons, civic responsibility, and social recognition out of a combination of public appreciation of the shared spaces and enhanced contact between people from diverse backgrounds. The quality of play among strangers is considered to be the key to civic becoming. Outcomes on the ground, however, as a rich archive of research on public spaces confirms, have been mixed – social indifference or hostility towards the stranger in some instances, self-interest or resigned tolerance in others, or glimmers of recognition in yet others.

I am less interested here in explaining this variety, than in asking whether the achievements (and disappointments) of urban public culture can be traced to *inter-human dynamics* in a city's public spaces. I have argued elsewhere that even when public spaces resonate with civic energy and mutual regard, for example, in the busy street, the noisy market, the multicultural festival, the well-used library, they do so because of largely pre-cognitive practices of human habitation of these spaces, experienced as negotiations of "situated surplus" rather than encounters between friendly/unfriendly strangers (Amin 2008). My claim is that the situation itself – characterized by many bodies and things placed in close juxtaposition, many temporalities, fixities and flows tangled together, many rhythms and repetitions of use, many visible and hidden patterns of ordering, many domestications of time, orientation, and flow, many framings of architecture, infrastructure, and landscape – profoundly shapes human conduct, including the balance between civic and non-civic behavior and belief. Accordingly, practices of recognition of the commons, curiosity for others, or civic responsibility may have more to do with the disciplines of presence and regulation in a plural space and with the everyday negotiation of ordered multiplicity (human and non-human) than has been hitherto recognized. The rhythms themselves of "throwntogetherness" (Massey 2005) might be at work in producing social affects such as sensing the crowd as safe, diversity as unthreatening, the commons as provisioning, individual claim as provisional and partial, and public presence as being among rather than with others.

In this reading of civic culture, the ways in which humans are entangled in the material culture of public space, in the rhythms of a given landscape, come to the fore. If this thesis has some merit, what are its implications for deliberative/humanist planning? I think it shows up the limitations of, and possibilities beyond, a focus on human deliberation and recognition as the staple of urban citizenship. It forces us to consider, for example, how the aesthetic of public space, manifest on billboards, public art, symbolic projections (e.g., advertising slogans and political manifestos), architectural style, landscape design, and so on, works upon public culture. Many a lament – often exaggerated – is heard about the manipulations of public culture by the spectacles of capitalism, fomenting consumerism, materialist escape, flight from the present, selfishness, and greed. But why not consider the possibility of alternative projections that work on the side of civic regard and living with difference or for the commons? This might involve experiments with public art and drama to expose the excesses of commodity fetishism, or visualizations – on the sides of buildings, through public performances – of the everyday multicultural city, the public goods that everyone benefits from, the hidden infrastructures that support collective wellbeing.

The hidden infrastructures – the elaborate technologies that regulate public space, from traffic flow systems to surveillance technologies and network cables – are centrally implicated in the formation of urban public culture. Some of the connections are recognized, so for example, humanist planning is quick to condemn the excesses of urban surveillance and control and keen to rebalance the relationship between rule by technological or bureaucratic systems and urban governance through extensive public deliberation. It would be odd indeed to fault this concern in our times of excessive, unaccountable, and often unnecessary public surveillance, ritually targeting the vulnerable and defenseless. Yet, it is also interesting that humanist planning does not recognize how the "technological unconscious" (Thrift 2005) contributes to urban civic culture in positive ways, by keeping things on the move, ensuring rapid recovery from urban breakdown or disaster, making public spaces safe and intelligible, holding the complex urban system together, facilitating communication across time and space, supplying the basics of life and communal existence, and so on. This silent machinery of regulation is more than just that. It also shapes collective understanding of the well-functioning and livable city, everyday expectation in public life, the possibilities on offer in a given urban environment, and more. At most times, these social perceptions are latent and barely acknowledged, but in times of infrastructural collapse or threat, they can come to the fore as the consequences of urban malfunction become all too clear.

Deliberative planning can do much in building public awareness of the technological unconscious that supports social wellbeing, urban democracy, and civic culture. These are two examples of possibility beyond the canons of deliberative planning, and in just one sphere of urban life. No doubt there are other possibilities, but the point is clear. Liberated from an idea of the good city as the product of closer ties between strangers, new openings involving the material culture of the city become immediately available for practical consideration.

Programmatic Planning

To return, however, to the problem of acting in an uncertain world, awareness of the urban as an assemblage of human and non-human entanglements also forces recognition of the limits of managing uncertainty. If situated surplus, the city formed as a meshwork, and the collective urban unconscious, possess an actancy of their own, the engineering of certainty – top-down or deliberative, through humans or non-humans – is rendered an imprecise art. The urban assemblage generates its own rhythms, rules, and surprises. Its machinery may, for example, slow down or dampen the impact of external shocks, perhaps even dissipate the impact of unforeseen or large shocks such as a pandemic or natural disaster. This machinery can "domesticate" change, absorb a shock, fold newness into the everyday. It can also affect the efficacy of emergency or disaster planning: a city's sanitation or sewage system will reveal its agency in responses to flood risk or global pandemics, as will the density of build and topography of streets in effective use of digital technologies to combat door-to-door urban warfare (Graham 2009). Similarly, the meshwork of nodes, lines, and flows in which a city and its parts find themselves located is a formative ecology in its own right, constantly producing both repetitions and surprises out of its multiple combinations and interactions, including unanticipated emergencies such as digital infestations or pollution fogs. The urban meshwork itself is a source of uncertainty in an uncertain world.

In these complex circumstances of trans-human formation, urban generative power, and heightened environmental uncertainty, does it suffice for urban planners to act as listening intermediaries? Do the circumstances not demand more, for example, an urgency and power that work the grain, strategic interventions that make the most of professional expertise, or alterations to material culture that enhance human wellbeing? Or is the urban machinery so strong and so independent that all that remains open to influence from planners are the micro-spaces in which squabbles between humans still count (e.g., in the schoolyard, town hall, housing estate, public amenity)? Could it be that inadvertently the epistemological shift from the knowing to the deliberative tradition has occurred because of some inadvertent recognition of the limits to planning?

Deliberative planners are by no means against strategic planning (see especially Healey 2007), but are wary of comprehensive, expert-driven, urban plans. Their emphasis, instead, falls on motivating visions, scenarios, and diagrams of possibility placed under democratic scrutiny. The strategic role of the planner is not to draw up a plan for implementation, but to offer a vision, to map alternatives. I wonder, however, if something has been lost of the knowing tradition in this otherwise laudable attentiveness to urban complexity and multiplicity; a certain programmatic

clarity over the overall aims and priorities of urban living, made all the more necessary in a context of radical uncertainty. Is it not possible for planners to draw up
an urban program without the pretensions of total vision, teleological fulfillment
and systemic certitude, offering a clear diagnosis of the threats that cities face, the
matters of collective concern that must be addressed, the goals that must be defended
to improve urban living for the many and not the few? Has the attentiveness of
deliberative planners to procedures of decision-making compromised the necessity
to know about substantive matters of urban change and wellbeing?

It is an irony that US pragmatist thought of the early twentieth century that
inspired deliberative planning theory during its formative years in the 1980s and
which has been revisited for new inspiration more recently (Healey 2009; see also
Bridge 2005) was pretty clear about the substantive goals of an emerging democracy
that faced turbulent and uncertain times. The criticisms of James, Peirce, and Dewey
of logical positivism, structuring totalities, and rational planning, their theorization
of non-linearity, incertitude, and emergence in complex open systems, their commitment to radical pluralism, did not prevent them from outlining a new model for
a just and democratic America. Their principled attachment to a politics of attention, that is, to addressing pressing issues of the day and making visible latent social
concerns and harms, went hand in hand with a clear and coherent program of
reform. The campaigns launched by the pragmatists on, say, anti-trust legislation,
welfare reform, mass education, anti-poverty, legal and institutional protection of
rights, regulated capitalism, participatory democracy, anti-corporatism, urban wellbeing, and ethical responsibility, were simultaneously issue-specific and threads of
a particular model of future promise. This was a model of equity-enhancing, participatory, and regulated capitalism, posited as a distinctive alternative to socialism
or corporatist capitalism (Amin and Thrift forthcoming). Awareness of the unexpected novelties of a plural order, of democracy as multiple becomings and belongings, of radical uncertainty in an America facing major changes (due to mass
migration, urbanization, and capitalist transformation) did not get in the way of
articulating a coherent vision and program of practical reforms, to be pursued with
urgency through a variety of means (from legislation and government to popular
mobilization and organized opposition).

In many respects, early twentieth-century America faced as uncertain a world as
we do today, but while the pragmatists managed to draft manifestos out of their
substantive, procedural, and methodological concerns, contemporary urban pragmatists seem to have lost clarity over the devils of urban living and the fundamentals
of the good life in the equitable and just city. If Healey (2007) and Hillier (2007)
are right in asking planners to articulate "motivating visions" and "scenarios of
possibility," what should these look like, and with what order of priority or urgency
placed on the proposals? Is it time to balance the progress made by deliberative
planners on matters of procedure and practice with more of the substantive certitude
that characterized the knowing tradition?

If so, a first step might be to critically evaluate the urban implications – substantive and political – of major social transformations said to be under way, such as
the rise of liquid modernity (Bauman 2000), the end of craft culture (Sennett 2008),
the clashes and entanglements of territorial and network power (Sassen 2006), the
emergence of risk society (Beck 1992), the urbanization of war (Graham 2007), the

associations between soft capitalism, heterarchical organization, and distributed power (Thrift 2005; Stark 2009; Lazzarato 2004), the financialization and digitalization of the economy (MacKenzie 2006; Knorr Cetina and Bruegger 2002), the extensions of biopolitics and related modes of human classification and control (Rose 2007; Diken and Laustsen 2005), the rise of hyper-individualism and new mobilizations of community based on ethnicity and religion (Connolly 2008; Žižek, 2008), the jostle between local, national, and new transnational modes of governance and interest (Slaughter 2004), the threats of ecological and environmental failure. These transformations, summarized only cursorily here, signal a profound alteration of the world and its orderings, and necessitate new analysis of the ways in which urban life is being recomposed and the challenges of social cohesion and equity associated with these transformations. This will help to identify the issues and interests to be championed, their urgency, and their place in a comprehensive vision of urban wellbeing.

This is a challenge for all urban actors, not just urban planners, let alone deliberative planners. But, given the explicit call of some deliberative planners for visionary designs and scenarios and given the uncertain implications of the above social transformations and also warnings of mounting global hazard and risk, an exercise that would focus attention is the imagination of an *emergency* urban plan. If Callon and others are right that contemporary uncertainty comes with potentially drastic outcomes, a "catastrophe audit" of cities would help to sharpen thinking on the urban fragilities – the threats to sustained collective wellbeing – that need to be tackled. Some are already well known, and they include the steady privatization and fragmentation of urban public culture, the intensification of social intolerance, poverty, and vulnerability, the rudimentary nature of risk assessment and catastrophe management procedures, muted response to climate change and environmental destruction, heightened vulnerability in the face of economic and financial globalization, growing infrastructural stress and militarization (after 9/11), continuing urban sprawl, spatial disconnection and social polarization, and the trend towards elite- or growth-driven governance of cities. The audit of these fragilities, grasped and contextualized with the help of appropriate theorizations of contemporary social transformation, would act as a call to attention, a solicitation for rapid response from those with the relevant powers, an opportunity to make things public and mobilize publics.

Such moves would return planning to the heart of programmatic urbanism, expecting planners not only to use the tools of their trade to find solutions to the fragilities and challenges identified, but also to use their substantive knowledge and insight to help outline the shape of the new house on the hill. Modernist planning – in the worst cases – went too far in trying to spell out every detail of the house, the journey up the hill, and the kinds of inhabitants expected. It laid itself open to the risk of disappointment and criticisms of vanity, false promise, and authoritarianism. The outline I have in mind here is different. It is one that offers clarity on the values and expectations of the city that works for the benefit of all its citizens (human and non-human), as it does on the ethical orientations of such an urbanism, explaining how the proposals address contemporary global hazard and risk (in all its varieties) and contemporary social transformation (in all its dimensions). The imperative, thus, is to trace the outline of the city that is able to build resilience against unfolding threat and instability (as far as is possible in a system of multi-nodal and distributed power), in ways that do not compromise the commons or collective wellbeing, explaining why this kind of city is to be valued or necessary.

Programmatic acting in an uncertain, and, we can add, trans-human world, however, cannot mean returning to the logic of linear rationality and intentionality. Instead, it means openly accepting that the realization of strongly held values, aims, and visions, is a journey freighted with contingency, constraint, and surprise, and therefore in need of continual audit, update, and adjustment. This requires cultivating expert judgment, anticipatory intelligence, contingency planning, and responsiveness to new and unexpected developments. It requires a particular kind of leadership; one that is steadfast about overall goals, but open-minded about methods and the debris thrown up by contingency and evolving developments, one that knows when expert judgment and deliberative democracy must be combined or traded off, and one that accepts that the relationship between urban legacy, policy intentionality, and meshwork agency is one of progression through durations, spirals, and jumps. Above all, it requires knowing what to make of the potency of matter, about how the urban environment and non-humans shape human behavior and intentionality, and about how to harness, for example, the technological unconscious, the object-world, the built and natural landscape, to make humans feel and act differently, to stop the urban process from drifting towards danger, division, and discord.

Conclusion

Arguing for a change in direction along these lines, to return to the question posed at the start of this chapter, is not to diminish the value of deliberative planning or multiple knowledges in an uncertain world. Instead, it is to ask for more in the context of heightened hazard and risk (e.g., programmatic expertise and clarity of purpose) and for less in the context of non-human agency (e.g., moderating the possibilities of human intentionality). Relational planners could helpfully take a lead in imagining an urbanism able to work its way through uncertainty, hazard, and risk without compromising collective wellbeing and security, and in mobilizing the unconscious, symbolic, aesthetic, material, and intentional to this end.

There is no shortage of emergency planning in the urban arena, but how far openness to the unknown and the emergent or unassimilated remains in efforts to deal with uncertainty almost always read as threat, is questionable. The risk posed by a governmentality based on elaborate forecasting intelligence, disaster simulation exercises, extensive and intrusive surveillance and control, a filigree of covert actions, and the cultivation of public suspicion in face of hazards such as pandemics, natural disasters, economic meltdowns, technological failures, or warfare and attack, is that exceptional forms of intervention that prey on fear and anxiety, compromise democracy, and legitimate authoritarian rule become the norm (Ophir 2007). Emergency planning, by dint or design, becomes reason to suspend civil liberties, the principle of the open society, and public accountability and trust. It slides into a state of emergency, allowing the state and others in power to deal with uncertainty in ways that close down that which is unilaterally – and often vicariously – deemed alien or undesirable.

There are, of course, dangers in drawing parallels between the suspension of democratic procedure, on the one hand, in action against pandemics or natural and economic disasters that require quick and effective response, and, on the other hand, in action against threats of terror, war, or sedition, when direct or collateral damage is inflicted to citizens and strangers whose guilt has yet to be proven. The point of the comparison, however, is to note that once the emergency state becomes legitimated, a single mindset towards uncertainty can prevail, one that considers it reasonable – in the process of dealing with suspected threat – to stifle due process or criticism, justify harsh measures and consequences in the name of emergency planning, and apportion blame or claim victory with little regard for accuracy.

Might there be a role for urban planners in helping to develop an alternative approach that responds quickly and effectively to uncertainty without compromising the principles of universal obligation, public accountability, and measured response? This would require mobilizing independent expertise on impending threats and vulnerabilities, using it to expose the dangers of the solutions offered by the emergency state, harnessing it to an ethos of risk aversion based on prevention, precaution, and minimized harm, and building momentum around a response to uncertainty that draws on distributed resilience and fortitude rather than hysteria and suspicion.

Such an approach would stay close to the causes of danger and harm, doing everything possible to tackle them, or when this is not possible, building resistance without punitive overload. It would – through and beyond the urban – invest in universal welfare, multicultural understanding, an efficient and inclusive technological unconscious, hope in the open society, an active public culture and strong sense of shared commons, security for the weak, vulnerable, and exposed, extensive regulation of risk, modes of discipline harnessed to principles of just and fair retribution, robust risk monitoring and mitigation systems, and distributed resilience. It would understand that tackling risk and hazard requires mobilization across a broad spectrum, including in arenas yet to be seen as essential for urban security and wellbeing in an uncertain age. It would accept that acting in a turbulent environment to preserve the open and inclusive city is partly a matter of building human equivalence and solidarity, and partly a matter of enrolling the non-human infrastructure to that effect.

References

Amin, A. (2007) Rethinking the urban social. *City* 11 (1): 100–14.
Amin, A. (2008) Collective culture and urban public space. *City* 2 (1): 5–24.
Amin, A., and Thrift, N. (2002) *Cities: Re-imagining the Urban*. Cambridge: Polity Press.
Amin, A., and Thrift, N. (forthcoming) *Political Openings: Recovering Left Political Will*. Durham, NC: Duke University Press.
Amoore, L., and de Goede, M. (2008) *Risk and the War on Terror*. London: Routledge.
Bauman, Z. (2000) *Liquid Modernity*. Cambridge: Polity Press.
Beck, U. (1992) *Risk Society: Towards a New Modernity*. London: Sage.
Bridge, G. (2005) *Reason in the City of Difference*. London: Routledge.
Callon, M., Lascoumes, P., and Barthe, Y. (2009) *Acting in an Uncertain World*. Cambridge, MA: MIT Press.

Connolly, W. (2008) *Capitalism and Christianity, American Style*. Durham, NC: Duke University Press.

De Landa, M. (2006) *A New Philosophy of Society*. London: Continuum.

Diken, B., and Laustsen, C. (2005) *The Culture of Exception: Sociology Facing the Camp*. London: Routledge.

Dillon, M. (2008) Underwriting security. *Security Dialogue* 39 (2–4): 309–32.

Graham, S. (2007) War and the city. *New Left Review* 44: 121–32.

Graham, S. (2009) *Cities Under Siege: The New Military Urbanism*. London: Verso.

Healey, P. (2007) *Urban Complexity and Spatial Strategies*. London: Routledge.

Healey, P. (2009) The pragmatic tradition in planning thought. *Journal of Planning Education and Research* 28 (3): 277–92.

Hillier, J. (2007) *Stretching Beyond the Horizon*. Aldershot: Ashgate.

Knorr Cetina, K., and Bruegger, U. (2002) Global microstructures: the virtual societies of financial markets. *American Journal of Sociology* 107 (4): 905–95.

Lazzarato, M. (2004) *Les révolutions de capitalisme*. Paris: Les Empêcheurs de Penser en Rond.

MacKenzie, D. (2006) *An Engine, not a Camera: How Financial Models Shape Markets*. Cambridge, MA: MIT Press.

Massey, D. (2005) *For Space*. London: Sage.

Ophir, A. (2007) The two-state solution: providence and catastrophe. *Journal of Homeland Security and Emergency Management* 4 (1): 1–44.

Rose, N. (2007) *The Politics of Life Itself*. Princeton, NJ: Princeton University Press.

Sassen, S. (2006) *Territory, Authority, Rights*. Princeton, NJ: Princeton University Press.

Sennett, R. (2008) *The Craftsman*. London: Allen Lane.

Slaughter, A.-M. (2004) *A New World Order*. Princeton, NJ: Princeton University Press.

Stark, D. (2009) *The Sense of Dissonance: Accounts of Worth in Economic Life*. Princeton, NJ: Princeton University Press.

Thrift, N. (2005) *Knowing Capitalism*. London: Sage.

Žižek, S. (2008) *Violence*. London: Profile Books.

Chapter 56

The Three Historic Currents of City Planning

Peter Marcuse

Introduction

Three quite different approaches characterize the mainstream of modern planning: a technical one, a social reform one, and a social justice one. Each is prominent at a particular time and place, forming three identifiable approaches in planning history, in most but not all cases with the simultaneous presence of the others. The three approaches thus often mix, sometimes conflict, are rarely pure, but differ significantly in their methods and goals.

The deferential technicist approach, going back millennia, builds on the urban work of engineers, and is necessarily responsive to those in power that have the authority and resources to commission the work. In modern history it developed out of a concern with the inefficiencies, initially mainly the physical, in the organization of the new industrial economy, inefficiencies which inhibited economic growth and prosperity. It did not question, but rather deferred to, the maintenance of existing institutional relationships, and focused on the value of efficiency, taking the continuance of those relationships for granted. It thus had primary support from established political, economic, and social groups. Technicist planning is inherently, in this definition, subservient to the power structures of the status quo.

The social reform approach similarly developed out of a concern with the externalities of industrialization, but with their social welfare aspects: health, crime, unsanitary housing, social unrest, pollution, not with their economic processes. It approached those issues in the spirit of reform, expecting to, and often succeeding in, remedying social problems within the existing structures of power. Its view of social problems was generally from outside and above, from how they might affect the health and wellbeing of those benefiting from existing established economic and

The New Blackwell Companion to the City   Edited by Gary Bridge and Sophie Watson
© 2011 Blackwell Publishing Ltd

political relationships, not from those suffering from them. It prioritized evaluating results in terms of the extent to which needs were satisfied rather than the cost efficiency of the methods, although the latter also continued to play a role. Its definition of social was a narrow one, focusing on the disadvantaged, the weak, the poor, the minority, the excluded, rather than seeing the problems of such groups as aspects of the broad social system in which they occur, which includes dealing with those that take advantage as well as the disadvantaged, with the majority as well as the minority, the excluders as well as the excluded – in other words, seeing the social as the entire set of interpersonal and inter-group relations that constitute a society.[1]

The social justice approach arose out of concern with the human costs to those adversely affected by rapid urbanization and industrialization, visible in the burgeoning cities and slums with their impoverished populations. It was broadly critical of existing urban social and institutional relationships, proposing sweeping alternatives, and seeing the physical as ancillary to broader social change. It saw social issues from the point of view of those suffering from them, from below, and had broad but varying levels of support from the poor and oppressed.

This essay attempts to define the separate approaches in broad terms, and for each to give selected examples from their history and evolution. Attention will be drawn to two aspects in each, as they appear: (1) critical vs. deferential attitudes towards existing relations of power and (2) social vs. efficiency concerns. It concludes with the suggestion that the main approaches are in tension today, a tension visible in both planning theory and planning practice, and contends that a recent partial resolution of the tension, undertaken without widespread and explicit discussion, was a missed opportunity to advance the cause of planning generally.

The discussion relies on and is in counterpoint to, three classic treatments of planning's history: Leonardo Benevolo's *The Origins of Modern Town Planning*,[2] Peter Hall's *Cities of Tomorrow*,[3] and Mel Scott's *American City Planning*.[4] As will be clear, it draws heavily on their research but attempts to extend their discussion to paint a broader picture of key underlying trends and tensions in that history.

Deferential Planning ("Technicist Planning")

Deferential or technicist is the term used here for planning devoted to maximizing the efficiency of whatever system or place is being planned. Efficiency is of course a goal of virtually any form of planning; certainly no plan is so framed as to be inefficient, just as no plan is framed so as to be unsustainable. Thus planning in the critical social justice approach is expected to be efficient in the service of its purposes also. But deferential technicist planning, as used here, elevates the use of the technical tools of planning, those aspects devoted to efficiency, to be its characteristic and driving force. It sees the planner as a professional, an expert, a technician with a special training and knowledge, capable of using a bag of tools in which he or she has had specific technical training. It is formulated thus in the Green Book, often taken as the leading manual for professional planners:

> The central aim [of planning] is to muster the best knowledge, skill, and imagination in solving complex problems and in making the solutions work. The active client sets

the priorities among problems, judges whether the best effort has been used, and in addition judges whether the solution is effective, whether its cost is too high, and whether the solution gets in the way of other good things.[5]

Karl Polanyi said it well: the role of planning has been to embed the market in society. The market militates against the production of equity or justice; indeed, it does not claim otherwise. Even its strongest defenders, such as Hayek, concede that the market should not be looked to for social ends, and will not do what it does best if it is interfered with by the state (or planners working for the state) in the interests of social objectives. Thus, one of the three streams of planning action that I want to identify, the technicist, is inherently conservative: it is to serve an economic and social and political order in which its role is to make that order function smoothly. The social component of planning enters in only to the extent necessary to permit the market to function efficiently. Thus planning needs to provide infrastructure, needs to avoid clashing land uses that interfere with economic efficiency, and needs to regulate social abuses to the extent they may interfere with order. The City Scientific is the clearest historical expression of that stream of planning activity, and it is in practice mainstream. Planning's function in this view is akin to engineering: not to ask why something is built, but to build it well. So this is the first stream of planning: efficient functioning. It is a technical view of planning – or, since all planning is by its very nature technical, it is "technicist," making planning *only* the technical, ignoring all other considerations.[6]

In terms of the interests supporting such a technicist planning approach, Mel Scott's history is replete with narratives of the extent to which established groups in positions of power played a decisive role: business groups, chambers of commerce, and real-estate interests were prime movers, from the White City Exposition in Chicago to the adoption of zoning in New York City to the urban redevelopment and urban renewal programs of the post-World War II years. Indeed, one line of analysis argues that it was precisely the role of planning to smooth out the contradictions of economic growth and urban development under advancing capitalism that required the development of planning and a planning profession.[7]

Within deferential technicist planning three variations may be differentiated: "scientific" planning, designer planning, contractual planning, and process planning. Efficiency is the central concern. But where planning is defined simply as problem-solving, leaving the statement of the problem and the goals to be sought to others, efficiency becomes not merely a criterion to judge the quality of planning in the pursuit of its goals, but the goal itself. Planning theory offers a variety of models suggesting principles for professionals to use in efficient planning practice.

"Scientific" planning

"Scientific" planning views the function of planning as producing the scientifically most efficient machine through which to perform the activities of the current city, whatever they happen to be. It is concerned with efficiency, but it makes efficiency the master, not the servant, itself the goal, not one criteria of measures to reach a goal generated elsewhere. The city, working efficiently like a machine or a natural organism, becomes the norm, and planning is dedicated to ensuring that it does in fact work efficiently. Problems are technical, physical, primarily civil engineering, planning as urban engineering. There is no critical edge to the approach, and the social is, if mentioned at all, one subcategory analogous to transportation or sewage disposal, not an overriding goal. The process goal of planning is to garner support for that vision, and the planner should try to convince his or her client of the validity and feasibility of that vision.[8] Mel Scott speaks of it alternately as "the City Efficient or the City Functional."[9]

We find this view at the very beginnings of planning as a profession in the United States. Nelson Lewis, author of the ground-breaking *The Planning of the Modern City*, put it this way in 1912: "The creation of a city plan is … essentially the work of the engineer, or rather of the regular engineering staff of the city."[10]

Frederick Law Olmsted, Jr., in 1910, compared the city to "one great social organism,"[11] a vision of a city without conflicts of interest, in which planners could act to the benefit of all its residents – implicitly affirming the continuance of existing and established relations of power.

The engineering approach to city planning evident in the origins of the profession in the United States has been broadened over the ensuing years to become a fuller technicist view, which goes beyond the physical focus of the earlier approach to apply technical solutions to social matters also, in a deferential manner that avoids criticism but attempts to ameliorate the undesired social consequences of existing arrangements without questioning their source. Technicist social planning thus becomes very similar to the reform element in social justice planning. The difference lies in the extent to which criticism is explicit, the extent to which the support for the initiatives comes from established groups concerned to protect the status quo, and the extent to which technical expertise is seen as a central element in addressing social concerns. Thus recommendations such as those of Castells and Borja for a management approach to city planning[12] strike some critics as technicist,[13] although social issues are certainly important among their concerns.[14]

Designer planning

Designer planning elevates the role of the planner to one which, because of outstanding technical competence and/or perhaps imaginative genius, enables the planner to develop a unique vision of the most desirable design for what should be built. It is typically unconcerned with process, and sees physical designs as resulting in, rather than stemming from, the social and individual characteristics of its users. It shares with much of reform planning an appreciation of the need for change, an implicit criticism of particular aspect of the current situation, but sees the imaginative solutions of the designer planner as providing the answer.

Le Corbusier is perhaps the primary example of such an approach, although more socially oriented planners, such as Ernst May or Bruno Taut, were not dissimilar in their view of the importance of their own expertise in formulating plans, and similarly were rarely concerned with the participation of their intended beneficiaries in the planning of their new developments. Today, the term "designer planner," with all its overtones, may well be applied to "star" architects such as Frank Gehry, Rem Koolhas, or Lord Norman Foster, who take the position that the solution to social problems is not their concern. As one journalist has it:

Lord Foster is not a social critic; his job, as he sees it, is to create an eloquent expression of his client's values. What he has designed is a perfect monument for the emerging city of the enlightened megarich: environmentally aware, sensitive to history, confident of its place in the new world order, resistant to sacrifice.[15]

While designer planners tend overwhelmingly to be architects, this is not a criticism of architecture as such, but does have to do with the disciplinary boundaries among the professions, and the priority given to imaginative design for its own sake in some of professional education in architecture, with only secondary attention devoted to social concerns. The scale of the urban design they are often empowered to practice may not be called "planning," although it often is,[16] but what it does is in the mainstream of deferential technicist planning.[17]

Contractual planning

In contractual planning, deferential technicist planners see themselves simply as obedient servants of their employer, bringing to the job the special skills, training, and experience of professional planners, with a kit of tools that experience and training have provided, to accomplish those purposes for which they are hired. There is of course a difference between a planner who is an independent contractor and one who is an employee, but both are subject to contractual terms that require loyalty, subjection to the interests of the client or employer, confidentiality of the work, etc. For purposes of this account, the key question relates to the independence of the planner on matters having to do with the objectives of the plan. Good planning of any sort requires clarity as to its objectives, and a deferential technicist planner will indeed press a client or an employer to clarify their stated goals, often in the process needing to question the beginning statement provided him or her. But the questioning is only to clarify, not to question the ethics, the morality, the ultimate vision, towards which the employer desires. Thus in narrowly contracted planning, alternate visions of the purpose of planning are irrelevant, excluded. In the various Codes of Ethics of planners and civil servants, the point is sometimes acknowledged, but issues of contractual obedience are stated as formal and enforceable requirements of the profession, whereas adherence to substance goals, principles, values, visions, may be included but as aspirational rather than enforceable.[18]

Contractual planning is not only relevant in the private sector; it is also a pervasive aspect of public planning, although the client is a public employer. Case study and practitioner accounts one after another reveal the tensions that arise when planners ignore the restrictions on what they are expected to do, and show how they succeed when they act within those expectations.[19]

Process planning

Much, perhaps most, of planning theory is theory as to how deferential planning really works or how it should work. It is not concerned with what the goals of planning should be, except in process terms. It suggests that planning should make certain that the client, who establishes its goals, has thought through what is desired and clarified what goals should be pursued. It sees planning as a method of problem-solving, and concerns itself with how that process, as a method of work, can most efficiently function. It is critical only to the extent that it may highlight the gap between what it claims it is doing and what is actually done.[20] Primarily, however, it analyzes the procedures used in deferential planning, and does it in the context of established planning practices and for the benefit of their established clients.

Social Reform Planning

Social reform planning constitutes by far the largest channel into which concern with social issues in planning has flowed, although it is indebted to utopian forerunners, where, it will be argued below, social criticism of urban conditions first developed. Urban reform in its modern sense began well before there was such a concept as urban planning, or a profession called "planning." Concern with hygiene and the avoidance of epidemics was an early central part of this movement for public regulation of urban development.

Reform planning of one kind or another has played a role in much of modern planning. Even when its focus has been purely on the physical aspect of urban space, on harmony or beauty or order, it has seen those characteristics as requiring changes in the urban environment contributing to general human welfare, and as requiring changes in conditions as they are with that purpose in mind. As with utopian planning, there is a grounding in social ideas and values, but, as opposed to utopian planning, the changes viewed as needed are not fundamental but are capable of being accomplished within the framework of the existing social, political, and economic order, even if they may lead to or be dependent on changes in that order at the margins. Thus the scope, the depth, of reform is limited, both in nature and in scale, in most reform endeavors.

Some, indeed, have aspirations that are large in scale and, if carried to their logical conclusions, might be fully utopian. The City Beautiful movement in the United States, for instance, set its sights on characteristics of the city over its entire expanse, but it saw its goals in terms of physical improvements, avoiding the social, political, and economic issues that a broad adoption of aesthetics as a criterion of urban development might entail. And its implicit critique of the day-to-day ugliness of the industrial city was one that emerged for a predominantly upper-class milieu, of which social reform was not a part. The parks movement, of which Frederick Law Olmsted Sr.'s Central Park in New York City was a model, had a similar social base, and its social justice and reformist concerns did not extend to those displaced by its construction.[21]

Concern for environmental sustainability, often if not always linked to environmental justice, is a growing component of the reform approach in planning today. Green planning is reformist, and shares social values with much of traditional reform planning, simply giving greater emphasis to respect for nature and ecological balance as values in themselves, sometimes, as in hard ecology, raising such values to foundational levels, akin to the values and orientation for fundamental change of utopian planning. "Sustainable" planning, if it means anything other than ecologically sensitive planning, is a misnomer. No planning is intended to be unsustainable; every plan, except perhaps those to deal with temporary emergencies, is intended to be sustainable in pursuit of its own objectives.[22]

In the United States, the Society for Decongestion of the Population and the movement for reform of the tenement house laws and the National City Planning Conference were originally substantially joint affairs; they separated out only in 1910[23] in a series of events that signaled the separation of the reform from the deferential technicist approaches of planning. Zoning had its origins in a concern with the negative impact of nuisances; it may appropriately be considered deferential technicist planning, interested in the efficient use of land and the correction of inefficiencies, and closely related to issues of traffic and congestion, avoiding undesired social mix that interfered with the efficient rationalization of land values. Housing planning separated from this stream and moved to social reform concerns.

Public participation in planning, its democratization, became a main ingredient of almost all reform planning in the mid-1960s, largely in the context of the civil rights movement, and became embodied in law in the War on Poverty and Model Cities programs, and is continued in the Empowerment Zone legislation in effect today. Sherry Arnstein laid out the spectrum of participation in a leading article in 1969.[24] The distinction between participation and democratic decision-making has been highlighted since.[25] Participation is not power; its reform is not radical. Virtually no significant planning project today can be undertaken without some form of participation, although democratic processes of decision-making lagged behind. Participation is a reform that, at least in name, seems firmly embedded as a commitment of the profession today. In the new revision of the AICP Code of Ethics the first rule reads:

> 1. We shall not deliberately or with reckless indifference fail to provide adequate, timely, clear and accurate information on planning issues.[26]

Equity planning, a term associated with the work of Norman Krumholz in Cleveland between 1969 and 1979,[27] is perhaps as comprehensive a formulation of the goals of reform efforts in the profession as we have seen to date. Krumholz was elected President of both the American Planning Association and the American Institute of Certified Planners, and thus played a role significantly different from those of most of the otherwise ideologically related planners of the social justice approach next taken up here; in content it was very closely allied to that more critical view of existing realities.

Social Justice Planning

Most social reform planning is professional planning, advocates' planning, experts' planning, planning within established bureaucratic/legal structures. Paralleling such planning is social justice planning based on grass-roots groups, which at their strongest become social movements. Such groups have been major actors in obtaining planning decisions reflecting social justice concerns. Sometimes they have worked within and/or used existing structures, as those described by Leonie Sandercock and Tom Angotti;[28] sometimes they have been deliberately outside of and disruptive of such structures, as those Frances Piven and Richard Cloward describe in *Poor Peoples' Movements*.[29] Their planning, and that of their supporters, differs from social reform planning in its direct confrontation with issues of power, putting the interests of social justice ahead of competing claims on planning oriented towards efficiency as the primary goal.

I mean by social justice the complex of goals and values, changing over time, that center about human development, the expansion of capabilities, values such as equity, equality, diversity, caring.[30] Historically, social justice approaches are supported by a different array of groups, interests, and advocates than the deferential technicist approaches.[31] More than deferential technicist planning and most social reform planning, it calls, not merely for participation, but for decision-making from below on issues of planning.

Ethical/cultural principles planning

The most recent approach to planning, and one as yet lodged primarily in planning theory discussions, might be called principles planning. It is planning that would put ahead of any immediate target of planning action the fundamental principle or principles that should be applied in the situation, and require any proposed action towards the immediate target to meet the requirements imposed by that principle. Its origins lie in a variety of socially oriented criticisms of conventional planning, which argue that particular approaches are undemocratic, opaque, unfair or unjust, productive of inequality, disrespectful of individual differences, directed at growth without regard to human consequences, unsustainable. In response, proposals are made for alternate approaches, under names such as transactive planning,[32] just city planning,[33] communicative planning,[34] planning for sustainability, planning for diversity, multi-cultural planning,[35] planning for the full development of human capabilities, and others.

The extent to which these various forms of principles planning have made their way into the actual practice of the profession is variable. Thus far, most remain either in the realm of planning theory, where they are recognized, for instance in the American Institute of Certified Planners (AICP) qualifying exam for certification,[36] or they are dedicated to the procedures and methods of planning, rather than posing substantive issues going beyond a single objective, e.g., ecological sustainability, as their subject-matter. They are thus far virtually ignored in the newly adopted Code of Ethics of the AICP, where words such as "justice," "diversity," and "culture" do not appear.

Community-based planning

Another channel towards the radical side of the social justice stream of planning, combines elements of the utopian (below) and the reform. It shares with the utopian the concern with the ideal, but it moves towards the reform and shares with the reform the concern with the practically possible. Its most visible manifestation today is probably in community-based planning, a movement given substantial impetus in the United States by the anti-poverty and model cities legislation of the 1960s, which in turn received their impetus from the civil rights movement and political unrest of the 1960s,[37] in opposing discrimination and supporting integration, supporting public housing and its expansion, staffing community design centers under the War on Poverty program, espousing advocacy planning both in theory and in practice,[38] and most recently, if still largely at the level of theory, in the growing discussions around planning for empowerment,[39] insurgent planning,[40] indigenous planning, feminist planning, and critical planning.[41]

Radical or critical planning

Radical or critical planning adopts the core principles of social justice planning, but differs from ethical or community-based planning in its insistence on pressing its underlying analysis to confront the functioning of the social, economic, and/or political system that gives rise to the particular issues a planning effort confronts. In so doing it sees power not as something to be dealt with tactically, to successfully implement immediate gains, but as something that must be confronted in most cases more fundamentally and long-range. In examining what needs to be done in dealing with the impact of Hurricane Katrina on the residents of New Orleans, for instance, technicist planning focuses on the most efficient way of determining how and whether low-lying areas should continue to be occupied and how and where dykes should be fortified; social reform planning focuses on how most fairly to distribute the available federal aid and how to give priority assistance to the poor and minority occupants of flooded areas and aid them to return to better planned neighborhoods (stressing the involvement of their residents in the planning process). Critical planning, however, would also examine the structure of the planning process itself in New Orleans and highlight the unjust distribution of power underlying the decision-making process in the city, while pointing out the responsibility of the real-estate industry, tourist businesses, and shipping concerns for the ecological damage that permitted the flooding in the first place.[42]

Utopian planning

Utopian thinking is concerned with ideal end states or proposals leading to ideal states, and places them in critical contrast to existing realities.[43] It addresses issues of power only by implication; by pressing proposals that amount to a complete overhaul, and indeed rejection, of existing arrangements, it by implication rejects the systems of power on which such arrangements rest, although how explicitly it raises the issue of power varies. But there are variations within utopian thinking that have to do with the extent of the focus on the built environment, the forms and shapes of utopias, and the aspects as to which they stand in critical contrast.

There are three main variations of utopian thinking. The first, design utopias, address directly ideals of a perfect society but are little concerned with its physical form. The second, symbolic utopias, use the forms of the built environment simply to illustrate broad social concepts of such a society. The third, physical utopias, see defining forms of the built environment as in fact decisively incorporating the desired ideal. While abstract utopias have a long history, as concrete planning proposals aimed at the improvement of the built environment they are of relatively recent vintage.

Design utopias are oldest, going back millennia. They focus at the societal scale, are sharply critical of existing forms, and share with other utopias a lack of concern with implementation, developing instead ideal models, not so much concerned with physical arrangements, urban or rural, as with the social, with relationships of government, or among individuals, or between individuals and society. Plato might be an early contributor, Thomas More's *Utopia*, Thomas Campanella's *City of the Sun*, St. Augustine's *City of God*, are among others.

Symbolic utopias, deceptively related to the structuring of the built environment, used physically shaped proposals to illustrate graphically, or symbolize, desired social arrangements. Butler's *Erewhon*, H. G. Wells's *A Modern Utopia*, Edward Bellamy's *Looking Backward*, Jack London's *Iron Heel*, George Orwell's *1984*, are examples. Both of these types are what David Harvey would call utopias of process.[44] The third type of utopian planning is what Harvey would call utopias of product: planning whose primary focus is affecting spatial and physical relationships.

Applied utopias are those often seen as being in a direct line from the early utopias, although their social justice edge is often implicit rather than explicit – the proposals for the design of city forms and social relationships, such as Ebenezer Howard's Garden Cities proposals. They are physical utopias and share the heart of utopianism, the grounding in ideals involving fundamentally different new social, economic, or institutional arrangements, derived from a critical view of the existing society. But they make serious physical proposals as the way to those changes, rather than seeing physical changes as the result or simply accompaniment of broader social changes. It may well be that such proposals entered the imagination only at the point when physical changes in the organization of urban life began to appear as something subject to public control.

Garden Cities ideas have had wide popularity, and have been implemented to varying degrees. The ideas of the Regional Planning Association of America in the United States, the new towns developments in the United Kingdom and in the Scandinavian countries, the housing developments of the between-wars periods in Germany, all owe much to analogous thinking. None has produced developments operating at the scale of the large city or the megalopolis, although they were centrally concerned with issues of regionalism, and all have been severely limited by the dependence on national political and economic structures that have curtailed the resources available to their full development. The abortive New Towns initiative in the United States in the 1970s is a classic example of the limitations within a broader national context little focused on social justice ideals.

What is important about all of these evolutions that social justice planning took from its roots in the early utopian schemes is their central concern with the social and their critical view of the existing conditions, both aspects of which vary from one to the other in their scale, their depth, and their concern with implementation, but not in their willingness to challenge the conventional and the established in their efforts.

Conclusion

So there have been three different approaches in the history of planning, each with multiple differing aspects. They range from the technicist to the social, running sometimes parallel, almost always mixing to some degree, often in tension with each other. Their separate natures can be formulated in many different ways. Their difference is analogous to that between substantive rationality and instrumental rationality in Habermasian terms, between conventional planning and justice planning in the current discussions about the Just City.[45] Israel Stollman, the well-respected long-time leader of both the American Planning Association and the American Institute of Certified Planners, phrased it as the tension between planners following the precepts of their clients and planners asserting their own values.[46]

Thus this essay should not be taken as suggesting a moral judgment on the actions of individual planners, but rather as an attempt to highlight the divergent roles that planning has been asked to play historically in the shaping of cities. The interplay between what is wanted, and by whom, and what is possible, between what is just and what is realistic, creates a constant tension in city development. Clarity on the causes of that tension and attention to the alternatives for its resolution ought to be an on-going mandate for those concerned about the future of cities.

Notes

1 The difference between the two definitions roughly corresponds to the uses of the word "social" in schools of social work and in departments of sociology. As planners use the term, it often corresponds to the "soft" concerns of planning, as opposed to the "hard" of physical concerns.

2 Leonardo Benevolo (1967) *The Origins of Modern Town Planning*. Trans. Judith Landry. London: Routledge and Kegan Paul.

3 Peter Hall (2001) *Cities of Tomorrow: An Intellectual History of Urban Planning and Design in the Twentieth Century*. 3rd edn. Oxford: Basil Blackwell.

4 Mel Scott (1969) *American City Planning*. Berkeley: University of California Press.

5 Israel Stollman (1979) The values of the city planner. In *The Practice of Local Government Planning*, ed. Frank So and Israel Stollman, American Planning Association, *et al.* Washington, DC: International City Management Association in cooperation with the American Planning Association (hereafter "The Green Book"), 7. Subsequently, Stollman talks explicitly about the values of "the planner," but of the planner as an individual, not of planning as a profession.

6 Both Coke in the first ICMA Green Book (James G. Coke (1968) Antecedents of local planning. In *Principles and Practice of Urban Planning*, ed. William I. Goodman and Eric C. Freund. Washington, DC: International City Managers' Association, 5–28) and David Harvey (1978) On planning the ideology of planning. In *Planning for the '80s: Challenge and Response*, ed. J. Burchall. New Brunswick, NJ: Rutgers University Press, separate out that component of planning that is technical.

7 See for instance David Harvey (1976) Labor, capital, and class struggle around the built environment in advanced capitalist societies. *Politics & Society* 6: 265–95; Edmond Preteceille (1976) Urban planning: the contradictions of capitalist urbanization. *Antipode* March: 69–76; Richard E. Foglesong (1986) *Planning the Capitalist City: The Colonial Era to the 1920s*. Princeton, NJ: Princeton University Press; Christine Boyer (1983) *Dreaming the Rational City*. Cambridge, MA: MIT Press.

8 T. J. Schlereth (1981) Burnham's Plan and Moody's Manual: city planning as progressive reform. *Journal of the American Planning Association* 47 (1981): 70–82.

9 Scott, *American City Planning*, 123.

10 *Proceedings of the Engineers' Club of Philadephia* July 1912: 198–215 at p. 201.

11 In 1910 before the Second National Conference on City Planning and Congestion of Population, reprinted as F. L. Olmsted (1910) The basic principles of city planning. *American City* 3: 6772.

12 M. Castells and J. Borja, in collaboration with Belil Mireira and Benner Chris (1997) *Local and Global. The Management of Cities in the Information Age.* United Nations Centre for Human Settlements (Habitat). London: Earthscan Publications Ltd.

13 Peter Marcuse (2002) Depoliticizing globalization: from neo-Marxism to the network society of Manuel Castells. In *Understanding the City*, ed. John Eade and Christopher Mele. Oxford: Blackwell, 131–58.

14 Castells and Borja, *Local and Global.*

15 Nicolai Ouroussoff (2006) Injecting a bold shot of the new on the Upper East Side. *New York Times* October 10. Available online at www.nytimes.com/2006/10/10/arts/design/10fost.html?scp=1&sq=ouroussoff%20Upper%20East%20Side%20October%2010%202006&st=cse (accessed October 21, 2010).

16 See, for instance, the columns of Nicolai Ouroussoff, architect critic of the *New York Times*. On Gehry in particular, see (with a symptomatic headline "What will be left of Gehry's vision for Brooklyn?") *New York Times* March 21, 2008: E25.

17 The most recent examples run from downtown Los Angeles to Atlantic Yards in Brooklyn, New York.

18 For a more detailed discussion of the multiple roles of planners in practice, see Peter Marcuse (1976) Professional ethics and beyond: values in planning. *Journal of the American Institute of Planners* 42 (3): 254–74. Reprinted in *Public Planning and Control of Urban and Land Development: Cases and Materials*, ed. Donald Hagman. 2nd edn. Minneapolis, MN: West Publishing Co. (1980), 393–400.

19 See, for instance, the accounts collected in Bruce W. McClendon and Anthony James Catanese (1996) *Planners on Planning: Leading Planners Offer Real-Life Lessons on What Works, What Doesn't, and Why.* Jossey-Bass Public Administration Series. San Francisco: Jossey-Bass Publishers.

20 Bent Flyvbjerg (1998) *Rationality and Power: Democracy in Practice.* Chicago: University of Chicago Press.

21 See Elizabeth Blackmar and Roy Rosenzweig (1992) *The People and the Park: A History of Central Park.* Ithaca, NY: Cornell University Press.

22 Peter Marcuse (1998) Sustainability is not enough. *Environment and Urbanization* 10 (2): 103–12. Also in *The Future of Sustainability*, ed. Marco Keiner. Heidelberg: Springer Verlag (2006), 55–68.

23 See Peter Marcuse (1980) Housing in early city planning. *Journal of Urban History* 6 (2): 153–76, reprinted in slightly different form as Peter Marcuse (1980) Housing policy and city planning: the puzzling split in the United States, 1893–1931. In *Shaping an Urban World*, ed. Gordon E. Cherry. London: Mansell.

24 S. Arnstein (1969) The ladder of citizen participation. *Journal of American Institute of Planners* 35 (4): 216–24.

25 Peter Marcuse (1970) *Tenant Participation – for What?* Washington, DC: The Urban Institute, Working Paper No. 112–20, July 30.

26 As adopted by the American Institute of Certified Planners, March 19, 2005. The full text, and its history, is available at www.planning.org/ethics/ethicscode.htm (accessed October 21, 2010).

27 Norman Krumholz and John Forester (1990) *Making Equity Planning Work. Leadership in the Public Sector*, foreword by Alan A. Altshuler. Philadelphia: Temple University Press; Norman Krumholz and Pierre Clavel (1994) *Reinventing Cities: Equity Planners Tell Their Stories.* Philadelphia: Temple University Press.

28 Leonie Sandercock (ed.) (1998) *Making the Invisible Visible*. Berkeley: University of California Press; Thomas Angotti (2008) *New York for Sale: Community Planning Confronts Global Real Estate*. Cambridge, MA: MIT Press.

29 Frances Fox Piven and Richard A. Cloward (1977) *Poor People's Movements: Why They Succeed, How They Fail*. New York: Pantheon Books.

30 In Amartya Sen and Martha Nussbaum's sense of the term: Martha C. Nussbaum and Amartya Sen (1993) *The Quality of Life*. Oxford: Oxford University Press.

31 This characteristic needs to be spelled out in more detail. It is intuitively likely that working-class groups, immigrants, minority group members, women, non-conformists in lifestyle or ideology, are to be found active within or supportive of critical social justice planning, but the detailed evidence remains to be marshaled. It is one of the lacunae in existing research that this has not yet been done systematically.

32 John Friedmann (1987 [1973]) *Retracking America: A Theory of Transactive Planning*. Garden City, NY: Doubleday; John Friedmann (1987) The social mobilization tradition of planning. In *Planning in the Public Domain: From Knowledge to Action*. Princeton, NJ: Princeton University Press, 225–310.

33 Susan Fainstein (2009) Planning and the just city. In *Searching for the Just City*, ed. Peter Marcuse, James Connolly, Johannes Novy, Ingrid Olivo, Cuz Potter, and Justin Steil. New York and London: Routledge, 19–39.

34 John Forester (1989) *Planning in the Face of Power*. Berkeley: University of California Press.

35 Michael Burayidi (ed.) (2000) *Urban Planning in a Multicultural Society*. Westport, CT: Praeger, 225–34.

36 Clare G. Hurley (1999) Planning theory … approaching the millennium … *Study Manual for the Comprehensive AICP Exam of the American Institute of Certified Planners*. Chapter President's Council, the American Planning Association.

37 Angotti, *New York for Sale*, and James DeFilippis (2004) *Unmaking Goliath: Community Control in the Face of Global Capital*. New York: Routledge.

38 Paul Davidoff (1965) Advocacy and pluralism in planning. *Journal of the American Institute of Planners* 31: 331–8; Linda Davidoff and Nel Gold (1974) Suburban action: advocacy planning for an open society. *Journal of the American Institute of Planners* 40: 12–21.

39 June Thomas (1998) Racial inequality and empowerment: necessary theoretical constructs for understanding US planning history. In Sandercock (ed.), *Making the Invisible Visible*, 198–208.

40 Sandercock, *Making the Invisible Visible*.

41 Peter Marcuse (2007) Social justice in New Orleans: planning after Katrina. *Progressive Planning* summer: 8–12.

42 The argument is developed in P. Marcuse (2005) Katrina disasters and social justice. *Progressive Planning, the Magazine of Planners Network* 165 (fall): 1, 30–5.

43 For background, I have found Malcolm Miles (2007) *Urban Utopias: The Built and Social Architectures of Alternative Settlements*. London: Routledge, exceptionally useful. There is a Society for Utopian Studies, whose website has links to a substantial bibliography.

44 David Harvey (2000) *Spaces of Hope*. Berkeley: University of California Press.

45 See Peter Marcuse, James Connolly, Johannes Novy, Ingrid Olivo, Cuz Potter, and Justin Stein (eds.) (2009) *Searching for the Just City: Debates in Urban Theory and Practice*. Oxford: Routledge.

46 Stollman, The values of the city planner, 8.

Chapter 57

Photourbanism: Planning the City from Above and from Below

Anthony Vidler

Photography shows cities in aerial shots, brings crockets and figures down from the Gothic cathedrals. All spatial configurations are incorporated into the central archive in unusual combinations which distance them from human proximity.

(Siegfried Kracauer, Photography.[1])

Aerial photography, in its context as an extension of the traditional "view from above" as it had been established in Paris from the first balloon flights of the 1780s to the photographic surveys from balloon by the photographer Nadar, served from the outset as at once a machine of the "real" and agent of the surreal, an increasingly privileged instrument of the double desire of planners – utopian and projective.[2] As Kracauer noted, this viewpoint, entirely distanced from the ground, tended necessarily to increase the natural "distance" inherent in the photographic medium, and thus to increase its assumed objectivity and of course its inherent manipulability devoid of the difficult and intractable individual or social subject.

And yet, the camera, with its real effect, is also a primary instrument of resistance to this view from above, and, building on the tradition of street photos, after the rediscovery of Atget in the 1920s increasingly served to counter the aerial views of planners with the "on the ground" views of radicals and nostalgics who called for the art of city planning to recognize the historical and social context. In this sense the debates and uses of photography in urban planning replayed in a new key the debates over demolition and reconstruction that had begun long before Baron Haussmann. Here I want to focus on two moments in the modernist history of this discussion (which still goes on): that of the confirmation of the aerial view in its planning role by Le Corbusier in the 1920s and 1930s, and that of the not entirely successful opposition to this vision in the 1950s and 1960s.

The New Blackwell Companion to the City   Edited by Gary Bridge and Sophie Watson
© 2011 Blackwell Publishing Ltd

Chapter 29

The New Blackwell Companion to the City   Edited by Gary Bridge and Sophie Watson
© 2011 Blackwell Publishing Ltd

Harvey, D. (1973) *Social Justice and the City*. London: Edward Arnold.

Jacobs, J. (1969) *The Economy of Cities*. New York: Random House.

Kling, R., Olin, S., and Poster, M. (eds.) (1991) *Postsuburban California: The Transformation of Orange County Since World War II*. Berkeley and Los Angeles: University of California Press.

Knox, P. L. (2008) *Metroburbia, USA*. Piscataway, NJ: Rutgers University Press.

Mackenzie, E. (1994) *Privatopia: Homeowner Associations and the Rise of Residential Private Government*. New Haven, CT and London: Yale University Press.

McDonald, John F. (1997) *Fundamentals of Urban Economics*. New York: Prentice-Hall.

Sassen, S. (2001) *The Global City*. Princeton, NJ: Princeton University Press.

Soja, E. W. (1989) *Postmodern Geographies: The Reassertion of Space in Critical Social Theory*. Oxford and Malden, MA: Blackwell.

Soja, E. W. (2000) *Postmetropolis: Critical Studies of Cities and Regions*. Oxford and Malden, MA: Blackwell.

Soja, E. W. (2002) The new regionalism: a conversation with Edward Soja. Interview by R. Ehrenfurt. *Critical Planning* 9: 5–12.

Soja, E. W. (2008) Taking space personally. In *The Spatial Turn: Interdisciplinary Perspectives*, ed. Barney Warf and Santa Arias. New York and London: Routledge, 11–34.

Soja, E. W. (2009) Regional planning and development theories. In *The International Encyclopedia of Human Geography*, ed. N. Thrift and R. Kitchin. Amsterdam: Elsevier, 259–70.

Soja, E. W., and Kanai, J. M. (2008) The urbanization of the world. In *The Endless City*, ed. R. Burdett and D. Sudjic. New York and London: Phaidon, 54–69.

Soureli, K., and Youn, E. (2009) Urban restructuring and the crisis: a symposium with Neil Brenner, John Friedmann, Margit Meyer, Allen J. Scott, and Edward W. Soja. *Critical Planning* 16: 34–60.

Storper, M. (1997) *The Regional World: Territorial Development in a Global Economy*. New York: Guilford Press.

Chapter 60

Invisible Architecture: Neighborhood Governance in China's Cities

John Friedmann

This chapter explores the invisible architecture of local governance in Chinese cities. By making this structure visible, we may discover what makes urban China "Chinese" after all, not just a slightly skewed mirror image of the west. The structure of local governance in China is a mix of the old and the new. The old is the authoritarian, top-down system of administration, running from Beijing down to the lowliest neighborhood and village. In this respect, little has changed. But the new is indeed very new, dating back to the 1980s and the start-up of the so-called reform period, when the government opened China to the world and, step-by-step, abandoned its system of central economic planning in favor of the free market. This process of change is still ongoing; while we can trace its evolution, the overall pattern that we glimpse is only of the moment; ten years from now, it will almost certainly be different.

The system of local governance allows us to look at the process of urban transformation. My focus here will be on the central government's attempt to devolve certain service delivery systems to its lowest governmental presence in cities, the sub-district or street offices and more particularly, to the numerous grass-roots neighborhood organizations called residents' committees which were organized after the assumption to power of the Communist regime in 1949. These committees, now upgraded and renamed *sheque* residents' committees, have been assigned a new role in the development of China's rapidly growing cities. The entire program is known as *shequ jianshe* or neighborhood construction and has been under way across the country for about a decade.

To tell this story, I will proceed in four stages. First, I will cast a backward glance at the Maoist period (1949–77) during which a new institutional framework for

The New Blackwell Companion to the City   Edited by Gary Bridge and Sophie Watson
© 2011 Blackwell Publishing Ltd

China's governance was put in place. This will serve as a comparison for the reform era that followed (1978 and continuing). The second stage will look at both the changes and the continuities in this framework and their consequences for urban management with particular focus on the lowest level of urban governance, the residents' committee (*jumin weiyuanhui*) and its gradual restructuring through the national program of "neighborhood construction" promoted by Beijing's Ministry of Civil Affairs (MCA). This program will first be described in its ideal formulation, where a neighborhood unit (*shequ*) is understood to be an administratively designated area that is articulated through a neighborhood service center. In the third stage, we will look at the actual implementation of this program based on a small number of empirical studies in key cities, and the challenges the program has encountered with regard to its legal status, the role of the Chinese Communist Party (CCP) in its realization, hoped-for civic participation, and financial viability. A brief concluding section will assess the evidence in terms of what the neighborhood construction program portends for the future of China's cities.

Maoist Era: Laying the Institutional Foundations (1949–77)

When the People's Republic of China (PRC) was proclaimed on October 1, 1949, no one could have foreseen that 60 years on, this poor, war-torn country would become a major economic and political player in the world. Ninety percent of its population, mostly illiterate, were farmers. After decades of war, civil war, and revolutionary struggle, China had hit rock bottom. New institutions of governance would have to be put in place to provide the scaffolding for the social order to come.

China had survived decades of social turmoil and now, unified again, was finally at peace. Political power would henceforth be concentrated in the CCP, while a parallel system of bureaucratic power (the state) would carry out its mission according to a series of five-year national plans. Headed by the State Council in Beijing, China would in future be guided by the collective leadership of the Party. Both, however, were ultimately accountable, at least in principle, to the People's Congress, a representative body organized at each hierarchical level of administration, rising from urban district, municipality, and province, to culminate in a National Assembly. In practice, People's Congresses have served as a legitimizing device for Party rule, though in recent years they show signs of slowly evolving into more deliberative forums (O'Brien 2009).

Reaching down into the nooks and crannies of family, farm, and factory in all parts of the country, Party control was and continues to be ubiquitous. In principle, the Party was subject to the "mass line" which Mao Zedong explained as the only source of "correct leadership":

> In all practical work of our party, all correct leadership is necessarily "from the masses to the masses." This means: take the ideas of the masses (scattered and unsystematic ideas) and concentrate them (through study turn them into concentrated and systematic ideas) then go to the masses and propagate and explain these ideas until the masses embrace them as their own, hold fast to them and translate them into action, and test the correctness of these ideas into such action. (Saich 2004: 44)

Mao called this a "Marxist theory of knowledge." In theory, writes Saich, "the 'mass line' is about consultation, education, persuasion and eliciting an enthusiastic response" (Saich 2004: 44). This formula may have made sense in a nation of illiterate small farmers concentrating on their survival from harvest to harvest. In the increasingly stratified, urbanized, and educated populace of today, with widespread access to multiple media and the internet, mass line rhetoric is an anachronism that continues to justify the vanguard dictatorship of the Party.

During Chairman Mao's rule, China's economy was centrally planned using a version of the Soviet Union's method of "material balances."[1] The official *renminbi* or "people's currency" was reduced to a unit of accounting. Commodity markets were abolished (including for land and labor), and prices no longer reflected the balance between supply and demand but were set by bureaucratic fiat. For planning purposes, calculations were made in terms of bushels of grain and tons of steel.

Along with these fundamental changes in governance and the economy came two important institutions meant to serve a dual purpose: to increase production (while holding down consumption) and to teach people how to live frugally according to the new precepts of collective life. People's communes were established as large collective farms that were further broken down into "production brigades" and "production teams." A block of agricultural land to be farmed collectively was assigned to each production team, comprising a village neighborhood that contained some 10 to 50 households (Unger 2002: 10). Sharing in the proceeds from their work, everyone would enjoy a basic level of security, even the poorest members of the collective such as orphans, widows, and the childless elderly. The head of the production team was either elected or chosen by acclamation. On the other hand, what crops should be grown and how their village should be run was a matter for superior authorities to decide in conformity with the specific targets of the current five-year plan.

The functional equivalent of the rural commune was the urban "work unit" or *danwei*. David Bray calls it "the basic unit of urban social [and spatial] organization" in the post-1949 period (2005: 124). By the mid-1970s, nearly 80 percent of urban workers belonged to a *danwei* which offered a whole way of life and nourished a sense of personal identity. For more and more urbanites, it was a place where you lived, worked, and died alongside neighbors and workmates just like yourself. All state and collective enterprises such as factories, universities, hospitals, railways, and similar organizations including the military were designed as gated compounds that comprised, in addition to work spaces, housing, recreation facilities, kindergartens, primary schools, canteens, and health centers for their workforce and families (if any). Indeed, one could say that the *danwei* was a city-in-miniature – a model of the socialist city of production – that promised a basic livelihood, a steady job, neighborliness, friendship, and security in old age. *Danwei* people had minimal private possessions, and essential life spaces including kitchens, toilets, and bath houses, were shared by small clusters of households. Although the traditional city continued to house large numbers of people – the building of *danwei* was a gradual, project-by-project process – it no longer required city-wide land use planning. Bray puts it well when he writes: "The Chinese city was to develop more as a collection of self-contained and spatially defined communities than as an integrated urban network" (2005: 124). Consequently, from 1960 onwards, city planning was suspended. Though sporadically resumed in the early 1970s, it did not regain its full influence and power until the following decade when China, in another historical turn, was in a rush to "marketize" its economy.

Those who lived beyond the walls of *danwei* compounds – and by the end of the Mao period there were still many – were subject to other forms of regulation. Below the district level, two organizations deserve mention: the street office (*jiedao banshichu*) and the residents' committee (*jumin weiyuanhui*). According to Bray,

> Although these organizations operated as a kind of parallel system to the *danwei*, they were designed as a temporary solution to an urban problem, and it was always assumed that they would wither away as the process of socialist construction progressively absorbed the remaining urban population into a socialist *danwei* of one sort or another. (2005: 100–1)

But this was not to be. Essentially, street offices (SOs) were neighborhood branches of the district bureaucracy, the district being the lowest hierarchical level of government (each district also had a People's Congress or legislative assembly). On the other hand, as a mass-line organization, residents' committees (RCs) were classified as autonomous bodies of the people, each responsible for some 100 to 700 households. RCs thus became a basic link between the grassroots and the hierarchy of state and Party. Their job was to mobilize the local population when called upon, to ensure the full implementation of the one-child-per-family and similar policies, and to assist Public Security in maintaining public order. Elected members to an RC were often retired women, who enjoyed the confidence of the local Party branch and SO cadres. But as it turned out, far from being the temporary stop-gap institutions originally imagined, SOs and RCs would come to play significant new roles in the *shequ*-construction movement that began in the final years of the twentieth century.

One more institutional innovation with major impacts on both urban and rural development was the household registration or *hukou* system (Dutton 1992; Wang 2005). Given antecedents that reached back to the Qin dynasty more than 2,000 years ago, its reincarnation in the latter half of the1950s was not an especially remarkable event. Indeed, many people welcomed what they saw as a step towards the recovery of civic order after decades of turmoil. Administered by the Ministry of Public Security, households would be registered according to their actual place of residence or birth. Two types of *hukou* were issued: agricultural and non-agricultural. The system, devised principally to restrict unauthorized migration, particularly from rural areas to the city, was enforced in two ways: first by a system of ration cards that entitled *hukou* holders to basic necessities such as grain, oil, and cotton cloth, but only in their area of official residence, and second by the requirement that anyone wanting to move away from there to anywhere else would have to obtain official permission from their commune or *danwei* of record as well as the local police. Like European guest workers in the 1960s, rural migrants under contract to urban work units were expected to return home at the end of their contracted period. Forbidden to remain in the *danwei*, and with a family that usually continued to be domiciled in their home village, few workers succeeded in making a permanent move from rural to urban.

Figure 60.1 Chinese courtyard. Photo S. Watson.

The Reform Era: Key Institutional Changes

The reform era is usually dated back to the Third Plenum of the 11th Central Committee of the CCP in 1978 which, two years after Mao's death, endorsed Deng Xiaoping's reform proposals. The way forward would be rocky, and great efforts were made to stress the ideological continuities in China's revolutionary tradition. Even so, the changes were every bit as dramatic as those which Mao had introduced following his accession to supreme power in the People's Republic. Here I will restrict myself to the briefest outline of these revolutionary "reforms," concentrating on the transformations in some of China's key institutions, changes that, despite much talk of gradualism, actually occurred with lightning speed during the 1980s. Some fundamentals of China's governance system, however, remained unchanged, most importantly, the CCP's monopoly hold on power. Although Mao's giant portrait continued to look down benignly from Tiananmen Gate to the people gathered in the square below, his charisma was now little more than a memory, albeit for large numbers of people a bitter one. The Great Helmsman had dreaded bureaucracy, not least the bureaucracy of his own Party. A revolutionary his whole life, he believed (like Thomas Jefferson) in the *permanent* revolution. But his leadership faltered badly when, with great cunning, he launched the Great Proletarian Cultural Revolution in 1966 against those whom he suspected of plotting a return to the "bad old days" of the bourgeois republic. Many still refer to the "lost decade" of the 1960s and 1970s when the PRC almost self-destructed. Rising to power in 1978, Deng Xiaoping, himself an old-guard revolutionary, succeeded in setting China on a completely new course.

The system of "material balances" which had been the soft technology of China's centrally planned economy was abandoned. With far-reaching implications, this simple act redefined relations between the central state and the multiple local economies throughout China's vast territory. Power was devolved to provincial and municipal governments in order to promote, in whatever ways they saw fit, their own development as platforms of export-led economic growth. Foreign investments (especially from east and southeast Asia) were eagerly sought to partner with Chinese firms, and money resumed its traditional role as an indicator of relative scarcity. By the mid-1980s, the commune system was dismantled, and land divided into small household plots that would be farmed under a "responsibility system" that required delivery of a certain quantity of grain at prices fixed by the government in advance of harvest. The communes themselves were turned into township administrations and became the last outposts of the CCP in rural areas. As long as land continued to be held collectively, village committees could decide how to use it. Especially in coastal areas, many villages decided to augment their incomes by starting up small industries or simply renting out their land for urban uses, such as golf courses or manufacturing plants. In time, these industries would make up a full third of China's industrial product.

The urban *danwei*, which had long been a huge drain on the fiscal capacity of the state, were also "marketized." With few strategic exceptions, they were told that henceforward they, too, would have to compete internationally. The result of this mandate was that unless a *danwei* could modernize its production system, unless it learned how to market its products overseas, unless it got rid of its surplus of labor power, and unless it could free itself of its many social obligations – in short, unless it ceased to be a socialist city-in-miniature – it would go bankrupt. And this is indeed what happened to many state-owned enterprises. With few prospects of re-employment in the short term, as many as 50 million workers lost their jobs and hard-earned pensions (Naughton 2007: 185–9). One of several strategies devised to mitigate urban unemployment on such a massive scale was for the local state to promote housing construction. Under Mao, housing had met the austere needs of the period, but a huge pent-up demand for a more commodious sort of housing was building up. In response, high-rise developments sprang up throughout urban China, especially in suburban and peri-urban areas, many of them developed by companies that had spun off from *danwei*, channeling profits to the work unit to which they were still, if tenuously, linked. This housing boom created large numbers of jobs not only directly but also in industries producing the sort of stuff new home-owners looked for to furnish their empty apartments still smelling of paint.

The return to family farming in the countryside together with the new rural industries, many of them producing for export markets, raised household incomes but also created new demands that could no longer be satisfied by working locally. The *hukou* system was, of course, still in place. But already there were cracks in the dam, and the first small trickles of urban-bound migrants in the 1980s eventually swelled to an irreversible tide. The government tried to steer migration away from burgeoning coastal cities to smaller cities and towns, but the temptation to make money in the new urban economy, especially in the large coastal cities, was too powerful. At the turn of the millennium, the census counted 145 million people who had lived away from their hometown for a period of at least six months (Lin 2007). Very likely, this was a significant under-count.

Cities themselves expanded at an unbelievable pace. At the beginning of the reform period, China's urban population accounted for about 18 percent of the total. By 2004, it had ballooned to 42 percent of a much larger population, more than a three-fold increase since 1978. In absolute numbers, the State Statistical Bureau estimated urban population (minus legal and illegal migrants) at 543 million in 2004, a truly astounding number, given that many people still thought of China as a society of peasants (Wu *et al.* 2007: 3). All this growth, whether of people, urban spatial extent, production, or household income, created enormous pressures for a restructuring of urban space. As the city expanded outward into adjacent rural areas, it swallowed up entire villages that would eventually be leveled and re-urbanized. Land itself was treated as a virtual commodity, and soon central cities had to plan for massive redevelopments, as skyscraping office buildings vied to outdo their competitors in height. In the mid-1980s, planning, which had been put on ice during the Cultural Revolution, was revived because the new cities required plans and spatial ordering.

The *Danwei* Is Dead; Long Live the *Shequ*: Controlling Urban Populations

But physical planning wasn't the only thing the new city needed. Around the same time that planning returned to the scene, the Ministry of Civil Affairs in Beijing started to worry about social chaos (*luan*), which, in light of their history, most Chinese dread as potentially the greatest calamity that could befall them. More specifically, ministry officials were concerned with the imminent restructuring of the *danwei* as a total institution and the social consequences that "marketization" would bring. Not only would its workforce cease to live inside the compound (where everyday behavior could easily be monitored), but the whole social security system managed by the *danwei* would be dismantled. In addition, downsizing and bankruptcies would pour millions of unemployed workers into the street. From the Party's perspective, the problem was therefore seen to be two-fold: how to deliver social services to those needing them and how to maintain social stability in the new spatial order – or rather perceived disorder – where people worked in one place but lived in another. A related concern was the new mobility, as millions of migrants streamed into cities and their peripheries; displaced central city inhabitants looked for suburban housing; rural villages were suddenly engulfed by creeping urbanism; and the newly rich were enticed by luxury suburban life styles.

What emerged over the next decade and a half of discussions and policy experiments was the new model of neighborhood construction, or *shequ jianshe*. A *shequ* (pronounced *sher-chü*) was defined as an officially designated neighborhood unit focused upon a physical facility or service center. Under this model, the *shequ* neighborhood unit would assume some of the social functions of the old work unit or *danwei*, and over time (so ministry officials hoped), people (*ren*) would adopt a new social identity. Former *danweiren,* would become *shequren* or "neighborhood people" (Bray 2005: 183). With neighbors acquiring new identities, order would be restored to the city.

But *shequ* was a neologism in the official lexicon, whereas RCs were already functioning "communities" whose existence (and role) was acknowledged in the constitution. The new *shequ* would thus be presented as a reinvention of the RC *on a larger scale.* Like the RC, it would still be an "autonomous" mass-line organization or social collective, the hierarchical equivalent of an administrative village in the countryside. Whereas the old RC was responsible for only a few hundred households, the new *shequ*/RC would be enlarged, for a total population of between 8,000 and 10,000.

The vision of the Chinese city in this model was thus of a network of neighborhoods integrated with, but separate from, the administration of district and subdistrict that, for its part, would provide core funding to make the *shequ* centers in their area viable service organizations. Once the initial investments in *shequ* service infrastructure had been made, the ongoing costs would not presumably be very large. According to the population size of each *shequ,* no more than three to seven professionals would be required (it was thought) to run the place, with the rest of the staff comprised of volunteers. But since operating funds would be needed to carry out its multiple functions, *shequ* would be authorized to set up small collective enterprises, a portion of whose profits (if any) could then be applied to finance a range of services to poor and vulnerable members of the community.

As the reform movement swept throughout China, the idea of such an organization corresponded to a slogan used with increasing frequency: "Small Government, Big Society." As a social collective, the *shequ* committee would be elected by either direct or indirect vote, and once constituted, would select the professional staff of the center. *Shequ* functions would encompass the administration of social services, the promotion of cultural activities and socialist educational work, sanitation and health care (including family planning), conflict resolution, and public order. Finally, *shequ* would coordinate and liaise with various other organizations, such as the street office, the local Party organization, and home-owners' associations in their area of jurisdiction.

To capture the flavor of Chinese-style community building, one needs to look very closely at the way the system is expected to work. One of the main jobs of *shequ* officials is to mobilize a network of volunteers to assist them in their daily tasks. According to the standard model, volunteers will be organized in military fashion into a hierarchy, at the top of which stands the "compound leader" who supervises a number of "building leaders." Each building, in turn, has several "unit leaders," and at the bottom of this system are the residents' representatives. "Together," writes Bray, they provide a comprehensive network for ensuring that all aspects of *shequ* life are kept under close scrutiny … In theory, at least, it is the volunteer network that links the *shequ* population to the organizational structure and binds its territory into one seamless unit" (Bray 2005: 188).

After 14 years of discussions and a series of important experiments in various cities, *shequ jianshe* was finally adopted as official policy in the millennial year. Explicitly embraced by the CCP, a section of the tenth five-year plan was devoted to it. What remains to be asked is, how well has this governance system worked?

Has the neighborhood unit fulfilled its promise of replacing the *danwei* as the new cell of urban society in China?

Shequ under Implementation

Not enough time has passed to assess the successes and failures of the *shequ* movement. What might have been called a social movement in the west originating in civil society, is a government-inspired and now mandated movement in China which falls under the Ministry of Civil Affairs and its branches at provincial municipal, district, and sub-district levels. One hesitates to use an expression such as "community development" for what is perhaps better translated as "neighborhood construction," the term I have used here. Nevertheless, it is clear that on the government's part, there is genuine concern with the social dimensions of the vast changes that have left cities, towns, and villages at the mercy of social forces that even the omniscient State Council, with all of its expertise, probably doesn't quite understand. To an outside observer, it seems incomprehensible how one can foist a new governance structure down to the neighborhood level on an urban population of over 500 million within a matter of a few years. And yet, it has happened, and in most large cities, the new *shequ* centers are already staffed and fully operational.

What we learn from the existing literature is something about the process of institutional innovation in China, for instance, its grounding in actual experiences, its tolerance of variations on a basic policy theme, and the willingness of the MCA to bide its time rather than insist on immediate results. There is also the curious amalgam of *shequ*/RC, which allowed an existing mass-line organization to be taken as the frame for molding the incipient neighborhoods, a case of "new wine in old bottles." The old RCs were simply enlarged, consolidated, and charged with a new mission that would be entrusted to a new type of modernizing leadership (Pan 2005). Meanwhile, existing RCs were left to atrophy as mini-neighborhood committees in the older parts of the city.

In its formal policy paper circulated in 2000, widely known as the 23rd Document, the MCA put forward five principles of community construction (Yan and Gao 2005: 226–7). The fourth of these principles was that "residents' self-governance must be allowed through the expansion of local democracy." Was this principle taken to heart in the implementation of the policy on community construction? As a mass-line organization, RCs had always been thought of as having "autonomy." And when, in 1989, the Chinese government enacted legislation for the organization of urban RCs as "self-managing, self-educating, self-servicing, self-governing grass-roots institutional entities" it was merely confirming existing understandings (Yan and Gao 2005: 231). Only a few urban communities, however, have actually experimented with new forms of democratic process (p. 231). Local elections in Shenyang were one of the earliest of these. As candidates were nominated through a group process (instead of being nominated by the district or street office, or the local CCP branch), and suffrage was extended to all households in the new neighborhood unit, old habits were abandoned (p. 232). However, as the authors of this study comment, people's response to democratic elections has been "lukewarm" on the whole. Urban residents who often do not live where they work, are detached from their *shequ* and may not even be aware of the full range of local services available to them.

They also quite accurately assess the true power of their vote to influence outcomes, since *shequ* are still under the direct control of the state bureaucracy and, in any case, the local CCP branch is expected to take a leading role in their management.

As one ponders this contradiction between, on the one hand, "four levels of implementation" and, on the other, "grassroots democratization," both of which are true to an extent, and both of which have been promoted as "models," one can only conclude that this contradiction is in fact willed, reflecting a deeply held belief in the unity of opposites (*yin* and *yang*), where two dynamics are nearly always in tension or disequilibrium, with *yang* forces in the ascendant but *yin* forces nevertheless assertive of some power to constrain their opposite, awaiting the moment when the balance of power might be reversed in the future.

Conclusions

This story of neighborhood governance is without a neat conclusion. Whether *shequren* will eventually turn into *shehuiren,* or people of (civil?) society, as an outcome of these experiments with "community construction" and as Ministry of Civil Affairs policy analysts hope for and, indeed, expect, only time will tell. There are inherent problems with this model, however, and I will conclude this chapter with a few personal remarks.

In my view, the neighborhood construction program is based on a model with which the MCA analysts were already familiar, that of the "large public family" of the *danwei* which I have called a socialist city-in-miniature. But the contemporary post-socialist city is something very different. It is no longer composed of hundreds of self-governed, self-managed, self-reliant "cells." In the *danwei*, people "lived under the same roof and ate from the same pot." In today's city, they no longer do that. The "iron rice bowl" has been smashed; life has again become mobile and precarious. People can lose their jobs, they can switch jobs, and they can be fired. Work is of course important, but when they are not working, people's time is largely their own, and everyone uses the city in their particular ways.

The whole top-down system of neighborhood construction, beginning with the definition of what a "neighborhood" is or should be, the quasi-professionalization of *shequ* staff, the government's overriding concern with social stability, the omnipresence of the Party, the quasi-military organization of "volunteers," all these raise questions about the future of the neighborhood construction movement. The present system may work well enough as a method of local governance and control; whether it will also help to shape a new "neighborhood person" or *shequren* or, indeed, an autonomous civil society, thus avoiding further social fragmentation, remains to be seen.

Acknowledgments

The present version of this chapter is a shortened version of a paper originally written under contract for a book on Chinese architecture to be published by the Cooper-Hewitt National Design Museum. This publication never eventuated, however. I would like to thank Timothy Cheek, Zhong Sheng, Leslie Shieh, Chen

Fang, Leonie Sandercock, and Matilda McQuaid for their comments and suggestions on earlier drafts.

Note

1   Material balances refers to a technique developed in the Soviet Union for determining physical input requirements for a given quantity of output. Also known as a primitive form of input/output analysis – primitive, because it used prices only as an accounting convention – it was a primary tool of central planning and was adapted for use in China's command economy.

References

Bray, David (2005) *Social Space and Governance in Urban China*. Stanford, CA: Stanford University Press.

Dutton, Michael R. (1992) *Policing and Punishment in China: From Patriarchy to "the People."* Cambridge: Cambridge University Press.

Lin, George C. S. (2007) Chinese urbanism in question: state, society, and the reproduction of urban spaces. *Urban Geography* 28 (1): 7–29.

Naughton, Barry (2007) *The Chinese Economy: Transitions and Growth*. Cambridge, MA: MIT Press.

O'Brien, Kevin (2009) Local People's Congresses and governing China. *China Journal* 61 (January): 131–41.

Pan, Tianshu (2005) Historical memory, community building and place-making in neighborhood Shanghai. In *Restructuring the Chinese City: Changing Society, Economy and Space*, ed. Laurence J. C. Ma and Fulong Wu. London: Routledge, 122–37.

Saich, Tony (2004) *Governance and Politics of China*. 2nd edn. New York: Palgrave Macmillan.

Unger, Jonathan (2002) *The Transformation of Rural China*. Armonk, NY: M. E. Sharpe.

Wang, Fei-Ling (2005) *Organizing Through Division and Exclusion: China's* Hukou *System*. Stanford, CA: Stanford University Press.

Wu, Fulong, Xu, Jiang, and Gar-On Yeh, Anthony (2007) *Urban Development in Post-Reform China: State, Market, and Space*. London and New York: Routledge.

Yan, Miu Chung and Gao, Jian Guo (2007) Social engineering of community building: examining policy process and characteristics of community construction in China. *Community Development Journal* 42 (2): 222–36.

Chapter 61

Retreat from a Totalitarian Society: China's Urbanism in the Making

Fulong Wu

An Earth-Bounded Society

Fei Xiaotong, a renowned Chinese sociologist, described the foundations of Chinese society as "earth-bounded" (Fei 1992). He further elaborated that in such an earth-bounded society the social structure is characterized by the order of so-called *chaxugeju* (the differential model of association), which is the basic organization principle of rural China. Different from clearly defined social boundaries in western society, the Chinese traditional society is "just like the circles that appear on the surface of a lake when a rock is thrown into it. Everyone stands at the centre of the circles produced by his or her own" (Fei 1992: 62). The rural society is essentially a society of acquaintance, in which one is "differentially associated" with the inner circle of family members, then the outer circle of extended family members, and further the ring of villagers. These differential associations integrate individuals into a society with social networks. Because of close but varying association, the rural villages are governed by social norms rather than laws or regulations.

In the imperial period, China was predominantly rural (Esherick 2000). The city was mainly an administrative center; but the feudal system primarily relied on rural villages' self-containment and self-governance (the mechanism is the *baojia* system, see discussion later). As the seats of administration and local political power, the cities had the most salient spatial element: the government buildings (*yamen*) served as the nerve center of a city (Ma 2009). Apart from this administrative role, other activities such as commerce were suppressed, and the Confucian elites all preferred to pursue their career in the government rather than becoming merchants (Ma 2009). While in the Song dynasty (960–1279) China saw an embryonic urban

The New Blackwell Companion to the City   Edited by Gary Bridge and Sophie Watson
© 2011 Blackwell Publishing Ltd

culture brought about by booming commerce, the city as a civil society was absent in a modern sense.

As an administrative center, the Chinese city was in contrast with what Max Weber called the Occidental City in sixteenth-century Europe; Weber believes "in Europe citizens participated in the local administration, in China urban dwellers belonged to their families and native villages, while in India urban dwellers were members of different castes." In other words, the development of city in the west represents the advancement of modernism. The implication of modernization on everyday life is the so-called "bureaucratization of social relationships." Such an urbanized life inside the city wall became the "breeding ground for the new mode of production – capitalism – and Occidental modernity" (Haussermann and Haila 2005: 51).

Socialist Totalitarianism

The features of rural society have been continued and even strengthened by so-called "communist neo-traditionalism" (Walder 1986). In the planned economy, the state organized collective consumption through state work-units. These work-units are more than production units; they are "total social entities" carrying out service provision, housing development and distribution, and social management (Whyte and Parish 1984). Chinese sociologist Sun Liping argues that Chinese society was a totalitarian society because social relations were totalized. He describes such a totalitarian society as a society with "under-differentiated social structure," in which "the state controls the economy and monopolizes all social resources. Further, politics, society and ideology are highly overlapped with each other" (2004: 31). Such a totalitarian society was effective in terms of social mobilization.

The totalitarian society was strengthened by state housing provision. The work-unit compound is a unique built form of state-led industrialization (Wu 1996) and thus a territory of governance combined with hierarchical state control and residential management (Bray 2005). In other words, the work-unit compound is a combination of workplace and living-place, resulting in a relatively under-differentiated socio-spatial pattern in urban China, which has been mainly based on occupational types (Yeh *et al.* 1995) rather than socioeconomic or class division. With the decline of the *danwei* system, however, a new pattern of spatial differentiation based on housing tenure began to emerge (Li and Wu 2008). In the remainder of this chapter, we focus on the social implications of this new residential pattern.

Absence of Urbanism

The state plays a dominant role in production as well as reproduction. The redistributive state (Nee 1991) is mainly achieved through omnipotent and self-contained work-units. An important feature of this totalitarian society is that individual members of the work-unit form a comprehensive relation, rather than a partial relation such as an employer–employee relation.

Because investment in consumption was believed wasteful and unproductive, the state constrained consumption and emphasized the production role of the city. In addition, through the household registration system (*hukou*), rural to urban migration was controlled, and the spontaneous inflow into cities was prohibited (Chan 1994). Up to economic reform in 1978, the level of urbanization, i.e., the proportion of urban population, was suppressed below 18 percent (Zhou and Ma 2003). In contrast to the "hyper-urbanization" in developing countries, the ratio of urban population to total population lagged behind the respective level of industrialization in China. In other words, the socialist city was "under-urbanized" (Szelenyi 1996). China achieved "industrialization without urbanization."

Similar to other socialist cities in central and eastern Europe, the state workplace played a dominant role in everyday life (Stenning 2005). Production, consumption, and reproduction were intertwined at the local scale of workplace community. Szelenyi (1996) argued that the socialist city typically lacked "urbanism"; the trait of diversity, heterogeneity, and anonymity of the modern metropolis was absent. The landscape was monotone, with standard multi-story walk-ups for industrial workers. Except for monuments and public buildings, there was no skyscraper to break up the skyline. The crime rate was low; beggars and homeless were absent. There was no urban vice typically associated with urbanism. Uniformity and collectivity were the basic features of Chinese urbanism in state socialism.

Market Reform and Emerging Residential Diversity

Market-oriented reform has brought about new freedom to middle-class consumers. Coincident with the disillusion of socialist utopia after the failure of the "Great Proletarian Revolution," a "dystopia" has been developed; the residents escape the public realm and search for a new good life of their own. Instead of seeking social mix, they tend to choose gated suburbia as a new fantasy. As a result, these gated communities have auspicious names such as Orange County, Yosemite, Beverly Hills, Fontainebleau, and Thames Town (Wu 2005). Some of these new residences are decorated ostentatiously with neo-classical building styles (Figure 61.1).

The development of the commodity economy transformed urban spaces (Davis *et al.* 1995; Ma and Wu 2005), leading to greater diversity and autonomy. The consumer revolution unleashed the process of individualization, in which individual residents can choose their place of living according to their preferences rather than being allocated designated state-owned flats. Residential mobility increases (Li and Wu 2004), with millions of people relocated to the suburbs, leading to rapid urban expansion and suburbanization (Feng *et al.* 2008).

Rather than following the preset technical design norms of the socialist period, the design standards become more differentiated to suit different consumer groups (Wang and Murie 2000). Developers boast that their products are now tailor-made or purpose-built (*du sheng da zao*, a term used in Chinese real estate which literally means "measuring your body to make it just for you") and therefore distinguish themselves from the products of mass consumption. In contrast to social and spatial proximity in traditional neighborhoods, these new places are built into more individualistic forms (Doulet 2008: 7), sometimes with luxury amenities such as golf courses and club houses (Giroir 2007). Changing residential styles are not a trivial matter. It will have profound social implications, as real-estate developers put forward a slogan: "living transforms China" (*juzhu gaibian zhongguo*).

Figure 61.1 An up-market villa compound in a premium location between the Summer Place and the hill of Yuquanshan where the leaders of Chinese government reside; the figure shows the club house, served by professional domestic servants in a noble style. Author's photo.

Uprooted Communities

Urban villages

With the influx of migrants, villages near the city became migrant settlements. Under state socialism the rural population was not entitled to public housing. Rural migrants are therefore not eligible for public housing allocation. When public housing of state work-units was privatized, sitting tenants became property-owners. But they usually do not have spare property to rent. When migrants came to the city in the post-reform period, they could not find sufficient private rentals in work-unit compounds. Rather, they had to find accommodation at the periphery of the city, usually farmers' housing or self-developed housing by local farmers for migrant workers.

In Chinese, villages encircled by the city are called "urban villages" (*chengzhong-cun*). But they are significantly different from defensive village space in the UK (Biddulph 2000) or ethnic enclaves described by Gans (1962) in the US. Urban villages in China are literally migrant settlements, providing low-cost housing to migrant workers (Zhang *et al.* 2003). But the quality of housing is poor. Many migrants and their families have to share apartments and even subdivided rooms.

In urban villages, the migrant population well exceeds that of local farmers. For example, in the Anlian village of Shenzhen, the population size in the household registration system is 4,042, while migrant population reaches 93,000; the ratio of migrant population to the local reaches 23:1.

While the original village is a rural society integrated by family ties, the arrival of migrant population breaks up the traditional structure. Within these urban villages, the division between the rural and urban areas has been transformed into new duality between the renter and proprietor classes. Whereas for original villagers their membership of the village gives them entitlement to the village sharehold company, most migrants are excluded from any decision-making, leading to fragmentation of social space in *chengzhongcun*. While migrants may stay in the city for years, they are still sojourners in these villages because they do not belong to the community.

Migrants are extremely mobile in terms of their residential location, constantly adjusting their residences according to their job location. The informal rental market plus informal employment render tenancy unstable, although migrants from the same native place tend to cluster in the same area, creating places nicknamed by the place of origin such as Zhejiang village (Zhang 2001), Henan village, Xinjiang village. But these villages are significantly different from an established rural society.

Traditional neighborhoods

Rapid urban redevelopment, especially with the property-led approach, creates profound impacts on traditional neighborhoods in China. In fact, before they were demolished, traditional neighborhoods had been less incorporated into the state system than their counterparts in work-unit residential areas. In terms of housing tenure, a large proportion was public housing converted from pre-1949 private housing but under the management of municipal housing bureaux. This is a relatively inferior type of public housing (Wu 1996).

In terms of governance, traditional neighborhoods were less bureaucratized because the organization was more or less organized by the street offices and their subsidiary mass organization called residents' committees (*juming weiyuanhui*) rather than state workplaces and their formal government (Wu 2002). Because residents stay in these communities for a long time, they develop an intimate relationship and are familiar with each other. Courtyard housing (*hutong*) in Beijing and lane houses or alleyway houses (*longtang*) in Shanghai all present a picture of close neighboring and intense social interaction.

Increasingly these traditional neighborhoods see a changing social composition. When wealthier residents moved out to suburban commodity housing, they sold out their street-front housing to retail premises or rented them to migrant workers. The building density of inner-city housing increased, especially when residents self-built extensions in the communal area. The courtyard therefore is turned into a "jumble yard." Surprisingly, even with many families living close together in the same courtyard, the traditional neighborhood ties declined because of high mobility and changing in tenancy.

Now many traditional neighborhoods are "razed to make way for garish high-rise office buildings, in town luxury apartments, Hong Kong-style malls, and five-star hotels that might be anywhere and nowhere" (Friedmann 2007: 271). In fact, even before large-scale real-estate development, state-organized urban renewal in the early years of reform in the 1980s with high-rise residential buildings, and large residential districts had already reduced neighborhood interaction (Wu and He 2005). From the design perspective, the modern style of building could be blamed for reducing physical interaction between neighbors, but the new design is a response to the increasing demand for privacy by residents themselves. Property-led redevelopment accelerates the process of residential relocation, and replaces inner-city residents with commodity housing buyers of higher socioeconomic status (He and Wu 2007). Many traditional communities have vanished, and the Chinese city witnesses a dynamic process of the "erasure and rebuilding of place-based communities" (Friedmann 2007: 275).

Property-Based Interests and the Private Sphere

When inner-city residents were uprooted from their territorial communities, they began to form new social relations in gated communities. These new communities have been there for a very limited time and are not "memorable places" (Tomba 2005: 939), thus lacking complex social networks of social interaction. Mostly these estates are developed from scratch by real-estate developers, providing new appealing lifestyle models but at the same time sorting social strata in the post-*danwei* era (p. 939). Nevertheless, residents in these gated communities are all home-owners. Home-ownership provides a new foundation for them to form "communities of consumers." Home-owners' associations have been set up, initially encouraged by the government because they help to mediate between residents, developers, and service providers such as property management companies and thus enhance social stability without incurring a cost to the government.

The emergence of home-owners' associations adds to the complexity of neighborhood governance because traditionally neighborhoods are governed by the street offices and residents' committees (Read 2003). To defend their common property-based interests, residents use home-owners' associations as a space of their own – a relatively autonomous space. In this space, the role of traditional neighborhood organizations is waning. Recently there have been increasing disputes over land uses in gated communities such as preservation of green space and problems of noise and pollution. With identity based on property ownership, residents in gated communities are associated through property rights rather than entitlement and membership of the work-unit.

Professionalization of Social Services and Community Governance

In response to rising social mobility and an emerging sphere outside the state sphere, the state reinvented community governance and started an agenda of "professionalization of social services." In the imperial period, China was governed by a neighborhood watch system, known as the *baojia* system; it is essentially a system of community-based law enforcement and civic control, invented by Wang Anshi of the Song dynasty (960–1279). One *jia* consisted of 100 households, and 10 *jia*s formed one *bao*. The leaders of *baojia* took responsibility for social order, while the households within the same *baojia* shared community duties. This system was replaced by the *danwei* (work-unit) system in the socialist period. In the post-reform period, however, the state began to recognize the importance of community organizations, and to consolidate smaller residents' committees into larger *shequ* (community) committees. The budget of these committees is allocated by the street office, though it is relatively modest. *Shequ* committees often operate community services as a sideline business to subsidize operational costs, but more recently the state requires these businesses to be stripped off from the community organization, changing the latter into more or less a pure government agency.

The changing population composition challenges neighborhood management. Rapid neighborhood changes create difficulties of maintaining social cohesion in these places. New residents in gentrified areas belong to a higher social stratum. They are in full employment and are very busy. They are reluctant to participate in neighborhood activities. This is in sharp contrast with the close relationship among original residents. For original residents, the residents' committee, often served by retired people and housewives similar to themselves, is a more amiable association to exchange information and seek help. In upper-market housing areas, many properties are vacant, because they were bought for the purpose of investment, and many buyers do not actually live there.

Although some inner-city residents are relocated to suburbs, they still manage to retain their household registration status in the old neighborhoods. Because the services such as schooling are better in the central area than in suburbs, the residents want to access the services based on the catchment area. They strive to maintain their registration location in the central area. In Shanghai, for example, along the route of elevated ring roads built in the 1980s, thousands of residents are still registered in these sub-districts. This creates a unique phenomenon in Chinese cities: the separation between *hukou* registration place and actual living place (*renhu fenli*), which creates a problem for neighborhood management.

Heterogeneity, Anonymity, and Diversity

The socialist city was socially engaged. The private realm was reduced by state-organized collective consumption. In the work-unit compound, residents were familiar with each other because they were affiliated to the same workplace. In traditional neighborhoods, former single family houses were converted into multiple tenements. The privacy of courtyard living was eroded because of increasing living density and multiple occupancies. Residents often had to share facilities and communal spaces. In a sense, the socialist city was a totalitarian society, because everyday life was totalized into a public sphere.

The development of commodity housing provides a chance for the new middle class to escape from the totalitarian society. The aspiration of the new middle class for social engagement in the neighborhood is low. Rather than seeking a community life, they desire a good environment with higher privacy. For them these gated communities maintain certain anonymity. Thus, relocating into these places gives them a sense of freedom, escaping from intense social engagement, control, and monitoring in traditional neighborhoods. Although the property management company sometimes promotes neighborhood activities, residents are generally willing to keep a comfortable distance from each other. Professional services can be provided by property management companies rather than neighbor assistance. Their places thus are purified living space, without too much uncertain interaction between neighbors or nuisance uses.

When Chinese city streets were lit up by electricity in the late imperial period, the available public facilities symbolized the arrival of modernism. But after an ephemeral period of prosperous urban culture in the 1920s and 1930s (Lee 1999), which in many ways resembled a lively urbanism, city life was interrupted by Japanese invasion and World War II. It was not until the late 1970s when China started economic reform that the neon lights began to glow again. With frontloading the market in everyday life, the new private sphere has begun to emerge. With the development of commodity housing, a home of one's own is becoming possible. The accumulation of wealth and increasing income has revived urban commerce. Commercial streets become prosperous; and some streets are converted into pedestrian streets and street malls. Shopping places are more differentiated nowadays, with franchised and luxury outlets comparable to the most expensive ones in global cities such as London, New York, Tokyo, and Hong Kong.

Figure 61.2 Xintiandi in Shanghai, an up-market and trendy shopping and entertainment district adaptively built in preserved housing of stone-portal gate style. Author's photo.

Among the premium consumption locations are Shanghai's Xintiandi (literally "New Heaven and Earth") (Figure 61.2). This project was a joint venture between Hong Kong property developer, Shui On, and Luwan district, using an approach of property-led redevelopment (He and Wu 2005). The terrace housing in colonial Shanghai was adaptively converted into boutiques, bars, and restaurants. The building style, known as *shikumen*, or stone-portal gate, is preserved, while the place is becoming a trendy consumption and entertainment quarter of Shanghai. Places like Xintiandi are not an "ordinary space" of shopping or eateries – they want to assume new identities for particular places. Xintiandi is engineered and grafted into Shanghai's "upper corner" from the colonial era (Pan 2005). Together with the calendar with pop stars and the café, the terraced housing style forms "Shanghai nostalgia" which romanticizes colonial days. Most importantly, the products in these trendy places represent a new taste, distinguishing themselves from standard goods of mass consumption.

Conclusion: Urbanism in the Making, but a New Social Mentality?

Market-oriented reform has brought about profound social changes in China. Before the communist revolution, China had been largely an earth-bounded rural society; state-led industrialization has been initiated since 1949, but through work-unit social organization and the "totalization" of state–society relations, China achieved "industrialization without urbanization." Urbanism was absent, and some traits of the traditional society remained. This stable social order has been broken by the introduction of the market. Post-reform urban development has been driven by the political economy of marketization on the one hand, and rising consumer revolution (Davis 2000) and individualism on the other.

Large-scale rural to urban migration has significantly increased the size of the de facto urban population. The social bonding of migrant workers begins to loosen out, and they become sojourners; more than that, through rapid urban redevelopment and demolition of traditional neighborhoods, the whole urban population is uprooted and become literally a "floating population," customarily in China only referring to migrants. The rootless situation is physically due to rising residential mobility and metaphorically because of the relaxed relation with place-based communities. Meanwhile, responding to new aspirations of privacy and the private life, gated communities are built and widely spread. Urban China is thus becoming more diversified and heterogeneous. In a sense, the making of urbanism in China is a result of the retreat from a totalitarian society that has existed in Chinese history for many dynasties.

In response to increasing social complexity, the state strives to maintain a governable society by downloading administrative tasks to the community (Wu 2002), hoping to impose a new spatial order through rebuilding place-based communities, under the name of "community construction" (Friedmann 2007). But this is not equivalent to re-establishing a totalitarian society. First and foremost, commodification has profoundly changed social relations. Community services are commodified and provided through so-called "property management companies." The management of neighborhoods is also "professionalized," because the retirees and housewives of residents' committees are replaced by professional social workers. The organization of the street office evolves into a level of government, with officials on the payroll of civil servants. At the community level, property owners form home-owners' associations, but their relationships are based on property interests, and thus are more rational and partial than the more comprehensive relations in a totalizing work-unit environment. Over time, newly built neighborhoods may mature and social relations may be strengthened. But it is unlikely that urban China will return to its totalitarian past.

In short, urban China under market reform presents an unprecedented level of diversity and heterogeneity, in terms of both spaces and social classes. Treating market development as the driver for social progress, the state has necessarily to manage newly acquired social complexity, division, and mobility. This increasingly forces the state itself to be separated from society, becoming the state apparatus in its modernist sense. The consequence is professionalization of social management; and recent increases in social expenditure can be read from this trend of the modern state. What we will see in urban China is modernization of society as well as the state, much in line with bureaucratization of social life, predicted by Max Weber. The state thus can no longer be embedded within society, as it was in a totalitarian society. The state has to stand on the opposite side of society and mediate various social contentions and conflicts, rather than acting as a direct resource allocator. Thus, returning to the classic concern of urbanism and mental life (Simmel 1903), an intriguing question would be, to what extent is this newly made urbanism shaping a different social mentality and a new personality?

References

Biddulph, M. (2000) Villages don't make a city. *Journal of Urban Design* 5 (1): 65–82.

Bray, D. (2005) *Social Space and Governance in Urban China: The* Danwei *System from Origins to Reform*. Stanford, CA: Stanford University Press.

Chan, K. W. (1994) *Cities with Invisible Walls*. Hong Kong: Oxford University Press.

Davis, D. S. (ed.) (2000) *The Consumer Revolution in Urban China*. Berkeley: University of California Press.

Davis, D. S., Kraus, R., Naughton, B., and Perry, E. J. (eds.) (1995) *Urban Space in Contemporary China: The Potential for Autonomy and Community in Post-Mao China*. Cambridge: Cambridge University Press.

Doulet, J.-F. (2008) Where are China's cities heading? Three approaches to the metropolis in contemporary China. *China Perspectives* 4: 4–14.

Esherick, J. W. (ed.) (2000) *Remaking the Chinese City: Modernity and National Identity, 1900–1950*. Honolulu: University of Hawaii Press.

Fei, X. (1992) *From the Soil: The Foundations of Chinese Society (Xiangtu Zhongguo)*. Trans. Gary G. Hamilton and Wang Zhen. Berkeley: University of California Press.

Feng, J., Zhou, Y., and Wu, F. (2008) New trends of suburbanization in Beijing since 1990: from government-led to market-oriented. *Regional Studies* 42 (1): 83–99.

Friedmann, J. (2007) Reflection on place and place-making in the cities of China. *International Journal of Urban and Regional Research* 31 (2): 257–79.

Gans, H. (1962) *The Urban Villagers*. New York: Free Press.

Giroir, G. (2007) Spaces of leisure: gated golf communities in China. In *China's Emerging Cities: The Making of New Urbanism*, ed. F. Wu. Abingdon: Routledge, 235–55.

Haussermann, H., and Haila, A. (2005) The European city: a conceptual framework and normative project. In *Cities of Europe*, ed. Y. Kazepov. Oxford: Blackwell, 43–64.

He, S., and Wu, F. (2005) Property-led redevelopment in post-reform China: a case study of Xintiandi redevelopment project in Shanghai. *Journal of Urban Affairs* 27 (1): 1–23.

He, S., and Wu, F. (2007) Socio-spatial impacts of property-led redevelopment on China's urban neighbourhoods. *Cities* 24 (3): 194–208.

Lee, L. O. F. (1999) Shanghai modern: reflections on urban culture in China in the 1930s. *Public Culture* 11 (1): 75–107.

Li, S.-M., and Wu, F. (2004) Contextualizing residential mobility and housing choice: evidence from urban China. *Environment and Planning A* 36 (1): 1–6.

Li, Z., and Wu, F. (2008) Tenure-based residential segregation in post-reform Chinese cities: a case study of Shanghai. *Transactions of the Institute of British Geographers* 33 (3): 404–19.

Ma, L. J. C. (2009) Chinese urbanism. In *Encyclopaedia of Human Geography*, ed. R. Kitchin and N. Thrift. Oxford: Elsevier, 65–71.

Ma, L. J. C., and Wu, F. (eds.) (2005) *Restructuring the Chinese City: Changing Society, Economy and Space*. London: Routledge.

Nee, V. (1991) Social inequalities in reforming state socialism: between redistribution and markets in China. *American Sociological Review* 56: 267–82.

Pan, T. (2005) Historical memory, community-building and place-making in neighborhood Shanghai. In *Restructuring the Chinese City: Changing Society, Economy and Space*, ed. L. J. C. Ma and F. Wu. London: Routledge, 122–37.

Read, B. L. (2003) Democratizing the neighbourhood? New private housing and home-owner self-organization in urban China. *China Journal* 49 (1): 31–59.

Simmel, G. (1903 [2005]) The metropolis and mental life: the sociology of George Simmel. In *The Urban Sociology Reader*, ed. Jan Lin and Christopher Mele. London: Routledge, pp. 23–31.

Stenning, A. (2005) Post-socialism and the changing geographies of the everyday in Poland. *Transactions of the Institute of British Geographers* 30: 113–27.

Sun, Liping (2004) *Transformation and Division: Changing Social Structure since Economic Reform*. Beijing: Tsinghua University Press (in Chinese).

Szelenyi, I. (1996) Cities under socialism – and after. In *Cities After Socialism: Urban and Regional Change and Conflict in Post-Socialist Societies*, ed. G. M. Andrusz, M. Harloe, and I. Szelenyi. Oxford: Blackwell, 286–317.

Tomba, L. (2005) Residential space and collective interest formation in Beijing's housing disputes. *China Quarterly* 184: 934–51.

Walder, A. G. (1986) *Communist Neo-Traditionalism: Work and Authority in Chinese Industry*. Berkeley: University of California Press.

Wang, Y. P., and Murie, A. (2000) Social and spatial implications of housing reform in China. *International Journal of Urban and Regional Research* 24 (2): 397–417.

Whyte, M. K., and Parish, W. L. (1984) *Urban Life in Contemporary China*. Chicago: University of Chicago Press.

Wu, F. (1996) Changes in the structure of public housing provision in urban China. *Urban Studies* 33 (9): 1601–1627.

Wu, F. (2002) China's changing urban governance in the transition towards a more market-oriented economy. *Urban Studies* 39 (7): 1071–93.

Wu, F. (2005) Rediscovering the "gate" under market transition: from work-unit compounds to commodity housing enclaves. *Housing Studies* 20 (2): 235–54.

Wu, F., and He, S. (2005) Changes in traditional urban areas and impacts of urban redevelopment: a case study of three neighbourhoods in Nanjing, China. *Tijdschrift voor Economische en Sociale Geografie* 96 (1): 75–95.

Yeh, A. G. O., Xu, X. Q., and Hu, H. Y. (1995) The social space of Guangzhou city, China. *Urban Geography* 16 (7): 595–621.

Zhang, L. (2001) *Strangers in the City: Reconfiguration of Space, Power, and Social Networks Within China's Floating Population*. Stanford, CA: Stanford University Press.

Zhang, L., Zhao, S. X. B., and Tian, J. P. (2003) Self-help in housing and Chengzhongcun in China's urbanization. *International Journal of Urban and Regional Research* 27 (4): 912–37.

Zhou, Y., and Ma, L. J. C. (2003) China's urbanization levels: reconstructing a baseline from the fifth population census. *China Quarterly* 173: 176–96.

Chapter 62

Transnational Urban Political Ecology: Health and Infrastructure in the Unbounded City

Roger Keil

Introduction

> There were mornings when Alex turned on his radio with the thought, almost the assumption, that he would hear about a major terrorist attack in one of the central cities, London or Paris or Los Angeles. Somehow it was not a thought that brought any sense of fear with it, nothing much stronger than curiosity, and up to this point he had never actually been proved right. But it had been that way since what happened in New York; any daily routine, now, could contain this news.
>
> (Helwig 2008: 177)

The experience of global simultaneity and contiguity is typical for the transnational period of urbanization in which we find ourselves today. The historical distinctness of place, reinforced by national difference and regional path-dependencies, is increasingly qualified in the light of overarching developments in economic, technological, political, and ecological space which penetrate traditional separations of global capitalism's time-space matrix. Of course, globalization has, as many participants in the debate have shown, not made all places alike. By contrast, it has thrived on a perhaps unprecedented unevenness and diversity among places. But this difference is now not a result of disconnectedness of more and less developed worlds as it was the case in the classical periods of imperialism and colonialism when metropolitan and dependent regions drifted apart into fatefully intertwined but tragically oppositional trajectories. Today's world is one of connectivity where the constitution of one implies the constitution of other places, spaces, scales, to a degree yet unseen. "Precisely as interconnections among dispersed spaces around the globe are thickened, geographical differences are becoming more rather than less profound, at once in everyday life and in the operation of social, political, and economic power"

The New Blackwell Companion to the City   Edited by Gary Bridge and Sophie Watson
© 2011 Blackwell Publishing Ltd

(Brenner 2009: 27). The profound spatial reordering due to globalization, including most prominently the puncturing of the system of Westphalian nation-states, has multiplied the interrelationships (dependencies and conflicts) among supra- and subnational spatial entities and highlighted their differences (Mahon and Keil 2009: 3). Such unevenness leads to dramatic interterritorial and intra-network struggles at various scales of the global order as Amin (2002: 396) submits:

> those concerned with the politics of regulation and governance associated with globalization ... are right to stress that globalization ... has unleashed a rigorous restructuring of the rationale and spaces of formal politics ... including the rise of new forms of economic and political regionalism, experiments to regulate a new global regime of capital accumulation, [and] the reorganization of the state towards the imperatives of global competition ... All of these aspects do represent a politics mobilized around redrawn institutional boundaries and fixities, including scalar ones.

We can speak, therefore, of a new transnational urbanism, which is by no means free from spatial constraints but is rather conditioned by their variety and by their parameters.

Transnational urbanism has been a term most associated with the seminal work of Michael Peter Smith (2001) who has pioneered a view of the global city as constituted not just by structural flows of capital and culture but also by the agency of marginalized, yet transnationally active communities. Smith (2005: 236) notes that "globalisation and transnationalism can be characterised as multidimensional discourses about complex connectivity and network forms of social organisation" but also identifies differences between the two processes whereas transnational urbanism represents a critique of both the first generation proponents and critics of globalization. Smith by contrast focused on "transnational interconnectivity because it captured a sense of distanciated yet situated possibilities for constituting and reconstituting social relations" (2005: 237). Conradson and Latham (2005: 227) have added that the notion of transnationalism "enables us to consider what it means to live in an interconnected, topologically complex world without resorting to overly abstract or grand narratives of global transformation to describe that connectivity." At the same time, Yeoh (2005: 412) has cautioned that

> [a]cknowledging the "politics of simultaneity" and giving weight to the ability of "ordinary people to think and act simultaneously at multiple scales" (Smith 2001:164) to push their projects at several sites at once does not annihilate the "frictional distance" and "cost" in moving bodies to localities. Even with artificially enabled presences such as the internet or telephone, it is still impossible to be really in two places at one time, and even if one is a cosmopolitan elite with plenty of resources, the grounding of the body in locality means that mobility entails a cost, not simply in the economic sense, but also in physiological, social and emotional terms.

In this chapter I argue that transnational urbanism has to be viewed against a background of a double constitution and destruction of the urban. Those advocating for a perspective that engages transnational urbanism have prioritized its capacity for enabling new, either polarized or "middling" political relationships (Conradson and Latham 2005). I add to this view a more sinister notion of threats entailed by the transnational connectivity for the political ecologies of the transnational urban.

It has been argued that the city has been destroyed both from the inside and from the outside (Mongin 2005). The internal destruction refers to the classical pessimism in urban theory that cities are bad places, that they are dis-orderly, unruly, and chaotic. Deservedly or not, Mike Davis's work (1990, 1998, 2005) is often cited in this context. The external destruction speaks to yet another stereotype deployed in the history of urban thinking: the inevitable dissolution of the city into the countryside, the urban into the social, and the local into the global (Lefebvre 2003). Much of this has been reinforced by the notion of a networked (urban) world to which we will say more below. For French commentator Olivier Mongin, then, cities today are confronted by a stark reality:

> Yesterday's network city, the trading cities of the first globalization did not intend to fence in spaces or to close in sites. On the contrary, the network-city, not unlike the refuge-city, assured the capacity to enter and to exit. The intention is not to blur the boundaries and the thresholds, but to ensure an unstable equilibrium between the process of territorialization and that of deterritorialization. Today, we are left with no other choice but to be deterritorialized or over-territorialized, an exterior prisoner with no way in or an interior hostage with no escape. This is what the underpinnings of the urban contemporary network teach, a network that participates in an economic chain, one that is mobile, flowing and fluid like the open seas and financial flows. (Mongin 2005: 176)

Next to the megacity, the global city has been one of pervasive figures of today's urbanization (Mongin 2005; Brenner and Keil 2006). Both share a certain preoccupation with superlatives. Megacities – those urban agglomerations with populations above five million (Planet Earth 2005) – are seen as the inevitable consequence of generalized urbanization dynamics, underdevelopment, and agricultural failure. Against the idea of classifying cities by their alleged importance in a global hierarchy or network, Jenny Robinson has set the notion of the "ordinary city": "In a world of ordinary cities ways of being urban and ways of making new kinds of urban futures are diverse and are the product of the inventiveness of people in cities everywhere" (2006: 1). Robinson's intellectual maneuver "implies a stronger reterritorialization of the imagination of urban studies around the individual city, or city-region, rather than its immersion in recounting transnational flows" (2006: 10). There is clearly a tension, then, between the dynamics of networked connectivities and the territorialized practices which are no less dependent on more than local dynamics. This idea is taken up by Ananya Roy in her plea for a rethinking of the theoretical geographies of urban studies. She suggests "a rather paradoxical combination of specificity and generalizability: that theories have to be produced *in* place (and it matters *where* they are produced), but that they can then be appropriated, borrowed, and remapped. In this sense, the sort of theory being urged is simultaneously located and dis-located" (Roy 2009: 820). In practical terms, this dynamic relationship between specificity and generalizability, expounded here for theoretical and practical purposes by Robinson, Roy, and others, refers back, to some degree, to the necessity for global cities to manage two divergent dynamics: the city's internal contradictions and the cities' external integration (Kipfer and Keil

2002). Without watering this agenda down, it is appropriate to point at the fact that these problematiques have now become standard reference points in a more popular discourse as witnessed in this quote from international strategy consultant Jeb Brugmann's book: "It is the fundamental challenge to the global City's coherence: the reconciliation of the local citysystem with the foreign city model: the local *city of places* with the extended *city of flows*" (Brugmann 2009: 246).

This is the starting point: we see that urban realities are constituted through the transnational networks but only realized through place-specific, path-dependent processes of multi-scalar interaction. This takes place through a host of spatial relationships (and failures of those): hierarchies, networks, scales, and hub-like condensations like urban centers.

We will begin to approach these relationships through the prism of urban political ecology (UPE) which has created a productive framework for the study of the metabolic relationships of cities. It is concerned with the regulation of the societal relationships with nature in cities (Keil 2003, 2005). The main focus of both theoretical work and empirical studies has been on particular cases that reflect the general insight that "the daily replenished food bays in our supermarkets and endless water fountains that spring from our showerheads, highlight momentarily that our urban lives depend most fundamentally on global ecologies and the political economies that uphold them," not to speak of the perennial urban "crises (in the fields of energy provision, health, water, etc.)" (Keil 2003: 723; see also Swyngedouw and Heynen 2003). New urban challenges in the field of urban political ecology are now emerging in an age of climate change and catastrophic failure in urban–nature relations (Hurricane Katrina stands as the prime example here). A politics of resilience has begun to recognize the complexity of these relations (Keil and Whitehead forthcoming).

But most research, while recognizing the globalized societal relationships with nature that constitute urban life today, and the complex governance processes that regulate them, has looked at individual or comparative case studies, not at the networked matrix itself on which urban–nature relations are made and unmade. Research inspired by actor–network theory has enriched the body of work provided by Marxist UPE (Castree 2002; Holifield 2009). Two areas have been particularly affected by this conversation: thinking about the boundaries between humans and non-human nature and the globally networked condition of their constitution. It is the latter in particular which we will pursue further in this chapter.

Some work has been done specifically on the societal relationships with nature in global cities (Desfor and Keil 2004; Keil 1995; Luke 2006; Schroeder and Bulkeley 2009). Most of this work has been concerned with the effects of globalization on particular places or it has treated the globalized aspect of a particular city as a mere background to the constitution of socio-environmental relations there. Luke's work stands out in pointing out that the urban built environments of the global system of cities "constitute much of the world-wide webs of logistical flows which swamp the conventional boundaries between the human and the natural with a new biopolitics of urbanism" (Luke 2006: 277). In this most radical view of the urban political ecology of today's global cities which complements well the critique mounted by Robinson and Roy above we see the precondition for a different, transnational perspective on UPE.

Looking through the lens of UPE allows us ultimately to see metaphors of connectivity being turned into a symbolic web of vulnerability. From the unboundedness (Amin 2004) of urban regions to a new claustrophobia that is to do with the very vulnerability of cities' networked condition is now increasingly on the agenda of urban governance and politics. Once imagined mostly in flows of capital and labor, connectivity has been studied through relationships of flows among cities, their nodality and cliquishness, as well as their topological relationality (Alderson and Beckfield 2004; Brenner and Keil 2006; Derudder and Taylor 2003; Knox and Taylor 1995; Taylor *et al.* 2007; Taylor 2004).[1] Eschewing the view that " 'space' is a surface, across which investments/migrants/connections flow and forces march" Massey (very much in line with the argument forwarded by Robinson and Roy) sees in these views an underlying "colonial space" of central to peripheral distribution at work which denies "the dimension of coexisting actors, the dimension that precisely enables (and requires) their multiplicity" (Massey 2007: 22).

The crucial aspect that makes cities global is that they are constituted in a network and that they are constitutive of a complex, multi-scaled, and topologically entwined network space. Yet, the global network city is hierarchically segmented and globalized cities articulate national and regional economies into the world economy. Some global urban networks are tangible and material, others are virtual (Graham 2006: 119). The global connectivity created polarization and social differentiation at home. Yet, besides the insistence in some of the literatures on global cities that each city's integration into the global city network and hierarchy entailed polarization, the downsides of this connectivity have been of little concern. Neither the boosterist nor the dystopian literatures say much about the pitfalls that lie in the network itself. Much has been written about social class divisions in global cities, ethnic diversity, ecological and health issues of social polarization, and the like. But we have no sustained understanding of the dangers and opportunities that lie in being networked per se. It is to this issue of networked vulnerability that this chapter speaks: the relationship of systemic networked connectivity with new forms of vulnerability in the global city system.

When we recalibrate our optics to move from the positive views of global city connectivity to the potentially negative consequences caused by relationalities in and of the network, we can borrow from recent work by Ulrich Beck who speaks of transnational actor-networks of risk definition and distribution and opts for "analyses that are not global, not national, but are rather oriented transnationally/regionally" (Beck 2007: 309). He adds: "Transnational cooperation of states is precisely the condition for successful national and local management of risk" (p. 313). Beck talks further about an " 'internal globalization' of the national politics of risk. Inside and outside, Us and Them cannot be clearly separated from one another" (pp. 314–15). And, finally: " 'Social vulnerability' cannot be demarcated temporally and spatially but results methodologically from the cosmopolitan gaze" (p. 319).

The context of the shift from connectivity to vulnerability is set by the instabilities and disruptions of neoliberalization, a process to which "[t]he rise of global cities has been integral" (Massey 2007: 211; see also Purcell 2008: 170). In the process, and especially during the global financial crisis of 2009/10, the economic, social, and ecological externalities of capitalist accumulation have been shifted to the poor and vulnerable in our cities. Ecological modernization, the progressive politics of environmental justice, and urban political ecology have provided a broad agenda for community action (Desfor and Keil 2004) and now we are moving into a more generalized politics of vulnerability and risk. As the crisis continues to spread, new challenges have arisen for urban regions in which the contradictions of neoliberalism come into full relief. Moreover, the urban political ecology of globalizing cities is more than ever affected by the rising vulnerabilities in the network itself, particularly in the areas of infectious disease transmission and attainment and networks of infrastructures in metropolitan regions. The former case focuses on the urban political ecology of bodies in cities; the latter case concentrates on the urban political ecology of societal relationships of technology and infrastructure.

Health

> Across the city, harmless bacteria passed between individuals, carried by airborne particles or traces of saliva or the touch of a hand, our lives marked always by the proximity of others. And on this night or some night close in time, a germ woke up and began to inhabit someone's blood, in a way that was no longer innocent.
>
> (Helwig 2008: 128)

The arrival of Severe Acute Respiratory Syndrome (SARS) in Toronto in March 2003 signaled a fundamental crisis of the way that Canadian city saw its place in the global network of cities (Ali and Keil 2008). A financial center of secondary importance in the global hierarchy of such centers, Toronto had seen its position reinforced through the recovery of the Canadian economy in the late 1990s. The newly amalgamated metropolitan region seemed to be set to play a growing role in the expanding North American economy and appeared to benefit both from European and Asian economic articulations with Canada. This was clear notwithstanding the impeding dynamics of an aggressively neoliberal regime in the province of Ontario which had severely undermined the social and health safety net in Toronto and had casualized much work in the health and related sectors. When SARS struck – it had traveled to Toronto from a superspreader in the Metropole Hotel in Hong Kong – a network of connectivity was revealed which tied together a clique of cities such as Singapore and Hong Kong with Toronto. The connecting tissue was not capital, information, or culture but the bodies of migrating and oscillating family members in all cities.

When the SARS epidemic burnt out in the summer of 2003, 44 people had died and about 250 had been infected by a virus that, at times, tested severely the surge capacity and normal functioning of Toronto's hospital system. Worldwide, 8,000 people were infected and about 770 succumbed to the disease. In terms of numbers of victims, SARS was not as grave a disease as even seasonal influenza and nothing in comparison with HIV/Aids or malaria. But its effects were noteworthy nonetheless: it disrupted local and global economic, transportation, and cultural flows for a considerable time, and it tied up enormous segments of the medical system locally in global cities in east Asia and Canada. What SARS demonstrated in a few short weeks is that the transnationality of networks had a materiality which had been mostly overlooked. The virus exposed the vulnerability of bodies traveling in transnational pathways and lodging in particular hubs of human activity, such as Toronto, Hong Kong, or Singapore.

But the fact that some networks that coincided in 2003 were transnationalized was both a problem and a solution in the crisis around SARS. On the one hand, there were now open boundaries in spatial and temporal terms through which infected bodies could move rather unrestrictedly. The rapidity of the spread was surprising even to those who had predicted fast diffusion through the dense accelerated flight patterns that span the globe. On the other hand, the global network of index laboratories that worked with the World Health Organization (WHO) around the clock through email and phone conferencing was able to quickly identify the corona virus behind SARS and allowed medical staff everywhere to focus their attention on measures specific to this type of germ and to move away from the unspecific specter of "atypical pneumonia" which had haunted communities previously. Schillmeier observes: "thanks to the risk of a pandemic spread, highly effective and successful networks were assembled. These networks imitated the trans-continental circulation of the SARS virus by building up a complex set of connections between socio-technical, political, medical and economic dimensions to contain the circulation of the disease" (2008: 191). This meant that SARS pointed to transnationalism as both problem and solution.

Further, the virus also demonstrated the disproportional vulnerability of particular groups in the global urban world. In Toronto, SARS both localized and threw into stark relief transnational workers in various sectors. While much attention was on the Chinese community, with rampant racialization of the disease (Keil and Ali 2006), two groups of workers were strongly affected by SARS. First there were the hospital workers, often immigrant women in precarious work, who took the brunt of the infection as two of them died, dozens were infected, and all of their lives were in disarray. Secondly, there was the group of hotel and restaurant workers who were suffering from layoffs and job insecurities caused by poor economic performance in their sector during and after the SARS crisis (Major 2008; Major and Keil forthcoming).

After SARS, the attention of the medical community moved from mopping up to preparedness. In this process it became clear that populations that normally appear as profoundly localized perhaps are not. Homeless people and aboriginal populations, for example, who are among the most ghettoized groups in the Canadian urban landscape, are also among the most mobile both in their microcircuits of everydayness on the streets of the city and in their relationships with external communities in other cities and countries and on reserves. Both populations have also been rated as highly vulnerable to avian or swine flu pandemics. Preparations to stem the disease have concentrated on housed and resident populations as well as workplace protocols, where as the specific issues related to the contradictory (im)mobility of homeless people and aboriginals have often slipped through the conceptual nets spanned by pandemic preparedness plans at all governmental levels.

A world away from the mean streets of Toronto, in the meantime, in Geneva, Switzerland, and Lyon, France, public health experts brought together by the WHO have taken the relationship between cities, infectious disease, and global management of pandemic outbreaks as the starting point for ongoing consultations on how to bring cities – rather than nation states – into the picture of dealing with public health crises. This debate now goes beyond the common recognition that urbanization causes and deepens public health conditions (Patel and Burke 2009) and begins to view the networked nature of cities itself. A report based on a consultation in the fall of 2008 concludes:

> However much cities may differ, cities in one country also have many things in common with cities in another country – sometimes more so than with other areas of their own country. The consultation participants proposed that a forum for sharing the experience of cities in dealing with emergencies would be a valuable resource for helping to avoid mistakes and for promoting good practice in the future. Recommending the establishment of such a forum was beyond the terms of reference of the Lyon consultation, but the idea remains as an issue worth revisiting. Cities, wherever they are, have a lot to learn from each other in many ways – and if they can share information that helps protect the health of their citizens in a public health emergency, the effort would be worthwhile indeed. (Lyon Biopole and WHO 2009: 28)

It is with this kind of acknowledgment that a new global urban political ecology – or better, pathology – develops that sees a shift from a "national-geopolitical to an urban-geopolitical" governance framework emerge (Keil 2008: 37; Keil and Ali 2007).

Infrastructure

> "It's stupid," said the girl. "Forget it. It's probably just like, they have a problem with the pipes in the subway or something, they just don't want to admit it so they blame the, you know, terrorists or somebody. That's probably, that's probably it."
> (Helwig 2008: 110)

At the basis of today's urban political ecology in a transnational world is the assumption that there is a greater degree of "connectivity" than ever before. Connectivity is tied up with notions of technological advances and social possibility. The network society has supposedly arrived largely because of the rapid and ubiquitous spread of spaces of flows in concrete networked grids of electronic information (Castells 2000). Rapid technological change has had significant impact on the political ecologies of cities in a global age (Monstadt 2009). Advances in transportation and information and communication technologies are seen as crucial to the increased connectivity of human societies across continents and globally but also internally. Infrastructure development is central to most current elite scenarios for urban regions as "splintering" and "rebundling" have become the choice methods through which urban political economies have restructured the provision of basic and ancillary services in urban regions, although the terms have been shown to be more applicable in the west than in the global south (Graham and Marvin, 2001; Kooy and Bakker 2008). Steve Erie (2004) has argued in the case of Los Angeles that the success of the southern California metropolis in global interurban competition has to be credited to a large degree to the urban region's massive infrastructure investments both at the local/regional (transit, rail-corridor) and suprametropolitan (airport, port) scales. Simplistic interpretations of technological change as social change must be rejected though. Networked connections in the age of the cybercity may be more, rather than less socially just, spatially even, and politically democratic (Graham and Marvin 2001; Graham 2000; for a critique see Coutard 2002; Graham 2002). Saskia Sassen has pointed to the necessity of viewing technological and informational connectivity as embedded in social processes: "One fact that has become increasingly evident is that to maximize the benefits of the new information technologies, you need not only the infrastructure but a complex mix of other resources" (2000: 108).

Infrastructures are now transnationally financed and contextualized. But they are fully subject to local trappings. Financing major infrastructures (airports, roads, megaprojects, etc.) is now an internationalized affair. As Morag Torrance has shown, in a case study of the private Highway 407 in Toronto, for example:

> Non-local owners, through abiding by contractual obligations, play an increasing role in the governance of infrastructure projects at the urban scale. "Glocal" products, owned by global owners and regulated by local actors are developing, forging new styles of "glocal" governance. This governance is based on the rule of law, through which global players own and manage infrastructure assets in various countries in just one portfolio. (Torrance 2008: 2)

As the financing is glocalized, or effectively transnationalized, these infrastructures are for transnational use as much as for local use. Global city transportation has to hold the balance between those poles. This means that even the global, exchange value oriented superstructures like airports and private highways are shared, at some point by diaspora populations on their way "home" and business travelers on their way "abroad" (or the other way around). The transnational class crosses paths with the transnational outcasts in the same airport lobbies and at the same luggage carousels. In the ways in which infrastructural vulnerabilities are distributed between mobilities and immobilities, it becomes clear that transnationalization contributes or leads to new kinds of localization. As ever faster and more efficient hardwares are produced to connect places in the global city, the soft tissue of social and public service infrastructure comes under increasing attack.

In an era of transnationalized splintering urbanism (Graham and Marvin 2001) urban political ecology is characterized by the tendency that many urban areas may have at once too much and too little infrastructure. Hyperconnected, fast, and expensive spaces are close to spaces that are not connected, slow, and cheap. The politics that produced such contradictions and the ways in which infrastructures have been designed result in residents and users either getting stuck in marginality or hooked up to other prime networked spaces. The proximity and even simultaneity of fast and hyperconnected with slow (or stuck) and disconnected is remarkable. The premium Highway 407, for example, originally built by the Province of Ontario but subsequently sold to a multi-national private consortium, offers fast east–west travel to toll-paying drivers while the publicly owned non-tolled Highway 401 runs roughly parallel to 407.

Close to the prime networked space of the 407 city, low-income single parents will continue to travel with their infants in strollers on overcrowded buses operated by an underfunded public transit system on pot-holed streets. They will do so in sight of huge tractor-trailer trucks fitted with state-of-the-art GPS that are monitored 24/7 from a nationally important logistics complex a few kilometers northwest of Toronto. Above the slowly moving buses, a steady stream of aircraft prepare to land at Toronto Pearson International Airport, recently rebuilt at a cost of $4.4 billion (Young and Keil 2009; Keil and Young 2008).

Conclusion: Governance Revisited

> So it was like that now, catastrophe inevitable at the most empty moments. Everyone waiting, almost wanting it, a secret, guilty desire for meaning. Their time in history made significant once by that distant wall of black cloud.
>
> (Helwig 2008: 177)

Transnational realities call for new forms of governance. In the field of global environmental politics, multi-scalar arrangements have begun to span the globe as municipal governments have entered the stage as forerunners of urban sustainability efforts and as climate change actors. Cities are described here as influenced by both the multi-level governance structure that conditions their politics and by their networked nature (Bulkeley 2005; Bulkeley and Betsill 2005). To some, urban political ecological governance is now characterized paradigmatically by security concerns (Hodson and Marvin 2009). As we can see, the WHO goes global and local at the same time by transcending state power both sub-nationally and super-nationally in fighting infectious disease spread through urban networks.

For our purposes here, we note that the metabolic relationships with nature at the two interfaces of the city with the living body and with the technological base of transnational urbanism (infrastructure) are profoundly affected by these changes. For the former case, we can conclude:

> In sum, the second-order risk scenarios initiated by the transcontinental spread of SARS uncovered the cosmo-politics of SARS, i.e. the re-mapping of local/global, human/non-human and culture/nature assemblages that questioned, disrupted and altered common modes, forms and limits of local and global, individual and sociocultural calculations, rationalities, values, perceptions and practices. (Schillmeier 2008: 193).

Ultimately, the two cases demonstrate that (a) places have to be understood in their specificity (even originality) in a globalized environment (including the global cities) but they also demonstrate that there are generalizable tendencies; (b) the transnational constitution of the urban, while not leading to equalization, makes other sites than just the privileged global cities accessible and vulnerable to the transgressions inherent in the global urban. The ordinary city is clearly also a transnational city.

Both examples of shifts in the transnational urban political ecology – of health and infrastructure – give a glimpse into a rapidly recombinant world in which cities are major waystations. Capital, labor, technologies, and germs reposition themselves in and through urban life. The governance of these new relationships can be called transnational urban political ecology (or in the SARS case additionally transnational urban political pathology).

Note

1 This section borrows from Keil (forthcoming).

References

Alderson, A. S., and Beckfield, J. (2004) Power and position in the world city system. *American Journal of Sociology* 109: 811–51.

Ali, S. H., and Keil, R. (eds.) (2008) *Networked Disease: Emerging Infections in the Global City*. Oxford: Wiley-Blackwell.

Amin, A. (2002) Spatialities of globalization. *Environment and Planning A* 34: 385–99.

Amin, A. (2004) Regions unbound towards a new politics of place. *Geografiska Annaler series B Human Geography* 86: 33–44.

Beck, U. (2007) *Weltrisikogesellschaft*. Frankfurt: Suhrkamp.

Brenner, N. (2009) A thousand leaves: notes on the geographies of uneven spatial development. In: *Leviathan Undone? Towards a Political Economy of Scale*, ed. R. Keil and R. Mahon. Vancouver: University of British Columbia Press, 27–50.

Brenner, N., and Keil, R. (2006) *The Global Cities Reader*. New York: Routledge.

Brugmann, J. (2009) *Welcome to the Urban Revolution: How Cities are Changing the World*. Toronto: Viking Canada.

Bulkeley, H. (2005) Reconfiguring environmental governance: towards a politics of scales and networks. *Political Geography* 24: 875–902.

Bulkeley, H., and Betsill, M. (2005) Rethinking sustainable cities: multilevel governance and the "urban" politics of climate change. *Environmental Politics* 14 (1): 42–63.

Castells, M. (2000) *The Information Age: Economy, Society and Culture*, vol. I: *The Rise of the Network Society*. 2nd edn. Oxford: Blackwell.

Castree, N. (2002) False antitheses: Marxism, nature and actor-networks. *Antipode* 34: 111–46.

Conradson, D., and Latham, A. (2005) Transnational urbanism: attending to everyday practices and mobilities. *Journal of Ethnic and Migration Studies* 31 (2): 227–33.

Coutard, O. (2002) Premium networked spaces: a comment. *International Journal of Urban and Regional Research* 26 (1): 166–74.

Davis, M. (1990) *City of Quartz*. New York and London: Verso.

Davis, M. (1998) *Ecologies of Fear*. New York: Metropolitan Books.

Davis, M. (2005) *Planet of Slums*. London: Verso.

Derudder, B., and Taylor, P. J. (2003) The cliquishness of world cities. *GaWC Research Bulletin* no. 113. Available online at www.lboro.ac.uk/gawc (accessed October 14, 2010).

Desfor, G., and Keil, R. (2004) *Nature and the City: Making Environmental Policy in Toronto and Los Angeles*. Tucson: University of Arizona Press.

Erie, S. P. (2004) *Globalizing LA. Trade, Infrastructure, and Regional Development*. Stanford, CA: Stanford University Press.

Graham, S. (2000) Constructing premium network spaces: reflections on infrastructure networks and contemporary urban development. *International Journal of Urban and Regional Research* 24 (1): 183—200.

Graham, S. (2002) On technology, infrastructure, and the contemporary urban condition: a response to Coutard. *International Journal of Urban and Regional Research* 26 (1): 175–82.

Graham, S. (2006) Global grids of glass: on global cities, telecommunications and planetary urban networks. In *The Global Cities Reader*, ed. Neil Brenner and Roger Keil. London and New York: Routledge, 118–25.

Graham, S., and Marvin, S. (2001) *Splintering Urbanism: Networked Infrastructures, Technological Mobilities and the Urban Condition*. London: Routledge.

Helwig, M. (2008) *Girls Fall Down*. Toronto: Coach House Books.

Hodson, M., and Marvin, S. (2009) "Urban ecological security": a new urban paradigm? *International Journal of Urban and Regional Research* 33 (1): 193–215.

Holifield, R. (2009) Actor–network theory as a critical approach to environmental justice: a case against synthesis with urban political ecology. *Antipode* 41 (4): 637–58.

Keil, R. (1995) Environmental problematics in world cities. In *World Cities in a World-System*, ed. P. L. Knox and P. J. Taylor. New York: Cambridge University Press, 280–97.

Keil, R. (2003) Urban political ecology. *Urban Geography* 24 (8): 723–38.

Keil, R. (2005) Progress report – urban political ecology. *Urban Geography* 26 (7): 640–61.

Keil, R. (2008) Urban politics and public health: what's urban, what's politics? *Urban Geography* 30 (1): 36–9.

Keil, R. (forthcoming) Global cities: connectivity, vulnerability and resilience. In *Global Cities*, ed. B. Hahn and M. Zwingenberger. Heidelberg: Universitätsverlag Winter.

Keil, R., and Ali, S. H. (2006) Global cities and the spread of infectious disease: the case of severe acute respiratory syndrome (SARS) in Toronto, Canada. *Urban Studies* 43: 491–509.

Keil, R., and Ali, S. (2007) Governing the sick city: urban governance in the age of emerging infectious disease. *Antipode* 39: 846–73.

Keil, R., and Whitehead, M. (forthcoming) Cities and the politics of sustainability. In *The Oxford Handbook of Urban Politics*, ed. Karen Mossberger, Susan E. Clarke, and Peter John. Oxford: Oxford University Press.

Keil, R., and Young, D. (2008) Transportation: the bottleneck of regional competitiveness in Toronto. *Environment and Planning C; Government and Policy* 26: 728–51.

Kipfer, S., and Keil, R. (2002) Toronto Inc.? Planning the competitive city in the new Toronto. *Antipode* 34 (2): 227–64.

Knox, P. L., and Taylor, P. J. (eds.) (1995) *World Cities in a World-System*. New York: Cambridge University Press.

Kooy, M., and Bakker, K. (2008) Splintered networks: the colonial and contemporary waters of Jakarta. *Geoforum* 39: 6.

Lefebvre, H. (2003) *The Urban Revolution*. Minneapolis: University of Minnesota Press.

Luke, T. W. (2006) "Global Cities" vs. "global cities": rethinking contemporary urbanism as public ecology. In *The Global Cities Reader*, ed. N. Brenner and R. Keil. New York: Routledge, 275–81.

Lyon Biopole and WHO (2009) *Report: Cities and Public Health Crises*. Lyon: World Health Organization Office.

Mahon R., and Keil, R. (2009) *Leviathan Undone: Towards a Political Economy of Scale*. Vancouver: University of British Columbia Press.

Major, C. (2008) Affect work and infected bodies: biosecurity in an age of emerging infectious disease. *Environment and Planning A* 40 (7): 1633–46.

Major, C., and Keil, R. (forthcoming) SARS and service work: infectious disease and racialization in Toronto. In *Great White North: Race, Nature and the Geographies of Whiteness in Canada*, ed. A. Baldwin, L. Cameron, and A. Kobayashi.

Massey, D. (2007) *World City*. London: Polity Press.

Mongin, O. (2005) *La condition urbaine: la ville à l'heure de la mondialisation*. Paris: Édition du Seuil.

Monstadt, J. (2009) Conceptualizing the political ecology of urban infrastructures: insights from technology and urban studies. *Environment and Planning A* 41 (8): 1924–42.

Patel, R. B., and Burke, T. F. (2009) Urbanization – an emerging humanitarian disaster. *New England Journal of Medicine* 361: 8.

Planet Earth (2005) *Megacities – Our Global Urban Future*. Leiden, The Netherlands: Earth Sciences for Society Foundation.

Purcell, M. (2008) *Recapturing Democracy*. New York: Routledge.

Robinson, J. (2006) *Ordinary Cities*. New York: Routledge.

Roy, A. (2009) The 21st-century metropolis: new geographies of theory. *Regional Studies* 43 (6): 819–30.

Sassen, S. (2000) *Cities in a World Economy*. 2nd edn. Thousand Oaks, CA: Pine Forge Press.

Schillmeier, M. (2008) Globalizing risks – the cosmo-politics of SARS and its impact on globalizing sociology. *Mobilities* 3 (2): 179–99.

Schroeder, H., and Bulkeley, H. (2009) Global cities and the governance of climate change: what is the role of law in cities? *Fordham Urban Law Journal* 36 (2): 313–59.

Smith, M. P. (2001) *Transnational Urbanism: Locating Globalisation*. Oxford: Blackwell.

Smith, M. P. (2005) Transnational urbanism revisited. *Journal of Ethnic and Migration Studies* 31 (2): 235–44.

Swyngedouw, E., and Heynen, N. C. (eds.) (2003) Urban political ecology in advanced capitalist countries. *Antipode* 35 (5): 898–918.

Taylor, P. J. (2004) *World City Network: A Global Urban Analysis*. New York: Routledge.

Taylor, P. J., Derudder B., Saey P., and Witlox, F. (eds.) (2007) *Cities in Globalization: Practices, Policies and Theories*. New York: Routledge.

Torrance, M. (2008) Forging glocal governance? Urban infrastructures as networked financial products. *International Journal of Urban and Regional Research* 32 (1): 1–21.

Yeoh, B. S. A. (2005) Observations on transnational urbanism: possibilities, politics and costs of simultaneity. *Journal of Ethnic and Migration Studies* 31 (2): 409–13.

Young, D., and Keil, R. (2009) Seeking the urban in-between: tracking the urban politics of infrastructure in Toronto. Paper presented at the Association of American Geographers Annual Meeting, Las Vegas, March.

Chapter 63

Entrepreneurial Urbanism, Policy Tourism, and the Making Mobile of Policies

Kevin Ward

A colloquium held at Orleans in 1985 brought together academics, businessmen, and policymakers from eight large cities in seven advanced countries ... The charge was to explore the lines of action open to urban governments in the face of widespread erosion of the economic and fiscal base of many large cities in the advanced capitalist world. The colloquium indicated a strong consensus: that urban government had to be much more innovative and entrepreneurial, willing to explore all kinds of avenues through which to alleviate their distressed condition and thereby secure a better future for their populations.

(Harvey 1989: 4)

The cumulative effect of a range of developments – the internationalization of consultancy firms; the broadening of policy remits of trans-national institutions; the formation of new policy networks around think tanks, governmental agencies and professional associations; and the growth of international conferencing and "policy tourism" – has been to proliferate, widen and lubricate channels of cross-border policy transfer.

(Peck 2003: 228–9)

Intellectual Context

For David Harvey (1989: 1) it was a New Orleans colloquium that embodied the shift towards entrepreneurialism in urban politics. The content and the context of this event were, as Harvey has argued, "symptomatic of a reorientation in attitudes towards urban governance." It would probably not have surprised Harvey that New Orleans was not the only city hosting such an event at the time. I am sure there were lots across many industrialized countries of the global north and global south. I came across one in my analysis of the redevelopment pathways of Birmingham, Leeds, and Manchester in England (K. Ward 2000).

The Birmingham City Centre Challenge Symposium (known locally as the Highbury Initiative as it took place at the former home of Joseph Chamberlain, the city's most famously progressive politician) took place in March 1988, three years after the New Orleans Colloquium. The participants came from a wide range of geographical and occupational backgrounds. In attendance were architects, artists, economic development and management consultants, land-owners, local media and politicians, planners, and surveyors. Many of the sorts of actors that might appear in Logan and Molotch's (1987) urban growth machine or Stone's (1989) urban regime. They came from different parts of the world: the east and the west coasts of the US, Japan, Holland, West Germany (as it was then known), as well as elsewhere in the UK. At this two-day symposium were laid the foundations for the transformation of the city center which has taken place in the 20 plus years since (Loftman and Nevin 1996, 1998; K. Ward 2003).

The overarching theme of the weekend was the "city as theatre," pre-empting by almost a decade the "experience economy" thesis (Pine and Gilmore 1999) which has underpinned a number of North American cities' downtown strategies in the 2000s, particularly those pursued through Business Improvement Districts and influenced by the drive to produce, in the words of Florida (2002: 7) "a good 'people' or 'creative' climate" – or what Harvey (1989: 47) termed a "good living environment." The emphasis was on making Birmingham an "attractive exciting, comfortable place," akin to the "live, work and play" ethos espoused by many US Business Improvement Districts (K. Ward 2007a). The strategies those in attendance deemed necessary to effect this transformation were considered comparable to putting on a show. Six working groups were established. Each one was charged with a different aspect of the show: "producing the show," which focused on the role of the city center and resources; "setting the stage," which focused on urban design and landscape; "casting the roles," which focused on user perception; "directing the actors," which focused on movement and transportation; and "managing the stage," which focused on management and maintenance. The schedule consisted of formal talks, informal dinners, and walking tours. Existing sites around the city were visited, touched, photographed, and talked about. At the end of the weekend a number of future initiatives were hatched, most noticeably around the marketing of the city, pedestrian access to the center, and public transport. In the years since this symposium *it* – the event itself – and the outcomes have proved influential in how the city has been developed (Loftman and Nevin 2003).

These two examples – New Orleans and Birmingham – are revealing in a number of ways. In both cases it was not just local political officials involved in strategizing the future of the city. A range of "experts" brought their accounts, experiences, and knowledge to the symposium: academics, architects, development consultants, engineers, and planners. That is not to claim that the state was not involved. It was, but in a qualitatively different manner, as its involvement in economic and social governance was subject to restructuring from inside and outside (Peck 2003). The focus of both events was not just economic development narrowly defined. In both cases there was an attention to the emotional and symbolic as well as the material urban economy, and how the three might be co-constitutive. In both cities there was a concern to better market or promote the city. While in the US there has been a long history of cities boosting their economies through these sorts of activities, this has been less so in the case of the UK. An attention to the built environment and how it might be remade in order to attract back capital and people to the city center was also high on the agendas of both cities.

Of course, much of this should come as no surprise to those readers versed in urban and regional political economy since the late 1980s. Much has been written about the changing nature of urban governance and economic development in industrialized cities of the global north in this period (Lauria 1996; Hall and Hubbard 1998; Jonas and Wilson 1999; Brenner and Theodore 2002). What is perhaps surprising is that neither Harvey (1989) nor many who have worked in this field subsequently have picked up on the importance of these types of events: colloquiums, conferences, seminars, and symposiums – events in which geographically unevenly situated individuals come together to learn about one another's cities. It was at the New Orleans Colloquium that expertise and knowledge from a number of cities was brought to bear on the problem facing urban governments in general (and in turn constructing it as a common problem, of course): how best to map out a future growth trajectory? Experts of one sort or another visited a city, bringing with them historically and geographically specific "evidence" that they could impart through interacting with one another, and shaping the ways in which that city may or may not evolve. At the Birmingham Symposium the emphasis was on how this particular city should go about its future. However participants themselves would not have been unaffected. It is likely that they would have returned to their own places of work and have been influenced by the experiences shared at the symposium.

Nor has there been much reflection in the entrepreneurial urbanism literatures on how Baltimore – Harvey's then home town – became a model of waterfront redevelopment, one that could be replicated by other cities around the world, including Birmingham some years later (S. Ward 2006). Of course the city was not alone. Cities such as Amsterdam, Barcelona, Dubai, Los Angeles, Manchester, New York, and Vancouver have become known as success stories in one area of urban policy or another (McCann and Ward 2010a, 2010b): geographically uneven sets of global circuits of different sorts of knowledges, in and through which these cities are cast as models to be copied, imitated, or replicated. Each one has been visited by actors from other cities, so that they can compare and replicate, returning home to put into action the lessons they have learnt. Those involved in their "successes" have moved from one city to another, speaking about their achievements. The "demand" and the "supply" side are mutually constituted and constitutive. Taken together these two examples – New Orleans and Birmingham – speak to the growth in the circuits, the networks, and the webs that connect together cities with often quite different histories. They are deeply interconnected: the expansion in the means through which policies are made mobile, on the one hand, and the making up of what might be thought of as *imitable cities* on the other, feed off and reinforce one another.

In this chapter I do two things. First, I consider ways of conceptualizing contemporary patterns and processes of urban governance. I argue that the last three decades have been witness to a profound series of transformations in the way cities of the global north are governed and these have been well captured by the rise across the social sciences in work on entrepreneurial urbanism. Second, I turn to suggest that an important factor in geographically disparate cities seemingly undertaking similar redevelopment programs is the role played by *policy tourism*. This is important in making cities imitable. Study tours or visits in and through which actors in one city learn about another city, either by visiting it or by being visited by representatives of it, are on the increase. It is one of the reasons behind what Harvey (1989: 10) observed as the "repetitive and serial reproduction of certain patterns of development." In the conclusion, the chapter reiterates its two main points: first, during the 1990s and 2000s many cities of the global north have been witness to the variegated forms, patterns, and processes of entrepreneurial urbanism and second that working within this frame of analysis there remains a need to explicate the means through which policies are made mobile. This demands an attention both to the various techniques used to incentivize comparisons between cities (such as auditing, benchmarking, league tables, and key performance indicators) and the geographically uneven systems that connect (and disconnect) "local" governance regimes. In this the chapter speaks to a growing literature in critical human geography (Peck and Theodore 2001, 2010; K. Ward 2006, 2007b, 2010a, 2010b; Cook 2008; McCann 2008, forthcoming; McCann and Ward 2010a, 2010b; Robinson 2010).

Entrepreneurial Urbanism: Scale, Spatiality, States, Strategies

Since the late 1970s a large and intellectually diverse body of work has been produced on the changing political economies of North American and western European cities. Particular attention has been paid to the ways in which public, private, and third sectors have worked in unison to oversee a transformation in the ways in which cities are governed. Cox (1993) has argued this constitutes the emergence of a "new urban politics." Writing more than twenty years ago, Harvey (1989: 4) argued that we had witnessed the emergence of "a general consensus ... throughout the advanced capitalist world that positive benefits are to be had by cities taking an entrepreneurial stance to economic development."

Through seeking to understand the interrelationship between the process of urbanization and capitalist social relations and accumulation, this foundational work rested on three claims over the changes witnessed in Baltimore (and beyond, certainly in the UK and elsewhere in the US) (Harvey 1989). First, public–private partnerships were increasingly working alongside local governments to boost and market local economies (Leitner 1991; Hall and Hubbard 1998). It was argued that this mode of organization was becoming hegemonic. This did not mean there was no role for local government but rather that increasingly other "local" – as understood both territorially and, increasingly, relationally – stakeholders, in addition to elected local officials, were in positions to affect the ways in which cities developed. Second, the practices and policies of public–private partnerships were entrepreneurial in so far as they were innovative in design and delivery, in many cases taking a lead from the private sector. For Hall and Hubbard (1996: 155) "[i]ncreasingly ... the line between the public and private sectors has become blurred," with the result being not a reduction in the state per se but rather the emergence of new forms of statecraft (Peck 2003; Coleman *et al.* 2005). It was argued that fundamental to these new forms are the ways in which scale is understood to be constituted through the struggles over entrepreneurial strategies, rather than as a cartographic given (Brenner 1999). Based on their analysis of Hong Kong, Jessop and Sum (2000: 2295) suggest the term "glurbanization," by which they mean entrepreneurial strategies that are concerned to secure the most advantageous insertion of a given city into the changing interscalar division of labor in the world economy.

The third claim made by Harvey (1989) was that in and through entrepreneurial urbanism the emphasis of local government switched from an attention to territory – and associated housing, education, and social policies – to a focusing on place – and on particular civic projects. This claim was bound up with one about the move away from social redistribution. Local government no longer solely acted on behalf of those who voted it into power. Rather, it was placing increasing attention – and spending more resources – on levering in various forms of attention-seeking investments. Examples that are often cited include conference centers, cultural centers, heritage parks, museums, shopping malls, science parks, sports stadia.

Drawing upon and extending Harvey's (1989) hugely influential work, a series of subsequent studies have sought to examine conceptually, empirically, and methodologically the variegated ways in which this generalized transformation has occurred – contradictions and all – in localities across the cities of the industrialized global north. Five themes are worth further elaboration in this chapter. The first is the significant literature on the changing spaces, scales, and subjects of the state. Rejecting claims about the "hollowing out" of the state, this work has sought to underscore the ways in which recent decades have witnessed a qualitative process of state restructuring. The edges of the state have been renegotiated as its various elements have become involved in a myriad of alliances and partnerships, particularly but not exclusively in the field of economic development. Drawing a firm line around where the state starts and stops has become increasingly complicated, it has been argued. Activities that were once performed inside the state are now just as likely to be done outside. Instead the state's role has been redefined as one of a facilitator, with a whole array of indicators designed to evaluate performance, often at a distance. Internally the state has also been restructured. More traditional ways of decision-making have been replaced by new ways of organizing activities. New teams and units have been formed, in the process challenging traditional ways of working, such as through formal committees. Some professional demarcations have been transgressed, with elements of traditional jobs such as architecture, engineering, and planning combined to form new types of entrepreneurial "redevelopment" officials (Painter 1998).

The second theme in this work is that which details the nature and extent of the changes in the institutional arrangements in place to govern cities (Boyle and Hughes 1994; Goodwin and Painter 1996; Cochrane 1999; Imrie and Raco 1999; K. Ward 2000), both in terms of a quantitative detailing of those involved in the redevelopment process, and more qualitatively, the particular ideological underpinnings of the urban agendas as "policy ... fit[s] itself to the grooves already established by the market" (Smith 2002: 94). Related to this second theme, the third one in this literature emphasizes the changing agenda, interests, and identities involved in territorial coalitions, partnerships, and regimes, and the theoretical convergences and differences between these terms (Cox and Mair 1988; Imrie *et al.* 1995; Cochrane *et al.* 1996; Jessop *et al.* 1999; Peck and Tickell 1995). This draws attention to the discourses and representations, and the politics over their mobilization and use, associated with contemporary entrepreneurial modes of urban governance (Jessop 1997, 1998; McCann 2002; Ward 2003; Wilson 1996, 1998). Indicative of the wider "cultural turn" in human geography and beyond, those working on issues of urban governance have become increasingly sensitized to the non-materiality of political practices: or put another way, on the extra-economic dimension of economic development, exploring "the relations between the political economy of place and the cultural politics of place" (Hall and Hubbard 1996: 162). The re-imaging of cities has involved urban leaders spending more time on place promotion, investing in new cultural projects, and focusing on selling the city in terms of new lifestyles and experiences, cajoling, manipulating, and stimulating the attachments and emotions individuals feel towards cities.

The fourth theme in this literature is the increasingly diverse scales represented and entangled in "urban" governing formations (Amin and Graham 1997; Brenner 1999). On the one hand, work has sought to reveal the range of geographical scales present in the "urban" entrepreneurial governance arrangements that characterize many industrialized cities of the global north. This takes as its point of departure Harvey (1989: 6) which argued that "The shift towards entrepreneurialism in urban governance has to be examined ... at a variety of spatial scales – local neighbourhood and community, central city and suburb, metropolitan, region, nation state, and the like."

This work in human geography has overlapped with that in political science on multi-level governance, which has sought to unpack the multi-scalar processes behind contemporary expressions of "urban" governance (Sellers 2002, 2005). On the other hand there have been a more recent series of contributions that have sought to rethink the language of geographical scale. Bound up in a wider debate between those who propose alternative ways of theorizing space, this work has highlighted the increasingly open, porous, and interconnected configuration of territorial entities. As MacLeod and Jones (2007: 1186) put it, "all contemporary expressions of territory ... are, to varying degrees, punctuated by and orchestrated through a myriad of trans-territorial networks and relational webs of connectivity." So, for Allen and Cochrane (2007: 1163) it is important to appreciate both the relational as well as the territorial elements bound up in the production of something called the "urban" scale:

it would seem that there is little to be gained by talking about ... [urban] governance as a territorial arrangement when a number of the political elements assembled are not particularly ... [urban] ... in any traditional sense. Many are "parts" of elsewhere, representatives of political authority, expertise, skills, and interests drawn together to move forward varied agendas and programmes. The sense in which these are ... [urban] ... assemblages, rather than geographically tiered hierarchies of decision-making, lies with the tangle of interactions and capabilities within which power is negotiated and played out.

The fifth theme running through this work has been that of the restructuring of the urban built environment. New kinds of landscapes have been produced as part of the geographically uneven process of entrepreneurial urbanism. Emphasis in some of the literature has been on ways in which strategies to market and promote cities necessarily have an urban design element. As Hubbard (1996: 1444) puts it, "place marketing is inevitably accompanied by a fabrication of the landscape, which can therefore be seen as both an expression and a consequence of attempts to re-image the city." New downtown redevelopments puncture many industrialized cities of the global north. Think not only of the iconic developments in some of the major capitals but also of other significant constructions. They reflect the attracting of inward investment, the capturing of value in the downtowns, and are examples of how cities have used the redesigning of the built environment as a means of placing themselves globally.

What these five themes reflect are the ways in which the intellectual agenda first hatched by Harvey (1989), which itself built on earlier contributions (Fainstein *et al.* 1983), has developed into a significant body of academic scholarship. Emphasis has been on the territorial nature of the state restructuring that is both cause and effect of the process of entrepreneurial urbanism. What, at its core, has been argued is a quite fundamental recalibration of the relationship between the neoliberal capitalist system and the urban condition. Less well understood is the means through which policies are made mobile and the role of different types of events in this process. Why is it, for example, that we see similar types of urban policy developments taking place the world over? All cities are not becoming the same – this is not some crude globalization thesis. However, there is empirical evidence to suggest that if it was ever enough to stop at the city limits when seeking to account for changes in urban development pathways, and trajectories, then that time has now passed. One city and its experiences appear to be increasingly implicated or entangled in another. How this comes about – what sorts of spatial infrastructure exists to facilitate the making mobile of certain sorts of knowledge – remains an under-explored issue in the existing literature. It is the one I turn to next.

Policy Tourism: Circuits, Networks and Webs of Urban Policy Mobility

> Cities that become popular destinations for incoming delegations of policy actors develop protocols and packaged narratives for dealing with their visitors in a way that is efficient for the host and also edifying and enjoyable for the guests.
>
> (McCann forthcoming: 22)

The holding of colloquiums, conferences, seminars, and workshops and the visits and tours of cities that accompany them is just one of a series of examples that speaks to how different ways of "doing" economic development – from design through to evaluation – are being circulated amongst different types of policy actors in different cities around the world (McCann 2008, forthcoming; K. Ward 2006, 2007b; Robinson 2010). There is of course nothing new about these types of events in which different types of policy actors come together to share information and knowledge: architects, consultants, designers, economists, engineers, and planners. Professional organizations of various sorts have long had a record of organizing such events and in bringing together different sorts of urban stakeholders to share knowledge and to exchange examples of "good practice" policy (for the example of planning see S. Ward 2000). Despite this history it does appear that in recent years there has been a growth in these types of events and their importance, as part of a wider expansion in the mechanisms that connect cities and in and through which many of their leaders and officials learn. Some occur through existing formal channels, such as the sister cities programs in the US or the twinning programs across Europe and beyond, while others stem from informal connections or gatherings.

It is possible to discern two types of policy tourism. These do not cover all types but are merely suggestive. On the one hand *event-led policy tourism* refers to events such as the New Orleans Colloquium. Policy actors of various stripes are invited to share their experiences. Some will speak about their involvement in their own city's redevelopment strategies. Urban managers will spell out the details of their city's success stories, pointing to examples of how areas have been redeveloped. Others fulfill slightly different roles. Professionals such as architects, economists, engineers, designers, and planners will bring their specific, technical knowledge to bear, sharing examples of cases in which they have been involved. Finally, "international" policy actors participate, using their distant geographical location as a means of widening the terms of discussion and debate and of legitimizing their approaches. At these events the format includes presentations, panels, question and answer sessions, and of course tours to key locations. Participants learn from one another, although there is often a hierarchy amongst them with the expertise and knowledge of some more valued than others. Handouts are circulated, photographs are taken, and recordings are made. In and through coming together temporarily – for anything between a day and a week – participating policy actors learn from each other and the speakers. They then return to their respective cities to translate what they have heard or read at the event into actionable and achievable goals or objectives. These can then form the basis of a localized approach to economic development, albeit one of which the history is as much relational as it is territorial.

On the other hand *visit-led policy tourism* involves visiting and touring cities that have become known for their successful approaches. Groups of policy actors from one city visit another city to see and to learn from its own policy actors about "the processes, challenges, and benefits of the formulation and realization of particular policy models" (McCann forthcoming: 22). Tours take in key sites or spaces: major infrastructure developments, new public spaces, residential developments in particular – physical examples of the host city's successes. By being there and seeing "evidence," policy actors are able to distil and interpret the possible lessons to be learnt for their own cities. Show-and-tell tours, walk-and-talk activities, and before-and-after visual displays serve to reinforce the means through which visiting policy actors can translate the evidence they have generated – photographs, notes, etc. – into tangible suggestions. These are then relayed back to other policy actors in their home cities. The general knowledge acquired on the visit is translated into something more appropriate to the specific needs of their city.

Conclusion

> If my memory serves, the weekend of March 25–27, 1988, was … the historic weekend when around 80 people with some kind of professional interest in Birmingham's city centre assembled for an event which was arguably one of the most important watersheds in the city's history.
>
> (Grimley 2008: 1)

So wrote a local journalist who had attended the Birmingham Symposium. He was writing on the eve of a twentieth anniversary event to mark its lasting legacy on Birmingham. A visit to the center of the city will confirm how it has been transformed in the interim. Much of the built environment of the 1980s either no longer exists or has been remade to the point that it is almost beyond recognition. Of course a lot of local time and effort of community representatives, politicians, policy-makers, and so on has been invested into delivering the newly revalorized city of Birmingham. However, policy tourism has continued to play a part in shaping the city's development. Over the last twenty years different city leaders have visited many other European and North American cities with a view to learning how better to develop and govern Birmingham. At the same time, representatives from other cities have visited Birmingham to learn from it. Only in 2009 there was a series of visits between Birmingham and Chicago around the role of housing and redevelopment.

This chapter has reviewed the literatures on entrepreneurial urbanism. It has highlighted five features that characterize much of the existing work. This has generated a series of insights into the contemporary urban condition (particularly as it is experienced in industrialized cities of the global north). However it has been relatively quiet on the mechanisms in and through which policies are made mobile. *Policy tourism* refers to the different types of ways in which policy actors in one city visit and learn from policy actors in another. While not without its historical precedents, this chapter has argued that since the late 1980s there has been a growth in the number of events and visits that take place, facilitating the movement of policies from one city to another. A range of different policy actors, many with clear territorial remits, are involved in the process of making policies mobile. All of which adds further intellectual weight to the argument that future research into cities needs to be sensitive to both the territorial and relational geographies that are behind their constitution.

Acknowledgements

The author acknowledges a Philip Leverhulme Prize (2005) which supported the writing of this chapter, the supportive comments of the editors, and the more general intellectual debts to Eugene McCann. The usual disclaimers apply.

References

Allen, J., and Cochrane, A. (2007) Beyond the territorial fix: regional assemblages, politics and power. *Regional Studies* 41: 1161–75.

Amin, A., and Graham, S. (1997). The ordinary city. *Transactions of the Institute of British Geographers* n.s. 22: 411–30.

Boyle, M., and Hughes, G. (1994) The politics of urban entrepreneurialism in Glasgow. *Geoforum* 25: 453–70.

Brenner, N. (1999) Globalisation as reterritorialisation: the re-scaling of urban governance in the European Union. *Urban Studies* 36: 431–51.

Brenner, N., and Theodore, N. (eds.) (2002) *Spaces of Neoliberalism: Urban Restructuring in North American and Western Europe.* Oxford: Blackwell.

Cochrane, A. (1999) Redefining urban politics for the twenty-first century. In *The Urban Growth Machine: Critical Perspectives Two Decades Later*, ed. A. E. G. Jonas and D. Wilson. Albany: SUNY Press, 109–24.

Cochrane, A., Peck, J., and Tickell, A. (1996) Manchester plays games: exploring the local politics of globalisation. *Urban Studies* 33: 1319–36.

Coleman, R., Tombs, S., and Whyte, D. (2005) Capital, crime control and statecraft in the entrepreneurial city. *Urban Studies* 42: 2511–30.

Cook, I. (2008) Mobilising urban policies: The policy transfer of US Business Improvement Districts to England and Wales. *Urban Studies* 45: 773–95.

Cox, K. R. (1993) The local and the global in the new urban politics: a critical review. *Environment and Planning D: Society and Space* 11: 433–48.

Cox, K., and Mair, A. (1988) Locality and community in the politics of local economic development. *Annals of the Association of American Geographers* 78: 307–25.

Fainstein, N., Fainstein, S., Hill, R. C., Judd, D., and Smith, M. P. (1983) *Restructuring The City: The Political Economy of Urban Redevelopment.* New York: Longman.

Florida, R. (2002) *The Rise of the Creative Class: And How It's Transforming Work, Leisure, Community and Everyday Life.* New York: Basic Books.

Goodwin, M., and Painter, J. (1996) Local governance, the crises of Fordism, and the changing geographies of regulation. *Transactions of the Institute of British Geographers* n.s. 21: 635–48.

Grimley, T. (2008) Birmingham's long road to renewal. *Birmingham Post* March 31. Available online at www.birminghampost.net/news/newsaggregator/2008/03/31/birmingham-s-long-road-to-renewal-65233-20697493/ (accessed October 13, 2010).

Hall, T., and Hubbard, P. (1996) The entrepreneurial city: new urban politics, new urban geographies. *Progress in Human Geography* 20: 153–74.

Hall, T., and Hubbard, P. (1998) *The Entrepreneurial City: Geographies of Politics, Regime and Representation.* Chichester: John Wiley & Sons.

Harvey, D. (1989) From managerialism to entrepreneurialism: the transformation of urban governance in late capitalism. *Geografiska Annaler* 71B: 3–17.

Hubbard, P. (1996) Urban design and city regeneration: social representations of entrepreneurial landscapes. *Urban Studies* 33: 1441–61.

Imrie, R., and Raco, M. (1999) How new is the new local governance? Lessons from the United Kingdom. *Transactions of the Institute of British Geographers* n.s. 24: 45–64.

Imrie, R., Thomas, H., and Marshall, T. (1995) Business organizations, local dependence and the politics of urban-renewal in Britain. *Urban Studies* 32: 31–47.

Jessop, B. (1997) The entrepreneurial city: re-imaging localities, redesigning economic governance or restructuring capital. In *Transforming Cities: Contested Governance and New Spatial Divisions*, ed. N. Jewson and S. MacGregor. London: Routledge, 28–41.

Jessop, B. (1998) The narrative of enterprise and the enterprise of narrative: place marketing and the entrepreneurial city. In *The Entrepreneurial City: Geographies of Politics, Regime and Representation*, ed. T. Hall and P. Hubbard. Chichester: John Wiley & Sons, 77–102.

Jessop, B., and Sum, N. L. (2000) An entrepreneurial city in action: Hong Kong's emerging strategies in and for (inter) urban competition. *Urban Studies* 12: 2287–313.

Jessop, B., Peck, J., and Tickell, A. (1999) Retooling the machine: economic crisis, state restructuring, and urban politics. In *The Urban Growth Machine: Critical Perspectives Two Decades Later*, ed. A. E. G. Jonas and D. Wilson. Albany: SUNY Press, 141–59.

Jonas, A. E. G., and Wilson, D. (eds.) (1999) *The Urban Growth Machine: Critical Perspectives Two Decades Later*. Albany: SUNY Press.

Lauria, M. (ed.) (1996) *Reconstructing Urban Regime Theory: Regulating Urban Politics in a Global Economy*. London: Sage.

Leitner, H. (1991) Cities in pursuit of economic growth. *Political Geography Quarterly* 9: 146–70.

Loftman, P., and Nevin, B. (1996) Going for growth: prestige projects in three British cities. *Urban Studies* 33: 991–1019.

Loftman, P., and Nevin, B. (1998) Pro-growth local economic development strategies: civic promotion and local needs in Britain's second city, 1981–1996. In *The Entrepreneurial City: Geographies of Politics, Regime and Representation*, ed. T. Hall and P. Hubbard. Chichester: John Wiley & Sons, 129–48.

Loftman, P., and Nevin, B. (2003) Prestige projects, city centre restructuring and social exclusion: taking the long term view. In *Urban Futures: Critical Commentaries on the City*, ed. T. Hall and M. Miles. London: Routledge, 76–91.

Logan, J., and Molotch, H. (1987) *Urban Fortunes: The Political Economy of Place*. Berkeley: University of California Press.

MacLeod, G., and Jones, M. R. (2007) Territorial, scalar, networked, connected: in what sense a "regional" world? *Regional Studies* 41: 1177–91.

McCann, E. (2002) The cultural politics of local economic development: meaning-making, place-making, and the urban policy process. *Geoforum* 33: 385–98.

McCann, E. (2008) Expertise, truth and urban policy mobilities: global circuits of knowledge in the development of Vancouver, Canada's "four pillar" drug strategy. *Environment and Planning A* 40: 885–904.

McCann, E. (forthcoming) Urban policy mobilities and global circuits of knowledge: towards a research agenda. *Annals of the Association of American Geographers*.

McCann, E., and Ward, K. (eds.) (2010a) *Mobile Urbanism: Cities and Policy-making in the Global Age*. Minneapolis: University of Minnesota Press.

McCann, E., and Ward, K. (2010b) Relationality/territoriality: towards a conceptualization of cities in the world. *Geoforum* 41: 175–84.

Painter, J. (1998) Entrepreneurs are made, not born: learning and urban regimes in the production of entrepreneurial cities. In *The Entrepreneurial City: Geographies of Politics, Regime and Representation*, ed. T. Hall and P. Hubbard. Chichester: John Wiley & Sons, 259–74.

Peck, J. (2003) Geography and public policy: mapping the penal state. *Progress in Human Geography* 27: 222–32.

Peck, J., and Theodore, N. (2001) Exporting workfare/importing welfare-to-work: exploring the politics of Third Way Policy Transfer. *Political Geography* 20: 427–60.

Peck, J., and Theodore, N. (2010) Recombinant workfare, across the Americas. *Geoforum* 41: 169–74.

Peck, J., and Tickell, A. (1995) Business goes local: dissecting the "business agenda" in Manchester. *International Journal of Urban and Regional Research* 19: 55–78.

Pine, J. H., and Gilmore, B. J. (1999) *The Experience Economy: Work Is Theatre and Every Business a Stage*. Boston, MA: Harvard Business School.

Robinson, J. (2010) The spaces of circulating knowledge: city strategies and global urban governmentality. In *Mobile Urbanism: Cities and Policy-making in the Global Age*, ed.

E. McCann and K. Ward. Minneapolis: University of Minnesota Press.

Sellers, J. (2002) The nation-state and urban governance: toward multilevel analysis. *Urban Affairs Review* 37: 611–41.

Sellers, J. (2005) Re-placing the nation: an agenda for comparative urban politics. *Urban Affairs Review* 40: 419–45.

Smith, N. (2002) New globalism, new urbanism: gentrification as global urban strategy. In *Spaces of Neoliberalism: Urban Restructuring in North America and Western Europe*, ed. N. Brenner and N. Theodore. Oxford: Blackwell, 80–103.

Stone, C. (1989) *Regime Politics: Governing Atlanta 1946–1988*. Lawrence: University of Kansas Press.

Ward, K. (2000) A critique in search of a corpus: re-visiting governance and re-interpreting urban politics. *Transactions of the Institute of British Geographers* n.s. 25: 169–85.

Ward, K. (2003) The limits to contemporary urban redevelopment: "doing" entrepreneurial urbanism in Birmingham, Leeds and Manchester. *City* 7: 199–212.

Ward, K. (2006) "Policies in motion," urban management and state restructuring in the trans-local expansion of Business Improvement Districts. *International Journal of Urban and Regional Research* 30: 54–75.

Ward, K. (2007a) "Creating a personality for downtown": Business Improvement Districts in Milwaukee. *Urban Geography* 28: 781–808.

Ward, K. (2007b) Business Improvement Districts: mobile policies, state edges and urban liveability. *Geography Compass* 1: 657–72.

Ward, K. (2010a) Entrepreneurial urbanism and Business Improvement Districts in the state of Wisconsin: a cosmopolitan critique. *Annals of the Association of American Geographers* 100 (5): 1177–96.

Ward, K. (2010b) Towards a relational comparative approach to the studying of cities. *Progress in Human Geography* 34: 471–87.

Ward, S. V. (2000) Re-examining the international diffusion of planning. In *Urban Planning in a Changing World: The Twentieth Century Planning Experience*, ed. R. Freestone. London: Spon, 40–60.

Ward, S. V. (2006) "Cities are fun": inventing and spreading the Baltimore model of cultural urbanism. In *Culture, Urbanism and Planning*, ed. J. Monclús and M. Guardia. Aldershot: Ashgate, 271–85.

Wilson, D. (1996) Metaphors, growth coalition discourses and black poverty neighborhoods in a US city. *Antipode* 28: 72–96.

Wilson, D. (1998) Progress report: the politics of urban representation. *Urban Geography* 19: 531–42.

Chapter 64

Making Up Global Urban Policies

Allan Cochrane

Most people live their lives in cities of one sort or another, but it is their political and social significance that matters as much as any argument about numbers. Rhetorically and practically, cities have been imagined "spaces of hope" (maybe even sites of revolutionary engagement), while at the same time being machines for the reproduction of inequality and division (Davis 2006; Harvey 2002; Lees 2004; Lefebvre 1996; Wacquant 2007). It is this that helps to make urban policy and the politics of urban policy significant, as contested arenas in which the tensions and contradictions are negotiated and potentially resolved.

In this context, the practices of actually existing urban policy can seem rather disappointing because they often appear mundane, technicist, and localist. They reflect a strong policy focus on the identification of carefully delimited and specified *urban* problems deemed suitable for intervention and spatial targeting. There has been a strong emphasis on looking for "what works," so that supposedly grand claims are eschewed in favor of pragmatic claims about the potential of particular initiatives. Much writing in the field has focused on the identification and discussion of particular projects and the sharing of "best practice" – often reflected in a series of stories or case studies. Sometimes, looking at the practice of urban policy, it is hard to get away from the detailed case studies and the particular initiatives.

In that sense paradoxically, despite the political tensions identified above, they could be seen as prime examples of what Erik Swyngedouw has identified as a post-political turn (Swyngedouw 2007; see also Baeten 2009). Indeed, it has been strongly argued that at the heart of urban policy is a concern with the management of "troublesome populations," through a process of sanitization and depoliticization, whether through the fostering of community and neighborhood initiatives, housing

The New Blackwell Companion to the City   Edited by Gary Bridge and Sophie Watson
© 2011 Blackwell Publishing Ltd

renewal, redevelopment and gentrification, or simply the identification (and effective segregation) of particular populations as suitable for the attention of welfare and policing agencies (see, e.g., Allen 2007; Dikec 2009; Haylett 2003; Mooney 2008; Wacquant 2007).

However, the broad contours of urban policy as it has developed over time also reflect changing understandings of cities and their role in economic and social development, as well as the way in which understandings of social policy have changed in the context of global neoliberalism and its local variants. Elsewhere (Cochrane 2007), I have focused on the role of urban policy in the reshaping of national welfare regimes. The development of urban policy as a distinctive field helped to constitute (as well as reflecting) the policy upheavals and state restructuring that characterized the fraying of the Keynesian welfare state and the unsettling of the political, economic, and welfare settlement implied by it. By the late 1970s and 1980s, at least in the US and the UK, urban policy was explicitly being mobilized as part of a wider strategy directed towards building "a market-led path to post-industrial society" (Barnekov et al. 1989: 5).

Here I am concerned with something rather different, namely the way in which urban policy can be seen as part of a wider political reframing in a world of fast policy transfer and policy mobilities (Peck 2002; McCann 2008; Ward 2006), in which formal and informal institutions nevertheless play a key role in shaping policy (see, e.g., Deacon et al. 1997). If urban policy emerged in the context of the crisis of national Keynesian welfare states, it has been transformed by the impact of, and has helped to shape the politics of, (neoliberal) globalization. The new emphasis on urban competitiveness, whether expressed in the development of mega projects, cultural initiatives, place marketing, or the provision of social and economic infrastructure, has been part of the process of redefining "welfare" in terms that stress the importance of economic success for cities and access to employment for urban residents.

The drive for the "competitive city" has become an apparently ubiquitous – global – policy phenomenon. The rise of mega-projects, the re-imagination of cities as cultural centers and "global cities" is marked in Pacific-Asia, South America, and even sub-Saharan Africa as much as in the US and western Europe. In this context the purpose of urban policy is redefined – instead of being the locus of decline, decay, and disorder, here cities become potential (and actual) sources of growth and development as long as the right policies are adopted. They are "the engines of growth" (Hall and Pfeiffer 2000: 51). It is, according to the OECD, a "well-established fact that cities are locomotives for national economic growth" (OECD 2003: 128).

The core message of contemporary urban policy is an explicitly globalized one, precisely because it is rooted in an emphasis on notions of economic competitiveness, or what has been described as the "new conventional wisdom" (Buck et al. 2005). According to this set of understandings (which can be seen as a particular expression of neoliberalism), because economic development is the basic underpinning of collective local prosperity, the key tasks of urban policy-makers are: to foster urban competitiveness and enable the competitiveness of business within their territories; to build effective and market-friendly forms of governance, with a strong role for non-state actors in the delivery of services; to maintain social cohesion, whether by fostering forms of community self-discipline or, if necessary, through punitive policing. Environmental sustainability has also been identified as an aspect of this policy vision both because it makes cities more attractive to the knowledge workers and managerial strata they wish to retain or bring in, and because it is likely to underpin continued growth, enabling cities to move into a virtuous circle of self-sustaining growth (see, e.g., the report prepared by Hall and Pfeiffer 2000 for a Global Conference on the Urban Future, sponsored by a network of national governments from global north and south).

It sometimes appears as if these ways of thinking about urban development and urban policy have simply emerged from a more or less organic process of reflection and the exchange of ideas between those working in the field – that the rise of a neoliberal sensibility is a more or less natural process. Work on tracing the ways in which transnational policy learning has taken place through complex lattices of interaction is important and revealing, however, in highlighting the ways in which urban policy is actively assembled (see, e.g., McCann and Ward forthcoming). It is actively constructed by a range of actors and Jennifer Robinson helpfully suggests that urban policy is "developed through the loose and relatively unpredictable networks of political influence, policy circulation, and financial enticement" (Robinson forthcoming). Here I want briefly to focus on just one aspect of this by considering the role of some agencies that have a strong claim to having helped to produce a globalized urban policy, recognizing the unpredictability of the process, but also setting out to explore some of the ways in which attempts have been made to assemble rather more coherent frameworks within which others may be expected to operate. This is not a straightforward hierarchical process, but one in which the supposedly local is made up of actors from a range of levels, including apparently global ones (see Allen and Cochrane 2010 for a discussion of similar relationships in the regional context).

Polycentric Urbanism and the European Union

The case of the European Union highlights some of the uncertainties of the process, but also indicates some of the ways in which urban policy may be fostered across levels of government. Formally the European Commission has not been given any specific competency for urban policy by the European Union's member states. But a range of policies is explicitly oriented towards cities and incorporates a set of understandings about urban policy and what it might be expected to achieve. From the late 1990s it is possible to identify a more or less distinctive approach to urban policy and urban development in a cluster of documents, strategies, and conferences associated with various EU institutions (see, e.g., among many others, CEC 1997, 1998, 2007, 2008; Committee on Spatial Development 1999; European Commission 2003). Rob Atkinson has described this as a process by which an "urban agenda," if not yet a fully fledged "urban policy," has been developed for the EU (Atkinson 2001).

The emphasis is placed on the need to support economic prosperity and generate employment in urban areas, but also to promote social cohesion through improving the urban environment and contributing to good urban governance. According to one of these reports (and similar statements could be drawn from all of them),

"Cities and metropolitan areas are the engines of Europe's economic development. They are also the frontline in the battle against obstacles to growth and employment – especially social exclusion and environmental degradation" (CEC 2008: 3). The key policy challenges are identified as finding ways of reinforcing the competitiveness of cities, of challenging social exclusion and building community capacity, and of achieving physical and environmental regeneration (European Commission 2003: 6 and 26). Meanwhile the European Spatial Development Perspective (agreed at a meeting of ministers responsible for planning, but with no formal authority) explicitly sets out a polycentric vision of Europe's urban system, seeking to resist concentration in global cities and aiming to encourage more balanced growth (Committee on Spatial Development 1999).

Here urban policy retains an explicit economic cast, which is consistent with the more explicit neoliberal formulations discussed above, but in this case social policy intervention is justified as delivering broader economic, that is competitive, benefits. In other words, old models of welfare are more or less explicitly inverted, so that urban policy has the task of providing the social infrastructure required to sustain the competitiveness of business. It is possible to be skeptical about the various ambitions set out in these documents, and the extent to which they are consistent with each other, but the policy drive is clear enough.

So, for example, an urban dimension of the European Regional Development Fund has increasingly been emphasized (see, for example, CEC 2008) and the URBAN program (whose second phase came to an end in 2006) was directly targeted on urban areas. Here the aim was not so much to deliver major EU-funded projects, but, rather, to look for ways of generating "innovative" models for economic social and economic regeneration. The URBAN projects were supposed to foster new ways of participative involvement by communities, as well as partnerships between agencies from public, voluntary, and private sectors (including different levels of government as well as the European Commission). Partnership and the sharing of good practice are described as "the URBAN method" (European Commission 2003: 16).

The emphasis of the Commission on partnership initiatives at local and regional levels (since it has no agencies capable of direct involvement) has reinforced the spread of partnership approaches within urban policy (see, e.g., Geddes 2000 for a discussion of EU-based social exclusion policies and the rise of local partnerships). At the same time initiatives such as the Urban Audit and the State of European Cities Report that arose from it (CEC 2007) present data about cities across Europe in ways that are intended to encourage national and local policy-makers to learn from the experience of others and to locate themselves within a wider set of European networks and hierarchies. In other words, they are intended to encourage self-activity at local level through an engagement with professional networks (see, e.g., the response of Manninen 2008) as well as wider networks such as Eurocities.

The recognition that the EU cannot take a lead role in the direct delivery of urban policy across the member states is reflected in the emphasis placed on finding ways of sharing best practice of regeneration and sustainable development (CEC 2002; European Commission 2003). Urban policy (or an "urban agenda") has, in other words, been developed through a variety of "soft" means, rather than any attempt to implement a top-down program of action. However, that does not mean it has been ineffective. So, for example, even the EU sponsored selection of European Capital of Culture (which has no direct funding implications) can be seen to have added "fuel to culture city competition, whilst at the same time celebrating an official version of the European urban renaissance" (Evans 2003: 426). The example of the European Union and the European Commission is, of course, a particular one, but some of the issues it highlights – above all the way in which approaches to urban development and urban policy are promoted through a range of initiatives, but without the expectation that the EC will actually be the delivery agent – highlight the extent to which similar methods are used by other agencies in different contexts. In the next section the focus of this chapter shifts to consider some of the ways in which the new conventional wisdom has been translated into policies of "slum up-grading" in the cities of the global south.

Slum Upgrading and the World Bank

Traditionally, those living in urban slums have been identified in academic and policy literatures as problem people, that is, people who need to change their behavior if any positive development is to take place (see, e.g., Mooney 2008). They are said to be trapped in a "culture of poverty" (Lewis 1975). While Mike Davis (2006) has a very different starting point, his conclusions are similarly bleak, since he emphasizes the extent to which the informal workers of the slums are overwhelmingly focused on finding ways of daily survival. He quotes a report prepared by the United Nations Centre for Human Settlements (UN-HABITAT), which suggests that "instead of becoming a focus for growth and prosperity, the cities have become a dumping ground for a surplus population working in unskilled, unprotected and low wage informal service industries and trade" (UN-HABITAT 2003: 46).

All this sits uneasily with the wider belief that cities are key drivers of growth and development. The World Bank explicitly questions the European Union's commitment to polycentric growth, by contrast placing great stress on the perceived benefits of uneven development and economic concentration in big cities (World Bank 2008: 39). Even within the same broad competiveness paradigm, in other words, it is possible to have a different emphasis. The World Bank has, at least since the early 1970s (see, e.g., World Bank 1991) emphasized the role that cities can play in driving wider development. The Bank's urban strategy focuses on cities as propulsive agents in delivering national growth, and the purpose of the strategy is identified as being to ensure "that countries extract the most benefit from urbanization" (World Bank Infrastructure Group Urban Development 2000: 6). The general (universal, transhistorical) rule is stated simply: "As countries become richer, economic activity becomes more densely packed into towns, cities, and metropolises" (World Bank 2008: 48).

In the Bank's developmentalist approach (at least as expressed in its *World Development Report 2009*), it is argued the slums of the global south are simply a repeat of what happened in the industrializing cities of the global north in the nineteenth century (World Bank 2008: 68–71). For "world" cities such as London, New York, Paris, Singapore, and Tokyo, we are told, "slums can, with the benefit of hindsight, be viewed as part of their 'growing pains'" (World Bank 2008: 68). The "problem" of the slums is explained as one of "dysfunctional land markets" so that as the market adjusts the problem will disappear (World Bank 2008: 68). So, "the correct response ... is to tackle dysfunctional land markets ... inefficient land markets, often thanks to misguided urban planning and zoning, produce only a limited and unresponsive supply of affordable, legal land sites for building housing to keep pace with the demand" (World Bank 2008: 69).

But the reinterpretation of the slums has gone beyond this, with some (whose work has been widely taken up through the networks sponsored by the World Bank) suggesting that they are spaces within which "the entrepreneurial ingenuity of the poor has created wealth on a large scale" (de Soto 2006: 32). The shift in understanding implied by this approach is hard to overstate: slum-dwellers are no longer understood as passive victims, but as active agents who are also responsible for managing their own lives. Instead of identifying the survival strategies of the poor as necessarily condemning them to a culture of poverty, they are seen to provide evidence that poor people can be major sources of energy and vitality, potential drivers of development, rather than brakes on it.

In its *World Development Report 2009*, the World Bank notes that "slum dwellers in developing countries are often productively taking advantage of the economic opportunities the city offers" suggesting that "slums arise in many developing countries as low-income households take advantage of spatially concentrated employment opportunities and as businesses take advantage of their location in a land-constrained environment" (World Bank 2008: 68–9). The accuracy of this analysis may be questionable (see Davis 2006 for a critique) but it is being translated into the practices of urban policy.

In policy terms these understandings found an expression in the formation of the Cities Alliance in 1999 which brought together the World Bank and UN-HABITAT in a "multidonor partnership," with an emphasis on supporting the development of city development strategies (discussed by Robinson forthcoming) and "scaled up programs for the poor" (or slum-upgrading). Plans for developing "slum upgrading" strategies were launched in 1999 and endorsed at the UN Millennium Summit in 2000. These approaches identified "wellsprings of entrepreneurial energy" within the slums while recognizing that, "their brutal physical conditions limit residents' ability to realize welfare improvements from their own efforts alone" (Cities Alliance 1999: 2). "Slums," it has been suggested (in the same report quoted by Davis and referred to above), "can be divided into two broad categories: slums of hope; and slums of despair" (UN-HABITAT 2003: 9) and it is the identification and fostering of the former that is the task of policy. In this particular reinterpretation and reworking of the new conventional wisdom, with its stress on self-help and local entrepreneurialism, the poor both become more active players in determining their own lives and are somehow expected to take on greater responsibility for doing so.

It is, of course, dangerous to suggest that there has been any straightforward translation from these broad shifts in the policy approaches of global agencies and the detailed practices of urban policy in particular places. But, as in the case of the European Union and with more direct leverage through project funding of one sort or another, the "soft" approach represented by the big reports (like the *World Development Report*) and the boxed case studies of best practice sponsored through the Cities Alliance (see, e.g., also Mitlin and Satterthwaite 2004, which presents a series of case studies highlighting the potential of local initiatives to begin to challenge forms of urban poverty), are important in helping to frame the context for policy development.

Conclusion

Jennifer Robinson emphasizes the need to pay "attention to the range of sites and the diversity of tracks which compose a globalized field of urban development knowledge. This includes the dense associations represented by agencies and donor groupings, or by the networks of consultants and theorists as well as the city-specific, territorialized, agents involved in policy circulation" (Robinson forthcoming). Here I have just tried to explore one set of agencies that might be involved in this process. What is clear is that this is no process of top-down imposition, but one in which the global institutions play a significant part, not above the fray, but actively involved in it; neither handing down policy from above, nor simply leaving it to others to develop their own initiatives.

It is also clear that there is no single agenda shared by the global agencies themselves. Within a broad competitiveness paradigm, the EC's stress on polycentric and balanced urbanism contrasts significantly with the World Bank's emphasis on concentration and its celebration of uneven development as a driver of development. This is a battle of ideas as the global agencies seek to set agendas, to create conventional wisdoms of one sort or another. But is not just a debate between those agencies. Urban policy cannot just be taken for granted as an organic outcome of some shared understanding of the problem. A limited set of visions may currently be available and widely circulated, but this merely confirms the need to develop alternatives.

References

Allen, C. (2007) *Housing Market Renewal and Social Class*. Abingdon: Routledge.

Allen, J., and Cochrane, A. (2010) Assemblages of state power: topological shifts in the organization of government and authority. *Antipode* 42 (5): 1071–89.

Atkinson, R. (2001) The emerging "urban agenda" and the European Spatial Development Perspective: towards an EU urban policy. *European Planning Studies* 9 (3): 385–406.

Baeten, G. (2009) Regenerating the South Bank: reworking community and the emergence of post-political regeneration. In *Regenerating London. Governance, Sustainability and Community in a Global City*, ed. R. Imrie, L. Lees, and M. Raco. Abingdon: Routledge, 237–53.

Barnekov, T., Boyle, R., and Rich, D. (1989) *Privatism and Urban Policy in Britain and the United States*. Oxford: Oxford University Press.

Buck, N., Gordon, I., Harding, A., and Turok, I. (eds.) (2005) *Changing Cities. Rethinking Urban Competitiveness, Cohesion and Governance*. Basingstoke: Palgrave Macmillan.

CEC (1997) *Towards an Urban Agenda in the European Union*. Communication from the Commission. Brussels: Commission of the European Communities.

CEC (1998). *Sustainable Urban Development in the European Union: A Framework for Action*. Brussels: Commission of the European Communities.

CEC (2002) *The Programming of the Structural Funds 2000–2006: An Initial Assessment of the Urban Initiative*. Brussels: Commission of the European Communities.

CEC (2007) *State of European Cities Report. Adding Value to the Urban Audit*. Brussels: Commission of the European Communities, Directorate-General Regional Policy.

CEC (2008) *Fostering the Urban Dimension. Analysis of the Operational Programmes co-financed by the European Regional Development Fund (2007–2013)*. Brussels: Commission of the European Communities, Directorate-General Regional Policy.

Cities Alliance (1999) *Cities Without Slums. Action Plan for Moving Slum Upgrading to Scale*. Washington, DC: The World Bank/UNCS (HABITAT).

Cochrane, A. (2007) *Understanding Urban Policy. A Critical Approach*. Oxford: Blackwell.

Committee on Spatial Development (1999) *ESDP. European Spatial Development Perspective. Towards Balanced and Sustainable Development of the European Union*. Luxembourg: Office for the Official Publications of the European Communities.

Davis, M. (2006) *Planet of Slums*. London: Verso.

Deacon, R., with Hulse, M., and Stubbs, P. (1997) *Global Social Policy. International Organizations and the Future of Welfare*. London: Sage.

de Soto, H. (2006) *The Mystery of Capital. Why Capitalism Triumphs in the West and Fails Everywhere Else*. London: Black Swan.

Dikec, M. (2009) *Badlands of the Republic. Space, Politics and Urban Policy*. Oxford: Blackwell.

European Commission (2003) *Partnership with the Cities: the URBAN Community Initiative*. Luxembourg: Office for the Official Publications of the European Communities.

Evans, G. (2003) Hard branding the cultural city – from Prado to Prada. *International Journal of Urban and Regional Research* 27 (2): 417–40.

Geddes, M. (2000) Tackling social exclusion in the European Union? The limits to the new orthodoxy of local partnership. *International Journal of Urban and Regional Research* 24 (4): 782–800.

Hall, P., and Pfeiffer, U. (2000) *Urban Future 21: A Global Agenda for Twenty-First-Century Cities*. London: Spon.

Harvey, D. (2002) *Spaces of Hope*. Edinburgh: Edinburgh University Press.

Haylett, C. (2003) Culture, class and urban policy: reconsidering equality. *Antipode* 35 (1): 55–73.

Lees, L. (ed.) (2004) *The Emancipatory City? Paradoxes and Possibilities*. London: Sage.

Lefebvre, H. (1996) *Writings on Cities*. Trans. and ed. E. Kofman and E. Lebas. Oxford: Blackwell.

Lewis, O. (1975) *Five Families. Mexican Case Studies in the Culture of Poverty*. New York: Basic Books.

Manninen, A. (2008) Monitoring urban change and identifying future potentials: the case of the European Urban Audit and the State of European Cities Report. *Urban Research and Practice* 1 (3): 222–9.

McCann, E. (2008) Expertise, truth, and urban policy mobilities: global circuits of knowledge in the development of Vancouver, Canada's "four pillar" drug strategy. *Environment and Planning A* 40 (4): 885–904.

McCann, E., and Ward, K. (eds.) (forthcoming) *Mobile Urbanism: Cities and Policymaking in the Global Age*. Minneapolis: University of Minnesota Press.

Mitlin, D., and Satterthwaite, D. (eds.) (2004) *Empowering Squatter Citizen. Local Government, Civil Society and Urban Poverty Reduction*. London: Earthscan.

Mooney, G. (2008) "Problem" populations, "problem" places. In *Social Justice: Welfare, Crime and Society*, ed. J. Newman and N. Yeates. Maidenhead: Open University Press, 97–128.

OECD (2003) *Urban Renaissance: Glasgow. Lessons for Innovation and Implementation.* Paris: Organisation for Economic Co-operation and Development.

Peck, J. (2002) Political economies of scale: fast policy, interscalar relations, and neoliberal workfare. *Economic Geography* 78: 331–61.

Robinson, J. (forthcoming) Mobility and differentiation in international urban policy: the case of city development strategies. In *Mobile Urbanism: Cities and Policymaking in the Global Age*, ed. E. McCann and K. Ward. Minneapolis: University of Minnesota Press.

Swyngedouw, E. (2007) Impossible "sustainability" and the post-political condition. In *The Sustainable Development Paradox: Urban Political Ecology in the US and Europe*, ed. R. Krueger and D. Gibbs. New York: Guilford Press, 13–40.

UN-HABITAT (2003) *The Challenge of the Slums: Global Report on Human Settlements* London: Earthscan.

Wacquant, L. (2007) *Urban Outcasts. A Comparative Sociology of Advanced Marginality.* Cambridge: Polity Press.

Ward, K. (2006) "Policies in motion," urban management and state restructuring: the translocal expansion of Business Improvement Districts. *International Journal of Urban and Regional Research* 30 (1): 54–75.

World Bank (1991) *Urban Policy and Economic Development. An Agenda for the 1990s.* A World Bank Policy Paper. Washington, DC: The World Bank.

World Bank (2008) *World Development Report 2009. Reshaping Economic Geography.* Washington, DC: World Bank.

World Bank Infrastructure Group Urban Development (2000) *Cities in Transition. World Bank Urban and Local Government Strategy.* Washington, DC: The World Bank.

Chapter 65

Urban Governance in Europe: What Is Governed?

Patrick Le Galès

The urban government/governance debate has proved quite fruitful in contributing to the understanding of the transformation of cities. By contrast to classic views about local government, scholars from various origins have tried to understand the political capacity of groups within cities to steer, pilot, change the urban society, to adapt to outside pressure, to be transformed by new state policies or by market competition logics.

In the European context, the urban governance/urban regime debate was particularly useful in understanding new modes of governance (John 2001) (through democratic participation or networks) and to contrast different explanatory models of transformation. Opposition between urban governance models based upon transformation of the state in relation to new demands of globalized capitalism (Brenner 2004) and those based upon the lesser constraint of the state allowing some cities to develop collective actor strategies in the logic of the Weberian European city has been drawn and sometimes exaggerated (Bagnasco and Le Galès 2000; Kazepov 2005; Giersig 2008).

Classically, the literature on urban governance (or urban regimes or urban growth coalitions) aimed at pointing towards various mechanisms to create collective capacity to go beyond market and state failures (Stone 1989; Logan and Molotch 1987). Political scientists working on urban governance have rightly emphasized government/governance as capacity to change urban society on the one hand, and to raise democratic issues and the participation of inhabitants on the other (Heinelt and Kübler 2005; Denters and Rose 2005). This has proved particularly relevant to the case of European cities which were originally mostly cities that represented points of articulation between trade, culture, and a form of political autonomy.

The New Blackwell Companion to the City   Edited by Gary Bridge and Sophie Watson
© 2011 Blackwell Publishing Ltd

However, as Jessop suggested, and beyond the rhetoric of governance used by political actors, there was no reason to believe that governance failures would not be as spectacular as government failures (Jessop 2004). In other words, governance and government are not linear, and if analyzed as process are always incomplete. Urban societies are more or less governed over different periods. Studying the limits and discontinuities of government and governance is therefore particularly interesting for urban scholars, a classic way of thinking for scholars working on the large metropolis. In this chapter governance is defined as a process of coordinating actors, social groups, and institutions to attain particular goals, discussed and defined collectively in fragmented, uncertain environments (Le Galès 1998). Thus, governance relates to all the institutions, networks, directives, regulations, norms, political and social usages, and public and private actors that contribute to the stability of a society and of a political regime, to its orientation, to its capacity to direct, and to its capacity to provide services and ensure its own legitimacy. In other words, this conceptualization based upon regulation is useful to answer the question "Who governs when nobody governs?" In other words, the point has been made that governments do not govern all the time. On the other hand, there is rarely no government at all, more or less strong, precise, codified, forms of government. Some sectors of the city can classically be organized and steered according to market logics and actors who may, or may not be dependent upon government resources to develop their project. But market regulations can be combined with other types of regulation.

This chapter reviews arguments about the governance of European cities and then suggests new avenues for urban governance research.

Government of European Cities

The argument of the modes of governance of European cities has been developed to make sense of the remaining strength and collective capacities of European medium-size cities. It started from the limits of urban governments in order to make sense of what was observed in a number of cities.

Urban governments are classically defined, first, as political arenas and instruments for enhancing democracy and participation and steering local societies and, second, in terms of service provision and public policy. Urban governments are usually related to the nation state in terms of democratization and legitimation of forms of territorial management.

European cities are back on the political agenda of Europe, not as the old medieval cities, but as more autonomous political authorities within a European governance in the making. They make a fairly general category of urban space, relatively original forms of compromise, and aggregation of interest and culture which bring together local social groups, associations, organized interests, private firms, and urban governments. However, the pressures created by property developers, major groups in the urban services sector, and cultural and economic globalization processes, provoke reactions and adaptation processes of actors within European cities.

The modernized myth of the European city remains a very strongly mobilized resource, and is strengthened by growing political autonomy and transverse mobilizations. It is based on the medieval autonomous cities of the Middle Ages analyzed by Max Weber. Urban governments played a key role in providing basic utilities and services such as water, sewage, street lighting, later gas and electricity, fire services, and transport not to mention the slaughterhouse. Urban government pioneered policy programs in housing, planning, basic elements of welfare, and education. This development was diverse, fragmented, and contested between a conservative petty bourgeoisie and the municipal socialism movement, and more consistent in the north of Europe than in the south. Most local government in Europe gained legal recognition in the second part of the nineteenth century. Gradually, a professional local bureaucracy emerged to deal with those developments. The rise of urban government was not just a local or national phenomenon. Exchanges of experiences of ideas, for instance in planning and social housing, were crucial.

Urban governments were understood either as a functional entity to deliver services, in particular welfare services (hence the long lasting debate on size and amalgamation) or as a political unit. In their classic comparative research, Goldsmith and Page (1987) have suggested that local government autonomy in Europe should be analyzed in terms of autonomy through two major criteria which encompass or are closely related to other dimensions: legal status and political status. That analysis clearly stressed the differences between the welfarist northern European urban governments and the more political (sometimes clientelistic) southern European urban governments.

Urban governments were contested in the 1970s and 1980s by urban social movements. The bureaucratization, hierarchies, urban regeneration projects, and complex and fragmented decision-making processes of urban government were attacked in cities all over Europe. Conflicts entered the realm of urban politics in relation to housing, planning, large infrastructure projects, economic crisis, and cultural issues. New groups, beyond class basis, organized to raise new issues (quality of life, democracy and participation, economic development, and culture) and to promote urban change against elected urban leaders. New middle classes were gradually incorporated within political parties (social democratic and green) and played an important role in many European cities to promote a new set of urban policies to deal with those issues. In the most radical cases, squatters in Amsterdam or Berlin for instance, urban government officials have learned to cooperate, to provide sources of funding, and to incorporate those groups in more loosely defined structures of governance. Preventing large social conflicts and including various groups have become the norm for urban governments. Urban governments in Europe were also facing political pressure related both to the restructuring of the state and to questions about representative democracy and changes of political culture (Hoffman-Martinot and Sellers 2005).

These movements, and changing patterns of governing elites, led both to structural changes and experiences in urban governments all over Europe. Beyond the UK, market friendly ideas associated to "new public management" are having an impact in urban government, in particular in the north of Europe. Issues of citizen participation in urban governments were associated with growing issues of management efficiency in the delivery of services to customers. The restructuring of the public sector led to increased confusion in public policies and the fragmentation of urban governments (Pierre 1999), hence the growing interests for issues of leadership, management, coordination, and governance (Borraz and John 2004). The fragmentation of urban government was also accelerated by the large privatization movement in infrastructures.

European cities are not immune nowadays to common pressures in terms of immigration, rising inequalities, suburban sprawl, and network fragmentation. However, European cities remain strong within metropolitan areas in the making; governance issues are now more visible within European cities, as are interdependence and interrelation between different actors and organizations – all things that used to be represented and made visible on the national and European scene. This new-found visibility of interdependence gives opportunities to social and political actors to be involved in modes of urban governance or, by contrast, to increase the fragmentation and dislocation of European cities. European cities have not been dislocated and they have considerable resources, including strong urban governments, which they can draw on in adapting to or resisting the new frame of constraints and opportunities.

Every city is characterized first and foremost by structural conditions that relate to the market, to the state, or to civil society, as well as by a culture and an identity that are more or less established and congruent. To avoid the stumbling-block of fetishizing the local requires, for example, consideration of the situation of each city in relation to the market and to conditions of economic development, which will vary according to period (Harding 1997). Modes of governance of European cities can vary along four dimensions: (1) variables in the structure of local society; (2) political orientation; (3) the institutionalization of collective action; and (4) results or outcomes.

What Is Governed?

Governments govern of course, like workers work, but what exactly? Classical thinking about the government meant looking at either the formal apparatus of government, the institutions, or at the general functions and activities. Governments are defined in terms of rules of the game, constitutions, organizations, and actors, processes of aggregation and segregation, and outputs (Leca 1996). The governance debate started from the limits of government. This debate has led to a dynamic governance research domain, beyond the "who governs?" question, organized around the following questions: Can government govern, steer or row (Peters 1997)? Could cities be considered as collective actors with governance capacities (Pichierri 1997; Le Galès 2002)? Do governments always govern? What do they govern, and how? What is not governed (Crosta 1998)? Can we identify dysfunctions of governments over time? Can groups or sectors escape from governments (Mayntz 1993)? Who governs when governments do not govern? Can governance replace government or will governance failure replace government failures (Jessop 2004)? How does government or governance operate (Lascoumes and Le Galès 2007)? What does it mean to govern complex urban societies and networks of cities (Pierre and Peters 2005; Perulli 2000)? Do utilities networks govern large cities (Le Galès and Lorrain 2004)? What sort of framework is constructed through governance (Bevir 2010)?

James Scott's famous *Seeing Like a State* (1999) underlined the role of planning and the creation of street maps as examples of rational modern government aiming at making society, including the urban society, "legible" so that it could be governed. Tax could be raised and men mobilized for war. Some activities of government take place routinely. However, most government activities are not continuous (Favre 2003: 165). What is governed is a key question. That may change over time. In period of war, governments increase their control on a range of activities and sectors. There is a massive increase of public policies, tax, and control. By contrast, when times are more peaceful and security threats are not on the radar, when there is no massive economic crisis or threat to social and political order (secessionist movements, waves of riots) governmental activities may be far less important. Similarly, some sectors, some domains, are heavily governed with dense public policies and laws. By contrast some sectors are not governed at all or weakly governed. As became obvious in the recent period, loans for housing and sub-primes were weakly governed and regulated. As is well known, many groups and individuals in societies spend considerable time and energy in avoiding being governed, hence a famous question on the ungovernability of societies (Mayntz 1993). It is also worth mentioning that regulation is only one part of government. In some cases, regulation may not mean much more than setting the rules of the game for the actors without giving a direction, without the steering element.

In urban terms, this question is particularly interesting. What part, sectors or groups of the city are really governed? What is weakly governed? What is left out? What is escaping government? Historically, the rise of urban governments was about the institutionalization of governments against illegal activities, slums, mobile populations, rejected poor neighborhoods. Analyzing a city requires not just focusing on governments but also on the understanding of the illegal side of the city, the invisible activities, from undocumented immigrants in clandestine rooms to gangs controlling drug traffic or private developers illegally financing political activities in order to build new developments. This is not just some dark side of the city which will disappear on the road to rational progress but an irreducible part of any city.

In her book *Ordinary Cities* (2005), Robinson calls for more systematic comparison of cities from the north and the south. Governance could well travel in those terms, as suggested by McCartney and Stren in particular (2003). In his wonderful book on "the city yet to come," Simone's characterization of African cities as "work in progress" (2004: 1) is a good reminder that what is not governed in a classic governmental rational way may be more central to understand what works in a city. Following Robinson's suggestion, the governance of European cities should also be understood in relation to what is illegal, what is clientelism, what is not governed. This may take different forms from illegal activities to suburbanization and the limits of metropolitan governments and governance.

However, who is governed in the city? Government or governance is a two-way process. Whatever government processes may be depends a lot upon the population which is governed. Governing a large city is a difficult task because the population is so fluid and diverse.

Urban riots now take place regularly. Reports after the riots usually signal the failures of local schools and of social services, discrimination against young people from immigrant background on the labor market, isolation of some ethnic groups, police violence, the rise of illegal trafficking, and the absence of legality in some neighborhoods. In other words, some sections of European cities are not really governed. Some inner cities and some outer city developments are not completely left out but many have weak infrastructures and public services support. Drug trafficking and informal markets are also part of the urban life. In some neighborhoods, the police are not welcome and only intervene when problems emerge and then with significant numbers of police. Waves of riots in the UK, France, and sometimes Germany, the Netherlands, and Italy, point to the development of parallel lives between immigrants and their children and the rest of the population. Analysis points to discrimination, intense segregation in some cities, and the lack of policies to integrate some of those groups (Garbaye 2010; Lagrange and Oberti 2006; Waddington *et al.* 2009).

Are those neighborhoods governed? More or less, it depends. In France or Britain, the making of large outer-city social housing schemes in the 1960s was not matched by services to the population. In French poor suburbs where some estates concentrate the poorest populations and recent immigrants, local authorities did not have resources, social services, police, or schools and transport systems were very weak. Those places were not governed, or only weakly governed. The development of public policies to integrate and incorporate different groups leads to some success and many failures – governance failures. In most cities, the question of how to provide services to those populations, how to include them in the democratic debate, how to help children to do well, but also how to control these groups and neighborhoods, how to make the law respected, is very high on the agenda. In the American case, Jones-Correa and his colleagues show the challenge of ethnic diversity in *Governing American Cities* (2001). Similar challenges are very much at stake in European cities and there are numerous cases of problems and lack of governance capacity in relation to ethnic groups in particular.

The "who is governed question?" can also be linked to questions of mobility. In his seminal contribution, Martinotti (1993) identified different groups of city users beyond the classic groups of those who work and live in the same place, a minority in most cities. By contrast he pointed not only towards the classic regular suburbanite working in the city center but also the rise of occasional "city users," visitors, with different levels of professional constraints or levels of segregation at a different scale. A wide literature has developed on "cities and visitors" (Hoffmann *et al.* 2003). The literature on immigration (Favell and Smith 2006) has also pointed to the development of transnational networks and the mobility of groups between two places. Who governs transnational networks of retired Moroccan, Pakistani, Senegalese, or Turkish pensioners who spend half the year in the home country where they build a house and half a year in a host country where the children have organized their life? John Urry's "sociology of mobility" (2000) points to the end of a form of a "garden state," when people travel or become more mobile. Census agents have more problems with those students, families, or often pensioners, traveling, or organizing their life in two different places for a number of years or immigrating for a number of years. Who governs mobile populations? This raises numbers of questions about the provision of services, about tax avoidance, about school populations, or the provision of housing. As Scott and Foucault argued, the rise of modern governments was related to the development of new technologies of government to make society "legible." One could argue that increased mobility of different sorts make urban society less legible and therefore far more difficult to govern.

Regulating is not governing. However, the economic sociology of regulation is helpful to understand regulations. In analytical terms, cities are more or less organized around markets or governments, in more or less conflictual or combined ways. Regulations can be seen as mechanisms of governance and defined on the basis of three dimensions: (1) the mode of co-ordinating diverse activities or relationships among actors; (2) the allocation of resources in relation to these activities or these actors; and (3) the structuring of conflicts (prevented or resolved). Consequently, the word "regulation" can be used, for example, when highlighting relatively stabilized relationships between actors or social groups, relationships which allow the distribution of resources according to explicit or implicit norms and rules (Lange and Regini 1989). Three ideal types are usually defined. The first is state regulation (frequently identified with hierarchical or political regulation), where the state structures conflicts, distributes resources, and coordinates activities and groups. This type of regulation implies domination and control as well as the capacity to sanction. This description can also fit certain large, hierarchized organizations where authority is the principal moving force, even if only informally. The second is market regulation. Since the emergence of capitalism, this type of regulation has played a growing role in organizing exchanges between supply and demand, adjusted through prices (or sometimes through volume). The third is cooperative/reciprocal regulation (sometimes called regulation through social or political exchange) based on values and norms, on a single identity, and on the trust that expresses forms of exchange and/or solidarity between the members of a community, a clan, a family, or a district (Crouch *et al.* 2001).

The three types of regulation are mixed in the governance of cities. Governments never completely govern a city because they have to deal with market forces (private developers in urban growth coalitions), and with religious groups, familial interest, social movements, or non-governmental organizations.

A classic form of regulation in the third category (exchange reciprocity) is clientelism, patronage, corruption. An underdeveloped research agenda has in particular suggested to take seriously cooperation/reciprocity regulation beyond the "enchanted" view of governance through traditional regulation. Patronage is defined as: "the complex social arrangements known as patron–clients relations denote, in their fullest expression, a distinct mode of regulating crucial aspects of institutional order: the structuring of the flow of resources, exchange and power relations and their legitimation in society" (Eisenstadt and Roniger 1984: 209). Corruption is classically defined as a system of exchange whereby public officials obtain financial resources in exchange for decisions. The "community" or "cooperative/reciprocal" regulation is also a broad church where one can at least distinguish between the logic of reciprocity and the logic of social/political exchange. As far as urban politics is concerned, the latter is more relevant. There is a long tradition of research to examine patronage and corruption as one type of social or political regulation in anthropology in particular, and later in sociology and political science, particularly taking into account the bureaucracy or factions in urban political machines. In urban politics, classics include, in the US, Banfield and Wilson, *City Politics* (1963) or Percy Allum's monograph on Naples (Allum 1973). In the last two decades in many European cities, some forms of patronage, clientelism, or corruption have been identified for instance with the *mani pulite* operation in Italy seeing the demise of the socialist domination of Milan; in Paris several leaders of the Chirac post-Gaullist party were condemned by the courts; and also in the northeast of England or in Liège in Belgium. In other words, part of the city is regulated according to non-classic governmental principles but with the participation of governmental actors.

Who governs when nobody governs? Corrupt elite networks sometimes do. Illegal organizations are also a classic case where they can "run," organize, possibly govern, some sectors, some neighborhoods, some part of the city. The case of the Camorra in Naples has become a classic, but more limited examples could be found in different settings.

Finally, urban governance, and most public policies, are part of the world of overlapping powers within the global and regional (such as European) governance in the making: municipalities, metropolitan authorities, regions sometimes, federal states or autonomies, the nation state, the EU and sometimes the OECD urban group, the UN (Habitat Summit) with international rules comprising environmental norms, can all play a role in urban policies. There are endless cases of urban policies where the norm is now for the overlapping funding and influence of different levels of government, for better (i.e., more targeted and coordinated effort), or worse (more piecemeal fragmented actions). In most countries, the territorial organization of the nation state has been facing serious reshaping, an ongoing process which leads to the pluralization of territorial interests within the state. Associations, voluntary sector organizations, from neighborhood groups to giant utility firms, have a say and some power in urban policies. Urban policy therefore covers a wide range of actors from different sectors of societies, with different status, acting at different levels. Emerging problems raise questions which cross horizontally over bureaucracies and sectors, and vertically over different levels of government. In that world, one wonders if governance is more than the aggregation of various incremental choices, and random developments.

Territories of Urban Governance: Uncertain Metropolitan Governments

What is governed and what is not governed should also be considered in relation to local government boundaries. The city is proving more elusive, populations more diverse, but governments are being rescaled and new modes of governance are being structured.

The classic European city, contained within city walls, has disappeared a long time ago. Although the city in a classical sense has remained relatively robust, suburbanization has also developed all over eastern and western European cities. In territorial terms, what is governed is everything but an obvious question. This is a classic theme in the urban literature. Those writing on megacities, gigacities, or the rise of global urban regions (Scott 2001), point to the rise of networks and governance failures related to obsolete governmental boundaries. Another way to think along the same lines relates to the idea of the end of cities and the triumph of urban sprawl, in other words the suburbanization of cities and the urbanization of suburbs (Dear 2000). In that line of analysis, the dissolution of the city is taking place within a large fragmented, chaotic, unstable urban world which is not governed. Is the urban world becoming ungovernable? A classic argument dismisses this view because the relatively stable core of Europe's urban system is made up of medium-sized and reasonably large cities, which are fairly close to one another, and a few metropolises. The importance of regional capital cities, of medium-sized cities (200,000 to two million inhabitants), remains a major feature of contemporary European societies (Le Galès 2002). However, there is also serious suburbanization (Phelps *et al.* 2006) based upon the departure of population from both the city and the metropolitan area because of deindustrialization, for instance, and the rise of the metropolitan area (in the case of London and Paris for instance, or Brussels, Milan, Marseille, or Lisbon). Increasing urban concentration has been accompanied by apparently inescapable, unlimited dispersal into conurbations and urban regions with fluctuating outlines. Cities have expanded, fragmented, and sometimes organized into networks like those in northern Italy or the Netherlands, and this is said to be rendering traditional urban governments obsolete. Europe is made of few declining cities, many dynamic medium-size and large cities, and two dynamic large global cities, whatever that means. European cities make a fairly general category of urban space, relatively original forms of compromise, aggregation of interest and culture, which bring together local social groups, associations, organized interests, private firms, and urban governments. The pressures created by property developers, major groups in the urban services sector, and cultural and economic globalization processes, provoke reactions and adaptation processes of actors within European cities, defending the idea of a fairly particular type of city that is not yet in terminal decline. The modernized myth of the European city remains a very strongly mobilized resource, and is strengthened by growing political autonomy and transverse mobilizations.

Despite sprawling movements in most European cities, the resistance of the old city centers epitomizes their peculiarity. Lévy (1997) takes the example of large public collective transport (in particular the tramway) together with pedestrian areas and cycle paths to demonstrate the remaining strength of the idea of European city. There is a continuing representation of the city as a whole; Crouch (1999) suggests a "Durkheimian" view of the city which still exists in Europe. The increased legitimacy of political urban elites sustains and reinvents this presentation. European cities are still strongly regulated by public authorities and complex arrangements of public and private actors. European cities appear to be relatively robust, despite pressures from economic actors, individuals, and states (including welfare states) being reshaped within the European Union. Processes of exclusion, strengthening and transformation of inequalities, segregation, and domination are also unfolding in these cities. The development of residential suburbs separated from the city and of polycentric cities; the isolation of disadvantaged districts; the development of cultural complexes, leisure facilities, and shopping centers, as well as diverse cultural models and migrations, all clearly demonstrate the pressures exerted on the traditional medium-sized city. The urban regions of Milan and the Randstadt are good examples of more polycentric structures and interdependent dynamics between the city center and other cities.

These developments have led in most countries towards never-ending debates about the rescaling of metropolitan governments, the making and unmaking of metropolitan governments (Lefèvre 1998), and the developments of all sorts of collaborative forms of governance, including private–public partnership, charters, plans, contracts, or joined-up government.

In most places in Europe, the reorganization of urban governments has given salience to the particular status of (big) cities, now comprised in terms of metropolitan areas and often organized under state pressure (Brenner 2004). Firstly, in comparison with a century or 50 years ago, the larger European cities have more autonomy and much more vigorous local leadership (Borraz and John 2004). The major capital cities of Europe have only in the last years or decades had an elected unified government and mayor (Paris in 1977, London in 2001). Despite some resistance, a metropolitan government is being recreated in Britain, and slowly, in Italy. In France too, the restructuring of local government based on a mix of direct constraints and strong financial incentives is creating an original and powerful structure of inter-municipal urban government benefiting from strategic and public policy delivery powers together with important financial and human resources. Metropolitan government emerged in the Stockholm area in the 1970s and has developed in the other Nordic capital regions too. In Eastern Europe, reforms of local government in the 1990s led to a differentiated set of legal statuses, in particular for the capital. During the negotiations for these countries to join the EU, a particular emphasis was put on decentralization reforms supposed to undermine existing bureaucracies and to reinforcing the democratization of the political regimes. Within that decentralization trend, cities did particularly well in terms of new powers. In the Hungarian two-tier system, the capital has been granted a special legal status with specific powers given to the district government of Budapest and the urban mayors are directly elected. The same applies to the Czech Republic where the 2002 restructuring of local government applies a special status to Prague and to 19 statutory cities. In Poland too, 65 cities were given county status. Relatively high levels of devolution were also granted to Baltic state cities.

To conclude, there is a good deal of urban governance going on in European cities but not all the time, not for all groups, not for all neighborhoods, and not so much for the peripheries of the city. That feeds the rise of new policy instruments to increase governing capacity (Pinson 2009; Lascoumes and Le Galès 2007). Governance discontinuities should therefore be analyzed more systematically.

References

Allum, P. (1973) *Politics and Society in Post-War Naples*. Cambridge: Cambridge University Press.

Bagnasco, A., and Le Galès, P. (eds.) (2000) *Cities in Contemporary Europe*. Cambridge: Cambridge University Press.

Banfield, E. C., and Wilson, J. Q. (1963) *City Politics*. Cambridge, MA: Harvard University Press.

Bevir, M. (2010) Interpretive theory. In *The SAGE Handbook of Governance*, ed. M. Bevir. London: Sage.

Brenner, N. (2004) *New State Spaces: Urban Governance and the Rescaling of Statehood*. Oxford: Oxford University Press.

Borraz, O., and John, P. (2004) Symposium on the transformation of urban political leadership in Western Europe. *International Journal of Urban and Regional Research*: 11–26.

Crosta, P. L. (1998) *Politiche. Quale conoscenza per l'azione territoriale.* Milan: Franco Angeli.

Crouch, C. (1999) *Social Changes in Western Europe.* Oxford: Oxford University Press.

Crouch, C., Le Galès, P., Trigilia, C., and Voelzkow, H. (2001) *Local Industrial Systems in Europe, Rise or Demise?* Oxford: Oxford University Press.

Dear, M. (2000) *The Postmodern Urban Condition.* Oxford: Blackwell.

Denters, B., and Rose, L. (eds.) (2005) *Comparing Local Governance: Trends and Developments.* Basingstoke: Palgrave Macmillan.

Eisenstadt, N., and Roniger, L. (1984) *Patrons, Clients and Friends: Interpersonal Relations and the Structure of Trust in Society.* Cambridge: Cambridge University Press.

Favell, A., and Smith, P. (eds.) (2006) *The Human Face of Global Mobility: International Highly Skilled Migration in Europe, North America and the Asia-Pacific.* New Brunswick, NJ: Transaction Publishers.

Favre, P. (2003) *Comprendre le monde pour le changer. Epistémologie du politique.* Paris: Presses de Sciences Po.

Garbaye, R. (2010) *Emeutes urbaines et diversité ethnique en Grande-Bretagne.* Paris: Presses de Sciences Po.

Giersig, N. (2008) *Multilevel Urban Governance and the "European City": Discussing Metropolitan Reforms in Stockholm and Helsinki.* Wiesbaden: VS Verlag.

Goldsmith, M., and Page, E. (eds.) (1987) *Central Local Relations in Western Europe.* London: Sage.

Harding, A. (1997) Urban regimes in a Europe of cities? *European Urban and Regional Studies* 4 (4): 291–314.

Heinelt, H., and Kübler, D. (eds.) (2005) *Metropolitan Governance.* London: Routledge.

Hoffmann, L., Fainstein, S., and Judd, D. (eds.) (2003) *Cities and Visitors.* Oxford: Blackwell.

Hoffmann-Martinot, V., and Sellers, J. (eds.) (2005) *Metropolization and Political Change.* Wiesbaden: VS Verlag.

Jessop, B. (2004) Multilevel governance and multilevel meta-governance. In *Multilevel Governance*, ed. I. Bache and M. Flinders. Oxford: Oxford University Press, 49–75.

John, P. (2001) *Local Governance in Western Europe.* London: Sage.

Jones-Correa, M. (ed.) (2001) *Governing American Cities: Inter-Ethnic Coalitions, Competitions, and Conflict.* New York: Russell Sage Foundation.

Kazepov, Y. (ed.) (2005) *Cities of Europe.* Oxford: Blackwell.

Lagrange, H., and Oberti, M. (eds.) (2006), *Émeutes urbaines et protestations.* Paris: Presses de Sciences Po.

Lange, P., and Regini, M. (eds.) (1989) *State, Market and Social Regulation.* Cambridge: Cambridge University Press.

Lascoumes, P., and Le Galès, P. (2007) From the nature of instruments to the sociology of public policy instrumentation. *Governance* 20 (1): 1–21.

Leca, J. (1996) La gouvernance de la France sous la Vème République: une perspective de sociologie comparative. In *De la Vème République à l'Europe*, ed. F. d'Arcy and L. Rouban. Paris: Presses de Sciences Po.

Lefèvre, C. (1998) Metropolitan government and governance in western democracies: a critical review. *International Journal of Urban and Regional Research* 22 (1): 9–25.

Le Galès, P. (1998) Regulation, territory and governance. *International Journal of Urban and Regional Research* 3: 482–506.

Le Galès, P. (2002) *European Cities, Social Conflicts and Governance.* Oxford: Oxford University Press.

Le Galès, P., and Lorrain, D. (2004) Gouverner les très grandes métropoles. Institutions et réseaux techniques. *Revue Française d'Administration Publique* 107: 307–20.

Lévy, J. (1997) *Europe, une géographie.* Paris: Hachette.

Logan, J., and Molotch, H. (1987) *Urban Fortunes. the Political Economy of Place.* Berkeley: University of California Press.

Martinotti, G. (1993) *Metropoli.* Bologna: Il Mulino.

Mayntz, R. (1993) Governing failures and the problem of governability. In *Modern Governance*, ed. J. Kooiman. London: Sage, 9–20.

McCartney, P., and Stren, R. (eds.) (2003) *Governance on the Ground: Innovations and Discontinuities in Cities of the Developing World.* Baltimore: Johns Hopkins University Press.

Perulli, P. (2000) *La città delle reti: forme di governo nel postfordismo.* Turin: Bollati Boringhier.

Peters, G. (1997) Shouldn't row, can't steer: what's a government to do? *Public Policy and Administration* 12 (2): 51–61.

Phelps, N. A., Parsons, N., Ballas, D., and Dowling, A. (2006) *Post-Suburban Europe: Planning and Politics at the Margins of Europe's Capital Cities.* Basingstoke: Palgrave Macmillan.

Pichierri, A. (1997) *Città stato. Economia e politica del modello anseatico.* Venice: Marsilio.

Pierre, J. (1999) Models of urban governance: the institutional dimension of urban politics. *Urban Affairs Review* 34 (3): 372–96.

Pierre, J., and Peters, G. (2005) *Governing Complex Societies.* Basingstoke: Palgrave Macmillan.

Pinson, G. (2009) *Gouverner les villes par projet.* Paris: Presses de Sciences Po.

Robinson, J. (2005) *Ordinary Cities.* London: Routledge.

Scott, A. J. (2001) *Global City-Regions.* Oxford: Oxford University Press.

Scott, J. (1999) *Seeing Like a State.* New Haven, CT: Yale University Press.

Simone, A. (2004) *The City Yet to Come.* Durham, NC: Duke University Press.

Stone, C. (1989) *Regime Politics, Governing Atlanta, 1946–1988.* Lawrence: University Press of Kansas.

Urry, J. (2000) *Sociology Beyond Societies: Mobilities for the Twenty First Century.* London: Routledge.

Waddington, D., Jobard, F., and King, M. (eds.) (2009) *Rioting in the UK and France: A Comparative Analysis.* Portland, OR: Willan Publishing.

Index

The New Blackwell Companion to the City   Edited by Gary Bridge and Sophie Watson
© 2011 Blackwell Publishing Ltd